HARRY C. TREXLER LIBRARY

Gift of

Dr. & Mrs. Bernard Frank

American Jewish Year Book

American Jewish Year Book 1990

VOLUME 90

Prepared by THE AMERICAN JEWISH COMMITTEE

Editor
DAVID SINGER

Executive Editor
RUTH R. SELDIN

THE AMERICAN JEWISH COMMITTEE
NEW YORK
THE JEWISH PUBLICATION SOCIETY
PHILADELPHIA

COPYRIGHT © 1990 BY THE AMERICAN JEWISH COMMITTEE
AND THE JEWISH PUBLICATION SOCIETY

All rights reserved. No part of this book may be reproduced in any form without permission in writing from the publisher, except by a reviewer who may quote brief passages in a review to be printed in a magazine or newspaper.

ISBN 0-8276-0359-2

Library of Congress Catalogue Number: 99-4040

PRINTED IN THE UNITED STATES OF AMERICA
BY THE HADDON CRAFTSMEN, INC., SCRANTON, PA.

Preface

This year's volume features a major study of Ashkenazi and Sephardi Jews in Israel. In "Ethnic Differences Among Israeli Jews: A New Look," U.O. Schmelz, Sergio DellaPergola, and Uri Avner document demographic and sociocultural changes that have occurred over the past four decades among Jews of Asian-African and European-American extraction. The authors—leading Israeli demographers—report growing similarity between the two main origin groups in many respects, but with significant gaps in educational attainment at higher levels. In the crucial area of voting behavior, the authors find social class to be a stronger factor in party preference than ethnic background.

The volume also includes Ralph Mandel's regular article on Israel, this year providing extensive coverage of the *intifada* and the 1988 elections.

Regular articles on Jewish life in the United States are "Intergroup Relations," by Earl Raab and Douglas Kahn; Lawrence Grossman's "Jewish Communal Affairs"; and "The United States, Israel, and the Middle East," by Kenneth Jacobson. Updated estimates are provided for Jewish population in the United States and in the world.

This year's reports on Jewish life around the world include articles on Canada, the USSR, Western and Eastern Europe, and Australia.

We gratefully acknowledge the assistance of Terry Smith, Diane Hodges, and many colleagues at the American Jewish Committee, especially Cyma M. Horowitz and Michele Anish of the Blaustein Library, and Lotte Zajac.

THE EDITORS

Contributors

URI AVNER: Director, Department for Labor and Social Statistics and member of the directorate, Central Bureau of Statistics, Jerusalem, Israel.

HENRIETTE BOAS: journalist, Amsterdam, Holland.

Y. MICHAL BODEMANN: associate professor, sociology, University of Toronto, Canada; visiting professor, Freie Universität, Berlin, West Germany.

SERGIO DELLAPERGOLA: associate professor and director, Division of Jewish Demography and Statistics, Institute of Contemporary Jewry, Hebrew University of Jerusalem, Israel.

SIMONETTA DELLA SETA: Middle East correspondent, *Il Giornale* (Milan, Italy); researcher in modern Jewish history, Hebrew University of Jerusalem, Israel.

ZVI GITELMAN: professor, political science, and Preston R. Tisch Professor of Judaic Studies, University of Michigan.

LAWRENCE GROSSMAN: director of publications, American Jewish Committee.

KENNETH JACOBSON: director, international affairs, Anti-Defamation League of B'nai B'rith.

DOUGLAS KAHN: executive director, Jewish Community Relations Council, San Francisco.

LIONEL E. KOCHAN: Oxford Center for Post-Graduate Hebrew Studies, England.

MIRIAM KOCHAN: writer, translator, Oxford, England.

BARRY A. KOSMIN: director, North American Jewish Data Bank, Graduate School, City University of New York.

SAM LIPSKI: editor, *Australian Jewish News,* Melbourne, Australia.

RALPH MANDEL: journalist, translator, Jerusalem, Israel.

ROBIN OSTOW: Canada Research Fellow in sociology, McMaster University, Hamilton, Ontario, Canada.

EARL RAAB: director, Nathan Perlmutter Institute for Jewish Advocacy, Brandeis University.

JEFFREY SCHECKNER: administrator, North American Jewish Data Bank, Graduate School, City University of New York.

U.O. SCHMELZ: professor emeritus, Jewish demography, Institute of Contemporary Jewry, Hebrew University of Jerusalem, Israel.

MASSIMO TORREFRANCA: researcher, musicology, Hebrew University of Jerusalem, Israel; contributor, Italian Radio cultural programs.

HAROLD M. WALLER: chairman, department of political science, McGill University, Montreal, Canada; director, Canadian Center for Jewish Community Studies.

Contents

PREFACE ... v
CONTRIBUTORS ... vii

SPECIAL ARTICLES

Ethnic Differences Among
   Israeli Jews: A New Look   *U.O. Schmelz, Sergio DellaPergola, and Uri Avner*   3

UNITED STATES

CIVIC AND POLITICAL
Intergroup Relations   *Earl Raab and Douglas Kahn*   207

The United States, Israel, and
   the Middle East   *Kenneth Jacobson*   228

COMMUNAL
Jewish Communal Affairs   *Lawrence Grossman*   258

DEMOGRAPHIC
Jewish Population in the United
   States, 1989   *Barry A. Kosmin and Jeffrey Scheckner*   278

OTHER COUNTRIES

CANADA	*Harold M. Waller*	301
WESTERN EUROPE		
Great Britain	*Lionel and Miriam Kochan*	321
The Netherlands	*Henriette Boas*	335
Italy	*Simonetta Della Seta and Massimo Torrefranca*	345
CENTRAL EUROPE		
Federal Republic of Germany	*Y. Michal Bodemann*	356
German Democratic Republic	*Robin Ostow*	371
EASTERN EUROPE		
Soviet Union	*Zvi Gitelman*	378
Eastern European Countries	*Zvi Gitelman*	389
AUSTRALIA	*Sam Lipski*	393
ISRAEL	*Ralph Mandel*	401
WORLD JEWISH POPULATION, 1988	*U.O. Schmelz and Sergio DellaPergola*	514

DIRECTORIES, LISTS, AND OBITUARIES

NATIONAL JEWISH ORGANIZATIONS
United States 535
Canada 582

JEWISH FEDERATIONS, WELFARE FUNDS, COMMUNITY COUNCILS
United States 585
Canada 596

JEWISH PERIODICALS
United States 597
Canada 605

OBITUARIES: UNITED STATES 606

SUMMARY JEWISH CALENDAR,
5750–5754 (Sept. 1989–Aug. 1994) 618

CONDENSED MONTHLY CALENDAR,
1989–1992 (5749–5752) 620

SELECTED ARTICLES OF INTEREST IN RECENT VOLUMES
OF THE AMERICAN JEWISH YEAR BOOK 648

INDEX 651

Special Articles

Ethnic Differences Among Israeli Jews: A New Look

by U.O. SCHMELZ, SERGIO DELLAPERGOLA, and URI AVNER

ISRAEL'S JEWISH POPULATION is made up of immigrants and their descendants from all over the world, most of whom came to the country only in the last few decades. Within this societal mosaic the meeting of the two major origin groups of Jews—Asian-African and European-American—is of particular significance and has attracted widespread attention by researchers.[1]

During the early statehood period, the two groups exhibited strong dif-

---

Note: The research reported in this study was carried out under the auspices of the Division of Jewish Demography and Statistics, the Institute of Contemporary Jewry, the Hebrew University of Jerusalem. All statistics were derived from published or unpublished data compiled by Israel's Central Bureau of Statistics or from computer files deposited by the bureau with the Hebrew University's Data Bank. Numerous special tabulations were made from these files. The responsibility for the findings rests exclusively with the authors. U.O. Schmelz wrote the introduction and the sections on immigration, population size and structure, residential distribution, interethnic marriage, and fertility; Uri Avner wrote the section on education; Sergio DellaPergola wrote the section on voting behavior and the conclusion. Benjamin Anderman, Zvi Richter, Nitza Genuth, Judith Even, and Arin Poller ably assisted in preparing this study.

[1]In the vast literature dealing with the problems discussed in the present study, see the following general works: Carl Frankenstein, ed., *Between Past and Future* (Jerusalem, 1953); S.N. Eisenstadt, *The Absorption of Immigrants* (London, 1954); Judah Matras, *Social Change in Israel* (Chicago, 1965); Moshe Lissak, *Social Mobility in Israel Society* (Jerusalem, 1969); *Mizug Galuyoth—The Integration of Immigrants from Different Countries of Origin in Israel* (in Hebrew; Jerusalem, 1969); S.N. Eisenstadt, Rivka Bar Yossef, Chaim Adler, eds., *Integration and Development in Israel* (Jerusalem, 1970); Michael Curtis and Mordecai Chertoff, *Israel: Social Structure and Change* (New Brunswick, 1973); Roberto Bachi, *The Population of Israel* (Jerusalem, 1977); Sammy Smooha, *Israel: Pluralism and Conflict* (London, 1978); Ernest Krausz, ed., *Migration, Ethnicity and Community, Studies of Israeli Society*, 1 (New Brunswick and London, 1980); Moshe Lissak and Nurit Ronel, eds., *The Ethnic Problem in Israel—Continuity and Change* (in Hebrew), *Megamot*, 25, 1984; Dov Friedlander and Calvin Goldscheider, *Israel Population: The Challenge of Pluralism*, Population Bulletin 39, 1984; Shlomo Deshen and Moshe Shokeid, eds., *Jews of the Middle East: Anthropological Perspectives on Past and Present* (in Hebrew; Tel Aviv, 1984); S.N. Eisenstadt, *The Transformation of Israeli Society: An Essay in Interpretation* (London, 1985); Alex Weingrod, ed., *Studies in Israeli Ethnicity* (London, 1985); Peter Y. Medding, ed., *Studies in Contemporary Jewry*, vol. 5 (New York, 1989).

ferences in many areas: demographic patterns and family organization, educational attainment, occupational skills, consumption patterns, degree of religiosity, and so on. The impact of these objective differentials was exacerbated by the existence of psychological barriers, such as the perception by each group that the other had "a different mentality" and the accumulated resentment of Asian-Africans toward the dominant European-Americans over initial absorption difficulties. At the same time, a broad diversity prevailed within each of the major groupings with respect to country of origin, mother tongue, and societal background abroad. Later arrivals among European Jews did not show the strong commitment to social experimentation and change that was evident among European immigrants of the pre-1948 period.

This diversity notwithstanding, there existed strong commonalities among Israel's Jews, in particular a shared Jewish heritage—the ancestral religion and history, some international contacts in matters of rabbinical learning, and the perennial experience of minority status in the Diaspora, which had recently been underscored by the Holocaust in Europe and nationalistic violence against Jews in Arab lands. Most of the immigrants in their countries of origin had been town-dwellers with urban occupations, and the Jewish men, at least, had been better educated than their non-Jewish counterparts. In addition, most Jews arriving in Israel shared the feature of being destitute refugees.[2]

In Israel itself, the members of the two origin groups were brought closer together by such existential factors as smallness of the country, residential proximity of many people of different backgrounds and characteristics, dependence on the same institutions, such as schools, and the impact of common legal obligations, especially compulsory military service. Another unifying factor was the emergence of Hebrew as the *lingua franca* of a population made up of Jews of diverse mother tongues.[3] Commonly shared experiences, often under conditions of war and national emergency, have served as powerful unifying bonds. Moreover, unlike in the early period of the state, most Israeli Jews are now native-born, and their proportion is growing.

The ethnic factor has shown itself to be a key dynamic element of Jewish society in Israel. The coexistence, interaction, and interpenetration of the main origin groups, as well as the changes which their members have

---

[2]U.O. Schmelz, *Jewish Refugee Immigration to Israel 1932–1980*, Hebrew University, Division of Jewish Demography and Statistics, Occasional Paper no. 8, 1989; a Hebrew version was published earlier.

[3]U.O. Schmelz and R. Bachi, "Hebrew as Everyday Language of the Jews in Israel—Statistical Appraisal," in *Salo Wittmayer Baron Jubilee Volume*, vol. 2, American Academy for Jewish Research, 1974, pp. 745–785.

experienced personally and intergenerationally, are major themes of Israeli social history. At the same time, the actual processes of evolution in each origin group as well as the differences between groups have tended to vary a great deal in different spheres—a point that is often not appreciated.

This study will concentrate on the analysis of origin differentials in selected subject fields. The aim is to elucidate the empirical patterns of these differentials and their transformations over time, to document the prevailing diversity, and to contribute to the in-depth analysis of the selected subject fields. Viewed overall, the investigation of these evolutionary patterns sheds light on the main challenges and problems involved in the task of contemporary nation-building by Israel's diverse Jewish population.

Background

Prior to the Holocaust, world Jewry consisted of several principal groupings, differing in geographical location, sociodemographic, and sociocultural characteristics—particularly the degree of modernity—as well as in modes of Jewishness and religiosity. The bulk of European Jewry lived in Eastern Europe, one of the less developed regions of the continent, where it was subject to strong economic and nationalistic pressures. Previously this had been a traditional Jewry of the Ashkenazi type. However, two powerful trends made for change: in the Soviet Union, the Pale of Settlement and the *numerus clausus* were abolished, giving Jews opportunities for geographical relocation and careers in the framework of a Communist regime; in the East European countries outside the USSR, modernization and industrialization advanced during the interwar period. Central and West European Jewries, with the exception of some recent immigrants from Eastern Europe, had become so modernized that they anticipated and actually exceeded the demographic dynamics currently characteristic of both the general populations of highly developed countries and the contemporary Diaspora. They exhibited negative population growth, low levels of Jewishness, and frequent mixed marriage. The recently established Jewish populations in the Americas, South Africa, and Australia were striking roots in these surroundings and setting out on the road to their remarkable present success in the economic and social spheres. The age-old Jewries of the Middle East and North Africa shared in the cultural and material stagnation of their countries of residence, most of which, in the mid-20th century, were just experiencing the early stages of sociodemographic change. Finally, the Jewish population of the Land of Israel (Palestine) during the Mandatory period was still of modest size, mostly of European provenance, with its majority ideologically oriented toward Zionist pioneering.

The Holocaust wiped out most of European Jewry, whether traditional or modern. The remnants from Europe—excluding for a considerable time the Soviet Union—and the Jews of the Islamic countries made up the bulk of the immigrants to the new State of Israel. Most came as refugees.

The dominant societal constellation in the early phase of the State of Israel resulted from the meeting of three sectors: the preexisting *yishuv*, new immigrants from Europe, and new immigrants from Asia-Africa. The latter two groups were newcomers, but conditions had changed utterly for the old-timers (themselves mostly foreign-born) as well. Since the old-timers and the immigrants from Europe had the same background, in sociodemographic terms the picture was reduced to the coexistence of two main origin groups—European-American and Asian-African. The two groups differed sharply in most respects.

Contents of Study

This study will analyze the ethnic dimension among Israel's Jews in the following areas:

Immigration. In the first four decades of Israel's existence the contribution of the two main origin groups has been roughly equal in terms of the number of immigrants to Israel. However, the potential for Jewish migration from Asia and North Africa is now almost exhausted. Any substantial future *aliyah* will have to come from Europe, the Americas, South Africa, or Australia.

Population Size and Structure. The changing proportions of the two main origin groups will be traced up to the point where they reached the approximate numerical balance that prevails at present. Asian-African Jews have drawn close to European-American Jews with regard to age structure.

Residential Distribution. In Israel's early period, marked dissimilarities arose between the origin groups with regard to both territorial dispersion and individual areas of residence within towns. However, in many of the newer housing areas and among the better educated, these dissimilarities have been greatly reduced.

Interethnic Marriage. Increasingly frequent marriages in which husband and wife are of different origins are a prime mechanism for the integration of Israel's Jewish population.

Fertility. The previously high mortality of Jews who lived in Asia-Africa was rapidly reduced after their arrival in Israel. Processes of demographic convergence have resulted in similarity of nuptiality and fertility patterns between the main origin groups in Israel.

Educational Attainment. Striking differences between the origin groups, by sex, prevailed among immigrants in the past. Great progress in education is a general feature of Israeli society, but there are still differences in the highest educational levels reached by the young of the main origin groups.

Voting Behavior. Ethnic voting patterns have shown considerable shifts in recent elections. In the political sphere, Asian-African Jews have become increasingly prominent.

Conclusion. A final section will summarize salient findings and briefly discuss their implications.

This study focuses entirely on behavioral patterns; it does not discuss policies relating to the ethnic situation or the psychological aspects. The analysis is based on statistical data, which are presented in tables in an appendix following the text.

Concepts and Terminology

In keeping with the usage in Israel's official statistics, foreign-born Jews will be divided by continent and, where feasible, by country of birth, and the Israeli-born by father's continent or country of birth. The Israeli-born whose fathers were also born in Israel are not further subdivided. From this division according to continents/countries of birth a classification by origin is derived, grouping together persons born in a certain continent or country with the Israeli-born whose fathers were born in that same continent or country. "European origin" thus means the natives of that continent and the sons or daughters born in Israel to European-born fathers.

Israeli origin consists only of the Israeli-born whose fathers were also born in the country. Thus, each foreign-origin group comprises more persons than the corresponding category by continent or country of birth, because the respective Israeli-born are likewise included. In contrast, the Israeli origin group is much smaller than the total number of Israeli-born, because it includes only those whose fathers were also born in Israel but not the Israeli-born of foreign paternity. The advantages of this approach are the objective and immutable[4] nature of a person's own and paternal country of birth throughout his/her lifetime. It should also be mentioned that countries are classified in their entirety. Hence, the Soviet Union together with its Asian territories is included in Europe, while Turkey is included in Asia despite Istanbul's location in Europe.

In Jewish sociological writing on Israel, as well as in popular literature, an origin division of the Jews according to *edot* (communities) has often been made, primarily into Ashkenazim and Sephardim, but also a variety of Eastern, or Oriental, communities. In fact, however, there is no generally accepted classification of *edot*. Confusion prevails between narrow use of

---

[4] Except where changes of frontiers occurred. In this case the current boundary division is reflected in the statistics.

the term "Sephardim," signifying descendants of exiles from Spain and Portugal, and its wider use embracing all non-Ashkenazi Jewish communities. There is thus excessive room for subjective and inconsistent personal responses when individuals are questioned about their *edah*. This is all the more true among the offspring of interethnic marriages, who are quite numerous in Israel.

Use of the loosely applied terms "Western" and "Eastern" to denote the origin composition of Israel's Jews disregards the geographical realities of the Diaspora. While the expression *edot hamizrah* ("Oriental" communities) is often employed in Hebrew as a generic name for Asian-African Jews, it is understood to exclude the Sephardim. The majority of so-called Western Jews actually come from the eastern portion of Europe, while the most numerous subgroup of allegedly Eastern Jews is the Moroccan community, which hails from the western corner of North Africa and whose very name in Hebrew, *ma'aravim*, signifies "people of the west." At any rate, the considerable body of Balkan Sephardim were sociodemographically Europeans at the approach of the Holocaust, while the Jews of South Africa are Ashkenazim.

When the Asian-African and European-American origin groups are compared in this article, particularly in the statistical tables, two situations are distinguished. The term "major groups" indicates that the Israeli origin group has been omitted from the data presented; "dichotomous groups" is used when the members of the Israeli origin group have been included and divided according to ultimate origin abroad.

Time Perspective

The analysis presented here will be confined to the period of Israel's statehood, from 1948 onward. In fact, it will often start only from 1961, for two reasons: by then most of the Holocaust survivors and the early Asian-African immigrants had arrived in the country, creating the initially striking origin differentials that will be followed up here; in addition, the detailed population census conducted in Israel in 1961 provided the first major reading of the situation that had arisen.

From one perspective the four decades since 1948 may appear a substantial period of time, considering that the great majority of Jews now living in Israel either immigrated or were born after the establishment of the state. From a different perspective, however, the four decades are but a short time span. Since the focus of this study is on origin-group differentials, it should be realized that those immigrants who arrived in the first years of statehood as young children are now only in their 40s. Even the adolescents and young adults of the period of mass immigration, who clearly remember the hardships of their early absorption, are now aged about 60 and may still be in the labor force. Consequently, their permanent characteristics, such as amount of schooling received abroad, may continue to affect the overall summaries for the existing Jewish population. Moreover, such persons still exert direct social influence.

In terms of the future, it should be recognized that the four decades under review constitute a large proportion of the period for which it is possible at all to investigate the differentials between the main origin groups with relative certainty. As noted, official statistics divide the foreign-born according to region of birth and the first generation of Israeli-born by father's birth region. However, the Israeli-born whose fathers were also born in the country are not subdivided. They amounted to only 8 percent of all Israeli Jews in 1972, but more than 21 percent in 1988. Unless a large wave of immigration arrives in the future, their proportion is bound to increase rapidly.

Furthermore, marriages involving couples in which one is of Asian-African origin and the other of European-American origin already constitute about a quarter of current marriages. The proportion of new matches between spouses from different countries of origin is even greater. The offspring of such marriages will be of mixed origin and will appear in the official statistics as follows: if the father is foreign-born, according to his birth region, while that of the mother will remain unrecorded;[5] if the father is Israeli-born, in that category whose origin is unspecified. Obviously, the specification of origin cannot be a simple and unequivocal matter when each parent and perhaps as many as 3–4 grandparents stem from different countries. Due to further growth in the proportions of persons who are of mixed parentage or who have been many generations in Israel, study of the subject based on statistics of the existing type will become increasingly inconclusive.

Sources

This study chiefly uses data from the official statistics of Israel; the few exceptions are duly noted. The official statistics in question consist of population censuses as well as statistics on immigration, vital events, school and university studies, parliamentary elections, and so on. Four national population censuses have been held so far in Israel: 1948, 1961, 1972, and 1983. In the main, reference will be to the last three, because the earliest census

---

[5]The origin division of the Israeli-born in the official statistics (and also here) is determined according to only one parent, the father. There are practical reasons for this method. The underlying demographic assumption is that the total offspring of origin-mixed Jewish marriages are divided rather evenly according to the respective origins of fathers and mothers.

essentially reflected the situation prior to the mass immigration that quickly changed the size and composition of Israel's Jewish population and launched the processes that are examined here. Moreover, the 1948 census did not divide the Israeli-born by father's country of birth, a fact that is necessary to establish the origin composition of Israel's Jews.

IMMIGRATION

Approximately 90 percent of the Jewish immigrants to Palestine during the Mandatory period whose country of provenance was recorded came from Europe.[6] Even if some adjustment is made for unrecorded cases, the European proportion remains as high as 88 percent.[7]

Table 1 reviews the course of immigration into the State of Israel according to previous continent of residence.[8] It shows strong variations over time both in the overall volume of immigration and in the geographical composition of the immigrants. The figures relate to gross immigration, without deducting any individuals who emigrated from Israel. (See Appendix for tables.)

The first few years of the new state (May 1948–1951) witnessed a major influx of 687,000 Jews as compared to 650,000 who lived there when independence was proclaimed. The first newcomers arrived primarily from Europe, as displaced persons or other survivors of the Holocaust. Soon, however, the proportion of Asian-Africans rose and by 1951 became preponderant, in part because of a ban on Jewish emigration from the Soviet satellite countries of Eastern Europe during Stalin's last years. For the whole of this brief period the percentages of arrivals from Europe and from Asia-Africa were virtually balanced. A striking feature in this situation was the transplantation to Israel of the overwhelming majority of certain Diaspora Jewries, the outstanding instances being Iraq (123,300 persons during 1948–1951), Yemen and Aden (48,400), Bulgaria (37,200), and Libya (30,900). By the end of 1951 the Arabic-speaking countries of Asia had been nearly emptied of Jews, and the potential subsequently remaining in this continent for migration to Israel was limited. Most of the large immigration of Asian-African provenance that continued in the following dozen years actually came from North Africa, especially from Morocco and Tunisia.

After a relative lull during 1952–1954, when African Jews predominated among the comparatively few arrivals, a second, though far more modest,

---

[6]Including less than 2 percent classifed under America and Oceania.

[7]U.O. Schmelz, "Mass Aliyah from Asia and North Africa: Demographic Aspects" (in Hebrew), *Pe'amim*, no. 39, 1989, p. 19f.

[8] For May 1948–1950, according to continent of birth.

immigration wave—165,000—came during 1955–1957. It comprised an African majority, but also included many Jewish migrants from Eastern Europe during the post-Stalinist thaw and after the abortive Hungarian uprising of 1956.

The years 1958–1960 saw another reduction in the number of immigrants, with a majority of arrivals coming from Europe. A renewed rise of the wave during 1961–1964 brought 228,000 persons to Israel, including most of the Jews who had until then remained in Morocco, as well as numerous Romanians.

The mid-1960s were a watershed in Israel's immigration history in that they marked the termination of the great exodus of Jews from Asia and Africa, where comparatively few Jews remained. After a few more years (1965–1968), another tide of immigration ensued during 1969–1974. There were two main tributaries: Soviet Jews who, in limited numbers, were allowed to leave for the first time in more than 40 years; and Jews from North America, Latin America, Western Europe, and elsewhere, who, in the optimistic atmosphere following the Six Day War, decided on *aliyah* (immigration) in larger numbers than before.[9] This tide terminated, however, in the aftermath of the Yom Kippur War of 1973.

In the following years (1975–1988), small, and on the whole decreasing, annual numbers of Jewish immigrants came to Israel. An interrelated phenomenon was the exit of Jews from the Soviet Union, holding Israeli visas but actually heading to other destinations. The immigration of some Iranian and Ethiopian Jews did not make up for the falloff elsewhere.

The data in table 1 report on the absolute numbers of immigrants. If their relative numbers per 1,000 Jews in Israel are considered, the declining trend of immigration is more strongly emphasized. Since the total of Jews in Israel has grown markedly, the same absolute number of immigrants corresponds now to a lower immigration rate than in the past. In the peak year 1949, when 240,000 Jews arrived, the rate of immigration was 266 per 1,000 of Israel's average Jewish population (including the Israeli-born) in that year. Relative to the number of Jews already living in Israel at the beginning of 1949, the increment was, of course, even greater: 316 per 1,000. In contrast, for the average of recent years (1985–1988) the yearly immigration rate was only 3 per 1,000.

The data in table 1 are, as noted, gross immigration figures. By deducting emigration of Jews from Israel, the net total of external migrations is obtained. In the past, most emigrants were the backwash of recent immigra-

---

[9] In 1969 a special visa category of "potential immigrants" was created in order to encourage *aliyah* from Western countries. These persons are included in the figures of table 1, but remigration has been considerable among them, especially among those coming from the United States.

tion. Today, when the majority of younger Jewish adults in Israel are native-born, they also constitute the majority of emigrants. During the 40 years 1948–1988 a gross total of 1,800,000 immigrants arrived, while the net total of external migrations of Jews to and from Israel amount to about 1,400,000.[10] In the mid-1980s the annual net balance of external migrations of Israel's total Jews was barely positive.

Jewish immigration to Israel, like many international migration streams, presents a wavelike pattern, with shorter spells of highs and lows in the first two decades of statehood and longer ones afterward. During 1948–1951 there was a massive wave of immigration, but ever since, the long-term trend has been sloping downward. This is because of—as noted earlier—the gradual exhaustion of migratory potentials in Asia, North Africa, and the Soviet satellite countries, and also because of the lack of enthusiasm of Jews from Western countries, particularly the United States, for moving to Israel.[11] As for the future, sizeable potentials for further immigration exist in the Soviet Union, on the one hand, and in the Western countries, on the other. The great changes now occurring in the USSR, which include more liberal emigration laws, compounded by the new regulations in the United States restricting the entry of Soviet Jews, are now producing another wave of Jewish migration from the USSR to Israel.

During the whole period 1948–1988, a modest majority of the gross immigration came from Europe and America. The difference between this percentage (56) and that of the arrivals from Asia-Africa (44) would be reduced if only net immigrants were considered, since emigration, including remigration, has been relatively larger among European-Americans than Asian-Africans. Hence *aliyah* of the two main origin groups has been roughly balanced during the state's first 40 years. However, the time-bound character of this balance should be appreciated. If the perspective were widened to include the whole of Zionist immigration over the last hundred years, a considerable European majority would result. Similarly, since any further immigration of considerable size can only come from the Soviet Union or the Western countries, the proportion of European-Americans would rise accordingly.

Jews from the Americas and Oceania amounted to only 9.5 percent of gross immigration during 1948–1988 and have been concentrated in the last two decades. Their share among net immigrants was even smaller, because of particularly strong remigration.

---

[10]The figure includes children born abroad to returning Israelis; see Central Bureau of Statistics (hereafter, CBS), *Statistical Abstract of Israel*, 1989, p.39.

[11]Sergio DellaPergola, "Aliya and Other Jewish Migrations: Toward an Integrated Perspective," in U.O. Schmelz and G. Nathan, eds., *Studies in the Population of Israel in Honor of Roberto Bachi*, Scripta Hierosolymitana, vol. 30 (Jerusalem, 1986), pp. 172–209; idem, "Mass Aliyah—A Thing of the Past?" *Jerusalem Quarterly*, no. 51, 1989, pp. 96–114.

The distribution of Israel's foreign-born Jews by period of immigration—which indicates their duration of residence in Israel—changed in the course of time. The passing of the years added new immigration waves, while deaths, some emigration, and the arrival of new immigrants reduced the absolute or relative numbers of veteran residents (table 2). By 1988 only 13 percent of the foreign-born had arrived before independence. The period of mass immigration and its immediate aftermath (1948–1954), which had accounted for more than half of all foreign-born Jews in the 1961 census, made up scarcely a third by 1988.

Because of the changing geographical composition of the immigrants, Jews born in the various continents are differently distributed according to immigration periods. The European-American-born have been the most veteran group, in keeping with the situation in the Mandatory period. However, since the late 1960s, they have also comprised an above-average share of recent immigrants. Among the Asian-born, large proportions came in the period of mass migration, and among the African Jews, many arrived around 1960. In the not too distant future, the Asian-African-born, especially the former, will constitute the most veteran of the continental groups among Israel's foreign-born Jews.

Table 3 displays the distribution of the foreign-born by principal countries of birth and immigration periods as of 1983.[12] It shows the heaviest concentration of pre-independence arrivals among Jews born in Germany and Austria, most of whom arrived before World War II. The relatively strongest concentrations of immigrants are from those Diaspora countries whose Jews participated in the mass transfers of the time: Iraq, Yemen, Libya, Bulgaria (the latter lumped together in the table with Greek Jewry, which in Israel is chiefly represented by Holocaust survivors). Two-thirds of Moroccan Jews arrived around 1960. In 1983 the majority of Soviet Jews living in Israel were relative newcomers; the same was true of Jews from the "other Europe" (Western Europe), the Americas, and the "other Africa" (mainly South Africa and Ethiopia).

POPULATION SIZE AND STRUCTURE

Origin Composition

During the Mandatory period, the Jewish population of Palestine grew rapidly—from less than 60,000 at the end of World War I to 650,000 by May 1948. Among the foreign-born, those from Europe (and America)

---

[12]Data on the distribution of foreign-born Jewish residents in Israel, by provenance and immigration period, have been officially updated since the 1983 census only on the continental level but not according to individual countries.

constituted 68 percent in the census of 1931 and 85 percent in that of November 1948.

The total number of Jews in Israel jumped from 650,000 in May 1948 and 717,000 in November of that year to 1,404,000 at the end of 1951; it has grown gradually since then to 3,659,000 at the end of 1988. This amounts to a 5.6-fold growth during slightly more than 40 years, or an average annual growth rate of 44 per 1,000. However, the rate of annual growth has slackened strikingly over time, as immigration has shrunk. Concurrently, the relative importance of external migration balance vis-à-vis natural increase as a factor in Jewish population growth has declined (table 4).

The changes that have taken place in the composition of Israel's Jews, by region of birth and origin, since the beginning of statehood, are documented in tables 5–7, by absolute numbers and percentages. At the time of the census of 1948, 35 percent of the country's total Jews had been born there. Mass immigration reduced this proportion to 25 percent at the end of 1951. It has grown ever since, exceeding half the Jewish population as from 1975. By 1988 it had reached 63 percent (table 6). The number of Israeli-born whose fathers were born in the country amounted to 107,000 in 1961. It rose to 786,000 in 1988. Correspondingly, the proportion of this group among all Israeli-born increased from 15 to 34 percent over the same years, and its percentage among the country's total Jews from 5.5 to 21.5. The share of Israeli-born rose between 1961 and 1988 as follows: all Jews— from 38 to 63 percent; European origin group—from 33 to 44 percent; Asian-African origin group, from 35 to 61 percent (see lower part of table 7).

The absolute number of foreign-born rose dramatically in the first two decades of the state, due to strong immigration. It did not increase much in the census interval 1972–1983, and it has declined in recent years because of the paucity of new immigrants as well as deaths and some emigration. The proportion of foreign-born among Israel's total Jews declined from 65 percent in 1948 and even 75 percent in 1951 to 37 percent by 1988. Among all foreign-born Jews, the share of Europeans and Americans dropped from 85 percent in 1948 and 63 percent in 1951 to 56 percent in the census of 1961. Since the 1972 census, the share of Europeans and Americans has maintained itself at about 55 percent, with limited fluctuations. Thus a small majority of Europeans and Americans has prevailed among the total of foreign-born Jews in Israel during the last three decades (table 6).

Considering the Israeli-born whose fathers were born abroad, a majority (54 percent) of the fathers were from Europe-America as late as 1961. Since then the initially high fertility in Israel of the large body of post-1948 immigrants from Asia-Africa has made itself felt: 58 percent of Israeli-born Jews with foreign-born fathers originated from Asia-Africa in 1972 and 61 percent in 1983–1988. Grouping together the foreign-born and the Israeli-born of foreign paternity,[13] one finds an analogous picture: a majority of European-American origin up to the 1961 census, a majority of Asian-African origin as from the 1972 census.[14]

To distribute the whole Jewish population dichotomously into two major origin groups according to geographical origin from Asia-Africa or Europe-America, the fast-growing category of Israeli-born with Israeli-born fathers needs to be divided. While this is not done in the official population statistics, there are birth statistics starting from the early 1950s that specify, in cases where the newborn's father is himself Israeli-born, the birth region of the paternal grandfather. The origin proportions of foreign-born grandfathers of the newborn have changed markedly in the course of time: from about two-thirds Europeans and Americans until the early 1970s to about 45 percent in the mid-1980s.

Only a few numerically limited subgroups remain indeterminate according to origin and thus subject to conjectural distribution: persons born in the country before the 1950s;[15] those born afterward whose paternal grandfathers were already Israeli-born; and infants whose paternal grandfathers' region of birth failed to be recorded. These were all assigned to the two origin groups on the strength of the amply documented fact that the majority of the Jewish population of Palestine toward the end of the Ottoman period, and even more so in the Mandatory period, originated in Europe, and that a marked fertility differential between the origin groups developed in Palestine only in the early Mandate period. By use of this procedure the following percentages of total Israeli-born with Israeli-born fathers were assigned to the European-American origin group: 1961 and 1972—about two thirds; 1983—60 percent; 1988—56 percent.

The division of all Israeli Jews according to the two origin groups is obtained by combining the foreign-born, the Israeli-born with foreign-born fathers, and the Israeli-born of Israeli paternity. In fact, it consists of the weighted averages of the respective shares of each origin group in these component subgroups. The overall percentages of European-Americans, as shown in the section "origin, dichotomous" of table 7, were (in rounded figures): 1961—56, 1972—50, 1983—50, 1988—48. The resultant finding is thus a rather balanced distribution of Israel's Jews according to the two main origin groups during the last two decades. At ages 15 and over, the

---

[13]As from 1984 the number of Israeli-born with foreign-born fathers has exceeded that of foreign-born Jews.

[14]The percentages of persons of European origin among all Jews of foreign origin were: 1961—55.2, 1972—48.2, 1983—47.5, 1988—46.3.

[15]Persons born in the country before 1950 amounted, in 1988, to only 9.6 percent of all Israeli-born or 6.0 percent of total Jews.

dichotomous origin division in 1988 turned out to be 50 percent for either group; at ages 18 and over the proportion of Asian-Africans was slightly below half. Thus, despite the common assumption to the contrary, the Asian-African origin group does not at present constitute a clear majority of Israel's Jews. Insofar as this belief is based at all on the inspection of statistics, it can be rationalized only by disregard of the Israeli-born of Israeli paternity (whose ultimate origin is not apparent from the official data but can be reconstructed; see above).

In terms of the near future, it should be noted that official population projections exist for Israel until the beginning of the 21st century. However, they do not provide the breakdown of children to be born in Israel during the projection period (from 1985 onward) by father's region of birth. Information on this matter was omitted because of the difficulty of making assumptions about the extent of new interethnic marriages and the number of children expected therefrom. Accordingly, tables 5–7 present data as of the year 2000 only for persons aged 15 and over. In order to permit relevant comparisons, analogous data for ages 15 and above are also given as of 1988. The medium version of the projections, shown here, assumes a zero balance of external migrations by Jews to and from Israel, in approximation to the situation of the mid-1980s.

According to these projections, at ages 15+ the total number of Jews in Israel will grow by 20 percent, the Israeli-born by 58 percent, and the Israeli-born with Israeli-born fathers by 153 percent, whereas the number of foreign-born will go down by 17 percent. According to the percentage distribution of the 15+-year-old Jews in the year 2000 by birth region, the share of all Israeli-born will rise from 49 to 65 percent, that of Israeli-born of Israeli paternity will increase from 9.5 to 20 percent and the Israeli-born of foreign paternity from 40 to 45 percent, while the total of foreign-born might drop from 51 to 35 percent. No marked changes would occur, according to these projections, in the continental distribution of the Israeli-born with foreign-born fathers and of the foreign-born themselves (table 6). However, due to the strong increase of the Israeli origin group, the proportion of the other origin groups—Asian-African and especially the more aged European-American—would be reduced (table 7).

As indicated, if the 15+-year-old Israeli-born with Israeli-born fathers are divided dichotomously, as of 1988 the total comprises equal shares of Asian-African and European-American origin.[16] By the year 2000 the Asian-African share might increase somewhat to 52 percent, because of a 25-percent growth in the absolute number of this origin group as compared

---

[16]As compared to nearly 52 percent of Asian-African origin among the Jews of all ages in 1988, since this origin group is younger than the European-Americans; see below, particularly table 13.

to only a 16-percent growth of the European-American group, according to these projections.

Two points should be added that go beyond the formal projection results: (a) Assuming that the external migration balance of Israel's Jews until the year 2000 will be nil, as was done in the projections, the origin composition in all ages together (including 0–14) will give a somewhat larger surplus to the Asian-African group than is shown in table 7 for ages 15+. Such a moderate surplus is already found for all ages in 1988, and its somewhat augmented continuation would be due, under the now prevailing conditions of rather similar fertility in both origin groups, to some majority of Asian-African origin among those in the most reproductive age groups during 1988–2000 (cf. table 13). (b) Hypothetical immigration potentials from the Diaspora are now located almost exclusively in Europe, America, South Africa, and Australia. A substantially positive migration balance would therefore strengthen the European-American origin group. Indeed, it might reverse the origin proportions in Israel's Jewish population that have of late leaned somewhat in the direction of an Asian-African surplus. According to the dichotomous computations, the surplus of Asian-Africans in 1988 amounted to approximately 120,000. This difference, as well as the effects mentioned in the previous paragraph, might be reduced or cancelled by not unrealistically large figures of future immigrants and their anticipated natural increase in Israel.

Thus, the main finding of this analysis is the existence and probable persistence in the near future of an approximate numerical balance between the two main origin groups of Israeli Jews.

Only continental birth or origin groups have been considered so far. Table 8 gives a succinct picture of the population evolution from 1961 to 1988 according to principal countries of birth or origin, including but distinguishing between two generations—the foreign-born and the Israeli-born offspring of foreign-born fathers. This breakdown provides a sense of the changes that have occurred both chronologically and intergenerationally. The three leading birth countries of the foreign-born in 1961 were Poland (17.2 percent), Romania (12.9), and Iraq (10.3); in 1988, Morocco (14.6), USSR (13.5), and Romania (12.0). Natives of Morocco and the USSR recorded rises above 60 percent in their numbers in Israel, though the greatest relative increases actually occurred with regard to countries with much smaller numbers of Jews in Israel. The three leading countries of origin among the Israeli-born with foreign-born fathers in 1961 were Poland (19.6), USSR (12.6), and Iraq (10.0); in 1988, Morocco (19.3), Iraq (11.3), and Poland (10.1). The advance of the Moroccans to first place according to origin reflected both their strong participation in the immigration flow of the early 1960s and their initially high fertility; the number of

Israeli-born with Moroccan fathers increased more than fivefold.

Table 8 also indicates the percentages of Israeli-born among Jews whose fathers were born in the various countries. These percentages rose in accordance with fertility and/or duration of residence in Israel. The first factor partly accounts for the high percentages found among Yemenites in both years, though they were also a group of comparatively long residence in Israel. The operation of length of residence in Israel is evidenced by the considerable percentages of Israeli-born in 1988 among Jews originating from European countries that were significantly represented only among immigrants of the Mandatory period and early statehood (e.g., Poland and Central European countries). In contrast, the more recent immigration from the USSR around 1970 led to a reduction in 1988 of the share of Israeli-born among the Jews originating from that country.

Table 8 also shows the small share among Israel's Jewish population of persons born in the Americas and Oceania, though their numbers increased in the period following the Six Day War. At the time of the 1983 census, persons born in these regions numbered 75,400 and those born in Israel to fathers from these origins numbered 28,300. The corresponding figures for the United States were 32,300 and 9,100.[17]

Age Composition

The age structure of a population is largely determined by past and current fertility. In Israel, it has also been significantly influenced by the specific age distributions of the large immigration during the early decades of the state.

Table 9 shows the age composition at time of arrival in Israel of Jewish immigrants who were born in Asia-Africa or Europe-America. The Asian-African group was consistently younger, but the differences narrowed after the large immigration waves of 1948–1964. The immigrants from Asia-Africa during 1961–1964, consisting mostly of Moroccans, were even somewhat younger than during the mass influx of 1948–1951; this may have been partly due to lowered child mortality and less selective representation of young adults among the immigrants. After the mid-1960s, immigrants from these continents had a less youthful age structure, which may be attributable to declining fertility and to more selective *aliyah* of young adults. The change may also be related to the fact that the children born in France to

---

[17]The main reason for the discrepancy between these figures and those of table 8, as compared to table 1, is remigration. The figures here and in table 8 relate to country/continent of birth, while those in table 1 relate to continent of last residence before *aliyah*. More immigrants to Israel from America and Oceania were born elsewhere than were born in America or Oceania and moved elsewhere before immigrating to Israel.

North African Jews who first migrated to that country and only afterward to Israel were not classified in the birth-region statistics together with their parents, but as European-born.

The age composition of immigrants from Europe showed strongly the irregular course of fertility which is characteristic of the group as well as the loss of children in the Holocaust. Three chronological stages of reproductivity can be distinguished up to the mid-1950s, whose impact could be seen first in the lower age groups and subsequently in the higher ages as time went on: depressed birthrates in the 1930s and the first half of the 1940s, compounded by child mortality in the Holocaust; a "baby boom," especially in the second half of the 1940s; and a renewed fertility recession afterward. The above-average survival of younger adults in the Holocaust is clearly exemplified in the European mass immigration of 1948–1951. The large percentages of 15–24 or 15–34-year-olds among the immigrants from Europe-America during the last two decades point to selective immigration of younger adults. Increased shares of the elderly are found among more recent immigrants from Europe-America, indicative both of the aging of the Diaspora and of a specific phenomenon of old-age *aliyah*.

In Israel itself, the age structures of Asian-Africans and European-Americans evolved due to the following major influences: the youthful character of the *yishuv* as a whole toward the end of the Mandatory period, mainly due to the arrival of pioneers and, afterward, of Holocaust survivors; the initially high but rapidly decreasing fertility of Asian-African Jews in Israel, though the latter trend was somewhat offset by improved child survival; and a rise in the fertility of European-born Jews after immigration to Israel.

The official population statistics of Israel divide Jews into foreign-born and Israeli-born. All children born in Israel to immigrants are classified as Israeli-born, separate from their parents. This leads to artifacts in the respective age distributions: as a group, the Israeli-born appear inordinately young, while the foreign-born have an elderly bias. Any birth-region group that has received recent migratory reinforcements may have relatively more young children than an equally or even more fertile group that has not absorbed many immigrants of late. Table 10 illustrates the biases due to immigration chronology in the officially published age statistics, when European-Americans are compared with Asian-Africans, and even when Africans are compared with the Asians as of 1988.

Tables 11–13 present the more realistic age distributions of origin groups in dichotomous division. The median ages of the European-American group in Israel have remained rather stable during the considerable span 1961–1988 and are projected to continue at approximately the same level for ages 15 and over, until the year 2000 at least (table 11). This is essentially due to comparatively limited fluctuations of fertility. In contrast, median ages have risen markedly in the Asian-African origin group and are projected to continue to rise, primarily because of fertility decline.

The basic finding of this section, then, is that the origin differentials in age distribution among Israel's Jews are diminishing, as Asians and Africans move more closely to the European-American pattern. Such a process, however, must take considerable time, since current fertility levels make themselves felt at the bottom of the age pyramid, through the relative size of newborn cohorts, while the age pyramid as a whole reflects the demographic experiences of the entire population, including the elderly.

Table 12 shows these developments in greater detail for three points of time: 1961, 1988, and 2000 (the latter only with regard to ages 15 and over). Among European-Americans no marked changes have occurred or are foreseen in the proportions of children and younger adults, which is indicative of the rather stable fertility that has prevailed among this origin group in Israel. The small cohorts born and surviving from the 1930s and the Holocaust in Europe made themselves particularly felt in 1961 at ages 15–24, as compared to the large "baby boom" cohort then aged 5–14; by 1988 these groups had advanced to ages 45–54 and 35–44, respectively. The percentage of elderly (aged 65 and over) among the European-American origin group rose between 1961 and 1988 from 6 to 15 percent. However this was not due to declining fertility, as is now usual when aging takes place in developed countries and as happens also among Asian-Africans in Israel. Rather, the bulges of young adults that had arrived from Europe during the Mandatory period and early statehood eventually reached old age. No augmentation in the proportion of elderly among European-Americans is foreseen until the year 2000, when the decreasing cohorts born in the 1930s will enter the elderly age range.[18]

In the Asian-African origin group, aging processes due to decreasing fertility have manifested themselves. The median age rose and is projected to continue doing so (the latter is substantiated in tables 11–12 for ages 15 and over). The percentages of children declined between 1961 and 1988, while those for persons above age 15 went up. Similarly, the percentages of 15–24-year-olds among all adults will have dropped by the year 2000, while the proportions of the 65+-year-olds are gradually expanding.

Table 13 indicates the proportions of dichotomous origin groups in Israel's total Jewish population age-specifically. In 1961 persons of Asian-African origin accounted for a much greater proportion of children than of middle-aged persons and especially of the elderly. At present, while Asian-Africans still make up a moderate majority of children, the percentage has declined (due to fertility reduction). The peak proportions of this origin

---

[18]U.O. Schmelz, *Aging of World Jewry* (Jerusalem, 1984).

group are now reached among younger adults (aged 15–34), while its share in the older ages continues to diminish strongly. For the year 2000, the largest proportion of Asian-Africans is foreseen in ages 35–44, with relatively less diminution in the later ages. The bulge of greatest Asian-African representation among the cohorts born around 1960, when this origin group was already large in Israel and its fertility still high, is moving up the age pyramid. Thus, if separate age groups of Israel's Jewish population are considered, their division by dichotomous origin is also becoming more balanced.

RESIDENTIAL DISTRIBUTION

Determinants of Evolution

Israel is a small country with a relatively dense network of roads in its inhabited areas. This facilitates commuting by those who work outside their place of residence as well as travel within the country for other purposes. Still, great practical importance with regard to economic, social, and cultural matters attaches to the spatial distribution of the population according to large territorial divisions, individual localities, and neighborhoods within towns. The degree of intermingling between the two major origin groups in small residential areas is a basic aspect of their interrelationship.

After Israel's War of Independence in 1948 and the exodus of most Arabs from the new state, large parts of the country were virtually uninhabited. This applied not only to the Negev in the south, but also to sizeable stretches of land within the Jewish settlement area as it had crystallized in the late Mandatory period, and the de facto frontiers.[19] In order to take effective possession of these parts of the country for security and other reasons, it was seen as imperative to establish Jewish settlements there. Precisely at this juncture in the earliest years of the state, mass immigration took place. A great many of the new immigrants were placed in temporary accommodations that were hastily set up; later they were moved to permanent housing. These factors together led to the extensive and rapid establishment of new localities in the countryside and new residential neighborhoods in existing towns.

Of the 1,034 Jewish localities[20] that were officially counted in Israel as of 1988,[21] 291 existed in 1947, while as many as 383 were set up in the short

---

[19]The "Green Line" according to the armistice agreements of 1949.
[20]This includes nine "mixed localities" with a sizeable Arab sector in the population; eight of these are urban, including the three major cities.
[21]These and the following data are from the Central Bureau of Statistics. Over the years

span 1948–1954. Of these latter, about half were located in the Northern and Southern districts, and another tenth in the Jerusalem district so as to strengthen the "corridor" between the capital city and the bulk of the state. After this early formative phase of striking relative growth, both in the size of the Jewish population and in the number of Jewish localities, the tempo slackened. Sixty localities were established during 1955–1959, half in the south, and only 48 throughout the 1960s. In the changed geopolitical conditions following the Six Day War, 98 Jewish localities were founded in the 1970s and another 154 during 1980–1988. Of these 252 recently created localities, more than half were situated in the administered areas or the Golan (incorporated into Israel as of 1982). The second largest concentration was in the Northern district (outside the Golan), where the relative proportions of Jewish and Arab population and landholding were a matter of concern to Jews.

Of Israel's 89 urban Jewish localities—defined as each having more than 2,000 population—in 1988 only 56 had over 10,000 inhabitants. A total of 44 urban localities—30 with a population above 10,000—were settled by Jews prior to independence. The last category included all cities currently over 100,000, except Beersheba.

The expansion of Israel's urban sector expresses itself in population size rather than number of towns. Since the 1960s, about 90 percent of Israel's Jews have been living in localities classified as urban. Between the censuses taken in November 1948 and the end of 1955, the Jewish population of the three main cities rose as follows: Jerusalem—from 83,000[22] to 144,000; Tel Aviv-Yafo—from 245,000 to 354,000; and Haifa—from 86,000 to 150,000.

The immigrants were first placed in abandoned Arab houses, e. g., in Jaffa, which had been a separate town and was now incorporated into the enlarged Tel Aviv-Yafo municipality, and the southern quarters of the Israeli part of divided Jerusalem. Subsequently, over a period of many years, public housing projects were set up at the ever-widening perimeters of the built-up areas of cities and towns, and newly arriving immigrants were accommodated in them. Date of immigration thus became a prominent factor in the residential location of people. Much later, higher-quality housing was also constructed on the outskirts of the built-up urban territories, attracting young couples from among the longer-resident population of Israel who strove to improve their quality of life and conditions for child rearing outside residentially congested or commercial areas.

The suburbanization of the population of large cities assumed two partic-

---

changes occurred in the total number of Jewish localities not only through establishment of new ones but also through merger, division, or abandonment of existing localities.

[22]Thousands of self-declared Jerusalem inhabitants were actually absent from the city when it was besieged during the 1948 war.

ular forms. First, around Tel Aviv-Yafo—and to a far lesser extent around Haifa—a metropolitan area took shape that comprised many administratively separate localities. Families moved from the core city or inner localities to localities further out.[23] What is defined for statistical purposes as the Tel Aviv conurbation in 1988 comprised 1,632,000 Jews or 45 percent of Israel's Jewish population. Second, in recent years there has been a marked tendency for people to transfer themselves from large towns to rural localities or to new and small-sized urban localities that have sprung up near the pre-1967 frontiers (the Green Line) in proximity to the Tel Aviv conurbation or in the administered areas.

As to the geographical location within Israel of Jews from different origin groups, several major determinants can be pointed out:

a. Immigration chronology was a crucial factor. At the end of the Mandatory period, the Jewish community as a whole and the populations of most Jewish localities were preponderantly European. This applied in particular to the kibbutzim and moshavim, which had an almost exclusively agricultural character. It has been shown above that during the period of mass immigration (1948–1951), the proportions of European and Asian-African groups were balanced. Yet a look at the annual figures reveals a strongly rising trend among the latter group. The percentage of Asian-Africans among all Jewish immigrants increased as follows: May to December 1948—14; 1949—47; 1950—50; and 1951—72 percent. From 1951 to 1956 a strong Asian-African majority prevailed among Jewish immigrants. Moreover, whereas Asian immigrants outnumbered Africans 2½-fold during 1948–1951, a strong surplus of Africans over Asians was typical of immigration in the following years, until the end of the large influx from these continents in the mid-1960s. During the period of most intensive settlement activity, from 1948 until the mid-1950s, the numerical majority in the yearly immigration contingents thus shifted from European to Asian and then to African Jews. This had important consequences in the context considered here.

The earliest arrivals, Europeans and Asians, could still be housed in existing localities, in dwellings deserted by Arab residents. The somewhat later arrivals, including relatively more African Jews, had to content themselves with temporary camp accommodations before moving to newly established localities or urban housing projects. At a subsequent stage, when immigration came largely from Africa, the new arrivals were directed straightaway to new localities or urban neighborhoods, which were at the

---

[23]The city of Tel Aviv-Yafo has lost Jewish population through outmovement, primarily within its own metropolitan area, since 1963, when it numbered 388,000 Jews. By 1988 it had only 307,000 Jewish residents. Its daytime population, on the other hand, has grown considerably.

time under construction. Whereas the early new localities were often established in semiperipheral areas, e.g., the margins of the Central district or the Jerusalem district, the later new localities were founded to an increasing extent at the periphery of the country, in the Southern and Northern districts.

b. The educational and occupational qualifications of the origin groups played an important role. Many of the new immigrants from Asia and Africa arrived with deficient schooling and a lack of modern occupational skills. Because the State of Israel as a whole was still in its early stages of industrialization and unable to absorb many factory hands, a portion of these immigrants were slated by the settlement authorities for agricultural work in new or already existing rural localities. Most immigrants from Asia and Africa—with the exception of many Yemenites and Kurds and some Jews from the Atlas mountains—had in fact been town dwellers before and, however backward the urban conditions in their former countries of residence, were not accustomed to farming. The sudden transfer to isolated rural localities therefore led to hardships of adjustment. Adding to this was the fact that manual labor and agricultural work suffered a loss of status as the fledgling Jewish state moved toward industrialization.

c. New rural localities in Israel were small and were thus often settled by immigrants from only one or two countries, sometimes those arriving together. Often family relationships or other preexisting affinities existed among the new inhabitants, and were accepted by the settlement authorities as given facts. Similar phenomena occurred when groups of new immigrants were placed in urban housing. All this made for segregation[24] by origin groups.

d. Another factor that had the same effect in the rural sector was ideology. The kibbutzim and prestate moshavim had been set up by European Jews imbued with socialist ideals that were alien to most of the new immigrants. Hence these existing localities did not attract many new immigrants, especially those of Asian-African origin. Whereas kibbutzim had been a little more than half of all rural Jewish localities at the end of the Mandate, by 1988 they amounted to only 30 percent. More tellingly, of the 1988 total of 267 kibbutzim, 133 had been established by 1947, another 80 in 1948–1954, and only 54 during the lengthy period 1955–1988. The localities set up after 1948 were mostly publicly sponsored "new immigrant moshavim," while a considerable proportion of the more recent ones have been sponsored by politically right-wing and/or religious groups.

---

[24]The word "segregation" is used in this article descriptively, without a negative connotation, to indicate marked residential separation between ethno-religious groups. Such segregation has been traditional in Palestine/Israel not only between different communities of Jews but also between Jews and Arabs, and Muslims and Christians.

All these developments have produced three often overlapping cleavages in the rural and semirural sector. They run according to origin group, organizational pattern, and sometimes also employment status, since old-established localities hire workers for agriculture and new industrial or service enterprises from the rural localities or "development towns" originally set up for new immigrants. In consequence, a considerable amount of residential segregation according to origin prevails in the rural sector. This applies not only to continents but also to individual countries of origin. Moreover, once a population is settled in a rural locality in Israel, its distinctive origin composition is more likely to be perpetuated than in urban neighborhoods without a communal framework or joint activities, and where changes of resident families may be more frequent.

The long-established towns mostly had a majority of Jews of European origin at the end of the Mandate period. Where neighborhoods of Asian-African Jews existed, for instance in Jerusalem, they tended to be subdivided according to particular ethnic backgrounds. In the decades of statehood, the general change in the origin composition of the Jewish population through strong additions of Asian-African Jews made itself felt in all urban localities, though to varying degrees. In some towns the longer-resident elements were flooded by newcomers, many of them from Asia-Africa; in some new "development towns" this origin group was dominant. Moreover, as public housing projects were set up and populated by evacuees from temporary camps or fresh arrivals from abroad, the initial inhabitants tended to comprise higher or lower proportions of Jews of Asian-African or European origin, depending on the origin composition of the immigrants at the time. Since immigration came largely from Asia-Africa during the 1950s and early 1960s, and from the USSR during the early 1970s, a great deal of origin-specific spatial segregation eventuated as a by-product of these public-housing activities.

The subsequent spatial evolution has been determined by a variety of factors. Regarding types of demographic dynamics, the following are most important: internal migration; place of settling by the immigrants who continued to arrive; and differential natural increase. A background factor of particular importance is the widespread improvement in living conditions and the quest for better-constructed housing, as seen, for example, in the publicly supported "Project Renewal" *(shikum hashekhunot)* activity. Other significant factors have been the strong differences in prices of land and housing in various geographical locations, as well as the establishment of Jewish localities, with comparatively inexpensive housing, in the administered areas.

Internal migration takes place between localities as well as within towns and cities. There is also much residential movement between localities of the same metropolitan area in Israel, especially the Tel Aviv conurbation. A three-phase pattern is strongly evident in the geographical mobility of the population: new immigrants were often placed initially in peripheral localities; many of them as well as persons of longer residence in Israel moved to the Greater Tel Aviv area,[25] the economic heart of the country; that area itself experienced successive suburbanization both within the municipal or metropolitan boundaries and beyond them. There has also been strong residential mobility in the towns and cities outside the Tel Aviv conurbation. Older and lower-class neighborhoods, which are often centrally located and can be converted to commercial and institutional functions, have been deserted by residents, especially of the younger generation, who move to newer, better-situated areas in or beyond the municipal boundaries. In terms of residential origin composition, these moves have often been from strongly segregated neighborhoods to others where the origin groups are more balanced.

Differential natural increase operated toward more-than-average growth of Asian-African neighborhoods as long as their inhabitants were very fertile. It continues to have this effect in ultra-Orthodox neighborhoods where great fertility persists. The city centers that are being abandoned by young residents turn into areas with elderly population remnants and experience a great drop in natural increase.

The discussion that follows will focus on the residential distribution patterns of the two major origin groups and on the evolution of these patterns over time.

Major Spatial Divisions

The state territory of Israel is divided into 6 administrative districts and 15 subdistricts, including the Golan.[26] There are, in addition, Jewish localities in the administered areas.[27]

The main outlines of the spatial distribution of the origin groups took shape as early as the mid-1950s. Tabulations of the official Population

---

[25]The area defined for statistical purposes as the Tel Aviv conurbation has grown rapidly. It now extends not only over the whole Tel Aviv district but also comprises most of the population, Jewish and general, of the Central district.

[26]Some demographic data for subdistricts and other geographical divisions are to be found in the following publications: CBS, *Statistical Abstract of Israel*, various issues; CBS, 1983 census, vol. 12; D. Friedlander, E. Ben-Moshe, Y. Schelekens, *Regional Demographic Changes in Israel* (in Hebrew), Research Report, Jerusalem Institute for Israel Studies, 1989; U.O. Schmelz, "Population," in *Atlas of Israel*, 3rd ed., 1985.

[27]The proportion residing in the administered areas among Israel's total Jews rose from 0.7 percent in 1983 (table 14) to 1.8 percent in 1988.

Register records of September 1953[28] already show the essential features of variation in the proportion of Asian-Africans among all Jews, by district and subdistrict, that on the whole persist to this day. With regard to the data in table 14, it should be noted that definitions changed in the course of time: the figures for 1953 and 1961 relate to the percentages of Asian-Africans among all foreign-born Jews, while those of 1983 refer to the percentages of the Asian-African origin group of ascertained origin abroad (i.e., the foreign-born and the Israeli-born of foreign paternity, to the exclusion of the Israeli-born of Israeli paternity).[29] The figures for the same geographical unit in the three years indicated are therefore not exactly comparable, but the essential features of geographical variation in each year are documented and can be safely compared.

In the whole of Israel the proportion of Asian-Africans increased markedly during the 30 years covered by table 14 (cf. tables 5–7). Comparatively elevated levels of Asian-African representation in all the three years reported are found in the Southern district, in the Kinneret, and, as from 1961, also in the Zefat subdistricts on the outskirts of the Northern district, as well as in Ramla subdistrict. Medium levels have prevailed in most of the Central district, in some parts of the Northern district, and more recently also in the Jerusalem district. Regarding the last, since the Six Day War, the state capital has absorbed relatively more new immigrants from Europe and America than has the country as a whole. Low representation of Asian-Africans has been characteristic for the (sub)districts comprising the cities of Tel Aviv-Yafo and especially Haifa, as well as for the Golan and the administered areas. As a consequence, in comparison to all European-Americans in Israel, a higher percentage of all Asian-African Jews live in the Southern district, but also in the Northern, Central, and Jerusalem districts. On the other hand, the Tel Aviv and Haifa districts—in the case of the latter the Haifa subdistrict in particular—account for larger shares of the country's European-Americans.

If a distinction is made between Jews of Asian and African origin—who form groups of almost equal size in Israel as a whole—the more central location of the former and the more peripheral of the latter becomes evident. Table 15 shows this for 1983. The largest proportions—around 30 percent—of Asians among all Jews were found in the bloc formed by the

---

[28] See Benjamin Z. Gil, *Settlement of New Immigrants in Israel 1948–1953*, Preliminary Report, Falk Project for Economic Research and Central Bureau of Statistics, 1957.

[29] The Israeli origin group, whose ultimate provenance abroad is unrecorded, has been excluded from the determination of origin composition in all the statistical tables and from the analysis of residential distribution of the different origin groups. However, the data on residential distribution of the total Jewish population in tables 17 and 19–21 include the Israeli origin group.

Jerusalem, Central, and Tel Aviv districts, which together comprise the majority of Israel's Jewish population. In contrast, the largest proportions of African Jews—around 50 percent—were located in the Zefat and Kinneret subdistricts to the North as well as in the Southern district.

The continental origin figures so far reported constitute weighted averages of the actual distributions of Jews from different countries. In many instances the country-of-origin distributions conform in essential features to what has been stated above regarding continents of origin, but there are exceptions. Thus, relatively large representations of Jews from the following countries are found in subdistricts that are not typical of their continent of origin: Iraq—Kinneret; Tunisia and Algeria—Ramla, Zefat; Libya—Sharon, Hadera. Table 16 highlights these points, indicating for each principal country of origin (or group of less frequent countries, cf. table 8) the three subdistricts with the highest concentrations of Jews from particular countries. For comparison, the percentage of Jews in all Israel from each of these countries is also indicated. As can be seen from table 16, the ratio between the country's highest percentage in a subdistrict and its percentage in Israel as a whole can vary considerably. Thus, the picture of the actual origin mosaic prevailing in Israel is more complex than the continental data alone indicate. Of course, if a country of origin is relatively overrepresented in some subdistricts, it must be underrepresented in others.

The recent dispersion of the two major origin groups is shown in greater territorial detail in table 17, where Israel as of 1983 is divided into 45 "natural regions."[30] In 26 of them the proportions of the Asian-African and European-American origin groups ranged between 35 and 65 percent of all Jews, i.e., the origin groups were roughly balanced.[31] These regions accounted for the great majority (82 percent) of all Jews in Israel. In 10 regions, which comprised somewhat more than half (54 percent) of the country's Jews, the origin groups were more closely balanced: 45–55 percent of Asian-African origin, at a time when this proportion amounted to 52 percent in the country as a whole. The 5 regions with less than 35 percent of Asian-Africans were constituted all of kibbutz concentrations in the Northern district and together accounted for only half of 1 percent of Israel's total Jews. The 14 natural regions with a considerable majority of Asian-African Jews (above 65 percent) formed two main nuclei, in the Southern and Northern districts, respectively; the former accounted for

---

[30]The natural regions constitute a subdivision, for statistical purposes, of the administrative districts and subdistricts. They are geographically, socioeconomically, and demographically more homogeneous than the subdistricts, but are of very unequal population size. For a recent locality list by natural regions, see 1983 census, vol. 6.

[31]In table 17 and the others of this type (19–25), if the proportion of Asian-Africans in an area ranges between 35 and 65 percent, the proportion of European-Americans must range inversely between 65 and 35 percent.

more than half of that category's Jewish population. In two regions in the south, the Jewish population was more than 80 percent of Asian-African origin. The differences between the natural regions in location and composition of the population according to Jews and Arabs, as well as in origin proportions of the Jews, are associated with other sociodemographic and socioeconomic differentials.[32]

Most of Israel's Jewish population lives in urban localities (table 18), which have here been uniformly defined as having a population exceeding 2,000.[33] The respective percentages were 87 and 90 in the censuses of 1961 and 1983. Hence the proportions of Asian-African origin among urban Jews (43 and 53 percent in these two censuses) came quite close to those among total Jews in the same years in Israel (43 and 52 percent). There is a good deal of difference in this respect between the three main cities, however. Jerusalem has the highest percentage of Asian-Africans, though this did not grow between 1961 and 1983 and closely corresponded in the latter year to the country average.[34] Tel Aviv-Yafo is in an intermediate position, but clearly below the country average, while Haifa has a particularly strong majority of European-Americans. All the other urban localities considered together somewhat exceed the average proportion of Asian-Africans in Israel as a whole.

In 1983, unlike 1961, total rural localities had a lower proportion of Asian-Africans than total urban localities. The change was due primarily to a decline of this proportion in the "other rural localities," which are neither kibbutzim nor moshavim and comprise many of the recently established settlements. Kibbutzim have particularly low shares of Asian-African Jews in their populations. The opposite is true of moshavim as a whole, due to those originally set up as "new immigrant moshavim." The latter differ in many respects from the long-established moshavim that preceded the creation of the state and whose origin composition is more similar to that of the kibbutzim. As a consequence, while the overall division of both major origin groups into residents of urban and rural localities comes quite close, Asian-Africans comprise notably greater shares living in "other towns" (i.e., outside the three main cities) and in moshavim, while European-Americans are relatively more represented in Tel Aviv-Yafo, Haifa, and the kibbutzim.

Table 19 analyzes the Jewish localities with more than approximately

---

[32]See Gabriel Lipshitz, "Inter-regional Inequality in Israel" (in Hebrew; Ph.D. thesis, Hebrew University, Jerusalem, 1982); 1961 census, vol. 42; 1983 census, vol. 5.

[33]At the time of the 1961 census, some Jewish localities above 2,000 were still considered as rural ("large villages"). They have here been reclassified according to the practice now current in the official statistics.

[34]The explanation was already given above, in the passage on subdistricts.

10,000 inhabitants[35] according to the percentages of Asian-Africans in 1961 and 1983. However, definitions of the available data differ. The 1961 figures relate to immigrants from Asia-Africa among foreign-born Jews,[36] whereas those of 1983 relate to the major origin groups. The number of localities with a population above 10,000 grew between the censuses of 1961 and 1983. In both censuses about half of these localities had a roughly balanced composition of Jews according to provenance from abroad, but the distribution of the aggregate populations changed drastically. In 1961 more than half of this population still lived in localities with a strong majority of European-Americans. By 1983, in contrast, almost three-quarters resided in localities with a roughly balanced origin distribution. In 1961 most of the prestate ("old") Jewish towns had strong local majorities of European-Americans, while most of the towns settled after 1948 ("new")[37] comprised more than 55 percent Asian-Africans. It may be added that this difference was associated with lower locality sizes in the second category.

The 1983 data in table 19 underscore this point more clearly. The three main cities had the following percentages of Asian-African origin in their Jewish populations: Jerusalem—53, Tel Aviv-Yafo—41, Haifa—28 (see table 18).[38] The great majority of Jews in the other cities above 50,000 inhabitants (all of which fell much short of the 200,000 mark) lived in rough origin balance. In the localities numbering between 20,000 and fewer than 50,000 inhabitants, only a small majority of the population lived in rough origin balance, and the proportions of those residing in marked concentrations of either the European-American or the Asian-African origin group were of similar size. However, in the localities of 10,000 to nearly 20,000 (table 19) and 2,000 to nearly 10,000 inhabitants (see "semi-urban" in table 21), the situation was quite different. In these size categories—comprising most of the "development towns"[39]—the great majority of Jews lived in

---

[35]Actually, the cities and towns that were divided into statistical areas, see below.

[36]More precisely, the percentages of immigrants from main birth countries in Asia and Africa among all Jews from main birth countries abroad (i.e., excluding those from minor birth countries). In the full enumeration of the 1961 census only main birth countries abroad were specified and can be grouped according to continent, and only such data were published for individual localities. In the 20-percent sample enumeration of 1961, all countries were specified, and such data are available for larger geographical aggregates (see tables 14 and 18; and cf. 1961 census, vol. 25).

[37]Several towns that were established before 1948 but whose populations received relatively very large additions of immigrants in the first years of the state were classified in the "new" category in the 1961 statistics.

[38]In 1983 the three main cities had the following numbers of Jews (total population in parentheses) according to the census: Jerusalem—306,300 (428,700); Tel Aviv-Yafo—317,800 (327,300); Haifa—208,400 (225,800).

[39]No agreed-upon list of development towns exists, although economic advantages are variously bestowed by government agencies under this title. The small urban localities estab-

localities with a strong preponderance of Asian-Africans. Of the 22 Jewish localities above 2,000 population that comprised at least 65 percent Jews of Asian-African origin in 1983, 20 had fewer than 20,000 inhabitants.

Two main patterns with regard to residential distribution emerge from the above analysis. As is the case for total Jews in the country, an approximate balance of the major origin groups is found in the 1983 census data for most subdistricts, and also among the great majority of the Jewish population according to natural regions, types of localities, and towns above 20,000 inhabitants. At the same time there do exist marked instances of origin differentiation. Strong concentrations of European-Americans persist in Haifa and the prestate rural localities; they are also found in the later established kibbutzim and in the Golan and the administered areas. On the other hand, heavy concentrations of Asian-Africans are found particularly in the Southern district and outlying parts of the Northern district, in those rural localities that used to be called "new immigrant moshavim," as well as in most development towns with populations ranging from 2,000 to fewer than 20,000 inhabitants.

Small Area Statistics

Since the 1961 census, Israeli towns of more than 10,000 inhabitants have been divided into "statistical areas" for purposes of data analysis (tables 20–21).[40] This circumstance makes it possible to present in table 21 statistics on origin composition of the Jewish population as of 1983 in the smallest

---

lished in the period of statehood, many of them in outlying places and with high proportions of Asian-African Jews, are generally described by this name.

[40]Some of the studies utilizing the division into urban statistical areas for research purposes are the following: Yehuda Gradus, "The Spatial Urban Ecology of Metropolitan Haifa, Israel—A Factorial Approach" (Ph.D. thesis, University of Pittsburgh, 1971); Vivian Z. Klaff, "Ethnic Segregation in Urban Israel," *Demography*, vol. 10, no. 2, 1973, pp. 161–184; Leah Shanan, "The Social Ecology of Jerusalem 1961" (in Hebrew; M.A. thesis, the Technion, Haifa, 1975); Sara Hershkovitz, "The Spatial Structure of the Population of Tel Aviv Metropolitan Area 1961–1972" (in Hebrew; Ph.D. thesis, Hebrew University, Jerusalem, 1979); E. Borukhov, Y. Ginsberg, and E. Werczberger, "The Social Ecology of Tel Aviv: A Study in Factor Analysis," *Urban Affairs Quarterly*, vol. 15, no. 2, 1979, pp. 183–205; Amiram Gonen, "A Basic Pattern in the Social Geography of Israeli Cities," in U.O. Schmelz, P. Glikson, and S. DellaPergola, eds., *Papers in Jewish Demography 1977* (Jerusalem, 1980), pp. 351–366; U.O. Schmelz, "Aging Areas in Jerusalem: Geography and Characteristics" (in Hebrew), *Gerontologia*, no. 9, 1977, pp. 22–33; Amiram Gonen, "The Changing Ethnic Geography of Israeli Cities," in Alex Weingrod, ed., *Studies in Israeli Ethnicity*, 1985, pp. 25–37; Amiram Gonen and Michael Sonis, "Dynamic Spatial Patterns of Age Structure in Metropolitan Tel Aviv," in U.O. Schmelz and G. Nathan, eds., *Studies in the Population of Israel in Honor of Roberto Bachi*, Scripta Hierosolymitana, vol. 30 (Jerusalem, 1986), pp. 362–380; Arie Shahar, "Urban Ecology of the Israeli Metropolitan Areas," in Schmelz and Nathan, *Studies in the Population of Israel*, ibid., pp. 381–414.

geographical units for which such information is available from the census files as processed—statistical areas within cities and towns that have been thus divided,[41] and smaller localities in their entirety.[42] It should be understood, however, that considerable variation according to actual population size exists in each of these two categories and between them. The average number of inhabitants per urban statistical area has exceeded 3,000, while it has amounted to only a few hundred per locality below 10,000 population. In 1983 the urban statistical areas comprised 86 percent of Israel's total Jewish population. As in the case of the larger urban localities (table 19 above), the population of the statistical areas was divided into Asian-Africans and European-Americans according to the foreign-born alone in 1961,[43] but according to major origin groups in 1983. More detailed information on the Jewish population in urban statistical areas, cross-classified with additional characteristics, is presented in tables 22–25.

The number of statistical areas in the Jewish cities and towns of Israel grew by about two and a half times from 1961 to 1983, due both to the increase in the number of localities concerned and the expansion of their populations. As was shown above for these towns when each was considered in its entirety (table 19), a shift toward a more balanced origin composition is evident from 1961 to 1983 if they are disaggregated into a considerable number of statistical areas. This is chiefly due to a reduction in the relative frequency and population share of statistical areas with a high representation of European-Americans, as against strongly increased instances of more limited differences between the origin groups in the statistical areas. This basic finding is abundantly clear from the data, beyond any possible influence of the disparate definitions (bigenerational origin groups versus foreign-born) between the two censuses.

The data in tables 20–21 also show that in the three main cities larger proportions of the Jewish population resided in statistical areas comprising relatively few Asian-Africans than was the case in other towns above 10,000 population. This was due to the influence of Haifa and Tel Aviv-Yafo

---

[41]The division into statistical areas is made prior to a census, before its results are known. This explains why in 1961 three towns somewhat above 10,000 inhabitants failed to be divided. Nor are they included in our table 19. In 1983, on the other hand, three towns, each of which turned out to comprise a population somewhat below 10,000, were divided. In tables 19 and 21 they and their statistical areas have been included in the "10,000–19,999" category and excluded from the "semi-urban" category.

[42]The results were obtained from tabulations specially undertaken for this article. The tabulations for 1961 were effected from data of the full enumeration, those of 1983 from the 20-percent sample that formed part of the census. Statistical areas below 20 Jews in 1961 as well as localities and statistical areas below 100 Jews in 1983 were excluded from the data presented here.

[43]See note 36 for specification.

among the main cities. Yet the trend toward a more balanced origin distribution is quite clear in both these urban categories of main cities and other towns. The relative frequency of areas where the Asian-Africans and European-Americans each accounted for 35–65 percent increased; so did the corresponding proportions of the aggregate populations of the areas. The proportion of Jewish population living in roughly origin-balanced statistical areas rose as follows from 1961 to 1983: main cities—17 to 37 percent; other towns—35 to 47 percent. This change was mainly effected by a strong reduction in the proportion of urban population dwelling in areas predominantly inhabited by European-Americans, while the population share of preponderantly Asian-African areas increased somewhat.

Table 21 also shows analogous data for smaller localities in 1983. The proportions of localities and of their aggregate populations characterized by a high concentration of Asian-Africans were particularly great in the semi-urban category (2,000–9,999 inhabitants). Within the rural sector (below 2,000 inhabitants), this proportion decreased from the total of moshavim to "other rural localities" and was insignificant in kibbutzim, most of which had an overwhelmingly European-American population. Close parallelism of these differentials was found between the distribution of the smaller localities themselves and the distribution of their aggregated populations (in the upper and lower parts, respectively, of table 21) according to the proportion of Asian-Africans in each locality. Moreover, these observations fit the findings for the entire population of these locality types (table 18 above). Studied at the local level, 85 percent of the smaller localities and 80 percent of their aggregate populations were markedly origin-segregated. Half of the smaller localities in question[44] had a clear majority of European-Americans, under the influence of the kibbutzim as well as of parts of the long-established moshavim and "other rural localities." Most semi-urban localities on the other hand, being development towns, had a strong majority of Asian-Africans. Since the semi-urban localities have by definition more inhabitants than the rural localities, the population distribution of all the smaller localities together turned out symmetrical—40 percent each with a clear majority of either European-Americans or Asian-Africans, and a minority of only 20 percent with a roughly balanced origin composition.

A differently symmetrical distribution by origin composition in the respective residential areas (urban statistical areas or small localities) was found for Israel's entire Jewish population as of 1983: 42 percent in the roughly balanced central categories and 27–31 percent each with a predominance of one of the two major origin groups.

From the 1961 census, only loosely comparable data are available for

---

[44]Excluding localities with less than 100 Jews; see note 42 above.

smaller localities. They relate to the percentages of Asian-African-born who immigrated since 1948 among all foreign-born Jews.[45] Here again, there were high concentrations of Asian-Africans in the semi-urban category, in moshavim, but then also in "other rural localities," whereas the kibbutzim were chiefly populated by European-Americans. Nor is the resultant parallelism with the solid data of 1983 surprising. It was noted above that most smaller Jewish localities in Israel were already set up prior to 1961, and that once such a locality was established, the origin composition of its population was more likely to persist than in the expansive and dynamic urban sector.

Attention will now be given to the distribution of each of the two major origin groups separately across the urban statistical areas in 1983, by extent of residential (de)segregation[46] and according to explanatory characteristics. Retrospective variables will render it possible to examine trends. The extent of segregation will be measured by the percent of Asian-Africans living in an area (as was done in tables 17 and 19–21).[47] Distinguishing the three main cities from other towns is important because the former contain significant concentrations of European-Americans. Under the prevailing conditions of upward social mobility, residential convergence of the major origin groups can be achieved in two ways: by moves of Asian-Africans into predominantly European-American areas whose origin composition is thus changed in the process, entailing the taxonomic shift of the areas into the "roughly balanced" category; or when members of both origin groups move into a newly populated area in proportions that ensure approximate balance between them.[48]

Table 22 examines the effects of period of entry of households[49] into the dwellings they occupied in 1983. It is seen that the later the entry the greater is the proportion living in a roughly balanced origin composition. In all statistical areas together, these proportions rose between the years prior to 1964 and 1974–1983 from 30 to 46 percent for Asian-Africans and from 39 to 52 percent for European-Americans. Essentially the same trend manifested itself in the three main cities as well as in the other towns that were divided into statistical areas. Of the Asian-African Jews in both types of towns, the proportions living in preponderantly Asian-African areas de-

---

[45]More precisely, immigrants since 1948 from the main birth countries of Jews in Asia-Africa per 100 foreign-born Jews (including those from minor birth countries). See 1961 census, vol. 28.

[46]See note 24.

[47]Excluding the Israeli origin group; see note 29.

[48]Those moving in may have departed from other areas of the same municipal or metropolitan territory, from elsewhere in Israel, or can be new immigrants from abroad taking up residence in Israel for the first time.

[49]According to year of entry of household head into the apartment.

clined, while those in roughly balanced areas increased. On the other hand, growing proportions of European-American Jews tended to move into areas that were classified as origin-mixed in 1983. There was thus a convergence of both origin groups. Table 22 also shows greater, though decreasing, residential segregation of European-Americans in the main cities than in other towns; in contrast, there was greater, albeit declining, segregation of Asian-Africans in the towns outside the three main cities.

The trend toward increasing residence in origin-balanced statistical areas appears even more saliently when the Asian-Africans and European-Americans are divided according to whether they inhabited old or new neighborhoods in 1983 (table 23). "New neighborhoods" are defined as those statistical areas where, at the time of the 1983 census, at least half of the Jewish population was living in dwellings constructed recently (1975–1983), while the other statistical areas are classified as "old neighborhoods." Altogether the proportions living in roughly origin-balanced statistical areas (35 and 65 percent of Asian-African and of European-American Jews, respectively) were greater in the new than the old neighborhoods, as follows: Asian-African origin—60 as compared to 39 percent; European-American origin—64 as against 44 percent. Very considerable convergence thus took place in this respect too.

Among Asian-Africans, the relative increase of those inhabiting roughly origin-balanced neighborhoods was effected outside the main cities through a great decline of those living in high concentrations of their own origin group, while in the three main cities it was due to some proportional shift away from old areas with strongly European-American populations to more balanced new areas. Among European-Americans, the change was rendered possible by a marked reduction of the proportion residing in high concentrations of their own origin group in the three main cities, but elsewhere by moderate diminution of the proportions resident in areas that were either strongly European-American or Asian-African.

Table 23 makes it clear that the greater origin balance in new areas is not the result of extended and gradual penetration by one origin group into areas where the other origin group was previously preponderant. Since new areas exclusively are considered, it must mainly be due to more or less synchronous and quantitatively balanced moves by members of both origin groups into the same areas. This is evidence of an actual convergence pattern. In fact, everyday experience shows a tendency for younger people of both origin groups—especially couples that have recently married or are raising children—to move from centrally located and residentially unattractive urban areas to housing projects and villas nearer the municipal outskirts. These new residential neighborhoods tend to be origin-mixed.

The trend toward more balanced origin composition in the urban sector was shown above for entire towns (table 19) as well as through the respective changes that occurred in the statistical areas from 1961 to 1983 (tables 20–21). It has now been confirmed by comparison of longtime residents with more recent entrants into apartments and of residents of older neighborhoods with those of newly established ones (tables 22–23).

If the residential distribution of the urban Jewish population aged 15 and above is examined according to origin group and educational attainment in 1983 (table 24), it is found that with rising education the proportions of people living in statistical areas of Asian-African predominance decreased, while the proportions inhabiting preponderantly European-American areas increased. This holds good for both origin groups. It should be noted, though, that persons with less than nine years of schooling are now a restricted and dwindling minority among European-American Jews. At the higher educational levels, Jews of Asian-African origin tended to live to an increasing extent in chiefly European-American areas of the three main cities, and in similar but more often in roughly origin-balanced areas of the other towns. There was no marked difference between European-Americans with 9–12 years of schooling and those with 13+ years, in their distribution in residential areas in the three main cities. The majority resided in areas predominantly populated by their own origin group. In the other towns, the majority of European-Americans lived in approximately origin-balanced areas, while the proportion residing in chiefly European-American areas rose with education.

What appears to be the basic residential pattern as education rises— relatively more Asian-Africans in European-American settings but fewer European-Americans amid Asian-African Jews—corresponds to the finding that emerges (see next section) concerning marriage between the major origin groups in Israel. The propensity toward origin-specific outmarriage is positively associated with educational attainment among Asian-African Jews but negatively among the European-American Jews. It is possible that some sort of causal connection exists between the two phenomena.

Based on the results of the 1983 census, a socioeconomic score was computed by the Central Bureau of Statistics for each urban statistical area through factor analysis.[50] The score rises with socioeconomic level. Values below the country average are expressed by negative figures. Birth region and origin group were not included among the restricted number of census variables selected for the final stage of the factor analysis because preliminary screenings showed them to be highly correlated with other variables that had a stronger direct influence on the socioeconomic profile of the statistical areas.

---

[50]See 1983 census, vol. 15. No score was computed for statistical areas with a population smaller than 1,000 and/or with less than 50 percent living in private households.

The relationships between four characteristics are examined here: two for individuals (origin group and educational attainment) and two for the population in the statistical area of residence (origin composition of Jews and socioeconomic score). For brevity, table 25 presents only the average scores of groups of persons defined by combinations of the other three characteristics mentioned. The average scores declined rather regularly as the percentage of Asian-Africans increased in the statistical areas.[51] This applied to persons of each origin group and educational attainment. At each percentage frequency of Asian-African origin in the statistical areas, the average scores rose moderately according to education among persons of each origin. However, at the same educational level there was little difference between the average scores of Asian-Africans and European-Americans in the various columns of table 25. This was particularly evident at the highest educational level indicated: 13+ years of study. There are thus two principal findings: the origin composition of the residential areas was strongly associated with their socioeconomic profiles as epitomized by the scores; and persons who lived in areas with approximately the same origin composition shared on the average a similar socioeconomic profile, rather irrespective of their personal origin.

We have seen that residential interpenetration of origin groups increases in new urban neighborhoods and also with higher education levels. Since new neighborhoods are continually being created or expanded, and the educational level is rising in both origin groups—both trends affecting the younger generation in particular—the expectation is that residential intermingling will intensify.

INTERETHNIC MARRIAGE

Marriages between spouses belonging to different origin groups are a prime mechanism for the gradual integration of Israel's Jewish population and are thus of profound social importance. This section will trace the evolution of interethnic marriage among the Jewish population of Israel, point to the marked increase of the phenomenon, and consider the determinants and patterns of this trend, especially in relation to educational attainment of spouses.[52]

---

[51] Weighted for population size of the areas. The strongly negative correlation factor between these variables amounted countrywide to -.72.

[52] Studies relating to interethnic marriage among Israeli Jews include the following: Zvi Eisenbach, "Marriage and Fertility in the Process of Integration: Intermarriage Among Immigrant Groups in Israel," paper presented to IUSSP Conference, New Delhi, 1989; Judah Matras, *Families in Israel*, part 2, Israel Central Bureau of Statistics, vol. 39 of 1961 census publication series, 1968; Judah Matras and Kelvin Selbee, "On Marriage, Social Stratification

Since Israel's Jewish population is very mixed according to geographical origin and also of rather recent formation, it is to be expected that many people have social affinities with those who share the same origin background. This tendency is intensified by the fact that persons of the same geographical origin often belong to common networks of relatives or acquaintances in Israel.

Mate selection and matchmaking are complicated processes, especially in the modern world. With regard to the situation in Israel the following needs to be kept in mind:

a. In terms of statistical probabilities, the larger a group, the greater is the chance that its members will contract their marriages homogamously within the group.

b. Empirical experience confirms the commonsense assumption that marriages outside any origin group become more frequent the longer the group has, on average, been in Israel. Duration of residence and proportion of Israeli-born in an origin group are positively connected with opportunities for social contacts with members of other origin groups. Contrariwise, if an origin group is reinforced by a relatively large influx of new immigrants, the prospects of new marriages being formed within the group are enhanced.

c. It is usual for grooms to be a few years older than brides. Thus, what matters regarding prospects of matchmaking is not the numerical balance of the sexes at the same ages, but at several years of age apart. In a situation of sex imbalance between somewhat older men and somewhat younger women in the principal age range of first marriage, one speaks of a "squeeze" for the sex that has a surplus so that its members encounter difficulties in finding mates. Such squeezes can be wholly or partly counteracted by changes in the mean age difference at first marriage between the sexes and, in case of groups within a population, by marriage with a partner outside the specific group.

Marriage squeezes have occurred in Israel in both major origin groups. Asian-Africans experienced high fertility abroad and for a time in Israel; hence each successive birth cohort was larger than its predecessor. This made for surpluses of would-be brides over grooms, especially when young men born abroad prior to the period of mass immigration confronted young women already born in Israel soon after that immigration. Not only was the fertility of the Asian-African group in Israel high, but the sudden reduction of child mortality among the immigrants resulted in greater survival of the newborn than had been the case abroad.

---

and Mobility in Israel," in U.O. Schmelz, P. Glikson, and S. DellaPergola, eds., *Papers in Jewish Demography 1977* (Jerusalem, 1980), pp. 283–300; U.O. Schmelz, "Marriages of Jews of Different Origin and Different Duration of Stay in Israel (Report)," in 6th Ford Foundation Project in Israel, Israel Foundation Trustees, Tel Aviv, 1974, pp. 1342–1345.

The situation among European-Americans has been more complicated and unstable. A surplus of somewhat older men prevailed as long as the members of both sexes belonged to the decreasing cohorts resulting from the fertility slump of the 1930s and early 1940s. When the large cohorts of women born in the "baby boom" after World War II faced the small cohorts of men born during or just before the war, European-American women underwent an intensive squeeze. Both of these stages were exacerbated by the effects of the Holocaust on the birth and survival of young children among post-World War II immigrants from Europe to Israel. Subsequently the situation was reversed once again, though less drastically, as smaller cohorts of women born after the "baby boom" faced larger cohorts of men still born during that phase of enhanced natality. A similar constellation continued for some time afterward, because of further decreasing birth cohorts.

The following simple presentation illustrates the occurrence and intensity of successive demographic squeezes at prime marriageable ages in the two major origin groups (excluding the Israeli-born of Israeli paternity):

| Year | Men per 100 Women at the Age Interval Indicated ||||||
| | Men Aged 30–34 Women Aged 25–29 || Men Aged 25–29, Women Aged 20–24 || Men Aged 20–24, Women Aged 15–19 ||
	Asian-African Origin	European-American Origin	Asian-African Origin	European-American Origin	Asian-African Origin	European-American Origin
1961	86	103	99	103	91	76
1972	83	61	73	72	86	132
1983	89	119	104	123	104	122

d. Interethnic marriage can be both a result of, and a mechanism for, social mobility. In Israel the European-American origin group has so far enjoyed a more favorable socioeconomic position. Hence, individuals of Asian-African origin, of either sex, who have advanced educationally, tend more than others of their group to marry European-American partners.

e. For simplicity of exposition, the frequencies and determinants of interethnic marriage among the Jews of Israel are presented for the country as a whole. In actuality, matters are far more complicated. Though Israel is a comparatively small country, there is no nationwide "marriage-market"; contacts leading to marriage often occur in one's own locality or neighborhood or in nongeographical frameworks, such as the army.

f. We can only mention here that the social networks and mechanisms through which potential marriage partners become acquainted and the decision is made to marry vary according to origin group and have undergone rapid change in Israel during recent decades.

"Interethnic marriage," "origin-specific heterogamy," and "outmarriage" of Jews in Israel all have the same meaning. For conciseness of expression the term outmarriage will usually be used here.

Attention will be given to the proportions outmarrying, according to origin, among Jewish couples and individual spouses. Methodologically, this is unlike the situation customary in the demographic study of Diaspora Jews. In the case of the latter, the "individual rate" of the outmarrying per 100 Jewish spouses is compared to a "couple rate" indicating the proportion outmarrying among all the couples with 1–2 Jewish spouses. In the tables in this article, the "couple rate" indicates the proportion contracting interethnic marriages among all Jewish couples that married in Israel during a given period. This couple rate must be smaller than the previously mentioned one. In terms of Diaspora Jewish demography, the rate used here concerning Israel would correspond to the proportion of couples with outmarrying Jewish spouses among all couples marrying in the entire population of a Diaspora country (including the wholly non-Jewish couples). Appended is a numerical illustration; the total in the last row is the weighted average of the origin groups.

In addition, indexes of ingroup marital attraction will be employed that take into account the size of the various origin groups among Jews who

Type of Data	Percent of Jews Outmarrying in Israel by Origin (Major Groups), 1974–1983		
	Total	Asia-Africa	Europe-America
Outmarrying per 100:			
Spouses of origin group			
Total	21.0	17.6	26.1
Husbands	21.0	16.0	28.1
Wives	21.0	19.1	24.0
Total Jewish couples	21.0	21.0	21.0
Couples with 1–2 spouses of origin group	(34.7)	29.9	41.4

married at given times in Israel and the consequent statistical probabilities of origin-specific inmarriage.[53]

All the data relate to Jewish couples in first marriages, and consisting of a household head and his wife (these form the overwhelming majority of existing couples). The data were collected in the censuses of 1961 and 1983; they are retrospective, specifying period of marriage.[54]

Major Origin Groups

The official statistics of Israel, as we have seen, make it possible to distinguish between those of Asian-African, European-American, and Israeli origin. The first two groups comprise the respective foreign-born together with the Israeli-born whose fathers were born in the same continent abroad. The Israeli origin group consists of the Israeli-born of Israeli paternity.

The Israeli origin group has so far accounted for no more than a small minority of Jewish spouses of either sex marrying in Israel. Moreover, the available statistics do not provide information about ultimate origin abroad. For these reasons, and because of the greater ease of dealing with two rather than three origin groups of the two spouses in couples—that is, with two rather than six possible outmarriage combinations—the data presented here will be only for those couples whose spouses are of overtly Asian-African or European-American origin. Excluded are couples with 1-2 spouses classified in the statistics as being of Israeli origin. The percentage of total Jewish marriages contracted in Israel that is lost is small. Still, it should be borne in mind that this approach leads to some underrepresentation of the levels of origin-specific outmarriage among Israel's Jews. A section below

---

[53]This is the attraction index of Benini, which ranges between .000 in the absence of attraction and 1.000 if attraction is maximal (there is also a repulsion index, with negative values down to -1.000). Applied to marriage, the maximum value means complete inmarriage, while the lower the positive index, the greater is the relative extent of outmarriage. The index is represented by the formula $(a-e)/(m-e)$; "a" denotes the actual number of homogamous marriages in a given group, "e" their expected number according to statistical probability alone, and "m" whichever of the total numbers of grooms and brides of the group is the smaller (this is the upper limit of homogamous unions possible among the given spouses of the group). If there are only two categories, such as the major origin groups of Jews in Israel, the index assumes an equal value for both (in tables 26, 27, and 32, contrasted with table 30).

[54]Coming from censuses, the data relate to "surviving" couples, i.e., the original number minus those that were severed by death or divorce or where the couple emigrated. Nevertheless, table 27 shows good agreement between corresponding cohorts of the 1961 and 1983 censuses. Corresponding data exist from yearly statistics of new marriages, but they contain neither the breakdown of Israeli-born grooms and brides by father's country of birth (as distinct from only the birth continent of the father) nor any information on the educational level of the spouses.

will substantiate this statement and provide further information on the matter.

When the two main origin groups being considered are viewed overall by means of the attraction index, it can be seen that outmarriage decreased in the transition from Mandatory times to the period of great immigration during early statehood, but has been increasing substantially ever since (tables 26–27). The index of marital attraction rose at first but then fell from .854 for marriages contracted in the years 1949–1953 to .560 in 1979–1983 and only .490 by 1987.[55] As noted above, this is related to the fact that the mass influx of immigrants tended very strongly at first to marry within their own groups. In the course of time, the proportions outmarrying have grown substantially due to the operation of several factors: mutual acquaintance and adjustment; the rise in the proportion of Israeli-born at marriageable ages within each origin group; upward social mobility of persons of Asian-African origin; and demographic squeezes, especially in the European-American origin group.

When each origin group is examined separately, one finds a marked reduction in outmarriage among Asian-Africans in the first years of the state, when large immigration waves flooded the small previous population of that origin, a part of which had educationally and socially acculturated to European models during the Mandatory period. A rise in outmarriage by Asian-Africans in Israel took place in the 1960s, coinciding with the end of large-scale immigration from those continents, and has been followed by rather stable proportions outmarrying, especially among men. In the European-American origin group a gradual increase in outmarriage for both sexes has occurred since Mandatory times, when its level was very low. The proportion outmarrying in Israel has been greater in the European-American than in the Asian-African origin group: among husbands since the mid-1950s, among wives since the mid-1960s. The relative difference in this respect has increased in the course of time, until around 1980 the proportion outmarrying among European-American men was twice that among Asian-African men. On the whole, the percentages outmarrying have been somewhat greater for women than men in the Asian-African group, while the opposite ranking of outmarriage proportions—men exceeding women—has prevailed in the European-American group, except toward the end of the 1960s. According to the census data presented, as many as 32 percent of the men and 27 percent of the women in the European-American group married a spouse of other origin around 1980; the corresponding percentages for the Asian-African group were 16 and 20, respectively.

These disparities in the evolution of mate selection by origin group and

---

[55]Computed from yearly marriage statistics and including remarriages.

sex are better understood when viewed against the demographic background (table 29). Asians and Africans were but a small minority among the Jews of Palestine in general, and the Jewish newlyweds in particular, during the late Mandatory period. Their proportion increased dramatically under the impact of mass immigration, reached the 50-percent mark of new spouses before the end of the 1950s, and somewhat exceeded 60 percent around 1980.[56] Thus, the Asian-African origin group has been a majority of all newly married Jews in Israel for the last 30 years. Consequently, any given absolute number of marriages between the two origin groups must involve a greater proportion of total European-American spouses than of total Asian-African spouses. Besides, until the 1970s, European-Americans comprised a larger proportion of the Israeli-born among marrying individuals. The Israeli-born, being best adjusted to the origin-mixed Jewish society of Israel, are shown by the data to have usually been more amenable to origin-specific outmarriage than the foreign-born. Moreover, the European-American group has had on the whole a surplus of men over women among marrying individuals, while the opposite sex ratio has prevailed among the Asian-African newlyweds.

These origin-specific sex differentials can be understood in terms of what has been stated above regarding demographic marriage squeezes. When European-American women were most subjected to a squeeze toward the end of the 1960s, the numerous girls of early marriageable age who were born after the mid-1940s did not find sufficient partners among the relatively few men of their own origin group who had been born during World War II. As a result, the usual numerical relationships were temporarily reversed. Only in the late 1960s were more women than men married in the European-American group, but more men than women among Asian-Africans. Likewise, only in the late 1960s were the proportions marrying outside their origin group greater for women than men in the European-American group but smaller for women than men in the Asian-African group.

The proportion of Israeli-born among marrying spouses has risen strikingly since the early years of the state (table 29), in line with the general evolution of Israel's Jewish population. Around 1980 this proportion already reached two-thirds of newlyweds. Until the mid-1970s it was higher in the European-American than the Asian-African origin group, because of the predominantly European character of the *yishuv* in Mandatory times. Around 1980 the positions of the origin groups were reversed, due both to the great initial fertility of Asian-African immigrants and to the cessation

---

[56]The respective proportions of Asian-African origin in table 29 are somewhat higher than at prime marriageable ages of the Jewish population according to table 13, because the Israeli origin group which in its majority was ultimately assigned to the European-American group (see above) has here been omitted.

of large-scale immigration from these continents in the 1960s. As a rule, the Israeli-born were relatively more frequent among wives than husbands, with only a few exceptions in the European-American origin group (not shown in table 29). The usual situation is due to the fact that wives are on average younger than husbands, and in Israel's adult Jewish population the lower the age the greater the proportion of Israeli-born.

Within the Asian-African group, the percentages of persons contracting origin-specific outmarriages have been consistently greater for both sexes among the Israeli-born as compared to the foreign-born (table 28). The same has often also applied to both sexes of European-American spouses. Exceptions were found among men during 1954–1968. European-American men born in Israel or abroad were on a par regarding the proportion outmarrying in 1969–1973; the same applied to European-American women during 1964–1973. The last-mentioned fact was perhaps due to the great marriage squeeze among European-American women at that time. The low proportions outmarrying among the Israeli-born men of this origin group in the 1950s and most of the 1960s might be conjecturally attributed to a tendency toward social seclusion on the part of Israeli-born young adults at the time. On the whole, however, it would seem that the native-born have been readier to disregard spouse's origin in mate selection, the more so as deeper analysis shows that the Israeli-born largely marry Israeli-born spouses, whatever their origin.

Considering all Israeli-born and all foreign-born, the indexes of marital attraction have been as follows: according to the 1961 census—.218 until 1945, .451 in 1946–1955, and .543 in 1956–1961; according to the 1983 census—.414 in 1964–1973 and .364 in 1974–1983. These indexes have evolved in a similar manner to those of the two origin groups abroad, but at a lower level. There has been a greater propensity for marriage between Israeli-born and foreign-born, irrespective of origin, than between Asian-Africans and European-Americans irrespective of birthplace.

Countries of Origin

So far, interethnic marriages have been considered only according to the two major origin groups. Table 30 presents indexes of marital attraction for the principal countries of origin,[57] by period of marriage in Israel. Persons born in any given country have been combined into one group with the Israeli-born whose fathers were born in the same country; couples comprising 1–2 Israeli-born of Israeli paternity are again excluded from the analysis. Similarly to what was found on the continental level, inmarriage

---

[57]In some rows of tables 30–31 the data do not relate to individual countries but to wider geographical regions that are comparatively little represented among Israel's Jews.

increased for persons originating from some of the countries in the transition from the Mandatory period to the period of mass immigration during early statehood. This applied especially to countries in Asia, North Africa, and the Balkans, though not to most European countries. Since the period of the great influx of immigrants, the indexes of marital attraction have declined with regard to all countries. This conforms to the expectation that comparatively large immigrant contingents of different provenance would at first tend to keep together socially in a new country, but would gradually come closer to the preexisting population and to one another.

The indexes of marital attraction were on the whole higher for Jews from Asian and African countries than from the European countries. In the main this reflects the fact that the propensity for marriage between persons originating from different countries within the Asian-African aggregate has been smaller than within the European-American aggregate. The country groups from Asia-Africa which attained especially high indexes in the early period of statehood—Yemen, Iraq, Iran, as well as Morocco, Tunisia, and Algeria—were very distinct not only from European Jews, but also from one another. It is noteworthy, however, that of the country groups with initially high levels of inmarriage, only Jews from India,[58] Yemen and, to a lesser degree, Morocco continue to display comparatively elevated, though already considerably reduced, indexes of marital attraction. The rather recent rise of inmarriage among Jews originating from the Soviet Union has been connected with the wave of new migration from that country since the 1970s and corresponds to similar phenomena that occurred in other country groups at the time of mass immigration into the young State of Israel.[59]

The last two columns of table 30 show the percentages of outmarrying husbands and wives in Israel during the recent period 1974–1983, by country of origin. The countries with the lowest indexes of attraction attained the highest proportions of outmarrying persons. These proportions reached about 90 percent for some European countries from which immigration virtually stopped in the early years of Israel's existence, such as Czechoslovakia, Hungary, Germany, and Austria. Table 31, which also relates to 1974–1983, divides the outmarrying husbands and wives of the various countries of origin according to spouse's continent of origin.[60] A considerable majority of individuals of either sex from European countries found a spouse from another European-American country of origin. In contrast, outmarrying Asians of either sex chose their spouses in not very different

---

[58] Most of the Jews from India immigrated to Israel only as from the 1960s.
[59] The Soviet immigration was not all composed of European Jews, but included Jews of Asian communities such as Grusinians and Bokharians.
[60] Not accounting for size of the groups in Israel's Jewish population.

proportions from another Asian country, from Africa, or from Europe-America; the same pattern held for outmarrying African Jews. Intercountry attraction within Asia and Africa was comparatively limited.

Computed comprehensively for all the 22 principal countries (or regions) of origin that are listed in tables 30–31, the index of marital attraction in 1974–1983 was .316, and the proportion outmarrying as high as 64 percent. The results would have gone even beyond these figures with a more detailed breakdown of countries or if the Israeli origin group were included. Recent Jewish marriages in Israel have been preponderantly mixed, if investigated by countries of origin rather than only for the two large bicontinental origin groups. Within these origin groups, inmarriage according to country has been more persistent among Asia-Africans than European-Americans.

Import of Education

The educational level of each spouse is an important factor in the formation of marriages within or outside an origin group. Educational level has been measured in tables 32–36 by number of years of study according to the 1983 census.[61] It can also serve as a proxy for socioeconomic status in general.[62] Viewed comprehensively by means of an attraction index, there is a tendency in the two major origin groups and both sexes together for outmarriage to increase with rising education of husbands and wives (table 32). The general outmarriage tendency can be observed from its somewhat increased level in the late Mandatory period through its reduction during the period of great migration into Israel and into its gradual extension in recent decades.

However, if the tendency to outmarriage by educational attainment is examined separately for each of the two major origin groups and by sex, a more complex picture is revealed. Table 33 compares the educational distribution of inmarrying and outmarrying husbands and wives, by origin group and period of marriage in Israel. In the Asian-African group, the educational attainment of those outmarrying was considerably higher than that of the inmarrying, while the outmarrying European-Americans had a lower educational profile than the inmarrying of their group. These findings applied both to husbands and wives of each origin group, though to a lesser degree to European-American wives married before 1960. Moreover, the

---

[61]The years of study have been grouped into three major strata so as to avoid an excessive number of categories in the cross-classified data for husbands and wives together. These strata correspond to primary (and junior high) school, high school, and college or above. The lumped category "9+ years of study" is used here in order to account for the fact that husband's education often exceeds that of the wife.

[62]Census data on couples do not usually supply information on the family background of the spouses prior to marriage.

educational differences between the inmarrying and outmarrying of each origin group were considerable in most instances—across the general rise in educational levels at marriageable ages that is reflected in table 33. The educational differences between the origin groups were maximal for the inmarried.

In the past, outmarrying Asian-African husbands had received more education than their European-American counterparts, but recently the educational levels of outmarrying men of either origin group have become rather similar, while both are topped by the superior education of inmarrying European-American men. Outmarrying Asian-African women have generally studied fewer years than corresponding European-American women, whereas since the 1960s the latter's education has been markedly exceeded by that of inmarrying European-American women. Generally, since the 1960s, the sex differential in education for each of the groups, i.e., the inmarrying and outmarrying of each origin, has become smaller.

Table 34 shows the cross-classified education of husbands and wives together. The most frequent marriages were between spouses in the same category of years of schooling—with differences according to origin and whether inmarrying or not. Admittedly, the categories of years of study as used here are wide, but they do characterize low, medium, and advanced education. Within spouses' origin combinations, the frequent combinations by years of study rose on the educational scale in the course of time.

The proportion outmarrying was positively associated with rising education among persons of both sexes of Asian-African origin, but tended to be inversely related to educational attainment among both sexes of European-American origin (table 35). This again is observable in all periods of marriage, though the inverse relation of education and outmarriage among European-Americans of both sexes has become more marked in recent decades.[63]

Finally, table 36 shows that the proportion of outmarrying husbands in the Asian-African group rose not only with their own education but also, within each educational level, it corresponded to rising education of the wives. In contrast, the proportion outmarrying among European-American husbands varied not only inversely to their education at 9–12 and 13+ years of their own studies, but also tended to drop with increases in the wives' education. The highest, though gradually decreasing, rates of outmarriage among Asian-African husbands were found when both they and their wives had 13+ years of study, while the highest rates of outmarriage by husbands of European-American origin were obtained when both they

---

[63]Since there are now few European-Americans with only 0–8 years of education, their number is also small among those contracting a first marriage in recent years. Therefore the respective outmarriage data in table 35 are to be treated with reservation.

themselves and their wives had only 0–8 years of study. The same situation applies to wives. The proportions outmarrying rose among Asian-African wives in accordance with their own and their husbands' education. Among European-American wives with above 8 years of study, in recent times these proportions varied inversely to their own and their husbands' education. In the course of time, the proportions of outmarrying European-American husbands and wives rose markedly at all levels of their own and their spouses' education. The proportions of outmarrying Asian-African husbands and wives within specific educational levels tended to decline, but overall this was more than compensated for by the fact that these proportions remained much greater at higher educational levels and that the share of better-educated Asian-African Jews in Israel expanded markedly.

The influence of education on origin-specific outmarriage levels of Jews in Israel is thus seen to be vigorous as well as rather consistent over time. The most educated persons of European-American origin of both sexes strongly tend to marry within their origin group. The most educated persons in the Asian-African group display a marked tendency to outmarriage, probably as part of upward social mobility. Conversely, the least educated European-Americans outmarry more than others of their group, while the least educated of either sex in the Asian-African group show a strong propensity to marry a partner of their own origin. These tendencies have prevailed since Mandatory times and can be observed across the general rise in origin-specific outmarriage among Israel's Jews that has manifested itself in recent decades.

Looking into the future, it should be noted that new spouses in first marriage with only 0–8 years of education are a rapidly diminishing category. The constant improvement in the educational attainment of Asian-Africans will continue to strengthen the better-educated sections among them, which have so far shown a greater tendency to outmarry. It is true that opposite education-specific differentials in outmarriage propensities have prevailed among European-Americans. Nevertheless, their propensities have increased considerably in the course of time at all educational levels, including the uppermost, resulting in a marked rise in the overall proportions of outmarrying European-American husbands and wives. This trend might be sustained in the future by the continuous growth of the upper educational stratum of Asian-Africans, who will provide enlarged opportunities for marriage of educated Europeans and Americans with Asian-African partners of their own standing. The rise of average duration of residence in Israel among the country's Jewish population and the increase in the percentages of Israeli-born should supply further sociodemographic incentives for an increase of marriages between members of the two major origin groups from abroad. The anticipated substantial growth of the

Israeli origin group will effectively add to this tendency. Large waves of *aliyah*, if and when they occur, might delay these developments but are not likely to change the basic trend toward increased interethnic marriage among Israel's Jews.

The Israeli Origin Group and Interethnic Marriage

It has been explained above that couples with 1–2 spouses of Israeli origin have been excluded from the data presented in the tables and from the discussion in the body of the text. If they were included in the analysis, the following findings would emerge.

Persons of Israeli origin have so far been no more than a very small proportion of Jewish spouses of either sex marrying in Israel—5–8 percent from late Mandatory times until the 1983 census. Their great majority—between 65 and 82 percent—appear in the statistics as outmarrying, i.e., marrying a partner of overtly Asian-African or European-American origin. The indexes of marital attraction in the Israeli origin group have consequently been very low: according to the 1961 census—.310 until 1945, .251 during 1946–1955 and .244 during 1956–1961; according to the 1983 census—.136 during 1964–1973 and .159 during 1974–1983.

These marital peculiarities of the Israeli origin group are attributable to two basic facts: it is both the Jewish group of longest residence in this country and is itself mixed according to whether the most recent foreign-born ancestor (generally in the male line) was a native of either Asia-Africa or Europe-America. In addition, the ancestry of persons in the Israeli origin group may actually be origin-mixed because of outmarriages in the parental or previous generations, which have not been infrequent in Palestine/Israel. On the other hand, not all unions with one spouse of Israeli origin are substantively outmarriages. They really are inmarriages, if the Israeli-origin person in question belongs by descent to the same origin group abroad (Asia-Africa or Europe-America) as his/her partner, even though this fact cannot be ascertained in the available statistics.

The exclusion of couples with 1–2 spouses of Israeli origin reduces the measured levels of outmarriage, though the extent of underrepresentation cannot be accurately ascertained because of the indeterminate composition of the Israeli origin group. In 1974–1983, for instance, the percentage of outmarrying couples was 29.9 according to the three origin groups, but only 21.0 according to the two origin groups overtly from abroad. The actual level must have fallen between these two values, since only a portion of the unions of Asian-African or European-American spouses with those of so-called Israeli origin are, as just explained, substantively outmarriages. It can therefore be estimated that the actual level of outmarriage in terms of ultimate dichotomous origin groups abroad was already as high as about a quarter of all new couples around 1980.[64]

FERTILITY

The natural movement of a population comprises fertility and its corollary natality, as well as mortality, marriage, and divorce. These, together with migration and, if applicable, assimilation, directly determine the changes in the size of a population or subpopulation. In the context of this article, the major types of natural movement are of considerable relevance and illustrate well the diversity of evolutionary patterns.

Asian-Africans have increased their marriage age, especially for girls, while European-Americans have reduced theirs, adopting a common mode of conduct in this regard. In addition, both origin groups have somewhat reduced their previously very high marriage propensities and raised their marriage ages in recent years. The fertility convergence of the origin groups is so far advanced that the wide gap that was prevalent at the time of the period of mass immigration has been virtually closed. Mortality, which was high in the Jewries of Asia and North Africa, has been reduced for these groups in Israel with remarkable speed, furnishing yet another example of Asian-Africans becoming more like their European-American counterparts.[65]

The discussion which follows will focus on fertility, using the following measures and drawing upon the following data sources:

a. Total fertility rate (TFR), which indicates the average number of children per woman in a population, irrespective of marital status, on the assumption that the age-specific birthrates throughout the fecund life span are the same as in the year(s) studied. This is a measure of "period fertility," i.e., current fertility, that synthesizes the behavior of different birth cohorts.[66] In Israel it is computed annually by the Central Bureau of Statistics

---

[64]If the method of computation customary in Jewish Diaspora statistics were applied to the tripartite origin scheme of Israel's Jews, the couple rate of outmarriage during 1974-1983 would be 46 percent—as compared to 35 percent according to the two major origin groups. If the overt but excessive outmarriage figures of the Israeli origin group are revised downward, a rate of about 40 percent could be estimated.

[65]Remaining morbidity and mortality differentials, including those between the Jews from various Asian and African countries, are of obvious interest to epidemiologists but of minor consequence in the overall sociodemographic assessment.

[66]TFR has the advantage of being rapidly available but is affected by changes and inconsistencies in the fertility behavior of the various cohorts synthesized. Cohort statistics of fertility, following up separate birth or marriage cohorts, also exist in Israel from the following: special fertility surveys (Dov Friedlander and Calvin Goldscheider, "Immigration, Social Change and Cohort Fertility in Israel," *Population Studies*, vol. 32, no. 2, 1978, pp. 299-317); aggregate

from the birth and population data of the most recent year. If TFR remains roughly constant for a sufficient number of years, it approximates completed cohort fertility.

The net reproduction rate (NRR) is derived from the TFR. It indicates the average number of girls that will replace a woman intergenerationally, accounting for mortality. NRR = 1.00 means maintenance of existing population size after the lapse of a generation. At minimal empirical mortality, the TFR required for bare demographic replacement amounts to 2.1. At higher mortality levels the required TFR is accordingly greater.

b. Census data on cumulative fertility up to the age or marriage duration at the time of a census. Such data will be presented for Jewish women in first marriage from the Israeli population censuses of 1961, 1972, and 1983, according to various demographic and socioeconomic characteristics.

c. Data on expected fertility of married women from two specific interview surveys on fertility that were conducted by researchers in Israel in 1974–1975 and 1987–1988.

d. Data on fertility differentials among Jews according to religiosity, obtained from interview surveys or through an ecological method.

Fertility Levels

During the 1920s and 1930s, the Jewish population of Palestine, which was predominantly of European provenance, experienced a strong fertility decline (table 37), in keeping with the general trend in Europe and North America at that time. Around 1940, TFR went down to approximately 2.35, corresponding to an NRR of no more than about 1.00.[67] However, the youthful age structure of that population kept the crude birthrate above 2 percent per annum.[68] At the end of World War II, a "baby boom" set in—again in conformance with the general trend in developed countries—which lasted until the beginning of the 1950s. Meanwhile, mass immigration was taking place and the new immigrants exhibited strikingly different fertility patterns. Europeans came with low fertility, something that the horror of the Nazi period had only intensified. Except for the Balkan countries, the completed fertility of European women immigrating near age 50 fell somewhat short of the replacement level, and that of the younger

---

follow-up of the births to marriage cohorts (CBS, *Statistical Abstract*); and record linkage of women and their children enumerated in censuses (U.O. Schmelz, "Fertility Follow-Up of Marriage Cohorts in Israel," paper presented to the 10th World Congress of Jewish Studies, Jerusalem, 1989). In the context of origin-group differentials, however, these data do not add much to the figures presented here.

[67]Bachi, *Population of Israel*, p. 225.

[68]The crude birthrate is determined both by the fertility level and the age structure of a population. Youthfulness of the population raises the birthrate; aging depresses it.

women was very low. On the other hand, until their mass immigration, Asian and African Jews had on the whole high completed fertility—approximately 6 children per woman—with marked differentials between countries of origin according to levels of modernization. Jewish fertility was particularly high (about 7 children) in Northwest Africa, Iran, and Yemen; it was somewhat lower in Iraq, and comparatively reduced in Egypt and Turkey.

Already in the Mandatory period, a ranking of Jewish fertility according to region of birth had taken shape in Palestine as follows (in descending order, table 37): Asia-Africa, Israel, Europe-America. The Israeli-born were of mixed origin, so that this three-tier ranking implied intergenerational fertility convergence.[69] Since Asian-African fertility in the last decade of the Mandate was considerably lower than during the subsequent period of mass immigration, some decline had probably taken place in this group,[70] implying a convergence tendency between the origin groups already at that time. The renewed fertility rise during the "baby boom" in the closing years of the Mandate was relatively much stronger in the European-American than the Asian-African group and thus also produced a convergent effect on the respective fertility levels.

From the period of mass immigration on, origin-specific convergence has been the dominant pattern in the fertility evolution of Israel's Jews. Asian-Africans reduced their fertility consistently and rather rapidly, from 6 children on average in the early 1950s to slightly above 3 in the 1980s. This accorded with the world trend toward fertility reduction under conditions of sociodemographic modernization,[71] but was undoubtedly accelerated by departure from a Muslim environment and joint life with European Jews in the modern and open society of Israel.

Fertility evolution among the European-Americans has been more remarkable. They raised their fertility during the "baby boom" around 1950 to levels—a TFR slightly above 3 children—which considerably surpassed that of the Diaspora Jewries in the respective continents. Though some recession took place around 1960, the TFR of European-Americans in Israel—fluctuating around 2.5 children—remained even then distinctly above the replacement minimum of 2.1. In subsequent years, an important peculiarity manifested itself. While fertility declined strongly throughout the advanced countries of the world and since the 1970s has been below

---

[69]This was compounded by the fact that the adult Israeli-born comprised relatively more religious persons than the European-born, which raised their fertility.

[70]However, the composition of the Asian-African immigrants by countries of birth changed in the course of time.

[71]Fertility reduction need not occur quickly when technological modernization is imported, as illustrated by some Muslim populations.

replacement needs in nearly all of them, Israel's European-American-born Jews have not participated in this widespread trend. About 1970 they even raised their TFR slightly and have maintained it at a level around 2.7 children until now.[72] The decline of fertility on the part of Asian-Africans and its rise among European-Americans, as compared to the Diaspora, constitutes conspicuous evidence of origin-group convergence in Israel.

The above findings derived from the current TFR are fully confirmed by data from the three population censuses of 1961, 1972, and 1983 on cumulative fertility up to given ages or marriage durations. For economy of space, table 39 presents only selected data, according to these two approaches: women aged 30–34 and 45–49 or married 10–14 and 25–29 years respectively. The first category according to either approach relates to women sufficiently advanced in age or length of marriage to clearly show intergroup differentiation; the second category comprises women of virtually completed fertility. Table 39 shows again that the descending fertility ranking of the birth regions is Asia-Africa, Israel, and Europe-America, and that the dissimilarities between these groupings have much narrowed in the course of time. The latter trend is seen particularly among younger or shorter-married women.

Regarding foreign-born Jewish women, tables 39 and 40 make it possible to discern several other important features of fertility evolution:

a. In keeping with the basic pattern of fertility convergence, it is found that with longer stay in Israel fertility tended to decline among Asian-Africans but rise among the European-Americans. Table 40 divides the women born in each continent abroad according to periods of immigration, but presents only strongly populated categories, selecting the periods shown for Asian-African women in conformance with immigration chronology. All three censuses document a tendency for Asian-Africans to have lower fertility the earlier their arrival in Israel—the longer they had been exposed to Israeli conditions until each census. The opposite tendency obtained with regard to the European-Americans who immigrated until the 1960s. However, the fertility of those who arrived around 1970 was slightly greater than that of the preceding immigrants from these continents. There is no conclusive information on the causes of this slight change in trend. Conjecturally, it might be attributed to the considerable proportion of Asian Jews (Grusinians, Bokharians) among Soviet immigrants at that time and/or to religious elements among the selective Jewish immigrants from Western countries.

b. The influence of prolonged stay in Israel on the fertility of foreign-born Jewish women could make itself felt both among those who had married

---

[72]However, there has been some postponement of childbearing until later ages, due to an increase in age at first marriage (see below).

while still abroad and those marrying in Israel (possibly with the husband of longer residence in Israel or perhaps even from another origin group). Table 40 gives some data (where possible) on fertility by place of marriage, when birth continent, immigration period, and marriage duration are kept constant. The available data show a tendency among Asian-African women who arrived in the mass influx after 1948 to have reached lower fertility when married in Israel rather than abroad. The corresponding picture for European-American women is not consistent, but at any rate the fertility differences by place of marriage were small and therefore liable to be more easily confounded by artifacts.[73]

c. In terms of continental aggregates, African-born women in Israel have consistently displayed somewhat higher fertility than their Asian-born counterparts. This was already the case with regard to the fertility abroad of the women who immigrated during 1948–1954 (table 38). Moreover, large-scale immigration from Asia stopped as early as 1951, while that from Africa continued until the mid-1960s. In recent years Asian-born women of fertile age, much more than corresponding African-born women, have belonged to small and selective immigration contingents that have arrived in Israel. The convergence motif has been carried forward by the total Israeli-born women whose fertility has always been intermediate between the Asian-Africans and the European-Americans. In the Mandatory period their own fertility was nearer to the former group; in the period of statehood it has been much closer to that of the European-Americans. This may be attributable both to the coming of age of children born in Palestine to the relatively many European immigrants who arrived during the Mandatory period and also to social developments, such as reduced religiosity, compared to the past.

To clinch the convergence argument, table 39 disaggregates Israeli-born women by father's region of birth. It is found that in all the three censuses the fertility ranking by paternal birth region paralleled that of foreign-born women: Asia-Africa, Israel, Europe-America, in descending order. For 1983, sufficient numbers of Israeli-born women of African paternity were already available to distinguish their slightly greater fertility from that of the Israeli-born of Asian paternity among younger or shorter-married women. Altogether the fertility differentials among the Israeli-born by father's birth region strongly narrowed in the course of time, but the accustomed ranking persisted until the 1983 census.

Given the special interest in the fertility evolution of European-American

---

[73]For instance, European-American women who immigrated during 1972–1974 and married in Israel had maximally little more than 11 years of marriage by the time of the 1983 census, while the corresponding group of women married abroad could have been fully 10–14 years past their weddings. The latter had the opportunity to attain a greater average number of children.

women, the relevant data are displayed more fully in table 41 for immigrants up to the mid-1960s, who overwhelmingly came from Europe, excluding the Soviet Union. The table documents the rise of fertility with lengthening stay in Israel according to four measurements (where feasible): at immigration and up to the 1961, 1972, and 1983 censuses respectively. The table compares the women according to their age at immigration or at the time of any of the censuses available. Obviously the women of a given age at these separate occasions were not the same women but belonged to different birth cohorts that were followed up to a common age. For instance, regarding each immigration period, the 30–34-year-olds in 1983 were born 11 years after their counterparts of 1972 and 22 years after the corresponding women of 1961; their average age at immigration and length of exposure to Israeli conditions varied accordingly. This lengthening of stay in Israel, in fact, is a plausible explanation for the observed fertility increases.

On the whole, table 41 documents the fact that each immigration contingent raised its fertility in Israel, and the earlier the contingent arrived the greater was the average fertility reached by the time of each census. The fertility increase in Israel, compared to the Diaspora ("at immigration"), was particularly impressive with regard to immigrants around 1960, who arrived a considerable time after the upheaval of World War II, most of them from Communist-ruled countries such as Romania, Poland, and Hungary. However at least two special matters require mention. The oldest women at arrival or in the 1961 census still showed traces of the higher fertility preceding the historic fertility depression around the 1930s; their levels must not be confused with the renewed and continual rise subsequently occurring in Israel, which is our concern here. The disturbing effects of World War II made themselves felt and must be isolated in interpreting table 41; e.g., concerning 1948–1954 immigrants aged 45–54 in 1961 or the 55–64-year-olds in 1972, who immigrated after the war. Part of the findings from census data presented above can be checked against period fertility measurements (TFRs), and both kinds of data are found to confirm one another in essentials.

Asian-African TFR tended to decline with lengthening stay in Israel, at least with regard to the immigrants of the period of mass influx. The maximum difference was measured in 1951, when the TFR of Asian-African immigrants since 1948 was computed as 6.9, compared to 5.1 among the earlier arrivals. The corresponding figures for European-Americans at that time of "baby boom," notably among the old-timers, were 3.5 for those who arrived before the establishment of the state and 2.8 among 1948–1951 immigrants.[74] The further course of European TFR in Israel by period of immigration was not very regular, though a somewhat increased level

---

[74]CBS, *Statistical Abstract*, various issues.

among the arrivals around 1970 is also noticeable from these data.

For the years 1985–1988, the TFR by women's origin and birthplace ranked as follows: total—2.81; Africa, born abroad—3.36; Africa, born in Israel—2.98; Asia, born abroad—2.86; Europe-America, born in Israel—2.82; Asia, born in Israel—2.80; Europe-America, born abroad—2.69; Israel, father also born in Israel—2.62. Insofar as recent period fertility is concerned, the Israeli-born of European-American paternity have caught up with the Israeli-born of Asian paternity, while the Israeli-born of Israeli paternity have for the time being slightly dropped below all the other categories. However, with the exception of the African-born, the fertility differentials between all the other categories have been small. The Israeli-born comprised 68 percent of all Jewish women who had live births during 1985–1988; the African-born constituted only 12 percent.[75]

Completed fertility can be empirically known only when women reach or come near the end of their fertile life span. In order to anticipate such information, it is usual in fertility studies to ask younger women about the final number of children they expect or would like to have. The conjectural nature of such replies requires that they be used with reservation, and actually discounted according to the respondents' age, marital status, etc. It is also possible to inquire about the number of children which the interviewed women consider to be the societal norm. The two major fertility surveys conducted in Israel in the 1970s and 1980s have yielded such information, which is epitomized in table 42.[76] Three facts emerge from these data: The origin differentials narrowed from the 1970s to the 1980s in these areas, just as they did for TFR and cumulative fertility up to given ages or marriage durations according to censuses. The reported levels of fertility desired, seen as ideal, or perceived as normative exceeded the fertility empirically observed at the particular time. Beyond their unusually high empirical fertility level among the developed countries of the world, Israel's Jews evince a considerable demand for children, much in excess of bare replacement needs. This applies to all origin groups, including European-Americans.

A recent development in the fertility pattern of Israel's Jews, common

---

[75]CBS data.

[76]The questions asked in the surveys and their nomenclature in table 42 are as follows: 1974–1975 survey: ("ideal") "If you had the medical and economic possibilities of having the number of children that would be most appropriate to you, what would that number be?"; ("Israeli norm") "What do you think is the most appropriate number of children for the average Israeli family?" 1987–1988 survey: ("desired") "How many children do you want?"; ("ideal") "If you had the medical and economic possibility to have the number of children that suits you best, what would that number be?" See Calvin Goldscheider and Dov Friedlander, "Reproductive Norms in Israel," in U.O. Schmelz and G. Nathan, eds., *Studies in the Population of Israel in Honor of Roberto Bachi*, *Scripta Hierosolymitana*, vol. 30 (Jerusalem, 1986), pp. 15–35; Eric Peritz, "Fertility Patterns in the Jewish Population of Israel—Results from a Sample Survey," research report, 1989, publication in preparation.

to all origin groups, is a tendency to somewhat delay reproduction in keeping with somewhat later age at first marriage. The age-specific birthrates changed in the short span from 1980-1984 to 1985-1988, as set out in table 43. The rates declined below age 25, especially at ages 20-24, but rose at later ages, especially ages 25-39. This occurred simultaneously among all origin groups and in all of them with hardly any change in the respective TFR.

Socioeconomic Characteristics and Fertility

If the origin groups in the population censuses of 1961, 1972, and 1983 are divided by educational attainment, a strong and rather consistent pattern becomes evident—that fertility varies inversely with education; the higher the educational level, the lower the fertility level. Table 44 presents the data by six educational levels and selectively for two marriage durations. The greater was the cumulative fertility of an origin group overall, the larger was the ratio between the higher fertility associated with low education and the reduced fertility at advanced education. Accordingly, the ratios were greater at 25-29 years of marriage duration than at 10-14 years. The fertility comparisons between the origin groups are somewhat handicapped at the educational extremes by the paucity of European-Americans with no or little schooling and Asian-Africans with 13 or more years of study. If inspected vertically, table 44 supplies evidence that at virtually each educational level the basic fertility ranking by birth regions—Asia-Africa, Israel, Europe-America—was preserved. Regarding the more detailed origin groups, the usual fertility ranking, expressed by descending rows of table 44, is on the whole preserved, though with irregularities. Education-specifically, a strong narrowing of fertility differences between the origin groups is evident, especially among women married only 10-14 years by 1983.

Table 45 carries this socioeconomic analysis one step further, separately investigating the fertility of women in the labor force and those out of it, by origin-birthplace and educational attainment. The data presented here are confined to women married 10-14 years, according to each of the three censuses. It should be noted that labor-force participation relates here to work in the 12 months preceding each census ("annual labor force"). Women who were in the labor force 10-14 years after marrying need not have been so earlier in their married life, and vice versa. However, such are the census data available, and there is probably some correlation between working by comparatively young women (10-14 years of marriage duration) and working at different preceding stages of their life cycle.[77]

Table 45 essentially confirms the inverse relationship between fertility

---

[77]This could be checked from the file of the 1987-1988 fertility survey.

and education for both working and not-working women. A strong though not quite regular tendency has prevailed for fertility to decline with rising education in each category, by origin, labor-force participation, and census in question. Table 45, however, adds a new finding: for each origin group generally, as well as by educational attainment, and according to each census, women classified as not being in the labor force tended to have somewhat greater fertility than their otherwise comparable counterparts in the labor force. This tendency has been rather consistent. Of course, the absolute differences between the fertility averages of the working and not-working women, measured here after only 10–14 years of marriage, were smaller in those origin groups that had comparatively limited fertility anyway, especially among the European-Americans.

For women both in and out of the labor force, at each educational level, and according to each census, fertility by birth region declined in the order Asia-Africa, Israel, and Europe-America. Less regularly, lower fertility figures were found among the more detailed origin groups presented in table 45 in conformance with the descending order of the rows. The table also corroborates, by labor-force participation and education, the basic trend of narrowing fertility differentials between origin groups over the course of time.

Religiosity and Fertility

A notable concentration of religious Jews, including ultra-Orthodox circles, is found in Jerusalem. Results of two large-scale studies on religiosity and fertility in Jerusalem are summarized in tables 46 and 47. The first was a maternity-ward interview survey (1975–1976); the second was an ecological investigation assigning to each woman the religiosity level of her immediate neighborhood, as ascertained from the proportions of votes cast for the various religious parties in the parliamentary elections of 1984.[78] The data relate to women who gave birth during the years indicated.[79] Though the ecological approach of the later study has obvious limitations, the results cannot be easily dismissed: they rely on numerous cases, are clearcut, and accord with nonstatistical evidence.

While both studies found rising religiosity to be strongly associated with increased fertility, there was a difference. In the maternity-ward survey, origin-specific fertility variation among the ultra-Orthodox was rather limited; the ecological survey found greater fertility of the European-American

---

[78]U.O. Schmelz, "Religiosity and Fertility Among the Jews of Jerusalem," in U.O. Schmelz and S. DellaPergola, eds., *Papers in Jewish Demography 1985* (Jerusalem, 1989), pp. 157–185.
[79]Unlike the census data reported here, which relate to all women in first marriage, and unlike the TFR, which relates to all women in a population, irrespective of marital status.

and Israeli origin groups as against the Asian-Africans. The general fertility survey of 1987–1988 came up with a similar finding.

A negative relationship of fertility with women's education and engagement in gainful work[80] is found at various religiosity levels. This also applies to most origin groups within each religiosity level, as far as is ascertainable from the data (table 47). However, these effects are minor as compared to the overriding influence of fertility differentiation according to religiosity levels. Unlike among total Jews in Jerusalem, at higher religiosity levels the fertility of women in the European-American and Israeli origin groups clearly tended to exceed that in the Asian-African group. Analogous results have been found in B'nei Berak, another large center of ultra-Orthodox Jews in Israel.

In sum, whereas origin-specific fertility convergence has been the rule for the total of Israel's Jews, some fertility differentiation according to origin manifests itself at higher religiosity levels. Contrary to the overall trends in the past, however, at higher religiosity levels, the fertility of European-Americans now exceeds that of Asian-Africans.

Size of Households

Size and composition of households are of great demographic, social, and economic importance. Private households (as distinct from institutions) are defined in Israel's official statistics as groups of persons living in the same dwelling who consume major meals together, as well as persons living alone in a dwelling.

The major determinant of household size in a population is the level of fertility, and for this reason the subject is included in this part of the study. However, the overall determinants of household size are complex, involving other aspects of natural movement (marriage, divorce, mortality) as well as changing habits of coresidence between persons not belonging to a nuclear family. Coresidence in turn is influenced by the availability of dwellings and thus by building intensity.

As long as the fertility of Asian-African Jews in Israel was high, the average number of persons in households headed by individuals of this origin group was markedly greater than in the European-American group. With the decline of Asian-African fertility and the increase in building activity in Israel connected with improved living conditions, these differences have narrowed. Since household size is associated with the age of the household head—it peaks at about age 35–44, when most children of exist-

---

[80]The information in these surveys, addressing themselves to women who had just given birth, did not conform to strict definitions of labor-force participation but related more loosely to whether these women had a gainful occupation or not.

ing couples are already born but have not yet left the parental home to start living on their own—both kinds of figures are shown.

Age of Household Head and Year	Average Number of Persons per Household			
	Origin of Household Head			
	Jews Total	Asia-Africa	Israel	Europe-America
All households				
1961	3.6	4.8	3.6	3.1
1983	3.2	3.8	3.3	2.8
Head aged 35–44				
1961	4.6	5.5	4.3	3.7
1983	4.5	4.9	4.4	4.2

Sources: CBS: 1961 census, vol. 36; 1983 census, vol. 8.

The above data actually give only a partial picture of the change that is taking place in origin-specific differentials in household size. An important further drop in Asian-African fertility, bringing it close to the persistent European-American level, occurred in Israel only in the 1980s (table 37). Since children in Israel tend to stay with their parents until the late teens, the full effect of the recent diminution of interorigin fertility differentials will make itself felt only in the future, at the turn of the century. Here then is an instance of near-equalization in one demographic aspect—fertility—with delayed repercussions in another—household size—as well as socioeconomically.

EDUCATIONAL ATTAINMENT

This section will examine differences between the main origin groups with respect to levels and types of education. A major distinction in what follows is between Israeli-educated adults, whether born in Israel or elsewhere, and immigrants educated abroad. This distinction is necessary for an understanding of the sources of the educational discrepancies between the origin groups, as well as for the prospects of bridging them.[81] A focal point in the

---

[81]See Roberto Bachi, *The Population of Israel* (Jerusalem, 1977), Ch. 15; M. Inbar and Ch. Adler, *Ethnic Integration in Israel: A Comparative Case Study of Moroccan Brothers Who Settled in France and in Israel* (New Brunswick, 1977); Y. Nahon, *Patterns of Educational*

following review concerns the persistence of considerable differentials between origin groups with regard to the proportions of highly educated people, even though the proportions of adults with secondary-school education exhibit a convergent rising trend.

Patterns of educational attainment in Israel are related to three sets of factors: (a) institutional arrangements, such as compulsory education and a tracking system at the secondary-school level;[82] (b) behavioral patterns, such as those reflected in age-specific rates of noncompulsory school attendance; (c) compositional factors, such as the sociodemographic structure of the population by age, country of origin, or age at immigration, which indicate whether the acquisition of education occurred before or after arrival in Israel.

Educational expansion owing to either institutional or behavioral change is relatively slow, since it occurs mainly through the regular school system. On the other hand, compositional changes occur independently of the national education system and may thus more rapidly alter the educational level of the population as a whole, either in an upward or downward direction. Such changes may also affect the relative position of different groups with respect to educational attainment.

Attention will first turn to an overall review of the educational attainment of the main origin groups as recorded in the 1983 population census, disregarding place of education. This will be followed by an analysis of Israeli-educated and foreign-educated adults of different origin groups with respect to some selected educational indicators. Next comes a look at the main changes that occurred within each group during the 1961–1983 period, using mainly data of three population censuses as well as some survey findings and educational statistics. Finally, some basic features of the Israeli education system will be examined, concentrating on those relevant to the analysis of differential attainment among the Israeli-educated, by origin.

Origin-Group Differences in Educational Attainment

Table 48 combines Israeli-born and foreign-born adults into three origin groups: Asia, Africa, and Europe-America. For each group, cross-classified by sex and age, several educational indicators are presented, ranging from the lowest to the highest levels of educational attainment, as recorded by

---

Expansion and the Structure of Occupational Opportunities: The Ethnic Dimension (in Hebrew), Jerusalem Institute for Israel Studies, 1987.

[82]Upon completing elementary school, Israeli pupils who continue their studies are directed into general or vocational education within either separate secondary schools or "tracks" in comprehensive schools. After the school reform measures of 1969 (see below), this tracking took place at the end of the final (9th) grade of the lower-stage of secondary education.

the 1983 population census. Ratios between the figures for Asia and Africa, on the one hand, and Europe-America, on the other, were calculated for each cell as indices of the educational differentials between the groups. The figures for Europe-America were given the value of 1.00 for this purpose. Thus, the closer the ratios are to 1.00, the smaller the educational differentials are between the origin groups. The Israeli-born of Israeli paternity are omitted from the analysis since they cannot be classified according to origins.

Several points emerge from the figures in table 48. In all three origin groups, younger cohorts of both genders have considerably higher educational attainment than older ones, and there is among them much more equality between the sexes in this respect. All educational indicators bear out this relationship. Thus, the medians of school years for men of Asian origin range from 5.3 among the 75+-year-olds to 12.0 among the 15-24 age group, compared with a 4.1-11.7 differential for men of African origin and a much smaller one (8.9-12.3) for men of European-American origin.[83] Substantially greater discrepancies exist among women of Asian and African origin. Their median years of schooling for the oldest and youngest age groups range from 0.7 to 12.1, compared with a range of 8.7 to 12.4 for women of European-American origin.

The percentages of people with at least some higher education (13+ years) likewise exhibit a pattern of age differentials: 5 percent for the 75+-year-olds as against 17 to 20 percent for the 25-34 age group among men of Asian or African origin, compared with a 19-54 percent range for men of European-American origin; from 1 to 19-20 percent, among women of Asian or African origin, and from 11 to 57 percent among women of European-American origin. (The figures for the 14-25 age group are relatively low, since they are too young to have acquired higher education.) Likewise, the proportions of total or functional illiterates (0-4 years of schooling) are significantly lower among younger persons of Asian-African origin, especially women. These patterns indicate compositional changes, with young and relatively well-educated cohorts replacing old and relatively poorly educated ones. The changes operated toward raising over time the educational level of all origin groups.

Controlling for age and sex, the wide educational discrepancies which prevail between the origin groups become clear. Thus, men aged 35-44 of European-American origin have a median of 13.7 years of schooling compared to only 10.6 years among their Asian-African peers, while 31 percent of the former are university graduates as compared to about 6 percent of the latter. Among women of these ages the differentials are still larger: 13.5

---

[83]It should be recalled that the median, a useful measure that refers to the midpoint of a distribution, is insensitive to its extremes. Therefore, medians should be treated with caution.

years of schooling for European-Americans compared with 10 years for Asians and Africans, and 23 percent of university graduates compared to 3 percent, respectively.

Since the ratios for Asians and Africans are quite similar, the two groups may be combined and compared with European-Americans. As the ratios show, different conclusions may be drawn regarding the magnitude and patterns of discrepancies between the origin groups depending on the measure chosen for comparison. With regard to median years of schooling, the medians for men and women aged 15+ of Asian-African origin are only 13–16 percent lower than the medians for European-Americans. Moreover, the discrepancies between origin groups, as measured by age-specific ratios based on the medians, grow substantially with age. For the youngest age group (15–24), the medians are only a few percentage points apart, while the differentials increase to 30–50 percent among elderly men (aged 65+) and even more than 90 percent among elderly women.

In comparison with the medians, much wider differentials exist at either extreme of the distribution of all adults by educational attainment. The percentages of functional illiterates among Asian-Africans are twofold to fourfold higher than among European-Americans (for men of all ages, 9–10 percent for Asia-Africa compared to 4 percent for Europe-America; for women—18–20 percent against 5 percent, respectively). Since the lack of even some education adversely affects life chances, the older age groups (ages 45+) of Asian-Africans and their dependents were clearly disadvantaged in comparison with their peers of European-American origin.

As one moves up the educational ladder the ratios decline, i.e., the differences between the origin groups tend to grow. Thus the percentages of Asian-Africans with completed education at the secondary-school level or higher are nearly 2/3 as high as those of European-Americans (ratios of .63 to .67). But the ratios expressing the gap between the origin groups drop to 1/3 for the percentages with 13+ years of schooling (equivalent to at least some postsecondary education) and down to 1/5–1/6 for the proportions with academic degrees (both sexes and all ages).[84]

For the proportions of people with secondary-school or higher certificates, the age-specific differentials between origin groups show an orderly pattern of decline as we proceed from older to younger age groups (see table 48, ratios). The percentage of holders of secondary or higher certificates among persons of Asian-African origin aged 15–24 reached 75–87 percent of the level found among persons of European-American origin, compared to 50 percent or less among those aged 45 or more, especially women. In

---

[84]Postsecondary training in Israel (for elementary-school teaching, nursing, practical engineering, etc.) usually extends for 2–3 years of full-time study, whereas university undergraduate education requires at least 3–4 years, or in sum, 15–16 years of schooling.

contrast, the pattern of age-specific differentials in the proportions of persons with 13+ years of schooling or academic degrees is more distinct. The highest proportions of people with 13+ years of schooling were found for the 25–34 and 35–44 age groups, but even among them, the percentages for persons of Asian-African origin do not amount to more than 2/5 of the corresponding ones for individuals of European-American origin, and the origin-related ratios pertaining to the proportions of university graduates at these ages stand around the 1/5 level.

Distinguishing the Israeli-educated from the Foreign-educated

How are the Israeli-educated and the foreign-educated to be distinguished? In the absence of direct information on the matter, it is necessary to work with data on place of birth and, for the foreign-born, age at immigration.

Israeli-born and immigrants who arrived at the age of 14 or below will be considered as Israeli-educated, since it seems safe to assume that they spent most of their formative years in Israel and thus acquired all or most of their schooling through the local education system. It is assumed also that the majority of immigrants who came to Israel at the age of 25 or more, if they ever studied at all, were old enough at immigration to have completed abroad their highest level of education, including university education. These, then, will be considered foreign-educated. Those who were 15–24 years old at immigration will generally be left aside in the following analysis since they constitute an intermediate group with respect to the place of their education.

To compare educational attainment between the Israeli-educated and the foreign-educated it is necessary to control for actual age in order to capture and isolate possible life-cycle and cohort effects. For the foreign-born, it is also necessary to control for age at immigration as a proximate measure of the length of exposure to the local educational system. A chronological dimension, such as period of immigration, should be added because institutional and other types of changes could have occurred during different periods—either in Israel or in the country of origin, and various waves of immigration differed by size and composition. The relationship between these variables may be expressed as follows: age at census = age at immigration + time elapsed since immigration. Thus, for instance, when actual age is controlled, the higher the age at immigration, the shorter is the stay in Israel and vice versa. In other words, the foreign-educated, as defined above, immigrated later than their Israeli-educated age-peers who were also born abroad. This relationship should be borne in mind as the analysis moves forward.

A quite developed system of Jewish education already existed under the

British Mandate and even before. With the establishment of the State of Israel, a Law of Compulsory Education was enacted (1949), stipulating a compulsory period of 9 years of schooling for all, free of charge, starting at age five. This period was lengthened in 1969 to 11 years. Elementary schools were opened in each rural locality and in every urban neighborhood. In 1969 school-reform measures were introduced, aimed at improving the scholastic achievement of pupils of disadvantaged backgrounds, this by placing them in "integrative" schools, where pupils of different backgrounds would attend the same classes.

A factor that greatly hampered the social mingling of pupils was the dissimilar geographic dispersion of the various origin groups. Another was the relatively stronger inclination for religious education among families of Asian-African origin. In 1983–84, 33 percent of the pupils of this background in primary education studied in religious (state or other) schools, compared with only 19 percent of the pupils of European-American origin. Nearly half of the pupils in state religious schools in the same year studied in relatively homogeneous schools, namely, schools with a majority of 65 percent and over of pupils of Asian-African origin, as compared with only 14 percent of the pupils in state nonreligious schools. On the other hand, 43 percent of the pupils in state nonreligious schools attended schools where pupils of Asian-African origin comprised a minority of less than 35 percent of total pupils. These figures illustrate the difficulties with which the Israeli school system had to cope in implementing social integration policies.[85]

Various measures were taken to motivate pupils of postcompulsory ages to prolong their studies, such as the development of a counseling and guidance system at the "gates" leading from the lower stage of secondary education (the "intermediate schools") to the upper stage; the elimination of all fees for the whole of secondary-school education; the introduction of a flexible tracking system into vocational schools; and later on, increasing differentiation of the curricular demands for matriculation. All these contributed not only to raising the rates of attendance among the relevant cohorts—first at the elementary-school level and then at secondary schools—but also to improving the prospects for entering higher education by obtaining a matriculation certificate.

How did the various origin groups fare in the context of the expanding

---

[85]For data on origin-group composition of the religious and nonreligious educational systems, see CBS, *Statistical Abstract of Israel*, no. 36, 1985, p. 628. On educational integration policies, see Y. Amir and S. Sharan, eds., *School Desegregation: Cross-Cultural Perspective* (Hillsdale, N.J., and London, 1984). On origin, scholastic achievement, and school integration, see A. Minkowich, D. Davis, and J. Bashi, *Success and Failure in Israeli Elementary Education* (New Brunswick, 1982). For an evaluative review of 15 years of Israeli research, as from the early 1970s, on the scholastic effects of integration, see Y. Dar and N. Resh, "Educational Integration and Scholastic Achievements: Summary and Evaluation of Research in Israel" (in Hebrew), *Megamot*, 31, 1988, pp. 180–207.

Israeli educational system? To answer this question, attention will first be given to the educational attainment of those who were born in Israel and then to that of the foreign-born who were young enough at immigration to be educated in Israel.

Educational Attainment of the Israeli-born

Three groups of Israeli-born adults are distinguished in table 49 by the father's continent of birth—Asian, African, and European-American. The data are median years of schooling and the ratios thereof based on the 1961, 1972, and 1983 censuses. As the table shows, in 1983 the medians for both sexes (all ages) were just above 12 years, reaching nearly 13 years for European-Americans compared to 11.5–12.0 years for Asians and Africans. In other words, nearly half the Israeli-born, of all origin groups, attained an educational level equivalent to a complete secondary-school education or higher. The lowest medians were found among the elderly of Asian-African origin (8.5 years for men and 5.3–6.4 years for women aged 65+), and the highest (14 years) among the Israeli-born of European-American origin aged 25–44.

During the two decades between 1961 and 1983, the medians for all the Israeli-born taken together increased by 1.5–2.0 years of schooling. All groups among the Israeli-born (gender, age, and origin) improved their education impressively, the most dramatic changes occurring in the educational levels of middle-aged and elderly women, whose medians in 1983 amounted to 12.2 years for the 45–64 age group and 8.6 years for those aged 65+, up from 7.3 and 1.0, respectively, in 1961. These figures reflect not only the institutional improvement of the Jewish educational system during the Mandatory period as compared to the late Ottoman period but also the effects of a normative change favoring equal education for both sexes.

Did the origin-group discrepancies narrow during this process of basic educational improvement? As far as median years of schooling are concerned, the answer is affirmative for both sexes: in 1983 the ratio of medians among Asian-Africans versus European-Americans (all ages) reached .90, compared to .70 in 1961 (table 49, ratios). This trend is going to continue in the future, since the origin differentials for the younger age groups are much smaller than for the older ones. The origin-specific ratios for the 15–24 age group in 1983 ranged for both sexes between .94 to .97, compared with .75 for men and .53 to .64 for women aged 65+.

Do origin-group discrepancies in the percentages of the highly educated show themselves for the Israeli-born? Table 51 sheds light on this question, relying on data from two post-censal surveys of university graduates.[86] The

---

[86]CBS, *Persons with Academic and Post-Secondary Education, 1974*, Special Series no. 643, 1981, p. 63; *University and Post-Secondary Education Graduates, 1984*, vol. B, 1988, p. 57.

ratio between the origin-specific percentages of university graduates in 1984 was just .15, up from .06 in 1974. While the ratios tend to be somewhat higher among the younger age groups, the figures seem to indicate that if there exists a process of narrowing of differentials, it is a very slow one.

Educational Attainment of Foreign-born Educated in Israel

From its inception, the Israeli education system had to cope with the challenge of absorbing young immigrant pupils. Considering the origin-group differentials in educational attainment reviewed above, it is interesting to explore whether any specific requirements or problems pertaining to the immediate postimmigration situation of these children (and their families) could have contributed to this effect. To cite just one example, many of the newly arrived pupils, particularly those of Asian-African origin, were absorbed in lower school grades than were suitable for their ages, in an attempt to compensate for the curriculum they had missed. Did this "grade retardation" or any other factor related to school experience hamper their chances for postcompulsory education?

The matter may be approached by examining the cross-section data of the 1983 census (table 52). Since individuals normally achieve their highest educational attainment around age 30, attention is given to the 25-34 and 35-44 age groups, presenting for them origin-specific median years of schooling and percentages of university graduates among the Israeli-born in comparison with the foreign-born, while controlling for age at the census and age at immigration. For both age groups, the two educational indicators are much higher among European-Americans than among Asians or Africans. The percentages of university graduates, for instance, are 24-34 percent as against 4-10 percent, respectively. The percentages for those aged 35-44 are higher than those of the younger age group, since the latter has not yet exhausted its chances for university graduation.[87]

Controlling for age at the census, the foreign-born of all origin groups show higher medians as well as higher percentages of university graduates among those who were older at immigration, i.e., who immigrated later. The highest medians and percentages were found among those who were 25+ years old at immigration. The lowest medians and percentages were observed among those who immigrated as young children (aged 0-14), their educational attainment being poorer than that of their age peers born in Israel, especially for the European-American origin group. For example, the percentage of university graduates among Israeli-born men aged 35-44 of European-American origin was 34 percent compared with 22 percent for those who immigrated from Europe-America at ages 0-14 (table 52). Dis-

---

[87]Compulsory army service in Israel, beginning at age 18, extends for two years for women and three years for men. Many sign on for even longer periods.

crepancies of similar order were also found for women.

Table 53 makes it clear that length of exposure to the Israeli educational system is an important factor affecting the amount of education finally acquired. This is indicated by the differentials in educational attainment between immigrants who came at ages 0–4 and 10–14, for instance. Among those who arrived in the period of mass immigration (1948–1954), the differentials in terms of median years of schooling in favor of those who came younger amount to 2.1 years for Asia, 1.5 years for Africa, and 0.9 years for Europe-America. Differentials with regard to university graduates were 2.8, 0.5, and 8.7 percentage points, respectively. Differentials in the opposite direction were recorded for those coming in later immigration waves, but as already noted, these belong to younger age-at-census groups.

It seems, therefore, that young immigrants—at least those who were already of school age upon arrival—were, indeed, relatively disadvantaged with respect to the development of their educational careers. Still, this group resembles the Israeli-born as far as the origin differentials are concerned; the ratios of both groups are similar and indicate wider discrepancies between origin groups than those of the foreign-educated (table 52).

Educational Attainment of Adults Educated Abroad

The data in the 1983 census make clear the relatively higher educational attainment of the foreign-educated, aged 25–44, of both origin groups, as well as the smaller educational differentials between them. This section presents a more detailed discussion of the foreign-educated as defined above—aged 25+ at immigration (tables 52 and 54).

In 1983 this population amounted to nearly 550,000 persons (table 54), two-thirds of whom were born in Europe-America and the rest, in equal parts (1/6 each), in Asia or Africa. The largest component came between 1948 and 1954 (31 percent); the second largest between 1955 and 1964 (24 percent); and the third largest between 1965 and 1974 (20 percent). Smaller groups came before 1948 (9 percent) and between 1975 and 1983 (14 percent).

The origin groups differ substantially in their breakdown by period of immigration: the foreign-educated who came in 1948–1954 comprised in 1983 more than half the Asian group (56 percent) but just 22 percent of the African group and 28 percent of the European-American group. The proportions of the 1955–1964 immigrants were 12 percent, 54 percent, and 19 percent, respectively. In contrast, 41 percent of European-Americans arrived after 1965 compared with only 22–23 percent of Asian-Africans. A large majority (80 percent) of the more recent immigrants came from Europe-America.

Immigration from Asia-Africa decreased sharply from the mid-1960s on. Therefore, in 1983 the proportion of the foreign-educated of Asian-African origin was found to be considerably lower than the corresponding one for European-Americans; their age composition was also somewhat older. Of the foreign-born aged 25+ of each origin, only 31 percent of Asians and 32 percent of African origin were foreign-educated as defined, compared to 51 percent among European-Americans. Calculating their proportions of the total numbers of the 25+-year-olds of each origin (including the Israeli-born), the figures are 21 percent for Asia, 26 percent for Africa, and 38 percent for Europe-America. Clearly, the differential immigration patterns rendered the educational composition of Asian-Africans as a whole significantly more dependent on education acquired in Israel than that of European-Americans.[88]

Those who immigrated at the age of 25+ constituted in 1983 a relatively mature population of which about 30 percent were 55–64 years old and 47 percent were aged 65+. Their proportions among the total Jewish population (Israeli-born included) varied according to age as follows: from 76 percent of the elderly aged 65+ and 58 percent among those aged 55–64 to only 3 percent of the 25–34 age group. This has contributed to the rising importance of the Israeli educational system in shaping the educational attainment of the population as a whole. The inverse relationship between educational level and age, noted above, reflects not only the pattern of intergenerational differentials in educational attainment but also the increasing weight of the foreign-educated among older age groups. The latter factor accentuated the general pattern, since for all origin groups it was found that among the older age groups the educational level of the foreign-educated majority was far lower than that of the Israeli-born. Thus, comparing median years of schooling for ages 65+, for Israeli-born men of Asian-African origin (a relatively small group), the median amounted to .75 of the median for European-Americans, compared to only .68 for those educated abroad. The largest differentials between the origin-specific medians were found among women; the ratios to Europe-America being .53 for Asia and .64 for Africa among the Israeli-educated, as against 0.8 and .09, respectively, for the foreign-educated. This reflects the very high percentage of illiterates among elderly women who immigrated as adults from Asia-Africa (tables 49 and 54).

Table 54 summarizes several educational indicators for sex–age–origin groups of the foreign-educated. On all indicators, the educational attainment of each origin group (men and women alike) improves substantially

---

[88]Of the total numbers of the 15+-year-olds of each origin group in 1983, the proportions of Israeli-educated (Israeli-born + foreign-born who were 0–14 years old at immigration) were for Asia—71 percent, Africa—66 percent, and Europe-America—49 percent.

when passing from older to younger age groups. Focusing on the older age groups, the effects of their differential backgrounds on their education are discernible. Thus, 29–32 percent of the men aged 55–64 and 44–46 percent of the men aged 65+ of Asian or African origin were functionally illiterate, compared with only 9 percent and 14 percent, respectively, among European-Americans. The percentages of functional illiterates among women of Asian-African origin amounted to 61 percent of the 55–64 age group and to 71–73 percent of those aged 65+, compared to just 9 percent and 17 percent, respectively, among European-Americans.

As with the Israeli-educated, so also with the foreign-educated, at the extremes of the distribution by education—i.e., below or above secondary education—origin group differentials are wider than at the middle. This relationship does not apply to foreign-educated women because of the dominance of illiteracy among them. For men the median schooling years of Asian-Africans was about 3/4 (ratios of .71–.76) that of European-Americans, while the percentages of functional illiterates were more than three times higher, and the percentages of university graduates reached just 1/5 (table 54, ratios).

The 1983 census shows that, for the foreign-educated, recent immigrants have a much younger age composition than those who came earlier. Bearing this in mind, it is seen (table 55) that, except for 1948–1954 for Asia and Europe-America and 1955–1964 for Africa, the later the period of immigration, the higher the educational attainment acquired abroad. The exceptions relate to periods of mass or relatively large immigration involving whole communities whose educational attainment tended to be lower than that of more selective immigrations that came earlier or later. Furthermore, origin-group differentials regarding education acquired abroad tend to narrow among those who came more recently. Thus, the percentages of university graduates among all men educated abroad were 4 percent for Asian-Africans, compared to 16 percent for European-Americans, but among those immigrating in 1975 or after, these figures were higher (14 percent for Asia, 22 percent for Africa, and 31 percent for Europe-America), and the origin differentials were smaller. Findings in a similar direction were observed for women as well (table 55).

The educational differentials between groups of immigrants varying by period of immigration are not just artifacts of their different age compositions. Table 56 shows, as of 1983, that for the foreign-educated who came from Europe-America, controlling for age, the later the period of immigration, the higher was the proportion of university graduates (e.g., among the 45–54 age group the proportion amounts to 33 percent of the 1975+ immigrants compared to only 16 percent of those who came during 1955–1964). The same is true for the other origin groups. The origin-specific differentials are generally smaller for those who immigrated since 1965 (table 55) compared to those for the whole Jewish population (table 48). For instance, among men who immigrated between 1965 and 1974 from Asia or Africa, the percentage of university graduates was .31 as high as that for Europe-America and even higher among those who immigrated from 1975 on (Asia—.47; Africa—.73), as compared to only about .20 among all Jewish men of Asian-African origin. This analysis indicates that the educational differentials in Israel reflect not only differences between immigrants from different countries but also the changing size of immigration waves and their composition by countries of origin. As future immigration will be composed mainly of relatively well-educated European-Americans, it may be expected to widen the gap in educational attainment between the main origin groups (especially if all adult ages are considered together).

This argument puts additional weight on the functioning of the Israeli education system, as future patterns of educational differentials between origin groups will depend to a great extent on its success or failure in achieving more equality with regard to the highest educational attainment of its graduates of different origins. We turn our attention now to some basic features of the Israeli education system.

Origin-Group Differentials and the Israeli Education System

The census data reviewed above indicate that for the Israeli-born, educational discrepancies between origin groups at the secondary-school level were almost completely closed during the 1961–1983 period. At the same time, considerable gaps persist at the postsecondary and university levels. In the following, attention will be given to some aspects of the functioning of the Israeli secondary and postsecondary school systems which possibly contributed to the persistence of the remaining origin-group differentials.[89]

Entrance to postsecondary education depends on formal completion of a secondary school. In addition, psychometric and other types of examinations are used to further select between prospective candidates. Only a matriculation certificate, of either a general or vocational school, which testifies to success in the nationwide examinations administered by the Ministry of Education, is accepted for candidacy for university studies.[90]

---

[89]See Ch. Adler, "Jewish Education in Israel: A Sociological Perspective," in H.S. Himmelfarb and S. DellaPergola, eds., *Jewish Education Worldwide: Cross-Cultural Perspectives* (Lanham, 1989), pp. 485–503; A. Yogev and D. Kfir, "Determinants of Tracking in Israeli Secondary Education: Ability Groupings and Sponsorship in the Educational System" (in Hebrew), *Megamot*, 27, 1981, pp. 139–153; Y. Shavit, "Tracking and Ethnicity in Israeli Secondary Education," *American Sociological Review*, 49, 1984, pp. 210–220; Nahon, *Patterns of Educational Expansion*.

[90]Matriculation certificates in relatively small numbers may also be obtained through an

During the first decade of its existence, the young State of Israel succeeded in absorbing growing numbers of children into its rapidly expanding education system. The Law of Compulsory Education, governing children ages 5 to 13, had fully achieved its goals by the end of the 1950s; in 1961-62, 98 percent of the 6-13 age group was attending school.[91] Since the early 1960s, raising the participation in the educational process of youth beyond these ages has been a cornerstone of educational policy. This was to be achieved through inducing more graduates of elementary schools to enter some type of secondary school—normally at age 14—as well as improving school-retention rates of pupils in secondary schools. The measures necessary for these purposes were to be geared mainly to the needs of youth of Asian-African origin, since their scholastic achievement was considerably lower than that of European-Americans.

To facilitate the entrance of youth of Asian-African origin into secondary schools, their scores in a nationwide aptitude test taken at the end of elementary school were intentionally up-scaled to improve their chances in the competitive selection process. A system of gradual exemption from school fees allowed all pupils to pay less or nil according to their socioeconomic backgrounds, thus alleviating the economic burden of prolonged studies. The number and geographic dispersion of secondary schools grew, and within them an increasingly differentiated number of programs was offered to pupils, mainly through two- to four-year curricula in a large variety of vocational tracks. Underachieving pupils were also offered various types of tutoring and supportive extra lessons.

In 1969 a school-reform plan was introduced, aimed mainly at advancing social integration within schools as well as improving the scholastic achievement of pupils of disadvantaged backgrounds. The education system underwent a structural change whereby a three-tier system was established, starting with six years of elementary school, followed by a three-year intermediate division—the lower stage of the secondary school—leading to the final three years of upper-stage secondary school. The intermediate stage included preparatory as well as diagnostic and sorting functions in order to improve counseling and guidance for graduates regarding their choices at the upper stage, which were expected in turn to raise their prospects for completing secondary education successfully.[92] The number of years of

---

"external" procedure in which personal registration for examinations is not mediated through any regular secondary school. "Preparatory pre-academic classes," mostly sponsored by the universities, constitute yet another avenue of approach to higher education. Finally, Everyman's ("Open") University admits candidates regardless of their previous educational attainments, and its academic degrees are fully recognized. Important as these "second chance" options may be for improving the prospects of various social groups to attain some higher education, quantitatively their impact has been limited.

[91] CBS, *Statistical Abstract*, no. 16, 1965, p. 548.

[92] The counseling and guidance services in Israel have attracted some research efforts during

tuition-free obligatory education was raised to include the final year of the intermediate school (in sum, ten years between the ages of 5 and 14) and then also the first year of the upper stage (age 15). School fees through the whole of secondary education were abolished in 1978.

How effective were all these measures? The available figures show that considerable progress has been made since the early 1960s. Starting with entrance to secondary education, at age 14 the rates of enrollment in any type of secondary school increased significantly even before the school-reform program, from 51 percent in 1961–62 to 64 percent in 1968–69.[93] The rise continued, and ten years later, 87 percent of children aged 14 were attending a secondary school.[94]

Following initiation of the school-reform program, retention rates also improved significantly, since more pupils were oriented to four-year programs and their dropout rates were reduced. This is reflected in the rising proportion of pupils graduating from elementary school (8th grade) who, four years later, were studying in the final year of secondary school (12th grade)—from 40 percent to 53 percent of the 1965–66 and 1972–73 elementary-school graduation cohorts, respectively. Analyzing the age-specific data on enrollment rates by type of school and origin group, it becomes clear that expanding vocational education played a major role in increasing the entrance rates as well as in prolonging secondary-school studies. About 85 percent of the increase in the enrollment rates at age 14 during the period 1963–64 to 1968–69 was related to rising participation in vocational programs. The proportions of this age group studying in vocational schools, including a small minority of pupils in agricultural schools, grew from 16 to 28 percent, whereas the proportions of those studying in general schools increased only from 34 to 36 percent.[95] The yearly figures on composition by type of curriculum of 9th-grade pupils (the first grade of secondary school before the reform plan) show that between 1961–62 and 1968–69 the proportion of those studying in vocational-agricultural schools increased from 26 to 48 percent (from 37 to 57 percent for boys and from 16 to 39 percent for girls).

The contribution of vocational education to the growth of the enrollment rates among 14-year-olds was far more important for Asian-Africans than for European-Americans. Thus, between 1963–64 and 1966–67 the overall enrollment rate for Asian-Africans grew by 14 percentage points (from 30 to 44 percent), of which 8 percent was recorded for vocational schools (from

---

the last decade, specifically with regard to their impact on differential tracking of ethnic groups through secondary education. See Yogev and Kfir, "Determinants of Tracking"; Shavit, "Tracking and Ethnicity."

[93]CBS, *Statistical Abstract*, no. 20, 1969, p. 559. The selection of years for the following comparisons was partly dictated by the availability of data.

[94]Ibid., no. 30, 1979, p. 628.

[95]CBS, *Statistical Abstract*, no. 17, 1966, p. 598; ibid., no. 20, 1969, p. 559.

14 to 22 percent), compared to 3 percent of an overall increase of 10 percentage points for European-Americans (from 18 to 21 percent in vocational schools, and from 65 to 75 percent in secondary schools generally).

Another achievement, also related to vocational schools, was the increasing school-retention rate. This is clearly reflected in the data available for two points in time around 1969.[96] Of the 9th-grade cohort of pupils, the proportions of those who prolonged their studies to the 12th grade of vocational education grew nearly 2.5 times between the 1965–66 and 1972–73 cohorts (from 10.5 to 24.8 percent), whereas the corresponding proportions for general education remained stable at 28–29 percent. Furthermore, the data confirm that vocational education was instrumental in prolonging the studies of both origin groups, particularly the Asian-African. The percentages of 9th-grade beginners who "survived" to the 12th grade among Asian-Africans grew between these cohorts from 23 to 44 percent, and most of the increase was related to developments in vocational education (from 9 to 27 percent as compared to 14 percent and 17 percent, respectively, in general education). The corresponding figures for European-Americans, including a small minority of Israeli-born of Israeli paternity, were 12 and 22 percent for vocational education, and 45 and 44 percent for general education.

As entrance and retention rates rose, increasing rates of secondary-school completion were to be expected. In the absence of a suitable time series on graduates, these may be traced approximately through the rates of enrollment—normally at the final (12th) grade—of the 17-year-olds. The figures presented in tables 57 and 58 indicate that since the mid-1960s the origin-group differences in prospects for graduating from secondary school have been reduced remarkably, but more for girls than for boys. During the period 1966–67 to 1981–82, the overall rates of enrollment at age 17 increased for boys from 34 to 60 percent and for girls from 40 to 78 percent; by 1987–88, the rates had further increased to 72 percent for boys and 88 percent for girls. Some boys opt out of school earlier than girls, either to other kinds of studies (short vocational courses or *yeshivot*) or to work. Still, the great majority of both sexes today complete a full secondary-school education.

Did the two origin groups benefit equally from this process? The figures in table 57 indicate that the advance of Asian-Africans from the previous low position was relatively much greater than that of European-Americans: between 1966–67 and 1981–82, the rates at age 17 increased from 21 to 63 percent for the former, compared to 50 and 73 percent, respectively, for the

---

[96]CBS, *Society in Israel: Statistical Highlights, 1980*, p. 181. Retention rates through secondary school are estimates based on gross numbers of pupils in each of the relevant grades, irrespective of changes due to immigration, class repetition, etc.

latter. The ratio between enrollment rates of the origin groups increased from .41 in 1966–67 to .85 in 1981–82 for all 17-year-olds, from .44 to .78 for boys, and from .39 to .91 for girls (1.00 representing parity of enrollment rates, table 58).

Two periods are discernible in the data. During the first, from the mid-1960s to the mid-1970s, the major growth factor was the expansion of vocational education, whereas during the following period—from the mid-1970s on—a more even growth of vocational as well as general education was recorded. Enrollment rates at age 17, by type of school, reflect these changes. Between 1965–66 and 1974–75 the rates for vocational education more than doubled (from 11 to nearly 25 percent), whereas the rates for general education rose minimally (from 26 to 28 percent). During the period 1974–75 to 1987–88, the rates for both types of education grew by 50 percent (from 25 to 37 percent for vocational education and from 28 to 43 percent for general education; table 58).

The rising rate of growth of general secondary-school education in the later period seems to be clearly related to the reform in the matriculation examinations that was introduced during the late 1970s. The reform aimed at increasing the variety and flexibility of the curricular program and of the examination requirements as well. The reasoning was that a redesign of general education in this direction might enable it to cater to a larger sector of the relevant age groups.

Table 58 presents data on origin-specific rates of enrollment in general and vocational education of youth aged 17, through the period 1966–67 to 1981–82. These figures shed some light on the impact that the changing features of the educational system may have had on the graduation prospects of the origin groups. In 1966–67, only 21 percent of 17-year-olds of Asian-African origin (20 percent of the boys and 22 percent of the girls) were studying in secondary schools (whether general or vocational) for four-year certificates (matriculation or others) compared with 50 percent of those of European-American origin (45 percent of the boys and 55 percent of the girls). The ratio between these values amounted to .41 (.44 among boys and .39 for girls; table 58). Whereas among the Asian-Africans the relatively low rates of enrollment in general and vocational education were quite similar (12 percent and 9 percent; 10 percent and 9 percent, respectively, for boys; 14 percent and 8 percent for girls), among European-Americans much higher rates of enrollment in general education were recorded—38 percent compared with only 12 percent in vocational education (30 percent and 15 percent, respectively, for boys; 47 percent and 9 percent for girls).

In 1974–75, both origin groups showed moderately higher rates for general education (Asia-Africa—16 percent, Europe-America—45 percent), but considerably higher rates for vocational education, with a threefold increase among Asian-Africans (from 9 to 26 percent; boys—from 9 to 24 percent, girls—from 8 to 29 percent) and a twofold increase among European-Americans (from 12 to 23 percent; boys—from 15 to 27 percent; girls—from 9 to 18 percent). This development brought closer the overall enrollment rates in secondary education of the two origin groups (Asia-Africa—42 percent, Europe-America—68 percent) and decreased the discrepancy between them (the ratios grew from .41 to .62).

By 1981–82, the overall enrollment rates rose to 63 percent for Asian-Africans and 73 percent for European-Americans, thus reducing further the discrepancy between the origin groups (the ratio grew to .85). The enrollment rates in vocational education continued to grow faster among Asian-Africans than among European-Americans (from 26 to 38 percent compared with 23 percent and 27 percent, respectively), and the discrepancy between them increased as the ratios grew from 1.16 to 1.39 (both above parity). It is interesting to note the same relative advance of the Asian-Africans in general education as well. Their enrollment rate grew from 16 to 24 percent, whereas that of European-Americans remained almost constant at 45–46 percent, thus reducing the discrepancy between them for this type of education (the ratios grew from .35 to .53).

These findings indicate not only the important role which vocational education played since the early 1960s in raising the prospects for completing secondary school among the Asian-African origin group, but also that the reform in general education was particularly beneficial for this group, as from the late 1970s.

Did the processes that reduced origin-group discrepancies in secondary-school completion also affect their differential prospects of winning matriculation certificates? Cross-section data shed some light on the matter.

The origin-specific rates for 17-year-olds in 1981–82, shown in table 60, indicate that the rates of enrollment in matriculation tracks amounted to only 46 percent among Asian-Africans compared to 66 percent among European-Americans, the difference reflecting mainly their lower representation in general secondary education. Among pupils aged 17 of Asian-African origin, only 73 percent were in matriculation tracks compared with 90 percent of European-Americans. Among the pupils in these tracks of Asian-African origin, 54 percent studied in general schools and 46 percent in vocational schools, compared with 69 percent and 31 percent, respectively, among the European-Americans. Since a smaller proportion of pupils in the vocational track actually sat for the examinations (73 percent compared to 93 percent in the general track in 1985–86), this factor too lowered the chances of Asian-African pupils acquiring a matriculation certificate. For both origin groups, the rates of pupils in matriculation tracks—and the percentages studying in general secondary schools—are higher for girls than for boys. Still, both sexes exhibit similar origin differentials.

The success rate in the matriculation examinations in 1986–87 was about a third lower in the vocational track than in the general one (45 percent vs. 70 percent; table 61). In both tracks the rates for examinees of Asian-African origin were relatively lower than those for European-Americans: 62 percent against 76 percent in the general track, and only 39 percent against 53 percent in the vocational one. The overall success rate was 53 percent for Asian-Africans, about a quarter lower than the 70-percent rate for European-Americans. The proportion of 17-year-olds (per 100 in the specified population) who acquired matriculation certificates in 1986–87, after completing studies in either track, is estimated to be about 23 percent for Asian-Africans compared to 42 percent for European-Americans.

In the light of the data presented above, it seems that this difference reflects the combined effects of factors involved in the streaming of pupils of various sociocultural backgrounds through the secondary schools, as well as of other factors determining their motivation and achievement all along the way.

Were the graduates of secondary schools of both origin groups equally inclined to enter university studies? Table 48 shows that among the 25–44 age group in the 1983 census, the percentages with any kind of secondary-school or higher certificates were in the range of 40–53 percent for men and 32–58 percent for women of Asian-African origin, as compared with 77–82 percent and 79–84 percent, respectively, for European-Americans. It seems that among these secondary-school graduates, who were mostly Israeli-educated (table 52), the majority of the European-Americans pursued higher studies, whereas only a minority of Asian-Africans did so. This is indicated in the data by differentials between the following proportions: (a) the percentage with certificates from a secondary school (including nonmatriculation) or higher education (i.e., 13+ years); (b) the percentage with some postsecondary or academic education; and (c) the percentage with an academic degree. The (b)/(a) ratios range from only .34 to .42 for Asian-Africans as compared with .66 to .70 for European-Americans, with very small differentials between the sexes. The differences in the proportions of secondary-school graduates who gained academic degrees are still larger: the (c)/(a) ratios among men aged 24–45 range from .12 to .15 for Asian-Africans as compared with .31 to .40 for European-Americans. Lower values were recorded for women: .08 for Asian-Africans and .29 to .30 for European-Americans, respectively (table 48).

Table 62 shows that during the period 1964–65 to 1988–89, the rates for university students in the 20–29 age group more than doubled, increasing from 3.8 to 8.2 percent. The rates for Asian-Africans were significantly lower than those for European-Americans, but since they grew faster, the ratios between the origin-specific rates—expressing the extent of similarity between the groups of origin—rose for the Israeli-born from .15 to .43 and for the foreign-born from .15 to .34. The considerable discrepancy which still persists reflects, as already noted, the lower proportion among Asian-Africans of graduates in matriculation tracks (see also table 59).

Another possible factor is a relatively lower inclination of Asian-African youth, even those with matriculation certificates, to turn to higher education. The 1983 census data indicate whether or not people who attained such a certificate—and for whom the information could be checked—attempted (either at the census date or before) to pursue further studies. Table 63 shows for men aged 25–34 that 35–37 percent of Asian-Africans, compared with 46 percent of European-Americans, studied at a time for higher certificates but had not (yet) graduated (for women—21–25 percent and 35 percent, respectively). This discrepancy between origin groups pertains mainly to university studies, whereas their representation in other types of postsecondary (mostly technical or semiprofessional) education is rather similar.

A follow-up survey of candidates who applied for university studies in 1981–82 found these proportions failing to be accepted: among the Israeli-born—27 percent for Asian-Africans compared to only 17 percent for European-Americans, and among the foreign-born—31 percent and 21 percent, respectively. Another follow-up survey, of a cohort of first-year students starting their studies in 1976–77, found that during the ensuing five-year span, about a quarter (27 percent) prematurely discontinued their studies, 34 percent among Asian-Africans compared to 24 percent among European-Americans.[97]

It has been suggested that excessive institutional intervention, involving a guided "streaming" of pupils into the various tracks of study in secondary schools, might have exerted a deterrent effect on pupils of Asian-African origin, more of whom, in a less selective school system, might have been motivated to attain higher education. However, the data reviewed in this section consistently indicate relatively lower rates of success in matriculation examinations for the Asian-African origin group, a weaker tendency for prolonging studies in any type of postsecondary education on the part of those who have acquired a matriculation certificate, lower success rates in the competition for admission to university studies, and, finally, lower graduation rates among those who start such studies. In a recent study of

---

[97]CBS, *Candidates for First Degree Studies at Universities in 1981/82*, Special Series no. 819, 1988, p. 65.; CBS, *Course of Studies of University First Degree Students: 1976/77 to 1980/81*, Special Series no. 772, 1986, p. 56.

pupil achievement in intermediate schools—i.e., before tracking takes place—significantly lower attainments were recorded for pupils of Asian-African origin on three different tests (IQ, science, and reading comprehension), controlling for socioeconomic status.[98] These findings point to somewhat differential prospects between origin groups with regard to the course of studies they are likely to follow at the upper stage of secondary education.

Along with the already noted trend of educational expansion over time among the Israeli population in general, the educational attainment of younger cohorts of parents is rising among all origin groups. In the long run, this process may be assumed to bring about profound change in home environment and familial socialization patterns in ways conducive to raising children's scholastic achievement and their motivation to prolong studies. It may also be expected to contribute to a further future narrowing of educational gaps between the young of the different origin groups.

VOTING BEHAVIOR

An assessment of voting behavior is indispensable to a broader understanding of Israeli society, particularly regarding the character and evolution of the ethnic dimension within it.[99]

Sharp polarization along ethnic lines has been repeatedly attributed to the Israeli political system, especially since the major political upheaval of 1977. In that election, the conservative-nationalist Likud party, backed by voters of Asian-African origin, for the first time took away the premiership from the Labor party. Subsequently, during the 1981 and 1984 electoral campaigns, instances of ethnic tension intensified, leading some observers to conclude that ethnic cleavages were widening and becoming a predominant factor in the Israeli political process.

In seeking to assess the role of the ethnic dimension in Israeli voting behavior, the general outlines of the evolution of the Israeli party system will first be traced. Attention will then turn to the question of how political

---

[98]The main findings were reported by investigators Y. Dar and N. Resh of the Hebrew University, during the annual conference of the Israeli Sociological Association, February 1990. See also their paper "Learning Achievements in Junior High Schools in Reading Comprehension and Science" (in Hebrew), Research Institute for Innovation in Education, Hebrew University, no. 121, 1989.

[99]Peter Medding and Abraham Diskin read an earlier draft of this section and offered invaluable criticism. Any responsibility for what follows is solely the author's, however. For recent overviews of the subject see Ernest Krausz, ed., *Politics and Society in Israel, Studies of Israeli Society*, 3 (New Brunswick and Oxford, 1985); Itzhak Galnoor, "Israeli Democracy in Transition," in Peter Medding, ed., *Studies in Contemporary Jewry*, 5, 1989, pp. 126–147.

parties explicitly focusing on ethnic issues have succeeded with voters. This will be followed by an examination of the connections between ethnic origin and other background characteristics and the Israeli party configurations that prevailed from the mid-1950s to the late 1980s. After that, the political map that emerged from the 1988 Knesset election will be analyzed in detail in an attempt to draw further conclusions about the relative weight of the major socioeconomic and sociocultural variables—ethnicity, socioeconomic status, religiosity, etc.—as determinants of political choice. Finally, attention will be given to those elected to public office, to measure the extent to which there is a trend toward equal political participation and representation of the major origin groups.

Background of the Israeli Party System

The origins of the Israeli political party system can in large part be traced to past Diaspora experience.[100] A great variety of ideological orientations existed among Jews in the Diaspora before Israel's independence. A major political divide concerned the basic analysis of the Jewish question, and of the solutions to be provided for it—whether through Zionism and the struggle to create an independent Jewish state, local Jewish autonomism in the Diaspora, or otherwise. In addition, Jewish political participation in the Diaspora tended to reflect the attraction of Jews toward general ideologies prevailing in the surrounding societies, such as liberalism, socialism, nationalism, and the like. Jewish political responses, then, emphasized a great variety of conflicting ideologies and interests. These diverse political backgrounds were gradually transfused by Jewish immigrants into the political reality of the prestate *yishuv* and provided the foundation of the major political camps that still operate in the contemporary Israeli political arena. In turn, the changing characteristics, needs, and experiences of Israel's population, along with evolving local political realities, stimulated continuous adjustments—and great fragmentation—in the Israeli party system.

According to Israel's electoral law, the 120 seats in the Knesset are divided proportionally according to the vote won by each party. Only parties failing to reach a minimum of 1 percent of the national vote are excluded. One result of the system is to permit political representation of relatively small sociopolitical groups, thus enabling virtually all significant minorities to be heard. Since no single party has ever won an absolute majority of the votes, government has been possible only on a coalition basis. As a result, tiny political factions occasionally gain disproportionate power.

---

[100]A broad historical and sociological outline is to be had in S.N.Eisenstadt, *The Transformation of Israeli Society* (London,1985); see also Dan Horowitz and Moshe Lissak, *The Origins of the Israeli Polity: Palestine Under the Mandate* (Chicago, 1978).

The Israeli party system accommodates a variety of competing ideological orientations. Prominent tensions exist, first, between different positions with regard to the Israeli-Arab conflict and, second, between various approaches to the question of religion and secularism. A further factor making for political cleavage, common to almost every other political system, is social class.[101] While many issues, taken individually, tend to generate political confrontation with little room for compromise, national defense, religious, and socioeconomic platforms, as expressed by the different parties, do not overlap according to rigid and constant patterns. Each party has worked out its own particular combination of issue positions. This composite political pluralism ensures governability by way of a variety of possible coalition agreements on selected and specific portions of each party's program. This also means that voters usually have a range of choice among several parties, parts of whose programs are sufficiently close to one another.

Since this article is concerned with the relationship between the ethnic dimension and voting behavior rather than politics per se, the following analysis will selectively consider the results of past Israeli political elections. The four elections examined are those of 1955 (3rd Knesset), the first vote after the end of the period of mass immigration; 1965 (6th Knesset), a time of consolidation in Israeli society, and the last election held before the Six Day War; 1977 (9th Knesset), which saw the rise of the Likud party; and 1988 (12th Knesset), the most recent election.

Results of Knesset Elections, 1955–1988

Table 64 presents a synopsis of selected election results, showing the percentage distribution of votes obtained by all parties which won at least one seat. For ease of presentation, the parties have been regrouped into five major political sectors—Labor, Liberal-Radical, Religious, Center-Right to Right, and Communist and Arab—also showing in greater detail changes within each sector.[102] When one considers the momentous events that occurred during this period, what is perhaps most striking is the comparative paucity of major changes in the basic balance of the Israeli party system.

---

[101]See Benjamin Akzin, "The Role of Parties in Israeli Democracy," in Eisenstadt, Bar Yossef, Adler, eds., *Integration and Development in Israel*, pp. 9–46; Emanuel Gutmann, "Parties and Camps—Stability and Change" (in Hebrew), in M. Lissak and E. Gutmann, *The Israeli Political System* (Tel Aviv, 1977), pp. 122–170; Yonatan Shapiro, "Political Sociology in Israel: A Critical View," in Krausz, *Politics and Society in Israel*, pp. 6–16.

[102]Somewhat different typologies of the Israeli party system have been proposed by various scholars. See, e.g., Dan Horowitz and Moshe Lissak, "Authority Without Sovereignty: The Case of the National Centre of the Jewish Community in Palestine," *Government and Opposition*, 8, 1973, pp. 48–71; Daniel J. Elazar, "Israel's Compound Polity," in H.R. Penniman, ed., *Israel at the Polls: The Knesset Elections of 1977* (Washington, 1979), pp. 1–38.

The more significant quantitative shifts, which in turn determined important changes in Israeli leadership, concerned the gradual shift of political hegemony from the Labor to the Center-Right sector.

As table 64 makes clear, the Labor sector reached a peak in 1965—indeed, an absolute majority of the vote if its different and rival factions are counted together. (In 1964, Mapai, the main Labor party, merged with the smaller Ahdut Ha'avoda to form the Ma'arakh, or Labor Alignment.) By 1977, the Labor camp, including Mapam, had lost over half of its support, part of which it recovered in subsequent elections. Several mergers and splits that occurred over the years involving the Labor sector attracted a great deal of the public's attention, perhaps diverting it from the major ongoing political trend of the gradual erosion of the Labor sector as the numerically predominant segment of the Israeli polity. Such a trend can clearly be traced to the early 1960s,[103] but it was not fully realized until the 1977 election. Significant changes also occurred in the internal distribution of the vote within the Labor sector, where the share of Mapam-United Workers' party, to the left of the Labor party, tended to decline significantly.

The Center-Right to Right sector started growing significantly after the 1965 election, reaching a peak in 1977 (the actual high was in 1981), which, however, was significantly lower than Labor's during the 1960s. In retrospect, a most significant change in the Israeli party structure was the creation in 1965 of Gahal from the fusion of the right-wing Herut and the center-right Liberal (formerly General Zionist) parties. While until then Mapai (the Israel Labor party) was the only large party around which a viable coalition could assemble, Gahal, which later evolved into the Likud, constituted a formation whose size was sufficiently large to offer a viable alternative. In 1977 the Likud was able to form a coalition with the decisive support of the religious parties. Within the Center-Right to Right sector, the share of the parties to the right of Likud—such as Tehiya, Tzomet, and Moledet in 1988—tended to increase.

One of the more important deviations from the predominant Israeli pattern of long-term, gradual political change was the formation in 1977 of the short-lived Dash party (Democratic Movement for Change) led by Yigael Yadin. Dash helped promote the shift between the two major parties at the core of Israeli political life. Dash took most of its own votes from the

---

[103]See Amiram Gonen, "A Geographic Examination of Electoral Competition Between the Ma'arakh and the Likud in Jewish Cities in Israel, 1965–1981" (in Hebrew), *Medinah, Mimshal Veyahasim Beinleumiim*, 19–20, 1982, pp. 63–87; Amiram Gonen, "A Geographical Analysis of the Elections in Jewish Urban Communities," in D. Caspi, A. Diskin, and E. Gutmann, eds., *The Roots of Begin's Success* (London-Canberra-New York, 1984), pp. 59–88; Abraham Diskin, *Elections and Voters in Israel* (in Hebrew; Tel Aviv, 1986; American edition forthcoming), pp. 76–80.

Labor Alignment, though it also attracted voters from the Likud and from its own neighbor parties within the Liberal-Radical sector. It was the political defeat of the Labor Alignment, determined by Dash, far more than the relative success of the Likud in 1977, that caused the end of Labor's hold on power. It should be noted, though, that even if Dash's votes are counted with the Labor sector, rather than in the Liberal-Radical sector, a consistently declining trend in the Labor grouping since the 1960s is still evident.

The weight of the religious sector has not changed much over time, remaining steady at just below 15 percent of the total vote. Research on religious attitudes and behavior of Israelis indicates that the proportion of voters for religious parties is substantially smaller than that of Jews defining themselves as very religious or religious. Thus, in a 1979 national survey of the Jewish population aged 14 and older, conducted by Israel's Central Bureau of Statistics, 6 percent said they were very religious, 18 percent religious, 37 percent not very religious, and 39 percent not religious.[104] In a 1988 study of marriage and fertility patterns, and limited to married Jewish women aged 22–39 in localities of 5,000 inhabitants and over,[105] 4 percent reported themselves to be very religious, 10 percent religious, 36 percent traditional, and 50 percent secular. Asked about parental home, 4 percent of the same women reported it as being very religious, 25 percent religious, 32 percent traditional, and 39 percent secular.

Religious behaviors were still significantly associated with countries of origin, especially among older age groups. In 1979, 33 percent of Jews born in Asia-Africa reported themselves as religious or very religious, as against 19 percent born in Europe-America and 14 percent of the Israeli-born. At the opposite end of the spectrum, 20 percent of the Asian-African born, 51 percent of the European-American born, and 62 percent of the Israeli-born defined themselves as nonreligious.[106]

Overall, these various findings, and research based on earlier data,[107] indicate a significant process of secularization among younger adult Israelis, although a minority kept to strong religious patterns and was sustained by the higher birthrate of the more religious sector of Israel's Jewish population. At the same time, there was an increased tendency toward ideological polarization between the extremely religious and the extremely secular in Israel. This reflected radicalization within the religious sector itself. Indeed,

---

[104]See Uri Avner, "Investigation of Attitude to Religion in Surveys" (in Hebrew), Jerusalem, 1982, mimeo.

[105]Eric Peritz et al., "Family Formation and Fertility in Israel," Hebrew University, Jerusalem, 1988, research in progress.

[106]See Avner, "Investigation of Attitude to Religion."

[107]See Yehuda Ben Meir and Perry Kedem, "Index of Religiosity of the Jewish Population of Israel" (in Hebrew), *Megamot*, 24, 1979, pp. 353–362; Calvin Goldscheider and Dov Friedlander, "Religiosity Patterns in Israel," AJYB 1983, vol. 83, pp. 3–39.

since the 1981 elections, remarkable changes have occurred within the religious electorate. The relatively moderate Mafdal-National Religious party (NRP)—formerly Mizrachi-Hapoel Hamizrachi, once the leading force among religious voters—lost much of its support. Instead, the more strictly Orthodox forces came to dominate numerically the religious political sector. Overall, Agudat Israel kept its share of the vote, while Shas (Sephardi Torah Guardians) emerged as a significant political force. Degel Hatorah emerged as yet another Orthodox faction in the 1988 Knesset.

The total weight of the Communist and Arab sectors of the Israeli party system was rather stable, despite moderate declines. The Communist party constituencies usually included both Jewish and Arab voters. The largest one was the Israeli Communist party, which split during the 1960s into two parties, one mostly Jewish and the other mostly Arab. The Jewish extreme Left continued to appear under changing party labels until the late 1970s. Later on, it virtually disappeared as a separate political force. Some of its voters joined the Arab-Jewish Progressive List for Peace, others moved to the Liberal-Radical and Labor sectors of the Israeli party system. The small political sector composed of parties exclusively aiming at the Arab electorate tended to decline over time. In the past these included various minorities' lists associated with the Labor movement and, in 1988, the Arab Democratic party. Their decline reflects a strengthened support of Arab voters for the extreme Left political sector, as well as a considerable diffusion of the Arab vote throughout all the Jewish parties.

In retrospect, election results over the years indicate a remarkable flexibility on the part of the Israeli political system in incorporating vast numbers of new voters without repeatedly incurring radical structural changes. This held true even as Likud replaced Labor as the leading political force. The number of voters grew nearly fivefold between 1949 and 1988 and nearly trebled between 1955 and 1988. Absorption of new immigrants, the overwhelming majority of whom had never voted anywhere before, also meant providing them with the basic elements of political education. The party structure as it existed since 1948, and its subsequent gradual evolution, evidently succeeded in providing the outlets for political expression within Israeli society.

Changing Weight of Ethnic Parties Within the Israeli Political System

Beginning with the elections to the 1st Knesset (1949), some Israeli parties openly sought the support of an ethnic constituency. As already noted, these were chiefly parties addressing the non-Jewish sectors of Israeli society. Ethnic parties addressing a Jewish constituency appealed mostly, though not exclusively, to voters of Asian and African origins. Often—though not always—they emphasized the traditional-religious aspects of a given group's cultural inheritance. Their share of the vote in national elections was generally very small; most failed to attain the 1 percent minimum legally required to win at least one seat in the Knesset. The fragmented nature of ethnicity and the narrow and particularistic programs usually advocated by ethnic parties evidently conflicted with the need to reach an audience sufficiently large and differentiated to build up a stable base of political influence.

Overall, the vote for ethnic parties tended to decline from about 5 percent of all votes in the 1st Knesset to about 1 percent or less throughout the 1950s and 1960s. Since the 1970s there has been a limited revival, though it has taken place through repeated substitutions of one ethnic party for another, with each displaced party quickly disappearing from the scene. The ethnic parties collectively obtained roughly 2–4 percent of the total votes in elections held during the 1970s and early 1980s. Among those succeeding in getting Knesset seats, Shmuel Flatto-Sharon's ephemeral Development and Peace list was followed by Aharon Abuhatzeira's Tami (Movement for Israel's Tradition), which in turn was replaced by Shas (Sephardi Torah Guardians). Led by former Sephardi chief rabbi Ovadia Yosef, and inspired by the leader of Lithuanian yeshivahs, Rabbi Menachem Eliezer Schach, Shas combined support for the religious traditionalism of Asian-African Jewish communities with an image actually close to that of the Ashkenazi ultra-Orthodox. It obtained the most impressive success ever by an ethnic political movement, with 4.7 percent of the vote and 6 seats in the 12th Knesset (1988). In the same election, less than one additional percent of the vote was gathered overall by several other splinter ethnic lists.

The vast majority of the Israeli electorate has thus never emphasized ethnic allegiance as the primary determinant of political choice. Actually, Shas's comparatively successful vote reflects a more complex balance of factors than mere ethnicity, being also strongly tied to ideological (religious) preferences and other social factors (see below). It should be noted, however, that the constituencies of several other political parties tended to be overwhelmingly homogeneous with regard to the geographical origins of voters, although ethnic issues were not openly addressed in the platform of such parties. Thus, as a kind of counterpart to the just mentioned concentration of votes by Asian-African origin groups, the constituencies of Agudat Israel, the Independent Liberals, and Dash in the past, or, more recently, Shinui (Center Movement) and Ratz (Citizens' Rights Movement, CRM), tended to be overwhelmingly European. An intriguing question is whether strongly homogeneous ethnic support can be, and in fact is, attracted in the

Israeli political system by way of subtle, symbolic communication, rather than by an explicit call to ethnic traditions and feelings.

The fact that openly ethnic lists have played a relatively marginal role on the Israeli political scene is not sufficient evidence to dismiss the possibility that ethnicity is significant in national political processes. Indeed, of the two major parties, Labor voters comprise a clear majority of European-Americans and the Likud a majority of Asian-Africans. Moreover, the fact that the 1981 and 1984 electoral campaigns to the Knesset were loaded with ethnic symbols and accompanied by episodes of violence with an ethnic undertone aroused fears of a potentially disruptive outburst of ethnic tension.[108] (These tensions were significantly weaker, if at all visible, during the 1988 electoral campaign.) Thus, the actual relationship between ethnicity and voting patterns calls for further careful assessment.

Social Structural Correlates of Voting Patterns, 1955–1988

METHOD

Direct data on the relationship between personal characteristics of voters and party preferences are not easily available. Given the secret ballot, information can be gathered only indirectly through general sample investigations of political attitudes over time or through exit polls. These indirect sources provide a wealth of interesting information and have been incorporated in the vast research literature which deals with elections and political behavior in Israel.[109] However, the approach adopted here is the analysis of actual vote returns, by aggregate characteristics of voters. The advantage of such an approach is that it relies on actual electoral results rather than on more or less perfect proxies. It also allows for homogeneous comparisons over extended periods of time for which other, more disaggregated, data are not available. The disadvantage lies in the risk that the analysis of electoral results for aggregate units of investigation, such as small geographical areas, may lead to different conclusions than would be obtained by focusing on individual voters.[110]

---

[108]Zeev Shavit, *Ethnic Connotations and Symbols of Ethnicity in Electoral Propaganda to the 10th and 11th Knesset* (in Hebrew), Jerusalem Institute for Israel Studies, no. 28, 1986.

[109]Detailed analyses of Israeli political elections, relying on a variety of sources, have been released periodically. See, e.g., Asher Arian, ed., *The Elections in Israel—1969* (Jerusalem, 1972); idem, *The Elections in Israel—1973* (Jerusalem, 1975); idem, *The Elections in Israel—1977* (Jerusalem, 1980); idem, *The Elections in Israel—1981* (Tel Aviv, 1983); Penniman, *Israel at the Polls . . . 1977*; Howard R. Penniman and Daniel J. Elazar, eds., *Israel at the Polls 1981: A Study of the Knesset Elections* (Bloomington, 1986); Diskin, *Elections and Voters in Israel*.

[110]See the technical discussions in W.S. Robinson, "Ecological Correlations and the Behavior of Individuals," *American Sociological Review*, 15, 1950, pp. 351–357; Laura Irwin Langbein

Keeping in mind these basic conceptual limitations, the aim is to find possible similarities and dissimilarities among Israeli political parties in order to discover basic patterns of linkage between the party configuration and selected sociodemographic characteristics of voters. Provided that strong and consistent patterns emerge over time, the ground will be set for formulating at least some promising research hypotheses, if not definitive conclusions. The procedure followed here is to compare the results obtained by each party at each of the four elections already discussed above (1955, 1965, 1977, and 1988).[111] The data were processed through Smallest Space Analysis (SSA), a standard nonmetric multivariate analysis technique.[112] The data input consists of the proportion of votes obtained by each party in each different type of Jewish locality. Based on the standard Central Bureau of Statistics classifications, the following typology of localities was used: Jerusalem, Tel Aviv, Haifa, other veteran cities, other new cities, veteran urban settlements, new urban settlements, veteran villages, new villages, veteran moshavim, new moshavim, kibbutzim, and other rural settlements.[113] The terms "veteran" and "new" refer to the date of a locality's settlement by Jewish inhabitants, whether before or after 1948.

---

and Allan J. Lichtman, *Ecological Inference* (Beverly Hills and London, 1978). The ecological approach has been usefully applied by various researchers to the study of Israeli elections. See, e.g., Matras, *Social Change in Israel*, pp. 113–130; Diskin, *Elections and Voters in Israel*, pp. 65–80.

[111]The official election results quoted throughout this article appear, respectively, in Central Bureau of Statistics, Ministry of the Interior—Inspector General of Elections, Office Mechanization Center, *Results of Elections to the Third Knesset and to Local Authorities 26.7.1955* (in Hebrew; Jerusalem, 1956), Central Bureau of Statistics, Special Series no. 51; Central Bureau of Statistics, Inspector General of Elections, Office Mechanization Center, *Results of Elections to the Sixth Knesset and to Local Authorities 2.11.1965*, vol. 1 (in Hebrew; Jerusalem, 1967), Central Bureau of Statistics, Special Series no. 216; Central Bureau of Statistics, Inspector General of Elections, Office Mechanization Center, *Results of Elections to the Ninth Knesset 17.5.1977* (in Hebrew; Jerusalem, 1977), Central Bureau of Statistics, Special Series no. 553; Central Bureau of Statistics, Ministry of the Interior—Inspector General of Elections, Malam Systems Ltd., *Results of Elections to the Twelfth Knesset 1.11.1988*, vol. A (in Hebrew; Jerusalem, 1989), Central Bureau of Statistics, Special Series no. 855. See also Central Bureau of Statistics, *Statistical Abstract of Israel* (Jerusalem, 1989).

[112]The technique is described in Louis Guttman, "A General Nonmetric Technique for Finding the Smallest Coordinate Space for a Configuration of Points," *Psychometrika*, 33, 1968, pp. 469–506. For an earlier discussion and application of the SSA technique to the study of the Israeli party system, see Diskin, *Elections and Voters in Israel*, p. 73.

[113]There were minor differences in the Central Bureau of Statistics' classification of localities at the various dates considered here. In 1955, the category of *ma'abarot* (transit camps) was also taken into account to determine the proportion of voters in new localities. In 1988, fewer types of localities were separately detailed, and the category of "development towns" was used to represent new localities (see table 65). For the purpose of SSA analyses, it would be better to examine more disaggregated data, e.g., by ballot districts or even by single ballot. Yet, previous ecological analyses of election results indicate that the degree of data disaggregation does not necessarily affect the main conclusions. See Diskin, *Elections and Voters in Israel*, p. 74.

Each type of locality represents an aggregate of voters of varying size and composition. It is assumed here that types of localities—or, more generally, homogeneous residential areas—represent a highly meaningful intermediate variable in the study of the Israeli societal structure. Beyond different geographical locations, the various types of localities reflect the chronology and changing composition of immigration, trends in urbanization and other aspects of socioeconomic change, and ideational differences within the Jewish population. It can be reasonably assumed that the different demographic, socioeconomic, and sociocultural characteristics of the inhabitants of different types of localities are reflected in their political preferences. In the particular context of our analysis, it should be stressed that new localities absorbed a disproportionate share of the mass immigration wave of 1948–1951, and to some extent of subsequent immigration, with a strong predominance of Jews of Asian and African origins. Patterns of political behavior in new localities can more generally be posited as a proxy for patterns among the Asian-African-born segment of the Jewish population. (For a more detailed discussion of ethnic patterns in residential distribution, see the section on this subject earlier in this study.)

Table 65 exemplifies the data input shaping the following analysis. It shows the distribution of votes obtained by major parties in the 1988 elections, by type of locality. Considerable variation characterizes the bases of power of different parties. The strongest polarization appears between mostly Jewish and mostly Arab parties, thus testifying to the social-structural and political cleavages that are known to exist between Jews and Arabs in Israel. Since this study focuses on the relevance of the ethnic dimension among Israel's Jews, the following analysis only refers to parties with a clear majority of Jewish voters and to mainly Jewish localities, thus excluding most of what was referred to above as the Communist and Arab sectors of the Israeli political spectrum. Kibbutzim—comprising an average of 3–4 percent of the total Jewish population—were also excluded from the analysis, the main reason being the skewed vote distribution there. Throughout the period of over 30 years examined here, two parties in particular, Ahdut Ha'avoda and Mapam, stand out for the high share of their total vote obtained in kibbutzim. This, by the SSA procedure, would result in a contraposition between these two parties and an analytically meaningless cluster of all of the other parties.

Diagrams 1, 2, 3, and 4 present the results of SSA analyses for the elections of 1955, 1965, 1977, and 1988, respectively. SSA computes a matrix of intercorrelations out of the original data input, transforms the numerical correlations into Euclidean distances, and produces maps in which each variable (political party) is represented by a point. The smaller or greater distances between points plotted reflect the similarity or dissimilarity in the distribution of votes for the various parties across the different types of localities considered. Having established the relative positions of different parties on a two-dimensional map, the two dimensions then need to be interpreted. It is assumed here that the two major latent dimensions in the Israeli party configuration are, on the one axis, a measure of religiosity, and on the other axis, a measure of ethnicity, namely the amount of support won by each party among voters of Asian-African origin.[114] In agreement with previous statements about the overall stability of the Israeli party system, it is suggested that a persistent set of sociodemographic factors has been associated with the Israeli political party system from the 1950s through the 1980s. In fact, the same structural interpretation applies to the four elections examined here, in spite of their being spread over 33 years and in spite of the significant differences in the respective electoral returns.

The diagrams' vertical dimension rates a party's religiosity in three categories: high, intermediate, and low. Such classification is highly consistent with what is known about the parties' programs on religious issues and about the religious characteristics of the respective constituencies. It is corroborated by the percentages of the respective total vote obtained by the various parties in cities like Jerusalem (see again table 65) or B'nei Berak, which have large shares of religious voters. The diagrams' horizontal dimension rates party support among voters of Asian-African origin as high, intermediate, and low. Ex-post-facto empirical validation of the latter criterion was obtained by computing the actual share of the total vote obtained by each party in new localities. As already noted, these places include high proportions of voters of Asian-African origin and are here considered a reasonable proxy for those origin groups on the whole. The vertical divisions in the diagrams reflect the results of such validation.

It should be stressed that the grid of diagonal and vertical lines in the diagrams was somewhat arbitrarily traced; no excessive significance should be attributed to their distances from the points each representing a different party.[115] The lines are only intended to help read the diagrams, by better characterizing the meaning of their two dimensions. Moreover, it should be emphasized again that, given the highly aggregate character of the data

---

[114] Clearly, alternative interpretations could be suggested about the meaning of the diagrams' two dimensions. Other relevant variables in the definition of the horizontal axis could be a measure of some demographic characteristic, such as the voters' age distribution or seniority of residence in Israel; a measure of educational attainment; or a measure of political orientation, ranging from most hawkish to most dovish.

[115] In comparing the four diagrams, it should be kept in mind that the respective scales are not necessarily the same. Diagram 4, in particular, is affected by the very eccentric position of one party, Degel Hatorah, which influences the respective positions of all the other parties, making them apparently very close one to another (see below).

DIAGRAM 1. SMALLEST SPACE ANALYSIS OF DISTRIBUTION OF VOTE FOR JEWISH PARTIES, BY TYPE OF LOCALITY—JEWISH LOCALITIES WITHOUT KIBBUTZIM, 1955

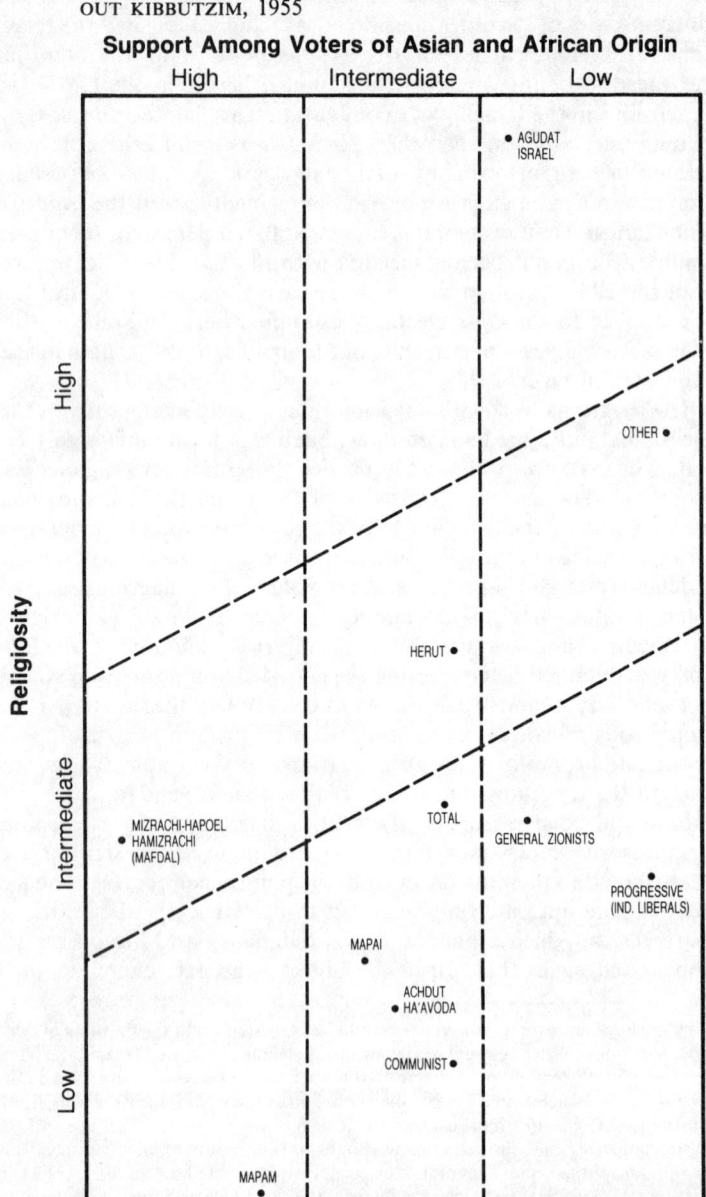

input and the roughness of a two-dimensional representation, results of the following analysis can only be considered exploratory and suggestive.

RESULTS

Along with clear signs of overall structural stability in the party configuration, several important changes should be noted among the four elections examined here. These variations reflect: (a) changes in the respective proportions of different types of localities out of Israel's total Jewish population; (b) demographic changes in the electoral body; (c) actual shifts in each party's share of the total vote; and (d) the drift of some of the parties across the sociopolitical space schematically represented in the diagrams.

Politically, the most significant aspects relate to the position of the point representing "Total" voters in the party configuration, and the proximity of the position of any single party to that of Total voters. Total is consistently plotted in an area characterized by low but not extremely low religiosity, and with intermediate support among Asian and African voters. This correctly describes the overall or "average" characteristics of the Israeli voter. If anything, in the course of time, Total tends to move slowly toward an area closer to a more Asian-African electorate (strong in new localities). Again, this aptly reflects changes in the demographic composition of the electorate between 1955 and 1988.

Closeness to Total reflects a balanced representation of a party in each type of locality—and, by implication, among each type of voter. The further a party is from Total, the more it is concentrated in one or a few types of localities, thus revealing a narrower and more particularistic constituency. Consistent with the election returns, the largest parties are closer to Total: this was the case with Mapai and the Alignment in 1955 and 1965, and with Likud in 1977 and 1988. (In 1955, the General Zionists, later to join Herut in eventually forming the Likud, were actually closer structurally to Total voters than Mapai was.)

The changing position of each individual party in the sociopolitical space defined by religiosity and support among Asian-African voters is also worthy of attention. Changes affecting the position of Likud among the Israeli electorate, as reflected in diagrams 1–4, are particularly significant. In 1955 the Herut and General Zionist parties were separate and had distinctly different constituencies: the former, moderately traditional and ethnically blended, the latter, distinctly secular and mostly of European origin. After the merger of these two parties in 1965, Likud (then Gahal) appeared to be still markedly associated with a secular constituency, with intermediate support among voters of Asian-African origin. In 1977 Likud had moved significantly closer to an electorate of Asian-African origin and one that was

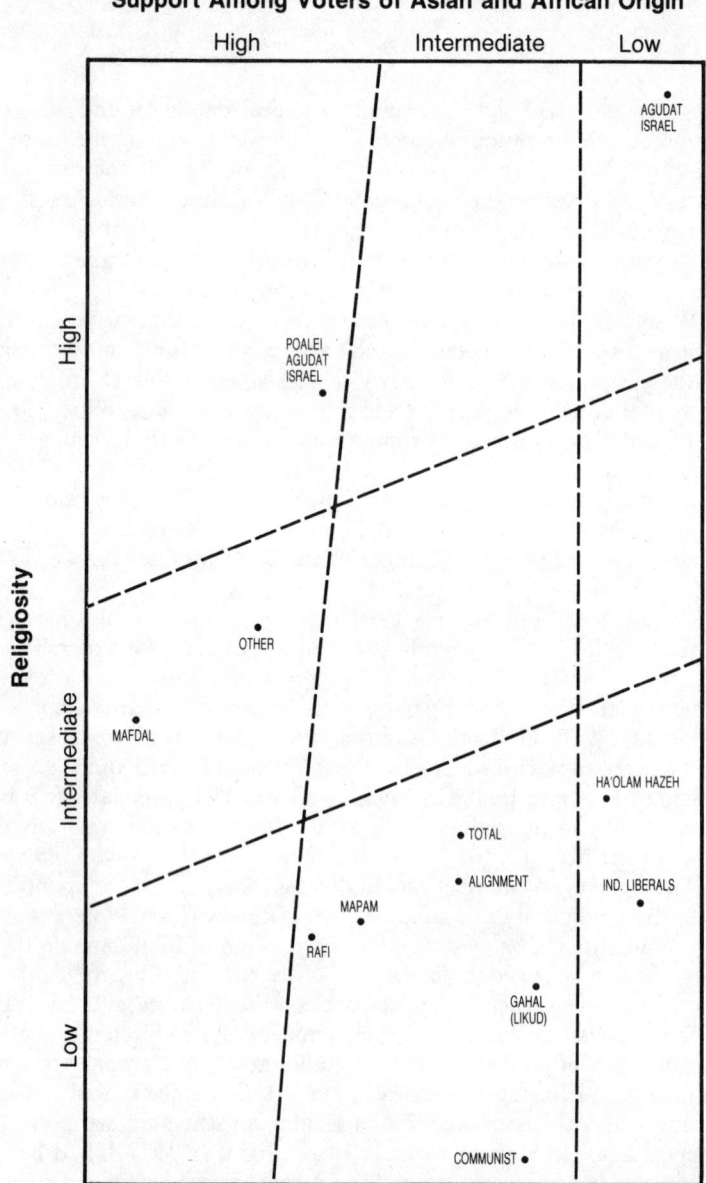

DIAGRAM 2. SMALLEST SPACE ANALYSIS OF DISTRIBUTION OF VOTE FOR JEWISH PARTIES, BY TYPE OF LOCALITY—JEWISH LOCALITIES WITHOUT KIBBUTZIM, 1965

close to moderately religious. The same trend appears to have continued in 1988, when the Likud's share among Asian and African voters grew above average. [116]

In a sense, an opposite trend characterizes the changing position of the Labor sector and its various components in the party configuration. Although Mapai had been for many years the dominant political force of the new State of Israel, playing an important role in the political absorption of large and heterogeneous groups of Jewish immigrants,[117] it appears that in 1955 its voters featured somewhat distinctive characteristics from those of the total electorate. Mapai's successor, the large Labor Alignment (Ma'arakh) party, reached a much closer relationship to Total voters in 1965—hence implying greatest extension and socioeconomic and ethnic heterogeneity. Later on, however, Labor tended to move to a more marginal position in the sociopolitical space, becoming associated with a more definitely secular, and somewhat more markedly European, electorate. It may be noted that of the original components of the Alignment, Mapai and Ahdut Ha'avoda in 1955 appealed to voters with very similar social characteristics, while the more left-wing Mapam—except for its strong kibbutz base—received stronger support among Asian-African voters. Also of interest in the diagrams is the apparent passage of Mapam's urban voters[118] from a strongly secular stance in the 1950s to a more central position in the religiosity continuum during the 1980s.

The already mentioned important role of Dash in promoting the Labor movement's defeat in 1977 clearly appears in diagram 3 to have been mostly determined by a secular and European-American electorate. At the same time, about the same proportion of voters of Asian-African background left the Alignment in 1977 for a variety of other political formations.[119] The secularization and Europeanization of the Alignment appears to have continued in the 1988 elections, as indicated by the lower location of this party in diagram 4 as compared to 3.

A further intriguing finding concerns the social-structural similarity of Shlomzion—the list headed by Ariel Sharon in 1977 and the Alignment (see diagram 3). It seems not impossible that Sharon, who soon after his election merged with the Likud, attracted some of the more hawkish voters who had previously been part of the Labor movement. Shlomzion's voters were not markedly concentrated among the Asian-African origin group. Not incon-

---

[116] The slight deviation in one vertical line in diagram 4 had to be introduced to accurately reflect the support of voters of Asian and African origin for the various parties.
[117] See Peter Y. Medding, *Mapai in Israel: Political Organization and Government in a New Society* (Cambridge, 1972).
[118] Kibbutzim are excluded from the present analysis.
[119] See Diskin, *Elections and Voters in Israel*, pp. 125–131.

DIAGRAM 3. SMALLEST SPACE ANALYSIS OF DISTRIBUTION OF VOTE FOR JEWISH PARTIES, BY TYPE OF LOCALITY—JEWISH LOCALITIES WITHOUT KIBBUTZIM, 1977

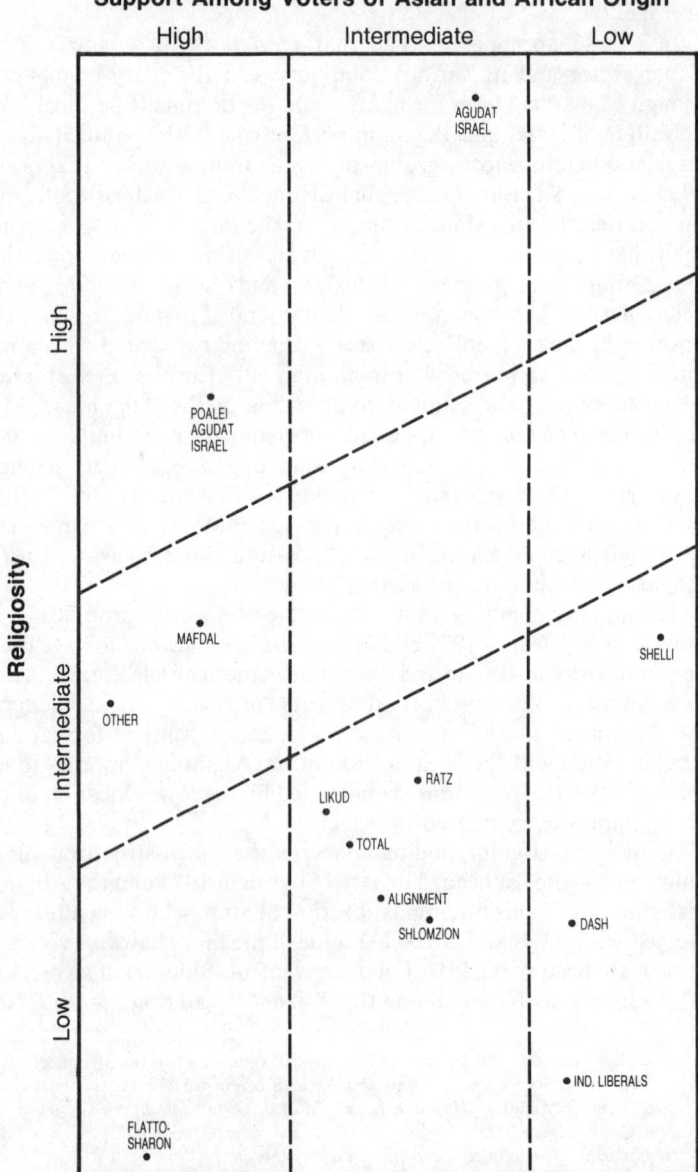

sistently, in the 1965 elections, Rafi—born of the split from the mainstream Labor movement of David Ben-Gurion and his younger and activist followers—occupied about the same ethnic position in the party configuration that was later to be taken by the Likud (diagrams 2 and 3). As a party Rafi eventually returned to the fold of unified Labor and the Alignment, but it would appear from these analyses that many of its supporters were left behind.

Among other interesting changes of position in the Israeli sociopolitical space, one of the more remarkable is that of Agudat Israel. Its constituency, while remaining within the religious sector, passed from low support among Asian-African voters throughout the 1955, 1965, and 1977 elections, to high support in 1988. This transition was helped by periodic association with the smaller Poalei Agudat Israel party (in 1955 and 1988), whose political base was comparatively strong in new localities. Even more significantly, in 1988, together with a new association with the Lubavich movement, Agudat Israel came to appeal to an electorate of Asian-African origins quite similar to that of the highly ethnic Shas party. On the other hand, Degel Hatorah seems to have taken over in the 1988 election some of the political space occupied by Agudat Israel between the 1950s and the late 1970s. Because of its strong concentration in Jerusalem and B'nei Berak, Degel Hatorah's actual position in the party configuration is extremely eccentric, which makes all the other parties appear much more clustered than in the preceding diagrams. It should be stressed that this is an artifact of the particular method of data processing used here and not a real change in the nature of the party configuration. Diagram 4 actually displays a modified SSA in which a substantial empty area between Degel Hatorah and all other parties was cut away to facilitate the reading of the results.

Other political drifts—at the European end of the ethnic continuum—concern the increasingly secular basis of the Independent Liberals, associated with Shinui-Center in 1988, and Ratz (CRM). The last party, originally an outgrowth of the Labor Alignment, subsequently developed a more radical stance on issues of civil rights and separation between religion and state. Conversely, the Mafdal–National Religious party (NRP) incurred important electoral losses but kept basically the same structural position over the years.[120] The small aggregate of "other" parties that did not achieve any Knesset seats tended in 1965 and 1977 to be composed of voters with characteristics similar to those of the NRP. Prominent among this heterogeneous political element were the already mentioned small ethnic lists which unsuccessfully represented a variety of Asian and African

---

[120]The NRP indeed lost many of its voters of Asian-African origin. Its actual strength in new localities, reflected in the party's position in diagram 4, may well derive from support among European-American voters in new localities.

DIAGRAM 4. SMALLEST SPACE ANALYSIS OF DISTRIBUTION OF VOTE FOR JEWISH PARTIES, BY TYPE OF LOCALITY—JEWISH LOCALITIES WITHOUT KIBBUTZIM, 1988

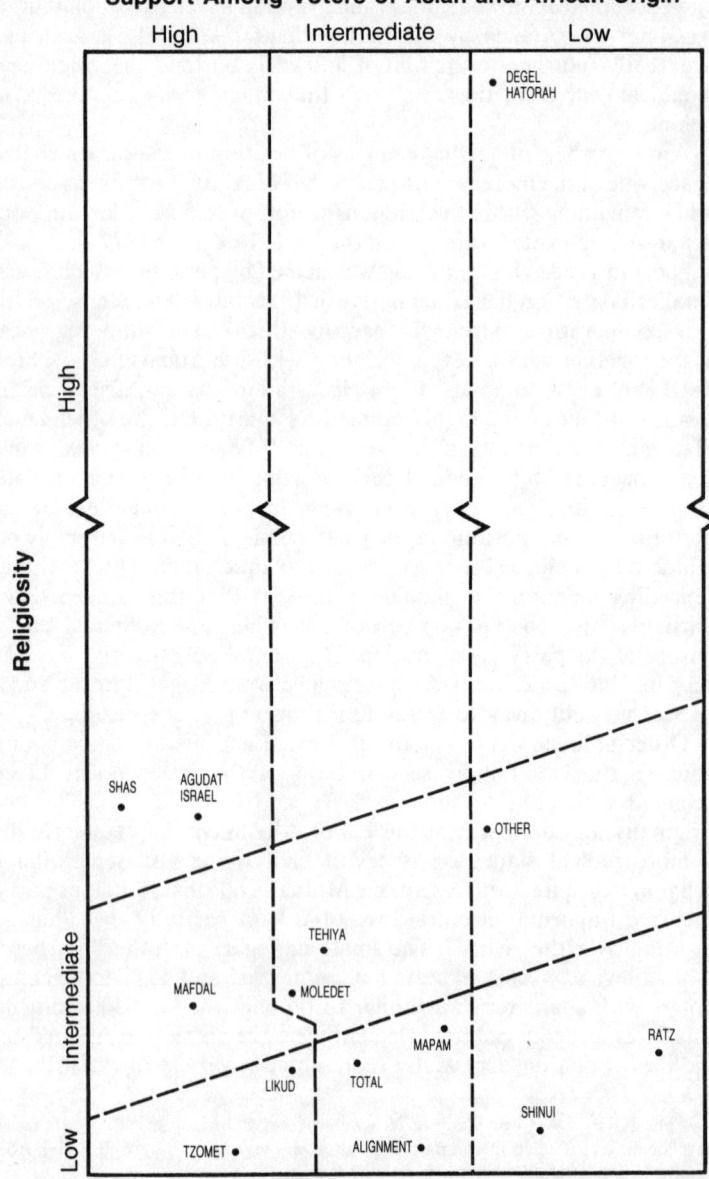

origin groups. In 1988, though still tangentially associated with the moderately religious party area, "other" parties obtained most of their support among voters of European and American origin.[121]

At the extremes of the ideological spectrum, there was never any significant Jewish support for the Communist Left among Asian-African voters, in spite of attempts to incorporate protest movements such as the Black Panthers during the early 1970s (see diagrams 1-3). Right-wing parties such as Tehiya, Tzomet, and Moledet (which latter probably absorbed most of the votes that might have gone to Meir Kahane's outlawed extreme-right Kach movement) in 1988 each appealed to somewhat different constituencies, ranging from moderately religious to secular, and from average to more strongly Asian-African (diagram 4). Looking across the four elections reported here, the combination of low religiosity and strong Asian-African support was infrequent, but it appeared from time to time under different political banners.

Finally, it can be noted that most parties—with the prominent exception of the ultra-Orthodox—appear to be plotted along a diagonal pattern cutting across the interpretative grid. It can be assumed that the observed diagonal ranking roughly indicates a measure of social status of the respective party constituencies, from lowest at the upper-left end of the diagonal to highest at the bottom-right end (see further discussion below). Such an assumption is consistent with the previously mentioned relationship between levels of educational attainment and ethnic origin group, namely, the lower socioeconomic status of the Asian-African group as compared to the European-American group, and the higher socioeconomic status of the younger and more secular Israeli-born as compared to the foreign-born.

Keeping in mind the tentative and exploratory nature of this analysis, a few significant conclusions can be drawn. First, ecological segregation—here expressed through different types of localities—plays an important role in Israeli society as an intermediate variable associated with political identity and behavior. Changes in spatial segregation, discussed earlier in this study, may prove important to the mutual relationship with political behavior. Second, several of the features described here point to considerable dynamism and fluidity of voting choices in Israel, within the context of rather static and lasting political coordinates. It is true that, so far, certain social-structural characteristics of the electorate, such as religiosity and ethnic origin, have provided the basic defining dimensions of the Israeli party configuration. Yet, the analysis clearly indicates that in Israel it is not always possible to easily deduce ideological differences between parties from the sociodemographic characteristics of their voters.

---

[121]The two lists which attracted the most votes among the "Other" group in 1988 were the Pensioners' party and Meimad, a moderate religious list. Both appealed mainly to voters of European-American origins.

Ethnic Origin vs. Socioeconomic Status in 1988 Elections

Twelve mostly Jewish parties and three mostly Arab parties won at least one seat apiece in the 12th Knesset. Given this situation, it is noteworthy that in about one ballot district out of four that were located in areas with Jewish majorities (1,094 out of 4,380 ballot districts), one single party won an absolute majority of the vote. This again points to the very significant homogeneity of political preferences within small geographical areas, also hinting at residential homogeneity according to other sociodemographic characteristics.

Following this ecological approach, table 66 offers a closer look at the amount of ethnic-origin and social-class differentiation among parties in the 12th Knesset election of November 1988. The data relate to the votes given to the main parties in 810 statistical areas in urban Jewish localities of over 10,000 inhabitants, each area being composed of several contiguous ballot districts. Residential areas of voters were classified according to the predominance of one or more origin groups among the resident population. Thus, by way of aggregate data, some inference can be drawn about the relationship between the ethnic backgrounds of voters and their party preferences. The same urban areas were also classified according to the predominant socioeconomic status of the inhabitants, providing a further aggregate frame of reference for the interpretation of electoral results.[122]

As already noted, correlation between ethnic origin and party preference appears to be substantial in Israel, though rather fluid. With regard to the Jewish vote, in 1988 the most ethnically homogeneous parties were Shinui and Ratz (CRM), each of which garnered about three-quarters of the respective votes in urban areas with a plurality of Jews of European-American origin. The newly formed Orthodox religious party Degel Hatorah followed closely, with over 70 percent of its votes in predominantly European-American areas. At the opposite end of the ethnic continuum, the Orthodox religious Shas party obtained nearly 73 percent of its votes in residential areas with Asian-African Jewish majorities. These four political movements, relying mostly on highly homogeneous ethnic precincts, together received 15 (13 percent) of the 114 Knesset seats won by Jewish parties. (Of the total 120 seats, 6 were won by parties with a predominantly Arab constituency; see table 65.)

---

[122]Geographical definitions of urban areas and classifications of the characteristics of their inhabitants were based on the results of the 1983 population census. For more technical explanations and the original data, see Uri Avner, "Voting in the Elections for the 12th Knesset in Comparison to Previous Elections" (in Hebrew), in Central Bureau of Statistics, Ministry of the Interior—Inspector General of Elections, Malam Systems Ltd., *Results of Elections to the Twelfth Knesset 1.11.1988*, vol. A (Jerusalem, 1989), Central Bureau of Statistics, Special Series no. 855, pp. 25–42.

Voters for other parties, including the two largest ones, Likud and Labor, featured lesser deviations from the overall ethnic background distribution of total voters. Yet, Labor and Mapam clearly appealed more to voters of European-American origin (close to 65 percent), while the Likud obtained greater support in predominantly Asian-African areas (57 percent). Substantial support among Asian-African voters (52 percent) was also won by Agudat Israel, in spite of its overwhelmingly Ashkenazi leadership. The smallest deviations from the mean, indicating fairly balanced representation among all major origin groups, appeared among the religious Mafdal (NRP), and among the three right-wing lists of Moledet, Tehiya, and Tzomet. Overall, in terms of their relationship to the ethnic background of voters, these results point to a continuum in the transition of party constituencies from mostly European-American to mostly Asian-African, rather than to the contraposition of two ethnic blocs of voters with distinctly different political orientations. It also appears that in 1988 the Labor Alignment was somewhat more European-American than the Likud was Asian-African.

Political cleavages associated with social-class stratification appear to be stronger than those just observed in relation to the ethnic origin of voters. Once again, based on an analysis of electoral results for small areas in Jewish urban localities, by aggregate characteristics of the resident population, the relationship between party preference and socioeconomic status of the area is examined in table 66. Five distinct clusters of parties emerge: (a) strongest in urban areas characterized by higher-than-average social status the Liberal-Radical parties Shinui-Center and Ratz (CRM), which obtained about 70 percent of the respective votes in the two highest socioeconomic quintiles and over 40 percent in the top one; (b) the Labor party and Mapam followed (over 50 percent of votes in the two highest quintiles); (c) somewhere socially intermediate—tending to a higher-middle social status—were the three kindred right-wing movements of Tehiya, Tzomet, and Moledet; and (d) tending to a lower social status, the Likud and Mafdal (NRP); (e) strongest in lower-than-average social status areas were the three religious parties of Shas, Agudat Israel, and Degel Hatorah (over 50 percent of votes in the two lowest quintiles).

A comparison of the 1988 vote with the previous election of 1984 highlights the strengthening or weakening of the major groups of parties in different ethnic and socioeconomic contexts (table 67). With regard to the ethnicity of voters, the Likud together with the kindred Tehiya, Tzomet, and Moledet made substantial gains, or incurred relatively minor losses, in predominantly European-American Jewish urban areas. These same parties obtained less remarkable gains, or suffered comparatively more important losses, in neighborhoods with a predominantly Asian-African electorate. In turn, Labor together with the left-of-center kindred parties (Mapam, Ratz, Shinui) won modest net gains in European-American-origin precincts, but incurred more substantial net losses in predominantly Asian or African areas. The religious parties overwhelmingly improved their standing in any type of neighborhood, regardless of origin of voters, though more strikingly so in predominantly Asian-African areas.

An examination of gains and losses of major party groupings between 1984 and 1988 elections, by social status of urban areas (see table 67), confirms that socioeconomic characterization of small residential areas is a much better predictor of voting behavior than ethnic composition of the same areas. Interestingly, there was a similarly positive correlation between electoral gains and an area's socioeconomic status for both the Center-Right to Right (Likud and kindred parties) and the Center-Left to Left (Labor and Liberal-Radical parties) political sectors, though that association was stronger for the former group of parties. Clearly, in 1988 the two major parties were competing directly for the votes of the same higher-than-average socioeconomic groups. This may have implied a certain similarity in electoral strategies and, possibly, a certain convergence of the two major parties toward the center of the political spectrum. On the other hand, for the aggregate of religious parties, the association between electoral gain and an urban area's socioeconomic status was significantly negative. Thus, the religious parties successfully competed for both the Likud's and the Alignment's lower socioeconomic strata.

The associated effects of ethnic origin and socioeconomic status on party preference are shown in table 68. The figures reported are indexes of vote concentration for the major parties or groups of parties, by combined characteristics of statistical areas in Jewish urban localities. In each cell, indexes above 100 indicate overrepresentation of voters with the indicated combination of characteristics; indexes below 100 indicate underrepresentation. Ratios between maximum and minimum indexes in each row and column of table 68 help to evaluate the amount of voter diffusion or polarization prevailing among each party or group of parties. Lower ratios indicate that a party's constituency is sociodemographically more balanced.

The least tendency toward vote concentration appears for the Likud, whose voters are comparatively more spread out across the different ethnic groups and social strata than is the case for other parties. Likud voters display the weakest social-class concentration, after controlling for ethnic origin. As already noted, social diffusion and heterogeneity of voters are consistent with a party's preponderant role in the political system. Kindred parties of the Right political sector appear, too, to be appealing to a quite heterogeneous constituency. Besides their weakness in the lowest socioeconomic quintile, these parties display weakest ethnic-origin concentration, after controlling for social status.

Far greater concentration appears among the other groups of parties examined in table 68. Trends among the religious parties appear to be antithetical to those among Labor and kindred parties of the Center-Left to Left. The former are strongest in areas combining lowest socioeconomic status and strongest Asian or African origin-group concentration; the latter emerge as strongest in areas combining a predominantly European-American background with high socioeconomic status. The socioeconomic base of the Labor Alignment in 1988 was intriguingly narrow, especially in view of the far larger extension of sociological boundaries of the Labor movement in the past.

Wishing to reduce the description of sociodemographic correlates of the Israeli party system to its bare minimum, a tripartite division can be suggested. It would appear that the Center-Left to Left parties, including the Alignment, stand diametrically opposed to the religious parties, while the Center-Right to Right parties, including the Likud, occupy an intermediate position. These findings confirm the suggestions concerning the social profile of party constituencies advanced in the preceding analysis of Israeli party configurations. Contraposition of the Alignment and the Likud, routinely mentioned in discussions of Israeli politics, does not capture the essential relationship between Israel's party system and sociological realities.

It is of particular relevance that the voting patterns of upwardly mobile Jews of Asian-African origin—those concentrated in upper-status residential areas—tend to resemble more the patterns of their European-American peers than those of voters of their own ethnic origin group who belong to lower socioeconomic strata. On the other hand, it seems plausible that the lowest social strata of the Jewish electorate found some of the religious parties more appealing than either of the two major political forces, whether at the left or the right of the political center. These findings tend to indicate that social class is significantly stronger than ethnic background as a correlate of party preferences. At the same time, a considerable number of voters of each major origin group shifted their party preferences from one election to another. Some of these moves probably reflected the changing personal characteristics and political perceptions and interests of the electorate; some were related to the changing issue positions and public images of the competing political parties. The data suggest a substantial fluidity of voting patterns, in marked contrast with deterministic interpretations of the role of ethnicity in the Israeli political process (see below).

Ethnic Background, Political Participation, and Representation

Another important aspect of the role of ethnicity in the political sphere—complementary to that of party preference—is the amount of active participation and share of leadership attained by each origin group. Elite formation and power sharing, in fact, constitute fundamental tests of the amount of ethnic integration attained in society.

Looking at the ethnic background of ruling elites in Israeli society over the years, one finds an overwhelming preponderance of European-born persons.[123] Where sectors such as academic and technical professions, private industry management, or even the judiciary or the military are concerned, such a European preponderance was the natural result of the deep inequalities in wealth, educational attainment, work experience, and seniority of residence in the country that prevailed among the different origin groups during the years of mass immigration and soon afterward. Mechanisms of cooptation into the upward echelons of such specific socioeconomic sectors would have to take into account a candidate's fitness by very stringent professional criteria as well as the existing relational network of the more veteran and established sections of the population. Therefore, there could be no reasonable expectation that in the short run the process of substitution of the entrenched senior personnel would involve significant ethnic change.

With regard to access to public office, and more particularly to elective office, however, it could be presumed that sooner or later the system would have to adapt itself to represent population composition more accurately, particularly in regard to ethnic background. Although persons of Asian-African origin were underrepresented among senior political figures since the onset of statehood, their share of total national officeholders could be expected to increase steadily.

A fundamental parameter in the process of integration is the ability of each ethnic group to produce from its ranks leading role-holders in the public institutional system, even if this does not occur with the same frequency as would be expected from a consideration of the group's numerical size. From this point of view, there was great symbolism attached to the fact that the highly honorific position of president of the state was filled by the Asian-African origin group at least once (Itzhak Navon), as was the crucially important position of chief of staff of the military (Moshe Levy). Several Knesset Speakers have been of Asian-African origin, as were the two vice-prime ministers in the government that was formed after the 1988 elections (Navon and David Levy), and the Histadrut secretary-general (Israel Kesar). The process of ethnic integration cannot be said to be completed, however, unless fairly large representation is simultaneously attained at all levels of the political system.

At what is generally considered to be the most senior political level in

---

[123]Yuval Elizur and Eliahu Salpeter, *Who Rules Israel?* (New York, 1973).

Israel, that of government member, between 1949 and 1958 the Asian-African origin group (including the Israeli-born) regularly obtained one single post out of a total ranging between 12 and 16 ministers (corresponding to 6–8 percent of ministerial posts).[124] Between 1959 and 1973 the number of ministers of Asian-African origin rose to 2 out of a total ranging between 15 and 24 (8–13 percent of ministerial posts). By 1989 their share in the government had increased to 9 out of a total of 26 (35 percent).

In the Knesset (constantly set at 120 members since 1948), the number of Jews of Asian-African origin (again including those born in Israel) grew from 8 in 1949 to 19 in 1973—an increase of from 7 to 17 percent, respectively, of the Jewish Knesset members.[125] In 1988 the number of Knesset members of Asian-African origin had grown to 38 (33 percent of total Jews in the House).

As to the ethnic composition of the central party committees of the two major parties, Labor and Herut (the major component of the Likud), it has evolved to be not significantly different.[126] The shares of those of Asian-African origin were 37 percent and 34 percent, respectively, in 1986. Herut had a comparatively higher share of Israeli-born activists of Israeli paternity, some of whom were of Asian-African origin (these are not included in the preceding percentages). The share of the Asian-African origin group was comparatively much larger among officeholders at the municipal level and among national and local trade-union leaders. In 1955, 26 percent of mayors and local council members were of Asian or African origin, this share growing to 47 percent in 1965, and 51 percent in 1983.[127] The proportion of Asian-African origin among members of the Histadrut central council grew from 9 percent in 1955, to 17 percent in 1965, and to 41 percent in 1983.

These trends are visible among both major parties and are further enhanced through the presence in the political system of forces even more attuned to an Asian-African electorate. The implications in the longer run may be quite significant, since local authority and trade-union frameworks may constitute important channels of recruitment for the national political leadership. In turn, structural similarity at the level of second- or third-rank party leadership is consistent with the already noted striving of both major parties to win the confidence of large and ethnically heterogeneous constitu-

---

[124] Smooha, *Israel: Pluralism and Conflict*, p. 310.
[125] Ibid., p. 311.
[126] Hana Herzog, Michal Shamir, and Alan Zuckerman, *The Israeli Politician: Social and Political Profiles of Activists of Labor and Herut Parties* (in Hebrew), Jerusalem Institute for Israel Studies, no. 34, 1989.
[127] Szewach Weiss, *Local Government in Israel: A Study of Its Leadership* (in Hebrew; Tel Aviv, 1972); Lev Grinberg, *Political Activists in Local Authorities and Trade Unions: The Ethnic Dimension* (in Hebrew), Jerusalem Institute for Israel Studies, no. 33, 1989.

encies. It is interesting to note, though, that the party preferences of a majority of the Asian-African origin group have not been influenced by the exact share of candidates of the same origins in the competing lists. This again tends to confirm that ethnic cleavages have not constituted the main factor in the contraposition of the major parties, as may instead have been the case with social-class and ideological differences.

It is also significant that basically the same amount of representation has been achieved by the Asian-African origin group at different levels of the national political system, from the lower one of central party committee, up to Knesset and government member. Results at the top of the system seem therefore to reflect basically what is developing at the bottom in terms of recruitment of political leadership from the rank and file of party supporters. The latter process is highly selective and tends to allocate more space to middle- to upper-middle-class elements[128] whose relative weight, as already noted, is not the same among the different origin groups.

CONCLUSIONS

Mechanisms of mass and selective migration brought to Israel sections of the Jewish Diaspora that had been quite differently affected by processes of modernization. Immigrants from more than fourscore countries possessed distinctive clusters of demographic characteristics, levels of education, social status, religiosity, and other cultural traits. While the different immigrant groups shared a common history and religion and the experience of being minorities in often hostile surrounding societies, their great diversity contained considerable potential for conflict. This was chiefly along lines of religion and secularity, socioeconomic status and interests, and cultural premises and intellectual traditions.

It is important to note that while Israel's creation was largely the product of an idealistic movement of national revival, the "fathers of Zionism" apparently gave little thought to the ramifications of immigrant absorption and ethnic stratification. The two pillars of Zionist thought, *kibbutz galuyot*, the ingathering of the exiles, and *mizug galuyot*, the fusion of the exiles, fundamentally imply homogeneity and egalitarianism in the new Jewish society. This is expressed in Israel's Declaration of Independence, which ensures social justice and equal opportunity to all its citizens. However, while the melting pot would ultimately seem to be the preferred model in the Zionist vision of nation building, there was always a latent, yet sufficiently clear preference for conformity to a predetermined ideal type—in

---

[128]See Diskin, *Elections and Voters in Israel*, p. 159.

this case, Western and European—because of the intellectual frame of reference of the movement's major leaders and because of the perceived need to build a nation that could hold its own with the leading nations of the world.

The process of mass immigrant absorption occurred in a very compressed period of time, one in which Israeli society was largely dominated by problems of defense and security. This placed a heavy drain on national resources, contributing to competition and inequities. At the same time—and this is what distinguishes the ethnic picture in Israel from that elsewhere—the conflict has been moderated, at least in part, by a sense of solidarity, a recognition that, as Jews, all confront common problems and share the same fate.

This implies that general theories of ethnic stratification may only have partial applicability within the limits of the present study. While the Israeli case should be studied in the larger context of ethnicity patterns in immigrant-absorbing countries, the attempt to deduce straightforward comparisons between ethnic processes among Jews in Israel and among Jews or other groups elsewhere may be deceiving. Keeping this in mind, some broader perspective needs to be provided for the empirical findings.

Observation of countries that have experienced large-scale, heterogeneous immigration—whether or not in the presence of veteran, "native" populations—has led to the formulation of alternative theories of the ethnic dimension in society. Central to the debate on the ever-changing salience of ethnicity is the assessment of the respective role and possible overlap of its social-structural and cultural components. Based on a variety of historical analyses, theoretical assertions, and empirical findings, various analysts have expressed quite different positions, affirming, respectively, the "twilight," "revival," or "transformation" of ethnicity in contemporary societies. These models may be viewed, and have actually served from time to time, as mere descriptions of the present situation, or theoretical expectations, or even normative ideals in relation to the future development of society.[129]

The Israeli case naturally offers ideal ground for confrontation between these different conceptualizations. Israeli society has often been referred to as an "ethnic mosaic" or even a "human laboratory" in which the unfolding of complex social processes tied to ethnicity can be routinely observed in

---

[129] From the classic formulation by Milton Gordon, *Assimilation in American Life* (New York, 1964), onward. See, for example, the different positions of: Michael Novak, *The Rise of the Unmeltable Ethnics* (New York, 1972); Richard D. Alba, *Italian Americans: Into the Twilight of Ethnicity* (Englewood Cliffs, 1985); and William L. Yancey, Eugene Ericksen, and Richard N. Juliani, "Emergent Ethnicity: A Review and Reformulation," *American Sociological Review*, 41, 1976, pp. 391–403.

daily life. This obviously reflects the seminal importance of large and heterogeneous immigration in the formative process of the Jewish population, as well as the presence of diverse non-Jewish religious, cultural, and social sectors in Israeli society. Numerous studies have addressed demographic, socioeconomic, and sociocultural differentials connected with origin group among Israel's Jewish population, generating a rich and lively theoretical debate.[130]

Among the major analytical perspectives suggested in the literature dealing with ethnic diversity in Israel, much emphasis used to be placed on the process of nation-building. Israel's success in developing the basic societal infrastructure—legal, institutional, motivational, cultural, economic—in a relatively short span of years and despite enormous difficulties seemed to proponents of this approach more significant than the issues of internal differences, inequality, and even conflict that developed. Much recent research is concerned with the effects of institutional interventions on the unfolding of individual and group mobility processes among immigrants and their children. A prominent point of view perceives the significance of ethnicity to be mainly along cultural lines, and thus of transient salience in an Israeli society that is striving toward greater uniformity. An opposite view stresses ethnic cleavages in Israeli society as fundamentally overlapping with social-class divisions and conflicts. At the extreme of this position, an exploitative interpretation of existing inequalities has been suggested. A further perspective, in a sense intermediate between the two preceding ones, recognizes the existence of various types of stratification—religious, social class, and ethnocultural—as a fundamental characteristic of a pluralistic Israeli society.[131]

Our study has attempted to contribute to these debates by providing some historical background and much substantive and updated evidence concerning the ethnic dimension in contemporary Israeli society.

---

[130]Moshe Lissak, "Research on the Ethnic Problem—An Overview" (in Hebrew), in N. Cohen and O. Ahimeir, eds., *New Directions in the Study of Ethnic Problems,* Jerusalem Institute for Israel Studies, no. 8, 1984, pp. 13–22; Sammy Smooha, "Three Perspectives in the Sociology of Ethnic Relations in Israel" (in Hebrew), in *The Ethnic Problem in Israel—Continuity and Change, Megamot,* 25, 1984, pp. 169–206; S. N. Eisenstadt, *The Development of the Ethnic Problem in Israeli Society,* Jerusalem Institute for Israel Studies, no. 17, 1986.

[131]Yaacov Nahon, *Trends in Occupational Status—The Ethnic Dimension* (in Hebrew), Jerusalem Institute for Israel Studies, no. 10, 1984; Nahon, *Patterns of Educational Expansion;* Eliezer Ben Rafael, *The Emergence of Ethnicity: Cultural Groups and Social Conflict in Israel* (London, 1982); S. Svirsky, *Not Deprived But Dispossessed* (in Hebrew; Haifa, 1981); Smooha, *Israel: Pluralism and Conflict.*

Summary of Major Findings

GENERAL ASPECTS

This study has presented a selective yet diversified overview of the changing role and mutual relationship of the two main origin groups of Israeli Jews. The topics have included immigration, population composition, spatial distribution, marriage, fertility, educational attainment, and political behavior. The emphasis in each case has been on aspects that lend themselves to quantitative measurement, even though it is clear that quantifiable aspects alone do not exhaust a very complex subject, whose subtle psychosocial and symbolic connotations require additional investigative approaches.

The major conclusion to be reached from the overview is that no single type of process characterizes recent trends in the demographic, socioeconomic, and sociopolitical evolution of the major Jewish origin groups in Israel. A surprisingly large number of different patterns appear to coexist regarding the changing presence of the ethnic factor. The starting date, rhythm, and consistency of each of the evolutionary patterns have been different. Consequently, no simple or single conclusion can be drawn about the role of ethnicity in the ongoing process of coalescence of the Jewish sector of Israeli society. While definite and sometimes dramatic changes have appeared in the course of a relatively brief time span of 40 years in each of the areas reviewed in this study, different judgments can be reached about the main thrust of the long-term process of immigrant absorption and integration, depending on which particular process is being examined. In a sense, the emerging trends demonstrate the inadequacy of the basic question which, in its simplest formulation, runs: "Are ethnic-related gaps among Israeli Jews narrowing or widening over time?"

One fundamental element of change in Israeli society over the last decades has been the growing share of Asian-Africans in the total Jewish population. In theory, this might have generated a variety of results ranging between the extremes of a much intensified concentration of the Asian-Africans in segregated areas and strata of society, or a much intensified dispersal throughout areas and strata with a strong presence of European-Americans. Keeping this in mind, the analysis of most demographic processes points to declining differences between the major origin groups, whether through mutual intermingling of persons belonging to the different groups (homogenization), intense accession of members of the Asian-African origin group to more favorable patterns that previously were typical of the European-American group (catching-up), or mutual reduction of previous gaps (convergence). In other areas of Israeli society, the major origin groups are characterized as well by processes of simultaneous but not necessarily equal improvement (convergent, parallel, or divergent rises), by crystallization in different patterns not involving a clear hierarchy of statuses (specialization), or by actual increases in social distance (polarization).

DEMOGRAPHIC ASPECTS

Homogenization involves achieving the same goal—reduced ethnic diversity—through intensive intermingling with persons of different backgrounds. An example is provided by the continuously increasing proportion of interethnic marriages, which are assumed to be a main factor in reducing the salience of ethnicity among the generation born of such marriages. A further example concerns intense residential mobility into ethnically mixed new residential neighborhoods.

Catching-up involves behavioral stability among the higher status group and upward change or other types of improvement among the lower status group. This pattern is exemplified by the changing spatial distribution, when upward mobility of Asian-Africans has been accompanied by a substantial penetration into existing residential areas which formerly were more exclusively European-American, or by improving local quality of life, through urban renewal projects. This does not mean that identical residential distributions were attained, nor that such a goal was attainable. The patterns of initial settlement of new immigrants in Israel, both nationally and locally, involved a high degree of ethnic homogeneity, sometimes described as a "mosaic of segregated groups."[132] Still, in spite of the considerable residential segregation which persists, a powerful trend toward achieving more equal environments, with regard to both a neighborhood's ethnic composition and amenities, has been at work. A different but conceptually analogous process was the rapid improvement of health standards among Asian-Africans during the early years of statehood and their achieving virtual parity with the longevity patterns of European-Americans.

Convergence involves achieving the same gap-reduction goal through opposite strategies. This was the case with family formation and fertility levels, in which substantial modernization and westernization of behaviors among members of the Asian-African group, leading to fertility reduction, was matched by a significant increase in familism, including some fertility increases, among members of the European-American group.

All of these different patterns point to the gradual formation of a more homogeneous or unitarian approach in the basic demographics of Jewish Israelis. At a minimum, the trends indicate that origin, as distinct from social class, has tended to become less influential in determining preferences

---

[132]Vivian Klaff, "Residence and Integration in Israel: A Mosaic of Segregated Groups," *Ethnicity*, 7, 1977, pp. 103–121.

related to basic family processes and choice of places of residence. It needs to be added here that these family norms and behaviors stand in striking contrast to those now prevailing in most developed countries, and even more so among the Jewish populations of those countries. Developed countries have experienced over the past 15 years an unprecedented general erosion of family processes, whose most conspicuous result has been a fertility level much below generational replacement. Judging by their still considerably high propensity to marry and their moderately high fertility levels, Israelis have developed a distinctive demographic environment which may be seen as the product of ethnic integration, at least as one among several other contributing factors.

SOCIOECONOMIC ASPECTS

The leading trends in educational attainment, as well as other socioeconomic trends not discussed in this study, can be defined as *simultaneous rises* in the standards of all major origin groups. The relative amounts of rise have varied considerably, thus generating patterns of *convergent, parallel, or divergent rises*. General improvement appears especially in enrollment patterns at the primary and secondary levels and partly at higher educational levels. Catching-up of the Asian-African group was virtually completed by the mid-1980s for the amount of schooling attained at age 20, but significant gaps between the major origin groups persist in the types of secondary schools attended and the frequency of enrollment in college and university studies. In many respects, by the late 1980s these gaps could be operationally defined as a time lag (roughly corresponding to about 20 years) in the educational attainment of Asian-Africans as compared to European-Americans. The data indeed indicate that the educational characteristics of Jews of Asian-African origin in the 1980s stood at the same, or even a slightly better, level than that of Jews of European-American origin during the 1960s.[133] In the 1960s the relative disadvantage of Asian-Africans was substantially greater. Catching-up has been more rapid among women than among men.

Considering the initial social characteristics of Asian-African immigrants during the late 1940s and early 1950s, these are remarkable achievements. At the same time, European-Americans have not been immobile. Consequently, the absolute gap between the two origin groups at the higher end of the educational attainment scale remained very large in the 1980s and was in fact only moderately smaller than in the 1960s, though at a much improved level for all.

---

[133]See also Nahon, *Patterns of Educational Expansion*, pp. 31–32.

Comparisons of the educational achievement of the foreign-born and the Israeli-born reveal one of the critical human cost factors of Israeli society, especially for young male adults raised and educated locally. Israeli-educated young adults are shown to be impaired in their higher-education achievements, especially when compared with education achieved abroad by the more recently immigrated foreign-born of the same origin group. An insuperable constraint here seems to be connected with the different positions of the Jews as a minority and a majority, respectively, in the Diaspora and Israel. In the Diaspora, under the prevailing conditions of status as a small minority, universal or quasi-universal academization of the Jewish young adult generation has been a long-standing normative goal, attained by a majority. In Israel, academization can actually be accomplished only by a more or less substantial minority, considering the much more complex labor-force requirements of a country which must take care of all of its necessities, including agriculture, industrial production, and military service.

This is the more so since Israel has adopted selective criteria of admission to its higher education system—in accordance with the prevailing system in some Western and Central European countries and unlike the open and less selective practice in other developed countries, such as the United States. Under these circumstances, many more academics of one group may imply somewhat fewer academics of another group and competition may become intense (unless the state enforces negative quotas on the higher-status group—which seems operationally quite unfeasible in Israel). So far, then, the more favorable initial characteristics of European-Americans have clearly permitted them to continue keeping a conspicuous relative advantage, though Asian-Africans have been slowly improving their relative standing.

Somewhat similar trends (not discussed in detail in this study) appear in the occupational sphere. There, however, the patterns are more complicated. Rather than reflecting one linear and absolute criterion—years of study or educational degrees attained—the possible occupational patterns are much more flexible and multiform. Various trade-offs between occupational prestige, decisional power, and income are conceivable. Options for upward occupational mobility may exist, regardless of educational attainment.[134] An appropriate description of the difference between the major origin groups may be, again, a time lag to the advantage of European-Americans. This refers in particular to the growing percentage of the labor force in academic, technical, and managerial occupations, and to declines in agriculture and semiskilled or nonskilled production work. Yet, it is not self-evident that the same final distributions should be expected for the two

---

[134]Nahon, *Trends in Occupational Status.*

origin groups. As in any societal setup involving the presence of different groups, some amount of group occupational specialization is likely to develop and is in fact occurring in Israel.

At the same time, the very processes of ethnic gap reduction just described in the demographic and socioeconomic areas have tended to produce some increased *polarization*. The fact that among persons of Asian-African origin marriage with European-American spouses and residential mobility into ethnically mixed localities and neighborhoods have been associated with upward mobility implies leaving behind the nonmobile, the downwardly mobile, or those, e.g., the elderly, whose mobility opportunities are exhausted. Therefore, given the asymmetric socioeconomic stratification of European-Americans and Asian-Africans, the bottom social strata have tended to remain homogeneously ethnic, namely, Asian-African. Nationally, this situation involves a minority of the total population, and even a minority of the Asian-African group. Yet, the pattern itself cannot be ignored in the global assessment of the role of gaps in Israeli society.

It is with regard to socioeconomic processes that the polarization trend seems to be of greatest significance. The process in which the least socially mobile are left behind and become ethnically more homogeneous has sometimes been referred to as generating a deprived "ethnoclass." This corresponds to the lower stratum of the Asian-African origin group, including its Israeli-born descendants. Its possible isolation from ongoing processes of sociodemographic mobility and ethnic equalization constitutes the very problematic hard core of the ethnic problem among Israel's Jews.

Viewed through the prism of social indicators, however, the overall socioeconomic position of the major origin groups is not one of real polarization but rather of unequal representation on the rungs of the social ladder. One can see this clearly by looking at the varying weight of each origin group within income deciles. The following are the percentages of Asian-African-born out of all foreign-born Jewish heads of households in urban households, by deciles of net income per capita in 1986–87:[135]

Total	Highest Decile	9th	8th	7th	6th	5th	4th	3rd	2nd	Lowest Decile
44	18	25	28	40	46	55	53	60	60	68

[135]CBS, *Statistical Abstract of Israel*, 1989. Jews born in Israel and non-Jews were excluded from the following calculations.

In comparison to their percentage among total urban households (44 percent), Asian-Africans are clearly underrepresented—but not absent—in the three upper-income deciles, and clearly overrepresented—but not alone—in the three lower deciles.

POLITICAL ASPECTS

One of the most interesting patterns has emerged in the political sphere. The findings discussed above indicate clearly that rather than being characterized by a simple bivariate mechanism, the relationship between ethnic origin group and ideological preferences—as expressed in party choices—appears to be strongly mediated by the socioeconomic status of voters. Ethnic, socioeconomic, and political characteristics of the population, as already noted, are related to a great deal of ecological concentration. As shown earlier in this study, the ethnic composition of different social strata among the Jewish population is quite different. Lower social strata still have a predominantly Asian-African origin, while the majority in higher social strata have a European-American background. Similar relationships exist between religiosity levels and ethnic origins. These overlaps between social, ideological, and ethnic differentiations may lead to some confusion with regard to the real motives behind political choices, especially in relation to the role played by the voting patterns of main ethnic groups in determining the balance between major political forces in the country. The question refers in particular to the shift to the Likud of sections of the electorate of Asian-African origin, large parts of which had previously supported the leading Mapai party and its Labor Alignment successor.

Deterministic political interpretations tend to attribute the major thrust of Israeli political changes to shifts in the demographic composition of the population, namely, the changing weight of different ethnic groups. Assuming rather stable political allegiances within each major origin group, and each group's alleged differential rate of growth in the voting population, the current and future trends in Israeli politics are presumed to depend primarily on the changing demographic balance between ethnic groups.[136] The political choices of Israelis, particularly of those of Asian-African origin, are attributed, by such reasoning, to primordial sociocultural allegiances rather than to substantive political considerations. Such an argument, promoted by the Likud's electoral increases during the late 1970s and early 1980s, seems to downplay the fact that Israeli voters of all origins actually showed a substantial amount of party mobility over the last 30 years.

---

[136]Yochanan Peres and Sara Shemer, "The Ethnic Factor in the Elections to the Tenth Knesset" (in Hebrew), in *The Ethnic Problem in Israel—Continuity and Change*, Megamot, 25, 1984, pp. 316–331.

Indeed, the same Likud, or more significantly the whole Center-Right to Right political sector, after reaching a peak in 1981, tended to decline through 1988, in spite of the continuing moderate increases in the percentage of Asian-Africans out of the total Jewish population.

Even more interesting, though, is the fact that the decisive event at the turning point of the 1977 elections was not the Likud's plurality of votes, but rather the fact that many of Labor's former voters opted out. It was this virtual split of the predominantly European-American Labor camp that dramatically modified the parliamentary balance and coalition-making opportunities in Israel. These voting shifts reflected the dissatisfaction—in the context of the mid-1970s—of large strata of Israeli society with the party that had ruled the country since independence and before. At the same time, these changes seem to have reflected the Likud's shift, from being largely European, middle-class, and rather secular, to being populist, interclassist, and not antireligious. This combination of factors apparently was particularly appealing to middle-lower socioeconomic strata in the population, disappointed with the Labor movement, seeking a strong national image, and asking for more active participation in the political system. Many of these voters were of Asian-African origin.

It would appear, then, that in the Israeli political system, beyond narrow group interests the major determinants of political behavior have been rationally motivated political choices, which in turn reflected the different existential experiences of different strata of the electorate. Party shifts by large sections of certain ethnic groups may have occurred much more on the grounds of general, national political goals and aspirations than in relation to particularistic, ethnic-related interests.[137] It appears that the same political causes sometimes determined different political choices among ethnically different people. Ethnic allegiances functioned as an important contributing factor in Israeli politics primarily to the extent that ethnic origin partly overlapped with two other major explanatory variables of political behavior—socioeconomic status and religious-national ideology. There is no point in denying some independent effects of ethnicity in the party choices of Israelis, but overall such effects were secondary as compared to other factors.

In the Israeli experience, the possibly common normative goal of more equal power sharing between major origin groups conflicts with what is essentially a zero-sum situation: in spite of the continuous significant expansion in the number and types of public offices available, more power to one group means less power to some other group. Hence, the existing veteran, overwhelmingly European political elites demonstrated a great slowness, if

---

[137]Hanna Herzog, "Political Ethnicity in Israel" (in Hebrew), in *The Ethnic Problem in Israel*, ibid., pp. 332–352.

not reluctance, in allowing greater access to power to the emergent strata of the newer Asian-African groups. As a reaction, a circumventing strategy was enacted by members of the Asian-African group, mainly through the maneuvering space offered by the veteran party system, and to some extent with the flanking assistance of smaller and ethnically militant political new formations. The results achieved, in terms of percentages of political elite positions now held by Asian-Africans, are superior to those just demonstrated with regard to the upper-income strata, and by implication, occupational elites.

It may be legitimate to assume that the progress attained in the political sphere will influence, at least indirectly, the further chances for advancement and gap reduction of Asian-Africans in the socioeconomic sphere, through the emerging network of personal contacts and through legislation or other interventions. In any event, it has been shown earlier in this study that political behavior reflects the socioeconomic stratification of origin groups more than ethnicity per se. Proof is to be had in the overwhelming vote for extremely religious parties with a strong ethnic appeal among the lower socioeconomic strata, possibly including some cases of actual downward mobility, and the vote for either of the two major parties or for smaller formations to the left-of-center among the higher strata of each origin group.

OTHER SOCIOCULTURAL ASPECTS

Even in the sociocultural sphere, independent processes of ethnic equalization are clearly visible. Religiosity patterns have evolved to be quite independent of ethnic background.[138] A similar continuum from most to least religious now obtains among younger cohorts within each major origin group, in contrast to a previous generation in which Asian-Africans were much more traditional than most European-Americans—with the exception of an ultra-Orthodox minority of mostly European background. Moreover, on a more general plane, the differences in socioeconomic stratification, personal experience, and related personal satisfaction of Jews of Asian-African and European-American origins do not seem to have produced significantly different cognitive attitudes about the reality of Israeli society.[139] Rather, people belonging to each origin group appear to have quite similar perceptions of the mutual relationships and contradictions between the major social, economic, legal, political, and attitudinal

---

[138]Goldscheider and Friedlander, "Religiosity Patterns in Israel," pp. 3–39.

[139]Zeev Ben-Sira, *Alienated Identification in Jewish-Israeli Society: Interethnic Relations and Integration* (in Hebrew; Jerusalem, 1987), especially pp. 58–88 and 129–137.

variables at work in Israeli society and of their possible effects on the widening or narrowing of social gaps. Perhaps the most significant implication of this relative uniformity of perceptions and mental maps is that it narrows the ground for possible ethnic tensions in Israeli society based on an organic combination of conflicting socioeconomic interests with hostile ethnic stereotypes.

Role of Ethnicity in Social Stratification

In conclusion, a few remarks should be added about the changing role of ethnicity in the Jewish sector of Israeli society. As in any other society, but perhaps more distinctly so in the Israeli case, there coexist multiple bases of identification between individual and society. Ethnicity, which is fundamentally a derivative of geographical background abroad and of the cultural and socioeconomic traits associated with countries of origin, is only one of them. Two other highly relevant variables are socioeconomic status and ideological orientation, the latter itself a complex of variables, including mostly, but not exclusively, religiosity.

Ascription to a given origin group is a primordial, transmitted characteristic. Overall, little statutory legitimation is given to communities of origin in the Israeli social system. The major exception is represented by the Chief Rabbinate, and more generally by the set of national and local institutions which deal with religious matters, including personal status. In these matters, separate branches of the same institution provide services to Ashkenazim and Sephardim (in the wide sense of the latter term). True, the process of immigrant absorption often resulted in geographic concentration of immigrants from the same place of origin; however, this more often reflected contingent expedients rather than a clear ideological directive. In more recent years, greater recognition and legitimation have been awarded to *edot* as intermediate social frameworks, the main rationale being that ethnic-group identification may help the individual process of emotional identification with society at large. But it is practically impossible to establish an accepted hierarchy of origin groups—apart from the respective socioeconomic and religious correlates—or criteria for mobility between groups.

In comparison, social class provides a conventional criterion for social stratification, the belonging to which is more flexible and which definitely allows for internal mobility. At least ideally, no legitimation is provided in Israeli society for social-class divisions and inequality. Yet, the socioeconomic fabric includes important sectors—namely, the Histadrut and its numerous associated social and industrial institutions—which, at least nominally, are supposed to care primarily for the interests of the working class or other particular socioeconomic groups. In any event, the amount of social conflict related to economic interest and to class solidarity seems to be more diffuse and persistent than ethnic conflict in Israeli society.

Segregation and cleavages connected with religious attitudes and practices probably are even more intense and durable. Divisions based on religion are, indeed, officially sanctioned within the Israeli social system. For example, separate educational systems are available to *haredi* (ultra-Orthodox), religious, and secular Jews. The choice to belong to any of these educational systems is the sole prerogative of citizens—in fact, of the pupils' parents. But once the choice is made, the likelihood of significant interaction between youth belonging to each of these educational systems becomes reduced until a later stage in life, be it military service or, even later, participation in the labor force. Separate and parallel tracks, characterized by different religious content, thus direct the main stages of socialization of the new generation of Israelis.

Another stratification factor that was powerfully at work in the past was *vetek*—seniority in the country. During the British Mandate and during the early statehood period, *vetek* often was the sole status differentiator among people, mostly refugees, who, for the most part, lacked any economic means and whose familiarity with the local language and culture was extremely limited. In the course of time, with the decline of immigration and with the gradual growth to numerical predominance of the local-born sector of the Jewish population, the societal relevance of seniority has tended to decline.

Several mechanisms of social change, already mentioned in the preceding analysis, have directly or indirectly affected the ethnic dimension in Israeli society. Three different factors of transformation call for particular attention.

Institutional interventions: the introduction of laws and regulations affecting the whole population or very large sections of it. Relevant examples are the introduction of compulsory education and the lengthening of its duration; regulations establishing the basic approach and technical standards concerning the absorption of new immigrants; regulations affecting the labor market and the main patterns of economic activity; compulsory national insurance and transfer payments; compulsory military service; official recognition of the role of religion in society; and other broad interventions of the institutional system in the life of the individual.

Compositional changes: sociodemographic trends affecting variations in the size of successive birth or marriage cohorts, the size and composition of immigration waves, the size of cohorts joining the educational system and the labor force, and the like. By affecting the basic size and composition of the population, and the environments within which each specific process occurred, these changes powerfully determined the constraints and opportunities that were available over time to each individual and to society globally.

Behavioral changes: widespread changes in the attitudes of, or opportunities available to, the public at large. Changes in the country's economic position, whether due to its intrinsic productive capacity, foreign help, or other factors, led to widespread changes in patterns of income and consumption and to general changes in the standard of living of the population. Changes in educational attainment, namely, the general diffusion of elementary and secondary schooling, fundamentally affected the training patterns of the younger generation toward meeting the manpower needs of an industrialized nation.[140] Large-scale changes in values and norms of the population took place as a result of continued exposure to mass-communication channels, whether originating from within or outside the country. The results of these changes can be observed in many areas, such as preferred family size, propensities to attend school at various educational levels, occupational preferences reflecting the evolving prestige of different occupations, individual attitudes toward religion, political behavior, and so on.

One further significant factor of social change, whose impact goes beyond its basically compositional nature, has been the role of Israeli non-Jews in processes of Jewish immigrant absorption, ethnic integration, and socioeconomic stratification. While these effects could not be dealt with in any detail in this study, it is quite obvious that Jews in Israeli society do not live in a vacuum. The presence of relatively important Arab minorities within the State of Israel inside the pre-1967 Green Line and, even more significantly, the contiguity with a large Arab population in the areas administered since 1967, deeply impinged on socioeconomic and political processes among the Jewish population. The major effect probably was the sudden availability of a relatively large and unsophisticated labor force that could fulfill roles at the bottom of the social ladder, thus enabling the lower sectors of the Jewish labor force (mostly of Asian-African origin) to move toward other endeavors. Further important effects concerned the definition of Jewish group identity and that part of political behavior more directly connected with identificational factors.

These varied and complementary factors of change exerted conflicting effects on the characteristics and trends of the Jewish population. Some of these factors, e. g., laws aiming at equalization, probably tended to reduce preexisting gaps. Other factors, such as mass immigration or even certain mechanisms inherent in a free-market society, at times enhanced inequality. In particular, the shock of the mass immigration experience appears to have

---

[140]Adler, "Jewish Education in Israel: A Sociological Perspective," pp. 485–504.

had longer-term effects on life chances among the immigrants themselves, as well as among their children. In the final analysis, what can be evaluated is the product of the continuing interactions between these different factors of change and the ever evolving social reality.

The product seems to be an ethnicity which, much less than in the past, constitutes a universal and primordial differentiator of Israel's Jewish population. Varying intensities of the ethnic factor coexist today in society, ranging from a relative minority for whom homogeneous cultural and socioeconomic environments reinforce the permanence of a strong and nearly all-encompassing ethnic bond; through a majority for whom ethnic origin is a definite frame of reference and an enriching element but which nevertheless is oriented toward more neutral and homogeneous Israeli socioeconomic goals and cultural ways of expression; down to a further group for whom any cultural remnant of, or interest in, the past ethnic origin has been completely lost (whether or not that origin can be genealogically traced). These various coexisting situations define, respectively, a coherent and cohesive ethnic community, a meaningful social group, or a mere statistical category.

While the effects of time and generation operate toward enhancing the presence of the weaker types just listed, the role of ethnicity is not bound to be lost completely. Different cultural traditions and tastes, different modes of functioning in familial and other social networks, and other similar variables continue to operate as significant factors of differentiation in Israeli society.[141] To this must be added the factor of rising expectations. Whatever social equality among Israeli ethnic-origin groups has been achieved might strengthen the demand for even greater parity. At the same time, a possibility remains that ethnic-origin stereotypes will become somewhat associated with social status. If this were to happen, the socially mobile Israeli-born of Asian-African origin, or more significantly the mobile children of interethnic marriages, might come to be identified by themselves or by others according to a neutral Israeli identity, while their socially stagnant or downwardly mobile homologues might be perceived as of Asian-African origin. To what extent this type of crystallization, which currently exists at the margins of the ethnic stratification system, might persist or intensify is difficult to say at this point.

It may be expected that the further evolution of the ethnic dimension, whether toward greater equalization or in the opposite direction, will reflect the nature of overall developments in the Israeli economy and the availabil-

---

[141]Pnina Morag-Talmon, "The Integration Processes of Eastern Jews in Israeli Society, 1948–1988," in Medding, ed., *Studies in Contemporary Jewry*, vol. 5, pp. 25–38; Eliezer Ben-Rafael, "The Changing Experience, Power and Prestige of Ethnic Groups in Israel: The Case of the Moroccans," in Medding, ed., ibid., pp. 39–58.

ity of socioeconomic opportunities. Judging from developments over the last few decades, relative prosperity and stability may be conducive to a continuation of integrative trends, thanks especially to the crucial catching-up pattern on the part of Asian-Africans. On the other hand, economic or political crises and the consequent public tensions and competition for limited resources may lead to intensification of the persisting potentialities for ethnic polarization and conflicts. In this respect, the present prospect for intensified immigration from Eastern Europe may well constitute a test of existing trends. At any given time, people belonging to different origin groups in Israel may perceive that their socioeconomic characteristics and interests differ. In considering the future of the ethnic dimension in Israeli society, it is the objective socioeconomic situations underlying such diverging perceptions—much more than ethnic attitudes per se—that seem to constitute the main focus for concern and possible public intervention.

In any event, as Israeli society continues to evolve, the ethnic dimension will continue to represent one of the constituting factors, and not the least one, of the ongoing transformations. Several more generations may be necessary before the final results of the whole saga of Jewish immigration and absorption in Israel, and the consequent long-term processes of ethnic and social stratification, can be appropriately assessed.

APPENDIX

Statistical Tables

CONTENTS	TABLES
Immigration	1–3
Population size and structure	4–13
Residential distribution	14–25
Interethnic marriage	26–36
Fertility	37–47
Educational attainment	48–63
Voting behavior	64–68

NOTE ON TERMINOLOGY

"Origin" refers to the regional division used in Israel's official statistics: Israel, Asia-Africa (or each of these continents separately), and Europe-America. "Major origin groups" means Asian-African and European-American, omitting the Israeli origin group. "Dichotomous origin groups" likewise means Asian-Africans and European-Americans, but with the Israeli origin group having been divided according to ultimate origin abroad.

NOTATION

— No respective cases exist.
·· Cases exist but their number is not known.
() Data are derived from small numbers of cases or are otherwise of limited reliability, such as estimates.
x Even smaller numbers of cases are available, which cannot be relied on for meaningful results.

Because of rounding of figures, particular items may not add to a given (sub)total.

TABLE 1. JEWISH IMMIGRANTS,[a] BY CONTINENT OF LAST RESIDENCE AND PERIOD OF IMMIGRATION, 1948[b]–1988

Period of Immigration	Total in Period	Cumulative	Annual Average	Total	Asia-Africa Total	Asia	Africa	Europe-America Total	Europe	America-Oceania
1948[b]–1988										
In thousands	1,804.4	1,804.4	44.4	1,804.4[d]	784.7	357.3	427.4	994.4	824.6	169.8
Percent				100.0	44.1	20.1	24.0	55.9	46.4	9.5
1948[b]–1951	686.7	686.7	189.2	100.0	50.0	35.8	14.2	50.0	49.3	0.7
1952–1954	54.1	740.8	18.0	100.0	76.4	24.6	51.8	23.6	18.1	5.5
1955–1957	164.9	905.7	55.0	100.0	68.3	5.3	63.0	31.7	29.5	2.2
1958–1960	75.5	981.2	25.2	100.0	36.1	17.6	18.5	64.0	59.2	4.8
1961–1964	228.0	1,209.2	57.0	100.0	59.5	8.6	50.9	40.5	34.0	6.5
1965–1968	81.3	1,290.5	20.3	100.0	49.7	18.5	31.2	50.3	38.9	11.4
1969–1971	116.5	1,407.0	38.8	100.0	27.4	17.0	10.4	72.5	43.3	29.1
1972–1974	142.8	1,549.8	47.6	100.0	9.2	4.4	4.8	90.8	72.0	18.8
1975–1979	124.8	1,674.6	25.0	100.0	14.3	9.5	4.8	85.7	62.1	23.6
1980–1984	83.6	1,758.2	16.7	100.0	27.1	8.3	18.8	72.9	42.6	30.3
1985–1988	46.2	1,804.4	11.5	100.0	24.4	11.7	12.7	75.7	42.8	32.9

[a] As from 1970 including non-Jewish family members of immigrants.
[b] As from May 15, 1948.
[c] Except for first line.
[d] Including "unknown" cases.
Source: Israel Central Bureau of Statistics (hereafter, CBS), *Statistical Abstract of Israel,* 1989.

TABLE 2. FOREIGN-BORN JEWS, BY CONTINENT OF BIRTH AND PERIOD OF IMMIGRATION, 1961–1988 (PERCENT)

Period of Immigration	Total	Asia-Africa Total	Asia	Africa	Europe-America
		1961			
Total	100.0	100.0	100.0	100.0	100.0
Up to 1947	26.6	10.2	16.0	2.8	39.5
1948–1954	53.6	63.5	76.0	47.2	45.8
1955+	19.8	26.2	8.0	50.0	14.7
		1972			
Total	100.0	100.0	100.0	100.0	100.0
Up to 1947	19.4	7.0	12.4	2.1	30.4
1948–1954	40.0	46.1	65.2	28.8	34.5
1955–1964	27.5	35.3	11.8	56.6	20.6
1965+	13.1	11.6	10.6	12.5	14.5
		1983			
Total	100.0	100.0	100.0	100.0	100.0
Up to 1947	15.4	6.5	11.1	2.2	22.3
1948–1954	34.0	43.7	61.3	27.6	26.5
1955–1964	23.7	33.4	11.2	53.6	16.1
1965–1974	16.3	11.9	11.0	12.6	19.8
1975+	10.6	4.6	5.3	3.9	15.3
		1988			
Total	100.0	100.0	100.0	100.0	100.0
Up to 1947	13.4	5.8	10.3	2.0	19.6
1948–1954	32.4	41.9	60.4	25.8	24.7
1955–1964	23.2	32.6	11.3	51.1	15.6
1965–1979	22.3	14.0	14.4	13.6	29.1
1980+	8.6	5.6	3.6	7.4	11.0

Sources: CBS: 1961 census, vol. 13; 1972 census, vol. 10; 1983 census, vol. 7; Special Publication 215; *Statistical Abstract of Israel,* 1989; unpublished data.

TABLE 3. FOREIGN-BORN JEWS, BY COUNTRY OF BIRTH AND PERIOD OF IMMIGRATION, 1983 (PERCENT)

Country of Birth	Total	Up to 1947	1948–1954	1955–1964	1965–1974	1975+
Total	100.0	15.4	34.0	23.7	16.3	10.6
Asia, total	100.0	11.1	61.3	11.2	11.0	5.3
Turkey	100.0	13.3	47.5	16.1	17.2	5.8
Syria, Lebanon	100.0	41.9	18.0	16.2	15.1	8.7
Iraq	100.0	6.0	90.1	1.8	1.8	0.3
Yemen, S. Yemen	100.0	20.6	76.3	2.1	0.7	0.3
Iran	100.0	4.0	37.0	26.3	17.4	15.4
India	100.0	0.7	14.8	24.7	50.2	9.7
Other Asia	100.0	18.8	54.2	10.6	9.6	6.7
Africa, total	100.0	2.2	27.6	53.6	12.6	3.9
Morocco	100.0	0.8	17.0	67.2	13.6	1.5
Tunisia, Algeria	100.0	1.5	34.4	44.4	14.5	5.2
Libya	100.0	3.8	85.2	3.4	7.1	0.5
Egypt, Sudan	100.0	11.5	46.8	35.9	4.6	1.3
Other Africa	100.0	3.3	6.2	14.3	20.8	55.4
Europe-America, total	100.0	22.3	26.5	16.1	19.8	15.3
USSR	100.0	15.5	7.3	7.3	40.9	29.1
Poland	100.0	43.1	35.8	14.8	4.3	1.9
Czechoslovakia	100.0	37.9	49.5	4.1	6.4	2.0
Hungary	100.0	26.2	41.8	23.6	5.0	3.4
Romania	100.0	9.8	37.2	35.0	12.8	5.2
Bulgaria, Greece	100.0	26.4	67.6	3.2	1.7	1.0
Germany, Austria	100.0	60.3	25.7	3.7	5.7	4.5
Other Europe	100.0	10.2	21.7	14.7	23.9	29.6
North America, Oceania	100.0	2.7	3.4	6.2	36.1	51.6
Latin America	100.0	1.6	5.4	20.3	37.8	34.8

Source: CBS, 1983, census vol. 7.

TABLE 4. GROWTH OF JEWISH POPULATION, BY COMPONENTS, 1948[a]–1988

Period[b]	Annual Growth Rate (per 1,000)	Components of Growth (%) Migration Balance	Natural Increase
1948[a]–1988	44	46.2	53.8
1948[a]–1960	92	68.9	31.1
1961–1971	30	45.0	55.0
1972–1982	21	25.1	74.9
1983–1988	15	5.4	94.6

[a]As from May 15, 1948.
[b]Approximately corresponding to intervals between censuses (except for last line).
Source: CBS, *Statistical Abstract of Israel,* 1989.

TABLE 5. JEWISH POPULATION, BY REGION OF BIRTH OR ORIGIN, 1948–2000 (IN THOUSANDS)

Region	1948	1961	1972	1983[a]	1988	% Change 1961–88	1988	2000[b]
				All Ages			Ages 15+	
				Region of Birth				
All Jews	716.7	1,932.4	2,686.7	3,371.0	3,659.0	89.4	2,577.1	3,103.3
Israeli-born, total	253.7	730.4	1,272.3	1,946.1	2,315.9	217.1	1,273.8	2,016.4
Father born in:								
Israel	..	106.9	225.8	540.0	786.3	635.5	245.0	619.9
Asia-Africa	..	288.5	608.9	863.4	940.3	225.9	618.0	863.3
Asia	..	189.8	339.8	446.8	468.7	146.9	339.8	436.8
Africa	..	98.7	269.1	416.6	471.6	377.8	278.2	426.5
Europe-America	..	335.0	437.6	542.7	589.4	75.9	410.8	533.1
Foreign-born, total	468.0	1,201.9	1,414.4	1,424.9	1,343.1	11.7	1,303.2	1,087.0
Asia-Africa	70.0	529.8	665.0	622.9	601.3	13.5	591.9	485.9
Asia	57.8	300.1	316.1	297.3	278.8	−7.1	276.1	216.3
Africa	12.2	229.7	348.9	325.6	322.5	40.4	315.8	269.6
Europe-America	393.0	672.1	749.4	802.0	741.8	10.4	711.3	601.1

TABLE 5.—(Continued)

Region	1948	1961	1972	1983[a]	1988	% Change 1961-88	1988	2000[b]
			All Ages				Ages 15+	
				Origin, by Region of Birth				
All Jews	..	1,932.4	2,686.7	3,371.0	3,659.0	89.4	2,577.1	3,103.3
Israel	..	106.9	225.8	540.0	786.3	635.5	245.0	619.9
Asia-Africa, total	..	818.3	1,273.9	1,486.3	1,541.6	88.4	1,209.9	1,349.2
Foreign-born	..	529.8	665.0	622.9	601.3	13.5	591.9	485.9
Israeli-born	..	288.5	608.9	863.4	940.3	225.9	618.0	863.3
Asia, total	..	490.0	655.9	744.1	747.5	52.6	615.9	653.1
Foreign-born	..	300.1	316.1	297.3	278.8	-7.1	276.1	216.3
Israeli-born	..	189.9	339.8	446.8	468.7	146.8	339.8	436.8
Africa, total	..	328.3	618.0	742.2	794.1	141.9	594.0	696.1
Foreign-born	..	229.7	348.9	325.6	322.5	40.4	315.8	269.6
Israeli-born	..	98.6	269.1	416.6	471.6	378.3	278.2	426.5
Europe-America, total	..	1,007.1	1,187.0	1,344.7	1,331.2	32.2	1,122.1	1,134.2
Foreign-born	..	672.1	749.4	802.0	741.8	10.4	711.3	601.1
Israeli-born	..	335.0	437.6	542.7	589.4	75.9	410.8	533.1
				Origin, Condensed				
All Jews	—	1,932.4	2,686.7	3,371.0	3,659.0	89.4	2,577.1	3,103.3
Israel	—	106.9	225.8	540.0	786.3	635.5	245.0	619.9
Asia-Africa	—	818.4	1,273.9	1,486.3	1,541.6	88.4	1,209.9	1,349.2
Europe-America	—	1,007.1	1,187.0	1,344.7	1,331.2	32.2	1,122.1	1,134.2
				Origin, Dichotomous				
All Jews	—	1,932.4	2,686.7	3,371.0	3,659.0	89.4	2,577.1	3,103.3
Asia-Africa	—	841.3	1,346.5	1,700.7	1,889.3	124.5	1,287.9	1,612.6
Europe-America	—	1,091.1	1,340.2	1,670.3	1,769.7	62.2	1,289.2	1,490.7

[a]Adjusted census data.
[b]Projection.

TABLE 6. JEWISH POPULATION, BY REGION OF BIRTH, 1948–2000 (PERCENT)

Region	All Ages					Ages 15+	
	1948	1961	1972	1983[a]	1988	1988	2000[b]
				Region of Birth			
All Jews	100.0	100.0	100.0	100.0	100.0	100.0	100.0
Israeli-born, total	35.4	37.8	47.4	57.7	63.3	49.4	65.0
Father born in:							
Israel	··	5.5	8.4	16.0	21.5	9.5	20.0
Asia-Africa	··	14.9	22.7	25.7	25.7	24.0	27.8
Asia	··	9.8	12.7	13.3	12.8	13.2	14.1
Africa	··	5.1	10.0	12.4	12.9	10.8	13.7
Europe-America	··	17.3	16.3	16.1	16.1	15.9	17.2
Foreign-born, total	64.6	62.2	52.7	42.3	36.7	50.5	35.1
Asia-Africa	9.8	27.4	24.8	18.5	16.4	22.9	15.7
Asia	8.1	15.5	11.8	8.8	7.6	10.7	7.0
Africa	1.7	11.9	13.0	9.7	8.8	12.2	8.7
Europe-America	54.8	34.8	27.9	23.8	20.3	27.6	19.4
			Foreign-born, by Region of Birth				
Total	100.0	100.0	100.0	100.0	100.0	100.0	100.0
Asia-Africa	15.1	44.0	47.0	43.7	44.8	45.4	44.7
Asia	12.5	24.9	22.3	20.9	20.8	21.2	19.9
Africa	2.6	19.1	24.7	22.8	24.0	24.2	24.8
Europe-America	84.9	55.9	53.0	56.3	55.2	54.6	55.3
			Israeli-born, by Father's Region of Birth				
Total	··	100.0	100.0	100.0	100.0	100.0	100.0
Israel	··	14.6	17.7	27.7	34.0	19.2	30.7
Asia-Africa	··	39.5	47.9	44.4	40.6	48.5	42.9
Asia	··	26.0	26.7	23.0	20.2	26.7	21.7
Africa	··	13.5	21.2	21.4	20.4	21.8	21.2
Europe-America	··	45.9	34.4	27.9	25.4	32.2	26.4

[a], [b] See notes a and b to table 5.
Source: Same as table 5.

TABLE 7. JEWISH POPULATION, BY ORIGIN AND REGION OF BIRTH, 1961–2000 (PERCENT)

Origin, Region of Birth	All Ages 1961	All Ages 1972	All Ages 1983[a]	All Ages 1988	Ages 15+ 1988	Ages 15+ 2000[b]
Origin						
All Jews	100.0	100.0	100.0	100.0	100.0	100.0
Israel	5.5	8.4	16.0	21.5	9.5	20.0
Asia-Africa, total	42.3	47.4	44.0	42.1	46.9	43.5
Asia	25.3	24.4	22.0	20.4	23.9	21.1
Africa	17.0	23.0	22.0	21.7	23.0	22.4
Europe-America, total	52.1	44.2	39.9	36.4	43.5	36.6
Origin, Dichotomous						
All Jews	100.0	100.0	100.0	100.0	100.0	100.0
Asia-Africa	43.5	50.1	50.4	51.6	50.0	52.0
Europe-America	56.5	49.9	49.6	48.4	50.0	48.0
Region of Birth, by Dichotomous Origin						
Israeli-born, father born in Israel[c]	100.0	100.0	100.0	100.0	100.0	100.0
Asia-Africa	32.9	32.2	39.7	44.2	31.8	42.5
Europe-America	67.1	67.8	60.3	55.8	68.2	57.5
Israeli-born, father foreign-born	100.0	100.0	100.0	100.0	100.0	100.0
Asia-Africa	46.2	58.2	61.4	61.4	60.0	61.8
Europe-America	53.7	41.8	38.6	38.5	39.9	38.2
Foreign-born	100.0	100.0	100.0	100.0	100.0	100.0
Asia-Africa	44.0	47.0	43.7	44.8	45.4	44.7
Europe-America	55.9	53.0	56.3	55.2	54.6	55.3
Percent Israeli-born, by Origin						
All Jews	37.8	47.4	57.7	63.3	49.4	65.0
Israel	100.0	100.0	100.0	100.0	100.0	100.0
Asia-Africa	35.2	47.7	58.1	61.0	51.1	64.0
Asia	38.8	51.8	60.0	62.7	55.2	66.9
Africa	30.0	43.5	56.1	59.4	46.8	61.3
Europe-America	33.3	36.9	40.4	44.3	36.6	47.0

[a], [b] See notes a and b to table 5.
[c] Origin distribution partly conjectural.
Source: Same as table 5.

TABLE 8. JEWISH POPULATION,[a] by Country of Origin and Place of Birth, 1961 and 1988

Country	In Thousands 1988 Total	Foreign-born	Israeli-born	Percent Distribution 1961 Total	Foreign-born	Israeli-born	1988 Total	Foreign-born	Israeli-born	% Israeli-born 1961	1988	% Change 1961–1988 Total	Foreign-born	Israeli-born
Total	2,872.7[a]	1,343.1	1,529.6[a]	100.0	100.0	100.0	100.0	100.0	100.0	34.2	53.2	57.4	11.7	145.3
Asia, total	747.5	278.8	468.7	26.9	24.8	30.4	26.0	20.7	30.7	38.8	62.7	52.5	−7.1	146.7
Turkey	90.4	39.5	50.9	3.6	3.4	3.8	3.2	2.9	3.3	36.3	56.3	38.7	−4.8	114.9
Iraq	264.7	92.5	172.2	10.2	10.3	10.0	9.2	6.9	11.3	33.6	65.0	42.3	−25.1	175.1
Yemen, S. Yemen	163.1	47.2	115.9	6.7	5.1	9.7	5.7	3.5	7.6	49.5	71.1	33.0	−23.7	90.8
Iran	130.6	57.4	73.2	3.3	3.1	3.7	4.5	4.3	4.8	38.1	56.0	115.8	53.3	217.0
India	98.8	19.4	56.5	3.1	0.5	3.2	3.4	1.4	3.7	35.6	57.2	77.1	196.0	184.2
Other		22.9			2.4			1.7					−22.0	
Africa, total	794.0	322.5	471.5	18.0	19.2	15.8	27.6	24.0	30.7	30.0	93.4	141.9	40.4	378.6
Morocco	491.7	195.9	295.8	9.1	9.9	7.5	17.1	14.6	19.3	28.1	60.2	197.0	64.6	535.0
Tunisia, Algeria	126.1	48.9	77.2	3.3	3.6	2.8	4.4	3.6	5.0	29.3	61.2	108.8	14.6	335.4
Libya	76.6	24.4	52.2	2.7	2.6	3.0	2.7	1.8	3.4	38.0	68.1	52.7	−21.6	174.0
Egypt	64.9	26.9	38.0	2.7	2.9	2.3	2.2	2.0	2.5	28.9	58.6	32.2	−23.0	168.0
Other	34.6	26.4	8.2	0.2	0.2	0.2	1.2	2.0	0.5	32.3	23.7	1,051.4	1,197.9	744.5

TABLE 8.—(Continued)

Country	In Thousands 1988 Total	In Thousands 1988 Foreign-born	In Thousands 1988 Israeli-born	Percent Distribution 1961 Total	Percent Distribution 1961 Foreign-born	Percent Distribution 1961 Israeli-born	Percent Distribution 1988 Total	Percent Distribution 1988 Foreign-born	Percent Distribution 1988 Israeli-born	% Israeli-born 1961	% Israeli-born 1988	% Change 1961–1988 Total	% Change 1961–1988 Foreign-born	% Change 1961–1988 Israeli-born
Europe-America, total	1,331.2	741.8	589.4	55.1	55.9	53.7	46.4	55.2	38.6	33.3	44.3	32.2	10.4	75.9
USSR	293.8	181.6	112.2	10.4	9.3	12.6	10.2	13.5	7.3	41.2	38.2	54.1	62.2	42.7
Poland	290.6	136.4	154.2	18.1	17.3	19.6	10.1	10.2	10.1	37.1	53.1	−11.9	−34.3	26.1
Romania	274.2	161.2	113.0	10.6	12.9	6.2	9.6	12.0	7.4	20.0	41.2	41.1	3.6	191.3
Bulgaria, Greece	62.8	29.6	33.2	3.7	4.1	3.1	2.2	2.2	2.2	28.7	52.9	−8.2	−39.3	69.1
Germany, Austria	89.2	40.5	48.7	4.7	4.5	5.2	3.1	3.0	3.2	37.2	54.6	3.3	−25.3	51.4
Czechoslovakia	84.6	19.3	43.9	2.2	2.1	2.4	3.0	1.4	2.9	36.3	51.9	1.4	−24.9	54.9
Hungary		21.4		2.4	2.4	2.2		1.6		31.8			−27.1	
Other Europe	235.9	59.4	84.2	2.2	2.4	1.8	8.2	4.4	5.5	28.1	35.7	337.3	108.2	456.7
North America-Oceania		48.5		0.8	0.9	0.6		3.6		27.9			796.4	
Latin America		43.8						3.3						

[a]Excluding the Israeli origin group (i.e., Israeli-born whose father was also born in this country).
Sources: CBS: 1961 census, vols. 13, 22; Special Publication 274; *Statistical Abstract of Israel*, 1989.

TABLE 9. JEWISH IMMIGRANTS,[a] BY CONTINENT OF BIRTH AND AGE, SELECTED IMMIGRATION PERIODS, 1948–1988 (PERCENT AND MEDIAN)

Age	1948–1951 Asia-Africa	1948–1951 Europe-America	1961–1964 Asia-Africa	1961–1964 Europe-America	1969–1972 Asia-Africa	1969–1972 Europe-America	1984–1988 Asia-Africa	1984–1988 Europe-America
Total	100.0	100.0	100.0	100.0	100.0	100.0	100.0	100.0
0–4	12.9	10.5	14.0	6.3	6.4	6.6	9.9	8.1
5–14	24.2	9.3	29.5	15.1	19.0	14.6	20.3	10.8
15–24	23.8	15.9	19.5	14.1	27.0	24.4	24.4	23.0
25–34	13.6	19.6	10.8	10.9	13.9	15.0	15.7	22.7
35–44	10.0	18.0	10.0	16.3	10.6	11.5	8.9	10.8
45–54	7.6	13.2	7.5	16.8	9.3	10.5	5.6	5.4
55–64	4.4	8.3	5.4	12.6	7.4	8.6	7.1	7.9
65–74	2.4	3.9	2.5	5.7	4.6	6.4	5.3	6.8
75+	1.0	1.2	0.7	2.3	1.7	2.4	2.7	4.5
Median age	20.0	31.8	17.8	37.3	24.0	27.5	23.0	28.0

[a]As from 1970 including non-Jewish family members of immigrants.
Sources: CBS: Special Publications 489, 777, 790, 808, 833, 858.

TABLE 10. JEWISH POPULATION, BY REGION OF BIRTH AND AGE, 1988 (PERCENT AND MEDIAN)

Age	All Jews	Israel	Asia-Africa Total	Asia	Africa	Europe-America	% All Jews Born in Israel
All ages	100.0	100.0	100.0	100.0	100.0	100.0	63.3
0–4	10.2	18.2	0.1	0.1	0.2	0.7	98.4
5–14	19.4	31.8	1.4	0.8	1.9	3.4	95.2
15+, total	70.4	50.0	98.5	99.1	97.9	95.9	49.4
15–24	16.4	24.6	3.4	2.9	3.7	6.5	88.6
25–34	14.4	15.7	12.4	6.7	17.3	9.5	72.4
35–44	13.6	6.3	25.3	23.0	27.4	16.1	45.5
45–54	8.1	1.8	22.4	24.7	20.4	10.9	27.3
55–64	7.6	1.0	18.5	21.4	16.0	17.9	12.8
65–74	6.0	0.4	10.6	12.3	9.2	19.5	4.8
75+	4.2	0.2	5.8	8.0	3.9	15.5	3.4
Median age	27.8	13.0	48.2	51.6	44.8	56.8	

Sources: CBS, *Statistical Abstract of Israel,* 1989; unpublished data.

TABLE 11. MEDIAN AGE OF JEWISH POPULATION, BY ORIGIN (DICHOTOMOUS) AND SEX, 1961–2000

Year	Asia-Africa Total	Males	Females	Europe-America Total	Males	Females
All ages						
1961	19.0	18.7	19.3	32.9	33.0	32.8
1972	20.4	20.0	20.8	32.8	31.2	34.2
1983[a]	23.6	23.1	24.2	32.5	31.3	33.7
1988	24.8	24.2	25.4	32.2	30.5	33.9
Ages 15+						
1961	32.4	32.4	32.4	42.7	43.5	41.9
1972	31.8	31.4	32.3	43.6	43.1	44.1
1983[a]	33.1	32.6	33.6	42.9	41.2	44.4
1988	34.4	34.0	34.9	41.8	40.8	42.9
2000[b]	37.2	36.6	37.9	41.2	39.8	42.7

[a]Adjusted census data.
[b]Projection.
Source: Same as table 5.

TABLE 12. JEWISH POPULATION, BY ORIGIN (DICHOTOMOUS) AND AGE, 1961, 1988, 2000 (PERCENT AND MEDIAN)

Age	All Ages						Ages 15+			
	Asia-Africa		Europe-America				Asia-Africa		Europe-America	
	1961	1988	1961	1988	1988	2000[a]	1988	2000[a]		
All ages	100.0	100.0	100.0	100.0						
0–4	15.3	11.1	7.9	9.2						
5–14	27.2	20.7	20.9	18.0						
15+, total	57.5	68.2	71.2	72.8	100.0	100.0	100.0	100.0		
15–24	17.4	18.5	12.0	14.1	27.2	24.1	19.4	21.7		
25–34	14.9	16.5	11.9	12.2	24.1	21.7	16.8	18.9		
35–44	9.8	12.9	14.9	14.4	18.9	18.8	19.8	15.1		
45–54	7.1	8.3	16.3	7.9	12.1	15.9	10.9	17.5		
55–64	4.8	6.5	9.9	8.9	9.5	9.3	12.2	9.4		
65–74	} 3.6	3.6	} 6.2	8.6	5.3	6.7	11.7	8.7		
75+		1.9		6.7	2.8	3.4	9.2	8.7		
Medians:										
All ages	19.0	24.8	32.9	32.2						
Ages 15+	32.4	34.4	42.7	41.8	34.4	37.2	41.8	41.2		

[a]Projection.
Source: Same as table 5.

TABLE 13. PERCENTAGE OF ASIAN-AFRICAN ORIGIN IN THE JEWISH POPULATION (DICHOTOMOUS ORIGIN GROUPS), BY AGE, 1961–2000

Age	1961	1972	1983[a]	1988	2000[b]
All ages	43.5	50.1	50.4	51.6	—
0–4	60.0	60.5	55.9	56.5	—
5–14	50.1	64.0	56.4	55.1	—
15+, total	38.4	44.8	48.0	50.0	52.0
15–24	52.6	54.9	60.7	58.3	54.6
25–34	49.1	53.0	54.1	59.0	55.4
35–44	33.7	51.1	49.5	48.8	57.5
45–54	25.1	36.7	49.1	52.7	49.5
55–64	27.2	27.4	35.4	43.7	51.7
65–74		27.3	26.6	30.9	45.4
75+	30.7	29.2	24.4	23.6	30.0

[a], [b] See notes a and b to table 11.
Source: Same as table 5.

TABLE 14. JEWISH POPULATION, BY REGION OF BIRTH/ORIGIN GROUP[a] AND SUBDISTRICT, 1953, 1961,[b] AND 1983 (PERCENT)

District and Subdistrict	Geographical Distribution Total 1961	1983[c]	Origin, 1983 Asia-Africa	Europe-America	Percent of Asian-African Jews in (Sub) District 1953	1961	1983
Total	100.0	100.0	100.0	100.0	36.1	43.1	52.4
Jerusalem district	9.7	10.4	10.2	8.8	50.7	57.0	56.2
Northern district	10.0	9.8	10.7	8.6	43.1	53.2	57.6
Zefat sd.	2.2	1.8	2.3	1.1	47.7	64.2	69.2
Kinneret sd.	1.8	1.4	1.6	0.8	58.8	60.3	67.6
Yizreel sd.	3.4	3.4	3.6	3.4	40.4	47.3	53.6
Akko sd.	2.6	2.9	3.1	3.1	33.9	48.0	52.4
Golan sd.	—	0.2	0.1	0.2	—	—	39.4
Haifa district	16.7	13.9	10.7	17.8	23.5	28.9	39.9
Haifa sd.	13.3	11.1	7.8	15.2	17.6	25.7	36.2
Hadera sd.	3.4	2.7	2.9	2.6	44.0	41.9	55.0
Central district	19.7	22.8	23.9	21.3	46.7	50.6	55.3
Sharon sd.	4.4	4.5	4.8	4.4	44.7	44.9	54.6
Petah Tiqwa sd.	6.8	8.5	8.5	8.1	44.5	48.3	53.8
Ramla sd.	3.3	2.9	4.0	2.0	51.5	62.7	68.4
Rehovot sd.	5.2	6.9	6.6	6.8	46.6	50.0	51.7
Tel Aviv district	35.9	29.5	25.8	33.6	27.1	34.4	45.9
Southern district	8.0	12.9	18.2	9.2	62.2	69.1	68.6
Ashqelon sd.	3.9	6.0	8.6	4.4	61.5	67.0	68.4
Beer Sheva sd.	4.1	6.9	9.6	4.8	63.1	70.9	68.6
Judea, Samaria, Gaza	—	0.7	0.5	0.7	—	—	43.5

[a]1953 and 1961—foreign-born only; 1983—according to origin groups (here and in all analogous data for 1983 in tables 15–25, excluding Israeli origin).
[b]From 20-percent sample.
[c]Including the Israeli origin group.
Sources: CBS: 1961 census, vol. 22; 1983 census, vol. 12; B. Gil (see note 28 to text).

TABLE 15. JEWISH POPULATION, BY ORIGIN GROUP AND SUBDISTRICT, 1983 (PERCENT)

District and Subdistrict	Row Percentages Total[a]	Asia	Africa	Europe-America	Column Percentages Total[a]	Asia	Africa	Europe-America
Total	100.0	26.3	26.1	47.6	100.0	100.0	100.0	100.0
Jerusalem district	100.0	31.9	24.3	43.8	9.5	11.5	8.8	8.8
Northern district	100.0	17.2	40.4	42.4	9.7	6.3	15.0	8.7
Zefat sd.	100.0	15.4	53.8	30.8	1.8	1.0	3.6	1.1
Kinneret sd.	100.0	22.7	45.1	32.3	1.2	1.1	2.1	0.8
Yizreel sd.	100.0	19.0	34.7	46.3	3.5	2.5	4.6	3.4
Akko sd.	100.0	13.8	38.6	47.6	3.1	1.6	4.6	3.1
Golan sd.	100.0	19.1	20.3	60.6	0.2	0.1	0.1	0.2
Haifa district	100.0	15.0	24.9	60.1	14.1	8.1	13.4	17.8
Haifa sd.	100.0	13.2	23.0	63.8	11.3	5.7	9.9	15.2
Hadera sd.	100.0	22.4	32.6	45.0	2.8	2.4	3.5	2.6
Central district	100.0	32.9	22.4	44.7	22.7	28.4	19.5	21.3
Sharon sd.	100.0	25.0	29.6	45.4	4.6	4.4	5.2	4.4
Petah Tiqwa sd.	100.0	39.1	14.7	46.2	8.3	12.4	4.7	8.1
Ramla sd.	100.0	28.7	39.7	31.6	3.1	3.3	4.7	2.0
Rehovot sd.	100.0	32.5	19.2	48.3	6.7	8.3	4.9	6.8
Tel Aviv district	100.0	31.8	14.1	54.2	29.5	35.7	15.9	33.6
Southern district	100.0	18.0	50.6	31.4	13.9	9.5	27.0	9.2
Ashqelon sd.	100.0	18.9	49.5	31.5	6.6	4.7	12.5	4.4
Beer Sheva sd.	100.0	17.1	51.5	31.4	7.3	4.8	14.5	4.8
Judea, Samaria, Gaza	100.0	22.3	21.2	56.5	0.6	0.5	0.5	0.7

[a]Excluding the Israeli origin group.
Source: CBS, 1983 census, vol. 12.

TABLE 16. JEWS, BY COUNTRY OF ORIGIN AND SUBDISTRICT (THREE SUBDISTRICTS WITH HIGHEST REPRESENTATION OF COUNTRY IN THEIR JEWISH POPULATIONS, AND TOTAL ISRAEL), 1983 (PERCENT)

Country of Origin	Highest Subdistrict	Percent	2nd Highest Subdistrict	Percent	3rd Highest Subdistrict	Percent	Israel (percent)
Turkey	Ramla	5.5	Tel Aviv	5.0	Petah Tiqwa	4.0	3.3
Syria, Lebanon	Tel-Aviv	2.4	Haifa	2.0	Golan	1.7	1.4
Iraq	Kinneret	15.4	Jerusalem	13.4	Tel Aviv	12.8	9.4
Yemen	Petah Tiqwa	14.9	Rehovot	13.8	Sharon	10.2	5.8
Iran	Jerusalem	8.1	Zefat	5.4	Tel Aviv	5.3	4.3
India, Pakistan	Ramla	6.0	Beer Sheva	4.9	Ashqelon	3.3	1.3
Morocco	Zefat	37.7	Beer Sheva	33.8	Ashqelon	33.1	16.2
Tunisia, Algeria	Beer Sheva	12.5	Ramla	11.0	Zefat	10.5	4.3
Libya	Sharon	11.5	Hadera	5.6	Ashqelon	5.1	2.7
Egypt	Tel Aviv	3.3	Beer Sheva	2.7	Haifa	2.5	2.3
USSR	Haifa	13.6	Ramla	13.4	Yizreel	12.5	10.5
Poland	Tel Aviv	16.6	Haifa	15.0	Golan	12.8	11.3
Romania	Haifa	19.2	Akko	13.4	Rehovot	11.6	10.0
Bulgaria, Greece	Tel Aviv	4.8	Rehovot	2.6	Ramla	2.5	2.4
Germany, Austria	Golan	7.5	Judea, Samaria	5.5	Haifa	4.8	3.3
Czechoslovakia	Golan	3.0	Sharon	2.5	Haifa	2.1	1.5
Hungary	Golan	3.3	Judea, Samaria	2.9	Jerusalem	2.2	1.6
North America	Judea, Samaria	11.0	Golan	6.3	Jerusalem	6.0	1.7
Latin America	Golan	3.8	Yizreel	3.2	Beer Sheva	3.2	1.9

Source: Same as table 15.

TABLE 17. NATURAL REGIONS AND THEIR JEWISH POPULATION BY DISTRICT AND PERCENTAGE OF ASIAN-AFRICAN ORIGIN IN JEWISH POPULATION, 1983

District	Percentage of Asian-African Origin					
	Total	Up to 34.9	35.0–64.9			65.0+
			Total	35.0–44.9	45.0–54.9	55.0–64.9	

Natural Regions

District	Total	Up to 34.9	Total	35.0–44.9	45.0–54.9	55.0–64.9	65.0+
Total	45	5	26	7	10	9	14
Jerusalem	2	—	1	—	1	—	1
Northern	19	5	9	3	3	3	5
Haifa	5	—	5	1	1	3	—
Central	6	—	5	1	3	1	1
Tel Aviv	1	—	1	—	1	—	—
Southern	10	—	3	1	—	2	7
Judea, Samaria, Gaza	2	—	2	1	1	—	—

Jewish Population

	Total	Up to 34.9	Total	35.0–44.9	45.0–54.9	55.0–64.9	65.0+
Total (in thousands)	3,350.0	16.4	2,824.6	597.8	1,803.7	423.1	509.0
Percent	100.0	0.5	84.2	17.8	53.8	12.6	15.2

Source: Same as table 15.

TABLE 18. JEWISH POPULATION, BY REGION OF BIRTH/ORIGIN GROUP[a] AND TYPE OF LOCALITY, 1961[b] AND 1983 (PERCENT)

Type of Locality	Geographical Distribution Total 1961	Geographical Distribution Total 1983[c]	Origin, 1983 Asia-Africa	Origin, 1983 Europe-America	Percent of Asian-African Jews in Type of Locality 1961	Percent of Asian-African Jews in Type of Locality 1983
Total	100.0	100.0	100.0	100.0	43.1	52.4
Urban, total	87.0	90.2	91.8	90.2	42.7	52.9
Jerusalem	8.5	9.1	8.3	8.2	52.4	52.9
Tel Aviv-Yafo	19.7	9.5	7.4	11.9	29.9	40.8
Haifa	9.0	6.2	3.4	9.3	20.2	28.4
Others	49.8	65.4	72.7	60.8	50.2	56.8
Rural, total	13.0	9.8	8.2	9.8	46.7	48.0
Moshavim	6.4	4.5	5.4	3.2	57.7	65.3
Kibbutzim	4.0	3.4	1.0	5.0	12.4	18.0
Others	2.6	1.9	1.8	1.6	68.4	54.7

[a]1961—foreign-born only; 1983—according to origin groups (excluding Israeli origin).
[b]From 20-percent sample.
[c]Including the Israeli origin group.
Sources: CBS: 1961 census, vol. 22; 1983 census, vol. 12.

TABLE 19. URBAN JEWISH LOCALITIES WITH 10,000+ INHABITANTS[a] AND THEIR JEWISH POPULATION, BY TYPE OF LOCALITY AND PERCENTAGE OF ASIAN-AFRICAN JEWS,[b] 1961 AND 1983

Type of Locality	Percentage of Asian-African Jews						
	Total	Up to 34.9	35.0–64.9				65.0+
			Total	35.0–44.9	45.0–54.9	55.0–64.9	
Localities							
1961, total	30	5	19	9	4	6	6
Main cities	3	2	1	—	1	—	—
Other towns	27	3	18	9	3	6	6
Old	13	2	11	8	3	0	0
New	14	1	7	1	0	6	6
1983, total	56	6	28	8	10	10	22
Main cities	3	1	2	1	1	—	—
Other towns	53	5	26	7	9	10	22
100,000–199,999	7	—	7	—	5	2	—
50,000–99,999	5	—	3	2	1	—	2
20,000–49,999	20	4	11	3	3	5	5
10,000–19,999	21	1	5	2	—	3	15
Jewish Population (Percent)							
1961, total	100.0	47.9	43.7	19.3	18.0	6.4	8.4
Main cities	100.0	77.2	22.8	—	22.8	—	—
Other towns	100.0	18.8	64.4	38.5	13.1	12.8	16.8
Old	100.0	26.2	73.8	53.3	20.5	—	—
New	100.0	5.6	47.8	12.2	—	35.6	46.6
1983, total	100.0	12.0	72.3	21.1	36.0	15.2	15.7
Main cities	100.0	25.2	74.8	38.1	36.7	—	—
Other towns	100.0	6.6	69.0	13.8	34.7	20.5	24.5
100,000–199,999	100.0	—	100.0	70.9	29.1	—	—
50,000–99,999	100.0	—	66.1	48.0	18.1	—	33.9
20,000–49,999	100.0	20.4	57.0	16.2	15.4	25.4	22.5
10,000–19,999	100.0	3.8	25.5	9.8	—	15.7	70.6

[a]See note 41 to text.
[b]1961—foreign-born only (for specification see note 36 to text); 1983—according to origin groups.
Sources: Computations from 1961 census data, vol. 12; and special tabulations from 1983 census file.

TABLE 20. URBAN STATISTICAL AREAS[a] AND THEIR JEWISH POPULATION, BY TYPE OF LOCALITY AND PERCENTAGE OF ASIAN-AFRICAN JEWS,[b] 1961

Type of Locality	Total	Up to 34.9	35.0–64.9 Total	35.0–44.9	45.0–54.9	55.0–64.9	65.0+
Statistical Areas (Percent)							
Total	100.0	51.6	25.9	9.0	9.5	7.4	22.5
Main cities	100.0	62.5	18.7	5.8	8.0	4.9	18.7
Other towns	100.0	36.7	35.5	13.3	11.4	10.8	27.7
Old	100.0	52.5	33.3	13.1	12.1	8.1	14.2
New	100.0	13.5	38.7	13.4	10.4	14.9	47.8
Jewish Population (Percent)							
Total	100.0	52.7	26.1	10.0	9.3	6.8	21.2
Main cities	100.0	66.6	16.9	6.3	6.8	3.8	16.5
Other towns	100.0	38.9	35.3	13.7	11.8	9.8	25.8
Old	100.0	53.5	32.2	13.6	13.0	5.6	14.3
New	100.0	12.8	40.9	13.8	9.7	17.4	46.3

[a]Excluding areas with fewer than 20 Jews.
[b]Foreign-born only (for specification see note 36 to text).
N: Statistical areas—390; Jewish population—1,440,400.
Source: Computations from 1961 census data, vol. 12.

TABLE 21. SMALL RESIDENTIAL AREAS[a] AND THEIR JEWISH POPULATION, BY TYPE OF LOCALITY AND PERCENTAGE OF ASIAN-AFRICAN ORIGIN IN JEWISH POPULATION, 1983

Type of Locality	Total	Up to 34.9	35.0–64.9 Total	35.0–44.9	45.0–54.9	55.0–64.9	65.0+
Small Areas (Percent)							
Total	100.0	36.9	30.8	12.1	9.9	8.8	32.3
Urban statistical areas:							
Total	100.0	26.5	43.3	15.7	14.6	13.0	30.3
Main cities	100.0	43.6	37.3	13.0	14.2	10.1	19.1
Other towns	100.0	16.7	46.6	17.2	14.8	14.6	36.6
100,000–199,999	100.0	13.6	61.8	22.0	22.0	17.8	24.6
50,000–99,999	100.0	26.3	37.4	14.1	8.1	15.2	36.4
20,000–49,999	100.0	22.3	40.2	14.7	13.0	12.5	37.5
Up to 19,999	100.0	3.3	30.0	13.3	6.7	10.0	66.7
Small localities:							
Total	100.0	50.3	14.9	7.5	4.0	3.4	34.8
Semi-urban	100.0	(9.1)	(30.3)	(9.1)	(3.0)	(18.2)	(60.6)
Rural, total	100.0	52.2	14.2	7.4	4.1	2.7	33.7
Moshavim	100.0	37.2	13.2	7.0	3.9	2.3	49.6
Kibbuzim	100.0	86.9	12.2	8.1	2.7	1.4	0.9
Others	100.0	33.6	22.1	7.7	7.7	6.7	44.2
Jewish Population (Percent)							
Total	100.0	27.4	41.6	15.3	13.8	12.5	31.0
Urban statistical areas:							
Total	100.0	25.5	44.9	16.5	15.1	13.3	29.6
Main cities	100.0	44.3	37.6	12.9	14.7	10.0	18.0
Other towns	100.0	17.9	47.8	17.9	15.3	14.6	34.2
100,000–199,999	100.0	13.3	61.7	21.7	21.8	18.2	24.9
50,000–99,999	100.0	28.3	40.5	16.3	8.8	15.4	31.2
20,000–49,999	100.0	24.9	41.7	15.8	13.9	12.0	33.4
Up to 19,999	100.0	3.2	30.0	13.6	7.3	9.1	66.8

TABLE 21.—*(Continued)*

Type of Locality	Percentage of Asian-African Origin					
	Total	Up to 34.9	35.0–64.9			65.0+
			Total	35.0–44.9	45.0–54.9	55.0–64.9	

Small Localities:						
Total	100.0	39.8	20.1	7.6	5.1	7.4	40.0
Semi-urban	100.0	6.8	31.7	8.7	6.0	17.0	61.4
Rural, total	100.0	54.5	15.1	7.2	4.7	3.2	30.4
Moshavim	100.0	34.8	14.1	7.1	4.7	2.3	51.1
Kibbuzim	100.0	89.9	9.4	6.5	2.2	0.7	0.7
Others	100.0	32.6	29.4	8.9	9.8	10.7	38.0

[a]Urban statistical areas and Jewish localities with fewer than 10,000 inhabitants (see note 41 to text); excluding areas and localities with fewer than 100 Jews.
N: Total small areas—1,701; Jewish population—3,329,000; urban statistical areas—955; Jewish population—2,880,400.
Source: Special tabulations from 1983 census file.

TABLE 22. JEWISH POPULATION IN URBAN STATISTICAL AREAS,[a] BY TYPE OF LOCALITY, ORIGIN (MAJOR GROUPS), PERIOD OF ENTRY INTO DWELLING,[b] AND PERCENTAGE OF ASIAN-AFRICAN ORIGIN AMONG JEWS OF STATISTICAL AREA, 1983

Origin of Persons and Period of Entry into Dwelling	Total	Up to 34.9	35.0–64.9 Total	35.0–44.9	45.0–54.9	55.0–64.9	65.0+
All Statistical Areas (Percent)							
Asia-Africa, total							
Total[c]	100.0	11.2	42.2	12.3	14.6	15.3	46.5
Until 1963	100.0	7.4	29.9	7.5	9.9	12.5	62.6
1964–1973	100.0	11.2	41.6	12.2	14.7	14.7	47.1
1974–1983	100.0	12.1	46.4	13.3	16.4	16.7	41.4
Europe-America, total							
Total[c]	100.0	38.8	47.1	20.0	15.9	11.2	14.0
Until 1963	100.0	47.9	38.9	16.5	13.6	8.8	13.1
1964–1973	100.0	40.7	45.2	18.9	15.2	11.1	14.1
1974–1983	100.0	33.6	52.0	21.8	17.8	12.4	14.4
Main Cities (Percent)							
Asia-Africa, total							
Total[c]	100.0	22.1	43.5	12.1	17.5	13.9	34.3
Until 1963	100.0	20.7	34.3	10.0	12.8	11.5	45.0
1964–1973	100.0	21.0	40.6	10.3	17.1	13.2	38.2
1974–1983	100.0	23.6	45.9	11.3	19.5	15.1	30.5
Europe-America, total							
Total[c]	100.0	61.0	31.9	12.6	12.5	6.8	7.0
Until 1963	100.0	70.2	24.9	10.2	10.2	4.5	4.7
1964–1973	100.0	65.3	27.1	10.0	11.3	5.8	7.6
1974–1983	100.0	56.1	35.9	13.1	14.5	8.3	7.8

TABLE 22.—*(Continued)*

Origin of Persons and Period of Entry into Dwelling	\multicolumn{7}{c}{Percentage of Asian-African Origin in Area}
	Total	Up to 34.9	\multicolumn{4}{c}{35.0–64.9}	65.0+
			Total	35.0–44.9	45.0–54.9	55.0–64.9	

Other Towns (Percent)

	Total	Up to 34.9	Total	35.0–44.9	45.0–54.9	55.0–64.9	65.0+
Asia-Africa, total							
Total[c]	100.0	8.1	41.9	12.4	13.8	15.7	50.0
Until 1963	100.0	3.7	28.6	6.8	9.0	12.8	67.6
1964–1973	100.0	8.2	41.9	12.8	13.9	15.2	49.9
1974–1983	100.0	9.1	46.7	13.9	15.6	17.2	44.2
Europe-America, total							
Total[c]	100.0	27.6	54.8	23.7	17.7	13.4	17.6
Until 1963	100.0	28.9	50.8	21.8	16.6	12.4	20.3
1964–1973	100.0	29.1	53.7	23.1	17.0	13.6	17.1
1974–1983	100.0	24.7	58.3	25.3	19.0	14.0	17.0

[a]Excluding areas with fewer than 100 Jews.
[b]According to head of household.
[c]Including unspecified period of entry.
Source: Same as table 21.

TABLE 23. JEWISH POPULATION IN URBAN STATISTICAL AREAS,[a] BY TYPE OF LOCALITY, ORIGIN (MAJOR GROUPS), PERIOD WHEN MOST DWELLINGS IN AREA WERE CONSTRUCTED,[b] AND PERCENTAGE OF ASIAN-AFRICAN ORIGIN AMONG JEWS OF STATISTICAL AREA, 1983

Origin of Persons and Period of Construction of Area	Total	Up to 34.9	35.0–64.9 Total	35.0–44.9	45.0–54.9	55.0–64.9	65.0+
All Statistical Areas (Percent)							
Asia-Africa, total	100.0	11.2	42.2	12.3	14.6	15.3	46.5
Old areas	100.0	11.4	39.4	11.2	13.1	15.1	49.3
New areas	100.0	10.3	60.0	19.2	24.1	16.7	29.7
Europe-America, total	100.0	38.8	47.1	20.0	15.9	11.2	14.0
Old areas	100.0	41.0	44.2	18.4	14.6	11.2	14.9
New areas	100.0	26.8	64.2	29.1	23.7	11.4	9.0
Main Cities (Percent)							
Asia-Africa, total	100.0	22.1	43.5	12.1	17.5	13.9	34.3
Old areas	100.0	23.1	42.3	12.0	17.1	13.2	34.6
New areas	100.0	15.1	51.8	12.8	20.5	18.5	33.1
Europe-America, total	100.0	61.0	31.9	12.6	12.5	6.8	7.0
Old areas	100.0	62.8	30.4	12.2	12.0	6.2	6.7
New areas	100.0	46.2	44.6	16.3	16.7	11.6	9.3
Other Towns (Percent)							
Asia-Africa, total	100.0	8.1	41.9	12.4	13.8	15.7	50.0
Old areas	100.0	8.0	38.5	11.0	11.9	15.6	53.5
New areas	100.0	9.1	62.1	20.8	25.1	16.2	28.8
Europe-America, total	100.0	27.6	54.8	23.7	17.7	13.4	17.6
Old areas	100.0	29.0	51.6	21.8	15.9	13.9	19.4
New areas	100.0	21.1	69.9	32.8	25.7	11.4	9.0

[a]See note a to table 22.
[b]"New areas"—if more than half of the 1983 Jewish population lived in dwellings whose construction terminated during 1975–1983; "old areas"—all other areas.
Source: Same as table 21.

TABLE 24. JEWISH POPULATION (AGED 15 AND OVER) IN URBAN STATISTICAL AREAS,[a] BY TYPE OF LOCALITY, ORIGIN (MAJOR GROUPS), YEARS OF STUDY, AND PERCENTAGE OF ASIAN-AFRICAN ORIGIN AMONG JEWS OF STATISTICAL AREA, 1983

Origin of Persons and Years of Study	Percentage of Asian-African Origin in Area						
	Total	Up to 34.9	35.0–64.9				65.0+
			Total	35.0–44.9	45.0–54.9	55.0–64.9	
All Statistical Areas (Percent)							
Asia-Africa, total	100.0	11.5	41.9	12.1	14.6	15.2	46.6
0–8	100.0	7.2	37.8	9.5	13.4	14.9	55.0
9–12	100.0	11.9	43.6	12.9	15.0	15.7	44.5
13+	100.0	23.2	47.0	16.9	16.4	13.7	29.7
Europe-America, total	100.0	40.2	46.2	19.7	15.7	10.8	13.6
0–8	100.0	31.6	48.1	18.2	17.4	12.5	20.2
9–12	100.0	39.6	46.5	19.6	15.7	11.2	13.8
13+	100.0	46.8	44.3	20.8	14.4	9.1	8.9
Main Cities (Percent)							
Asia-Africa, total	100.0	22.4	42.5	11.6	17.5	13.4	35.0
0–8	100.0	14.1	40.6	10.0	17.0	13.6	45.1
9–12	100.0	23.2	43.8	12.1	17.6	14.1	32.9
13+	100.0	40.2	43.0	13.9	18.4	10.7	16.7
Europe-America, total	100.0	62.8	30.4	12.0	12.1	6.3	6.8
0–8	100.0	54.4	34.8	13.6	13.6	7.6	10.6
9–12	100.0	64.5	28.7	11.1	11.6	6.0	6.7
13+	100.0	65.4	29.7	12.0	11.8	5.9	4.8
Other Towns (Percent)							
Asia-Africa, total	100.0	8.1	41.7	12.3	13.7	15.7	50.2
0–8	100.0	5.0	36.9	9.4	12.3	15.2	58.1
9–12	100.0	8.7	43.5	13.1	14.3	16.1	47.8
13+	100.0	15.8	48.8	18.2	15.5	15.1	35.4
Europe-America, total	100.0	27.8	54.8	23.9	17.6	13.3	17.4
0–8	100.0	21.4	54.2	20.4	19.1	14.7	24.4
9–12	100.0	27.6	55.1	23.8	17.7	13.6	17.2
13+	100.0	33.4	54.7	27.1	16.2	11.4	11.9

[a]See note a to table 22.
Source: Same as table 21.

TABLE 25. AVERAGE SOCIOECONOMIC SCORES[a] OF JEWISH POPULATION (AGED 15 AND OVER) IN URBAN STATISTICAL AREAS,[b] BY ORIGIN (MAJOR GROUPS), YEARS OF STUDY, AND PERCENTAGE OF ASIAN-AFRICAN ORIGIN AMONG JEWS OF STATISTICAL AREA, 1983

Origin of Persons and Years of Study	Percentage of Asian-African Origin in Area								
	5–14.9	15–24.9	25–34.9	35–44.9	45–54.9	55–64.9	65–74.9	75–84.9	85–94.9	95.0+
Asia-Africa, total	1.18	1.17	0.82	0.46	0.44	0.18	−0.12	−0.14	−0.48	−0.95
0–8	1.09	0.97	0.60	0.24	0.23	0.04	−0.23	−0.19	−0.54	−0.95
9–12	1.20	1.17	0.84	0.49	0.50	0.24	−0.05	−0.11	−0.42	−0.95
13+	1.21	1.31	1.02	0.75	0.73	0.36	0.13	0.01	−0.32	−0.95
Europe-America, total	1.19	1.16	0.86	0.46	0.45	0.20	−0.10	−0.08	−0.44	−0.95
0–8	1.12	0.87	0.46	0.05	0.03	−0.04	−0.31	−0.20	−0.55	−0.95
9–12	1.18	1.11	0.85	0.37	0.44	0.14	−0.13	−0.11	−0.46	−0.95
13+	1.23	1.33	1.05	0.76	0.71	0.41	0.19	0.10	−0.30	—

[a]See CBS, 1983 census, vol. 15.
[b]Excluding areas with small Jewish population in private households.
Source: Same as table 21.

TABLE 26. JEWISH MARRIAGES IN ISRAEL, BY ORIGIN (MAJOR GROUPS) OF SPOUSES AND PERIOD OF MARRIAGE

Origin	1961 Census			1983 Census	
	Until 1945	1946–1955	1956–1961[a]	1964–1973	1974–1983[a]
	Couples (Percent)				
Total	100.0	100.0	100.0	100.0	100.0
Inmarried, total	95.0	91.4	87.4	82.3	79.0
Both Asia-Africa	9.9	29.7	45.5	44.2	49.3
Both Europe-America	85.1	61.7	41.9	38.1	29.7
Outmarried, total	5.0	8.6	12.6	17.7	21.0
Husband Asia-Africa	2.4	3.2	4.1	9.0	9.4
Husband Europe-America	2.6	5.4	8.5	8.7	11.6
	Spouses (Percent)				
Husbands, total	100.0	100.0	100.0	100.0	100.0
Asia-Africa	12.3	32.9	49.6	53.2	58.7
Europe-America	87.7	67.1	50.4	46.8	41.3
Wives					
Total	100.0	100.0	100.0	100.0	100.0
Asia-Africa	12.5	35.1	54.0	52.9	60.9
Europe-America	87.5	64.9	46.0	47.1	39.1
	Percentages of Outmarrying Spouses				
Husbands, total	5.0	8.6	12.6	17.7	21.0
Asia-Africa	19.5	9.7	8.2	16.9	16.0
Europe-America	3.0	8.0	16.9	18.6	28.1
Wives					
Total	5.0	8.6	12.6	17.7	21.0
Asia-Africa	21.0	15.3	15.7	16.5	19.1
Europe-America	2.7	4.9	8.9	19.1	24.0
	Index of Marital Attraction[b]				
Asia-Africa/Europe-America[c]	.777	.851	.821	.648	.590

[a]Here as well as in tables 27–29: until May 1961 and until May 1983, respectively.
[b]See explanations in note 53 to text.
[c]If there are only two groups, the index is equal for both.
Sources: Computations from 1961 census data, vol. 36; and special tabulations from 1983 census file.

TABLE 27. OUTMARRIAGE AMONG JEWS IN ISRAEL, BY ORIGIN (MAJOR GROUPS) OF SPOUSES AND PERIOD OF MARRIAGE

Period of Marriage	Couples	Husbands Asia-Africa	Husbands Europe-America	Wives Asia-Africa	Wives Europe-America	Index of Marital Attraction
			1961 Census			
Total	8.7	10.1	8.1	16.1	4.9	.847
Up to 1945	5.0	19.5	3.0	21.0	2.7	.777
1946–1955	8.6	9.7	8.0	15.3	4.9	.851
1956–1961	12.6	8.2	16.9	15.7	8.9	.821
			1983 Census			
Total	16.2	14.7	17.7	16.9	15.4	.695
Up to 1948	6.2	19.6	3.8	21.6	3.4	.769
1949–1953	8.4	9.2	7.9	13.6	5.2	.854
1954–1958	11.8	9.1	14.4	14.1	9.4	.809
1959–1963	13.1	9.5	17.5	13.4	12.6	.773
1964–1968	15.9	15.8	16.0	13.8	18.3	.698
1969–1973	19.0	17.8	20.4	18.4	19.7	.624
1974–1978	20.1	16.0	25.8	18.7	22.3	.609
1979–1983	22.3	16.0	31.8	19.6	26.7	.560

Source: Same as table 26.

TABLE 28. PERCENTAGES OUTMARRYING AMONG JEWISH SPOUSES IN ISRAEL, BY ORIGIN (MAJOR GROUPS), REGION OF BIRTH, AND PERIOD OF MARRIAGE

Period of Marriage	Husbands					Wives				
	Asia-Africa		Europe-America		Asia-Africa		Europe-America	
	Israeli-born	Foreign-born	Israeli-born	Foreign-born	Israeli-born	Foreign-born	Israeli-born	Foreign-born
				1961 Census				
Total	21.4	8.6	10.6	7.6	31.2	13.6	8.0	4.0
Up to 1945	20.7	19.2	10.9	2.4	23.7	19.8	6.0	2.4
1946–1955	22.6	8.1	10.4	7.7	32.5	12.7	7.4	4.3
1956–1961	21.0	6.8	10.7	19.9	34.5	13.4	9.4	8.4
				1983 Census				
Total	19.2	12.7	22.6	14.3	21.5	13.8	19.4	12.2
Up to 1948	25.4	17.8	8.6	3.4	22.3	21.3	6.9	2.9
1949–1953	18.3	8.4	9.8	7.7	29.8	11.8	6.8	4.9
1954–1958	28.3	7.4	12.7	15.0	37.4	11.2	10.9	8.5
1959–1963	24.2	7.8	13.2	20.3	29.4	11.1	13.0	12.3
1964–1968	30.5	13.9	13.8	17.9	24.8	11.6	18.0	18.4
1969–1973	22.9	16.4	20.4	20.4	21.5	16.3	19.6	19.9
1974–1978	17.2	14.8	28.4	21.4	20.2	16.1	23.4	20.5
1979–1983	16.7	14.7	35.6	24.5	20.0	18.5	28.7	23.7

Source: Same as table 26.

TABLE 29. DEMOGRAPHIC COMPOSITION OF JEWISH SPOUSES IN ISRAEL, BY ORIGIN (MAJOR GROUPS) AND PERIOD OF MARRIAGE

Period of Marriage	Percentage of Asian-African Origin Among Spouses — Husbands	Percentage of Asian-African Origin Among Spouses — Wives	Percentage of Israeli-born in Origin Group — Asia-Africa	Percentage of Israeli-born in Origin Group — Europe-America	Husbands Less Wives (Percent Difference) — Asia-Africa	Husbands Less Wives (Percent Difference) — Europe-America
			1961 Census			
Total	31.9	34.2	14.2	19.4	−6.7	3.5
Up to 1945	12.3	12.5	27.6	9.0	−1.9	0.3
1946–1955	32.9	35.1	13.2	17.7	−6.2	3.4
1956–1961	49.6	54.0	11.7	40.3	−8.2	9.6
			1983 Census			
Total	50.5	51.8	36.3	43.9	−2.6	2.8
Up to 1948	14.7	15.1	28.0	20.5	−2.4	0.4
1949–1953	35.7	37.5	9.9	15.8	−4.9	2.9
1954–1958	49.2	52.1	10.4	31.0	−5.4	5.9
1959–1963	55.6	58.1	12.1	45.2	−4.3	5.9
1964–1968	54.3	53.0	14.6	47.5	−2.4	−2.7
1969–1973	52.4	52.8	31.6	56.5	−0.8	0.8
1974–1978	57.2	59.1	57.0	63.4	−3.2	4.6
1979–1983	60.8	63.5	70.6	64.8	−4.3	7.4

Source: Same as table 26.

TABLE 30. JEWISH MARRIAGES IN ISRAEL, BY COUNTRY OF ORIGIN AND PERIOD OF MARRIAGE

Country of Origin	Index of Marital Attraction					Percent Outmarrying, 1974–1983	
	Total	Until 1948	1949–1963	1964–1973	1974–1983	Husbands	Wives
Turkey	.354	.463	.569	.288	.201	80.7	78.8
Syria-Lebanon	.269	.579	.380	.215	.111	89.2	88.6
Iraq	.524	.736	.796	.508	.293	65.4	65.8
Yemen, South Yemen	.652	.865	.826	.657	.511	48.1	48.0
Iran	.505	.553	.679	.509	.426	56.7	61.7
India	.657	—	.732	.715	.612	40.1	40.0
Rest of Asia	.182	.529	.353	.094	.112	89.5	88.7
Morocco	.570	.428	.701	.606	.458	46.0	50.6
Tunisia, Algeria	.372	x	.630	.380	.222	74.8	76.2
Libya	.423	.681	.733	.402	.255	74.4	72.6
Egypt	.274	(.212)	.440	.249	.169	83.3	82.1
Rest of Africa	.218	x	x	(.266)	.222	79.5	83.4
USSR	.354	.427	.230	.216	.517	49.1	46.9
Poland	.355	.526	.443	.261	.230	75.6	71.2
Czechoslovakia	.156	.376	.240	.103	.061	93.9	93.0
Hungary	.188	.312	.336	.131	.094	90.7	90.0
Romania	.407	.474	.534	.423	.267	73.4	69.8
Bulgaria, Greece	.377	.661	.544	.208	.139	88.0	85.6
Germany, Austria	.207	.492	.228	.094	.099	90.2	88.8
Rest of Europe	.146	.253	.213	.125	.097	88.8	91.2
North America	.256	x	(.241)	.215	.266	75.7	84.2
Latin America	.360	—	.427	.409	.301	70.2	73.9

Source: Special tabulations from 1983 census file.

TABLE 31. OUTMARRYING JEWISH SPOUSES IN ISRAEL, BY COUNTRY OF ORIGIN OF ONE SPOUSE AND CONTINENT OF ORIGIN OF THE OTHER (PERCENT)

Country of Origin	Outmarrying Husbands, by Wife's Continent				Outmarrying Wives, by Husband's Continent			
	Total	Asia	Africa	Europe-America	Total	Asia	Africa	Europe-America
Turkey	100.0	34.2	35.6	30.2	100.0	31.3	33.7	34.9
Syria-Lebanon	100.0	39.1	30.0	30.9	100.0	35.2	26.2	38.6
Iraq	100.0	27.3	44.0	28.7	100.0	27.5	37.5	35.0
Yemen, South Yemen	100.0	33.4	44.7	21.9	100.0	33.3	34.5	32.2
Iran	100.0	35.4	39.0	25.6	100.0	37.2	36.7	26.1
India	100.0	44.2	34.0	21.8	100.0	31.1	32.9	36.0
Rest of Asia	100.0	40.0	18.2	41.8	100.0	38.8	19.7	41.4
Morocco	100.0	41.3	28.3	30.4	100.0	42.1	27.1	30.8
Tunisia, Algeria	100.0	30.6	47.8	21.6	100.0	29.0	44.6	26.4
Libya	100.0	38.0	40.7	21.3	100.0	40.9	33.7	25.4
Egypt	100.0	35.9	32.8	31.3	100.0	32.9	27.8	39.2
Rest of Africa	100.0	24.4	19.8	55.8	100.0	20.5	18.8	60.7
USSR	100.0	19.5	15.7	64.8	100.0	19.6	13.7	66.7
Poland	100.0	21.3	18.4	60.3	100.0	17.4	15.3	67.4
Czechoslovakia	100.0	13.4	12.1	74.5	100.0	8.3	10.7	81.0
Hungary	100.0	17.7	17.0	65.3	100.0	14.9	15.9	69.2
Romania	100.0	19.1	21.6	59.3	100.0	18.0	17.4	64.6
Bulgaria, Greece	100.0	31.9	25.6	42.5	100.0	38.4	19.7	41.8
Germany, Austria	100.0	17.0	13.5	69.5	100.0	14.2	13.4	72.4
Rest of Europe	100.0	21.6	31.2	47.2	100.0	19.2	30.9	49.8
North America	100.0	15.7	12.2	72.2	100.0	17.7	16.7	65.6
Latin America	100.0	18.9	20.2	60.9	100.0	14.7	18.9	66.3

Source: Same as table 30.

TABLE 32. INDEXES OF MARITAL ATTRACTION IN JEWISH MARRIAGES IN ISRAEL, BY ORIGIN (MAJOR GROUPS), YEARS OF STUDY OF SPOUSES, AND PERIOD OF MARRIAGE

Years of Study[a]		Period of Marriage				
Husbands	Wives	Total	Until 1948	1949–1963	1964–1973	1974–1983
Total	Total	.695	.769	.814	.648	.590
0–8	Total	.773	.843	.872	.562	.513
9–12	Total	.664	.690	.780	.600	.532
13+	Total	.541	.444	.672	.545	.513
Total	0–8	.820	.848	.869	.547	.612
Total	9–12	.665	.575	.755	.602	.528
Total	13+	.532	.428	.515	.512	.513
0–8	0–8	.834	.868	.883	.514	.601
0–8	9–12	.696	.581	.826	.592	.447
9–12	0–8	.791	.765	.838	.561	.605
9–12	9–12	.651	.655	.743	.584	.502
9–12	13+	.540	.787	.496	.479	.514
13+	9–12	.612	.429	.685	.561	.549
13+	13+	.474	—	.504	.470	.455
9+	0–8	.654	.596	.730	.593	.534
13+	9–12	.521	.348	.634	.528	.508

[a]Combination of 0–8 and 13+ years of study by husbands and wives respectively were not listed, because of small absolute numbers.
Source: Same as table 30.

TABLE 33. INMARRYING AND OUTMARRYING JEWISH SPOUSES IN ISRAEL, BY ORIGIN (MAJOR GROUPS), YEARS OF STUDY, AND PERIOD OF MARRIAGE (PERCENT)

Origin	\multicolumn{4}{c}{Husbands}	\multicolumn{4}{c}{Wives}
	Total	0–8	9–12	13+	Total	0–8	9–12	13+
\multicolumn{9}{c}{Total Periods}
Asia-Africa, total	100.0	33.3	51.7	15.0	100.0	33.8	51.5	14.7
Inmarrying	100.0	36.6	51.7	11.7	100.0	37.8	51.3	10.9
Outmarrying	100.0	14.2	51.6	34.2	100.0	17.4	54.8	27.8
Europe-America, total	100.0	13.8	44.4	41.8	100.0	14.3	45.5	40.1
Inmarrying	100.0	13.4	42.2	44.4	100.0	13.7	43.6	42.8
Outmarrying	100.0	15.8	54.8	29.4	100.0	10.9	52.3	36.8
\multicolumn{9}{c}{Until 1948}
Asia-Africa, total	100.0	64.8	27.3	7.9	100.0	74.7	21.1	4.2
Inmarrying	100.0	71.7	23.6	4.7	100.0	83.0	15.2	1.8
Outmarrying	100.0	36.4	42.4	21.2	100.0	55.6	36.3	8.1
Europe-America, total	100.0	28.4	47.8	23.7	100.0	33.7	51.6	14.6
Inmarrying	100.0	27.7	48.4	23.9	100.0	32.9	52.2	14.9
Outmarrying	100.0	47.1	33.6	19.3	100.0	40.9	45.4	13.6
\multicolumn{9}{c}{1949–1963}
Asia-Africa, total	100.0	53.9	35.7	10.3	100.0	64.3	29.9	5.8
Inmarrying	100.0	57.2	34.6	8.1	100.0	68.6	28.1	3.4
Outmarrying	100.0	21.6	46.9	31.5	100.0	41.0	44.2	14.8
Europe-America, total	100.0	24.2	45.1	30.8	100.0	24.3	46.7	29.0
Inmarrying	100.0	22.4	44.8	32.8	100.0	21.8	47.1	31.1
Outmarrying	100.0	36.3	46.4	17.3	100.0	22.8	48.1	29.1
\multicolumn{9}{c}{1964–1973}
Asia-Africa, total	100.0	32.6	51.5	15.9	100.0	32.8	52.6	14.6
Inmarrying	100.0	36.5	51.6	11.9	100.0	37.4	52.6	10.0
Outmarrying	100.0	13.8	50.7	35.4	100.0	14.8	56.0	29.2
Europe-America, total	100.0	6.4	43.2	50.4	100.0	5.8	44.7	49.4
Inmarrying	100.0	4.9	40.0	55.0	100.0	3.8	42.2	54.0
Outmarrying	100.0	12.7	56.8	30.4	100.0	10.3	52.7	37.0
\multicolumn{9}{c}{1974–1983}
Asia-Africa, total	100.0	18.6	63.6	17.7	100.0	12.5	66.2	21.3
Inmarrying	100.0	20.3	65.3	14.4	100.0	14.0	68.6	17.5
Outmarrying	100.0	10.1	54.8	35.1	100.0	5.7	60.2	34.1
Europe-America, total	100.0	4.3	43.4	52.3	100.0	4.0	42.3	53.7
Inmarrying	100.0	3.5	37.4	59.1	100.0	3.3	35.3	61.4
Outmarrying	100.0	6.2	58.7	35.1	100.0	4.8	53.9	41.2

Source: Same as table 30.

TABLE 34. JEWISH COUPLES MARRYING IN ISRAEL, BY ORIGIN (MAJOR GROUPS), YEARS OF STUDY OF SPOUSES, AND SELECTED PERIODS OF MARRIAGE (PERCENT)

Years of Study Husbands	Wives	Total	Inmarrying Asia-Africa	Inmarrying Europe America	Outmarrying Husband's Origin Asia-Africa	Outmarrying Husband's Origin Europe-America
				Total Periods		
Total	Total	100.0	100.0	100.0	100.0	100.0
0–8	0–8	14.9	24.5	7.6	5.8	9.0
	9–12	7.9	11.2	5.0	7.1	6.0
	13+	0.9	0.9	0.9	1.3	0.7
9–12	0–8	8.2	12.0	5.0	4.5	7.3
	9–12	31.2	34.3	26.0	34.4	36.8
	13+	8.7	5.3	11.2	12.6	10.7
13+	0–8	1.1	1.2	1.0	0.6	1.1
	9–12	9.5	5.8	12.6	10.8	11.9
	13+	17.7	4.7	30.7	22.9	16.4
				1949–1963		
Total	Total	100.0	100.0	100.0	100.0	100.0
0–8	0–8	29.2	48.6	13.3	12.9	24.2
	9–12	8.1	8.1	7.7	7.2	10.6
	13+	1.0	0.6	1.4	1.5	1.4
9–12	0–8	12.2	17.6	7.3	8.8	14.4
	9–12	22.3	15.7	27.4	28.9	25.5
	13+	6.1	1.3	10.2	9.3	6.5
13+	0–8	1.8	2.4	1.3	1.1	2.4
	9–12	8.4	4.2	12.0	12.0	8.1
	13+	10.8	1.4	19.5	18.3	6.9
				1974–1983		
Total	Total	100.0	100.0	100.0	100.0	100.0
0–8	0–8	4.5	7.4	1.4	2.3	1.9
	9–12	7.4	11.9	1.7	6.5	3.9
	13+	0.8	1.0	0.4	1.2	0.5
9–12	0–8	4.2	6.2	1.6	2.3	3.4
	9–12	39.6	50.0	21.8	37.9	42.8
	13+	11.4	9.1	14.0	14.6	12.5
13+	0–8	0.3	0.4	0.2	0.1	0.5
	9–12	9.3	6.7	11.8	9.5	13.5
	13+	22.5	7.4	47.1	25.5	21.1

Source: Same as table 30.

TABLE 35. PERCENTAGES OUTMARRYING AMONG JEWISH SPOUSES IN ISRAEL, BY ORIGIN (MAJOR GROUPS), YEARS OF STUDY, AND PERIOD OF MARRIAGE

Origin	\multicolumn{7}{c}{Years of Study}
	Husbands				Wives			
	Total	0–8	9–12	13+	Total	0–8	9–12	13+

Total Periods

Asia-Africa	14.7	6.3	14.7	34.6	16.9	8.6	17.8	34.1
Europe-America	17.7	20.2	21.8	12.4	15.4	12.7	17.9	13.6

Until 1948

Asia-Africa	19.6	11.0	30.5	52.5	21.6	15.6	39.7	54.5
Europe-America	3.8	6.3	2.7	3.1	3.4	4.2	3.0	3.1

1949–1963

Asia-Africa	9.3	3.7	12.2	28.4	13.7	8.6	20.0	41.1
Europe-America	13.0	19.5	13.4	7.3	8.8	9.2	9.0	8.3

1964–1973

Asia-Africa	16.9	7.2	16.7	37.8	16.5	7.2	17.3	36.5
Europe-America	18.6	37.1	24.5	11.2	19.1	39.2	22.8	13.9

1974–1983

Asia-Africa	16.0	8.7	13.8	31.7	19.1	8.8	17.2	31.5
Europe-America	28.1	41.1	38.0	18.9	24.0	31.7	32.6	17.5

Source: Same as table 30.

TABLE 36. PERCENTAGES OUTMARRYING AMONG JEWISH SPOUSES, BY ORIGIN (MAJOR GROUPS), YEARS OF STUDY OF SPOUSES, AND SELECTED PERIODS OF MARRIAGE

Years of Study[a]		Outmarrying per 100 Husbands of—					
		Asian-African Origin			European-American Origin		
Husbands	Wives	Total Periods	1949–1969	1974–1983	Total Periods	1949–1969	1974–1983
0–8	0–8	3.9	2.6	5.7	20.4	21.4	34.2
0–8	9–12	9.8	8.3	9.5	20.7	17.0	47.0
9–12	0–8	6.1	4.9	6.7	23.7	22.8	44.6
9–12	9–12	14.7	15.9	12.6	23.3	12.2	43.4
9–12	13+	29.1	42.0	23.4	17.0	8.7	25.9
13+	9–12	24.4	22.6	21.4	16.9	9.1	31.0
13+	13+	45.7	56.5	39.8	10.3	5.0	14.9

Years of Study[a]		Outmarrying per 100 Wives of—					
		Asian-African Origin			European-American Origin		
Wives	Husbands	Total Periods	1949–1963	1974–1983	Total Periods	1949–1963	1974–1983
0–8	0–8	7.0	7.3	5.6	12.3	8.6	34.6
0–8	9–12	11.0	11.5	11.2	14.0	10.5	31.2
9–12	0–8	9.9	17.2	7.1	20.6	8.2	54.8
9–12	9–12	17.9	20.5	16.8	19.4	9.2	35.4
9–12	13+	29.6	23.1	32.3	13.4	8.9	20.4
13+	9–12	29.0	43.9	24.4	17.1	8.1	24.8
13+	13+	41.5	43.0	40.4	11.9	8.3	14.6

[a]Combinations of 0–8 and 13+ years of study by husbands and wives respectively were not listed, because of small absolute numbers.
Source: Same as table 30.

TABLE 37. TOTAL FERTILITY RATES OF JEWISH WOMEN IN ISRAEL BY REGION OF BIRTH, 1926–1988

Year	Total	Asia-Africa	Israel	Europe-America
1926–1927	3.86	..	..	..
1928–1930	3.35	..	..	..
1931–1933	2.84	..	..	..
1934–1936	2.67	..	..	..
1937–1939[a]	2.35	4.55	3.94	1.82
1940–1942	2.36	..	..	..
1943–1945[b]	3.35	4.79	3.68	2.91
1946–1947	3.44	..	..	..
1948–1949	3.25	4.47	3.57	3.20
1950–1953	3.94	6.09	3.52	3.10
1954–1957	3.63	5.61	2.83	2.64
1958–1960	3.46	5.11	2.76	2.39
1961–1964	3.37	4.68	2.73	2.42
1965–1969	3.36	4.35	2.83	2.59
1970–1974	3.28	3.92	3.05	2.83
1975–1979	3.00	3.40	2.91	2.80
1980–1984	2.80	3.09	2.82	2.76
1985–1988	2.81	3.17	2.84	2.69

[a]1938–1940 for separate regions of birth.
[b]1944–1945 for separate regions of birth.
Sources: R. Bachi, *The Population of Israel* (Jerusalem, 1977), p. 196.; CBS, *Statistical Abstract of Israel,* 1989.

TABLE 38. AVERAGE NUMBER OF CHILDREN BORN ABROAD PER MARRIED[a] JEWISH WOMAN (IMMIGRATED 1948–1954), BY SELECTED COUNTRIES OF BIRTH AND AGES AT IMMIGRATION, 1961

Country of Birth	Age at Immigration		
	30–34	40–44	45–49
Asia-Africa, total	4.0	5.7	6.1
Thereof:			
Turkey	2.5	3.9	4.0
Iraq	4.0	6.3	6.4
Yemen, South Yemen	4.5	6.4	6.8
Iran	4.8	5.6	7.1
Morocco, Tunisia, Algeria	5.6	6.1	7.5
Libya	4.8	7.0	7.5
Egypt	2.5	4.2	(6.2)
Europe-America, total	1.3	1.8	1.9
Thereof:			
Bulgaria, Greece	1.4	2.1	2.2
USSR	1.3	1.8	1.6
Poland	1.3	1.9	2.1
Romania	1.1	1.6	1.8
Hungary	1.2	(1.5)	(1.8)
Czechoslovakia	1.1	(1.6)	(1.9)
Germany, Austria	0.8	1.5	1.9

[a]Here and in tables 39, 40, 41, 44, and 45: women married in first marriage.
Sources: CBS, 1961 census, vol. 32; and special tabulations from 1961 census file.

TABLE 39. AVERAGE NUMBER OF CHILDREN PER MARRIED JEWISH WOMAN, BY WOMAN'S ORIGIN, REGION OF BIRTH, SELECTED AGES, AND MARRIAGE DURATIONS, 1961, 1972, 1983

Origin	Region of Birth	Age 30–34	Age 45–49	Duration of Marriage 10–14	Duration of Marriage 25–29
		1961 Census			
Total		2.98	3.12	2.71	3.36
Africa	Abroad	4.82	6.74	4.29	7.07
Asia	Abroad	3.98	5.81	3.71	6.20
Asia[a]	Israel	3.09	5.11	3.20	5.51
Israel	Israel	2.59	3.40	2.65	3.61
Europe-America	Israel	2.18	2.88	2.29	2.86
Europe-America	Abroad	2.05	2.15	1.99	2.24
		1972 Census			
Total		3.10	3.36	2.97	3.01
Africa	Abroad	4.08	6.26	3.71	6.44
Asia	Abroad	3.45	5.03	3.36	5.02
Asia[a]	Israel	2.83	4.23	2.93	3.95
Israel	Israel	2.72	3.21	2.80	3.20
Europe-America	Israel	2.44	2.62	2.57	2.62
Europe-America	Abroad	2.29	2.16	2.22	2.05
		1983 Census			
Total		2.61	3.64	2.77	3.49
Africa	Abroad	3.11	5.22	3.18	5.13
Asia	Abroad	2.89	4.26	3.00	4.12
Africa	Israel	2.82	3.06	3.03	x
Asia	Israel	2.60	3.48	2.88	3.50
Israel	Israel	2.50	3.23	2.72	3.24
Europe-America	Israel	2.37	2.92	2.59	2.93
Europe-America	Abroad	2.33	2.56	2.44	2.42

[a]Including some Israeli-born women of African origin.
Sources: Special tabulations from 1961 and 1972 census files; CBS, 1983 census, vol. 14.

TABLE 40. AVERAGE NUMBER OF CHILDREN PER MARRIED FOREIGN-BORN JEWISH WOMAN, BY WOMAN'S REGION OF BIRTH, PERIOD OF IMMIGRATION, PLACE OF MARRIAGE, AND SELECTED MARRIAGE DURATIONS, 1961, 1972, 1983

Region of Birth	Period of Immigration	\multicolumn{3}{c	}{Duration of Marriage 10–14}	\multicolumn{3}{c}{25–29}
		Total	Married Abroad	In Israel	Total	Married Abroad	In Israel
\multicolumn{8}{c}{1961}
Africa	1948–1954	4.31	4.66	3.52	7.28	7.28	—
	1955–1961	4.45	4.45	—	7.11	7.11	—
Asia	Up to 1947	3.13	3.00	3.13	5.79	5.61	6.00
	1948–1954	3.80	4.02	3.15	6.37	6.37	—
Europe-America	Up to 1947	2.09	2.27	2.08	2.33	2.27	2.40
	1948–1954	1.96	1.94	1.99	2.02	2.02	—
	1955–1961	1.77	1.77	—	2.08	2.08	—
\multicolumn{8}{c}{1972}
Africa	1948–1954	3.60	—	3.60	6.42	6.42	—
	1955–1960	3.66	3.96	3.64	6.39	6.39	—
	1961–1964	3.99	4.06	3.08	7.44	7.44	—
Asia	Up to 1947	2.79	—	2.79	4.04	3.94	4.07
	1948–1954	3.43	—	3.43	5.40	5.40	—
Europe-America	Up to 1947	2.27	—	2.27	2.23	2.27	2.21
	1948–1954	2.32	—	2.32	2.04	2.04	—
	1955–1960	2.16	2.27	2.13	2.00	2.00	—
	1961–1964	2.01	2.02	1.91	1.68	1.68	—
	1965–1972	2.21	2.21	—	1.95	1.95	—
\multicolumn{8}{c}{1983}
Africa	1948–1954	3.21	—	3.21	4.69	5.79	4.67
	1955–1960	3.14	—	3.14	5.14	5.35	4.91
	1961–1964	3.31	—	3.31	6.39	6.39	—
Asia	Up to 1947	2.95	—	2.95	3.50	—	3.50
	1948–1954	3.03	—	3.03	4.17	6.00	4.17
Europe-America	Up to 1947	2.49	—	2.49	2.55	—	2.55
	1948–1954	2.65	—	2.65	2.44	3.21	2.43
	1955–1960	2.50	—	2.50	2.63	2.51	2.95
	1961–1964	2.32	—	2.32	1.80	1.80	—
	1965–1971	2.44	2.62	2.40	2.25	2.25	—
	1972–1974	2.38	2.38	2.35	2.55	2.55	—
	1975–1983	2.25	2.25	—	2.40	2.40	—

Source: Same as table 39.

TABLE 41. AVERAGE NUMBER OF CHILDREN PER MARRIED EUROPEAN-AMERICAN-BORN JEWISH WOMAN, BY SELECTED PERIODS OF IMMIGRATION AND AGE, 1961, 1972, 1983

Period of Immigration	Reference Date	20–24	25–29	30–34	35–39	40–44	45–49	50–54	55–59	60–64	65+
Up to 1947	At immigr.[a]	0.20	0.54	1.22	1.91	2.28	2.74	2.92	3.11	x	x
	1961	0.90	1.81	2.18	2.34	2.34	2.30	2.10	2.14	2.42	3.18
	1972	1.38	1.68	2.55	2.71	2.49	2.44	2.38	2.19	2.05	2.11
	1983	—	—	—	3.00	2.89	2.91	2.51	2.41	2.35	2.21
1948–54	At immigr.[a]	0.59	0.95	1.29	1.59	1.80	1.92	2.37	2.81	3.14	3.58
	1961	1.01	1.68	2.01	2.11	2.00	1.93	1.83	2.02	2.46	3.11
	1972	1.10	1.66	2.38	2.49	2.36	2.13	1.92	1.76	1.67	2.08
	1983	—	1.80	2.58	2.78	2.87	2.62	2.37	2.17	1.93	1.83
1955–60	At immigr.[a]	0.47	1.15	1.65	1.71	1.87	1.66	1.49	1.96	2.39	2.90
	1961	0.88	1.33	1.79	1.87	1.99	1.87	1.64	1.89	2.28	3.17
	1972	0.91	1.62	2.41	2.52	2.16	2.09	1.88	1.79	1.58	1.75
	1983	1.34	1.79	2.38	2.65	2.98	2.75	2.34	1.97	1.95	1.79
1961–64	At immigr.[b]	0.41	0.93	1.38	1.48	1.53	1.32	1.54	1.60	2.09	3.58
	1972	0.91	1.65	2.05	2.04	1.74	1.65	1.47	1.39	1.81	3.11
	1983	0.87	1.59	2.36	2.58	2.67	1.90	1.73	1.72	1.55	2.08

[a] According to 1961 census.
[b] According to 1972 census.
Source: Same as table 39.

TABLE 42. ATTITUDES OF MARRIED JEWISH WOMEN, BY ORIGIN, CONCERNING NUMBER OF CHILDREN, 1974–1975 AND 1987–1988

Survey and Type of Information	Total	Asia-Africa	Israel	Europe-America
	Average Number of Children per Woman			
1974–1975				
Ideal number	4.3[a]	5.0	—	3.7
Israeli norm	3.8[a]	4.1	—	3.5
1987–1988				
Desired number	3.5	3.7	3.6	3.2
Ideal number	4.2	4.4	4.1	4.0

[a]Excluding Israeli origin group.
Source: See note 76 to text.

TABLE 43. AGE-SPECIFIC BIRTHRATES OF JEWISH WOMEN, BY REGION OF BIRTH, 1980–1984 AND 1985–1988

Age	Total 1980–1984	Total 1985–1988	Asia-Africa 1980–1984	Asia-Africa 1985–1988	Israel 1980–1984	Israel 1985–1988	Europe-America 1980–1984	Europe-America 1985–1988
Up to 19	22.8	14.8	44.4	42.2	18.4	12.1	53.6	35.3
20–24	156.3	135.4	183.4	167.8	151.9	132.2	159.9	138.8
25–29	181.5	191.9	184.0	196.4	183.5	193.6	168.9	177.4
30–34	127.0	137.6	129.7	141.2	132.9	140.3	111.5	123.4
35–39	60.8	68.0	64.0	71.2	65.5	75.4	50.7	52.0
40–44	10.5	13.3	12.2	14.8	10.9	13.8	6.9	10.5
45–49	0.6	0.9	0.8	1.2	0.6	0.7	0.4	0.7
TFR	2.80	2.81	3.09	3.17	2.82	2.84	2.76	2.69

Source: CBS, Statistical Abstract of Israel, and unpublished data.

TABLE 44. AVERAGE NUMBER OF CHILDREN PER MARRIED JEWISH WOMAN, BY WOMAN'S ORIGIN, REGION OF BIRTH, YEARS OF STUDY, AND SELECTED MARRIAGE DURATIONS, 1961, 1972, 1983

Origin	Region of Birth	Total	0–4	5–8	9–10	11–12	13–15	16+
				MARRIED 10–14 YEARS				
				1961 Census				
Total		2.71	4.04	2.51	2.18	2.05	2.03	1.76
Africa	Abroad	4.29	4.97	3.94	3.18	2.44	2.30	x
Asia	Abroad	3.71	3.69	3.08	2.74	2.71	2.45	x
Asia[a]	Israel	3.20	4.29	3.08	2.86	2.52	x	x
Israel	Israel	2.65	3.04	2.89	2.56	2.37	2.23	x
Europe-America	Israel	2.29	x	2.48	2.23	2.29	2.20	2.03
Europe-America	Abroad	1.99	2.13	2.03	1.97	1.88	1.91	1.67
				1972 Census				
Total		2.97	4.00	3.29	2.73	2.56	2.50	2.33
Africa	Abroad	3.71	4.51	3.84	3.13	2.87	2.96	2.39
Asia	Abroad	3.36	3.95	3.36	2.98	2.76	2.62	x
Asia[a]	Israel	2.96	3.15	3.13	2.89	2.96	2.65	x
Israel	Israel	2.80	x	3.07	2.74	2.75	2.67	2.63
Europe-America	Israel	2.57	1.43	2.75	2.48	2.64	2.56	2.41
Europe-America	Abroad	2.22	2.04	2.16	2.31	2.21	2.26	2.25
				1983 Census				
Total		2.77	3.33	3.24	2.90	2.69	2.65	2.46
Africa	Abroad	3.18	3.52	3.46	3.19	3.06	2.85	2.81
Asia	Abroad	3.00	3.11	3.27	2.98	2.82	2.94	2.77
Africa	Israel	3.03	(3.44)	3.38	3.02	2.88	2.76	2.47
Asia	Israel	2.88	(3.69)	3.09	2.94	2.73	2.90	2.51
Israel	Israel	2.72	x	3.18	2.91	2.61	2.73	2.51
Europe-America	Israel	2.59	x	2.92	2.58	2.56	2.67	2.50
Europe-America	Abroad	2.44	(2.63)	2.75	2.50	2.43	2.44	2.35

TABLE 44.—*(Continued)*

Origin	Region of Birth	Total	0–4	5–8	9–10	11–12	13–15	16+
					Years of Study			

MARRIED 25–29 YEARS
1961 Census

Origin	Region of Birth	Total	0–4	5–8	9–10	11–12	13–15	16+
Total		3.36	5.89	2.86	2.35	2.14	2.13	1.83
Africa	Abroad	7.07	7.80	6.15	5.21	3.47	x	x
Asia	Abroad	6.20	6.66	4.89	4.39	3.39	x	x
Asia[a]	Israel	5.51	5.85	5.70	x	x	x	x
Israel	Israel	3.61	5.77	3.97	2.26	2.27	x	x
Europe-America	Israel	2.86	x	3.02	2.55	2.40	2.60	x
Europe-America	Abroad	2.24	2.86	2.28	2.14	2.07	2.10	1.74

1972 Census

Origin	Region of Birth	Total	0–4	5–8	9–10	11–12	13–15	16+
Total		3.01	5.35	2.76	2.39	2.12	2.09	2.00
Africa	Abroad	6.44	7.45	5.92	5.19	3.49	3.77	x
Asia	Abroad	5.02	6.06	4.13	3.48	3.14	3.21	x
Asia[a]	Israel	3.99	4.90	3.95	4.08	2.57	x	x
Israel	Israel	3.20	4.88	3.47	2.93	2.70	2.44	2.31
Europe-America	Israel	2.62	x	2.75	2.64	2.51	2.62	2.64
Europe-America	Abroad	2.05	2.14	2.12	2.08	1.92	1.92	1.86

1983 Census

Origin	Region of Birth	Total	0–4	5–8	9–10	11–12	13–15	16+
Total		3.49	5.26	3.79	3.20	2.87	2.75	2.53
Africa	Abroad	5.13	6.48	4.97	4.48	4.12	3.72	(3.22)
Asia	Abroad	4.12	5.05	3.99	3.39	3.26	3.12	2.59
Asia	Israel	3.50	(3.61)	3.77	3.61	3.18	2.52	(2.81)
Israel	Israel	3.24	(3.25)	3.71	3.23	2.98	3.23	2.76
Europe-America	Israel	2.93	(3.80)	3.36	2.75	2.88	3.03	2.85
Europe-America	Abroad	2.42	2.54	2.47	2.57	2.34	2.38	2.30

[a]Including some Israeli-born women of African origin.
Sources: Special tabulations from 1961 and 1972 census files; CBS, 1983 census, vol. 14.

TABLE 45. AVERAGE NUMBER OF CHILDREN PER JEWISH WOMAN MARRIED 10–14 YEARS, BY WOMAN'S ORIGIN, REGION OF BIRTH, SELECTED YEARS OF STUDY, AND LABOR-FORCE PARTICIPATION, 1961, 1972, 1983

Origin	Region of Birth	Total	5–8	9–10	11–12	13–15
1961 CENSUS — In Labor Force						
Total		2.22	2.24	2.09	1.98	1.97
Africa	Abroad	3.56	3.37	3.31	2.35	2.33
Asia	Abroad	3.12	2.88	2.30	2.32	x
Asia[a]	Israel	2.63	2.62	2.40	2.50	x
Israel	Israel	1.70	2.60	2.38	2.00	2.19
Europe-America	Israel	2.22	2.24	2.23	2.32	2.12
Europe-America	Abroad	1.91	1.97	1.95	1.82	1.89
Not in Labor Force						
Total		2.86	2.56	2.22	2.10	2.12
Africa	Abroad	4.41	4.02	3.14	2.48	2.27
Asia	Abroad	3.79	3.11	2.84	2.87	2.93
Asia[a]	Israel	3.33	3.17	3.04	x	x
Israel	Israel	2.80	2.93	2.63	2.60	2.33
Europe-America	Israel	2.35	2.53	2.23	2.26	2.33
Europe-America	Abroad	2.02	2.04	1.99	1.91	1.93
1972 CENSUS — In Labor Force						
Total		2.48	2.95	2.40	2.34	2.38
Africa	Abroad	3.07	3.47	2.77	2.40	2.85
Asia	Abroad	2.79	3.02	2.43	2.40	2.42
Asia[a]	Israel	2.54	2.52	2.48	2.72	2.52
Israel	Israel	2.51	3.05	2.37	2.42	2.55
Europe-America	Israel	2.47	2.44	2.20	2.57	2.49
Europe-America	Abroad	2.08	2.22	2.21	1.99	2.09
Not in Labor Force						
Total		3.24	3.37	2.89	2.74	2.74
Africa	Abroad	3.90	3.91	3.28	3.21	3.09
Asia	Abroad	3.49	3.42	3.09	2.98	3.00
Asia[a]	Israel	3.16	3.25	3.10	3.19	3.00
Israel	Israel	3.01	3.07	2.95	3.01	2.89
Europe-America	Israel	2.69	2.81	2.66	2.71	2.72
Europe-America	Abroad	2.35	2.14	2.36	2.38	2.60

TABLE 45.—*(Continued)*

Origin	Region of Birth	Total	5–8	9–10	11–12	13–15
		\multicolumn{5}{c}{Selected Years of Study}				

Origin	Region of Birth	Total	5–8	9–10	11–12	13–15
			1983 CENSUS			
			In Labor Force			
Total		2.57	3.04	2.67	2.54	2.57
Africa	Abroad	2.87	3.12	2.92	2.81	2.76
Asia	Abroad	2.82	3.22	2.78	2.67	2.90
Africa	Israel	2.75	3.12	2.79	2.68	2.65
Asia	Israel	2.73	3.08	2.83	2.59	2.77
Israel	Israel	2.60	2.79	2.64	2.52	2.70
Europe-America	Israel	2.51	2.84	2.45	2.47	2.60
Europe-America	Abroad	2.32	2.56	2.29	2.32	2.34
			Not in Labor Force			
Total		3.07	3.31	3.07	2.91	2.97
Africa	Abroad	3.45	3.58	3.36	3.38	3.18
Asia	Abroad	3.17	3.29	3.11	3.00	3.06
Africa	Israel	3.27	3.47	3.19	3.10	3.14
Asia	Israel	3.03	3.10	3.01	2.91	3.26
Israel	Israel	2.94	3.34	3.14	2.74	2.83
Europe-America	Israel	2.79	2.94	2.69	2.71	2.97
Europe-America	Abroad	2.74	2.84	2.76	2.66	2.83

[a]Including some Israeli-born women of African origin.
Source: Same as table 44.

TABLE 46. AVERAGE NUMBER OF CHILDREN PER JEWISH WOMAN (AGED 30–34 AND CURRENTLY GIVING BIRTH), BY WOMAN'S ORIGIN, REGION OF BIRTH, AND RELIGIOSITY: JERUSALEM, 1975–1976 AND 1983–1984

Indicators of Religiosity	Total	Asia-Africa Abroad	Asia-Africa Israel	Israel Israel	Europe-America Abroad	Europe-America Israel
		Maternity Ward Interview Study, 1975–1976				
Total	3.7	4.1	3.3	4.2	3.2	3.3
Woman does not go to mikveh	3.0	3.6	3.0	2.9	2.4	2.6
Woman goes to mikveh and husband is:						
not in yeshivah	4.3	4.5	3.8	4.4	4.0	3.8
in yeshivah	5.2	4.7	(5.6)	5.5	5.3	4.9
		Ecological Study, 1983–1984				
Religiosity of residential region:						
Total	3.8	3.5	3.3	4.5	3.8	4.1
Very low	3.0	3.3	3.2	2.8	2.8	2.6
Rather low	3.7	3.6	3.1	3.6	3.6	3.9
Rather high	5.1	4.8	3.7	5.7	5.4	5.1
Very high	5.9	4.8	5.3	6.0	6.0	6.0

Source: U.O. Schmelz (see note 78 to text).

TABLE 47. AVERAGE NUMBER OF CHILDREN PER JEWISH WOMAN (AGED 30–34 AND CURRENTLY GIVING BIRTH), BY WOMAN'S ORIGIN, REGION OF BIRTH, YEARS OF STUDY, WORK STATUS, AND RELIGIOSITY[a]: JERUSALEM, 1983–1984

Origin, Birth Region, and Selected Years of Study	Working, by Religiosity				Not-Working, by Religiosity			
	Very Low	Rather Low	Rather High	Very High	Very Low	Rather Low	Rather High	Very High
Total	2.6	3.2	4.6	5.0	3.7	4.3	5.6	6.3
9–12	2.9	3.2	4.7	5.2	3.7	4.1	5.7	6.4
13+	2.5	3.3	4.5	4.9	3.3	4.5	5.2	6.0
Asian-African origin								
Born abroad	2.9	3.4	4.0	(3.8)	3.9	4.0	5.4	5.5
9–12	2.9	(3.4)	x	x	3.9	(4.0)	x	(5.4)
13+	2.7	(3.5)	(4.1)	x	3.2	(3.9)	x	x
Born in Israel	2.8	2.7	(3.8)	3.9	3.7	3.5	3.7	6.1
9–12	2.9	2.8	x	x	3.7	(3.6)	(3.4)	(5.7)
13+	2.6	2.7	x	(4.2)	x	x	x	(6.7)
Israeli origin	2.6	2.9	5.1	5.4	3.4	(5.4)	6.2	6.2
9–12	2.7	x	x	(4.8)	3.6	x	(6.3)	5.9
13+	2.5	3.0	5.0	5.7	(3.3)	x	(5.9)	6.0
European-American origin								
Born abroad	2.5	3.5	4.3	4.9	3.7	4.3	5.9	6.4
9–12	2.8	x	x	x	4.0	(4.5)	(6.9)	7.2
13+	2.4	3.5	4.2	4.1	3.5	4.1	5.0	5.6
Born in Israel	2.4	3.4	4.7	5.2	3.1	4.8	5.9	6.5
9–12	2.8	(3.8)	x	x	3.4	(4.5)	(6.4)	6.7
13+	2.4	3.4	4.5	5.0	2.9	4.8	5.4	6.0

[a]Religiosity of residential area.
Source: Same as table 46.

TABLE 48. JEWS AGED 15+, BY SEX, ORIGIN, AND AGE—SELECTED EDUCATIONAL INDICATORS, 1983

Origin and Age	Total (Thousands)	% 0–4	% 13+	Median	% with Secondary or Higher Certific. (A)	% with Academic Degree (B)
Men						
Asia						
Total	276.6	10.2	12.7	10.8	40.5	3.8
15–24	72.4	0.9	8.1	12.0	50.9	0.3
25–34	66.6	1.7	19.7	11.6	53.5	6.5
35–44	47.4	4.5	16.8	10.6	41.0	6.2
45–54	39.6	18.3	10.2	8.8	26.2	3.8
55–64	26.1	25.9	9.4	8.3	24.0	3.4
65–74	15.4	38.1	7.5	6.9	16.2	2.5
75+	9.0	48.9	4.6	5.3	9.6	1.0
Africa						
Total	252.7	9.2	11.8	10.8	39.4	3.0
15–24	79.2	1.2	7.2	11.7	46.7	0.3
25–34	66.0	2.2	17.4	11.3	50.6	4.7
35–44	38.8	5.2	16.7	10.6	39.9	5.5
45–54	30.6	17.3	10.9	8.9	25.6	3.3
55–64	21.5	27.7	8.7	8.4	19.1	2.6
65–74	12.0	40.4	7.4	6.9	12.8	2.0
75+	4.6	57.3	5.2	4.1	9.3	1.5
Europe-America						
Total	535.1	4.3	35.5	12.4	60.7	17.4
15–24	79.7	0.6	20.5	12.3	61.9	1.9
25–34	107.8	0.6	54.1	13.5	81.6	25.7
35–44	84.3	0.9	54.6	13.7	77.1	31.1
45–54	67.9	4.3	38.4	12.4	61.0	23.2
55–64	80.4	6.3	24.6	10.8	45.5	12.6
65–74	73.2	9.2	21.4	10.5	40.4	9.9
75+	41.7	14.7	18.6	8.9	33.3	9.4

TABLE 48—*(Continued)*

Origin and Age	Total (Thousands)	% 0–4	% 13+	Median	% with Secondary or Higher Certific. (A)	% with Academic Degree (B)
				Women		
Asia						
Total	279.8	20.0	11.0	10.3	37.9	1.9
15–24	68.0	0.6	11.5	12.1	57.8	0.9
25–34	68.4	1.6	20.4	11.8	58.3	4.6
35–44	48.4	9.6	12.7	10.0	34.4	2.7
45–54	40.7	38.1	4.1	7.1	14.8	0.7
55–64	27.6	54.8	2.7	4.0	11.1	0.6
65–74	17.3	68.4	2.1	0.8	6.7	0.4
75+	9.5	79.2	1.1	0.7	3.6	0.1
Africa						
Total	258.8	18.0	10.9	10.5	38.0	2.0
15–24	75.4	1.0	10.6	12.0	54.2	0.9
25–34	68.7	2.4	18.9	11.4	52.7	4.1
35–44	40.7	11.9	11.0	9.8	31.8	2.7
45–54	32.6	40.7	5.2	7.7	16.2	1.1
55–64	22.9	57.7	2.7	1.0	10.8	0.9
65–74	13.4	66.2	2.2	0.8	6.4	0.6
75+	5.1	76.4	1.2	0.7	4.6	0.4
Europe-America						
Total	583.6	5.4	32.6	12.2	60.2	12.8
15–24	74.8	0.7	27.3	12.4	66.5	4.3
25–34	113.4	0.6	57.3	14.1	84.5	25.0
35–44	89.3	1.0	53.5	13.5	78.6	22.7
45–54	76.3	5.5	31.6	12.1	57.6	12.7
55–64	97.1	7.0	16.6	10.3	41.6	6.5
65–74	85.3	11.2	13.8	10.1	39.6	4.8
75+	47.3	18.3	10.9	8.7	34.1	4.7

TABLE 48—*(Continued)*

Origin and Age	Years of Schooling % 0–4	% 13+	Median	% with Secondary or Higher Certific.	% with Academic Degree

Origin-Specific Ratios (Europe-America = Base 1.00)

Men

Asia					
Total	2.37	.36	.87	.67	.22
15–24	1.50	.40	.98	.82	.16
25–34	7.50	.36	.86	.66	.25
35–44	5.00	.31	.77	.53	.20
45–54	4.26	.26	.71	.43	.16
55–64	4.11	.38	.77	.53	.27
65–74	4.14	.35	.66	.40	.25
75+	3.33	.25	.60	.29	.11

Africa					
Total	2.14	.33	.87	.65	.17
15–24	2.00	.35	.95	.75	.16
25–34	3.67	.32	.84	.62	.18
35–44	5.78	.31	.77	.52	.18
45–54	4.02	.28	.72	.42	.14
55–64	4.40	.35	.78	.42	.21
65–74	4.39	.35	.66	.32	.20
75+	3.90	.28	.46	.28	.16

Women

Asia					
Total	3.70	.34	.84	.63	.15
15–24	.86	.42	.98	.87	.21
25–34	2.67	.36	.84	.69	.18
35–44	9.60	.24	.74	.44	.12
45–54	6.92	.13	.59	.26	.06
75–64	7.83	.16	.39	.27	.09
65–74	6.11	.15	.08	.17	.08
75+	4.33	.10	.08	.11	.02

TABLE 48—*(Continued)*

Origin and Age	Years of Schooling % 0–4	Years of Schooling % 13+	Median	% with Secondary or Higher Certific.	% with Academic Degree
Africa					
Total	3.33	.33	.86	.63	.16
15–24	1.43	.39	.97	.82	.21
25–34	4.00	.33	.81	.62	.16
35–44	11.90	.21	.73	.40	.12
45–54	7.40	.16	.64	.28	.09
55–64	8.24	.16	.10	.26	.14
65–74	5.91	.16	.08	.16	.12
75+	4.17	.11	.08	.13	.09

Source: CBS, 1983 census, vol. 10.

TABLE 49. MEDIAN YEARS OF SCHOOLING AMONG ISRAELI-BORN JEWS AGED 15+,[a] BY SEX, AGE, AND ORIGIN,[b] 1961, 1972, 1983

Age	Men Total[c]	Men Asia	Men Africa	Men Europe-America		Women Total[c]	Women Asia	Women Africa	Women Europe-America
					1961				
Total	10.7		8.3	11.4		10.4		8.0	11.4
14–29	10.9		8.6	11.4		10.8		8.7	11.5
30–44	10.1		7.6	11.6		9.7		7.0	11.3
45–64	9.3		7.4	10.5		7.3		5.4	8.6
65+	8.5		(6.1)	10.9		1.0		(0.8)	5.9
					1972				
Total	11.3	10.0	9.6	12.3		11.4	10.2	9.9	12.4
14–29	11.1	10.1	9.6	12.2		11.4	10.3	9.9	12.4
30–44	12.3	9.9	10.1	12.8		12.2	8.9	10.3	12.8
45–64	10.7	8.7	8.7	11.9		9.8	8.2	8.4	11.8
65+	9.0	(8.2)	(8.4)	10.4		8.1	(0.8)	(3.0)	8.5
					1983				
Total	12.2	11.6	11.5	12.8		12.3	12.0	11.8	12.9
15–24	12.1	11.9	11.6	12.3		12.2	12.1	11.9	12.5
25–44	12.5	11.5	11.4	13.7		12.7	11.8	11.7	14.2
45–64	12.3	10.1	10.2	12.8		12.2	8.8	8.8	12.8
65+	10.5	8.6	(8.5)	11.5		8.6	5.3	(6.4)	10.0

TABLE 49—*(Continued)*

Age	Men Asia	Men Africa	Women Asia	Women Africa
	Origin-Specific Ratios (Europe-America = Base 1.00)			
		1961		
Total		.73		.70
14–29		.75		.76
30–44		.66		.62
45–64		.70		.63
65+		(.56)		(.14)
		1972		
Total	.81	.78	.82	.80
14–29	.83	.79	.83	.80
30–44	.77	.79	.70	.80
45–64	.73	.73	.69	.71
65+	(.79)	(.81)	(.09)	(.35)
		1983		
Total	.91	.90	.93	.91
15–24	.97	.94	.97	.95
25–44	.84	.83	.83	.82
45–64	.79	.80	.69	.69
65+	.75	(.74)	.53	(.64)

[a]1961, 1972—ages 14+.
[b]In parentheses—cells with N < 500.
[c]Including Israeli-born, father also born in Israel.
Sources: CBS, 1961 census, vol. 15; 1972 census, unpublished tabulations; 1983 census, vol. 10.

TABLE 50. MEDIAN YEARS OF SCHOOLING AMONG FOREIGN-BORN JEWS AGED 15+,[a] BY SEX, AGE, AND ORIGIN, 1961, 1972, 1983

Age	Men Total	Men Asia	Men Africa	Men Europe-America	Women Total	Women Asia	Women Africa	Women Europe-America
1961								
Total	8.4	6.9		9.5	7.3	3.7		8.8
14–29	8.4	7.7		9.9	7.8	6.7		9.8
30–44	8.4	6.8		9.4	7.5	1.4		8.8
45–64	8.6	5.5		9.5	7.3	0.7		8.7
65+	7.3	2.5		8.4	4.0	0.6		6.4
1972								
Total	9.7	8.5	8.8	10.8	8.8	6.7	8.3	10.3
14–29	..	10.1	10.0	12.2	..	9.6	9.7	12.3
30–44	..	8.5	8.6	11.6	..	6.5	7.8	10.8
45–64	..	7.2	7.7	10.4	..	0.8	0.9	9.7
65+	..	3.0	1.0	8.9	..	0.6	0.6	8.5
1983								
Total	10.8	9.1	10.3	12.0	10.2	8.2	8.9	11.2
15–24	12.2	12.2	12.1	12.2	12.3	12.2	12.2	12.3
25–44	12.0	10.8	10.9	13.5	11.8	10.2	10.5	13.3
45–64	10.2	8.5	8.7	11.3	8.7	5.2	5.6	10.6
65+	8.8	6.3	6.2	10.2	8.5	0.7	0.8	9.0

TABLE 50—*(Continued)*

Age	Men Asia	Men Africa	Women Asia	Women Africa
	Origin-Specific Ratios (Europe-America = Base 1.00)			
		1961		
Total		.73		.42
14–29		.78		.68
30–44		.72		.16
45–64		.58		.08
65+		.30		.09
		1972		
Total	.79	.81	.65	.81
14–29	.83	.82	.78	.79
30–44	.73	.74	.60	.72
45–64	.69	.74	.08	.09
65+	.34	.11	.07	.07
		1983		
Total	.76	.86	.73	.79
15–24	1.00	.99	.99	.99
25–44	.80	.81	.77	.79
45–64	.75	.77	.49	.53
65+	.62	.61	.08	.09

[a]1961, 1972—ages 14+.
Sources: Same as table 49.

TABLE 51. ISRAELI-BORN JEWS AMONG ACADEMIC GRADUATES, BY SEX, AGE, AND ORIGIN, 1974 AND 1984 (RATES PER 1,000 IN SPECIFIED POPULATION GROUP)

Sex and Age	Total[a]	Asia-Africa (A)	Europe-America (B)	Ratio[b] (A)/(B)
1974				
Both sexes, total	73	7	119	.06
Thereof:				
20–24	7	—	15	—
25–29	125	19	172	.11
30–34	163	18	225	.08
35–44	135	12	195	.06
45–54	77	(15)	122	x
1984				
Both sexes, total	107	29	197	.15
Thereof:				
20–24	17	8	29	.28
25–29	93	38	171	.22
30–34	145	45	248	.18
35–44	205	37	278	.13
45–54	171	49	236	.21
Men, total	115	32	216	.15
Thereof:				
20–24	8	(2)	(18)	x
25–29	85	31	160	.19
30–34	148	62	241	.26
35–44	246	53	331	.16
45–54	239	(86)	329	x
Women, total	99	27	178	.15
Thereof:				
20–24	27	14	41	.34
25–29	102	46	182	.25
30–34	141	28	255	.11
35–44	165	(22)	226	x
45–54	105	(14)	146	x

[a]Including Israeli-born, father also born in this country.
[b]Ratios per 1.00.
Sources: CBS, *Persons with Academic and Post-Secondary Education, 1974,* Special Series, no. 643, 1981; *University and Post-Secondary Education Graduates, 1984,* vol. B, Special Series, no. 820, 1988.

TABLE 52. JEWS AGED 25–44, BY SEX, ORIGIN AND REGION OF BIRTH, AGE AT CENSUS, AGE AT IMMIGRATION, AND EDUCATION, 1983

Origin and Age at Census	Total	Israeli-born	Foreign-born Who Immigrated at the Age of: 0–14	15–24	25+
			MEN Thousands		
Asia					
25–34	66.6	48.9	14.2	2.9	0.6
35–44	47.4	9.2	32.5	3.6	2.1
Africa					
25–34	66.0	28.5	33.6	3.2	0.7
35–44	38.8	1.4	22.3	12.9	2.1
Europe-America					
25–34	107.8	67.9	18.4	14.6	6.9
35–44	84.3	34.4	25.8	9.3	14.8
		Median Years of Schooling			
Asia					
25–34	11.6	11.6	11.3	12.2	(14.2)
35–44	10.6	11.0	10.5	10.5	11.8
Africa					
25–34	11.3	11.4	11.1	12.4	(12.9)
35–44	10.6	11.3	10.5	10.6	12.5
Europe-America					
25–34	13.5	13.4	12.9	13.9	15.7
35–44	13.7	14.2	12.8	13.5	15.0
		Percentage of University Graduates			
Asia					
25–34	6.5	5.8	6.2	14.2	(33.6)
35–44	6.2	6.0	5.5	5.8	17.7
Africa					
25–34	4.7	3.6	4.2	13.9	(32.4)
35–44	5.5	10.0	4.6	4.5	19.8
Europe-America					
25–34	25.7	24.4	20.8	27.5	47.5
35–44	31.1	34.1	22.4	24.8	43.2

TABLE 52—*(Continued)*

Origin and Age at Census	Total	Israeli-born	Foreign-born Who Immigrated at the Age of: 0–14	15–24	25+

MEN

Origin-Specific Ratios of Median Years of Schooling[a]

Asia					
25–34	.86	.87	.88	.88	(.90)
35–44	.77	.77	.82	.78	.79
Africa					
25–34	.84	.85	.86	.89	(.82)
35–44	.77	.80	.82	.79	.83

Origin-Specific Ratios of Percentages of University Graduates[a]

Asia					
25–34	.25	.24	.30	.52	(.71)
35–44	.20	.18	.25	.23	.41
Africa					
25–34	.18	.15	.20	.51	(.68)
35–44	.18	.29	.21	.18	.46

WOMEN

Thousands

Asia					
25–34	68.4	49.9	14.3	3.5	0.7
35–44	48.4	10.3	31.3	4.1	2.7
Africa					
25–34	68.7	28.6	35.1	4.2	0.9
35–44	40.7	1.5	22.3	14.6	2.2
Europe-America					
25–34	113.4	67.9	18.7	19.6	7.2
35–44	89.3	35.6	26.0	11.8	16.0

Median Years of Schooling

Asia					
25–34	11.8	12.0	10.9	11.5	(12.2)
35–44	10.0	10.9	9.0	9.0	9.8
Africa					
25–34	11.4	11.7	11.0	12.2	(12.8)
35–44	9.8	11.4	9.4	9.2	12.0

TABLE 52—*(Continued)*

Origin and Age at Census	Total	Israeli-born	Foreign-born Who Immigrated at the Age of: 0–14	15–24	25+

WOMEN

Europe-America
25–34	14.1	14.2	12.9	13.9	15.5
35–44	13.5	14.2	12.7	13.0	14.2

Percentage of University Graduates

Asia
25–34	4.6	4.6	3.4	7.3	(12.4)
35–44	2.4	3.2	1.9	2.8	5.1

Africa
25–34	4.1	3.8	2.7	14.6	(22.4)
35–44	2.7	7.9	1.7	2.1	12.7

Europe-America
25–34	25.0	24.0	19.2	26.7	45.2
35–44	22.3	23.1	15.1	20.7	35.6

Origin-Specific Ratios of Median Years of Schooling[a]

Asia
25–34	.84	.84	.84	.83	(.79)
35–44	.74	.77	.71	.69	.69

Africa
25–34	.81	.82	.85	.88	(.83)
35–44	.73	.80	.74	.71	.84

Origin-Specific Ratios of Percentages of University Graduates[a]

Asia
25–34	.18	.19	.18	.27	(.27)
35–44	.11	.14	.13	.14	.14

Africa
25–34	.16	.16	.14	.55	(.50)
35–44	.12	.34	.11	.10	.36

[a]Europe-America = base 1.00.
Source: Special tabulations from 1983 census file.

TABLE 53. FOREIGN-BORN JEWS EDUCATED IN ISRAEL,[a] BY REGION OF BIRTH, PERIOD OF IMMIGRATION, SELECTED AGES AT IMMIGRATION, AND EDUCATION, 1983

Region of Birth and Period of Immigration	Median Years of Schooling 0–4	Median Years of Schooling 10–14	% of University Graduates 0–4	% of University Graduates 10–14
Asia, total	10.7	8.8	4.1	2.1
Thereof:				
1948–1954	10.6	8.5	4.5	1.7
Africa, total	11.4	10.4	2.6	3.1
Thereof:				
1948–1954	10.4	8.9	2.9	2.4
1955–1964	12.0	10.4	2.2	2.7
Europe-Amer., total	12.6	12.2	16.0	11.7
Thereof:				
1948–1954	12.9	12.0	20.5	11.8
1955–1964	12.8	12.7	13.1	18.8
1965–1974	11.3	12.6	0.2	10.6
	Origin-Specific Ratios[b]			
Asia, total	.85	.72	.26	.18
Thereof:				
1948–1954	.82	.71	.22	.14
Africa, total	.91	.85	.16	.26
Thereof:				
1948–1954	.81	.74	.14	.20
1955–1964	.94	.82	.17	.14

[a]Immigrated at the ages of 0–4 or 10–14.
[b]Europe-America = base 1.00.
Source: CBS, 1983 census, vol.10.

TABLE 54. FOREIGN-BORN JEWS WHO IMMIGRATED AT THE AGE OF 25+, BY SEX, REGION OF BIRTH, AGE AT CENSUS, AND EDUCATION, 1983

Age at Census	Men			Women		
	Asia	Africa	Europe-America	Asia	Africa	Europe-America

Thousands

Total	41.7	43.6	168.0	46.5	51.2	196.2
25–34	0.6	0.7	6.9	0.7	0.9	7.2
35–44	2.1	2.1	14.8	2.7	2.2	16.0
45–54	3.8	8.3	19.2	4.8	11.5	22.4
55–64	14.9	16.6	41.6	15.9	19.1	54.7
65+	20.3	15.9	85.6	22.4	17.5	95.9

Percentage with 0–4 Years of Schooling

Total	34.1	34.4	10.4	60.1	58.7	12.1
25–34	(1.7)	(18.6)	0.5	(5.0)	(15.6)	0.6
35–44	7.3	9.6	2.2	12.8	12.0	1.8
45–54	18.1	24.6	7.1	30.7	47.9	8.9
55–64	29.4	31.6	9.2	60.9	61.3	9.3
65+	44.4	46.5	13.9	73.2	71.0	17.0

Median Years of Schooling

Total	7.6	8.2	10.7	0.9	0.9	10.2
25–34	(14.2)	(12.9)	15.7	(12.3)	(12.8)	15.5
35–44	11.8	12.5	15.0	9.8	12.0	14.2
45–54	8.9	8.7	12.6	7.2	6.1	12.1
55–64	8.1	8.3	10.5	0.9	0.9	10.1
65+	6.1	6.0	8.9	0.7	0.8	8.8

Percentage of University Graduates

Total	4.2	3.9	17.9	1.0	1.7	11.9
25–34	(33.6)	(32.4)	47.5	(12.4)	(22.4)	45.2
35–44	17.7	19.8	43.2	5.1	12.7	35.6
45–54	6.3	5.1	30.8	1.9	1.5	21.4
55–64	3.9	2.2	14.0	0.6	0.7	7.9
65+	1.8	1.8	10.0	0.3	0.5	5.3

TABLE 54—(Continued)

Age at Census	Men Asia	Men Africa	Women Asia	Women Africa
\multicolumn{5}{c}{Origin-Specific Ratios (Europe-America = Base 1.00)}
\multicolumn{5}{c}{Percentage with 0–4 Years of Schooling}
Total	3.28	3.31	4.97	4.85
25–34	(3.40)	x	(8.33)	x
35–44	3.32	4.36	7.11	6.67
45–54	2.55	3.46	3.45	5.38
55–64	3.20	3.43	6.55	6.59
65+	3.19	3.35	4.31	4.18
\multicolumn{5}{c}{Median Years of Schooling}
Total	.71	.76	.09	.09
25–34	(.90)	(.82)	(.79)	(.83)
35–44	.78	.83	.69	.85
45–54	.71	.69	.60	.50
55–64	.77	.79	.09	.09
65+	.68	.67	.08	.09
\multicolumn{5}{c}{Percentage of University Graduates}
Total	.23	.22	.08	.14
25–34	(.71)	(.68)	(.27)	(.50)
35–44	.41	.46	.14	.36
45–54	.20	.17	.09	.07
55–64	.28	.16	.08	.09
65+	.18	.18	.06	.09

Source: Special tabulations from 1983 census file.

TABLE 55. FOREIGN-BORN JEWS WHO IMMIGRATED AT THE AGE OF 25+, BY SEX, REGION OF BIRTH, PERIOD OF IMMIGRATION, AND EDUCATION, 1983

Period of Immigration	Men Asia	Men Africa	Men Europe-America[a]	Women Asia	Women Africa	Women Europe-America[a]
			Thousands			
Total	41.7	43.6	157.0	46.5	51.2	183.3
Up to 1947	3.0	0.5	22.3	3.1	0.5	21.7
1948–1954	23.9	10.1	47.2	26.0	10.8	53.8
1955–1964	4.8	23.2	29.7	6.1	27.8	37.6
1965–1974	6.7	7.0	33.7	7.4	8.8	40.9
1975+	3.4	2.8	24.1	3.9	3.3	29.3
			Percentage with 0–4 Years of Schooling			
Total	34.1	34.4	10.4	60.1	58.7	12.1
Up to 1947	39.6	(26.5)	5.3	72.6	50.5	6.7
1948–1954	41.4	35.0	11.8	73.7	65.2	13.9
1955–1964	31.5	40.2	15.4	52.9	65.6	15.1
1965–1974	18.6	21.2	9.9	32.4	42.6	11.7
1975+	12.6	18.7	7.3	24.8	22.7	9.9
			Median Years of Schooling			
Total	7.7	8.2	10.5	0.9	1.0	10.1
Up to 1947	6.6	(8.5)	10.7	0.8	(4.9)	10.5
1948–1954	6.5	8.0	8.9	0.7	0.9	8.8
1955–1964	7.2	7.4	9.0	4.3	0.8	8.8
1965–1974	8.9	9.4	11.4	7.4	7.0	10.5
1975+	10.7	12.3	12.6	8.5	10.8	11.6
			Percentage of University Graduates			
Total	4.2	3.9	15.6	1.0	1.7	10.1
Up to 1947	0.7	(2.1)	11.0	0.5	(3.0)	6.9
1948–1954	2.5	1.7	6.0	0.4	0.5	2.5
1955–1964	3.1	1.6	12.3	0.3	0.4	6.3
1965–1974	7.4	7.5	23.9	2.3	2.9	16.5
1975+	14.4	22.4	30.8	4.1	12.9	21.9

TABLE 55—*(Continued)*

Period of Immigration	Men Asia	Men Africa	Women Asia	Women Africa
	Origin-Specific Ratios (Europe-America = Base 1.00)			
	Percentage with 0–4 Years of Schooling			
Total	3.28	3.31	4.97	4.85
Up to 1947	7.47	(5.00)	10.84	(7.54)
1948–1954	3.51	2.97	5.30	4.69
1955–1964	2.05	2.61	3.50	4.34
1965–1974	1.88	2.14	2.77	3.64
1975+	1.73	2.56	2.51	2.29
	Median Years of Schooling			
Total	.73	.78	.09	.09
Up to 1947	.63	(.79)	.08	(.47)
1948–1954	.73	.90	.08	.10
1955–1964	.80	.82	.49	.09
1965–1974	.78	.82	.70	.67
1975+	.85	.98	.73	.93
	Percentage of University Graduates			
Total	.27	.25	.09	.17
Up to 1947	.06	(.19)	.07	(.43)
1948–1954	.42	.28	.16	.20
1955–1964	.25	.13	.05	.06
1965–1974	.31	.31	.14	.18
1975+	.47	.73	.19	.59

[a]Small discrepancies in comparison with table 54 are due to the different sources.
Source: CBS, 1983 census, *Educational and Socio-Economic Characteristics of the Population* (in preparation).

TABLE 56. PERCENTAGES OF ACADEMIC GRADUATES AMONG FOREIGN-BORN JEWS WHO IMMIGRATED FROM EUROPE-AMERICA AT THE AGE OF 25+, BY AGE AT CENSUS AND PERIOD OF IMMIGRATION, 1983

Period of Immigration	Total	25–34	35–44	45–54	55–64	65+
Total	14.7	46.3	39.2	25.7	10.5	7.6
Up to 1947	9.1	—	—	—	4.9	9.6
1948–1954	4.4	—	—	—	4.6	4.3
1955–1964	9.5	—	(14.3)	16.0	9.3	7.2
1965–1974	22.3	(37.4)	37.2	28.1	18.5	10.2
1975+	30.1	46.7	42.2	32.7	19.2	12.4

Source: Same as table 55.

TABLE 57. ENROLLMENT RATES IN SECONDARY SCHOOLS AMONG JEWS AGED 17, BY SEX AND ORIGIN, 1966–67, 1974–75, 1981–82[a]

Sex and Origin	1966–67	1974–75	1981–82
		Total	
Total	37.0	52.9	68.8
Israel	45.6	66.6	82.7
Asia-Africa	20.7	42.0	62.6
Europe-America	50.1	67.8	73.4
		Boys	
Total	33.7	46.7	60.2
Israel	40.9	63.7	76.1
Asia-Africa	19.8	35.0	52.4
Europe-America	44.9	61.4	67.1
		Girls	
Total	40.5	59.7	77.8
Israel	50.3	69.5	89.8
Asia-Africa	21.8	49.4	73.3
Europe-America	55.5	74.7	80.2

[a]Rates per 100 in specified population group. The rates for 1987–88 were: total—79.9%; boys—72.0%; girls—88.3%.
Source: CBS, *Statistical Abstract of Israel,* no. 36, 1985, p. 621, table 12.

TABLE 58. ENROLLMENT RATES[a] IN SECONDARY SCHOOLS AMONG JEWS AGED 17, BY SEX, ORIGIN, AND TYPE OF SCHOOL, 1966–67, 1974–75, 1981–82

Sex and Origin	General School			Vocational or Agricultural School		
	1966–67	1974–75	1981–82	1966–67	1974–75	1981–82
Total						
Total	25.8	28.2	35.2	11.2	24.7	33.6
Israel	33.3	44.8	54.8	12.3	21.8	27.9
Asia-Africa	12.0	15.6	24.5	8.7	26.4	38.1
Europe-America	38.2	45.1	45.8	11.9	22.7	27.5
Boys						
Total	20.5	21.1	25.6	13.2	25.6	34.6
Israel	26.4	36.0	42.7	14.5	27.7	33.4
Asia-Africa	10.3	10.7	16.6	9.5	24.3	35.8
Europe-America	30.0	34.2	34.1	14.9	27.2	33.0
Girls						
Total	31.5	36.0	45.3	9.0	23.7	32.5
Israel	40.3	53.5	67.6	10.0	16.0	22.1
Asia-Africa	13.9	20.8	32.8	7.9	28.6	40.6
Europe-America	46.9	57.1	58.5	8.6	17.6	21.7

TABLE 58—*(Continued)*

Year	Type of School Specific Ratios[b]				Origin-Specific Ratios[c]		
	Total	Israel	Asia-Africa	Europe-American	Total	General	Vocational or Agricultural
				Total			
1966–67	.43	.37	.73	.31	.41	.31	.73
1974–75	.88	.49	1.69	.50	.62	.35	1.16
1981–82	.95	.51	1.56	.60	.85	.53	1.39
				Boys			
1966–67	.64	.55	.92	.50	.44	.34	.64
1974–75	1.21	.77	2.27	.80	.57	.31	.89
1981–82	1.35	.78	2.16	.97	.78	.49	1.08
				Girls			
1966–67	.29	.25	.57	.18	.39	.30	.92
1974–75	.66	.30	1.38	.31	.66	.36	1.62
1981–82	.72	.33	1.24	.37	.91	.56	1.87

[a]Rates per 100 in specified population group. The rates for 1987–88 were for general schools: total—42.7%; boys—33.5%; girls—52.6%; for vocational and agricultural schools: 37.2%, 38.6% and 35.7%, respectively.
[b]General schools = base 1.00.
[c]Europe-America = base 1.00.
Source: Same as table 57.

TABLE 59. ADULT JEWS OF SELECTED AGE GROUPS, BY SEX, ORIGIN, AND TYPE OF LAST SCHOOL ATTENDED, 1972 AND 1983

Sex and Origin	Total (Thousands)	Rates by Type of School[a] General (A)	Vocational or Agricultural (B)	Ratio (B)/(A)
		1972, Ages 14–29		
Men, total[b]	387.8	22.9	35.3	1.54
Thereof:				
Asia	102.5	16.9	37.4	2.21
Africa	97.8	16.2	35.8	2.21
Europe-America	162.9	29.7	33.5	1.13
Women, total[b]	375.5	32.5	23.3	.72
Thereof:				
Asia	99.9	25.7	28.7	1.12
Africa	93.6	24.6	26.7	1.09
Europe-America	159.2	40.0	18.3	.46
		1983, Ages 15–24		
Men, total[b]	273.1	28.1	44.1	1.57
Thereof:				
Asia	72.5	20.9	53.8	2.57
Africa	79.3	19.8	51.9	2.62
Europe-America	79.7	35.0	32.9	.94
Women, total[b]	257.4	40.2	32.1	.80
Thereof:				
Asia	68.0	35.2	41.2	1.17
Africa	75.4	32.7	41.5	1.27
Europe-America	74.8	44.5	20.0	.45

[a]Rates per 100 in specified population group.
[b]Including Israeli-born, father also born in this country.

TABLE 60. ENROLLMENT RATES[a] IN SECONDARY SCHOOLS AMONG JEWS AGED 17, BY SEX, ORIGIN, AND COURSE OF STUDIES, 1981–82

Sex and Origin	Total (A)	Studying for Matriculation Certificate Total (B)	Studying for Matriculation Certificate General (C)	Studying for Matriculation Certificate Vocational (D)	Studying for Other Certificates	Ratios (B)/(A)	Ratios (C)/(B)
Total							
Total	68.9	56.2	35.4	20.8	12.7	.82	.63
Israel	83.1	75.4	55.3	20.1	7.8	.91	.73
Asia-Africa	62.6	45.9	24.6	21.3	16.7	.73	.54
Europe-America	73.6	66.4	46.1	20.3	7.1	.90	.69
Boys							
Total	60.5	47.3	25.9	21.4	13.1	.78	.55
Israel	76.7	67.5	43.4	24.1	9.3	.88	.64
Asia-Africa	52.5	36.1	16.8	19.3	16.4	.69	.47
Europe-America	67.4	58.7	34.4	24.3	8.7	.87	.59
Girls							
Total	77.9	65.7	45.5	20.2	12.2	.84	.69
Israel	90.0	83.8	68.0	15.8	6.2	.93	.81
Asia-Africa	73.3	56.3	32.9	23.4	17.1	.77	.58
Europe-America	80.2	74.8	58.7	16.1	5.5	.93	.78

[a]Rates per 100 in specified population group. Small differences in comparison with tables 57 and 58 are due to different sources.
Source: CBS, unpublished data.

TABLE 61. PERCENTAGES OF SUCCESS IN MATRICULATION EXAMINATIONS, BY COURSE OF STUDIES AND ORIGIN, 1986–87 (PERCENT)

Origin	Total (A)	General (B)	Vocational (C)	Ratio (C)/(B)
Total examinees	62.8	70.5	45.4	.64
Israel	71.2	76.2	54.2	.71
Asia-Africa	53.3	62.3	38.8	.62
Europe-America	69.8	76.3	53.4	.70
Ratio: Asia-Africa/Europe-America	.76	.82	.73	

Source: CBS, *Matriculation Examinations, 1986–87* (in preparation).

TABLE 62. JEWISH STUDENTS AT UNIVERSITIES, BY ORIGIN, 1964–65 TO 1988–89

Origin	1964–65	1969–70	1974–75	1984–85	1988–89
	\multicolumn{5}{c}{Rates per 100 Jews Aged 20–29 in Specified Population Group}				
Total	3.8	6.3	7.2	7.6	8.2
Israeli-born, total	8.1	9.9	9.5	8.2	11.3
Father born in:					
Israel	5.2	7.5	10.0	13.4	15.2
Asia-Africa (A)	1.6	2.5	3.0	3.7	6.6
Europe-America (B)	10.7	12.6	14.0	14.9	15.3
Born in Asia-Africa (C)	0.8	1.6	2.1	2.8	2.8
Born in Europe-America (D)	5.3	9.8	8.4	8.3	8.2
	\multicolumn{5}{c}{Origin-Specific Ratios}				
(A)/(B)	.15	.20	.21	.25	.43
(C)/(D)	.15	.16	.25	.34	.34

Sources: CBS, *Statistical Abstract*, no. 40, 1989, p. 613, table 14; for 1988–89—*Statistical Abstract*, no. 41 (in preparation).

TABLE 63. JEWISH ADULTS AGED 25–34 WITH MATRICULATION CERTIFICATES,[a] WHO CONTINUED STUDIES, BY SEX, ORIGIN, AND TYPE OF LAST SCHOOL ATTENDED, 1983

Type of Last School Attended	Men Asia	Men Africa	Men Europe-America	Women Asia	Women Africa	Women Europe-America
Rates of Study in Specified Last School[b,c]						
Total	35.2	37.0	45.9	21.2	25.1	35.3
Postsecondary	9.3	8.6	9.3	8.0	11.7	11.2
University	25.9	28.4	36.6	13.2	13.4	24.1
Origin-Specific Ratios[d]						
Total	.77	.81		.63	.71	
Postsecondary	1.00	.92		.71	1.04	
University	.71	.78		.55	.56	

[a] Highest certificate attained at census date.
[b] Per 100 holders of matriculation certificates in specified population group.
[c] Attended at census date or before.
[d] Europe-America = base 1.00.
Source: Same as table 55.

TABLE 64. VOTES FOR MAIN PARTIES, KNESSET ELECTIONS, 1955, 1965, 1977, 1988 (PERCENT)

Major Political Sectors and Parties[a]	3rd Knesset 1955	6th Knesset 1965	9th Knesset 1977	12th Knesset 1988
Eligible voters	1,057,795	1,499,709	2,236,293	2,894,267
Percent actual voters	82.8	83.0	79.2	79.7
Valid votes	853,219	1,206,728	1,771,726	2,283,123
Total	100.0	100.0	100.0	100.0
Labor	47.7	51.2	24.6	32.5
Mapam (United Workers' party)	7.3	6.6	—	2.5
Ma'arakh (Alignment)—Israel Labor party	32.2[b]	36.7	24.6	30.0
Achdut Ha'avoda (Unity of Labor)	8.2	—	—	—
Rafi (Israel Workers' List)	—	7.9	—	—
Liberal-Radical	4.7	5.0	15.6	6.0
Independent Liberal party—Progressives	4.7	3.8	1.2	—
Center Movement—Shinui (Change)	—	—	—	1.7
Dash (Democratic Movement for Change)	—	—	11.6	—
Ratz (Citizens' Rights Movement)	—	—	1.2	4.3
Ha'olam Hazeh (This World)	—	1.2	—	—
Shelli (Peace for Israel)	—	—	1.6	—
Religious	13.8	14.0	13.9	14.6
Mafdal (National Religious party)	9.1	8.9	9.2	3.9
Agudat Israel (United Orthodox Religious)	4.7	3.3	3.4	4.5
Poalei Agudat Israel (Agudat Is. Workers)	—	1.8	1.3	—
Shas (Sephardi Torah Guardians)	—	—	—	4.7
Degel Hatorah (Torah Flag)	—	—	—	1.5

TABLE 64—*(Continued)*

Major Political Sectors and Parties[a]	3rd Knesset 1955	6th Knesset 1965	9th Knesset 1977	12th Knesset 1988
Center-Right to Right	22.8	21.3	37.3	38.1
General Zionists-Liberal party	10.2	—	—	—
Herut (Freedom)	12.6	—	—	—
Likud—Herut/Liberal party	—	21.3[c]	33.4	31.1
Shlomzion (Peace to Zion)	—	—	1.9	—
Flatto-Sharon	—	—	2.0	—
Tehiya (Renaissance)	—	—	—	3.1
Tzomet (Zionist Renewal Movement)	—	—	—	2.0
Moledet (Homeland)	—	—	—	1.9
Communist and Arab	8.9	7.2	6.0	6.4
Maki (Israel Communist party)	4.5	1.1	—	—
Rakah—Hadash—Israel Communist party	—	2.3	4.6	3.7
Progressive List for Peace	—	—	—	1.5
Minorities' List	4.4	3.8	1.4	—
Arab Democratic party	—	—	—	1.2
Other[d]	2.4	1.3	2.9	2.3

[a]Parties listed separately won at least one seat. Several parties changed their names from election to election. In general, the first name listed is the most recent version.
[b]Mapai.
[c]Gahal.
[d]Won no seats.
Source: CBS, *Statistical Abstract of Israel,* 1989.

TABLE 65. DISTRIBUTION OF VOTES FOR MAIN PARTIES, BY TYPE OF LOCALITY, 12TH KNESSET (1988) (PERCENT)

Party[a]	No. of Seats Won	Total Valid Votes	Jerusalem	Tel Aviv	Haifa	Development Towns	Other Urban	Moshavim	Kibbutzim	Other Rural	Urban	Other
Total	120	100.0	7.6	9.2	6.1	9.2	49.5	3.9	3.3	1.8	7.8	1.5
Mapam	3	100.0	5.2	6.8	3.8	5.0	25.5	1.6	37.1	0.8	9.2	4.9
Alignment—Labor	39	100.0	5.0	10.4	8.1	7.1	52.2	4.5	6.0	1.4	4.1	1.2
Shinui	2	100.0	7.2	12.2	8.8	3.6	46.1	3.6	1.8	1.9	12.4	2.3
Ratz	5	100.0	10.0	14.3	8.3	4.2	43.3	3.4	5.0	2.0	7.4	2.1
Mafdal	5	100.0	8.9	5.6	4.3	10.5	48.6	8.2	1.5	5.0	5.6	1.7
Agudat Israel	5	100.0	14.6	6.9	3.3	15.0	53.3	4.8	0.3	1.4	0.3	0.1
Shas	6	100.0	13.6	8.1	2.5	16.6	52.0	4.6	0.1	1.6	0.7	0.2
Degel Hatorah	2	100.0	32.7	2.8	2.6	4.2	53.4	1.7	0.1	1.1	1.2	0.3
Likud	40	100.0	7.5	10.2	5.5	12.0	57.5	3.3	0.2	1.7	1.5	0.6
Tehiya	3	100.0	9.5	8.7	5.4	7.7	55.9	5.1	1.5	5.7	0.4	0.1
Tzomet	2	100.0	7.2	7.5	8.5	12.3	52.0	7.1	1.5	3.1	0.6	0.2
Moledet	2	100.0	9.4	8.6	5.7	9.9	55.6	5.6	0.7	3.9	0.2	0.4
Rakah—Hadash	4	100.0	0.5	2.3	5.0	4.0	4.3	0.0	0.1	0.1	78.1	5.7
Progressive List for Peace	1	100.0	0.9	1.4	2.2	3.3	2.3	0.1	0.3	0.1	84.5	4.9
Arab Democratic party	1	100.0	0.8	2.1	2.2	0.9	5.1	0.1	0.0	0.1	65.1	23.6
Other	—	100.0	12.3	9.4	6.5	6.0	45.4	4.6	2.6	1.9	7.5	3.8

[a] Listed in the same order as in table 64.

Source: Adapted from Uri Avner, "Voting at the Elections for the 12th Knesset in Comparison to Previous Elections" (in Hebrew), CBS, Ministry of the Interior—Inspector General of Elections, Malam Systems Ltd., *Results of Elections to the Twelfth Knesset 1.11.1988, Vol. A*, 1989; CBS, Special Series, no. 855, pp. 25–42.

TABLE 66. VOTES FOR MAIN PARTIES, BY ORIGIN (MAJOR GROUPS) AND SOCIOECONOMIC STATUS OF POPULATION IN URBAN JEWISH LOCALITIES,[a] 12TH KNESSET (1988) (PERCENT)

Party[b]	Total Valid Votes	Origin of Majority of Area's Inhabitants (Major Groups)					Area's Socioeconomic Status (Quintiles)				
		Europe-America	Asia-Africa[c]	Asia[d]	Africa[e]	1 (Highest)	2	3	4	5 (Lowest)
Total	100.0	53.2	10.8	15.3	16.8	21.4	19.2	20.7	20.5	18.2
Shinui	100.0	76.0	7.4	7.7	5.3	46.7	24.2	15.9	9.3	4.0
Ratz	100.0	74.1	7.9	8.1	5.8	43.7	25.0	16.6	10.3	4.4
Degel Hatorah	100.0	71.1	5.1	13.9	8.5	7.0	10.8	16.4	38.6	27.3
Alignment—Labor	100.0	64.8	10.0	10.7	10.4	29.1	23.5	22.0	15.9	9.5
Mapam	100.0	64.1	9.7	10.6	11.1	29.8	24.2	19.6	16.5	9.9
Tsomet	100.0	56.2	12.0	12.7	15.2	22.6	21.9	22.7	19.7	13.2
Tehiya	100.0	54.2	11.6	16.7	13.1	23.3	21.7	22.3	19.0	13.8
Moledet	100.0	50.5	12.1	16.8	15.9	20.2	20.6	23.2	20.5	15.5
Mafdal	100.0	50.3	9.8	16.6	20.2	17.0	18.9	21.1	21.8	21.3
Agudat Israel	100.0	48.1	9.9	16.5	22.8	7.1	11.5	18.9	29.4	33.2
Likud	100.0	43.0	12.3	19.2	21.5	16.1	16.9	21.1	22.8	23.0
Shas	100.0	27.1	11.8	24.9	33.1	5.1	10.0	17.7	28.8	38.5

[a]Based on a total of 810 statistical areas in urban Jewish localities over 10,000 inhabitants. See also note 41 to text.
[b]Parties with a majority of Jewish voters, ranked according to proportion of party's votes obtained in residential areas with plurality of Jews of European-American origins.
[c]Asian-African origins combined include larger share of total population than European-American origins, without either Asia or Africa alone reaching a plurality.
[d]Plurality of Asian origin alone.
[e]Plurality of African origin alone.
Source: Same as table 65.

TABLE 67. PERCENT OF CHANGE IN VOTE FOR MAJOR GROUPS OF PARTIES IN STATISTICAL AREAS IN URBAN JEWISH LOCALITIES,[a] BY ORIGIN (MAJOR GROUPS) AND SOCIOECONOMIC STATUS OF POPULATION, 12TH KNESSET (1988) IN COMPARISON TO 11TH KNESSET (1984)

Group of Parties[b] and Percent of Change, 1984–1988	Total	Origin of Majority of Area's Inhabitants (Major Groups)[c]				Area's Socioeconomic Status (Quintiles)				
		Europe-America	Asia-Africa	Asia	Africa	1 (Highest)	2	3	4	5 (Lowest)
No. of statistical areas	810	417	88	123	149	157	154	165	165	169
Alignment—Labor, Mapam, Ratz, Shinui	100.0	100.0	100.0	100.0	100.0	100.0	100.0	100.0	100.0	100.0
Lost 10% or more	26.4	19.0	21.6	30.8	48.3	3.8	6.5	18.7	42.4	57.4
Stabled	50.4	53.0	53.4	53.7	36.3	49.1	61.1	67.3	44.3	31.4
Gained 10% or more	23.2	28.1	25.0	15.4	15.4	47.1	32.4	13.9	13.3	11.2
Religious parties	100.0	100.0	100.0	100.0	100.0	100.0	100.0	100.0	100.0	100.0
Lost 10% or more	3.8	7.0	1.1 —	0.6	12.7	5.8	0.6 —	0.6	—	—
Stabled	11.2	19.4	2.3	3.3	0.7	27.4	20.1	4.2	1.8	4.2
Gained 10% or more	85.0	73.6	96.6	96.7	98.7	59.9	73.1	95.2	98.2	95.2
Likud, Tehiya, Tzomet, Moledet	100.0	100.0	100.0	100.0	100.0	100.0	100.0	100.0	100.0	100.0
Lost 10% or more	12.4	9.1	7.9	15.4	22.8	1.9	4.5	6.6	12.8	34.9
Stabled	41.7	37.0	38.6	50.4	52.4	26.8	38.3	37.6	53.9	50.9
Gained 10% or more	45.8	53.9	53.4	34.2	24.8	71.3	57.1	55.7	33.3	14.2

[a] Based on a total of 810 statistical areas in urban Jewish localities.
[b] Does not include parties which did not win seats in the 12th Knesset, or parties which won seats in the 11th Knesset and did not participate in the 12th Knesset elections.
[c] See notes c, d, e to table 66.

TABLE 68. INDEXES OF VOTE CONCENTRATION FOR MAJOR GROUPS OF PARTIES, BY ORIGIN (MAJOR GROUPS) AND SOCIOECONOMIC STATUS OF POPULATION IN URBAN JEWISH LOCALITIES,[a] 12TH KNESSET (1988)

Parties and Origin of Majority of Area's Inhabitants (Major Groups)[b]	Total	1 (High)	2	3	4	5 (Low)	Row Max/Min Ratio[c]
Alignment—Labor							
Total	100	136	122	106	77	52	2.6
Europe-America	122	**139**	127	115	76	50	2.8
Asia-Africa	93	68	102	100	92	65	1.6
Asia	70—	84	95	74	**48**		2.0
Africa	62—	87	87	69	53		1.6
Column max/min ratio[d]	2.0	2.0	1.5	1.3	1.3	1.4	**2.9**[e]
Mapam, Ratz, Shinui							
Total	100	243	110	84	57	30	8.1
Europe-America	141	**243**	135	87	49	**28**	8.7
Asia-Africa	77	123	112	83	61	35	3.5
Asia	57—	121	83	62	30		2.0
Africa	42—	99	70	51	29		3.4
Column max/min ratio[d]	3.4	2.0	1.5	1.2	1.3	1.3	**8.7**[e]
Religious parties							
Total	100	41	66	90	139	173	4.2
Europe-America	83	**39**	63	97	214	**307**	7.9
Asia-Africa	93	88	82	83	92	146	1.8
Asia	125—	88	77	117	166		2.2
Africa	144—	110	106	129	160		1.5
Column max/min ratio[d]	1.7	2.3	1.7	1.4	2.3	2.1	**2.9**[e]

TABLE 68—*(Continued)*

Parties and Origin of Majority of Area's Inhabitants (Major Groups)[b]	Area's Socioeconomic Status (Quintiles)					Row Max/Min Ratio[c]
	Total	1 (High)	2	3	4	5 (Low)	

Likud

Total	100	75	88	102	111	126	1.7
Europe-America	81	74	85	90	80	**73**	1.2
Asia-Africa	114	115	102	110	120	126	1.2
Asia	125—	108	118	124	132		1.2
Africa	128—	106	117	124	**133**		1.3
Column max/min ratio[d]	1.6	1.6	1.3	1.3	1.6	1.8	**1.8**[e]

Tehiya, Tzomet, Moledet

Total	100	104	112	109	96	77	1.5
Europe-America	100	101	109	104	79	**52**	2.1
Asia-Africa	109	**162**	119	117	99	72	2.3
Asia	101—	121	127	107	89		1.4
Africa	87—	108	104	99	76		1.4
Column max/min ratio[d]	1.3	1.6	1.1	1.2	1.4	1.7	**3.1**[e]

[a]Based on a total of 810 statistical areas in urban Jewish localities. Each cell in this table represents a given combination of the predominant origin (major group) and socioeconomic status of the voters in such areas. Indexes of vote concentration are ratios between the percent of votes won by a given group of parties in the statistical areas included in a given cell of the table and the percent of votes obtained nationally by the same parties. Indexes above 100 indicate overrepresentation of voters with the indicated combination of origin and socioeconomic status among voters for a given party; indexes below 100 indicate underrepresentation. The highest and lowest indexes of vote concentration for each party appear in bold.
[b]See notes c, d, e to table 66.
[c]Ratio between highest and lowest index of vote concentration in each row.
[d]Ratio between highest and lowest index of vote concentration in each column, relative to given party or group of parties.
[e]Ratio between highest and lowest index of vote concentration, relative to given party or group of parties.
Source: same as table 65.

Review of the Year

UNITED STATES

Civic and Political

Intergroup Relations

THE 1988 PRESIDENTIAL ELECTION campaign raised troubling questions about Jewish status in America and led to increased tensions with the black community. In addition, relations between the U.S. government and Israel were strained by Israel's handling of the *intifada*, the Palestinian Arab uprising. Otherwise, matters relating to American Jewish security were essentially variations on familiar themes.

1988 Elections

If political equality and efficacy are prime tests of a minority group's status, the general election year of 1988 was a rigorous testing period for American Jews. Both personalities and party politics posed potential threats to Jewish interests.

The personalities in question, at the beginning of the year, were the Reverend Jesse Jackson, a Democratic party presidential candidate, and the Reverend Pat Robertson, a Republican party presidential candidate. A question repeatedly raised was whether Jackson or Robertson would cost his respective party more Jewish votes. In a national survey carried out in the spring by Steven M. Cohen for the American Jewish Committee,[1] 59 percent of Jews said that Jesse Jackson was anti-Semitic; 41 percent said that Pat Robertson was anti-Semitic. Jackson's burden, as far as Jews were concerned, was a record of some anti-Semitic references in the past and an association with Arab-American causes and forces in this country. Robertson's burden was the fact that he was a fundamentalist preacher with a strong belief in the primacy of Christianity.

In a *Los Angeles Times* survey carried out early in the year, about 3 percent of American Jews said they would vote for Jackson in the primaries, and less than 1 percent said they would vote for Robertson. Cohen's national survey came up with approximately the same results. In the latter, which was conducted in April and May, about a quarter of the Jews said they would vote for the Democratic ticket if Jackson were the vice-presidential candidate—fewer than half of Democratic-

---

[1]Published under the title *The Dimensions of American Jewish Liberalism* (New York, 1989).

leaning Jews. About 10 percent of the Jews said they would vote for the Republican ticket if Robertson were on it—a little more than half of otherwise Republican-leaning Jews. Although both candidates were widely considered inimical to Jewish interests, Jackson received the most attention, partly because the Democratic party was the traditional political home for most Jews.

REACTION TO JACKSON

New York City mayor Edward Koch became a lightning rod for these attitudes when he said, in April, that any Jews who supported Jackson "have got to be crazy, in the same way that they'd be crazy if they were black and voted for someone who was praising Botha and the racist supporters of the South African administration." Faced with a torrent of angry reaction from blacks, and some from Jews, Koch apologized, weakly, later in the month, saying, "If I was carried away in my language, it was because of what I perceived to be a danger at hand." While many Jews apparently agreed with Koch's sentiments, most Jewish community leaders were nervous about the bluntness of his style. David Pollock, an official of the Jewish Community Relations Council of Greater New York, said, "We are concerned about the community relations impact, and hope there's not a fallout." Seen as at risk were not only black-Jewish relations in general but the Jewish relationship to the Democratic party.

Throughout the remainder of the election year, there were constant attempts by both the Jackson forces and Jewish leadership to patch up relations. In April, while Koch's remarks still resounded, Jackson met with a selected group of Jewish leaders in New York, including Rabbi Gilbert Klaperman, president of the Synagogue Council of America. At the meeting, Jackson was asked about his past association with Muslim leader Louis Farrakhan, who had in previous years called Judaism "a gutter religion" and Adolf Hitler a "great" man. Jackson reportedly held to the position that he disavowed the sin but not the sinner, believing in "forgiveness," and indicated that he had had no recent contact with Farrakhan. He also said that he opposed any resolution equating Zionism with racism.

Rabbi Klaperman stated that he was not "completely satisfied" with Jackson's responses and was particularly disappointed that Jackson had been unwilling to meet with any major Jewish groups as such. Jackson was the only Democratic presidential candidate to decline an invitation, issued six months before, to speak in New York at a preprimary meeting of the Conference of Presidents of Major American Jewish Organizations. Jackson's reluctance to meet with Jewish organizations was still the subject of comment in August, when he held a meeting with Israeli ambassador Moshe Arad. Morris Abram, chairman of the Conference of Presidents, said that Jackson's meeting with Arad was "appropriate," but "is not a substitute for a meeting with representatives of the American Jewish community."

During this period, Jackson addressed the question of black-Jewish friction in generally conciliatory terms. In an interview with the *New York Times* in April, after Mayor Koch's initial strong remarks, he called for the Jews to be more willing to share power with the blacks and suggested that Jewish unwillingness to share power was itself a source of tension. He said that Jews "have no basis for being afraid of sharing power with blacks or of my leadership. I genuinely respect and care for Jewish people." In May Jackson placed a wreath at a statue honoring Holocaust victims, in a park overlooking the Statue of Liberty, saying that "the sons and daughters of the Holocaust and grandsons and granddaughters of slavery must find common ground to end racism and anti-Semitism forever." And in November, speaking at a *Kristallnacht* commemoration of the Union of American Hebrew Congregations in Washington, D.C., Jackson called for Jews and blacks to work together for social justice as they had during the 1960s civil rights movement.

Despite these expressions of rapprochement, most American Jews regarded as inseparable Jackson's attitude toward them and his attitude toward Israel. He made the connection explicit, for example, when, in the *New York Times* interview, he described the "Israel–South Africa connection" as a major source of "tension" between blacks and American Jews. An extensive document distributed to delegates at the Democratic National Convention spelled out in detail Jackson's long and close association with activist Arab-American groups. In April Abdeen Jabara, president of the American-Arab Anti-Discrimination Committee—while chiding Jackson for saying that he would not, as president, sit down with Yasir Arafat— pointed out that "virtually every Arab-American looked to [Jackson] as the one symbol of strength in a field of political candidates who are notorious for their unwillingness to stand up to the pro-Israel lobby."

After Jackson garnered 55 percent of the Democratic primary vote in Michigan in late March, Mark Siegel, a Democratic party consultant and Jewish liaison in the Carter administration, said that the Jewish community had a "good deal of concern about the possibility" that Jackson might become the Democratic candidate. At the end of 33 state primary votes, as recapitulated by the *New York Times* on June 13, Jackson had received well over six million votes, 29 percent of the total, compared with 28 percent for all other candidates except Dukakis, who had received 43 percent. Although blacks provided him with two-thirds of those votes, Jackson's share of the white vote had tripled since the election of 1984. Jews, who generally voted in much higher numbers for black gubernatorial and mayoralty candidates around the country than did other white, and even Hispanic, voters, went against this trend: only 8 percent of Jewish primary voters chose Jackson, as against 12 percent of white non-Hispanic voters and 30 percent of Hispanic voters.

It did not help that forces associated with Jackson's "Rainbow Coalition," as Mayor Koch pointed out in July, were instrumental in the promulgation of pro-Palestinian statements in seven Democratic party state platforms, although the national platform finally eliminated those statements. The same forces helped launch pro-Palestinian referenda in two California and two Massachusetts cities. Three of the four referenda were ultimately defeated after strenuous campaigns.

The initiatives in San Francisco and Newton, Massachusetts, called for Palestinian statehood and safeguarding the security of Israel and a Palestinian state. Both were defeated by more than 2–1 margins. A resolution on the Berkeley, California, ballot called for making Jabaliya refugee camp in Gaza a "sister city" of Berkeley. It too was defeated by more than 2–1. The Cambridge-Somerville (Mass.) initiative called upon Congress and the president to demand Israel's withdrawal from occupied territories, to stop spending U.S. taxpayer money for the occupation, and to support establishment of a Palestinian state. It passed by a narrow margin.

JEWS AND REPUBLICANS

Meanwhile, the Republican party was having its own problems with Jewish concerns. Early in the year, the source of the tension was the candidacy of evangelist Pat Robertson and his explicitly "Christian" views. Robertson used a half-hour TV program in March to deny that, as president, he would seek to impose his religious views on others, and one of his press secretaries maintained that there was no contradiction in campaigning on religious values while vowing to keep church and state separate. Nevertheless, the fact that as a Christian evangelist he did advocate religious values made Jews—as well as many other Americans—nervous. (His basic stump speech carried the line, "I want to see a time when little children can once again pray in the schools of America.")

Robertson faded as a serious presidential candidate, but the ultimate Republican candidate, George Bush, developed problems of his own. In September the *Washington Jewish Week* revealed that a campaign "ethnic outreach" committee appointed by Bush included a Holocaust revisionist and people with fascist connections. A cochairman of the committee, Jerome Brentar, had been active in groups that denied the Holocaust. Florian Galdau, honorary chairman, a Romanian Orthodox priest, was described by Nazi hunter Simon Wiesenthal as New York chief of the Iron Guard, Romania's anti-Semitic, pro-Nazi movement. A vice-chairman of the committee, Philip Guarino, was listed as a member of P-2, a conspiratorial Italian fascist group. Radi Slavoff, national chairman of Bulgarians for Bush, reportedly had served in a national front aligned with the Nazis. Lazio Pasztor had served as an official in Hungary's anti-Semitic, pro-Nazi Arrow Cross. Ignatius Bilinsky and Bohdan Fedorak had been leading critics of the Justice Department's investigations of Nazi war criminals living in the United States.

These seven members of the ethnic panel resigned before the end of the month, at the urging of the Bush campaign. Nevertheless, the Democratic party, worried about "the Jackson effect" on Jews, played up the revelations. Michael Dukakis said, "I think this raises continuing questions about Mr. Bush's judgment." And Hyman Bookbinder, a special adviser to Dukakis on Jewish matters, said that while it was "unfair" to suggest that Bush knew beforehand about the background of the resignees, it was not unfair to ask why "they chose Bush as the person they want to support." In the same month, Frederic V. Malek, a top adviser to Bush, resigned from a senior position at the Republican National Committee after admitting that in 1971, after twice refusing to do so, he had finally made a count of ranking Jewish officials at the Bureau of Labor Statistics, at President Richard Nixon's request. Nixon had made this request of Malek after complaining that a "Jewish cabal" in the bureau was trying to undermine him. A couple of Jewish officials at the bureau were reassigned after Malek made his report.

ELECTION RESULTS

Whether or not these incidents made an impression on Jewish voters, and whether or not Jewish voters were reassured by the pointed distance which Dukakis kept between himself and Jesse Jackson after he became the Democratic candidate, Jews voted overwhelmingly for Dukakis, in about the same proportion that they had voted for Walter Mondale four years before. The three major national exit polls—CBS News/*New York Times*, NBC News/*Wall Street Journal*, ABC News/*Washington Post*—respectively counted the Jewish vote for Dukakis as 65 percent, 71 percent, and 72 percent.

The election results in general reassured Jews that their position in the political arena had not diminished. At election's end, the House of Representatives had an all-time high of 31 Jewish members, and there continued to be 8 Jewish senators. In short, the proportion of Jews in the U.S. Congress was about three times higher than the proportion of Jews in the population. While it is true that congressional candidates tend to come from the higher educational and occupational brackets in the population, in which Jews are disproportionately represented, the figures are meaningful because most of these identifiably Jewish lawmakers were elected by overwhelmingly non-Jewish constituencies. It should also be noted that no significant expressions of anti-Semitism were reported in the course of the campaigns.

At the same time, the prime consensual agenda of the organized Jewish community promised to be treated sympathetically by the new body of public officials. Despite concerns about the *intifada*, in October Congress had approved a $3-billion grant to Israel—almost one-quarter of its total foreign-aid measure. It was passed by a voice vote in the Senate and a 327–92 vote in the House. Jewish Congress-watchers anticipated that, all things remaining even, the newly elected Congress would be just as supportive.

As for the White House, some concerns were expressed by Jewish organizations at the appointment of New Hampshire governor John H. Sununu as Bush's chief of staff. Sununu, once a member of the National Association of Arab Americans, had refused to join all other governors in 1987 in condemning the UN resolution equating Zionism with racism. However, in a meeting with a delegation of Jewish organizational leaders in November, Sununu explained his action as merely a technical matter and willingly discussed his attitudes about the Middle East. At the end of the meeting, Theodore Ellenoff, president of the American Jewish Committee, said that Sununu's explanations "satisfied the group. There was a measurably higher comfort level achieved."

Reactions to the Intifada

The Palestinian Arab uprising in the occupied territories of Israel caused the Jewish community considerable uneasiness in 1988. The daily media images of Palestinian youths being injured and killed by Israeli soldiers in the West Bank and Gaza raised fears of a public-opinion backlash and the effect of such a backlash on American-Israeli relations.

In March, 30 U.S. senators, including 5 Jews and a number of others historically friendly to Israel, signed a letter accusing Israel of being inflexible over the terms of a possible peace settlement. In June the State Department unsuccessfully urged Israel not to deport Mubarak Awad, a controversial Palestinian-American who had been living in the West Bank and who was accused of supporting the *intifada*. In August the State Department said that the United States was "shocked" at Israel's decision to expel 25 Palestinians from the West Bank and Gaza. In the same month, the Israeli government and American Jewish groups expressed dismay at U.S. Trade Representative Clayton Yeutter's decision to accept an American-Arab Anti-Discrimination Committee petition for him to investigate Israel's treatment of Palestinian laborers. In September the State Department criticized Israel's use of plastic bullets. And, most significantly, in December the administration announced that it would hold a "substantive dialogue" with the PLO, a radical reversal of the American policy dating from 1975 that had ruled out any discussion with that organization. (See "The United States, Israel, and the Middle East," elsewhere in this volume.)

In addition to these U.S. government rebuffs, some American religious groups intensified their attacks on Israel's treatment of the Palestinians. In June a committee of the Presbyterian Church (USA) charged Israel with "a repressive policy." And for the second consecutive year, in the spring the American Friends Service Committee, with two other organizations, placed 200 posters on Boston's subways depicting a Palestinian locked in the grip of a helmeted Israeli soldier. The same type of campaign was mounted by the American-Arab Anti-Discrimination Committee in the Metro in the nation's capital, in July.

PUBLIC OPINION

Concerned over possible growing animosity in America, not just toward Israel but toward the American Jewish community as well, the major Jewish public-affairs organizations commissioned special surveys of the American population. Since public opinion on topical issues such as the Israeli-Palestinian clashes is notoriously volatile, it is not surprising that the surveys showed an increasing sympathy for the Palestinians. At the same time, they also showed a continuing "bedrock of support" for Israel among Americans. At a panel discussion arranged in September by the Conference of Presidents of Major Jewish Organizations, the Penn and Schoen organization reported on the survey it conducted for the Anti-Defamation League the previous January. It found that there had been little erosion of American public support for Israel up to that time. By contrast, a Roper poll conducted for the American Jewish Committee in March found that American support for Israel had declined since the beginning of the *intifada*, although basically, "as a group," the American public still supported Israel. The Martilla and Kiley organization reported on a survey conducted for the American Jewish Congress in April. It found that the American public registered "strong and secure" support for Israel and was by a large margin still "more sympathetic" to Israel than to either the Arab states or the Palestinians.

In short, these surveys and others conducted during the year found the level of American support for Israel more unsteady than it had been for years, although still much higher than for the Arab states or the Palestinians. Within that design, however, a large part of the American public was uniformly critical of Israel's actions in the West Bank and Gaza, finding them "too harsh." And while the PLO remained very low in American popularity, sympathy for the Palestinians in the West Bank and Gaza seemed to be on the increase. Surveys also found that about a quarter of the American people believed, in one wording or another, that "most American Jews are more loyal to Israel than to the United States." That figure was no higher than it had been in recent years, perhaps suggesting that no special backlash had set in against American Jews as a result of current events. Still, none of the surveys gave great comfort to American Jews, since political criticism of Israel often faulted the American Jewish community for allegedly walking in lock-step with Israeli foreign policy.

College campuses saw an increase in anti-Israel hostility and a number of overt anti-Semitic incidents during the year. At the University of Arizona, for example, a shot fired into the window of a Hillel lounge was linked to ABC-TV *Nightline* broadcasts about the *intifada*. The letters "PLO" were spray-painted in front of the Hillel building at one of the campuses of the University of Minnesota. Among the worst campus-based anti-Semitic incidents to take place during the 50th anniversary of *Kristallnacht* was the spray-painting of slogans, including "Kill the Kikes" and "Zionazi racists" on the wall of the Jewish Student Center at SUNY Binghamton. Although many of the campuses involved had substantial numbers of Arab students, which presumably accounted for the anti-Israel sentiment, there was concern about the wider effects of this activity on the thinking of other students, the potential future leadership of this country.

A related concern expressed by a number of Hillel directors was how the backlash was affecting Jewish college students. One Jewish Telegraphic Agency roundup in May reported that "some Hillel directors worried that Jewish students seemed slow to defend Israel, and expressed fear that these future leaders of tomorrow may be turning away from the pro-Israel position." This alleged weakening of Jewish college-student support of Israel reflected the widely asserted allegation that Jews in general were seriously split on the subject of Israel. The effect of such allegations on American Jewish status was problematic. On the one hand, an American Jewish split on Israel might presumably help to destroy both the image of a monolithic Jewish community and the notion that Jews were primarily loyal to Israel. On the other hand, any suggestion that American Jews were abandoning Israel might damage the still existing American consensus of support for Israel. That, in turn, apart from its effect on Israel, might accelerate an American public backlash against a Jewish population that continued to battle politically for Israel. As the substantial surveys of the *Los Angeles Times* and Steven Cohen both demonstrated, while American Jews were split in their opinions about Israeli strategy, they were still strongly consensual in their will to do political battle for American support of Israel. (See also "Jewish Communal Affairs," elsewhere in this volume.)

Hate Groups

Small but often connected anti-Semitic and racist groups continued to operate in America, and efforts continued to prosecute them when they crossed the line to violence. The Anti-Defamation League reported that some 70 such organizations were active and increasingly violent, although small in membership numbers.

The U.S. Justice Department reported that, from 1979 to 1985, more than 150 individuals had been prosecuted for racially motivated violence. In December 1987, five top leaders of the Order, an offshoot of the notorious racist group Aryan Nations, were sentenced to long prison terms. However, efforts to contain the extremist movement were set back when 13 white supremacists were acquitted of seditious conspiracy and other charges by a federal court in Arkansas, in April. (A 14th defendant had been acquitted earlier by the judge, for insufficient evidence.) The defendants—among whom were the five already jailed—were charged with conspiring to overthrow the government by force; conspiring to murder a federal judge and an FBI agent; and other charges, such as transporting stolen money. Those on trial, aside from being members of the Order, had variously been leaders or members of the Ku Klux Klan and of groups such as Identity and the Covenant, Sword and the Arm of the Lord, which subscribed to a doctrine of religious and racial superiority.

The accused uniformly held that they had only been exercising their constitutional rights to free expression and free association, and the judge frequently called the prosecution to task for presenting "hearsay" evidence. Groups that monitor right-wing activity saw the acquittal as a victory for the white supremacist movement, with its leaders now free to rebuild their organizations.

Of continuing concern were teenaged "skinhead" gangs, whose members shaved their heads, often wore swastikas, and were prone to engage in violent activity directed against Jews, blacks, or other minorities. An Anti-Defamation League (ADL) report released in March claimed that about two dozen such groups operated in a dozen states, with a combined membership of 1,000–1,500. Skinheads were arrested in many of these states for vandalism and assault. The skinheads seemed to epitomize the chief concern about extremist groups in America: not so much their membership numbers, which did not seem to increase significantly, but their apparently increasing propensity for overt action and violence. The ADL report also warned that skinheads were graduating into the network of adult white supremacist groups.

LYNDON LAROUCHE

Despite the fact that he himself was under indictment for fraud, Lyndon LaRouche's organization, the National Democratic Policy Committee, known for its anti-Semitic and other conspiracy theories, placed a number of political candidates in the field at the beginning of the year. In April, for example, it was revealed by unhappy Democratic party officials that 16 LaRouche members had filed for various state legislative and U.S. congressional seats to be decided at the June Democratic primary in Iowa. In the end, no LaRouche candidates were elected in any primary, except where uncontested, and none was elected to political office. The ADL reported that the LaRouche organization had expanded into Latin America, under the name of Partido Laboral. A former Panamanian consul-general in New York charged that General Manuel Noriega had given funds to the LaRouche organization, which then proceeded to attack U.S. senators who had been critical of Noriega. In December LaRouche and six of his top officials were convicted by a federal jury of conspiracy to defraud the Internal Revenue Service as well as a number of people who had loaned him millions of dollars.

Anti-Semitism

Even taking skinhead activity into account, the Anti-Defamation League's 1988 "Audit of Anti-Semitic Incidents" concluded that, while there had been an increase in reported incidents, "anti-Semitic vandalism, overwhelmingly, is not the work of organized hate groups." The audit reported 823 episodes of vandalism and desecration, fewer than in 1981 and 1982, but substantially higher than in 1987. The number of violent crimes, 28, was more than twice as many as in 1987; it included 7 cases of arson, 7 cases of attempted arson, 1 bombing, and 13 cemetery desecrations. About 60 percent of these acts of vandalism occurred in three states: New York and Florida, where the number of incidents had increased, and California, where it had decreased.

There were also reported 458 acts of anti-Semitic harassment, threats, and assaults against Jewish individuals and institutions, again the highest figure since 1982.

Of those, 21 were physical assaults against Jewish individuals. The most serious occurred in New York, in November, when a 19-year-old Yeshiva University student was beaten, stabbed, and robbed by a teenaged gang, to the accompaniment of anti-Semitic epithets.

In its audit of anti-Semitism, the ADL reported that "this year, for the first time, an external political event—namely, the West Bank/Gaza Palestinian 'uprising'—was clearly related to a high number of anti-Semitic incidents in the U.S." The perpetrators of almost 10 percent of reported anti-Semitic incidents, including bomb threats, vandalism, and other harassment, indicated explicitly that their actions were motivated by anti-Israel sentiments related to the Palestinian Arab *intifada*. In previous years, fewer than 1 percent of the episodes had revealed an anti-Israel connection. In this count, anti-Israel expressions were not in themselves considered anti-Semitic. It was only when, for example, synagogues were vandalized in company with anti-Israel graffiti, or harassment was accompanied by anti-Israel statements, that the acts were counted as anti-Semitic. It was not known how many more anti-Semitic incidents may have been rooted in anti-Israel animosity but not so labeled. Nor was it known how many of these anti-Israel references were simply used as a matter of convenience by perpetrators who would have engaged in anti-Semitic actions in any case.

In the week commemorating the 50th anniversary of *Kristallnacht* (November 9), when the media and Jewish agencies turned public attention to that night of ominous Nazi savagery, a substantial rise in anti-Semitic incidents was noted. According to the ADL, more than 60 incidents involving anti-Semitic graffiti and threats were reported during the week of November 6–13. An average weekly total was about 15.

"JAP"-BAITING

Reports continued of "JAP-baiting" on a number of college campuses, as did debate over the causes, seriousness, and implications of the phenomenon. It appeared that long-popular and relatively harmless (if still offensive) "JAP" (Jewish American Princess) jokes, which made fun of Jewish women for being pampered and materialistic, had escalated into something more ominous—abusive language and behavior. Jewish women at some university football games were heckled with shouts of "JAP! JAP!" and were exposed to "JAPS Do Not Enter" signs with swastikas, vulgar graffiti in libraries, and similar occurrences. A nationally distributed guide to campuses, produced by the *Yale Daily News*, referred to the prevalence of JAPS at certain schools.

Dr. Gary Spencer, a Syracuse University sociology professor who had made a study of the subject, said, "We have documented incidents at approximately 100 different institutions. This is not solely a campus phenomenon. It reflects what is occurring in the larger community." Indeed, the stereotype was perpetuated by some Jews as well. Two Jewish male student disk jockeys at the radio station of American University ran a "Biggest JAP on Campus" contest, and a Jewish fraternity offered "Slap-a-Jap" T-shirts at a college carnival. In Coral Gables, Florida, the Jewish owner of a boutique called PAJ (JAP spelled backwards), offered a "JAP discount" in newspaper ads. When Jewish groups remonstrated with her, she said: "I'm fulfilling my lifelong dream (to be a Jewish American Princess) and I don't understand why my own are trying to take it away from me."

The existence of the problem was first exposed in the Fall 1987 issue of *Lilith*, a Jewish feminist magazine, and through a press conference convened jointly by the magazine and the American Jewish Committee in September of that year. Social analysts saw the emergence of hostile JAP stereotyping—at a time when Jewish women were increasingly career-oriented and the "princess" had virtually disappeared—as an outlet for several attitudes: hostility of Jewish men toward Jewish women, Jewish self-hatred, sexism, and anti-Semitism. They noted that precisely because overt expressions of anti-Semitism were now regarded as taboo, the JAP stereotype offered an ideal vehicle for anti-Jewish feelings, socially sanctioned precisely because it was started by Jews and perpetuated by them.

In an article in *Newsweek* (May 23, 1988), Laura Shapiro wrote that "until recently Jewish organizations have been reluctant to confront the problem, partly because it was seen as a women's issue and hence unimportant, and partly because the earliest jokes and images originated with Jews themselves. . . ." Jewish feminists and their supporters sought to raise public consciousness of the problem through articles, conferences, media interviews, and other means. Hillels and other Jewish organizations did their best to discourage offensive graffiti and T-shirts and other expressions of the JAP stereotype. But they still had to overcome some reluctance to regard JAP-baiting and JAP jokes as a serious issue.

EVALUATING ANTI-SEMITISM

If most of the anti-Semitic vandalism and violence was "not the work of organized hate groups," what did it represent? Was a tidal wave of popular anti-Semitic sentiment gathering force among Americans? Judging from public-opinion polls, there was no evidence of such a rising tide in the expressed attitudes of Americans. The *Los Angeles Times* survey asked the question usually considered key to ferreting out serious anti-Semitic animosity: "Do the Jews have too much power?" About 15 percent of Americans answered affirmatively, a proportion at the lower end of responses elicited by that question in recent years. In April the Roper Organization asked the same question in a multiple-choice design: "Which groups do you believe have too much power in the U.S.?" About 8 percent of Americans designated the Jews, the usual multiple-choice level in recent years. But more than 8 percent of Americans said they believed that the Catholic Church, the blacks, and the Orientals each had too much power, and about 20 percent said that Arab interests had too much power. Cohen's American Jewish Committee survey found that white non-Jewish Americans felt just as "favorable" toward Jews as they did toward Catholics and mainstream Protestants and about twice as "favorable" toward Jews as toward fundamentalist Protestants.

According to the Anti-Defamation League, some 80 to 90 percent of those apprehended for anti-Semitic violence were teenagers, which raised the possibility that if there was in fact a new "wave" of hostility toward Jews, it might be found among adolescent Americans. Indeed, much attention was given to racial and anti-Semitic incidents on the campuses of colleges and universities. The National Institute Against Prejudice and Violence said that it had recorded incidents motivated by racial or religious prejudice at 81 institutions of higher learning since the fall of 1986.

However, despite the JAP phenomenon and incidents of anti-Semitism on at least several dozen major campuses around the country, public-opinion surveys showed no evidence of increased anti-Semitism in the expressed attitudes of young Americans. When, for example, the response elicited by the Roper Organization on Jewish power was broken down by age, the negative response by younger Americans was a bit lower than that of other age groups and showed no signs of having increased from the past.

The hypothesis prevailed, as it had in recent years, that the phenomenon at hand was not so much an increase in the ranks of attitudinal anti-Semites as a rise in the level of licentious violence, a continuing breakdown in civility among the young in general. For example, various law enforcement agencies, as well as the Anti-Defamation League, cautioned that while all skinheads had a potential for violence, they were not all overtly anti-Semitic or racist. In Milwaukee, members of a local group calling itself the Skinhead Army of Milwaukee were described by a local Jewish official as being more "thugs" than white supremacists. Their violence had, so far, not been directed at Jewish or black individuals or institutions.

A general decline in civility was suggested on many levels. In June the National Gay and Lesbian Task Force recorded a 42-percent rise in reported incidents directed against homosexuals in the country. Over 7,000 such incidents, "ranging from verbal abuse to murder," had been reported in the preceding year. And heightened teenage gang violence in general was noted in every large city, typically associated with drug traffic. Young bigots also presumably participated in this permissive climate, expressing their bigotry more violently. Conversely, bigotry—including anti-Semitism—presumably served to provide a specific edge to generalized violent activity, as it had in the past.

There were, however, reassuring signs. In this election year, Jewish candidates for office, as detailed above, did not meet anti-Semitic opposition, nor were they shunned by overwhelmingly non-Jewish constituencies. And governments—federal, state, and local—responded swiftly and positively to anti-Semitic incidents. (Police departments in 19 states reported 124 arrests in connection with such incidents.) In addition, hate-crimes laws were promulgated in a number of localities around the country. In June President Ronald Reagan signed into law a bill passed by the U.S.

Congress to provide criminal penalties for damage to religious property. The new law imposed fines of up to $250,000 and/or ten years in prison for anyone convicted of causing more than $10,000 in damage to a religious institution or cemetery, or causing serious bodily injury to anyone trying to exercise his or her religious beliefs.

Another bill introduced this year would require the Justice Department to gather statistics and report annually on crimes against persons or property because of race, religion, ethnic origin, or sexual orientation. The need for such an annual report was emphasized by a study released in January by the Center for Democratic Renewal. The study indicated that about 3,000 prejudice-related incidents had taken place in the United States between 1980 and 1986 but noted that this figure was based mainly on unofficial sources, because only Virginia, Maryland, and Pennsylvania kept careful official figures on hate crimes. Rabbi James Rudin, director of interreligious affairs for the American Jewish Committee, supported the need for a federal reporting procedure, saying that the hate crime "is not a regional issue—as some might have thought years ago—it is a national issue." He added that such a reporting procedure would be "like tracking a disease."

The federal reporting bill was passed by the House of Representatives in May, 383-29. It also passed the Senate Judiciary Committee, but did not pass in the full Senate and was expected to be reintroduced in the next congressional session. Meanwhile, 5 more states passed hate-crime laws, lifting to a total of 43 the number of states that had passed such legislation.

Soviet Jewry

The American Jewish community had no serious reason this year to doubt its political status or influence with respect to American policy on Soviet Jews, although some difficulty did develop over immigration policy.

In the aftermath of the December 1987 rally, held on the eve of a Reagan-Gorbachev summit, when more than 200,000 people attended the largest ever Soviet Jewry event in Washington, D.C., the American government continued to press the Soviet government for increased emigration. Thus, in May, President Reagan made a point on his first trip to the Soviet Union to hold a highly visible meeting with refuseniks and dissidents, clearly offending his hosts in the process. Yuli Kosharovsky, one of the leading refuseniks, addressed the president at that meeting, which helped focus international attention on the emigration issue. In fact, emigration increased during the year and Jewish cultural opportunities were expanded, leading some to conclude that the overall situation for Soviet Jews had improved significantly.

In the wake of these developments, the Israeli government renewed its pressure on the American government not to allow Soviet Jews who had received Israeli visas to come to the United States under "refugee" provisions. While the American Jewish community was, by and large, sensitive to Israel's concern—the proportion of Soviet Jews choosing America over Israel reached 95 percent some months—it was also committed to the principle of freedom of choice. As evidence grew that the Soviets would allow increased applications to the United States, and in order to avoid the potential for rancorous debate, American Jewish leaders began promoting a dual-track system. Soviet Jews seeking to come to the United States would be encouraged to apply directly for American visas, and Soviet Jews with Israeli visas would be required to go directly to Israel.

Ironically, as American Jews began to spread the word about the dual-track system, and as emigration of Soviet Jews increased significantly, the American government, for the first time, began denying refugee status to a number of individual Soviet Jews seeking to immigrate to the United States. Funds for refugee resettlement were exhausted, and the American government had begun to take a closer look at whether every Soviet Jew had a "well-founded fear of persecution." A backlog began to build of thousands of applicants waiting to be processed by an American embassy officer in Moscow. Near Rome, a colony of Soviet Jews waiting for permission to enter the United States began to swell in numbers. At year's end, the American Jewish community and the American government were amicably seeking some way to reduce the numbers of people waiting and to resolve the question of refugee status. (See also "Jewish Communal Affairs," elsewhere in this volume.)

Holocaust-Related Matters

In January the Vatican announced that Pope John Paul II would meet with Austrian president Kurt Waldheim during a visit to Austria in June. For American Jews this announcement rekindled the controversy with the Catholic Church dating from the pope's warm embrace of Waldheim at their meeting in Rome a year earlier.

A month later, the international commission of historians established by the Austrian government to investigate Waldheim's wartime activities issued its report. Although it concluded that "no proof" was found that Waldheim had committed war crimes, the report criticized him sharply for failing to intervene in, or protest, mass deportations and atrocities that he knew were occurring. The panel head, Swiss military historian Rudolff Kurz, said that Waldheim had concealed and lied about his wartime activities. Israeli panel member Prof. Yehuda Wallach maintained that the report contained enough information to bring criminal proceedings against Waldheim for being a participant in illegal activities. In the wake of calls for his resignation, Waldheim defended himself yet again and added that "it must be our holy obligation to do everything to see that the crimes of that time will not be repeated."

When the pope met with Waldheim in Vienna in June, a small group of American Jewish demonstrators, dressed in concentration-camp uniforms, protested outside the Austrian leader's office. The pope's failure to mention Jews in remarks made on a visit to Mauthausen concentration camp, and his reference to Austria as a victim of Nazism, provoked strong condemnation from American Jewish leaders. Elie Wiesel, summing up the feelings of many, wrote in the *New York Post* (June 28) that the pope wanted to "de-Judaize the Holocaust" with his "strange and offensive behavior whenever he is confronted by the cruelest event in recorded history. . . . It is now clear: This pope has a problem with Jews, just as Jews have a problem with him. His understanding for living Jews is as limited as his compassion for dead Jews. . . ."

FORMER NAZIS

This year saw the conclusion of the trial in Jerusalem of John Demjanjuk, for his participation in the murder of some 800,000 Jews killed in the gas chambers at Treblinka death camp. (Demjanjuk had been stripped of his U.S. citizenship and extradited to Israel in 1986.) On April 18, he was found guilty of crimes against humanity, war crimes, crimes against the Jewish people, murder, and other offenses. The court concluded that the cumulative evidence furnished proof that the 69-year-old retired automobile worker from Cleveland, Ohio, was in fact "Ivan the Terrible," who brutalized Jews as he herded them into the gas chamber. On April 25, he was sentenced to death under the 1950 Nazi and Nazi Collaborators Law. (Adolf Eichmann was the only other former Nazi ever sentenced to death by an Israeli court, in 1962.) Defense attorney Yoram Sheftel appealed the verdict, citing insufficient evidence and a lynch-mob atmosphere.

In the United States, legal proceedings against ex-Nazis continued. In a rare case, in February a 76-year-old Jew from Brooklyn was stripped of his American citizenship for collaborating with the Nazis and brutalizing Jewish concentration-camp inmates. Jacob Tannenbaum confessed to having been a kapo at the Goerlitz concentration camp in Germany. Tannenbaum, whose parents, five sisters, first wife, and their baby were killed in the Holocaust, and who was in ill health, was not deported.

In a report issued in June, the Justice Department admitted that convicted Nazi war criminal Robert Jan Verbelen—a resident of Austria—and at least 13 other former Nazis had worked for the U.S. Army's Counter Intelligence Corps in Vienna from 1946 to 1956, but claimed it had no evidence of Verbelen's true identity before mid-1956.

Controversy surrounded the case of 83-year-old Boleslav Maikovskis, a Long Island resident who had served as police chief in Nazi-occupied Latvia, where hundreds of civilians were murdered. In October it was discovered that he had secretly fled to West Germany in 1987, presumably to avoid deportation to the Soviet Union, which had sentenced him to death in absentia in 1965. The Anti-Defamation League accused the Justice Department—which denied the charge—of covering up his flight. West German authorities arrested Maikovskis soon after his arrival, on war-crimes charges.

On another front, in October the U.S. Congress finally passed a bill making genocide a crime in the United States. The bill, named the Proxmire Act after the senator who had led the ratification fight for 20 years, implemented the United

Nations Convention Against Genocide. Anyone convicted of "incitement to genocide" would face a fine of up to $500,000 and/or 5 years in prison—and a fine of up to $1 million and/or 20 years in prison if the act resulted in death.

In other government action, the U.S. Environmental Protection Agency barred scientists, on ethical grounds, from including data from Nazi medical experiments in a report on the effects of a toxic gas. And the National Jewish Commission on Law and Public Affairs (COLPA) challenged the decision of the Internal Revenue Service to grant tax-exempt status to the German American Information and Education Association, a group which denied that the Holocaust took place.

HOLOCAUST EDUCATION

Meanwhile, government-assisted efforts to foster awareness of the Holocaust continued. The Department of Defense distributed a book entitled *Days of Remembrance* to American armed forces, urging that programs and ceremonies be planned during the week of remembrance in the spring. In October President Reagan dedicated the cornerstone of the U.S. Holocaust Memorial Museum on the National Mall in Washington, D.C. At the ceremony he stated that "the Jewish people will never stand alone against tyranny." The museum, scheduled for opening in late 1990, had embarked on a $170-million fund-raising campaign.

Finally, it was reported in October that, as part of a growing trend, eight states—New York, California, Pennsylvania, New Jersey, Ohio, Tennessee, Virginia, and Connecticut—and a number of cities had adopted curricula for teaching about the Holocaust to high-school students.

All 50 governors and over 150 mayors issued proclamations to commemorate the 50th anniversary of *Kristallnacht*, urging their constituents to "always strive to overcome prejudice and inhumanity through understanding, vigilance and resistance."

Black-Jewish Relations

The Jesse Jackson phenomenon was a prominent element in the year's black-Jewish relations, but Jews and blacks viewed him in different contexts. Jews tended to see Jackson as inseparably anti-Israel and anti-Semitic, and were particularly bothered in 1988 by his political stand on the Middle East. Blacks did not see Jackson primarily in the context of the Middle East. Roper's survey in April found that while 29 percent of white Americans found Israel's response to the Palestinian uprising "too harsh," only 27 percent of black Americans agreed, even though Jackson referred often to what he considered Israel's harsh response. In short, while most Jews tended to see Jackson as primarily reflecting a black point of view on Israel, most blacks tended to see Jackson as primarily reflecting a black point of view on domestic affairs. It was not clear what the long-range effect of Jackson's candidacy would be on black-Jewish relations.

Otherwise, 1988 was a mixed year for black-Jewish relations, beginning and ending with calls for cooperation and reconciliation, but with a number of tense encounters in between.

In April it was learned—through some tapes acquired by the Anti-Defamation League—that Steve Cokely, an aide to Chicago's mayor Eugene Sawyer, had delivered a series of virulently anti-Semitic speeches to the Nation of Islam, headed by Louis Farrakhan. Among the accusations he made were that Jews were conspiring to rule the world and that "the AIDS epidemic is a result of doctors, especially Jewish ones, who inject AIDS into blacks." Sawyer hesitated nearly a week before firing Cokely. Jewish leaders were outraged over the slow response by Sawyer and other black leaders, especially as only 3 of the 18 black aldermen on the Chicago City Council called for Cokely's dismissal. Some black leaders, in turn, were upset over the dismissal of Cokely as a perceived result of Jewish pressure. In a piece in the *New York Times* (July 26), Prof. Eugene Kennedy of Loyola of Chicago wrote: "Virulent anti-Semitism has gripped Chicago's black community. Nobody morally powerful enough to try to combat it, including the Rev. Jesse Jackson, who lives here has attempted to do so."

Jewish leaders in Chicago took a less alarmist view than Kennedy, pointing to a *Chicago Tribune* poll which indicated that only 8 percent of blacks thought Cokely should have been kept in office. In the ensuing weeks and months, clergy and lay leaders representing Chicago's black and Jewish communities cooperated on joint statements denouncing "all expressions of anti-Semitism, racism and other forms of bigotry, to prevent them from gaining legitimacy," and in a series of meetings in churches and synagogues to stress the "historic ties" between the two groups.

Several other incidents around the country also aggravated black-Jewish relations. In April a speech at the University of Pennsylvania by Louis Farrakhan, in which he blamed Jews for instituting black slavery in America, was protested by more than a thousand Jewish students. At the University of Massachusetts, Julius Lester, a black professor of Afro-American studies and a convert to Judaism, who criticized black author James Baldwin for anti-Semitic remarks he had made, was forced out of the department in a unanimous vote of its faculty members. The move to oust Lester from that department actually began after the publication in 1987 of his book *Lovesong*, which chronicled the steps leading to Lester's conversion, and was brought to a head over the Baldwin issue. Many saw the ouster as a blow to academic freedom. In the meantime, Lester joined the university's department of Judaic studies.

In Los Angeles, a racist memo laying out a plan for a Jewish-financed campaign to defeat black mayor Tom Bradley was made public in August. The memo, prepared by two political campaign professionals for Jewish city councilman Zev Yaroslavsky, said in part, "You've got 50 IQ points on him (and that's no compliment). . . . But your IQ advantage is of no electoral use if you don't use it." Yaroslavsky immediately dissociated himself from the memo, emphasized his "high personal regard" for the mayor, and ultimately dropped out of the race.

These incidents were offset by an equal number of new attempts to reaffirm the importance of the traditional black-Jewish alliance. In January the Israel embassy in Washington held its fourth annual observance of Martin Luther King, Jr.'s birthday. Some 300 Jews and blacks attended the event, although some black leaders stayed away in protest of Israeli policies in the West Bank and Gaza. Ambassador Moshe Arad said, "We fervently hope that the spirit of peace and reconciliation exemplified in Dr. King's life and work will overcome the forces of evil and hatred and violence in the world today. This has always been the hope of the Jewish people."

In April boxing promoter Don King contributed $75,000 to be administered by B'nai B'rith to launch the Don King Center for Black-Jewish Relations in Washington, D.C. "Blacks and Jews have both known discrimination and oppression," King said. "Blacks and Jews have much to gain from cooperation and much to lose from antagonism."

In Oklahoma, in May, in the aftermath of a resurgence of anti-Semitic and racist graffiti, black and Jewish groups organized a "Say No to Hate" campaign. Black and Jewish groups had been working closely in the state to combat anti-Semitism among farming families.

In October the American Jewish Committee's National Leadership Conference on Black-Jewish Relations sponsored a conference at Wingspread in Wisconsin for religious, political, academic, and business leaders from the Jewish and black communities. At a follow-up meeting it was agreed that a "code of community conduct" should be developed. The code would offer guidance "so that all aspects of social and economic life can proceed with a minimum of racism, bigotry and discrimination."

Finally, in November Jewish and black veterans of early civil-rights battles came together in Atlanta, Georgia, for a reunion and a reaffirmation of their commitment to the cause. Nearly 100 civil-rights veterans spent two days at the gathering, called "The Black-Jewish Alliance: Reunion and Renewal," which was videotaped as part of a planned archive of black-Jewish history. Among the recollections recorded was that of Jewish community-relations official Charney Bromberg on meeting an elderly black woman in Mississippi in 1963. She immediately said she knew he was Jewish, "because Jews are the best Christians."

Civil Rights

Affirmative-action controversies, which sometimes exacerbated Jewish-black relations, continued to occupy the courts. In June the Supreme Court expanded the use of statistical evidence by employees to prove bias (*Watson v. Ft. Worth*). A black woman in Texas had been barred by a lower court from using "disparate-impact" statistics to prove that she was discriminated against because she was black. (In most cases, "disparate impact," demonstrated by statistical patterns of employment, is easier to prove than "disparate treatment," or intentional discrimination.) The

Justice Department argued against the acceptance of a "disparate-impact theory," saying that it would lead to quotas. But the main Court opinion, written by Justice Sandra Day O'Connor, held that statistics could be used as a factor in determining discrimination.

The Supreme Court also upheld a 1984 New York City law aimed primarily at requiring the admission of women to private clubs that presumably had a role in business life. The Court left open the possibility that certain genuinely private clubs had a constitutional right to discriminate with respect to race, sex, or other characteristics, under the First Amendment freedom of association.

Interreligious Matters

One issue in the area of interreligious relations that captured public attention in 1988 was a Hollywood film, *The Last Temptation of Christ*, which was released in late summer and received mixed, though largely favorable, reviews from the critics. Primarily because it portrayed Jesus imagining himself—in his final moments—living a normal family life, including sexual relations, the film was accused by some Christians of being blasphemous. It was denounced prior to its screening by major fundamentalist and other religious leaders around the country who called for picket lines and boycotts.

Some of the protests focused on Lew Wasserman and other Jewish principals in the MCA company that owned Universal Pictures, the distributor of the film, and warned of a "backlash against Jews." The fact, well advertised, that the film was directed by a Roman Catholic (Martin Scorsese) and based on a book by a Greek Orthodox (Nikos Kazantzakis), did not stop several ugly anti-Semitic incidents, including a demonstration on July 20, led by Rev. Robert Hymers, head of the Baptist Tabernacle of Los Angeles, outside Lew Wasserman's home.

The Campus Crusade for Christ at the University of Georgia agreed not to seek out Jews specifically for conversion. The Jews for Jesus organization sued the Jewish Comunity Relations Council in New York, alleging that the JCRC threatened a boycott against a Catskill Mountains country club unless it backed out of a contract with Jews for Jesus. A Presbyterian nursery school in Los Angeles told its Jewish teachers that they would be dismissed unless they expressed their faith in Jesus. This led a number of parents, non-Jews as well as Jews, to withdraw their children. And the California State Supreme Court ruled in October that two former members of the Unification Church could sue the church on grounds of deception and brainwashing, "because freedom of religion does not protect fraudulent recruiting."

A number of American rabbis refused to attend a scheduled meeting with Joseph Cardinal Ratzinger on January 27 because of his earlier statement that the proper Christian approach to dialogue was to maintain that Judaism finds its fulfillment in Christianity. Among those who declined the invitation to meet with Cardinal Ratzinger, a close adviser to Pope John Paul II, were Rabbi Wolfe Kelman, executive vice-president of the Rabbinical Assembly, Rabbi Henry Michelman, executive vice-president of the Synagogue Council, and Rabbi Marc Tanenbaum of the American Jewish Committee, who said that the cardinal's expressed view on dialogue "calls for the most thorough examination and reflection."

At a news conference the next day, however, Cardinal Ratzinger stated that Catholics should "respect the point of view of our Jewish brothers. . . . We must be able to read the Old Testament the way the Jews read the Old Testament, rather than always looking at it from a Christian perspective." Other attempts to repair relations included an announcement at the end of the year that a Jewish-Vatican conference would be organized to explore the roots of Christian anti-Semitism.

Church-State Issues

At the beginning of the year, the U.S. armed services agreed to permit Jewish personnel to wear yarmulkes routinely, following the signing of an amendment to that effect in the Defense Authorization Law. Rep. Stephen Solarz (D., N.Y.) led the effort in the House and Sen. Frank Lautenberg (D., N.J.), in the Senate.

In a widely publicized matter, Sen. Daniel Inouye (D., Hawaii) acknowledged that he had made a mistake in judgment in sponsoring an $8-million appropriation for the Jewish education of North African refugees in France. The project was supported by a campaign contributor, but opposed by the State Department, the UN refugee agency, and the French government. Following public criticism (although most American Jewish groups remained silent), Inouye moved to rescind the appropriation.

In February the Supreme Court refused to hear an appeal from fundamentalist Christian families in Tennessee who objected to some of the textbooks used in their children's elementary school. The U.S. Court of Appeals ruling that the children must use the books taught in school (*Mozert v. Hawkins County Public Schools*) thus stood. Objections had been made against books ranging from *The Wizard of Oz* to *The Diary of Anne Frank*.

In March the New York State Court of Appeals dismissed an appeal challenging the constitutionality of an *eruv* in Belle Harbor, Queens. (An *eruv* is an unobtrusive boundary marker around an area that permits observant Jews within its limits to carry objects on the Sabbath.) In the initial ruling, Justice Aaron Goldstein held that the *eruv* was a valid accommodation of the religious needs of a minority.

In April a federal appeals court in New York overturned a lower court's ruling that would have required a school in North Babylon, Long Island, to accommodate the religious beliefs of David Smith, an Orthodox Jew, by not holding its high school graduation on a Saturday. The court decided that Smith would not be denied his diploma by reason of not attending the graduation ceremony and therefore "the burden being placed on David Smith's free exercise of his religious belief simply makes the practice of his religion more difficult than the practice of other religions."

In October the Supreme Court agreed to hear its first case involving the constitutionality of a Hanukkah menorah display. At issue was the display of an 18-foot-high menorah standing alongside a Christmas tree, on the steps of Pittsburgh city hall. In this case (*ACLU et al. v. County of Allegheny and City of Pittsburgh*), the Chabad organization (Lubavitcher Hassidim), which owned the menorah, joined with the city and county in filing an appeal. They jointly argued that it was not only constitutionally permissible for the city to permit display of a menorah alongside a Christmas tree, but the city might be required to ensure such equal treatment of majority and minority religions. In the 1986 suit brought by the ACLU, the U.S. Court of Appeals for the Third Circuit ruled earlier in the year that the Constitution barred both the 18-foot-high menorah at city hall and a nativity scene placed on a staircase landing inside the Allegheny County courthouse near city hall, because the displays were evidence of unconstitutional establishment of religion.

The Supreme Court also agreed to hear the case of an Illinois man (*Frazee v. Department of Employment Security*) who claimed he was denied state unemployment benefits as a result of his refusal to work on Sunday, his Sabbath. The court was to decide whether an individual must demonstrate that he is a member of a formal religious group which requires strict Sabbath observance. In this case, the man belonged to no organized church or denomination.

Throughout the year, President Reagan continued to endorse the concept of a constitutional amendment permitting school prayer, but there was no serious activity in response.

Among the most difficult issues for the American Jewish community was the matter of church-state separation and child-care legislation. The organized Jewish community actively supported, in concept, major national legislation to provide funding for child care. Since church-based centers, as major providers of child care, would be among the chief recipients of federal funds, debate ensued about how to build in protections to ensure separation of church and state. Open controversy on this issue broke out in late August and September as House and Senate committees debated a proposed $2.5-billion child-care measure. As originally drafted, the bill not only barred church-based centers from engaging in "any sectarian purpose or activity" if they accepted federal funds but also required the removal of all religious symbols and the hiring of all staff members without regard to their religion. The U.S. Catholic Conference found these last two provisions unacceptable, and they were removed from the bill. As a result, other members of the coalition supporting the bill, including the National Education Association, the National PTA, a Baptist committee, and the American Jewish Committee, now also found the bill unacceptable.

EARL RAAB
DOUGLAS KAHN

The United States, Israel, and the Middle East

THE YEAR 1988 WAS unusual in America's relations with Israel and the Middle East: It was characterized by frenetic diplomatic activity during a period when both the United States and Israel were conducting national elections. The pattern during the previous decade had been that elections, either in the United States or Israel, signaled a time for pause. Not so in 1988.

What was different this time? Principally, it was the new ingredient in the Arab-Israeli cauldron, the *intifada*. Begun in December 1987, the uprising in the Israeli-occupied territories of the West Bank and Gaza became the overarching event of 1988, its impact felt strongly in Israel, in Jordan, among the Palestinians, in the United States, and within the American Jewish community.

While there was a rising feeling among many of the concerned parties that, as a result of the uprising, the status quo was no longer viable, the implications of the new situation were seen differently by them. For some in Israel it implied the need for Israel to make a new peace offer involving major territorial concessions; for others it offered evidence that Jews and Arabs could not live together and that some movement of population was necessary. For King Hussein of Jordan, it meant a reassessment of his relationship to the Palestinians and the West Bank. For Yasir Arafat, it raised new questions about his relations with Israel, the residents of the territories, and the United States. And for the United States, there was a new urgency based not so much on the fundamental interests that had impelled American involvement in the 1970s—matters of oil supplies and the U.S. conflict with the Soviet Union—but on the perception that the *intifada* was both a heightening of the conflict and a moment of opportunity.

November elections in the United States and Israel brought new governments into office, but if they differed significantly from their predecessors, this was not immediately apparent. The *intifada* continued unabated. Only at the end of the year did the landscape change dramatically, by virtue of one event. This was the American decision to open a dialogue with the Palestine Liberation Organization (PLO), following a series of statements by its head, Yasir Arafat, which were interpreted as meeting U.S. demands that the PLO accept Israel and renounce terrorism.

The Intifada *and U.S.-Israeli Relations*

As the year began it became clearer that the rioting in the territories that had started on December 9, 1987, was qualitatively different from previous waves of unrest there during the 21 years of Israeli occupation. Apart from being increasingly well organized and involving all segments of Palestinian society, the depth of feeling expressed seemed to ensure that the violence would endure for some time. This was a new factor to be reckoned with in assessing possible resolutions of the Arab-Israeli, and more specifically the Palestinian-Israeli, conflict.

The uprising took on a predictable pattern. Demonstrators, sometimes in Gaza, sometimes in the West Bank, sometimes in both places, would confront Israeli soldiers daily, burning tires, setting up barricades, throwing rocks or firebombs. Israel reacted with a variety of measures—shooting at attackers, firing tear gas, arresting demonstrators. Boycotting Palestinian shopowners were forced to reopen their shops. Israel's military and police forces were reinforced. Alleged leaders of the uprising were arrested and deported. By the end of 1987 more than 20 Palestinians had been killed and 1,200 Palestinians detained. (By the end of 1988, some 300 Palestinians had been killed, according to the Israel Defense Forces count, and over 5,000 were in jail, including 1,500 under administrative detention.)

Israel's handling of the *intifada* was a source of continuing tension between Washington and Jerusalem during the year. While American policymakers took a much more balanced approach to events in the territories than did the rest of the world, there were continuing exchanges, if not confrontations, between the two governments concerning the situation. Overall, the United States tended to focus on specific Israeli abuses, rather than engage in broad condemnation. Even when reservations were expressed about Israel's use of violence, there was also recognition of Israel's right and responsibility to restore law and order. However, when Israel's defense minister spoke of a policy of "beatings" or of using plastic bullets to deter the demonstrators, American officials reacted with criticism.

American objections were strongest in regard to one issue: Israel's decision to expel those it considered leaders of the *intifada*. The U.S. administration repeatedly expressed opposition to these deportations; voted with the other Security Council members on one resolution speaking to this matter; and hinted that should Israel expand its deportation policy, the fundamental U.S.-Israeli relationship could be damaged.

Israel's response to U.S. reactions reflected the many dilemmas embodied in the relationship. Israelis felt under siege—from the Palestinians, from the media, from the international community—and looked to the United States for support. When it came, such as in the U.S. refusal to go along with many UN resolutions condemning Israel, or when the American president defended Israeli actions at a televised press conference, Israel welcomed it. On the other hand, when the United States once voted with the other Security Council members in condemning Israel, or when a strong State Department letter was conveyed to Israel about its behavior, Israeli officials expressed surprise and disappointment. Still, all in all, at year's end the relationship remained fundamentally intact, its true strength reflected in its ability to withstand the many emotional exchanges caused by Israel's anxieties and U.S. concerns.

AMERICAN RESPONSES TO ISRAELI ACTIONS

The administration had expressed unreserved opposition in late December 1987 to proposed Israeli expulsions of Palestinian activists. On January 3, Israel announced that it would expel nine Palestinians, five from the West Bank and four from Gaza, who were described as the "chief instigators" of the uprising and senior organizers of the PLO and Muslim fundamentalist groups in the territories. The nine Palestinians were allowed to appeal their expulsions to a military review board and, if that failed, to the Israeli Supreme Court. Within Israel there was virtually no criticism of the expulsion order.

On January 5, the United States joined with the rest of the UN Security Council in unanimously adopting a resolution calling on Israel to drop plans to deport the Palestinians. This was the first time the U.S. delegate had voted in favor of a Security Council resolution criticizing Israel's handling of the uprising. Indeed, the last time the United States had voted in favor of a Security Council measure against Israel was in 1982, during Israel's siege of Beirut. Before that, in 1981, the United States backed two such resolutions, one declaring Israel's annexation of the Golan Heights "null and void," the other criticizing Israel for bombing the Iraqi nuclear reactor. On the latest occasion, U.S. deputy representative Herbert S. Okun indicated that his government opposed deportation of Palestinians and believed that Israel had used unnecessarily harsh measures to restore order in the territories. The following day, Israel expressed "regret and disappointment" over the U.S. vote, and an Israeli Foreign Ministry official expressed surprise: "We thought they would just abstain." The State Department immediately played down the significance of the vote, denying that it represented any deterioration in U.S.-Israeli relations. State Department spokesman Charles Redman described the relationship as "very strong" and said the U.S. action was in direct "continuity" with its long-standing opposition to the Israeli practice of deportations. Secretary of State George P. Shultz was reported to have reassured a delegation representing American Jewish organizations that the vote did not mark any shift in the relationship.

On January 13, Israel carried out the deportation of four of the Palestinians, after they had withdrawn their appeals on the grounds that they were denied access to evidence they contended had been arbitrarily ruled secret. An Israeli army helicopter flew the four from a prison in Nablus to an area in southern Lebanon, just north of Israel's security zone on the border. The State Department said it was an action "we deeply regret." The following day the Security Council adopted a second resolution, calling on Israel to cancel the deportations and to allow those already deported to return home. This time the United States abstained. American ambassador to the UN Vernon A. Walters indicated that while the administration of President Ronald Reagan remained opposed to the deportations, it would abstain, because repeatedly raising the issue did not help the situation. Reports indicated that following the prior vote the administration had decided to avoid associating itself with any further council criticism of Israel's handling of the riots and would make its views known directly to Israel.

Defense Minister Yitzhak Rabin of Israel indicated in an interview on January 18 that the disturbances were the most difficult and widespread Israel had yet faced but vowed to bring the unrest to a "manageable" level. He described the protests as difficult because of "the number, frequency, and the simultaneous public disorders." Most significantly, he said that "whatever started it, it started without any instructions from outside. It took the PLO leadership two to four days to catch up." Rabin said Israel would continue to use tough measures, such as curfews, curbs on the press, and large troop deployments, but he emphasized that restoring law and order was only an interim measure and that political negotiations among Israel, Jordan, and Palestinians from the territories would be necessary for a long-term solution.

The following day Rabin announced a new policy to deal with the uprising: "The first priority is to use force, might, beatings." A senior Israeli military source explained that the new policy was meant as a substitute for using live ammunition. The State Department's Redman indicated that the United States was "disturbed by the adoption of a policy . . . that calls for beatings as a means to restore or maintain order."

The reaction to Rabin's words and to stories of some 200 Palestinians being treated for broken bones or other serious injuries from beatings in the first few days after Rabin's announcement was one of widespread criticism. Israel's ambassador to Washington, Moshe Arad, appearing on Israeli television, said that the damage to Israel was most heavy and had "hurt Israel's image of being an enlightened country." Other criticism came from the American Jewish community, including Morris Abram of the Conference of Presidents of Major American Jewish Organizations and Alexander Schindler of the Union of American Hebrew Congregations. Israel's police minister, Haim Bar Lev, said on January 24, following a cabinet meeting, "There is no beating. This is an unfortunate term." Despite the criticism, Rabin said on January 25 that he still believed the beatings policy in general was "the right one" and that it helped produce "a relative calm." He explained that the beatings were to be used only against rioters and only "while the violence is going on—not after, not before."

Although the outside world was harsh in its condemnation of Israel's conduct, there was little public debate on the subject in Israel. Pollster Hanoch Smith explained that "the riots have aroused hostility on the part of the Israeli population," and "when these eruptions take place, it presses people to take a harder stand." At the same time, Israeli officials increasingly talked of "the other war," the struggle over media coverage. Complaints were voiced about oversaturated coverage—there were between 600 and 700 foreign reporters, cameramen, soundmen, photographers, editors, and television producers in the country—and about a high degree of anti-Israel bias.

In February Deputy Chief of Staff Ehud Barak told foreign journalists that "unacceptable" behavior by Israeli soldiers, such as the attempt to bury alive four Palestinians, would be punished, but that the army had no choice but to use force since it was something "forced upon us by the situation." On Friday, February 19,

Attorney General Yosef Harish instructed Rabin to issue strict written guidelines prohibiting soldiers from using physical force except when dispersing riots or making arrests.

On the evening of February 24, in a televised press conference, President Reagan claimed that outside agitators were behind the uprising: "There's every evidence that these riots are not just spontaneous and homegrown." The president went on to say, "We have intimations that there have been certain people suspected of being terrorists, outsiders coming in not only with weapons but stirring up and encouraging the trouble in those areas." Reagan also declined to criticize Israel's response to the riots. The following day, Secretary Shultz, on the way to Israel, modified the president's remarks. He said that the "fundamental origins" of the violence were "essentially indigenous. There is an underlying problem consisting of a large number of people in occupation who haven't had the basic rights of governance."

In March the focus shifted to talk of Israel restricting press coverage on the West Bank. On March 4, the entire area was closed. Israel claimed this represented no change in policy, but was the decision of the commander in charge who expected disturbances in the area. On March 25, Charles Redman of the State Department expressed U.S. "regrets" concerning Israeli restrictions on the West Bank, including sealing off the area and limiting media access. He added, "We hope these restrictions will be lifted quickly and not resumed." At the same time, Assistant Secretary of State for Human Rights and Humanitarian Affairs Richard Schifter told a House of Representatives hearing, "In our view, Israel clearly has not only the right, but the obligation, to preserve or restore order in the occupied territories and to use appropriate levels of force to accomplish that end." Schifter indicated that the administration had protested "regularly and consistently" to "the highest level of the Israeli government" about abuses. But, he noted, "there is a sharp difference between a peaceful march in which slogans might be displayed or shouted and acts of violence. While we must insist on human rights grounds on respect for the right of peaceful assembly, this does not extend to assembly for the purpose of throwing rocks and firebombs."

MORE DEPORTATIONS

On April 11, Israel expelled eight more Palestinian activists; once again, the State Department condemned the expulsions. The expulsions were seen as designed to deflect public criticism that the army had been too soft on the uprising. The eight deportees were described as main organizers for the PLO and Islamic fundamentalist groups in the territories. Four days later the Security Council considered another resolution urging Israel to return deported Palestinians and calling for a Middle East peace settlement under UN auspices; 14 members voted in favor but the United States vetoed it. U.S. delegate Okun called the resolution "redundant and inappropriate" and said "its broad and sweeping condemnation of Israel contains not a scintilla of balance."

The next day, news came of the slaying in Tunis of the PLO's military commander, Abu Jihad, which was attributed to Israel. (See below.) Palestinians in the territories poured into the streets following the first news broadcasts, shouting: "We will take revenge." By day's end, 14 Palestinians had been killed, the highest toll since the beginning of the uprising. The previous single-day high was 6 killed.

On April 19, Israel deported 8 more Palestinians, raising the total to 20. Again the U.S. government criticized the Israeli action, labeling it "counterproductive, in violation of the fourth Geneva Convention," and sure to "inflame further passions." Meanwhile, in an Israeli Supreme Court ruling on April 10, Israel's deportation policy was upheld as not being in violation of the Geneva Conventions.

On May 6, Israeli prime minister Yitzhak Shamir ordered the expulsion of Mubarak Awad, a Palestinian-American activist who preached civil disobedience against Israeli rule in the territories. The United States strongly protested the decision, the State Department describing him as an "American citizen, born in Jerusalem, who espouses nonviolence and reconciliation between Palestinians and Israelis." U.S. officials said that he "should not be forced to leave without due process of law." On June 5, the Israeli Supreme Court upheld the government's decision, not by addressing the government's assertion that Awad was a mastermind of the uprising, but because his visa had expired and Israel had the right to refuse to give him a new one. Awad, who lived in the United States from 1970 to 1983, had argued that because he was born in Jerusalem before the State of Israel was founded, the government had no authority to deport him. Israel's Foreign Ministry explained the government's decision: "There is a widespread conviction that Mubarak Awad is a dedicated disciple of Mahatma Gandhi and Martin Luther King, Jr., and that he is committed to the philosophy, practice, and support of nonviolence. This belief is a misconception, based on lack of familiarity with his fundamental views." Eight days later, Israel deported Awad; he was placed on a flight to New York. Charles Redman, speaking for the State Department, repeated the U.S. view that Awad was an authentic voice of political moderation who deserved Israeli encouragement, not deportation.

ONGOING DIFFERENCES OVER HUMAN RIGHTS

On June 14, another *intifada*-related issue arose between Washington and Jerusalem. On Sunday, June 12, Rabin had told the cabinet that civilians in the territories were free to shoot Palestinians seen with firebombs; firebomb attacks had increased in the weeks before. The State Department urged Israel to rescind the shoot-on-sight policy, in these words: "We believe that Israeli civilians should not be given the authority to maintain law and order. That requires proper training and is the province of the police authority."

U.S. concern about human-rights abuses in the territories surfaced again the same month following a visit to the area by Schifter. He indicated on his return that there had been "clear human rights violations" resulting from excessive use of force, and he said Israel should create a special court of appeals for the territories because there were "very limited opportunities" for Palestinians to appeal through the existing military court system there. He indicated that Israel and the United States had recently agreed on "a joint effort to monitor" conditions in the territories, through U.S. ambassador to Israel Thomas R. Pickering and Israel's chief administrator of the territories, Shmuel Goren.

Late in June, on the occasion of Defense Minister Rabin's visit to the United States, the Reagan administration told him that the "preservation of order in the territories must neither provide a justification for civilian lawlessness nor act as an excuse for avoiding political discourse with the Palestinians of the West Bank and Gaza." Rabin, when asked about U.S. criticism (he met with Reagan, Bush, Powell, and others), said: "I explained Israeli policy. I am not saying that everyone here is in agreement with our policy, but we are a free, independent state."

The expulsion policy continued. On July 8, Israel announced plans to expel 10 more Palestinians; 8 were deported on August 1. Four more were expelled on August 17, while orders had been issued for 25 others. The army saw this as an intensification of the crackdown on the *intifada*'s leadership—the so-called popular committees—and Israel indicated that the measure was the most effective means of deterring violence. Since the start of the uprising, 33 Palestinians had been deported.

On August 23, Washington made a new strong protest to Israel, Acting Secretary of State John Whitehead reportedly telling Israeli representatives in Washington that the administration would not veto future attempts in the Security Council to censure Israel for expulsions. The following day the administration said it was "deeply concerned" over Israel's expanding use of expulsions and "shocked" by the decision to expel 25 more Palestinians. Israeli officials were quoted as saying that the U.S. protest was "very harsh," but they denied any crisis in relations over the issue. The *Jerusalem Post* on August 24 published a text of a U.S. protest in which the administration told Israel that expelling Palestinians "has reached the point that an increasing number of Americans are wondering what Israel is doing." The United States further warned Israel that, if the expulsions continued, "damage to our bilateral relations will occur," and the U.S. government would oppose the policy "in the UN and elsewhere."

U.S. criticism of Israel was voiced again on September 6, by Assistant Secretary of State for Near Eastern Affairs Richard Murphy, who told the biennial convention of B'nai B'rith International that "Israel's attempts to end the Palestinian uprising have been ineffective, and at times counterproductive. Force is not the answer. Intimidation is not the answer. Deportation of Palestinians is not the answer."

In its continuing efforts to put down the uprising, Israel announced in September a decision to use plastic bullets, which could be fired at longer range and with greater accuracy than rubber bullets, against Palestinian rioters. The State Department said on September 28 it saw "no justification" for such a decision and was "disturbed" by the recent rise in Palestinian casualties. Rabin, in explaining the use of plastic bullets, said "our aim is to hit those involved" in demonstrations "but not to kill them." His statement was seen as a desire to demonstrate toughness in Israel's election campaign.

On December 8, the beginning of the second year of the uprising, Palestinian leaders acknowledged that the revolt had grown stagnant, that a certain inertia had set in, partly because various factions had extreme differences of view on how to proceed. Some urged more violence, others less. Still others wanted a more political approach. And the feeling was articulated by its leaders that the uprising had lost its ability to achieve its principal aim, exciting public opinion in the territories and abroad.

The Peace Process

In 1988 Secretary of State George Shultz conducted himself in a significantly different manner in regard to the Middle East than he had previously. Up to that time he had consistently expressed an unwillingness to take risks before the parties themselves were ready to do so. In 1988, pushed by the *intifada* and the criticism, whether justified or not, that U.S. inaction had been harmful, Shultz repeatedly put himself on the line—against what many saw as impossible odds. He paid four visits to the Middle East; at one point he even set a deadline for the parties to respond to his initiative; and he was more blunt about his differences with Yitzhak Shamir than he had ever been. Clearly, as his own remarks indicated, the stepped-up activity reflected not only the pressure of the *intifada* but the fact that his own days in office were winding down.

The year began with a flurry of activity reflecting the new sense of urgency generated by the *intifada*. Israel's foreign minister, Shimon Peres, and Jordan's prime minister, Zaid al-Rifai, in separate interviews, called for the convening of an international peace conference. Rifai, speaking to the BBC, asserted that the violence in the territories offered "another proof of the necessity of keeping the peace process alive. As long as there is no chance of a settlement in sight on the West Bank and Gaza, this is only the beginning." In line with King Hussein's long-standing policy, the Jordanian called for a conference attended by all parties to the conflict, as well as the five permanent members of the Security Council, to be held under UN auspices. Peres, too, continued to speak in behalf of a conference, in opposition to Prime Minister Shamir, but the conference he envisioned had clear parameters not spelled out by the Jordanian. Speaking on ABC's "This Week," on January 3, Peres said: "I would not mind seeing the Russians participate in the conference if the conference does not have any authority to impose a solution or to intervene in the negotiations."

Meanwhile, Hosni Mubarak, president of Egypt, told the Kuwaiti newspaper *Al-Anba,* on January 6, "I fail to understand why we have turned Camp David into . . . a problem." He noted that the autonomy agreement "provides the general framework for solving the Palestinian problem in all its aspects . . . it is a method for a solution." Mubarak went on to say, "If we would have continued with the talks on the second framework [the autonomy proposal], we would have been in a better situation. . . ." Several days later, Shamir referred with satisfaction to Mubarak's comments about Camp David and indicated that he would turn to Mubarak and tell him, "You yourself said that you were sorry that the negotiations were broken off. So let's resume them." In the same interview, in what was read as possibly a new direction in Likud thinking, Shamir said that he did "not object to the idea" of bilateral talks with the inhabitants of the territories on the implementation of the autonomy proposals of Camp David, if Egypt and Jordan refused to participate. Long-time Likud policy pointed to talks with Palestinians of the territories only in the context of talks with Egypt and Jordan.

Soon calls began to be heard for movement toward an international peace conference. The conventional wisdom that nothing could be done to launch the peace process until after the 1988 elections in the United States and Israel was held to be no longer valid because of the uprising. The *Jerusalem Post* reported that UN officials had decided to launch a new diplomatic initiative to reinvigorate the peace process and to fill the void created by U.S. inactivity. It was reported in the Arab press on January 14 that Prime Minister Margaret Thatcher of Great Britain and Claude Cheysson, European Community commissioner, had joined the call for an international conference. In a January 19 letter to UN Secretary-General Javier Pérez de Cuéllar, Foreign Minister Eduard Shevardnadze of the Soviet Union proposed that the Security Council discuss convening an international conference.

The Reagan administration entered into internal deliberations on whether to take a more active and visible role in pursuing peace efforts. A State Department official told the *New York Times* on January 21 that the "violence, so intense and so prolonged as it has been confirms that the status quo is not sustainable and there is an even more urgent need to identify the problems and get the peace process going." But, he added, "the more we look at it, the more we realize that the fundamental elements that made it difficult to move over recent years have not changed, so I think progress is unlikely." On the subject of sending an envoy to Israel, which Labor party representatives had recommended, there was little interest in Washington: "There's the old idea that you can send an envoy out and beat up on all sides until they come around. Frankly, that doesn't sound very appealing to the Administration." American officials pointed out that neither Shamir nor King Hussein had called for increased American activity. They noted as well that Israeli elections might work against Israeli flexibility because Shamir would not want to be outflanked on the right by Ariel Sharon and others.

On January 21, in an interview with the *Washington Post*, Mubarak rejected Shamir's call for a renewal of Camp David, saying that events had overtaken the 1979 accord. Instead, he said, he would launch a peace initiative urging the Palestinians to stop all acts of violence against Israelis in return for agreement by Israel to halt new Jewish settlements in the territories, to move toward an international peace conference, and to "respect and strictly observe the political rights and freedoms of the inhabitants of the West Bank and Gaza" over the next six months. Mubarak emphasized that he saw an international conference as a ceremonial prelude to direct negotiations: "If the Israelis want direct negotiations, I'm telling them, an international conference will start and the negotiations will be bilateral." He said there would be no attempt to impose any solution and he offered no specific details on how the problem of Palestinian representation at such a conference would be resolved.

The following day, Pérez de Cuéllar called on the Security Council to begin an urgent effort to end the Arab-Israeli conflict, saying a political solution was the only way to ensure the safety of Palestinians in the occupied West Bank.

The pressure on the Reagan administration to do something continued. At a briefing on Friday, January 22, White House press secretary Marlin Fitzwater defended the administration's Middle East record against the charge that it was not aggressive enough. "From day one," Fitzwater said, the administration had "a pretty high profile in the area." He cited the visits to the region by Assistant Secretary of State for Near Eastern Affairs Richard Murphy, Secretary of State George Shultz, and Vice-President George Bush. "On all of these occasions we expressed U.S. interest in being helpful in any way possible. It's just that nothing has materialized. If there is a new opening here, we certainly will take it, and we'll be an active participant in the process."

On January 23, the Arab League's representative in the United States and senior diplomats from Jordan, Tunisia, and Kuwait met with Richard Murphy in Washington and urged the administration to endorse a broad international peace conference that would have substantive authority to determine the outlines of a settlement of the Arab-Israeli conflict. Late in January, Mubarak arrived in Washington for three days of talks. After a meeting at the White House, President Reagan said that the Palestinian problem should not be allowed to "fester" any longer and called for "practical, not merely rhetorical, steps" to restart the stalemated peace process. Reports indicated that U.S. and Egyptian officials were discussing new ways to begin negotiations on local autonomy for the West Bank and Gaza as a step toward a peace settlement.

On January 30, without any prior announcement, special envoy Philip C. Habib met with King Hussein in Amman. State Department officials said Habib's objective was to bring Hussein into the process. Apparently Shultz had concluded that the dispute over an international conference was so intractable and the demand for positive movement so intense that Washington had to explore transitional arrangements. These would seek to improve the living conditions and increase self-government for Palestinians in the territories as well as to look at the territories' final status at the end of an interim period—in other words, to focus on substance as well as procedure. King Hussein reacted negatively, calling the U.S. proposal "just a variation of Camp David."

SHULTZ INITIATIVE

Within days, however, this approach was being labeled a new U.S. initiative, one described by an administration official as aimed at providing "some kind of interim arrangement that would give the Palestinians a stake in their future." The United States had outlined the plan to Israeli representatives Eli Rubinstein of Likud and Nimrod Novik of Labor, and to President Mubarak. At the same time, the United States vetoed a Security Council resolution that would have formalized a UN role in negotiating a settlement.

The Shultz plan called for Israel and Jordan, working through a shuttling U.S. mediator, to agree by September on limited Palestinian self-rule in the territories, with direct negotiations on the final status to follow in December. The plan, which Shultz called "a blend of ideas," was based on Camp David but greatly accelerated the timetable of a five-year interim autonomy period. The quickened pace was intended as an inducement to King Hussein to take part in negotiations.

On a trip to Bonn (February 9), Hussein said he welcomed the new U.S. engagement but added that any attempt to arrive at "piecemeal" solutions short of eventual Israeli withdrawal from the occupied areas was doomed to failure. On the same day, Shamir sharply criticized the idea of accelerating the Camp David plan for autonomy. Foreign Minister Peres, however, took a different tack: "Why again tell Washington 'nyet'? Even if this is a one-in-a-hundred chance, it is worth investigating." Assistant Secretary Murphy, who met with Shamir, Peres, Hussein, Syrian president Hafez al-Assad, Mubarak, and King Fahd of Saudi Arabia during a special mission to the region, told reporters on February 10 that he had found "a sense of eagerness and enthusiasm in each place that I visited."

Shamir, however, demurred from another aspect of the Shultz plan. Shultz had referred to the new initiative as being based on the "territory for peace" formula. Ehud Olmert, visiting Washington in mid-February as an envoy for Shamir, told the administration that this could not be a basis for talks.

To follow up on the U.S. initiative, Secretary Shultz decided to visit the region himself, following a trip to Europe. In a news conference in Brussels two days before his visit, Shultz said, "It's going to be tough." But, he added: "I believe that if there are chances, even if the chances are small, it's worthwhile trying. You can't be too afraid of failing. Suppose I go and I don't succeed? What am I saving myself for? So we'll try, and people want to have the United States come, and maybe we'll get somewhere."

Arriving in Jerusalem on February 25, Shultz called on Israel to make "decisions of historic proportions" to help change the status quo. Warning that the status quo was "not a stable option for any of the parties," he said he was bringing "a workable proposal" that addressed both Israel's security concerns and the Palestinians' need for "legitimate rights." Speaking with reporters on the plane before arrival, he warned that the plan would not work if each party simply picked one part it liked and discarded the others. Other remarks were seen as directed to Prime Minister Shamir. Shultz indicated that it was essential to get into discussion of final-status issues promptly and said the "fundamental touchstone here is Resolution 242." He noted that having a large number of people under occupation for a long time was "just inherently not a stable situation."

On February 26, Shamir and Shultz met and, not surprisingly, reports indicated that Shamir resisted two elements of the plan—an international conference as a framework for negotiations and giving up land for peace. Shultz was also planning to meet with local Palestinian representatives on the same day at the American Colony Hotel in East Jerusalem, but under instructions from the PLO, none of the Palestinians showed up. In a statement, Shultz said that "Palestinian participation is essential to success in the peace process."

The following day, Shultz flew to Amman and Damascus, where both governments resisted Shultz's plan as offering only a partial solution. Following a two-and-a-half-hour meeting in Amman, there was little evidence of any fundamental progress. Jordan's foreign minister, Taher al-Masri, repeated past Jordanian positions, namely, that "the only way to arrive at a peaceful settlement is through the convening of an international conference," including participation of the PLO, and the basis for a settlement "must be withdrawal of Israel from the occupied territories." Foreign Minister Farouk al-Sharaa of Syria made similar remarks after his meeting with Shultz, adding that "partial and unilateral solutions would only complicate the situation rather than solving it." The visit of Shultz to Damascus was significant in that it was his first since 1983, when he tried in vain to persuade President Assad to accept a U.S.-negotiated security agreement between Israel and Lebanon. When a reporter on his plane leaving Damascus asked whether he had made progress, Shultz laughed and said, "I'm overwhelmed by your sense of humor." He added that the "idea of negotiations of this kind is to get people to be realistic. We are not there yet."

The secretary had better luck in Cairo, where his plan received Egyptian endorsement. With Egyptian foreign minister Esmat Abdel Meguid standing by his side and indicating agreement, Shultz said, after three hours of talks with President Mubarak, that "we both feel we have a package and it's promising. Whether anybody else will think it's promising is a question." On February 29, Syrian foreign minister al-Sharaa called Shultz's proposal a "fig leaf" to keep Palestinians "under Israeli hegemony." Like the others, however, in not wanting to appear rejectionist, he expressed a desire for further U.S. contact on the matter.

The issue of Palestinian representation became a more serious stumbling block than it had been previously when Shultz paid a second visit to Jordan on February 29. Jordanian officials suggested they would support the PLO's demand for a separate seat at any peace conference. Previously, in order to get around the U.S. and Israeli ban on dealing with the PLO, the United States and Jordan had talked of a joint delegation made up of Jordanians and Palestinians approved by the PLO. The PLO was said to have told Jordan it was no longer interested in a joint delegation, reflecting the feeling that its diplomatic hand had been strengthened by the continuing uprising.

Leaving Israel for Europe on March 1, Shultz could only say that no one had rejected the plan outright: "No one has signed our proposals, but everybody wants us to keep working. So we'll keep working." In London, he met with King Hussein. The following day in Brussels, President Reagan, attending a meeting of NATO, announced that Shultz would return to the region to devote two more days to his peace mission: "It's clear that all countries in the region believe it is useful for the United States to remain engaged in this process. We will spare no effort in our search for a comprehensive settlement." Describing his objectives, Shultz said, "In a way, the more important negotiations go on within each constituency. As you operate on the tip of the iceberg, which is what I do, what you are doing is you are saying to people, 'You better go back and try to condition your constituency along certain lines or try something out on them and so on.'"

Returning to the region on March 4, Secretary Shultz paid short visits to Jerusalem, Damascus, and Cairo, where he met Shamir, Peres, Assad, and Mubarak. In each place he delivered letters spelling out the American peace plan and requested all parties to make their views known to him "in the next week and a half or so." He indicated that, at the very latest, he wanted their answers before he met with Shamir in Washington on March 16. Shultz discussed with reporters several aspects of the process. He said that he continued to favor a joint Jordanian-Palestinian delegation; indicated that Hussein "continues to believe that's the way to go," but conceded it would not be easy to resolve the issue if the PLO continued to oppose the joint delegation. He said his "time line" for the peace plan was "very ambitious" and that the next administration might be responsible for implementing part of the plan. But he insisted that giving the parties a deadline was a good way "to get people to make up their minds."

On Shultz's return to Washington on March 5, more details of his proposal appeared in the press. Under the plan, according to State Department officials, negotiations would begin May 1 on an interim phase of self-administration for Palestinians living in the territories, to include election of an administrative council by the Palestinians. An international conference, involving Israel, Syria, Egypt, a Jordanian-Palestinian delegation, and the five permanent members of the Security Council, would convene two to four weeks before these talks. The conference would have a continuing role but could not veto or impose a settlement. The negotiations on self-administration would last six months. By December, talks would begin between Israel and a Jordanian-Palestinian delegation on the final status of the territories; the interim phase would not go into effect until those talks were under way. The final talks would last one year, and whatever solution they produced would take effect three years after the interim phase began.

Shultz returned to Washington to find a letter, written to him March 3, from 30 U.S. senators, including some of Israel's staunchest supporters, criticizing Shamir, suggesting he could be obstructing efforts for peace. Although the letter also criticized Arab states—excluding Egypt—for not committing themselves to guarantee recognition and peace for Israel, the fact that it criticized Shamir's position and sided with Peres was unprecedented. Declaring support for Shultz's recent peace efforts, in particular the concept of "land for peace," the senators said they were "dismayed to read in the *New York Times* of February 26 that Prime Minister Shamir had said that 'this expression of territory for peace is not accepted by me.'" The letter also said that "peace negotiations have little chance of success if the Israeli Government's position rules out territorial compromise." The letter was circulated by Senators Carl Levin (D., Mich.) and Rudy Boschwitz (R., Minn.). Other signers included Edward Kennedy (D., Mass.), Alan Cranston (D., Calif.), Daniel Patrick Moynihan (D., N.Y.), Howard Metzenbaum (D., Ohio), and Frank Lautenberg (D., N.J.). On March 7, White House spokesman Marlin Fitzwater said that the administration "welcomed" the letter.

PRIME MINISTER SHAMIR'S U.S. VISIT

In advance of Shamir's visit, Minister Without Portfolio Moshe Arens met with Shultz in Washington, conveying the Israeli prime minister's opposition to the proposal for an international conference because he feared it would have too much authority and result in "extreme positions." With criticism of Shamir mounting on the eve of his visit, Shultz met with members of the House, urging them not to pressure Israel publicly to accept the U.S. plan. He indicated that Israel was a friend and ally and that the administration would not push her into a corner. The impression was left that Shultz would seek to convince Shamir to accept the plan through persuasion and the assurance that the United States would not desert Israel, rather than through coercion. Shamir himself responded to the 30 senators on March 9 in identical letters to Boschwitz and Levin. He wrote, "We were astonished by the words of criticism you leveled at us" and said that Israel had complied and remained committed to the Camp David accords.

Shultz continued to press forward in his effort to generate an atmosphere for a breakthrough. At a hearing of the House appropriations subcommittee on foreign operations on March 10, he urged Israel to rethink its concept of defense and to address the "ticking demographic time bomb." Clearly, this was part of Shultz's strategy of friendly but firm appeals designed to maneuver Shamir into making the necessary compromises to get negotiations under way.

On March 11, Shamir struck back. In an interview with *Ha'aretz* in which he used unusually strong language, he said, "The only word in the Shultz plan I accept is his signature." The document "does not serve the cause of peace or advance it even by one centimeter," he asserted. He told the *Jerusalem Post* that these proposals "harbor grave dangers for the future of Israel. It obligates me to resist them with all my power. And my power to resist is very great." Shamir reiterated his objection to "the very convening of an international conference" and said he would seek changes in the American position. Of Shultz's proposals he said, "The whole thing is an attempt to satisfy the Arabs. It has been done in a way that eliminates every element favorable to Israel while emphasizing and making permanent all that is comfortable to the Arabs."

Yitzhak Shamir arrived in Washington on March 14 for four days of talks. Tension was high, because of the Shultz-Shamir differences, as well as the criticism of Shamir from the senators and some in the American Jewish community. By the end of his stay, the perception was that Shamir had quieted the waters, at least for the time being, mainly because the U.S. administration was unwilling to push him into a corner where he would have no choice but to reject the plan. As it was, Shamir managed to avoid outright rejection, while expressing his own strong objections. Shamir and Shultz met on March 14 and 15, and on March 16, Shamir and Reagan met for two hours. The president indicated after his session that the United States "will not slice this initiative apart and will not abandon it." With Shamir standing by his side, Reagan said: "Those who will say 'no' to this plan—and the Prime Minister has not used this word—need not answer to the United States. They'll need to answer to their people why they turned down a realistic and sensible plan to achieve negotiations."

Shamir, meanwhile, continued to focus his opposition on the international conference proposed by Shultz. "We are interested, first of all, to negotiate directly with all the parties concerned. We don't see any positive role for an international conference." At the same time it was reported that Shamir offered an alternative approach involving the construction of 41,000 apartments in Gaza and the West Bank for 280,000 Palestinians living in refugee camps, the funding to come from the international community; a peace treaty and diplomatic relations with Jordan at the beginning—not the end—of negotiations on the final status of the territories; and support for the Camp David accords.

In addition to his meetings in Washington, Shamir spent much time with Jewish groups to shore up his perceived weaknesses there. On March 14, he told the UJA Young Leadership Conference that the *intifada* was aimed not just against the occupation but "against the existence of the State of Israel."

Shortly after Shamir ended his visit, Shultz, appearing before the Senate Budget Committee, gave a lengthy rebuttal to Shamir's contention that an international conference would be stacked against Israel's interests: "The United States opposes, and will not participate in, an international conference designed to replace bilateral negotiations. . . . The conference will be specifically enjoined from imposing solutions or vetoing what had been agreed bilaterally." Shultz also echoed the president's statement to Shamir that the administration would not abandon its plan: "The strength of the American approach is its integrity; no individual aspect of it can be extracted, finessed or ignored without sacrificing its balance. The United States will not permit any aspect of its proposal to be eroded or compromised."

When asked in an interview with Reuters whether the initiative was on the brink of failure, Shultz said, "No . . . because it's the only game in town." Reflecting the effort to remain intensively engaged, the administration sent Philip Habib to the region to talk with leaders in Jordan, Egypt, Saudi Arabia, and Morocco. On Habib's return several days later, the State Department announced that Shultz would return to the region on April 3 in a new attempt to gain acceptance for his plan. When asked by reporters why Shultz was going back, spokesman Charles Redman said: "No one has said no. Our proposal is still on the table. People are actively and seriously considering it."

SHULTZ'S THIRD AND FOURTH TRIPS

Stopping off in Rome on the way to the Middle East, Secretary Shultz indicated on April 2 that he expected his talks to produce "a little progress—measured in small increments." In talking with reporters, he said that the United States "would keep working for peace," but conceded that he had given up hope of getting the quick "yes" or "no" answers to the plan that he had said he would insist on when he began his personal involvement in the new peace effort.

This time the Shultz shuttle lasted five days, including visits to Israel, Jordan, Syria, Egypt, and Saudi Arabia, but at its end had little to show for the effort. In Israel, Peres continued to back the plan, while Shamir again avoided rejecting the plan outright though reiterating his specific criticisms. In Jerusalem, Shultz pointedly emphasized that his plan was based on "land for peace." In Amman, where he lauded Hussein's "constructive" approach to peace, it was significant that Jordanian TV refused to air an interview with Shultz. Officials were reportedly offended by the American's strong defense of Israeli security needs, his rejection of a PLO role, and his warning to Jordan that it could not expect to get back all the territories.

Despite the lack of progress, Shultz would not give up. On his return to Washington he said that he wanted to "leave something constructive for my successors" and promised that he would be back again during the remaining months of the Reagan administration. When asked why he was willing to commit so much time to this seemingly intractable problem, he responded: "What am I saving myself for?"

On May 9, the State Department announced that Shultz would return to the region in June. In mid-May, Peres visited Washington, and President Reagan lavished praise on the foreign minister for supporting American peace efforts. On the same day, May 17, the White House issued a statement praising Peres for displaying a "positive attitude toward peace," while criticizing "those leaders who are negative, consistently reject new ideas and fail to exploit realistic opportunities to bring about negotiations."

Earlier, Secretary Shultz, at a luncheon for Peres, agreed with him that the status quo "is not only unsatisfactory," but would not last: "As you once told me, the status quo now is like a pregnant woman. It is not an option; something is going to change. The question is whether it is going to change for better or worse, whether it is going to change in response to conscious efforts to work at it, or whether it will simply be allowed to take whatever course it takes." Peres said that "without the U.S. initiative" and without America's strong support for Israel, "the Middle East today might already be torn to pieces."

During this period, there was a great deal of discussion about how a changing

Soviet Union under Mikhail Gorbachev would relate to the Middle East. President Reagan, in an interview with European journalists at the White House in late May, shortly before his departure for a summit meeting in Moscow, insisted that the USSR would have to restore formal diplomatic relations with Israel before it could participate in an international peace conference. On June 1, following the Reagan-Gorbachev meetings in Moscow, Gorbachev reiterated his support for an international conference, while calling for recognition of Israel's "right to security" as well as the Palestinians' right to "self-determination." In reviewing the summit, American officials indicated satisfaction over discussions concerning the Middle East, citing greater Soviet flexibility on the nature of an international conference and how the Palestinians would be represented.

Between June 3 and June 7, Shultz tried personal diplomacy one more time. His refrain was familiar. In Israel, he warned that the occupation was "a dead-end street" that only increased the threat of war. In Cairo, he called on both sides to "lay aside prejudices, hatred and overblown dreams in favor of a negotiated settlement." And while there was no reported progress, in public remarks Shultz continued to take heart that none had rejected his overtures out of hand.

The last day of his visit to the region also saw the opening of an emergency Arab summit meeting in Algiers. Labeled the *intifada* summit, it was a marked contrast in focus to the last summit in November 1987 in Amman, where Iran was the central issue. A resolution vowed "all possible support by all possible means" to the uprising, but there was no public pledge of the financial aid sought by the PLO. And although the final communiqué called for a Palestinian state and affirmed the PLO as the sole representative of the Palestinians, Arab leaders did not accede to Arafat's request to disavow the U.S. peace plan, which neither recognized the PLO nor envisioned an independent state.

As Shultz returned from his fourth trip to the region since the uprising began, observers in Washington speculated that he was unlikely to make any more.

HUSSEIN'S SURPRISE MOVE

If the *intifada* was the spur for increased peace efforts, it became clear on July 31 that it also had forced King Hussein of Jordan to reconsider his own involvement. On that day, in a television address to his nation, the king announced that his government would cut its legal and administrative ties to the Israeli-occupied West Bank, thereby surrendering its claims to the territory to the PLO. The move seemed to surprise all the interested parties, though there had been forewarnings just a few days earlier. On July 28, Jordan canceled a $1.3-billion economic development plan for the West Bank; on July 30, the king dissolved the lower house of Jordan's Parliament, half of whose 60 members represented West Bank districts.

In his address, Hussein said he recognized the right of the PLO "to secede from us in an independent Palestinian state," which would be "established on the occupied Palestinian land after its liberation." Focusing on Jordan's own independence, and evidently trying to warn away any who hoped to establish the independent Palestinian state on the East Bank, Hussein stressed that "Jordan is not Palestine" and that "there should be a separation of the West Bank from the Hashemite Kingdom of Jordan." The address provoked much analysis. Some saw it as merely a tactic, the king gambling that the West Bankers would turn to him once they realized that the PLO could not fill the void left by Jordan's disengagement. In this view, the announcement was not an irreversible step. However, regardless of Hussein's intent, the action was undeniably a blow to the peace efforts of both George Shultz and Shimon Peres, both of which sought to deal with the Palestinian problem by negotiating with Jordan.

In August, when it was already evident that the peace process was slowing down, Shultz sent Assistant Secretary Murphy to the region, rather than going himself. After Murphy met in Israel on August 7 with Shamir and Peres, an Israeli Foreign Ministry official said, "It's clear to the United States and to Israel that nothing will happen in the peace process until after November," the time for elections in both countries. Murphy himself, however, denied that the process was in a "holding pattern." The following day, Murphy called on Israeli leaders to increase their contacts with "moderate Palestinians." His remarks were seen as a reaction to King Hussein's drastic move, with its implication that Israel had no choice but to negotiate the future of the territories with the Palestinians.

U.S. and Israeli Elections

As the fall advanced, and elections in the two countries drew closer, politics intruded into everything. Thus, when it became known that President Reagan had invited the foreign ministers of Israel and Egypt to meet with him in New York on September 26, supporters of Yitzhak Shamir charged that Washington was trying to boost the election chances of Shimon Peres, whose views on a settlement were far closer to those of Ronald Reagan and George Shultz. U.S. sources described the meetings as merely intending to discuss the next moves, in light of Hussein's decision to step back.

On September 16, in a speech at a conference sponsored by the Washington Institute for Near East Policy, Shultz laid out his views on the process and substance of future peace efforts. He warned, "Peace cannot be achieved through creation of an independent Palestinian state or through permanent Israeli control or annexation of the West Bank" and asserted that the status of the territories "cannot be determined by unilateral acts of both sides, but only through a process of negotiations." He was blunt in telling the Arabs that they could not now get what they had turned down in the 1940s, namely, the partition of Palestine into Jewish and Arab states, nor for security reasons could they expect Israel to surrender all the territory captured in the 1967 war. On the other hand, he called on Israel, as he had done in the past, to withdraw from some of the occupied land. Israel "must find a way to respond to expressions of Palestinian grievances," he maintained. "It cannot claim there is no one to talk to while suppressing political expression and arresting or deporting those who speak out—even those who speak in moderate terms."

On September 26, Reagan, Shultz, Peres, and Egyptian foreign minister Abdel Meguid met in New York. Not surprisingly, there was no breakthrough, and some indeed saw the meeting as an effort by the United States and Egypt to boost Peres's chances in the coming election.

The month of October was a time of waiting. The sensitivities relating to Israel's approaching election were highlighted when King Hussein appeared on the ABC News "Nightline" program, on October 20, reportedly as a result of arrangements by a Peres political adviser, and said that should Shamir win, "the whole area is threatened, and I cannot begin to imagine what the end results will be." Shamir issued a statement the next day expressing "regret and dismay" over Hussein's appearance and saying Labor's involvement was "a sign of a lack of national pride." Officials of Labor claimed that the Hussein comments would demonstrate to undecided Israeli voters that there was a realistic basis for Peres's proposal that Israel and a joint Jordanian-Palestinian delegation begin negotiations under the auspices of an international conference.

The Israeli election on November 1 proved inconclusive, with the Likud bloc winning 40 seats and Labor, 39. However, the ballot was immediately seen as a defeat for Labor, because of the increased number of seats won by the religious parties, who were viewed as most likely to join a Likud coalition. The official Washington response was that the United States would "work closely with whatever government is formed" in Israel, noting that relations were based on "the mutual interests of our two countries, not on the leadership."

While Israeli politicians went through the long, tortuous process of forming a new government, the U.S. elections on November 8 produced a clear-cut winner, George Bush. By early December there were reports of discussions by key Bush advisers on the new administration's Middle East focus come January 1989. Dennis Ross, the director of national security affairs for Bush's transition team, a man expected to have an important role in the new administration's foreign-policy decision making, indicated the need for swift U.S. diplomacy to promote the peace process.

On December 19, following a month and a half of intense wrangling, a coalition government was agreed upon in Israel. It would have Shamir remaining as prime minister, Rabin at Defense, Moshe Arens at the Foreign Ministry, and Peres heading the Ministry of Finance.

The month of December was chiefly notable, however, for a development that had the potential to change fundamental conditions that had long been taken for granted in the Arab-Israeli conflict. This was the decision by the United States, on December 14, to begin a dialogue with the Palestine Liberation Organization.

U.S.-PLO Relations

When the *intifada* began, it was unclear what its impact would be on the PLO's standing. On the one hand, the fact that it thrust the Palestinian issue to the fore seemed to work to the PLO's advantage. On the other hand, since the uprising was a phenomenon overwhelmingly generated by the residents of the territories themselves and not by the leadership of the PLO residing elsewhere, the possibility existed that the PLO would lose influence in the territories to indigenous forces.

At the beginning of 1988 not much had changed in the U.S. attitude toward the PLO since the day in 1975 when Henry Kissinger reached agreement with Israel that the United States would not deal with the PLO until it recognized Israel and renounced terrorism. Over the years there had been many reports of secret American-PLO talks—all denied; many reports that the PLO itself was going to move—never realized; and reports that the United States might abandon its commitment—which never occurred.

Early signs were that 1988 would be no different. In Baghdad, on January 14, Arafat said that before he would recognize Israel's right to exist, Israel and the United States had to accept PLO participation in an international conference and UN resolutions supporting Palestinian rights to an independent homeland. An aide to Shamir said, "There is nothing new in what Arafat proposes." There was no U.S. response.

When the PLO tried to arrange for a ship to carry back to Israel Palestinians deported since the beginning of the uprising—a reenactment of the 1947 sailing of the *Exodus* with Jewish refugees—the publicity effort collapsed when the ship was sabotaged in a Cypriot port. This took place on February 15, one day after three senior PLO military officers were killed by a bomb in Cyprus. Although the perpetrators of neither act were identified, Arafat not only blamed Israel but threatened to revoke a PLO declaration made in Cairo in 1985, committing the organization to limit guerrilla attacks to Israel and the occupied territories. Several days later, however, the PLO seemed to back off this threat as Abu Iyad, the head of the PLO's counterintelligence unit, told reporters in Tunis, "We will answer inside the occupied territories and we will not be dragged outside." The shift was seen as a response to an Egyptian warning to the PLO to "err on the side of caution" in public statements relating to the current crisis.

It became increasingly clear that the *intifada* had strengthened the PLO vis-à-vis Jordan as the focal point of West Bank activity. Thus, when Shultz visited the region on his first trip in February, his invitation to meet with Palestinians met with rejection on orders from the PLO. Late in March the State Department announced that Shultz would meet with Edward Said and Ibrahim Abu Lughod, professors and U.S. citizens who were members of the Palestine National Council (PNC), the PLO's unofficial government in exile. Shamir told U.S. ambassador to Israel Thomas Pickering that he viewed such a meeting "with grave and serious concern because the United States guaranteed in 1975 it would not meet PLO members barring certain conditions which have not been met." The U.S. position, not accepted by Israel, was that these individuals were not technically members of the PLO and did not fall under the 1975 agreement. According to the State Department, the Shultz decision signified "no change in U.S. policy on negotiating with or recognizing the PLO. That policy remains as it has been since 1975." After the disputed meeting, held on Saturday, March 26, State characterized it as "a routine consultation with prominent Palestinians."

In April Soviet leader Gorbachev urged Arafat to grant formal recognition of Israel's right to exist as an important step toward peace. At a meeting of the two in Moscow, Gorbachev said the Palestinians had broad support for "self-determination," but added that "in the same way, recognition of the state of Israel, consideration of its security interests . . . is a necessary element for the establishment of peace."

On April 16, Abu Jihad (Khalil al-Wazir), the PLO's senior military figure, was gunned down at his home in Tunis. The PLO accused Israel of the killing; Israel withheld formal comment. In March Israeli officials had accused Abu Jihad of organizing the hijacking of a bus in Israel which resulted in the deaths of three Israelis. Within days of Abu Jihad's death there were reports based on comments by Israelis with access to government officials that Israel had decided to kill him because they believed he was directing the uprising in the territories. The government, however, remained silent.

The situation took a surprising turn in June, when an aide to Arafat issued a statement calling for negotiations with Israel and a referendum in the territories. The aide, Bassam Abu Sharif, circulated his statement, which was also sent to the State Department, at the Arab summit conference in Algiers June 7–9. The document was signed by Abu Sharif, but the Beirut daily *As Safir* quoted him as saying in an interview that the document had been drawn up and approved by Arafat. In the statement, Abu Sharif maintained that the time had come to invest the gains of the uprising in a political settlement. He said that the Palestinians "would be making a big mistake if they thought they could solve their problem without talking directly with Israel," adding that the PLO should be prepared to talk to Israel in the framework of an international conference.

Abu Sharif's comments were condemned by various Palestinian guerrilla organizations, including one within the PLO, the Popular Front for the Liberation of Palestine. When Arafat was asked, while on a visit to Belgrade, whether Bassam Abu Sharif's statement was authoritative or personal, Arafat said: "I will not tell this to you, but only to an American representative." He indicated that he was "ready to meet an official American representative and discuss the solution of the Palestinian question and the crisis in the Middle East." State Department spokeswoman Phyllis Oakley praised the Abu Sharif statement for its "constructive tone" and "positive points," but added: "If the PLO is serious about moderating its positions so as to make a practical solution to the peace process, it can do so in an authoritative way. We have yet to see an authoritative statement." Another State

Department official was quoted as describing the document as "the clearest, best-formulated indication of a willingness to meet with Israelis or negotiate with Israel." Some administration officials reportedly attributed the PLO's movement to Soviet pressure on Arafat to moderate his position.

When King Hussein made his dramatic announcement on July 31 severing his ties to the West Bank, which seemed to leave the PLO as the dominant force in the territories, speculation mounted as to how the United States would proceed. The next day, the administration indicated that there was no basis for it to change its conditions for dealing with the PLO, but that the administration would put new pressure on the PLO, through intermediaries, to accept these conditions.

Reports soon began to circulate that the PLO was considering plans to form a government in exile, because of the vacuum created by Hussein's withdrawal. On August 9, Arafat confirmed the reports and indicated that the PNC would officially consider such a plan within a month. Meanwhile, pro-PLO figures in the West Bank prepared a document detailing a plan to establish a Palestinian state unilaterally, within the partition boundaries determined in 1947. An American Jewish peace activist, Jerome Segal, professor of philosophy at the University of Maryland, was said to have inspired this statehood plan through his own proposals, including specific steps leading to the establishment of a state, which had been widely circulated among Palestinian circles in East Jerusalem and the West Bank.

The pot continued to boil in mid-August, with reports that the PLO, under pressure from the clandestine leadership of the *intifada,* was considering a plan for Arafat to declare a provisional government explicitly recognizing Israel. The plan would be announced in mid-September, when Arafat would attend a European Community meeting in Strasbourg, and would be swiftly followed by ratification by the PNC.

Shultz indicated in an interview with CBS News on August 17 that he would welcome a decision by the PLO to recognize Israel's right to exist, but maintained that the establishment of an independent Palestinian state "doesn't make sense as far as I can see." Asked about rumors that the PLO was about to recognize Israel, he said that "before anyone takes the [PLO] statement seriously, it needs to be an official, full statement."

While there were reports that a critical PNC meeting would convene in Algiers in mid-September, the meeting was put off because of what were said to be fierce internal debates on how to proceed. The fundamental conflict was between those who wished to condemn terrorism and opt for support of a two-state solution and the more radical PLO elements that threatened to destroy the organization should the PLO adopt such an approach.

Despite the built-up expectations, Arafat's speech on September 13 at Strasbourg offered no breakthrough. As in the past, he accepted UN Resolutions 242 and 338, but only in the context of all other UN resolutions on the conflict. The United States had long maintained that PLO acceptance of 242 and 338 should be unconditional and not part of a blanket acceptance of all Security Council resolutions on Arab-

Israeli issues. On the question of the formation of a Palestinian provisional government, Arafat said that such an action could be taken only by the PNC, but indicated that King Hussein's renunciation of Jordanian claims to the West Bank had brought the search for Middle East peace to a "crucial stage" calling for new initiatives from the PLO leadership.

Meanwhile, Egyptian minister of state for foreign affairs Butrus Ghali was quoted as saying that his government had urged Palestinian leaders to delay a decision on their next political moves until after the Israeli and U.S. elections. His aim with regard to the United States was "to avoid giving either candidate for the United States presidency the chance to bid for Jewish votes by making pledges it would be hard for the new administration to ignore." As to Israel, he said, "a premature Palestinian decision on the next steps could also reinforce the Israeli extremist wing."

PLO WINS U.S. ACCEPTANCE

On October 20, the PLO, under pressure not to inflame the Israeli election process, decided to delay the PNC meeting in Algiers to November 12–14, after both elections. The meeting opened on the 12th with a speech by Arafat appealing to President-elect Bush to formulate a new U.S. policy of "justice and fairness" toward Palestinians. Two days later, by a vote of 253 to 46, the PNC formally approved a policy document that called for an international conference to be held under the auspices of the UN Security Council on the basis of "Resolutions 242 and 338 and the assurance of the legitimate national rights of the Palestinian people," starting with the "right to self-determination." It "rejected terrorism in all its forms, including state terror" and renewed the council's commitment to previous related UN resolutions, which confirmed the right of people to struggle against foreign occupation. It called for "the escalation and continuation of the *intifada.*" On November 15, Arafat read the PNC's declaration of independence of a Palestinian state: "The Palestine National Council, in the name of God, and in the name of the Palestinian Arab people, hereby proclaims the establishment of the state of Palestine on our Palestinian territory, with holy Jerusalem as its capital."

Israeli leaders of both major parties were unimpressed. Shamir called the unilateral declaration of independence "another step in the war of the Arab terrorist organizations against the existence and independence of the state of Israel." Peres said that the PNC's supposed recognition of Israel was so hedged with "ambiguity and double talk" as to be essentially meaningless. On the same day, the White House rejected the PNC's independence proclamation but saw "positive elements" in the apparent acceptance of 242 and 338. Reagan said he saw "some progress," while President-elect Bush said, "I think the jury is still out."

The following day the State Department issued a formal reaction after studying the text of the PNC document. State Department spokesman Redman called the

PNC resolutions "an advance over previous efforts," but said that "possibly implied or indirect reference to Israel's right to exist is not sufficient."

Amidst the controversy over what the PNC meeting did or did not do arose another issue of contention. Back on November 9, Arafat, in a move that had been rumored for months, asked the United States for a visa so that he could address the UN General Assembly in New York later in the year. Secretary of State Shultz, whose decision it was whether to grant the visa, had received a letter on September 29 signed by 51 senators, including vice-presidential candidates Lloyd Bentsen and Dan Quayle, urging the administration to deny Arafat's expected visa request. By the third week of November, a major debate was reported to be taking place within the State Department on this issue. The Bureau of Near Eastern and South Asian Affairs was said to be arguing in favor of granting Arafat a visa, in order to avoid stalling the Middle East peace process. The Bureau of International Organization Affairs and the Office of Counter-Terrorism were reportedly opposed to Arafat's entry.

On November 26, after listening to both sides, Shultz denied Arafat a visa because of his "associations with terrorism." A State Department statement explaining the decision cited a U.S. law that "excludes members of the PLO from entry into the United States by virtue of their affiliation in any organization that engages in terrorism." The only question was whether to grant Arafat a waiver; State decided not to do so because it had "convincing evidence that PLO elements have engaged in terrorism against Americans and others," and that Arafat, as chairman of the PLO, "knows of, condones, and lends support to such acts." The statement also cited the presence at the Algiers PNC session of Mohammed Abu al-Abbas, the PLO executive committee member implicated in the 1986 *Achille Lauro* hijacking in which an American citizen, Leon Klinghoffer, was murdered.

The decision caused an international uproar, and Arab nations immediately moved to shift the UN meeting to Geneva so that Arafat could participate. On November 26, a White House spokesman indicated that the president was aware of the Shultz decision but had no role in it; the following day, Reagan said he "agreed very much" with it. Asked if the decision would send a signal that the United States was obstructing the peace process, Reagan replied: "I think the other way would have sent out the wrong signal. That we were patsies." Two days later, Shultz defended his decision, saying that "it's too easy for people to forget" the serious threat that terrorism posed to "civilized society." On December 2, the General Assembly overwhelmingly voted to move the session of the Palestine debate to Geneva, on December 13–15.

The turbulence surrounding U.S.-PLO relations continued when a group of five American Jews, acting on their own initiative, met with Arafat in Stockholm on December 6 and 7. (The five were Rita Hauser, Drora Kass, Stanley Sheinbaum, Menachem Rosensaft, and Avraham Udovitch. See "Jewish Communal Affairs" article elsewhere in this volume.) At the conclusion of the discussions, Arafat and the Jewish delegation issued a four-point statement clarifying what they said were the stands taken at the PNC's Algiers meeting. These were that the PNC had "established the independent state of Palestine and accepted the existence of Israel as a state in the region" and that it had "declared its rejection and condemnation of terrorism in all its forms, including state terrorism." Afterward, at a news conference, Arafat added: "The PNC accepted two states, a Palestinian state and a Jewish state, Israel. Is that clear enough?"

Israel quickly dismissed Arafat's words, Shamir saying the declaration "doesn't add anything because the philosophy of the PLO has not changed—that is, the destruction of Israel." Peres called Arafat's remarks "a cunning explanation" and "a postulation in theory." Nor was Shultz ready to accept the contention that the PLO had satisfied U.S. conditions for acceptance: "I have read the reports from Stockholm and it seems to be a little bit further clarification, and I welcome that. But there's still a considerable distance to go." Shultz went on to say that the PLO had to accept 242 and 338, explicitly recognize the existence of Israel, and renounce terrorism "directly, not inferentially or partially. They haven't met our conditions yet."

On December 13, Arafat addressed the UN General Assembly in Geneva. He delivered an 80-minute speech in Arabic, dressed in his checkered headdress and khaki uniform, but without the pistol holder that had caused controversy in his 1974 address to the assembly. He proposed a three-point plan, including an international conference to be attended by "the state of Palestine, Israel, and other neighbors" that would seek a comprehensive settlement based on 242 and 338. He called on the "leaders of Israel to come here, under the sponsorship of the United Nations, so that we can forge that peace." On terrorism, he said, "I condemn terrorism in all its forms, and at the same time salute those sitting before me in this hall who, in the days when they fought to free their countries from the yoke of colonialism, were accused of terrorism by their oppressors."

The American reaction was that, once again, Arafat had not gone far enough. Charles Redman said that the speech "contained some interesting and some positive developments," but "it continued to be ambiguous on the key issues . . . as a consequence the speech did not meet our conditions." President-elect Bush, in much the same vein, said the United States needed "a much clearer statement of everything." These reactions were seen as particularly significant because there had been reports—in the days before the speech—that, through intermediaries, Arafat had received the exact wording that would be necessary to enable the United States to end its boycott of the PLO.

According to reports, immediately following the speech and the U.S. reaction, a number of those intermediaries, particularly a team of Swedish diplomats, went to work relaying U.S. demands to the PLO and the PLO's responses back to Washington, all with the purpose of gaining U.S. acceptance of the PLO. The following day, December 4, Arafat called a news conference, at which, apparently as a result of the hectic diplomatic exchanges, he modified his language slightly. He affirmed "the right of all parties concerned in the Middle East conflict to exist in peace and security, including the state of Palestine, Israel, and their neighbors." He omitted his usual reference to the Palestinian right to self-determination when declaring his acceptance of 242 and 338, and further stated—a State Department precondition—that the PLO "renounces" rather than merely "condemns" all forms of terrorism.

A few hours later the White House issued a statement from Reagan saying that the PLO had met American conditions and authorizing "the State Department to enter into a substantive dialogue with PLO representatives." Reagan emphasized that the PLO still had to "demonstrate that its renunciation of terrorism is pervasive and permanent." Simultaneously, Shultz announced that he had designated the American ambassador to Tunisia, Robert H. Pelletreau, Jr., to carry out the dialogue with the PLO. He also stressed that the United States "does not recognize the declaration of an independent Palestinian state."

Seeking to reassure Israel, the president said that the U.S. government's "special commitment to Israel's security and well-being remains unshakeable." The following day, he said that the United States would "certainly break off communications" with the PLO if it broke its vow on terrorism. And U.S. officials were quick to point out that while the American aim was ultimately to bring Israelis and Palestinians together in direct talks, the administration would not simply "deliver" Israel to the PLO.

On December 15, Pelletreau telephoned PLO headquarters to arrange a meeting. The first talks with the PLO team, which was led by executive committee member Yasir Abed Rabbo, took place the next day and lasted 90 minutes. Pelletreau said the talks were "practical and characterized . . . by seriousness of purpose"; Abed Rabbo called them "constructive and fair."

Shamir called the U.S. decision a "grave mistake" that "will have an impact" on U.S.-Israeli relations. Peres was more restrained, saying bilateral relations were "as friendly, as deep, as meaningful" as ever, despite disappointment over the issue. American Jewish reaction was subdued, Jewish leaders apparently showing little inclination to criticize Shultz or Reagan, who were viewed as strong supporters of Israel.

The American decision was warmly received on the international level. The General Assembly ended its special session by adopting two resolutions—one calling for an international peace conference, the other changing the designation of the PLO's observer mission at the UN from "PLO" to "Palestine." Only the United States and Israel voted against the two resolutions, although a large bloc of Western nations abstained in the voting for the second measure.

In the final analysis, it could be seen that the *intifada* had not only moved the PLO to center stage but had induced it to utter the magic words it had resisted for so many years. The result was a new relationship with the United States, an astonishing development, but one whose future direction remained uncertain.

U.S.-Israeli Bilateral Relations

During all the difficult moments between the United States and Israel in 1988—centering on controversies involving the *intifada*, the peace process, and U.S.-PLO relations—George Shultz was fond of saying that American-Israeli relations had never been so strong and that all the controversies would have no impact on that strong relationship. Shultz had every right to reach such a conclusion, since he had been the key figure in building up bilateral relations ever since he took over as secretary of state in 1983. While the United States had for a long time had "special relations" with Israel, the Shultz tenure was unique in displaying fewer inhibitions than its predecessors about developing more intimate ties, lest the United States be perceived as too close to Israel.

Strategic, economic, and trade relations between the two countries underwent dramatic change during the Shultz years. Strategic cooperation was transformed into a living reality, with greater information sharing, visits of American forces to Israeli facilities, training of forces, and so on. Economic assistance not only increased but was converted entirely into grants, rather than the previous arrangement of part loans. During Israel's economic crisis of 1984–85, Shultz got personally involved and was responsible for providing the emergency U.S. aid that helped Israel recover. Free trade was becoming a reality through the Free Trade Act (FTA) of 1985, which offered possibilities of substantial business dealings between American and Israeli companies. All this took place amidst continuing diplomatic conflict, whether it was Israeli opposition to the Reagan plan, the Pollard case, or the Iran-*contra* fiasco.

STRATEGIC COOPERATION

The fundamental reason that U.S.-Israeli strategic cooperation survived successive diplomatic disputes through the Reagan years was the perception—different from that of the Carter administration—that ties with Israel were in America's interest rather than being merely a reward for diplomatic concessions. Thus, the strategic theme ran on a separate track from the diplomatic relationship and evolved on its own terms. As developments during 1988 indicated, the administration still preferred to keep the tracks separate. At no point during Shultz's critique of Shamir's policy or of the administration's unhappiness with the deportation of *intifada* leaders were there threats of cutbacks in the strategic area; all the areas of cooperation, including the regular forum of the Joint Political Military Group—to identify areas of common interest largely in connection with the external threats to the eastern Mediterranean area—continued to function as before.

Even further steps in cooperation were taken this year. Of particular importance, on April 21, the two countries signed a five-year agreement formalizing their cooperation on a range of military, economic, political, and intelligence matters. The document, known as a memorandum of understanding, was signed by Reagan in the White House and Shamir in his office in Jerusalem. On Israeli television, Shamir said that it was "very significant indeed that we give today special expression to this unique partnership in common values, in interests and in the desire for peace." The agreement, which had been completed early in April in Shultz-Shamir meetings and was signed to coincide with Israel's 40th-anniversary celebration, formalized the variety of cooperative arrangements that had evolved over the years. The preamble welcomed the "achievements made in strategic, economic, industrial, and technological cooperation" and took note that Israel was designated "as a major non-NATO ally" of the United States. It went on to say that the parties wished "to enhance their relationship through the establishment of a comprehensive framework for continued consultation and cooperation."

Following were four articles spelling out the agreements. The first recognized the value in continuing, frequent consultations and periodic meetings between the top officials of the two nations. The second spelled out plans for regular meetings—called a Joint Political Consultation (JPC)—between the director-general of the Israeli Foreign Ministry and the U.S. under secretary of state for political affairs. It also called for periodic meetings between representatives of the Agency for International Development and Israel's Division of International Cooperation to "coordinate and facilitate programs of cooperative assistance to developing countries." The third article spelled out and reaffirmed the importance of existing joint groups, including the Joint Political Military Group (JPMG), the Joint Security Assistance Planning Group (JSAPG), and the Joint Economic Development Group (JEDG).

JPMG was described as the forum for discussions of joint cooperative efforts such as combined planning, joint exercises, and logistics. It met biannually, alternating between the United States and Israel, and was cochaired by the director-general of Israel's Ministry of Defense and the U.S. assistant secretary of state for politico-military affairs.

JSAPG was described as the forum in which the two states would review Israel's requests for security assistance, as well as discuss industrial and technological cooperation and cooperative research and development related to Israel's designation as a non-NATO ally. JSAPG met annually in Washington and was cochaired by the director-general of Israel's Ministry of Defense and the U.S. under secretary of state for security assistance, science, and technology.

JEDG was described as the forum for discussions of Israel's economy, with a view to stimulating economic growth and self-reliance, and evaluating Israel's requests for U.S. economic assistance. The JEDG met annually, alternating between the United States and Israel, and was cochaired by the director-general of the Israel Ministry of Finance and the U.S. under secretary of state for economic affairs.

The fourth article of the memorandum of understanding stated that the agreement was in force for an initial period of five years and would be renewed for additional periods of five years, unless either party indicated that it wished to terminate the agreement.

Speaking to a meeting of AIPAC (American Israel Public Affairs Committee) one month after the signing of the agreement, Secretary of Defense Frank Carlucci indicated that strategic cooperation was moving ahead. He said, for example, that Israel's weapons sales to the United States rose from $9 million in 1983 to $250 million in 1987 and would "continue to grow." Carlucci described Israel as "a faithful friend in a turbulent region" and said that Israel would "remain an important source of weapons systems that are proven and ready in some cases, saving the United States the time and expense of developing its own." He indicated that the Pentagon spent 54 percent of its budget allocation for the evaluation of foreign weapons on testing weapons made in Israel. And he noted that Israel was one of four U.S. allies working on the Strategic Defense Initiative, building the experimental antitactical ballistic missile known as the Arrow.

The issue of the Arrow took on new significance in light of the spread of ballistic missiles in the Middle East. In March it was disclosed that Saudi Arabia had purchased a mobile Chinese ground-to-ground missile system. When Shamir aide Yosef Ben-Aharon declared in Los Angeles that "the possibility always exists" that Israel might strike at the missile sites, the administration approached the Israeli government and expressed its "serious concern." On March 25, Reagan urged Israel to refrain from any military action against the Saudi missiles, saying that "we would be totally opposed to any such thing and hope that they are not considering any such action."

On Tuesday, June 28, following a visit by Israeli defense minister Rabin to the White House, Reagan issued a statement saying he was troubled by "ominous new military developments" in the region, including the spread of ballistic missiles and chemical weapons. Reagan said that the situation called for international efforts to stop the spread of the weapons and made continued U.S.-Israeli defense cooperation imperative.

On June 29, the United States and Israel signed a memorandum of understanding to develop and produce jointly the new defensive missile, the Arrow. Under the agreement, the United States would pay 80 percent of research costs of the Arrow. The new antitactical ballistic missile was under development in Israel, but additional U.S. funding and technology were needed. According to Defense Minister Rabin, Israel proposed to demonstrate the Arrow's usefulness "within two to three years," by showing that it was capable of intercepting an incoming missile that had a range of 625 miles. Rabin told the National Press Club the same day that the action amounted to a decision to allow Israel "to develop the technical feasibility to intercept tactical ballistic missiles." At a news conference on that day, Shultz said that the development of a defensive ballistic system was "very desirable" and a major contribution to the deterrence of war. Shultz, as was often the case, was able to put himself in Israel's place: "I suppose if you happen to be sitting in Israel with ballistic missiles—in this case, shorter-range ballistic missiles, but nevertheless ballistic missiles that are hard to defend against—around you, you feel very strongly the importance of learning how to defend yourself against them."

On Monday, July 11, one more example of increasing strategic cooperation took place when the U.S. aircraft carrier *Eisenhower* of the Sixth Fleet began an exercise with the Israel Navy. The first such joint activity was reported to involve mock combat and refueling of the *Eisenhower* by Israeli naval vessels.

FREE TRADE

The Free Trade Agreement (FTA) between Israel and the United States, signed in 1985, went through some difficult days in 1988. In June it was reported that Washington had protested trade taxes levied by Israel that it said violated the FTA. The taxes, an import price-equalization tax and purchase taxes, were said to have raised the prices of U.S. manufactured goods to uncompetitive levels. U.S. ambassador to Israel Thomas Pickering was reported to have written a tough letter to Israel's Trade and Industry minister, Ariel Sharon, complaining of "artificial steps and arbitrary taxes" to make U.S. imports more expensive. Sharon dismissed the American criticism as "economic pressure," and a spokesman for the Trade and Industry Ministry indicated that in an upcoming meeting of the Free Trade Area Consultative Group, Israel would raise its "concern with the intensifying protectionist policies, as reflected in the new American trade law and in different procedures of the American government."

Despite these differences, American and Israeli officials tried to minimize the extent of the tension caused by the implementation of the FTA accord. At the same time, in New York on June 6, an international trade specialist involved in drafting the FTA accord warned that Israel was endangering the agreement through "unfair business practices." Harold Paul Luks, speaking at a symposium on America-Israel Economic Relations, said that Israeli government attempts to bypass the agreement by imposing various taxes and subsidizing exports could eventually create a backlash. He emphasized that the agreement was not a charity, "but a bilateral, reciprocal agreement." Luks did, however, see a brighter side as well, predicting that there were still many advantages Israel could reap from the FTA. In particular, he pointed out that Israeli exporters should be looking ahead to January 1989, when Taiwan, Korea, Hong Kong, and Singapore would lose their preferential treatment in the U.S. market.

Meanwhile, it was reported that under the FTA, U.S. exports to Israel increased by 40 percent in 1987, while imports increased by 9 percent.

KENNETH JACOBSON

Communal

Jewish Communal Affairs

IN 1988 AMERICAN JEWS continued to worry about the ongoing violence in Gaza and the West Bank. They were caught between the need to help Israel defend itself against its enemies and a distaste for some of the actions that Israel took to quell the uprising. The year saw American Jewry's long-standing advocacy of the cause of Soviet Jewry finally bear fruit as increasing numbers were allowed to leave the USSR, although the question of their destination aroused great controversy. Also in 1988, the centrality of the Holocaust in American Jewish life became more evident than ever before, the presidential election encouraged a reexamination of Jewish political preferences, Jewish organizational life confronted new difficulties, and the revival of efforts to amend the Israeli Law of Return aroused unprecedented anger among American Jews.

Reaction to the Intifada

Differences among American Jews over Israel's handling of the Palestinian *intifada* were sharpened in January 1988 by Defense Minister Yitzhak Rabin's announcement of a policy of beatings to put down the violence.

Those individuals and organizations already skeptical about Israel's course reacted with dismay. Rabbi Alexander Schindler, head of the Union of American Hebrew Congregations, cabled the president of Israel to urge a halt to "indiscriminate beating of Arabs," which Schindler considered "an offense to the Jewish spirit." A high-level American Jewish Congress delegation, after a fact-finding mission to Egypt, Jordan, and Israel, issued a denunciation of Israel's "brutalization of innocents." The organization's executive director, Henry Siegman, explained "that there are certain lines that no civilized society can allow itself to cross, even in the face of extreme provocations." The *New York Times* published an op-ed piece by Woody Allen (January 28) in which the actor and film director stated that he was "appalled beyond measure by the treatment of the rioting Palestinians by the Jews," and advocated "every method of pressure—moral, financial and political—to bring this wrongheaded approach to a halt."

Other elements of American Jewry disagreed. Burton Levinson, national chairman of the Anti-Defamation League of B'nai B'rith, declared himself "sick and tired of American Jews who take their case [against Israeli policy] to the general press," and he cited a new ADL poll indicating that Americans were as supportive of Israel as ever. On January 24, more than 500 Jews, organized by the Zionist Organization of America, picketed ABC headquarters in New York City to protest what they considered the network's bias against Israel in its coverage of the uprising. The ZOA also held a rally across the street from the Israeli consulate in New York at which over 350 people demonstrated support for Israel. Orthodox groups backed Israeli actions as well: the National Council of Young Israel criticized Schindler and the AJCongress for "hurling damaging invectives against Israel's policy in Judea and Samaria," while the president of the Rabbinical Council of America noted that "self-defense, even including the use of a pre-emptive strike, is fully justified in biblical and talmudic tradition."

The Conference of Presidents of Major American Jewish Organizations convened an emergency meeting to hammer out a consensus position for the organized Jewish community. What enabled it to do so was a message from Israeli prime minister Yitzhak Shamir stating that force was not being used indiscriminately, but only against violent demonstrators and those resisting arrest. The Conference of Presidents issued a statement on January 27 pointing out that "in every country, including our own, police officers are equipped with weapons, including billy clubs, to maintain order and to protect the lives and property of local residents against mob rule." It called on "non-violent" Palestinians to enter into negotiations with Israel. A few days later the conference released another statement, this one signed by 51 organizations—including those that had been critical of the beatings—that reiterated American Jewish support for Israel. And in February American Jewish leaders expressed relief when the results of the United Jewish Appeal Super Sunday "phone-athons" around the country showed no drop-off in contributions.

American Jewish attention now turned to the peace process. On February 27, a plenary meeting of the National Jewish Community Relations Advisory Council—the coordinating body for Jewish community relations in the United States—endorsed the Reagan administration's peace initiative, which envisioned limited autonomy for the Palestinians, local elections, followed by talks aimed ultimately at the final status of the territories, capped by an international conference.

However, a 60-person delegation from the Conference of Presidents arriving in Israel two days later quickly saw that Israel's government, bitterly divided between Labor and Likud, lacked the ability to speak coherently about the proposal. After hearing presentations by representatives of each bloc, Albert Vorspan, senior vice-president of the UAHC, remarked, "If there is a schizophrenia on the highest level in Israel, what expectations can we have from the Presidents Conference?" But conference president Morris Abram remained optimistic, expressing "confidence in the overall moral authority of the government in respect to its defense policy," and suggesting that American Jewish leaders critical of Israeli actions should express their views privately to the Israeli government and not publicize them.

On March 7, 30 U.S. senators—including several longtime supporters of Israel—sent a letter to Secretary of State George Shultz that criticized Israeli prime minister Yitzhak Shamir for impeding progress on the land-for-peace formula. The Rabbinical Council of America (Orthodox) denounced the letter as "an unwarranted and outrageous interference in Israel's internal politics," the Zionist Organization of America charged that it would "only serve to embolden the enemies of Israel," and Morris Abram denied that Shamir was an obstacle to peace.

That sympathy for Shamir's hard line was widespread among American Jews seemed evident when he made a four-day trip to the United States a week after the release of the senators' letter. About 100 enthusiastic supporters met him at dawn at Kennedy Airport, bursting into "Hatikvah" when they saw him alight from his plane. Though his meetings at the State Department brought no diplomatic movement, his speeches before Jewish audiences evoked enthusiasm. In Washington, a crowd of 3,000 at the National Young Leadership Conference of the United Jewish Appeal repeatedly interrupted Shamir with applause and cheers as he reiterated his refusal to cede territory in exchange for peace; in New York, close to 1,000 pro-Shamir demonstrators rallied across the street from his hotel; and in Los Angeles, despite a boycott by some community leaders who disagreed with his views, 1,600 people turned out to hear the prime minister speak, and others had to be turned away. So powerful was his impact on American Jewry that a meeting in New York called by the North American Friends of Peace Now to counteract Shamir was scarcely noticed. Upon his return to Israel, a happy Shamir reported that "the vast majority" of American Jewry "enthusiastically and faithfully supports Israel and stands by the government of Israel unreservedly."

Was Shamir's assessment correct? On April 13, the *Los Angeles Times* published the results of a survey of Jewish (and non-Jewish) opinion on the Middle East which suggested that American Jews were rather more ambivalent than the Israeli prime minister assumed. Over 60 percent of Jews surveyed backed an international peace conference (opposed by Shamir), though a plurality—45 percent to 29 percent—opposed a Palestinian homeland. Thirty-five percent of the Jews agreed that continued occupation of the territories "will erode Israel's democratic and humanitarian character," but 45 percent denied this. While the Jews divided just about evenly over whether Jews "should support Israel in public even when they disagree in private," younger Jews approved of public criticism by a three-to-two margin.

Indeed, buoyed by the support of Israeli finance minister and Labor bloc leader Shimon Peres, who visited the United States in May, American Jews who considered the Shamir stance overly intransigent became quite vocal during the spring and summer. On April 24, more than 2,000 New Yorkers demonstrated at a "Rally for Peace" sponsored by about 20 Jewish organizations seeking to move Israeli policy in a more dovish direction. One rally organizer, Mark Gold, of the Americans for Progressive Israel, explained that the event was intended to give the lie to Shamir's assertion that American Jewry backed him. Two days later, Menachem Rosensaft, the newly elected president of the Labor Zionist Alliance, claimed that more American Jews actually sided with the Labor party's views on peace than agreed with Shamir, and asserted that "it is the responsibility of those in the leadership of the liberal organizations to make our views heard" in Israel. The May 5 issue of the *New York Times Magazine* carried excerpts from Albert Vorspan's personal diary—entitled "Soul Searching"—that sharply attacked most American Jewish leaders for stifling their real doubts about Israel's course in order not to offend the Israelis. And in July, newly appointed American Jewish Committee executive head Ira Silverman asserted that he believed in "stating plainly our view about how best to achieve a peace for Israel," a "view that may differ from the view of the prevailing Israeli government administration at any given time."

In November the Palestine National Council—the policy-making body of the PLO—met in Algiers and agreed to accept UN Security Council Resolution 242, in the context of other UN resolutions on the Middle East. Did this constitute acceptance of the State of Israel, the necessary first step toward negotiations? American Jewish organizations were skeptical. AJCommittee president Theodore Ellenoff considered this "so-called recognition of Israel's right to exist" too "vague and ephemeral" to have any meaning. Morris Abram saw "nothing positive" in the PNC statement. Seymour Reich, president of B'nai B'rith International, called it "a triumph of style over substance."

On December 5, it became known that a group of American Jews was planning to meet with Yasir Arafat in Stockholm. Malcolm Hoenlein, executive director of the Conference of Presidents, could not think of "any responsible or representative American Jewish leaders" who would do such a thing. The next day, the five-person delegation—Menachem Rosensaft of the Labor Zionist Alliance, Rita Hauser, a New York attorney, Drora Kass of the Israel Center for Peace in the Middle East, Stanley Sheinbaum, an economist and publisher, and Abraham Udovitch, chairman of the Near Eastern studies department at Princeton University—met with Arafat for six and a half hours. After the session, a joint statement was issued in which the PNC agreed to renounce terrorism and explicitly recognize Israel "as a state in the region" alongside a projected Palestinian state.

Most American Jewish leaders were less than enthusiastic. In the eyes of ZOA president Milton Shapiro, the Jews who met with Arafat were simply "renegades." Morris Abram, remaining "highly suspicious of Arafat's true intent," castigated the five Jews for giving "aid and comfort" to the enemy. Abraham Foxman, the Anti-Defamation League's national director, declared that the PLO still "failed to meet the need for clear recognition of Israel, clear repudiation of terrorism and a clear commitment to negotiate peace." Yet a number of influential Jews who had previously called on Israel to soften its position on the Palestinians expressed guarded optimism: for Alexander Schindler, this was "a step in the right direction," while Henry Siegman perceived a "new willingness" on the part of the PLO to move toward peace.

For a while, Arafat seemed determined to prove the pessimists correct. In a

90-minute speech to the UN General Assembly (held in Geneva because the United States refused to grant him a visa), Arafat moved away from the moderate line he had taken with the American Jewish delegation in Stockholm. But when Arafat was more forthcoming at a news conference the next day, U.S. Secretary of State Shultz considered his change of position enough to warrant the start of direct substantive negotiations between the United States and the PLO.

The American Jewish community, which had come to see Shultz as a bastion of support for Israel, tried to make the best of the situation. All of the mainstream organizations declared that Shultz's move was acceptable, though they insisted that the PLO's actions should be made to conform to Arafat's moderate words. Even the ZOA, which had consistently backed the Shamir hard line against the PLO, could only describe the new American position as "troublesome" and a "sobering reality." (See also "The United States, Israel, and the Middle East," elsewhere in this volume.)

Memorializing the Holocaust

In January 1988, over 300 children of Holocaust survivors met in Los Angeles for a three-day conference about "Jewish Identity in the 21st Century: A Challenge for the Post-Holocaust Generation." The very name of the gathering indicated the extent to which many American Jews had come to see the Nazi Holocaust as the appropriate context for discussions of the Jewish future. The featured speakers drew a series of practical implications from the destruction of European Jewry: not to allow the Catholic Church to obscure its record during the Holocaust; to effect a massive *aliyah* of American Jews to Israel; to keep Judaism alive by combating assimilation on college campuses; not to let Israel become the sole source of Jewish identification; not to let the Holocaust become a substitute religion.

Events during 1988 not only underlined the Holocaust's centrality in the American Jewish consciousness but also indicated widespread non-Jewish recognition of Jewish sensitivities on the matter. Jewish hostility to President Kurt Waldheim of Austria for his SS past helped ensure that the United States—and other Western governments—would treat him as a diplomatic pariah. Jewish interest in disseminating understanding about the Holocaust induced the U.S. Department of Defense to set the week of April 10–17 as a period of Holocaust remembrance for the armed forces, and to issue a 96-page booklet, prepared by the Anti-Defamation League, about how to organize Holocaust commemorations. After participating in one such event at an army base in White Sands, New Mexico, the executive director of the El Paso Jewish federation expressed a common Jewish justification for such activities, saying, "I think the ceremony led to a better understanding. The Holocaust is not something we want to see happen here, and we hope to find out how to prevent that from happening again." Senate passage in October of a bill finalizing American acceptance of the international treaty against genocide, and President Ronald Reagan's approval of it in November, also symbolized Jewish success in interpreting such concerns to the nation at large. "I am delighted to fulfill a promise made by Harry Truman to all the peoples of the world—and especially the Jewish people," announced Reagan.

On May 19, the U.S. Holocaust Memorial Council—itself testimony to government sympathy with the American Jewish interest in remembering the past—announced that it had raised over $50 million from private philanthropy. This sum would be used to begin construction of a Holocaust museum on federally donated land in Washington, D.C. Preliminary plans called for a three-story structure, the first devoted to the years 1933–39, the second to the Holocaust itself, and the third to an assessment of its legacy. On October 5, President Reagan dedicated the museum's cornerstone with a promise that "the Jewish people will never stand alone against tyranny" and an attack on those guilty of "minimizing or even denying the truth of the Holocaust."

Another aspect of American Jewish Holocaust consciousness was support for bringing to justice those guilty of Nazi war crimes. In April, when John Demjanjuk, a native Ukrainian and retired auto worker from Cleveland, was convicted in an Israeli court of operating the gas chamber at the Treblinka death camp, American Jewish organizations approved, despite the resentment the verdict aroused among some East European ethnic groups in the United States. When Demjanjuk was sentenced to death, ADL's Abraham Foxman, expressing the consensus of American Jewish leadership, asked rhetorically, "What other penalty would be appropriate" for such crimes?

Jewish sensitivities to the Holocaust played a role in the presidential election campaign. Allegations of anti-Semitism and sympathy for Holocaust revisionism led Republican candidate George Bush to fire several campaign workers. Both Mr. Bush and Kitty Dukakis, the Jewish wife of his Democratic opponent, Michael Dukakis, visited the Holocaust memorial in Skokie, Illinois, where neo-Nazis had marched ten years before.

November 9–10, 1988, was the 50th anniversary of *Kristallnacht*, the night on which the Nazis vandalized and destroyed synagogues and other Jewish-owned buildings all over Germany. In preparation for the occasion, Ronald Lauder, the multimillionaire former ambassador to Austria, funded a publicity campaign organized around the theme that *Kristallnacht* marked the beginning of the Holocaust. Under Lauder's sponsorship, over 1,000 commemorative activities were held in the New York area alone. The Synagogue Council of America and the United Jewish Appeal, cooperating with Lauder, asked synagogues, churches, and other public institutions to leave lights on for 24 hours on November 9.

Similar events took place around the country, even in communities with few Jews. At the last minute, even Jesse Jackson—who was not exactly known for his close ties to the Jewish community—acknowledged the significance of the day by deciding to speak at a memorial meeting in Washington. Governors of all 50 states issued proclamations commemorating *Kristallnacht*. Throughout the week of the anniversary, television networks and radio stations featured programming on the Holocaust. On November 9, many newspapers published news stories about *Kristallnacht* observances, interviews with people who lived in Germany at the time, and op-ed pieces assessing the long-term significance of that night a half-century ago and deriving lessons from it.

A new book published in December—*The Jewish Way*—by Rabbi Irving Greenberg, president of the Center for Jewish Learning and Leadership (CLAL), showed how deeply the Holocaust experience had affected Jewish theology. After an extensive analysis of the ways in which the cycle of Jewish holidays can speak meaningfully to contemporary men and women, Greenberg suggested that the Holocaust had shattered traditional conceptions of God's covenantal benevolence to the Jewish people. From that time on, he wrote, Jews were no longer bound to follow God's way; those persisting in doing so were taking on the burden of the covenant voluntarily.

Whatever the merits of Greenberg's view—and he had his critics—his book articulated a pervasive sense within the Jewish community that the Holocaust bore an essential message for Judaism. Non-Jews could not help but notice. As New York's Cardinal O'Connor remarked on the anniversary of *Kristallnacht*, "To say to Jews, 'forget the Holocaust' is to say to Christians, 'forget the Crucifixion.' "

Soviet Jewry

In January 1988, Jerry Goodman announced that he would resign as executive director of the National Conference on Soviet Jewry (NCSJ), an organization that he helped found in 1971. Explaining why he had chosen just this time to make the decision, Goodman suggested that a phase of the Soviet Jewry movement was ending. Citing the successful mobilization for Soviet Jewry held in Washington, D.C., on December 6, 1987, as the symbolic turning point, he said, "This is a time of change. We are on the threshold of new developments." Indeed, as 1988 unfolded, American Jews scrambled to keep up with dramatic changes in Soviet policy, even as they began to face up to the new problems they raised.

On January 4, the National Conference reported that 8,155 Jews had left the Soviet Union in 1987, the most in any one year since 1981. Two weeks later, the USSR granted permission for an Israeli diplomatic mission to visit. And on January 28, the board of governors of the U.S.-based B'nai B'rith International decided to test the limits of *glasnost* by seeking to be the first "outside" Jewish organization to open a branch in the Soviet Union (it would take them all year, but by December they succeeded).

Yet through the early months of 1988, American Jewish activists tried to counter the euphoria that these events—especially against the backdrop of the Washington mobilization—might have induced. A drop in the January emigration figures— attributed to a Soviet policy of strict adherence to a rule that only those with first-degree relatives in Israel could get visas to go there—elicited American Jewish protest. When intervention by Secretary of State Shultz induced the Kremlin to waive the "first-degree" rule for 1988, the National Conference warned that similar pledges in the past had not been honored.

In March President Reagan announced that he would go to Moscow at the end of May for a summit meeting with Mikhail Gorbachev. NCSJ chairman Morris Abram declared that "if the deliberations in Moscow are to be considered fruitful, and if we are to be able to believe Soviet promises on the whole range of issues, the Moscow meeting must result in the adoption of a program that will lead to sustained, systematic and substantial Jewish emigration."

Although confrontational rhetoric continued, it was clear that change was in the air when, in April, the Coalition to Free Soviet Jews announced cancellation of the Solidarity Sunday March for Soviet Jewry, an annual event in New York City for the previous 16 years. "You don't hold a demonstration because you have nothing else to do," explained the coalition's executive director. Most of the organizations involved in the Soviet Jewry movement now felt that *glasnost* had made the strategy of mass rallies obsolete. As Lynn Singer, executive director of the Long Island Committee for Soviet Jewry put it, "To all intents and purposes, the community feels that the problem is no longer the problem of the 1970s and 1980s. The 'names' have been released and we have to go through a new education process."

The Student Struggle for Soviet Jewry (SSSJ), however, considered cancellation of the rally "an absolute outrage," and, in cooperation with other like-minded groups, sponsored a demonstration on May 1. It featured an emotional appeal by former prisoner of Zion Yosef Begun, who called for putting unremitting pressure on the USSR until all refuseniks were allowed to leave the country. SSSJ leader Rabbi Avi Weiss insisted that *glasnost* was a hoax. "Tell Gorbachev we will not be fooled; we will not be silent," he said.

As President Reagan prepared for the Moscow summit, the mainstream and militant wings of the Soviet Jewry movement pursued different strategies. A delegation of the former—organized by the National Conference—met for 20 minutes with Mr. Reagan on May 12, getting a pledge from him that human rights would be high on the summit agenda. The National Conference also decided to send 50 prominent Americans to Helsinki—a stopover point for the president on his way to the USSR—for a silent vigil on behalf of Soviet Jews. In contrast, the SSSJ and the Union of Councils for Soviet Jewry (UCSJ) announced plans for more aggressive tactics in Helsinki: news conferences, a march to the Soviet embassy, and a mock "trial" of *glasnost*.

President Reagan turned out to be as good as his word, placing the human-rights agenda center-stage in the Moscow talks. American Jewish leaders were grateful. Said Jerry Goodman, "I am not surprised by the commitment. I am pleasantly surprised by the amount of exposure the administration gave to this issue." Buoyed by administration sympathy for their cause, 5,000 people filled Times Square in New York City on May 31 to rally for free emigration from the USSR. The next day came more good news: the total number of Jews leaving the Soviet Union in May was put at 1,146, the highest monthly figure in seven years.

Meanwhile, working on its own, the World Jewish Congress (WJC) reported more progress on the Soviet Jewry front. Two weeks before the Reagan-Gorbachev summit, WJC president Edgar Bronfman held discussions with Soviet foreign minister Eduard Shevardnadze. The latter told Bronfman that in light of "a new positive atmosphere," the Kremlin was willing to deal with the problem of Jewish emigration. Symbolizing the revolutionary new openness of the Soviet Union on Jewish issues, the press published reports of these talks, and Soviet television even broadcast parts of them.

Within the American Soviet Jewry movement, the long-felt need for better coordination was partially addressed, in June, by the board of directors of the Council of Jewish Federations and Welfare Funds (CJF), which funds the agencies involved. It was decided that the NCSJ would have full responsibility for setting policy in this area, and that the National Jewish Community Relations Advisory Council (NJCRAC) would maintain a "special relationship with the National Conference, helping coordinate the involvement of local Jewish communities with the national strategies."

Later in the year there were further signs that the plight of Soviet Jews was easing. In September—as a result of the initiative of Rabbi Arthur Schneier of New York—the USSR allowed two Jewish men to come to the United States to study the techniques of circumcision and kosher slaughtering. In the same month, Morris Abram termed "a hopeful sign" a *New York Times* report (September 29) that the Kremlin was about to ease considerably the remaining barriers to Jewish emigration. In October the Soviets gave permission for a Jewish cultural center in Moscow and legalized the teaching of Hebrew throughout the country. No wonder, then, that when Mikhail Gorbachev visited New York in December, the slogans uttered and the placards carried by Jewish demonstrators expressed not just the traditional demand to free Soviet Jewry but also some praise for what had already been accomplished.

EMIGRÉ DESTINATION

As *glasnost* seemed on its way to clearing up the Soviet Jewish emigration problem, the question of where these émigrés were to go—an ongoing bone of contention between Israel and Diaspora Jewry—assumed greater importance.

Israel, alarmed at the high percentage of "dropouts"—Jews who left the Soviet Union on Israeli visas but settled elsewhere—had long sought ways to attract a greater share of these Jews. Having failed in 1987 to get the U.S. government to deny refugee status to Soviet Jews, it announced a new policy on April 24, 1988: the invitations from Israel that Soviet Jews needed in order to obtain exit permits from their government would now direct that the emigrants go to Israel via Romania, not through Vienna, a favorite point for "dropping out" to the West. While this Israeli move did not technically *require* emigrants to take the new exit route, it was clearly intended to discourage Soviet Jews from settling anywhere else but Israel.

The American Soviet Jewry movement split over this decision. The National Conference—which had traditionally cooperated closely with Israel on such matters—announced its support on the ground that it conformed to the NCSJ's own two-track solution: Soviet Jews with Israeli visas should go to Israel, while those wishing to go to the United States should do so through U.S. government channels, without dealing with Israel at all. Noted Jerry Goodman, "Everyone supports the two tracks, as long as we make certain that those Jews who wish to come to America will not be hurt or prejudiced by it."

The Union of Councils for Soviet Jews argued that the new Israeli policy did indeed strip Soviet Jews of the "freedom of choice to emigrate directly to any country of their choice that will accept them." Furthermore, charged the UCSJ, by lowering the number of dropouts seeking asylum in the United States, the existence of the USSR–Romania–Israel route would have the effect of reducing American pressure on the Soviet Union to let more Jews out.

In June Israel went even further in its war on the dropout phenomenon. By a 16–2 vote, the cabinet decided that only those Soviet Jews seriously intending to settle in Israel would receive Israeli visas. The rationale for this action was that the Jewish state was under no obligation to assist Jews in exchanging one diaspora country for another; any Jew who wanted to go to America could seek an American visa.

The NCSJ once again went along with Israeli policy, pointing out that the Soviet Union had become increasingly willing to issue exit permits—without invitations from Israel—to Jews with relatives in the United States. Morris Abram suggested that the new Israeli system still preserved freedom of choice for the emigrants, except that, instead of being exercised in Vienna, the choice of destination would now be made before leaving the Soviet Union. But the UCSJ warned that "if Jews in the Soviet Union believe Israel is the only way out—after 40 years of anti-Israel propaganda and little knowledge of Israel except the terrible things they've heard—they may be discouraged from exercising their right to emigrate."

The two-track model for Soviet Jewish resettlement depended on continued American receptivity to those emigrants eager to come to the United States. But on July 10, the American embassy in Moscow suddenly suspended the issuance of refugee visas on the ground that funds were exhausted. The NCSJ, the Council of Jewish Federations, and the Hebrew Immigrant Aid Society (HIAS) drafted a joint statement urging that new money be found for this purpose. On July 18, the Reagan administration reversed course and announced that it would resume processing visa applications, though it called upon voluntary agencies to foot much of the bill. In response, American Jewish organizations asked Congress to authorize supplemental appropriations for refugee resettlement.

In the fall, Richard Schifter, assistant secretary of state for human rights and humanitarian affairs, spoke pessimistically before both the Union of Councils and the National Conference. He stated forthrightly that even if Congress did come up with more money, the primary financial burden for resettling Soviet Jews would rest with American Jewry. And he warned that "there may be limits as to the numbers of Jews allowed to emigrate to the United States, particularly when there is another country of refuge—Israel." Sure enough, on December 4, American immigration officials started challenging the refugee status of Soviet Jews seeking to enter the United States. With the liberalization of Soviet policy—so the argument ran—it could no longer be taken for granted that every Soviet Jew had the "well-founded fear of persecution" that was required for treatment as a refugee. From now on, such "fear" would have to be proven on a case-by-case basis.

Stunned by this move, American Jewish organizations insisted that, despite the changes wrought by *glasnost*, Soviet Jews as a group were still persecuted and merited refugee status. Following a December 6 meeting of a NCSJ delegation with Secretary of State Shultz for half an hour, Attorney General Richard Thornburgh announced that 2,000 Soviet emigrants per year could enter the country, not as refugees but under the parole power, which meant that they would not be eligible for government funds and could not become citizens unless they married Americans. The irony of the situation was inescapable; for its own budgetary reasons, by making it more difficult for Soviet Jews to enter the United States, the American government was now helping Israel manage its dropout problem.

Jewish Political Options

Early in 1988, Leonard Fein drew renewed attention to the liberal political preferences of American Jews in a new book, *Where Are We? The Inner Life of America's Jews*. Fein, the founder and first editor of *Moment* magazine, described it as a "book about the choices Jews make." Asserting that assimilation, religious Orthodoxy, Holocaust-centeredness, neoconservatism, Israeli chauvinism, and sheer survivalism were unsatisfactory choices, Fein argued that the quest for social justice remained the essence of the Jewish ethos. Speaking before the American Jewish Committee's annual meeting in May, Fein suggested that the bulk of American Jewry realized "that while one is permitted to be rich, one is not permitted—not in this oh-so-fractured planet—to be comfortable."

Fein, and other Jews who shared his views, criticized what they saw as a growing trend in the Jewish community to support candidates for public office solely on the basis of their stand on Israel, a strategy that could garner increased Jewish backing for conservative politicians. "For every ounce of protection we theoretically gain for Israel," warned Fein, "we will lose a pound of protection for pluralism." Writing in the Baltimore *Jewish Times* (March 11, 1988), Hyman Bookbinder, who had served for many years as the American Jewish Committee's Washington representative, claimed that one-issue politics would not, in the end, even help Israel: "It's because our whole Jewish community is active—not only in its pro-Israel activities, but on the civil rights front, and the social justice front—that we have such tremendous credibility. Because we've achieved credibility on the other issues, we've achieved enormous credibility on the issue of Israel."

Jewish neoconservatives—admittedly no more than a small minority of American Jews—strongly disagreed with the assumption that liberal policies were necessarily moral, reflected Jewish values, or were in the Jewish interest. The man most closely identified with the neoconservative movement, Irving Kristol, denied in the pages of *Moment* magazine (October 1988) that defection from the liberal cause connoted the triumph of self-interest over social conscience and called for an end to the "moral posturing" of the Jewish liberals. In his view, liberalism simply had not worked. And on the two major issues which Kristol considered crucial for American Jews—American support for Israel and affirmative action/quotas—he believed that the conservatives' preferences for a strong military and for meritocracy in employment and education were better for Jews than the liberal alternatives.

Since 1988 was a presidential election year, theoretical arguments over Jewish political allegiances were translated quickly into the jab and thrust of the political campaign. Those Jews already wary of liberalism had their suspicions confirmed by the degree of support in the Democratic primaries for Jesse Jackson, who was widely perceived as hostile to Jewish interests, if not an outright anti-Semite. And even though the Democrats ended up nominating Michael Dukakis and not Jackson—argued the noted Jewish theologian Richard Rubinstein in *Sh'ma* (October 14, 1988)—"Jackson has convinced the Democratic leadership that victory cannot be won without him . . . [which] has led them to pander to Jackson. The lesson of a Democratic victory would be that pandering pays."

Jewish liberals answered back. Writing in the same issue of *Sh'ma*, Leonard Fein pointed out that "Jackson is not the nominee of the Democratic party, nor is there any reason to suppose that he will be especially influential in the affairs of state if Dukakis wins." Rabbi Harold Schulweis, though disappointed that Jackson would not denounce concrete instances of black anti-Semitism, did not think that this merited Jewish abandonment of the Democratic party and its commitment to the poor and disadvantaged. "Those who counsel Jews to distance themselves from the anguish of other peoples," he wrote, "are ignorant of the Biblical, prophetic, rabbinic, and Jewish philosophic traditions that mandate an active empathy toward the submerged communities of non-Jews."

Despite Jewish concern over Jackson's potential power in a Dukakis administration, the result on election day indicated that Jewish liberalism was alive and well. The country at large gave Republican George Bush a substantial majority, but the Jews voted about two-to-one for the Democrat Dukakis; blacks were the only group that went more heavily Democratic than Jews.

The perceived influence of fundamentalist Christians on the Republican party and revelations about the anti-Semitic pasts of some Bush activists may have stiffened Jewish resistance to Republican blandishments; however, Hyman Bookbinder was surely correct in pointing out after the election that most American Jews had "remained loyal to their basic commitments." An AJCommittee survey of Jewish political attitudes taken in the spring of 1988 (and published the next year as *The Dimensions of American Jewish Liberalism*) showed that Jews were consistently more liberal than other white Americans on such vital issues as government responsibility for social welfare, church-state separation, civil rights, abortion, gay rights, and pornography. And a *Los Angeles Times* poll taken around the same time found that Jews perceived a connection between these views and their Jewishness. Asked, "As a Jew, which of the following qualities do you consider most important to your Jewish identity: a commitment to social equality, or religious observance, or support for Israel, or what?" fully half the sample chose "social equality," far more than for any other response.

Bitterly disappointed that George Bush could get no more than a third of the Jewish vote, Jewish neoconservatives could only conclude that Jews were, in the words of Prof. Jacob Neusner, "atavistic" in their liberalism, blind to their real interests (Jewish Telegraphic Agency, JTA, November 11, 1988). In the pages of *Commentary* (January 1989), Irving Kristol grumbled that "there is nothing 'Jewish' in the politics of modern liberalism."

Some Jews who identified with the political left believed it possible to transform widespread Jewish support for the Democrats into an organized movement of Jewish progressives. In December, 1,500 Jews gathered in New York City for a three-day conference on "Reconstituting the Progressive Tradition of American Jewish Intellectuals." The organizer was Michael Lerner, editor of *Tikkun* magazine, a liberal Jewish bimonthly that had been established in 1986 to counteract the influence of the neoconservative *Commentary*.

Lerner opened the conference by contrasting the overwhelming Jewish vote for the Democrats with "the conservative style and substance that many people experience as stultifying" and that, he claimed, characterized the mainstream organizations of American Jewry. Lerner indicted these organizations both for their reluctance to take progressive stands on American domestic issues and for their alleged acquiescence in Israel's "irrational and destructive" occupation of Gaza and the West Bank. While the participants—including such prominent figures as social theorist Michael Walzer, literary critic Irving Howe, feminist Letty Cottin Pogrebin, and Israeli statesman Abba Eban—agreed on the shortcomings of the "Jewish establishment," they reached no consensus on how to remedy the situation. Some agreed with Michael Lerner on the need to set up an alternative leftist Jewish organization, others urged liberals to work within the system to influence existing organizations. While one group at the conference expressed interest in developing the case for Jewish progressivism in intellectual terms, another preferred political action. And although some participants sought to combine leftist politics with some version of Jewish spirituality, others had no interest in religion.

The conference adjourned without agreeing to any program or course of action. The fact that it took place at all, however, showed, in Michael Walzer's words, that "there continues to be a large Jewish left, although it may be bruised and battered."

Jewish Organizational Life

One characteristic feature of the American Jewish community, its intricate network of organizations—unmatched in comprehensiveness and complexity by any other ethnic group—came under strain in 1988.

A number of organizations were experiencing fund-raising difficulties. In part the problem had to do with changes in the tax law, which reduced the financial incentive for philanthropy generally, but a study released in June indicated that the money problems of Jewish agencies had deeper roots. At a conference on "Jewish Philanthropy in Contemporary America," held at the City University of New York, Barry Kosmin, director of the North American Jewish Data Bank, discussed the findings of the study. Wealthy Jews, he said, were giving less and less of their charitable dollar to Jewish causes. In the early 1970s, 75 percent of the money contributed by Jews went to Jewish institutions; by 1988 it was around 50 percent. This was so, he explained, because younger givers were more assimilated and secularly oriented than their parents, and more inclined to join the boards of ballet companies and museums than to help fund national and local Jewish institutions.

The stability of the Jewish organizational structure was also threatened in 1988 by a perceived leadership "crisis." The firings in 1987 of the executive vice-presidents of the American Jewish Committee and B'nai B'rith International and the difficulty experienced by other Jewish organizations in attracting and retaining top-level professionals evoked concern: Why were these organizations, which had traditions of long tenure for their senior staff, hiring and firing so frequently?

Michael Berenbaum, a theologian and consultant to Jewish organizations, charged (*Sh'ma*, January 22, 1988) that the fault lay with the volunteer leaders, who, instead of being satisfied with supporting and encouraging the initiatives of staff, now wanted to control decision making. "Lay participation is essential to the success of an organization—lay participation, but not lay dominance." He argued that the continued success of AIPAC, the Simon Wiesenthal Center, and the Union of American Hebrew Congregations—all run, according to Berenbaum, by powerful professionals, with volunteers clearly subordinate—proved his point.

In the same issue of *Sh'ma*, others took issue with his diagnosis. Theodore Ellenoff, president of the American Jewish Committee, denied that there ever was a "golden age" when professionals ran the show. He cited the long tradition of powerful lay leaders in his own organization, from Jacob Schiff and Louis Marshall to more recent figures such as Judge Joseph Proskauer and Jacob Blaustein. Ellenoff felt that the current problem was that too many professionals, unwilling to cooperate with volunteers, preferred to engage in "wasteful arm-wrestles for domination."

Sanford Solender, who had served for many years as the professional head of New York UJA/Federation, also faulted Berenbaum's analysis. While agreeing that professional control and lay acquiescence might work for a while, he maintained that since the best volunteers will drop out, "the success is illusory and time-limited, and a prescription for long-term weakness and instability." Without such people, he maintained, organizations lose not only their financial support, but also "their special understanding of community interests . . . and their communal, business and professional expertise."

Ironically, AIPAC—the preeminent pro-Israel lobby—which Michael Berenbaum cited as one of the three most effective Jewish organizations, went through its own series of crises toward the end of 1988. On October 12, the *New York Times* published a front-page story about a critical letter from the top executives of the American Jewish Committee, American Jewish Congress, and the Anti-Defamation League to AIPAC. The three membership organizations complained that AIPAC had taken positions outside "the consensus of the organized Jewish community" and, according to the *Times*, they threatened to establish a rival "joint political committee" in Washington.

While AJCommittee, AJCongress, and the ADL acknowledged the existence of such a letter—which was intended to be confidential—they denied any intention of setting up their own lobbying body. All they sought, they claimed, was the opportunity for more consultation with AIPAC before the latter took public policy stands. For its part, AIPAC pointed out that the other organizations were already represented on its executive committee, which met quarterly. AIPAC nevertheless agreed to help develop new procedures for consultation with the "big three."

AIPAC suffered a worse blow on October 23, when the popular CBS-TV show "60 Minutes" subjected it to rough treatment. Under questioning by host Mike Wallace, some of those interviewed charged that AIPAC broke the law by instructing pro-Israel political action committees which candidates deserved their financial support. Indeed, former senator Charles Percy blamed his defeat for reelection on AIPAC, and former under secretary of state George Ball insinuated that it was American Jewry, through AIPAC, that had taken control of U.S. Middle East policy away from the American people. AIPAC responded that it did not funnel money to politicians, but, by making known the positions on Israel of candidates for office, it was "exerting a constitutional and legal right to participate in the democratic process." AIPAC complained that "60 Minutes" had twisted its legitimate support for Israel into "something negative and sinister."

The dust had hardly settled from this episode when, in December, AIPAC went through an internal shake-up. As reported by the JTA (December 22, 1988), Douglas Bloomfield, its legislative director, was asked to resign, as was the entire board of *Near East Report*, the organization's newsletter. Bloomfield's departure reportedly involved a conflict over whether AIPAC should concentrate on lobbying Congress, or give more attention to influencing the White House. The ousting of the *Near East Report* board resulted from its refusal during the presidential campaign to publish remarks by Max Fisher, a prominent Jewish Republican, in support of George Bush.

Religious Life

The steadily growing influence of the most traditional elements within American Orthodox Judaism led, in 1988, to the emergence of clear distinctions between different ideological streams that had long shared the Orthodox label. Three trends were discernible: a "right wing," the self-styled "centrists," and, to the left of them, those calling themselves "traditionalists."

On March 22, Norman Lamm, the president of Yeshiva University, delivered an address at the Fifth Avenue Synagogue in New York City that was reported the next day, in some detail, in the *New York Times*. His theme was "Centrist Orthodoxy: Agenda and Vision, Successes and Failures." Lamm, eager to counter what he considered the "triumphalism" of the right wing of his movement, took on the Orthodox extremists. "Moderation should never be confused with indecisiveness," he declared. "On the contrary, a lack of self-confidence in one's most basic commitments is often expressed in extremism. Only one who is sure of what he stands for can afford to be moderate."

After noting that the centrists shared with all Orthodox Jews an overarching commitment to Halakhah, traditional Jewish law, Lamm discussed three areas on which his vision diverged from the right wing: openness to secular culture, enthusiasm for Zionism, and tolerance of divergent opinions. He noted with pride that his institution, Yeshiva University, provided secular studies along with a Torah curriculum, and castigated those Orthodox elements that insisted on making an issue in Israel out of "Who is a Jew?" While acknowledging that he was unable to accept the legitimacy of non-Orthodox forms of Judaism, Lamm said he considered them "valid groupings" that "possess spiritual dignity" if they are "sincere in their commitments."

Such a public challenge to the Orthodox right wing—which drew immediate applause from Reform and Conservative leaders—evoked a strong counterattack. The *Jewish Observer*, the Agudath Israel's monthly magazine, published an "Open Letter to Norman Lamm" by Prof. Aaron Twerski of Brooklyn Law School (April 1988), who leveled a caustic attack on Lamm's tolerance for non-Orthodox Judaism. What did Lamm mean when he called the Reform and Conservative movements "valid"? Surely not valid according to Halakhah—perhaps the intention was to categorize them with "valid" secular organizations like B'nai B'rith? As for their "spiritual dignity," Lamm could hardly have meant that a Jew may pray in their synagogues—perhaps he meant that their rabbis shared the spiritual status "of a Jesuit priest, or . . . a Tibetan Monk?" In the name of "Torah Judaism," Twerski challenged Lamm: "The public has a right to know . . . are you there with us?"

Lamm responded in a conciliatory manner (*Jewish Observer*, Summer 1988). By "valid," he explained, he had in mind the Latin root of the word, which means "strong": the non-Orthodox groups were established facts that could not be wished away. And his attribution to them of "spiritual dignity" referred only to their sincerity—indeed comparable to that of Jesuit priests and Tibetan monks. "Yes,

Professor Twerski," he concluded, "I am there with you."

But Twerski was not satisfied. If Lamm really shared the right-wing perspective, why had he not protested to the *Times* for distorting his words? Twerski used the opportunity to express his contempt for the centrism that Lamm stood for: "If you are the center of normative Judaism," he sneered, "just exactly who represents the Left?"

That question was answered in September, at the first national conference of the Fellowship of Traditional Orthodox Rabbis. This group was organized by rabbis who felt that even the centrist Orthodoxy of Yeshiva University and the Union of Orthodox Jewish Congregations had drifted too far to the right. Indeed, these men felt that the very appellation "centrist," which had replaced "modern" in these circles, constituted a concession to the strict traditionalists.

The majority of rabbis in the new fellowship served synagogues that departed from Orthodoxy only in allowing men and women to sit together during services—a deviation that had long been tolerated by national Orthodox bodies but was now under attack. The Union of Orthodox Jewish Congregations had notified these synagogues that they would lose their membership unless they separated the sexes. Similarly, rabbinical graduates of Yeshiva University who formerly served these congregations would no longer accept such pulpits, fearful of being branded as less than fully Orthodox.

Conservative Judaism, which had undergone internal disputes between right and left over the religious role of women, and between rabbis and lay leaders over their respective places in the movement, sought in 1988 to articulate a unified, compelling vision for Jewish life. How well it succeeded was a matter of debate.

Emet Ve-Emunah, the first official statement of Conservative principles in the movement's history, was released at the annual meeting of the Rabbinical Assembly in March. The product of three years of work by a committee headed by Rabbi Robert Gordis, *Emet Ve-Emunah* sought to assert the authority of Jewish tradition while at the same time rejecting theological fundamentalism. The difficulty in doing so coherently led the drafting committee to assert the legitimacy of divergent approaches and to stress the importance of tolerating a variety of views. Thus, after articulating the centrality of belief in God, the document went on, "we have the right to challenge the existence of God." *Emet Ve-Emunah* urged greater attention to ritual practice in the home and advocated halakhic flexibility to enable Judaism to adapt to social change.

That conflicts within the movement would not necessarily be resolved by declarations of principle became clear at the annual meeting of the Conservatives' Cantors Assembly in May. Although the Rabbinical Assembly admitted female rabbis, although the Jewish Theological Seminary already granted cantorial diplomas to its female graduates, and despite a shortage of cantors in the movement, the Cantors Assembly voted 97–95 against admitting the first four female applicants (a two-thirds vote was required for acceptance). JTS chancellor Ismar Schorsch expressed his disappointment and predicted that the cantors would eventually change their minds. But the leader of the opposition in the Cantors Assembly called the vote "a victory for common sense, for *halakha*, and for due process."

The Conservative movement reacted with dismay, in June, when the official rabbinate in Jerusalem revoked the kosher certification of a Conservative youth hostel that had operated unhindered for 15 years. While the authorities had no complaints about the food, their discovery of Conservative sponsorship convinced them that the hostel was comparable to a "monastery," a place that "destroys the Jewish religion," and therefore unfit for a kosher certificate. "Issues of politics, not piety, are controlling the Jerusalem rabbinate," charged the president of the United Synagogue of America. "The Conservative movement will not accept second-class citizenship in Israel." This affair still rankled when the World Movement of Conservative Judaism and its constituent organizations convened in Jerusalem in July for the ordination of the first Israeli Conservative rabbis. The United Synagogue endorsed a petition to the Israeli Supreme Court calling for restoration of the kosher certificate, even if that meant overriding the rabbinate's authority. The Rabbinical Assembly passed a resolution urging the abolition of Israel's chief rabbinate, which, it claimed, "is not based on Jewish tradition."

Chancellor Schorsch of JTS saw Israeli Orthodox intransigence as part and parcel of a "messianic mindset" that affected the country's foreign policy as well. In September, in a widely reported speech, he came down squarely on the side of the Israeli Left's "land for peace" formula, warning that "Israel must not permit itself to be progressively recast in the image of an East European shtetl." He called for the drafting of yeshivah students into the Israeli military and urged a requirement that all rabbis and rabbinical court judges possess university training. Arguing that four decades of Orthodox power had not convinced the great majority of Israelis to abandon their secularism, Schorsch suggested that religious pluralism deserved a chance.

Compared to the ferment within Orthodoxy and Conservatism, little apparently disturbed the peace of Reform Jews in 1988. There was a flurry of interest at the beginning of the year over the publication in *Moment* (January-February 1988) of a report on a survey that asked Reform rabbis whether they performed intermarriages. Half said that they did, but more than half of those did not want their names publicized. According to Rabbi Irwin H. Fishbein, an outspoken advocate of rabbinic officiation who conducted the survey, "collegial pressure or fear that it will affect career opportunities" kept these rabbis in the closet. Moreover, according to his data, another 32 percent of Reform rabbis, while unwilling to officiate, would refer couples to more flexible colleagues. The article also mentioned the somewhat sobering findings of a recent American Jewish Committee study of 300 couples which found that rabbinic officiation had no discernible impact on the mixed-religion family's future Jewishness.

The impression conveyed that the great majority of Reform rabbis either performed or aided and abetted the performance of mixed marriages, struck a sensitive nerve in the movement. Rabbi Elliot Stevens, an official of the Central Conference of American Rabbis, wrote to counter Fishbein's claims (*Moment*, April 1988). Pointing out that over 60 percent of CCAR members did not respond to the survey, Stevens suspected that most of those were opponents of officiation who wanted nothing to do with a Fishbein project. Stevens claimed that the younger Reform rabbis were more reluctant to perform intermarriages than their older colleagues. He attributed this to their greater appreciation of ritual and tradition, buttressed by the year of study in Israel that had been a requirement of Hebrew Union College since 1970.

The CCAR's 1988 annual convention, which was held in Israel, showed that the movement had complex, indeed ambivalent, feelings about the role of the Jewish state in Reform Judaism. The rabbis sent a letter to Prime Minister Yitzhak Shamir denouncing the beating of Arab protesters "as beyond the bounds of Jewish moral values." CCAR president Eugene Lipman devoted his address to the thesis that one may be a good Zionist without living in Israel. Rabbi Simeon Maslin agreed, arguing that "*galut* [exile] is not a place, *galut* is the abandonment, willingly or unwillingly, of the Jewish mission."

"Who Is a Jew?" Once More

In December 1987, the American Jewish Committee hosted an all-day conference—in conjunction with CLAL and the City University of New York—on "Conflict, Schism or Division? Jewish Communal Antagonism Past, Present and Future." The sessions ranged from a debate over whether the Jewish people might soon split into two, to historical papers on previous internal Jewish conflicts, to practical suggestions for healing the current communal wounds. While opinions differed sharply over many issues, one fact was incontestable: conflict between the religious movements over "Who is a Jew?"—that is, what is a Jewish conversion—posed a powerful threat to the unity of the Jewish people.

That threat loomed larger in June of 1988, when Orthodox factions in the Israeli Knesset once again introduced an amendment to the Law of Return specifying that only those converts who entered into Judaism according to Orthodox practice could be considered Jews. Secular and non-Orthodox Jewish organizations in the United States worked hard to convince the Knesset not to back the bill. The Council of Jewish Federations and the United Jewish Appeal even took out ads in the major Israeli newspapers warning that the amendment would plant "seeds of discord between the Jews of Israel and of the diaspora." American Jewish pressure was given much of the credit for the defeat of the amendment on June 14.

With Israeli elections scheduled for November, American Jews worried that an indecisive result might give the Orthodox parties the balance of power necessary to amend the Law of Return. Anticipating trouble, the American Jewish Congress resolved at its October convention to urge Israeli parties to refrain from using "Who is a Jew?" as a political bargaining chip.

Sure enough, the Israeli elections brought not only a virtual dead heat between

Right and Left but also a much strengthened ultra-Orthodox contingent in the Knesset. Once again, non-Orthodox American Jewish organizations contacted Israeli political leaders in a desperate effort to prevent passage of the problematic amendment. "There will be hell to pay here," commented Rabbi Joseph Glaser, executive vice-president of the CCAR. A joint statement by American Conservative leaders warned that a change in the law "would inevitably lead to the deterioration of Israeli society and the rupture of its unity with the Diaspora." A hastily organized coalition of 27 organizations issued a statement on November 11 charging that acquiescence to the Orthodox "would inflict enormous danger, actual and symbolic, on the Jews of the Diaspora."

The threat of withdrawal of financial support from Israel also emerged. Local federation executives reported that some big givers were disenchanted at the prospect of giving money to a Jewish state that did not recognize their form of Jewishness. Peter Kalikow, publisher of the *New York Post*, threatened to stop buying Israel Bonds. "And I won't be the only one," he said.

The General Assembly of the Council of Jewish Federations, meeting in New Orleans, November 16–20, voted overwhelmingly that "Who is a Jew?" had to be removed from the Israeli political agenda. It sent a high-level delegation to Israel to press its point of view and initiated a petition drive in communities around the country. These steps were considered inadequate by some participants, who preferred a tougher line that would threaten a cutoff of financial support to Israel.

So deep was American Jewish feeling over this matter that it even influenced some of the Orthodox. The Rabbinical Council of America, the major centrist Orthodox rabbinic group in the country, denounced the "Who is a Jew?" amendment as a threat to Jewish unity, calling the matter of identity one that belonged in the hands of religious authorities, not the secular Knesset. Explaining how he reached this position, RCA president Max Schreier described the climate of opinion at the General Assembly as one "which was national and deep and widespread, and not phony." Yeshiva University president Norman Lamm publicly backed the RCA stand, even though Rabbi Aaron Soloveitchik, the senior Talmud professor at his own institution, flew to Israel to encourage passage of the amendment.

The formation in December of another broad-based national unity government, including both the Likud and Labor blocs, deprived the religious parties of their political leverage. A crisis in American Jewish-Israeli relations had been averted.

LAWRENCE GROSSMAN

Jewish Population in the United States, 1989

THE JEWISH POPULATION OF the United States in 1989 was estimated to be 5,944,000, which represents hardly any change from the figure reported for 1988. (The renewal of large-scale Soviet immigration that took place in 1989 will be reflected in next year's estimate.) The current estimate is for the resident Jewish population of the country, including that both in private households and in institutional settings. Non-Jewish family members have been excluded from this total.

While the Jewish federations are the chief reporting bodies, their service areas vary in size and may represent several towns, one county, or an aggregate of several counties. In some cases we have subdivided federation areas to reflect the more natural geographic boundaries. Some estimates, from areas without federations, have been provided by local rabbis and other informed Jewish community leaders. In still other cases, the figures that have been updated are from past estimates provided by United Jewish Appeal field representatives.

The state and regional totals shown in Appendix tables 1 and 2 are derived by summing the individual estimates shown in table 3 and making three adjustments. First, communities of less than 100 are added. Second, duplicated counts within states are eliminated. Third, communities whose populations reside in two or more states (e.g., Kansas City and Washington, D.C.) are distributed accordingly.

The reader should be aware that population estimating is not an exact science and that collection procedures can result in annual fluctuations in community or state totals. In most cases where a figure differs from that shown last year, the increase or decrease did not come about in one year but occurred over a period of time and has just now been substantiated. Similarly, the results of a completed local demographic study often change the previously reported Jewish population figure. This should be understood as either an updated calculation of gradual demographic change or a correction of a faulty older estimate.

In determining Jewish population, communities count both affiliated and nonaffiliated residents. In most cases, counts are made by households, with that number multiplied by the average number of self-defined Jewish persons per household. Most communities also include those born and raised as Jews but who at present consider themselves of no religion. As stated above, non-Jews living in Jewish households, primarily the non-Jewish spouses and any non-Jewish children, are not included in the 1989 estimates presented in the appendix below.

The community reporting the largest documented numeric gain since the last estimate was completed was Dallas, Texas, whose increase—based on a 1988 demographic survey—exceeded 10,000 persons. The Norfolk-Tidewater area of Virginia also raised its estimate, following a demographic survey. Four other southern communities—Atlanta, Georgia; Fort Worth, Texas; Raleigh, North Carolina; and Savannah, Georgia; and one other western community—Sacramento, California—have experienced recent growth and raised their estimates accordingly. Small but significant increases were also reported by Port Angeles and Bellingham, both in Washington State, and Ventura County and San Luis Obispo in California. The increase reported for Connecticut's Norwalk-Westport area is due to both real growth and expanded geographic parameters of that community. In Orange County, New York, the increase is due primarily to the growth of a Hassidic community near Monroe.

The Jewish population has grown in resort communities such as Palm Springs and Murietta Hot Springs, California; Port Charlotte-Punta Gorda, Florida; and the Pocono Mountain area (Pike and Wayne counties) of Pennsylvania. The latter is becoming an exurban extension of the New York City suburbs, as is Dekalb, Illinois, in relation to Chicago.

While the New York area's large numeric decline reported in last year's AJYB was due to the elimination of the non-Jews in Jewish households, this year's largest decline, that of 12,000 in Miami-Dade County, Florida, is the result of actual demographic change in recent years. The primary features of this change are an aging population, an increase in the numbers of non-Jewish immigrants settling in Jewish areas, and a preference by Jewish newcomers to Florida to locate further up the coast in Broward and Palm Beach counties.

More moderate declines have occurred in some of the older, medium- and small-sized cities in the Northeast and Midwest, part of a long-term trend in these regions. The affected communities include Evansville, Indiana; Wheeling and Huntington, West Virginia; Bayonne, New Jersey; Auburn and Cortland, New York; Mansfield, Ohio; and Wilkes-Barre, Pennsylvania. Declines reported for the aging resort towns of Elsinore and Sun City, California, were offset by growth in the aforementioned newer resort areas.

Finally, Hawaii's decrease is due to a correction of a previous overcount.

BARRY KOSMIN
JEFF SCHECKNER

APPENDIX

TABLE 1. JEWISH POPULATION IN THE UNITED STATES, 1989

State	Estimated Jewish Population	Total Population*	Estimated Jewish Percent of Total
Alabama	9,300	4,023,000	0.2
Alaska	2,400	525,000	0.5
Arizona	69,600	3,386,000	2.1
Arkansas	2,000	2,388,000	0.1
California	909,000	27,663,000	3.3
Colorado	49,000	3,296,000	1.5
Connecticut	115,000	3,211,000	3.6
Delaware	9,500	644,000	1.5
District of Columbia	25,400	622,000	4.1
Florida	585,300	12,023,000	4.9
Georgia	67,500	6,222,000	1.1
Hawaii	7,000	1,083,000	0.6
Idaho	400	998,000	0.1
Illinois	258,000	11,582,000	2.2
Indiana	18,300	5,531,000	0.3
Iowa	6,400	2,834,000	0.2
Kansas	14,000	2,476,000	0.6
Kentucky	11,800	3,727,000	0.3
Louisiana	15,800	4,461,000	0.4
Maine	8,500	1,187,000	0.7
Maryland	209,600	4,535,000	4.6
Massachusetts	276,000	5,855,000	4.7
Michigan	84,300	9,200,000	0.9
Minnesota	30,500	4,246,000	0.7
Mississippi	2,100	2,625,000	0.1
Missouri	61,700	5,103,000	1.2
Montana	450	809,000	0.1
Nebraska	7,400	1,594,000	0.5
Nevada	19,500	1,007,000	1.9
New Hampshire	7,000	1,057,000	0.7
New Jersey	411,000	7,672,000	5.4
New Mexico	6,400	1,500,000	0.4
New York	1,844,000	17,825,000	10.3

JEWISH POPULATION IN THE UNITED STATES

State	Estimated Jewish Population	Total Population*	Estimated Jewish Percent of Total
North Carolina	15,800	6,413,000	0.2
North Dakota	800	672,000	0.1
Ohio	130,900	10,784,000	1.2
Oklahoma	5,300	3,272,000	0.2
Oregon	12,300	2,724,000	0.5
Pennsylvania	345,800	11,936,000	2.9
Rhode Island	16,100	986,000	1.6
South Carolina	8,700	3,425,000	0.3
South Dakota	350	709,000	0.1
Tennessee	19,600	4,855,000	0.4
Texas	107,300	16,789,000	0.6
Utah	3,300	1,680,000	0.2
Vermont	4,600	548,000	0.8
Virginia	67,700	5,904,000	1.1
Washington	22,800	4,538,000	0.5
West Virginia	2,400	1,897,000	0.1
Wisconsin	35,800	4,807,000	0.7
Wyoming	450	490,000	0.1
U.S. TOTAL	**5,941,000	243,400,000	2.5

N.B. Details may not add to totals because of rounding.
*Resident population, July 1, 1987. (*Source:* U.S. Bureau of the Census, *Current Population Reports,* series p. 22, no. 26.)
**Exclusive of Puerto Rico and the Virgin Islands, which previously reported Jewish populations of 1,500 and 350, respectively.

TABLE 2. DISTRIBUTION OF U.S. JEWISH POPULATION BY REGIONS, 1989

Region	Total Population	Percent Distribution	Jewish Population	Percent Distribution
Northeast	50,278,000	20.7	3,028,000	50.9
New England	12,844,000	5.3	427,200	7.2
Middle Atlantic	37,443,000	15.4	2,600,800	43.8
North Central	59,538,000	24.5	648,450	10.9
East North Central	41,904,000	17.2	527,300	8.9
West North Central	17,634,000	7.2	121,150	2.0
South	83,884,000	34.5	1,165,100	19.6
South Atlantic	41,684,000	17.1	991,900	16.7
East South Central	15,290,000	6.3	42,800	0.7
West South Central	26,910,000	11.1	130,400	2.2
West	49,700,000	20.4	1,102,600	18.6
Mountain	13,167,000	5.4	149,100	2.5
Pacific	36,533,000	15.0	953,500	16.0
TOTALS	243,400,000	100.0	5,944,000	100.0

N.B. Details may not add to totals because of rounding.

TABLE 3. COMMUNITIES WITH JEWISH POPULATIONS OF 100 OR MORE, 1989 (ESTIMATED)

State and City	Jewish Population	State and City	Jewish Population	State and City	Jewish Population
ALABAMA		**CALIFORNIA**		Oakland (incl. in Alameda County)	
*Birmingham	5,100	Alameda County (listed under San Francisco Bay area)		Ontario (incl. in Pomona Valley)	
Decatur (incl. in Florence total)		Antelope Valley	700	Orange County	85,000
*Dothan	150	Bakersfield (incl. in Kern County)		Palmdale (incl. in Antelope Valley)	
Florence	150	Berkeley (incl. in Contra Costa County total)		Palm Springs[N]	9,600
Huntsville	750	*Chico	500	Palo Alto (incl. in South Peninsula)	
**Mobile	1,100	Contra Costa County (listed under S.F. Bay area)		Pasadena (also incl. in L.A. Metro area)	2,000
**Montgomery	1,300	Corona (incl. in Riverside total)		Petaluma (incl. in Sonoma County)	
Selma	100	***El Centro	125	Pomona Valley[N]	6,750
Sheffield (incl. in Florence total)		*Eureka	500	*Redding	145
Tuscaloosa	300	Fairfield	800	Riverside	1,620
Tuscumbia (incl. in Florence total)		Fontana (incl. in San Bernardino total)		Sacramento[N]	12,000
ALASKA		*Fresno	2,000	Salinas	500
**Anchorage	2,000	Kern County	1,400	San Bernardino area	2,800
***Fairbanks	210	Lancaster (incl. in Antelope Valley)		*San Diego	70,000
Juneau	100	Long Beach (also incl. in Los Angeles total)[N]	13,500	San Francisco Bay area[N]	196,000
Ketchikan (incl. in Juneau total)		Los Angeles Metro area	501,000	San Francisco	45,500
ARIZONA		Merced	170	N. Peninsula	22,000
*Flagstaff	250	*Modesto	450	S. Peninsula	19,500
*Phoenix	50,000	Monterey Peninsula	1,500	San Jose	32,000
Prescott	150	Murietta Hot Springs	400	Alameda County	30,500
*Tucson	19,000	*Napa	450	Contra Costa County	21,000
Yuma	100			Marin County	17,000
ARKANSAS				Sonoma County	8,500
Fayetteville	120				
**Ft. Smith	160				
Hot Springs	200				
**Little Rock	1,300				
Pine Bluff	100				

[N]See Notes below. *Includes entire county. **Includes all of 2 counties. ***Figure not updated.

State and City	Jewish Population
*San Jose (listed under San Francisco Bay area)	
*San Luis Obispo	1,500
*Santa Barbara	3,800
*Santa Cruz	1,200
Santa Maria	300
Santa Monica (also incl. in Los Angeles total)	8,000
Santa Rosa (incl. in Sonoma County)	
Sonoma County (listed under San Francisco Bay area)	
*Stockton	1,600
Sun City	200
Tulare & Kings counties	500
***Vallejo	400
*Ventura County	8,000

COLORADO
Aspen	250
Boulder (incl. in Denver total)	
Colorado Springs	1,500
Denver[N]	45,000
*Ft. Collins	1,000
Grand Junction	250
Greeley (incl. in Ft. Collins total)	
Loveland (incl. in Ft. Collins total)	
Pueblo	250
Vail	100

CONNECTICUT
Bridgeport[N]	18,000
Bristol	200
Cheshire (incl. in Meriden total)	
Colchester	575
Danbury[N]	3,500
Danielson	100
Darien (incl. in Stamford total)	
Greenwich	3,800
Hartford[N]	28,000
Hebron (incl. in Colchester total)	
Lebanon (incl. in Colchester total)	
Lower Middlesex County[N]	1,475
Manchester (incl. in Hartford)	
Meriden[N]	3,000
Middletown	1,300
New Britain (incl. in Hartford)	
New Haven[N]	28,000
New London[N]	4,000
New Milford	400
Newtown (incl. in Danbury)	
Norwalk[N]	9,500
Norwich (also incl. in New London total)	1,800
Putnam	100
Rockville (incl. in Hartford)	
Shelton (incl. in Valley area)	
Southington (incl. in Meriden total)	
Stamford/New Canaan	11,100
Storrs (incl. in Willimantic total)	
Torrington	560
Valley area[N]	550
Wallingford (also incl. in Meriden total)	500
Waterbury[N]	2,700
Westport (incl. in Norwalk total)	
Willimantic area	700

DELAWARE
Dover[N]	650
Wilmington (incl. rest of state)	9,500

DISTRICT OF COLUMBIA
Greater Washington	165,000

FLORIDA
Boca Raton-Delray Beach (listed under Southeast Fla.)	
Brevard County	3,000
*Crystal River	100
Dade County (listed under Southeast Fla.)	
**Daytona Beach	2,000
Fort Lauderdale (listed under Southeast Fla.)	
Fort Myers (incl. in Lee County)	
Fort Pierce	500
Gainesville	1,200
Hollywood (listed under Southeast Fla.)	
**Jacksonville	7,300
Key West	170
*Lakeland	800
Lee County	3,500
*Miami (incl. in Dade County)	
Naples	750
***Ocala	100
Orlando[N]	18,000
Palm Beach County (listed under Southeast Fla.)	
**Pasco County	1,000
**Pensacola	775
*Port Charlotte-Punta Gorda	400
**Sarasota	9,500

State and City	Jewish Population	State and City	Jewish Population	State and City	Jewish Population
*St. Petersburg (incl. Clearwater)....	9,500	Kuaii	100	Evansville	520
		Maui	210	Ft. Wayne	1,125
Southeast Florida	512,000			**Gary-Northwest Indiana	2,300
		IDAHO			
Dade County	226,000	**Boise	220	**Indianapolis...	10,000
Hollywood[N]	60,000	Lewiston	100	**Lafayette	500
		Moscow (incl. in Lewiston total)		Marion...........	100
Ft. Lauderdale[N]	116,000			*Michigan City.....	280
Boca Raton-Delray Beach	52,000	**ILLINOIS**		Muncie...........	160
		Aurora area.......	500	South Bend[N]	1,800
Palm Beach County (excl. Boca Raton-Delray Beach).	55,000	Bloomington-Normal	170	*Terre Haute.......	325
		Carbondale (also incl. in S. Ill. total)....	100	**IOWA**	
Stuart-Port St. Lucie	3,000	*Champaign-Urbana	2,000	Ames (also incl. in Des Moines total)	200
Tallahassee	1,500	Chicago Metro area[N]	248,000	Cedar Rapids	430
*Tampa	12,500	**Danville.........	130	Council Bluffs (also incl. in Omaha total)	150
Venice (incl. in Sarasota total)		*Decatur	210		
*Vero Beach	300	*DeKalb	200	Davenport (incl. in Quad Cities, Ill.)	
Winter Haven (incl. in Lakeland total)		East St. Louis (incl. in S. Ill.)		*Des Moines	2,800
		Elgin[N]	600	*Iowa City	1,200
GEORGIA		Freeport (incl. in Rockford total)		**Sioux City	630
Albany...........	400	Galesburg	100	*Waterloo	235
Athens...........	300	*Joliet	850		
Atlanta Metro area	60,000	Kankakee.........	200	**KANSAS**	
		*Peoria..........	1,000	Kansas City (incl. in Kansas City, Mo.)	
Augusta[N].......	1,400	Quad Cities[N]	1,350	Lawrence.........	175
Brunswick	100	**Quincy..........	125	Manhattan........	100
**Columbus	1,000	Rock Island (incl. in Quad Cities)		*Topeka...........	500
**Dalton	225			Wichita[N]	1,000
Fitzgerald-Cordele .	125	Rockford[N]......	1,000		
Macon	900	Southern Illinois[N]..	825	**KENTUCKY**	
*Savannah.......	2,750	*Springfield	1,000	Covington/Newport (incl. in Cincinnati, Ohio total)	
**Valdosta.........	110	Waukegan	500		
				Lexington[N]	2,000
HAWAII		**INDIANA**		*Louisville.......	9,200
Hilo	280	Bloomington	1,000	Paducah (incl. in S. Ill. total)	
Honolulu (includes all of Oahu) ...	6,400	Elkart (incl. in South Bend total)			

State and City	Jewish Population	State and City	Jewish Population	State and City	Jewish Population
LOUISIANA		**MASSACHUSETTS**		Lowell Area	2,000
Alexandria	350	Amherst	750	Lynn-North Shore area[N]	25,000
Baton Rouge[N]	1,200	Andover[N]	3,000	*Martha's Vineyard	260
Lafayette (incl. in S. Central La.)		Athol area (also incl. in Worcester County total)	300	New Bedford[N]	3,000
Lake Charles	300	Attleboro	200	Newburyport	280
Monroe	525	Beverly (incl. in Lynn total)		Newton (also incl. in Boston total)	34,000
**New Orleans	12,000	Boston Metro Region[N]	228,000	North Adams (incl. in N. Berkshire total)	
*Shreveport	1,000	Brockton[N]	8,000	North Berkshire County	750
South Central La.[N]	250	Brookline (also incl. in Boston total)	26,000	Northampton	700
Tallulah (incl. in Vicksburg, Miss. total)		Cape Cod (incl. all of Barnstable County)	2,900	Peabody (incl. in Lynn total)	
MAINE		Clinton (incl. in Worcester County total)		Pittsfield (incl. all Berkshire County)	3,100
Augusta	500	Fall River	1,780	Plymouth	500
Bangor	1,250	Falmouth (incl. in Cape Cod)		Provincetown (incl. in Cape Cod)	
Biddeford-Saco (incl. in So. Maine)		Fitchburg (also incl. in Worcester County total)	300	Salem (incl. in Lynn total)	
Brunswick-Bath (incl. in So. Maine)		Framingham[N]	10,800	Southbridge (also incl. in Worcester County total)	105
Lewiston-Auburn	500	Gardner (incl. in Athol total)		Springfield[N]	11,000
Portland	3,900	Gloucester (also incl. in Lynn total)	450	Taunton area	1,200
Rockland	110	Great Barrington (incl. in Pittsfield total)		Webster (also incl. in Worcester County total)	125
Southern Maine (incl. Portland)[N]	5,500	*Greenfield	900	Worcester area[N]	10,100
Waterville	300	Haverhill	1,500	*Worcester County	13,700
MARYLAND		Holyoke	550		
*Annapolis	2,000	*Hyannis (incl. in Cape Cod)		**MICHIGAN**	
**Baltimore	93,000	Lawrence (incl. in Andover total)		*Ann Arbor	4,500
Cumberland	265	Leominster (also incl. in Worcester County total)	700	Battle Creek	180
***Easton Park area[N]	100			Bay City	280
*Frederick	600			Benton Harbor	500
*Hagerstown	300			**Detroit	70,000
*Harford County	1,000			*Flint	2,000
Howard County	7,200			*Grand Rapids	1,500
Montgomery and Prince Georges counties	104,500				
Ocean City	100				
**Salisbury	400				
Silver Spring (incl. in Montgomery County)					

State and City	Jewish Population	State and City	Jewish Population	State and City	Jewish Population
**Jackson	325	NEBRASKA		Camden (incl. in Cherry Hill total)	
*Kalamazoo	1,000	Grand Island-Hastings (incl. in Lincoln total)		Cherry Hill[N]	28,000
*Lansing	2,100	Lincoln	1,000	Edison (incl. in Middlesex County)	
*Marquette County	150	Omaha[N]	6,500	Elizabeth (incl. in Union County)	
Midland	200				
**Mt. Clemens	500	NEVADA		Englewood (incl. in Bergen County)	
Mt. Pleasant[N]	120	Carson City (incl. in Reno total)		Essex County[N] (also incl. in Northeastern N.J. total)	76,200
*Muskegon	235	*Las Vegas	18,000		
*Saginaw	200	**Reno	1,400	North Essex	15,600
MINNESOTA		NEW HAMPSHIRE		East Essex	10,800
**Duluth	500	Bethlehem	100	South Essex	20,300
*Minneapolis	22,000	Claremont	200	Livingston	12,600
Rochester	400	Concord	450	West Orange-Orange	16,900
**St. Paul	7,500	Dover	450		
Winona (incl. in LaCrosse, Wis. total)		Hanover-Lebanon	360	Flemington	900
		***Keene	105	Freehold (incl. in Monmouth County)	
MISSISSIPPI		**Laconia	270	Gloucester (incl. in Cherry Hill total)	
Biloxi-Gulfport	150	Littleton (incl. in Bethlehem total)		Hoboken (listed under Hudson County)	
Clarksdale	100	Manchester	3,000		
**Cleveland	120	Nashua area	480	Hudson County (also incl. in Northeastern N.J. total)	13,750
**Greenville	480	Portsmouth area	1,100		
**Hattiesburg	120	Salem (also incl. in Andover, Mass. total)	150	Bayonne	2,500
**Jackson	700			Jersey City	5,500
**Vicksburg	105	NEW JERSEY		Hoboken	750
MISSOURI		Asbury Park (incl. in Monmouth County)		North Hudson County[N]	5,000
Columbia	350	*Atlantic City (incl. Atlantic County)	15,800	Jersey City (listed under Hudson County)	
Hannibal (incl. in Quincy, Ill. total)				Lakewood (incl. in Ocean County)	
Joplin	100	Bayonne (listed under Hudson County)		Livingston (incl. in Essex County)	
Kansas City Metro area	19,100	Bergen County (also incl. in Northeastern N.J. total)	85,000	Middlesex County[N] (also incl. in Northeastern N.J. total)	40,000
Springfield	285				
*St. Joseph	280	***Bridgeton	325		
**St. Louis	53,500	Bridgewater (incl. in Somerset County)		Millville	135
MONTANA					
*Billings	200				
Butte	110				
Helena (incl. in Butte total)					

State and City	Jewish Population	State and City	Jewish Population	State and City	Jewish Population
Monmouth County (also incl. in Northeastern N.J. total)	33,600	Toms River (incl. in Ocean County)		Fredonia (incl. in Dunkirk total)	
		Trenton[N]	8,500	Geneva	300
Morris County (also incl. in Northeastern N.J. total)	33,500	Union County (also incl. in Northeastern N.J. total)	30,000	Glens Falls[N]	800
				*Gloversville	420
				*Herkimer	180
Morristown (incl. in Morris County)		Vineland[N]	2,500	Highland Falls (incl. in Orange County)	
Mt. Holly (incl. in Cherry Hill total)		Warren County	400	Hudson	470
		Wayne (incl. in Passaic County)		*Ithaca	1,250
Newark (incl. in Essex County)		Wildwood	425	Jamestown	100
New Brunswick (incl. in Middlesex County)		Willingboro (incl. in Cherry Hill total)		Kingston[N]	4,500
				Lake George (incl. in Glens Falls total)	
Northeastern N.J.[N]	351,650	NEW MEXICO		Liberty (also incl. in Sullivan County total)	2,100
Ocean County (also incl. in Northeastern N.J. total)	9,500	*Albuquerque	4,500	***Massena	140
		Las Cruces	525	Middletown (incl. in Orange County)	
		Los Alamos	250		
Passaic County (also incl. in Northeastern N.J. total)	18,700	Santa Fe	900	Monroe (incl. in Orange County)	
		NEW YORK		Monticello (also incl. in Sullivan County total)	2,400
Passaic-Clifton (also incl. in Passaic County total)	8,000	*Albany	12,000		
		Amenia (incl. in Dutchess County)		New York Metro area[N]	1,671,000
Paterson (incl. in Passaic County)		Amsterdam	450	Bronx	85,000
Perth Amboy (incl. in Middlesex County)		*Auburn	175	Brooklyn	418,900
		Beacon (incl. in Dutchess County)		Manhattan	274,300
Phillipsburg (incl. in Easton, Pa. total)		*Binghamton (incl. all Broome County)	3,000	Queens	321,200
				Staten Island	31,000
Plainfield (incl. in Union County)		Brewster (incl. in Putnam County)		Nassau County	311,700
Princeton	2,600	*Buffalo	18,500	Suffolk County	106,200
Salem	100	Canandaigua (incl. in Geneva total)		Westchester County	122,600
Somerset County (also incl. in Northeastern N.J. total)	4,900	Catskill	200	New Paltz (incl. in Kingston total)	
		Corning (incl. in Elmira total)		Newark (incl. in Geneva total)	
Somerville (incl. in Somerset County)		*Cortland	200	Newburgh (incl. in Orange County)	
Sussex County (also incl. in Northeastern N.J. total)	4,100	Dunkirk	120		
		Ellenville	1,600		
		Elmira[N]	1,100		
		Fleischmanns	115		

State and City	Jewish Population
Niagara Falls	395
Olean	120
**Oneonta	250
Orange County	10,000
Pawling	105
Plattsburg	260
Port Jervis (also incl. in Orange County total)	560
Potsdam	250
*Poughkeepsie	6,500
Putnam County	1,000
**Rochester	23,000
Rockland County	60,000
Rome	205
Saratoga Springs	500
**Schenectady	5,200
South Fallsburg (also incl. in Sullivan County total)	1,100
Sullivan County	7,425
Syracuse[N]	9,000
Troy area	800
Utica[N]	1,900
Walden (incl. in Orange County)	
Watertown	170
Woodstock (incl. in Kingston total)	

NORTH CAROLINA
Asheville[N]	1,350
**Chapel Hill-Durham	2,800
Charlotte[N]	4,000
Elizabethtown (incl. in Wilmington total)	
*Fayetteville area	300
Gastonia	240
Goldsboro	120
*Greensboro	2,700
Greenville	300
Hendersonville	135
**Hickory	100
High Point (incl. in Greensboro total)	
Jacksonville (incl. in Wilmington total)	
Raleigh	2,500
Whiteville (incl. in Wilmington total)	
Wilmington area	500
Winston-Salem	440

NORTH DAKOTA
| Fargo | 500 |
| Grand Forks | 150 |

OHIO
**Akron	6,000
Athens	100
Bowling Green (also incl. in Toledo total)	120
Butler County	900
**Canton	2,400
Cincinnati[N]	23,000
**Cleveland[N]	65,000
*Columbus	15,000
**Dayton	6,000
East Liverpool	200
Elyria	250
Fremont (incl. in Sandusky total)	
Hamilton (incl. in Butler County total)	
*Lima	365
Lorain	600
Mansfield	250
Marietta (incl. in Parkersburg, W.Va. total)	
Marion	110
Middletown (incl. in Butler County total)	
New Philadelphia (incl. in Canton total)	
**Newark	105
Norwalk (incl. in Sandusky total)	
Oberlin (incl. in Elyria total)	
Oxford (incl. in Butler County total)	
**Sandusky	130
Springfield	250
*Steubenville	180
Toledo[N]	6,300
Warren (also incl. in Youngstown total)	400
Wooster	125
Youngstown[N]	4,000
*Zanesville	120

OKLAHOMA
Norman (also incl. in Oklahoma City total)	350
**Oklahoma City	2,300
*Tulsa	2,750

OREGON
*Corvallis	150
Eugene	2,300
**Medford	500
Portland	9,000
**Salem	250

PENNSYLVANIA
Allentown	6,000
*Altoona	480
Ambridge[N]	350
Beaver Falls (incl. in Upper Beaver County)	
Bethlehem	810
**Bradford	110
Brownsville (incl. in Uniontown total)	
Bucks County (lower portion)[N]	14,500

State and City	Jewish Population	State and City	Jewish Population	State and City	Jewish Population
*Butler	285	Pike County	300	Westerly (incl. in Washington County total)	
**Chambersburg	470	Pittsburgh[N]	45,000		
Chester (incl. in Phila. total)		Pottstown	700		
		Pottsville	250	**SOUTH CAROLINA**	
Chester County (also incl. in Phila. total)	4,000	*Reading	2,800	*Charleston	4,000
		*Scranton	3,150	**Columbia	2,000
Coatesville (incl. in Chester County total)		Shamokin (incl. in Sunbury total)		Florence area	210
Easton area	1,200	Sharon (also incl. in Youngstown, Ohio total)	260	Georgetown (incl. in Myrtle Beach total)	
*Erie	800			Greenville	800
Farrell (incl. in Sharon total)		State College	550	Kingstree (incl. in Sumter total)	
		*Stroudsburg	400		
Greensburg (also incl. in Pittsburgh total)	425	Sunbury[N]	160	**Myrtle Beach	425
		Tamaqua (incl. in Hazleton total)		***Orangeburg County	105
**Harrisburg	6,500				
Hazleton area	410	Uniontown area	290	Rock Hill (incl. in Charlotte total)	
Honesdale (incl. in Wayne County)		Upper Beaver County	200	*Spartanburg	320
		**Washington (also incl. in Pittsburgh total)	250	Sumter[N]	175
Jeanette (incl. in Greensburg total)					
		Wayne County	500	**SOUTH DAKOTA**	
**Johnstown	485	Waynesburg (incl. in Washington total)		Sioux Falls	135
Lancaster	2,100				
*Lebanon	400	West Chester (also incl. in Chester County)	300	**TENNESSEE**	
Lewisburg (incl. in Sunbury total)				Bristol (incl. in Johnson City total)	
		Wilkes-Barre[N]	3,500		
Lock Haven (incl. in Williamsport total)		**Williamsport	415	Chattanooga	2,000
		York	1,500	Jackson	100
McKeesport (incl. in Pittsburgh total)				Johnson City	210
		RHODE ISLAND		Kingsport (incl. in Johnson city total)	
New Castle	200	Cranston (incl. in Providence total)			
New Kensington (incl. in Pittsburgh total)				Knoxville	1,350
		Kingston (incl. in Washington County total)		Memphis	10,000
Norristown (incl. in Philadelphia total)				Nashville	5,520
		Newport-Middletown	700	Oak Ridge	200
**Oil City	145				
Oxford-Kennett Square (incl. in Chester County)		Providence area	14,200	**TEXAS**	
		Washington County	1,200	Amarillo[N]	190
Philadelphia area[N]	250,000			*Austin	5,000
				Bay City (incl. in Wharton total)	
Phoenixville (incl. in Chester County)				Baytown	300
				Beaumont	800

State and City	Jewish Population	State and City	Jewish Population	State and City	Jewish Population
*Brownsville	325	Newport (incl. in St. Johnsbury total)		**WASHINGTON**	
College Station-Bryan	400	Rutland	550	Bellingham	300
*Corpus Christi	1,400	**St. Johnsbury	100	Ellensburg (incl. in Yakima total)	
**Dallas	34,000			Longview-Kelso (incl. in Portland total)	
El Paso	4,800	**VIRGINIA**		Olympia	300
*Ft. Worth	5,000	Alexandria (incl. Falls Church, Arlington, and Fairfax counties)	35,100	Port Angeles	100
Galveston	800			Pullman (incl. in Moscow, Idaho total)	
Harlingen (incl. in Brownsville total)		Arlington (incl. in Alexandria total)		*Seattle[N]	19,500
**Houston[N]	42,000	Blacksburg	300	Spokane	800
Kilgore (incl. in Longview total)		Charlottesville	950	*Tacoma	1,100
Laredo	200	Chesapeake (incl. in Portsmouth total)		Tri Cities[N]	180
Longview	200	Colonial Heights (incl. in Petersburg total)		Vancouver (incl. in Portland total)	
*Lubbock	225	Danville	100	**Yakima	100
Lufkin (incl. in Longview total)		Fredericksburg	140		
Marshall (incl. in Longview total)		Hampton (incl. in Newport News)		**WEST VIRGINIA**	
*McAllen	475	Harrisonburg (incl. in Staunton total)		Bluefield-Princeton	250
Midland-Odessa	150	Lynchburg area	275	*Charleston	1,025
Paris (incl. in Sherman-Denison total)		**Martinsville	130	Clarksburg	115
Port Arthur	100	Newport News (incl. Hampton)[N]	2,500	Fairmont (incl. in Clarksburg total)	
San Angelo	100	Norfolk-Virginia Beach	18,000	Huntington[N]	275
*San Antonio	9,000	Petersburg area	550	Morgantown	150
Sherman-Denison	125	Portsmouth-Suffolk (also incl. in Norfolk total)	1,900	**Parkersburg	100
Tyler	450	Radford (incl. in Blacksburg total)		**Wheeling	300
Waco[N]	500	Richmond[N]	8,000		
**Wharton	130	Roanoke	1,050	**WISCONSIN**	
Wichita Falls	260	Staunton[N]	375	Appleton	250
		Williamsburg (incl. in Newport News total)		Beloit	120
UTAH		Winchester[N]	145	Green Bay	260
Ogden	150			*Kenosha	200
*Salt Lake City	3,000			LaCrosse	150
				*Madison	4,500
VERMONT				Manitowoc	100
Bennington	100			Milwaukee[N]	29,000
Brattleboro	150			Oshkosh	150
**Burlington	3,000			*Racine	375
Montpelier-Barre	500			Sheboygan	160
				Superior (also incl. in Duluth, Minn. total)	100

State and City	Jewish Population	State and City	Jewish Population	State and City	Jewish Population
Waukesha (incl. in Milwaukee total)		WYOMING		Laramie (incl. in Cheyenne total)	
Wausau[N]	240	Casper	100		
		Cheyenne	230		

Notes

CALIFORNIA

Long Beach–includes in L.A. County Long Beach, Signal Hill, Cerritos, Lakewood, Rosmoor, and Hawaiian Gardens. Also includes in Orange County Los Alamitos, Cypress, Seal Beach, and Huntington Harbor.

Palm Springs–includes Palm Springs, Desert Hot Springs, Cathedral City, Palm Desert, and Rancho Mirage.

Pomona Valley–includes Alta Loma, Chino, Claremont, Cucamonga, La Verne, Montclair, Ontario, Pomona, San Dimas, and Upland. Portion also included in Los Angeles total.

Sacramento–includes Yolo, Placer, El Dorado, and Sacramento counties.

San Francisco Bay area–North Peninsula includes northern San Mateo County. South Peninsula includes southern San Mateo County and towns of Palo Alto and Los Altos in Santa Clara County. San Jose includes remainder of Santa Clara County.

COLORADO

Denver–includes Adams, Arapahoe, Boulder, Denver, and Jefferson counties.

CONNECTICUT

Bridgeport–includes Monroe, Easton, Trumbull, Fairfield, Bridgeport, Shelton, Stratford, and part of Milford.

Danbury–includes Danbury, Bethel, New Fairfield, Brookfield, Sherman, Newtown, Redding, Ridgefield, and part of Wilton; also includes Brewster and Goldens Bridge in New York.

Hartford–includes most of Hartford County and Vernon, Rockville, Ellington, and Tolland in Tolland County.

Lower Middlesex County–includes Branford, Guilford, Madison, Clinton, Westbrook, Old Saybrook. Portion of this area also included in New London and New Haven totals.

Meriden–includes Meriden, Southington, Cheshire, and Wallingford. Portion also included in New Haven total.

New Haven–includes New Haven, East Haven, Guilford, Branford, Madison, North Haven, Hamden, West Haven, Milford, Orange, Woodbridge, Bethany, Derby, Ansonia, and Cheshire.

New London–includes central and southern New London County. Also includes part of Lower Middlesex County and part of Windham County.

Norwalk–includes Norwalk, Weston, Westport, East Norwalk, Darien, Wilton, part of Georgetown and part of New Canaan.

Valley area–includes Ansonia, Derby, Shelton, Oxford, Seymour, and Beacon Falls. Portion also included in Bridgeport and New Haven totals.

Waterbury–includes Middlebury, Southbury, Naugatuck, Watertown, Waterbury, Oakville, and Woodbury.

DELAWARE

Dover–includes most of central and southern Delaware.

DISTRICT OF COLUMBIA

Greater Washington–includes Montgomery and Prince Georges counties in Maryland; Arlington County, Fairfax County, Falls Church, and Alexandria in Virginia.

FLORIDA

Ft. Lauderdale–includes Ft. Lauderdale, Pompano Beach, Deerfield Beach, Tamarac, Margate, and other towns in northern Broward County.

Hollywood–includes Hollywood, Hallandale, Dania, Davie, Pembroke, and other towns in southern Broward County.

Orlando–includes all of Orange and Seminole counties and part of Lake County.

GEORGIA

Augusta–includes Burke, Columbia and Richmond counties and part of Aiken County, South Carolina.

ILLINOIS

Chicago–includes all of Cook and DuPage counties and Southern Lake County. For a total of Jewish population of the Chicago Metropolitan region, please include Northwest Indiana, Joliet, Aurora, Elgin, and Waukegan totals.

Elgin–includes Northern Kane County, Southern McHenry County, and western edge of Cook County.

Quad Cities–includes Rock Island, Moline (Ill.), Davenport, and Bettendorf (Iowa).

Rockford–includes Winnebago, Boone, and Stephenson counties.

Southern Illinois–includes lower portion of Illinois below Carlinville, adjacent western portion of Kentucky, and adjacent portion of southeastern Missouri.

INDIANA

South Bend–includes St. Joseph and Elkhart counties and part of Berrien County, Mich.

KANSAS

Wichita–includes Sedgwick County and towns of Salina, Dodge City, Great Bend, Liberal, Russel, and Hays.

KENTUCKY

Lexington–includes Fayette, Bourbon, Scott, Clark, Woodford, Madison, Pulaski and Jessamin counties.

LOUISIANA

Baton Rouge–includes E. Baton Rouge, Ascencion, Livingston, St. Landry, Iberville, Pt. Coupee, and W. Baton Rouge parishes.

South Central–includes Abbeville, Lafayette, New Iberia, Crowley, Opelousus, Houma, Morgan City, Thibadoux, and Franklin.

MAINE

Southern Maine–includes York, Cumberland, and Sagadahoc counties.

MARYLAND

Easton Park area–includes towns in Caroline, Kent, Queen Annes, and Talbot counties.

MASSACHUSETTS

Andover–includes Andover, N. Andover, Boxford, Lawrence, Methuen, Tewksbury, Dracut, and town of Salem, New Hampshire.

Boston Metropolitan region–includes all towns south and west of Boston within approximately 35 miles, and all towns north of Boston within approximately 20 miles.

Brockton–includes Avon, Brockton, Easton, Bridgewater, Whitman, and West Bridgewater. Also included in Boston total.

Framingham–includes Maynard, Stow, Hudson, Marlborough, Framingham, Southborough, Ashland, Hopkinton, Holliston, Milford, Medway, Millis, Medfield, Billingham, and Franklin. Also included in Boston total.

Lynn–includes Lynn, Saugus, Nahant, Swampscott, Lynnfield, Peabody, Salem, Marblehead, Beverly, Danvers, Middleton, Wenham, Topsfield, Hamilton, Manchester, Ipswich, Essex, Gloucester, and Rockport. Also included in Boston total.

New Bedford–includes New Bedford, Dartmouth, Fairhaven, and Mattapoisett.

Springfield–includes Springfield, Longmeadow, E. Longmeadow, Hampden, Wilbraham, Agwam, and West Springfield.

Worcester–includes Worcester, Northborough, Westborough, Shrewsbury, Boylston, West Boylston, Holden, Paxton, Leicester, Auburn, Millbury, and Grafton. Also included in the Worcester County total.

MICHIGAN

Mt. Pleasant–includes towns in Isabella, Mecosta, Gladwin, and Gratiot counties.

NEBRASKA

Omaha–includes Douglas and Sarpy counties. Also includes Pottawatomie County, Iowa.

NEW HAMPSHIRE

Laconia–includes Laconia, Plymouth, Meredith, Conway, and Franklin.

Manchester–includes Manchester, Hookset, Merrimac, Amherst, Goffstown, Auburn, Derry, and Londonderry.

NEW JERSEY

Cherry Hill–includes Camden, Burlington, and Gloucester counties.

Essex County–East Essex includes Belleville, Bloomfield, East Orange, Irvington, Newark, and Nutley in Essex County, and Kearney in Hudson County. North Essex includes Caldwell, Cedar Grove, Essex Fells, Fairfield, Glen Ridge, Montclair, North Caldwell, Roseland, Verona, and West Caldwell. South Essex includes Maplewood, Millburn, Short Hills, and South Orange in Essex County, and Springfield in Union County.

Middlesex County–includes in Somerset County, Kendall Park, Somerset, and Franklin; in Mercer County, Hightstown; and all of Middlesex County.

Northeastern N.J.–includes Bergen, Essex, Hudson, Middlesex, Morris, Passaic, Somerset, Union, Hunterdon, Sussex, Monmouth, and Ocean counties.

North Hudson County–includes Guttenberg, Hudson Heights, North Bergen, North Hudson, Secaucus, Union City, Weehawken, West New York, and Woodcliff.

Somerset County–includes most of Somerset County and a portion of Hunterdon County.

Trenton–includes most of Mercer County.

Union County–includes all of Union County except Springfield. Also includes a few towns in adjacent areas of Somerset and Middlesex counties.

Vineland–includes most of Cumberland County and towns in neighboring counties adjacent to Vineland.

NEW YORK

Elmira–includes Chemung, Tioga, and Schuyler counties. Also includes Tioga and Bradford counties in Pennsylvania.

Glen Falls–includes Warren and Washington counties, lower Essex County and upper Saratoga County.

Kingston–includes eastern half of Ulster County.

New York Metropolitan area–includes the five boroughs of New York City, Westchester, Nassau and Suffolk counties. For a total Jewish population of the New York metropolitan region, please include Fairfield County, Connecticut; Rockland, Putnam, and Orange counties, New York; and Northeastern New Jersey.

Syracuse–includes Onondaga County, Western Madison County, and most of Oswego County.

Utica–southeastern third of Oneida County.

NORTH CAROLINA

Asheville–includes Buncombe, Haywood, and Madison counties.

Charlotte–includes Mecklenberg County. Also includes Lancaster and York counties in South Carolina.

OHIO

Cincinnati–includes Hamilton and Butler counties. Also includes Boone, Campbell, and Kenton counties in Kentucky.

Cleveland–for a total Jewish population of the Cleveland metropolitan region, please include Elyria, Lorain, and Akron totals.

Toledo–includes Fulton, Lucas, and Wood counties. Also includes Monroe and Lenawee counties, Michigan.

Youngstown–includes Mahoning and Trumbull counties. Also includes Mercer County, Pennsylvania.

PENNSYLVANIA

Ambridge–includes lower Beaver County and adjacent areas of Allegheny County.

Bucks County (lower portion)–includes Bensalem Township, Bristol, Langhorne, Levittown, New Hope, Newtown, Penndel, Warrington, Yardley, Richboro, Feasterville, Middletown, Southampton, and Holland.

Philadelphia–includes Philadelphia City, Montgomery, Delaware County, Chester County, and central and upper Bucks County. For a total Jewish population of the Philadelphia metropolitan region, please include lower Bucks County; the Cherry Hill area and Salem and Mercer counties, New Jersey; and the Wilmington area of Delaware.

Pittsburgh–includes all of Allegheny County and adjacent portions of Washington, Westmoreland, and Beaver counties.

Sunbury–includes Shamokin, Lewisburg, Milton, Selinsgrove, and Sunbury.

Wilkes-Barre–includes all of Lucerne County except southern portion, which is included in Hazleton totals.

SOUTH CAROLINA

Sumter–includes towns in Sumter, Lee, Clarendon, and Williamsburg counties.

TEXAS

Amarillo–includes Canyon, Childress, Borger, Dumas, Memphis, Pampa, Vega, and Hereford in Texas; and Portales, New Mexico.

Houston–includes Harris, Montgomery and Ft. Bend counties and parts of Brazoria and Galveston counties.

Waco–includes Mclellan, Coryell, Bell, Falls, Hamilton, and Hill counties.

VIRGINIA

Newport News–includes Newport News, Hampton, Williamsburg, James City, York County, and Poquosson County.

Richmond–includes Richmond City, Henrico County, and Chesterfield County.

Staunton–includes towns in Augusta, Page, Shenendoah, Rockingham, Bath, and Highland counties.

Winchester–includes towns in Winchester, Frederick, Clark and Warren counties, Virginia; and Hardy and Jefferson counties, West Virginia.

WASHINGTON

Seattle–includes King County and adjacent portions of Snohomish and Kitsap counties.
Tri Cities–includes Pasco, Richland, and Kennewick.

WEST VIRGINIA

Huntington–includes nearby towns in Ohio and Kentucky.

WISCONSIN

Milwaukee–includes Milwaukee County, eastern Waukesha County, and southern Ozaukee County.
Wasau–includes Stevens Point, Marshfield, Antigo, and Rhinelander.

Review of the Year

OTHER COUNTRIES

Canada

National Affairs

DESPITE THE WARNING BELLS sounded by the stock-market crash in October 1987, Canada enjoyed a prosperous 1988: it saw its dollar appreciate from about 77 to about 83 U.S. cents, unemployment decline, and economic growth remain on a steady if unspectacular path. Most political attention focused on the November 21 general election, in which the Progressive Conservative party (PC) of Prime Minister Brian Mulroney sought a second mandate. Canadian Jews faced the election with some special concerns in addition to those shared with their fellow Canadians. Among these, fear that the Canadian position on the Middle East might deteriorate was foremost. In addition, many Jews held serious doubts about the wisdom of the Meech Lake agreement for constitutional change, which was signed in 1987 but still lacked the approval of two provinces.

The major issue in the federal election was free trade with the United States, which was the centerpiece of the PC program but was opposed by the Liberals and New Democrats (NDP). The strategy of stressing the trade issue, which evoked a strong emotional reaction in a country that at least in part defined itself in comparison with its large neighbor and strove to avoid domination by the U.S., was a risky one for Mulroney. Ultimately he swept to another strong victory and majority government, aided in part by the poor campaign conducted by the Liberals, traditionally the main alternative to the PCs.

Of the 1,577 candidates for the House of Commons, 15 were Jewish. There were Jewish candidates in Ontario, Quebec, British Columbia, Manitoba, Newfoundland, and Nova Scotia, including candidates for each of the three major parties. Of the 15, 6 were elected. Gerry Weiner, the first Jewish cabinet minister in a PC government, was handily reelected in his suburban Montreal district. Similarly, Liberal Sheila Finestone won a strong victory for a second term in Montreal's Mount Royal district. Liberal David Berger moved into a new constituency in Montreal because of redistricting and was returned to the House. In Ontario, two Liberal incumbents won easily, Herb Gray in Windsor and Robert Kaplan in Toronto. Dave Barrett, the former NDP premier of British Columbia, won a seat on his first attempt in federal politics. One incumbent Jewish MP who lost was David Orlikow, who held a Winnipeg seat for the NDP for 26 years. Among non-Jewish candidates, a significant loss from the Jewish perspective was Rev. Roland de Corneille, an MP from Toronto, who had failed in his bid for renomination as a Liberal in the spring. De Corneille had been outspoken on innumerable Jewish issues and was viewed by many Jews as one of the most valuable MPs. On the other hand, Bill Attewell, a PC and chairman of the Parliamentary Group for Soviet Jewry, was reelected, as was cabinet minister Barbara McDougall, also very popular with Jewish voters. Both held seats in the Toronto area. In a footnote to the campaign, Douglas Christie, an attorney who had represented anti-Semites James Keegstra and Ernst Zundel, garnered only 171 votes running as an independent in British Columbia.

Earlier in the year, Gerry Weiner, who had been minister of state for immigration in the federal cabinet, was appointed minister of state for multiculturalism. Subsequently, the post was upgraded by the creation of a Department of Multiculturalism and Citizenship headed by Weiner as a full minister.

In the Manitoba provincial election, held in April, Jim Carr, a Liberal, won a seat for the first time. Carr defeated NDP cabinet minister Roland Penner, also a Jew. Other Jews who lost their seats in Manitoba were Marty Dolin of the NDP and Abe Kovnats of the PCs.

Ontario held municipal elections just before the federal election. Mel Lastman, longtime mayor of North York, was reelected, as was City of York councillor Ben Nobleman. Howard Levine won a seat on the Toronto City Council.

MEECH LAKE

Aside from the election itself, a key political issue of concern to Canada's Jews was the Meech Lake accord, a constitutional amendment package that was criticized by many because it would enhance the power of the provincial governments at the expense of the federal government. Although it was quickly approved by the federal Parliament and eight of the ten provincial legislatures soon after the agreement was reached in 1987, New Brunswick and Manitoba were still withholding approval. Unless all the provinces approved by the middle of 1990, the agreement would lapse. Since the accord defined Quebec as a "distinct society," explicitly recognizing that province's right to cultural and linguistic particularism, advocates argued that if it was not put into effect, Quebec might eventually secede. Opponents, such as the Canadian Jewish Congress (CJC), Ontario Region, contended that Meech Lake was too high a price to pay to bring Quebec into the Constitution. They claimed that the accord weakened individual and minority rights and specifically threatened Quebec anglophones. Fears were expressed that the Jewish community of Quebec (about one-third of the Canadian total) might see its overall position weakened and its language rights further eroded.

Relations with Israel

Canadian supporters of Israel had reason to be concerned this year. The warning signals included indications of a possible policy shift by the government, adverse reactions to Israel's handling of the uprising of the Palestinian Arabs, troubling media coverage of Israel, divisions within the Jewish community regarding Israel's policies, and public criticism of Israel.

From the beginning of the uprising there were signs of division within the government as to how Canada should respond. Prime Minister Mulroney was perceived as less willing to criticize Israel than was his Department of External Affairs and its minister, Joe Clark. Mulroney's recognition of Israel's difficult situation and his praise of the country for showing restraint were applauded by the Canada-Israel Committee (CIC) and its constituent organizations. In contrast, External Affairs people reportedly complained to the Israeli ambassador about "Israel's excessive use of force against the Palestinians." Clark himself called in the Israeli ambassador during January to criticize various aspects of Israeli policy regarding the uprising. Later, in response to a reporter's question, Clark replied, "Certainly, human rights are being abused." In addition, both Clark and Mulroney endorsed the idea of an international peace conference, which was opposed by the Israeli government.

At the annual CIC Parliamentary Dinner in March, an occasion that was supposed to have been a celebration of 40 years of Israeli independence, Clark startled the assembled community representatives with a hard-hitting speech in which he used terms such as "unacceptable human rights violations," "illegal under international law," and "shocking" to characterize Israel's handling of the uprising. Clark was also rather blunt in assessing the occupation itself. He stated that "a policy of indefinite control over the land without an acknowledgement of the rights of its inhabitants has been proven a failure," calling upon Israel to withdraw if the Palestinian leadership recognized Israel's territorial integrity. In recapitulating the principles of Canadian foreign policy in the region, Clark emphasized the notion of mutual recognition between Israel and the Palestinians and a homeland for the latter, stopping just short of an overt call for a Palestinian state.

Jewish reaction to the Clark speech was generally quite antagonistic. His delivery was punctuated with boos, jeers, and catcalls. Some members of the audience even walked out on the minister. Immediately after the speech, CIC chairman Sidney Spivak publicly informed Clark that "we fundamentally disagree with your analysis and prescription." Later, the CIC executive, representing the organized Jewish community, stated that it was "appalled at the unbalanced and ill-informed statement." It accused Clark of suffering from a fundamental misunderstanding of the situation between the Arabs and Israel, of misrepresenting facts, and of reacting intemperately. CJC president Dorothy Reitman found it "grotesque that Mr. Clark should intimate that Israel is responsible for the ongoing conflict. . . ." Ralph Snow, president of B'nai Brith Canada, denounced Clark's approach as "ill-informed and unacceptable."

The leaders of the two opposition parties also spoke at the CIC dinner, although their remarks were overshadowed by the consternation caused by Clark's address. NDP leader Ed Broadbent reiterated his party's criticism of the "totally unwarranted" and sometimes "brutal" actions employed by Israel to deal with the *intifada*. John Turner, the Liberal party head, suggested that the occupied territories be placed under a new administration pending the convening of an international peace conference. Turner also restated his own and his party's commitment to Israel, receiving a standing ovation as he concluded.

Considerable community pressure was mounted in response to Clark's speech, with the CIC requesting a meeting with the minister in order to clarify the situation. The meeting between Clark and the executive was held about two weeks later, a day after the prime minister sent a reassuring letter to the CIC ("Israel is our friend"). However, despite the conciliatory comments that followed the meeting, a belief lingered among the CIC people that Clark may have been preparing the ground for a major shift in foreign policy.

Clark was able to mend some fences in an April speech to the Jewish community of Edmonton, a speech that differed markedly in both tone and content from his Ottawa speech. CIC chairman Spivak was pleased with the speech and noted the "constructive, balanced approach" taken by the minister, who stressed Canada's support for Israel's independence and integrity.

Criticism of Israel

Events in Israel had repercussions beyond government policymakers, in particular in the media. The *Toronto Star*, the country's largest circulation newspaper, carried an editorial in March praising Clark's speech to the CIC as "a necessary reminder to members of the Jewish community in Canada that they are citizens of Canada, not Israel." The raising of the dual-loyalty canard brought down an avalanche of criticism on the paper and a demand for an apology by the major national Jewish organizations. The *Star* held fast. Subsequently, after a concerned citizen in London, Ontario filed a formal complaint with the Ontario Press Council, the council found for the complainant, contending that the *Star* should have made clear that it was not referring to all Canadian Jews, only those who had walked out on Clark. The paper was obligated to publish the adjudication decision.

A systematic analysis of Toronto newspaper coverage of Israel and the Middle East was carried out by a media monitoring committee headed by York University professor Sally Zerker. By comparing headlines in the *Star* and the *Globe and Mail* with those in the *New York Times*, Zerker found that the Toronto papers conveyed a more hostile image of Israel than did the *Times*, generally covering only one side of a story. Zerker also observed that "the press is unreasonably persistent in its coverage of Israel," to the point of being obsessive.

In response to criticism of the media, Howard Bernstein, a CBC producer, remarked at a community forum that the Jews were unfairly blaming the messenger.

However, there was no denying that the news had an effect. A definite softening of the strong Canadian public support for Israel was reported by pollster Martin Goldfarb earlier in the year.

This could be seen as well in widening support for the Palestinian cause and increased public criticism of Israel and its policies. In April Shirley Carr, president of the Canadian Labor Congress, criticized violence by both the Israeli government and Palestinian terrorists, but also asserted that the PLO had the right to attend any peace conference on the future of the territories, a new position for her organization. In May the Canadian Council of Churches circulated a draft statement that asked its members to be aware of "the urgency and justice of the Palestinian cause, with consideration for the peace and security of Israel." It added that "the vicious circle of the victims becoming the oppressors must be broken once and for all . . ." and that Israel's annexation of East Jerusalem is a violation of international law and "as such is null and void." The council charged that its freedom of contact with Christians was limited by Israeli authorities, called for withdrawal of Israeli troops from the territories, and supported the creation of a Palestinian state. CJC prepared an elaborate critique of the statement in response.

Other Middle East-Related Issues

Throughout the year, the government pursued the case of Mahmoud Mohammad, a former Palestinian terrorist who immigrated to Canada in 1987 without disclosing his conviction in Greece in 1970 for a 1968 attack on an El Al airplane there that resulted in one death. When the government became aware of his past—including membership in the Popular Front for the Liberation of Palestine—it moved to deport him. After months of protracted hearings, the immigration department adjudicator ruled that Mohammad had lied about his past when he applied for immigrant status. However, he also ruled that Mohammad could not be deported because he had already applied for refugee status in Canada. It was unlikely that a deportation could be carried out until appeals of the immigration hearing and the full process of the refugee application were completed, which could take up to eight years.

Another national issue with a Middle East dimension involved the government's decision to acquiesce to a request excluding certain classes of people, namely Jews, women, and people of Arab extraction, from participation in the Canadian force of some 500 sent to monitor the ceasefire between Iran and Iraq with peacekeepers from 19 other countries. Following CJC charges that the policy was discriminatory, Defense Minister Perrin Beatty announced a review of the decision. He stated, however, that the policy reflected the UN practice of respecting the traditions, customs, religious practices, and beliefs of the host countries. The League for Human Rights of B'nai Brith Canada announced its intention to launch a lawsuit over the issue.

Anti-Semitism

The indefatigable Ernst Zundel spent several months in court again on the retrial of charges that he violated the criminal code by spreading false news, specifically by promoting Holocaust denial. (See "Canada" article, AJYB, annually, going back to 1983.) The prosecution had to prove that he knowingly published false information about the Holocaust that was likely to cause injury to the public interest. Zundel had been convicted on these charges in 1985, but the Ontario Court of Appeal vacated the conviction on technical grounds and ordered a new trial.

In a decision that significantly changed the legal framework from that of the original trial, the judge agreed to a Crown motion to take judicial notice of the Holocaust as an historical fact. This eliminated the necessity of rebutting defense testimony that the Holocaust had not occurred. Much of the trial focused on Zundel's pamphlet—*Did Six Million Really Die?*—the publication of which was the basis for the charge against him. Despite the judge's ruling, the defense concentrated on witnesses who questioned the veracity of accepted historical accounts of the Holocaust, or concurred in some of the defendant's negative views about Jews. One defense witness, Prof. Robert Faurisson, repeated his earlier assertions that no Jews were gassed at Birkenau. Another defense witness, historian David Irving, testified that perhaps as few as 100,000 Jews had been killed by the Nazis.

After some 15 weeks of testimony, the jury finally delivered a guilty verdict. They had heard the Crown prosecutor assert that Zundel published his pamphlet in order to get public attention and that he had anti-Semitic motives. The defense had argued that the pamphlet merely contained opinions, which were constitutionally protected. Zundel was sentenced to nine months in jail, but promised to appeal.

The other major national case involving anti-Semitism, that of former high-school social-studies teacher James Keegstra, continued to work its way through the courts. (See "Canada" article, AJYB 1989, 1988, 1987, 1986.) Keegstra's crime had been to teach his classes that Jews fomented revolution and wars, were evil, and had lied about the Holocaust. In a surprise decision, the Alberta Court of Appeal struck down the antihate law under which Keegstra was convicted and declared it unconstitutional. The fact that the law itself was invalidated was a source of distress to the Jewish community, especially the Jews of Alberta. The necessity for Supreme Court adjudication of the issue became clear when the Ontario Court of Appeal upheld the same law in a case involving the promotion of hatred against nonwhites. In fact, the Alberta attorney general decided to appeal to the Supreme Court of Canada, insuring that eventually the inconsistency between the positions of the Ontario and Alberta courts would be resolved.

Another teacher with allegedly anti-Semitic views was the subject of ongoing controversy in the eastern part of the country. Malcolm Ross of New Brunswick had been the target of accusations for years, for engaging in public anti-Semitic activities, including the publication of a book, *The Spectre of Power*, alleging a worldwide Jewish conspiracy. Although the provincial government had declined to prosecute, for various reasons, the New Brunswick Human Rights Commission, decided to investigate. When the commission was stymied in its investigation by the refusal of the New Brunswick school board to cooperate, a commission of inquiry was established by the government. At that point Ross retained B.C. lawyer Douglas Christie to represent him, adding himself to Christie's existing list of clients that included Zundel, Keegstra, and alleged war-crimes perpetrator Imre Finta. Subsequently, a court took jurisdiction of the case; however, when questions were raised about the commission of inquiry's jurisdiction, this delayed consideration of the substance of the case yet again.

In its report for 1986, B'nai Brith's League for Human Rights documented some 55 anti-Semitic incidents, a decline for the third consecutive year. However, preliminary figures for early 1988 showed an increase from previous years.

In Calgary, police arrested two supporters of the Ku Klux Klan in connection with a plot to murder a prominent Jewish businessman and blow up the Jewish Community Center. In Toronto, the Hillel House at the University of Toronto was vandalized; windows were broken and signs defaced twice within two weeks. Also in Toronto, in a downtown area with many Jewish businesses, a large sign appeared, displayed prominently: "Jews out of Gaza, out of Canada."

A Saint John, N.B., radio station was fined $5,000 for allowing anti-Jewish and antiblack comments on the air by a leader of the racist Aryan Nations group. After the Canadian Radio and Television Commission filed charges in court, the station pleaded guilty. Several Montreal synagogues suffered vandalism during the year. One synagogue, in an area where few Jews resided any longer, was heavily damaged in a fire that was most likely caused by arson. The synagogue had suffered other forms of vandalism in the past. In November there was a rash of anti-Semitic graffiti in the predominantly Jewish suburb of Cote St. Luc, at Jewish institutions and in public places.

Nazi War Criminals

In the aftermath of the Deschenes Report on Nazi war criminals living in Canada, bilateral agreements were concluded between Canada and such countries as Israel, the Netherlands, and the Soviet Union to facilitate cooperation on prosecutions. (See AJYB 1989, pp. 259–60.) Under the agreements, Canadian investigators could gather evidence in the other countries that would be admissible in Canadian courts, under Canadian rules of evidence.

Despite the signing of the agreements, the government was accused of dragging its feet in the pursuit of specific war criminals by David Matas, a lawyer acting on behalf of B'nai Brith Canada. Describing the government as "overcautious," he accused it of "not proceeding with a sense of urgency, enthusiasm, or commitment." Matas urged the government to spend less time negotiating evidentiary agreements and more time in actual prosecutorial activities. He pointed out that Justice Jules Deschenes had identified 20 individuals who merited prompt action, but by mid-

1988, only two cases were under way. Government spokesmen responded that, in light of their concern to bring only strong cases before the courts, they were making good progress.

The only case actually before the courts was that of Imre Finta, who was charged with forcible confinement, kidnapping, and manslaughter in connection with the deportation of over 8,000 Jews from his native Hungary in 1944. Due to delays in gathering evidence, the trial did not begin during the year, but prosecution and defense attorneys traveled to Hungary and Israel to interview witnesses.

In a noncriminal case, the government began proceedings to strip Jacob Luitjens of his citizenship on the grounds that he concealed his Nazi past when he immigrated from Paraguay (where he had taken refuge after the war) in 1961. Luitjens, convicted *in absentia* by Holland for his wartime collaboration activities, was a retired University of British Columbia botany professor. If the government succeeded in removing his citizenship, he would probably be deported to the Netherlands, which had requested his extradition in 1981. The citizenship hearing began in September, in Vancouver, where several witnesses appeared. Further testimony was expected to be heard in Holland.

Holocaust-Related Activity

The Toronto Jewish Congress cosponsored a conference for educators from across the country at the University of Toronto, in August, on "Teaching the Holocaust in the Canadian Context." Several Canadian scholars attended a major conference in Britain on "Remembering the Future: The Impact of the Holocaust and Genocide on Jews and Christians." Among those who presented papers were Profs. William Seidelman, John Conway, Alan Davies, Marilyn Nefsky, and Michael Marrus. Other educational programs included an educators' tour to the death camps and to meet survivors in Israel; the development of a new unit on *Kristallnacht* for Montreal Protestant high-school students; an in-service program on the Holocaust for New Brunswick high-school history teachers; and a lecture and film series, "Resistance, Rescue, and Moral Responsibility," held in Montreal.

The province of Manitoba decided to erect a memorial to the Jewish victims of the Holocaust on the grounds of the Legislature in Winnipeg. In the city of North York in the Toronto area, a Holocaust memorial was planned for a city park. It would consist of a 36-foot-high obelisk created by sculptor Ernest Raab.

Two films dealing with Holocaust themes were shown during the year. The Canadian Broadcasting Corporation (CBC) produced a television drama by Anna Sandor, *Two Men*, concerning a survivor who confronts one of his persecutors. The Canadian Jewish Congress released a documentary film, *Voices of Survival*, featuring interviews with Canadian survivors. It was shown on national television.

JEWISH COMMUNITY

Demography

Although Canada conducted a mid-decade census in 1986, the data on Jews may have raised more questions than they answered. Unlike the 1981 census, which included questions on both religion and ethnicity, the 1986 census had only a question on ethnic origin, allowing the individual to give multiple responses. The result was that 245,855 people listed only a Jewish ethnic origin, while an additional 97,655 people listed Jewish as one of two or more ethnic origins. These data yield a total of 343,510 people who might in some way be considered Jewish, though it is difficult to ascertain just how Jewish people with multiple ethnic origins might be. The confusion that results from the inconsistency in measurement of Jewish identity between the two censuses makes any comparisons difficult and perhaps not meaningful. What is known is that the number of Jews is somewhere between 245,000 and 343,000, but it is difficult to say just where. If one errs on the side of inclusion, it would be reasonable to estimate the number of Jews who identify as such to be between 315,000 and 330,000.

In the absence of any better figures, the populations of the three largest Jewish communities, using the total of single and multiple Jewish ethnic identifiers, were: Toronto—142,095; Montreal—96,475; and Vancouver—18,925. It should be noted that a more restrictive measure of the Montreal Jewish population during the early 1970s indicated about 115,000 people, suggesting a population loss since the advent of the Parti Québécois in 1976 of about 20,000 people or more.

Using the same criteria, the Jewish population by province was as follows: Newfoundland—540; Prince Edward Island—160; Nova Scotia—4,405; New Brunswick—1,515; Quebec—98,225; Ontario—176,535; Manitoba—18,270; Saskatchewan—2,610; Alberta—15,105; British Columbia—25,870; and Yukon and Northwest Territories—270. The major growth occurred in Ontario, particularly Metro Toronto, with additional growth in Alberta and British Columbia.

Winnipeg's community had been worried about population decline for some time. Because of losses to Ontario and other locales where economic opportunities were perceived to be better, a high proportion, about 27 percent, of Winnipeg's Jewish population was over age 65 (compared to about 20 percent in Montreal and less than 15 percent for Canadian Jewry as a whole). Also in Winnipeg, the abandonment by the younger part of the community of the traditional North End neighborhood, and its move to the South End, had implications for Jewish community institutions.

The census confirmed the long-term trend away from a Yiddish-speaking community. In 1986 there were only 22,700 Jews who listed Yiddish as their mother tongue, a decline from 32,800 in 1981. About two-thirds of those listing Yiddish as their mother tongue were over 60 years old.

The census also showed a higher socioeconomic status for Jews than the Canadian average, with higher incomes, more education, and higher-status jobs in general.

Communal Affairs

Events in Israel were the chief focus of community attention and concern during the year. At the request of Charles Bronfman, a highly influential behind-the-scenes community leader, virtually every national Jewish organization was represented at a September meeting in Toronto, to discuss the community's Israel-related issues, especially the uprising in the administered territories. At this and subsequent meetings, the role of each organization was examined in order to assign responsibilities more effectively and to try to develop a unified strategy. The convening of the meetings reflected a conviction that the community was not making the most of its resources, which in part was an organizational problem.

Criticism of Israel's policies in the territories was by no means limited to non-Jews. An organization called Jews for a Just Peace demonstrated in front of the Israeli consulate in Toronto in April. Its president, Yossi Schwartz, said that the government of Israel under Yitzhak Shamir "has a fascist vision which is leading the country into a Third Reich" and called for an end to the occupation. On a more moderate note, the Board of Trustees of Toronto's Holy Blossom Temple urged the Israeli government to exercise greater restraint, supported negotiations, and endorsed the idea of an international peace conference.

The question of Jews criticizing Israel publicly was the topic at a session of a CJC, Quebec Region, conference in November. Prof. Frederick Krantz argued vigorously about the need for Jews to close ranks publicly in time of crisis, while Prof. Blema Steinberg and writer Leon Wieseltier defended the integrity of those who did not agree with current Israeli policy while reaffirming strong commitments to Israel.

In November the Canadian Zionist Federation held a seminar in Montreal for community leadership. Participants discussed Middle East issues and methods of putting Israel's case to the Canadian public and to the rank and file of the Jewish community more effectively.

THE MONTEBELLO ISSUE

Significant community discord surfaced in connection with what came to be known as the Montebello issue. In April the Canadian Institute for International Peace and Security, a government-sponsored think tank, convened a two-day private seminar on issues relating to peace in the Middle East at Chateau Montebello, a resort near Ottawa. The impetus for the seminar came from Secretary of State for External Affairs Joe Clark, following up on a suggestion contained in the 1980 Stanfield Report. Its stated purpose was to stimulate dialogue and improve communication between Jews and Arabs. The Canadian participants—15 Jews and 15 Arabs—were reportedly asked to keep their identities secret, and the sessions were closed to the media. According to an institute spokesperson, they came as individuals rather than as representatives of organizations.

When details of the seminar eventually leaked out, the seminar itself and especially its Jewish participants—many of them prominent community leaders—came under attack. Critics contended that the participants were possibly being used by Clark, that the 15 Jews would be perceived as representatives of the Jewish community even though they claimed not to be, that the Jewish participants were selected in a manner that produced greater support for the idea of a Palestinian state than existed in the community, that the organized community was left out despite the participation of some of its leaders in personal capacities, and that secrecy was contrary to the community's interests. Supporters, including many of the participants, responded that the seminar was no more than what was officially claimed, that they attended on their own and represented no one, that the discussions were useful, and that media presence would have inhibited frank discussion.

Originally there were plans to hold a second seminar at the end of the summer. Ultimately, the sponsoring institute decided to postpone the second dialogue, which was never held. The residue within the Jewish community was that one segment, generally centrist to right politically, was satisfied that it had thwarted the continuation of what it considered to be a misguided effort. Another segment, generally leftist, though not exclusively so, was frustrated because an opportunity for productive Arab-Jewish dialogue had been torpedoed. This division reflected differences of opinion within the community regarding the appropriate path to the achievement of Arab-Israeli peace.

RELIGIOUS AND FUND-RAISING ISSUES

After the Israeli election on November 1, the Jewish community turned its attention to the negotiations over forming a new governing coalition. The main concern of most Canadian Jewish organizations was the proposed amendment by the Orthodox parties of the definition of Jewishness in the Law of Return in such a way as to offend non-Orthodox Diaspora Jewry. Representatives of the Toronto and Montreal federations joined their counterparts from five U.S. cities in meeting with key Israeli party leaders and other politicians to communicate their apprehension over the divisiveness that the proposed amendment would cause. The United Israel Appeal (UIA), Montreal Allied Jewish Community Services (AJCS), and Toronto Jewish Congress (TJC) also expressed opposition to the amendment.

A group of Orthodox rabbis and one lay leader, from Montreal and Ottawa, who backed the amendment to the law, denounced the federations for their stance and flew to Israel to express their views to Prime Minister Yitzhak Shamir. They carried with them a message of support from Chief Rabbi Pinchas Hirschprung of Montreal. However, their action was opposed by many of their colleagues, among them the Orthodox Rabbinical Council of Canada, Quebec Region, which, while adhering to the principle that conversions should follow Jewish religious law, did not agree that the public law of Israel was the proper vehicle to achieve that goal. The council advocated noninterference by Diaspora Jews in internal Israeli affairs.

Meanwhile, a delegation of 40 Reform Jewish leaders from across the country and a delegation representing major Canadian Jewish federations and national organizations met with the Israeli ambassador to voice their opposition to changes in the law and to ask that the issue be removed from the political agenda. The decision in Israel to forge a new national unity government, which effectively removed the "Who is a Jew?" issue from the agenda, obviated the need for further action.

The issue of how to allocate funds raised in local communities was a concern of the United Israel Appeal, which channeled money from annual drives to projects in Israel. Although there had been a gain in funds collected in the two major cities, Montreal and Toronto, it had been offset in recent years by declines in smaller communities. UIA president Martin Levine noted that in some cities as much as 93 percent of the campaign proceeds was retained for local needs, compared to the norm of about 50 percent, the balance going to Israel through the UIA.

Community Relations

The question of Sunday shopping continued to occupy a prominent position on the community's agenda with the government, especially in Ontario. A Toronto supermarket that catered to a Jewish clientele, Sunnybrook Foods, was found guilty of violating the Retail Business Holidays Act by being open on Sunday. A defense claim that the law was unconstitutional was rejected in provincial court. The store lost its first appeal but planned to appeal further.

In a major new development, the Ontario government introduced a bill in April that would exempt any Sabbath-observing store from the Sunday-closing rule if all stores owned by the company were closed on the same day. This was a big improvement over the previous law, which sharply limited the exemption. Furthermore, municipal or regional governments would be empowered to set their own rules. The move was welcomed by the Canadian Jewish Congress with one reservation, namely, that chains wanting certain stores closed on Sundays and others closed on Saturday would not be allowed to do so.

In Quebec, the Canadian Institute on Minority Rights urged the provincial government to stop enforcing Sunday-closing laws. The present law exempted only stores with fewer than four employees that had an affidavit from the CJC attesting to the religious commitment of the proprietor. The congress, which was not happy with its role, asked the government to be relieved of it. CJC's preference was that any retailer who closed on Saturday for religious reasons be permitted to open on Sunday.

SCHOOLS

Ontario's Jewish community continued its struggle to obtain government funding of its day schools. Organizations continued to lobby for funds, with CJC's Ontario

Region describing the issue as a matter of equity. Several of Montreal's Jewish day schools faced problems as a result of nonrenewal of leases or exorbitant rental increases during the next few years. The most pressing situation involved the end of the lease of the United Talmud Torahs (UTT) for the Merton School, owned by the Protestant School Board of Greater Montreal (PSBGM), which considered using the building for an alternative school. After a rancorous public campaign, the board was persuaded to extend the lease through the summer of 1990.

Despite pressure from the organized Jewish community, the Protestant School Board of Greater Montreal (PSBGM) opened an "alternative school" that offered some Hebrew instruction as an option, in addition to enriched programs in several academic subjects. Many people involved in Jewish education feared that the school, which charged a nominal fee for the optional studies, would siphon off students from Jewish day schools. The school opened with about 175 students, perhaps 150 of them Jewish, and most of the Jewish students did in fact transfer from Jewish day schools.

In a major decision, the Ontario Court of Appeal struck down a provincial regulation that required the daily recitation of a prayer—typically the Lord's Prayer—and reading from the Christian Bible in schools. Four of the five justices ruled that the regulation violated the religious freedom of non-Christians and atheists, despite a provision for opting out of the religious exercises. The case arose in Sudbury, where one of the three parental plaintiffs was Jewish. After deciding not to appeal the case to the Supreme Court, the Ontario government issued new guidelines which, rather than eliminating prayer in the classroom—as the Jewish organizations had urged—allowed a variety of prayers from many religious traditions. In another case, the Supreme Court of Ontario upheld religious instruction in the public schools, noting that children who objected could be exempted from such instruction.

THE OUTREMONT AFFAIR

The Vishnitzer Hassidim of the Montreal suburb of Outremont had an unpleasant encounter with their municipal government that mushroomed into a nasty episode of anti-Semitism. The city council twice rejected their petition to rezone an empty lot to allow the construction of a synagogue. Opposition to the Vishnitzers was spearheaded by Gerard Pelletier, head of the Parti du Renouveau Outremont and a member of the council. Expressing concern about how numerous the Hassidim might become, he spoke of the "fear" and "conflict" that can be created as a minority grows in a community.

The Outremont affair escalated significantly in September when one of Montreal's major daily newspapers, *La Presse*, ran a front-page story about the suburb's "Jewish problem." The story cited complaints from residents, published in a local Outremont paper, that the Hassidim were unfriendly, that they ignored parking regulations, and that they were buying up houses. Pelletier was also reported to have expressed fears that the Hassidim would soon outnumber the French Canadians in the town. (Currently the Hassidim constituted about 11 percent of the Outremont population.)

After Jewish community relations organizations denounced the article, *La Presse* apologized for using the term "Jewish problem" but stuck to the content of its story, the intercommunity tensions. Chief editorial writer Alain Dubuc wrote that the zoning issue masked a malaise that had to be reported and claimed that phrases that had offended Jewish sensitivities were really no more than another manifestation of "tensions between the francophone majority and groups that have chosen English as their language of usage." The CJC responded that Dubuc failed to deal with the religious prejudice of the original article and instead tried to turn it into a linguistic issue. In a companion piece to Dubuc's editorial, columnist Gerald LeBlanc blamed the Jews for the problem because they failed to integrate into the French milieu. He also castigated Jewish anglophones for allegedly opposing the survival and protection of the French society.

Quebec's immigration minister, Louise Robic, defended the Hassidim, praising them as hardworking, law-abiding citizens. Education Minister Claude Ryan also described them as exemplary citizens. Meanwhile several attempts at dialogue were under way in Outremont in an effort to defuse the situation.

Education

Data on Toronto's Jewish schools showed 14,750 enrolled in all types of schools in 1987–88. Of these, 8,600 were in day schools (7,539 in 12 elementary schools and 1,061 in 7 high schools). There were 35 supplementary schools with 6,427 students. The Associated Hebrew Schools was the largest day school on the continent, with about 3,000 students at the elementary level.

Some of the problems of the Montreal day schools were addressed in a study carried out for the Association of Jewish Day Schools. Approximately 60 percent of Jewish children attended at the elementary level, while about 40 percent went to Jewish high schools. Many of the schools had been losing students in recent years, mainly to the public schools. The ultra-Orthodox and francophone schools were gaining, while the mainstream anglophone day schools were losing students. The schools also faced dissatisfaction with rapidly rising fees, lack of facilities, and failure to keep up with the latest trends, according to Monette Malewski, director-general of AJDS.

One of the big success stories to come out of the Montreal day schools was the innovative Tal Sela Hebrew-language program, directed by Tova Shimon. It had been adopted by 140 schools across the continent, encompassing more than 12,000 students between grades 2 and 6, as well as by schools in Switzerland and South Africa.

Soviet Jewry

Canadian Jews continued to publicize the situation of Soviet Jews as part of the pressure campaign to enable as many as possible to emigrate. The policy question concerning the destination of the emigrants was discussed, but did not emerge as a significant community issue during the year. However, it was understood by community leadership that if the flow of emigrants were to increase substantially, this question would become more pressing.

The emotional highlight of the year was the visit of Yosef Begun, the former refusenik now residing in Israel. Begun's cross-country tour was a focal point in the effort to maintain the enthusiasm and commitment that had characterized the Soviet Jewry movement in the past. In his public remarks, Begun stressed the importance of Diaspora protests in obtaining both the release of Soviet Jews and greater cultural and religious rights for those remaining in the Soviet Union. He argued that *glasnost* had not yet brought about the fundamental change in the situation of Soviet Jews that so many had hoped for from it.

McGill University professor and human-rights activist Irwin Cotler established a Soviet branch of InterAmicus, the human-rights organization. The main functions of the Moscow office would be to advise and inform Soviet citizens on legal developments and the exercise of various human rights. Cotler argued in statements upon his return from a June visit to the Soviet Union that a legal revolution was taking place and that Soviet citizens could look forward to greater legal protection against government actions.

The theme of change within the Soviet system was also stressed by World Jewish Congress president Edgar Bronfman in a Toronto speech in December. In response to the improvements in Soviet life, he urged activists to be less confrontational in dealing with the Soviet Union. He also emphasized the need to achieve cultural and religious freedom for Jews who remained in the Soviet Union. As he put it, "Let my people be Jews" should be the movement's slogan.

Yakov Rabkin, a Université de Montréal professor who was born in the Soviet Union, was one of the signatories of an historic agreement to establish a Jewish studies program at the USSR's new Academy of World Civilizations. Along with Israeli rabbi Adin Steinsaltz, Rabkin's efforts were aimed at training a new generation of scholars to revive the once outstanding tradition of rabbinic scholarship. The program would be the first of its kind since the Russian Revolution.

Religion

There were signs in 1988 that the hostility characterizing relations between the Jewish religious movements in the United States was finding expression in Canada as well. An example of this was an initiative, in September, by the Union of Orthodox Rabbis of the United States and Canada (a right-wing group) to "alert the public to the dangers of Reform and Conservatism," ostensibly to combat intermarriage. The union's stand was attacked by Rabbi Dow Marmur of Toronto's Holy Blossom Temple (Reform), who questioned the integrity and honesty of the Israeli rabbis who stimulated the original stance. Marmur called on Orthodox rabbis and lay leaders to take a stand in favor of Jewish unity and to reject actions by some Orthodox leaders to deny the legitimacy of the other movements.

Questions about Orthodoxy in Israel were also raised by Chancellor Ismar Schorsch of the Jewish Theological Seminary in an address to the Canadian Council for Conservative Judaism in Toronto, in November. He criticized in particular the use of governmental power on behalf of ultra-Orthodox causes in Israel. Council delegates strenuously objected to Israeli proposals to amend the Law of Return in a manner "that would appear to deny the legitimacy of non-Orthodox forms of Judaism." They also heard a report on a survey of Canadian Conservative synagogues showing that most of those responding did not count women in a *minyan* or offer *aliyot* to women. Earlier in the year, the Conservative movement had opened its first permanent office in Canada, the Jewish Theological Society of Canada, located in Toronto.

A major point of contention between Orthodox and non-Orthodox in Toronto was access to a *mikveh* (ritual bath). Both Conservative and Reform leaders protested a decision to limit the use of the Koschitzky *mikveh* to women engaging in the monthly ritual bath and to bar its use for conversions. This was seen by the Conservative and Reform rabbinates as an attack on them, because Orthodox rabbis had access to other facilities for conversion purposes. As a result, some rabbis had to take converts out of town for the required immersion. Rabbi Lawrence Troster (Conservative) lamented the situation, claiming that it "reflects a polarization of the community." Similarly, in Winnipeg, the Lubavitch-owned *mikveh* was no longer available to non-Orthodox rabbis for conversions. The Canadian Council of Liberal Congregations (Reform), meeting in London, Ontario, in November, opposed amendments to the Law of Return and deplored the *mikveh* controversy in Toronto.

The role of women in Jewish religious life continued to be an important issue. Within Orthodoxy, Rabbi Moshe Stern of Toronto criticized his colleagues for not encouraging women to pursue the avenues of religious expression that were already permissible within Jewish law. Recognizing the effect of feminism even in Orthodox circles, Rabbi Stern argued that Orthodoxy need not be perceived as antifeminist and urged rabbis to take a more positive attitude toward women's religious needs. In Hamilton, Temple Anshe Shalom (Reform) engaged the city's first female cantor, Ruth Slater. She formerly held similar positions in two other Ontario cities.

On another issue involving women, a coalition pursuing civil remedies for women whose husbands refused to grant a religious divorce urged that Parliament amend the Divorce Act to prohibit the granting of civil divorce if a religious divorce had not been obtained. In the meantime, the practice of requiring a prenuptial agreement to grant a *get* (religious divorce) in case of civil divorce was gaining acceptance among Orthodox rabbis in Montreal.

For the first time in its history, the International Council of Christians and Jews held its international colloquium in Canada. The Montreal meeting, in August, dealt with interfaith dialogue throughout the world. The Jewish keynote speaker, Rabbi Howard Joseph of Montreal, called for "theological humility" on the part of all religions. ICCJ president Victor Goldbloom of Montreal urged participants to extend involvement in interfaith dialogue to a wider range of people rather than just specialists.

Culture

The Toronto Jewish Cultural Council, an arm of the Toronto Jewish Congress, established a competition to encourage the writing of plays with Jewish themes. An annual award was contemplated.

Basya Hunter's play *Johannes Reuchlin and the Talmud* opened in Toronto in March. In Montreal, a children's play about a Canadian girl who moves to Israel, *Aviva's Piano*, by Miriam Chaiken, was produced at the Saidye Bronfman Center. Children from day schools appeared in the play before audiences of their classmates. The new Winnipeg Jewish Theater presented its first play, *Hannah Senesh*, by David Schecter.

Toronto Jewish music audiences had an opportunity to attend "The Jewish Composer in Canada," a concert of instrumental, choral, and vocal works by several prominent Canadian Jewish composers, held in Toronto in January. The same month, *Shabbat Shirah* was the occasion for the premieres of new compositions of Jewish music by Gordon Kushner and Cantor Paul Kowarsky at Beth Tzedec Congregation in Toronto. Srul Irving Glick had two new works performed during the year. The Toronto Jewish Folk Choir presented "Four Yiddish Songs for Mixed Choir, Viola, and Piano" at a concert at the University of Toronto in May. In August Glick's "Visions Through Darkness: An Oratorio of Our Time" had its premiere. Winnipeg's *klezmer* group, Finjan, released its first record album, *From Ship to Shore*.

Two major exhibitions of Jewish interest appeared at leading Canadian museums during the year. The Montreal Museum of Fine Arts presented the largest exhibition of the works of Marc Chagall ever shown in Canada. The collection, brought over from Paris, included nearly 50 paintings and over 100 drawings, many on Jewish or biblical themes. In Toronto, the Royal Ontario Museum exhibited "Treasures of the Holy Land: Ancient Art from the Israel Museum."

Several films released during the year had a Canadian Jewish dimension. Actor Saul Rubinek made *So Many Miracles*, an account of his family's history, especially in Europe during the Holocaust. Another Holocaust film, *Dark Lullabies*, was produced by Irene Angelico and Abbey Neikik, with financial support from the Jewish Community Foundation of Greater Montreal. The film, which deals with the impact of the Holocaust on the postwar generation of Germans and Jews, won several international awards. *The Outside Chance of Maximilian Glick*, directed by Allan Goldstein, is based on a story by Toronto attorney and writer Morley Torgov.

The film is an account of a Jewish boy growing up in a small Canadian town, a theme with parallels in Torgov's own life.

Two radio and television productions are worth noting. The French CBC radio network presented a 13-part series on Israel in the spring, to commemorate Israel's 40th anniversary. CBC television carried a documentary in the fall entitled "Promises to Keep: The Canadians in Palestine," about foreign volunteers who fought for Israel in the War of Independence, among them several non-Jews.

Architect Moshe Safdie added to his internationally prominent reputation with two major new projects, the National Gallery in Ottawa and the Musée de la Civilisation in Quebec City, both of which opened this year.

A major symposium on Yiddish Montreal was held in March, with nearly 20 scholars participating. The major address was by Prof. David Roskies, of the Jewish Theological Seminary of America, a former Montrealer. The other participants included Zachary Baker, David Rome, Leo Davids, Eugene Orenstein, Pierre Anctil, and Marie Poirier. The themes covered ranged over language, literature, newspapers, demography, and education.

A new Hebrew-language newspaper, with sections in English and French, *Mabat*, made its appearance in Montreal and was distributed in other major cities as well.

Publications

Two new books by established Canadian Jewish authors were published this year. Ruth Wisse's *A Little Love in Big Manhattan: Two Yiddish Poets* is about Mani Leib and Moishe Leib Halpern and the interaction of their work with the environment in which they lived. Morton Weinfeld and Harold Troper deal with a topical issue in *Old Wounds: Jews, Ukrainians and the Hunt for Nazi War Criminals in Canada*.

The subject of Moroccan Jews and their adaptation to Canadian life is explored in *Sephardim d'hier et de demain* ("Sephardim of Yesterday and Tomorrow") by André Elbaz and *Juifs marocains à Montréal: Témoignages d'une immigration moderne* ("Moroccan Jews in Montreal: Recollections of Modern Immigration") by Marie Berdugo Cohen, Yolande Cohen, and Joseph Levy. The experience of Ashkenazi Jewish immigrants to Montreal is investigated in detail by the non-Jewish historian Pierre Anctil in two books, *Le Devoir, les Juifs et l'immigration: De Bourassa a Laurendeau* ("*Le Devoir*, Jews, and Immigration: From Bourassa to Laurendeau") and *Le Rendez-Vous Manqué: Les Juifs de Montréal face au Québec de l'entre-deux-guerres* ("The Missed Encounter: The Jews of Montreal and Quebec Between the Two Wars"). Anctil shows that Jewish immigration made French Quebecers question their identity and the limits of their ability to tolerate those who are different.

Two books that probe the diversity of Jewish life are *Voices of Canadian Jews* by Rachel Alkallay and Bryan Knight and *Les Juifs Progressistes au Québec* by Allan Gottheil. The former involves extensive interviews with a cross-section of the community. The latter contains portraits of ten Quebec Jews who have challenged the established order in one way or another.

Other new books of note on Jewish subjects included: *Development of Jewish Law: Concepts and History of Rabbinic Jurisprudence from Its Inception to Modern Times* by Rabbi Mendell Lewittes; *A Comprehensive Etymological Dictionary of the Hebrew Language for Readers of English* by Rabbi Ernest Klein (posthumously); *Just a Simple Pharmacist: The Story of Murray Koffler, Builder of the Shoppers Drug Mart Empire* by Frank Rasky; *When Paupers Dance* by Szloma Renglich; *A Soviet Odyssey* by Suzanne Rosenberg; *A Man of Little Faith* by Rick Salutin; *The Tree of Life* by Fredelle Bruser Maynard; and *Life Is a Dance—You Should Only Know the Steps*, translated by Katie Brown. Three important new works on general subjects by Jewish authors were *Sometimes a Great Nation: Will Canada Belong to the 21st Century?* by Peter C. Newman; *The Collins Dictionary of Canadian History* by J.L. Granatstein and David Bercuson; and *The Manipulators: Inside the Soviet Media* by Ilya Gerol and Geoffrey Molyneaux (not Jewish).

Personalia

The Order of Canada was conferred on Irving Guttman, a pioneering opera director in Western Canada. Stanley Hartt became chief of staff to the prime minister. Allan Gotlieb retired as ambassador to the United States and was appointed chairman of the Canada Council. Nancy Gay-Rotstein was appointed a member of the council. Nathan Nemetz retired as chief justice of British Columbia. Irwin Lampert was appointed judge in the New Brunswick provincial court. Joseph Blumer was named assistant deputy chairman of the immigration appeal division of the Immigration and Refugee Board. Alan Shefman became a member of the Ontario Human Rights Commission. Leo Yaffe won the Seaborg Medal of the American Nuclear Society. Chaim Niznik won the John Polanyi Prize in medicine and physiology. Michael Marrus won the Canadian Historical Association Ferguson Prize for *The Holocaust in History*. Phyllis Lambert was awarded three international medals for her achievements in architecture. Morris Perlis became the president of American Express Canada. Larry Grossman was appointed president of Counsel Financial Corporation. Brian Segal left the presidency of Ryerson Polytechnical Institute to become president of the University of Guelph, while Arnold Naimark, president of the University of Manitoba, was named chair of the Association of Commonwealth Universities.

Two Canadians, Peretz Miransky and Ruth Wisse, were awarded the Itzik Manger Prize, the most prestigious award in the field of Yiddish literature. Justice Irving Halperin was awarded the Samuel Bronfman Medal for Jewish Communal Service. Edward Bronfman received the Human Relations Award of the Canadian Council of Christians and Jews, and Marnie Paikin became president of the organization.

Within the Jewish community, Brian Feldman was elected president of B'nai Brith Canada, Neri Bloomfield became president of the Jewish National Fund, Sol Lederman became president of the United Israel Appeal of Canada, Baila Aspler was elected president of Emunah Women of Canada, and Edward Winant was elected president of Canadian Friends of Hebrew University. Bob Willmot was named national executive director of the Canada-Israel Committee, Gerry Koffman was appointed director of the Ottawa Jewish Community Center, Pearl Gladman became associate national director and Yechiel Glustein Quebec regional director of B'nai Brith, and Michael Crelinsten was appointed executive director of the Quebec Region of Canadian Jewish Congress. Internationally, Phil Granovsky was elected chairman and Jack Rose vice-chairman of the board of trustees of Keren Hayesod.

Among leading Jews who died in 1988 were the following: Joseph Gallay, former editor of the Yiddish newspaper *Kanader Adler*, in January, aged 82; urban planner Hans Blumenfeld, in February, aged 96; Kingston community leader Harry Abramsky, in February, aged 90; film producer Felix Lazarus, in March, aged 76; Rebbetzin Elsie Frank, in March, aged 81; public-relations man George Cohen, in March, aged 72; Dr. Arthur Vineberg, noted surgeon, in March, aged 84; real-estate broker Percy Caplan, in March, aged 80; congregational rabbi Haim Kemelman, in April, aged 62; political activist Joshua Gershman, in May, aged 84; physicist Lionel Goldfarb, in May, aged 61; Dr. Louis Harnick, radiologist, in May, aged 68; Toronto Symphony violinist Isadore Dubinsky, in June, aged 85; veterans organization leader Albert Caplan, in June, aged 67; Jewish community professional Harry Berger, in June, aged 78; criminologist Barbara Maslowsky, in June, aged 39; Dr. David Eisen, radiologist and Holy Blossom Temple archivist, in June, aged 87; Prof. Frank Talmage, Bible scholar and historian, in July, aged 50; Cantor Moses Oziel, in August, aged 74; Jonathan Roskies, community activist, in September, aged 32; Israel Bonds leader Chaim Lewin, in October, aged 78; Prof. Bernie Vigod, historian and community leader, in October, aged 42; educator Ruth Ashkenazy, in October, aged 52; summer-camp founder Chaim Pripstein, in November, aged 89; Joseph Joffre, the oldest Jew in Canada, in November, aged 113; pioneer social worker Ethel Shane Vineberg, in November, aged 86; Israel Nitikman, former Manitoba judge, in December, aged 83; Harry Binder, community worker and former Communist party activist, in December, aged 75; and Edward Barkoff, community leader, in December, aged 88.

HAROLD M. WALLER

Western Europe

Great Britain

National Affairs

SUPERFICIALLY, THE OVERALL PICTURE of a country dominated by the Conservatives remained unchanged throughout 1988. This was reflected, for example, in the relative tranquility of the labor front, where there were fewer strikes than in any year since the end of World War II.

Yet there were also signs of a shift in attitudes among Conservatives themselves, away from uncritical endorsement of the government's general policy and toward a measure of sympathy with the Labor opposition. The government's plans for the privatization of the water and electricity industries came under criticism from within its own ranks. There was also a massive revolt of Tory members of Parliament against the government's new regressive tax, the "community charge," also known as the "poll tax," on which issue the normal Conservative majority dropped from 101 to a mere 25.

But perhaps the most severe blow to Tory self-confidence came on the economic front. The chancellor's budget, issued in March, cut income tax by twopence on the pound. This, together with interest-rate cuts following the crash of October 1987, encouraged consumer demand; in the first nine months of the year economic growth was running at an annual 5 percent. This proved unsustainable, however; the budget and Tory economic policy in general lost their shine when interest rates had to be increased nine times in the last seven months of the year as a means to cope with a renewal of inflation and growing trade and balance-of-payments deficits.

By contrast, Labor leader Neil Kinnock was able to make progress in bringing his party's policies into harmony with the perceived outlook of public opinion. Labor accepted the need to come to terms with market forces and proposed to revise the party's defense policy away from unilateral nuclear disarmament, which Kinnock himself declared "redundant." Although Kinnock had no difficulty in securing reelection at the Labor party conference in October, he was defeated on the defense issue when the conference voted to maintain its policy on unilateral disarmament. In the meantime, the political center seemed to disintegrate when the Liberal and

Social-Democratic (SDP) parties voted in September to form the Social and Liberal Democrats. However, Dr. David Owen, former SDP leader, refused to accept the majority decision of his party and continued to lead a separate, much reduced SDP.

Relations with Israel

Although officials of both countries described British-Israeli relations as good, British criticism of Israeli actions in Gaza and the West Bank was frequent in the first six months of the year, eliciting protests from Israeli ambassador in London Yehuda Avner and from the Board of Deputies of British Jews. In January the Foreign Office minister in charge of the Middle East, David Mellor, on a visit to Gaza, challenged an Israeli officer after witnessing the arrest of an Arab youth. The condition of refugees in Jabaliya camp was "an affront to civilized values," he said. In April the Foreign Office voiced concern at the "disproportionate" severity of Israeli measures on the West Bank and Gaza. The same month Britain voted for a United Nations Security Council resolution condemning Israel's violation of Tunisia's territorial integrity in the alleged killing of PLO military chief Khalil al-Wazir (Abu Jihad). In May Foreign Minister Sir Geoffrey Howe called an Israeli attack on terrorist bases in South Lebanon "provocative."

A minor Israeli diplomat, Arie Regev, and a PLO member were ordered out of Britain, in June, after it was discovered that the Mossad, Israel's central intelligence agency, was running a double-agent intelligence operation. Ismail Sowan, a Jordanian, was found guilty of illegally possessing explosives and arms in Hull, which he was storing for the PLO. Sowan testified that he was employed by the Mossad to watch Abdul Mustapha, an alleged member of a PLO terrorist group who was wanted in Britain for the murder of Palestinian journalist Ali Adhami in London in July 1987. Whitehall was thought to be angered by the Mossad's failure to inform them of either Mustapha's movements or the arms cache.

In February it was announced that Jordan would buy eight British Tornado IDS aircraft; in July a deal with Saudi Arabia involving large quantities of sophisticated arms was reported. In September Israeli foreign minister Shimon Peres, after meeting in London with Prime Minister Margaret Thatcher, Foreign Office officials, and Anglo-Jewish leaders, said arms were the only difference marring the excellent relations between the two countries. He did not accept Mrs. Thatcher's claim that the weapons were defensive.

Prime Minister Thatcher continued to see an active role for Britain in the Middle East peace process. In January, meeting with President Hosni Mubarak of Egypt, she rejected his peace plan as insufficiently comprehensive but agreed with him on the need for an international conference to act as a framework for bilateral negotiations between Israel and the Arabs. In February Thatcher and King Hussein of Jordan held talks in London with U.S. secretary of state George Shultz, on his peace initiative.

Britain seemed to be trying to encourage the moderate elements in the PLO, though not without some ambivalence. In February the government stated officially that it did not regard the PLO umbrella group as a terrorist organization, while acknowledging that parts of it did engage in terrorism. In March Foreign Secretary Howe received an Arab League delegation, which included Prof. Walid Khalidi, a member of the Palestine National Council (PNC), the PLO government in exile, arguing that he was not a PLO representative but "a Palestinian chosen to be a member of the delegation." In December Foreign Office minister of state William Waldegrave, who succeeded David Mellor in July, met Bassam Abu Sharif, senior aide to Arafat, who indicated that he favored peace with Israel in accordance with UN Resolutions 242 and 338.

Britain abstained in a UN vote on an Arab-sponsored resolution condemning the United States for refusing to grant Arafat an entry visa to attend the UN General Assembly debate on the Middle East issue; however, it supported America's December decision to talk to the PLO. Howe, on a visit to the Persian Gulf states in December, said that Israel's leaders would be making a major mistake and harming Israel's long-term interests if it did not seize the chance to pursue a peace initiative. In Kuwait he said that Britain would "use every means at our disposal to urge Israel to recognize the need for a positive response" to the PLO.

British pressure on Israel to talk to the PLO intensified following the PNC's Algiers declaration in November, which implicitly recognized Israel, and Arafat's explicit acceptance of Israel as a state in December. However, Mrs. Thatcher gave assurances that the British government did not intend to recognize the independent state the PLO had proclaimed.

Thatcher's overtures to the PLO in no way lessened her benevolent attitude toward Israel. In March she informed the Zionist Federation's biennial conference that the government approached the task of bringing peace to the Middle East and ending violence in "a spirit of friendship for Israel." In October she accepted an honorary doctorate from the Hebrew University of Jerusalem, awarded in recognition of the "deep friendship she has shown toward the Hebrew University and the Jewish people." In November she sent good wishes to the "Heart of Israel" exhibition at London's Alexandra Palace, the concluding event of a year of celebration of the state's 40th anniversary and the largest Israel exhibition ever held in Britain. In December she wrote to Prime Minister Yitzhak Shamir congratulating him on the formation of his new government, hoping that he might visit London, "so that we can talk over issues of concern to us both."

Labor party leader Neil Kinnock visited Israel in February, where he criticized its handling of the unrest and urged Shamir to accept the idea of an international conference. On his return, he told the Board of Deputies that the Palestinians must publicly recognize "the permanence of the State of Israel" and put an end to terrorism. Shadow Foreign Secretary Gerald Kaufman, who over the year had talks with various Middle East leaders, consistently castigated Shamir and the Likud half of the Israeli government as the main obstacle to a peace conference. After visiting Jordan, Israel, and the occupied territories in January, he urged that maximum pressure be brought to convince Shamir to drop his resistance to the conference. In July Kaufman shared a platform with Farouk Kaddoumi, head of the PLO's political department.

The September Blackpool conference of the Democrats (formerly the Social and Liberal Democrats) called on the British government to support a UN-sponsored international conference to which the PLO and Israel would be invited. The motion recognized that both Israel and the Palestinians had a right to "statehood and self-determination."

Criticism of Israel and Anti-Semitism

Criticism of Israeli policies was voiced in various quarters outside the government. It was not always easy to differentiate between "legitimate" disapproval expressed by groups or persons otherwise sympathetic to Israel and statements masking deeper hostility to the Jewish state generally or to Jews as Jews.

In April the National Union of Journalists' annual conference voted unanimously to dissociate from the anti-Semitic publication *Holocaust News*. At the same time, it called on the British and Irish governments to press for a UN peace conference on the Middle East, with PLO participation. In May the Association of Cinematograph, Television, and Allied Technicians' annual conference condemned the assassination of Abu Jihad and "Israel's brutal acts of torture and murder of the Palestinians" and supported the uprising in the West Bank and Gaza. An anti-Israel motion proposed by the Society of Graphic and Allied Trades (SOGAT 82), and opposed by the Labor party leadership, was passed at the Labor party conference in October.

An official of the Union of Jewish Students (UJS) reported that anti-Zionist activity on the campus was "on a scale greater than I have ever seen before." By February 12, 49 colleges had passed anti-Zionist resolutions, many presented by the Socialist Workers' Students' Society, the General Union of Palestinian Students, and Students for Palestine. Leaflets calling for the removal of Zionist elements from the student union were distributed at Manchester University Institute of Science and Technology (UMIST). At University College, London, the Socialist Workers' party organized a meeting on "Gaza—Israel's Soweto."

Off the campus as well, anti-Israel and/or pro-Palestinian sentiment was in evidence. In February some 150 Muslims marched through Derby to protest the treatment of Arabs in Gaza. In May a memorial meeting for Abu Jihad was held under the auspices of the Marxist party, an offshoot of the Workers' Revolutionary party. An exhibition of Palestinian culture, "Arts Under Occupation," sponsored by the Palestinian Trade Union Federation, was shown in Glasgow in May and in Hounslow, London, in November. In May the right-wing National Front (NF) joined Asians and blacks in the annual "Al Kuds March," organized by the United Islamic Students' Association to mark the end of Ramadan.

There were varying assessments of the extent of actual anti-Semitic acts in Britain.

Barkingside police told the *Jewish Chronicle* that only 3 of the 27 incidents reported in that district in 1987 targeted Jews, but in July the Barnet community relations council reported that there had been more racial attacks on Jews and other minority groups in the borough in the first three months of 1988 than in all of 1987. The Board of Deputies, however, said it was unaware of any increase in racial attacks anywhere. The same month the board declared that Muslim fundamentalist anti-Israel propaganda was becoming increasingly anti-Jewish and called for tougher race-relations laws to curb anti-Semitic literature produced by right-wing racist groups and Muslim extremists.

Despite protests by the Board of Deputies, the American-based Templeton Prize for progress in religion was awarded to Muslim leader Inamullah Khan in Melbourne, in October, after being postponed in April for further investigation. The board claimed that Khan, the Pakistani-based director-general of the World Moslem Congress, helped finance anti-Semitic literature. Presumably to forestall future problems, in October the judging panel announced the appointment of Sir Sigmund Sternberg, chairman of the International Council of Christians and Jews, to a seat on the panel.

In May representatives of the Board of Deputies, the Union of Jewish Students, the Association of Jewish Sixth-Formers (AJ6), and the 45 Aid Society, an organization of Holocaust survivors, demonstrated at the first performance of *Perdition*. The controversial play by Jim Allen, which deals with alleged cooperation between Zionists and Nazis in wartime Budapest, was performed for a week at London's Conway Hall. An earlier production of the work in February 1987 was halted following an avalanche of protests. (See AJYB 1989, pp. 294–95.)

Nazi War Criminals

The establishment of the independent War Crimes Inquiry into alleged Nazi war criminals living in Britain was announced in the House of Commons in February, to be headed by Sir Thomas Hetherington, former director of public prosecutions, and William Chalmers, former Crown Agent in Scotland. The inquiry made a worldwide appeal for evidence in March, and Hetherington and Chalmers visited the Soviet Union, where the Russians agreed to let witnesses give evidence in the West. By July the inquiry team had drawn up a "prioritized" list of some 100 suspects.

Much of the impetus for the inquiry came from the parliamentary All-Party War Crimes Group (APWCG), which in January revealed details from British files compiled in 1948 of 3,000 former Nazis who had entered Great Britain after the war. The Simon Wiesenthal Center of Los Angeles also provided evidence on a number of suspects, and Wiesenthal himself visited England in June, in connection with the inquiry. Despite appeals from the APWCG and an amendment to the Criminal Justice Bill to allow the prosecution of alleged Nazi war criminals living in Britain—introduced in the Commons in March by the APWCG vice-chairman, Labor MP

Peter Archer—Minister of State at the Home Office John Patten told the House in April that the government could not consider changing the law until the inquiry's findings were known. The best-known Nazi suspect in Britain was Antanas Gecas, living in Edinburgh, who allegedly took part in mass shootings of Jews in Lithuania. In February the first Soviet war-crimes official to visit Britain since the Nuremberg trials said that at least 30 witnesses in the Soviet Union could testify against Gecas.

In a separate investigation to determine whether Austrian president Kurt Waldheim was associated with wartime killings, in February the government reopened the World War II files on six British commandos who were captured and executed in the Balkans, allegedly with his knowledge. Prime Minister Thatcher instructed the Ministry of Defense to examine any new evidence, and Ian Stewart, minister for the Armed Forces, appealed to British servicemen to assist in a review of Waldheim's wartime record. It was clear from a report of an independent international commission of historians, Stewart told the Commons, that a wide range of sources had not previously been available. By October the investigation had received so much information that its findings would not be published until early 1989, said historian and Conservative MP Robert Rhodes James. In May Thames TV presented a four-hour program featuring a commission of inquiry into Waldheim's wartime activities.

JEWISH COMMUNITY

Demography

The Jewish population of Great Britain was estimated at 330,000. Figures for provincial Jewry continued to fall. Local demographic surveys placed the total Jewish population of Liverpool at 4,400, one-third less than in 1965; of Leeds at 10,500, a fall of more than 7,000 over two decades (a finding challenged by the Board of Deputies research unit); and of Sheffield at about 800, a fall of over half during the past three decades.

Synagogue marriages continued to decline in 1987, falling to 1,046 from 1,097 the previous year and an annual average of 1,136.8 in 1982–86, according to the Board of Deputies' Community Research Unit annual report. Reform was the only group within the general total to register an increase: to 184 in 1987 from 160 in 1986 and an annual average of 174.2. But the Progressive grouping as a whole declined to 230 from 246 and an annual average of 244.6. Figures for Orthodox marriages solemnized in 1987 were 800 (against 867 and 892.2).

Burials and cremations under Jewish religious auspices fell to 4,486 in 1987 from 4,838 in 1986 and an annual average of 4,837.6 for 1982–86.

Anglo-Jewry and Israel

In January, in response to fears that growing criticism of Israel's handling of the *intifada* would increase anti-Zionism and anti-Semitism, a steering committee was formed of representatives from the Board of Deputies, the Zionist Federation (ZF), and Jewish student groups. The committee's task was to monitor the situation and coordinate Jewish public reaction.

Also in January, a widening rift within Anglo-Jewry over Israeli policy came to a head when June Jacobs, chairwoman of the Board of Deputies' foreign affairs committee, was criticized for voicing concern, on the radio, over the behavior of Israeli troops in the occupied territories. The matter was not fully resolved until October, when the board, which hitherto had expressed unqualified support of Israel at all times, passed a motion recognizing that members of the community had rights of dissent and freedom of speech. The motion went on to say that the board should "encourage dialogue, mutual respect and tolerance between Jews of differing views."

That differences existed was shown on numerous occasions. In January members of the Jewish Socialist Group joined a vigil, organized by Palestinians, outside St. James's Church, Piccadilly, London, condemning Israel's treatment of the Palestinians in the occupied territories. The Jewish Socialists also sponsored a meeting about Israel's handling of the West Bank and Gaza crisis, addressed by PLO's London representative, Faisal Oweida.

The split in the community was evident when the Zionist Federation's (ZF) biennial conference in March passed a resolution backing the Shultz peace formula. "The role of the Zionist organization in the diaspora is to be wholly supportive of the government democratically elected by the citizens of Israel," said the National Zionist Council (NZC), which included British Herut, and which had broken away from the ZF five years earlier. The NZC expressed regret that the ZF, which claimed to be an umbrella organization, lent support to one political faction. Mizrachi condemned the resolution as "counterproductive," but Poale Zion, the Labor Zionist group, said the ZF had "expressed the view of the overwhelming majority of the Jewish people."

Members of British Friends of Peace Now distributed leaflets outside a Board of Deputies meeting in May, calling on Israel to withdraw from the West Bank and Gaza. In June a leading West Bank Palestinian, Hanna Siniora, editor of the East Jerusalem newspaper *Al-Fajr*, addressed a meeting of Mapam, the socialist Zionist group, in London. In December Mapam called for an end to Israel's "policy of rejection" and for negotiations with the PLO to test its sincerity. The group sponsored meetings between Palestinian and Jewish women, to discuss coexistence and to promote peace.

In August Poale Zion proposed a resolution for presentation to the annual Labor party conference in October, supporting "the legitimate rights of the Palestinian people." The statement called on Israel to reject the concept of a greater Israel, and the PLO to renounce terrorism and the clauses in its national covenant calling for liquidation of the State of Israel.

In December the PLO sent letters to leading British Jewish and Zionist organizations, including the ZF, NZC, and the Board of Deputies, in an effort to persuade them that Arafat's recognition of Israel was genuine.

Communal Activities

The increased rationalization and professionalism that characterized welfare organizations in 1987 were reflected in the December announcement that the Jewish Welfare Board (JWB) and the Jewish Blind Society (JBS) had agreed to merge in January 1990. Together they would form one of the largest voluntary welfare organizations in Britain, with a total staff of some 900, 33 homes and day centers, and an annual budget of almost £13 million. The merger was expected to result in immediate annual savings of £250,000 through reduced overhead, as well as to serve the changing age profile of the community and to use resources more effectively.

The director of Norwood Child Care reported in February that the agency had a caseload of 400 families, or 1,600 children, in 1987. There were 120 cases where children had either been abused or were felt to be at risk of abuse; four years earlier Norwood did not have one such case. In December Norwood announced that Britain's first Jewish adoption agency would open in 1989, to prevent parentless Jewish children being lost to the community. It was estimated that a maximum of seven Jewish children were currently available annually for adoption, while hundreds of people wanted to adopt.

In December a new organization was formed to provide improved services for Jewish children with special educational needs. Called Binoh, the Jewish Special School Service, it combined the resources of three agencies: the United Synagogue, Norwood, and the existing Binoh organization.

Community Relations

In January the Jewish Council for Community Relations published a pamphlet, "Divided Families—Time We Acted," calling on Jewish organizations to protest the government's immigration bill, on grounds that it discriminated against blacks and others. The leaflet highlighted the plight of Asian families kept apart by the laws. The council also held a series of workshops in conjunction with Yakar, the independent Jewish study center in Hendon, North London, to explore aspects of immigration and refugee policy.

In March Chief Rabbi Immanuel Jakobovits appealed to South African president P.W. Botha to spare the lives of the "Sharpeville Six," six blacks who had been on death row for three years and were the focus of an international campaign for clemency. In August Jews Against Apartheid campaigned on behalf of jailed South African Jews David Bruce and Raymond Suttner and launched a trust fund to aid victims of apartheid. The group, which held its first open meeting in 1986 and sponsored an annual Freedom Seder outside London's South African embassy, had

200 members plus group affiliates, including the Jewish Socialist Group, Mapam (Socialist Zionists), the Jewish Council for Community Relations, the Reform Assembly of Rabbis, and the rabbinic conference of the Union of Liberal and Progressive Synagogues.

A letter issued in October by the Chief Rabbi's Office supported British Muslims protesting Salman Rushdie's controversial novel *Satanic Verses*. Rabbi Jakobovits deprecated "not only the falsification of established historical records, but the offense caused to the religious convictions and susceptibilities of countless citizens."

Soviet Jewry

All sections of the community continued to work in behalf of Jews wishing to leave the Soviet Union. University student groups organized meetings and rallies, as did the Zionist Youth Council, the United Synagogue, the Association of Jewish Sixth-Formers, and the 35s, the women's campaign for Soviet Jewry. Members of Middlesex New Synagogue, Harrow, lobbied European MPs in Strasbourg, in May, and a group called Refusenik: Public Action for Soviet Jews, which aimed to use modern advertising to capture increased public support, launched its first campaign in July. In December Vladimir Ivanov, minister at London's Soviet embassy, received a delegation from the Board of Deputies. The same month the board organized a lobby of MPs in conjunction with the National Council for Soviet Jewry. In December, too, the All-Party Parliamentary Committee for the Release of Soviet Jewry placed a full-page advertisement in the *Times*, signed by 170 MPs as well as by various organizations. The ad welcomed Soviet leader Mikhail Gorbachev's planned visit to England, but drew attention to Russia's human-rights restrictions.

A number of former refuseniks visited England during the year, among them composer and violinist Leonid Feigin, Naftaly Tsitverblit, Vladimir Slepak, and the families of Pavel Abramovitch, Vladimir Prestin, Leonid Volvovsky, and Alexander Kholmiansky. In June Ida Nudel, a guest of the Federation of Women Zionists, met with Margaret Thatcher. In July Natan Sharansky was in London to speak and to publicize his book *Fear No Evil*. In October Viktor Brailovsky addressed a symposium in Cambridge, organized by Scientists for the Release of Soviet Refuseniks. In November Prof. Alexander Lerner urged the Foreign Office to take up the cases of several refusenik scientists during Mr. Gorbachev's forthcoming visit.

In June the British government and the International Bar Association put strong pressure on Soviet authorities to reverse their refusal to grant entry visas to Israeli law professor Yoram Dinstein, Yaacov Rubin, president of Israel's Bar Association, and several British lawyers, so that they could attend a legal conference in Moscow. In December the Foreign Office announced that Britain had dropped its opposition to holding a Human Rights conference in Moscow in 1991, "providing recent progress on human rights in the Soviet Union" was maintained.

Religion

The New Year Honors bestowed a peerage on the chief rabbi. Immanuel, Baron Jakobovits of Regents Park in Greater London, suggested that he had been honored "for being true to my faith, for teaching Judaism in an unadulterated form, and for remaining loyal to my convictions." He made his maiden speech in the House of Lords in March, in a debate on the Immigration Bill.

Despite the national acclaim he received, Lord Jakobovits was again involved in controversy in the Jewish community, this year on the subject of abortion. The Halakhah, he argued, did not allow termination of pregnancies for "social" reasons. In February leading Jewish doctors protested his position; also in protest, the Union of Liberal and Progressive Synagogues (ULPS) issued a statement in April denying that "a Jewish view" on abortion existed.

Lord Jakobovits continued to reject Liberal rabbi Sidney Brichto's proposal, made in 1987, for resolving differences in Orthodox and Progressive conversion and divorce procedures. Writing in *L'Eylah*, published by the Chief Rabbi's Office and Jews' College, Jakobovits reiterated the view that demands for some form of Orthodox recognition of non-Halakhic conversions "can by definition never be met, and should therefore never be pressed in what can only be an incitement to divisiveness and rancor."

In July the chief rabbi was elected president of the New York-based Memorial Foundation for Jewish Culture.

With Jakobovits scheduled to retire at age 70 in February 1991, in October the search began for a successor. The United Synagogue (US) Council empowered its executive to call together the 200-odd members of the Chief Rabbinate Council, representing all congregations and those provincial communities that recognized the authority of the Chief Rabbi's Office and contributed to its upkeep. The council would elect a body of 35 people to make recommendations.

The founding of the Association of Synagogues in Berkshire, in April, by Reform and Orthodox congregations in Maidenhead and Reading and the Liberal Thames Valley congregation was the first move of its kind in Britain aimed at improving relations between religious communities holding different views.

It was reported in June that ULPS membership had fallen to about 10,000 from 12,000 ten years earlier, while membership in the Reform Synagogues of Great Britain (RSGB) had risen to 42,000 from 33,000. RSGB's most pressing problem was a shortage of rabbis: four rabbinic posts were vacant in its 33 congregations and 5 developing communities. A recruitment campaign was under way by the Leo Baeck College to add to its current enrollment of 18 students.

A Reform and Liberal Association of Mohelim (ritual circumcisers) was established in September to circumvent the problem faced by Progressive converts of possible rejection by Orthodox *mohelim*. The group, which had eight full and eight trainee members (including one woman), provided an alternative to the Initiation Society (Orthodox), which had trained and provided *mohelim* for British Jews for

243 years and which currently had 61 members. An estimated 1,750 religious circumcisions took place annually, 350 of them for children of Progressives.

The Marble Arch (US) and Western (independent) synagogues, both in Central London, agreed to form the merged Western Synagogue at Marble Arch, an independent congregation recognizing the chief rabbi's authority. The Western's building would be sold. In November the Belsize Square Synagogue withdrew from ULPS to become independent.

Education

To boost its education and youth funding, estimated at nearly £2 million, the United Synagogue entered into partnership with the Joint Israel Appeal (JIA) in the Kol Nidre appeal. Under the unprecedented agreement, JIA was to receive the first £500,000 raised, Jewish education the next £250,000, and any further proceeds would be shared. The US's own Rosh Hashanah appeal for Jewish education in 1987 had had only limited success.

A new Jewish secondary school for outer North-West London was scheduled to open in September 1990, with a capacity of 600 students. According to Simon Caplan, director of the Jewish Educational Development Trust (JEDT), the coeducational school would be fee-paying, although scholarships would fund 20 percent of the places. The syllabus would be "modern Orthodox, Zionist, and academically striving."

A half-million-pound program to train top-quality teachers for Jewish education was launched in June, funded by JEDT, the Israeli Ministry of Education's joint program for education, and the Jewish Agency. The organizers hoped to prepare candidates for the 60 senior teaching posts expected to fall vacant in the next three years. Jews' College announced in June that it would seek to attract women to its B.A. program in Jewish studies by offering a wider choice of rabbinic literature courses. This would enable women to compensate for inadequate preparation in Talmud, which was a major component of the curriculum. The college had 94 students this year, the largest enrollment in its 133-year history.

The Hebrew and Jewish studies department of University College, London, had 30 undergraduate and 10 postgraduate students. In August a B.A. program in Jewish history at London University was opened to nonmatriculated students. The Open University announced a new offering of a continuing education course in Jewish history, in cooperation with the Spiro Institute. In October it was reported that a professorship devoted to Judaism in the 20th century would be established at Manchester University, financed by the family trust of local businessman David Alliance. Britain's first Center for Holocaust Studies opened at Leicester University in December.

Publications

The winner in the nonfiction category of the H. H. Wingate Awards for 1988 was Anton Gill for *The Journey Back from Hell*, an oral history of concentration-camp experiences. Amos Oz won the fiction prize with *Black Box*, translated from Hebrew by Cambridge University lecturer Nicholas de Lange. *A Cup of Tears* by Abraham Lewin was commended.

Robert Maxwell, Mirror Newspapers Group owner, bought a 30-percent stake in Israel's Modi'in Publishing House, which published the Hebrew newspaper *Ma'ariv*, for his Pergamon Media.

Works on the current Arab-Israeli conflict published this year included *The Israeli Connection: Whom Israel Arms and Why* by Benjamin Beit-Hallahmi; *The Yellow Wind* by David Grossman; *Israel's Fateful Decisions* by Yehoshafat Harkabi; *Britain and the Arab-Israel Conflict* by Ilan Pappe; and *Israel, the Embattled Land: Jewish and Palestinian Women Talk About Their Lives* by Beata Lipman.

New books celebrating present-day Israel were *Israel at 40* by Julian J. Landau; *All Israel*, edited by Josephine Bacon; *Israel* by Frederic Brenner and A. B. Yehoshua; and *Israel: The First Forty Years*, a collection of photographs, with an introduction by Abba Eban and a commentary by William Frankel.

Books published during the year on modern Israeli history included *Geography and Politics in Israel Since 1967* by Elisha Efrat; *The Jews in Palestine, 1800–1882* by Tudor Parfitt; *Zionism: The Crucial Phase (1906–1920)* by David Vital; *Collusion Across the Jordan* by Avi Shlaim; *A Soldier in Search of Peace* by Avraham Tamir; *The Best of Enemies: Israel and Transjordan in the War of 1948* by Uri Bar-Joseph; *Israel, Turkey and Greece: Uneasy Relations in the East Mediterranean* by Amikam Nachmani; *The Impact of the Six-Day War: A Twenty-Year Assessment*, edited by Stephen J. Roth; *The Two Zions: Reminiscences of Jerusalem and Ethiopia* by Edward Ullendorff; *Domestic Politics and Regional Security. Jordan, Syria and Israel* by Valerie Yorke; *A Clash of Heroes: Brandeis, Weizmann and American Zionism* by Ben Halpern; *For Zion's Sake* by Yehuda Z. Blum, Israel's permanent representative at the UN between 1978 and 1984; and *Birth of Israel: Myths and Realities* by Simha Flapan.

New works on Judaism included *The Mishnah*, edited with the commentary "Koheleth Jacob" by the late Rabbi Jakob Kornberg; *The Jewish Law of Inheritance* by Dayan Dr. I. Grunfeld; *Home Ceremonies According to Sephardi Usage*, compiled by Dayan Pinchas Toledano; *Here and Hereafter (Blue Guide)*, an anthology by Lionel Blue with Jonathan Magonet; and *Blue Heaven* by Lionel Blue; *Daath Chachamim* by Joseph B. Weinstein, an anthology of midrashic, aggadic, and other homiletical material; and *1001 Questions and Answers About Judaism* by David C. Gross. *The Rylands Haggadah*, introduced, transcribed, and translated by Raphael Loewe, is a facsimile of the medieval Sephardi masterpiece. *Heine* by Ritchie Robertson, *Rashi* by Chaim Pearl, *Bialik* by David Aberbach, and *Buber* by Pamela Vermes were all published in the new Great Jewish Thinkers series.

Studies in local Jewish history were represented by *Go and Learn*, the story of Jews and medicine in Scotland, by Kenneth Collins; *Survivors: Jewish Refugees in Birmingham, 1933–1945* by Zoe Josephs and members of the Birmingham Jewish history research group; *The Federation of Synagogues, 1887–1987* and *London Jewry and London Politics, 1889–1986* by Geoffrey Alderman; *East End, 1888* by William J. Fishman; *History of the Board of Deputies* by Aubrey Newman; and *Volla, Volla, Jew Boy*, a portrait of traditional Jewish immigrant life in the East End, by Cyril Spector.

Among new works on general Jewish history were *The Jewish Presence in Latin America*, edited by Judith Laikin Elkin and Gilbert W. Merkx; *A Century of Ambivalence: The Jews of Russia and the Soviet Union* by Zvi Gitelman; and *The Transformation of German Jewry, 1780–1840* by David Sorkin.

Biographies and autobiographies published this year included *Backbencher* by Labor left-winger Ian Mikardo; *Fear No Evil* by Natan Sharansky; *Ben-Gurion* by Shabtai Teveth; *Gorbals Boy at Oxford* by Ralph Glasser; *Anne Frank Remembered* by Miep Gies with Alison Leslie; *The Footsteps of Anne Frank* by Ernst Schnabel; *Freud, A Life for Our Time* by Peter Gay; *Marks of Distinction: The Memoirs of Elaine Blond* by Barry Turner; *Rothschild: A Story of Wealth and Power* by Derek Wilson; *Begin, An Anatomy of Leadership* by Sasson Sofer; and *A Dream of Belonging: My Years in Postwar Poland* by Janina Bauman.

New studies of anti-Semitism and the Nazi period included *Fascism, A Reader's Guide*, edited by Walter Laqueur; *Mothers in the Fatherland: Women, the Family and Nazi Politics* by Claudia Koonz; *Atonement: From Holocaust to Paradise* by Ulrich Simon; *Art of the Holocaust* by Janet Blatter and Sybil Milton: *Born Guilty: Children of Nazi Families* by Peter Sichrovsky; *The Burning Bush—Anti-Semitism and World History* by Barnet Litvinoff; and *Identifying Ivan* by Willem A. Wagenaar. *The Directory of Holocaust-Related Activity, A Guide to Holocaust Education* was the first publication of the Holocaust Education Trust set up in 1988 under the chairmanship of Greville Janner.

Fiction of the year included *The Immortal Bartfuss* by Aharon Appelfeld; *Mother's Girl* by Elaine Feinstein; *The Catacomb* by Brian Glanville; *A Deputy Was King* by G. B. Stern; *Miriam's Tambourine*, Jewish folktales selected and retold by Howard Schwartz; *After the Dream* by Maisie Mosco; *Middlepost* by Antony Sher; *Latecomers* and *A Friend from England* by Anita Brookner; *Chateau Ella*, a family saga by Hilary Norman; and two books for younger readers, *Plots and Players* by Pamela Melnikoff, and Lynne Reid Banks's *Melusine*.

Poetry published this year included Gerda Mayer's *A Heartache of Grass*; *Selected Poems* by Jon Silkin; *Metro* by George Szirtes; *Barricades in West Hampstead* by Bernard Kops; *To Urania*, Joseph Brodsky's selected poems, 1965–1985; and *Selected Poems* by Ruth Fainlight.

Books on art included *Jewish Painters and Sculptors*, a directory compiled by Herbert Revesz, and *Jewish Ceremonial Embroidery* by Kathryn Salomon.

Origins of the Yiddish Language, Winter Studies in Yiddish, vol. l, edited by

Dovid Katz, was a collection of papers from the First Annual Oxford Winter Symposium on Yiddish Language and Literature, held in December 1985.

Personalia

In addition to the peerage bestowed on Chief Rabbi Jakobovits, Sally Oppenheim-Barnes, chairwoman of the National Consumer Council and minister of state for consumer affairs, 1979–87, was created a baroness. Knighthoods went to Nobel prize-winning scientist Aaron Klug; former chairman of the Prince's Youth Business Trust, Dr. Alcon Copisarow; David Alliance, chairman of Coats Viyella; Leon Brittan, former home secretary and now one of Britain's European commissioners; Peter Levene, chief of defense procurement at the Ministry of Defense; and Evelyn de Rothschild, chairman of N. M. Rothschild, bankers. Sir Ernst Gombrich, art historian and philosopher, was appointed a member of the Order of Merit.

Among British Jews who died in 1988 were Hugh Schonfeld, biblical scholar and historian, in January, aged 86; Solomon Cutner, the international pianist "Solomon," in February, aged 85; Marghanita Laski, writer, in February, aged 72; Lady Daphne Haddow, honorary president of WIZO, in February, aged 78; Avrohom Kohn, founder and principal of the Gateshead Teachers' Training College, in March, aged 83; Sir Rex Cohen, leading entrepreneur, in March, aged 81; Joseph Collins, show-business agent and impresario, in April, aged 85; Alfred Abrahams, Liverpool surgeon, in April, aged 75; Peter Wohlfarth, physics professor at Imperial College, London, in April, aged 63; Edward Walter Joseph, banker, in April, aged 79; Henry Oscar Joseph, banker and charitable worker, particularly associated with helping refugees, in April, aged 87; Ginette Spanier, fashion expert and writer, in May; George Trenter, Zionist leader, in May, aged 76; Israel Chayen, scientist and inventor, in May, aged 78; Dan Frankel, Labor politician, in May, aged 88; Leopold Muller, founder of the de Vere hotel group, in June, aged 86; George Theiner, editor of *Index on Censorship*, in July, aged 80; Charles Allchild, landlord of the West End Fitzroy Tavern in the 1930s, '40s, and '50s, and charity worker, in August, aged 81; Sydney, Lord Jacobson, journalist, former editor of the *Daily Herald* and *The Sun*, in August, aged 79; Samuel Charles, Lord Silkin of Dulwich, Labor party politician, attorney-general (1974–79), in August, aged 70; Sir John Hazan, High Court judge, in August, aged 61; Hans Gunther Adler, poet, author, and historian, in August, aged 78; Max Hamilton, professor of psychiatry at Leeds University, 1964–77, in August, aged 76; Joseph Cymerman, vice-president of the Federation of Synagogues, in September, aged 77; Leah Hertz, author and women's-rights activist, in September, aged 51; Naomi Birnberg, educator and political thinker, in September, aged 97; Rabbi Isaac Goss, former director, South African Board of Jewish Education, in November, aged 76; Roger Japhet, journalist, in November, aged 73; Dorothy de Rothschild, matriarch of the Rothschild family, in December, aged 93; Peter Morrison, philanthropist, in December, aged 94.

MIRIAM & LIONEL KOCHAN

The Netherlands

National Affairs

THE NETHERLANDS CONTINUED TO enjoy political stability and economic progress in 1988, under the second-term coalition government of Christian Democrats (CDA) and Liberals (VVD) headed by Premier Rudolf (Ruud) Lubbers (CDA).

One matter that occupied Parliament throughout much of the year was the so-called Passport Affair, involving delays and mismanagement in the production of a new fraud-resistant Netherlands passport to replace the one in use, which was easily counterfeited. A parliamentary commission of inquiry appointed to look into the matter presented its report in August, highly critical of all concerned. The parliamentary debates that followed led to the resignations of Defense Minister Willem F. van Eekelen (VVD), a former under secretary for foreign affairs, and Under Secretary for Foreign Affairs René van der Linden (CDA). Van Eekelen was succeeded as defense minister by Frits Bolkestein, likewise VVD, a highly respected senior political figure. By year's end there was still no prospect of a new fraud-resistant passport.

The economy continued to show an upward trend, growing by 2.75 percent over 1987, whereas inflation increased by only 0.7 percent. Industrial production rose 4 percent and exports 9 percent. Some 120,000 new jobs were created this year, thus increasing the total number of jobs by 2.6 percent to 4,830,000. Unemployment, however, remained relatively high, at some 500,000. The entry of increasing numbers of married women into the labor market was one factor. However, about half of those out of work were long-term unemployed, largely unskilled, and, in the case of immigrants from Third World countries, lacking both completed elementary education and knowledge of the Dutch language.

A continuing social problem was the growing ranks of persons seeking political asylum in the Netherlands, whose number rose from about 3,500 in 1987 to about 7,000 in 1988. Although 85 percent of all applications for asylum were rejected, very few actually left the country. Many were escorted by police across the border, only to return illegally. Others obtained residence permits by entering into fictitious marriages with Dutch nationals. It was estimated that in Amsterdam alone, one of every four marriages concluded in 1988 was in this category.

Another issue in the public spotlight was the demographic future of the Dutch population, which was becoming older, with fewer children being born, particularly in Dutch-born families. Ethnic minorities, by contrast, tended to have large families. In the large cities, such as Amsterdam and The Hague, over 50 percent (in some places as high as 80 percent) of elementary school pupils were of Surinamese, Turkish, Moroccan, or other foreign ethnic origin.

World War II Aftermath

This year saw the conclusion of the case of Flora Rost van Tonningen, the widow of a Dutch Nazi member of Parliament and herself an outspoken neo-Nazi, whose pension rights had been challenged. (See AJYB 1989, p. 316.) On September 13, the Second Chamber of Parliament rejected, 78 to 68, a private member's bill that would have withdrawn her pension. The vote, which cut across all political parties, effectively closed discussion on the subject.

The draft bill proposed by the Ministry for Social Welfare and Culture to simplify and coordinate payments to war victims was criticized by three organizations engaged in helping them, including the Jewish Social Welfare Foundation. The criticism focused on two provisions in particular: one that would end regular monthly payments for new cases of second-generation victims, though psychiatric help would be provided, when necessary; and one that would limit payments to those who had performed paid work before or during the war and become incapacitated as a result of wartime experiences.

The Jewish historian Louis de Jong (born in Amsterdam in 1914) completed his monumental *Geschiedenis van het Koninkrijk der Nederlanden tijdens de Tweede Wereldoorlog* ("History of the Kingdom of the Netherlands During the Second World War"), which numbered 13 volumes in 27 parts. De Jong, who had been director of the Netherlands State Institute from 1945 until his retirement in 1979, had spent some 40 years on the work. On the occasion of the completion of this *magnum opus*, a symposium was held in Utrecht, in October, organized by the Netherlands Society of Historians. The topic was the historiography of the Second World War, in particular the historiography of the German occupation of the Netherlands. De Jong was sometimes reproached by younger Dutch historians for viewing the events of 1940–1945 too much in terms of "good" and "bad" and for speaking of "collaboration," where they would prefer "accommodation."

Relations with Israel

Early in the year, questions were raised about Premier Lubbers's planned official visit to Israel on the occasion of its 40th anniversary, which many considered inappropriate in light of the *intifada*. The trip, which had been agreed upon several months earlier to take place in March or in May, was postponed a few times and finally scheduled for July 17–19. Instead of being purely ceremonial, as originally planned, it was changed to include official business, and Foreign Minister Hans van den Broek was added to the delegation. Lubbers and Van den Broek were instructed by Parliament to express criticism of Israeli government actions against the Palestinians and rejection of the PLO. Lubbers expressed his government's views during a dinner in his honor given by Premier Yitzhak Shamir, at which he urged Israel to agree to an international peace conference. Van den Broek met in East Jerusalem with a number of prominent Palestinian personalities and briefly visited the Kalandia refugee camp.

Premier Lubbers publicly criticized Israel at a Jewish community celebration, held on April 24, of Israel's 40th anniversary. Still, he and Mrs. Lubbers stayed at the gathering throughout the evening.

Two official visits were canceled in the wake of the *intifada*: one, by the minister of defense, in February, to the Dutch members of the UN Observers Force in Sinai, which was to have been followed by courtesy visits to the Egyptian and Israeli ministers of defense; the second, a cycling tour of Israel in the summer, by 120 well-known Dutchmen, including the under secretary for public health, as a tribute to Israel on its 40th anniversary.

The *intifada* received enormous attention in the news media, in particular during the first part of the year. Daily reporting by the 12 or so Dutch correspondents stationed in Israel (most of them Jews)—the largest contingent from any country except the United States—in the press and on television, was supplemented by news agency coverage and articles in foreign newspapers. In addition, several news organizations sent special correspondents to the occupied areas, sometimes accompanied by a Palestinian living in Holland, and always working through contact with a Palestinian press office in East Jerusalem. Their coverage was nearly always hostile to Israel.

At the invitation of the Dutch branch of the Friends of the Magen David Adom, the chairman of the Second Chamber of Parliament, Dr. Dick Dolman, attended the cornerstone-laying ceremony for a first-aid station in Petach Tikvah in April. Dolman expressed support for Israel but also criticism of its policies.

The government's annual statement of policy, issued in the third week of September, reiterated its continued support of the right of the State of Israel to secure and recognized borders and also recognition of the legitimate rights of the Palestinian people. With the other members of the European Community (EC), the Netherlands continued to advocate an international peace conference, based on the acceptance of UN Security Council Resolutions 242 and 338. It also pressed for the economic development of the occupied areas, beginning with the direct export of Palestinian agricultural products. To this end, the Netherlands had a major share in bringing about the export to the EC of citrus fruit from the Gaza Strip, making available a Dutch expert and facilitating an agreement between Israel and the EC on this matter. The arrival of the first shipment of Gaza citrus in Rotterdam, on December 16, was welcomed in person by all the Arab diplomats stationed in The Hague and the PLO representative there and received wide coverage in the media. However, due to problems not at all connected with Israel, this export effort largely failed.

Although the Netherlands still refused to grant full diplomatic status to the PLO representative in The Hague, the PLO office continued to function. Under its new incumbent, Afif Safieh, who had arrived there in the autumn of 1987, the office was much more active than under its predecessor. On November 24 it organized a "Day of International Solidarity with the Palestinian People," in The Hague, with the controversial Greek-Catholic bishop Hilarion Capucci as the main speaker. Among other groups active on behalf of the Palestinians was the Association of Palestinians in Holland, headed by Ibrahim al Baz, a deputy member of the Palestine National Council and a permanent resident of the Netherlands, a result of having married a Dutch woman from whom he was later divorced.

Much interest in the fate of the Palestinians was shown by the Netherlands Council of Churches, an affiliate of the World Council of Churches. Claiming that it acted at the request of the Council of Churches in the Middle East, the Dutch body appealed to Israel at the end of November—after the proclamation of a Palestinian state by the Palestine National Council meeting in Algiers—to recognize the rights of the Palestinians. A working group of the council, on "the Palestinians and Israel," strongly criticized a pamphlet published for the annual Israel Sunday of the Dutch Protestant Churches, on October 2, for being too pro-Israel and for ignoring the Palestinians. On the other hand, more fundamentalist Protestants, such as those in the Israel Committee Netherlands, Christians for Israel, and the Evangelical Broadcasting Company ("EO") were strongly pro-Israel. These groups, together with the Society Netherlands-Israel and the Netherlands Zionist Organization, organized a campaign at the end of December for the planting of a Dutch forest of 10,000 trees in Israel, to replace the trees lost by arson.

Jews who were vocal in their criticism of Israel were relatively few in number, and included individuals who had previously shown little or no interest in Israel or Jewish affairs. Groups expressing criticism included the left-wing Poale Zion, which had 47 of the 1,200 members of the Netherlands Zionist Organization, the Friends of Peace Now, a small group working for Palestinian-Israeli dialogue, and a number of left-wing journalists of Jewish origin. The latter, on the occasion of Israel's 40th anniversary, published *Israel After 40 Years*, a collection of essays aimed at showing how Israel had deviated from its original ideals.

At the annual meeting of the Netherlands-Israel Chamber of Commerce, on October 16, in the presence of the Dutch under secretary for trade and industry, Israel Trade Awards were presented by Ambassador Zeev Suffoth of Israel to representatives of 43 Dutch firms that had made outstanding contributions to promoting trade between the two countries. The total flow of trade between the two countries in 1987 amounted to $650 million, of which exports from Holland accounted for $300 million and exports from Israel, $350 million. The latter, in addition to citrus fruit, chemical products, and flowers, increasingly included high-technology products. A Dutch delegation representing firms in the high-technology field, led by former Minister of Economic Affairs G. van Aardenne, visited Israel in November to examine Dutch-Israeli cooperation in this field. Apart from oil imports, Israel was the most important trading partner of the Netherlands in the Middle East.

On April 12, Queen Beatrix attended the presentation of Yad Vashem awards in

Amsterdam by the Israeli ambassador to a group of 47 Righteous Gentiles who had saved Jewish lives during the German occupation of the Netherlands.

The Netherlands government continued to represent the interests of Israel in Moscow by issuing visas for Israel to Soviet Jewish emigrants. It refused, however, to issue visas for direct flights from Moscow to Israel via Bucharest instead of via Vienna, on the ground that the emigrants should be free to choose their destination.

Anti-Semitism

The theater was again a focus of controversy because of productions that were offensive to Jews. Following 1987's commotion over the planned performance of a play by Rainer Werner Fassbinder, as a result of which it was not performed in public (see AJYB 1989, pp. 319–20), the play's director, Johan Doesburg, produced a similarly disturbing work in 1988. This drama, *Mein Kampf*, by George Tabori, was presented in Dutch translation, by an Amsterdam company, in the fall. The same play had been performed in the original German in Amsterdam, in June, by the Wiener Burgtheater, within the framework of the annual Holland Festival. Also controversial was a work by the Dutch Jewish journalist, playwright, and minor actor Ischa Meijer, whose writings often expressed Jewish self-hatred. He wrote and staged a parody on the Fassbinder affair, *Our Village, Beauty and Life*, with himself in the part of the "rich Jew." A performance by a Dutch company of the play *Ghetto*, by Israeli playwright Yehoshua Sobol, was also viewed as problematic.

Apart from some minor incidents, anti-Semitism expressed itself this year mainly in the guise of anti-Israelism and an extreme concern for the Palestinians. The expression "The Jews who suffered so much at the hands of the Nazis now behave like Nazis themselves toward the Palestinians" was spoken or written frequently, mostly in left-wing circles.

JEWISH COMMUNITY

Demography

In the absence of any scientific census or survey, the number of Jews in the Netherlands was still estimated at about 25,000. Of these, 10,659 were considered official members of the Ashkenazi community (Nederlands Israelitisch Kerkgenootschap, NIK), distributed among 42 local communities throughout the country. Amsterdam, with nearly 8,000 registered members, The Hague, with 450 members, and Rotterdam, with 356 members, accounted for 82 percent of all NIK members. The Portuguese (Sephardi) community remained stable, with fewer than 1,000 members and one congregation, in Amsterdam; membership in the Liberal Jewish community was about 2,500, in six congregations. At least half of all persons of Jewish origin in Holland were not affiliated with the organized Jewish community.

Communal Affairs

The problem of finding suitable spiritual leadership for the Amsterdam Ashkenazi community—the largest Jewish community in the Netherlands—was resolved with the appointment of two new rabbis in July. They were Dutch-born Lody van de Kamp, aged 39, who had been Ashkenazi rabbi of The Hague since 1981, and Frank Lewis, aged 36, of London. The latter, who was to be responsible primarily for matters of Jewish law, only arrived to take up his post at the end of December, due to contractual obligations in London. To fill the vacancy in The Hague (450 members) created by the departure of Rabbi Van de Kamp for Amsterdam, Pinchas Meijers, aged 24, was appointed in December. Born in Holland of Dutch-born parents, from the age of 12 he attended yeshivahs of the Lubavitch movement in, successively, Paris, Jerusalem, and Montreal, where he was ordained.

After the return to Israel of Rabbi Dov Salzmann in February, the post of religious leader of the Rotterdam Ashkenazi community remained vacant. The same month, Willem van Dijk was appointed Jewish army chaplain, succeeding Michael Nagler, who had reached military retirement age. The Amsterdam Ashkenazi community ceased to employ a resident ritual slaughterer, but was served by a *shohet* who came over from London once a week. The Liberal Jewish community of Amsterdam appointed Peter Halpern of Rochester, N.Y., as its cantor, in July.

The protracted lawsuit brought by a Jewish father, Robert Brucker, against the Jewish Maimonides Lyceum in Amsterdam for refusing to admit his son Aram as a pupil, because his mother was not Jewish according to Jewish law, ended this year. (See AJYB 1989, pp. 321–22.) On January 22, the Supreme Court ruled that the school was entitled to refuse the boy, that under article 23 of the Dutch Constitution any denominational school had the right to decide its admission policy according to its own religious rules, and that no racial discrimination was involved. This effectively overturned earlier decisions of the Amsterdam Higher District Court which had ruled in the father's favor.

To mark its 40th anniversary, the Jewish Social Welfare Foundation (Joods Maatschappelijk Werk, JMW) presented a symposium in Amsterdam, on September 7, on the subject "Well-being in the Year 2,000." The symposium was officially opened by Minister of Social Welfare and Culture Elco Brinkman. The foundation had been established in September 1948 to enable the numerous Jewish organizations that were engaged in social welfare before 1940, and had lost most of their staff as a result of the German occupation, to join forces and resume functioning. JMW was subsidized by the Ministry of Social Welfare and Culture, the Ministry of Justice, and the municipalities of Amsterdam, Rotterdam, and The Hague. In recent years much of its activity had involved the processing of applications for payments under the WUV, the 1972 law on payments to war victims. Now that most of these applications had been dealt with, JMW wanted to direct its attention to strengthening Jewish identity among young Jews who were remote from Judaism.

The Foundation for Jewish Ambulatory Mental Health Services (JAGGZ) opened its new head office in Amsterdam on December 8 with a symposium on mental-health problems related to World War II. In addition to its head office, JAGGZ had seven branches in various parts of the country, in which it served about 1,000 persons a year, including some non-Jews, with a staff of 24. It was part of the Jewish Mental Health Foundation, which also included the Sinai Hospital in Amersfoort for chronic mental patients.

The Jewish National Fund in the Netherlands—which also directed its appeal to non-Jews, inter alia by a lottery—netted some $4 million in 1988, the highest per capita yield in any country. On November 15, the United Israel Appeal in the Netherlands presented a program with American diplomat Henry Kissinger as the speaker. He was flown to Amsterdam from the United States especially for the occasion. At the 85th Annual Conference of the Netherlands Zionist Organization (Nederlandse Zionisten Bond, NZB) held in February, Henoch Wajsberg, who had been chairman for four years and a member of the executive for six years before that, resigned. He was succeeded by Yitzhak Moed.

Education

The Jewish day schools in Amsterdam—kindergartens, elementary, and secondary schools—had a combined enrollment of over 600 pupils. In addition to the Rosh Pinah elementary school and kindergarten and the Maimonides Lyceum, Orthodox schools that dated from the 1920s, the ultra-Orthodox Cheder Foundation, founded in 1973, had added a secondary-school department and was attracting an increasing number of children from Orthodox homes away from Rosh Pinah and Maimonides. The Liberal Jewish day school in Amsterdam, the Leo Baeck School, which opened in 1986, had no more than 50 pupils, many of them children of mixed marriages who would not qualify for admission to the Orthodox schools. In Rotterdam, a Jewish day school, Beth Sefer Etgar, opened in September.

The Ashkenazi Teachers' and Rabbinical Seminary, which now trained few if any Jewish teachers or rabbis, introduced classes for lay students that proved to be very successful, in particular those on the liturgy of the High Holy Days.

Memorials and Restorations

A number of monuments or tablets in memory of Jews who perished during the Nazi occupation of the Netherlands were unveiled during the year. On October 16, in what was formerly the Jewish quarter of Amsterdam, a monument to Jewish wartime resistance was dedicated by Dick Dolman, chairman of the Second Chamber of Parliament, and the mayor of Amsterdam, Ed van Thijn. The project had been initiated in 1986 by the Jewish Wartime Resistance Foundation, headed by Benny Blum (who died before its completion), in order to refute the claim that Jews did not take part in wartime resistance. Paid for with contributions from the Dutch government, the Amsterdam municipality, and private persons, and created by

Belgian Jewish sculptor Josef Glatt, the monument was a rectangular column of black granite, four meters high, containing a Hebrew text and Jewish symbols. It is estimated that some 1,000 Jews participated in the Dutch resistance movement, of whom 500 lost their lives. The question of "Jewish resistance" was actually somewhat controversial, since many persons of Jewish origin participated in resistance groups not as Jews but as Dutch nationals. At the same time, there was no agreed-upon definition of who qualified as a resistance fighter.

Culture

The Jewish Historical Museum enjoyed a record number of visitors following its reopening in April 1987 in new, much more spacious premises in the former complex of Ashkenazi synagogues on Jonas Daniel Meijer Square in Amsterdam.

In addition to its permanent collection, the museum offered several temporary exhibitions, including some in connection with the 40th anniversary of the State of Israel. Among these were: "Forty Years of Israel Posters," on loan from the Art Library in West Berlin; "*Neroth Mitzvah*," modern Jewish ritual objects relating to light; and an exhibition of photographs of early Jewish Palestine by Yaakov Ben Dov. In connection with the "William and Mary Year," commemorating the tercentenary of the arrival in England of Stadtholder William III of Holland and his wife, Mary Stuart, which was celebrated both in England and the Netherlands, the Jewish Museum presented an exhibit on the Sephardi Suasso family, one of whose members, Francisco Lopez Suasso, had largely financed William's expedition against England. The first copy of a very fine catalog on the Suasso family, prepared by Daniel Swetschinski of Tucson, Arizona, and Loeki Schönduve, was presented to Princess Margriet, a sister of Queen Beatrix, who was the patron of the William and Mary celebration in the Netherlands.

The museum obtained on long-term loan a fine collection of Chagall prints that had been gathered by a Roman Catholic cleric, Father A. Reyers, of the Congregation of Missionaries of the Holy Family.

The Society for Jewish Genealogy, which was established in June 1987, had some 285 members, including many who were no longer Jews themselves but had Jewish ancestors. The society began publishing a quarterly, *Mishpoge*.

The fifth biennial Symposium on Dutch-Jewish History was held November 20–22, partly in Amsterdam and partly in The Hague. Since 1980 the conference site had alternated between the Netherlands and Israel. The theme of this year's symposium, which was not confined to Dutch-Jewish history, was "The Problem of Migration and Jewish Identity." Some 300 persons, both Jews and non-Jews, attended one or more lectures and workshops. At the Anne Frank Foundation—which is not under Jewish auspices—journalist Dick Houwaart, a Jew, was succeeded as chairman of the board of governors, after 12½ years in the position, by Johan Lammers, a non-Jew, governor of the province of Flevoland. The Anne Frank House was visited by some 560,000 persons in 1988, largely tourists from abroad.

In July the Anne Frank Medal was presented at Anne Frank House to Miep and Jan Gies, the non-Jewish couple who had helped the Frank family in hiding, from July 1942 to August 1944. The Anne Frank Foundation refused to join public protests of alleged racism in the State of Israel toward the Palestinians, stating that in its view no racism was involved.

Publications

A number of new works on Jews and Judaism in the Netherlands appeared this year. *Studies on the History of Dutch Jewry*, vol. 5, edited by J. Michman, was published (in Hebrew and English) by the Institute for the History of Dutch Jewry in Jerusalem. A jubilee volume on the 70th birthday of Dr. Jacques Baruch, *Benedictus Homini Homo*, included articles on his activities as a physician, as a municipal councillor of Amsterdam, as an MP, and as chairman of the Amsterdam Sephardi community.

Other new publications were: J. Lanser, ed., *Joodse identiteit in de geestelijke gezondheidszorg* ("Jewish Identity in Jewish Mental Health Care"); D. Michman, *Het Liberale Jodendom in Nederland 1929–43* ("Liberal Judaism in the Netherlands, 1929–43"); and Henk van der Molen, *Met de Joden op weg* (explanations of Judaism and Jewish customs for non-Jews).

Works on local history included Joel Cahen, ed., *Vier Eeuwen Waterlooplein* ("Four Centuries of the Waterlooplein"), about the area that was the heart of the Amsterdam Jewish quarter; Selma Leydesdorff, *Wij hebben als mens geleefd* ("We Lived as Human Beings"), about the poor living conditions in the Amsterdam Jewish quarter in the first two decades of the present century, based on interviews with persons who lived there as children; S. G. Derksen, *250 Jaar Joods Leven in Meppel* ("The Rise and Fall of the Jewish Community of Meppel"); and A. van den Berg and R. van den Berg, *De Joodse Gemeente van Oud Beijerland* ("The Jewish Community of Oud Beijerland"), a village near Rotterdam.

Two new works on the World War II period were Joop and Sofie Citroen, *Duet Pathétique*, about the couple's experiences during the German occupation, respectively, in concentration camps and in hiding; and Willy Lindwer, *De laatste seven maanden van Anne Frank* ("The Last Seven Months of Anne Frank"), based on interviews for a film documentary with six women who knew her in Westerbork, Auschwitz, and Bergen Belsen.

New books on Israel included Constant Vecht and Yael Koren, *Verzonken Heimwee* ("Subdued Nostalgia"), 16 interviews with Jews who remained in Holland and Dutch Jews who settled in Israel; and the Reverend G. H. Cohen Stuart, ed., *Het Volk Israel leeft. Am Yisrael Chai*, a volume in honor of Israel's 40th anniversary, with contributions by Jews from Holland who settled in Israel. Stuart was a Dutch Protestant clergyman residing in Jerusalem.

The year's new biographies included works on two Amsterdam Jewish historians: *Jacques Presser*, by Nanda van der Zee; and *Ben Sijes*, by Richter Roegholt.

In addition, there were a number of translations into Dutch of works by foreign Jewish authors, such as Saul Bellow, Philip Roth, Elie Wiesel, Primo Levi, Natan Sharanski, Pinchas Lapide, Harold Kushner, Amos Oz, Marek Halter, Lionel Blue, and David Grossman.

Personalia

Film director Willy Lindwer received an Emmy Award in New York, in November, for his documentary *The Last Seven Months of Anne Frank*, which was also published in book form. Judith Herzberg received the Charlotte Kohler Prize for her play *Leedvermaak* ("Schadenfreude"). The 85-year-old author Josepha Mendels, who had been living in Paris for over 50 years, received the feminist Anne Bijns Prize for her entire *oeuvre*.

Herman Loonstein, a 29-year-old Orthodox Jewish lawyer, was appointed professor extraordinary in Jewish law in the Theological Faculty of the Roman Catholic University of Nijmergen.

A number of prominent Dutch Jews died this year. Eva Halverstad Furth, aged 75, was the chairwoman and leading figure of the Netherlands Auschwitz Committee for nearly 40 years. Lin Jaldati, aged 76, died in East Berlin. Born Lin Brilleslijper in Amsterdam, she was a well-known performer of Yiddish songs, even after moving with her husband, Dr. Everhard Rebling, to East Berlin in 1945. Henny Kohnstamm-van Voolen, aged 79, was long active in the community, first in WIZO, then on behalf of State of Israel Bonds, and eventually, together with her late (second) husband, on the executive of the Netherlands-Israel Society.

Daniel da Silva Solis, aged 87, was the oldest member of the Sephardi community of Amsterdam. Hans Schrijver, aged 71, of The Hague, was a medical doctor active in many Jewish and Zionist organizations, including those for Jewish war victims. Friedrich Weinreb, aged 78, died in Zurich, where he had lived for the previous 20 years. The subject of great controversy in the late '40s and again in the late '60s over his activities during the German occupation of the Netherlands, in recent years he published rather abstruse interpretations of the Bible which were popular among certain groups of non-Jews. Simon A. Colthof, aged 84, was associated from 1928 until his retirement, with an interruption during the war years, with the Jewish secondary school in Amsterdam (Maimonides Lyceum), first as teacher of mathematics and then principal. He died in Jerusalem where he had settled after retirement.

HENRIETTE BOAS

Italy

THE ITALIAN JEWISH COMMUNITY was strongly affected in 1988 by the Palestinian revolt in Israel's occupied territories and the Israeli response to it. Anti-Semitism, almost insignificant in Italy up to a few years earlier, gained momentum, fueled by the general atmosphere of hostility toward Israel and Zionism. On the other hand, the Italian public showed increased interest in Jewish culture and related subjects, and relations between the Catholic Church and the Jews saw significant improvement.

National Affairs

Lack of stability continued to characterize the Italian political scene. The coalition government headed by Christian Democrat Giovanni Goria was almost completely paralyzed by the strong rivalry between the two main partners in the coalition, the Christian Democrats (DC) and the Socialists (PSI). After a crisis in February led Goria to resign, negotiations between the parties, lasting for two months, produced a new coalition government—similar in composition to the previous one—headed by DC party secretary Ciriaco De Mita. Despite the resolution of the immediate political crisis, tension between the Christian Democrats and the Socialists increased, and their inability to coexist peacefully seriously hampered government functioning.

The huge state deficit, a major national concern, reached a record high of over $700 billion. The deficit in the balance of trade, mostly due to energy imports, amounted to $1.17 billion, and inflation was about 5 percent, still twice as high as the European average. Private consumption increased by 3.8 percent, imports by 10 percent. Nationally, unemployment remained at its 1987 level of about 12 percent; however, while the number of unemployed continued to drop in northern Italy, it increased in the south. This negative data notwithstanding, 1988 was a positive year for the Italian economy, with GNP growing by 3.9 percent and exports by 6 percent. Italian industry continued its structural renovation, with the investment in updating plants, machinery, and technology increasing by 21 percent.

Relations with Israel

Following the outbreak of the Palestinian revolt in December 1987 and its continuation throughout the whole of 1988, Italy's long-standing sympathy for the Palestine Liberation Organization (PLO) resulted in increasing criticism of Israeli policy in the occupied territories. In an effort to convince the Italian public and

Italian political elements of Israel's will for peace, Prime Minister Yitzhak Shamir of Israel visited Italy February 15–17. Although the visit was not considered official, because the Goria government had resigned just a few days before, Shamir met with Italian president Francesco Cossiga, outgoing prime minister Goria, and acting foreign minister Giulio Andreotti. Cossiga expressed "the worries and concerns of the Italian public" over the situation in the occupied territories, while Goria and Andreotti confirmed the Italian government's commitment to the European Community (EC) position in favor of an international Middle East peace conference with the participation of all parties, including the PLO. Shamir met also with the president of the Chamber of Deputies, Nilde Iotti, and the president of the Senate, Giovanni Spadolini, and had long conversations with leaders of the main political parties, including the Communists. With the exception of Republican party secretary Giorgio La Malfa and major figures in the Radical party, all the Italian political leaders were critical of what they labeled "Israeli immobility."

A delegation of the Italian Chamber of Deputies' Foreign Affairs Commission, composed of representatives of all political parties, visited Israel February 29–March 4. The delegation was headed by the commission's president, MP Flaminio Piccoli (DC). In the course of the visit, Mario Capanna of the extreme left group Proletarian Democracy (Democrazia Proletaria) chained himself to a roadside pylon at the entrance to Ramallah, in the West Bank, and distributed leaflets condemning the "Israeli racist policy in the territories." The Italian delegation condemned Israel's handling of the situation and the lack of political initiative on the Israeli side.

The foreign policy of the De Mita government was identical to that of its predecessor, and Giulio Andreotti was again appointed minister of foreign affairs. With regard to the Arab-Israeli conflict, the Italian government maintained its commitment to a comprehensive resolution by means of dialogue and negotiation between Israel, the neighboring Arab countries, and the PLO, such dialogue and negotiation to take place in the framework of an international conference on peace in the Middle East. In May the Italian Parliament upgraded the PLO bureau in Rome, according it the status of "general legation."

In his capacity as president of the UN Security Council, Giulio Andreotti visited Israel November 8–9, where he held conversations with then acting prime minister Yitzhak Shamir and acting foreign minister Shimon Peres. When Andreotti told the Israeli leaders that PLO chairman Yasir Arafat was ready to initiate a special discussion on the Middle East in the UN Security Council, he received negative reactions from both Shamir and Peres.

In spite of its critical political attitudes toward Israel, the Italian government maintained a strong interest in cultural relations with the Jewish state. In February the two governments signed a new cultural agreement, the most extensive Israel had ever entered into with any European country. The agreement, which would be effective to 1991, incorporated exchanges of scholars and archivists, art exhibitions, language courses, art workshops, theatrical presentations, scholarship awards, and joint ventures between universities and research institutes.

Foreign Affairs Minister Andreotti took a strong personal interest in Rabbi Adin Steinsaltz's plans for opening a yeshivah and a center for Jewish studies in Moscow and for cataloging the huge treasure of Judaica in the Soviet Union. Beginning in October, Andreotti took several steps to advance Rabbi Steinsaltz's projects, including raising the subject in the course of meetings with top Soviet officials. As a result of Andreotti's interest, some important Italian cultural institutions, such as the Institute for the Italian Encyclopedia and the National Council for Research, became involved in Steinsaltz's activities in the Soviet Union.

RADICAL PARTY MEETING IN JERUSALEM

The Italian Radical party, known for civil-rights advocacy and the struggle against famine in the Third World, as well as for its firm support of Israel, decided to become a transnational political force and elected some non-Italian members to its Federal Council. After meetings of its representative body were held in Brussels, Madrid, and Rome during 1988, the party decided to hold a fourth meeting in Jerusalem, in October. The Radicals aimed to found an Israeli branch of the transnational party and to launch a campaign for European support for Israel, "the only democracy in the Middle East." They asked the European Community to admit Israel as a full member, maintaining that "the European framework is the only secure guarantee against Israeli fears, and the only possible context for the definition of a peaceful coexistence with the Palestinians." At the meeting of the Transnational Radical party in Jerusalem, October 21–25, which was covered extensively by the Israeli media, Member of Knesset Shulamit Aloni (Civil Rights Movement) and former Prisoner of Zion Ida Nudel announced that they were joining the group.

Anti-Israel Activity

The Italian press and government-run television were extremely hostile to Israeli policy in the West Bank and Gaza Strip and often depicted Israel as a colonialist entity. On the occasion of the 40th anniversary of Israel's independence, in May, many daily and weekly newspapers published partial or distorted versions of the history of the Jewish state. The negative evaluation of Israel's current policy sometimes led to strongly anti-Zionist statements, including questioning the very legitimacy of the Jewish state's existence. In many instances, anti-Zionist positions developed into anti-Semitic ones (on this, see below). In this atmosphere, a boycott of Israeli products was attempted—unsuccessfully—by extreme left organizations, chief among them Proletarian Democracy. Other groups chose the path of violent protest. In April leftists belonging to several student organizations occupied the Israel booth at the International Children's Book Fair in Bologna for several hours and effectively destroyed it. In the same month, an unknown "anarchist group" set fire to the Luxemburg bookshop in Turin, one of the biggest in that city. The arsonists described the bookshop as "a Zionist nest" and accused its non-Jewish owner, Angelo Pezzana, of being "a dirty Zionist." Pezzana, a lifelong friend of Israel, was a prominent figure in both the Radical party and the gay movement in Italy. The Luxemburg bookshop had a large Judaica section and annually published a catalog of books in Italian on Jewish subjects. A few days after the bookshop fire, an anonymous group announced that it had poisoned several tons of Jaffa grapefruits. Israeli grapefruits were then confiscated throughout Italy by the health authorities as a "precautionary measure"; however, though some poisoned grapefruits were actually found in a supermarket in Rome, the whole story proved to be a bluff.

Anti-Semitism

In the course of 1988 many Jews received anonymous threatening letters at home; others were the object of threats at their jobs. Copies of Jewish magazines mailed to subscribers were purposely damaged and even destroyed. In Rome, Milan, and Turin, shutters of shops owned by Jews were painted with slogans praising Hitler and his "final solution of the Jewish problem." Similar graffiti appeared several times on the walls of the Jewish school in Milan. At soccer games, fans frequently shouted anti-Semitic slogans at supporters of rival teams.

The most serious anti-Jewish episodes occurred at the beginning of the year. On two separate occasions in January, students participating in demonstrations against Israel's policy in the territories tried to reach the main synagogue of Rome, shouting anti-Israel and anti-Jewish slogans. On both occasions, the demonstrators clashed with the police and Jews living in the area close to the synagogue. At this point, feeling that their customary public denunciations were inadequate, officials of the Union of Italian Jewish Communities (UCII) and the community of Rome had a meeting with the minister of interior, at which they asked for harsher measures against those responsible for anti-Semitic acts and closer surveillance of synagogues and Jewish institutions.

Many newspapers and magazines made use of anti-Semitic arguments and stereotypes throughout the year. The most violent and coarse attack on the Jews was published by the monthly *Fotografare* in January. Chief editor Cesco Ciapanna wrote a long article depicting the Jews as a race of exploiters whose religious imperative was to dominate other people and classes, peasants in particular. No wonder, he asserted, that Israeli Jews were oppressing the Palestinian peasants in the occupied territories. According to Ciapanna, world finance was largely controlled by Jewish financiers, who provoked the stock-market crash in October 1987. Similar articles were published by other magazines, ostensibly as "historical background" to events in the West Bank and Gaza Strip.

Part of the Catholic press was particularly negative in its attitudes. In January *Il Sabato*, the widely read weekly of the influential fundamentalist movement

Comunione e Liberazione, published an editorial by Maurizio Blondet on the programs and powers of what the journalist called the "temple lobby," a group of wealthy Jews affiliated with freemasonry. The group, which, according to Blondet, was led by Edgar Bronfman, president of the World Jewish Congress, aimed to restore the temple in Jerusalem. Blondet claimed that the "lobby" influenced the American administration to soften its policy toward the USSR, in exchange for which the USSR would authorize a massive immigration of Soviet Jews to Israel, thereby strengthening the Jewish state. In Blondet's words, the "bloody repression" of the Palestinian uprising was just part of the lobby's plan for restoring the temple. He further contended that the same group had directed the "defamation campaign" against Austrian president Kurt Waldheim.

Other articles in the Catholic press, though not as blatant as Blondet's in their reliance on the "Protocols of the Elders of Zion," were nonetheless characterized by the use of old and new anti-Semitic stereotypes. In February, in the weekly *Segnosette*, journalist Massimo Giuliani defined Israeli policy toward Palestinians as a "genocide, carried out by yesterday's victims." Israeli concerns about the security of the Jewish state were described by the writer as "a form of idolatry." The whole situation is so serious, he said, "that we can understand Christians who are currently reconsidering the legitimacy of the reasons for the existence of the State of Israel, and the relations between the Christian and Jewish faiths."

In March the authoritative Jesuit monthly *Civiltà Cattolica* published an article by commentator Giovanni Rulli on the occupied territories. Israeli behavior toward Palestinians was termed "horrifying violence" justified by "strongly racist assumptions." "Israeli crimes" in the West Bank and Gaza Strip were similar to the ones "Jews suffered when it seemed that they were all fated to perish in the 'final solution,' " he asserted. Israel's intention, according to Rulli, was to subjugate and enslave Palestinians, making them work for Israel's security and well-being.

In March the professional association of Italian journalists censured Paolo Panerai for his anti-Semitic remarks in an article published by *Milano Finanza* in October 1987 (see AJYB 1989, p. 326). Since all journalists were required to belong to the association, it had considerable power, and its action was likely to deter other journalists from publishing similar ideas.

JEWISH COMMUNITY

Demography

An estimated 31,000 Jews were affiliated with one or other of the local Italian Jewish communities, with no significant change in number over the previous year.

Communal Affairs

On the occasion of Israeli prime minister Shamir's visit to Italy in February, some 500 Jewish personalities, mostly active members of their communities, signed a petition expressing "dismay" over Israel's policy in the territories and "worry" over its possible consequences. To prevent the media from using the document for anti-Israel propaganda, the petition was to be delivered directly to Prime Minister Shamir. However, it was leaked by a Jewish journalist to the daily *La Stampa*, which published it before it was handed to Shamir. Some 3,000 members of the Milan Jewish community reacted strongly to the document, signing a counter petition expressing full support for Israel. The Rome community, too, condemned the petition, arguing that at such a critical time Israel deserved the strongest support possible from the Diaspora. Conflict within the Italian Jewish community over differing views on Israel calmed down after a few weeks, at least outwardly.

In the course of 1987–88, Italian authorities finally decided to grant Italian citizenship to the Libyan Jews who had come to Italy after the expulsion in 1967 and enacted the necessary legislative and administrative measures. Some 3,500 Jews of Libyan origin currently lived in Italy. The few who already held Italian citizenship obtained it before World War II (Libya was an Italian colony from 1911 to 1943); others received it after several years of residence in Italy. Many Libyan Jews, however, were still stateless persons.

Italian Jewish organizations and institutions were active in the international Jewish forum. The UCII (Union of Italian Jewish Communities) participated in all the meetings held in 1988 by the European Jewish Congress (EJC), a body in which all the European communities were represented. Recent manifestations of anti-Zionism and anti-Semitism were discussed at a meeting in Milan, February 7–8, of the EJC's commission on anti-Semitism, organized by the Center for Contemporary Jewish Documentation (CDEC) in that city. Representatives of the various communities noted that the recent wave of anti-Semitism displayed common characteristics all over Europe and urged that strategies to fight it be coordinated on a continental level. The EJC executive gathered in Jerusalem, February 21–25, to discuss the current situation in Israel and the occupied territories and its implications for world Jewry.

The annual meeting of the EJC took place in Brussels, May 29–31. Among the topics discussed were the role of European Jewry in the process of growing European integration; the EC's policy toward Israel and the Middle East; recent developments in the Soviet Union; the prospects of better cooperation between international Jewish organizations; and the recent development of anti-Zionist and anti-Semitic manifestations in Europe. These subjects were considered again at the gathering of the EJC executive in London on November 13.

The president of the UCII, Tullia Zevi, participated in a meeting of the national executive of the American Jewish Committee in Boston on October 27. She reported on anti-Semitism in Italy and Europe and discussed possible responses by the Jewish communities of the world.

The legislative measures enacted by the Fascist regime in 1938, discriminating against Jews in all spheres of life, were the subject of an international conference held in Rome, October 17–18. Participants discussed the historical and ideological background of these measures, the political motivation behind them, their extent, how they were enforced, and their influence on Italian Jewry. The conference, which was organized by the Italian Parliament, the UCII, and the CDEC, was attended by a number of renowned scholars. *La Rassegna Mensile di Israel*, the Italian Jewish monthly, in collaboration with the CDEC, issued a special volume on the racial laws: *1938—Le leggi contro gli ebrei* ("1938—The Laws Against the Jews").

Nazi War Criminals

Jewish organizations tried to arouse public interest in two cases involving Nazi criminals. The first was that of Anton Malloth, a former SS guard in the Theresienstadt concentration camp, who had been sentenced to death in absentia by a Czechoslovakian court in 1948, for crimes against humanity. Later, criminal proceedings against him were also initiated by the tribunal in Dortmund, Germany, and by Austrian judicial authorities. From 1973 on, Malloth officially resided in Meran (Italian Southern Tyrol), where his wife was born. He actually lived in Italy for very short periods, however, having been declared *persona non grata* by Italian authorities. In August 1988 he was arrested by the Italian police and expelled to Germany by the judicial authorities of Bolzano (Italian Southern Tyrol).

Despite the urgings of the president of the Jewish community of Meran, Federico Steinhaus, UCII president Tullia Zevi, and Nazi hunter Simon Wiesenthal, a Czech offer to provide documentation on Malloth so that he could be brought to trial was declined by Italian, German, and Austrian authorities, each for different reasons. Most of the Italian press was indifferent to the case. Southern Tyrol newspapers were sympathetic to Malloth, whom they considered "just an old, sick man."

The second case involved Annalise Kappler, the widow of SS officer Herbert Kappler, who wanted to come to Italy to publicize her book about her husband's escape from the military jail in Rome in 1977. Herbert Kappler had organized the deportation of the Jews of Rome to the death camps in October 1943. He was also responsible for a reprisal action in 1944, following an attack by partisans on German troops, in which the Nazis killed more than 340 innocent people. Although he was sentenced to life imprisonment after the war, in 1977 Kappler managed to escape from the Rome prison and reached Germany, possibly with the complicity of some Italian authorities. He died shortly afterward. Annalise Kappler's planned tour of Italy seemed to Jewish and ex-partisan organizations to be an unacceptable provocation, and, as a result of pressure by them on Italian authorities, the Ministry of Interior barred her from entering Italy.

Jewish-Catholic Relations

In January UCII president Tullia Zevi wrote to Cardinal Johannes Willebrands to protest the anti-Semitic tone of many articles published in Catholic magazines. Cardinal Willebrands headed the Vatican's Commission on Religious Relations with the Jews. In March and April the chief rabbi of Rome, Prof. Elio Toaff, in several interviews and public statements, vehemently condemned anti-Semitic tendencies within the Catholic Church. He called for a clear rejection of any form of anti-Semitism by the highest spiritual authorities of the Church.

At the end of May, the Episcopal Conference of Italy (CEI), the decision-making body of the Italian Catholic Church, composed of all the bishops of the country, approved a document on anti-Semitism. In it the bishops made a clear distinction between Jews, Israelis, and the government of Israel, asked Catholics and the Italian public in general not to confuse the three, and warned against easy simplification and partisan interpretation of the situation in Israel and the occupied territories. They also expressed concern over recent manifestations of intolerance and anti-Semitism in Italy, which, they said, should not be considered a marginal phenomenon in Italian society. The bishops went on to remind Catholics that, according to the "Nostra Aetate" encyclical of the Second Vatican Council, Christians were tied to Jews in "spiritual brotherhood." In their document, the bishops quoted other, more recent, official Catholic statements about the Jewish people and anti-Semitism, affirming that Christians must relate to the Jews with "respect and love" and "deplor[ing] the hatred, the persecutions and all the manifestations of anti-Semitism initiated against the Jews by anyone at any time."

Both Tullia Zevi and Chief Rabbi Toaff applauded the bishops' document, Rabbi Toaff affirming that "now we can start our dialogue again." Zevi praised the content of the document and urged wider dissemination of its principles within the Catholic Church. "A survey conducted in 1985," she wrote, "showed that 66 percent of the priests, 68 percent of the nuns, 91 percent of the catechists, 97 percent of the teachers, and 78 percent of the students had not read the 'Nostra Aetate' encyclical." As a result, they were not yet aware of recent changes in the Catholic Church's attitude toward the Jews and Judaism.

At the end of September, Pope John Paul II publicly reaffirmed that "the Jews are not to be considered responsible for the death of Jesus."

Culture

The work of preserving Jewish monuments and artistic treasures in Italy showed continuing progress. In 1988 restoration was started on the Sephardic synagogue in Pesaro, one of the finest in Europe. In June the restoration of the Ashkenazi synagogue of Venice ("Schola Canton"), built in 1531–32, was completed, and the synagogue was opened to the public. The Jewish catacombs of Villa Torlonia in Rome were officially turned over to the Italian state by the Vatican in March.

According to the provisions of the new agreement between the Republic of Italy and the Union of Italian Jewish Communities, the UCII would share management of the catacombs with the Italian authorities.

Jewish monuments and works of art in Italy were still vulnerable, however. In March and April unknown persons stole capitals from the ruins of the synagogue in ancient Ostia (near Rome), which dates to the first century BCE. The dome of the Italian synagogue of Venice was destroyed by an accidental fire in April. The synagogue had just been restored and was about to be opened to the public. Repair of the dome would cost some $70,000.

Several international conferences and congresses on the history of the Jews of Italy were held during 1988. In May two conferences, in Jerusalem and Bertinoro, marked the 500th anniversary of the journey to Palestine of Rabbi Ovadiah ben Abraham Yare of Bertinoro. Ovadiah was an important scholar and author of a famous commentary to the Mishnah whose letters, written during his journey from Italy to Jerusalem, are an important source for the history of the Mediterranean countries and Jewish communities in that area. The conference in Bertinoro, organized by the local authorities of Emilia Romagna, focused on the history of the Jews of Italy of that time and on Ovadiah himself. The conference in Jerusalem, organized by the Ben Zvi Institute, the Hebrew University, and the Italian Synagogue of Jerusalem, was devoted to his contributions in the field of Jewish studies, as well as the life, culture, and customs of the Mediterranean Jewish communities.

"Leone De' Sommi and the Performing Arts in the Renaissance" was the subject of an international conference that took place in Tel Aviv June 4–6. The conference was organized by the Faculty of Visual and Performing Arts of Tel Aviv University and the Italian Cultural Institute. De' Sommi, a 16th-century Mantuan Jew, was an outstanding actor, director, dramatist, and theorist, who wrote the first known complete comedy in Hebrew and an important treatise on staging. The conference was attended by an international group of scholars in the fields of theater, dance, music, literature, and Jewish studies.

The 500th anniversary of the first printing of a Hebrew Bible, by the Soncino family, who took their name from the village of Soncino, near Milano, was marked by the issue of a new stamp by the Italian postal service. The famous family of printers and the beginning of Hebrew publishing in Italy were the subjects of a symposium held in Soncino on June 12.

As noted above, an international conference and a special volume of *La Rassegna Mensile di Israel* were devoted to the 50th anniversary of the Fascist racial laws. The meaning of the Holocaust was debated in a two-day meeting at Jesolo, near Venice, April 24–25. Organized by the Department for Cultural Assistance of the UCII, the conference focused on the "Memory and Mythology of the Holocaust" and was attended by rabbis and scholars from Italy and Israel.

Beth Hatefutsoth, the Museum of the Diaspora, in Tel Aviv, was responsible for an exhibition on the history and traditions of the Jews of Ethiopia that was shown to the public in Rome in May and later in other Italian towns.

The Jewish cultural program that most interested the Italian public was "Wonders of the Ghetto," an exhibit of ritual and daily objects from the Jewish Museum of Prague, shown in Ferrara, from September to the end of the year. In the same town, another interesting exhibition was mounted on the history and culture of the Jews of Emilia Romagna.

The Italian public took an interest in Israeli culture as well. The most significant recent Israeli movies were screened at a festival of Israeli cinema that took place in Milan, October 10–16. Also, two very different books by the Israeli journalist and writer David Grossman were among the best-sellers of the year: the novel *Vedi alla voce: amore* (*See Under: Love*), widely acclaimed by the critics, and a long report on the situation in the occupied territories, *Il vento giallo* (*The Yellow Wind*), which aroused controversy and debate.

Publications

Responding to the interest of the Italian public in Jewish subjects, publishing houses offered a large number of books on Judaica. Among the most significant recent ventures was the publication by the Carucci publishing house, which specialized in Judaica, of a new, corrected edition of the Italian *Mahzor*, the year-round prayer book according to the Italian rite. The first new *Mahzor* to appear since 1856, it would be published in three volumes, in Hebrew with Italian translation. The first volume, "Prayers of Yom Kippur," was released in 1988.

A facsimile of the 1856 edition of the *Mahzor*, known also as "*Mahzor ShaDaL*," the inititals of the author of the introduction, Shmuel David Luzzatto, was being published by the Italian Synagogue of Jerusalem. The second volume, "Prayers of Rosh Hashanah, Yom Kippur, and Sukkot," was made available before the penitential days in 1988.

Marietti, a small Catholic publishing house long interested in Judaica, published Rashi's commentary on Exodus, in the Italian translation by Rabbi Sergio Sierra. Forni of Bologna continued to publish books of historical interest on Judaica in facsimile form: in 1988 it offered *Paris un Vein*, a secular work by Elijah Bahur Levita, published in Yiddish (16th century). Giacoma Limentani, a writer and teacher in the field of Jewish studies, published *L'ombra allo specchio* ("The Shade in the Mirror"), a collection of tales and thoughts related to Midrash.

Personalia

Rabbi Mino Bahbout of Rome was awarded the special prize of the Israel Ministry for Religious Affairs for spiritual leaders of Jewish communities in Israel and the Diaspora. Bahbout, a physicist and a teacher at the Rabbinical College in Rome, was the director of the UCII's cultural affairs department.

Edoardo Vitta, a renowned professor of international law at several Italian universities and for many years head of the Jewish community of Florence, died in January at the age of 74. Vitta, author of several books on international law, lived in Israel during the 1940s, where he was an important official in the Ministry of Justice and a member of the commission on drafting a constitution.

Paolo Milano, a well-known literary critic, died in Rome, in April, at the age of 84. An anti-Fascist, Milano moved to Paris in 1938 after the enactment of the racial laws and in 1940 to New York, where he taught comparative literature at Queens College and the New School for Social Research and reviewed books for *Partisan Review*, the *Nation*, and other publications. Returning to Italy in 1956, he continued to write about literature, particularly in the highly regarded weekly *L'Espresso*.

Herbert Pagani, a versatile artist active in the fields of music, theater, and visual arts, died at the age of 44 in the United States, in August. Born in Tripoli, Libya, Pagani had lived in Italy, France, Germany, and the United States. In Italy, where he lived most of the time, he was a successful singer and songwriter in the late 1960s, early 1970s. He conducted several popular programs on Radio Montecarlo and wrote and directed the show *Megalopolis*, for which he also composed the music and lyrics and designed the scenery. A painter and sculptor as well, Pagani had come to the United States to prepare an exhibition. Pagani, who was well known in Israel, was to have been the host of the Israel Philharmonic Orchestra concert at Masada, in October 1988, which was part of Israel's 40th-anniversary celebration.

SIMONETTA DELLA SETA
MASSIMO TORREFRANCA

Federal Republic of Germany

For the Bonn government, 1988 was a relatively uneventful year, one in which some progress was made in easing tensions with the USSR, and the president of the Bundestag was forced to resign as a result of an ill-considered speech commemorating *Kristallnacht*. The Jews of West Germany were shaken this year by a major scandal involving the embezzlement of funds by the head of the community, though the consequences proved less damaging than originally feared.

National Affairs

Two major areas of foreign policy occupied the Bonn government in 1988: Eastern Europe, especially the USSR, and the apartheid regime in South Africa.

Several steps were taken this year to ease relations with the Soviet Union, which had been seriously strained since 1986, when Chancellor Helmut Kohl (Christian Democratic Union, CDU) in a *Newsweek* interview compared Mikhail Gorbachev to Nazi propagandist Josef Goebbels. First, in mid-January, Soviet foreign minister Eduard Shevardnadze paid a three-day visit to Bonn, where he discussed the status of West Berlin, disarmament, and various bilateral issues. Shevardnadze indicated that Gorbachev would not be able to visit Bonn in 1988, but did not exclude the possibility for a later time. Secondly, in February Lothar Späth, premier of Baden-Württemberg, met with Gorbachev in Moscow to discuss the improvement of economic relations. In the course of their meetings, which were described as very successful, the Soviets made clear that they recognized the economic importance of the West German state. Other Germans who traveled to the Soviet Union this year to meet with Gorbachev were Willy Brandt, honorary chairman of the Social Democrats (SPD), in April; Hans-Jochen Vogel, chairman of the SPD, in May; and later that month, Economics Minister Martin Bangemann. As for Eastern Europe, Foreign Minister Hans-Dietrich Genscher visited Poland and Hungary in order to strengthen relations with these countries.

The question of relations with South Africa evoked considerably more controversy within the government of the Federal Republic than did those with Eastern Europe. Differences developed during a meeting in Dakar, Senegal, in October 1987, at which German ambassadors to African states engaged in a general reappraisal of the FRG's policy vis-à-vis Africa with Foreign Minister Genscher. The subsequent flurry of African travel and travel plans by German politicians reflected the divisons within the Kohl cabinet: In late January 1988, Bavarian premier Franz-Josef Strauss made a tour of southern Africa that began in Johannesburg and continued to Mozambique and Namibia. Strauss's support for the South African regime, however, was opposed by Labor Minister Norbert Blüm, who had hoped to travel to South Africa as well, but was blocked by Chancellor Kohl. Strauss's visit led to a dispute in the CDU-FDP coalition government, but criticism came from the opposition SPD and the Greens as well.

At the beginning of March, siding with the liberal elements in the cabinet, President Richard von Weizsäcker embarked on a two-week tour of various African countries, not including South Africa. In his public remarks, von Weizsäcker voiced sharp criticism of apartheid, which in turn led to more acrimony inside the federal cabinet. Later that same month, two influential politicians in the Free Democrats (FDP), Gerhard Baum and Burkhard Hirsch, made their own tour of southern Africa, and on June 14, the president of the African National Congress, Oliver Tambo, was received by Genscher and von Weizsäcker in Bonn.

Two domestic issues in particular occupied national attention in 1988. One was a scandal related to improper disposal of nuclear waste at the Nukem plant in Hesse; the other, the landslide victory of premier-to-be Björn Engholm of the SPD, in the traditional CDU stronghold of Schleswig-Holstein. This upset was a direct consequence of the previous election campaign, in which charges of "dirty tricks" were made against former premier Uwe Barschel, who subsequently committed suicide. Another issue was a controversial speech delivered by Bundestag president Philipp Jenninger on the 50th anniversary of *Kristallnacht* (see below).

In Düsseldorf, in April, Abbas Hamadei, who was associated with the Lebanese Hezbollah group accused of holding Western hostages, was sentenced to 13 years in prison. The court established that Hamadei was involved in the kidnappings of two West German businessmen in January 1987 with the purpose of stopping West Germany from extraditing his brother, Mohammed Ali Hamadei, to the United States. Mohammed was sought for hijacking an American jetliner and murdering a passenger, a U.S. Navy diver, in June 1985. Mohammed's trial opened in Frankfurt in early July.

Relations with Israel

Foreign Minister Genscher paid a weekend visit to Israel late in January, to convey to the Israeli government the feelings of the European Community (EC) about the situation in the occupied territories. The European Parliament had adopted a resolution expressing its concern "over the measures of oppression with which the Israeli armed forces react against demonstrations of the Palestinian population."

On March 11, at the request of the Green party, the Bundestag (Federal Parliament) debated the situation in the Middle East, in light of the *intifada*. All parties agreed that the moderate forces on both sides had to be strengthened. At the same time, there was virtual consensus that it was unacceptable for Germans to equate the crimes of Nazism with the "brutalities committed against the Palestinians in the *intifada*."

The number of German tourists to Israel in 1987 was 195,000—30 percent more than in 1986. By contrast, the number of tourists from France and Britain increased by 14 percent each in the same period.

The German-Israeli Economic Association, founded by Dr. Kurt Moosberg of Tel Aviv and Walter Hesselbach of Frankfurt, celebrated its 20th anniversary this year. The current president was Dr. Ralf Krüger.

50th Anniversary of Kristallnacht

The anniversary of the pogroms of November 9, 1938 (the term *Pogromnacht* was now preferred by many Jews and their supporters to *Kristallnacht*, which they viewed as less accurate and even offensive) was commemorated widely in the Federal Republic—at the national and local levels, by official bodies as well as by private groups and individuals. It is no exaggeration to estimate that well over 10,000 separate commemorations—from exhibits in high schools to church-sponsored events—marked the anniversary. Activities included an all-night candlelight vigil by one man and a few supporters at Berlin's Kurfürstendamm, silent marches, street exhibits marking the sites of Jewish-owned stores and buildings that had been vandalized, discussions, and poetry readings, in addition to the big official events. (See also below, under "Jewish Community.") The major theme of all these commemorations was taken from words of the Hassidic master, the Baal Shem Tov: "Remembrance Is the Secret of Redemption." This motto was also used on the commemorative stamp issued for the anniversary.

The theme had been voiced in a speech by Elie Wiesel in late December 1987, in which he urged Germans to "accept the challenge of remembrance." German writer Siegfried Lenz echoed this motif on the occasion of his being awarded the Peace Prize of the German Booksellers Association in Frankfurt with a speech entitled "Auschwitz Is in Our Custody" (*Auschwitz bleibt uns anvertraut*). The same theme underlay the demand by the churches and the Berlin Jewish community that the Kinkelstrasse in the Berlin borough of Spandau be renamed Jüdenstrasse, its name until 1938.

The central memorial event arranged by the Jewish community took place in the Westend Synagogue in Frankfurt, on November 9. Those attending included President von Weizsäcker, Chancellor Kohl, Prime Minister Walter Wallmann of Hesse, Ignatz Bubis, head of the Frankfurt Jewish community, and Heinz Galinski, chairman of the Zentralrat der Juden in Deutschland (Central Council of Jews in Germany). Kohl's speech was repeatedly disrupted by young Jews shouting "Bitburg" and "lies."

THE JENNINGER SPEECH

The Bundestag's commemoration of the 50th anniversary of *Kristallnacht*, on November 10, was preceded by a dispute over whether or not Heinz Galinski, chairman of the Central Council, should speak to Parliament, as he had pushed for, with the support of members of the Green party. Others in the Jewish community opposed his participation, and a Bundestag committee had voted against it.

One reason why Galinski was not invited was Bundestag president Philipp Jenninger's own keen interest in being the keynote speaker at the memorial meeting. As it turned out, Jenninger's speech was a major fiasco that ignited a political storm and ultimately led him to resign. Jenninger tried to give a dispassionate account of the Nazi regime's rise to power, as it was seen by the average German at the time. He described the years between 1933 and 1938 as "fascinating," insofar as "history knows few parallels to Hitler's political triumphs during those early years.... For the Germans, who had experienced the Weimar Republic as a series of humiliations in foreign policy, all this had to appear as a miracle.... Mass unemployment had turned into full employment, mass misery had been replaced by something like well-being for the widest strata.... Did not Hitler make real what Kaiser Wilhelm II had only promised—to lead Germany into glorious times? ... And as far as the Jews were concerned: had they not in the past—as it was said then—usurped a role that was not becoming to them? ... Was it not right to set them certain limits? ... " Though Jenninger was not, in fact, expressing approval or attempting to justify those views, he failed to distinguish between what he was reporting and his own opinions. As a result, most listeners misinterpreted his remarks and were outraged.

Negative reactions, which came from all parties represented in the Bundestag and from broad segments of the German political leadership and intellectuals, led to Jenninger's resignation. Reactions abroad, especially from Jewish groups, were also critical, expressing astonishment that Jenninger, a strong supporter of Israel, would have made such a speech. Israeli prime minister Yitzhak Shamir's press secretary expressed astonishment, but hoped that this would remain a minor episode. After his resignation, urged by Chancellor Kohl, who was about to embark on a visit to the United States, Jenninger expressed regret at having hurt some people's feelings. "Not everything can be said aloud in Germany," he concluded.

One member of the Zentralrat directorate, Michael Fürst, of Hannover, dissented from the generally negative reaction, stating that he found the speech unobjectionable. Subsequently, he was forced to resign his seat in the council's directorate and, at Galinski's behest, was censured by its council of representatives.

Neo-Nazism and Anti-Semitism

The Frankfurt Jewish Community Center and the offices of Saudi Airlines were bombed in April. Damage to the center was estimated to be around $400,000. The chairman of the Central Council of Jews in Germany, Heinz Galinski, appealed to federal authorities to take greater responsibility for the security needs of Jewish institutions and individual Jewish citizens.

As in other Western countries, there was a notable increase this year in activities of the extreme Right in the FRG, even involving politicians from the established parties. Both Gerhard Mayer-Vorfelder (CDU), the minister of education in Baden-Württemberg, and Defense Minister Manfred Wörner (CDU) published articles in right-wing magazines (*Nation Europa* and *Mut*). Mayer-Vorfelder was also criticized for not having considered any form of commemoration of the November 1938 pogroms in the Baden-Württemberg school system, for which he was responsible. The neo-Nazi Freiheitliche Arbeiterpartei (Free German Labor party, FAP) began publishing a new paper, *Der Politische Soldat* ("The Political Soldier"). The *Freie Rundschau*, a right-wing newspaper published in Berlin, had links to other right-wing periodicals, such as *SIEG*, the NPD paper *Deutsche Stimme*, and *Nation Europa*.

The Mönch-Buchversand in Koblenz was part of a publishing group closely tied to the armaments industry and the West German army (Bundeswehr). Books offered by the firm included histories of various Waffen-SS divisions that were also sold by a publishing company linked to an SS veterans' association. The firm also distributed books published by right-wing organizations, as well as publications of the Bundeswehr, including a book authored by Defense Minister Wörner.

A study conducted at the University of Dortmund found that in 1987 the quantity of printed right-wing material increased by 14 percent. According to Michael Jäger, a researcher at Dortmund, new publications on the Right contrasted sharply with traditional neo-Nazi publications, officially disavowing the Third Reich and Hitler in order to make people more receptive to their ideas. Among the noteworthy magazines directed at the more intellectual right-wing reader were *Elemente* (fashioned after the French *éléments*) and *Mut*.

In early March, the German police raided residences of over 80 members of Die Bewegung (the Movement), considered to be a successor organization to the National Socialist Action Front (Aktionsfront Nationaler Sozialisten/Nationale Aktivisten, ANS/NA). This organization was also considered to be in close contact with the FAP.

On the anniversary of Rudolf Hess's death, 100 neo-Nazis, including Michael Kühnen, leader of the ANS/NA, led a demonstration in the town of Wunsiedel, where Hess is buried. The demonstration was authorized by the courts. Manfred Roeder, convicted of neo-Nazi activity in Hesse, was allowed by the authorities to continue his campaigns from jail. In Koblenz, Rudolf Koch, a school principal, was reinstated in his job by a higher court, after having been dismissed for telling students and colleagues that Auschwitz was an invention of the Americans and that no more than 40,000 Jews—if any at all—were killed under Nazism.

Another example of the leniency of West German courts in dealing with Nazi war criminals occurred in November, with the acquittal of Count Modest Korff, a former SS-Hauptsturmführer accused of having deported Jews from France to

Auschwitz. When the sentence was greeted by strong protests in the courtroom, the judge ordered the court cleared. In Dortmund, the trial of Anton Malloth was suspended because the defendant had a fatal illness. Malloth was accused of having personally killed more than ten people at the prison in the Theresienstadt concentration camp.

In Schleswig-Holstein, a former member of the Christian Democrats, Emil Schlee, had become active with the Republicans, a party established in the early '80s and headed by Franz Schönhuber, a former member of the Waffen-SS. Schlee was involved with Lyndon LaRouche's Patrioten für Deutschland. The other political parties in Schleswig-Holstein organized protests against the increase in right-wing activity. There were protests this year in Frankfurt against neo-Nazism, fascism, and racism. Over 2,500 people took part in a demonstration against a proposed meeting of the neo-Nazi NPD. The Green party, which had become active in issues related to anti-Semitism and racism, held a conference on anti-Semitism, with Heinz Galinski and the Israeli-German historian Dan Diner among the speakers. Similarly, a meeting of delegates from the OTV (Union of Public Employees) and other organizations warned against the growth of right-wing movements and stressed the importance of marches, vigils, demonstrations, and other protest activities.

On a more positive note, the Daimler Benz auto firm finally agreed to pay 20 million marks to the Conference on Jewish Material Claims Against Germany, the Red Cross, and other organizations, as compensation to former slave laborers. Daimler Benz also agreed to erect a monument to the memory of World War II slave laborers at its Stuttgart headquarters. Action was initiated to have the Volkswagen company pay compensation to female slave laborers in the so-called basement bunker, an underground production site at Wolfsburg.

A study on anti-Semitism in the FRG, carried out by the Allensbach Institute jointly with the Institute for the Study of Anti-Semitism at the Technical University in Berlin and commissioned by the Anti-Defamation League in the United States, found that 8 percent of the population were "committed" anti-Semites and another 7 percent were strongly anti-Semitic in orientation. Also, the respondents judged anti-Semitic were unevenly distributed across age groups: 27 percent of the oldest cohort, but only 9 percent of the 16–29-year-olds, fell into this category. Among all those questioned, 33 percent said Jews had too much influence in the world; 22 percent considered Jews partly responsible for being persecuted and hated.

In a Wickert Institute opinion poll, Jews fared somewhat better than other minority groups. The survey found 26 percent of Germans opposed to their child marrying a Jew, compared to 42 percent, a Turk, and 40 percent, a black. Similarly, 12 percent opposed having a Jew live in their building, 20 percent opposed having a Turk.

In mid-February it was learned that at least 80,000 documents had disappeared from the Berlin Document Center, the principal archive of Nazism, containing files of NSDAP members and other Nazi organizations. It was alleged that documents from the center had been sold, either to clear the records of former Nazis or to supply the market with Nazi memorabilia. A number of arrests were made, including that of an auctioneer and several traders of militaria. The first trial in the case started in November.

JEWISH COMMUNITY

Demography

As of January 1, 1989, the 66 local Jewish communities in the Federal Republic and West Berlin had a total of 27,552 members (the 1988 figure was 27,612). A closer analysis shows that despite the slight decline this year, the general trend toward demographic normalization, pointed to last year (see AJYB 1989, p. 341), was continuing. The number of those in the 0–15 age bracket increased to 3,853 in 1988 (3,668 in 1987); and the number aged 70 and over declined to 3,866 (4,103). Losses from deaths amounted to 458 (423); from membership cancellations, 93 (41); and from emigration 297 (231). Increases through conversion were 40 (43) and from immigration, 568 (546), both virtually unchanged. There was a noteworthy increase in the birthrate, however: 108, as against 11 the previous year. By and large, the smaller communities continued to decline, whereas most of the larger communities increased slightly.

Communal Affairs

THE NACHMANN SCANDAL

In the spring, the Jewish community was hit by a scandal of unprecedented dimensions when it learned that large sums of money intended for victims of the Holocaust had been embezzled by Werner Nachmann, chairman of the Zentralrat der Juden in Deutschland (Central Council of Jews in Germany). The facts began to unfold after Nachmann's death on January 21.

Born in 1925 in Karlsruhe into an old Baden merchant family, Nachmann had emigrated with his parents to France in the late thirties, returning in 1945 to Karlsruhe, where his father, Otto, operated a firm that processed used textiles and other scrap materials. After his father's death, Werner succeeded him both in the firm and in the Oberrat der Israeliten Badens (Council of Jews of the Land of Baden), originally cofounded by Otto Nachmann. Indeed, the entire family virtually monopolized Jewish affairs in Baden, which in the postwar period had a community of only a few hundred people. Otto's wife, Hertha, founded the women's association there, and no one other than the Nachmanns was ever known to speak for the Jews of Baden. In 1962 Nachmann was elected to the directorate of the Zentralrat, and in 1969 he became its chairman.

Nachmann was instrumental in the development of the Hochschule für Jüdische Studien (College for Jewish Studies) in Heidelberg, a school that was criticized in some Jewish quarters for being geared more to non-Jewish theology students than to prospective rabbis and teachers for the Jewish community. Active on the boards of various Jewish and German-Jewish institutions, his excellent contacts with mostly conservative German politicians helped ensure the financial stability of the Jewish community and made possible the erection, with state support, of a number of Jewish commmunity centers and synagogues. At the same time, he was often criticized for his opportunism and for what was seen as a servile attitude toward German politicians. He had made many friends in Germany, using as his slogan, "Why don't we live perfectly normally together?" Most offensive to many in the Jewish community was his defense of the former premier of Baden-Württemberg, Karl Filbinger, a fanatical Nazi who, as a military judge, had ordered the execution of German soldiers even after capitulation.

Nachmann had a clear understanding of the exculpatory role of Jews in the Federal Republic, which he used to gain advantage both for himself and the community. In a speech in 1986 he argued, "It is often forgotten that through our return [to Germany] we have helped the world to renew its trust in this democracy. Germany was thus reinstated into the association of free nations.... We returned as Jews and yet have become different from what we were, just as those are different who served or tolerated tyranny or who had fought it with bitter powerlessness...."

The recipient of numerous honors in Germany, Nachmann had recently become a vice-president of the European section of the World Jewish Congress.

Nachmann's funeral was a national event. From President von Weizsäcker to Chancellor Kohl and the president of the Federal Constitutional Court, virtually the entire German political elite was present. The highly laudatory eulogies delivered by various notables later came to be of considerable embarrassment. ("Nachmann ensured the coexistence of Jews with Germans; . . . I mourn for an outstanding personality and a humanist whose legacy of tolerance, of reconciliation and civic responsibility is an obligation to us all."—President von Weizsäcker. "Baden Württemberg loses a personality of great merit to our land. As a committed and successful entrepreneur, he acquired a high reputation in business circles. . . ."—Premier Späth. "The captain has left the boat, it is wandering about. We have all become orphans, the Jewish community in Germany is a widow."—Former Baden chief rabbi Peter Levinson.)

THE SCANDAL ERUPTS

In March Heinz Galinski, head of the West Berlin Jewish community, was elected to succeed Nachmann as chairman of the Central Council. The theft of well over DM 30 million ($15 million) became known to Galinski and others in early April. This amount constituted the interest accrued on accounts under Nachmann's control which came from two sources: (1) a special fund of DM 400 million established in 1980 by the West German government for Holocaust victims, mostly from Eastern Europe, who had not previously filed claims; and (2) a DM 40-million fund earmarked for needs of the Zentralrat. The investigation by Treuhand, the accounting firm engaged by the Central Council, revealed that although Nachmann forwarded the principal to an account of the Conference on Material Claims Against Germany in New York, he diverted the interest thereof to his own enterprises, including one operated with a female companion in Karlsruhe. Other funds ended up in banks in France, Italy, Spain, and possibly Israel.

Although Galinski informed members of the federal government of the investigation's findings in early April, they were kept confidential and became public only on May 17, by way of a report in the weekly *Sonntagsblatt*. Ten days later, Galinski declared that trust in the Jewish community in Germany had been "put in jeopardy." How was it possible, he asked, that the Zentralrat allowed such a large account—DM 400 million—to be established outside its own supervision? At this time, the council's general secretary, Alexander Ginsburg, who was now under suspicion as Nachmann's closest associate, officially requested a leave of absence from his duties. Unofficially, it became known that he had strongly resisted being forced out of office by Galinski. Galinski promised that a full investigation would be made public when completed and that there would be "personal consequences" for anyone found culpable.

Alexander Ginsburg resigned in September, under pressure. Only in December, although no charge or accusation had been made against other individuals, did several other members of the Zentralrat offer their resignations. The basic problem, as pointed out in an editorial in the conservative *Frankfurter Allgemeine Zeitung*, in May, was the council's failure to exert control over financial matters, especially since—as revealed by the Treuhand audit—its accounts had been in chaos at least since 1980, a fact that must have been known not only to Nachmann and Ginsburg but to several others as well. The Zentralrat leadership, however, appears to have decided to limit blame and investigation to the two key individuals. Galinski indicated that while the resignation of the entire directorate had been considered, it was decided that the body that shared responsibility for the developments of recent years should also be prepared to repair the damage that was caused. Galinski criticized the finance ministry in Bonn for refusing to publish its correspondence with Nachmann. (The government's role in the affair was never satisfactorily explained.) He also suggested that in the course of the current bankruptcy proceedings against Nachmann's estate, some of the money must have disappeared, probably into the pockets of relatives and former associates.

There were few immediate changes affecting the Central Council. Galinski initiated a redrafting of its constitution, and there was a realignment of forces in Nachmann's home power base, the Karlsruhe Jewish community. In Cologne, which he represented, Ginsburg was asked to resign, on September 4, by a large segment of the community. His supporters, on the other hand, praised his 30 years' service to the Cologne *Gemeinde*, the community organization. In the end, virtually all *Gemeinde* representatives resigned, to make way for a new leadership, and a new constitution was to be adopted, under an interim board.

To the astonishment of many observers and in contrast to the strong statements made in the Israeli press, the West German press was extraordinarily restrained. The many politicians who had only months earlier heaped praise on Nachmann in his grave understandably now found it difficult to condemn him. Few papers even hinted at questions about his private life that had emerged or looked at Nachmann's close personal ties to conservative West German politicians. With the exception of the neo-Nazi *National Zeitung*, virtually no anti-Jewish overtones were expressed anywhere in the media. As a result, the Nachmann scandal was quickly buried and never became a major issue in the FRG.

Cultural and Commemorative Events

The anniversary of the 1938 pogroms was used as an occasion to rededicate a number of new or restored synagogues, such as in Darmstadt and in Bad Nauheim, or to open Jewish cultural centers, such as the new Jewish Museum in Frankfurt. (The new Freiburg synagogue had been dedicated earlier.)

On November 9, Chancellor Kohl officially opened the Jewish Museum of Frankfurt, whose first exhibit dealt with synagogue architecture. Other exhibits of note were opened in Trier, Kaiserslautern, and Bad Vilbel (Jewish Diaspora Museum), and, in the framework of *Kulturwochen* or *Kulturtage*, in Frankfurt, Munich, Duisburg (*Duisburger Akzente*, dedicated to the memory of 200 years of creative activity of Jewish artists, writers, and scholars), and West Berlin. Among exhibits of note in Berlin was one on the Jewish history of the borough of Neukölln, "*Zehn Brüder waren wir gewesen*" ("We Had Been Ten Brothers") and one titled "*Aus Nachbarn wurden Juden*" ("When Neighbors Became Jews").

Memorial plaques were placed at sites throughout the country, including Allendorf and Hungen (both in Hesse), to honor the Jewish population there; in Cologne, in memory of the former Lützowstrasse Jewish public school and the "Kinderheim"; and at the site of the former synagogue in Nuremberg.

A movement had been under way in recent years among non-Jewish Germans to preserve or recover local Jewish heritage. Numerous town historical studies called attention to traces of local Jewish history, and a number of attempts were begun to catalog all former synagogues. In Darmstadt, with a minuscule Jewish community, the synagogue was rebuilt at the initiative of a non-Jewish citizens' coalition. Another such project was under way in Hechingen (Baden-Württemberg). In Ichenhausen, Bavaria, an intercultural meeting house (*Haus der Begegnung*) was created at the site of a former synagogue, at the initiative of the late Werner Nachmann. Similarly, the former Freudenthal Synagogue had been turned into the "Pädagogisch-Kulturelles Zentrum Freudenthal," an educational-cultural center. It was officially dedicated this year with a lecture by Rabbi Albert H. Friedlander, Director of the Leo Baeck Institute and School in London.

Some found it ironic that more money was available for memorializing Jews in places where they had long ceased to live or where they lived in tiny and dwindling communities than for the support of living Jewish communities and institutions. Thus, for example, Charlotte Knobloch, president of the Munich community, made an appeal for help in implementing plans to build a new Jewish community center there, calling on the government of Bavaria as well as the community for support. "A state that gives 3 million marks for the reconstruction of the synagogue of Ichenhausen, where not even a single Jew lives, should make it a priority to build a synagogue and community center in the [Bavarian] capital of Munich," she asserted. The Munich community had also long been demanding improved police protection for its properties and had so far been refused.

Emigré Visitor Programs

In recent years, numerous towns and cities had established programs to invite former citizens to visit the places from which they had to flee in the 1930s. Typically, these programs paid for transportation and accommodation for a week and included such events as exhibits, concerts, or plays with Jewish themes. Originally begun in cities with large prewar Jewish communities, such as Berlin, Hamburg, Cologne, and Frankfurt (Berlin this year was host to 200 of its former Jewish citizens and so far had welcomed 16,000 of them), other cities and small towns had also come to adopt the idea. This year the following cities received guests: Darmstadt (on the occasion of the dedication of the synagogue, 200 invited guests); Muhlheim/Ruhr (60 invited, 17 came); Leverkusen (17 of its former 150 Jewish inhabitants); Ulm (80 plus 70 accompanying persons). Other places included Freiburg, Karlsruhe (both in October and November), Neuss, Bonn, Meckenheim, Windecken, and the state of Schleswig-Holstein.

Jewish-Christian Relations

On the anniversary of *Kristallnacht*, the Central Committee of German Catholics issued a declaration that said, in part, "We cannot declare, on one hand, our allegiance to a community and on the other deny responsibility for what in the name of the community was done or was not done, just by referring to our own personal innocence. . . . The secret of redemption is remembrance."

The Federations of German Protestantism in West and East Germany adopted a joint resolution on the occasion of the upcoming anniversary of the pogroms: "Even if some individuals have paid for their deeds, if others have died, and if a new generation has grown up, we are nevertheless all responsible for the consequences of a past period of guilt."

This year's Brotherhood Week had as its theme "A Hope Come True: The 40th Anniversary of the State of Israel." The keynote speaker at the central event, in Fulda, was Asher Ben-Natan, the first ambassador of Israel to the FRG. On this occasion, the Buber-Rosenzweig Medal was awarded to the German committee coordinating an academic year-abroad program in Israel for Catholic and Protestant theology students, and the main speaker was Emil Fackenheim. Interfaith observances of Israel's Memorial Day and Independence Day were held in Cologne, Stuttgart, Frankfurt, Ingelheim/Mainz, Neuwied, Siegen, and Aachen.

Debate continued concerning the proposed youth center (*Jugendbegegnungsstätte*) at Dachau, near Munich. The city administration there was concerned that increased attention to the site of the former concentration camp would further damage the reputation of their city.

Relations with Jews in East Germany

In February, for the first time since 1952, the leader of the West Berlin Jewish community, Heinz Galinski, was invited by his counterpart in East Berlin, Peter Kirchner, a physician, to participate in a commemoration of the so-called *Fabrikaktion* of February 28, 1943, when mostly younger Jews working as slave laborers in war-related industries were rounded up and transported to the east. In the fall of the year, Galinski, now having become head of the Zentralrat, met with his counterpart, Sigmund Rotstein, president of the Jewish communities of the GDR. The two agreed to intensify contacts and work more closely together.

In early June, Galinski was invited to meet Erich Honecker, chairman of the East German Council of State. Items discussed included the establishment of an international committee on the restoration of the Great Synagogue (East Berlin) and of the Weissensee cemetery (one of the largest Jewish cemeteries in Europe); coordination of plans for the anniversary of the 1938 pogroms in both German states; efforts to bring about more accurate reporting on issues related to the Middle East; and compensation for Nazi victims living outside the GDR.

Subsequently, Galinski returned to the GDR to meet with Kurt Löffler, state secretary for church affairs. Löffler, who succeeded Klaus Gysi, a part Jew, promised to ensure more balanced reporting on the Middle East in GDR newspapers and to explore possibilities for more Jews to study at the College for Jewish Studies in Heidelberg. Also discussed were preparations for a commemoration of the 50th anniversary of the pogroms and recent anti-Semitic occurrences in Leipzig. For the first time, the chairman of the Zentralrat was invited to attend an official state event in the GDR—the memorial ceremony in the East German People's Chamber (parliament) commemorating *Kristallnacht*.

In October, at the invitation of the East Berlin community, the Jüdische Gruppen (see AJYB 1989, p. 343) held a weekend seminar to mark the anniversary of *Kristallnacht*. It was the first large joint gathering of Jews from East and West Germany since 1952.

Religion

On the occasion of the publication of an autobiography by a German female convert to Judaism, Rivka Richterich (*Mehr als tausend Schritte*, "More Than a Thousand Steps"), the *Allgemeine Jüdische Wochenzeitung* featured a series of articles on converts to Judaism in Germany that received considerable attention. In letters to the weekly, many converts and others interested in converting pointed to the reluctance of German rabbis to conduct classes for them. Several of those who had succeeded in getting instruction, or were in the process of conversion, complained about the rejection they experienced and the feeling of being isolated within the communities.

The First International Jewish Congress for Halakhah and Medicine was held in November in West Berlin. The largest gathering of Jewish physicians to be held in Germany since World War II, it was organized by Berlin physician and financier Roman Skoblo, under the aegis of the West Berlin Organization of Jewish Physicians and Psychologists. Skoblo noted that many scholars and physicians turned down the invitation to attend because they were committed to never setting foot on German soil.

Publications

Noteworthy new works on German Jewish history published in 1988 included Mordechai Breuer, *Jüdische Orthodoxie im Deutschen Reich 1871–1918. Die Sozialgeschichte einer religiösen Minderheit*. ("The Social History of German Jewish Orthodoxy"); Nachum T. Gidal, *Die Juden in Deutschland von der Römerzeit bis zur Weimarer Republik* ("Jews in Germany from Roman Times to Weimar"); Klaus Guth, with Eva Goiss-Lau and Ulrike Krzywinski, *Jüdische Landgemeinden in Oberfranken (1800–1942). Geschichte und Volkskultur* ("The History and Culture of Rural Franconian Jewish Communities"); Heinz Knobloch, *Herr Moses in Berlin* (about Moses Mendelssohn; 1987, a second revised edition); by the same author, *Berliner Grabsteine* ("Berlin Gravestones," about burial sites of famous Berlin Jews); and Ina Lorenz, *Die Juden in Hamburg zur Zeit der Weimarer Republik* ("Jews in Hamburg During the Weimar Republic").

Among new works on or relating to the Holocaust were two key texts by Ernst Nolte, the revisionist historian: *Der Europäische Bürgerkrieg 1917–1945. Nationalsozialismus und Bolschewismus* ("The European Civil War, 1917–1945: Nazism and Bolshevism"); and *Das Vergehen der Vergangenheit. Antwort an meine Kritiker im sogenannten Historikerstreit* ("The Passing of the Past: In Response to My Critics"). Other significant books on the World War II period published this year or last year were *Dachauer Hefte # 3: Opfer und Täterinnen* ("Women Victims and Female Guards in Concentration Camps"), by various contributors; Eberhard Jäckel and Jürgen Rohwer, eds., *Der Mord an den Juden im Zweiten Weltkrieg. Entschlussbildung und Verwirklichung* ("Decision-making Processes in the Murder of Jews in

WWII"); Barbara Just-Dahlmann and Helmut Just, *Die Gehilfen. NS Verbrechen und die Justiz nach 1945* ("How the Courts Helped to Carry Out Nazi Justice"); Hans Proligheuer, *Wir sind in die Irre gegangen—Die Schuld der Kirche unterm Hakenkreuz* ("The Church Under Nazism"; 1987); Ulrike Puvogel, ed., *Gedenkstätten für die Opfer des Nationalsozialismus—Eine Dokumentation* ("A Documentation of Memorial Sites for Victims of Nazism"; 1987); and Rita Thalmann and Emanuel Feinermann, *Die Kristallnacht*. Also of interest is Herbert A. Strauss et al., *List of Displaced German Scholars 1936*, a new edition edited at the Technische Universität Berlin (1987).

On more recent history, new works included Rolf Vogel, ed., *Der deutsch-israelische Dialog. Dokumentation eines erregenden Kapitels der deutschen Aussenpolitik* ("German-Israeli Relations," vol. 1); Dörte von Westernhagen, *Die Kinder der Täter—Das Dritte Reich und die Generation danach* ("On the Children of Nazis"); and Juliane Wetzel, *Jüdisches Leben in München, 1945–1951. Durchgangsstation oder Wiederaufbau?* ("Jewish Life in Munich in the Postwar Period").

Personalia

Schalom Ben-Chorin, a German-born writer living in Israel who writes in German, received an honorary doctoral degree from the University of Munich. On his 80th birthday, actor Curt Bois was nominated for the European Film Prize in Berlin for his performance in Wim Wenders' film *Himmel über Berlin* ("Sky over Berlin"). Henry Ehrenberg, an entrepreneur in the Swabian town of Knittlingen, was honored by the city with a square renamed for him. Sociologist Norbert Elias received the European Amalfi Prize awarded by the Italian Sociological Association. Eric M. Warburg received, from Atlantic-Brücke, a prize which bears his name.

Julius Carlebach, a sociologist at the University of Sussex in Brighton, England, was appointed the new head of the College of Jewish Studies at Heidelberg, filling a two-year-old vacancy. The acting director of the college during that period was the former president of Heidelberg University, Baron zu Putlitz.

Plaques were dedicated in Berlin in memory of Maximilian Harden (1861–1927), political journalist and writer, and Joseph Roth (1894–1939), novelist, essayist, and publisher. Arno Lustiger (a nephew of the cardinal of Paris) was elected chairman of the Zionist Organization of Germany. He replaced Maximilian Tauchner, who retired. Alfred Moos received the Citizens' Medal of Ulm on the occasion of the visit of former Jewish citizens to that city.

The Mendelssohn Prize was awarded in West Berlin to Helen Suzman, civil-rights and anti-apartheid activist in South Africa. Former recipients were Eva G. Reichmann of London and Sir Yehudi Menuhin. Klaus von Dohnanyi, Lord Mayor of Hamburg, received the Gold Medal of Bnai B'rith and of the local Joseph Carlebach Lodge.

Among German Jews who died in 1988 were a number of prominent and colorful personalities. Rose Ausländer, a German lyricist and poet, was born in 1901 in

Czernowitz, emigrated to the United States, returned in 1931 to Europe, lived in the States again between 1945 and 1965, and thereafter in Düsseldorf. Erich Fried, a noted poet and recent recipient of the Georg Büchner Prize, who emigrated to England from Vienna, died at the age of 67. The most political German poet in the postwar period, Fried was a fierce critic of conservative German governments and strongly attacked neo-Nazism and racism in the Federal Republic. He was also a harsh critic of Israeli policies vis-à-vis the Palestinians and a revered personality in German intellectual circles. Julius Günther, head of the Jewish community of Koblenz, died in February. Born in 1895 in the Moselle River region and a veteran of World War I, he was sent to Dachau after the 1938 pogroms, lived in Bolivia and Israel after the war, returning in 1957 to Germany and settling in Koblenz. He was elected president of the community in 1958.

Max Kaufmann, a member of the Aachen Jewish community, died in May. Born in 1909 into a Jewish merchant family in Kornelimünster near Aachen, and early active against Robert Ley, a leading Nazi, he was arrested in 1933 together with his father, but freed upon the intervention of local peasants. After serving in the French underground, he returned in 1945 to Aachen, where he helped rebuild the Jewish community.

Hans Rosenberg died in Freiburg in June, aged 84. After leaving Germany in the '30s, he taught at Brooklyn College and later at Berkeley. One of the most outstanding historians of Germany in this century, he authored several books, including the classic *Bureaucracy, Aristocracy and Absolutism in Prussia, 1660–1815*.

Wolf Weil was president of the community of Hof, where he died, aged 75. Born in Krakow, he escaped the Nazis with the help of Oskar Schindler. He was a cofounder of the community in Hof in 1945.

Rosi Wolfstein-Frölich died in December 1987, aged 99. A close associate of Rosa Luxemburg, she fled in 1933 to Belgium, then in 1941 to New York, later returning to the Federal Republic, where she became an active member of the SPD.

Y. MICHAL BODEMANN

German Democratic Republic

National Affairs

THE YEAR 1988 SAW TWO MAJOR developments in the GDR. At the international level, several steps were taken toward rapprochement with Western countries and integration into Western markets. This took place against the background of reductions of Soviet troops stationed in the GDR. Internally, the increasing frustration and impatience with the Erich Honecker government for its refusal to undertake political and economic reform could be seen in a series of unauthorized political demonstrations, massive resignations from the Socialist Unity party, and requests to leave the country. The government responded to this unrest with, on the one hand, heavy-handed procedures against those labeled as "dissidents" and, on the other, a mild liberalization in some areas of life—for example, cultural policy and travel privileges—for the rest of the population. Because the Protestant Church tried to protect many individuals and groups that became defined as opponents of the state, the social turmoil often took the form of church-state conflict. One result of this development was the retirement of Klaus Gysi, minister for church-state affairs, and his replacement by Kurt Löffler. Gysi, who was of partly Jewish descent, had favored a conciliatory policy toward the Church. He was also known as a friend of the Jewish communities.

Less visibly, but of equal importance, in 1988 close to 40,000 citizens of the GDR emigrated to the West, and 47,000 foreign workers from Vietnam, Mozambique, Angola, and Cuba were employed in East German industry. These demographic changes were accompanied, predictably, by increasing tensions between "Germans" and "foreigners."

This year saw the GDR's Jewish communities emerge from their previous isolation and into the public life of the state, as ties to institutions within and outside the country were strengthened. One important precondition for many of the new developments was the government's decision to make a "humanitarian donation" of $100 million to Jewish survivors of the Holocaust. As of September 1989 the details of this payment were being negotiated by GDR foreign minister Oskar Fischer and Rabbi Israel Miller of the Conference on Material Claims Against Germany.

The government's positive Jewish policy was seen by some observers as a means to facilitate GDR trade contact with Western countries and also to strengthen the "antifascist" tradition of the Socialist Unity party in the face of the new influence and muscle-flexing of the Protestant Church and increasing neo-Nazi manifestations (see below).

Relations with Israel

The GDR was still the only Eastern Bloc state with no official ties to Israel, though contacts had recently been made at several levels, and diplomatic relations were expected to develop within the foreseeable future. Beginning in 1987, increasing numbers of East German Jews—especially individuals below retirement age—were allowed to visit relatives in Israel, though not all Jews who applied were granted travel permits.

In 1988, for the first time in memory, public lectures and discussions of Israel and Zionism took place in packed halls of the Jewish communities of East Berlin and Dresden, and a slide show about Israel was arranged at the children's summer camp. Among the Israelis who lectured in the GDR in 1988 were the political scientist and former Foreign Ministry director-general Shlomo Avineri, and Meir Marcell Faerber of the Israeli chapter of PEN.

Toward the end of the year, Dr. Peter Kirchner, president of the East Berlin Jewish community, West German Jewish leader Heinz Galinski, and World Jewish Congress president Edgar Bronfman, among others, voiced strong public criticism of the coverage of Israel and the Middle East conflict in the GDR media. The reports, they claimed, were not balanced enough; in many instances causes and effects were not distinguished, and the Middle East conflict was overreported compared to other conflicts. Reports on Israel in the GDR media were subsequently toned down.

In connection with the GDR's increasingly relaxed attitude toward Israel, in December 1988, for the first time, a delegation of GDR state functionaries, led by Hermann Falk, director of the Artists Association, visited Israel to discuss the possible participation of the Berliner Ensemble in the Jerusalem Festival in 1989.

50th Anniversary of Kristallnacht

Literally the entire population of the GDR was mobilized by the government to commemorate the 50th anniversary of the pogroms of November 9, 1938 (*Kristallnacht*, or, as many Jews and sympathizers preferred to call it now, *Pogromnacht*). On November 8, there was a special session of the Volkskammer (Parliament) to honor the Jewish victims. The speeches given were translated into five languages (including Hebrew), for the benefit of the many foreign guests, and the entire session was broadcast on GDR television.

In East Berlin, a major exhibit about Jews in Berlin (see "Culture," below) was held, and 20 smaller exhibits about Jewish life were shown in other cities. For the anniversary, many synagogues were renovated or restored, including, among others, the small chapel in the Rykestrasse Synagogue and the Jewish Old Age Home in East Berlin, the synagogue in Dresden, and the former synagogue in Gröbzig, which was currently being used as a museum.

Over the summer, many Jewish cemeteries were cleaned up and restored by members of (GDR) Aktion Sühnezeichen (Operation Sign of Atonement), a Protestant group that had been working in Jewish cemeteries since the 1960s, and by university students, school classes, masons, members of the FDJ (Free German Youth, the state youth organization), and soldiers. For many years the international Jewish organizations had reproached the GDR for neglecting its Jewish cemeteries and letting them deteriorate.

On October 27, tens of thousands of members of the FDJ attended a commemoration of the November pogroms at the former concentration camp Ravensbrück. Smaller events were arranged by many organizations throughout the GDR, e.g., the Lawyers Association, the universities, the Association for the Administration of Public Monuments, and others. The Berliner Ensemble, the Deutsche Theater, the Leipzig Synagogue Choir, and other cultural institutions staged special commemorative performances. Plaques and monuments honoring the Jewish victims were unveiled in almost every city. Many special publications were issued. In October and November articles with Jewish content appeared in the media almost every day. It was difficult to assess the long-term meaning and effect of this sudden and massive national commemoration of Nazi Germany's crimes and the Jewish victims. They would undoubtedly become clearer in the course of the celebration of the 40th anniversary of the founding of the German Democratic Republic in fall 1989.

Attitudes Toward Jews

Although *Neues Deutschland* (New Germany), the major daily newspaper, and Siegmund Rotstein, president of the League of Jewish Communities of the GDR, regularly emphasized that Nazism and anti-Semitism in the GDR had been eliminated "down to the root," the reality was more complex. Certainly, attitudes toward Jews among the increasingly restless East German population seemed to be quite varied.

The existence of a positive interest in Jews and Judaism could be observed in the long lines of people who waited for hours in the November cold and damp to see the exhibit on Jews in Berlin. In general, cultural events with Jewish content were always well attended, perhaps viewed as something a bit extraordinary. Interestingly, of the 11 GDR musicians who publicly performed Yiddish music, only 2 were Jewish. Events organized by the Society for Christian-Jewish Cooperation of the Protestant Church were popular, as were the Christian-Jewish workshops at the annual Protestant Church conferences, where Jews from within and outside the GDR were invited as speakers.

On the other hand, in 1988 there were many reported incidents, in several cities, in which groups of up to 40 young men shouted Nazi slogans and attacked passersby. On most of these occasions the East German police intervened late, if at all. Those youths who were brought to trial were usually accused of "rowdiness" and "insulting the public." A major incident took place in East Berlin in late February–early March at the Jewish cemetery on the Schönhauser Allee. Over 200 tombstones and graves were desecrated, damaged, or destroyed. The five young men responsible for this shouted Nazi slogans, and three of the five also attacked people on the street. The culprits were all given prison sentences of two-and-a-half to six-and-a-half years.

Privately, many Jews and non-Jewish antifascists expressed fears that the massive commemorations in November and the sudden priority given to Jewish projects—in a country where shortages of basic commodities were a fact of life—could cause jealousy among less privileged groups and strengthen anti-Semitic tendencies.

JEWISH COMMUNITY

Demography

Approximately 400 Jews belonged to the eight organized Jewish communities in the GDR: 200 in East Berlin, 50 in Dresden, 40 in Leipzig, 30 in Erfurt, and very small groups in Karl-Marx-Stadt, Magdeburg, Halle/Saale, and Schwerin. An additional 2,000 to 3,000 GDR citizens of Jewish ancestry did not belong to any of the Jewish communities. Although no numbers were given, applicants were waiting to be admitted to almost all the Jewish communities, and complaints were heard in East Berlin, Dresden, and Leipzig that in several cases application procedures were being prolonged over several years.

Communal Affairs

Rabbi Isaac Neuman, the American rabbi sent to serve in East Berlin in September 1987, left in May, after eight months in office. He bitterly accused the board of directors of the East Berlin Jewish community of intercepting his mail, denying him a private telephone line, and generally frustrating his efforts to modernize religious observance in a rather traditional Jewish community. The board and many members of the congregation, in turn, accused the rabbi of spending too much time out of the country, not making himself available to the community, and orienting his activities toward the foreign media, rather than the congregation (they nicknamed him "the Hollywood rabbi"). Many observers close to the scene saw the rabbi's short and tempestuous term of office as a result of personality clashes and perhaps also unrealistic expectations on many sides. Rabbi Neuman's departure, though disappointing (his appointment was the result of several years of negotiations involving the GDR, the U.S. State Department, and the American Jewish Committee), did not damage the warm relationship between the Jewish communities of the GDR and the American and international Jewish organizations.

Within the GDR's Jewish communities, prayer services and cultural events were better attended than in previous years. For the first time in decades, a Jewish wedding and a bar mitzvah were conducted in East Berlin; and so many children were registered for the Jewish summer camp that some had to be turned away. Because many of the approximately 350 Jews who had in recent years begun to take an active interest in Judaism and frequent the Jewish communities considered themselves atheists, the developing Jewish consciousness took on a "national" dimension, one which had been long suppressed. Observers suggested that this development could eventually lead to demands for a redefinition of Jewishness and of the mandate of the Jewish communities in the GDR.

Warming relations with West German Jews and the international Jewish community were demonstrated in various ways. Heinz Galinski, president of the Central Council of Jews in West Germany and president of the West Berlin Jewish community, visited East Berlin and Dresden during the year. Two East German Jews attended a summer course at the College of Jewish Studies in Heidelberg (West Germany), and negotiations were initiated to set up regular exchanges of students and scholars. Arrangements were also made for Prof. Shlomo Tichauer of West Berlin to conduct a course in Jewish tradition for members of the East Berlin Jewish community. The GDR visits of Edgar Bronfman, president, and Rabbi Israel Singer, secretary general, of the World Jewish Congress, and of Ronald Lauder, former U.S. ambassador to Austria, resulted in pledges of American and WJC support for the Jewish communities of the GDR and the Honecker government's commitment to a payment of $100 million to Jewish survivors of the Holocaust (see above). These visits also strengthened the ties of the Jews in the GDR to the international Jewish organizations and to North American Jewry.

NEW SYNAGOGUE BERLIN–CENTRUM JUDAICUM

One of the most important long-term projects undertaken to strengthen Jewish life in the GDR was the establishment in 1988 of a foundation, the New Synagogue Berlin–Centrum Judaicum. The foundation, which was under the auspices of the GDR Ministry of Culture and was to be headed by Dr. Hermann Simon, vice-president of the East Berlin Jewish community, was to be financed partly by the state and partly by private donations from within the GDR and from abroad (presumably Jewish organizations in the West). The cost of establishing the foundation was estimated at 60 million East German marks, of which the GDR had committed itself to paying at least half.

The foundation was charged with carrying out various mandates: to commemorate the Jewish victims of German fascism, to provide a place for prayer, to preserve public awareness of Jewish scientific and cultural achievements as part of the German cultural heritage, to promote the preservation of Jewish culture, and to facilitate cooperative projects on Jewish themes, within the GDR and at the international level. For these purposes, the Centrum Judaicum would contain a Jewish museum, seminar rooms, a Jewish library, a chapel, and the Comprehensive Archives of the German Jews, which had been housed since the mid-1950s in the State Archives in

Potsdam. The Centrum would also issue publications, conduct conferences, and undertake cooperative projects with other Jewish institutions.

The name "New Synagogue Berlin—Centrum Judaicum" referred to plans for the foundation to be housed in the synagogue on the Oranienburgerstrasse in East Berlin, a bombed-out edifice that was to be restored, at great expense, and was slated to become a major architectural feature of East Berlin's downtown area. The building was once Berlin's most elegant and important synagogue and the first home of Reform Judaism.

Culture

"*Und lehrt sie: Gedachtnis*" ("And Teach Them Not to Forget") was the title of the largest and most comprehensive exhibit on Jews in Berlin to date. The display of approximately 600 objects was a cooperative effort involving the GDR Ministry of Culture, the Ministry for Church-State Affairs, and the League of Jewish Communities of the GDR. Many of the objects exhibited were loaned by individuals and institutions on two continents. The collection was shown in East Berlin in October and November 1988; its core would become part of the permanent exhibit at the Centrum Judaicum.

The announced restoration of the severely damaged Gesamtarchiv der deutschen Juden (Comprehensive Archives of the German Jews), to be housed in the new Centrum Judaicum, would afford GDR Jews new access to their history. One unresolved question was whether these documents would be made available to the entire scholarly community or only to a handful of official chroniclers.

In January the second Festival of Yiddish Culture—a four-day program of Yiddish poetry and music—took place in East Berlin. DEFA, the GDR state film corporation, released a 60-minute documentary—*Erinnern heisst leben* ("To Remember Is to Live")—about the role of Jews in the cultural history of Berlin, and also a feature film—*Die Schauspielerin* ("The Actress")—about the persecution of Jewish actors in Germany in the 1930s. The Theater der Freundschaft, the major children's theater in East Berlin, premiered *Geheime Freunde* ("Secret Friends"), a play about the persecution of a young Jewish girl by the Nazis. The play, based on Myron Levoy's novel *Alan and Naomi* (New York, 1977), had been performed in West Germany under another title.

Publications

Thirty-six books of Jewish interest were published in 1988 in the GDR. Among these, six were memoirs of Jewish antifascists, three were translations of American books, three were translations of Hebrew books, and another three had been previously published in West Germany.

Among the most important were the following: Horst Busse and Udo Krause, *Lebenslänglich für den Gestapokommissar* ("Life Sentence for the Gestapo Chief"), about the trial of the head of the Dresden Gestapo, SS-Obersturmführer Henry Schmidt, before the district court of Dresden, September 15–28, 1987; Bernd Engelmann, *Deutschland ohne Juden. Eine Bilanz* ("Germany Without Jews: A Balance"), an analysis of the effects of the Nazi persecution of the Jews on the development of the Federal Republic of Germany (published in the FRG in 1970); Stefan Heym, *Ahasver* ("The Wandering Jew"), a polemical novel by a major East German writer (published in the FRG in 1981); Abraham B. Jehoschua, *Der Liebhaber* ("The Lover"), an Israeli novel about relations between Jews and Arabs; Georg Lukacs, *Zur Kritik der faschistischen Ideologie* ("A Critique of Fascist Ideology"), containing two works written in exile: "How Did Fascist Philosophy Develop in Germany?" and "How Did Germany Become the Center of Reactionary Ideology?"; Kurt Pätzold and Irene Runge, *Kristallnacht. Zum Pogrom 1938* ("*Kristallnacht*: On the Pogrom of 1938"), a monograph on the place of *Kristallnacht* in the history of the Nazi persecution of the Jews.

ROBIN OSTOW

Eastern Europe

Soviet Union

National Affairs

MIKHAIL SERGEEVICH GORBACHEV continued in 1988 to introduce the most far-reaching changes the Soviet system had experienced since the beginning of the Stalin period. Yet, in the third year of his tenure it was still unclear how deeply his reforms had affected the system and society and whether they were being institutionalized. In 1988 *glasnost'*, or openness, went quite far. *Perestroika*, or restructuring, was being proposed and widely discussed, but was being implemented slowly or not at all. It proved difficult to alter habits of mind, patterns of behavior, and vested institutional and personal interests that had developed over many years. Opposition to Gorbachev came from those who felt the reforms had not gone far enough as well as those who felt they had gone too far. Intensive debate of political, cultural, and economic issues continued throughout the year with no clear resolution.

The nearly two million Jews of the USSR were affected by this debate in four ways. They were affected as individuals, in their economic, political, and cultural lives, and as members of a nationality. In addition, more than most of the over 100 officially recognized nationalities, Jews were affected by the vicissitudes of international relations, especially the Soviet-American relationship and, to a lesser extent, the Soviet-Israeli one. Finally, as had happened previously in Russian history, Jews and "the Jewish question" became symbols in the debate over the nature and future of the system. Rightly or not, "Jew" was used as a code word for an internationalist, liberal outlook, and the "Jewish question" became a surrogate for a broad range of issues. *Glasnost'* brought the Jewish issue into the open to a greater extent than at any time in the recent past, but the new openness turned out to cut both ways: it allowed more public expression of anti-Semitism as well as criticism of it.

Several times during the year Communist party secretary Gorbachev publicly expressed anger and frustration at the slow pace of reform, though on several occasions he criticized journalists and politicians who were, in his view, too impatient and demanding of results. The overall thrust of Gorbachev's economic reforms was to make the economy more efficient and competitive. This involved stimulating individual initiative, getting people to work harder, making more rational use of the country's immense natural and human resources, and eliminating or at least radically reducing corruption.

A major change in the political structure of the USSR was approved by a special party conference, the first such since 1941, held in June, and approved by the Supreme Soviet in late November. A new body, the Congress of Peoples' Deputies, would be constituted, composed of 2,250 delegates—1,500 to be elected from territorial and national districts and 750 from public organizations. This congress would then elect a smaller Supreme Soviet, consisting of only 400–500 members. The congress would also elect a president who would have broad powers in legislation, foreign policy, and defense. It was widely assumed that Gorbachev would be this president and would also continue as first secretary of the party, thus concentrating increased governmental and party powers in his hands. On the other hand, it was recommended that the party's role in economic life be reduced, and that a five-year maximum term of office be set for both party and government officials. Reflecting the controversial nature of the proposals and the fears of some that too much power was being concentrated in the hands of one man, 209 delegates to the conference voted against the proposals.

The new institutional arrangements were severely criticized by Andrei Sakharov, nuclear scientist and human-rights activist, who warned of the dangers of concentrating too much power in one person's hands. The arrangements were also criticized by representatives of the Baltic nationalities, especially the Estonians, who argued that the new system would allow the central authorities to override the republics on important issues and would thus destroy any vestige of federalism.

In September elections in the primary party organizations (the approximately 400,000 basic party units), about half the seats were contested and a substantial number of new leaders came into office.

Glasnost' moved ahead faster than *perestroika*. Emigré writers such as Vladimir Nabokov and Joseph Brodsky were published for the first time, as was Boris Pasternak's novel *Dr. Zhivago* and other works formerly banned. Some films made years ago but never released were shown to the public for the first time. Attacks on Stalinism continued unabated, but in the spirit of freer expression the media also carried defenses of Stalin and his policies. Nearly 700 victims of the purges were "rehabilitated" by a special commission appointed for that purpose.

Because of uncertainty as to the correct interpretation of recent historical events, especially those connected with the Stalinist period, no final examinations were given in history in the secondary schools. Instead, teachers substituted ungraded oral discussions of current events. This reflected both the uncertainty and fluidity of reevaluations of the system.

RELIGIOUS GROUPS AND NATIONALITIES

Strictures on religion were considerably relaxed during the year, perhaps because the Russian Orthodox Church, the largest denomination in the country, celebrated the millennium of Christianity in Russia, Ukraine, and Belorussia. The campaign against Islam, very militant in previous years, was somewhat toned down; Jewish religious groups were by and large allowed to function unharassed; and Christianity was treated with a respect it had not enjoyed since World War II. Konstantin Kharchev, the government official in charge of religions, claimed that in the first half of the year alone, almost 160 new religious congregations had registered with the authorities. Cathedrals in Klaipeda and Vilnius in the Baltic were returned to the Catholic Church after they had been used for other purposes during many years.

Problems with nationalities surfaced and loomed very large during the year, the most dramatic events taking place in the southern republics of Armenia and Azerbaijan and in the Baltic republics. In the former, there were violent clashes reflecting deep-seated ethnic tensions, traditionally denied by Soviet officials. As a result of the continuing unrest, thousands of Armenians from Azerbaijan took refuge in Armenia, and large numbers of Azerbaijanis fled the Armenian republic to their own. In addition to the pain caused to the nationalities involved, events in the Caucasus cast a long shadow on the myth of "friendship of the peoples" and embarrassed the Gorbachev leadership. Conservative critics suggested that the disorders were a direct result of *perestroika* and the forces it had unleashed. The devastating earthquake in Armenia on December 7, in which about 25,000 were killed and many more were wounded or made homeless, overshadowed the nationality frictions, at least temporarily.

Events in the Baltic republics posed a more direct political challenge. In Estonia, Latvia, and Lithuania, popular, officially recognized movements emerged demanding greater political, economic, and cultural autonomy from Moscow. Some suggested that the Baltic republics were the most likely venues of successful economic reform and that Gorbachev was willing to permit this spontaneous political and cultural activity in return for demonstrations of how successful economic *perestroika* could be.

Foreign Affairs

In order to revive the economy and breathe life into a political system that had lost its dynamism during the "years of stagnation"—the current euphemism for the Brezhnev era—Gorbachev tried to reduce Soviet commitments abroad as well as to divert resources going to the military toward the domestic economy. In May the pullout of Soviet troops from Afghanistan began, cutting a commitment first made in 1979. By the end of 1988 there were said to be 50,000 troops left there, down from 115,000 when the withdrawal began. For the first time the Soviets admitted the magnitude of their casualties: 13,310 killed and 35,478 wounded. An internal party circular acknowledged that fundamental errors had been made in the Afghan adventure.

Political prisoners were released and prominent refuseniks were permitted to emigrate, partly in order to remove the "human-rights obstacle" from relations with the West. In fact, Western Europe responded favorably to Soviet invitations to help the economy. The Federal Republic of Germany granted $1.6 billion in credits to help the consumer sector, and Western businesses eagerly sought opportunities in the huge Soviet economy.

An ideological rationale for these policies was given by Vadim Medvedev, promoted to the Politburo in October as its new ideological specialist. He said in a speech reprinted in *Pravda* that Soviet communism was in crisis and that it should borrow ideas from capitalist countries as well as socialist ones. He argued that universal values, such as avoiding wars and ecological catastrophes, had come to outweigh the class struggle in importance, and that peaceful coexistence would be a long-term proposition. This contrasted with statements by his predecessor, Yegor Ligachev, who warned that class struggle must not be abandoned even in periods of reform.

In May the U.S. Senate approved a treaty eliminating American and Soviet intermediate-range missiles. The following month another summit meeting took place between President Ronald Reagan and Gorbachev. Reagan met with dissidents in Moscow and addressed students at Moscow State University; however, little progress was made on arms control. Meetings between Reagan, Gorbachev, and President-elect George Bush at the United Nations were cut short when Gorbachev had to rush home to deal with the earthquake in Armenia; however, in his address to the UN, Gorbachev announced a unilateral deep cut in Soviet armed forces in Western Europe.

Relations with Israel

Relations with Israel improved as well. Consular delegations were exchanged, placing relations on a lower level than those of Israel with Poland and Hungary, but restoring a formal, albeit largely symbolic, relationship nonetheless. Six Israeli diplomats took up residence in Moscow in July. On several occasions Soviet representatives reiterated the view that a full restoration of relations could occur only "in the framework of a comprehensive Middle East settlement." Foreign Minister Eduard Shevardnadze, meeting in New York, in June, with Prime Minister Yitzhak Shamir of Israel, said about the restoration of relations that "when an effective international conference goes to work, the Soviet Union will be ready to resolve the issue."

During the course of the year, some 8,000–10,000 Soviet Jews visited Israel as tourists, hosted by family and friends. A large number also visited the United States. In July Rabbi Simcha Kook of Rehovot became the first Israeli rabbi since 1967 to pay an official visit to the USSR. In the same month, 70 people from eight cities set up a "Soviet-Israeli Friendship Society." By contrast, Evgeny Evseev, a well-known anti-Zionist writer often accused of anti-Semitism, established the "Committee of the Soviet Public Against the Establishment of Diplomatic Relations with Israel."

Israel sent two teams of over 40 persons each to assist the victims of the Armenian earthquake in December. They arrived in Israeli aircraft clearly marked as such. At the same time, five Soviet hijackers who had released their child hostages in return for a cargo plane and $3 million and who flew to Israel were arrested by the Israelis and returned to the USSR. Israel's action drew favorable comment in Soviet media.

In June the Israeli cabinet resolved that Soviet Jews wishing to emigrate could obtain their Israeli visas only in Bucharest and from there they would have to fly directly to Israel. This drew negative commentary from American and Soviet Jews and a mixed reception in the U.S. Department of State.

Anti-Semitism

Jews gained from *glasnost'* and *perestroika*, though there were some costs as well. On the one hand, improved relations with the West and Israel raised emigration levels significantly. Moreover, greater tolerance for religious and ethnic cultural expressions benefited Jews along with others. On the other hand, *glasnost'* permitted anti-Semitism to be expressed more widely. Pamiat', a Russian nationalist organization, expressed explicitly anti-Jewish sentiments in public meetings and publications, blaming Jews and Freemasons for most of the USSR's historic and contemporary problems. The rhetoric of Pamiat' was so strong that it drew public protests. *Pravda* (February 1) criticized Pamiat' for its anti-Semitism and for having become an "extremist, chauvinist organization." *Izvestiia* (February 27) also criticized the organization and mocked its claims of a Zionist-Masonic conspiracy that was trying to establish worldwide dominance.

The well-known "anti-Zionist" writers Yevseev, Begun, and Romanenko were criticized by the Yiddish monthly *Sovetish haimland* (No.12) for publishing works which "abound in a large number of various propositions and inaccuracies that make it possible to assess their works as unscientific and essentially disorienting to readers. . . ." Experts from the Soviet Institute of the USA and Canada who had been asked to study the works of these propagandists concluded that they contained distortions, exaggerations, and "juggling of facts." In their article for *Sovetskaia Kultura*, quoted in *Izvestiia* (February 27), they accused Begun of employing a "simple device: he replaces the word 'Jew' with the word 'Zionist' and then he follows the original [of *Mein Kampf*] verbatim, occasionally interspersing the text with pseudo-Marxist phraseology." This was one of the strongest criticisms seen in a Soviet publication of works which had long been viewed as anti-Semitic in the West but which the Soviets had insisted were merely anti-Zionist.

Reformist magazines also condemned anti-Semitism. Two authors writing in *Ogonyok* noted, "Unfortunately, in the recent past the criticism of Zionism was not always conducted from a class position in the works of certain Soviet authors. Scientific analysis was replaced by ambiguous hints, and the concepts 'Jew' and 'Zionist' were often confused. Anti-Semitism and its social roots were passed over in silence . . . or received an incorrect evaluation" and the influence of Zionism in capitalist countries was exaggerated. (Vladimir Nosenko and Sergei Rogov, "Beware: Provocation! Who Needs 'Black Hundreds' Myths!" *Ogonyok*, No. 23, June 4–11, 1988.)

In January *Sovetish haimland* (No. 1) translated a long critique by Andrei Tshervizov of Pamiat' and three well-known "anti-Zionist" writers who were accused of being anti-Semites. The May issue of the same journal (No. 5) published several letters from Jews concerned about open anti-Semitic expressions. In August *Izvestiia* published a letter by 59 staff members of the Leningrad division of the Academy of Sciences' Institute of Oriental Studies, protesting Pamiat's anti-Semitism and castigating it for blaming Jews and other non-Russians for Stalinist repressions and the destruction of Russian cultural monuments. A. Z. Romanenko's book *The Class Essence of Zionism* was criticized in at least three Soviet journals for inaccuracies and for conveying the mistaken impression that world Zionism was the chief enemy of revolutionary causes and the main proponent of war. The book was said to be "harmful to the internationalist upbringing of Soviet people," meaning that it aroused anti-Semitic feelings.

However, anti-Semitic motifs did not disappear from the press. Writing in *Pravda* (July 22) about Michael Dukakis, for example, V. Linnik said, "The Jewish bourgeoisie's money carries colossal weight in the Democratic party, and Dukakis's distinctly pro-Israeli stand is no accident." In an article that became a political *cause célèbre* (*Sovetskaia Rossiya*, March 13), Nina Andreevna, a chemistry teacher in Leningrad, attacked *perestroika* by linking it to Jews, lack of patriotism, and political liberalism. "Another special feature," she wrote, "of the views of the 'left-liberals' is an obvious or camouflaged cosmopolitan tendency, a sort of de-nationalized 'internationalism,' " citing Trotsky as the epitome of this tendency. Trotsky, she asserted, slighted Russian culture and the Russian proletariat. In case the Jewish connection was not clear enough, she suggested that "militant cosmopolitanism is now linked with the practice of 'refusenikism,' of refusing socialism." Refuseniks commit "outrages" by demonstrating publicly, she asserted. "Moreover, we are somehow gradually being trained to see this phenomenon as an almost inoffensive change of 'place of residence,' not as class and nationality betrayal by persons most of whom have been graduated from higher schools and graduate schools at public expense." She mocked "refusenikism" as "some kind of manifestation of 'democracy' and 'human rights.' "

So the connection was made between Trotsky—the cosmopolitan Jewish intellectual who had no regard for Russians—refuseniks, and democracy. Little wonder that rumors of anti-Semitic pogroms connected to the Church millennium spread among Jewish activist circles, especially after leaflets appeared in Leningrad calling for "Death to the Jews." The rumors proved unfounded.

Past episodes of anti-Semitism were also reconsidered. In April the magazine *Druzhba Narodov* ("Friendship of the Peoples") published 90-year-old Yakov Rapaport's memoir of the "Doctors' Plot" of 1953, when Kremlin doctors, most of them Jews, were accused of poisoning top Soviet leaders. This led to a pogrom atmosphere in the entire country, in which Jewish doctors such as Rapaport bore the brunt of popular rage. His daughter's memoir of the time was published simultaneously in *Yunost'*, a youth magazine. In July *Sovetskaia Kultura* published a long article on the death of Solomon Mikhoels, Yiddish actor and director, in 1948, admitting that he was murdered, that the murder was "sanctioned," and that the official version of his death was a fabrication.

Emigration

When a new emigration law went into effect in 1987, providing, among other things, that only first-degree relatives could invite Soviet citizens to join them abroad, many assumed that this would severely constrict Jewish emigration. In fact, since the law was only sporadically applied, Jewish emigration soared dramatically. Whereas in 1986 only 914 Jews left the USSR, in 1987 some 8,000 did so, and in 1988, 18,965 were permitted to leave. Among them were several hundred long-term refuseniks, including Yosif Begun and Pavel Abramovich, leading Hebrew teachers in Moscow; Naum Meiman, Alexander Yoffe, Feliks Kochubievsky, Alexander Lerner, Alexander Paritsky, Grigory Rozenshtain, and former prisoners Leonid Volvovsky, Alexei Magarik, and Alexander Kholmiansky. Among those still waiting for exit visas was Yuli Kosharovsky, in refusal for years. At the end of the year, however, Kosharovsky and three other refuseniks were notified that they were no longer considered to possess state secrets and thus were free to leave the country.

There were signs that the Soviets might in fact be changing their traditional hostility toward émigrés. A number of articles appeared in the press suggesting that people who emigrated were not necessarily hostile to the USSR and that they helped disseminate and promote Russian culture. A letter to the editor of a Lithuanian newspaper protested the exclusion of two Heroes of the Soviet Union from museum exhibits on World War II just because they had emigrated to Israel for family reasons. A Moscow theater staged a play titled *Benjamin the Third's Trip to the Holy Land*, despite its depiction of earlier generations of Jews wishing to leave for Israel.

A new kind of emigration problem arose midyear when the United States announced that the unexpectedly large emigration, mostly of Armenians, had exhausted the budgetary allocations for Soviet immigrants. In the next few months, the backlog of immigrants began to build, and many Jews found themselves stuck in Rome, awaiting transit to the United States, or having their refugee status challenged on the grounds that they could not prove that they were likely to be persecuted in the USSR. In December the U. S. attorney general agreed to exercise his "parole power" and admit more Soviet immigrants, but those admitted under such status would not enjoy the assistance offered to refugees. American Jewish organizations promised to press the matter with the new administration and Congress.

JEWISH COMMUNITY

Demography

The 1979 census had enumerated 1,811,000 self-identified Jews. The next census was planned for 1989 and was expected to show some decline in the number of Jews as a result of emigration and the aging of the Jewish population, as well as of low fertility rates.

Culture

In 1988 there emerged several "grassroots" Jewish cultural groups which were not necessarily religious or oriented toward emigration. In July the Jewish Cultural Club was formed in Riga, with B. Gaft as its coordinator. The Jewish Cultural Society was established in Estonia in March. *Literaturna Ukraina* (November 24) reported that a Jewish cultural society had been formed in Kiev, where a Jewish folk-song ensemble, Nigunim, was already performing. The founding of the society was welcomed by representatives of the Ukrainian Cultural Fund and by Aleksandr Levenbuk, director of the Shalom Theater in Moscow and a leader of a similar group in Moscow, one which, he said, was open to all and included Russians and Ukrainians. He was quoted as saying, "Our aim is to develop Jewish culture, to strengthen internationalism on the basis of the exchange of spiritual values with representatives of other nationalities" (Tass, October 28). The new Union of Lovers of Jewish Culture in Minsk, chaired by artist M. Dantsig, planned to feature local actors and dance groups, offer courses in Yiddish, and publish a yearbook in Yiddish and Belorussian. The organizers also expressed a desire to link up with similar groups inside and outside the USSR (Tass, October 18).

The Kishinev (Moldavia) municipal government announced that tuition-free Yiddish courses would be offered for adults and children. In Chernovtsy and Lvov in Ukraine, Yiddish courses were also announced, in the latter city organized by the newly formed Sholem Aleichem Society. *Sovetish haimland* (No. 11, p. 160) reported that a "large number of families have demanded that their children learn Yiddish language and literature in the schools" of Lvov. Even in cities with only a few thousand Jews, such as Ufa, Cheliabinsk, Kuibyshev, and Kherson, Jewish cultural associations were formed. Their main activities seemed to be lectures, musical and dance programs, and instruction in Yiddish or Hebrew. In Berdichev and Baku, Yiddish courses were announced. In Central Asia, a Bukharan Jewish section was created in the Union of Writers of Uzbekistan.

In Lithuania Jewish cultural activity was officially encouraged. The May issue of

Kommunistas (Lithuania) reported an order to party committees, trade unions, and the republic's Ministry of Culture to "devote constant attention to the development of the national cultures of the Polish and Jewish populations" and to provide for art exhibits, literary evenings, the expansion of Yiddish library holdings, and commemoration of Nazi victims, and to arrange wider local coverage of Jewish history, culture, and traditions. Jews and other national minorities were to be "guaranteed fair representation in party, government, Komsomol, trade union and economic organs, and in the ranks of the CPSU." Such a directive was unknown anywhere else or, for that matter, at any time in recent Soviet history. Indeed, the Group to Promote Jewish Culture was formed under the aegis of the Lithuanian Cultural Fund, and its representatives participated in the 45th-anniversary commemoration of the Warsaw Ghetto uprising.

The authorities were asked to reopen the State Jewish Museum of Culture in Vilnius, which had closed in 1949, but by year's end this had not happened. On the other hand, an exhibit of Lithuanian Jewish graphic art from the 17th through the 20th centuries opened in Kaunas in June and was then shown in Vilnius. Organizer of the exhibit was Emanuelis Zingeris, active in the promotion of Yiddish culture in Lithuania. In an article in *Sovetish haimland* (No. 7), Zingeris related that in 1942 the Nazis had gathered 100,000 Yiddish and Hebrew books in Lithuania, shipping about 20,000 to Germany and turning the rest into pulp. At the time of writing, the Lithuanian Book Palace held 20,705 works in Yiddish and Hebrew, mostly published in Lithuania in the last two centuries. There were also 21,420 Yiddish newspapers and journals in the collection.

The Yiddish Folk Theater of Vilnius gave 15 performances in Moldavia and several in Belorussia. A Jewish chamber ensemble from Vilnius performed in Georgia and Azerbaijan and also for five military units. Grigory Kanovitch, a novelist whose themes were Jewish life in Lithuania in the 19th and early 20th centuries, was awarded a republic prize for literature. Middle School No. 6 in Vilnius began offering Yiddish courses on three levels, and another school was scheduled to introduce similar instruction in the next academic year.

In Moscow, too, cultural activity picked up considerably, some claiming that 25 Jewish cultural groups were active there. World War II veteran Yuri Sokol opened a Jewish library in his apartment in Moscow and reported that 30 to 40 readers a week patronized it. He applied to the city soviet for official recognition of the library and for the establishment of a museum highlighting the role of Soviet Jews in World War II, but his application was denied. Mikhail Chlenov, an anthropologist, had founded a group for the historical and anthropological study of Jewry as far back as 1981. In March, along with two others, he began publishing a journal of general Jewish interest, *Shalom*. A second issue appeared in September. Altogether, about six journals of Jewish interest were being published (typed and inexpensively reproduced) in the USSR in 1988.

Aspects of Jewish culture that had been anathema in the past now seemed to gain legitimacy. *Sovetish haimland* (No. 1) devoted considerable space to the 115th anniversary of the birth of the Hebrew, Zionist poet, Chaim Nachman Bialik. One of his best-known poems was published in Yiddish translation, along with an appreciation of the poet written by Maxim Gorki.

Ilya Shifman published the *World of the Bible* in 200,000 copies, a work that included talmudic commentary as well as modern Israeli scholarship. Sixty Hebrew teachers from eight cities formed the National Hebrew Teachers Association headed by Lev Gorodetsky.

Rabbi Adin Steinsaltz of Israel announced in May that a Jewish religious training institute would open in Moscow in 1989, offering classical Jewish studies from an Orthodox viewpoint. The teachers would come initially from abroad. The institute was part of a broader agreement providing for Soviet-Western cooperation in surveying, preserving, and studying Judaica books and manuscripts in Soviet libraries and archives. The agreement was negotiated with Evgeny Velikhov, vice-president of the Soviet Academy of Sciences, acting on behalf of the Academy of World Civilizations.

Edgar Bronfman, president of the World Jewish Congress, announced in the fall that the WJC and the Jewish Agency had agreed to work with the Soviet Ministry of Culture to establish and help finance a Jewish cultural center at the site of the Jewish Musical Theater in Moscow. To be named the Solomon Mikhoels Culture Center and scheduled to open in February 1989, it would include a Judaica library, a museum, art gallery, and teaching areas. Bronfman further announced that Soviet authorities had agreed to allow the distribution of Jewish cultural and religious material. The building adjacent to the main Moscow synagogue was also to be turned into a museum of Jewish culture.

Holocaust-Related Matters

There were signs this year that Soviet reluctance to recognize the Holocaust as a specifically Jewish tragedy might be changing slightly. The Main Archival Administration of the USSR and the United States Holocaust Memorial Council signed an agreement in the summer to permit American researchers to copy documents in Soviet archives that related to the Holocaust. The copies would be deposited in the Holocaust Museum scheduled to open in Washington, D.C., in 1991.

Arbit Blatas, a Lithuanian-born sculptor living in the United States, was given permission to erect a monument to Holocaust victims in Vilnius, one that would have a specifically Jewish character and include the Hebrew word *"zakhor"* (remember). A commemoration of the 45th anniversary of the liquidation of the Lvov ghetto was held in that city on June 24. At the officially sanctioned meeting, which was conducted in Yiddish, Russian, and Ukrainian, speakers called for the preservation of Jewish cultural monuments, popularization of Yiddish language and literature, and the opening of Jewish schools and synagogues in Lvov. Luiza and Iosif Shternshtam, Lvov sculptors, presented a proposal for a monument to ghetto victims to the local soviet.

In a letter to the editor of a local newspaper, a Lithuanian wrote that before the war, "Lithuanian children played with Davids, Yoskes, Chashkes, Mirkes. But alien camps arrived who began to murder our good neighbors. That was not all. There were Lithuanian sons . . . who . . . joined the alien murderers." The writer called for a memorial to be erected to the Jewish children who died in the Holocaust (*Sovetish haimland*, No. 1, p. 128). Party veteran Solomonas Atamukas, a Jew, admitted that Jewish suffering and the role of Jews generally in Lithuanian history had been suppressed in the USSR.

In general, there were more public commemorations of the Holocaust, unimpeded by the authorities, than in previous years. Public observances of *Yom Hashoah* (Holocaust Memorial Day) were held in Vilnius and Leningrad. In Moscow and Kiev the anniversary of the massacre at Babi Yar was observed by Jewish groups. Delegations from Minsk and Vilnius attended ceremonies in Warsaw marking the anniversary of the ghetto uprising. In Minsk itself, however, a gathering at a monument to victims of the Nazis was dispersed by police. And in Lithuania it was pointed out that though nearly a third of the soldiers of the 16th Lithuanian Division had been Jews, their role in fighting the Nazis was not mentioned in Soviet media and literature. Finally, *Sovetish haimland* (No. 11) included an article stating clearly that writer Ilya Ehrenburg's attempts to publish testimonies about the Holocaust had been blocked by the authorities. The writer of the article called for publication of the "Black Book" in full, in line with the trend toward filling the "blank pages" in Soviet history. At least Vassily Grossman's monumental novel about World War II, *Life and Fate*, wherein the Jewish element is prominent, was finally published this year in the magazine *Oktiabr'*, long after it had become an underground classic.

Personalia

Several prominent cultural figures died in 1988. Among them were composer Zinovy Kompaneets, some of whose works were on Jewish themes. The deaths of Yiddish writers Note Lurie (aged 81) and Yosef Rabin (aged 87) in late 1987 were reported at the beginning of the year. Other writers who died were Buzi Miller (aged 75) of Birobidzhan and Khaskl Tabachnikov of Kiev. Scholar and author Leib Vilsker, formerly the curator of Judaica at the Saltykov-Shchedrin Public Library in Leningrad, died at age 69. Ilya Zilbershtain, a prominent literary figure who wrote in Russian, died at age 84.

ZVI GITELMAN

Eastern European Countries

Czechoslovakia

IN 1988 CZECHOSLOVAKIA showed only the faintest signs of political and economic reform, and its leadership remained unenthusiastic about changes taking place in the USSR. In October Prime Minister Lubomir Strougal, generally thought to be an advocate of economic reform, resigned, along with Deputy Prime Minister Petr Colotka. Both men also resigned from the Politburo, the leading organ of the Communist party. Ladislav Adamec succeeded Strougal as prime minister.

There were modest indications this year of some relaxation in Czechoslovakia's hostility to Israel. In September, at a meeting of the UN General Assembly in New York, Foreign Minister Shimon Peres of Israel met with his Czechoslovak counterpart, Bohuslav Chnoupek. Such a meeting had not taken place since 1967, when Czechoslovakia unilaterally broke relations with Israel, following the Soviet lead. It was agreed that Czechoslovakia would send two delegations to Israel, one economic and one to deal with consular matters.

JEWISH COMMUNITY

There were no significant changes in the position of the Jewish community, generally estimated to number about 5,000, though some maintained that there were another 10,000 people of Jewish origin who did not identify with the Jewish community. The community was served by a single rabbi, Daniel Meyer, in Prague. Some after-school classes for Jewish children were offered in that city.

Hungary

Hungarian political life was lively in 1988. In May Janos Kadar was removed as general secretary of the Hungarian Workers (Communist) party and was replaced by Prime Minister Karoly Grosz. Kadar had led the party since late 1956, when he entered the country with Soviet forces which overthrew the reformist regime of Imre Nagy. In the 1960s Kadar guided Hungary through economic reform and political liberalization, but by the late 1980s he was thought to be unsympathetic to further reform and both physically and mentally incapable of continuing his leadership. Grosz, a conservative reformer, took pains to point out on television that, despite his family name, he was not Jewish. In November Miklos Nemeth replaced Grosz as prime minister, the latter retaining the post of party leader.

In March an Israeli interests section was opened in Budapest, making Hungary the only East European country aside from Poland to reestablish some form of diplomatic relations with Israel. Israeli foreign minister Shimon Peres visited Budapest in May and met with party secretary Grosz. Peres's coalition partner, Prime Minister Yitzhak Shamir, did the same in September. While on an official visit to Israel, Minister of Cults Imre Miklos agreed to permit Israeli educators to come to Hungary to teach Hebrew and Jewish subjects. Israeli scholars would also be given access to Judaica materials in Hungarian libraries and archives.

JEWISH COMMUNITY

The Jewish population of Hungary, the largest in Eastern Europe, was estimated at between 35,000 and 100,000, the great majority not formally affiliated with the community.

Late in the year, the Center for Jewish Studies was inaugurated within the Hungarian Academy of Sciences. Initiated by the New York-based Memorial Foundation for Jewish Culture, which, together with the academy, provided it with financial assistance, the center was headed by Prof. Geza Komoroczy, a non-Jewish specialist in the ancient Near East who had been teaching biblical Hebrew for 26 years. The inauguration of the center was attended by U.S. ambassador Mark Palmer and the president of the Academy of Sciences, professor of history Ivan Berend. Several lectures on Judaic subjects were given by Hungarian and foreign scholars in connection with the inauguration. The center and the Hungarian Jewish community agreed to publish Judaica materials for adults, to supplement the work of the Aleph Library, which published similar materials for children. The first work to be published was *The Essential Talmud*, by Israeli scholar Rabbi Adin Steinsaltz.

The Memorial Foundation concluded an agreement with the Ministry of Cults enabling the Budapest Rabbinical Seminary, the only one of its kind in Eastern Europe, to train teachers of Judaica in addition to rabbis. It was also agreed that Hebrew would be taught in select secondary schools in Budapest.

The Federation to Maintain Jewish Culture in Hungary was founded this year. In contrast to the long-recognized religious community (Magyar Izraelitak Orszagos Kepviselete), this organization did not define itself in religious terms but stressed the ethnic dimension of Jewish identity. The organizers, who were from highly assimilated backgrounds, were led by Endre Rozsa, a well-known radio personality. Claiming over a thousand members, the federation lobbied for Jewish elementary schools and Hebrew instruction.

A privately sponsored journal of Jewish content made its appearance in 1988. Called *Mult es Jovo* (Past and Future), the journal featured works on Jewish themes by both contemporary and past writers.

The improved climate of Israeli-Hungarian relations enabled two Israeli *sofrim* (scribes) to visit Hungary and collect about 140 Torah scrolls from abandoned synagogues and Jewish communities. Most could not be refurbished, however, and were taken to Israel for burial.

Poland

Poland's economic and political situation continued to deteriorate. In February the prices of about half of Poland's goods and services were raised an average of 27 percent, and the currency was officially devalued. By April strikes broke out and were curbed only at the cost of wage increases. In August coal miners and dockworkers went on strike. After meeting with Interior Minister General Czeslaw Kiszczak to discuss the possibility of the government negotiating with the Solidarity union, Solidarity leader Lech Walesa called for an end to what were now nationwide strikes. Prime Minister Zbigniew Messner, whose government had failed to improve the economy, resigned in September and was succeeded by Mieczyslaw Rakowski. When the new government announced plans to begin closing the Lenin shipyards in Gdansk, a Solidarity stronghold, it was strongly condemned by that movement.

Polish-Israeli relations continued to expand. In June El Al Israel Airlines inaugurated direct flights from Tel Aviv to Warsaw. In October the Polish and Israeli foreign ministers, meeting in New York, agreed in principle to upgrade their diplomatic missions in Warsaw and Tel Aviv to make them independent, rather than have them operating under the diplomatic sponsorship of the Netherlands. Polish scholars were among the 300 people who attended a conference in February on the history and culture of Polish Jewry, held at the Hebrew University of Jerusalem, the latest in a series of such conferences that had taken place in Poland and the United States. At the conference, Prof. Jozef Gierowski of the Jagellonian University in Krakow announced that the Polish government would soon issue a statement on the anti-Semitic campaign and purges of 1968. The same month, the weekly *Polityka* called the campaign "infamous" and "an embarrassment" to Poland. However, the official statement, issued on March 2, in *Trybuna Ludu*, organ of the Polish United Workers party, while acknowledging that there had been an anti-Semitic campaign, asserted that "the overwhelming majority of party and state activists had nothing to do with anti-Semitism." It admitted that the campaign "brought harm to many people," but went on to say, "It should be strongly stated that the party as a whole and its leadership—although not always effective or timely—nevertheless tried to discourage an atmosphere of anti-Semitism." *Trybuna Ludu* admitted that 13,000 Jews left Poland in the period 1968–1971 and that the purge of Jews "caused harm to many people" and damaged Poland's intellectual life and image abroad.

The Warsaw Yiddish Theater toured Israel in February and the Mazowsze Folk Dance Troupe did the same in May. The renowned Polish director Andrzej Wajda directed a production of the classic Yiddish play *The Dybbuk* at Tel Aviv's Habimah Theater. In June Dr. Yossi Beilin, political director of the Israel Foreign Ministry, met with Polish foreign minister Tadeusz Olechowski in Warsaw.

JEWISH COMMUNITY

Most estimates agreed on about 5,000 Jews in Poland, fewer than half of them affiliated with the religious communities or the secular social and cultural society of Jews in Poland.

On the 45th anniversary of the Warsaw Ghetto revolt, commemorated in April, over 3,000 Jews from 35 countries came to Warsaw for the ceremonies. They included six members of the Israeli Knesset, Deputy Prime Minister Yitzhak Navon, and Justice Minister Avraham Sharir. In a ceremony at the Polish Parliament, 99 Poles who saved Jews during World War II were given "Righteous Gentile" awards by the Yad Vashem Institute. A newly erected memorial monument to those deported to death camps was dedicated by the authorities at Warsaw's Umschlagplatz, the point of embarkation on the death trains. One voice of protest was that of Marek Edelman, the only one of the leaders of the ghetto revolt still living in Poland and a Solidarity activist. Objecting to the fact that the ceremonies were arranged by a repressive government, he organized an alternative ceremony at the monument to the ghetto resisters, in which some 5,000 people participated. The unofficial commemoration also dedicated its own monument, a marker in the Jewish cemetery in honor of Viktor Alter and Henryk Erlich, leaders of the Jewish Labor Bund in prewar Poland, who were murdered in the Soviet Union on Stalin's orders after they had proposed the formation of a Jewish armed force to fight with the Soviet army against the German invaders.

Romania

U.S. deputy secretary of state John Whitehead met with President Nicolae Ceausescu in February to warn that Congress was displeased with Romania's human-rights record and could revoke Romania's status as a Most Favored Nation for trade purposes. Romania then announced that it was voluntarily relinquishing this status. It made no concessions on human rights.

JEWISH COMMUNITY

The Jewish community, declining steadily as a result of emigration and a preponderance of aged people, was estimated at about 20,000.

Chief Rabbi Moses David Rosen celebrated his jubilee as a rabbi and 40th year as the chief rabbi of Romania. The anniversary was marked in both Bucharest and Jerusalem.

ZVI GITELMAN

Australia

THE CELEBRATION OF AUSTRALIA'S bicentenary in 1988 focused the country's attention on the issues that would continue to determine its progress and shape its society into the 1990s and the 21st century. Uppermost in the bicentennial national debate were some controversial and interrelated questions: How much Asian immigration should this predominantly European society accept? As an immigrant society, should Australia pursue multiculturalism or a more assimilationist "One Australia" policy? How could an essentially hedonistic and relaxed business and trade-union culture remain competitive in the fast-growing Asia-Pacific region? And, by no means least, should there be a formal treaty, 200 years after the first European settlement of the continent, between the Australian government and the aborigines who, for the most part, still remained the underprivileged minority?

For Australian Jews, the bicentenary proved to be a kind of turning point, the beginning of an attempt to understand the emerging Australian Jewish identity. Uniquely among Jewish communities in the West, Australian Jews were "present at the creation." Between 8 and 14 Jews were among the convicts Britain sent with the First Fleet which, in 1788, established the penal colony at what was to become the city of Sydney. Thus, Jews had a sense of continuous participation in Australian history from its European origins; at the same time, they were aware that the majority of the community was of recent—post-World War II—vintage and was continuing to absorb new elements. The occasion of the bicentenary inspired a burst of cultural activity related to the Australian Jewish experience—exhibitions, museum displays, and theatrical events—as well as the introduction of new Jewish studies courses at colleges and universities. There was an upsurge of creativity among local Jewish artists, historians and other academics, writers, musicians, and filmmakers. Through this intense creative and intellectual self-examination, Australian Jews began to see themselves more clearly as a community with a distinctive identity, one no longer derived primarily from its immigrant antecedents. What all this meant for the future, especially in relation to the place of Israel in Australian Jewish life, was by no means clear, however.

National Affairs

Since winning the 1983 elections, the Labor government of Prime Minister Bob Hawke had maintained continuity in Australia's foreign policy, most notably in keeping and extending traditional ties with the United States in foreign policy and defense matters. Unlike New Zealand, which elected the Labor government of David Lange at much the same time as Hawke came to power in Australia, Australia continued to allow ship visits by American nuclear-powered and nuclear-armed ships. New Zealand's refusal to do so had led to the effective breakup of the ANZUS defense alliance, but the bilateral alliance between Canberra and Washington was developed and expanded. The same could not be said, however, in trade relations, where Hawke and other Australian ministers and officials attacked, often in outspoken terms, both the U.S. Congress and the administration for adopting various forms of protectionist subsidies to American wheat growers, which adversely affected Australia's wheat trade.

In the domestic economy, the Hawke government had managed an increasingly difficult balancing act. Its policy of deregulation and incentives to business won it plaudits from the private sector; at the same time, it had maintained an accord with the trade-union movement which conceded regular, if constrained, wage increases in return for a measure of industrial peace. By the end of 1988, however, looming problems threatened this precarious exercise in economic management. A sharp increase in interest rates to around 18 percent, inflation hovering at 8 percent, and an inability to do much to boost exports and thus stem the draining trade and payments deficits raised questions about Hawke's ability to win again at the polls. He had already won three elections in a row, unprecedented for an Australian Labor leader, and remained personally popular in the opinion polls. But the Labor party had alienated many of its traditional supporters, who had been forced to bear the brunt of the high-interest fiscal policies. Thus, most observers believed that, unless the Liberal-National opposition parties again fell victim to the internal divisions that had bedeviled their recent election campaigns, there could be a change of government in 1989 or 1990.

Relations with Israel

While Hawke had won an international reputation as an eloquent, often emotional, champion of Israel and had personally negotiated with President Mikhail Gorbachev on behalf of refuseniks and Soviet Jews generally, he was quick to welcome the December 1988 statements by the PLO's Yasir Arafat in Geneva as a significant breakthrough in the Middle East diplomatic impasse. In addition, the criticism of Israel by Australian delegates at the United Nations for its handling of the *intifada* in the territories became increasingly one-sided and vehement in 1988. What did become clear was that Hawke's view was not the result of pressure from his left wing, as had been feared when Labor first took office, but stemmed from his own belief that, as a friend of Israel, he had to exert pressure on it to accept the PLO as a partner for talks. Echoing language used by some American critics of Israeli policies a decade ago, Hawke's approach was seen in the Jewish community as an attempt "to save Israel in spite of herself."

Although the Liberal-National opposition queried the Hawke government about the speed and extent of its tilt toward the PLO, there were few indications that, in office, it would differ substantially. Once Washington had agreed to deal with the PLO and had accepted that Arafat had recognized Israel, it would be virtually impossible for any Australian government, but particularly a Labor government, to try to be more pro-Israel than the United States.

Nazi War Criminals

There was, however, one matter on which an incoming Liberal-National government might well take a markedly different attitude to that of the Hawke government—war-crimes trials. After lengthy and often acrimonious debate, the Australian Parliament, in early 1988, passed legislation to enable the investigation, trial, and punishment of Nazi war criminals found to be resident in Australia. As with the United States, Canada, and more recently Britain, the proposed legislation and subsequent investigations proved bitterly controversial in some sectors of public opinion. In the immediate aftermath of World War II, Australia had accepted hundreds of thousands of immigrants from Europe with demonstrably inadequate screening techniques. Government investigators estimated that hundreds of Nazi war criminals, many from East European countries, could have entered Australia. Although the government's investigations unit was said to be concentrating its inquiries on between 70 and 100 Australian residents, only a handful of prosecutions were likely to be undertaken.

When the Hawke government sought bipartisan support for its war-crimes initiative, the Liberal-National opposition said it favored the legislation—in principle. However, under pressure from East European émigré communities, who denounced the legislation as a group libel against them, it did not support the measure in practice. The opposition claimed that the war-crimes provisions could be misused against Australian ex-servicemen and that prosecutions would be too dependent on evidence from Soviet sources. The investigations unit, led by a senior civil servant, Robert Greenwood, was understood to be preparing to launch its first prosecutions in 1990, if legal challenges to the legislation did not succeed. But some observers believed that if a Liberal-National government came to office it would, over time, disband the investigations unit and drop the whole process of war-crimes inquiry.

Anti-Semitism and Anti-Zionism

The widespread and drawn-out debate over war-crimes legislation exposed Australian Jews to a virulent, and mostly unprecedented, anti-Semitic campaign emanating largely from some of the East European émigré groups. Anti-Jewish statements and cartoons also appeared in sections of the Christian church media, where Jews were portrayed as seeking revenge instead of forgiveness, and in the mainstream media, where some editorialists and columnists accused Jews of abusing their allegedly disproportionate political influence to push through the war-crimes legislation. In reality, while the Jewish leadership undoubtedly supported the government's decisions to proceed with the legislation, the recommendations to proceed were made at every point by non-Jewish senior civil servants, in many cases retired, who were largely immune to political lobbying. Even though the prosecution of ex-Nazis was presented to the government by its panel of investigators as a matter of law and justice, it was widely portrayed as a "Jewish issue." Some influential writers, especially among the conservative and neoconservative Right, who had traditionally been pro-Israel and sympathetic to Jewish concerns, not only attacked the war-crimes legislation but turned against Israel, world Jewry, and the local Jewish leadership. Jews were taken aback by the reversal, but it became clear that the critics were those with a strong anti-Soviet stance who identified with the émigré communities, such as the Australian-Ukrainian associations, who were the most opposed to the war-crimes legislation. The conflict led to bitter exchanges and the breakup of some informal political alliances which Jewish leaders and intellectuals had formed over the previous 25 years.

While there was an undoubted increase of "verbal" and "physical" manifestations of anti-Semitism—and in a country where such incidents had been rare they stood out—the evidence from public-opinion survey data continued to show that Jews were among the most accepted minorities in Australia. Still, the "old-style" anti-Semites, mostly organized around the League of Rights and its leader, Eric Butler, were using the growing resentment in some areas against Asian immigration to fuel anti-Semitism. The league's approach tried to exploit the worsening economic conditions, particularly in rural areas, and to blame them on various combinations of Asian immigration, Japanese investment, and the Jews. In some Australian states, particularly semitropical Queensland, which was often called "the deep North," the League of Rights had been successful in infiltrating some political parties. But it received a setback when a senior federal politician formerly associated with the group exposed its racist activities in a widely reported parliamentary statement.

Anti-Zionism, almost invariably spilling over into criticism of "Jewish influence" or "Jewish media control" or the "well-heeled Jewish lobby," remained a concern, heightened by the media coverage of the *intifada* during 1988. The growing sympathy for the PLO shown by the Australian government and the increase in propaganda activity by PLO supporters in key public-opinion areas, such as schools and universities, had led to wider acceptance by public opinion of a pro-Palestinian, anti-Israel viewpoint.

JEWISH COMMUNITY

Demography

The data from the 1986 national census showed an overall increase of some 12 percent, over the previous five years, in the Australian Jewish population. Allowing for those who did not reply to the elective question on religion, and the estimated increase in immigration since the census was taken, community demographers reached a figure of 90,000 for the total Jewish population. The estimated figures for the main cities were: Melbourne—42,000; Sydney—37,000; Perth—6,000; Adelaide—2,000; Brisbane and the Gold Coast—2,000.

The fastest growing community was Perth in Western Australia, whose size had almost doubled to 6,000 between 1986 and 1989. The growth was almost entirely due to immigrants from South Africa, who were attracted by Perth's Indian Ocean temperate climate, economic opportunities, life-style, and relative proximity to South Africa.

It was estimated that some 15,000 Jews from South Africa had migrated to Australia during the 1970s and '80s. Although more South African Jews were expected to seek entry, Canberra, ever sensitive to the political implications of its dealings with South Africa, had not made it easy for white Africans wanting to settle in Australia.

Russian Jews had also begun to come in growing numbers, after a decade of almost no migration from the Soviet Union. Communal welfare agencies were bracing themselves for a substantial increase in Russian Jews opting for Australia as an alternative to the United States or Canada. However, it was not certain how flexible the Australian immigration authorities would be toward those seeking entry visas outside the framework of family reunion and how liberally the refugee category would be applied, if at all.

Intermarriage rates remained relatively low—between 5 and 10 percent—in the main communities, though higher in the smaller centers. Although reliable figures on divorce were not available, the rate was widely assumed to be increasing, judging by the number of *gittin* (religious divorce decrees) given by the rabbinical courts and the evidence available from schools and welfare agencies. In a community still strongly influenced by traditional values, the agencies were just beginning to examine the implications of this trend.

Communal Affairs

Despite the downturn in the Australian economy, which was hard hit by the 1987 stock-market crash and a burgeoning balance-of-payments deficit, the Jewish communities in the main cities continued to expand their network of institutions, encouraged by the growth of some 12 percent in the Jewish population during the 1980s, due largely to the immigration of South African and Russian Jews.

Jews continued to make their mark in Australian public life, the professions, and business. In the latter field their success was particularly noteworthy, with at least 50 Jews reportedly among the 200 wealthiest Australians. The widely publicized success of many Jewish entrepreneurs was greeted with mixed feelings by the Jewish community as a whole. While Jews were generally better off than average, the community still had pockets of hardship, and many younger Jews were entering the salaried professions rather than going into business. But, taken as a whole, in economic terms, Australian Jews constituted a remarkable success story.

The Australian Jewish leadership and virtually all communal organizations remained strongly supportive of Israel, following the outbreak of the *intifada* in December 1987. There were some dissenting groups, based mainly around the Jewish Left, but they could muster only limited support in the community at large. Unlike American Jewry and, to an extent, some elements of European Jewry, no Australian Jewish leader of any standing publicly expressed criticism of Israeli government policies.

The coincidence of Australia's 200th anniversary and Israel's 40th formed the backdrop to many communal events during 1988. Among the more noteworthy was the reception, in August, to mark Israel's anniversary, organized by the House of Representatives and the Senate in the Australian Parliament. Arranged at the initiative of Mark Leibler, president of the Zionist Federation of Australia, the event was the first of its kind to be held in the new Parliament House after its opening by Queen Elizabeth in May 1988. It was attended by almost all of the more than 200 federal MPs, 20 ambassadors, and Jewish leaders from around Australia.

Although the South African influx caused a certain amount of tension between older residents and the newcomers, it transformed Perth's Jewish community, which had increasingly suffered from its static, no-growth limitations. The new migration—mostly younger people—boosted the number of students at Perth's Carmel School, the city's only Jewish day school, from 270 to 600 in two years. It was estimated that the school would have 1,000 pupils by 1992. South African Jews also made their impact in the main centers of Melbourne and Sydney. Coming from a community with a longer and more recognized tradition of Jewish professional service than in Australia, which had not yet produced its own cadre of Jewish civil servants, they were moving into senior communal service roles as rabbis, administrators, educators, welfare workers, and journalists.

The Jewish press experienced growth and change in the period under review. In August 1987, Melbourne businessman Richard Pratt bought the Melbourne-based weekly *Australian Jewish News* from the Rubinstein family, which had founded the paper and owned it for 53 years. In October 1987, the Melbourne paper joined the Sydney-based *Australian Jewish Times*, owned by the Klein family, in a joint venture to publish both newspapers. Over the next two years, both newspapers were redesigned and reorganized. The Melbourne paper, in addition to its English-language edition, also continued to publish *Die Yiddishe Neyess*, a 12-page weekly in Yiddish.

In Melbourne and Sydney, and to a lesser degree in the smaller cities, the Jewish community also had access to multilingual and community radio networks for the broadcast of programs of Jewish interest. In Melbourne, community programs were aired a total of eight hours a week in English, Hebrew, and Yiddish.

Nobel laureate and author Elie Wiesel made his first visit to Australia in November 1988, his public lectures drawing large audiences. In Melbourne, in March, the first Jewish Concert in the Park, a musical presentation of Jewish singers, dancers, and massed choirs, drew a crowd of 7,000.

Soviet Jewry

Australian Jewry had a long and active involvement in the Soviet Jewry movement, dating back to the early '60s when the Australian government was the first to raise the question of Soviet Jewry and human rights in the United Nations. Since then the campaign for Soviet Jewry in Australia had brought together communal leadership, synagogues, women's groups, and students to give Australian Jewry an unusually high profile internationally on the issue. In the period under review, that involvement culminated in a cultural agreement signed in Australia between the Soviet Ministry of Culture and the president of the Australian Jewish community, Isi Leibler. Leibler, a vice-president of the World Jewish Congress (WJC) and active in the international Soviet Jewry movement for more than 30 years, had campaigned for many years for the release of the refuseniks. After a number of the leading refuseniks were released in late 1987 and early 1988, some of them due to the direct intercession with Soviet leader Mikhail Gorbachev by Prime Minister Hawke, Leibler hosted 15 of them, who had come from Israel, at a gala reception in Melbourne in May. The evening—the undisputed highlight of the Jewish communal year—was attended by 3,000 guests, including Prime Minister Hawke, WJC president Edgar Bronfman, and many national and international dignitaries. As part of the program, a live radio-link to Moscow made possible a conversation between the Australian prime minister and remaining refuseniks.

The cultural agreement with Moscow, which followed a few months later, provided for the opening in the Soviet capital of the Solomon Mikhoels Cultural Center in February 1989, as a joint endeavor of Australian Jewry, the WJC, and the Soviet Ministry of Culture. The Mikhoels Center was to house a library, lecture hall, theatrical and musical facilities, and provide a meeting place for Moscow's Jews. It would also develop cultural exchange programs between Israel, world Jewry, and Soviet Jews.

Education

The emphasis on Jewish day-school education remained strong. A growing concern in Melbourne, where the Jewish day-school movement, with nine schools, was at its strongest, was the "drop-out factor" at high-school level. In recent years, even though an estimated 80 percent of the elementary-school-age population attended

Jewish schools, the figure had fallen to 50 percent in high school. Some Jewish educators expressed concern over the growing enrollment of Jewish students in private church schools. Although the reasons for this shift were not clearly understood, causative factors included dissatisfaction among parents and students over what was said to be excessive academic pressure in some Jewish day schools, the additional demands of Jewish studies, and in some cases the burden of high fees.

Despite these concerns, the overall picture was one of growth and development. Melbourne's Mount Scopus College,[1] with 2,500 students one of the largest Jewish schools in the world, launched a five-year campaign to raise A$20 million for the upgrading of facilities and the introduction of new educational projects. Sydney's Moriah College began building a new campus to accommodate 1,500 students. On Sydney's North Shore, the rapid influx of South African immigrants placed severe strains on Masada College's campus, which was expanded to cope with hundreds of new students. In Brisbane, the only main center of Jewish population without a day school, plans were under way to open the first such classes in 1990.

In common with the trend internationally, there was an upsurge in interest in Jewish studies at university and college level. Melbourne University appointed Mark Baker the first Arnold Bloch Memorial Lecturer in Jewish History, and there were moves to introduce similar courses at Monash University. Sydney University extended the range of Jewish courses available through the Department of Middle East Studies. Victoria College, also in Melbourne, offered a bachelor's degree in Jewish studies, and a growing number of other universities and colleges were introducing courses in Holocaust studies, Israel and the Middle East, Hebrew, and Yiddish. Interestingly, many of the courses were more popular with non-Jewish students than with Jewish undergraduates.

A three-day international conference on the future of Jewish education in Australia drew 1,000 teachers, educators, and academics from around the country and from Israel, the United States, and the Asia-Pacific region.

Personalia

Several prominent Australian Jews received the Order of Australia in 1987 and 1988: businessman and philanthropist Richard Pratt, lawyer and former president of the Executive Council of Australian Jewry Leslie Caplan, and lawyer and president of the Zionist Federation of Australia Mark Leibler.

SAM LIPSKI

---

[1]"College" is the term used for a privately funded primary and secondary school combined.

Israel

The Year of the Intifada

VIRTUALLY NO AREA of Israeli life was untouched, directly or indirectly, by the uprising in the occupied territories in 1988. The *intifada* (literally, "shaking off"), as the Palestinians in the territories called their multifaceted revolt against Israel's generation-long rule over them which began on December 9, 1987, impinged on the Israeli polity as few events had in the state's history, short of full-scale war. Ironically, the uprising occurred precisely in the year that Israel was celebrating the 40th anniversary of its establishment. The festivities went ahead largely as planned, but the tourists stayed home—a development that also contributed to the economic malaise, itself due in no small part to the *intifada*—and the general mood was muted.

Israel's major ally, the United States, tried to seize the opportunity to get Israel to embark on the road to a settlement with the Palestinians and Jordan as the first stage in a comprehensive Middle East settlement. However, the fact that 1988 was an election year both in Israel and the United States was not calculated to make Prime Minister Yitzhak Shamir and his colleagues forsake their status-quo politics. Movement, however, was visible on the other side, near the end of the year. PLO chairman Yasir Arafat recited the litany of declarations which the United States had demanded since 1975 as the condition for launching a dialogue with the organization. Arafat's move, and the PLO's earlier declaration of a Palestinian state in the territories, were both results of the pressures generated by the *intifada*.

The confusion, fears, and uncertainty that were pervasive in Israel in 1988 were clearly reflected in the results of the November general election. The new government, which was essentially the old government—reconstituted after six weeks of coalition give-and-take—appeared ill equipped to deal with the urgent problems on the national agenda.

THE *INTIFADA*

The First Phase: "Force, Might, and Blows"

In its initial phase the *intifada* was impelled by sheer force of numbers and the unleashing of pent-up fury. Throughout the territories, in cities and towns, in villages and refugee camps, tens of thousands of people took to the streets and engaged Israeli troops in mass confrontations. Briefly, around the beginning of January, when the demonstrations tapered off, the Israeli military thought their assessment had been vindicated that the huge and bloody demonstrations in December—in which 22 Palestinians had been killed and scores wounded by live fire—had in fact been one more "wave of riots," albeit on an unprecedented scale, such as the Israel Defense Forces (IDF) had coped with sporadically over the past two decades. On January 4, Prime Minister Shamir told Israel Radio: "I do not believe that the wave of disturbances will resume. . . . I do not believe that a new situation has been created. . . . [The Arab population in the areas] wants a return to normalcy, because it sees that these disturbances, acts of incitement and stone throwing do not lead anywhere."

Within days, however, of Shamir's reassuring statement, correspondents were describing the Gaza Strip as "looking like a war zone" after the army rushed in forces on a large scale, including armored personnel carriers, to put down a renewal of the violent mass demonstrations.

In addition, there were incipient signs that the uprising was seeking new directions, and that the demonstrations and riots were the prelude to more institutionalized forms of civil revolt. On January 7, Hanna Siniora, the editor of the East Jerusalem daily *al-Fajr*, urged the residents of the territories to launch a phased boycott of Israeli-made goods, culminating in a refusal to work for Israeli employers. Around the same time, the first leaflet of the "United National Command of the Uprising" was circulated in the West Bank and the Gaza Strip. It called on the population to observe a general strike from January 11–13, to "include all forms of revolutionary escalation." January 15, a Friday, the Muslim sabbath, was declared a "day of unity and solidarity," to be devoted to "commemorating the fallen of the uprising in requiem prayers and symbolic funerals." Thirty more leaflets were issued in 1988 by this shadowy leadership group, and all attempts by the security forces to put a stop to the phenomenon—by deportations, mass arrests, outlawing of organizations, and uncovering of clandestine printing presses—were unavailing.

The United National Command (UNC) was a coalition of Fatah, the Democratic Front for the Liberation of Palestine, the Popular Front for the Liberation of Palestine, and the Palestine Communist party. The group's close identification with the PLO was indicated by the motto that appeared at the head of each leaflet, beginning with the third one (January 18):

No voice rises above the voice of the uprising,
No voice rises above the voice of the Palestinian people
—the people of the Palestine Liberation Organization

Similarly, Hamas, the Gaza-based Islamic Resistance Movement, issued 33 leaflets in 1988, and occasional leaflets were issued by some of the smaller left-wing and religious organizations.

The ideological message of the leaflets was that the Palestinians could achieve their aim of hastening Israel's departure from the territories by engaging in a combination of violent and nonviolent activity. The former included stone-throwing, gasoline-bomb attacks, erecting barricades, the use of knives and axes, and actions against "collaborators." Nonviolent activity would include breaking off contact with Israel in the economic and service sectors, refusing to obey Israeli laws and regulations, and heightening internal solidarity.

In the first stage of the uprising, however, these long-term political objectives, whose culmination would be the establishment of an independent Palestinian state, were obscured by violence: a hail of rocks and other objects—often propelled with powerful slingshots from behind a thick curtain of acrid black smoke created by barricades of burning tires and accompanied by jeering, taunts, and curses—that greeted Israeli patrols in the territories. Israeli soldiers, unprepared and untrained in riot-control techniques, responded in the first instance with a liberal use of tear gas, including (as confirmed by Defense Minister Yitzhak Rabin in the Knesset) a more toxic type of gas than had previously been used by the IDF. Palestinians and groups such as Amnesty International alleged, and Israel denied, that tear gas was sometimes used in confined or semiconfined spaces, such as rooms in houses or schools, reportedly causing asphyxiation in some cases.

When tear gas failed to produce the desired effect, troops resorted to the use of live fire in "life-threatening situations." Rubber bullets, introduced in January, had no perceptible mitigating effect on the high casualty rates resulting from officers having to make instant interpretations of the phrase "life-threatening situation" when confronted with rampaging mobs who had lost all fear of the military and were masters of their own turf. It was in an effort to stem the tide of adverse media reports, domestic and external, that Defense Minister Rabin announced a new policy means to reduce the number of fatalities among Palestinian demonstrators. In the event, this proved even more controversial and more damaging to Israel's international image.

On January 19, during a tour of the West Bank, Rabin told reporters that the security forces' "top priority" was "to use force, might, and blows" [*makot*] to quell the violent demonstrations in the territories. A week later *Ha'aretz* quoted Rabin as telling defense reporters that the beatings policy had actually been in effect since January 4, and that, in combination with other measures including curfews and "hot pursuit" of demonstrators, it had "brought about calm which was more obvious in Gaza and less so in Judea-Samaria." In addition, Rabin said, this combination of measures had "created the impact we wanted: the fear of the population." Another, less fortuitous, result of the new approach was a surge in media reports about what were officially termed "deviations" or "excesses" perpetrated by soldiers against the local population. Rabin himself conceded that some soldiers were "keen to deliver beatings," but insisted that, overall, troops were obeying the orders prohibiting the use of force after a riot had been dispersed and its instigators apprehended.

The problem was that, by the time the orders filtered down to the field units, they had become diffuse and vague. Young officers and soldiers took advantage of the unwritten rules to vent on the local population their frustrations caused, in essence, by their being called on to act as policemen in situations for which nothing in their combat training had prepared them. A Health Ministry report, cited by the Citizens' Rights Movement, stated that by the end of April, nearly 2,000 persons had been treated in local hospitals in the territories, the majority suffering from broken bones, after being beaten with truncheons.

The backlash inside Israel was reflected in the relatively large attendance—an estimated 40,000 people—at a Peace Now rally held in Tel Aviv on January 23. Speakers at the gathering called for the renewal of the peace process and an end to the "iron fist" policy in the territories. On January 29, an unusual petition, signed by nearly 500 Israeli mental-health practitioners, appeared in the Hebrew press. The signatories asserted that beyond the "fear and humiliation" suffered by the Palestinians in the territories during the two decades of the occupation, the situation was having "a horrendous impact upon the Jewish population as well. . . . We are being swept into an existence marked by fear, violence and racism. We are losing our sensitivity to human suffering." In the same vein, 600 of the country's leading academics and intellectuals, including the sociologist Shmuel Eisenstadt, the historian Shmuel Ettinger, and the writers Amos Oz and A. B. Yeshoshua, signed a petition expressing "profound concern" about Israel's future, urging the government to "reevaluate" its policy.

Within the IDF, too, concern was voiced at the long-term effects, especially on young soldiers, of the behavioral norms they were internalizing due to the nature of their service in the territories. The IDF's chief education officer, Brig. Gen. Nehemiah Dagan, initiated an information campaign against the dehumanization of the Palestinians. At the end of January, the army's military advocate-general, Brig. Gen. Amnon Strashnow, stated that he had ordered investigations into "recent incidents in which troops went beyond the use of reasonable force." Maj. Gen. Amram Mitzna, the O/C Central Command (whose area of responsibility included the West Bank), told reporters that some soldiers had been court-martialed and reassigned for beating Palestinians indiscriminately.

Defense Minister Rabin, replying in the Knesset on February 16 to motions for the agenda submitted by Mapam and the Citizens' Rights Movement on the implementation of "manifestly illegal" orders in the territories, denied having used the phrase "to break bones" or having sanctioned beatings as a punitive measure. Rabin explained that the first priority was to prevent outbreaks of violence; if nevertheless a violent situation developed, tear gas was to be used in the first stage, then rubber bullets, and if these tactics failed, soldiers were to charge the rioters using force, including riot clubs. However, blows were to be administered only during the operation itself or during hot pursuit of rioters; if a stone thrower or other agitator took refuge in a house, soldiers were at liberty to enter that house, forcibly if necessary. Rabin acknowledged that "irregularities" had occurred and revealed that in two cases officers who had been involved in such incidents were under investigation. Rabin asserted that an "information campaign" had been launched in the IDF to ensure that soldiers understood the policy.

TWO CASES OF BRUTALITY

Nevertheless, "irregularities," "deviations," and "excesses" continued to be rumored and reported. (Some of the incidents became public knowledge only toward the end of the year, when those involved went on trial following lengthy Military Police investigations—see below.) Two of the most heavily publicized cases of brutality in the first part of the year occurred in February. In one, following a demonstration at the village of Kafr Salem, near Nablus, four young villagers were forced by soldiers to lie on the ground and were buried under a foot of wet earth by a bulldozer. They were dug out and revived by villagers after the troops left. General Mitzna, who did not learn about the incident until a week after it happened, was quoted as saying the incident was "beyond his worst dreams." (Three soldiers—two privates and a master sergeant from the Civil Administration, were tried in connection with the incident. The privates were sentenced on March 29 to four and five months, respectively, in prison. Their prison terms were halved by an appeals court on May 17, two days after the master sergeant received a four-month prison term and was demoted to the rank of private.)

The second incident was revealed to the world on February 25, when CBS-TV screened a report showing Israeli soldiers viciously beating two Arabs sitting helplessly on the ground, hands tied behind their backs. Israeli TV screened only a brief segment from the full CBS report, followed by an interview with General Mitzna, who said he had been "shocked" by the incident and wanted to assure the public that "this behavior is still the exception." Israeli embassies in Europe were deluged with protests from individuals, human rights organizations, and governments, and American Jewish leaders said it would be difficult to defend Israeli policy after this incident, which seemed to confirm the worst reports about what was going on in the territories. (An officer and two corporals faced trial in connection with the beating incident. As in the "burial" case, the charges against the three were mitigated in a plea-bargaining deal from "aggravated assault" to "shameful behavior" and "unbecoming conduct." In April the three received suspended sentences, and the two corporals, who had done most of the beating, were demoted to the rank of private. The three judges noted that, given the conditions in the territories, especially the provocative behavior of the local residents, "even the finest, the wisest and the most restrained of soldiers will find it difficult to muster the psychological strength and the forbearance enabling him to remain calm, cool and collected. . . .")

That such incidents, while extreme, were not as "exceptional" as Rabin and others claimed, was implicitly confirmed by Attorney General Yosef Harish. In a letter to the defense minister, made public on February 22, Harish wrote that the "large number of complaints about acts of abuse" in the territories received by his office "raises the suspicion that classification of these incidents as irregularities no longer reflects reality." Following the publication of Harish's letter, the chief of staff, Lt. Gen. Dan Shomron, broke the public silence he had maintained on the subject of the "aberrations." In a message to IDF commanders issued on February 23, Shomron noted that the "broad wave of violent riots and disturbances" in the territories had confronted the IDF with "one of the most complex and sensitive missions" it had ever faced. "The execution of this mission requires the use of force," Shomron continued, but its implementation must be tempered with the "self-control, restraint and sensitivity commensurate with the high norms of behavior incumbent upon IDF soldiers and commanders."

CONTINUING VIOLENCE; ESCALATING RESPONSE

Despite Defense Minister Rabin's declared justification for introducing the policy of beatings—that it would reduce the number of persons killed by firearms (and thus, it was hoped, lessen the pressure on Israel)—17 Palestinians were killed in January, 13 of them in the Gaza Strip, while February saw a dramatic increase to 32 deaths, this time the vast majority (27) occurring in the West Bank. One reason for the surge in casualties was that, in a concerted effort to break the uprising, more troops were dispatched to the territories with orders to confront Palestinian demonstrators more aggressively, as called for by the beatings policy, even in previously ignored remote villages, thus broadening and intensifying the cycle of violence.

March brought a rising number of Palestinian casualties and April even more; at least 40 Palestinians were killed by Israeli troops, including 16 on April 16, following the assassination in Tunis of Khalil al-Wazir, code-named "Abu Jihad," Yasir Arafat's deputy for military operations in Fatah. While the high number of casualties in April was in part a backlash from the Tunis operation, the surge in fatalities and wounding actually began during the final week of March as the Israeli authorities began to change their tactics in dealing with the uprising.

In mid-March, with firebomb attacks coming at an average rate of 4–5 a day, primarily in the West Bank, where settlers were more easily targeted, the regulations for opening fire in the territories were relaxed. Troops could now shoot at persons about to throw, or holding, or suspected of holding firebombs, on the ground that these devices were lethal weapons and hence constituted an immediate threat to soldiers' lives.

Another cause of the steep rise in Palestinian casualties was the new, explicit orders to officers to confront violent demonstrators "aggressively and assertively," not to back away from clashes with rioters even if this course of action placed the troops in a situation of concrete danger obligating them to open fire. This reversal of the previous policy, which had called for avoidance of confrontations with demonstrators, was meant to enable the security forces to demonstrate the qualities that had gained the IDF its reputation on the field of battle: tactical originality, improvisational ability, adherence to mission, and carrying the battle to the enemy.

The difference was that, in the occupied territories, as often as not, the "enemy" consisted of rock-throwing children. In an interview with *Davar* on March 18, Chief of Staff Dan Shomron articulated the dilemma facing the military: "[T]he long-term solution is entirely political," he explained. "There is no possibility of bringing about a solution through the use of military force, given the restrictions and limitations we have imposed on ourselves." Shomron added: "As long as we do not decide to alter the code of behavior of the State of Israel by employing firearms against unarmed civilians in the territories, there is no possibility of bringing about total calm through the use of the army."

CURFEW AND DEPORTATION

From the start of the uprising, one of the first Israeli countermeasures was to impose curfew on trouble spots, compounding the impact of the permanent commercial strike conducted by the Palestinians. Increasingly during the year, curfews, some continuing for extended periods and often aggravated by the authorities' severing of phone and other communications links to the outside, took on the character of a purely punitive measure and were utilized by the military to carry out search-and-arrest operations. Residents complained that they were prevented from receiving urgent medical treatment during curfews, and in some cases there were reports of food shortages, allegations that were denied by the IDF.

Probably there was not a curfew-free day in the territories during all of 1988. The Shati refugee camp in the Gaza Strip and the Tulkarm refugee camp in the West Bank spent 149 and 143 days, respectively, under full curfew. An indefinite night curfew (10 P.M. until 3 A.M.) was imposed on the entire Gaza Strip on March 14. The city of Nablus, with a population of more than 80,000, was under curfew for a total of more than two months in 1988. By the end of the year, even this measure was no longer a guarantee of quiet as it was increasingly defied, particularly by inhabitants of refugee camps.

A major cause of the renewed demonstrations in early 1988 was the IDF's announcement, on January 3, that deportation orders had been served that day to nine residents of the territories, five from the West Bank and four from the Gaza Strip. According to the communiqué, the nine were "leading activists and organizers involved in incitement and subversive activity on behalf of terrorist organizations." Ignoring both U.S. admonitions and a unanimous UN Security Council resolution adopted on January 5, citing the 1949 Fourth Geneva Convention on "the protection of civilian persons in time of war," and calling on Israel "to refrain from deporting any Palestinian civilian from the Occupied Territories," Israel on January 13 expelled four of those on the list to Lebanon, the first of 32 Palestinians deported from the territories during 1988 (see also below).

Among those in the January 13 group was Jibril al-Rujoub, aged 35, from the town of Doura, near Hebron, who was one of the 1,500 security prisoners released in the 1985 deal with the Ahmed Jibril organization in return for three Israelis; before becoming deputy editor of a West Bank women's magazine, he was employed at the Center for Palestine Studies, in East Jerusalem, where he became, according to an IDF communiqué, the "right-hand man" of the institution's director, Faisal al-Husseini, himself described as "a senior Fatah activist now under administrative detention."

The deportation triggered a second Security Council resolution (January 14), this one passed by a vote of 14–0 (the United States abstained) and expressing "deep regret" at Israel's "defiance" of the earlier resolution. A no-confidence motion against the government on the same issue submitted in the Knesset by four left-wing parties (Mapam, Citizens' Rights, Communists, Progressive List for Peace) had been resoundingly defeated by the coalition on January 6. (The other five persons on the list of nine were deported on April 11, some ten weeks after dropping their appeals to the High Court of Justice, a step they took, according to their lawyer, "in order not to legitimize the court's authority to decide their fate following the submission of secret evidence that they will not be allowed to see.")

Jerusalem—"Scars and Coexistence"

One of the entrenched Israeli conceptions undermined by the *intifada* was that of a reunited Jerusalem, its Jewish and Arab populations living in separate but equal—and peaceful—coexistence. (East Jerusalem was sovereign Israeli territory, having been formally annexed in 1967.)

Jerusalem had remained relatively quiet during the first month or more of the *intifada*. This situation came to a dramatic and violent end on Friday, January 15, when police and Border Police clashed with worshipers who streamed out of the Al Aqsa mosque on the Temple Mount, following the weekly prayers, chanting anti-Israel slogans, throwing rocks, and burning the Israeli flag. Police wearing gas masks and face shields fired dozens of canisters of tear gas at the rioters and charged them, riot clubs flailing. About 70 Palestinians and 6 policemen were hurt in the melee, and 8 demonstrators were arrested. The sensitivity of the site and the massive presence of the foreign media ensured that the event would receive extensive coverage abroad. Israeli officials vehemently denied reports that tear gas had been fired directly into the Al Aqsa mosque, although conceding that tear gas might have wafted into the building from outside.

A week later, on January 22, the previously unthinkable happened: for the first time since the Six Day War, curfew was imposed in one of the capital's neighborhoods, A-Tur, lying between Mount Scopus and the Mount of Olives. The step was especially galling for Mayor Teddy Kollek, as it was taken without informing him, via an emergency order issued by the O/C Central Command, General Mitzna, at the request of the police. At Kollek's urging, the curfew was lifted about 20 hours after being declared. It had been imposed after youngsters from the village blocked the road to the Al-Maqassed Hospital and the Intercontinental Hotel for four consecutive days by burning tires, erecting barriers, and stoning vehicles. While the curfew was in effect, all males in A-Tur between the ages of 10 and 50 were ordered to gather in the local schoolyard where they were checked by security personnel; four were arrested.

Sporadic violence continued throughout the year in East Jerusalem—whose status as sovereign Israeli territory ironically enabled it to become, in effect, the political-intellectual center of the uprising—and in outlying refugee camps and villages incorporated within the municipal boundaries after the 1967 war. The commercial strike in East Jerusalem intensified, although a leaflet issued by the leadership of the uprising permitted stores to open for three hours a day so that residents would not have to shop in the city's western section—where, just minutes from the Arab area, life went on normally, at least on the surface.

On February 5, the Jerusalem municipality decided, for the first time ever, to close down all 31 public schools in East Jerusalem for a week, due to their part in the unrest, low attendance by the 16,000 pupils, and threats to the lives of headmasters by the organizers of the commercial strike (private schools in East Jerusalem had been closed for some time).

Residents of some of the Jewish neighborhoods built after 1967 in former Jordan-held territory could corroborate Kollek's plaint that "coexistence in the city is collapsing." In East Talpiot, large numbers of police and Border Police fired tear gas canisters and rubber bullets on February 7 to repulse hundreds of youngsters who marched into the neighborhood from the adjacent Arab village of Jabel Mukaber, carrying Palestinian flags, chanting nationalist slogans, and throwing rocks through windows of houses and a school. A similar march by about 500 youngsters from the Shuafat refugee camp toward the nearby Pisgat Ze'ev neighborhood was forcibly broken up. The No. 25 bus, connecting the city to the Neve Ya'akov quarter on the road to Ramallah, was stoned 40 times in the first two months of the uprising.

Serious disturbances were also reported within the walls of the Old City. On July 3, workers in an archeological dig sponsored by the Ministry of Religious Affairs in the Western Wall area dug a hole on a Muslim Quarter street (adjacent to the Via Dolorosa, where Christian pilgrims were touring) to gain better access to a water tunnel from the Hasmonean period. Immediately, rumors spread—fanned by the *muezzin* using the powerful loudspeakers on the Temple Mount—that "the Jews" were trying to seize control of one of the gates to the mount and to undermine Muslim structures. Fifteen local residents and one policeman were injured in a fierce two-hour riot that ensued in the Old City.

On July 19, Jerusalem experienced its first fatal casualty of the uprising. Sixteen-year-old Nidal Rabadi, from the Old City's Christian Quarter, was shot and killed, reportedly after a bus was stoned on the Jerusalem-Ramallah road and passengers, including soldiers, opened fire at fleeing Arabs. Rabadi's funeral, held on Mount Zion following a procession through the Christian Quarter, triggered serious rioting. Attendance at the Western Wall for the traditional 9th of Av fast-day prayers (July 23–24) marking the destruction of the Temple was down by 80 percent as compared with previous years.

The statistics relating to Jerusalem were as astonishing as those for the territories. According to official data, Jerusalem—more specifically, East Jerusalem—in 1988 experienced 114 firebomb attacks, 283 cases of tire burning, 1,766 incidents of stone throwing, and 708 incidents of road blocking. Besides these 2,963 violent incidents (of which more than 20 percent occurred in the final month of the year, in a pattern similar to the events in the territories), on 1,229 occasions the Palestinian flag was hoisted in the capital.

In effect, Jerusalem in 1988 was once more a divided city. Few Jewish Jerusalemites or other Israelis ventured into the city's eastern section, including the Old City, and even at the Western Wall fewer worshipers turned up on holy days. Jerusalem also suffered in other ways from the *intifada*. The general decline in foreign tourism to Israel during the year affected Jerusalem disproportionately. But it was hard to blame foreigners when even Israelis stayed away—school trips to the capital from all over the country, a staple of the curriculum, were nearly all canceled under pressure from parents fearful for their children's safety. Businesses in the Jerusalem area that were dependent on workers from the territories, particularly garages and the construction industry, had to cope with frequent employee absenteeism due to curfews imposed by the military and/or general strikes called by the leadership of the uprising. Mayor Teddy Kollek seemed to be on the mark when he said, in mid-February, that the situation in the capital had "changed in a fundamental way," adding: "Coexistence is not dead, but I'm sure there will be deep scars left when this is over."

Israel's Image—The Media Connection

A mid-January meeting with President Chaim Herzog (scheduled before the uprising began) gave a delegation of the Foreign Press Association in Israel the opportunity to protest at the highest level against what they described as a "campaign of vilification" against foreign media representatives in Israel due to their reporting on the events in the territories. In part, they charged, Israeli government officials were the cause of this climate of opinion, which had resulted in physical attacks on journalists by settlers and soldiers. In his response, President Herzog voiced the long-standing Israeli complaint that media reporting did not provide the "full perspective" on the situation in the territories, such as the considerable rise in the living standard of the inhabitants there since 1967. Herzog noted further that the alternative was not between violence and negotiations, "but to contain the trouble and see that it does not get out of hand, or deteriorate into another Teheran or Beirut."

For Israeli policymakers, who feared in the initial phase of the *intifada* that the situation was about to lurch out of control, the media became a popular scapegoat. Thus, just days after the start of the uprising, Prime Minister Shamir suggested that a connection existed between the events and the presence of journalists in the territories. At that time, however, Chief of Staff Shomron came to the support of the press by persuading Shamir that closure of the territories to the press would be both impractical and counterproductive.

As the first serious attempt by the politico-military establishment to cope with the problem, on January 24 the defense establishment opened a "Media Information Center on Events in Judea, Samaria, and Gaza" to provide the Israeli press, but primarily the foreign media—the 200 correspondents regularly stationed in Israel and the more than 700 others who had arrived to cover the uprising—with "accurate and reliable information on the activity in the territories on a daily basis."

A practical problem was that information was to be given out only "after it had been corroborated by all relevant Civil Administration and IDF units," to ensure that information was both comprehensive and correct. In practice, the cumbersome army bureaucracy, compounded by stringent field-security considerations, often delayed official reactions to events, enabling Palestinian sources to put out their own versions of events first and meet journalists' deadlines. In some cases, the IDF Spokesman's Unit was itself the unwitting victim of false reporting and misinformation from the field. Thus, an initial denial about the "bulldozer burying incident" later had to be retracted. The Media Information Center operated for about seven weeks during the height of the mass violence (January 24–March 18), issuing a daily "Operational Update" sheet summing up the day's events in the territories. Such efforts, however well-intentioned, could not overcome the gap between official pronouncements and the situation in the field as it was documented by the media and other foreign observers.

The information center's closure came, coincidentally or not, in conjunction with a shift in the overall Israeli approach toward the uprising. In late March the army began imposing new, collective measures—emergency orders of various kinds—that impinged on journalists as well as on the Palestinian population.

In connection with Land Day—an annual event (March 30) on the calendar of Israeli Arabs, commemorating a violent general strike held in 1976 to protest land expropriations—residents of the territories would not be permitted to enter or leave Israel proper for three days, and a full curfew was imposed. Journalists could enter the territories and move about in them "only upon authorization of the IDF Spokesman's Office [and then] only if escorted by an IDF representative." Informally it was explained that media presence was known to trigger rioting. The IDF said that it would organize "press pools," an arrangement in which small groups of journalists could cover a story and share the material with their colleagues.

This unprecedented move, amounting to the reinstatement of the pre-1967 Green

Line, led the Foreign Press Association to take an unprecedented move of its own: the association petitioned the High Court of Justice against the IDF. The closure of the territories to the media, the petition argued, "constitutes a grave and unprecedented infringement of freedom of the press and the public's right to know." At the hearing, held on March 30, Nili Arad, from the State Attorney's Office, representing the IDF and the defense establishment, declared without embellishment, "This is a real war. The situation in the field is the same as in a war. Therefore the military commander found it necessary to close the area and declare it a military zone." The justices did not grant an interim order allowing the press into the territories that day, though they did commit the court to deal with the principles involved at a later date. Effectively, the army had its way.

In the event, neither the absence of the media from the territories on Land Day (with the exception of two pool teams totaling about 15 journalists), nor the stringent measures imposed by the military—including orders to the heavily reinforced troops to act "firmly and forcefully" against all attempts to disrupt public order—prevented the outbreak of widespread violent disturbances, particularly in the rural areas of the West Bank. The day's toll: 4 persons killed (all in West Bank villages) and at least 50 wounded in the West Bank and the Gaza Strip (where refugee-camp residents defied the curfew and demonstrated) by IDF gunfire. Six Israelis—three soldiers and three civilians—were injured by stones.

Besides the blanket sealing off of the area for several consecutive days at critical times—notably around Land Day and Independence Day, during the Palestine National Council session in November that proclaimed an "independent Palestinian State," and when Arafat appeared at the UN in December—curfew was routinely imposed over whole populations, and the authority to declare an area a "closed military zone" was granted to the "senior officer" at the site, whatever his rank, instead of "military commanders." This measure was frequently resorted to on an "instant" basis to keep the press at bay during disturbances: officers reportedly took to carrying closure orders prepared in advance, which they brandished at the first sign of trouble.

Palestinian Press

Paralleling the process through which the military exercised growing control over media access to the territories, the authorities continued to target, far more intensively than in past years, the East Jerusalem-based Palestinian press. Four of the 32 Palestinians deported in 1988 were journalists, including two, Bashir Nafeh (April 11) and Samir Sbeihat (August 1), from the East Jerusalem daily *al-Fajr*. The exponential increase in the recourse to "administrative detention" (arrest without trial based on classified material under the 1945 Defense [Emergency] Regulations promulgated by the British Mandate government and not repealed by Israel) to suppress the intellectual leadership of the uprising netted at least 20 Palestinian journalists.

Both the Gaza Press Service and *al-Awda* magazine were closed down by the authorities (the former for six months) in 1988, as were the English-language version of *al-Awdah* and its parent company, Palestine Press Services, for six months on March 31, extended for an additional year on September 30. The latter had been especially valued by the foreign press as a source of information about the territories. Several other press and information offices were also shut down for periods ranging from three months to a year. In all these cases, the authorities charged that the publications and information officers were "tools" or "fronts" for various Palestinian terrorist organizations and were funded by them.

Inside Israel, for the second year running, an Israeli-Palestinian publication based in West Jerusalem, legally registered with the Interior Ministry, abiding by military censorship regulations and supplying reliable information on the occupied territories, was shut down and its staff arrested and accused of security offenses. In 1987 this had been the fate of the fortnightly *News from Within*, published by the Alternative Information Center (see AJYB 1989, p. 376), while in 1988 the publication in question was a radical left-wing fortnightly called *Derekh Hanitzotz* ("by means of the spark") in its Hebrew version and *Tariq al-Sharara* in its Arabic version. On February 16, Ribhi Arouri, the paper's Palestinian editor, was arrested, interrogated for three weeks, and placed under administrative detention. Two days after his arrest the weekly was shut down by order of the commissioner of the Jerusalem District on the ground that it had ties with Nayef Hawatmeh's Democratic Front for the Liberation of Palestine (DFLP). However, only when the paper's Jewish editorial staff of four were detained one by one during April and May did the story make headlines in Israel.

The four, all in their 30s, were Ya'akov Ben-Efrat and his estranged wife, Roni Ben-Efrat; Michal Schwartz, the daughter of a distinguished Israeli historian, Prof. (emeritus) Yehoshua Arieli; and Assaf Adiv, who had been the paper's publisher and the brother of Ehud Aviv, paroled in 1985 after serving a lengthy prison term for spying on behalf of the Syrians. Like the case of the Alternative Information Center the previous year, the closure of *Derekh Hanitzotz* and the arrest of its editors attracted international attention and gave rise to charges that "national security" was being falsely brandished in order to stifle press freedom and deny the public information.

On May 25, the four Israelis under arrest were charged with a number of security violations, including membership in a terrorist organization and contact with a foreign agent. According to the charge sheet, they had made contact with DFLP personnel in London in late 1983 or early 1984 and had agreed to publish a paper in Israel with DFLP funding and to set up a Jewish-Arab political organization—as indeed they had done. On June 16, Supreme Court justice Aharon Barak accepted the appeal of the State and overturned a decision by the Jerusalem district court to release three of the four detainees on bail. Citing the extreme gravity of the charges, Barak ordered that all four be held in custody until the end of the proceedings against them. The trial began in September before a tribunal in the Jerusalem district court, with the prosecution announcing that it would call 29 witnesses, including 17 Shin Bet (General Security Service) agents whose testimony would be heard *in camera*, although the rest of the proceedings were open to the public.

Second Phase—Fighting the "Alternative Government"

By mid-March the emerging perception of the Israeli defense establishment was that in the territories Israel faced a situation of "war by other means." The ultimate aim of the uprising was, as the leaflets issued by the United National Command suggested, not to throw the Jews into the sea but to replace the Israeli administration in the territories with an "alternative government" run by the Palestinians. As early as March, Palestinian employees of the Civil Administration, particularly policemen and tax-department clerks, had obeyed the leadership's call to resign. Leaflet No. 10 (March 10, 1988), for example, declared: "We renew our call for merchants to refrain from paying taxes . . . . The popular committees, including the merchant committees, should supervise the implementation of this directive." Furthermore, "our shopkeepers" were urged "to boycott both Israeli and foreign products where there is a locally produced alternative." Businesses and professionals—doctors, pharmacists, and lawyers—were urged to lower their prices: "Now is the time for real solidarity between all sections of our society."

From the Palestinians' standpoint, a major achievement of the uprising was the forging of this sense of solidarity and of a shared destiny among all sectors of their society. The different political camps overcame their differences to form the United National Command of the Uprising, and virtually all the social strata in the territories took part in the insurrection, in one form or another. Writing in the *Jerusalem Post* in September, Shukri B. Abed, an Israeli Arab researcher at the Hebrew University's Truman Institute for the Advancement of Peace, argued that the events in the territories should be seen in part as a "social revolution" within Palestinian society:

> The *intifada* is a multifaceted phenomenon. It is, to be sure, a *political* phenomenon, an "uprising" against the long years of oppressive occupation. But it is also a *social and psychological* phenomenon: an awakening, a self-cleansing, a breaking away from the Palestinians' own past, from the heavy weight of inherited social structures that have outlived their usefulness. [Emphases in the original.]

It was the security forces' struggle against the growing manifestations of autonomy in the territories, chiefly through the use of bureaucratic and administrative measures, that dominated the second phase of Israel's struggle against the *intifada*.

PREVENTING CIVIL DISOBEDIENCE

On March 19, the Shabiba youth movement was outlawed in the territories, several hundred of its activists—nearly all from the West Bank—were arrested, and a number of youth clubs that had served as centers of activity for the Shabiba were closed down by administrative fiat. For some years, the Shabiba ("youth" in Arabic) had, in effect, filled the vacuum created by the absence of a recognized leadership in the territories. Over the years—well before the *intifada*—the Shabiba had become a dominant force in the territories, especially in West Bank high schools and refugee camps. In the camps, they engaged in communal and cultural activity, though this was tinged with heavy ideological-nationalist overtones.

According to the military, the Shabiba was outlawed because it was a "front organization" for Fatah, and its activists were instigators of violence. Beyond this, it was noted, the move was part of a concerted drive by the Israeli authorities to suppress attempts aimed at escalating the civil revolt and creating independent, Palestinian-run administrative structures as an alternative to the Civil Administration.

Exactly five months after the outlawing of the Shabiba movement, on August 18, the so-called popular committees that had sprung up in the territories were also declared illegal. Members of the committees, persons attending meetings sponsored by them, found in possession of leaflets issued by them, or donating money to them were liable to a ten-year prison term. Unlike the Shabiba, the popular committees were a distinctly *intifada*-related phenomenon, although in some cases their origins preceded the uprising. The committees, which had been set up in virtually every village, refugee camp, and urban neighborhood in the territories, were responsible at the grass-roots level for providing various social and communal services to the population in the emergency situation engendered by the uprising.

The legal problem faced by the authorities in combating these essentially mutual-aid activities was that they were not manifestly criminal or unlawful or violent in character. Thus, for example, "medical assistance committees" based in Ramallah, which had operated openly for some time before the uprising, expanded their work during the *intifada* within the framework of the popular committees. The popular committees also organized classes in private homes for school-aged children in the wake of the extended closure of the educational system in the territories.

What particularly troubled the defense establishment was the process by which these committees were undermining the Civil Administration by creating alternative institutions, in this case at the level of community services, and imbuing the population with a growing sense of independence. In an Israel Radio interview on August 18, Defense Minister Rabin—who on more than one occasion had complained that existing laws prevented the military from dealing with the uprising efficiently—stated that the outlawing of the popular committees (under a special order drawn up by defense establishment legal advisers based on the 1945 Defense [Emergency] Regulations) provided "a convenient legal tool" for dealing with the problem. Rabin explained that the security authorities had decided to act against the popular committees because "they constitute a basis for the continuation and institutionalization of the uprising."

In fact, the committees continued to function, as did two other bodies that were also banned: the "regional guidance committees," which organized demonstrations and disturbances against the Israeli authorities at the local level; and the "strike forces," groups of young toughs who acted as "enforcers" for the United National Command of the Uprising and operated against "collaborators" with the Israeli authorities. (A number of suspected or known "collaborators" were killed by other Palestinians during the year—see below.)

Other organizations targeted in 1988 included trade unions and various charitable societies. Such associations had been closed down sporadically in previous years, but as the uprising took root in the territories, the drive against them appeared to become more systematic. Among the charitable, social, and educational organizations closed down—on June 20, for a two-year period—was the In'ash al-Usra (family rehabilitation) society in the town of el-Bireh, the largest body of its kind in the West Bank. It had been operating for 23 years and was run by a well-known woman activist in the territories, Samiha Khalil, aged 65. The closure order (which excluded the orphanage and kindergarten) followed a raid on the organization's premises on June 8, while el-Bireh was under curfew, in which the Israeli authorities reported that they had seized inflammatory and anti-Semitic material, including videotapes and printed literature. In a press conference held on June 21, the society's staff denied all the charges and asserted that the closure would deprive thousands of Palestinian women of their earnings from various community projects and hundreds of underprivileged children of vital services. The society subsequently petitioned the High Court of Justice to rescind the closure order, shortly after Khalil was charged with incitement and distribution of "hostile material."

DEPORTATIONS

In addition to closing down institutions, the authorities also took administrative measures against individual activists. The harshest of these was deportation. As already mentioned, 32 Palestinians were deported in 1988—the most in a single year since 1972—and expulsion orders were pending against another 27 persons at year's end. Besides journalists, the list of deportees included trade-union and campus activists. Six of the eight persons expelled on April 19 were from the West Bank village of Beita, having been singled out for their involvement in the catastrophic incident there two weeks earlier (see below). The vast majority (25) of the still-pending deportation orders were against persons who, according to the IDF communiqué, were "directly involved in the actions and operations of the 'popular committees' according to instructions from the terrorist organizations, whose aim is for these committees to replace the Civil Administration in the territories."

The legal proceedings involving three of the deportees—Abd al-Nasser al-Affo, aged 32, Jamal Ahati al-Hindi, aged 30, both from Jenin and both activists at an-Najah University in Nablus; and Abd al-Aziz Uda Rafih, a leading "ideologue and spiritual mentor" of the Islamic Jihad movement in the Gaza Strip, according to the IDF—predated the *intifada*. They had appealed the expulsion order to the High Court of Justice (even though the High Court had never blocked a deportation order), arguing that deportations from the territories constituted a violation of Article 49 of the 1949 Fourth Geneva Convention.

In a benchmark decision handed down on April 10, the court, sitting in an expanded panel of five justices headed by Supreme Court president Meir Shamgar, dismissed the petition. The court found that the relevant paragraph of Article 49 had to be read in the context of the World War II situation. The idea, according to the Israeli justices, had been to prevent mass transfers such as those carried out by the Nazis for extermination or forced labor, and therefore Article 49 did not refer to expulsions for security reasons.

MUBARAK AWAD

The High Court was also called on to rule in a deportation case of a different category, one which became a cause célèbre. Mubarak Awad, aged 44, a self-proclaimed disciple of Mahatma Gandhi and Martin Luther King, and the director of the East Jerusalem-based Center for the Study of Nonviolence, had been targeted by the security authorities even before the *intifada* as a fomenter of unrest in the territories. However, there were both technical and political problems. Awad was a Jerusalem native who held American citizenship and enjoyed the protection of the American embassy and the intercession on his behalf of the highest levels of the State Department. In other circumstances Awad might have been left alone—especially as he was said to have little personal following in the territories—but with the *intifada* raging, his ideas could be depicted as helping to ignite a full-scale civil revolt.

As a native of Jerusalem, Awad had been granted permanent residence in Israel but had declined citizenship when East Jerusalem was annexed in 1967. In 1970 he went to study in the United States, eventually receiving a doctoral degree in psychology. He was granted resident status in 1973 and U.S. citizenship five years later. He visited Israel some 15 times after 1983, entering as a tourist on his U.S. passport, and in 1985 he established the Center for the Study of Non-Violence in East Jerusalem. On May 5, 1988, Prime Minister and Acting Interior Minister Yitzhak Shamir signed an order for Awad's deportation on the ground that Awad had been in the country illegally since November 1987, when his visa expired. Moreover, according to a May 6 communiqué issued by the prime minister's media adviser, Aviezer Pazner, via the Government Press Office—one of a series of position papers issued in the case, due to the American connection and intense media interest: "Awad caused harm to the security of the state and to public order," the center he headed "received [funds] from terror organization sources abroad," and its purpose was "to develop in Judea, Samaria and Gaza a widespread movement of 'passive resistance' that would stir up a civilian uprising and force Israel to retreat from these areas."

His avowed nonviolent philosophy notwithstanding, Awad was also accused of supporting the PLO's "armed struggle" and of "having contacts with the PLO leadership." He was described as being "one of the main contributors" to the uprising in the territories, having helped to draft leaflets of the United National Command.

Awad was arrested on May 6; on May 8 he appealed the deportation order to the High Court of Justice, but lost the appeal. Awad was deported to the United States on June 13, where he immediately became a media star, carrying his message to the American public. On June 15, *Ha'aretz* reported that the O/C Central Command, General Mitzna, then in the States on a lecture tour, had told Israeli embassy staff that it was difficult to know where Awad was doing more damage to Israel—in Jerusalem or in the United States.

ADMINISTRATIVE DETENTION

One of the principal measures resorted to by the authorities to eradicate the *intifada* involved the use of administrative detention on an unprecedented scale. Under the Israeli occupation, the practice had been widespread until the late 1970s but was nearly abandoned between 1980 and 1985. Moreover, in 1980 the procedures for implementing administrative detention were tightened in the wake of assurances given by Prime Minister Menahem Begin to U.S. president Jimmy Carter (at Egypt's request). Under the amended ordinance, only a "regional commander" (a major general) could issue an administrative-detention order (until then, this prerogative belonged to any "military commander" holding the rank of colonel or above), incarceration was limited to six months, and judicial review was provided for beyond what the Geneva Convention required.

Like other measures, such as deportations and house demolitions, reinstituted by Defense Minister Rabin after all but being jettisoned under the Begin government, administrative detention was restored as an active deterrent measure in mid-1985. Over 300 persons were administratively detained in the following 30 months, until the outbreak of the *intifada*, and some 70 persons were serving terms of detention on December 9, 1987, when the uprising began. On March 17, 1988 (the day before the Shabiba movement was outlawed), Chief of Staff Shomron approved a harsher version of the regulations governing administrative detention than that in force before 1980. Under the new rules, any military commander could issue an administrative detention order for a six-month period with the possibility of its extension. The entire judicial review process was abolished, and the detainee's only recourse was to appeal the order—at his own initiative—before a military appeals committee possessing limited powers.

Again Israel was willing to brave American and international criticism and to violate its own pronouncements concerning its principles in the territories—in this case, that administrative detention was an exceptional measure and was implemented, in accordance with the stipulates of the Geneva Convention, only in special cases—to achieve its goal of quelling the uprising. No fewer than 4,000 administrative-detention orders were issued in the course of 1988 (the figure was given by the military advocate-general, Brig. Gen. Amnon Strashnow, in an interview with the IDF weekly *Bamahaneh*, November 23), the vast majority against Palestinian intellectuals and professionals—lawyers, human-rights monitors, journalists, and campus, trade-union, and community activists. At year's end, some 1,500 persons were still being held in administrative detention, more than 20 times the figure on the eve of the uprising.

Once more, the most prominent Palestinian held in administrative detention was Faisal al-Husseini, who had been imprisoned without charge almost consecutively since April 1987. Husseini was released on June 9 from two successive periods of administrative detention totaling nine months, but was again detained, this time for six months, on July 31 by order of the defense minister. At the same time, the East Jerusalem-based Arab Studies Society founded and headed by Husseini was closed down for a year by order of the O/C Central Command under the 1945 Defense (Emergency) Regulations. According to the police announcement, Husseini had "renewed his subversive and hostile activities within the framework of the Fatah organization" immediately after being released in June, and had engaged in "coordination, incitement [and] institutionalization of the uprising." The Arab Studies Society was said to be "controlled and financed by Fatah" and to have served as the venue for "meetings of activists in terrorist organizations." Following a past pattern, Husseini's July arrest came four days after he spoke at a Peace Now meeting and advocated a two-state solution.

The huge number of arrests in 1988—in addition to the 4,000 administrative detainees, 17,000 other Palestinians were taken into custody at some point during the year (according to a briefing by Defense Minister Rabin to the Knesset's Defense and Foreign Affairs Committee on December 28)—placed a tremendous strain on the existing detention facilities in the territories. At any given time 5,000 persons were in prison for *intifada*-related offenses, of whom about a quarter were administrative detainees.

To cope with the overload, new military prisons were set up, including one in December 1987 at Dahariya, near Hebron, on the grounds of an IDF base, and in mid-March 1988 at Ketziyot, in the Negev desert—inside Israel proper—not far from the border with Egypt. Complaints about serious overcrowding at both installations as well as intolerable physical conditions and abusive treatment by prison guards were voiced frequently during the year.

On December 20, an officer and four soldiers, one of them a woman, were sentenced to prison terms after being convicted on 22 counts of assaulting and maltreating bound and blindfolded detainees at Dahariya in March. The court, basing itself on testimony given during the trial, concluded that abuse of prisoners was "the norm" at Dahariya. On December 28, the Association for Civil Rights in Israel made public a report on Dahariya drawn up following a visit by an ACRI delegation a month earlier. The group had found that, despite efforts to improve conditions, in its present state the facility remained "unfit for human beings."

At Ketziyot, where nearly all the administrative detainees were incarcerated, it took a visit by three Supreme Court justices before improvements were reported. On April 27, a petition to the High Court of Justice was filed by 14 administrative detainees at Ketziyot. They argued that their incarceration outside the occupied territories was unlawful because the order under which they were detained specified that the detention facility must be located in an area subject to military command—Israel in fact declared the detention site a "closed military area"—and violated Article 76 of the Fourth Geneva Convention, which prohibited the transfer of residents of occupied zones to the territory of the occupying power. The petition also referred to the "inhuman" physical conditions in the huge tent complex and the "brutal" behavior of the guards. The 14 were joined by 3 other detainees, incarcerated in the West Bank, who asked the court to block their transfer to Ketziyot.

On September 1, the three justices sitting in the case, led by Supreme Court president Meir Shamgar, took the unusual step of visiting the facility. Of the 2,750 prisoners there at the time, all but 312 were administrative detainees. The judges, attired in black suits despite the searing heat, heard inmates' complaints about living conditions, punishments for infractions of the rules, and the inability of the review boards to cope with the volume of appeals—fewer than half of the appeals submitted had been heard. In its decision, handed down on November 8, the High Court rejected the detainees' petition but was critical of the conditions at the facility and recommended establishment of an advisory committee to monitor conditions at the camp (this was duly set up, headed by a military judge).

COLLECTIVE MEASURES

The IDF consistently denied that it employed collective punishments (prohibited under the Geneva Convention) in the territories. When Chief of Staff Shomron was asked point-blank, in an interview (October 28) with Israel TV's Arabic Language Service, whether "the policy of collective punishment [will] continue," he declared unequivocally that "no policy of collective punishment exists." He then added: "Anyone who claims that this is a popular uprising should not be surprised if some of the punishments are directed against large groups. . . . Whoever contends that an entire village is involved in the uprising has to understand that, unfortunately, some [IDF] responses will entail harm to the entire village."

Probably the most sweeping and sustained action of this kind taken in the occupied territories, primarily in the West Bank, was the shutting down of the educational system for most of the year. To begin with, all the institutions of higher learning throughout the territories were closed early in 1988, "until further notice," and were not permitted to reopen for the rest of the year. This measure affected about 18,000 students in the West Bank and 3,500 in Gaza, as well as several thousand faculty and administrative staff. As in other spheres, the measures against this sector took to a logical extreme patterns that had evolved previously: in the years leading up to the *intifada*, the universities and colleges had been targeted with growing frequency by the military as "hotbeds of incitement."

Measures against the lower educational system, however, were implemented with a methodical intensity different from anything that had gone before. The 1,194 government (i.e., Civil Administration), private, and UNRWA schools in the West Bank—at the elementary, junior-high, and high-school levels—with a total enrollment of some 310,000 pupils, were closed down on February 4 and allowed to reopen (on a staggered basis) starting at the end of May, were shut down for two days in mid-June, and closed again from July 21 until November 30, reopening on December 1. Effectively, the entire 1987–88 school year was lost in the West Bank. By contrast, in the Gaza Strip the school system continued to function normally. Indeed, in Gaza an extra three weeks were added to the school year in June to partially compensate for the large number of days lost, even when schools were open, due primarily to extended curfews. Even in East Jerusalem, more than 35 different closure orders were issued, and for all but kindergarten and first-grade pupils the school year opened late in the fall of 1988.

To the Palestinians, at least, the most convincing proof that the Israeli claim that the closures were necessitated by security considerations was a mere pretext was the military's relentless drive against all forms of "alternative education" or "popular education." Troops raided small classes held in private homes, often arresting those present. Indeed, from this point of view, the shutting down of the educational system was counterproductive for the Civil Administration, since the establishment of independent educational frameworks helped the Palestinians cut themselves off from the Civil Administration. At the same time, the leadership of the uprising was also unhappy with this state of affairs. Even though three-quarters of the pupils in the West Bank attended government-run schools—run, that is, by the Civil Administration—Palestinians at all levels demanded the reopening of the schools to prevent what they feared would be irreversible damage to the young generation.

The Bureaucratic War

The Israeli authorities recognized that even if the struggle for the hearts and minds of the populace was a lost cause, the outward trappings of orderly relations had to be retained. This was essential, in the short term, to ensure the smooth functioning of the Military Government—including the collection of taxes from the residents, the Civil Administration's primary source of revenue. In the longer term, the authorities sought to prevent the creation of a vacuum that would be filled by the PLO and eventuate in the establishment of an independent Palestinian state.

COMMERCE; TAXES

The commercial sector was an early and ongoing arena of struggle. The commercial strike in the territories and in East Jerusalem, which was launched immediately after the start of the *intifada*, was one of the most blatant signs of the population's defiance of the authorities as well as of Palestinian solidarity. The defense establishment spared no efforts, therefore, to break the strike. Initially, methods used in previous years were tried: shopkeepers were ordered to open for business; if this failed to produce the desired result, troops forced open their shops and/or welded them shut. Various other tactics were tried during the year with equally little success.

Measures were taken by the Civil Administration to prevent the PLO from injecting funds into the territories in order to fuel the uprising and partially offset the self-inflicted economic hardships that affected all social levels in the territories. In February and March, the amount of money a person could bring in who entered the territories via the Jordan River bridges or an Israeli port of entry was drastically reduced; a permit was required in advance, and routinely refused, for sums exceeding about $1,000. Licensed Palestinian money changers were forbidden to visit Jordan. The authorities at Ben-Gurion International Airport seized $500,000 and opened 46 criminal files against incoming residents of the territories who were found in possession of sums exceeding the permitted amount. Palestinians claimed that the primary sufferers from these blanket sanctions would be, on the one hand, educational, health, and welfare institutions in the territories that received outside funding, and, on the other hand, the many families who were dependent on support from relatives working abroad.

The revenues collected by the Civil Administration from the local population plummeted. This was due primarily to outright refusals to pay taxes, especially VAT, and to the resignation of Palestinians employed in the Civil Administration's tax department, as well as to a ripple effect from the economic slowdown. As a result, essential services were cut and an intensive campaign was launched to offset the budget shortfall by other means. Thus, besides withholding salaries from teachers laid off by the school closures, the Civil Administration made sharp cuts in the health budget. More than 10 percent of all hospital personnel were dismissed, funds for treatment of Palestinians from the territories in Israeli hospitals were slashed by at least 80 percent, and patients admitted to government-run hospitals in the territories for treatment of wounds sustained in disturbances had to pay for three days of hospitalization in advance at about $150 per day. The whole sphere of tax collection in the territories became an arena of battle. With a shortfall of 40 percent in anticipated revenues from taxes in the first half of the year, administrative fiats were introduced to halt the tax revolt. The issuing of essential permits—drivers' licenses, birth certificates, ID cards, export-import licenses, and many others—was made contingent on proof of payment of all outstanding taxes, including income tax, VAT, property tax, municipal tax, and in some cases even traffic tickets. Cars of residents found to be in arrears to the authorities were impounded at roadblocks; tax-collection sweeps were carried out in which property of persons who could not prove payment of all taxes was confiscated or attached.

The most widely publicized case in this realm was that of Beit Sahour, an affluent town of some 9,000 Christian Arabs near Bethlehem. On July 7, the authorities mounted a large-scale tax-collection raid in the town, where some 300 residents had responded to tax claims by returning their government-issued ID cards to the municipality. A curfew imposed on Beit Sahour during the tax raid was lifted ten days later, shortly after the Association for Civil Rights in Israel informed the Central Command legal adviser that it intended to petition the High Court of Justice against the prolonged closure.

In a letter dated October 24 to the Ramallah-based al-Haq Law in the Service of Man group, which had charged that Israeli tax-collection tactics in the territories were "arbitrary" and "extra-judicial," the Judea and Samaria Region legal adviser, Col. David Yahav, wrote that soldiers accompanied tax collectors "only for security reasons" and that the Beit Sahour curfew had been imposed "only after a riot by the residents took place, for security reasons and to safeguard public order."

In the Gaza Strip a more comprehensive tactic was employed to facilitate control over the population. Beginning on May 10, the Civil Administration in Gaza began replacing the ID cards of some 450,000 adult local residents with new color-coded cards to make identification of the bearer easier at roadblocks or during search operations. The fact that access to Israel would be denied to those without cards guaranteed the success of the operation, since nearly 50 percent of Gaza's working population was employed in Israel, generally in menial labor. However, in order to receive a new card, residents had to pay a fee and show proof of payment of all taxes and other levies, and proof, in the form of a stamped document, that they were not wanted for questioning by the security forces.

One of the harshest punitive economic sanctions applied against the Palestinians in an effort to break the uprising was the issuing of sporadic bans on growing, harvesting, and/or exporting agricultural crops. Also, during prolonged curfews in a number of villages, crops rotted on the ground when residents were denied access to their fields. Most damaging were the measures taken against the West Bank's agricultural mainstay, the olive crop. On a number of occasions, the military uprooted olive trees, usually groves along roadsides which had been giving cover to persons throwing stones or firebombs at Israeli vehicles, or as sheer punishment, notably in the case of Beita, where some seven acres of trees were dug up following the incident there in April (see below). During the olive harvest itself, beginning in October, picking and marketing of the fruit were often prohibited, and olive presses were shut down in various locales, particularly in the Jenin area, following unrest or as a means of coercing villagers to cooperate with the Civil Administration.

FOREST FIRES

If the Israeli authorities uprooted trees, Palestinians burned them. In the period from May to September there were some 1,200 forest and brush fires throughout the country, which ravaged about 38,000 acres of woodlands, fields, and fruit orchards. This was four times the number of fires in 1987. At the height of the summer, the Jewish National Fund, the body responsible for planting and maintaining forests, had to cope with some 50 big fires a week. It was estimated that about half the fires were being deliberately set by hostile arsonists, in the main, Palestinians from the territories, though also some Israeli Arabs, often children—for nationalist reasons. On at least one occasion the United National Command of the Uprising urged the population to torch Israeli targets. Leaflet No. 19 of June 8 designated June 22 as a general-strike day and a "return to the land" on which the soil was to be "enriched and sown" and "enemy industrial and agricultural property is to be destroyed and burned."

In fact, although this "day of burnings," as it was dubbed in media headlines, did not produce many fires, it did have the effect of stretching Israeli resources and manpower to the limit. Anticipating intense arson efforts, the army and the police, along with about 1,500 staff and volunteers from the JNF and the Nature Conservation Authority, declared a countrywide alert. Ground and air patrols operated across broad areas. The day's count was 14 minor fires of which 8 were deliberately set—well below the average (in the week beginning June 12, 132 fires were reported in the country).

ECONOMIC EFFECTS

While the economic damage caused by forest fires was largely indirect and of a long-term character, the cumulative economic consequences of the actions and counteractions taken by the Palestinians and the Israeli authorities were direct and immediate for both Israel (see below) and the territories. Allowing for difficulties in collecting data in the territories, the Central Bureau of Statistics estimated that in 1988 in the West Bank, available per capita private income declined by 16 percent in fixed prices, following an increase of 12 percent in each of the two preceding years. The GNP in the West Bank fell by 12–15 percent after a per annum growth of 8 percent in 1986–1987; the figures for Gaza were substantially the same. Residents of the territories put in about 25 percent fewer workdays, both locally and in Israel, than in 1987. The decline in work hours in Israel was twice as high in industry (35 percent) as it was in agriculture (18 percent). In the West Bank itself, however, work in the agricultural sector increased by some 15 percent, as did agricultural production, reflecting both the drive toward self-sufficiency and sheer necessity. Agricultural production remained stable in the Gaza Strip, where topography and tradition precluded the option of the "return to the land" that existed in Judea and Samaria: fully 96 percent of the Gazans who worked in Israel had no recourse to agriculture that could sustain them without work in Israel, while the comparable figure in the West Bank was 68 percent.

Public consumption (the value of the services given by the Civil Administration and the local authorities) decreased by 16 percent in the West Bank, following 9-percent increases in each of the preceding two years, and by 3 percent in Gaza, following an average per annum increase of 11 percent in the previous two years. Likewise, investments in fixed assets fell by about a quarter in the West Bank after an average per annum increase of 15 percent in 1986 and 1987. A particularly steep decline—44 percent—occurred in investments by the Civil Administration and the local authorities (in road building, construction, and equipment), following a 26-percent growth in the previous two years. In the Gaza Strip, investments in fixed assets were off by 13 percent and in public investments by 28 percent. Industrial production in the West Bank dropped by 8 percent, but by 23 percent without the production of olive oil; the Gaza Strip registered a 20-percent fall in industrial production. Construction in the West Bank was down by about 30 percent, following a 12-percent growth in the two preceding years, while in Gaza it fell by 13 percent.

Compounding this already harsh state of affairs was a drastic decline of more than 40 percent in the value of the Jordanian dinar. The overall result was that the standard of living in the occupied territories fell by about a third in the course of a single year.

Terrorism and Vigilantism

Blood feuds and other forms of intracommunal violence were traditional in Palestinian society, and the uprising added to them a new element, political assassination. Primarily, this took the form of attacks against known or suspected "collaborators" with Israel by the "strike forces," the "commando" units of the popular committees, or by entire villages. As the uprising became more institutionalized, such assaults increased in frequency and intensified in brutality. For many Israelis the killings, and especially the savagery which attended them, tended to validate their perception of Arabs in general as violence-prone and confirmed their worst fears of what would be in store if an independent Palestinian state were established on Israel's doorstep.

Of the approximately 20 killings of Palestinians by Palestinians in 1988, virtually all in the West Bank, perhaps the most barbaric was the first, the lynching of a 42-year-old resident of the West Bank village of Kabatiya, Muhammad al-Ayed, said to have sired 15 children by three wives. On February 24, hundreds of villagers surrounded Ayed's home, shouting that he was a traitor and demanding that he come out. Ayed defended himself against the mob with an automatic weapon (issued to him, as to others who worked with the Israeli authorities, by the Shin Bet), killing a 14-year-old boy and wounding 15 other persons before he was seized and his home set ablaze. When Israeli security forces finally reached the scene they found Ayed's battered body hanging from an electricity pole with a Palestinian flag flying above. In a predawn punitive action the next day, troops and Shin Bet personnel arrested about 100 villagers suspected of participating in the murder and demolished the houses of the two main suspects.

Subsequently, two more houses were blown up and several hundred persons arrested. In an effort to deter more attacks on "collaborators," the IDF sealed Kabatiya from the outside world for 37 consecutive days, cut off its supplies of water, electricity, and cooking gas, and closed its principal source of revenue, stone quarries. Nevertheless, Israeli journalists who entered the town through back roads reported that morale was high and that the events had intensified the inhabitants' sense of solidarity. For subsistence they had resorted to the ways of their ancestors, drawing water from wells, using wood for fuel, living off the land, and employing medicinal herbs in the absence of proper medical treatment. They had also smuggled in supplies from nearby villages through the surrounding hills.

On March 2, Leaflet No. 9 of the United National Command of the Uprising congratulated "heroic" Kabatiya for "teaching a lesson to the betrayers of the homeland" and called on all Palestinian employees of the Civil Administration and all Palestinian policemen "to resign immediately and join the popular masses in their heroic struggle." Five days later a Jericho policeman was murdered near his home, evidently as an example to others. Some 300 policemen in the territories promptly resigned.

The first week of October saw the murder of three more "collaborators," including Mustafa Abu Bakr, the mukhtar (headman) of the village of Bidya, near Kalkilya, who was suspected by villagers of cooperating with the Israeli authorities and of being involved in land sales to Jewish buyers. Immediately after Bakr's killing, Bidya was placed under curfew for four days and the army blew up five houses of suspects. An IDF announcement on December 7—see also below—stated that members of a "local terrorist cell" had confessed to the crime. On the day of Bakr's murder a man from the village of Anin, near Jenin, was shot to death while sitting in a cafe in the Israeli-Arab town of Umm al-Fahm. Residents of Anin celebrated the murder of the "treacherous dog."

Settlers

The long-term significance of such attacks, the *Jerusalem Post*'s Yehuda Litani wrote after the Abu Bakr killing, was to "seriously impair Israel's ability to control the territories through surrogates." To no one did this development appear more menacing than to the Jewish settlers in the areas, whose sheer physical well-being depended on the Palestinians "knowing their place" as that conception dictated. The two types of Jewish settlers in the territories, those who were driven by a mystical, quasi-messianic yearning for the biblical Land of Israel and those—the overwhelming majority of the Jewish inhabitants of the territories—who had been lured there by government-subsidized housing, now found themselves locked into a true "pioneering" situation. The latter were for the most part nonreligious and cared little for abstract ideologies; they wanted only a quiet life in country villas set in tight-knit communities where the air was clean and the streets were safe and the children had space to grow—suburbia in Samaria. As for their indigenous neighbors, the Palestinian Arabs, the settlers were part of a generation of Jews that had become accustomed to looking at Arabs, if at all, as garbage collectors, construction workers, street sweepers, and dishwashers in restaurants. It came as a profound shock to the new suburbanites when these previously invisible Arabs suddenly turned into highly visible "Palestinians" and launched a concerted campaign to drive them out of their newfound Eden.

The ideological settlers of Gush Emunim, on the other hand, tended to view the Arabs as the incarnation of the biblical "Amalek," the adversary of the Hebrews who was to be expunged from the Land of Israel, or, at best, as bearing the halakhic status of "resident stranger." They also looked at the unfolding events as fulfilling the Divine Plan, perhaps the onset of the cataclysms traditionally associated with the "birth pangs of the Messiah." Therefore, taking a millenarian approach, they were able to evince a modicum of forbearance, at least in the early part of the uprising, certain that though their triumph might tarry, it would surely come.

By definition, the nonideological settlers lacked a sustaining vision of this kind. If the IDF, whose manifest task it was to keep the "locals" in place, could not or would not suppress the Arab troublemakers, then the settlers would fend for themselves. The upshot was that, as the *intifada* intensified, the nonideological settlers (along with the Kahanists of Kiryat Arba, who were beyond the pale even for the other groups) increasingly spearheaded "reprisals," "patrols," "vigilante" actions, and other aggressive "self-defense" tactics. Far more frequently than in past years, therefore, Israeli soldiers found themselves having to act as a buffer between enraged settlers and Palestinians. From this point of view, the situation was far more volatile in the West Bank than in the Gaza Strip, where fewer than 3,000 Jews, including children, resided in 14 settlements, and "bypass" roads enabled the settlers to reach their homes as though the local population did not exist. In the West Bank, however, many of the roads to Jewish settlements ran next to or through Arab towns and villages, and the potential for confrontation was ever present.

Another factor in the West Bank equation was the O/C Central Command, Maj. Gen. Amram Mitzna, who was said to be "soft" on Arabs—a reputation he had picked up in 1982, when he objected to IDF actions in Beirut during the Lebanon War. Six years later Mitzna served as a lightning rod for much of the settlers' wrath at what they believed was the military's deliberate refusal to stamp out the uprising. In the Gaza Strip, in contrast, the O/C Southern Command, Maj. Gen. Yitzhak Mordechai, a no-nonsense type who could "speak to the Arabs in their own language" and had a well-developed public relations sense to boot, was generally perceived to be the right person in the right place.

Toward the end of January, at the height of the stage of violent mass confrontations between Palestinians and Israeli troops, Yisrael Harel, editor of the settlers' journal *Nekudah*, told a *Jerusalem Post* reporter: "Everything has been going on during this period like always. . . . We've even had Arabs from the area coming to shop for food in our grocery because of the commercial strike which has kept [Arab businesses] shut down. For us, it's been business as usual." Yet within two weeks (February 4), a fellow resident of Harel's from the Gush Emunim settlement of Ofra, Meshulam Moskowitz, a 30-year-old immigrant from Brooklyn, suffered a fractured skull when he was hit by a rock in an ambush at Kafr Malik in Samaria. Four days earlier a 32-year-old Beit El man, Dov Kalmanovich, had suffered severe burns when a firebomb turned his car into a blazing inferno near el-Bireh. The two attacks were part of a pattern of escalating violence against Israeli vehicles in the West Bank.

When settlers warned that they would act on their own if they did not receive more protection, Defense Minister Rabin reiterated his stand that they should take an example from Israel's northern border settlements and restrain themselves. Rabin said, "It's impossible to station a soldier to guard every settler." Taking Rabin at his word, ultranationalist settlers from Hebron and Kiryat Arba, including activists from Meir Kahane's Kach movement, began operating night patrols in the area between Hebron and Jerusalem, claiming it was their right to employ legitimate self-defense in reaction to stoning or firebomb attacks.

As the settlers became more aggressive, mere rumors of raids by them were sufficient to trigger rioting in towns and villages. On February 4, loudspeakers of mosques in Tulkarm broadcast that Jewish settlers had kidnapped local residents and urged the population to protest. As a result, several thousand persons poured into the streets, erected barricades, burned tires and garbage bins, and attacked an IDF patrol. A 26-year-old local man was shot to death when he attacked an Israeli officer.

On March 22, Defense Minister Yitzhak Rabin told the Knesset's Defense and Foreign Affairs Committee that the permission granted soldiers to open fire on Palestinians throwing or apparently about to throw firebombs was valid also for the settlers, but "only in instances of danger to life and as long as that danger lasts." This further relaxation of the rules for opening fire followed a dramatic escalation in Palestinian violence against Jewish civilians in the territories and retaliations by settlers, on both an individual and an organized basis. According to data of the IDF Spokesmans's Office, the period from February 9 to March 8 saw 2,247 violent incidents (not including firebomb attacks or the use of firearms) perpetrated in the territories against the IDF and Israeli civilians—1,730 in the West Bank and 517 in the Gaza Strip—an average of more than 75 incidents per day, and an increase of nearly 1,000 incidents over the previous month.

While settlers were occasionally questioned following attacks on Arab property— most common were night raids in which Arab-owned vehicles were vandalized, primarily in the Hebron area—investigations were usually perfunctory and charges were rarely pressed. This and a number of serious incidents demonstrated that the "dual system of justice" in the territories, documented earlier in the decade in an official report by the State Attorney's Office (the "Karp Report"—see AJYB 1986, pp. 340–341), was still in force. Arabs who stoned Israeli vehicles in and around Jerusalem were theoretically liable for 20 years' imprisonment under the section of the penal code that was invoked in such cases, and throughout the territories stone-throwers were routinely given up to a year in prison and a stiff fine. Similarly, Arabs throwing firebombs with intent to maim and murder, even if no one was hurt in the attack, usually found themselves serving up to ten years in jail. Release on bail was unheard of.

In contrast, after Pinhas Wallerstein, aged 39, a leading Gush Emunim activist and the head of the Binyamin Regional Council, was detained for questioning on January 11 in connection with the shooting death that day of Rabeh Hussein Ghanem, aged 17, and the wounding of his cousin in the village of Beitin, near the settlement of Ofra, he was released on his own surety of NIS 5,000, apparently following the intervention of one or more cabinet ministers. Wallerstein was eventually charged with manslaughter and aggravated assault, though not before the High Court intervened and the attorney general heard arguments by Wallerstein's lawyer in a rarely used procedure. On October 11, exactly ten months after the incident, Wallerstein pleaded not guilty, by reason of self-defense, when his trial opened.

On September 30, Rabbi Moshe Levinger, leader of the Jewish community in Hebron and the spearhead of the entire settlement movement in the territories since 1967, was questioned briefly by police following an incident in the center of the city in which a shop owner was shot to death and at least one other person was wounded. Reportedly, when the car in which Levinger was traveling with other members of his family was stoned, he got out of the vehicle and opened fire with his pistol. On November 22, the police recommended that Levinger be charged in connection with the incident, but a week later the State Attorney's Office returned the file to the police saying that the evidence was insufficient.

In most cases the investigations into such incidents—some 15 Palestinians died at the hands of settlers during the year—either dragged on interminably or were eventually dropped for lack of evidence. The only Jewish civilian in the territories against whom legal proceedings were completed during the year in the wake of a shooting death was Israel Ze'ev, a 37-year-old American-born resident of the Shilo settlement. On May 5, Ze'ev killed a shepherd, Jouda Awad, from the nearby village of Turmus Ayya, and wounded another while they were grazing their flock just outside the settlement. Ze'ev claimed he had acted in self-defense. The investigation revealed that the Palestinians had done nothing to provoke the firing but also that Ze'ev had intended only to scare them off. On December 4, he was sentenced to three years' imprisonment and two years' suspended and ordered to pay the victim's widow NIS 30,000 in compensation. While this was considered a stiff sentence by the settlers, it fell far short of the maximum permitted—the charges were manslaughter and aggravated assault, for which Ze'ev could have received 20 and 6 years, respectively.

Despite the violence in the territories, the number of settlers continued to increase. Although nonsettler Israelis ceased almost entirely to travel to the territories, even to visit relatives and friends, about 1,000 families (4,000 persons) moved to the West Bank and Gaza during the year. While the 6.5-percent population growth was down from the previous year's 10.7-percent rise—and both of these figures represented major decreases from the early 1980s—the fact that any increase at all was registered in the conditions of 1988 was touted as a major accomplishment by the settlement leadership. At year's end the Jewish population of the territories stood at about 71,000 (at least half of them children), as compared with at least 1.5 million Arabs.

BEITA INCIDENT

One episode in particular in 1988 demonstrated how swiftly the volcanic passions of both Israelis and Palestinians could be unleashed, and how profound were the mistrust and blinkered perceptions on both sides. One Israeli and two Palestinians were killed in the incident, and three persons, including an Israeli guard, were seriously wounded.

On April 6, during the Passover holiday, a group of 16 teenagers from Elon Moreh, a Gush Emunim settlement in Samaria, set out on a walking hike through the surrounding countryside. The Elon Moreh hikers were accompanied by two armed escorts: Roman Aldoubi, aged 26, the founder of the yeshivah at "Joseph's Tomb" in Nablus, whose militancy had led to his banishment in 1987 from Nablus for six months under a special—and unprecedented—order of the O/C Central Command; and Menachem Ilan, aged 55, who in 1984 had been convicted of destroying evidence in a fatal shooting incident for which fellow settlement member Yosef Harnoi was sentenced to ten years in prison (see AJYB 1987, p. 311; in December 1988 the Supreme Court rejected Harnoi's appeal). It was Ilan who "initiated, planned and was responsible for the hike," according to the official IDF report on the events of that day (issued April 27), written by General Mitzna following the investigation by the police, the IDF, and the Shin Bet.

As the hikers, moving through a wadi, drew near the village of Beita, the loudspeakers of the local mosque blared out a warning of their approach. Villagers later said they thought a party of armed settlers was about to attack them. Stones were thrown at the hikers from a hilltop at a distance of about 100 meters. Aldoubi fired several shots at them with his Uzi submachinegun, and then, as more villagers appeared, he exchanged his weapon for Ilan's more accurate M-16 rifle and fired a "warning shot . . . at a distance of about 50 meters," killing Moussa Salah Daoud, aged 20, and wounding another man. Villagers now surrounded the hikers and "forced" them to enter the village, "albeit without employing physical violence." The hikers formed a protective circle around Aldoubi to prevent villagers from grabbing his rifle.

The situation erupted into what the report called a "mass riot" when Mounira

Daoud, the distraught sister of the dead man and wife of the wounded man, threw a rock that struck Aldoubi in the head. "In an instinctive reaction . . . Aldoubi fired several bullets while turning around"; more shots were fired "during a struggle over Aldoubi's weapon," and the second guard, Menachem Ilan, who had earlier tried to restrain Aldoubi, was knocked senseless. The riot that ensued, in which the hikers were attacked with rocks, clubs, "and anything within reach," ended within a few minutes, and many of the villagers involved in the melee fled into the hills. As the bruised and battered hikers picked themselves up, they saw to their horror that a 15-year-old girl named Tirza Porat, daughter of Rabbi Yosef Porat, a founder of Elon Moreh, had been killed—the first Israeli civilian death of the *intifada*. A villager, Hatam Ahmed al-Jaber, aged 22, also lay dead. A second villager had been injured, and Aldoubi was unconscious (he had suffered brain damage, and remained in a coma in the hospital following surgery).

The Israeli public in general, and the settlers in particular, were shocked and appalled by the events in Beita. However, the settlers forfeited some sympathy when it emerged that the group had failed to coordinate this hike with the IDF—indeed, it was remarked that parents who sent their children on an outing of this kind seemed willing to put their lives at risk just to prove that Jews could go wherever they pleased in the Land of Israel. Senior officers, including the chief of staff, also let it be known that, contrary to the version of events put out by the hikers, who claimed immediately after the event and in a subsequent press conference that Tirza Porat had been killed either by a rock or by villagers' gunfire, the actual cause of death was a bullet from the rifle of Roman Aldoubi, who had fired wildly when he was struck in the head.

Still, the army's report placed the brunt of the blame squarely on the villagers: "The motivation and aggression evinced by the local Arabs and their readiness to harm a group of Jewish hikers constitute the primary elements in the unfolding of the incident and its tragic ending." The conclusion, together with the atmosphere of hysteria in the settlements, virulent denunciations of senior IDF officers by right-wing politicians, and, as the chief of staff told the Knesset's Defense and Foreign Affairs Committee on April 12, a desire to deter other villages from harassing hikers, evidently constituted the rationale for the unprecedented punitive measures taken against Beita. The village and the surrounding area were declared a closed military zone and sealed off from the outside world for more than three weeks. In Beita a weeklong curfew was imposed. All the males in the village of some 4,200 residents were rounded up and about 60 were taken into custody, while the others were held in a local school for five days. Air Force helicopters were called in to flush out villagers hiding in the surrounding hills, and nearby villages were warned not to shelter the fugitives.

The Beita incident afforded right-wing politicians an opportunity to vent their frustration and rage. Justice and Tourism Minister Avraham Sharir (Likud-Liberal) called for Beita to be razed to the ground. Such sentiments found ready echoes at Tirza Porat's funeral, attended by thousands of settlers as well as the prime minister, five other cabinet ministers, and many MKs and public figures.

The security forces swiftly acted against villagers suspected of having been involved in the incident. In the two days following the events, the IDF blew up at least 13 houses in the village, including, accidentally, the house of one of the villagers who had come to the hikers' aid (it was announced that he would be compensated). Until this time, the High Court of Justice had consistently refused to intervene in house demolitions, not recognizing this measure as collective punishment. When the Association for Civil Rights in Israel on April 10 petitioned the High Court against further demolitions in Beita, pointing out that the military was acting solely on the basis of one side's version of the events, a panel of three justices engineered a compromise. The IDF agreed to give 48 hours' notice to any family in the village whose house was targeted for demolition so that it could turn to the court. (This applied exclusively to Beita—the army had no obligation to provide advance notification of intent to demolish a house, and in most cases the occupants were allowed a short time to remove personal effects.) One of the first houses to be demolished was that of Mounira Daoud, who had thrown the rock that struck Aldoubi in the head. (Daoud, who was nursing an infant at the time, was arrested and denied bail; on August 11 she was sentenced to eight months' imprisonment, including the four she had already spent in jail awaiting trial. Twenty other Beita residents went on trial in connection with the incident later in the year.)

Other Intifada-Related Violence

Inside Israel, on June 12, three firebombs exploded on the street after being thrown from the roof of the Dizengoff Shopping Center in the heart of Tel Aviv. The incident caused no interruption to the city's booming night life, which was, outwardly at least, unaffected by the uprising.

Elsewhere more vicious methods were employed. On June 20, Eli Cohen, a 33-year-old farmer from Moshav Shekef, in the Lachish district on the Israeli side of the Green Line near Kiryat Gat, died when he was savagely beaten and stabbed while working in his vineyard. When General Mitzna arrived at the settlement, residents lashed out at him, complaining that the army had taken no action despite a series of sabotage attacks on the area. About six weeks later, on August 3, a 69-year-old woman, Rachel Weiss, was found murdered in her home on Moshav Shafir, also in the Lachish district. Three youths from the Jebalya refugee camp in the Gaza Strip were arrested in connection with the attack.

The 2 Lachish district residents were among the 16 Israeli Jews who died in Israel and the territories in 1988 in *intifada*-related violence. (About 400 Jewish civilians, almost all of them settlers, were wounded, a few seriously, in attacks in the territories, the vast majority—370—in the West Bank.) The first Israeli death occurred on March 20 in Bethlehem when a reserve soldier, Moshe Katz, aged 28, was shot twice in the head at close range with a pistol while doing guard duty. On June 2, an 18-year-old yeshivah student, Eliezer Schlesinger, was shot to death while walking in a Jerusalem park with a fellow student after late-night studies; the assailant, who confessed to the crime, was a teenaged Arab prostitute. On August 15, the battered and partially burned body of Ziva Goldovsky, an 18-year-old high-school senior from Holon and an activist in a Jewish-Arab group who spent much time in the occupied territories, was found near Ramallah. The police arrested a 26-year-old man from el-Bireh with a criminal record, an acquaintance of the dead woman, who confessed to the murder, which he said was committed for "nationalistic" reasons.

In the year's worst outrage, perpetrated on the evening of October 30 (and which probably influenced the outcome of the Knesset elections, held two days later), several incendiary bombs were thrown into a Tiberias–Jerusalem bus as it passed through Jericho. Four persons died in the ensuing blaze—a Jerusalem woman, Rachel Weiss, and her three children, all under four years old. David Delarosa, a 19-year-old soldier who suffered critical lung damage when he reentered the bus in an effort to rescue Rachel Weiss, died on December 22 in a London hospital, before he could undergo lung-transplant surgery. Five other passengers were hospitalized. Within hours of the attack, three Jericho residents reportedly confessed to the crime. The following day the army blew up seven houses of suspects in Jericho and a nearby village; army bulldozers uprooted scores of fruit-bearing trees on both sides of the road in the vicinity from which the bombs were thrown.

A week after the bus incident, on November 7, a reservist, David Danieli, was stabbed to death while guarding the settlement of Massuah in the Jordan Rift Valley. The assailant was shot to death on the spot by a member of the settlement; his family's house, near Nablus, was demolished within hours of the murder. Another reservist, Arturo Herstig, aged 42, originally from Argentina, was killed on December 13 in the aftermath of an incident near the Samaria settlement of Har Bracha. A member of the settlement and an Arab shepherd were killed as a result of a quarrel between the two over the ownership of a disputed 300-acre plot of land. Herstig was killed when the army vehicle he was riding in was fired on by the shepherd.

Three Israeli civilians were killed in a terrorist attack of the classic kind, which was indirectly related to the *intifada*. On March 7, three heavily armed gunmen who had infiltrated across the border with Egypt commandeered a military car from five unarmed IDF officers near Mitzpe Ramon in the Negev. The gunmen broke through a police roadblock at Yeroham and then engaged a pursuing police van in a gun battle along the highway near Dimona, while firing at passing civilian vehicles. Finally, a police bullet hit one of the car's tires and the terrorists leaped out, just as a bus carrying staff workers to the nearby Nuclear Research Center came on the scene. The driver and most of his passengers managed to escape before the terrorists reached the bus, but some were trapped inside and held hostage. Negotiations began in which the gunmen demanded that Israel release Arab security prisoners. After more than two hours of give-and-take, shots were heard from the bus, and the order was given for the antiterrorist unit of the Border Police to storm the vehicle. The three gunmen, as well as two of the women hostages, were killed in the 30-second operation. Besides the two women who died—Miriam Ben-Yair, aged 42, mother of three, and Rina Shratzky, aged 30, mother of two—Victor Rahm, aged 38, a widower and father of three whose wife had recently died of cancer, was shot in cold blood by the gunmen.

Responsibility for the attack was claimed by PLO headquarters in Tunisia, which issued a communiqué that the organization's military wing had carried out "the heroic attack against the Zionist atomic scientists at Dimona." Most observers, however, believed the action's true purposes were to sabotage the Shultz peace mission (see below) and to demonstrate that the PLO based outside the territories was also actively involved in the *intifada*. The raid in fact followed a number of failed attempts by Arafat's Fatah organization to send murder squads into Israel via Lebanon, Jordan, and Egypt; a month earlier, another Fatah squad had been captured near Mitzpe Ramon after crossing the Egyptian border. For the PLO, however, the bus outrage proved counterproductive: it enabled Israel to score propaganda points by depicting the PLO as a terrorist organization, and hence the leadership of the uprising, who identified with the PLO, as terrorists by association, with all that this entailed.

Much of the hostile activity in Israel proper was perpetrated by Israeli Arabs. The most serious incident occurred on August 20, when 25 persons were wounded—one seriously, an 8-year-old boy who lost a leg—by a grenade that was thrown on Haifa's pedestrian mall. On December 6, it was announced that 13 Israeli Bedouin from Galilee villages, two of them soldiers, had been arrested and charged with organizing as a Fatah squad to perpetrate a series of terrorist attacks, including the Haifa operation. The group was also alleged to have torched parked buses and thrown incendiary bombs at buses traveling in the area.

The principal venue for such incidents was the Wadi Ara road, a major Galilee artery passing through an area populated almost exclusively by Israeli Arabs. Buses and other vehicles traveling on this highway were frequently attacked with stones or firebombs. Galilee forests were also a favorite target for arsonists, some of them Israeli Arabs. Other areas in which Israeli Arabs evinced solidarity with the *intifada* and hostility toward the Jewish population were around Mount Tabor and, in the Negev, near the large Bedouin villages and encampments in the Beersheba area. Overall, little physical damage and few injuries resulted from these incidents, which were perpetrated mainly by youths and children.

All told, 1,468 incidents of stone throwing were registered inside the Green Line, along with 169 firebomb attacks, 37 cases in which the Palestinian flag was raised, 94 of "incitement to rebellion," and about 80 cases in which roadblocks were erected. Besides these incidents, the Israel Police counted more than 400 instances of what the security forces termed "hostile terrorist activity" within the Green Line.

Antiterrorist Activity

The Shin Bet, which along with other Israeli security arms had been caught unprepared when the uprising erupted, reportedly improved its intelligence capabilities in the territories by adding a new department for situation appraisals. In the field, at all events, the Shin Bet scored some big successes in uncovering terrorist cells, although, without saying so, the defense establishment broadened the operative definition of "terrorism" to include attacks not only on Jewish civilians but also on other Palestinians and against the military. The weapons that were included under the revised rubric ranged from stones and incendiary bombs to grenades and firearms, but the new classification encompassed also the distribution of leaflets or even the scrawling of nationalist graffiti on walls. Similarly, after the popular committees and other forms of local organization were outlawed, they were added to the traditional list of PLO-affiliated groups who perpetrated "hostile terrorist activity."

Some of the successes involved incidents from the pre-*intifada* period. In January the security forces announced the capture of a terrorist cell suspected of murdering Yigal Shahaf in Jerusalem in October 1987 (AJYB 1989, p. 377); on February 17, the Lod military court sentenced an unrepentant 50-year-old-man, Wasfi Mansour, from the village of Tira, to life imprisonment for planting a bomb on an interurban bus just over a year previously, which exploded and injured nine persons (AJYB 1989, p. 377); the same sentence was imposed by the same court on May 8 against two Arab residents of the city, Muhammad Ziyada, aged 34, and Mukhias Bourgal, aged 26, for throwing a grenade at a bus on a highway near the city on June 5, 1987, the 20th anniversary of the outbreak of the Six Day War; and on November 1, a military court in the Gaza Strip sentenced a Rafah resident, Fat'hi Zakout, to five life sentences for planting bombs on Israeli buses on a number of occasions in 1987, one of which wounded a driver.

In May a Fatah cell was uncovered in the Gaza Strip while planning a suicide-bombing operation at the Tel Aviv central bus station. A Hebron gang caught in June was accused of employing violence against Palestinians going to work in Israel and against Israeli-appointed village council members. An Israel Police communiqué on June 26 announced the uncovering in Jerusalem of "terrorist cells affiliated with Naif Hawatmeh's Democratic Front for the Liberation of Palestine, and local groups with affiliation with the Islamic Jihad." Those detained were "suspected of having taken part in disturbances in Jerusalem, distributing leaflets, writing slogans [on walls] and of carrying out a series of attacks," including the throwing of a firebomb at the car of Industry Minister Ariel Sharon in the Old City. On August 16, the IDF spokesman announced the uncovering of a number of terrorist squads in the Hebron and Bethlehem areas suspected of belonging to Fatah/Arafat, Fatah/Abu Moussa, and Islamic Jihad. The gangs were accused of carrying out more than 20 attacks dating back to 1980.

One facet of the tight cooperation between the army and the Shin Bet in combating the uprising consisted of operations undertaken by the army against urban neighborhoods, villages, or refugee camps. The military usually moved in stealthily, in the predawn hours, to gain the element of surprise. Curfew was declared, all the males were ordered to assemble at a central place, house-to-house searches were conducted for suspects and weapons, and local residents were made to remove roadblocks, erase wall graffiti, and take down Palestinian flags from buildings and electricity poles (at least one youth was electrocuted during the year as a result of this practice). Generally, an informer, hooded to prevent identification, accompanied the troops to facilitate their seizure of "wanted" persons, based on lists prepared by the Shin Bet, whose agents were also present.

IDF-initiated operations were increasingly frequent in the second half of the year, after the mass demonstrations had declined. The biggest IDF operation of the kind took place—in the second week of September—in the town of Kalkilya (population 25,000), just across the Green Line from Kfar Sava. General Mitzna admitted that one reason for the big search-and-arrest action was complaints by Jewish settlers, who had to drive through the town to reach their homes, of unremitting harassment by stone-throwing youths. A bypass road was under construction but not yet serviceable, and a night curfew imposed in the two months preceding the operation had proved ineffective. The IDF decided to act. At 4 A.M. on September 6, Kalkilya was placed under total curfew, all roads to the town were blocked, and all phone lines cut off. Hundreds of troops moved in, armed with lists of wanted persons, and conducted house-to-house searches. Dozens of military vehicles took part in the sweep, along with helicopters, to locate suspects who took refuge in the countryside. Some 200 persons were arrested within 48 hours, including members of Hamas, the Gaza-based Islamic Resistance Movement. In the later stages of the operation, which lasted for more than a week (September 6–14), troops escorted personnel from internal revenue and other departments of the Civil Administration who collected overdue taxes, levies, fines, and other monies owed, or confiscated property in lieu of payment.

Some senior military sources professed to see the massive Kalkilya operation (and a parallel thrust in Gaza: see below) as a "turning point" in the IDF's battle against the uprising. However, no sooner had the curfew been lifted than violence erupted in large parts of the town, and on September 17, at least nine residents were wounded in clashes with troops in demonstrations to mark the sixth anniversary of the Beirut refugee-camp massacre in the Lebanon War.

By no means were all the operations of the security forces massive and overt. Persistent reports in 1988 suggested that in some instances the authorities resorted to "dirty tricks." One of these was the seizure of cars of local residents, bearing license plates from the territories, to be used, sometimes for an entire day, for a variety of missions before being returned to their owner. The primary reason for this ruse was to enable the security forces to gain unhindered access to locales where Israeli vehicles of any kind would inevitably receive a hostile reception. Israeli and especially foreign journalists complained that undercover agents were also posing as reporters to enter villages, not only giving the profession a bad name but placing genuine journalists in physical danger from jittery local residents.

Toward the end of the year, as the first anniversary of the uprising approached, preceded by the declaration of "Palestinian statehood" in Algiers in mid-November (see below), the apprehension of terrorist squads seemed to move into high gear. On December 7, two days before the first anniversary of the start of the *intifada*, the Defense Ministry announced that, during October and November, the security forces had uncovered no fewer than 93 terrorist cells—62 in Judea and Samaria, 27 in the Gaza District, and 4 inside Israel. A total of 610 persons were in custody, 310 in the West Bank, 283 in the Gaza Strip, and 17 in Israel. It was noted that "the large number of arrests was due to the extensive uncovering of 'popular committees' and 'shock units.' "

The Defense Ministry communiqué of December 7 provided a revealing breakdown of the organizational affiliation of the 93 terrorist cells: half of them (47), it turned out, were local, i.e., unaffiliated, and established at the initiative of local activists. In the West Bank, the proportion of local groups was even higher, with 39 of the 62 cells uncovered there falling into that category—while 23 were said to be affiliated with Fatah. Oddly, of the 27 cells uncovered in the Gaza Strip, where Islamic fundamentalism was dominant, fully half (13) were identified with Fatah, and 10 of those were popular committees or shock units. Hamas accounted for five cells, three in Gaza, and Islamic Jihad for another three, of which two were Gaza-based. (Hamas was established shortly after the start of the *intifada*, utilizing an already existing network of Islamic educational and cultural organizations in the Gaza Strip—which, ironically, had been encouraged to operate by the Israeli authorities in Gaza, as a countermeasure to the PLO. (According to its Covenant, published on August 18, 1988, Hamas was "a wing of the Muslim Brotherhood in Palestine" and "a link in the chain of *jihad* [holy war] against the Zionist invasion [of Palestine]"; its goal was "to unfurl the banner of Allah over every centimeter of Palestine.")

Arguably, the year's major antiterrorist action occurred far from Israeli shores. On Saturday, April 16, Khalil al-Wazir, better known by his *nom de guerre* Abu Jihad ("father of the holy war"), was gunned down by unknown assailants in Tunis. As Yasir Arafat's top lieutenant and as commander of the PLO's military arm and chairman of its Committee on the Occupied Territories, the 52-year-old Ramle-born al-Wazir was believed to be one of the masterminds of the *intifada*. His name was also linked with some of the most horrific atrocities perpetrated against Israel in recent years, including the Savoy Hotel attack in 1975, the coastal-road massacre in 1978, and, most recently, the takeover of a bus in the Negev five weeks before his assassination.

Although there was no official reaction of any kind from Jerusalem, observers claimed to detect several indicators possibly implicating Israel. About a week later the Government Press Office temporarily suspended the press credentials of two foreign correspondents, the Israel bureau chiefs of NBC and the *Washington Post*, for failing to submit to prior censorship reports about the assassination purporting to reveal details of how the Israeli politico-defense establishment had planned and executed the operation. Minister Without Portfolio Ezer Weizman, said to have voted against the operation, told Israel Army Radio: "If it had been up to me, it wouldn't have been done." Asked directly whether Israel was responsible for the assassination, Weizman replied: "Guess for yourself."

The Third Phase—Plastic Bullets and Politics

The major decision-making body dealing with the *intifada* was neither the cabinet (which did not hold a single comprehensive discussion on the subject) nor the General Staff, but an *ad hoc* group known as the "Territories Forum." Its 30 or so members, including senior General Staff officers, the military advocate-general and other legal advisers, the coordinator of activities in the territories, and regional heads of the Civil Administration, the director of the Shin Bet, a representative of the Israel Police, and the prime minister's military aide, convened once a week, usually on Friday, in the office of the defense minister. Defense Minister Rabin paid regular visits to the territories, had input even in minor decisions, and was the final arbiter on policy for combating the uprising. The defense minister was dubbed the "chief of staff" of the *intifada*—a state of affairs which did not seem to faze Chief of Staff Dan Shomron, who projected a pronounced sense of distaste for having to devote so much of his and the army's time to suppressing a civilian uprising.

It was the Territories Forum, presumably, which gave the go-ahead to the use of plastic bullets in the territories, beginning in the summer. (Except that their heads were made of hard plastic, these cartridges were identical to conventional ammunition. However, their muzzle velocity was lower than regular bullets and, while able to penetrate the body, they lacked the internal spin that was a major cause of serious injuries and fatalities.) The rationale for the move was explained by Yitzhak Rabin in a press conference at Beit El military HQ on September 27, some two months after the new ammunition had become standard issue for troops stationed in the West Bank and Gaza. "The problem we faced," Rabin said, "arose after it was found that clubs, tear gas and rubber bullets were inadequate in confrontations with stone throwers at a distance of 30–50 meters. We had to develop means which would be effective at this range but which would not have the lethal impact of live fire."

In fact, the number of Palestinian fatalities was reduced, or at least stabilized, following the introduction of plastic bullets in August; an average of about 20 Palestinians a month died at Israeli hands during the summer and fall months. However, the number of wounded climbed dramatically, running into hundreds a month—555 in September, up from 343 in August and 228 in July, according to official IDF statistics (which related only to gunfire wounds and even then were incomplete, since many residents chose not to be treated at hospitals to avoid registration). Many were critically hurt or maimed for life. It was the new ammunition's capacity to cause injury that had caused the military advocate-general—in his role as the IDF's legal adviser—to delay his approval for the use of plastic bullets. Indeed, if fired from too close, or if they hit a vital organ, plastic bullets could kill. Thus, the original orders accompanying their introduction as standard-issue ammunition stated that they could be fired only by an officer who had undergone special training or at his explicit instructions, and then only from a distance of at least 70 meters and only at the legs of perceived agitators.

As the efficacy of the plastic bullets in quelling demonstrations proved itself in the field, these directives were relaxed. The resulting quantum leap in casualties, far from upsetting the defense minister, prompted him to declare, in the press conference already mentioned, that he was "not concerned about the large number of persons who had been wounded, as long as [this occurred] as a result of their active participation in violent actions, whether as organizers, instigators or in the activity itself."

Others were less sanguine. "We can see no justification for a policy admittedly designed to cause an increase in casualties," the State Department spokeswoman said in Washington. Closer to home, the Association for Civil Rights in Israel on September 29 asked Attorney General Yitzhak Harish to examine the legality of the defense establishment's policy regarding the use of plastic bullets. ACRI's legal adviser told the press that if the new ammunition was being used as a punitive or deterrent measure, such a policy would be "manifestly illegal." In its letter to the attorney general, the civil rights group recalled that Harish's intervention earlier in the year regarding the beatings policy had resulted in the chief of staff's clarifying letter. However, on October 10, *Ha'aretz* reported that Harish had informed ACRI that "the orders issued to IDF commanders and soldiers [for the use of plastic bullets] underwent my prior examination and were given following my go-ahead."

On October 8, with the casualty rate in the territories spiraling upward, Rabin asserted: "In every confrontation with rioters we are interested not only in arresting whoever needs to be arrested, but if the violence persists, that they should emerge from it with scars, with casualties. I am the defense minister and I am responsible for the [policy]."

PUNISHMENT OF SOLDIERS

The question of responsibility became an acutely personal one for a few dozen soldiers in 1988. By year's end, some 45 soldiers and officers had been court-martialed or were facing military trial for offenses ranging from manslaughter and maltreatment of civilians to theft and causing property damage. Another 200–300 soldiers had been tried by their direct superiors in disciplinary hearings for so-called "excesses" or "deviations." One well-publicized incident occurred on November 20, when a bus carrying paratroopers from a squad commanders' course, who had just completed a period of service in the territories, was stoned while passing the Kalandia refugee camp north of Jerusalem. While pursuing the perpetrators, who slipped away, the paratroopers smashed car windshields and windows, vandalized property, entered houses, and reportedly also beat up some of the occupants. Five days later all those who took part in the incident were sentenced to 20 days' detention.

Asked about the event in a radio interview, the chief of staff said that these were "our finest youth" and that they had "gone a little too far" while giving chase—in itself, a laudable initiative. Backing him up, Defense Minister Rabin wrote to the worried parents of one of the paratroopers who had contacted him about the incident. In his reply, made public on November 29, evoking "the values which have always characterized the IDF in its combat missions," Rabin explained that "your son, together with his comrades, deviated from the norms of behavior that we demand from those in uniform" and was therefore punished. However, "this does not mean that your son is unworthy to hold a command post in the IDF. . . . I am certain that the unfortunate incident will not adversely affect your son's continued military service, and that after justice has been done and the punishment completed, things will return to normal."

The decision to make Rabin's letter public spoke volumes. At the same time, his and Shomron's implicit sanctioning of the paratroopers' action as a youthful letting off of steam may help account for the fact that, despite a growing number of reports about "irregularities," no officer holding a rank higher than captain was brought to trial. In addition, the military advocate-general, Brig. Gen. Strashnow, was said to be under pressure from his superiors to avoid court-martialing senior officers. Thus, in the case of "Colonel G.," as he was dubbed in the press, a brigade commander who had allegedly opened fire from a range of 200 meters at fleeing West Bank demonstrators after giving pursuit in a helicopter, killing a villager of Bani Na'im, near Hebron, Strashnow decided—following consultations with Defense Minister Rabin and others—not to court-martial the colonel for manslaughter. Instead, he was brought before the deputy chief of staff in a disciplinary proceeding, given a severe reprimand, and removed from his post. (He subsequently left army service.)

Some cases involving deaths of Palestinians began to reach the trial stage toward the end of the year, following lengthy Military Police investigations. The harshest sentence handed down in 1988 was against Private Eli Yedidya, who received 21 months' imprisonment and 24 months' suspended for killing a resident of Bidu village, near Ramallah, in a March incident. The court found that Yedidya had shot the victim in the head with a rubber bullet at a range of 20 centimeters, and that he had also perjured himself and suborned witnesses.

The most widely publicized case was that of four soldiers—a master sergeant and three privates—from the Givati infantry brigade, who went on trial for manslaughter in September. The charge sheet stated that on August 22, after stones were thrown at them in Gaza's Jebalya refugee camp, they forced their way into the home of the al-Shami family and brutally beat the father, Hani al-Shami, aged 41, a suspect, using rifle butts and a broom stick; they also kicked him and jumped on him from a bed. The victim died a few hours later at the Jebalya army base of internal wounds and massive hemorrhaging. In their defense, the four said that they had beaten the man because they were "uptight" and "to let off steam" after the stones were thrown. They also claimed that they had acted in accordance with explicit standing orders to beat suspects before detaining them "so the Arabs will learn not to riot." On December 8, after a pathologist testified that in his opinion the beating administered by the Givati soldiers had left the victim "half-dead" but that the fatal blows had been delivered at the Jebalya base, the four soldiers were released from custody, although the court recommended that they not be permitted to rejoin their unit "until the military court decides on the charge attributed to them."

At year's end (December 1), the military advocate-general, addressing cadets in an officers' course, found it necessary to remind them that soldiers were duty-bound not to obey a "manifestly illegal order," such as an order to beat innocent persons or to perform any action contravening fundamental moral values. General Strashnow said that no illegality attached to the current orders about when it was permissible to open fire or to strike demonstrators. "It is permitted to fire in order to kill during battle, but once the battle ends, wounded and prisoners must not be harmed," he explained. However, because the fight to suppress the *intifada* was by definition not a "battle" in the conventional sense, the IDF found itself in uncharted gray areas in which actions once considered "aberrations" gradually became the norm, and what seemed to be purely military operations ineluctably had political ramifications.

Thus, when Defense Minister Rabin was asked, in an interview with Israel TV's Arabic Service in December, on the eve of the first anniversary of the uprising, for his "interim assessment" of what the interviewer chose to call "the disturbances in the territories," three of the points he made were of a political nature. First, in an apparent turnaround from Jerusalem's long-standing official line that the Arab-Israeli conflict involved only the Arab states, and that the Palestinian issue was not the "heart of the conflict," Rabin acknowledged that in the 1980s, and more specifically in the aftermath of the peace treaty with Egypt and the Lebanon War, the conflict had become, essentially, a "Palestinian-Israeli confrontation." The Palestinians, by employing "civilian violence"—Rabin, again in contrast to Shamir, drew a distinction between this phase of the Israeli-Palestinian struggle and an earlier stage of "terrorism in the territories"—had once more placed the Palestinian issue high on the international agenda.

Second, the Palestinians were able to gain sympathy for their cause "because the Western democracies do not like to see clashes between women and children—civilians—and an army." Beyond these general outcomes of the first year of the uprising, Rabin pointed to a third, more concrete result. The Palestinians, he said, had succeeded in "forcing Jordan's hand." Their actions, combined with the failure of the U.S. diplomatic initiative, had brought about Amman's decision to disengage from the territories, thereby shifting the political spotlight to the PLO. Had Rabin been interviewed a week later he might have cited as perhaps the major achievement, however indirect, of the *intifada*, the U.S. decision to enter into a dialogue with the PLO in the wake of declarations made by Yasir Arafat (see below).

The Peace Process

The initiative of U.S. secretary of state George Shultz, which played itself out in the first half of the year, from late February until early June, was at least in part the victim of bad timing. As it happened, 1988 was an election year in both Israel and the United States, so that the secretary of state was perceived to represent a lame-duck administration, while the Israeli prime minister was less inclined than ever to budge from his status-quo politics. The basic problem, though, was that by the time the Shultz initiative got off the ground, it was an anachronism.

Shultz addressed himself to the pre-*intifada* situation; by February 1988 the territories had undergone a sea change. Shultz came to Israel at the height of the mass violence of the uprising's first phase, and his presence seemed only to intensify that violence. On the day of his arrival, February 25, three Palestinians were killed by IDF gunfire in clashes and at least ten wounded, the territories observed a complete general strike, the military began its punitive reprisals in Kabatiya, where villagers had lynched the local headman for "collaborating" with the security forces, and CBS-TV screened its report of Israeli soldiers brutalizing two hapless prisoners. The United National Command of the Uprising called for protest demonstrations against Shultz, and public figures in the territories refused to meet with him, saying that to do so would undercut the standing of the command.

The Israeli political establishment showed no sign of altering its views. Its right wing in particular seized on every negative security development, and the *intifada* was such a development *par excellence*, to dig in more deeply. An exchange of letters between Shultz and Prime Minister Yitzhak Shamir in mid-January had left the U.S. official in no doubt about what Shamir thought concerning key elements of his plan. These included the concept of "peace for territory," which, although it derived from UN Security Council Resolution 242, formally endorsed by Israel at the time of its passage in 1967, again in Resolution 338 of 1973, and a third time in the Camp David accords of 1978, was anathema to the entire Israeli Right-religious bloc; the idea of an "international opening" prior to direct talks between the sides, which Shamir had been fighting bitterly ever since the notion was advanced by Labor party leader and foreign minister Shimon Peres as the only means of bringing King Hussein to the negotiating table; and a new feature, the "telescoping" of the Camp David process from five years to nine months.

Furthermore, the atmosphere of mutual suspicion and mistrust that prevailed in Jerusalem was not conducive to a political breakthrough. Following talks held in Israel by U.S. assistant secretary of state Richard Murphy prior to Shultz's arrival, Shamir accused Peres, without naming him, of "run[ning] every day and every minute to the other side [i.e., the Americans] and say[ing]: 'Don't listen to what Shamir says, I'll sell it to you cheaper!'"

Nevertheless, upon his arrival in Israel—the first of four visits in 1988, each shorter than the last—Shultz exuded optimism, declaring that he had drafted a "workable plan" toward a settlement and adding: "If we can work together with commitment and determination, we can make 1988 a year of peace in the region." Shultz's first meeting with Shamir (February 26) demonstrated how far apart the two were. The Israeli leader again rejected the "peace for territory" principle which underlay the entire Shultz plan. Instead, he tried to sell the secretary of state the notion, concocted by the premier's aides and floated in the Israeli press, that Israel had already fulfilled the relevant article of Resolution 242 when it returned the Sinai, which constituted more than 90 percent of the territories captured in 1967, to Egypt. It followed, according to this logic, that the solution in the West Bank should not and could not be "territorial" but must be "administrative," meaning the "autonomy" regime stipulated in Camp David. Shamir also said no to the idea of an "interlock" between negotiations on an interim agreement and the start of the talks on the final status of the occupied territories, this as part of the "telescoping" process.

Besides Israel, the secretary of state's energetic pursuit of his mission took him, in the course of nine days, to Egypt, Jordan, Syria, London (where he met with King Hussein on March 1), Brussels (for consultations with President Reagan on March 2), London again, and then back for a second visit to Israel, Syria, and Egypt, all on March 4, where he formally presented his plan in writing to each country's leadership before leaving the region.

THE SHULTZ PLAN

Two days later the mass-circulation *Yediot Aharonot* published on its front page a photostat of Shultz's letter to Shamir. The document summarized in some detail the "statement of understandings" that had emerged from the talks Shultz held with "regional leaders" in order "to achieve the prompt opening of negotiations." The "agreed objective" of such talks was "a comprehensive peace providing for the security of all the States in the region and for the legitimate rights of the Palestinian people" (a concept Israel had accepted in the Camp David accords). Negotiations were to commence at "an early date"—May 1 was specified—between Israel "and each of its neighbors which is willing to do so." The parties to each set of bilateral talks "will determine the procedure and agenda of their negotiation." In an apparent endeavor to reassure King Hussein that the United States adhered to the "peace for territory" principle implicit in Resolutions 242 and 338, Shultz emphasized that each bilateral negotiation would be based on those two resolutions "in all their parts." This was reiterated in the context of the negotiations between Israel and "the Jordanian-Palestinian delegation," which, the letter said, "will be based on all the provisions and principles of . . . Resolution 242."

Shultz proposed that the first stage of the crucial Israeli–Jordanian/Palestinian negotiations last no longer than six months and that they should produce "arrangements for a transitional period." Then,

[s]even months after transitional negotiations begin [i.e., on December 1], final status negotiations will begin, with the objective of completing them within one

year. . . . Final status talks will begin before the transitional period begins. The transitional period will begin three months after the conclusion of the transitional arrangement and will last for three years. The United States will participate in both negotiations and will promote their rapid conclusion.

The letter made it plain that Shamir had failed to bring Shultz around to his view that an international conference constituted a threat to Israel; instead, clearly the secretary of state had been persuaded, whether by his Arab interlocutors or in recent talks with his Soviet counterpart, to overcome his reluctance to bringing the Soviet Union into the Middle East peace process. Thus, two weeks before the start of the negotiating process—i.e., on April 15, in just six weeks' time—an "international conference" was to be convened. The mechanics were simple: the UN secretary-general would issue invitations "to the parties involved in the Arab-Israeli conflict" and to the permanent members of the Security Council. All the participants would have to declare their acceptance of 242 and 338 "and renounce violence and terrorism"—a sop to Israel and an attempt to force the PLO's hand. Another Israeli fear was addressed when Shultz wrote that, while the sides could "refer reports on the status of their negotiations to the conference [forum] in a manner to be agreed," that forum "will not be able to impose solutions or veto agreements reached."

Shultz's explicit assertion that "[t]his statement of understandings is an integral whole" pulled the rug from under Shamir's contention that modifications were still possible. Shultz also stated that he "look[ed] forward to the letter of reply of the Government of Israel in confirmation of this statement"—by March 15, according to press reports. The pressure on Israel was heightened because Shamir was scheduled to leave on March 13 for a weeklong visit to the United States, including a meeting with President Reagan. On March 9, Shamir offered the reply of his wing of the "unity" government. Addressing the Likud Knesset caucus, the prime minister blasted the Shultz initiative, listing what he called "the sins of the American capitulation," above all Washington's "surrender" to the riots in the territories as viewed through the distorting prism of international public opinion. Earlier that day, in a meeting of the inner cabinet, the country's senior policy-making forum, Shamir had rebuffed the demand of the body's Labor ministers, supported by Housing Minister David Levy, of Herut, that the Shultz document be put to a vote so that Shamir could speak "with one voice" during his U.S. visit and prevent a crisis in relations with that country.

On March 11, *Ha'aretz* quoted Shamir as telling the country's leading political columnist, Yoel Marcus: "The only word I accept in the Shultz document is his signature." Israel's safety and security were not ensured in the plan, Shamir said, and the "whole thing [was] an attempt to placate the Arabs." More substantively, Shamir complained that the wording of Shultz's letter left the way open for the UN secretary-general to invite the PLO to the international conference; that Israel's right to exist was nowhere mentioned; and that nothing was said about "direct" negotiations.

At the cabinet meeting on March 13, in which Defense Minister Rabin informed the ministers that the situation in the territories would require army reservists to serve more days and necessitate an increase in the defense budget, Prime Minister Shamir gave each minister ten minutes to speak his piece about the Shultz plan and again declined to put it to a vote. Following the meeting, Foreign Minister Peres sent Shamir a letter, on behalf of the Alignment ministers, asserting that it was "essential" for Israel to accept the Shultz initiative at this "critical" stage in the peace process. Peres said that Shamir's refusal to call for a vote on the Shultz plan had created an "unconscionable situation" and that "in the absence of an Inner Cabinet decision, your stands on the issue of the Shultz initiative do not represent the position of the government of Israel." In his reply, Shamir said he intended to seek "further clarifications" from President Reagan and Secretary Shultz, and pledged that "proximate to my return I will bring the issue without delay for a decision by the Inner Cabinet or the Cabinet plenum. . . ."

With talk rampant of a looming government crisis and possible early elections, something of the polarization in the country was indicated by two big demonstrations, each of which drew tens of thousands of participants, held in Tel Aviv on successive nights. On March 12, a rally organized by Peace Now called for "a change of direction" and urged Shamir to say "yes to peace," while 24 hours later, in the same plaza, a rally sponsored by Gush Emunim and the political Right urged Shamir to stand firm and tell the American people that "we do not want to commit suicide."

In the United States, Shamir was able to reiterate his objections to the Shultz plan in his talks with both Reagan and Shultz—emphasizing, pointedly, that the international conference element would automatically give both the Soviet Union and Communist China a voice in the proceedings—but finally left matters hanging in the air by not actually rejecting the initiative. Shamir also complained that it was unfair to ask Israel to respond first, when not a single Arab state had replied to the Shultz letter. Speaking to reporters after his meeting with Shamir (March 16), President Reagan indirectly revealed something of the Israeli premier's arguments when he stated: "The U.S. will not slice this initiative apart and will not abandon it." With Shamir standing beside him, the president added, tellingly: "And those who say no to the plan—and the prime minister has not used this word—need not answer to us. They need to answer to themselves and their people as to why they turned down a realistic and sensible plan to achieve negotiations."

Observers described Shamir's talks in Washington (March 14–17) as "inconclusive." In terms of the Shultz initiative this was so. But for Shamir's purposes the very inconclusiveness of the talks demonstrated conclusively that, despite everything, the widely anticipated—and by no one more than Shimon Peres—crisis in Israeli-U.S. relations had been averted. Moreover, the administration's unwillingness, for whatever reason, to push Shamir to the wall meant, as the Israeli premier well knew, the conclusive end of the Shultz initiative in all but name. Thus Shamir was able to deflate the opposition at home by announcing the simple truth. "Nobody has imposed anything on us, including a timetable," he declared triumphantly on his arrival at Ben-Gurion Airport on March 22.

At the inner cabinet meeting the following day, instead of holding a vote on the

Shultz plan "without delay" upon his return, as he had pledged to Peres, Shamir had little trouble persuading the ministers that it was in Israel's best interest to wait until Shultz returned to the region and could inform Israel whether either the Arabs or the Soviets accepted his plan. In fact, Shamir told a meeting of Likud ministers, Shultz had personally assured him that "as long as I am secretary of state, we will not drag you by force into an international conference." As for Shimon Peres, he was in a bind: if he submitted a formal motion for a vote, the certain result would be a stalemate (the inner cabinet consisted of five Likud and five Alignment ministers) which, under cabinet rules, would mean the motion's defeat, a consummation not devoutly wished by the Labor party chairman. Again, the structure of the national unity government had proved that it was the ideal instrument for standing pat.

The full dimensions of the chasm separating Shultz and Shamir were exposed when the prime minister, in a rare Knesset appearance (March 28), revealed the principles he had put forward in Washington. Most striking was the disparity between Shultz's vision of a comprehensive regional settlement, including "the legitimate rights of the Palestinian people" and Shamir's version of the declared goal: "a peace treaty with Jordan, and the settlement of the problems of the Arabs in Eretz Israel." In line with this approach, Shamir asserted that the Palestinians in the Jordanian-Palestinian delegation "must be acceptable to the parties to the negotiations," meaning that Israel reserved the right to veto anyone considered to be associated with the PLO. Instead of an "international event," the most Shamir would accept was the "symbolic presence of the two superpowers at the opening of direct peace negotiations between the sides," an idea first broached by Shultz himself the previous October. Shamir then played his unvarying trump card. In Washington, he said, both the president and the secretary of state had stressed that the Israeli-U.S. alliance was "unshakable, even if we have differences over how to promote the peace process."

In his speech Shamir referred to one of those "differences" when he remarked on a meeting Shultz had held in Washington on March 26 with two prominent Palestinian Americans, Professors Edward Said and Ibrahim Abu-Lughod, both members of the Palestine National Council (the PLO's "parliament"). Shamir told the House that Israel would never conduct negotiations, "direct or indirect," with the PLO, and that "we take a grave view of American attempts to establish contacts with PLO members," including PNC delegates. If Shamir thought that the Shultz meeting indicated an evolving shift in U.S. policy and portended further developments in the same direction should the Shultz mission fail, he kept his apprehensions to himself. Indeed, Shultz's move and others like it in the international community played into Shamir's hands by enabling him to depict Israel as under threat from all quarters. Speaking to the Likud Knesset caucus, he warned that a "web of conspiracy" was being woven around Israel and "campaigns" were afoot which aimed to "dwarf" Israel and reduce it to "dimensions which would make its existence impossible."

Shultz himself was at extraordinary pains to deny that his plan was detrimental to Israel's security. Shortly after his arrival in Israel on April 3 to resume his mission, he addressed the editors of the Israeli press and told them that he accepted Shimon Peres's three "noes"—no to a Palestinian state, no to the PLO, and no to a return to the 1967 lines. (The first two positions were unacceptable to the Palestinians and the third, by leaving open the option of returning some land, was unacceptable to Shamir.) Shultz did nothing to ingratiate himself with the Shamir camp when, in an unprecedented step by a serving secretary of state, he took his case directly "to the Israeli people" by granting Israel TV two exclusive interviews within four days: one on the nightly news and the second on the prestigious weekly "*Moked*" (Focus) interview program. Although Shultz's performance had no perceptible impact, Shamir and his aides railed at Israel TV for "placing the screen at Shultz's disposal so he could make his pitch to the nation over the head of the prime minister."

Beyond Shultz's ability to make headway in Jerusalem, his failure to achieve progress in his talks with King Hussein in Amman and Hafez al-Assad in Syria contributed to the gathering sense of gloom about the fate of the initiative. A public statement of support for the plan from the vacillating Jordanian monarch was considered essential to swing public opinion in Israel. But Shultz left the region on April 7 in the same state as he had a month earlier. The traumatic Beita incident, which occurred the day before his departure, was not likely to induce flexibility among Israelis (see above).

In the meantime, Prime Minister Shamir was able to take advantage of the situation to persuade his erstwhile Herut ally, MK Moshe Arens, who had resigned from the cabinet to protest against the decision to scrap the Lavi aircraft project (AJYB 1989, pp. 394–396), to rejoin that body. Shamir, asserting that Arens's "skills and experience" were essential at this parlous juncture, thus bolstered his strength in the party with a view to the intraparty election of Knesset candidates, while Arens, as a minister, would be better placed to secure a higher ranking on the party's list. To maintain the sacred balance of the unity government, Shimon Peres approached Mordechai Gur, a former health minister, who had refused to serve under Shamir because of the latter's part in the No. 300 bus affair, with the same offer. Peres noted that Gur's "military experience"—he was a former chief of staff—was essential at this perilous moment, and Gur, like Arens, evidently decided that he had proved his point and that there was no reason to cut off his nose to spite his face. On April 18, following Knesset approval of a cabinet resolution of April 10, Arens and Gur became ministers without portfolio.

SHULTZ'S LAST TRIP

Such moves showed that the Israeli political level was already preoccupied with the looming election campaign. So it was not unexpected that Shultz's fourth—and last, as it turned out—visit to the region to promote his initiative was as unfruitful as the previous three. His arrival in Israel on June 5 for seven hours of talks, after already having met with the leaders of Egypt, Jordan, and Syria, triggered a three-day general strike in the occupied territories, motivated in part by the fact that June 5 was the 21st anniversary of the Six Day War.

Shultz arrived in the region after attending the Reagan-Gorbachev summit meeting in Moscow, but speculation that the superpowers had reached an understanding on the Middle East quickly proved unfounded. Shultz devoted a good deal of time during his one-day visit to Israel, notably almost the whole of his meeting with Defense Minister Rabin, to the issue of human rights in the territories. Accompanying Shultz this time was Assistant Secretary of State for Human Rights Richard Schifter, who, in the company of U.S. ambassador to Israel Thomas Pickering, toured the territories on June 6, after Shultz had left, hosted by the Coordinator of Government Activities Shmuel Goren. The Americans expressed special interest in judicial matters, arrest procedures, the imposition of curfew, and the use of tear gas. Shultz himself, before departing, reaffirmed in strong language Washington's long-standing position that Israel's "continued occupation of the West Bank and Gaza and the frustration of Palestinian rights is a dead-end street. The belief that this can continue is an illusion."

Yet by the terms of that very analysis, Shultz's peace plan was equally illusory. By relegating the Palestinians in the territories to a secondary role and continuing to exclude the PLO, Shultz ignored the very forces that had impelled his initiative. The inevitable demise of the Shultz initiative left the way clear for those forces to set in motion the series of events that culminated in the PLO's proclamation of the "State of Palestine" and, a month later, the U.S. decision to enter into a dialogue with the PLO.

A hint of the PLO's modified position surfaced at the Arab summit meeting in Algiers, which convened in June immediately after Shultz's departure from the region. As expected, the summit reaffirmed that the PLO was the sole legitimate representative of the Palestinian people, that as such it should participate as an equal in an international peace conference, and that the Palestinians had the right to establish an independent state. At the meeting, PLO representatives circulated copies of an article, originally published in the London-based *Middle East Mirror*, by the organization's spokesman and close adviser to Arafat, Bassam Abu Sherif. Sherif's article seemed to signal a radical PLO departure by calling for direct talks between Israel and the Palestinians in order to achieve a two-state solution. While Arafat, as usual, neither endorsed nor refuted the article, it was clear that it could not have been published without his approval.

U.S. assistant secretary of state Richard Murphy termed it "a contribution to a rational discussion of the problem," but in the recurring pattern of recent years, PLO hard-liners joined Israeli leaders in rejecting Sherif's ideas, the former because they were "deviationist" and the latter, including Shimon Peres, who was locked into a commitment to the Jordanian option, as an empty public-relations gimmick whose sole purpose was to secure U.S. recognition of the PLO. (In February Abu Sherif had been involved in the PLO's attempt to send a so-called "ship of return" carrying more than 100 Palestinians deported from the territories and a large contingent of journalists to Israel. The voyage, with its obvious evocation of the Jewish refugee ship *Exodus*, was intended to capitalize on the international sympathy for the Palestinians generated by the *intifada*. Jerusalem shrugged off the plan as a "propaganda stunt" but was sufficiently concerned to set up a ministerial committee to monitor the situation. In the event, an explosion that ripped through the vessel that had been chartered for the voyage, docked at Limassol, Cyprus, on February 15, a day after three senior PLO officials were killed in a car-bomb blast in the same city, persuaded the PLO to postpone the sailing. Both attacks were widely attributed to Israeli secret agents.)

HUSSEIN'S MOVE

Unexpectedly, it was the vacillating King Hussein who dropped the next bombshell. Taking his cue from the situation in the territories, the resolutions of the Arab summit, and emerging changes in the PLO, as indicated by Abu Sherif's article, Hussein went on Jordanian TV and radio on July 31 and announced that Jordan was disengaging from the West Bank and renouncing its claims to that territory. Amman's links with the area, both legal and administrative, were to be severed. Hussein had already canceled an ongoing five-year development scheme for the region and dissolved Jordan's lower house of Parliament, where half the members represented West Bank locales. As Prime Minister Shamir pointed out in a television interview the following day, Hussein's move "actually confirms the situation in the field—a situation in which the King of Jordan has no influence on developments" in the territories. More questionable was Shamir's standard conclusion—that "this step essentially changes nothing"—although this stance did enable him to reject demands by ultranationalist circles to take advantage of Hussein's move and annex the territories.

For the Palestinians in the territories, dependent on Jordan for key services (including international travel documents), and in thousands of cases for salaries, the move could hardly be said to have "changed nothing." On August 4, Amman decided to dismiss the more than 20,000 civil servants in the territories who were still on its payroll and to cease paying their salaries, which totaled some $40 million per year. This would clearly exacerbate the depressed economic situation in the areas and indirectly affect the Civil Administration, which relied on taxes collected from the inhabitants to maintain the civilian aspects of the occupation. Above all, however, Hussein's actions threw the ball squarely into the PLO court. That organization would henceforth be called upon to demonstrate that its designation by the Arab world as the "sole legitimate representative of the Palestinian people" was more than just words. In the meantime, Leaflet No. 23 of the United National

Command of the Uprising, issued on August 5, hailed Jordan's disengagement as "one of the most important achievements" of the uprising.

"STATE OF PALESTINE" PROCLAIMED

With the political field left completely to the PLO, all eyes were on Arafat, to see if he would articulate the words necessary to fulfill the conditions for American recognition. In mid-September he spoke about accepting Resolution 242 in a speech to the European Parliament at Strasbourg, but ambivalently, and this was deemed to be insufficient by Peres and Shultz when they met in New York later that month to attend the UN General Assembly session. On September 28, a trilateral meeting took place in New York between Peres, U.S. president Reagan, and Egyptian foreign minister Esmat Abdel Meguid. They agreed that, in the pursuit of peace, Egypt's role should be to "encourage the Palestinians to adopt reasonable positions," while Israel should "find a way to reach out to the Palestinians."

In the event, the next development was that Palestinians reached out to other Palestinians. On November 15, with the Israeli political establishment mired deep in a coalition tangle following another inconclusive general election, the 19th Palestine National Council, meeting in Algiers, proclaimed the independent "State of Palestine," albeit without defining its exact boundaries, and declared that it supported the holding of an international conference "on the basis of Security Council [Resolutions] 242 and 338." This, together with the PNC's 40-year-late endorsement in its "Declaration of Independence" of General Assembly Resolution 181 of November 29, 1947, which partitioned Palestine into two states, one Jewish and one Arab, led the White House to speak of "positive elements" at the PNC meeting but to reject the declaration of statehood due to Washington's opposition to "unilateral action[s]" which "purport to change the status of the occupied territories" without "direct negotiations."

Like Jordan's disengagement and the American readiness to talk to the PLO, the PNC move undermined ingrained Israeli assumptions about the Palestinians. In the territories, the military, not knowing what to expect, braced for the worst. On November 11, the IDF declared a total curfew "until further notice" on the Gaza Strip; lifted only five days later, it was the longest curfew on such a large population since 1967. In addition, all telephone lines to the territories were cut (with the exception of hospitals and elements connected with the Military Government), Arabs were barred from entering or leaving Jerusalem, hundreds of persons were placed under preventive detention, and roadblocks were set up throughout the areas as troops were rushed in on a massive scale. Nablus, the hotbed of Palestinian nationalism in the West Bank, was declared a closed military zone and placed off-limits to reporters. The curfew declared in Kalkilya, Tulkarm, the Balata refugee camp near Nablus, and elsewhere was utilized by the IDF to force residents to remove Palestinian flags and paint over nationalist graffiti. Helicopters and light planes flew reconnaissance missions over the territories. Nevertheless, at least four persons from two Gaza refugee camps were wounded by IDF gunfire on November 13, when residents defied the curfew and clashed with the army, and in the West Bank, one man was killed and a number of West Bank inhabitants were wounded in confrontations with soldiers.

On November 14, the announced date of the declaration of Palestinian statehood (the proclamation finally came after midnight, on the 15th), Yitzhak Shamir was chosen to form the new government; he stated that his government would make a "tremendous effort" to advance the peace process with the Arab states, thus continuing to ignore the Palestinians. The IDF announced that 19 terrorist cells had been uncovered in the West Bank and Jerusalem and that the houses of some of the suspects had already been demolished. In the Gaza Strip, one person was killed and a number wounded by gunfire and beatings in widespread clashes which erupted despite the curfew. Defense Minister Rabin toured the West Bank where four persons were wounded by IDF gunfire and a firebomb was thrown into an Israeli bus en route to the settlement of Shilo (alert passengers put it out with a fire extinguisher). Rabin told reporters that troop reinforcements had been brought in to suppress "any attempt to violate law and order" in the territories and would "employ every means to achieve that goal." He was probably reacting to a leaflet of the United National Command of the Uprising urging the population to celebrate statehood at 4 P.M. on November 15th by holding parades, singing the "national anthem" *"Biladi, Biladi"* ("My Country, My Country"), and hoisting Palestinian flags.

As a result of Rabin's measures, a million persons found themselves under curfew in the West Bank and Gaza, army patrols were beefed up with half-tracks (there were more troops in the areas than at any time since the immediate aftermath of the Six Day War), journalists were barred from entering the territories, the distribution of newspapers was banned, and, in a new twist, despite the bitter cold, the authorities cut off the power supply throughout the Gaza Strip and in most areas of the West Bank, including the entire cities of Nablus, Hebron, and Tulkarm and their adjacent refugee camps—thus to prevent inhabitants from viewing TV reports of the proceedings in Algiers. (No attempt was made to confiscate batteries to preclude the use of transistor radios.)

As it happened, at the defense minister's "request," Israelis too were permitted to see only a truncated report of the final PNC session and Arafat's concluding speech. The director-general of the State Broadcasting Authority, Uri Porat, a hard-line Likud appointee, explained that Rabin had "suggested" that coverage be muted after hearing IDF officers in the West Bank express their fear that televised reports of the Declaration of Independence ceremony from Algiers would inflame passions in the territories. (Porat made no reference to the fact that without electricity the Palestinians in the territories could not view the newscast in any case. He did, however, voice his concern that Israeli Arabs were liable to be influenced by Arafat's words.) Porat added a number of other restrictions on the news department's coverage of the Algiers meeting: reporters were not to say "Palestinian state" but "PLO state," the "PLO anthem" was not to be broadcast, speeches from the PNC session were to be paraphrased in the studio and not screened, and no expert commentators were to be brought in to analyze the events.

The massive IDF presence in the territories did its work, and although some 14 persons were wounded in incidents on November 15, the day passed relatively quietly. West Bank youths made a few feeble attempts to "celebrate" their "independence" in defiance of the curfew by scrawling a few slogans on walls, igniting fireworks, or floating balloons in the Palestinian colors, and elite IDF units chased children who lit firecrackers or sent aloft balloons. The IDF command in Gaza put out a leaflet prohibiting singing, dancing, or the use of noisemakers.

In Jerusalem the Foreign Ministry put out an official statement that accused the PLO of resorting to its traditional "ambiguity and double talk" in order "to obscure its advocacy of violence and terrorism." Prime Minister Shamir termed the PNC decisions "a deceptive propaganda exercise" with "no relevance to reality," and the cabinet, on November 20, called them "an additional attempt at disinformation [and] a jumble of illusions meant to mislead world public opinion."

Some opinion in Israel was shifting in response to events. The mainstream Peace Now organization, which had assiduously refrained from urging a dialogue with the PLO, now declared in newspaper ads that in Algiers the PLO had "forsaken the road of rejectionism and the Palestinian Covenant and embarked on the path of political compromise." The group called on the government to broaden "the opening to peace" and, explicitly, "to talk to the PLO." On November 30, hundreds of persons attended a public meeting in Jerusalem sponsored by Peace Now under the previously inconceivable slogan: "Talk peace with the PLO now." (On June 30, four peace activists who had met with PLO officials in Romania in November 1986 [AJYB 1988, p. 377] were sentenced to six months' imprisonment and a year suspended and fined NIS 3,000 each, for violating a controversial 1986 amendment to the Prevention of Terrorism Ordinance prohibiting contact with members of terrorist organizations. The four were permitted to do community service in lieu of serving time in jail, but the start of the sentences was deferred for appeal and the case seemed certain to reach the Supreme Court.)

ARAFAT INITIATIVE

For the remainder of 1988 the Israeli government was relegated to the sidelines as the PLO retained the political initiative by "talking peace" and achieving a long-held objective: the onset of an official dialogue with the Americans. Thirteen years earlier, on September 1, 1975, in a Memorandum of Agreement between the United States and Israel, Washington had pledged:

> The United States will continue to adhere to its present policy with respect to the Palestine Liberation Organization, whereby it will not recognize or negotiate with

the [PLO] so long as the [PLO] does not recognize Israel's right to exist and does not accept Security Council Resolutions 242 and 338. The United States Government will consult fully and seek to concert its position and strategy on this issue with the Government of Israel.

With the Israeli leadership unable or unwilling to respond to developments, the pragmatic wing of the PLO leadership was able to translate the accumulated momentum of the year-old *intifada*, the thwarted Shultz mission, and Jordan's disengagement from the territories into a major political and diplomatic coup on an international scale.

Having crossed the Rubicon by declaring a Palestinian state, PLO chairman Arafat met in Stockholm, on December 7, with a delegation of five Jews from the American branch of the Tel Aviv-based International Center for Peace in the Middle East. This encounter produced an untitled, unsigned document, ratified by Arafat but read out by Foreign Minister Sten Andersson of Sweden (who would play a key behind-the-scenes role in the events leading up to the U.S. decision to talk to the PLO), declaring that the recent PNC meeting in Algiers had accepted Israel's right to exist as an independent state, had committed the PLO to take part in an international peace conference on the basis of Resolutions 242 and 338, and had condemned and rejected terrorism "in all its forms," including state terrorism (a reference to Israeli activity in the occupied territories and in Lebanon). This statement sparked a mixed bag of reactions. Asked in an Israel TV interview (December 7) whether he saw any positive change in PLO policy in the wake of the Stockholm declaration, Prime Minister Shamir, while admitting that he had not seen the "complete text" of the statement, said: "I do not see such a change, nor do I expect that I will ever see a substantive change, since their *raison d'être* is Israel's destruction. On the day they conclude that this is not possible or desirable, they will have to disband."

The day, although not the outcome predicted by Shamir, was closer at hand than the Israeli political hierarchy had believed possible. On December 13, Arafat addressed the UN General Assembly, meeting in Geneva because the State Department had refused the PLO chairman a visa to enter the United States. The PLO leader declared before the world forum that the Palestine National Council had "reaffirmed its rejection of terrorism in all its forms, including state terrorism," and that he, "as chairman of the [PLO], hereby once more declare that I condemn terrorism in all its forms." Invoking General Assembly Resolution 181 of 1947, which "decided on the establishment of two states in Palestine, one Palestinian Arab and the other Jewish," Arafat presented a three-point "Palestinian peace initiative" calling for an international conference; the stationing of UN forces in "our occupied Palestinian land ... to protect our people and, at the same time, to supervise the withdrawal of Israeli forces from our country"; and a "comprehensive settlement among the parties concerned in the Arab-Israeli conflict, including the State of Palestine, Israel, and her neighbors, within the framework of the international conference for peace in the Middle East on the basis of Resolutions 242 and 338. . . ." Arafat called on "the leaders of Israel to come here under the sponsorship of the United Nations, so that, together, we can forge that peace."

It was still not enough for Washington. State Department spokesman Charles Redman said that, although Arafat's speech had contained "some interesting and positive developments... it continued to be ambiguous on the key issues which must be clearly addressed in order for the U.S. to enter a substantive dialogue with the PLO." Redman revealed that indirect contacts were under way between the United States and the PLO, with the Americans having conveyed "in very explicit, specific terms" to the PLO, through certain "third parties"—presumably Sweden—the conditions Arafat would have to meet before a dialogue with the United States could begin. Despite this coaching, Arafat had failed to deliver the goods.

In the territories, the Gaza Strip was again placed under total curfew prior to Arafat's speech, all telephone lines to the refugee camps were cut, and the power supply was turned off in some locales, although on nothing like the scale of the previous month. Five persons were wounded in clashes in the West Bank, three of them children aged 10, 13, and 16. Children in Gaza released balloons with Palestinian flags painted on them after Arafat's speech, and a few brief parades and demonstrations were held in the West Bank, primarily in the Nablus area.

In Jerusalem, within hours of Arafat's speech, Prime Minister Shamir released a statement describing Arafat's performance as "a monumental act of deception," and expressing his hope that "for the sake of promoting the chances of peace and advancing the struggle against terrorism and violence, the United States will never establish any contact with the PLO."

Defense Minister Rabin, who as prime minister in 1975 was a co-architect with then Secretary of State Henry Kissinger of the PLO clause in the Memorandum of Agreement, told Army Radio on December 14 that at that time Washington had committed itself, at Israel's behest, to "formulations which I did not believe the PLO was capable of accepting." Asked what would happen if the PLO were, nevertheless, to state its acceptance of those conditions, Rabin, too, offered a variation on Shamir's theme. "The PLO would cease being the PLO if it were to accept all these [stipulations]." Foreign Minister Peres, speaking in the Knesset on December 14, said Arafat had "performed acrobatics" at Geneva, so it was "no wonder that the tense anticipation in Washington yesterday before the speech quickly turned into immediate disappointment after they read the speech."

U.S. RECOGNIZES PLO

Before the day was out, however, Washington had reversed its stand of 24 hours earlier, in the process delivering to Israel what the daily *Hadashot* called "the most resounding diplomatic slap-in-the-face" in its history. U.S. officials were listening closely when Arafat, speaking at a previously scheduled but delayed press conference in Geneva on December 14, made an opening statement in which he "clarified" the crucial points in his General Assembly speech. (Reportedly, Arafat rescheduled the event so that he could confer with Swedish foreign minister Andersson, who was in touch with the State Department to ensure coordination regarding Arafat's terminology.)

Thus, Arafat declared that the Palestinians' "desire for peace is a strategy and not an interim tactic" and "[s]elf-determination means survival for the Palestinians. And our survival does not destroy the survival of the Israelis as their rulers claim." Concretely, Arafat explained that by the references in his speech to Resolution 181 and to "our acceptance of Resolutions 242 and 338 as the basis for negotiations with Israel" in an international conference,

> it was clear that we mean our people's right to freedom and national independence according to Resolution 181 and the right of all parties concerned in the Middle East conflict to exist in peace and security, and as I have mentioned including the State of Palestine and Israel and other neighbors according to the Resolution 242 and 338 [sic].

On the terrorism issue, Arafat said, "I renounced it yesterday in no uncertain terms and yet I repeat it for the record that we totally and absolutely renounce all forms of terrorism, including individual, group and state terrorism." (By adding the words "individual" and "group" Arafat had in fact significantly expanded his statement of the previous day.)

The *quid pro quo* was immediate. Within hours President Reagan declared:

> The Palestine Liberation Organization today issued a statement in which it accepted United Nations Security Council Resolutions 242 and 338, recognized Israel's right to exist and renounced terrorism. These have long been our conditions for a substantive dialogue. They have been met. Therefore I have authorized the State Department to enter into a substantive dialogue with PLO representatives. The [PLO] must live up to its statements. In particular it must demonstrate that its renunciation of terrorism is pervasive and permanent.

The president termed the U.S. decision "an important step in the peace process, the more so because it represents the serious evolution of Palestinian thinking towards realistic and pragmatic positions on the key issues." Israel was assured that the "special commitment" of the United States to its security "remains unshakable." Moreover, a "major reason" that the United States was commencing a dialogue with the PLO was "to help Israel achieve the recognition and security it deserves."

On December 15, Secretary of State Shultz sent identical letters to Shamir and Peres, explaining that after "stud[ying] the text of Arafat's remarks carefully," he had concluded that they "satisfie[d] the long-standing American conditions for opening a substantive dialogue." Shultz wrote that he was aware of "how sensitive an issue this is for you and the people of Israel," and that the U.S. decision "was not taken lightly." He too emphasized that Washington was motivated by "the desire to see a safe and strong Israel, living in peace with its neighbors. Nothing will shake the foundations of our relationship." Shultz promised that the United States would keep Israel "fully informed of what transpires in our [dialogue] with the

PLO," which was to be conducted solely by the U.S. ambassador to Tunisia. (Ambassador Robert Pelletreau held his first meeting with a PLO delegation in Tunis on December 16.)

When Shamir, stunned by Washington's decision, disappeared from public view for two days after the U.S. announcement, his spokesman, Aviezer Pazner, issued a statement (December 15) "very much regret[ting]" the U.S. decision, "which will not advance the cause of peace" in the region. "We believe that the United States will discover very soon the true face of the PLO," Pazner added. In the same vein, Foreign Minister Peres told Israel Radio on the same day, in reference to Arafat's renunciation of terrorism, that "in my opinion, if one Molotov cocktail is thrown today in the territories this will nullify his entire commitment." Peres termed the development "a sad day for all of us" and did not miss the chance to rub salt in the wounds of "those who opposed Jordan[ian participation] and an international conference [and thereby] paved the way for the PLO."

Shamir broke his silence in an interview on Israel Radio on December 17, with words that seemed to betray (at best) a sense of sheer bewilderment. Shamir invoked the usual formulation in cases of divergent Israeli and U.S. approaches—"allies can have serious disagreements, but [these] do not affect the alliance itself"—only to call it into question: "This week something happened that puts this principle to a very serious test. The U.S. decided to commence talks with Israel's arch enemy. It is no wonder that we are all trying to decide what happened, why it happened, and what we should do about it." However, within two days Shamir had recovered sufficiently to tell the First World Conference of Children of Holocaust Survivors in Jerusalem that the international community was now witnessing a "worldwide spectacle of deception" in which the PLO chairman and his cohorts were trying with "satanic intent" to achieve by "political cunning what they were unable to bring about by means of weapons, blood, terrorism and violence." Israel, however, would not be taken in by this "show" and would not talk to "terrorists whose one goal is to establish another Arab state . . . in place of the Jewish state."

Defense Minister Rabin linked the U.S. decision to the *intifada* when he told Israel TV on December 16 that Washington's decision was "grave and mistaken," and that its effect was to "give legitimization to the uprising in the territories." Earlier that day, five persons, aged 18–22, were killed by IDF gunfire and about 20 wounded—three of whom later died—in a series of incidents in Nablus, some of which revolved around the funeral of a 15-year-old boy who had died of wounds sustained three weeks earlier. Some saw the events in Nablus as a jittery reaction by the Israeli defense establishment to the unexpected developments in Geneva and Washington; military sources said the violence was the work of extremists who opposed the PLO's diplomatic moves. Local residents claimed that soldiers opened fire without provocation. A three-day general strike was called in the territories to protest the shootings in Nablus. On the same day a nine-month-old infant girl from the settlement of Dolev, near Ramallah, suffered severe head wounds when she was hit by a rock thrown at the car in which she was a passenger.

There was no letup in the violence. On December 17, a husband and wife from the settlement of Ginot Shomron in Samaria were seriously injured when a rock smashed through the windshield of their car near Kalkilya. On December 18, three Palestinians were shot and killed by Israeli troops in the territories—one of them when he was spotted on the roof of a building holding a concrete block to be hurled down at a passing soldier—and about 30 others were wounded. The cabinet, at its weekly meeting that day, rejected a proposal from Labor ministers Moshe Shahal and Gad Yaakobi to introduce "unilateral autonomy" in the territories in the wake of the new situation created by the PLO's revised stands and Washington's decision to start a dialogue with the organization. Prime Minister Shamir said that "the government cannot make decisions today, but they will be made soon."

This was the final cabinet meeting of the outgoing government. The new government was approved in the Knesset four days later. Following the U.S. decision on the PLO, Shamir engineered a breakthrough in the deadlocked coalition talks. Arguing convincingly that only another unity government could rebuff the challenges facing Israel, he successfully brought the second consecutive such government into being (see below).

On December 24, tens of thousands of Israelis attended a Peace Now rally in Tel Aviv at which speakers—including MKs from Labor, Mapam, Citizens' Rights, and Shinui—called on the government to launch a dialogue with the PLO in pursuit of peace and an end to the occupation. The previous day the mass-circulation *Yediot Aharonot* had carried a poll suggesting that 54 percent of Israelis favored talks with the PLO.

At year's end two of the main adversaries in the arena voiced ideas that were at bottom similar about a possible way out of the vicious cycle of violence. In an interview in *Ha'aretz* (December 30), Prime Minister Shamir referred to the possibility of holding "democratic elections" in the territories, as envisaged in the Camp David accords, with the Arab residents there electing an "administrative council to run their internal affairs" but which would also become "the legitimate representative of the Palestinians in negotiations" with Israel. On December 29, *Davar* quoted Faisal al-Husseini, the most prominent Palestinian public figure in the territories and a supporter of Arafat's Fatah organization, as saying that if Israel were to permit "free, democratic, unconditional elections, unrelated to the autonomy plan, it is probable that the majority of the residents of the territories would take part in them and [thus] elect their representation for political talks with Israel." Husseini made these remarks to MK Yair Tzaban (Mapam), who was visiting him in prison, where he was still being held under an administrative detention order.

The gap between those two positions was probably more easily bridged than the chasm of mistrust, enmity, and sheer hatred that was generated by IDF activity in the territories in 1988, involving unremitting friction between troops and Civil Administration officials and the Palestinians. According to B'Tselem, the Israeli Information Center for Human Rights in the Occupied Territories, 293 Palestinians were killed by the Israeli security forces in the first year of the uprising (December

9, 1987–December 8, 1988). There were 199 fatalities in the West Bank and 94 in the Gaza Strip. Of these, 270 resulted from shootings (including plastic and rubber bullets), 20 from beatings (13 cases in the Gaza Strip), and 3 from other causes. Over half (55.6 percent) of the fatalities were in the 17–24 age group; 18.8 percent were aged 25–35, 14.3 percent were 13–16 year old, and 9 deaths (3.1 percent) were of children below the age of 12. The number of wounded was not known, but ran into the thousands.

In April Chief of Staff Dan Shomron said that unduly harsh measures in the territories would only stiffen solidarity and resistance among the population, necessitating even more stringent actions. "Bear in mind that we will have to live with these people," he cautioned then. In November Shomron acknowledged the double-bind situation in which Israel found itself when he told the Knesset's Defense and Foreign Affairs Committee that "every measure we take [to lower the level of the uprising] causes long-term damage"—but that failure to take those measures would also cause long-term harm. The real problem the IDF and the State of Israel faced in combating the uprising was encapsulated by O/C Central Command Maj. Gen. Amram Mitzna in a November interview with the *Jerusalem Post*. "The *intifada*," he said, "is not so much throwing stones as it is a state of mind."

OTHER NATIONAL AFFAIRS

The Knesset Elections

Around the end of March, Labor party chairman Shimon Peres pronounced the Knesset elections scheduled for November 1 "the most important since the establishment of the state." Peres, who was addressing a meeting of Labor's Central Committee—which reelected him party chairman by acclamation—spoke against the background of nearly four months of violent mass demonstrations in the territories and the Shultz peace initiative, then at its height. His assumption that the peace question was the most crucial issue facing the country was broadly accepted. Peres himself hoped to ride the crest of the peace wave to victory in November or, alternatively, to score points by blaming the Likud for torpedoing the chance for peace.

THE PARTY LISTS

Both the Labor Alignment and Herut (the dominant element of the Likud) made efforts to rejuvenate their ranks and present a more attractive list of candidates. In Labor, a sweeping "democratization" process initiated largely by the party's general secretary, MK Uzi Baram, had eliminated many of the manifestations of internal "bossism" (although the first six slots were still reserved for the party's "elder statesmen"). On June 15, Labor's Central Committee exercised its new prerogatives, with the result that 17 of the party's MKs in the 11th Knesset were dropped (some by their own choice) from the 1988 ticket. They were replaced, in almost every instance, by young activists, many of Sephardi origin and some hailing from development towns. (Ultimately, of the 39 Labor candidates elected to the 12th Knesset, no fewer than 14 were new MKs.) Yet a price was paid: many Israelis, and not only Labor supporters, were shocked that the veteran parliamentarian and statesman Abba Eban was denied a realistic place on Labor's list—after 30 years in the Knesset and stints as education minister and foreign minister, acquiring in the process, as the *Jerusalem Post* noted, "an international reputation as Israel's most articulate spokesman." Similarly, women fared poorly in the final ranking, getting only 10-percent realistic representation (four places in the first 40).

Three weeks later (July 6), Herut's 2,100-member Central Committee, long since "democratized," put on a display of rough-and-tumble political infighting whose ultimate result, in the opinion of most observers, was to weaken the standing of party leader Yitzhak Shamir. In the jockeying for position by the three rival camps in the party, headed by David Levy, Ariel Sharon, and Shamir ally Moshe Arens, the Levy and Sharon blocs were able to unite long enough to outvote the Shamir camp and push Arens into fourth place behind Shamir, Levy, and Sharon. (In the final Likud ranking, about 10 percent of the slots went to Herut's Liberal party allies, and on August 25, the two parties formally merged, the new entity known as the "Likud National Liberal Movement.") New faces among the top ten on the Herut list were Binyamin Begin, the son of reclusive former prime minister Menachem Begin, and Benjamin Netanyahu, who at the end of March had abruptly resigned his post as UN ambasssador in order to stand for a place on the Likud list. Oddly enough, despite Herut's identification with the Sephardi and "oriental" Jewish communities, its list was top-heavy with Ashkenazim (in contrast to Labor). Besides this, only one woman (from the Liberals) was included among the first 40 candidates on the final Likud list and not a single Arab or Druze (Labor's list contained two Israeli Arabs).

Twenty-eight lists—many of them single-issue (and, it sometimes seemed, single-person) groups, seeking everything from abolition of the income tax to a better deal for pensioners/prisoners/development towns/demobilized soldiers/Yemenites—had officially applied to run by the registration deadline, September 27. However, only 27 survived the final cutoff. On October 5, the Central Elections Committee (composed of representatives from the parties in the outgoing Knesset and headed by Supreme Court justice Eliezer Goldberg) voted overwhelmingly, 28–5 with three abstentions, to bar MK Rabbi Meir Kahane's Kach party from running. The grounds adduced for the decision were that Kach incited to racism and rejected the "democratic character of the state," two of the criteria contained in a 1985 amendment to the Basic Law: Knesset—passed in the wake of Kahane's successful Knesset campaign in 1984—under which a list could be prevented from participating in Knesset elections. The votes against barring Kahane were cast by the religious parties—Kahane cited the Torah and Jewish religious law as the inspiration for his platform advocating a theocracy free of Arabs and "Hellenizing Jews"—while the abstentions came from the ultranationalist camp. Kahane was the only Kach MK in the outgoing Knesset, but he was given a good chance of winning at least three seats in 1988 because of an *intifada* backlash inside Israel in general and among Kahane's constituency in particular. Kahane lost no time in appealing the decision to the Supreme Court.

Following a pattern in recent years, every action taken by the Left against Kahane triggered measures by the Right against the Progressive List for Peace (PLP), an Arab-Jewish party advocating the creation of a Palestinian state alongside Israel. Thus, on the day following the vote to keep Kach out of the campaign, the Central Elections Committee voted on motions to similarly bar the PLP—but these were rejected, 20–19. The decisive vote was cast by Justice Goldberg, who was not persuaded by arguments that the PLP's platform "negated the existence of Israel as the state of the Jewish people," a provision of the 1985 amendment inserted at the demand of the religious–right-wing bloc and aimed explicitly at the PLP. However, in this case, too, the final decision was to rest with the Supreme Court, following a petition filed by the Likud, Tehiya, Agudat Israel, and the National Religious party to overturn the committee's decision.

In the event, the rulings by the Supreme Court, announced on October 18, upheld and mirrored the votes of the Central Elections Committee. Sitting in an expanded panel of five justices, the court voted unanimously to bar Kach from running and, 3–2, to allow the PLP to participate. The decision regarding Kach, which was written by Supreme Court president Meir Shamgar, rejected Kahane's contention that the Halakhah (Jewish religious law) was incompatible with a democratic Jewish state and found that Kach's goals and actions were "manifestly racist" in a manner that was "appallingly similar to the most horrific experience of the Jewish people." On the PLP petition, the court majority held that the written material submitted for its perusal in support of barring the list was insufficiently "clear, convincing, and unequivocal."

Although Kahane was out of the race, his ideas about Arabs were not. They were well represented in the form of the new Moledet (Homeland) party headed by Maj. Gen. (res.) Rehavam Ze'evi. Like Kahane, Ze'evi played on deep-rooted fears of Israeli Jews, and taking as his point of departure the need to preserve Greater Israel, carried to its logical extreme the solution of the demographic problem that confronted those who wished to retain the occupied territories but also prevent the emergence of a binational state. Ze'evi called for a so-called voluntary transfer of the Arabs from the territories to Arab states. Not surprisingly, since the start of the uprising in the territories, opinion polls suggested that ever more Israelis were willing to entertain such a notion. Opponents of the scheme argued that, beyond the moral principles involved—since the Palestinians would obviously not "volunteer" to leave their homes, especially after their national consciousness had been raised by the *intifada*—the "transfer" in question was a mere euphemism for outright expulsion.

Ze'evi's stance was utterly devoid of a religious dimension; instead, he professed to find his inspiration in the national-liberation movement of the Jewish people, Zionism. (See also the section on "Extremism," below.) Besides the absence of the "Judaic" dimension in Ze'evi's ideas, what differentiated him from Kahane was that he was an authentic insider in the Israeli establishment. With his military background, his friends in high places, and his directorship of the Eretz-Israel Museum in Tel Aviv, Ze'evi made his pitch to a very different element of the population than Kahane, although he undoubtedly picked up votes from Kahane supporters after Kach was barred from the elections.

THE CAMPAIGN

At all events, the impact of the Palestinian uprising ensured that the "Arab question," in one form or another, became the central theme of the election campaign. The problem was that where the occupied territories were concerned, neither major party offered substantive, realistic, or innovative solutions. Both Likud and Labor were locked into their traditional platforms and clearly felt that a general election was not a propitious time to rock the boat. The Likud again resorted to guilt-by-association tactics against its chief rival. Its allegations that Labor would make a deal with the abhorred PLO were intended to create in the public's mind an identification between Labor and the PLO in order to discredit and demonize Labor. The tone was set in an article by Ariel Sharon (*Hadashot*, October 2), who asserted that the "Labor party leadership is engaged in a consistent endeavor to legitimize the PLO as a negotiating partner with Israel"—and then went on to equate Arafat with Hitler and the PLO with the Third Reich. The reader was left to draw the inference.

Labor, which for years had advocated the "Jordanian option," was nonplussed by King Hussein's formal disengagement from the West Bank virtually on the eve of the election campaign. This forced the party to abruptly drop from its campaign two of its principal planks: negotiations with Jordan (rather than with the Palestinians) to resolve the West Bank question, and an international peace conference framework (which no longer had a rationale now that Hussein was out of the picture). Still unwilling to address the real issues, Labor dredged up the 20-year-old Allon Plan for a "territorial compromise" in the West Bank. To demonstrate that a desire for peace was not tantamount to "wimpishness," and that Labor would not let itself be outdone by the Likud in projecting a tough image, the party turned to recently retired generals, notably Avigdor Ben-Gal and Ori Orr, who came up with a document stating that "the area to be relinquished by Israel in return for peace will be surrounded by Israeli forces on the west, the north, the south, and the east." One Labor party TV ad showed an electronic fence that would separate Israel from the Palestinian "enclave." The "generals' plan," as it was dubbed, was meant to demonstrate that the Allon Plan, far from being a "compromise out of weakness," was a scheme "that traps the Palestinians between a rock and a hard place without their being annexed but with peace."

The Orthodox and ultra-Orthodox parties, wracked by infighting that produced splits and splinter groups, enlisted "generals" of a different stripe. Agudat Israel ads (in the written press only—the Aguda shunned TV as immoral) featured the Brooklyn-based Lubavitcher Rebbe. Also supporting the all-Ashkenazi Aguda was the "Baba Baruch," a "wonder-working" rabbi with a zealous following among Israel's large Moroccan community. Both Shamir and Peres paid highly publicized (and ultimately futile) visits to his headquarters in the Negev development town of Netivot. A new list, Degel Hatorah (Torah Flag), was formed by Aguda breakaways guided by the venerable Rabbi Eliezer Schach, a bitter enemy of the Lubavitcher Rebbe and the Habad movement and a mentor of Shas. The latter, originally a Sephardi breakaway from Agudat Israel, used former Sephardi chief rabbi Ovadia Yosef in its TV ads. Shas played up the ethnic issue for all it was worth, railed against the disintegration of moral values in the modern society, and called for a return to religious fundamentals. One Shas TV ad, which stunned secular viewers and seemed to reveal the mind-set of at least part of the Shas constituency, showed a group of rabbis, clothed in traditional garb, intoning ritual incantations which were meant to release from their vows all persons who had taken an oath to vote for a specific party (i.e., a party other than Shas).

The religious-Zionist bloc, which had seen its ranks decimated in recent years by defections to both Herut (under Menachem Begin) and ultra-Orthodoxy, was able to hold its ground but little more. The ethnic factor crept into the National Religious party's selection of candidates when Prof. Avner Shaki, the hawkish leader of the NRP's Sephardi wing, scored an upset win over Religious Affairs Minister Zevulun Hammer in the fight for the top slot on the party's Knesset list. Of the NRP's first five candidates, two others besides Shaki were strongly identified with the Greater Israel movement.

The NRP's continuing tilt to the right produced a dovish backlash in the form of Meimad, a list headed by Rabbi Yehuda Amital, the dean of the *hesder* yeshivah (religious studies combined with army service) in the West Bank settlement of Alon Shvut. Despite these credentials, Amital expressed a readiness for territorial concessions in the territories, was against coercive religious legislation, and warned against the consequences of extremism. The NRP waged a bitter campaign against the new movement. Meimad's failure to obtain enough votes to enter the Knesset (1 percent of the total cast) spoke volumes about the mood among the religious-Zionist public in the Israel of 1988.

Feuding was also rife in the Arab sector, where the Communist party and the PLP (both ostensibly Arab-Jewish parties but which in practice drew nearly all their support from Israel's Arabs) were unable to overcome their differences long enough to sign a surplus-vote agreement to ensure that one of them would benefit from leftover votes after the allocation of seats, if those votes added up to another seat. (In the event, this failure cost the Communists, and hence Israel's Arabs, a fifth

MK.) A new feature on the Arab scene and also a sign of the times was the appearance of an all-Arab list, the Arab Democratic party, founded and headed by MK Abdel Wahab Darousha, who left Labor in protest at Defense Minister Rabin's policy toward the *intifada*. The campaigns of all three parties were focused largely on the occupation and the uprising—indeed, one PLP ad was banned by Justice Goldberg because it included a segment with PLO chief Yasir Arafat.

The uprising also featured prominently in the campaigns of the small established parties to the left of Labor and to the right of Likud. The Citizen's Rights Movement (CRM), Shinui, and Mapam—the latter ran independently of Labor for the first time in 23 years and was outraged when Labor signed a surplus-votes agreement with the CRM—urged that concessions be made for the sake of peace and called for an end to the occupation. Tehiya and Tzomet (the latter headed by former chief of staff Rafael Eitan, who broke with Tehiya), as well as Moledet, called for annexation of the territories, massive Jewish settlement, and the "eradication" of the *intifada*. These parties, and particularly the two largest, the CRM and Tehiya, laid a claim to ideological "purity," contending that they represented the unadulterated Left and Right, respectively. To demonstrate the point, they pooled some of their allotted television time to screen a debate between their leaders, MK Shulamit Aloni of the CRM and MK Yuval Ne'eman of Tehiya.

Economic and social issues were relegated to a secondary place in the campaign, although the Likud pounced on the ills of the giant Koor concern, which was affiliated with the Labor party via the Histadrut (Federation of Labor), and the attendant large-scale layoffs. Mapam, which had worked hard since its break with Labor to reassert itself as a socialist party whose chief concern was the worker, reaped the rewards of its endeavors, thanks in large measure to MK Yair Tzaban, its popular prophet of social justice.

Overall, though, in stark contrast to the pronouncements about the overriding importance of the elections, and combined spending by the parties estimated at $100 million, the campaign failed to catch fire. This was perhaps not surprising, since the two big parties had just completed four years of generally close and mutually beneficial cooperation in a national unity government. To see them suddenly attacking each other strained credibility. The by-now traditional TV debate between the leaders of Likud and Labor did little to enlighten the supposed quarter of a million undecided voters who were once more the primary target of the campaigns waged by the two major parties. The debate itself, which was finally held on October 23, a week before the election, had been the object of much bickering. The main stumbling blocks were disagreement over the moderator and the Shamir camp's insistence that the questions be submitted to the participants in advance, a stipulation that the Peres camp rejected outright and on which Shamir yielded. A word count made after the debate found that the moderator, Dan Shilon, a well-known radio and TV personality, had spoken more words than either of the two debaters.

The uprising finally impinged directly on the campaign in a brutal and tragic manner. On the evening of October 30, about 36 hours before the polls opened, a young ultra-Orthodox mother and her three infant children were burned to death when the interurban bus on which they were traveling was firebombed in Jericho. Immediately after the election results became known, Shimon Peres claimed that this incident had cost Labor three seats—a contention intended to take the onus off Peres for Labor's second-place finish, but which was obviously impossible to prove. At all events, when Peres failed to turn up at Labor's final campaign rally in Pardes Katz, and rumors flew that he had decided not to make a public appearance for fear of violence against him by hotheads in the wake of the bus outrage, his aides let it be known that he was visiting casualties of the attack. Rabin, for his part, took the unusual step of ordering the gutted hulk of the bus removed without allowing media access, leading Ariel Sharon and others to accuse the defense minister of acting out of electoral considerations, but Rabin said he had been guided by reasons of national morale and a desire not to enflame passions in the territories. On election day itself, a car carrying Likud activists was hit with a gasoline bomb in East Jerusalem, and one woman suffered serious burns. Such incidents were not likely to induce Israelis to respond to Yasir Arafat's eve-of-election plea that they should vote for "peace-seeking" parties. Both Likud and Labor rejected Arafat's attempt to intervene in the elections. Earlier, Arafat had addressed a similar call to Israeli Arabs.

ELECTION RESULTS AND ANALYSIS

The fragmented outcome of the election, and especially the cynical horse-trading that characterized the coalition negotiations, prompted renewed calls for a change in the country's electoral system. (In June a private member's bill to modify the

ELECTIONS TO THE 12TH KNESSET
(November 1, 1988)
AND 11TH KNESSET (July 23, 1984)

	1988	1984
Eligible voters	2,894,267	2,654,613
Valid votes cast[a]	2,283,123	2,073,321
Valid votes cast for parties not qualifying[a]	55,505	58,978
Valid votes counting in allocation of seats[b]	2,227,618	2,014,343
Quota per Knesset seat[b]	18,563	15,312

[a]Only lists receiving at least 1 percent of the valid votes cast—i.e., 22,831 in 1988—are entitled to share in the allocation of seats.
[b]The quotient for one Knesset seat is the number of valid votes cast for the lists qualifying—i.e., 2,227,618 in 1988—divided by 120 (the number of Knesset seats). Thus the quotient in 1988 was 18,563.

Party	Popular Vote (%) 1988	Popular Vote (%) 1984	Net Gain or Loss	Knesset Seats 1988	Knesset Seats 1984	Net Gain or Loss
Likud	709,305 (31.1)	661,302 (31.9)	−(0.8)	40	41	−1
Alignment[a]	685,363 (30.0)	724,074 (31.9)	−(1.9)	39	44	−5
Sephardi Torah Guardians (Shas)	107,709 (4.7)	63,605 (3.06)	+(1.64)	6	4	+2
Agudat Israel	102,714 (4.5)	36,079 (1.7)	+(2.8)	5	2	+3
Citizens Rights and Peace Movement	97,513 (4.3)	49,698 (2.4)	+(1.9)	5	3	+2
National Religious	89,720 (3.9)	73,530 (3.5)	+(0.4)	5	4	+1
Democratic Front for Peace and Equality	84,032 (3.7)	69,815 (3.36)	+(0.34)	4	4	—
Tehiya[b]	70,730 (3.1)	83,037 (4.0)	−(0.9)	3	5	−2
Mapam[a]	56,345 (2.5)	—	—	3	—	—
Tzomet[b]	45,489 (2.0)	—	—	2	—	—
Moledet	44,174 (1.9)	—	—	2	—	—
Shinui	39,538 (1.7)	54,747 (2.6)	−(0.9)	2	3	−1
Degel Hatorah	34,279 (1.5)	—	—	2	—	—
Progressive List for Peace	33,695 (1.5)	38,012 (1.8)	−(0.3)	1	2	−1
Arab Democratic party	27,012 (1.2)	—	—	1	—	—
Pensioners	16,674 (0.7)	—	—	—	—	—
Meimad	15,783 (0.7)	—	—	—	—	—
Derech Eretz	4,253 (0.2)	—	—	—	—	—
Le'or	4,182 (0.2)	—	—	—	—	—
Just Society	3,222 (0.1)	—	—	—	—	—
Yishai	2,947 (0.1)	—	—	—	—	—
Ma'as	2,838 (0.1)	—	—	—	—	—
Tarshish	1,654 (0.07)	—	—	—	—	—
Quiet Force	1,579 (0.07)	1,472 (0.07)	—	—	—	—
Veterans	1,018 (0.04)	—	—	—	—	—
Yemenites Union	909 (0.04)	—	—	—	—	—
Achdut	446 (0.02)	733 (0.035)	−(0.015)	—	—	—

[a]In 1984 the Labor Alignment included Mapam. Ezer Weizman's Yahad party, which won 3 seats in 1984, merged with Labor and its candidates were part of the Alignment list in 1988.
[b]In 1984 Tehiya and Tzomet ran together on a single list.

absolute proportional system, sponsored by the Knesset's Constitution, Law, and Justice Committee, passed its first reading by 69–37—the first time such a proposal had garnered the 61-vote absolute majority required to amend the law. However, the bill was then effectively buried in the same Law Committee whose chairman, Eli Kulas from the Likud, bowed to pressure from Prime Minister Shamir to table the legislation because of objections by the religious parties.)

The big loser in the election was Shimon Peres, and the big winner was the ultra-Orthodox parties. Peres, who was the centerpiece of Labor's election ads no less than a presidential candidate in the United States and ran what amounted to a single-issue campaign on the "peace" question, lost or at least failed to win his fourth straight election. (Rabin also appeared on TV with some frequency, but others, such as the party's "new faces" or Histadrut secretary-general Israel Kesar, were rarely if ever seen.) Calls in Labor for Peres's replacement as party leader that were voiced immediately after the results became known were soon muted, but the real power in the party passed almost palpably into the hands of Yitzhak Rabin. It was Rabin who called the shots in the coalition bargaining that ensued, Rabin who virtually coerced Peres into accepting a portfolio he did not want, and Rabin who, together with Yitzhak Shamir, created the second consecutive national unity government—ensuring in the process his retention of the key defense portfolio.

The 18 seats won by religious lists, a dramatic gain of 50 percent as compared with 1984, restored the numerical representation religious parties had enjoyed in the 1960s and early 1970s. However, there was a crucial difference. At that time religious Zionist parties, led by the NRP, had obtained about two-thirds of all the religious votes. In 1988 the situation was more than reversed: 13 of the 18 Knesset seats secured by religious lists were won by *haredi*, or ultra-Orthodox, parties that espoused a fundamentalist approach to religion and a non-Zionist if not anti-Zionist world view. The three ultra-Orthodox parties that entered the Knesset—Shas, Agudat Israel, and Degel Hatorah—received almost 75 percent of the votes cast for religious parties, an improvement of nearly a third over the combined 1984 *haredi* showing. Manifestly, a sea change had occurred in the religious sector. The spectacular performance by the religious lists, with Shas becoming the third largest faction in the House, came as an even more severe jolt to the nonreligious sector, because the polls had consistently predicted that the religious bloc would not better its 1984 representation. (The pollsters somewhat lamely explained—after the fact—that the *haredi* population refused to participate in polls.)

The Likud, with just over 31 percent of the votes cast, remained the country's largest party, though just barely. Nothing better exemplified the political atomization in the country than the fact that even the leading party won less than a third of the popular vote. A comparative analysis of voting patterns in 1984 and 1988 by the Central Bureau of Statistics showed that, while the Likud held its ground overall in the Jewish urban sector (obtaining about 35 percent of the total vote in the cities and large towns), its support in the development towns declined by 5 percent. This was more than accounted for by the gains recorded in that sector by religious parties, particularly Shas and Agudat Israel, which took 21 percent of the vote of this largely underprivileged and largely Asian-African population, more than double their 1984 performance and only 2 percent less than Labor.

Labor lost ground almost everywhere. In the Jewish urban centers its percentage of the popular vote declined from 34 percent in 1984 to 30 percent in 1988; in the moshavim, from 42 percent to 34 percent; and in the kibbutzim, from 79 percent to 55 percent, this due to the separate appearance of Mapam, which took 28 percent of the kibbutz vote. Labor also suffered a falloff among the non-Jewish population, obtaining 17 percent of the votes of Israel's Arabs, down from 23 percent in 1984. The turnout in the Arab sector was comparatively low (about 74 percent), and although Israel's Arabs possessed the potential to elect 12 MKs (they constituted 18 percent of the country's population, but the majority were below the voting age of 18) and thus bring about a drastic realignment in the Knesset, the three parties identified with the country's Arab population returned only half that number, the same as in 1984. Likewise, as in 1984, one of every three votes cast in non-Jewish locales went to the Communists, the Democratic Front for Peace and Equality.

The small parties to the left of Labor—the CRM, Mapam, and Shinui—returned ten MKs, with the CRM nearly doubling its 1984 vote, and Mapam, with three MKs, succeeding beyond its own best hopes. Overall, however, the combined Labor-Left bloc decreased by 4 Knesset seats, from 59 to 55, as compared with 1984.

On the other side of the spectrum, the parties to the right of Likud—Tehiya, Tzomet, and Moledet—increased their representation in the House from six to seven MKs (and would have had eight had Tzomet and Moledet signed a surplus-vote agreement). The ultranationalist parties obtained 50,000 more votes than in 1984, increasing their strength throughout the country. Indeed, the only sphere that disappointed the Right was the one area in which they had felt confident of success—the army. Even though the Likud and the small right-wing parties together garnered more than half the votes in the IDF, and the parties to the right of the Likud outperformed the parties to the left of Labor by 16 percent to 11 percent, the votes were broadly distributed so that Tehiya, which had counted on the army vote for a fourth seat, had to settle for three.

Forming a Government

The one overriding fact that triggered the political wheeling and dealing of the 50 days following the election was that, of the 27 lists that had run, no fewer than 15 entered the Knesset, 6 of them with no more than two MKs. Furthermore, Labor and Likud had finished in a virtual dead heat, with the Likud one key seat ahead. Broadly speaking, the results were as inconclusive as they had been in 1984, and the religious bloc, especially the ultra-Orthodox parties, held the key to a narrow coalition, whether led by Likud or Labor. No one was more keenly aware of this situation and its ramifications than the ultra-Orthodox parties.

In the last analysis, however, the ultrareligious bloc overreached itself, and a series of ironic twists and reversals ensued. The inordinate terms put forward by the *haredi* parties, especially Agudat Israel, under the prodding of the Lubavitcher Rebbe, for joining a narrow coalition, spurred the overwhelming majority of organized American Jewry—affiliated with the Reform and Conservative movements—to mount an intensive lobbying campaign vis-à-vis the Israeli political establishment and triggered a secular backlash within Israel. The growing debate about whether

Diaspora Jewry had the "right" to express itself on key topics regarding Israel (see also AJYB 1989, pp. 424–425) was for all practical purposes resolved when the postelection lobbying of the American Jewish leadership played an instrumental, if indirect, role in the formation of the second national unity government; and not only the "Who is a Jew?" amendment but virtually all religious legislation was shelved for the foreseeable future.

The squabble between the Israeli political leadership and American Jewry over the religious issue occurred while the PLO was engaged in diplomacy geared to translate the *intifada* into political gains, including the start of a dialogue with the United States. Jerusalem's intense preoccupation with the complexities of coalition making, and the estrangement between Israel and the American Jewish leadership over the religious question, meant that Israel's ability to respond forcefully to events in the international arena suffered. Finally, the concrete onset of the U.S.-PLO dialogue, perceived by Prime Minister-designate Yitzhak Shamir as inimical in the extreme to Israeli interests, was seized upon by him as sufficient cause to abandon any notion of forming a right-wing–religious coalition and to make concessions to Labor in order to ensure the creation of a second national unity government, thus effectively putting the ultra-Orthodox bloc in the position of a fifth wheel.

Things looked somewhat different in the immediate aftermath of the election. The announced aversion of Likud and particularly Labor to another national unity government, as an opening gambit at any rate, automatically made the ultra-Orthodox parties kingmakers. The Aguda and Shas, controlling 11 seats between them, wasted little time in stating their price—in the form of monetary allocations and religious legislation—for joining a coalition. In an effort to extract additional concessions, they played both ends against the middle, negotiating with both Likud and Labor even though they were known to be more inclined to join a Likud-led government. Compounding the situation was the unbridled, and unconcealed, enmity between Shas and the Aguda. This mutual rancor derived from a feud dating back to 18th-century Eastern Europe between *hassidim* and *mitnagdim*, groups personified two centuries later by Rabbi Schneerson (the Lubavitcher Rebbe) and Rabbi Schach, a Shas mentor, respectively. Also part of the equation was the ethnic factor—Sephardim vs. Ashkenazim. (The third ultra-Orthodox party, Degel Hatorah, ostensibly associated with Shas, seemed to espouse more dovish views than either Aguda or Shas, and with only two seats was less peremptory in its demands.)

The demands of the ultra-Orthodox parties, and the apparent readiness of Peres and Shamir to accommodate them (some on the Left urged Peres to take advantage of the rivalries within the ultra-Orthodox camp and form a coalition with part of the religious bloc, even if this entailed certain concessions in the religious sphere) raised fears of "Khomeinism" among Israel's secular majority. Abba Eban encapsulated what many felt when he lashed out at the ultrareligious and ultranationalist worldviews that seemed to hold the key to a new Israeli government. Speaking at a ceremony sponsored by the Jerusalem Foundation, Eban (still formally an MK) declared: "Prophetic Judaism and classical Zionism as expressed in the Declaration of Independence are now challenged by superstition, intolerance, political unilateralism, xenophobia and adventurism which take us far away from the world in which Israel's flag first went aloft in its own name and pride 40 years ago."

President Chaim Herzog, also reportedly alarmed by the sweeping *haredi* demands and a mounting secular backlash, took the unusual move of holding informal meetings with representatives of the parties that would form the 12th Knesset even before the Central Elections Committee published the official results of the vote. This was the first of several unorthodox steps on Herzog's part in an effort to bring about what he believed was the only viable solution that could break the deadlock and mute the religious-secular cacophony—the formation of a second Likud-Labor coalition. Herzog also let it be known that his office had been deluged with calls and cables urging national unity and a change in the electoral system—70,000 such appeals would eventually reach the president. Herzog, while barred from actively intervening in politics, thus implicitly lent his support to a mass rally held in Tel Aviv on November 12, calling for an overhaul of the system.

On November 14, four days after the official publication of the election results and after holding formal consultations with all the parties elected to the 12th Knesset, Herzog announced that, since a majority of their representatives (including both Shas and the Aguda) had recommended that the Likud candidate form the new government, and since the Likud was the largest Knesset faction, he was accordingly entrusting Yitzhak Shamir with the task.

Herzog took the opportunity of the announcement to urge "a thorough examination of the Election Law in order to ensure the public its full democratic rights." The president also indicated his own preference when he noted that the "will of the people," as he understood it, "suggests a longing for unity in the face of the hazards that lie in wait for us from without and the threat of a schism from within." He also voiced his concern regarding the dangers facing both "our society's Zionist character" and "the unity of the Jewish people," pointing especially to the "unprecedented attack . . . [launched] on a segment of the population because of its religious character." In his reply, Prime Minister Shamir agreed that a "national unity government . . . can [still] provide an answer to the country's needs and problems." He also referred specifically to "the voices of concern and apprehension that are reaching us from diaspora Jewry, especially from U.S. Jewry . . . on the issue of [the "Who is a Jew?"] legislation."

Indeed, as early as November 9, 27 national Jewish organizations in the United States had issued a joint statement warning that passage of the amendment to the Law of Return, which was being demanded by elements among the ultra-Orthodox as a condition for joining a coalition, would do "enormous damage, actual and symbolic" to Diaspora Jewry. (The so-called Who is a Jew? amendment, which was periodically submitted to the Knesset and routinely defeated—most recently five months earlier, on June 14, by a vote of 60–53—would bar non-Orthodox converts to Judaism from gaining automatic entry to Israel under the Law of Return, thus implicitly but effectively delegitimizing Judaism's Conservative and Reform streams.) With the publication of the statement by the American Jewish groups, the battle line was definitively drawn between the Judaism that was dominant in the pluralistic American society and the establishment Judaism of the Israeli polity. The statement by the American Jewish groups took as its point of departure a reaffirmation of American Jewry's "devotion to the State and the people of Israel" and stressed that "we are one people, with a single destiny." It continued:

> We reject any effort to divide our people by legislative action of the Knesset. All Jews, including those of us who are not citizens of Israel, are affected by the possibility of a change in the definition of Who is a Jew under Israel law, either through amending the Law of Return or adoption of the Rabbinical Courts bill. [The latter would give the Orthodox rabbinical courts absolute sovereignty in all personal status matters, without the possibility of recourse to the civil courts.]

These were but two of the demands of the religious parties that would be agreed to by the Likud in the following weeks before Shamir made a last-minute switch and opted for a coalition with Labor—a move that infuriated the religious parties and left scars that would not easily heal. Other demands were for ministerial portfolios including education (a portfolio sought by both Shas and the NRP), housing, interior, labor, and religious affairs; the chairmanship of the powerful Knesset Finance Committee and a series of other appointments at the rank of deputy minister; "budgetary parity" in education and large-scale allocations to various *haredi* institutions, at an estimated cost of NIS 500 million to the Treasury; a law enabling local municipalities to regulate the opening of businesses on the Sabbath and holy days; a law, based on a British Mandate ordinance of 1919, under which religious conversion would require the approval of the head of the community which the convert was joining—i.e., the Orthodox Chief Rabbinate in the case of Jews; a law restricting missionary activity; a law prohibiting damage to burial sites (aimed at archaeological digs); a law granting amnesty to the members of the Jewish terrorist underground still in prison and to other Israelis who had attacked Palestinians in situations of "security distress" (a proposal also supported by MKs from the ultranationalist lists); passage of the "pork law"; enforcement of the abortions law; a commitment from the Likud not to change the electoral system; and assurance that the status quo pertaining to the Sabbath and to the drafting of yeshivah students would be upheld. Agudat Israel also let it be known that it had been promised the chairmanship of the State Lottery, whose revenues were earmarked for various deserving institutions.

Shamir found himself in deep water when it emerged that some of the demands put forward by Likud's natural allies in the ultranationalist camp were incompatible with ultra-Orthodox conditions. In the realm of military service, former chief of staff Rafael Eitan's small Tzomet party was vehement in its insistence that exemptions granted to yeshivah students be drastically reduced if not eliminated altogether. The ultranationalists' demand for new settlements in the occupied territories would add hundreds of millions of shekels to the "bill" submitted by the religious parties. Even within his own ranks Shamir faced patronage problems, notably how to divide the two senior portfolios of defense and foreign affairs among Ariel Sharon, David Levy, and Shamir's close ally Moshe Arens.

LABOR-LIKUD TALKS

It was in large measure to extricate himself from this mass of mutually irreconcilable claims and counterclaims that Shamir invited the Alignment to hold talks on the possible re-formation of the national unity government. The first meeting between the two sides, attended by both Shamir and Peres, took place on November 15—the same day, as it happened, on which the PLO declared the "State of Palestine" in Algiers.

Yet these negotiations too immediately floundered due to conflicting demands and personal animosities. Shamir would not agree to another rotation in the premiership and refused even to entertain the possibility of Peres's returning to the Foreign Ministry, a stance for which he found a perhaps not unexpected ally in Labor's Yitzhak Rabin. In an Israel TV interview on November 16, Rabin stunned the Peres camp by proposing not only that the Likud-Labor coalition be reconstituted under Shamir without rotation, but that the Likud should be given "a chance to implement its peace plan" and that to this end, for the sake of harmony, it would be preferable if the Likud held the foreign-affairs portfolio as well as the premiership. Peres was relegated to the Treasury. Rabin had consulted with no one in the party before making public his audacious proposal, but once a figure of his standing had revealed his terms to the entire nation, they could not easily be retracted.

However, another full month was required before Shamir accepted even this scheme. In the meantime, opposition in the American Jewish community to the "Who is a Jew?" amendment—which Shamir had assured Agudat Israel would be passed within six weeks of the government's installation—was fast becoming a groundswell. The *Jerusalem Post* reported that Israel's ambassador to the United States, Moshe Arad, who was the immediate target of the outraged reaction of American Jews, had taken the unusual move of attempting to intervene in internal policy-making. "I implore you to discuss and reassess the grave repercussions which the law would have on the relations between Israel and the Jewish community, and as a direct consequence, the ramifications on our standing in the United States," Arad cabled Shamir and Peres. Nor did the American Jewish community confine its protests to the United States or to backroom diplomacy, as in the past. In an effort to prevent what they feared would be an irrevocable schism, with unforeseeable consequences for both Israel and the entire Jewish people, the American Jewish leadership intervened openly in the formation of an Israeli government.

A large ad in the Israeli Hebrew press on November 21 declaring that "the unity of the Jewish people is in the balance" called on "all Members of Knesset and the political leadership in Israel not to pass any legislation that would change the definition of 'who is a Jew.' " The ad asserted bluntly, "Your activity will determine the future relationship between the people of Israel and the Jewish people in the diaspora." The signatories were the United Jewish Appeal of the United States and Canada, the Conference of Jewish Federations of North America, and the United Israel Appeal. On the same day a delegation of these organizations arrived in Israel for meetings with Israeli political and religious leaders. A communiqué issued by the Prime Minister's Office following Shamir's talk with the group (November 22) noted that they had expressed their "grave concern" at the proposed legislation and had "asked the prime minister to remove the issue from the political agenda." Shamir had replied that "there is no question whatsoever of disqualifying any Jew" and had attempted to reduce the issue to a mere technicality, devoid of implications: "The matter under consideration," he noted, "is the registration of converts from abroad." Two other high-powered delegations also arrived in Israel to lobby against the amendment.

On November 24, Labor's Leadership Bureau decided that no basis existed for entering into negotiations with the Likud on the formation of a new government and that any such negotiations would require the bureau's prior approval. Peres and his aides continued to hold contacts with the religious parties and came under fire from the Likud for trying to form a government even though the president had entrusted that task to Shamir. Again, the main beneficiaries of the competition were the religious parties.

On November 30, six days after its initial decision, Labor's Leadership Bureau voted—against the recommendation of both Peres and Rabin—to reject another offer by Prime Minister Shamir to enter into negotiations on forming a government in which Shamir would hold the premiership for the full four-year period. The vote was 61–57 with one abstention. The general bewilderment at the course of events was indicated by the conflicting analyses of what the vote meant. Some commentators read it as a blow to the veteran leadership, while others thought that Peres had engineered the outcome in order to improve his bargaining position vis-à-vis the Likud by playing "hard to get" and enabling him to demand a higher price for acquiescence—specifically, a rotation agreement.

It then emerged that Peres and his confidant, the newly elected MK Dr. Yosef Beilin, had concluded a secret deal with Agudat Israel which, while insufficient to enable Peres to form a government, would preclude a Shamir government without Labor. At a stormy meeting of Labor's outgoing ministers on December 2, an outraged Yitzhak Rabin pulled out two documents which he said were the secret agreements cooked up by Peres and Beilin with the Aguda behind the backs of the party's leadership and without its authorization. Peres's concessions to Agudat Israel rivaled those of Shamir, including a pledge to recommend favorably to the party's Central Committee legislation to amend the Law of Return, with a timetable for its implementation.

On December 5, Shamir asked for and received from President Herzog an additional three weeks to form a government. In his statement granting Shamir the extension, Herzog gave voice to the "sense of frustration, helplessness, humiliation and shame, as well as grave concern," that he said was felt by the "great majority" of Israelis in the face of the coalition negotiations. According to *Ha'aretz*, Herzog held intensive contacts with political leaders and private talks with both Peres and Labor-party secretary-general Uzi Baram, imploring them to overcome factional and party differences and resume negotiations with the Likud for a "unity" government. By this stage, Peres was more than willing, as it was clear that he could not form a government, but Baram was steadfast in his principled objection (he would later decline a ministerial portfolio for the same reason). Thus, as bickering among the religious parties themselves continued—the latest snag was that both the Aguda and Degel Hatorah insisted on heading a promised new Education Ministry department that was to control the ultra-Orthodox school system—and Shamir seemed ready to pay whatever price was demanded for joining the coalition, Labor's Central Committee voted on December 8 by a 2-1 margin (637–348) to renew the coalition talks with the Likud. President Herzog's public and private endeavors were instrumental in this development.

Nevertheless, two additional weeks were required to complete the negotiations—the very period in which the dramatic U.S.-PLO rapprochement was played out. Among the stumbling blocks that the Likud and Labor teams ran up against were Labor's insistence on receiving the chairmanship of the Knesset's Finance Committee in order to ensure a harmonious rapport with the Finance Ministry which Peres was destined to head; Labor's refusal to accept Likud's consent to the Tehiya plan for the establishment of ten settlements a year in the occupied territories (a major problem in the Likud-Labor talks was that until the very end the Likud wanted to retain the option of setting up a religious–right-wing coalition and had given dozens of undertakings to the parties in question which were unacceptable to the Alignment); and Labor's demand to retain the education portfolio, which Shamir had already earmarked for the NRP.

The one issue that was studiously avoided by Likud and Labor was the *intifada*. Yet it was Yasir Arafat's iteration of Washington's conditions for the start of a U.S.-PLO dialogue and Shultz's announcement on December 14 that such a dialogue would begin that provided the final catalyst for the conclusion of the coalition talks and the formation of a second consecutive unity government.

Symbolically, December 14 also saw another significant stage in the battle of U.S. Jewry against the mooted amendment to the Law of Return, a matter that was not resolved until the signing of the Likud-Labor coalition agreement five days later. On that day a petition decrying the amendment, sponsored by the Council of Jewish Federations and signed by 100,000 North American Jews, was presented to Prime Minister Shamir by a representative delegation from 12 American Jewish communities. When Shamir resurfaced 48 hours after disappearing from public view—in the immediate aftermath of Shultz's announcement—to rail against the American move, he was determined to conclude the coalition-making process and set up the broad government that he believed Israel needed. Such a coalition was essential, he told the Knesset when he presented the government for its approval the following week, in order to rebuff "the massive propaganda and diplomatic offensive being conducted against Israel in the international diplomatic arena by the terrorist organizations and their friends and supporters."

To rope in Labor, Shamir agreed to the establishment of eight new settlements instead of the 40 he had promised Tehiya; Labor received the chairmanship of the Finance Committee; and a series of checks and balances was instituted in order to ensure that no major policy decisions could be made by Likud without Labor's consent. A so-called parity committee composed of the three senior ministers of each party was to be established to oversee major policy decisions. This informal but institutionalized body would supplement both the 26-member cabinet and the 12-member inner cabinet. Likud and Labor agreed that, in the event of the government's being toppled by a vote of no confidence in the Knesset, neither party would attempt to form a new narrow-based government, but that a bill would be submitted jointly to dissolve the House and hold an election within 100 days. It was further stipulated that Prime Minister Shamir could not fire a Labor minister without first consulting with Vice Premier Shimon Peres. The coalition agreement was signed on December 19.

Stormy sessions ensued when the two parties' central committees convened to ratify the accord. On December 20, the Likud Central Committee approved the coalition agreement by a margin of 56–44 percent, though not before Ariel Sharon and Yitzhak Modai—both of whom stood to lose out in terms of prestigious ministerial portfolios in a broad coalition—had castigated Shamir for breaking written contractual agreements with the religious parties and for showing "moral turpitude" in not forming a narrow government. Labor's Central Committee, meeting the following day, easily approved the coalition agreement despite the impassioned opposition of the party's young doves, led by Secretary-General Uzi Baram, but the meeting degenerated into cacophonous name-calling when it emerged that Peres had failed to name a single woman among his party's cabinet ministers.

The ultra-Orthodox parties hurled a good deal of invective at Shamir, and Degel Hatorah actually initiated court proceedings over the Likud's "breach of contract"; while it dropped the case, the party refused to enter the coalition. Both Shas and Agudat Israel soon swallowed their pride and joined the coalition, as did the NRP, all hoping to cash in on their pledges from Shamir even though the rules of the game had suddenly changed. The ultranationalist bloc (from which only Tehiya had finalized an agreement with the Likud) joined the left-wing parties in the opposition—which totaled fewer MKs than there were ministers in the cabinet.

THE NEW GOVERNMENT

The Basic Guidelines of the new government, as presented for the Knesset's ratification by Prime Minister Shamir on December 22, were virtually a replay of the 1984 policy principles, despite the developments of the intervening years, particularly in the occupied territories. Following the most inconclusive election in the country's history and hard on the heels of bitterly divisive and rancorous coalition negotiations, Shamir declared that "we urgently need national unity." Israel, he pronounced, would "spare no effort" to advance the peace process, which could come about "only through direct dialogue." A peace settlement would have to ensure Israel's security—which ruled out "a complete withdrawal to the suffocating borders of 1967"—while enabling "the Arab inhabitants of Eretz-Israel . . . to conduct their affairs with as much freedom as possible." In the same vein, Shamir called on "the Arab residents of Judea, Samaria and the Gaza District" to desist from "violent means [which] will achieve nothing" and to join Israel in "seeking to create conditions of peaceful coexistence" that would "assure liberty and prosperity for you and your children."

At the same time, the prime minister asserted that the Jewish settlements in the territories "fulfill an important role in the realm of defense and in preventing the establishment of a PLO state in Eretz-Israel," apparently unwittingly contradicting himself, however, when he added that it was "imperative for the IDF and the [other] security branches to guaranteee their security." Shamir pledged that "we will expand settlement throughout Eretz-Israel." He also took the opportunity to express the government's disagreement with the U.S. decision to launch a dialogue with the PLO. "We continue to hope that the U.S. will reconsider its decision," he said, while lauding the "unprecedented developments" in Israeli-U.S. bilateral relations during the Reagan years.

On the "Who is a Jew?" question, Shamir described American Jewry as "a faithful and vital ally" but also reiterated his view that no more was involved than "registering converts." Even though he had signed an agreement with Agudat Israel pledging to pass the amendment to the Law of Return within six weeks, Shamir said that "false impressions" had been created that had generated concern among Diaspora Jewry. "It goes without saying," he said, "that there is no intention whatsoever of delegitimizing any Jew." He urged "all streams and elements" in the Diaspora to make a "special effort," adding that "with good will it is possible to find a basis on which we can all unite."

Although the 12th Knesset contained no fewer than 38 new members, including 7 from the Likud and 14 from Labor, the composition of the cabinet presented by Prime Minister Shamir evoked a sense of *déjà vu*, since the majority of the ministers had served in the outgoing government, many holding the same posts. Among the newcomers were Shas's Rabbi Arye Deri, aged 29—the youngest cabinet minister in the country's history (he was not an MK)—who took the helm at the powerful Interior Ministry from which his Shas colleague Rabbi Yitzhak Peretz, now relegated to the small Absorption Ministry, had resigned under the previous government for reasons of conscience; and the Likud's Dan Meridor, the new minister of justice, who, along with Binyamin Begin, Benjamin Netanyahu, Roni Milo, and Ehud Olmert was one of the so-called "princes" in the party who came from veteran

Herut families. Milo and Olmert also assumed ministerial rank for the first time, Milo heading a brand-new Ministry of Environmental Protection and Olmert given responsibility for the "Israeli-Arab sector." Labor, for all its vaunted overhaul and "young" image, fielded only two new ministers, neither of whom could by any stretch of the imagination be termed "a new face" (Avraham Katz-Oz, the outgoing deputy agriculture minister, took over that portfolio, and Rafael Edri, a veteran party functionary, was named minister without portfolio). In the NRP a mini-upheaval occurred when, on December 25, the party's Central Committee chose Zevulun Hammer, from the party's moderate wing, by a large margin over the party's number-one candidate in the elections, the hawkish Avner Shaki, to serve as religious affairs minister, the same post he had held in the outgoing government.

Within three days of the cabinet's installment, the coalition agreement was broken. The framers of that document, evidently seeking to achieve hyper-parity, had provided for deputy ministers from the Likud to serve in the finance and defense ministries, both held by Labor, and for a deputy minister from Labor to serve in the Foreign Ministry, held by a Likud appointee. However, Defense Minister Rabin balked at this arrangement, and the new cabinet, meeting for the first time on December 25, appointed Likud MK Benjamin Netanyahu, former ambassador to the UN, as deputy foreign minister and Peres's confidant, MK Yossi Beilin, as deputy finance minister. The cabinet also created the Ministry for Environmental Protection and appointed 11 of the 12 members of the inner cabinet (up from 10 in the previous government), 6 each from Likud and Labor to ensure perfect balance. The Likud appointees, besides Shamir, were Arens, Levy, Sharon, Modai, and Nissim; while Labor went with Peres, Rabin, Navon, Bar-Lev, and Weizman. The sixth Labor member was not appointed, as Peres had not yet decided between Moshe Shahal and Mordechai Gur. (Shahal later got the appointment.) On December 26, Peres suffered a setback within his own party when his candidate for chairman of the Knesset caucus, MK David Libai, was beaten by Haim Ramon, one of the young doves in the party who had opposed Labor's entry into the national unity government.

National Security

The deleterious impact of the *intifada* on Israel's national security was direct and immediate, with the indirect and long-term consequences not yet clear.

The first to be affected were reserve soldiers in combat units. On April 11, the deputy chief of staff, Maj. Gen. Ehud Barak, told reporters that such reservists would serve up to 62 days in 1988—double the normal yearly call-up—with most of the time allotted to duty in the occupied territories. Clearly this would affect the scheduled training program for the reserve forces, Barak explained, but the arrangement would result in minimal harm to the training and maneuvers of the regular forces. Barak said that the first four months of the uprising had already cost the IDF tens of millions of shekels which had not been taken account of in budgetary

THE NATIONAL UNITY CABINET
(installed on December 22, 1988)

Prime Minister	Yitzhak Shamir (Likud-Herut)
Vice Premier & Finance Minister	Shimon Peres (Labor)
Deputy Premier & Minister of Education and Culture	Yitzhak Navon (Labor)
Deputy Premier & Minister of Construction and Housing	David Levy (Likud-Herut)
Agriculture	Avraham Katz-Oz (Labor)
Communications	Gad Yaakobi (Labor)
Defense	Yitzhak Rabin (Labor)
Economy and Planning	Yitzhak Modai (Likud-Liberals)
Energy and Infrastructure	Moshe Shahal (Labor)
Environmental Protection[1]	Roni Milo (Likud-Herut)
Foreign Affairs	Moshe Arens (Likud-Herut)
Health	Yaakov Tzur (Labor)
Immigrant Absorption	Yitzhak Peretz (Shas)
Industry and Trade	Ariel Sharon (Likud-Herut)
Interior	Arye Deri (Shas)
Justice	Dan Meridor (Likud-Herut)
Labor and Social Affairs	Yitzhak Shamir[2]
Police	Haim Bar-Lev (Labor)
Religious Affairs	Yitzhak Shamir[3]
Science and Development	Ezer Weizman (Labor-Yahad)
Tourism	Gideon Patt (Likud-Liberals)
Transport	Moshe Katzav (Likud-Herut)
Without Portfolio[3]	Rafael Edri (Labor)
	Mordechai Gur (Labor
	Moshe Nissim (Likud-Liberals)
	Ehud Olmert (Likud-Herut)

[1] The establishment of this new ministry was ratified by the Knesset on December 27.
[2] Rabbi Moshe Ze'ev Feldman from Agudat Israel—which traditionally refused to participate in the cabinet—was appointed deputy minister for labor and social affairs on December 25 to run the ministry on a day-to-day basis, although Prime Minister Shamir formally bore ministerial responsibility for its functioning.
[3] On December 27, the Knesset endorsed Zevulun Hammer (NRP) as religious affairs minister and Avner Shaki (NRP) as minister without portfolio.

planning. His hope was that the cost of putting down the *intifada* would not affect the army's procurement and development plans.

However, in May, Maj. Gen. Uri Saguy, the chief of the Ground Forces Command (GFC), was quoted in the IDF's weekly *Bamahaneh* as stating that the ongoing deployment in the territories had "seriously impaired the basic-training level" of the IDF and that only a decline in the intensity of the uprising would enable the GFC to "stabilize the training schedule for the regular army." Two months later, the head of the Logistics Branch, Maj. Gen. Menahem Einan, stated that if the IDF did not receive a "special supplement" to its current budget "as compensation for expenses arising from the *intifada*," he would "recommend that the IDF's weapons procurement program be halted." Einan said that the IDF lacked funds to achieve even its "minimum essential goals" and warned against concentrating inordinately on the events in the territories and in southern Lebanon at the expense of maintaining war readiness.

Indeed, a major concern of the High Command was that the Arab states would perceive Israel's reaction to the uprising—the deliberate refusal to quell it swiftly and brutally using full-scale battlefield means—as a sign of weakness. This might undermine a pillar of Israel's national-security doctrine—the maintenance of a credible deterrence vis-à-vis the Arab states. In the territories themselves, the behavior of the population, their readiness to confront fully armed troops with stones, and in some cases to attack them at close quarters, showed that the Palestinians had overcome a fear barrier, with a concomitant erosion of Israeli deterrent capability. The IDF's response was to impose ever more stringent punitive measures. Furthermore, Israeli military planners would have to add to their various war scenarios the distinct possibility that the inhabitants of the territories would stage mass demonstrations and engage in various forms of violence during a full-scale war, forcing the IDF to commit troops to this "front" and reducing its potential for maneuver in the territories.

Already in 1988, General Barak told the Press Club on December 4, the IDF had committed an average of 10,000 troops per day to the territories, accounting for 3.5 million workdays of soldiers and officers. Barak added that the IDF's deployment in the territories was adversely affecting the training continuity of regular units and military exercises for the reserves. Nevertheless, he said, "We are convinced that the IDF's combat ability has not been harmed."

Barak and others on the General Staff also dismissed the phenomenon of refusal to serve in the territories for reasons of conscience as insignificant. Yesh Gvul (There Is a Border/Limit), the group formed during the Lebanon War, again took the lead among organizations advocating refusal to serve in the territories, maintaining a support system for those who were jailed for their action. Although only several dozen persons formally refused to do reserve duty in the territories, serving military-prison terms of up to a month—in some cases more than once—many others avoided duty in the territories through internal arrangements with their unit commanders, serving elsewhere instead. Toward the end of the year it was reported that the police were conducting a secret criminal investigation into the activities of Yesh Gvul on suspicion that the group was engaged in unlawful incitement. According to a local Jerusalem paper, the investigation had been ordered by the attorney general following a request by the legal adviser of the Shin Bet. The action was taken after Yesh Gvul published a booklet instructing soldiers how to proceed if conscience prevented them from serving in the territories. Left-wing MKs, most of whom disagreed with the tactics of Yesh Gvul, demanded that the investigation be halted, calling Yesh Gvul a legitimate protest group. On December 28, two of the organization's activists were interrogated by the police.

The debate over the territories also led to quasi-protest movements from within the establishment. At the end of March, a group of 34 major generals, 86 brigadier generals, 115 colonels—all retired from the IDF—and some 200 experts in related spheres formed the Council for Peace and Security, headed by former chief of military intelligence Aharon Yariv. This group, which claimed to be nonpartisan but was identified in the public mind with the Labor party, had as its slogan: "Israel's security depends on the IDF and not on the territories." The council ran ads in the Israeli press calling for a distinction to be drawn between a "security border" and a "political border." In their view, the continued occupation of the territories undermined the IDF's war preparedness, eroded the national consensus which was essential in a genuine war situation, and, by reducing the prospects for peace, heightened the likelihood of war. In August the inevitable countergroup was formed. As its name—Officers and Academics for Security and Peace—suggested, this group, which included another former chief of intelligence, MK Yehoshua Saguy (Likud), placed "security ahead of peace." The aim of this body was to convince the public of the "vital importance of Judea, Samaria, Gaza and the Golan Heights for Israel's security."

A public-opinion survey on national security sponsored by Tel Aviv University's Jaffee Center for Strategic Studies (of which Aharon Yariv was the director) found that 57 percent favored the annexation to Israel of the West Bank and Gaza (up from 54 percent in 1986)—part of what the survey directors (headed by Prof. Asher Arian of Tel Aviv University) described as "a somewhat more right-wing tendency" in the country as compared with the previous poll two years earlier. (The survey, which was published June 1, was conducted six months earlier, during the initial, mass-demonstrations stage of the *intifada*.) The proportion of those who thought Israeli policy in the territories was too soft was up by 6 percent from 1986 and stood at 51 percent. Overall, the survey concluded, while Israelis continued to believe "by a very large margin" that the country could successfully overcome the threats it faced, "clear evidence" existed of an "erosion of that confidence" as compared with the earlier poll.

Israelis' confidence may have been boosted by the launching, on September 19, of Ofek-1, described officially in a press release issued by Israel Aircraft Industries as "an experimental technological satellite," and by MK Prof. Yuval Ne'eman, chairman of the Israel Space Agency, as Israel's "calling card to the space age." The

150-kilogram octagonally shaped satellite, lifted into space by a three-stage Shavit rocket, orbited the earth elliptically once every 90 minutes, from a perigee of 250 km. (over the Middle East) to an apogee of 1,000 km. Israel thus joined a select group of countries with satellite-launching capability. According to Ne'eman, Ofek-1 was a strictly civilian project and was not a spy satellite. It was expected to burn up after some weeks in space, though not before feeding Israeli scientists a wealth of data. According to Reuven Pedatzur, a defense affairs analyst for *Ha'aretz*, with the launching of Ofek-1 Israel showed for the first time that it possessed medium-range ballistic missile capability.

LEBANON

Ballistic missiles could be of no help, however, in combating the numerous attacks and infiltration attempts in and from Lebanon in 1988. Security personnel pointed to the *intifada* to account for the upsurge in hostile activity from Lebanon during the year. The thinking was that the PLO and others wanted to demonstrate their solidarity with the uprising, and perhaps open a "second front" by stepping up their activity in Lebanon (as well as from Egypt and Jordan). Thus 1988 saw more than 630 incidents involving the IDF or the Southern Lebanon Army (SLA), the Israeli-supported militia in the security zone. (On November 7, SLA commander Gen. Antoine Lahad was seriously wounded when he was shot at close range by a 21-year-old woman from the Lebanese Communist party.) There were 24 infiltration attempts across the border from Lebanon into northern Israel, all of which were foiled either in the Israeli-declared "security zone" in southern Lebanon or at the security fence along the border; this compared with 10 attempts in 1987. Five of the forays were carried out by Yasir Arafat's Fatah organization, but no Fatah squads were involved in such incidents after November 24, as Arafat moved toward a dialogue with the United States. Katyushas were also fired sporadically into upper Galilee, and in one such incident (March 3), five persons were hurt when a rocket hit a house.

As in previous years, the Israel Air Force was the spearhead of antiterrorist activity in Lebanon. Besides the standard targets, on August 8, the IAF bombed a Voice of Palestine radio station in southern Lebanon that had been broadcasting instructions to the leadership of the *intifada*. The Israel Navy was also active, sinking or intercepting a number of vessels with terrorists aboard.

Israeli ground forces were more active in 1988 than at any time since the IDF's withdrawal from Lebanon in June 1985, and as a result sustained more fatalities. Three Israeli paratroopers, two of them officers, were killed and 17 others wounded in a two-tiered IDF sweep in southern Lebanon on May 2–4, aimed at restoring Israel's deterrent capability in the area following a series of attacks on the IDF and the SLA. The sweep operation included an attack on the village of Maidoun, some 3 kilometers north of the security zone in the Beka'a Valley, in an area occupied by Syrian forces and large numbers of Hezballah gunmen, including hundreds of Iranians. The village had been deserted by its inhabitants and transformed by Hezballah into a heavily fortified stronghold. All the IDF casualties in the operation occurred in the heavy fighting that erupted in Maidoun. After the raid, which received worldwide publicity when ABC-TV interrupted its regular programming to announce that 2,500 Israeli troops had entered Lebanon—a figure which turned out to be highly exaggerated—it emerged that Defense Minister Rabin had not informed anyone in the cabinet about the operation. Ministers from both Labor and Likud were critical of this state of affairs and called for a review of the procedures for decision making on military operations—particularly if the possibility, however hypothetical, existed of intervention by Syrian forces. Rabin said the raid had been carried out within the parameters of ongoing government policy and therefore needed no special approval.

Rabin himself was critical of the IDF's performance in the army's first deep-penetration raid since the early stages of the Lebanon War. On the night of December 8, navy commandos, along with troops from the elite Golani infantry brigade, struck at a base of Ahmed Jibril's Popular Front/General Command organization situated northeast of Damour, 19 kilometers south of Beirut. The troops were put ashore from the sea and were airlifted out the next morning by helicopter after killing some 20 terrorists, wounding dozens, and destroying a training site and an ammunition dump. An Israeli battalion commander was killed in the raid and three soldiers were wounded. Four Israeli soldiers were missing when Chief of Staff Dan Shomron, concerned about a possible clash with Syrian troops in broad daylight, gave the order to take the main force out. The four were later located and extricated in a daring helicopter operation. Shomron was criticized for violating a hallowed IDF tradition of never leaving soldiers behind in enemy territory. Rabin was quoted as telling the Knesset's Defense and Foreign Affairs Committee: "If I had known how the operation in Lebanon would develop, I would not have authorized it."

On December 18, the IDF announced that three days earlier yet another force had ventured outside the security zone, in the area of Tibnin, this time returning with four prisoners, including two senior commanders from the Believers Resistance Front, a radical Shi'ite group believed to have been involved in the kidnapping of two Israeli soldiers in 1986. Two of the four suspects were released on December 17 following their interrogation.

Other incidents in which Israeli soldiers were killed included the following: On February 4, two 19-year-old paratroopers, Eliezer Sheffer, a yeshivah student from Herzliyah, and Avshalom Bashri, from Moshav Kfar Zeitim, fell in a gun battle with terrorists on the Israel-Lebanon border near Kibbutz Yiftah; on February 22, Sgt. Gavriel Permutti, aged 20, from Herzliyah, and Cpl. Amir Siedner, aged 19, from Jerusalem, were killed and two other soldiers were wounded when their tank hit a powerful roadside bomb, responsibility for the attack being claimed by the Believers Resistance Front; and in the year's worst single outrage, eight soldiers were killed—ranging in age from 19 to 44 and in rank from private to major—and seven wounded, on October 19, when a Hezballah suicide car-bomber managed to get his vehicle to a point near the border checkpoint just outside Metullah. Two days after the car-bomb attack, the IAF struck heavily at Hezballah and Palestinian targets in southern Lebanon, and on the following day it was announced that the gang responsible for the attack had been captured following intensive intelligence work by the security forces aided by the SLA.

This and other incidents that followed in the coming days, evidently motivated by the impending Israeli and U.S. elections and the scheduled Palestine National Council meeting in Algiers, elicited calls for Israel to expand the security zone. However, this idea was rejected by Defense Minister Rabin, who told the Knesset's Defense and Foreign Affairs Committee on October 25 that to enlarge the zone would be counterproductive because it would exacerbate relations with the local population and upset the "delicate balance" in southern Lebanon.

SECURITY TRIALS

Two trials relating to national security were in the news in 1988. The trial of Mordechai Vanunu, a former technician at the Dimona Nuclear Research Center who was accused of passing top-secret information about the facility to the London *Sunday Times*, was concluded. (For the background, see AJYB 1989, pp. 390–392, and AJYB 1988, pp. 373–375.) Following additional testimony, including that of Foreign Minister Shimon Peres, one of the founders of the country's nuclear-research program, and by Prof. George Quester, of the University of Maryland, an expert on international nuclear policy, Vanunu was convicted of the charges against him on March 24 and sentenced to 18 years' imprisonment on March 27. The sentence was two years less than what the prosecution had demanded and 37 years less than the total maximum accumulated prison term that could have been handed down separately for each count of aggravated espionage, treason, and disclosing state secrets.

The entire seven-month trial was held *in camera*, and only one page of the 60-page verdict was made public. This made it clear that the judges had rejected the defense's argument that Vanunu had acted from ideological motives because, as they wrote, "some of the most appalling crimes in human history were perpetrated for ideological reasons," and "the danger posed by ideological criminals is perhaps even greater than that of other criminals." It was also noted that the very fact of Vanunu's having given information to an unauthorized source constituted a crime, irrespective of whether the information itself was correct. The judges explained their decision not to impose the full sentence requested by the prosecution by citing mitigating circumstances in Vanunu's favor: his full cooperation with the investigators, the fact that he had been held in total isolation since his arrest and was likely to remain so, and "traces of remorse" in Vanunu's final statement. On March 28, Vanunu's lawyer appealed the sentence to the Supreme Court.

On January 10, it was disclosed that a 42-year-old Tel Aviv businessman, Shabtai Kalmanovitch, had been arrested by the Shin Bet on December 23, 1987, on suspicion of engaging in espionage for the Soviet Union. Kalmanovitch, well-known in high social and political circles, had immigrated to Israel from Lithuania in 1971. In the 1970s he had been involved with the most senior levels in Israel that dealt with Soviet Jewry, and in his subsequent career as an international financier he had established contacts with cabinet ministers and former ranking military personnel. The news of his arrest stunned not a few members of the Israeli political establishment. On December 15, following a three-month trial held *in camera*, Kalmanovitch was sentenced to a nine-year prison term in a plea-bargaining deal in which he confessed to spying for the Soviet Union and having contact with a KGB agent.

International Relations

Israel had to cope with severe criticism in 1988 for its activities in the territories, but oddly, those voices were loudest from Israel's allies among the Western democracies, whereas countries in the Eastern bloc, traditionally hostile to Israel, muted their criticism and moved rapidly toward a normalization of relations.

UNITED STATES

Relations with Washington were dominated in the first half of the year by the peace initiative of Secretary of State George Shultz (see above for the details). The mission encountered fierce opposition from Prime Minister Yitzhak Shamir and the Likud and died a lingering death. Washington's year-end decision to talk to the PLO—a move whose logic contradicted the essence of the Shultz plan but seemed more in harmony with the unfolding events generated by the *intifada*—was hotly disputed by most of the Israeli political establishment.

Overall, as in past years, the attitude underlying U.S. policy toward Israel could be described as much bark but very little bite. The barking was once again triggered by Israeli actions in the territories, but was louder than in past years due to the uprising. Thus, the year began with the United States protesting Israel's deportation of Palestinians, voting in favor of a UN Security Council resolution warning Israel against carrying out expulsions (January 5), and then abstaining (January 14) in a council resolution condemning the expulsion of nine Palestinians which was passed 14–0. Following the first vote, the Foreign Ministry issued a statement expressing "regret and disappointment" at the U.S. stance on the resolution, "which does not contribute to the reestablishment of calm or to a furthering of the peace process." Foreign Minister Shimon Peres saw the vote as a "grave deviation" from the traditional U.S. position. However, in a typical pattern, Secretary of State Shultz himself assuaged such concerns, thus neutralizing whatever the intended effect of the U.S. vote had been, when he told a Washington press conference that "the U.S. regards its friendship and the strength of its relationship with Israel as a key and unshakable relationship. No one should interpret a vote as meaning anything else."

Shultz also took the opportunity to note that while it was manifestly Israel's "duty to maintain law and order" in the territories, Washington believed that this could be accomplished "without the use of lethal means." Late in the month the State Department expressed its concern over the new Israeli riot-control measures announced by Defense Minister Yitzhak Rabin, reiterating that Israel could achieve its goal by employing "humane measures which do not result in civilian casualties."

A rare concrete step taken by the State Department—an "advisory" cautioning tourists not to visit the West Bank or the Gaza Strip, issued on the eve of the Passover-Easter holiday season—infuriated Tourism (and Justice) Minister Avraham Sharir. He accused the United States of "once again stabbing tourism to Israel in the back."

In mid-April, following three visits by Secretary of State Shultz to the region in pursuit of his peace mission, the United States stepped up its rhetoric regarding Israeli actions in suppressing the *intifada*. Speaking at the Hebrew University of Jerusalem, U.S. ambassador to Israel Thomas Pickering asserted that if Israel wished to continue enjoying close ties with the United States, it was "critical" for "the primacy of the rule of law" to be upheld in the territories. In Washington, the State Department condemned the deportation of eight more Palestinians on April 11, an action which, in the U.S. view, contravened the Fourth Geneva Convention of 1949; however, in the Security Council, the United States vetoed a resolution calling on Israel to allow the deportees to return.

The most stinging attack to date on Israeli policy—and the bluntest warning of the possible consequences—came a week after the IDF had issued deportation orders to 25 more Palestinians. On August 23, Deputy Secretary of State John Whitehead told Oded Eran, a senior official in the Israeli embassy in Washington, that the United States considered expulsion an "unduly harsh punishment under any circumstances." If Israel did not "reconsider" the newly issued orders, or "refrain from carrying them out," and in general change its position on this issue, Whitehead said, "damage to our bilateral relations will occur." In response, Foreign Minister Peres stated that no "policy of deportation" existed, "only individual cases" necessitated by the security situation. (Nonetheless, there were no more deportations in 1988, although the orders against the 25 were not revoked.)

In mid-September—halfway between the collapse of Secretary of State Shultz's peace initiative and his decision to start talks with the PLO—the secretary took the opportunity of a speech marking the tenth anniversary of the Camp David accords to sum up the Reagan administration's policy on the Israeli-Palestinian conflict. While rejecting the idea of an independent Palestinian state, Shultz also ruled out Israel's retention of all the territories. Israel, he said, "must be prepared to withdraw—as Resolution 242 says—from territories occupied in the [1967 war]." On Israeli measures to suppress the uprising, the secretary of state acknowledged that even though it was Israel's "responsibility to maintain law and order" in the territories, this must be achieved within certain parameters of behavior. Specifically, Shultz asserted that the United States would "vigorously" oppose attempts to carry out a "transfer" of Arabs from the territories, and especially to Jordan, which had a "strong national identity of its own" and therefore was "not a Palestinian state." (Shultz was responding to calls from ultranationalist circles in Israel to solve the issue of the territories by declaring Jordan the Palestinian "homeland," since the majority of its population was already of Palestinian origin.) The secretary of state was unusually blunt in his criticism of some of the more severe measures resorted to by Israel in the territories, and of the logic underlying them: "[Israel] cannot claim there is no one to talk to, while suppressing political expression [in the territories] and arresting or deporting those who speak out—even those who speak in moderate terms."

Prime Minister Shamir played out his part in the ritual by responding that at bottom the United States and Israel agreed on the substantive goal—Shultz, he pointed out, had affirmed Israel's "right and duty" to restore order in the territories—but disagreed over how that goal should be achieved. Foreign Minister Shimon Peres, in contrast, called Shultz's speech "very balanced."

Peres's successor as foreign minister, Moshe Arens, saw fit to take Israel's major ally to task in his first public statement following his confirmation. On December 23, Arens said that the U.S. decision to hold a dialogue with the PLO, "the leading terrorist organization in the past 25 years," would only generate more extremism and hence more violence. The previous day, President Reagan had sent Shamir a message (not made public until December 28) explaining the U.S. move and stressing that "nothing in this decision should be construed as weakening the United States' commitment to Israel's security." Reagan also took the opportunity to encapsulate his perception of U.S.-Israeli relations under his administration:

> Building on our friendship and strengthening the close ties that bind us have been among my proudest achievements as president. . . . I am confident that through our joint efforts nothing can destroy the mutual trust, confidence and commitment we have built, and that the next U.S. administration will move quickly to work with your government toward our mutual goals.

Traditionally, many of those "mutual goals" centered on security and strategy, and despite the fundamental differences over policy in the territories, relations at the military-defense level remained strong in 1988. The Iran-*contra* affair was finally wiped off the agenda between the two countries when an agreement was signed (announced March 28) formalizing Jerusalem's cooperation with the U.S. independent counsel investigating the matter. The terms of the agreement were not divulged, but the hope was expressed that it would assure continued cooperation "to the mutual satisfaction of both sides."

Mutual satisfaction, particularly on the Israeli side, was also expressed at the signing, on April 21, Israel's 40th Independence Day, of a Memorandum of Agreement (MOA) between the two countries at ceremonies held in Jerusalem and Washington. The document broke little if any new ground. Its primary purpose was to reaffirm "the close relationship" between the two countries "based upon common goals, interests and values," and Israel's designation "as a major non-NATO ally of the United States." A White House statement explained that the agreement, valid for five years with an option for further five-year renewals, "formalizes and perpetuates the bilateral U.S. and Israeli consultative groups that meet periodically to discuss joint military-security assistance and economic development questions." However, a phone conversation between Reagan and Shamir to mark the signing was canceled for "technical" reasons, and observers noted that Washington had hardly gone out of its way to publicize the event. Shamir however, cited the new MOA—which was signed despite the virtual demise of Shultz's peace initiative and despite the volatile situation in the territories following the assassination five days earlier of the PLO's Abu Jihad—as proof of the enduring quality of "this unique partnership in common values and interests and in the desire for peace."

The MOA stated explicitly that the Joint Israel-U.S. Political-Military Group was responsible, among other tasks, for planning "joint exercises" between the armed forces of the two countries. One such exercise was held in July with the participation of the Israel Navy and vessels from the U.S. Sixth Fleet, including the nuclear-powered aircraft carrier USS *Eisenhower*. At a ceremony marking the conclusion of the maneuvers, Sixth Fleet commander Rear Admiral Kendall Moranville said he had "been given assurances" that U.S. marines would conduct land maneuvers in Israel "in the near future."

In November U.S. secretary of defense Frank Carlucci paid a three-day visit to Israel for talks on bilateral military and strategic cooperation and regional developments. Carlucci said that the continuing U.S. military and other support for Israel was a "clear sign to Israel's adversaries that there is no military option." Carlucci was returning a visit to the United States by Defense Minister Rabin in June during which the two countries signed an agreement for the joint development (with Washington to underwrite 80 percent of the $130-million price tag) of the Arrow anti-ballistic missile, an Israeli concept deriving from the Strategic Defense Initiative ("Star Wars") project in which Israel had agreed to take part. (When Under Secretary of State for Political Affairs Michael Armacost visited Israel in June, he said Washington was concerned about the burgeoning Middle East missile race, particularly China's sale of medium-range missiles to Saudi Arabia. Earlier in the year, the director-general of the Prime Minister's Office, Yosef Ben-Aharon, had made a veiled threat that Israel would attack the missiles in Saudi Arabia, leading President Reagan, Egyptian president Mubarak, and others to ask Israel to show restraint. A statement from Prime Minister Shamir said that Israel did not plan to strike at the missiles but was concerned about their deployment on Saudi soil.) Carlucci, at all events, said he had been impressed by the "high level of proficiency and morale" he found in the IDF and added that the level of cooperation between the two defense establishments "could not be better."

WESTERN EUROPE

This was hardly the case in Israel's relations with much of Western Europe in 1988. Governments of countries traditionally friendly to Israel expressed their intense disapproval of the IDF's handling of the uprising in the territories, often in deeds as well as words, and nightly TV images of the *intifada* caused Israel's popularity to plummet in public-opinion polls.

In January British minister of state for foreign affairs David Mellors, visiting the Gaza Strip, castigated an IDF officer for his behavior and told the BBC that conditions in Gaza were "an affront to civilized values." The following month, the leader of the British Labor party, Neil Kinnock, accused the IDF of using dumdum bullets (designed to explode internally) against Palestinians in the territories, a charge that was "categorically" denied by both the IDF and Israeli government officials. In July Israeli spokesmen pointed to Britain's huge arms deal with Saudi Arabia, while maintaining an arms boycott vis-à-vis Israel, as proof that the British stand on the Middle East was unbalanced. A better atmosphere prevailed when Foreign Minister Peres met with Prime Minister Margaret Thatcher (September 14), with the two agreeing that PLO chairman Arafat had still not demonstrated that he was serious about moving toward peace. A weeklong visit by British tourism minister John Lee (he arrived October 28) was welcomed by Israel, particularly after the Arab League had issued a statement warning that the visit would be considered a "provocation" against the Arab world and could produce "negative repercussions for Arab-British interests."

Following a 24-hour visit (January 23–24), West German foreign minister Hans-Dietrich Genscher told a press conference in Jerusalem that the European Community (EC)—which he currently chaired—considered it "urgent" to find a political solution to the Arab-Israeli conflict, and this could be done by convening an international conference. In the course of his visit Genscher met with seven prominent Palestinians from the territories, who handed him a letter urging "international protection" for the Palestinians against Israeli policy in the territories.

A visit to France by Foreign Minister Shimon Peres (September 23–24) took place not long after French foreign minister Roland Dumas had met with PLO chief Yasir Arafat during the latter's visit to Strasbourg to address the European Parliament. Dumas briefed Peres, who also met with President François Mitterrand, on the meeting. President Chaim Herzog, making the first state visit by an Israeli head of state to France (October 17–21), devoted much of his time to explaining the situation in the territories. He also visited the Normandy coast, where he had landed as a soldier in the British expeditionary force on D-Day, June 6, 1944.

Netherlands prime minister Ruud Lubbers expressed his country's "concern" at Israeli actions and policies in the territories during a three-day visit in July, the first ever by a Dutch premier. Lubbers, who was accompanied by Foreign Minister Hans van den Broek, expressed Holland's "commitment to the Jewish people and the future of Israel," but also called for an international peace conference and urged

Israel to recognize Palestinian rights. Another major talking point between the two sides concerned the Israeli decision to seek direct flights from the USSR to Israel for new immigrants. The Dutch, who represented Israeli interests in Moscow and hence issued Israeli visas to Jews wishing to leave the Soviet Union, opposed the Israeli decision because it abridged freedom of choice. The two countries agreed to form a committee to study the matter. The Dutch foreign minister met with a group of leading PLO supporters from the territories and toured the Kalandia refugee camp near Jerusalem.

A blunt message was received from Foreign Minister Sten Andersson of Sweden during a two-day visit (March 7–9). Following a tour of Bethlehem and the adjacent Deheishe refugee camp, he told reporters that he did not see how Israel could continue to exist without solving the Palestinian problem. Andersson also met with nine leading Palestinians from the territories and was at loggerheads with his Israeli interlocutors on the question of PLO participation in an international conference.

On his return home following a visit to Italy (February 15–17), Prime Minister Shamir said that Israel's image in the Italian media is "very poor," but that "when one digs deeper, one reaches the conclusion that the media do not reflect the true state of public opinion." *Ha'aretz*'s Rome correspondent described Shamir's talks with Italian leaders, dominated by the issue of the occupied territories, as "a polite dialogue of the deaf."

Some scheduled visits did not take place at all due to the *intifada*, particularly in the early part of the year when the mass violence, and consequently the mass-media coverage, were at their height. Belgium canceled planned visits to Israel by its defense minister and a purchasing mission. A Swiss Army mission did likewise. Two Dutch high schools refused to host a youth delegation organized by the Israeli Foreign Ministry. In January the Foreign Ministry condemned as "totally unjustified and extremely offensive" a statement attributed to Prime Minister Andreas Papandreou of Greece in which he spoke of Israel's "fascist occupation." Even the Norwegian ambassador to Israel, Torleiv Anda, had to be berated—by Deputy Foreign Minister Yosef Beilin—after he drew a comparison between German actions in Norway in World War II and IDF measures in the territories. Anda, who had been incarcerated in Buchenwald, told Beilin he regretted making the remark, which, he said, had been distorted and misunderstood.

Concrete economic damage was inflicted on some branches of Israeli agriculture, notably flower growing, by the European Parliament's repeated postponement of ratification of trade protocols with Israel. As a result of the inaction, Israeli exporters were forced to continue paying high customs levies, which severely reduced their income and undercut their competitive ability. Although technical reasons were cited, an angry Prime Minister Shamir told the Knesset's Defense and Foreign Affairs Committee in January, after the European Parliament passed a resolution calling on Israel to desist from its "reprisals" against the Palestinians in the territories, that the real reason for the delay was political and was tantamount to "blackmail."

One demand of the Europeans which Israel had thus far refused to accept was to allow residents of the territories to export agricultural produce independently of Israel. It was not until October 12, after Palestinian farmers in the territories were permitted to export citrus fruit under their own label and independently of the Israeli marketing mechanism, that the European Parliament ratified the protocols. In December the first such shipment—"Gaza Top" grapefruits—was sent to Europe where it would compete with Israeli produce.

EASTERN EUROPE

Israel's relations with Eastern Europe continued to develop rapidly, despite the moral and material support the countries of that region had traditionally proffered to the Arabs in general and the PLO in particular. The major event in the continuing Israeli-Soviet rapprochement was the arrival in Moscow of an Israeli consular delegation on July 28. The six-member team was headed by a career diplomat, Russian-born Meron Gordon, plucked from his current posting in Rome, and included Yaakov Kedmi, formerly Yasha Kazakov, a former refusenik and one of the initiators of the emigration movement among Soviet Jewry in the 1970s. Like their Soviet counterparts who had been in Israel since July 1987 (AJYB 1989, p. 406), the Israeli diplomats were officially in the USSR (where they were hosted by the Netherlands embassy) solely for the technical purpose of inspecting the former Israeli embassy building in Moscow. Israel had been paying rent on the building, reportedly $100,000 a year, since it was shut down 21 years earlier after relations were severed by the Russians. At the end of October the Soviets approved the posting of a ranking Israeli diplomat, Arie Levin, the head of the Foreign Ministry's research section, to head the consular mission, a move seen as an implicit upgrading of its diplomatic status.

Israel's stock in the Soviet Union got a further boost as a result of two events late in the year. On December 2, a Soviet airplane, hijacked during an internal Russian flight, landed at Ben-Gurion Airport. Israel's smooth handling of the crisis, including the detention and deportation to the USSR of the hijackers (none of them Jewish) the next day, won high praise from Moscow and produced a diplomatic breakthrough in the form of a meeting between Soviet foreign minister Eduard Shevardnadze and Arie Levin. The Tass news agency quoted Shevardnadze as thanking Israel for its "goodwill" and lauded the "norms of civilized intergovernmental relations" displayed during the incident. Several days later Soviet president Mikhail Gorbachev personally thanked Israel's UN envoy, Yochanan Bein, for Jerusalem's help, during a reception at the UN in New York. The Soviet consular mission in Israel was also involved in dealing with the crisis.

On December 11, an Israel Air Force Boeing 707 landed in Yerevan, the capital of the Armenian Republic, carrying a rescue team and medical personnel to help in the aftermath of a devastating earthquake. The mission was led by Brig. Gen.

Aharon Vardi, head of the IDF's Civil Defense Corps. A second team, comprising 46 military and civilian medical personnel, arrived five days later and set up a field hospital at Kirovakan, where they treated some 2,400 persons in two weeks. The Israeli efforts drew praise in *Izvestia* and from Soviet officials.

On September 30, Israel and Poland moved a step closer to diplomatic relations when each country's "interests section" was elevated to independent status. The upgrading was announced in New York in a meeting between Foreign Minister Shimon Peres and his Polish counterpart, Tadeusz Olechowski. Earlier in the year, the head of the Israeli mission in Warsaw, Mordechai Palzur, had had occasion to protest a statement by Polish government spokesman Jerzy Urban that Israel's handling of the uprising in the occupied territories was an insult to the memory of the Warsaw Ghetto defenders. The Polish statement came just days after 2,000 Jewish youths from Israel and the Diaspora, joined by Education Minister Yitzhak Navon, Justice Minister Avraham Sharir, Jewish Agency chairman Simcha Dinitz, six MKs, and dozens of other Israeli officials participated in a "March of the Living" at Auschwitz-Birkenau to mark the start of weeklong ceremonies and events commemorating the Warsaw Ghetto uprising 45 years earlier. It was the first visit to Poland by elected Israeli representatives in 20 years; in another first, Israel Radio broadcast the event live.

Israel's relations with Hungary moved forward. On March 14, the two countries established interests offices in Budapest and Tel Aviv, and on May 8, Foreign Minister Peres became the most senior Israeli official to visit an Eastern bloc country (other than Romania) since 1967, when he arrived in Budapest for talks with Prime Minister Karoly Grosz and Foreign Minister Peter Varkonyi. However, neither this visit nor one by Prime Minister Shamir in mid-September produced a further breakthrough in relations in 1988. For their part, the Hungarians dispatched Church Affairs Minister Imre Miklos to Israel in September, and the following month Tourism Minister Avraham Sharir and Hungarian Trade Minister Miklos Andriko signed a tourism agreement during the latter's visit to Israel. About 30,000 Israelis visited Hungary in 1988.

Other notable events in 1988 included the visit to Belgrade in August by Jewish Agency chairman Simcha Dinitz for a meeting with Foreign Minister Budimir Loncar, the first visit by a senior Israeli political figure to Yugoslavia in 20 years; and the first meeting of its kind between Foreign Minister Peres and his Czech counterpart, Bohuslav Chnoupek, held in September at UN headquarters in New York. Relations with Bucharest continued to flourish: in May, Romanian deputy premier Nikolai Konstantin visited Israel and in a meeting with Prime Minister Shamir the two countries agreed to arrange mutual visits by cabinet ministers. Industry and Trade Minister Ariel Sharon visited Romania in July, and in November he and his Romanian counterpart, Johan Ongor, signed various trade protocols during the latter's visit to Israel. (Sharon also visited Poland and Bulgaria in 1988, but on an unofficial basis.)

AFRICA, ASIA, LATIN AMERICA

On December 23, Kenya became the fifth African state to renew diplomatic relations with Israel in recent years. The Kenyan Foreign Ministry explained that the move followed the PLO's acceptance of "the two crucial United Nations resolutions leading to Middle East peace through direct negotiations." Extensive economic ties between Kenya and Israel had been maintained since Nairobi broke relations in 1973. Another African country, Zaire, went public—at a press conference on June 29 in Jerusalem, called by Foreign Ministry director-general Avraham Tamir and Zaire's ambassador to Israel, Lamponda Wa Botende—with a list of its disappointed expectations from its renewal of relations with Israel. In July Israel showed that it had gotten the message when Tamir signed a protocol in Zaire assuring additional Israeli military aid, an $8 million loan, and agricultural help.

In Asia the picture was mixed. In March Prime Minister Rajiv Gandhi of India personally prohibited his country's Davis Cup tennis team from playing in Israel as a protest against Israeli "atrocities" in the territories. However, in July India agreed to upgrade the level of the head of Israel's legation in the country from deputy consul to consul.

In February Foreign and Trade Minister Bill Hayden of Australia signed a trade agreement during a three-day visit to Israel and urged Israel to withdraw from the Gaza Strip, which he called "a demographic time-bomb."

Foreign Minister Sousuke Uno of Japan, on a Middle East tour in June, became the highest-ranking official from his country ever to visit Israel. His 24-hour stay (June 26–27) included meetings with the president, the prime minister, and the vice-premier as well as visits to East Jerusalem and refugee camps. Foreign Ministry director-general Tamir said Israel could not accept Japan's linkage of investments and joint projects with intensified peace efforts. In a message to Shamir (July 4), Foreign Minister Uno described his visit as "moving" and "most beneficial for further political dialogues between our two countries."

Ties with China inched forward. In March, the leader of the left-wing Mapam party, Elazar Granot, paid an official visit to China, noting that Mapam was the first Zionist party ever invited to send a representative to that country. In September Foreign Minister Peres met at the UN in New York with his Chinese counterpart, Qian Qichan, and was told that the establishment of diplomatic relations between the two countries depended on progress toward peace in the Middle East. A Chinese trade mission visited Israel in October, followed in November by the arrival of a permanent tourism representative.

Relations with Latin America continued strong, unaffected by the *intifada*. Visitors to Israel in 1988 included the commander of the Argentinian army, Gen. Jose Dantecaridi, in January; Colombian defense minister Gen. Rafael Samudio Molina, in October, who signed a deal worth $200 million for 13 Israeli-made Kfir jet fighters; and Bolivian foreign minister Guillermo Bedregal Gutierrez, in December.

Israel's skeptical view of the UN was reinforced when the world body's under secretary-general, Marrack Goulding, said in January, following a visit to the occupied territories in order to prepare a report for the Security Council, that the violence there was the result of Israeli policies which had engendered "despair and hopelessness." Goulding met with Foreign Minister Peres, but Prime Minister Shamir rejected a request for a meeting on the ground that Goulding was interfering in Israel's internal affairs. The report itself, issued by UN secretary-general Javier Pérez de Cuéllar in January, accused the IDF of using "disproportionate force" to put down disturbances in the territories and called on Israel "to change its position as to the applicability" of the Fourth Geneva Convention in the areas.

EGYPT

Developments in two spheres—the Palestinian uprising and the Taba arbitration talks—dominated relations between Israel and Egypt in 1988. On May 15, in Geneva, a five-member panel of international arbitrators, including one representative each from Egypt and Israel, began deliberating on the Taba issue after last-ditch compromise efforts by U.S. State Department legal adviser Abraham Sofaer had failed. (Taba, a tiny and nonstrategic strip of coastline just south of Eilat, on which stood an Israeli luxury hotel and a holiday village, was the last unresolved territorial element in the implementation of the 1979 Israeli-Egyptian peace treaty.) Talks between Israel and Egypt aimed at working out a solution both sides could live with continued, largely at the behest of the United States, which feared that the arbitrators' decision—which was binding—might spark a crisis in relations between the two countries. However, the politics of national unity proved a major stumbling block in the compromise efforts, the Likud and Alignment advocating diametrically opposed approaches to the problem. The director-general of the Foreign Ministry wanted to accept the U.S. proposal, which took as its starting point Egyptian sovereignty over Taba, and extract maximum concessions in the field; while the director-general of the Prime Minister's Office refused to concede Egyptian sovereignty and espoused what was, at bottom, an all-or-nothing approach.

On September 29—one month before the Knesset elections—the arbitration panel, as expected, basically gave all to Egypt and nothing to Israel. After an initial flurry of mutual recriminations over "who had lost Taba," Labor and Likud tacitly agreed not to make the matter a campaign issue. Two months to the day after the arbitration decision, Israeli and Egyptian representatives, meeting in Rome at the headquarters of the Sinai Multinational Force, reached agreement on the technical implementation of the decision. On December 15, as stipulated in the accord, Israeli and Egyptian military teams began "construction of the boundary pillars of the recognized international boundary" as determined by the arbitrators.

As it had been during the Lebanon War, official Egyptian reaction to Israel's handling of the uprising in the territories was relatively muted. Sporadic protests were made by President Hosni Mubarak and other senior officials, and the Egyptian embassy in Tel Aviv did not hold its traditional reception on Egypt's national day (although the Israeli chargé d'affaires in Cairo was invited to the official reception there). But when Egypt recognized the "State of Palestine" declared by the Palestine National Council in mid-November, Foreign Minister Peres himself summoned Egyptian ambassador to Israel Muhammad Bassiouny to his office and, according to a statement issued by the Foreign Ministry, informed him "that Egypt's recognition of the Palestinian state as declared in Algiers is not consistent with the principle of a negotiated settlement of the conflict to which both Egypt and Israel are committed." Peres expressed his "regret" at Cairo's move and asked Bassiouny to convey Israel's "concern at this development" to the Egyptian government.

In the meantime, diplomatic relations proceeded at lower levels: on September 19, the new Israeli ambassador to Egypt, Prof. Shimon Shamir, an orientalist from Tel Aviv University, presented his credentials to President Mubarak. He was then invited for a private 90-minute meeting with the Egyptian leader, during which the peace process and bilateral relations were discussed.

The Economy

The economy slumped badly in 1988, particularly in the second half of the year, when recessionary indicators, including rising unemployment, became apparent. This was due in part to the *intifada*, which had both direct and indirect effects, and in part to the standstill approach adopted by the Treasury, where measures taken (or not taken) by Finance Minister Moshe Nissim were influenced by the fact that 1988 was an election year.

According to most estimates, the uprising in the territories caused a direct loss of at least 1.5 percent of the GNP, or about $600 million, as compared with economic performance in 1987. Of this, approximately a quarter was due to civilian workdays lost because of call-ups for reserve duty and operational military expenditures. Defense expenditures as a percentage of Gross Domestic Product (GDP) increased for the first time since 1982 (the Lebanon War) and stood at 10.3 percent, which was 0.5 percent more than the state budget had allowed for. Following protracted discussions, the Treasury in September agreed to compensate the IDF to the tune of NIS 180 million for unbudgeted costs incurred in the *intifada*, even though the Defense Ministry estimated the actual cost to be in excess of NIS 400 million and had requested NIS 263 million.

Beyond this, the pervasive uncertainty caused by the government's vacillations in dealing with the peace process and with the *intifada* eroded confidence and created a climate that was not conducive to economic growth. The figures themselves could not tell the whole story since they did not take into account the high growth expectations that had been held for 1988 in various sectors, primarily because of events and programs which had been planned to coincide with Israel's 40th-anniversary celebrations. Hardest hit from this point of view was the tourism industry, which suffered a direct decrease of 15 percent in arrivals as compared with

1987 (1,169,000 in 1988 vs. 1,379,000 the previous year). In fact, the blow was even worse because the industry had invested in infrastructure and development in anticipation of a boom year, and because the decline was at its most intense in the peak summer months due to booking cancellations caused by media reports of the uprising's mass-demonstrations stage in the first quarter of the year.

Israeli "exports" to the occupied territories decreased by approximately 31 percent in real terms as compared with 1987. This was due to the drastic self-imposed economic slowdown in the territories and the boycotting of Israeli goods. The export of agricultural produce from Israel to the territories fell by some 60 percent, and factories in Israel which had manufactured products in high demand in the territories suffered. Overall, industrial production fell by more than 3 percent in 1988, following an increase of 5 percent in 1987 and 3.5 percent in 1986. One result was that the number of persons employed in industry declined by 3.5 percent, following a rise of 2 percent in 1987.

Particularly hard hit were the textile industry—a falloff of 15 percent in production—due in part to relatively high worker absenteeism; agriculture (a 7-percent production decline, caused in part by bad weather which nearly wiped out the avocado crop, after a growth of 8 percent in 1987); and construction (which managed to register a barely perceptible growth of about 1 percent, following a rise of 9 percent in 1987). All three sectors relied heavily on cheap labor from the territories. In January, Education Minister Yitzhak Navon ordered an emergency mobilization of high-school students "in order to help save the citrus crop," which was rotting due to the absence of workers from the territories. Labor and Social Affairs Minister Moshe Katzav authorized the import of about 550 workers from southern Lebanon for the harvest (citrus production was down 22 percent in 1988), alluding to the effect of the occupation on the original Zionist ethos when he declared that Jews must be encouraged to do manual labor. Indeed, some experts thought that, in the long term, *intifada*-related economic developments might prove salutary by forcing Israeli manufacturers to seek new markets for their products, both domestic and foreign, and by compelling labor-intensive industries such as construction to modernize and become more efficient, thus reducing housing costs and perhaps attracting more Israelis to an industry in which workers from the territories comprised about half the labor force.

Many Israelis found themselves forced out of the labor market altogether in 1988. When Finance Minister Nissim presented a budget of NIS 52.1 billion for fiscal year 1988–1989 on January 26 (with the uprising already six weeks old) in the Knesset, he made a virtue of restraint, arguing that since in 1987 his noninterventionist tactics had stimulated the business sector, generated higher exports, brought about increased investments, lowered inflation, and decreased unemployment, 1988 would see more of the same. The budget was passed on March 23, but virtually every Treasury forecast for 1988 turned out to be over-optimistic.

The GDP grew by only 1.5 percent, the lowest gain since 1982, as compared with increases of 5 percent in 1987 and 3–4 percent each in 1986 and 1985. Growth in the business sector was below 1 percent and was at a total standstill in the second half of the year. Private consumption, reflecting the living standard, rose by a modest 1.5 percent per capita, as compared with 7 percent in 1987 and 12 percent in 1986. Public consumption remained stable as compared with 1987, at about 3 percent (excluding defense imports). The overall unemployment rate stood at 6.4 percent at year's end, slightly higher than in 1987 (6.1 percent); however, in the second half of the year unemployment climbed to 7 percent (despite the shortfall in workers from the territories).

In June Histadrut's giant Koor concern, whose diverse firms employed one of every three Israeli industrial workers and accounted for 12 percent of the country's industrial product, announced losses of NIS 389 million for 1987, the worst single performance in Israeli industrial history. The conglomerate's managing director, Yeshayahu Gavish, had already resigned in March and been replaced by Benny Gaon, the successful director of another Histadrut enterprise, the Co-Op retail chain. Gaon, who likened Koor to "a plane without a pilot cruising aimlessly by night without a compass," launched a recovery program involving mass dismissals, plant closings, and the selling of assets.

One of the first problems Gaon faced was a liquidation threat by some of Koor's foreign creditors, including the U.S.-based Bankers Trust and Manufacturers Hanover Trust. On December 20, the Tel Aviv district court removed the danger of liquidation for at least a month, during which the sides were to endeavor to work out an arrangement acceptable to all parties involved. Explaining his decision, Judge Eliahu Winograd said that Koor's collapse would have a devastating ripple effect throughout the entire Israeli economy. In the meantime, the first to feel the effects of the concern's streamlining efforts were the workers, 4,760 of whom lost their jobs in the second half of the year as Koor-owned firms were scaled down, shut down, sold, or placed in receivership. Another labor-movement conglomerate, Milouot, comprising 13 food-processing plants in the country's north and owned by the kibbutz movement, was revealed to have debts of NIS 400 million.

Given this picture, it was perhaps not surprising that agricultural and industrial exports, excluding diamonds, were down by about 4 percent, due primarily to the steep decline in exports to the territories. Diamond exports rose by 2 percent, well below the increases of the previous three years. Civilian imports registered no change as compared with 1987. Nevertheless, imports of automobiles were up 21 percent as compared with 1987 and approached the peak year of 1983. All told, net civilian imports were higher by $2.8 billion than net exports, a 13-percent improvement as compared with 1987; the overall trade deficit stood at $5.3 billion, an 8-percent fall as compared with 1987, due to a drop in defense imports. Israel's total foreign debt at the end of 1988 was $24.4 billion, down by $1 billion from 1987. Export profitability showed a steady decline throughout the year, due in large part to the fixed exchange rate.

As the date of the general election approached, expectations of a devaluation of the shekel intensified, triggering mass purchasing of dollars and a call from Bank of Israel governor Michael Bruno for a devaluation. This trend was halted in the immediate aftermath of the election when Finance Minister Nissim—as he still was during the coalition negotiations—made it clear that he was against a devaluation. However, as those who had purchased dollars did not reconvert them to shekels, the banks faced an immediate liquidity crisis, and the interest rate for borrowers of "scarce" shekels soared to more than 30 percent. Shimon Peres, immediately upon his confirmation as finance minister, launched feverish meetings with representatives of the Histadrut and the Manufacturers Association in an effort to work out a package deal to spur economic growth. However, as it was widely believed that this would include a devaluation, another run on the dollar began which eventually totaled some $2.5 billion, most of it purchased by the business sector in the hope of an easy profit. At midday on December 12, the shekel was devalued by 5 percent against the dollar, but this failed to halt the dollar-buying spree as a second devaluation was expected. On December 29 (a Thursday), trading in foreign currency was halted for the remainder of the year. At midnight on December 31, the prices of basic commodities were hiked when the subsidies on them were slashed by 12–26 percent, the third such cut in 1988 (in May subsidies were reduced by 15–32 percent—for the first time since January 1987—and in October, less than a month before the elections, by 8–14 percent). Peres was to announce a new economic plan early in 1990.

The consumer price index for 1988 was 16.1 percent, down a full 3.6 percent from 1987, and including four months in which inflation was below 1 percent. The basket of goods that the Central Bureau of Statistics used to determine the CPI was revised in 1988—based on a survey of public consumption conducted in 1987—to make it conform with current Israeli expenditures. Thus the proportion allotted to most commodities or services was changed—the housing element decreased from 20 percent to 16.5 percent, clothing and shoes now accounted for 7.25 percent of the CPI basket, and so forth—and some new items were added, such as computers and VCRs. However, such calculations were largely irrelevant for the 634,000 Israelis who, the National Insurance Institute said, were below the poverty line, including nearly one of every three Israeli children, Jewish or Arab.

Extremism and Violence

In the view of some experts, the violence and extremism that had become increasingly pervasive in Israeli society were linked in some degree to Israel's suppression of the growing unrest in the occupied territories during the 1980s and particularly since the Lebanon War. One manifestation of these trends was the public's willingness to tolerate the dissemination of ideas that once were almost universally rejected as anathema. Thus, a public-opinion poll conducted in June by the Israel Institute of Applied Social Research and the Communications Institute of the Hebrew University found that 49 percent of Jewish Israeli adults thought that "causing the Arabs from the territories to leave" would "allow the democratic and Jewish nature of Israeli society to be maintained." The "transfer option" was chosen by two-thirds of persons who said they would vote Likud and by one-third of persons who said they would vote Labor. Concluded Prof. Elihu Katz, the poll's scientific director, "The subject of transfer is no longer taboo; it has gained legitimacy, become a focus of public discussion and swept through the [political] right."

The appearance on the political stage of the Moledet (Homeland) party, headed by a retired major general, Rehavam Ze'evi, which openly espoused the "voluntary transfer" of the Arabs in the territories, helped to legitimize the idea as a topic of debate. Unlike Meir Kahane, Ze'evi was flesh of the flesh of the Israeli establishment—nowhere was this better seen than in President Herzog's meeting with Ze'evi at the President's Residence as part of the postelection process, in striking contrast to Herzog's refusal to receive Kahane under the same circumstances four years earlier. Significantly, his arguments drew not on an interpretation of the Torah and the forefathers of the Jewish people but, ostensibly, on the roots of Zionism and the founding fathers of the Jewish state.

In an article in *Ha'aretz* (August 17), Ze'evi sought to refute contentions that the transfer idea was immoral. After quoting David Ben-Gurion and mentioning past Labor luminaries such as Moshe Sharett and Berl Katznelson, Ze'evi wrote: "If [the transfer idea] is not moral, then the whole of Zionism and its realization in the course of more than a hundred years is not moral. The settlement enterprise in Eretz-Yisrael and our War of Independence are studded with operations in which Arabs were transferred from their villages." Yet underlying the cool rationalism in which Ze'evi couched his arguments was another message, indistinguishable from Kahane's appeal to dark passions. A week after the appearance of his article in *Ha'aretz*, Ze'evi told a meeting of about 300 supporters in Tel Aviv: "The Palestinians in Judea-Samaria and Gaza are a festering sore, and in order to finish it—this cancer—it must not be allowed to develop."

On the night of August 8, in the town of Ohr Yehuda, near Tel Aviv, three Arab workers from Gaza were burned to death when the shack they were sleeping in was torched after the door had been locked from the outside. (Workers from the territories were not allowed to remain in Israel overnight, but thousands slept in makeshift shelters, in abominable conditions, the authorities generally turning a blind eye to the phenomenon.) The incident touched off riots in Gaza and several local youths were arrested. Toward the end of August, three other Ohr Yehuda residents, aged 20, 21, and 31, were arrested on suspicion of committing arson and conspiracy to commit murder after firebombs were thrown at a Jewish home in the town. The three had evidently planned a replay of the August 8 attack but had backed off at the last minute and had tried to create a "provocation" for which Arabs would be blamed. The mayor of Ohr Yehuda, Yitzhak Bukozba, paid a condolence visit to the family of one of the three workers who were burned to death, in Gaza. There were several incidents in which Arabs were beaten by Jews in Tel Aviv during August.

According to police statistics for 1988, the incidence of serious crime rose by 28.8

percent, and crimes involving violence were up by 5.7 percent. Of the offenders arrested inside the Green Line, 66 percent were Jews, 27 percent were Israeli Arabs (well above their proportion in the population), and 6.5 percent were Palestinians from the territories. The preoccupation of the police with *intifada*-related matters, primarily in Jerusalem and in Galilee, meant that fewer efforts could be devoted to other urgent matters, such as the war on drugs or efforts to reduce road accidents.

Observers on the Left professed to see an indirect endorsement of extremism in President Herzog's continued commuting of prison terms meted out to the members of the Jewish terrorist underground. On April 1, Yitzhak Ganiram and Ira Rappaport were released from prison after Herzog reduced their sentences by five-and-a-half and four-and-a-half months, respectively, along with a one-third reduction for good behavior. In this as in all the previous instances, the president explained his action by noting that the two had expressed "sincere contrition." Barak Nir, one of the five underground members who remained in prison (three of them serving life sentences for murder, which Herzog had reduced to 24 years), finished serving his four-year term, after getting a third off, on April 26. A private member's bill to further reduce the sentences of the underground members in prison by legislative fiat was narrowly defeated (58–53) in the Knesset on June 14; a previous attempt, about half a year earlier, had gained the support of only 40 religious and right-wing MKs.

Prime Minister Shamir, who voted in favor of both bills, on August 1 received in his office a delegation of the "Temple Mount Faithful," a small but highly vocal ultranationalist group that sought to restore "Jewish sovereignty" on the Temple Mount. According to a press release issued by the prime minister's media adviser, Shamir told the delegation that "he respects the struggle and persistence of the Temple Mount Faithful" and called for East Jerusalem to be "massively settled with Jews." Shamir added: "I am sure that many of your demands will be fulfilled in the coming years."

Religious Issues

The usually dormant issue of the exemption from military service of yeshivah students made headlines in 1988, perhaps due to the increased call-ups of reservists to deal with the *intifada*. On June 12, the High Court of Justice ruled that the Defense Ministry was empowered to defer the military service of yeshivah students, an arrangement dating back to 1948. Critics charged that over time the original intention—"deferral"—had in fact become "evasion." In 1988 the situation was that no more than 2 percent of those who received such deferrals actually did military service at a later stage. A division-sized body of yeshivah students, totaling some 20,000, was thus in practice exempted from serving in the IDF; defense establishment sources estimated that within five years this number would grow to 30,000, or 5.5 percent of Israel's military strength. In July the proposals of a subcommittee of the Knesset's Defense and Foreign Affairs Committee, headed by MK Rabbi

Menahem Hacohen (Labor), for slashing the number of yeshivah students eligible for draft exemptions, were endorsed by the committee's plenum. However, the prospects for passage of the legislation required to implement this plan were poor, particularly after the gains made by the ultra-Orthodox parties in the Knesset elections. In the aftermath of those elections, on November 29, with the coalition talks—and the demands of the religious bloc—at their height, thousands of people attended a rally organized by 66 senior reserve officers against draft exemptions. This was followed some days later by a counterdemonstration of hundreds of ultra-Orthodox Jews who had done military service.

Other issues involving the religious-secular rift also cropped up in 1988. In May the High Court of Justice ruled that a woman appointed to serve on a local Religious Council could in fact serve. The case was that of Leah Shakdiel, an Orthodox woman from the Negev development town of Yeroham, whose installation on the council had been held up solely because of her sex. On October 25, Shakdiel became the first woman in Israel ever to take part in the meeting of a Religious Council as a full member. The country's (Orthodox) rabbinical establishment, in the form of the Supreme Rabbinical Council, railed against the decision, as it did against another High Court ruling under which the new Ashkenazi chief rabbi of Tel Aviv was elected by a body including women members. (For additional details on both cases, see AJYB 1989, pp. 418–419.)

The indirect clash between the two court systems, the religious and the secular, was also in evidence on the vexed issue of personal status, on which neither the executive nor the legislative branch was able or willing to take a definitive stance. On January 31, the High Court of Justice decided by a vote of 4–1 to accept the announcement of the attorney general that, with the Shoshana Miller case as a precedent, he had no objections to the Interior Ministry's registering as Jews three recent immigrants converted abroad by Reform rabbis. (For additional background, see AJYB 1989, pp. 417–418.) The three, Gail Moscowitch from the United States and Julia and Claudio Varella, a Brazilian couple, became the first Reform converts to be registered as Israelis under the Law of Return (Shoshana Miller left Israel before receiving her ID card, although legal efforts were under way to have her name entered in the Israeli population registry). In the meantime, the High Court began hearing a petition by two "messianic Jews," Jerry and Shirley Beresford, new immigrants from Zimbabwe, whom the Interior Ministry had also refused to register as Jews under the Law of Return.

Efforts by Minister Without Portfolio Yitzhak Peretz (Shas; he had resigned as interior minister over the Shoshana Miller case) to block the introduction of summer daylight-saving time were thwarted when the cabinet voted on February 14 for five months of an extra hour of daylight (April 10–September 4). Peretz had wanted summer time to end on August 13, since on the following day—the first day of the Hebrew month of Elul—Sephardi Jews began reciting the predawn daily prayers of penitence preceding the High Holy Days, several weeks before Ashkenazi Jews.

A long-standing issue was finally and formally resolved when the cabinet on May

8 approved the leasing of the land on Mount Scopus on which the Mormons' Jerusalem Center for Near Eastern Studies had been built. The approval, by a vote of 11–4 (three religious ministers and Ariel Sharon), followed the government's acceptance of the contract with the Mormons under which they promised not to engage in missionary activity. The institution, a branch of Brigham Young University, had already begun operating. (See also AJYB 1989, p. 419.)

Israel and World Jewry

THE DEMJANJUK TRIAL

On January 25, the prosecution began a weeklong summation of its case against Ukrainian-born John Demjanjuk, a 68-year-old retired auto worker from Cleveland who had been extradited from the United States, accused of being the notorious "Ivan the Terrible" (*"Ivan Grozny"*) of the Treblinka death camp, where some 850,000 Jews had perished. Demjanjuk was charged on four counts under Israel's Nazi and Nazi Collaborators Punishment Law of 1950, which carried a maximum penalty of death. The defendant admitted all the facts of the case but denied that he was Ivan. (For further background and a summary of the trial proceedings, see AJYB 1988, pp. 405–406, and AJYB 1989, pp. 419–422.) The prosecution devoted considerable efforts to establishing the authenticity of the ID card which placed Demjanjuk at the SS training camp at Trawnicki and later at Sobibor, although it did not mention Treblinka.

On April 18, the tribunal—Supreme Court Justice Dov Levin and two district court judges, Dalia Dorner and Zvi Tal—pronounced John Demjanjuk guilty as charged on all four counts: crimes against humanity, crimes against the Jewish people, war crimes, and crimes against persecuted persons. Taking turns, the judges took ten hours to read the 444-page verdict, at the end of which Justice Levin declared: "Therefore we have found that the accused is 'Ivan the Terrible.' " The judgment was based "first and foremost on the testimonies and statements of the identifying witnesses," the judges wrote, backed up by the Trawnicki ID card and "the false alibi and other lies of the accused and his incriminating behavior and statements." The judgment was delivered in the defendant's absence: Demjanjuk remained in his cell, saying he had severe back pains. However, his immediate family was present, every seat in the courtroom was taken, and the world media were present in force.

A week later, on April 25, Demjanjuk was brought to the court in a wheelchair to hear sentence pronounced. Judge Zvi Tal, himself a Holocaust survivor, read out the verdict. "Even a thousand deaths will not atone for [the defendant's] deeds," he asserted. "For such crimes there is no statue of limitations and no forgiveness." Tal concluded:

> True, the accused is not Eichmann, he did not initiate the Holocaust and he did not organize the slaughter of millions. But he served as chief executioner and with

his own hands killed tens of thousands and willingly tortured, humiliated, abused, debased and persecuted these wretched people. Therefore, for the crimes he committed and for which he was convicted, we sentence him to death. . . .

The rest—in which Judge Tal announced that the accused had the right, and under Israeli law in the case of the death penalty, the obligation, to appeal the verdict—was drowned out as the packed courtroom erupted into a grotesque crescendo of applause, cries of "Death!" curses directed at defense lawyer Yoram Sheftel, the frenzied singing of "I Believe in the Coming of the Messiah" and *"Am Yisrael Chai"* ("Israel Lives"), and even dancing.

On June 30, the final day permitted under the law, Demjanjuk's lawyers filed a formal appeal in the Supreme Court against both the sentence and the verdict. Among the points adduced in the 100-page appeal were "press incitement" and a "lynch atmosphere," hostile statements by cabinet ministers and other public figures, the bench's interference in the defense's cross-questioning, and the failure of some survivors to identify the defendant. The bottom line, Sheftel and Paul Chumak argued, was that their client's guilt had not been proved "beyond a reasonable doubt."

However, on November 29, just days before the Supreme Court was scheduled to begin hearing the appeal, one of the defense lawyers, Dov Eitan, a 53-year-old former judge, leaped to his death from a Jerusalem office building. At Eitan's funeral two days later, a 70-year-old Jerusalem man, Israel Yehezkeli, whose family had perished at Treblinka, threw acid at Sheftel, injuring him in his left eye. As a result of these events, the Supreme Court postponed the hearing of Demjanjuk's appeal for six months, rescheduling it for May 4, 1989.

IMMIGRATION TO ISRAEL

In what Immigrant Absorption Minister Yaakov Tzur termed a "historic" decision, the Jewish Agency Board of Governors decided in February to accept the principles of a report recommending that the Israeli government assume full responsibility for all matters pertaining to the absorption of immigrants in Israel. The report had been drawn up by a committee chaired by Dr. Israel Katz, director of the Center for Social Policy Studies in Israel, and the underlying aim of the recommendations was to streamline the absorption process by eliminating duplication and reducing bureaucracy.

In the meantime, the Absorption Ministry was hardly overburdened: according to the Central Bureau of Statistics, 13,034 *olim*, or new immigrants, arrived in Israel in 1988, approximately the same number as in the previous year. Some 42 percent of these arrivals—virtually all of them from Western democracies—were classified as "potential immigrants." One country from which immigration did increase was Argentina, by about 50 percent, to 1,546 persons, a development that was attributed to that country's economic crisis.

Arrivals from Africa numbered 1,334, of whom about a third were from the South

African Jewish community. In Israel, the last of the vexed personal-status problems that had plagued another African community, the Ethiopian Jews, since their arrival via "Operation Moses," was apparently resolved, though not without a further intervention by the judiciary. On October 23, the High Court of Justice accepted the petition of the Ethiopians' Beta Yisrael organization and ordered the Ministry of Religious Affairs and the Absorption Ministry to establish within 90 days the Institute for the Heritage of Ethiopian Jewry. The court was critical of the foot dragging of the authorities on this matter, since agreement had been reached some three years earlier on the institute's creation as part of an arrangement by which Ethiopian Jews could forego ritual immersion (thus symbolically "converting" to Judaism at the demand of the Orthodox rabbinical establishment) before being allowed to marry. Following the court's ruling, the Chief Rabbinate appointed Rabbi David Chelouche, Sephardi chief rabbi of Netanya, as the marriage registrar for Ethiopian Jews. In early December Rabbi Chelouche conducted the ceremony at which Shlomo Akale married Makdes Mekonen Hiale, signifying the official integration of the Ethiopian Jewish community in Israel.

Soviet Jewish *olim* accounted for 2,283 of the new immigrants in 1988, slightly more than in the previous year, but constituting only about 11.5 percent of all the Jews who left the USSR during the year. A number of leading Soviet Jewish activists arrived in 1988, and by year's end virtually all the longtime refuseniks and former Prisoners of Zion had left the USSR. Yosef Begun, a 16-year refusenik and former Prisoner of Zion, was accorded a gala welcome at Ben-Gurion Airport on January 19; in February he was given a check for $43,000 at a ceremony in the Prime Minister's Office, as a winner (along with Sen. Henry Jackson of the United States and France's Simone Veil) of the 1983 Defender of Jerusalem Prize awarded him at the time *in absentia*. The distinguished mathematician Prof. Alexander Yoffe, a 12-year refusenik who had been given a professorship by the Haifa Technion in 1978, arrived in February, as did Prof. Alexander Lerner, aged 74, a world-class cybernetics specialist, who was appointed professor emeritus by the Weizmann Institute of Science in Rehovot, and Alexei Magarik, a 29-year-old cellist and Hebrew teacher, believed to be the last Prisoner of Zion—he had been released in September 1987. March saw the arrival of Prof. Nahum Meiman, aged 77, a physicist whose knowledge of "state secrets" had been cause enough for the Soviets to prohibit his leaving; Lev Shapiro, aged 48, an electrical engineer and 11-year refusenik; and Ari and Ludmilla Volvovsky, 14-year refuseniks whose 19-year-old daughter had preceded them to Israel by four months. In July Gershon Zvi Rosenstein, a 15-year refusenik and a biophysicist who was known as the Habad ultra-Orthodox movement's "chief of operations" in the USSR, came to Israel.

In May Israel's large (196,000-strong) Russian-Jewish community formed a body named the Zionist Forum of Soviet Jewry to promote the interests of Russian immigrants, newcomers, and veterans, and to present a united front vis-à-vis the Israeli government and the Jewish Agency. The chairman of the new group was Natan Sharansky, and the executive included such well-known figures as Ida Nudel,

Yosef Begun, Rabbi Eliahu Essas, and Yuli Edelstein. Later in the year, Sharansky and Nudel were involved in an exchange with the new Jewish Agency treasurer, former Herut MK Meir Shetreet. When the two former Prisoners of Zion had some stinging words for immigrant-absorption arrangements, Shetreet labeled them "slanderers" and perhaps revealed something of the gut feelings of many Israelis when he suggested that the money earmarked for Soviet immigrants could be better spent in preventing veteran Israelis from becoming emigrants.

A controversial issue was the decision by the cabinet on June 19 (by a vote of 16–2 and three abstentions) to compel Jews leaving the USSR with Israeli visas to proceed directly to Israel, with Bucharest named as the likely transit stop. The idea behind the move was to put a stop to what Absorption Minister Yaakov Tzur, speaking in the Knesset a few days before the vote, described as the "disgrace" of the "dropout" phenomenon—Soviet Jews who upon arrival in Vienna opted for destinations other than Israel. (In Bucharest this option would not exist.) However, the new arrangements remained largely on paper as they were opposed by the Netherlands, which represented Israeli interests in Moscow and issued the Israeli visas, and by the Soviet Union itself.

The Jewish Agency Assembly, meeting in Jerusalem in early July, unanimously endorsed a resolution "welcom[ing] the government of Israel's decision and initiative to secure direct flights from the Soviet Union to Israel for Soviet Jews who request an exit permit in order to reach Israel." However, this was largely neutralized when the assembly, taking note of "the Soviet policy on behalf of family reunifications," urged other governments to press Moscow to abide by its commitment to the Helsinki accords and "other international agreements regarding the right to leave." Such accords precluded the possibility of compelling immigrants to proceed to a specific destination, such as Israel. Many leading American Jewish organizations also objected to the Israeli cabinet decision.

AMERICAN JEWRY

Several issues produced strains in the relations between the American Jewish community and the Israeli political establishment in 1988. The aftermath of the Knesset elections, when ultra-Orthodox elements demanded passage of the "Who is a Jew?" amendment to the Law of Return as part of their price for joining either a Likud or Labor coalition, caused alarm and consternation among the overwhelming majority of American Jewry. (See the section on the election campaign, above, and "Jewish Communal Affairs," elsewhere in this volume.) Participants in the First International Jewish Feminist Conference, organized by the American Jewish Congress and held in Jerusalem in November, took the opportunity to express their opposition to the proposed change in the Law of Return by holding a demonstration in front of the Prime Minister's Office. Such legislation, the conference said, "would have particularly serious ramifications for Jewish women" because "the conversion of women to Judaism by non-Orthodox rabbis would render them and their children ineligible for [Israeli] citizenship under the Law of Return."

In conjunction with its first world gathering, held in Jerusalem in July, the Conservative movement asked the High Court of Justice to order the Jerusalem Religious Council to overturn its recent decision to withhold a *kashrut* permit from the movement's local youth hostel. On the Tisha be'Av fast day the conference delegates demonstrated outside the headquarters of the Chief Rabbinate. The Conservative movement's Rabbinical Assembly, which ordained the first four graduates of its Seminary of Judaic Studies in Jerusalem during the conference, urged the Knesset to abolish the Chief Rabbinate on the ground that it was a body alien to the Jewish tradition.

Israel's handling of the Palestinian uprising in the occupied territories also aggravated relations, especially in the early part of the year when Defense Minister Yitzhak Rabin introduced a policy permitting soldiers to beat demonstrators with truncheons. The officially declared policy appalled large numbers of American Jews, and many American Jewish leaders felt compelled to break with tradition and speak out publicly against the Israeli military actions they saw nightly on the TV news. Among the leaders who spoke out were Bertram Gold, acting executive vice-president of the American Jewish Committee, who deplored the use of "brute force" which "evokes other times and places when it was used against us"; Hadassah president Ruth Popkin, who said she was having a "hard time believing Rabin would have said something like that. . . . That is not the Israeli way and it is not the Jewish way"; and four intellectuals—Rabbi Arthur Hertzberg, the writer Irving Howe, the economist and former dean of Harvard University Henry Rosovsky, and the political scientist Michael Walzer—who sent a letter to the *New York Times* stating that they had "read with shame reports of house to house beatings of hundreds of people, leading to broken bones and hospitalization of the aged and children."

Rabbi Alexander Schindler, president of the Union of American Hebrew Congregations, fired off a cable to President Chaim Herzog in which he said he was "deeply troubled and pained" but could not "remain silent" in the face of a policy that was "self-defeating and, therefore, counterproductive." In a letter of response to Rabbi Schindler (January 25), President Herzog asserted that there had been "no order to beat indiscriminately," and that "steps [had] been taken to ensure" that any possible "divergences and irregularities" would not recur. Herzog then linked the events in the territories to "the wave of Khomeinism which threatens our area" and drew a comparison between Israeli actions and measures taken by other countries, both in the Middle East and by Western democracies such as Britain (in Northern Ireland) and the United States (Kent State, Watts County, and Newark). "The issue is a far wider one than that of Israel's image," Herzog wrote, adding that "the picture as reflected by the all too simplistic presentation on the television screens abroad evades the issue."

More blunt was the Israeli consul-general in New York, Moshe Yegar, who said that criticism of Israel by American Jews was an "unfriendly" act and belied protestations by such critics that they were "friends of Israel and strong Zionists." In an effort to tone down the debate, the Conference of Presidents of Major American Jewish Organizations and nine other groups, a total of 51 bodies, issued a somewhat equivocal statement, on the one hand supporting Israel's "legitimate efforts to oppose terrorism and violence" and accepting the concept that the uprising was part of the decades-long pattern in which "the Palestinian Arabs have been exploited and victimized by the Arab world"; but on the other hand noting that both President Herzog and Prime Minister Shamir had given "assurances . . . that the policy of restraint continues." The signatories said they had conveyed their "concern" to the Israeli government over "any departures in contradiction of this long-standing policy and practice."

In early March, when a delegation of the Presidents' Conference visited Israel, Prime Minister Shamir was on the eve of a crucial visit to Washington at the height of his efforts to stifle the peace initiative of Secretary of State Shultz. Shamir sought to convince the group that American Jewry must muzzle itself. American Jews, he told the 44-member mission, must not permit themselves "to be used in the campaign against us," irrespective of their opinions. Such criticism would play straight into the hands of Israel's enemies, Shamir warned, and the Arabs would turn it to their advantage by "driving a wedge between Israel and American Jewry" and ultimately between Israel and the United States. In an interview in the *Jerusalem Post* two days before his trip, Shamir reaffirmed the principle of nonintervention by the Diaspora in Israeli affairs: "Israel and its citizens alone must decide on fateful diplomatic and security matters."

At all events, on March 14, Shamir could well believe that his message had sunk in, and both he and the U.S. administration could believe that American Jewry was solidly behind him, as 3,000 young UJA fund-raisers gave him a resounding welcome at a banquet held in the Washington Hilton two days before his meeting with President Reagan. Shamir told the enthusiastic gathering that the violence in the territories was in fact an all-out "war," adding that only Israel's citizens could determine their destiny.

Other Domestic Matters

POPULATION

Israel's population stood at approximately 4,472,000 at the end of 1988, comprising 3,656,000 Jews (81.8 percent), 633,000 Muslims (14.2 percent), 105,000 Christians (2.3 percent), and 78,000 Druze and members of other faiths (1.7 percent). The total population increased by 1.5 percent, as compared with 1.7 percent in 1987.

Data released by the Central Bureau of Statistics in conjunction with Israel's 40th anniversary showed that the largest ethnic group among Israeli Jews was the Moroccan community, totaling 488,000 persons, followed by persons of Polish (297,000), Romanian (277,000), and Iraqi (266,000) origin. Those who warned of the so-called "demographic threat," notably a Committee on the Demographic Problem that was formed in August with the participation of former Foreign Ministry director-general David Kimche and former cabinet secretary Arye Naor, with the aim of countering the public's "terrible ignorance" in this area, pointed to the fact that in Israel and the territories combined, Arab children aged eight and under already outnumbered Jewish children by 40,000 (630,000 to 590,000), and that by the end of the century there would be more Arabs under the age of 18 than Jews (1.4 million to 1.3 million). Even in Israel proper, fully half the Muslim population was below the age of 17, and whereas the number of Jewish births in 1988 remained stable at 74 percent of the total, the number of Muslim births increased by 10 percent during the year due to the ongoing increase in the number of Muslim women of child-bearing age.

HEALTH-CARE CRISIS

In 1988 Israel's once vaunted public health-care system experienced the culmination of a deep structural crisis that had been building up for some years. A strike in early February—at a time when some medical professionals had already been "working to rule" for some time—by clerks, sanitation workers, and lab workers in 32 government hospitals, created chaotic and unsanitary conditions that lasted for the better part of the month. Doctors stepped up their sanctions in March, and hospital directors warned that the system was on the verge of collapse.

Doctors in hospitals run by Kupat Holim Clalit (the Histadrut-run medical insurance scheme which covered the majority of Israelis) performed only emergency operations. They were protesting the Treasury's refusal to accept a pay-raise agreement they had signed with the Kupat Holim management, which had triggered sanctions by surgeons in government-run hospitals who demanded equal terms. The feeling in the Labor party was that Finance Minister Moshe Nissim was out to "break" Kupat Holim, the Histadrut's flagship (all persons covered medically by Kupat Holim Clalit were compelled to become Histadrut members) for political purposes. By April, Kupat Holim hospitals were operating on a strictly emergency basis and the sanctions by doctors in government hospitals were in their fourth month. On June 5, the cabinet decided to establish a judicial commission to examine the entire structure of the health-care system and make recommendations.

In the meantime, the sanctions by hospital staff continued unabated, with doctors insisting on a permanent second-shift arrangement that would both eliminate the backlog of operations and other medical procedures and augment their salaries. Besides the hospital sanctions, services by Magen David Adom came to a near standstill as 900 MDA personnel protested the nonpayment of their wages, and 3,000 nurses began a "collective summer vacation" to prod the government into upholding an earlier agreement with them. On July 10, 12 MKs began a seven-day hunger strike to demonstrate their outrage at the government's "indifference to the collapsing health care system." On July 15 the doctors rejected a proposal for a temporary second shift, but did agree to enter into negotiations with the Health Ministry and gradually abandoned their sanctions. On October 6, doctors in the 14 Kupat Holim hospitals said they were returning to a normal schedule after getting a "commitment" from management that a second-shift schedule would soon be introduced. The following day a delegation of doctors from government hospitals met with Finance Minister Nissim to seek wage parity with their colleagues in Kupat Holim.

The restoration of regular hospital service came not a moment too soon, as September and October saw a polio scare and it was decided to vaccinate everyone in Israel and the territories below the age of 40. The polio virus was found in the sewage of 27 of 70 localities examined. The outbreak, which claimed one life and infected 11 other persons, and was apparently caused or exacerbated by the country's inadequate sewerage system, was officially declared over in mid-November, after nearly 3.5 million Israelis and another million people in the territories had been vaccinated.

ISRAELI ARABS

Israel's Arab population was in the news in 1988 primarily because of its declared solidarity—which sometimes went beyond mere words—with the uprising in the territories. (See the section on the *intifada*.) Various politicians and "security sources" warned of "irredentist tendencies" among the country's Arab population that were being intensified by the uprising. At a mass rally in Nazareth on January 23, Labor MK Abdel Wahab Darousha called Defense Minister Rabin a "murderer" and announced his resignation from the Labor party; he was later elected to the Knesset at the head of an all-Arab party. In March the Communist party's Nazareth-based daily *al-Ithihad* was shut down for a week by the Interior Ministry, ostensibly for publishing "inflammatory articles." However, as this measure was enacted six days before the annual Land Day general strike, some observers saw it as an attempt to prevent possible incitement connected with that day. Land Day itself was relatively quiet in Israel, in striking contrast to the situation in the territories.

That Israel's Arabs had legitimate grievances of their own was documented in a comprehensive report issued by the International Center for Peace in the Middle East. Summing up the results of a study conducted by a Jewish-Arab research team headed by Prof. Henry Rosenfeld of Haifa University, the report, entitled *The Condition and Status of the Arabs in Israel*, found that their condition was generally deplorable and their status second-class.

"Startling and alarming" was the report's description of the situation in the realm of social welfare. Fully 40 percent of all Israeli Arab families were found to be subsisting below the poverty line, with many homes lacking even the most basic facilities. (Following the polio outbreak, the deputy mayor of the Galilee village of Rama, Basep Ghattas, told a Technion symposium on the state of the country's sewerage systems that because the government had failed to approve building plans, public sanitation in Arab villages had deteriorated to "catastrophic" levels and the polio rate among Israeli Arabs was 17 times higher than among Israeli Jews.) The dropout rate from the educational system was 46 percent for Israeli Arab teenagers leaving school (despite the existence of the compulsory education law), as compared with 6.3 percent for Jewish teenagers. The disparity between the country's majority and minority population groups was equally pronounced in housing. While only 1.1 percent of Israeli Jews lived in conditions of severe overcrowding, in Arab locales the figure was 26.4 percent.

The report's most damning finding was that in many cases these conditions were the result of deliberate government policy which in practice resulted in discrimination. The lack of government-approved master plans for Arab villages had already been addressed in the Markowitz Report in 1987 (AJYB 1989, p. 429). In 1988, about 460 illegally constructed buildings, many of them dwellings, were demolished in the Arab sector. When 15 such structures were demolished in the village of Taibe on a single day, November 7, three days of rioting ensued, followed by a general strike of the country's entire Arab population on November 15. Israeli Arab leaders reiterated their long-standing contention that the government's land-expropriations policy, combined with the absence of master plans for towns and villages, had left the Arab population no choice but to build "illegal" homes. A statement released by the Interior Ministry on November 7 said that the structures that had been demolished in Taibe had been built "on agricultural land where construction is prohibited and thus constituted a provocation against the rule of law."

40TH-ANNIVERSARY CELEBRATIONS

The muted atmosphere in Israel caused by the *intifada* had its effect on the planned events and celebrations to mark the 40th anniversary of the state's establishment. Aggravating the gloomy mood was a steep decline in incoming tourism. In the evening of Independence Day some 45,000 people gathered at Ramat Gan National Stadium to view a pageant staged by the IDF which was also televised live. Among the winners of the Israel Prize for lifetime achievements—traditionally awarded on Independence Day evening—were Jerusalem mayor Teddy Kollek, the Talmud scholar Rabbi Adin Steinsaltz, the educator and community activist Arye Lova Eliav, and the veteran singer Shoshana Damari. The original Declaration of Independence was on display at the Knesset, and in Tel Aviv the document's signing in 1948 was reenacted.

An extravaganza to mark the closing of the 40th-anniversary celebrations (October 13) was a performance at the foot of Masada of Mahler's Second (*Resurrection*)

Symphony by the Israel Philharmonic Orchestra under the baton of Zubin Mehta. Gregory Peck, Yves Montand, and other notables also took part. Four thousand tickets were available, from $150 and up, and the majority were sold abroad. The biggest scheduled event of all, a performance of Verdi's opera *Nabucco* outside the walls of the Old City of Jerusalem, at a cost of $11.5 million within the framework of the Israel Festival/Jerusalem, was canceled, reportedly because the *intifada* had deterred financial backers, though production problems were also cited.

Culture

THE ARTS

As part of the country's 40th-anniversary celebrations, the Tel Aviv Municipality and the Ministry of Education and Culture sponsored a Festival of Original Plays composed of seven new productions and eight revivals of classic Israeli dramas. The most controversial of the new works was Yehoshua Sobol's *Jerusalem Syndrome*, ostensibly about ultranationalist extremism during the Jewish revolt in 70 CE but with clear allusions to modern-day Israel. Sobol, some of whose plays, notably *A Jewish Soul* and *The Palestinian Woman*, had infuriated the Israeli Right in the past, said the new production was meant as a statement about nationalist fanaticism as such. When Herut and Tehiya hotheads tried to shout down the performers at a performance in Tel Aviv on January 9, fistfights and heated verbal exchanges broke out in the audience. About a week later both Sobol and Gedalia Besser, the artistic directors of the Haifa Municipal Theater, announced their resignation because of "unrelenting interference by politicians" in their work.

The year's major sustained cultural offering, the Israel Festival/Jerusalem (May 14–June 11), sold 100,000 tickets of the 130,000 available—a percentage that the festival's artistic director, Oded Kotler, said was more than creditable given the distinctly unfestive atmosphere generated by the Palestinian uprising, and nowhere more so (in Israel) than Jerusalem. The festival offerings included a Habimah production of *The Dybbuk* directed by Poland's Andrzej Wajda and a staging of the classic Yiddish play in dance form by the Maurice Bejart Ballet.

At the 5th International Jerusalem Film Festival, organized by the Israel Film Archive/Jerusalem Cinematheque, more than 100 films were screened in ten days (June 30–July 9). Filmmakers from Asia (including Korea, Taiwan, and Hong Kong), Africa (Tanzania, Mali, and Senegal), and Eastern Europe (notably the USSR, which also sent an official delegation, the first Soviet cultural delegation to visit Israel since 1967) were represented. The 19 Israeli feature films released in 1988 drew about two million viewers, or 16 percent of the total number of tickets sold to films in Israel during the year (12.5 million). Two of the most interesting Israeli features were *Avia's Summer*, set in Palestine under the British Mandate, and based on the childhood experiences of the film's star and director, the veteran actress Gila

Almagor, who had already scored major local successes with book and stage versions; and *Because of That War*, a powerful documentary directed by Orna Ben-Dor Niv, relating the stories of two Holocaust survivors, one from Warsaw and the other from Salonika, and the devastating effect their wartime experiences had on their children, Yehuda Poliker, an Israeli rock star, and Ya'acov Gilad, a producer/songwriter who was Poliker's collaborator. In 1987 Poliker had released an extraordinary album called *Ashes and Dust* which sold 50,000 copies in Israel despite—or, some would say, because of—its theme: the Holocaust and its impact on the "second generation."

In October the Interior Ministry's Film and Theater Censorship Board banned Martin Scorsese's film *The Last Temptation of Christ* for screening in Israel. The vote was 16–3 and followed heavy pressure exerted by local Christian activists and pro-Israeli fundamentalist groups abroad. The producers and the local distributors were expected to appeal the banning to the Supreme Court.

A musical event that seemed to have carved out a solid niche for itself, both locally and internationally, was the Red Sea Jazz Festival, held in Eilat at the end of August. Some 15,000 tickets were sold for the four-day event, which featured 21 groups and individual artists, a third of them from abroad. In the realm of classical music, a major event was the first-ever visit to Israel by the Vienna Philharmonic Orchestra, an event whose political overtones were unmistakable, given the cool relations between Israel and Austria since the Waldheim election. Jerusalemites accorded the orchestra no more than a "correct" reception—despite the fact that the guest conductor was Leonard Bernstein, an immensely popular figure in Israel—but in Tel Aviv, where the audiences were apparently less politically motivated, the orchestra's performances of Mahler's Sixth Symphony drew rapturous ovations.

JUDAICA

April saw the opening of a spacious new wing for Jewish ceremonial art at the Israel Museum, where viewers could marvel at the 500-year-old "Rothschild Miscellany" and rare items from the fabled Stieglitz collection. In June the museum exhibited part of the "Aleppo Codex," the earliest known manuscript of the full text of the Bible, compiled in Tiberias more than a thousand years ago. The "Codex" survived the upheavals in the Middle East over the centuries, being housed in Jerusalem, Cairo, and finally in Aleppo, Syria, where it was thought to have been destroyed when a mob set fire to the Aleppo synagogue in 1947, in the wake of the UN resolution to partition Palestine. However, although about a quarter of the priceless document had been ravaged, the remnant was smuggled into Israel via Turkey in 1958 and presented to then President Yitzhak Ben-Zvi.

The Second International Judaica Fair, held in May at the Jerusalem Convention Center, drew enthusiastic crowds to view ritual objects, manuscripts, paintings, and other items. The fair culminated in an auction conducted by Sotheby's at which collectors spent a total of about $1 million, including $92,000 for an 18th-century German spice box and $47,300 for an illuminated 1732 *ketubah* (marriage contract) from Padua—the highest price ever paid at auction for a *ketubah*.

On August 30, the Israel Museum announced that it had received from an anonymous donor a tiny ivory pomegranate, 1.68 inches high, which was apparently in use in King Solomon's Temple nearly three millennia ago—the first relic ever attributed to the First Temple. The pomegranate, which bore an incised inscription in ancient Hebrew script ("Belonging to the Temple of the Lord, holy to the priests"), was probably carried on a scepter as part of the Temple ritual. It was purchased as a gift to the museum for $550,000 by "an anonymous friend of Israel from Basel, Switzerland," in the words of a Tourism Ministry press release.

ARCHAEOLOGY

In April the Israel Museum mounted a major exhibition of finds from the Chalcolithic period in the area of present-day Israel. Many of the 6,000-year-old items were on public display for the first time. In October the Hebrew University of Jerusalem announced that a team headed by Prof. Amihai Mazar of the university's School of Archaeology and Prof. Pierre de Miroschejdi of the French Research Center in Jerusalem had discovered the remains of a 5,000-year-old temple near the town of Beit Shemesh, southwest of Jerusalem. The temple and its associated cultic objects were expected to help further the understanding of the development of religion and society in the area some 2,000 years before the appearance there of the people of Israel as a nation. The excavation was funded by the National Geographic Society.

In May the extensive ruins of the Roman and Byzantine city of Beit She'an, featuring a large and well-preserved Roman amphitheater, were officially opened to the public. Local promoters were heartened by forecasts that the site would eventually draw half a million tourists a year, who would provide a much-needed economic injection for a sleepy town best known as the home of Herut's David Levy and as a way station between the Jordan Rift Valley and the country's north—its strategic location, indeed, having been the reason for its importance to the ancients.

Egypt demanded that Israel give back all the archaeological finds, apparently numbering in the thousands, which it had removed from the Sinai desert during the Israeli occupation of the peninsula from 1967–1982. In the meantime, the *Jerusalem Post* reported, quoting the director of the Israeli Academic Center in Cairo, that Egypt was prohibiting Israeli archaeologists from conducting excavations in the Sinai and even from taking part in international digs.

Personalia

On February 23, President Chaim Herzog was reelected for a second (and final) five-year term by the Knesset, by a vote of 82–2 in a secret ballot. A surprisingly large number of MKs (18) chose to cast blank ballots. Herzog took the oath of allegiance on May 9, officially beginning his new term.

Two key appointments were made in the security sphere. On April 1, the interim Shin Bet director appointed following the resignation of Avraham Shalom in the wake of the No. 300 bus scandal was replaced by a permanent chief. The name of the Shin Bet's director would not be made public while he held office, but it was revealed that the interim head for 18 months had been Yosef Harmelin, who had previously headed the Shin Bet from 1964–1975. The resignation of Amiram Nir, the prime minister's antiterrorism adviser who was implicated in the Iran-*contra* affair, also took effect on April 1. Nir, who had been appointed by Shimon Peres and had held the post for more than three years, was replaced a month later by Col. Yigal Carmon, a former intelligence officer who had also served in the Civil Administration in the occupied territories. (On December 1, Nir, aged 38, was killed in a plane crash in Mexico.)

Changes also occurred in the Supreme Court. On April 26, Justice Menachem Eilon was named the court's deputy president, replacing Justice Miriam Ben-Porat who retired at the mandatory age of 70. However, Justice Ben-Porat did not remain inactive for long: on June 14, she was elected state comptroller by the Knesset (the vote was 67–16, and 13 abstentions), following the resignation from that post of Judge Yaakov Malz (May 15)—after only a year—in order to be appointed a Supreme Court justice. Ben-Porat took up her duties as state comptroller and ombudswoman on July 4.

Personalities who died during the year included Prof. Ze'ev Vilnai, an Israel Prize winner who was a renowned geographer, veteran guide, and prolific author about the Land of Israel, on January 21, aged 88; Ilona Feher, famed violin teacher whose pupils included Shlomo Mintz and Shmuel Ashkenazi, on February 1, aged 86; Rafi Nelson, colorful founder of the Eilat holiday village near Taba, on February 6, aged 58; Prof. Yosef Nedava, historian of the Revisionist movement and a founding member of the Greater Israel Movement and the Tehiya party, on February 18, aged 73; Yehoshua Rotenstreich, an eminent lawyer who served as chairman of the Israel Press Council and was a senior member of the commission of inquiry into the Pollard affair, on March 10, aged 78; Alexander Bein, Israel Prize laureate in Zionist historiography and Israel's first State Archivist (1956–1971), on June 21, aged 85; Ya'ir Hurvitz, a major Israeli poet of the 1970s and 1980s who was awarded the Alterman Prize and the Prime Minister's Prize for Creativity, on July 26, aged 49; Zerubavel Gilad, a veteran poet who wrote the "anthem" of the prestate Palmach underground, on August 12, aged 75; Prof. Akiva Ernst Simon, Israel Prize laureate for education and an activist in promoting Jewish-Arab coexistence, on August 18, aged 89; Siona Tagger, a veteran artist who blended Western impressionism with a distinctive vision of the orient, on June 15, aged 89; Prof. Shmuel Ettinger, renowned historian who carried out path-breaking studies of anti-Semitism, president of the Israel Historical Society, and director of the Center for Research and Documentation of East European Jewry, on September 22, aged 69; Oved Ben-Ami, a leading industrialist who was considered the father of the Israeli diamond industry and who founded the city of Netanya and served as its mayor for 42 years, on October 17, aged 83; Menachem Savidor, the Speaker of the 10th Knesset and a longtime Liberal-party activist, on November 2, aged 70; Baruch Venger, who presided over the growth of the Galilee development town of Carmiel to a booming city of 20,000, serving as mayor since 1973, on November 22, aged 58; and Bernard Cherrick, longtime vice-president of the Hebrew University of Jerusalem, who was dubbed "Mr. University" for his tireless efforts on its behalf, on November 22, aged 74.

RALPH MANDEL

World Jewish Population, 1988

Updated Estimates

THIS ARTICLE PRESENTS UPDATES, for the end of 1988, of the Jewish population estimates for the various countries of the world.[1] The estimates reflect some of the results of a prolonged and ongoing effort to study scientifically the demography of contemporary world Jewry.[2] Data collection and comparative research have benefited from the collaboration of scholars and institutions in many countries, including replies to direct inquiries regarding current estimates. It should be emphasized, however, that the elaboration of a worldwide set of estimates for the Jewish populations of the various countries is beset with difficulties and uncertainties. Information on the quality of the estimate for each country is provided below, through a simple accuracy rating scale.

Over 96 percent of world Jewry is concentrated in ten countries. The aggregate of these ten major Jewish population centers virtually determines the assessment of the size of total world Jewry. The figures for 1988 have been updated from those for 1986 in accordance with the known or estimated changes in the interval—vital events (i.e., births and deaths), identificational changes (accessions and secessions), and migrations. In addition, some corrections have been introduced in the light of newly accrued information on Jewish population. Corresponding corrections have also been applied retrospectively to the 1986 figures, which appear below in revised summary (see table 1), so as to allow for comparison with the 1988 estimates.

The 1988 estimates were compiled in 1989, toward the end of the decade of the 1980s. By now, a new round of decennial population censuses is under way throughout the countries of the world. Those countries which include information on religion and/or ethnic group (or ancestry) in their census, specifying the Jews as a separate category, are expected to furnish updated counts of their self-declared Jews. The most important instance is the Soviet Union, which took its new census some-

---

[1]The previous estimates, as of 1986, were first published in AJYB, vol. 88, 1988, pp. 412–27, and reprinted in a condensed version in AJYB, vol. 89, 1989, pp. 433–41.

[2]Many of these activities have been carried out by, or in coordination with, the Division of Jewish Demography and Statistics at the Institute of Contemporary Jewry, the Hebrew University of Jerusalem.

what earlier, in January 1989, though no results by ethnic group (religion is not inquired into) had been released by the time of this writing. Other countries from which new census figures on national Jewish populations are expected include Canada, Brazil, Switzerland, South Africa, and Australia.

In addition, the world's largest Jewish population—that of the United States—will be investigated in 1990 by means of a scientifically designed national sample survey, under the auspices of the Council of Jewish Federations. The feasibility of Jewish-sponsored national sample surveys is being considered in other countries as well. Thus, while many of the estimates presented here for 1988 are updates ultimately traceable to data collections conducted around 1980 or even earlier, this new round of basic information intake is expected to provide the needed empirical data for several prominent Diaspora populations. This documentation will be duly taken into account in compiling our future sets of Jewish population estimates.

Israel took its latest census in 1983, but has constantly updated statistics of its Jewish population size.

Jewish Population Trends

Diaspora Jews are highly dispersed. In most countries their number is now rather small, and they constitute no more than a minute fraction of the entire population. Consequently, though Jews tend to cluster in large cities, they are greatly exposed to assimilation. While the assimilatory process leads to demographic losses for the Jewish population, there may also be gains through accession of persons who were born as non-Jews. It is the net balance of the identificational changes that matters demographically; in the longer run, though, the cohesion of a Diaspora population may be affected as well.[3]

The Jews in most countries of the Diaspora are demographically characterized by very low fertility, considerable outmarriage (which may involve losses of children to the Jewish population),[4] some other net assimilatory losses, and great aging. Since an increased proportion of elderly in the population usually implies not only many deceased but also a reduced proportion of persons of reproductive age—and therefore relatively fewer births—the aging of a population has the effect of reducing the birthrate and raising the death rate. There are differences in the levels of these demographic factors among the Jews in various regions and countries. In all major Diaspora populations, the joint balance of the natural and identificational changes is now close to nil or outrightly negative, with the Jewish deceased frequently outnumbering newborn Jews. These negative tendencies have been taken into account in updating the estimates of Jews in many countries.

---

[3]A fuller discussion of the subject can be found in U.O. Schmelz, "Jewish Survival: The Demographic Factors," AJYB, vol. 81, 1981, pp. 61–117. See also *Aging of World Jewry* (Jerusalem, 1984), by the same author.

[4]If less than half of the children of the outmarried are themselves Jews.

With regard to the balance of external migrations, there is no regularity among the various Diaspora populations or even in the same population over time. Where the migratory balance is positive—e.g., in North America—it counteracts or even outweighs any numerically negative influence of internal demographic developments. Where the migratory balance is negative, it may cause, or aggravate, the decrease of a Jewish population. In 1987–1988, the overall volume of international migrations of Jews was rather modest, primarily because of the restricted outflow of Jewish emigration from the Soviet Union.

In contrast, Jews in Israel incur virtually no outmarriages and direct assimilatory losses. Moreover, until the early 1980s they tended to have a positive migration balance. They have a younger age structure than Diaspora Jews and the general populations of the developed countries and exhibit a fairly high level of fertility. The previously substantial fertility differentials between Jews in-gathered in Israel from Asia-Africa and Europe-America are no longer in evidence. Remarkably, European Jews in Israel have not participated in the drastic fertility decline that has characterized the developed nations and particularly the Diaspora Jews during the last few decades, but have actually raised their fertility somewhat. In recent years, both major origin groups among Israel's Jews have displayed a fertility level surpassing not only the vast majority of Diaspora Jewry but also the general populations in the developed countries.

In the overall demographic balance of World Jewry, the natural increase of Israel has, so far, made up for losses in the Diaspora. But such compensation will not be possible for much longer. As a consequence of the intensifying demographic deficit in the Diaspora, a trend for some reduction in the total number of the world's Jews may soon be setting in.[5] The relative share of Israel among world Jewry is on the increase.

Difficulties in Estimating Jewish Population Size in the Diaspora

Some of the difficulties involved in estimating the size of Jewish Diaspora populations are common to all aspects of the study of Diaspora demography.[6] They are mainly due to the great geographical scattering of Jews—a factor that makes multiple data collection mandatory but also hinders its feasibility; to their unusually strong demographic dynamics in many respects—migrations, social mobility, family formation patterns (including outmarriage), etc.; and to lacunae of available demographic information, which is deficient in both quantity and quality.

More specific difficulties in estimating the up-to-date size of Jewish populations are due to conceptual and measurement problems.

---

[5]*Aliyah* and *yeridah*—immigration to, and emigration from, Israel—obviously constitute only internal transfers within the global Jewish framework.

[6]Reliable figures are currently forthcoming for the Jews of Israel from official statistics which need not be discussed here.

When mixed couples and households are not infrequent, it is necessary to distinguish between the "actually Jewish population" and the "enlarged Jewish population." The latter comprises also the non-Jewish household members (spouses, children, etc.) of the Jews. However socially significant the non-Jewish household members (and more distant non-Jewish relatives) of the Jews may be, they should not be included in a count of Jews. The paradoxical situation that exists is that growth of an enlarged Jewish population may be associated with contraction of the respective actually Jewish population.

Another vexing problem is identificational changes among Jews. Under present conditions, there are Jews who have not formally embraced another religion, yet are either very estranged ("marginal") or have even become resolutely alienated from Judaism and the Jewish community and, if questioned, disclaim being Jews any longer. When a census or survey is taken which inquires into religion or ethnicity, these individuals have an opportunity to define their current status subjectively.[7] In general, the practice of self-determination is followed in all relevant censuses and surveys.[8] This applies to marginal individuals, converts to Judaism (although some of the conversions may be contested between the various ideological trends—Orthodox, Conservative, and Reform), and to all other persons who claim to be Jews. In estimating the size of a Jewish population, it is usual to include, in principle, all marginal individuals who have not ceased to be Jews.

Particular difficulties exist with regard to the countries of Eastern Europe, whose Jewish populations were drastically reduced during and after World War II. Prolonged antireligious policies in these countries have had a negative effect on the identity of genealogically Jewish persons, many of whom may have severed—insofar as it depends on themselves—all links with Jewishness. The resulting uncertainties have led to wishful thinking and account for the widely differing estimates of Jews that have been circulated for these countries.

Not a few Jews (like other persons) have some residential status in more than one country.[9] This may be due to business requirements, professional assignments in foreign countries, climatic differences between countries, migrants staying temporarily in prolonged transit, etc. The danger of double-counting or omissions is inherent in such situations. The situation is particularly critical regarding some countries in Central and tropical South America, Africa, and East Asia, where the relatively few Jews living permanently may be outnumbered by a floating Jewish population of people who are not tourists but who are in residence for temporary periods. As far as possible, we have tried to account for such persons only once, giving precedence to the usual country of residence.

---

[7] Misreporting of Jews in official censuses is a different issue; see below.

[8] Persons who disclaim being Jews at some stage of life may change their minds later.

[9] The problem is even more acute with regard to residential status in more than one locality of the same country. This may adversely affect the accuracy of Jewish population reporting for individual countries through omissions or, more likely, double-counting.

Figures on Jews from population censuses are unavailable for most Diaspora communities, though they do exist for some important ones. Even where census statistics on Jews are forthcoming, they are usually scant, because the Jews are a small minority. There have been instances where detailed tabulations on Jews have been undertaken, through Jewish initiative, from official census material; examples are Canada, South Africa, and Argentina. In some countries serious problems exist, or are feared to exist, in the reporting of Jews as such: individuals may prefer not to describe themselves as Jews, or non-Jews may be erroneously included as Jews (as has happened in some Latin American countries). These problems require statistical evaluation whose feasibility and conclusiveness depend on the relevant information available.

Surveys are the only way of obtaining comprehensive information on Jewish population in the absence of official censuses. Jewish-sponsored surveys have the additional advantage of being able to inquire into matters of specifically Jewish interest, e.g., Jewish education, observances, and attitudes. However, since they address themselves to a small and scattered minority with identification problems, surveys are not easy to conduct competently and may encounter difficulties with regard to both coverage and response, especially with regard to marginal Jews. Again, these aspects require evaluation. Countrywide surveys have been undertaken in the United States, South Africa, France, Italy, Netherlands, etc. Local surveys have been carried out in many U.S. cities, in the United Kingdom, Latin America, Australia, etc. However, these local initiatives have so far been uncoordinated with regard to content and method.

In certain countries or localities, Jewish community registers include all, or the largest part, of the Jewish population. Often the same communities keep records of Jewish vital events—especially marriages performed with a Jewish ceremony and Jewish burials. However, communal registers tend to cover mixed households insufficiently. In addition, although the amount and quality of updating vary from place to place, community registers generally lag behind the actual situation of the respective Jewish populations.

Many estimates of Jewish populations for which no solid data from censuses or surveys exist are regrettably of unspecified or dubious source and methodology.

Besides the conceptual and measurement difficulties affecting the figures for a Jewish population at any base date, similar problems recur with regard to the updating information which should account for all the various types of changes in the time elapsed since that base date. For vital events and identificational changes, age-sex-specific models can be of use; these may be applied after studying the evolution of the respective or similar Jewish populations. With regard to the migratory balance in any updating interval, concrete information must be gathered, because of the above-mentioned irregularity, over time, in the intensity of many migratory streams.

Presentation of Data

The detailed estimates of Jewish population distribution in each continent (tables 2–6 below) refer to residents in countries with at least 100 Jews. A residual estimate of "other" Jews living in smaller communities, or staying temporarily in transit accommodations, supplements some of the continental totals. For each of the reported countries, the four columns in the table provide the United Nations estimate of midyear 1988 total population,[10] the estimated end-1988 Jewish population, the proportion of Jews per 1,000 of total population, and a rating of the accuracy of the Jewish population estimates.

There is wide variation in the quality of the Jewish population estimates for different countries. For many Diaspora countries it would be best to indicate a range (minimum-maximum) rather than a definite figure for the number of Jews. It would be confusing, however, for the reader to be confronted with a long list of ranges; this would also complicate the regional and world totals. Yet, the figures actually indicated for most of the Diaspora countries should be understood as being the central value of the plausible range. The relative magnitude of this range varies inversely to the accuracy of the estimate.

ACCURACY RATING

The three main elements that affect the accuracy of each estimate are the nature of the base data, the recency of the base data, and the method of updating. A simple code combining these elements is used to provide a general evaluation of the reliability of the Jewish population figures reported in the detailed tables below. The code indicates different quality levels of the reported estimates: (A) base figure derived from countrywide census or relatively reliable Jewish population surveys; updated on the basis of full or partial information on Jewish population movements in the intervening period; (B) base figure derived from less accurate but recent countrywide Jewish population investigation; partial information on population movements in the intervening period; (C) base figure derived from less recent sources, and/or unsatisfactory or partial coverage of Jewish population in country; updating according to demographic information illustrative of regional demographic trends; and (D) base figure essentially conjectural; no reliable updating procedure. In categories (A), (B), and (C), the years in which the base figures or important partial updates were obtained are also stated.

For countries whose Jewish population estimate of 1988 was not only updated but also revised in the light of improved information, the sign "X" is appended to the accuracy rating.

---

[10]See United Nations, Department of International Economic and Social Affairs, Statistical Office, *Population and Vital Statistics Report: Data Available as of July 1, 1989*. Statistical Papers, ser. A, vol. 41, no. 3 (New York, 1989).

Distribution of World Jewish Population by Major Regions

Table 1 gives an overall picture for 1988 as compared to 1986. For 1986 the originally published estimates are presented along with somewhat revised figures that take into account, retrospectively, the corrections made in 1988 in certain country estimates, in the light of improved information. These corrections resulted in a net increase of world Jewry's estimated size by 4,500. Some explanations are given below for the relevant countries.

The size of world Jewry at the end of 1988 is assessed at 12,979,000, or slightly below 13 million. According to the revised figures, the estimated growth between 1986 and 1988 was negligible—only 6,600 people, or about three per 10,000 annually. Despite all the imperfections in the estimates, it is clear that world Jewry is in the state of "zero population growth," with the natural increase in Israel compensating for demographic decline in the Diaspora.

The number of Jews in Israel rose from a figure of 3,562,500 in 1986 to 3,659,000 at the end of 1988, a change of +1.3 percent annually. In contrast, the estimated Jewish population in the Diaspora declined from 9,409,900 (according to the revised figures) to 9,320,000, a change of -0.5 percent annually. These changes were almost entirely due to internal demographic evolution, since the net migratory balance between the Diaspora and Israel amounted to no more than 3,300 during these two years (Israel gained migrants on balance). By the end of 1988, Israel's Jews constituted about 28.2 percent of total world Jewry.

About half of the world's Jews reside in the Americas, with 46 percent in North America. Twenty-eight percent live in Asia—excluding the Asian territories of the USSR and Turkey—nearly all of them in Israel. Europe—including the Asian territories of the USSR and Turkey—accounts for 20 percent of the total. The proportions of the world's Jews who live in Africa and Oceania are very small.

Among the major geographical regions listed in table 1, the number of Jews in Israel—and, in consequence, in total Asia—increased by more than 2 percent in the two-year span 1987–1988. The total number of Jews estimated for North America virtually did not change. The total estimate for Oceania increased by nearly 3 percent. Most other regions sustained decreases in Jewish population size.

World Jewry constitutes about 2.5 per 1,000 of total world population. One in about 395 people in the world is a Jew.

Individual Countries

THE AMERICAS

In 1988 the total number of Jews in the American continents was somewhat less than six and a half million. The overwhelming majority (93 percent) reside in the United States and Canada, less than 1 percent live in Central America—including

TABLE 1. ESTIMATED JEWISH POPULATION, BY CONTINENTS AND MAJOR GEOGRAPHICAL REGIONS, 1986 AND 1988

Region	1986 Original	1986 Revised Abs. N.	1986 Revised Percent	1988 Abs. N.	1988 Percent	% Change 1986–1988
Diaspora	9,405,400	9,409,900	72.5	9,320,000	71.8	−1.0
Israel	3,562,500	3,562,500	27.5	3,659,000	28.2	+2.6
World	12,967,900	12,972,400	100.0	12,979,000	100.0	+0.1
America, Total	6,454,700	6,453,200	49.8	6,447,600	49.7	−0.1
North[a]	6,010,000	6,010,000	46.3	6,010,000	46.3	0.0
Central	45,500	45,500	0.4	45,500	0.4	0.0
South	399,200	397,700	3.1	392,100	3.0	−1.4
Europe, Total	2,685,900	2,688,900	20.7	2,607,500[b]	20.1	−3.0
EC	1,005,100	1,005,100	7.7	1,000,400	7.7	−0.5
West, other	43,200	43,200	0.3	43,200	0.4	0.0
East and Balkans[c]	1,637,600	1,640,600	12.6	1,553,900	12.0	−5.3
Asia, Total	3,598,000	3,598,000	27.7	3,692,400	28.4	+2.6
Israel	3,562,500	3,562,500	27.5	3,659,000	28.2	+2.6
Rest[c]	35,500	35,500	0.3	33,400	0.2	−5.9
Africa, Total	145,200	145,200	1.1	141,900	1.1	−2.3
North	15,200	15,200	0.1	12,700	0.1	−16.4
Central	13,800	13,800	0.1	14,100	0.1	+2.1
South	116,200	116,200	0.9	115,100	0.9	−0.9
Oceania	84,100	87,100	0.7	89,600	0.7	+2.8

[a]U.S.A. and Canada.
[b]Including 10,000 Jews in transit.
[c]The Asian territories of USSR and Turkey are included in "East Europe and Balkans."

Mexico, and about 6 percent live in South America, where Argentina and Brazil have the largest Jewish communities (see table 2).

During the period reviewed here, 1986 to 1988, the balance of Jewish population changes in the United States as a whole probably was close to nil. Several local surveys taken in recent years provided evidence of very low "effectively Jewish" birthrates and of increasing aging among the Jewish population. Thus, it is possible that the influence of internal evolution on the size of U.S. Jewry may be negative, though there is no consensus with regard to this assessment. Any negative internal balance in U.S. Jewish population was generally offset by an undoubtedly positive balance of external migrations. In earlier years, the international migration balance of U.S. Jewry often resulted in actual increases of Jewish population size. However, the volume of Jewish international migration during most of the mid-1980s was very small, and only toward the end of 1988 did a significant increase begin to appear. The major determinant of these trends in recent years was the changing volume of Soviet Jewish immigration.

Our 1988 estimate of 5,700,000 Jews in the United States cautiously repeats the figures reported for the previous years, and differs slightly from the new estimates prepared by the research team of the North American Jewish Data Bank (NAJDB) which are reported elsewhere in this volume.[11] NAJDB estimated the U.S. Jewish population in 1986 at 5,814,000, including "under 2 percent" non-Jewish household members. This was very close to our own estimate of 5,700,000. For 1987, the NAJDB estimate was revised to 5,943,700, which was to be understood not as actual sudden growth but as a result of changes made in the figures for several local communities. For 1988, the NAJDB estimate was revised to 5,935,000, which again reflects corrections of data rather than actual decline. A nationwide sample survey of U.S. Jewry, scheduled for 1990—conducted by the NAJDB with the sponsorship of the Council of Jewish Federations—is expected to provide benchmark information and the basis for updates in subsequent years.

In Canada an official population census held in 1981 enumerated 296,425 Jews according to religion. If the persons are added who responded "Jewish" as a *single* reply to the census question on ethnic origin, while not indicating any religion (i.e., they were not Christians, etc.), the figure rises to 306,375. There were additional persons who did not indicate religion but mentioned "Jewish" as part of a *multiple*

---

[11]The new U.S. Jewish population estimates first appeared in Barry A. Kosmin, Paul Ritterband, and Jeffrey Scheckner, "Jewish Population in the United States, 1986," AJYB, vol. 87, 1987, pp. 164–91. The 1988 update, by the same authors, appeared in AJYB, vol. 89, 1989, pp. 233–52. See also U.O. Schmelz, *World Jewish Population: Regional Estimates and Projections* (Jerusalem, 1981), pp. 32–36; U.O. Schmelz and Sergio DellaPergola, "The Demographic Consequences of U.S. Jewish Population Trends," AJYB, vol. 83, 1983, pp. 141–87; by the same authors, *Basic Trends in U.S. Jewish Demography*, Jewish Sociology Papers, American Jewish Committee (New York, 1988); and Sidney Goldstein, "American Jewish Demography: Inconsistencies That Challenge," in U.O. Schmelz and S. DellaPergola, eds., *Papers in Jewish Demography 1985* (Jerusalem, 1989), pp. 23–42.

response to the question on ethnic origin. It is likely that some of them were merely thinking in terms of ancestry but did not actually consider themselves as Jews at the time of the census. By including a reasonable proportion of those who were identified in the census as Jews by multiple ethnicity only, a round total estimate of 310,000 was arrived at for 1981.

The population census held in Canada in 1986 provided new data on ethnic origins but not on religious groups. A total of 245,855 persons reported being Jewish as a *single* reply to the question on ethnic origin, as against 264,020 in the same category in 1981. A further 97,655 mentioned a Jewish origin as part of a *multiple* response to the 1986 question on ethnic origin, as compared to possibly 30,000 to 40,000 in 1981. Thus, a substantial increase in the number of Canadians reporting partially Jewish ancestry appeared to offset the decline in the number of those with a solely Jewish identification according to ethnic criteria. Changes in the wording of the relevant questions in the two censuses, no less than actual demographic and identificational trends, are responsible for these variations in the size of the Canadian "ethnically" Jewish population. It should be noted, too, that an unknown number of "ethnic" Jews identify with a non-Jewish religion. This occurs comparatively more frequently among those reporting multiple ethnic origins than among those identifying only with the Jewish ethnic group. (These "ethnic" Jews who identify with another religion are not included in our estimate.) Finally, census data suggest that about 9,000 Jews migrated to Canada between 1981 and 1986.

In the light of this admittedly partial evidence, and considering the increasingly aged Jewish population structure, it is suggested that a migratory surplus may have roughly offset the probably negative balance of internal evolution since the 1981 census. Consequently, the figure of 310,000 was adopted for 1988 as well. The next census, as of 1991, is again expected to include a question on religion, thus providing a better baseline for a revised estimate of Canada's Jewish population.

The estimate for Mexico has been kept unchanged at 35,000. While the official Mexican censuses have given widely varying figures—17,574 in 1950; 100,750 in 1960; 49,277 in 1970; 61,790 in 1980—it is generally admitted that the last three censuses erroneously included among the Jews many thousands of non-Jews living outside the known regions of Jewish residence in that country.

The Jewish population of Argentina is marked by a negative balance of internal evolution. In the past, the balance of external migrations was strongly negative; but since the restoration of a democratic regime, emigration has diminished and there has been some return migration. Assuming a moderately negative migratory balance, the estimate has been reduced from 224,000 in 1986 to 220,000 in 1988.

The official population census of Brazil in 1980 showed a figure of 91,795 Jews. Since it is possible that some Jews failed to declare themselves as such in the census, a corrected estimate of 100,000 was adopted for 1980, and has been kept unchanged for 1988, assuming that the overall balance of vital events and external migrations was close to zero. The 100,000 figure fits the admittedly rough estimates that are available for the size of local Jewish communities in Brazil.

On the strength of fragmentary information that is accumulating, the admittedly quite tentative estimates for Uruguay and Chile—as well as the figure for Peru—were reduced, while that for Venezuela was not changed.[12]

EUROPE

Of Europe's estimated 2,607,500 Jews, 40 percent live in Western Europe and 60 percent in Eastern Europe and the Balkan countries, including the Asian territories of the USSR and Turkey (see table 3).

The twelve countries that form the European Community (EC) contain a total Jewish population of one million. Economic integration between these countries will be greatly enhanced after the end of 1992, following the implementation of existing treaties. This will most likely stimulate occupationally motivated geographical mobility, with possible effects on the distribution of Jews among the EC's different countries.

France has the largest Jewish population in Western Europe, estimated at 530,000. Monitoring of the plausible trends in the internal evolution and the external migrations of Jews in France —including a new study conducted in 1988 at the initiative of the Fonds Social Juif Unifié—suggests that there has been little net change in Jewish population size since the major survey that was taken in the 1970s.[13]

A reestimation of the size of British Jewry was carried out by the research unit of the Board of Deputies, based on an analysis of Jewish deaths during 1975–1979. The revised population figure for 1977 was 336,000 with a margin of error of $+/-$ 34,000.[14] Allowing for an excess of deaths over births, some assimilatory losses, and emigration, the update for 1984, as elaborated by the board's research unit, came to 330,000. The update for 1986 was 326,000; continuation of the same trends suggests an estimate of 322,000 for 1988.

West Germany, Belgium, Italy, and the Netherlands each have Jewish populations ranging around 30,000. There is a tendency toward internal shrinkage of all these Jewries, but in some instances this is partly offset by immigration. The West German Jewish community records—which are among the most complete and up-to-date available—point to a modest Jewish population increase between 1986

---

[12] For a more detailed discussion of the region's Jewish population trends, see U.O. Schmelz and Sergio DellaPergola, "The Demography of Latin American Jewry," AJYB, vol. 85, 1985, pp. 51–102. See also Sergio DellaPergola, "Demographic Trends of Latin American Jewry," in J. Laikin Elkin and G.W. Merks, eds., *The Jewish Presence in Latin America* (Boston, 1987), pp. 85–133.

[13] Doris Bensimon and Sergio DellaPergola, *La population juive de France: socio-démographie et identité* (Jerusalem and Paris, 1984).

[14] Steven Haberman, Barry A. Kosmin, and Caren Levy, "Mortality Patterns of British Jews 1975–79: Insights and Applications for the Size and Structure of British Jewry," *Journal of the Royal Statistical Society*, ser. A, 146, pt. 3, 1983, pp. 294–310.

TABLE 2. ESTIMATED JEWISH POPULATION DISTRIBUTION IN THE AMERICAS, 1988

Country	Total Population	Jewish Population	Jews per 1,000 Population	Accuracy Rating
Canada	25,950,000	310,000	11.9	B 1981–86
United States	246,329,000	5,700,000	23.1	C 1986
Total Northern America		6,010,000		
Bahamas	244,000	300	1.2	C 1973
Costa Rica	2,851,000	2,000	0.7	C 1986
Cuba	10,402,000	700	0.1	D
Dominican Republic	6,867,000	100	0.0	D
Guatemala	8,681,000	800	0.1	A 1983
Jamaica	2,446,000	300	0.1	B 1988
Mexico	82,734,000	35,000	0.4	C 1980
Netherlands Antilles	188,000	400	2.1	D
Panama	2,322,000	3,800	1.6	C 1986
Puerto Rico	3,606,000	1,500	0.4	C 1986
Virgin Islands	110,000	300	2.7	C 1986
Other		300		D
Total Central America		45,500		
Argentina	31,963,000	220,000	6.9	C 1960–88
Bolivia	6,993,000	600	0.1	C 1986
Brazil	144,428,000	100,000	0.7	C 1980
Chile	12,748,000	15,000	1.2	C 1988 X
Colombia	30,241,000	6,500	0.2	C 1986
Ecuador	10,204,000	900	0.1	C 1985
Paraguay	4,039,000	900	0.2	C 1984
Peru	21,256,000	3,500	0.2	B 1985
Suriname	392,000	200	0.5	B 1986
Uruguay	3,060,000	24,500	8.0	D
Venezuela	18,751,000	20,000	1.1	D
Total Southern America		392,100		
Total		6,447,600		

and 1988. In Italy, until 1984, Jews were legally obliged to register with the local Jewish communities. Since then membership in the community has become voluntary. Although most Jews reconfirmed their membership, the looseness of the new legal framework may reduce both the completeness of the communal registers and, in the long run, the cohesion of the community.

Other EC member countries have smaller and, overall, slowly declining Jewish populations. An exception may be Spain, whose Jewish population is very tentatively estimated at 12,000.

Other Western European countries which are not EC members account for a cumulative Jewish population of 43,200. Among these, Switzerland's Jews are estimated at below 20,000. While there is evidence of a negative balance of births and deaths, connected with great aging and frequent outmarriage, immigration may have offset the internal losses. The Jewish populations in Scandinavian countries are, overall, numerically stable.

Eastern European Jewry is characterized by particularly low levels of effectively Jewish fertility, connected with a frequent and prolonged practice of outmarriage, and by heavy aging. The shrinking of the Jewish population in those countries must be comparatively rapid, therefore.

By far the largest Jewish population in Eastern Europe is concentrated in the Soviet Union, including its Asian territory. In 1987–1988, Jewish emigration from the USSR resumed and gained momentum: 8,100 Jews left in 1987 and 19,300 in 1988, as against only about 2,000 during 1985–1986. In the interim, the heavy deficit of internal population dynamics must have continued and even intensified, due to the great aging which is known to prevail. This can only have been exacerbated by the comparatively younger age composition of the emigrants.[15] On the strength of these considerations, the estimate has been reduced from 1,515,000 in 1986 to 1,435,000 in 1988.

Our estimates for Soviet Jewry are updates of the figures from three population censuses (1959, 1970, and 1979). These were rather consistent among themselves, considering the probable evolution in the intervals. Our reservation about Soviet Jewish population figures in previous AJYB volumes bears repeating: While some underreporting is not impossible, it cannot be quantified and should not be exaggerated. Data on nationalities from the Soviet Union's official population census, carried out in January 1989, will eventually provide a better basis for revised estimates of Jewish population size.

During the period reviewed here, the choice of country of destination by Jews leaving the Soviet Union followed the same pattern it had for the preceding few years. A minority went to Israel (12 percent of the total emigrants in 1987–1988), while a majority chose to settle in Western countries. However, because of the strong

---

[15]U.O. Schmelz, "New Evidence on Basic Issues in the Demography of Soviet Jews," *Jewish Journal of Sociology*, 16, no. 2, 1974, pp. 209–23. See also Mordechai Altshuler, *Soviet Jewry Since the Second World War: Population and Social Structure* (Westport, 1987).

TABLE 3. ESTIMATED JEWISH POPULATION DISTRIBUTION IN EUROPE, 1988

Country	Total Population	Jewish Population	Jews per 1,000 Population	Accuracy Rating
Belgium	9,925,000	31,800	3.2	D
Denmark	5,130,000	6,500	1.3	C 1988
France	55,874,000	530,000	9.5	C 1972–88
Germany, West	61,199,000	33,000	0.5	B 1988
Great Britain	57,077,000	322,000	5.6	B 1988
Greece	10,013,000	4,900	0.5	B 1986
Ireland	3,538,000	1,900	0.5	B 1988
Italy	57,441,000	31,500	0.5	B 1986
Luxembourg	375,000	700	1.9	C 1970
Netherlands	14,758,000	25,800	1.7	C 1988
Portugal	10,408,000	300	0.0	B 1986
Spain	39,053,000	12,000	0.3	D
Total European Community		1,000,400		
Austria	7,595,000	6,300	0.8	A 1986
Finland	4,951,000	1,300	0.3	A 1987
Gibraltar	30,000	600	20.0	B 1981
Norway	4,196,000	1,000	0.2	A 1987
Sweden	8,436,000	15,000	1.8	C 1986
Switzerland	6,509,000	19,000	2.9	B 1980
Total other Western Europe		43,200		
Bulgaria	8,995,000	3,100	0.3	D
Czechoslovakia	15,620,000	8,000	0.5	D
Germany, East	16,666,000	500	0.0	D
Hungary	10,596,000	58,500	5.5	D
Poland	37,862,000	4,200	0.1	D
Romania	23,048,000	20,000	0.9	B 1988 X
Turkey[a]	52,422,000	20,000	0.4	C 1988
USSR[a]	283,682,000	1,435,000	5.1	C 1979
Yugoslavia	23,559,000	4,600	0.2	C 1986
Total Eastern Europe and Balkans		1,553,900		
In transit		10,000		A 1988
Total		2,607,500		

[a]Including Asian regions.

TABLE 4. ESTIMATED JEWISH POPULATION DISTRIBUTION IN ASIA, 1988

Country	Total Population	Jewish Population	Jews per 1,000 Population	Accuracy Rating
Hong Kong	5,681,000	1,000	0.2	D
India	796,596,000	5,000	0.0	B 1981
Iran	52,522,000	20,000	0.4	D
Iraq	17,656,000	200	0.0	D
Israel	4,476,800[a]	3,659,000	817.3	A 1988
Japan	122,613,000	1,000	0.0	C 1988
Korea, South	41,975,000	100	0.0	D
Lebanon	2,827,000	100	0.0	D
Philippines	58,721,000	100	0.0	D
Singapore	2,647,000	300	0.1	C 1984
Syria	11,338,000	4,000	0.4	D
Thailand	54,536,000	300	0.0	D
Yemen	7,534,000	1,000	0.1	D
Other		300		D
Total		3,692,400		

[a]End 1988.

TABLE 5. ESTIMATED JEWISH POPULATION DISTRIBUTION IN AFRICA, 1988

Country	Total Population	Jewish Population	Jews per 1,000 Population	Accuracy Rating
Egypt	51,897,000	200	0.0	C 1988
Ethiopia	47,882,000	12,000	0.2	D
Kenya	23,882,000	400	0.0	B 1988
Morocco	23,910,000	10,000	0.4	D
South Africa	33,747,000	114,000	3.4	C 1980
Tunisia	7,809,000	2,500	0.3	D
Zaire	33,458,000	400	0.0	D
Zambia	7,531,000	300	0.0	D
Zimbabwe	8,878,000	1,100	0.1	B 1988
Other		1,000		D
Total		141,900		

preference for settling in the United States and that country's selective immigration policies, there were more emigrants than available immigration permits. Consequently, by the end of 1988, about 10,000 Soviet Jews were in transit in temporary accommodations, mostly in Italy and Austria. The relevant figure is shown separately in table 3.

The Jewish populations in Hungary and Romania and the small remnants in Poland, East Germany, Czechoslovakia, Bulgaria, and Yugoslavia are all reputed to be very overaged. Their inevitable numerical decline is reflected in reduced estimates.

The size of Hungarian Jewry—the largest in Eastern Europe outside the USSR— is quite insufficiently known. Our estimate only attempts to reflect the declining trend that prevails there too, according to the available indications. Comparatively large emigration of Jews continued to take place from Romania, whose Jewish population declined to 20,000 in 1988, according to the community records available there.

The Jewish population of Turkey, where a surplus of deaths over births is reported, has been estimated at about 20,000.

ASIA

Israel accounts for 99 percent of all the Jews in Asia, excluding the Asian territories of the USSR and Turkey (see table 4). Israel's Jewish population grew over 1987–1988 by about 97,000. Nearly all this growth was due to natural increase, since the migration balance was very small (+3,300) in 1987–1988.

It is difficult to estimate the Jewish population of Iran for any given date, but it continues to dwindle. The updated estimate for 1988 has been put at 20,000.

In other Asian countries with smaller, long-standing communities—such as India and Syria—the Jewish population tends to decline slowly. Very small communities, partially of a transient character, exist in several countries of Southeast Asia.

AFRICA

About 142,000 Jews are estimated to remain now in Africa. The Republic of South Africa accounts for 80 percent of total Jews in that continent (see table 5).

In 1980, according to the official census, there were about 118,000 Jews among South Africa's white population.[16] Substantial Jewish emigration since then has been compensated in good part by Jewish immigration. Considering a moderately negative migration balance, and an incipient negative balance of internal changes, the Jewish population estimate for 1988 was reduced to 114,000.

According to recent reports, the Jews remaining in Ethiopia may be very roughly

---

[16]Sergio DellaPergola and Allie A. Dubb, "South African Jewry: A Sociodemographic Profile," AJYB, vol. 88, 1988, pp. 59–140.

estimated at 12,000. The remnant of Moroccan and Tunisian Jewry continued to shrink through emigration. It should be pointed out, though, that not a few Jews have a foothold both in Morocco (or Tunisia) and in France, and their geographical attribution is uncertain.

OCEANIA

The major country of Jewish residence in Oceania (Australasia) is Australia, where 95 percent of the estimated total of nearly 90,000 Jews live (see table 6).

The estimate for Australian Jewry has been raised. The 1986 census of Australia, with an optional question on religion, enumerated 69,065 declared Jews. It also indicated that about 25 percent of the country's whole population either did not specify religion or stated explicitly that they had none. This large group must be assumed to contain some persons who identify in other ways as Jews. In addition, Australian Jewry has received migratory reinforcements during the last decade, especially from South Africa. At the same time, there are demographic problems linked to strong aging, low or negative natural increase, and assimilation. Therefore, we offer a provisional estimate of 85,000 for 1988—pending clarification of population trends since previous censuses.

The Jewish community in New Zealand—now estimated at 4,500—attracted some immigrants, too, but incurred a negative migration balance with Australia.

TABLE 6. ESTIMATED JEWISH POPULATION DISTRIBUTION IN OCEANIA, 1988

Country	Total Population	Jewish Population	Jews per 1,000 Population	Accuracy Rating
Australia	16,532,000	85,000	5.1	C 1986 X
New Zealand	3,292,000	4,500	1.4	C 1988
Other		100		D
Total		89,600		

Dispersion and Concentration

Table 7 demonstrates the magnitude of Jewish dispersion. The individual countries listed above as each having at least 100 Jews are scattered over all the continents. More than half (43 out of 75 countries) have fewer than 5,000 Jews apiece.

In relative terms, too, the Jews are now thinly scattered nearly everywhere in the Diaspora. There is not a single Diaspora country where they amount even to 3

TABLE 7. DISTRIBUTION OF THE WORLD'S JEWS, BY NUMBER AND PROPORTION (PER 1,000 POPULATION) IN VARIOUS COUNTRIES, 1988

	Jews per 1,000 Population					
Number of Jews in Country	Total	Below 1	1–5	5–10	10–25	25+
			Number of Countries[a]			
Total	75	50	14	7	3	1
Below 1,000	25	20	4	—	1	—
1,000–5,000	18	16	2	—	—	—
5,000–10,000	5	4	1	—	—	—
10,000–50,000	16	9	6	1	—	—
50,000–100,000	2	—	—	2	—	—
100,000–1,000,000	6	1	1	3	1	—
1,000,000 and over	3	—	—	1	1	1
		Jewish Population Distribution (Absolute Numbers)				
Total	12,979,000[b]	367,300	257,100	2,675,000	6,010,600	3,659,000
Below 1,000	11,700	9,400	1,700	—	600	—
1,000–5,000	46,900	38,600	8,300	—	—	—
5,000–10,000	32,300	25,800	6,500	—	—	—
10,000–50,000	344,600	193,500	126,600	24,500	—	—
50,000–100,000	143,500	—	—	143,500	—	—
100,000–1,000,000	1,596,000	100,000	114,000	1,072,000	310,000	—
1,000,000 and over	10,794,000	—	—	1,435,000	5,700,000	3,659,000
		Jewish Population Distribution (Percent of World's Jews)				
Total	100.0	2.9	2.0	20.7	46.3	28.2
Below 1,000	0.1	0.1	0.0	—	0.0	—
1,000–5,000	0.4	0.3	0.1	—	—	—
5,000–10,000	0.2	0.2	0.0	—	—	—
10,000–50,000	2.7	1.5	1.0	0.2	—	—
50,000–100,000	1.1	—	—	1.1	—	—
100,000–1,000,000	12.3	0.8	0.9	8.3	2.4	—
1,000,000 and over	83.2	—	—	11.1	43.9	28.2

[a]Excluding countries with fewer than 100 Jews.
[b]Total includes 10,000 Jews in transit in Europe.

TABLE 8. TEN COUNTRIES WITH LARGEST JEWISH POPULATIONS, 1988

| | | | \% of Total Jewish Population | | | |
| | | Jewish | In the Diaspora | | In the World | |
Rank	Country	Population	%	Cumulative %	%	Cumulative %
1	United States	5,700,000	61.2	61.2	43.9	43.9
2	Israel	3,659,000	—	—	28.2	72.1
3	USSR	1,435,000	15.4	76.6	11.1	83.2
4	France	530,000	5.7	82.3	4.1	87.3
5	Great Britain	322,000	3.4	85.7	2.5	89.8
6	Canada	310,000	3.3	89.0	2.4	92.2
7	Argentina	220,000	2.4	91.4	1.7	93.9
8	South Africa	114,000	1.2	92.6	0.9	94.8
9	Brazil	100,000	1.1	93.7	0.8	95.6
10	Australia	85,000	0.9	94.6	0.6	96.2

percent of the total population. In most countries they constitute a far smaller fraction. Only three Diaspora countries have 10–25 Jews per 1,000 of total population; and only ten countries have more than 5 Jews per 1,000 of population. The respective ten countries are, in descending order of the proportion of their Jews (but regardless of the absolute number): United States (23.1), Gibraltar (20.0), Canada (11.9), France (9.5), Uruguay (8.0), Argentina (6.9), Great Britain (5.6), Hungary (5.5), USSR (5.1), and Australia (5.1). This list includes all the Diaspora countries with Jewries of 100,000 or more, except for South Africa and Brazil (in the latter's large population the Jews form only 0.7 per 1,000).

In the State of Israel, by contrast, the Jewish majority amounted to 81.7 percent in 1988, against 82.2 percent in 1986 (not including the Arab population of the administered areas).

While Jews are widely dispersed, they are also concentrated to some extent (see table 8). In 1988 over 96 percent of world Jewry lived in the ten countries with the largest Jewish populations; 83 percent lived in the three countries that have at least a million Jews each (United States, Israel, Soviet Union). Similarly, the United States alone accounted for over 61 percent of total Diaspora Jewry; two countries (United States and Soviet Union) for 77 percent; and the nine leading countries together comprised about 95 percent of the Diaspora Jewish population.

U.O. SCHMELZ
SERGIO DELLAPERGOLA

Directories
Lists
Obituaries

National Jewish Organizations[1]

UNITED STATES

Organizations are listed according to functions as follows:

Community Relations	535
Cultural	539
Overseas Aid	544
Religious, Educational	546
Social, Mutual Benefit	565
Social Welfare	566
Zionist and Pro-Israel	570

Note also cross-references under these headings:

Professional Associations	580
Women's Organizations	581
Youth and Student Organizations	581

COMMUNITY RELATIONS

AMERICAN COUNCIL FOR JUDAISM (1943). PO Box 9009, Alexandria, VA 22304. (703)836–2546. Pres. Alan V. Stone; Exec. Dir. Allan C. Brownfeld. Seeks to advance the universal principles of a Judaism free of nationalism, and the national, civic, cultural, and social integration into American institutions of Americans of Jewish faith. *Issues of the American Council for Judaism; Special Interest Report.*

AMERICAN JEWISH ALTERNATIVES TO ZIONISM, INC. (1968). 501 Fifth Ave., Suite 2015, NYC 10017. (212)557–5410. Fax: (212)867–5166. Pres. Elmer Berger; V.-Pres. Mrs. Arthur Gutman. Applies Jewish values of justice and humanity to the Arab-Israel conflict in the Middle East; rejects nationality attachment of Jews, particularly American Jews, to the State of Israel as self-segregating, inconsistent with American constitutional concepts of individual citizenship and separation of church and state, and as being a principal obstacle to Middle East peace. *Report.*

AMERICAN JEWISH COMMITTEE (1906). Institute of Human Relations, 165 E. 56 St., NYC 10022. (212)751–4000. FAX: (212)-319–0975. Pres. Sholom D. Comay; Exec. V.-Pres. Ira Silverman. Seeks to prevent infraction of civil and religious rights of Jews in any part of the world; to advance the cause of human rights for people of all races, creeds, and nationalities; to interpret the position of Israel to the American pub-

---

[1] The information in this directory is based on replies to questionnaires circulated by the editors.

lic; and to help American Jews maintain and enrich their Jewish identity and, at the same time, achieve full integration in American life. Includes Jacob and Hilda Blaustein Center for Human Relations, William E. Wiener Oral History Library, William Petschek National Jewish Family Center, Jacob Blaustein Institute for the Advancement of Human Rights, Institute on American Jewish–Israeli Relations. AMERICAN JEWISH YEAR BOOK (with Jewish Publication Society); *Commentary; AJC Journal; Capital Update.* Published in Israel: *Alon Yedi'ot,* a monthly bulletin of the Institute on American Jewish-Israeli Relations.

AMERICAN JEWISH CONGRESS (1918). Stephen Wise Congress House, 15 E. 84 St., NYC 10028. (212)879–4500. Pres. Robert K. Lifton; Exec. Dir. Henry Siegman. Works to foster the creative cultural survival of the Jewish people; to help Israel develop in peace, freedom, and security; to eliminate all forms of racial and religious bigotry; to advance civil rights, protect civil liberties, defend religious freedom, and safeguard the separation of church and state. *Congress Monthly; Judaism; Boycott Report.*

ANTI-DEFAMATION LEAGUE OF B'NAI B'RITH (1913). 823 United Nations Plaza, NYC 10017. (212)490–2525. Chmn. Burton S. Levinson; Dir. Abraham H. Foxman. Seeks to combat anti-Semitism and to secure justice and fair treatment for all citizens through law, education, and community relations. *ADL Bulletin; Face to Face; Fact Finding Report; International Reports; Law Notes; Rights; Law; Research and Evaluation Report; Discriminations Report; Litigation Docket; Dimensions; Middle East Notebook; Nuestro Encuentro.*

ASSOCIATION OF JEWISH CENTER PROFESSIONALS (1918). c/o JCC, 3505 Mayfield Rd., Cleveland Heights, OH 44118 (216)-382–4000. Pres. Avrum I. Cohen; Exec. Sec. Paulette Buchler. Seeks to enhance the standards, techniques, practices, scope, and public understanding of Jewish Community Center and kindred agency work. *Kesher.*

ASSOCIATION OF JEWISH COMMUNITY RELATIONS WORKERS (1950). 443 Park Ave. S., 11th fl., NYC 10016. Pres. Jerome Levinrad. Aims to stimulate higher standards of professional practice in Jewish community relations; encourages research and training toward that end; conducts educational programs and seminars; aims to encourage cooperation between community relations workers and those working in other areas of Jewish communal service.

CENTER FOR JEWISH COMMUNITY STUDIES (1970). 1017 Gladfelter Hall, Temple University, Philadelphia, PA 19122. (215)787-1459. Jerusalem office: Jerusalem Center for Public Affairs. Pres. Daniel J. Elazar. Worldwide policy-studies institute devoted to the study of Jewish community organization, political thought, and public affairs, past and present, in Israel and throughout the world. Publishes original articles, essays, and monographs; maintains library, archives, and reprint series. *Jerusalem Letter/Viewpoints; Survey of Arab Affairs; Jewish Political Studies Review.*

COMMISSION ON SOCIAL ACTION OF REFORM JUDAISM (1953, under the auspices of the Union of American Hebrew Congregations). 838 Fifth Ave., NYC 10021. (212)249–0100. Chmn. Harris Gilbert; Dir. Albert Vorspan; Assoc. Dir. Rabbi David Saperstein. Policy-making body that relates ethical and spiritual principles of Judaism to the problems of today's world; implements resolutions through the Religious Action Center of the UAHC via advocacy, development of educational materials, and congregational programs. *Briefings.*

CONFERENCE OF PRESIDENTS OF MAJOR AMERICAN JEWISH ORGANIZATIONS (1955). 515 Park Ave., NYC 10022. (212)-752–1616. Chmn. Seymour D. Reich; Exec. Dir. Malcolm Hoenlein. Seeks to strengthen the U.S.-Israel alliance and to protect and enhance the security and dignity of Jews abroad. Toward this end, the Conference of Presidents speaks and acts on the basis of consensus of its 46 member agencies on issues of national and international Jewish concern. *Annual report.*

CONSULTATIVE COUNCIL OF JEWISH ORGANIZATIONS-CCJO (1946). 420 Lexington Ave., Suite 1733, NYC 10170. (212)808–5437. Pres.'s Adolphe Steg, Clemens Nathan, Joseph Nuss; Sec.-Gen. Warren Green. A nongovernmental organization in consultative status with the UN, UNESCO, ILO,UNICEF, and the Council of Europe; cooperates and consults with, advises and renders assistance to the Economic and Social Council of the UN on all problems relating to human rights and economic, social, cultural, educational, and related matters pertaining to Jews.

COORDINATING BOARD OF JEWISH ORGANIZATIONS (1947). 1640 Rhode Island Ave., NW, Washington, DC 20036. (202)-857–6545. Pres.'s Seymour D. Reich (B'nai B'rith), Leonard Kopelowitz (Board of Deputies of British Jews), David K. Mann (South African Jewish Board of Deputies); Exec. V.-Pres. Thomas Neumann (U.S.); Dir. Internatl. Council Warren Eisenberg. As an organization in consultative status with the Economic and Social Council of the UN, represents the three constituents (B'nai B'rith, the Board of Deputies of British Jews, and the South African Jewish Board of Deputies) in the appropriate UN bodies for the purpose of promoting human rights, with special attention to combating persecution or discrimination on grounds of race, religion, or origin.

COUNCIL OF JEWISH ORGANIZATIONS IN CIVIL SERVICE, INC. (1948). 45 E. 33 St., Rm. 604, NYC 10016. (212)689–2015. Pres. Louis Weiser. Supports merit system; encourages recruitment of Jewish youth to government service; member of Coalition to Free Soviet Jews, NY Jewish Community Relations Council, NY Metropolitan Coordinating Council on Jewish Poverty, Jewish Labor Committee, America-Israel Friendship League. *Council Digest.*

INTERNATIONAL CONFERENCE OF JEWISH COMMUNAL SERVICE (*see* World Conference of Jewish Communal Service)

JEWISH LABOR COMMITTEE (1934). Atran Center for Jewish Culture, 25 E. 21 St., NYC 10010. (212)477–0707. Pres. Herb Magidson; Exec. Dir. Martin Lapan. Serves as liaison between the Jewish community and the trade-union movement; works with the AFL-CIO to combat anti-Semitism and engender support for the State of Israel and Soviet Jewry; strengthens support within the Jewish community for the social goals and programs of the labor movement; supports Yiddish cultural institutions. *Jewish Labor Committee Review; Alumni Newsletter.*

———, NATIONAL TRADE UNION COUNCIL FOR HUMAN RIGHTS (1956). Atran Center for Jewish Culture, 25 E. 21 St., NYC 10010. (212)477–0707. Chmn. Sol Hoffman; Exec. Sec. Michael Perry. Works with the American labor movement in advancing the struggle for social justice and equal opportunity and assists unions in every issue affecting human rights. Fights discrimination on all levels and helps to promote labor's broad social and economic goals.

JEWISH PEACE FELLOWSHIP (1941). Box 271, Nyack, NY 10977. (914)358–4601. Pres. Rabbi Philip Bentley; Sec. Naomi Goodman. Unites those who believe that Jewish ideals and experience provide inspiration for a nonviolent philosophy and way of life; offers draft counseling, especially for conscientious objection based on Jewish "religious training and belief"; encourages Jewish community to become more knowledgeable, concerned, and active in regard to the war/peace problem. *Shalom/ Jewish Peace Letter.*

JEWISH WAR VETERANS OF THE UNITED STATES OF AMERICA (1896). 1811 R St., NW, Washington, DC 20009. (202)265–6280. Natl. Exec. Dir. Steve Shaw. Seeks to foster true allegiance to the United States; to combat bigotry and prevent defamation of Jews; to encourage the doctrine of universal liberty, equal rights, and full justice for all; to cooperate with and support existing educational institutions and establish new ones; to foster the education of ex-servicemen, ex-servicewomen, and members in the ideals and principles of Americanism. *Jewish Veteran.*

———, NATIONAL MEMORIAL, INC. (1958). 1811 R St., NW, Washington, DC 20009. (202)265–6280. Pres. Robert Zweiman. Operates a museum and archives commemorating the activities and service of American Jews in the armed forces of the U.S. *Routes to Roots.*

NATIONAL CONFERENCE ON SOVIET JEWRY (formerly AMERICAN JEWISH CONFERENCE ON SOVIET JEWRY) (1964; reorg. 1971). 10 E. 40 St., Suite 907, NYC 10016. (212)679–6122. Chmn. Shoshana Cardin; Exec. Dir. Martin A. Wenick. Coordinating agency for major national Jewish organizations and local community groups in the U.S., acting on behalf of Soviet Jewry through public education and social action; stimulates all segments of the community to maintain an interest in the problems of Soviet Jews by publishing reports and special pamphlets, sponsoring special programs and projects, organizing public meetings and forums. *Newsbreak; annual report; action and program kits; Wrap-Up Leadership Report.*

———, SOVIET JEWRY RESEARCH BUREAU. Chmn. Charlotte Jacobson. Organized by NCSJ to monitor emigration trends. Primary task is the accumulation, evaluation, and processing of information regarding Soviet Jews, especially those who apply for emigration.

NATIONAL JEWISH COALITION (1980). 415 2nd St., NE, Suite 100, Washington, DC 20002. (202)547-7701. Hon. Chmn. Max M. Fisher; Cochmn. Richard J. Fox, George Klein; Exec. Dir. Benjamin Waldman. Promotes Jewish involvement in Republican politics; sensitizes Republican leaders to the concerns of the American Jewish community; promotes principles of free enterprise, a strong national defense, and an internationalist foreign policy. *NJC Bulletin; NJC for the Record.*

NATIONAL JEWISH COMMISSION ON LAW AND PUBLIC AFFAIRS (COLPA) (1965). 450 Seventh Ave., Suite 2203, NYC 10123. (212)563-0100. Pres. Allen L. Rothenberg; Exec. Dir. Dennis Rapps. Voluntary association of attorneys whose purpose is to represent the observant Jewish community on legal, legislative, and public-affairs matters.

NATIONAL JEWISH COMMUNITY RELATIONS ADVISORY COUNCIL (1944). 443 Park Ave. S., 11th fl., NYC 10016. (212)-684-6950. Chmn. Arden E. Shenker; Sec. Barry Ungar; Exec. V.-Chmn. Albert D. Chernin. National coordinating body for the field of Jewish community relations, comprising 11 national and 114 local Jewish community relations agencies. Promotes understanding of Israel and the Middle East; freedom for Soviet Jews; equal status for Jews and other groups in American society. Through the NJCRAC's work, its constituent organizations seek agreement on policies, strategies, and programs for effective utilization of their resources for common ends. *Joint Program Plan for Jewish Community Relations.*

NEW JEWISH AGENDA (1980). 64 Fulton St., #1100, NYC 10038. (212)227-5885. Cochmn. Tom Rawson, Kate Harris; Exec. Dir. Annette Jaffe. Founded as "a progressive voice in the Jewish community and a Jewish voice among progressives." Works for nuclear disarmament, peace in Central America, Arab-Jewish reconciliation, feminism, and economic justice, and against anti-Semitism and racism. *Agenda In-Brief.*

SHALOM CENTER (1983). 7318 Germantown Ave., Philadelphia, PA 19119. (215)247-9700. Pres. Ira Silverman; Bd. Chmn. Viki List; Exec. Dir. Arthur Waskow. National resource and organizing center for Jewish perspectives on preventing nuclear holocaust and ending nuclear arms race. Trains community organizers, holds conferences, assists local Jewish committees and coalitions on nuclear weapons issues. Sponsors Sukkat Shalom. Provides school curricula, sermon materials, legislative reports, adult-education texts, and media for Jewish use. *Shalom Report.*

STUDENT STRUGGLE FOR SOVIET JEWRY, INC. (1964). 210 W. 91 St., NYC 10024. (212)799-8900. Natl. Dir. Jacob Birnbaum; Natl. Coord. Glenn Richter; Chmn. Avraham Weiss. Provides information and action guidance to adult and student organizations, communities, and schools throughout the U.S. and Canada; assists Soviet Jews by publicity campaigns; helps Soviet Jews in the U.S.; aids Romanian Jews seeking emigration; maintains speakers bureau and research documents. *Soviet Jewry Action Newsletter.*

UNION OF COUNCILS FOR SOVIET JEWS (1970). 1819 H St., NW., Suite 230, Washington, DC 20006. (202)775-9770. Pres. Pamela B. Cohen; Natl. Dir. Micah H. Naftalin. With 50 local councils and 100,000 members throughout the U.S., the largest grassroots human-rights organization in the world devoted exclusively to gaining freedom of emigration and cultural rights for Soviet Jews. Supports and protects Soviet Jews by gathering and disseminating news on the condition and treatment of Soviet Jews, advocacy of Soviet Jewry policy and priorities to the administration, Congress, and instrumental agencies and forums; publications; educational programs, including briefings and policy analyses; rallies, demonstrations, and vigils; and travel to the Soviet Union to meet with Soviet Jewish leaders and senior officials of the Soviet Foreign Ministry. *UCSJ Quarterly Report; Refusenik Update; Congressional Handbook for Soviet Jewry.*

NATIONAL JEWISH ORGANIZATIONS / 539

WORLD CONFERENCE OF JEWISH COMMUNAL SERVICE (1966). 15 E. 26 St., NYC 10010. (212)532–2526. Pres. Arthur Rotman; Sec.-Gen. Solomon H. Green. Established by worldwide Jewish communal workers to strengthen their understanding of each other's programs and to communicate with colleagues in order to enrich the quality of their work. Conducts quadrennial international conferences in Jerusalem and periodic regional meetings. *Proceedings of international conferences; newsletter.*

WORLD JEWISH CONGRESS (1936; org. in U.S. 1939). 501 Madison Ave., 17th fl., NYC 10022. (212) 755–5770. Pres. Edgar M. Bronfman; Chmn. N. Amer. Branch Leo Kolber (Montreal); Chmn. Amer. Sect. Rabbi Wolfe Kelman; Sec.-Gen. Israel Singer; Exec. Dir. Elan Steinberg. Seeks to intensify bonds of world Jewry with Israel as central force in Jewish life; to strengthen solidarity among Jews everywhere and secure their rights, status, and interests as individuals and communities; to encourage development of Jewish social, religious, and cultural life throughout the world and coordinate efforts by Jewish communities and organizations to cope with any Jewish problem; to work for human rights generally. Represents its affiliated organizations—most representative bodies of Jewish communities in more than 70 countries and 35 national organizations in Amer. section—at UN, OAS, UNESCO, Council of Europe, ILO, UNICEF, and other governmental, intergovernmental, and international authorities. Publications (including those by Institute of Jewish Affairs, London): *Christian Jewish Relations; Coloquio; News and Views; Boletín Informativo OJI; Batfutsot; Gesher; Patterns of Prejudice; Soviet Jewish Affairs.*

CULTURAL

AMERICAN ACADEMY FOR JEWISH RESEARCH (1920). 3080 Broadway, NYC 10027. (212)678–8864. Pres. David Weiss Halivni; V.-Pres. & Treas. Arthur Hyman. Encourages Jewish learning and research; holds annual or semiannual meeting; awards grants for the publication of scholarly works. *Proceedings of the American Academy for Jewish Research; Texts and Studies; Monograph Series.*

AMERICAN BIBLICAL ENCYCLOPEDIA SOCIETY (1930). 24 W. Maple Ave., Monsey, NY 10952. (914)352–4609. Exec. V.-Pres. Irving Fredman; Author-Ed. Rabbi M. M. Kasher. Fosters biblical-talmudical research; sponsors and publishes *Torah Shelemah* (Heb., 39 vols.), *Encyclopedia of Biblical Interpretation* (Eng., 9 vols.), *Divrei Menachem* (Heb., 4 vols.), and related publications. *Noam.*

AMERICAN JEWISH HISTORICAL SOCIETY (1892). 2 Thornton Rd., Waltham, MA 02154. (617)891–8110. FAX: (617)899–9208. Pres. Phil David Fine; Dir. Bernard Wax. Collects, catalogues, publishes, and displays material on the history of the Jews in America; serves as an information center for inquiries on American Jewish history; maintains archives of original source material on American Jewish history; sponsors lectures and exhibitions; makes available historic Yiddish films and audiovisual material. *American Jewish History; Heritage.*

AMERICAN JEWISH PRESS ASSOCIATION (1943). c/o Northern California Jewish Bulletin, 88 First St., San Francisco, CA 94105. (415)957–9340. Pres. Marc S. Klein. Natl. Admin. Off.:11312 Old Club Rd., Rockville, MD 20852–4537. (301)-881–4537. Exec. Dir. L. Malcolm Rodman. Seeks the advancement of Jewish journalism and the maintenance of a strong Jewish press in the U.S. and Canada; encourages the attainment of the highest editorial and business standards; sponsors workshops, services for members. *Membership bulletin newsletter; Roster of Members.*

AMERICAN SOCIETY FOR JEWISH MUSIC (1974). 155 Fifth Ave., NYC 10010. (212)-533–2601. Pres. Paul Kavon; V.-Pres. David Lefkowitz; Sec. Hadássah B. Markson. Seeks to raise standards of composition and performance in Jewish liturgical and secular music; encourages research in all areas of Jewish music; publishes scholarly journal; presents programs and sponsors performances of new and rarely heard works and encourages their recording; commissions new works of Jewish interest. *Musica Judaica.*

ASSOCIATION FOR THE SOCIAL SCIENTIFIC STUDY OF JEWRY (1971). City University of New York, 33 W. 42 St., NYC 10036. (212)642–2180. Pres. Rela Geffen Monson; V.-Pres. Steven M. Cohen; Sec.-Treas. Esther Fleishman. Arranges academic sessions and facilitates communication among social scientists studying Jewry through meetings, newsletter, and related materials. *Contemporary Jewry; ASSSJ Newsletter.*

ASSOCIATION OF JEWISH BOOK PUBLISHERS (1962). 838 Fifth Ave., NYC 10021. (212)-249-0100. Pres. Charles D. Lieber. As a nonprofit group, provides a forum for discussion of mutual problems by publishers, authors, and other individuals and institutions concerned with books of Jewish interest. Provides national and international exhibit opportunities for Jewish books. *Combined Jewish Book Catalog.*

ASSOCIATION OF JEWISH GENEALOGICAL SOCIETIES (1988). 1485 Teaneck Rd., Teaneck, NJ 07666. (201)837-2700. Pres. Gary Mokotoff. Confederation of over 30 Jewish Genealogical Societies (JGS) in the U.S. and Canada. Encourages Jews to research their family history, promotes membership in the various JGS, acts as representative of organized Jewish genealogy, implements projects of interest to persons researching their Jewish family history. Annual conference where members learn and exchange ideas. Each local JGS publishes its own newsletter.

ASSOCIATION OF JEWISH LIBRARIES (1965). c/o National Foundation for Jewish Culture, 330 Seventh Ave., 21st fl., NYC 10001. (212)427-1000. Pres. Marcia W. Posner; V.-Pres. and Pres.-Elect Linda P. Lerman. Seeks to promote and improve services and professional standards in Jewish libraries; disseminates Jewish library information and guidance; promotes publication of literature in the field; encourages the establishment of Jewish libraries and collections of Judaica and the choice of Judaica librarianship as a profession; cocertifies Jewish libraries (with Jewish Book Council). *AJL Newsletter; Judaica Librarianship.*

B'NAI B'RITH KLUTZNICK MUSEUM (1956). 1640 Rhode Island Ave., NW, Washington, DC 20036. (202)857-6583. Chmn. Museum & Art Comm., Murray H. Shusterman; Dir. Gayle Weiss. A center of Jewish art and history in nation's capital, maintains temporary and permanent exhibition galleries, permanent collection of Jewish ceremonial and folk art, B'nai B'rith International reference archive, outdoor sculpture garden, and museum shop. Provides exhibitions, tours, educational programs, research assistance, and tourist information. *Semiannual newsletter; permanent collection catalogue; exhibition brochures.*

CENTER FOR HOLOCAUST STUDIES, DOCUMENTATION & RESEARCH (1974). 1610 Ave. J, Brooklyn, NY 11230. (718)338-6494. Dir. Yaffa Eliach. Collects and preserves documents and memorabilia, oral histories, and literary works on the Holocaust period for purposes of documentation and research; arranges lectures, exhibits, drama and music performances, and exhibitions of Holocaust art; conducts outreach programs to schools; develops Holocaust curricula, conducts teacher training; maintains speakers bureau, oral history publication series, and audiovisual department. *Newsletter; Bibliography Series; Education Series.*

CENTRAL YIDDISH CULTURE ORGANIZATION (CYCO), INC. (1943). 25 E. 21 St., 3rd fl., NYC 10010. (212)505-8305. Mgr. Jacob Schneidman. Promotes, publishes, and distributes Yiddish books; publishes catalogues.

CONFERENCE ON JEWISH SOCIAL STUDIES, INC. (formerly CONFERENCE ON JEWISH RELATIONS, INC.) (1939). 2112 Broadway, Rm. 206, NYC 10023. (212)724-5336. Publishes scientific studies on Jews in the modern world, dealing with such aspects as anti-Semitism, demography, economic stratification, history, philosophy, and political developments. *Jewish Social Studies.*

CONGREGATION BINA (1981). 600 W. End Ave., Suite 1-C, NYC 10024. (212)873-4261. Pres. Elijah E. Jhirad; Hon. Pres. Samuel M. Daniel; Exec. V.-Pres. Joseph Moses. Serves the religious, cultural, charitable, and philanthropic needs of the Children of Israel who originated in India and now reside in the U.S. Works to foster and preserve the ancient traditions, customs, liturgy, music, and folklore of Indian Jewry and to maintain needed institutions. *Kol Bina.*

HEBREW ARTS CENTER (1952). 129 W. 67 St., NYC 10023. (212)362-8060. Chmn. Lewis Kruger; Pres. Alvin E. Friedman; Exec. Dir. Lydia Kontos. Offers instruction in music, dance, art, and theater to children and adults, combining Western culture with Jewish heritage. Presents in its

Merkin Concert Hall and Ann Goodman Recital Hall frequent performances of Jewish and general music by leading artists and ensembles. The Birnbaum Library houses Jewish music scores and reference books. *Newsletter,* bimonthly calendars.

HEBREW CULTURE FOUNDATION (1955). 515 Park Ave., NYC 10022. (212)752-0600. Chmn. Milton R. Konvitz; Sec. Herman L. Sainer. Sponsors the introduction and strengthening of Hebrew language and literature courses in institutions of higher learning in the United States.

HISTADRUTH IVRITH OF AMERICA (1916; reorg. 1922). 1841 Broadway, NYC 10023. (212)581-5151. Pres. Dr. David Sidorsky; Exec. V.-Pres. Aviva Barzel. Emphasizes the primacy of Hebrew in Jewish life, culture, and education; aims to disseminate knowledge of written and spoken Hebrew in the Diaspora, thus building a cultural bridge between the State of Israel and Jewish communities throughout the world. *Hadoar; Lamishpaha.*

HOLOCAUST CENTER OF THE UNITED JEWISH FEDERATION OF GREATER PITTSBURGH (1980). 242 McKee Pl., Pittsburgh, PA 15213. (412)682-7111. Pres. Holocaust Comm. Jack Gordon; Pres. UJF David Shapira; Dir. Linda F. Hurwitz. Develops programs and provides resources to further understanding of the Holocaust and its impact on civilization. Maintains a library, archive; provides speakers, educational materials; organizes community programs.

HOLOCAUST MEMORIAL RESOURCE & EDUCATION CENTER OF CENTRAL FLORIDA (1981). 851 N. Maitland Ave., Maitland, FL 32751. (407)628-0555. Pres. Dr. Earl Scarbeary; Exec. V.-Pres. Tess Wise. An interfaith educational center devoted to teaching the lessons of the Holocaust. Houses permanent multimedia educational exhibit; maintains library of books, videotapes, films, and other visuals to serve the entire educational establishment; offers lectures, teacher training, and other activities. *Newsletter.*

INTERNATIONAL JEWISH MEDIA ASSOCIATION (1987). U.S.: c/o St. Louis Jewish Light, 12 Millstone Campus Dr., St. Louis, MO 63146. (314)432-3353. Israel: PO Box 92, Jerusalem (02)533296. Pres. Robert A. Cohn; Exec. Sec. Asher Weill; Staff Consultant Malcolm Rodman. A worldwide network of Jewish journalists in the Jewish and general media, which seeks to provide a forum for the exchange of materials and ideas, and to enhance the stature of Jewish media and journalists. *Presidents Bulletin; proceedings of international conferences on Jewish media.*

JEWISH ACADEMY OF ARTS AND SCIENCES, INC. (1926). 888 Seventh Ave., Suite 403, NYC 10106. (212)757-1627. Act. Pres. Milton Handler; Hon. Pres. Abraham I. Katsh; Dir. Benjamin Saxe. An honor society of Jews who have attained distinction in the arts, sciences, professions, and communal endeavors. Encourages the advancement of knowledge; stimulates scholarship, with particular reference to Jewish life and thought; recognition by election to membership and/or fellowship; publishes papers delivered at annual convocations.

JEWISH MUSEUM (1904, under auspices of Jewish Theological Seminary of America). 1109 Fifth Ave., NYC 10128.(212)860-1889. Dir. Joan H. Rosenbaum; Chmn. Bd. of Trustees Morris W. Offit. Repository of the largest collection of Judaica—paintings, prints, photographs, sculpture, coins, medals, antiquities, textiles, and other decorative arts—in the Western Hemisphere. Includes the National Jewish Archive of Broadcasting. Tours of special exhibitions and permanent installations; lectures, film showings, and concerts; special programs for children. *Special exhibition catalogues; annual report.*

JEWISH PUBLICATION SOCIETY (1888). 1930 Chestnut St., Philadelphia, PA 19103. (215)564-5925. Pres. Edward E. Elson; Exec. V.-Pres. Rabbi Michael A. Monson. Publishes and disseminates books of Jewish interest for adults and children; titles include contemporary literature, classics, art, religion, biographies, poetry, and history. AMERICAN JEWISH YEAR BOOK (with American Jewish Committee).

JUDAH L. MAGNES MUSEUM—JEWISH MUSEUM OF THE WEST (1962). 2911 Russell St., Berkeley, CA 94705. (415)849-2710. Pres. Gary J. Shapiro; Dir. Seymour Fromer. Collects, preserves, and makes available Jewish art, culture, history, and literature from throughout the world. Besides permanent collections of fine and ceremonial art, a library of rare Judaica, and the Western Jewish History Center, the museum has changing exhibits, traveling exhibits, docent tours, lectures and special events, numismatics and poetry series and award, a museum shop. *Magnes News; special exhibition catalogues.*

JUDAICA CAPTIONED FILM CENTER, INC. (1983). PO Box 21439, Baltimore, MD 21208–0439. Voice (after 4 PM) (301)922–0905; TDD (301)655–6767. Pres. Lois Lilienfeld Weiner. Developing a comprehensive library of captioned and subtitled films and tapes on Jewish subjects; distributes them to organizations serving the hearing-impaired, including mainstream classes and senior adult groups, on a free-loan, handling/shipping-charge-only basis. *Quarterly newsletter.*

JWB JEWISH BOOK COUNCIL (1943). 15 E. 26 St., NYC 10010. (212)532–4949. Pres. Abraham J. Kremer; Dir. Paula Gribetz Gottlieb. Promotes knowledge of Jewish books through dissemination of booklists, program materials; sponsors Jewish Book Awards, Jewish Book Month; presents literary awards and library citations; cooperates with publishers of Jewish books. *Jewish Book Annual; Jewish Books in Review; Jewish Book World.*

JWB JEWISH MUSIC COUNCIL (1944). 15 E. 26 St., NYC 10010. (212)532–4949. Chmn. Leonard Kaplan; Coord. Paula Gribetz Gottlieb. Promotes Jewish music activities nationally; annually sponsors and promotes the Jewish Music season; encourages participation on a community basis. *Jewish Music Notes* and numerous music resource publications for national distribution.

JWB LECTURE BUREAU (1922). 15 E. 26 St., NYC 10010–1579. (212)532–4949. Chmn. Mark S. Mandell; Dir. Sesil Lissberger. A nonprofit program service of JWB providing lecturers and performers from a broad range of Jewish and public life; also offers photo exhibits to stimulate Jewish programming of communal organizations. *The Jewish Arts—A Listing of Performers; Learning for Jewish Living—A Listing of Lecturers; Available Lecturers from Israel; Lecturers on the Holocaust.*

LEAGUE FOR YIDDISH, INC. (1979). 200 W. 72 St., Suite 40, NYC 10023. (212)787–6675. Pres. Sadie Turak; Exec. Dir. Mordkhe Schaechter. Promotes the development and use of Yiddish as a living language. *Afn Shvel.*

LEO BAECK INSTITUTE, INC. (1955). 129 E. 73 St., NYC 10021. (212)744–6400. Pres. Yosef Haim Yerushalmi; Dir. Robert A. Jacobs. A library, archive, and research center for the history of German-speaking Jewry. Offers lectures, exhibits, faculty seminars; publishes a series of monographs, yearbooks, and journals. *LBI Bulletin; LBI News; LBI Yearbook; LBI Memorial Lecture; LBI Library & Archives News.*

A LIVING MEMORIAL TO THE HOLOCAUST-MUSEUM OF JEWISH HERITAGE (1982). 342 Madison Ave., Suite 717, NYC 10173. (212)687–9141. Cochmn. George Klein, Hon. Robert M. Morgenthau, Peter Cohen, Sen. Manfred Ohrenstein; Museum Dir. David Altshuler. The museum will be New York's principal public memorial to the six million Jews murdered during the Holocaust. Scheduled to open in 1992, will include permanent and temporary exhibition galleries, a computerized interactive learning center, a memorial chamber, and education facilities. *Brochure; bimonthly newsletter.*

MAALOT (1987)1719 Wilmart St., Rockville, MD 20852. (301)231–9067. Pres./Exec. Off. David Shneyer. A nontraditional school established in order to train individuals in Jewish music, cantorial, and liturgical arts. Offers classes, seminars, and institutes throughout the year. Though based in the Washington, D.C. area, its faculty travels to communities throughout the U.S. and Canada.

MARTYRS MEMORIAL & MUSEUM OF THE HOLOCAUST (1963; reorg. 1978). 6505 Wilshire Blvd., 12th fl., Los Angeles, CA 90048. (213)651–3175. Chmn. Jack I. Salzberg; Dir. Michael Nutkiewicz. Seeks to commemorate the events and victims of the Holocaust and to educate against future reoccurrences; maintains permanent and traveling exhibits, sponsors public lectures, offers school curricula and teacher training. West Coast representative of Israel's Yad Vashem; affiliated with the Jewish Federation Council of Greater Los Angeles.

MEMORIAL FOUNDATION FOR JEWISH CULTURE, INC. (1964). 15 E. 26 St., NYC 10010. (212)679–4074. Pres. the Right

Hon., the Lord Jakobovits; Exec. V.-Pres. Jerry Hochbaum. Through the grants that it awards, encourages Jewish scholarship and Jewish education, supports communities that are struggling to maintain their Jewish identity, makes possible the training of Jewish men and women for professional careers in communal service in Jewishly deprived communities, and stimulates the documentation, commemoration, and teaching of the Holocaust.

NATIONAL FOUNDATION FOR JEWISH CULTURE (1960). 330 Seventh Ave., 21st fl., NYC 10001. (212)629-0500. Pres. George M. Zeltzer; Exec. Dir. Richard A. Siegel. Coordinates the activities of the Council of American Jewish Museums, the Council of Archives and Research Libraries in Jewish Studies, and the Council of Jewish Theaters; supports Jewish scholarship through Doctoral Dissertation Fellowships; publishes resource guides for traveling exhibitions, Jewish theaters, and Jewish archives; administers the Joint Cultural Appeal on behalf of the federated communities for support of national cultural institutions; organizes special conferences, symposia, and festivals in the arts and humanities.

NATIONAL HEBREW CULTURE COUNCIL (1952). 14 E. 4th St, NYC 10012. (212)-674-8412. Cultivates the study of Hebrew as a modern language in American public high schools and colleges, providing guidance to community groups and public educational authorities; annually administers National Voluntary Examination in Hebrew Culture and Knowledge of Israel in the public high schools. *Hebrew in Colleges and Universities.*

NATIONAL YIDDISH BOOK CENTER (1980). Old East Street School, PO Box 969, Amherst, MA 01004. (413)256-1241. Pres. Gail L. Perlman; Exec. Dir. Aaron Lansky. Collects used and out-of-print Yiddish books to distribute to individuals and libraries worldwide; provides resources to make Yiddish culture accessible to a new generation. *Yiddish Book News; Der Pakn-treger/The Book Peddler; Yiddish Bibliographic Notes.*

RESEARCH FOUNDATION FOR JEWISH IMMIGRATION, INC. (1971). 570 Seventh Ave., NYC 10018. (212)921-3871. Pres. Curt C. Silberman; Sec. and Coord. of Research Herbert A. Strauss; Archivist Dennis E. Rohrbaugh. Studies and records the history of the migration and acculturation of German-speaking Jewish Nazi persecutees in various resettlement countries worldwide, with special emphasis on the American experience. *International Biographical Dictionary of Central European Emigrés, 1933-1945; Jewish Immigrants of the Nazi Period in the USA.*

ST. LOUIS CENTER FOR HOLOCAUST STUDIES (1977). 12 Millstone Campus Dr., St. Louis, MO 63146. (314)432-0020. Chmn. Fred Katz; Dir. Rabbi Robert Sternberg. Develops programs and provides resources and educational materials to further an understanding of the Holocaust and its impact on civilization. *Audio Visual and Curriculum Resources Guides.*

SEPHARDIC HOUSE (1978). 8 W. 70 St., NYC 10023. (212)873-0300. Exec. Dir. Janice Etzkowitz Ovadiah; Bd. Chmn. Rabbi Marc D. Angel. Conducts research and promotes Sephardic culture through courses, lectures, concerts, conferences, film programs, etc.; has an active publication program. *Sephardic House Newsletter.*

SKIRBALL MUSEUM, Los Angeles, CA (*see* Hebrew Union College-Jewish Institute of Religion)

SOCIETY FOR THE HISTORY OF CZECHOSLOVAK JEWS, INC. (1961). 87-08 Santiago St., Holliswood, NY 11423. (718)468-6844. Pres. and Ed. Lewis Weiner; Sec. Joseph Abeles. Studies the history of Czechoslovak Jews, collects material and disseminates information through the publication of books and pamphlets. *The Jews of Czechoslovakia* (3 vols); *Review I; Review II.*

UNITED STATES HOLOCAUST MEMORIAL COUNCIL (1980). 2000 L St., NW, Suite 588, Washington, DC 20036. (202)653-9220. Chmn. Harvey M. Meyerhoff. Established by Congress as an independent federal establishment, to plan, build and operate the United States Holocaust Memorial Museum in Washington, D.C., and to encourage and sponsor observances of an annual, national, civic commemoration of the victims of the Holocaust known as the Days of Remembrance. Also engages in Holocaust education and research programs. Composed of 55 members of all faiths and backgrounds appointed by the president, plus five U.S. senators and five members of the House of Representatives.

Newsletter (monthly); *Directory of Holocaust Institutions in the U.S. and Canada* (annual).

YESHIVA UNIVERSITY MUSEUM (1973). 2520 Amsterdam Ave., NYC 10033. (212)-960-5390. Chmn. Bd. of Govs. Erica Jesselson; Dir. Sylvia A. Herskowitz. Collects, preserves, and interprets Jewish life and culture through changing exhibitions of ceremonial objects, paintings, rare books and documents, synagogue architecture, textiles, decorative arts, and photographs. Oral history archive. Special events, holiday workshops, live performances, lectures, etc. for adults and children. Guided tours and workshops are offered. *Seasonal calendars; special exhibition catalogues.*

YIDDISHER KULTUR FARBAND—YKUF (1937). 1133 Broadway, Rm. 1023, NYC 10010. (212)691-0708. Pres. and Ed. Itche Goldberg. Publishes a monthly magazine and books by contemporary and classical Jewish writers; conducts cultural forums; exhibits works by contemporary Jewish artists and materials of Jewish historical value; organizes reading circles. *Yiddishe Kultur.*

YIVO INSTITUTE FOR JEWISH RESEARCH, INC. (1925). 1048 Fifth Ave., NYC 10028. (212)535-6700. Chmn. Dr. Arnold Richards; Exec. Dir. Samuel Norich. Engages in social and humanistic research pertaining to East European Jewish life; maintains library and archives which provide a major international, national, and New York resource used by institutions, individual scholars, and laymen; trains graduate students in Yiddish, East European, and American Jewish studies; offers exhibits, conferences, public programs; publishes books. *Yidishe Shprakh; Yivo Annual of Jewish Social Science; Yivo Bleter.*

———, MAX WEINREICH CENTER FOR ADVANCED JEWISH STUDIES (1968). 1048 Fifth Ave., NYC 10028. (212)535-6700. Provides advanced-level training in Yiddish language and literature, ethnography, folklore, linguistics, and history; offers guidance on dissertation or independent research. *The Field of Yiddish; Jewish Folklore & Ethnology Newsletter.*

OVERSEAS AID

AMERICAN ASSOCIATION FOR ETHIOPIAN JEWS (1969). 1836 Jefferson Place, NW, Washington, DC 20036. (202)223-6838. Pres. Nathan Shapiro; Exec. Dir. William Recant. Informs world Jewry about the plight of Ethiopian Jews; advocates reunification with family members in Israel as a major priority; provides aid in refugee areas and Ethiopia; and helps resettlement in Israel. *Release; Newsline.*

AMERICAN FRIENDS OF THE ALLIANCE ISRAÉLITE UNIVERSELLE, INC. (1946). 420 Lexington Ave., Suite 1733, NYC 10170. (212)808-5437. Pres. Henriette Beilis; Exec. Dir. Warren Green. Participates in educational and human-rights activities of the AIU and supports the Alliance System of Jewish schools, teachers' colleges, and remedial programs in Israel, North Africa, the Middle East, Europe, and Canada. *Alliance Review.*

AMERICAN JEWISH JOINT DISTRIBUTION COMMITTEE, INC.—JDC (1914). 711 Third Ave., NYC 10017. (212)687-6200. Pres. Sylvia Hassenfeld; Exec. V.-Pres. Michael Schneider. Provides assistance to Jewish communities in Europe, Asia, Africa, and the Mideast. Current concerns include Soviet Jewish émigrés; Israel's social needs; nonsectarian development and disaster relief in Armenia, Ethiopia, and elsewhere; and *glasnost*-facilitated program expansions in Eastern Europe, particularly in the USSR and Hungary. *Annual report; JDC World; Historical Album.*

AMERICAN JEWISH PHILANTHROPIC FUND (1955). 386 Park Ave. S., NYC 10016. (212)OR9-0010. Pres. Charles J. Tanenbaum. Provides resettlement assistance to Jewish refugees primarily through programs administered by the International Rescue Committee at its offices in Western Europe and the U.S.

AMERICAN ORT FEDERATION, INC.—ORGANIZATION FOR REHABILITATION THROUGH TRAINING (1924). 817 Broadway, NYC 10003. (212)677-4400. Pres. David B. Hermelin; Exec. V.-Pres. Donald H. Klein. Provides vocational/technical education to over 195,000 students at ORT schools and training centers in 35 countries, with the largest program in Israel serving 96,000 students. Teaching staff numbers 6,200. Annual cost of program is about $137 million. *American ORT Federation Bulletin; ORT Yearbook.*

———, AMERICAN AND EUROPEAN FRIENDS OF ORT (1941). 817 Broadway, NYC 10003. (212)677-4400. Pres. Simon

Jaglom; Hon. Chmn. Jacques Zwibak. Promotes the ORT idea among Americans of European extraction; supports the Litton ORT Auto-Mechanics School in Jerusalem and the ORT School of Engineering in Jerusalem. Promotes the work of the American ORT Federation.

———, AMERICAN LABOR ORT (1937). 817 Broadway, NYC 10003. (212)677-4400. Chmn. Sam Fine. Promotes the vocational/technical training of more than 200,000 young people with the marketable skills they need to become productive members of society. Promotes the work of the American ORT Federation in 35 countries around the world.

———, BUSINESS AND PROFESSIONAL ORT (1937). 817 Broadway, NYC 10003. (212)-677-4400. Pres. Rose Seidel Kalich. Promotes work of American ORT Federation.

———, NATIONAL ORT LEAGUE (1914). 817 Broadway, NYC 10003. (212)677-4400. Pres. Judah Wattenberg; First V.-Pres. Tibor Waldman. Promotes ORT idea among Jewish fraternal *landsmanshaften* and individuals. Promotes the work of the American ORT Federation.

———, WOMEN'S AMERICAN ORT (1927). 315 Park Ave. S., NYC 10010. (212)505-7700. Pres. Reese Feldman; Exec. Dir. Benjamin Hirsch. Represents and advances the program and philosophy of ORT among the women of the American Jewish community through membership and educational activities; materially supports the vocational training operations of World ORT; contributes to the American Jewish community by encouraging participation in ORT campaigns and through general education to help raise the level of Jewish consciousness among American Jewish women; through its American Affairs program, cooperates in efforts to improve the quality of education and vocational training in the U.S. *Women's American ORT Reporter; Close-Ups.*

CONFERENCE ON JEWISH MATERIAL CLAIMS AGAINST GERMANY, INC. (1951). 15 E. 26 St., Rm. 1355, NYC 10010. (212)-696-4944. Pres. Israel Miller; Sec. and Exec. Dir. Saul Kagan. Monitors the implementation of restitution and indemnification programs of the German Federal Republic (FRG) arising from its agreements with FRG. Administers Hardship Fund, which distributes DM 400,000,000 appropriated by FRG for Jewish Nazi victims unable to file timely claims under original indemnification laws. Also assists needy non-Jews who risked their lives to help Jewish survivors.

HIAS, INC. (HEBREW IMMIGRANT AID SOCIETY) (1880; reorg. 1954). 200 Park Ave. S., NYC 10003. (212)674-6800. Pres. Ben Zion Leuchter; Exec. V.-Pres. Karl D. Zukerman. International Jewish migration agency with headquarters in the U.S. and offices, affiliates, and representatives in Europe, Latin America, Canada, Australia, New Zealand, and Israel. Assists Jewish migrants and refugees from Eastern Europe, the Middle East, North Africa, and Latin America. Via U.S. government-funded programs, assists in the resettlement of Indo-Chinese and other refugees. *HIAS Reporter; annual report.*

JEWISH RESTITUTION SUCCESSOR ORGANIZATION (1947). 15 E. 26 St., Rm. 1355, NYC 10010. (212)696-4944. Sec. and Exec. Dir. Saul Kagan. Acts to discover, claim, receive, and assist in the recovery of Jewish heirless or unclaimed property; to utilize such assets or to provide for their utilization for the relief, rehabilitation, and resettlement of surviving victims of Nazi persecution.

NORTH AMERICAN CONFERENCE ON ETHIOPIAN JEWRY (NACOEJ) (1982). 165 E. 56 St., NYC l0022. (212)752-6340. Pres. Jonathan Giesberg; Exec. Dir. Barbara Ribakove Gordon. Provides assistance to Ethiopian Jews in Ethiopia and in Israel; informs American and other Jewish communities about their situation; works to increase involvement of world Jewish communities in assisting, visiting, and learning about Ethiopian Jews. *Lifeline* (membership newsletter).

RE'UTH WOMEN'S SOCIAL SERVICE, INC. (1937). 240 W. 98 St., NYC 10025. (212)-666-7880. Pres. Ursula Merkin; V.-Pres. Ilse Rosenbaum. Maintains in Israel subsidized housing for self-reliant elderly; old-age homes for more dependent elderly; Lichtenstadter Hospital for chronically ill and young accident victims not accepted by other hospitals; subsidized meals; Golden Age clubs. *Annual dinner journal.*

THANKS TO SCANDINAVIA, INC. (1963). 745 Fifth Ave., Rm. 603, NYC 10151. (212)-486-8600. Natl. Chmn. Victor Borge;

Pres. and Exec. Off. Richard Netter. Provides scholarships and fellowships at American universities and medical centers to students and doctors from Denmark, Finland, Norway, and Sweden in appreciation of the rescue of Jews from the Holocaust. Informs current and future generations of Americans and Scandinavians of these singular examples of humanity and bravery; funds books about this chapter of history. *Annual report; books, pamphlets.*

UNITED JEWISH APPEAL, INC. (1939). 99 Park Ave., Suite 300, NYC 10016. (212)-818-9100. Natl. Chmn. Morton A. Kornreich; Chmn. Bd. of Trustees Martin F. Stein; Pres. Stanley B. Horowitz. The annual UJA/Federation Campaign is the primary instrument for the support of humanitarian programs and social services for Jews at home and abroad. In Israel, through the Jewish Agency, campaign funds help absorb, educate, and settle new immigrants, build villages and farms in rural areas, support innovative programs for troubled and disadvantaged youth, and promote the revitalization of distressed neighborhoods. UJA/Federation funds also provide for the well-being of Jews and Jewish communities in 33 other countries around the world through the American Jewish Joint Distribution Committee. Constituent departments of the UJA include the Rabbinic Cabinet, University Programs Department, Women's Division, Young Leadership Cabinet, the Women's Young Leadership Cabinet, and the Business and Professional Women's Council.

RELIGIOUS AND EDUCATIONAL

AGUDATH ISRAEL OF AMERICA (1922). 84 William St., NYC 10038. (212)797-9000. Pres. Rabbi Moshe Sherer; Exec. Dir. Rabbi Boruch B. Borchardt. Mobilizes Orthodox Jews to cope with Jewish problems in the spirit of the Torah; sponsors a broad range of projects aimed at enhancing religious living, education, children's welfare, protection of Jewish religious rights, outreach to the assimilated, and social services. *Jewish Observer; Dos Yiddishe Vort; Coalition.*

———, AGUDAH WOMEN OF AMERICA–N'SHEI AGUDATH ISRAEL (1940). 84 William St., NYC 10038. (212)363-8940. Presidium Esther Bohensky, Aliza Grund. Organizes Jewish women for philanthropic work in the U.S. and Israel and for intensive Torah education.

———, CHILDREN'S DIVISION—PIRCHEI AGUDATH ISRAEL (1925). 84 William St., NYC 10038 (212)797-9000. Natl. Dir. Rabbi Joshua Silbermintz; Natl. Coord. Rabbi Mordechai Mehlman. Educates Orthodox Jewish children in Torah; encourages sense of communal responsibility. Branches sponsor weekly youth groups and Jewish welfare projects. National Mishnah contests, rallies, and conventions foster unity on a national level. *Darkeinu; Leaders Guides.*

———, GIRLS' DIVISION—BNOS AGUDATH ISRAEL (1921). 84 William St., NYC 10038. (212)797-9000. Natl. Dirs. Devorah Streicher and Leah Zagelbaum. Sponsors regular weekly programs on the local level and unites girls from throughout the Torah world with extensive regional and national activities. *Newsletters.*

———, YOUNG MEN'S DIVISION—ZEIREI AGUDATH ISRAEL (1921). 84 William St., NYC 10038. (212)797-9000. Pres. Avrohom Biderman; Dir. Rabbi Labish Becker. Educates youth to see Torah as source of guidance for all issues facing Jews as individuals and as a people. Inculcates a spirit of activism through projects in religious, Torah-educational, and community-welfare fields. *Zeirei Forum; Am Hatorah; Daf Chizuk; Ohr Hakollel.*

AGUDATH ISRAEL WORLD ORGANIZATION (1912). 84 William St., NYC 10038. (212)-797-9000. Cochmn. Rabbi Moshe Sherer, Rabbi Yehudah Meir Abramowitz. Represents the interests of Orthodox Jewry on the national and international scenes. Sponsors projects to strengthen Torah life worldwide.

AMERICAN ASSOCIATION OF RABBIS (1978). 350 Fifth Ave., Suite 3308, NYC 10001. (212)244-3350. Pres. Rabbi Richard Smith; Sec. Rabbi Sidney Vineburg. An organization of rabbis serving in pulpits, in areas of education, and in social work. *Bimonthly newsletter; semiannual journal.*

ANNENBERG RESEARCH INSTITUTE (formerly DROPSIE COLLEGE FOR HEBREW AND COGNATE LEARNING) (1907; reorg. 1986). 420 Walnut St., Philadelphia, PA 19106. (215)238-1290. Dir. Bernard Lewis; Assoc. Dir. David M. Goldenberg. A center for advanced research in Judaic and Near Eastern studies at the postdoctoral level. *Jewish Quarterly Review.*

ASSOCIATION FOR JEWISH STUDIES (1969). Widener Library M., Harvard University, Cambridge, MA 02138. Pres. Robert Chazan; Exec. Sec. Charles Berlin. Seeks to promote, maintain, and improve the teaching of Jewish studies in American colleges and universities by sponsoring meetings and conferences, publishing a newsletter and other scholarly materials, setting standards for programs in Jewish studies, aiding in the placement of teachers, coordinating research, and cooperating with other scholarly organizations. *AJS Review; newsletter.*

ASSOCIATION OF HILLEL/JEWISH CAMPUS PROFESSIONALS (1949). 6300 Forsyth Blvd., St. Louis, MO 63105. (314)726-6177. Pres. Barbara Bomze; Exec. Dir. Rabbi James S. Diamond. Seeks to promote professional relationships and exchanges of experience, develop personnel standards and qualifications, safeguard integrity of Hillel profession; represents and advocates before National Hillel Staff, National Hillel Commission, B'nai B'rith International, Council of Jewish Federations. *AHJCP Bulletin.*

ASSOCIATION OF ORTHODOX JEWISH SCIENTISTS (1948). 1364 Coney Island Ave., Brooklyn, NY 11230. (718)338-8592. Pres. Seymour Applebaum, M.D.; Bd. Chmn. Allen J. Bennett, M.D. Seeks to contribute to the development of science within the framework of Orthodox Jewish tradition; to obtain and disseminate information relating to the interaction between the Jewish traditional way of life and scientific developments—on both an ideological and practical level; to assist in the solution of problems pertaining to Orthodox Jews engaged in scientific teaching or research. Two main conventions are held each year. *Intercom; Proceedings; Halacha Bulletin; newsletter.*

BALTIMORE HEBREW UNIVERSITY (1919). 5800 Park Heights Ave., Baltimore, MD 21215. (301)578-6900. Pres. Leivy Smolar; Bd. Chmn. Irving F. Cohn. Offers PhD, MA, and BA programs in Jewish studies, biblical and Near Eastern archaeology, philosophy, literature, history, Hebrew language and literature; Joseph Meyerhoff Library.

——,BERNARD MANEKIN SCHOOL OF UNDERGRADUATE STUDIES. Dean Judy Meltzer. BA program; the Isaac C. Rosenthal Center for Jewish Education; on-site courses in Maryland and Jerusalem; interdisciplinary concentrations: contemporary Middle East, American Jewish culture, and the humanities.

——,PEGGY MEYERHOFF PEARLSTONE SCHOOL OF GRADUATE STUDIES. Dean Robert O. Freedman. PhD and MA programs; MA and MSW with University of Maryland School of Social Work and Community Planning in federation, community organization, center, and family services; MA and MEd in Jewish education and double MA in journalism with Towson State University; MA program in the study of Christian-Jewish relations with St. Mary's Seminary and University; MA program in community relations with University of Maryland Graduate School.

——,BALTIMORE INSTITUTE FOR JEWISH COMMUNAL SERVICE. Joint certification program with University of Maryland, Towson State University, the Associated Jewish Charities and Welfare Fund, the UJA/Federation of Greater Washington, and B'nai B'rith International sponsoring field work, seminars, and overseas study.

BETH MEDROSH ELYON (ACADEMY OF HIGHER LEARNING AND RESEARCH) (1943). 73 Main St., Monsey, NY 10952. (914)356-7065. Bd. Chmn. Emanuel Weldler; Treas. Arnold Jacobs; Sec. Yerachmiel Censor. Provides postgraduate courses and research work in higher Jewish studies; offers scholarships and fellowships. *Annual journal.*

B'NAI B'RITH HILLEL FOUNDATIONS, INC. (1923). 1640 Rhode Island Ave., NW, Washington, DC 20036. (202)857-6560. Chmn. B'nai B'rith Hillel Comm. David Bittker; Internatl. Dir. Richard M. Joel. Provides cultural, social, community-service, educational, and religious activities for Jewish college students of all denominational backgrounds. Maintains a presence on 400 campuses in the U.S., Canada, and overseas. Sponsors National Leaders Assembly, Public Policy Conference, targeted Israel missions, National Jewish Law Students Network. *Mekorot; Igeret; Jewish Life on Campus: A Directory of B'nai B'rith Hillel Foundations and Other Jewish Campus Agencies.*

B'NAI B'RITH YOUTH ORGANIZATION (1924). 1640 Rhode Island Ave., NW, Washington, DC 20036. (202)857-6633. Chmn. Youth Comm. Edward Yalowitz; Internatl. Dir. Sidney Clearfield. Helps Jewish teenagers achieve self-fulfillment and make a maximum contribution to the Jewish community and their country's culture; helps members acquire a greater knowledge and appreciation of Jewish religion and culture. *D'var; Monday Morning; Shofar; Hakol; Kesher.*

BRAMSON ORT TECHNICAL INSTITUTE (1977).6930 Austin St., Forest Hills, NY 11375. (718)261-5800. Dir. Howard S. Friedman. A two-year Jewish technical college offering certificates and associate degrees in high technology and business fields, including computer programming, electronics technology, business management, word processing, and ophthalmic technology. Houses the Center for Computers in Jewish Education.

BRANDEIS-BARDIN INSTITUTE (1941). 1101 Peppertree Lane, Brandeis, CA 93064. (818)348-7201. Pres. John Rauch; Exec. V.-Pres. Alvin Mars. A pluralistic, nondenominational Jewish institution providing programs for people of all ages: Brandeis Camp Institute (BCI), a leadership program for college-age adults; Camp Alonim, a positive Jewish experience for children 8-16; House of the Book *shabbat* weekends for adults 25+, at which scholars-in-residence discuss historical, cultural, religious, and spiritual aspects of Judaism. *Brandeis-Bardin Institute Newsletter; BCI Alumni News.*

BRANDEIS UNIVERSITY(1948). 415 South St., Waltham, MA 02254. (617)736-2000. Bd. Chmn. Louis Perlmutter; Pres. Evelyn E. Handler. Founded under Jewish sponsorship as a nonsectarian institution offering to all the highest quality undergraduate and graduate education. The Lown School is the center for all programs of teaching and research in the areas of Judaic Studies, Ancient Near Eastern Studies, and Islamic and Modern Middle Eastern Studies. The school includes the Department of Near Eastern Studies, the Hornstein Program for Jewish Communal Service, and the Cohen Center for Modern Jewish Studies. The Department of Near Eastern and Judaic Studies offers academic programs in the major areas of its concern. The Hornstein Program is a professional training program leading to the degree in Jewish communal service. The Cohen Center conducts research and teaching in contemporary Jewish studies, primarily in the field of American Jewish studies. *Various newsletters, scholarly publications.*

CANTORS ASSEMBLY (1947). 150 Fifth Ave., NYC 10011. (212)691-8020. Pres. Robert Kieval; Exec. V.-Pres. Samuel Rosenbaum. Seeks to unite all cantors who adhere to traditional Judaism and who serve as full-time cantors in bona fide congregations to conserve and promote the musical traditions of the Jews and to elevate the status of the cantorial profession. *Annual Proceedings; Journal of Synagogue Music.*

CENTRAL CONFERENCE OF AMERICAN RABBIS (1889). 192 Lexington Ave., NYC 10016. (212)684-4990. Pres. Rabbi Samuel E. Karff; Exec. V.-Pres. Rabbi Joseph B. Glaser. Seeks to conserve and promote Judaism and to disseminate its teachings in a liberal spirit. *Journal of Reform Judaism; CCAR Yearbook.*

CLAL—NATIONAL JEWISH CENTER FOR LEARNING AND LEADERSHIP (1974). 47 W. 34 St., 2nd fl., NYC 10001. (212)279-2525. Pres. Irving Greenberg; Exec. V.-Pres. Paul Jeser. Dedicated to preparing Jewish leaders to respond to the challenges of a new era in Jewish history; challenges which include the freedom to accept or reject one's Jewish heritage, the liberty to choose from an abundance of Jewish values and life-styles, and the exercise of Jewish power after the Holocaust and the rebirth of the State of Israel. *News & Perspectives.*

CLEVELAND COLLEGE OF JEWISH STUDIES (1964). 26500 Shaker Blvd., Beachwood, OH 44122. (216)464-4050. Pres. David S. Ariel; Bd. Chmn. Donna Yanowitz. Provides courses in all areas of Judaic and Hebrew studies to adults and college-age students; offers continuing education for Jewish educators and administrators; serves as a center for Jewish life and culture; expands the availability of courses in Judaic studies by exchanging faculty, students, and credits with neighboring academic institutions; grants bachelor's and master's degrees.

COALITION FOR THE ADVANCEMENT OF JEWISH EDUCATION (CAJE) (1976). 261 W. 35th St., #12A, NYC 10001. (212)-268-4210. Chmn. Betsy Katz; Dir. Eliot

G. Spack. Brings together Jews from all ideologies who are involved in every facet of Jewish education, and are committed to transmitting Jewish knowledge, culture, and experience; serves as a channel of communication for its membership to share resources and methods, and as a forum for exchange of philosophical and theoretical approaches to Jewish education. Sponsors annual conference on Alternatives in Jewish Education. *Bikurim; Crisis Curricula; Mekasher; CAJE Jewish Education News.*

CONGRESS OF SECULAR JEWISH ORGANIZATIONS (1970). 1130 S. Michigan Ave., #2101, Chicago, IL 60605. (312)922-0386. Chmn. Karen Levy; Exec. Dir. Gerry Revzin. An umbrella organization of schools and adult clubs; facilitates exchange curricula and educational programs for children and adults stressing our Jewish historical and cultural heritage and the continuity of the Jewish people. *Newsletter.*

COUNCIL FOR JEWISH EDUCATION (1926). 426 W. 58 St., NYC 10019. (212)713-0290. Pres. Reuven Yalon; Consultant Philip Gorodetzer. Fellowship of Jewish education professionals—administrators and supervisors and teachers in Hebrew high schools and Jewish teachers colleges—of all ideological groupings; conducts annual national and regional conferences; represents the Jewish education profession before the Jewish community; cosponsors, with the Jewish Education Service of North America, a personnel committee and other projects; cooperates with Jewish Agency Department of Education and Culture in promoting Hebrew culture and studies; conducts lectureship at Hebrew University. *Jewish Education; Sheviley Hahinnukh.*

DROPSIE COLLEGE FOR HEBREW AND COGNATE LEARNING (*see* Annenberg Research Institute)

FEDERATION OF JEWISH MEN'S CLUBS, INC. (1929). 475 Riverside Dr., Suite 244, NYC 10115. (212)749-8100. Pres. Lawrence Allen; Exec. Dir. Rabbi Charles Simon. Promotes principles and objectives of Conservative Judaism by organizing, sponsoring, and developing men's clubs or brotherhoods; supports OMETZ Center for Conservative Judaism on campus; promotes Home Library of Conservative Judaism and the Art of Jewish Living series;

sponsors Hebrew literacy adult education program; presents awards for service to American Jewry. *Torchlight.*

GRATZ COLLEGE (1895). Old York Rd. & Melrose Ave., Melrose Park, PA 19126. (215)635-7300. Bd. Chmn. Stephen Saks; Pres. Gary S. Schiff. Offers a wide variety of bachelor's, master's, teacher-training, continuing-education, and high-school-level programs in Judaic, Hebraic, and Middle Eastern studies. Grants BA and MA in Jewish studies, MA in Jewish education, MA in Jewish music, certificates in Judaica librarianship, Jewish communal studies, Jewish chaplaincy and other credentials. Joint bachelor's programs with Temple University and Beaver College and joint graduate program in Jewish communal service with U. of Pennsylvania. *Various newsletters, a yearbook, and scholarly publications.*

HEBREW COLLEGE (1921). 43 Hawes St., Brookline, MA 02146. (617)232-8710. Pres. Samuel Schafler; Bd. Chmn. Herbert L. Berman. Provides intensive programs of study in all areas of Jewish culture from high school through college and graduate-school levels, also at branch in Hartford; offers the degrees of MA in Jewish studies, Bachelor and Master of Jewish education, Bachelor of Hebrew letters, and teacher's diploma; degrees fully accredited by New England Assoc. of Schools and Colleges. Operates Hebrew-speaking Camp Yavneh in Northwood, NH; offers extensive Ulpan program and courses for community. *Hebrew College Today.*

HEBREW THEOLOGICAL COLLEGE (1922). 7135 N. Carpenter Rd., Skokie, IL 60077. (312)267-9800. Pres. Rabbi Don Well; Bd. Chmn. Colman Ginsparg. An institution of higher Jewish learning which includes a division of advanced Hebrew studies, a school of liberal arts and sciences, a rabbinical ordination program, a graduate school in Judaic studies and pastoral counseling; the Fasman Yeshiva High School; a high school summer program combining Torah studies and computer science courses; and a Jewish studies program. *Or Shmuel Torah Journal; quarterly newsletter.*

HEBREW UNION COLLEGE-JEWISH INSTITUTE OF RELIGION (1875). 3101 Clifton Ave., Cincinnati, OH 45220. (513)221-1875. Pres. Alfred Gottschalk; Exec.

V.-Pres. Uri D. Herscher; V.-Pres. Academic Affairs Eugene Mihaly; V.-Pres. Paul M. Steinberg; Chmn. Bd. of Govs. Richard J. Scheuer. Academic centers: 3101 Clifton Ave., Cincinnati, OH 45220 (1875), Kenneth Ehrlich, Dean; 1 W. 4 St., NYC 10012 (1922), Norman J. Cohen, Dean; 3077 University Ave., Los Angeles, CA 90007 (1954), Lee Bycel, Dean; 13 King David St., Jerusalem, Israel 94101 (1963), Michael Klein, Dean. Prepares students for Reform rabbinate, cantorate, religious-school teaching and administration, community service, academic careers; promotes Jewish studies; maintains libraries and a museum; offers master's and doctoral degrees; engages in archaeological excavations; publishes scholarly works through Hebrew Union College Press. *American Jewish Archives; Bibliographica Judaica; HUC-JIR Catalogue; Hebrew Union College Annual; Studies in Bibliography and Booklore; The Chronicle.*

———, AMERICAN JEWISH ARCHIVES (1947). 3101 Clifton Ave., Cincinnati, OH 45220. (513)221-1875. Dir. Jacob R. Marcus; Admin. Dir. Abraham Peck. Promotes the study and preservation of the Western Hemisphere Jewish experience through research, publications, collection of important source materials, and a vigorous public-outreach program. *American Jewish Archives; monographs, publications, and pamphlets.*

———, AMERICAN JEWISH PERIODICAL CENTER (1957). 3101 Clifton Ave., Cincinnati, OH 45220. (513)221-1875. Dir. Jacob R. Marcus; Codir. Herbert C. Zafren. Maintains microfilms of all American Jewish periodicals 1823-1925, selected periodicals since 1925. *Jewish Periodicals and Newspapers on Microfilm (1957); First Supplement (1960); Augmented Edition (1984).*

———, EDGAR F. MAGNIN SCHOOL OF GRADUATE STUDIES (1956). 3077 University Ave., Los Angeles, CA 90007. (213)-749-3424. Dir. Stanley Chyet. Supervises programs leading to PhD (Education), DHS, DHL, and MA degrees; participates in cooperative PhD programs with the University of Southern California.

———, JEROME H. LOUCHHEIM SCHOOL OF JUDAIC STUDIES (1969). 3077 University Ave. Los Angeles, CA 90007. (213)749-3424. Dir. David Ellenson. Offers programs leading to MA, BS, BA, and AA degrees; offers courses as part of the undergraduate program of the University of Southern California.

———, NELSON GLUECK SCHOOL OF BIBLICAL ARCHAEOLOGY (1963). 13 King David St., Jerusalem, Israel 94101. Dir. Avraham Biran. Offers graduate-level research programs in Bible and archaeology. Summer excavations are carried out by scholars and students. University credit may be earned by participants in excavations. Consortium of colleges, universities, and seminaries is affiliated with the school.

———, RHEA HIRSCH SCHOOL OF EDUCATION (1967). 3077 University Ave., Los Angeles, CA 90007. (213)749-3424. Dir. Sara S. Lee. Offers PhD and MA programs in Jewish and Hebrew education; conducts joint degree programs with University of Southern California; offers courses for Jewish teachers, librarians, and early educators on a nonmatriculating basis; conducts summer institutes for professional Jewish educators.

———, SCHOOL OF EDUCATION (1947). 1 W. 4 St., NYC 10012. (212)674-5300. V.-Pres. and Dean of Faculty Paul M. Steinberg; Dean Norman J. Cohen; Dir. Kerry M. Olitzky. Trains teachers and principals for Reform religious schools; offers MA degree with specialization in religious education; offers extension programs in various suburban centers.

———, SCHOOL OF GRADUATE STUDIES (1949). 3101 Clifton Ave., Cincinnati, OH 45220 (513)221-1875. Dean Samuel Greengus. Offers programs leading to MA and PhD degrees; offers program leading to DHL degree for rabbinic graduates of the college.

———, SCHOOL OF JEWISH COMMUNAL SERVICE (1968). 3077 University Ave., Los Angeles, CA 90007. (213)749-3424. Dir. Gerald B. Bubis. Offers certificate and master's degree to those employed in Jewish communal services, or preparing for such work; offers joint MA in Jewish education and communal service with Rhea Hirsch School; offers MA and MSW in conjunction with the University of Southern California School of Social Work, with the George Warren Brown School of Social Work of Washington University, and with the University of Pittsburgh School of Social Work; offers joint master's degrees in conjunction with USC in public administration or gerontology.

———, SCHOOL OF JEWISH STUDIES (1963). 13 King David St., Jerusalem, Israel, 94101. (02)20333. Dean Michael Klein; Assoc. Dean Rabbi Shaul R. Feinberg. Offers first year of graduate rabbinic, cantorial, and Jewish education studies (required) for American students; program leading to ordination for Israeli rabbinic students; undergraduate semester in Jerusalem and one-year work/study program on a kibbutz in cooperation with Union of American Hebrew Congregations; public outreach programs (lectures, courses, concerts, exhibits).

———, SCHOOL OF SACRED MUSIC (1947). 1 W. 4 St., NYC 10012. (212)674–5300. Dir. Israel Goldstein. Trains cantors and music personnel for congregations; offers MSM degree. *Sacred Music Press.*

———, SKIRBALL MUSEUM (1913; 1972 in Calif.). 3077 University Ave., Los Angeles, CA 90007. (213)749–3424. Dir. Nancy Berman; Curator Barbara Gilbert. Collects, preserves, researches, and exhibits art and artifacts made by or for Jews, or otherwise associated with Jews and Judaism. Provides opportunity to faculty and students to do research in the field of Jewish art. *Catalogues of exhibits and collections.*

HERZLIAH-JEWISH TEACHERS SEMINARY (1967). Division of Touro College. 844 Ave. of the Americas, NYC 10001. (212)-447–0700. Pres. Bernard Lander; Dir. Jacob Katzman.

———, GRADUATE SCHOOL OF JEWISH STUDIES (1981). 30 W. 44 St., NYC 10036. (212)447–0700. Pres. Bernard Lander; Dean Michael A. Shmidman. Offers courses leading to an MA in Jewish studies, with concentrations in Jewish history or Jewish education. Students may complete part of their program in Israel, through MA courses offered by Touro faculty at Touro's Jerusalem center.

———, JEWISH PEOPLE'S UNIVERSITY OF THE AIR. (212)447–0700. Dir./Producer Jacob Katzman. The educational outreach arm of Touro College, it produces and disseminates Jewish educational and cultural programming for radio broadcast and on audio-cassettes.

INSTITUTE FOR COMPUTERS IN JEWISH LIFE (1978). 845 N. Michigan Ave., Suite 843, Chicago, IL 60611. (312)787–7856. Pres. Thomas Klutznick; Exec. V.-Pres. Irving J. Rosenbaum. Explores, develops, and disseminates applications of computer technology to appropriate areas of Jewish life, with special emphasis on Jewish education; provides access to the Bar-Ilan University Responsa Project; creates educational software for use in Jewish schools; provides consulting service and assistance for national Jewish organizations, seminaries, and synagogues. *Monitor.*

JEWISH CHAUTAUQUA SOCIETY, INC. (sponsored by NATIONAL FEDERATION OF TEMPLE BROTHERHOODS) (1898). 838 Fifth Ave., NYC 10021. (212)570–0707. Pres. Richard D. Karfunkle; 1st V.-Pres./ Chancellor Alvin R. Corwin. The society's six-point interreligious educational program provides for visiting rabbi lecturers to colleges and schools, resident lectureships (endowed courses on Judaism taught by rabbis), book grant package programs for colleges and schools, film and tapes, Interfaith Institutes, and a secondary-school interfaith program. *Brotherhood.*

JEWISH EDUCATION IN MEDIA (1978). PO Box 180, Riverdale Sta., NYC 10471. (212)362–7633. Pres. Bernard Samers; Exec. Dir. Rabbi Mark S. Golub. Devoted to producing radio, television, film, videocassette and audio-cassette programming for a popular Jewish audience, in order to inform, entertain, and inspire a greater sense of Jewish identity and Jewish commitment. "L'Chayim," JEM's weekly half-hour program, airs on WOR Radio in New York and in radio and television syndication; it features outstanding figures in the Jewish world addressing the issues and events of importance to the Jewish community.

JEWISH EDUCATION SERVICE OF NORTH AMERICA (JESNA) (1981). 730 Broadway, NYC 10003. (212)529–2000. Pres. Bennett Yanowitz; Exec. V.-Pres. Jonathan Woocher. Coordinating, planning, and service agency for Jewish education in bureaus and federations; offers curricular advisement and maintains a National Educational Resource Center; runs regional conferences; conducts surveys on Jewish education; engages in statistical and other educational research; provides community consultations; sponsors the National

Board of License; administers Fellowships in Jewish Educational Leadership training program (FIJEL); provides placement of upper-level bureau and communal school personnel and educators; maintains an Israel office. *Pedagogic Reporter; TRENDS; Media "Meida"; Information Research Bulletins;* annual report.

JEWISH MINISTERS CANTORS ASSOCIATION OF AMERICA, INC. (1896). 3 W. 16 St., NYC 10011. (212)675–6601. Pres. Cantor Nathan H. Muchnick. Furthers and propagates traditional liturgy; places cantors in synagogues throughout the U.S. and Canada; develops the cantors of the future. *Kol Lakol.*

JEWISH RECONSTRUCTIONIST FOUNDATION (1940). Church Rd. and Greenwood Ave., Wyncote, PA 19095. (215)887–1988. Pres. Rabbi Elliot Skiddell; Exec. Dir. Rabbi Mordechai Liebling. Dedicated to the advancement of Judaism as the evolving religious civilization of the Jewish people. Coordinates the Federation of Reconstructionist Congregations and Havurot, Reconstructionist Rabbinical Association, and Reconstructionist Rabbinical College.

———, FEDERATION OF RECONSTRUCTIONIST CONGREGATIONS AND HAVUROT (1954). Church Rd. and Greenwood Ave., Wyncote, PA 19095. (215)887–1988. Pres. Roger Price; Exec. Dir. Rabbi Mordechai Liebling. Services affiliated congregations and havurot educationally and administratively; fosters the establishment of new Reconstructionist congregations and fellowship groups. Runs the Reconstructionist Press and provides programmatic materials. Maintains regional offices in New York, Los Angeles, and South Bend, Ind. *Reconstructionist;* newsletter.

———, RECONSTRUCTIONIST RABBINICAL ASSOCIATION (1974). Church Rd. and Greenwood Ave., Wyncote, PA 19095. (215)576–0800. Pres. Rabbi Sandy Sasso; Admin. Michael M. Cohen. Professional organization for graduates of the Reconstructionist Rabbinical College and other rabbis who identify with Reconstructionist Judaism; cooperates with Federation of Reconstructionist Congregations and Havurot in furthering Reconstructionism in N. America. *Raayanot;* newsletter.

———, RECONSTRUCTIONIST RABBINICAL COLLEGE (*see* p. 556)

JEWISH TEACHERS ASSOCIATION—MORIM (1931). 45 E. 33 St., NYC 10016. (212)-684–0556. Pres. Phyllis L. Pullman; V.-Pres. Eli Nieman. Protects teachers from abuse of seniority rights; fights the encroachment of anti-Semitism in education; provides legal counsel to protect teachers from discrimination; offers scholarships to qualified students; encourages teachers to assume active roles in Jewish communal and religious affairs. *Morim Jewish Teachers Association Newsletter.*

JEWISH THEOLOGICAL SEMINARY OF AMERICA (1886; reorg. 1902). 3080 Broadway, NYC 10027–4649. (212)678–8000. Chancellor Ismar Schorsch; Bd. Chmn. Stephen M. Peck. Operates undergraduate and graduate programs in Judaic studies; professional schools for training Conservative rabbis and cantors; a pastoral psychiatry center; Melton Center for Jewish Education; the Jewish Museum; and such youth programs as the Ramah Camps and the Prozdor high-school division. Produces the "Eternal Light" radio and TV programs. *Academic Bulletin; Seminary Progress; The Second Century.*

———, ALBERT A. LIST COLLEGE OF JEWISH STUDIES (formerly SEMINARY COLLEGE OF JEWISH STUDIES-TEACHERS INSTITUTE) (1909). 3080 Broadway, NYC 10027. (212)678–8826. Dean Anne Lapidus Lerner. Offers complete undergraduate program in Judaica leading to BA degree; conducts joint programs with Columbia University and Barnard College enabling students to receive two BA degrees.

———, CANTORS INSTITUTE AND SEMINARY COLLEGE OF JEWISH MUSIC (1952). 3080 Broadway, NYC 10027. (212)678–8038. Dean Rabbi Morton M. Leifman. Trains cantors, music teachers, and choral directors for congregations. Offers fulltime programs in sacred music leading to degrees of MSM and DSM, and diploma of *Hazzan.*

———, DEPARTMENT OF RADIO AND TELEVISION (1944). 3080 Broadway, NYC 10027. (212)678–8020. Dir. Marjorie Wyler. Produces radio and TV programs expressing the Jewish tradition in its broadest sense: The "Eternal Light" weekly radio program on NBC network; one hour-long documentary on NBC-TV; TV program on ABC. Distributes cassettes of programs at minimum charge.

NATIONAL JEWISH ORGANIZATIONS / 553

———, GRADUATE SCHOOL (formerly INSTITUTE FOR ADVANCED STUDY IN THE HUMANITIES) (1968). 3080 Broadway, NYC 10027. (212)678-8024. Dean Shaye J. D. Cohen. Graduate programs leading to MA, DHL, and PhD degrees in Jewish studies, Bible, Jewish education, history, literature, ancient Judaism, philosophy, rabbinics, and medieval studies; dual degree with Columbia University School of Social Work.

———, JERUSALEM CAMPUS, JTS (1962). PO Box 196, Jerusalem, Israel 91001. (02)-631121. Head of Campus Shamma Friedman. Offers year-in-Israel programs for college and postgraduate students seeking to combine Jewish studies with a community supportive of religious commitment and observance (Midreshet Yerushalayim). Academic and residential center for JTS rabbinical and cantorial students. Provides final year of training for rabbinical students of the Seminario Rabbinico of Argentina.

———, JEWISH MUSEUM (see p. 541)

———, LIBRARY OF THE JEWISH THEOLOGICAL SEMINARY. 3080 BROADWAY, NYC 10027. (212)678-8080. Librarian Mayer E. Rabinowitz. Contains one of the largest collections of Hebraica and Judaica in the world, including manuscripts, incunabula, rare books, and Cairo *Geniza* material. The 260,000-volume collection is housed in a state-of-the-art building and is open to the public.

———, LOUIS FINKELSTEIN INSTITUTE FOR RELIGIOUS AND SOCIAL STUDIES (1938). 3080 Broadway, NYC 10027. (212)678-8815. Dir. Wolfe Kelman. A scholarly and scientific fellowship of clergy and other religious teachers who desire authoritative information regarding some of the basic issues now confronting spiritually minded individuals.

———, MELTON RESEARCH CENTER FOR JEWISH EDUCATION (1960). 3080 Broadway, NYC 10027. (212)678-8031. Dirs. Eduardo Rauch, Barry W. Holtz. Develops new curricula and materials for Jewish education; recruits and prepares educators through seminars and in-service programs; maintains consultant and supervisory relationships with a limited number of pilot schools; sponsors "renewal" retreats for teachers and principals. *Melton Journal.*

———, NATIONAL RAMAH COMMISSION (1951). 3080 Broadway, NYC 10027. (212)678-8881. Pres. Irving Robbin; Dir. Sheldon Dorph. Sponsors 7 overnight Conservative Jewish camps in U.S. and Canada; offers opportunities for qualified college students and older to serve as counselors, administrators, specialists, etc. Offers special programs in U.S. and Israel, including Weinstein National Ramah Staff Training Institute, Ramah Israel Seminar, Ulpan Ramah Plus, and Tichon Ramah Yerushalayim. Summer day camp in Israel for Americans.

———, PROZDOR (1951). 3080 Broadway, NYC 10027. (212)678-8824. Principal Michael Panitz. The high-school department of JTS, it provides a supplementary Jewish education for students who attend a secular (public or private) full-time high school. Classes in classical Jewish studies, with emphasis on Hebrew language, meet twice a week. *Prozdor Pages.*

———, RABBINICAL SCHOOL (1886). 3080 Broadway, NYC 10027. (212)678-8816. Dean Gordon Tucker. Offers a program of graduate and professional studies leading to the degree of Master of Arts and ordination; includes one year of study in Jerusalem and an extensive field-work program.

———, SAUL LIEBERMAN INSTITUTE OF JEWISH RESEARCH (1985). PO Box 196, Jerusalem, Israel 92102. (02)631121. Dir. Shamma Friedman; Dir.-Gen. Shmuel Glick. Engaged in preparing for publication a series of scholarly editions of selected chapters of the Talmud. The following projects support and help disseminate the research: Talmud Text Database; Bibliography of Talmudic literature; Catalogue of Geniza Fragments; Teachers Training and Curriculum Development in Oral Law for Secondary Schools.

———, SCHOCKEN INSTITUTE FOR JEWISH RESEARCH (1961). 6 Balfour St., Jerusalem, Israel, 92102. (02)631288. Dir. Shamma Friedman; Dir.-Genl. Shmuel Glick. Comprises the Schocken collection of rare books and manuscripts and a research institute dedicated to the exploration of Hebrew religious poetry (piyyut). *Schocken Institute Yearbook (P'raqim).*

———, UNIVERSITY OF JUDAISM (1947). 15600 Mulholland Dr., Los Angeles, CA 90077. (213)879-4114. Pres. David L.

Lieber; Sr. V.-Pres. Max Vorspan. West Coast affiliate of JTS. Serves as center of undergraduate and graduate study of Judaica; offers preprofessional and professional programs in Jewish education, nonprofit management, and allied fields, including a prerabbinic program and joint program enabling students to receive BA from UCLA and BHL from U. of J. after four years of undergraduate study. Offers degree programs in Jewish and Western studies as well as a broad range of adult education and Jewish activities. *Direction Magazine; Bulletin of General Information.*

MACHNE ISRAEL, INC. (1940). 770 Eastern Pkwy., Brooklyn, NY 11213. (718)493–9250. Pres. Menachem M. Schneerson (Lubavitcher Rebbe); Dir., Treas. M.A. Hodakov; Sec. Nissan Mindel. The Lubavitcher movement's organ dedicated to the social, spiritual, and material welfare of Jews throughout the world.

MERKOS L'INYONEI CHINUCH, INC. (THE CENTRAL ORGANIZATION FOR JEWISH EDUCATION) (1940). 770 Eastern Pkwy., Brooklyn, NY 11213. (718)493–9250. Pres. Menachem M. Schneerson (Lubavitcher Rebbe); Dir., Treas. M.A. Hodakov; Sec. Nissan Mindel. The educational arm of the Lubavitcher movement. Seeks to promote Jewish education among Jews, regardless of their background, in the spirit of Torah-true Judaism; to establish contact with alienated Jewish youth; to stimulate concern and active interest in Jewish education on all levels; and to promote religious observance as a daily experience among all Jews. Maintains worldwide network of regional offices, schools, summer camps, and Chabad-Lubavitch Houses; publishes Jewish educational literature in numerous languages and monthly journal in five languages. *Conversaciones con la juventud; Conversations avec les jeunes; Schmuessen mit Kinder un Yugent; Sihot la-No-ar; Talks and Tales.*

MESIVTA YESHIVA RABBI CHAIM BERLIN RABBINICAL ACADEMY (1905). 1593 Coney Island Ave., Brooklyn, NY 11230. (718)377–0777. Pres. Sol Eiger; Exec. Dir. Y. Mayer Lasker. Maintains fully accredited elementary and high schools; collegiate and postgraduate school for advanced Jewish studies, both in America and Israel; Camp Morris, a summer study retreat; Prof. Nathan Isaacs Memorial Library; Gur Aryeh Publications.

NATIONAL COMMITTEE FOR FURTHERANCE OF JEWISH EDUCATION (1941). 824 Eastern Pkwy., Brooklyn, NY 11213. (718)735–0200. Pres. J. James Plesser; Natl. Pres. Joseph Fisch; Exec. V.-Pres. Rabbi Jacob J. Hecht. Seeks to disseminate the ideals of Torah-true education among the youth of America; provides education and compassionate care for the poor, sick, and needy in U.S. and Israel; provides aid to Iranian Jewish youth through the Iranian Children's Fund; sponsors Camp Emunah and Camp Emunah Tiny Tots for girls; Camp Shaloh for college youth; Operation Survival, War on Drugs; Hadar HaTorah, Machon Chana, and Ivy League Torah Study Program, seeking to win back college youth and others to Judaism; maintains schools and dormitory facilities, family and vocational counseling services. *Panorama; Passover Handbook; Seder Guide; Cultbusters; Intermarriage; Brimstone & Fire.*

NATIONAL COUNCIL OF YOUNG ISRAEL (1912). 3 W. 16 St., NYC 10011. (212)929–1525. Pres. Ruben Gruenbaum; Exec. V.-Pres. Rabbi Ephraim H. Sturm; Natl. Dir. Isaac Hagler. Maintains a program of spiritual, cultural, social, and communal activity aimed at the advancement and perpetuation of traditional, Torah-true Judaism; seeks to instill in American youth an understanding and appreciation of the ethical and spiritual values of Judaism. Sponsors kosher dining clubs and fraternity houses and an Israel program. *Viewpoint; Hashkafa series; Masorah newspaper.*

———, AMERICAN FRIENDS OF YOUNG ISRAEL SYNAGOGUES IN ISRAEL (1926). 3 W. 16 St., NYC 10011. (212)929–1525. Chmn. Jack Forgash; Cochmn. Michael Krengel. Promotes Young Israel synagogues and youth work in synagogues in Israel.

———, ARMED FORCES BUREAU (1912). 3 W. 16 St., NYC 10011. (212)929–1525. Advises and guides the inductees into the armed forces with regard to Sabbath observance, *kashrut*, and Orthodox behavior. *Guide for the Orthodox Serviceman.*

———, EMPLOYMENT BUREAU (1929). 3 W. 16 St., NYC 10011. (212)929–1525. Project Dir. Fed. Program Rabbi Ephraim H. Sturm; Project Dir. NYC Program Lisa S. Shmidman. Under federal contract in Cleveland and St. Louis and under contract to New York City, operates employment referral service for unemployed people, offering OJT (On-The-Job-Training; no classroom training). Counsels on job-search techniques. Low income limit. Serves all adults, including Sabbath observers. Reimbursement incentives available to employers.

———, INSTITUTE FOR JEWISH STUDIES (1947). 3 W. 16 St., NYC 10011. (212)929-1525. Pres. Ruben Gruenbaum; Exec. V.-Pres. Rabbi Ephraim H. Sturm. Introduces students to Jewish learning and knowledge; helps form adult branch schools; aids Young Israel synagogues in their adult education programs. *Bulletin.*

———, YOUNG ISRAEL COLLEGIATES AND YOUNG ADULTS (1951; reorg. 1982). 3 W. 16 St., NYC 10011. (212)929-1525. Chmn. Kenneth Block; Dir. Richard Stareshefsky. Organizes and operates kosher dining clubs on college and university campuses; provides information and counseling on *kashrut* observance at colleges; gives college-age youth understanding and appreciation of Judaism and information on issues important to Jewish community; arranges seminars and meetings, weekends and trips; operates Achva summer mission to Israel for ages 18–21 and 22–27.

———, YOUNG ISRAEL YOUTH (reorg. 1968). 3 W. 16 St., NYC 10011. (212)929-1525. Dir. Richard Stareshefsky. Fosters a program of spiritual, cultural, social, and communal activities for the advancement and perpetuation of traditional Torah-true Judaism; strives to instill an understanding and appreciation of the high ethical and spiritual values and to demonstrate compatibility of ancient faith of Israel with good Americanism. Operates Achva Summer Mission study program in Israel. *Monthly newsletter.*

NATIONAL JEWISH CENTER FOR LEARNING AND LEADERSHIP (see CLAL)

NATIONAL JEWISH HOSPITALITY COMMITTEE (1973). 201 S. 18 St., Rm. 1519, Philadelphia, PA 19103. (215)546-8293. Pres. Rabbi Allen S. Maller; Exec. Dir. Steven S. Jacobs. Assists persons interested in Judaism—for conversion, intermarriage, or to respond to missionaries. *Special reports.*

NATIONAL JEWISH INFORMATION SERVICE FOR THE PROPAGATION OF JUDAISM, INC. (1960). 3761 Decade St., Las Vegas, NV 89121. (702)454-5872. Pres. Rabbi Moshe M. Maggal; V.-Pres. Lawrence J. Epstein; Sec. and P.R. Dir. Rachel D. Maggal. Seeks to convert non-Jews to Judaism and return Jews to Judaism; maintains College for Jewish Ambassadors for the training of Jewish missionaries, and the Correspondence Academy of Judaism for instruction on Judaism through the mail. *Voice of Judaism.*

NER ISRAEL RABBINICAL COLLEGE (1933). 400 Mt. Wilson Ln., Baltimore, MD 21208. (301)484-7200. Rabbi Yaakov S. Weinberg, Rosh Hayeshiva; V.-Pres. Rabbi Herman N. Neuberger. Trains rabbis and educators for Jewish communities in America and worldwide. Offers bachelor's, master's, and doctoral degrees in talmudic law, as well as teacher's diploma. College has four divisions: Mechina High School, Rabbinical College, Teachers Training Institute, Graduate School. Maintains an active community-service division. Operates special program for Iranian Jewish students. *Ner Israel Update; Alumni Bulletin; Ohr Hanair Talmudic Journal; Iranian B'nei Torah Bulletin.*

OZAR HATORAH, INC. (1946). 1 E. 33 St., NYC 10016. (212)689-3508. Pres. Joseph Shalom; Sec. Sam Sutton. An international educational network which provides religious and secular education for Jewish youth worldwide.

P'EYLIM—AMERICAN YESHIVA STUDENT UNION (1951). 3 W. 16 St., NYC 10011. (212)989-2500. Pres. Jacob Y. Weisberg; Dir. Avraham Hirsch. Aids and sponsors pioneer work by American graduate teachers and rabbis in new villages and towns in Israel; does religious, organizational, and educational work and counseling among new immigrant youth; maintains summer camps for poor immigrant youth in Israel; belongs to worldwide P'eylim movement which has groups in Argentina, Brazil, Canada, England, Belgium, the Netherlands, Switzerland, France, and Israel; engages in relief and educational work among North African immigrants in France and Canada, assisting them to relocate and reestablish a strong Jewish community life. *P'eylim Reporter; News from P'eylim; N'shei P'eylim News.*

RABBINICAL ALLIANCE OF AMERICA (IGUD HARABONIM) (1944). 3 W. 16 St., 4th fl., NYC 10011. (212)242-6420. Pres. Rabbi

Abraham B. Hecht; Menahel Beth Din (Rabbinical Court) Rabbi Herschel Kurzrock. Seeks to promulgate the cause of Torah-true Judaism through an organized rabbinate that is consistently Orthodox; seeks to elevate the position of Orthodox rabbis nationally, and to defend the welfare of Jews the world over. Also has Beth Din Rabbinical Court for Jewish divorces, litigation, marriage counseling and family problems. *Perspective; Nahalim; Torah Message of the Week; Registry.*

RABBINICAL ASSEMBLY (1900). 3080 Broadway, NYC 10027. (212)678–8060. Pres. Rabbi Irwin Groner; Exec. V.-Pres. Rabbi Joel H. Meyers. Seeks to promote Conservative Judaism and to foster the spirit of fellowship and cooperation among rabbis and other Jewish scholars; cooperates with the Jewish Theological Seminary of America and the United Synagogue of America. *Conservative Judaism; Proceedings of the Rabbinical Assembly; Rabbinical Assembly Newsletter.*

RABBINICAL COLLEGE OF TELSHE, INC. (1941). 28400 Euclid Ave., Wickliffe, OH 44092. (216)943–5300. Pres. Rabbi Mordecai Gifter; V.-Pres. Rabbi Abba Zalka Gewirtz. College for higher Jewish learning specializing in Talmudic studies and rabbinics; maintains a preparatory academy including a secular high school, postgraduate department, teacher-training school, and teachers seminary for women. *Pri Etz Chaim; Peer Mordechai; Alumni Bulletin.*

RABBINICAL COUNCIL OF AMERICA, INC. (1923; reorg. 1935). 275 Seventh Ave., NYC 10001. (212)807–7888. Pres. Rabbi Max N. Schreier; Exec. V.-Pres. Rabbi Binyamin Walfish. Promotes Orthodox Judaism in the community; supports institutions for study of Torah; stimulates creation of new traditional agencies. *Hadorom; Record; Sermon Manual; Tradition.*

RECONSTRUCTIONIST RABBINICAL COLLEGE (1968). Church Rd. and Greenwood Ave., Wyncote, PA 19095. (215)576–0800. Bd. Chmn. Samuel Blumenthal; Genl. Chmn. Aaron Ziegelman; Pres. Arthur Green. Coeducational. Trains rabbis for all areas of Jewish communal life: synagogues, academic and educational positions, Hillel centers, federation agencies; confers title of rabbi and grants degrees of Master and Doctor of Hebrew letters. *RRC Report.*

RESEARCH INSTITUTE OF RELIGIOUS JEWRY, INC. (1941; reorg. 1964). 471 W. End Ave., NYC 10024. (212)874–7979. Chmn. Rabbi Oswald Besser; Sec. Marcus Levine. Engages in research and publishes studies concerning the situation of religious Jewry and its problems all over the world.

SHOLEM ALEICHEM FOLK INSTITUTE, INC. (1918). 3301 Bainbridge Ave., Bronx, NY 10467. (212)881–6555. Pres. Burt Levey; Sec. Noah Zingman. Aims to imbue children with Jewish values through teaching Yiddish language and literature, Hebrew and the Bible, Jewish history, the significance of Jewish holidays, folk and choral singing, and facts about Jewish life in America and Israel. *Kinder Journal* (Yiddish).

SOCIETY FOR HUMANISTIC JUDAISM (1969). 28611 W. Twelve Mile Rd., Farmington Hills, MI 48018. (313)478–7610. Pres. Lynne Master; Exec. Dir. Miriam Jerris; Asst. Dir. M. Bonnie Cousens. Serves as a voice for Jews who value their Jewish identity and who seek an alternative to conventional Judaism, who reject supernatural authority and affirm the right of individuals to be the masters of their own lives. Publishes educational and ceremonial materials; organizes congregations and groups. *Humanistic Judaism* (quarterly journal); *Humanorah* (quarterly newsletter).

SOCIETY OF FRIENDS OF THE TOURO SYNAGOGUE, NATIONAL HISTORICAL SHRINE, INC. (1948). 85 Touro St., Newport, RI 02840. (401)847–4794. Pres. Bella G. Werner. Helps maintain Touro Synagogue as a national historic site, as designated by the U.S. Dept. of the Interior in 1946; preserves and publishes its historical material; promotes public awareness of its preeminent role in the tradition of American religious liberty; annually commemorates George Washington's letter of 1790 to the Hebrew Congregation of Newport. *Society of Friends of Touro Synagogue Update.*

SPERTUS COLLEGE OF JUDAICA (1925). 618 S. Michigan Ave., Chicago, IL 60605. (312)922–9012. Pres. Howard A. Sulkin; Bd. Chmn. William Gofen; V.-Pres. for Academic Affairs Byron L. Sherwin. Provides Chicago-area colleges and universities with specialized undergraduate and graduate programs in Judaica and serves as a department of Judaic studies to these colleges and universities; serves as Midwest Jewish information center, through its Asher Library, Spertus Museum of Judaica, Katzin Memorial Rare Book Room, Chicago Jewish Archives, and Rosenbaum Artifact Center. Grants degrees in Jewish education, Jewish studies, and Jewish communal service. Four bachelor's and five master's degree programs. Has community outreach/extension studies program for adults.

SYNAGOGUE COUNCIL OF AMERICA (1926). 327 Lexington Ave., NYC 10016. (212)-686-8670. Pres. Rabbi Joel H. Zaiman; Exec. V.-Pres. Rabbi Henry D. Michelman. Serves as spokesman for, and coordinates policies of, national rabbinical and lay synagogal organizations of Conservative, Orthodox, and Reform branches of American Jewry.

TORAH SCHOOLS FOR ISRAEL—CHINUCH ATZMAI (1953). 40 Exchange Pl., NYC 10005. (212)248-6200. Pres. Abraham Pam; Exec. Dir. Henach Cohen. Conducts information programs for the American Jewish community on activities of the independent Torah schools educational network in Israel; coordinates role of American members of international board of governors; funds special programs of Mercaz Hachinuch Ha-Atzmai B'Eretz Yisroel. *Israel Education Reporter.*

TORAH UMESORAH—NATIONAL SOCIETY FOR HEBREW DAY SCHOOLS (1944). 160 Broadway, NYC 10038. (212)227-1000. Pres. Sheldon Beren; Bd. Chmn. David Singer; Exec. V.-Pres. Rabbi Joshua Fishman. Establishes Hebrew day schools in U.S. and Canada and provides the gamut of services, including placement and curriculum guidance; conducts teacher-training on campuses of major yeshivahs as well as seminars and workshops; publishes textbooks, workbooks, charts, and reading books. Runs Shabbatonim, extracurricular activities. National PTA groups; national and regional teacher conventions. *Olomeinu-Our World; Visions; Parshah Sheets.*

———, INSTITUTE FOR PROFESSIONAL ENRICHMENT (1973). 75 Varick St., Rm. 205, NYC 10013. (212) 941–9044. Dir. Bernard Dov Milians. Provides enriched training and upgraded credentials for administrative, guidance, and classroom personnel of Hebrew day schools and for Torah-community leaders; offers graduate and undergraduate programs in affiliation with accredited universities, which award full degrees: MA in early childhood and elementary education; MS in special education, reading.

———, NATIONAL ASSOCIATION OF HEBREW DAY SCHOOL ADMINISTRATORS (1960). 1114 Ave. J, Brooklyn, NY 11230. (718)258–7767. Pres. David H. Schwartz. Coordinates the work of the fiscal directors of Hebrew day schools throughout the country. *NAHDSA Review.*

———, NATIONAL ASSOCIATION OF HEBREW DAY SCHOOL PARENT-TEACHER ASSOCIATIONS (1948). 160 Broadway, NYC 10038. (212)227-1000. Exec. Sec. Mrs. Samuel Brand. Acts as a clearinghouse and service agency to PTAs of Hebrew day schools; organizes parent-education courses and sets up programs for individual PTAs. *Fundraising with a Flair; Monthly Sidrah Series Program; PTA with a Purpose for the Hebrew Day School.*

———, NATIONAL CONFERENCE OF YESHIVA PRINCIPALS (1956). 160 Broadway, NYC 10038. (212)227-1000. Pres. Rabbi Yitzchok Merkin; Bd. Chmn. Rabbi Baruch Hilsenrath; Exec. V.-Pres. Rabbi A. Moshe Possick. A professional organization of primary and secondary yeshivah day-school principals which seeks to make yeshivah day-school education more effective. *Newsletter; Directory of High Schools.*

———, NATIONAL YESHIVA TEACHERS BOARD OF LICENSE (1953). 160 Broadway, NYC 10038. (212)227-1000. Dir. Rabbi Yitzchok Merkin. Issues licenses to qualified instructors for all grades of the Hebrew day school and the general field of Torah education.

TOURO COLLEGE (1970). 844 Sixth Ave., NYC 10001. (212)575–0190. Pres. Bernard Lander; V.-Pres. Academic Affairs Solomon Simonson; Bd. Chmn. Max Karl. Chartered by NY State Board of Regents as a nonprofit four-year college with business, Judaic studies, health sciences, and liberal arts programs leading to BA, BS, and MA degrees; emphasizes relevance of Jewish heritage to general culture of Western civilization. Also offers JD degree and a biomedical program leading to the MD degree from Technion-Israel Institute of Technology, Haifa.

———, BARRY Z. LEVINE SCHOOL OF HEALTH SCIENCES AND CENTER FOR BIOMEDICAL EDUCATION. (1970) 135 Common Rd., Bldg. #10, Dix Hills, NY 11746. (516)673–3200. Dean Dr. Joseph Weisberg. Along with the Manhattan campus, offers 5 programs: Five-year program leading to MA from Touro and MD from Faculty of Medicine of Technion-Israel Institute of Technology, Haifa; BS/MA—physical therapy and occupational therapy programs; BS—physician assistant and health-information management programs.

———, COLLEGE OF LIBERAL ARTS AND SCIENCES. 844 Sixth Ave., NYC 10001. (212)575–0196. Exec. Dean Stanley Boylan. Offers comprehensive Jewish studies along with studies in the arts, sciences, humanities, and preprofessional studies in health sciences, law, accounting, business, computer science, education, and finance, health sciences, and law.

———, GRADUATE SCHOOL OF JEWISH STUDIES (1981) 844 Sixth Ave., NYC 10001. (212)575–0190. Pres. Bernard Lander; Dean Michael A. Shmidman. Offers courses leading to an MA in Jewish studies, with concentrations in Jewish history or Jewish education. Students may complete part of their program in Israel, through MA courses offered by Touro faculty at Touro's Jerusalem center.

———, INSTITUTE OF JEWISH LAW. Based at Fuchsberg Law Center, serves as a center and clearinghouse for study and teaching of Jewish law. Coedits *Dinei Israel* (Jewish Law Journal) with Tel Aviv University Law School.

———, JACOB D. FUCHSBERG LAW CENTER (1980). Long Island Campus, 300 Nassau Rd., Huntington, NY 11743. (516)421–2244. Dean Howard A. Glickstein. Offers studies leading to JD degree.

———, JEWISH PEOPLE'S UNIVERSITY OF THE AIR. (1979). 844 Sixth Ave., NYC 10001. (212)447–0700. Producer/Dir. Jacob Katzman. Produces and disseminates courses in Jewish subject matter for radio broadcasting and on audio-cassettes.- Printed course outlines for all courses and discussion-leader's guides for some.

———, SCHOOL OF GENERAL STUDIES. 240 E. 123 St., NYC 10021. (212)722–1575. Dean Stephen Adolphus. Offers educational opportunities to minority groups and older people; courses in the arts, sciences, humanities, and special programs of career studies.

———, SHULAMITH SCHOOL. (1929). 1277 E. 14 St., Brooklyn, NY 11230. (718)338-4000. Pres. Sy Knapel; Exec. Dir. Rabbi M. Zwick. Religious Hebrew preschool, elementary, and high school.

UNION OF AMERICAN HEBREW CONGREGATIONS (1873). 838 Fifth Ave., NYC 10021. (212)249–0100. Pres. Rabbi Alexander M. Schindler; Bd. Chmn. Allan B. Goldman. Vice-Pres. Albert Vorspan and Rabbi Daniel B. Syme. Serves as the central congregational body of Reform Judaism in the Western Hemisphere; serves its approximately 815 affiliated temples and membership with religious, educational, cultural, and administrative programs. *Keeping Posted; Reform Judaism.*

———, AMERICAN CONFERENCE OF CANTORS (1956). 1 Kalisa Way, Suite 104, Paramus, NJ 07652. (201)599–0910. Pres. Edward Fogel; Exec. V.-Pres. Raymond Smolover; Admin. Nancy Hausman. Members receive investiture and commissioning as cantors at ordination-investiture ceremonies at recognized seminaries, i.e., Hebrew Union College–Jewish Institute of Religion, Sacred School of Music, or Jewish Theological Seminary, as well as full certification through HUC-JIR-SSM. Through Joint Cantorial Placement Commission, serves Reform congregations seeking cantors and music directors. Dedicated to creative Judaism, preserving the best of the past, and encouraging new and vital approaches to religious ritual, music and ceremonies. *Koleinu.*

———, COMMISSION ON JEWISH EDUCATION OF THE UNION OF AMERICAN HEBREW CONGREGATIONS, CENTRAL CONFERENCE OF AMERICAN RABBIS, AND NATIONAL ASSOCIATION OF TEMPLE EDUCATORS (1923). 838 Fifth Ave., NYC 10021. (212)249–0100. Chmn. Rabbi Jonathan A. Stein; Cochmn. Robert E. Tornberg; Dir. Rabbi Howard I. Bogot. Long-range planning and policy development for congregational programs of lifelong education; network projects with affiliates and associate groups including:

special needs education, Reform Jewish outreach, and Reform Day Schools; activities administered by the UAHC Department for Religious Education.

———, COMMISSION ON SOCIAL ACTION OF REFORM JUDAISM (see p. 536)

———, COMMISSION ON SYNAGOGUE MANAGEMENT (UAHC- CCAR) (1962). 838 Fifth Ave., NYC 10021. (212)249–0100. Chmn. Paul Vanek; Dir. Joseph C. Bernstein. Assists congregations in management, finance, building maintenance, design, construction, and art aspects of synagogues; maintains the Synagogue Architectural Library.

———, NATIONAL ASSOCIATION OF TEMPLE ADMINISTRATORS (NATA) (1941). c/o Reform Congregation Keneseth Israel, York Rd. & Township Line, Elkins Park, PA 19117. (215)887–8700. Pres. William Ferstenfeld. Prepares and disseminates administrative information and procedures to member synagogues of UAHC; provides training of professional synagogue executives; formulates and establishes professional standards for the synagogue executive; provides placement services. *NATA Journal; Temple Management Manual.*

———, NATIONAL ASSOCIATION OF TEMPLE EDUCATORS (NATE) (1955). 707 Summerly Dr., Nashville, TN 37209–4218. (615)352–0322. Pres. Zena W. Sulkes; Exec. Sec. Richard M. Morin. Represents the temple educator within the general body of Reform Judaism; fosters the full-time profession of the temple educator; encourages the growth and development of Jewish religious education consistent with the aims of Reform Judaism; stimulates communal interest in and responsibility for Jewish religious education. *NATE News; Compass.*

———, NATIONAL FEDERATION OF TEMPLE BROTHERHOODS (1923). 838 Fifth Ave., NYC 10021. (212)570–0707. Pres. Richard D. Karfunkle; Exec. Dir. Lewis Eisenberg. Seeks to strengthen Judaism through family programming, by reaching out to college youth, and by promoting adult Jewish education. Through service programs, deals with current concerns of the changing Jewish family. Sponsors the Jewish Chatauqua Society, the brotherhoods' interfaith educational program. *Brotherhood.*

———, NATIONAL FEDERATION OF TEMPLE SISTERHOODS (1913). 838 Fifth Ave., NYC 10021. (212)249–0100. Pres. Judith Hertz; Exec. Dir. Eleanor R. Schwartz. Serves more than 640 sisterhoods of Reform Judaism; promotes interreligious understanding and social justice; awards scholarships and grants to rabbinic students; provides braille and large-type Judaic materials for Jewish blind; supports projects for Israel, Soviet Jewry, and the aging; is an affiliate of UAHC and is the women's agency of Reform Judaism; works in behalf of the Hebrew Union College–Jewish Institute of Religion; cooperates with World Union for Progressive Judaism. *Leaders Line; Notes for Now.*

———, NORTH AMERICAN FEDERATION OF TEMPLE YOUTH (NFTY; formerly NATIONAL FEDERATION OF TEMPLE YOUTH) (1939). 838 Fifth Ave., NYC 10021. (212)249–0100. Dir. Rabbi Ramie Arian; Pres. Roxanne Schneider. Seeks to train Reform Jewish youth in the values of the synagogue and their application to daily life through service to the community and congregation; runs department of summer camps and national leadership training institute; arranges overseas academic tours, work-study programs, international student exchange programs, and college student programs in the U.S. and Israel, including accredited study programs in Israel. *Ani V'Atah; The Jewish Connection.*

UNION OF ORTHODOX JEWISH CONGREGATIONS OF AMERICA (1898). 45 W. 36 St., NYC 10018. (212)563–4000. Pres. Sidney Kwestel; Exec. V.-Pres. Rabbi Pinchas Stolper. Serves as the national central body of Orthodox synagogues; sponsors Institute for Public Affairs; National Conference of Synagogue Youth; LAVE—Learning and Values Experiences; Our Way program for the Jewish deaf; Yachad program for developmentally disabled youth; Israel Center in Jerusalem; *aliyah* department; national OU *kashrut* supervision and certification service; Marriage Commission, Taste of Torah radio program; provides educational, religious, and organizational programs, events, and guidance to synagogues and groups; represents the Orthodox Jewish community in relation to governmental and civic bodies and the general Jewish community. *Jewish Action magazine; OU Kosher Directory; OU*

Passover Directory; OU News Reporter; Synagogue Spotlight; Our Way magazine; Yachad magazine; Luach Limud Torah Diary Home Study Program.

———, NATIONAL CONFERENCE OF SYNAGOGUE YOUTH (1954). 70 W. 36 St., NYC 10018. (212)244-2011. Pres. Alyson Maslansky; Dir. Rabbi Raphael Butler. Central body for youth groups of Orthodox congregations; provides educational guidance, Torah study groups, community service, programs consultation, Torah library, Torah fund scholarships, Ben Zakkai Honor Society, Friends of NCSY; conducts over 300 national and regional events including weeklong seminars, Travel America with NCSY, Israel Summer Seminar for teens and collegiates, and Camp NCSY East Teen Torah Center. Divisions include Senior NCSY in 18 regions and 465 chapters, Junior NCSY for preteens, Our Way for the Jewish deaf, Yachad for the developmentally disabled, Mesorah for Jewish collegiates, Israel Center in Jerusalem, and NCSY in Israel. *Keeping Posted with NCSY; Face the Nation—President's Newsletter; Oreich Yomeinu—Education Newsletter; Mitsvah of the Month.*

———, WOMEN'S BRANCH (1923). 156 Fifth Ave., NYC 10010. (212)929-8857. Pres. Gitti Needleman. Seeks to spread the understanding and practice of Orthodox Judaism and to unite all Orthodox women and their synagogal organizations; services affiliates with educational and programming materials, leadership, and organizational guidance, and has an NGO representative at the UN. Supplies candleabra for Jewish patients in hospitals and nursing homes; supports Stern and Touro College scholarship funds and Jewish braille publications. *Hachodesh; Hakol.*

UNION OF ORTHODOX RABBIS OF THE UNITED STATES AND CANADA (1902). 235 E. Broadway, NYC 10002. (212)964-6337. Dir. Rabbi Hersh M. Ginsberg. Seeks to foster and promote Torah-true Judaism in the U.S. and Canada; assists in the establishment and maintenance of *yeshivot* in the U.S.; maintains committee on marriage and divorce and aids individuals with marital difficulties; disseminates knowledge of traditional Jewish rites and practices and publishes regulations on synagogal structure; maintains rabbinical court for resolving individual and communal conflicts. *HaPardes.*

UNION OF SEPHARDIC CONGREGATIONS, INC. (1929). 8 W. 70 St., NYC 10023. (212)873-0300. Pres. Rev. Dr. Salomon Gaon; Bd. Chmn. Victor Tarry. Promotes the religious interests of Sephardic Jews; prints and distributes Sephardic prayer books; provides religious leaders for Sephardic congregations.

UNITED LUBAVITCHER YESHIVOTH (1940). 841-853 Ocean Pkwy., Brooklyn, NY 11230. (718)859-7600. Pres. Eli N. Sklar; Chmn. Exec. Com. Rabbi S. Gouraty. Supports and organizes Jewish day schools and rabbinical seminaries in the U.S. and abroad.

UNITED SYNAGOGUE OF AMERICA (1913). 155 Fifth Ave., NYC 10010. (212)533-7800. Pres. Alan Tichnor; Exec. V.-Pres./CEO Rabbi Jerome M. Epstein. International organization of 850 Conservative congregations. Maintains 12 departments and 20 regional offices to assist its affiliates with religious, educational, youth, community, and administrative programming and guidance; aims to enhance the cause of Conservative Judaism, further religious observance, encourage establishment of Jewish religious schools, draw youth closer to Jewish tradition. Extensive Israel programs. *United Synagogue Review; Program Suggestions; Yearbook Directory & Buyers' Guide; Book Service Catalogue of Publications.*

———, COMMISSION ON JEWISH EDUCATION (1930). 155 Fifth Ave., NYC 10010. (212)260-8450. Cochmn. Harry S. Katz, Miriam Klein Shapiro; Dir. Rabbi Robert Abramson. Promotes higher educational standards in Conservative congregational schools and Solomon Schechter Day Schools and publishes material for the advancement of their educational programs. Provides guidance and resources for adult-education programs; publishes the *Jewish Tract* series; distributes El-Am edition of Talmud and black-and-white and color films of "Eternal Light" TV programs on Jewish subjects. *Tov L'Horot; Your Child; Kol Bana'yikh.*

———, COMMITTEE ON SOCIAL ACTION AND PUBLIC POLICY (1958). 155 Fifth Ave., NYC 10010. (212)533-7800. Cochmn. Rabbi Zachary Heller, Scott Kaplan; Dir. Robert Blumenthal. Develops and implements positions and programs on issues of social action and public policy for the United Synagogue of America; represents these positions to other Jewish and civic organizations, the media, and government; and provides guidance, both informational and programmatic, to its affiliated congregations in these areas.

———, JEWISH EDUCATORS ASSEMBLY (1951). 15 E. 26 St., NYC 10010. (212)-532-4949. Pres. Rabbi Marim D. Charry; Exec. Dir. Benjamin Margolis. Advances the development of Jewish education on all levels in consonance with the philosophy of the Conservative movement. Promotes Jewish education as a basis for the creative continuity of the Jewish people. Serves as a forum for the exchange of ideas, programs, and educational media. *Bulletins; newsletters.*

———, KADIMA (formerly PRE-USY; reorg. 1968). 155 Fifth Ave., NYC 10010. (212)-533-7800. Exec. Dir. Rabbi Paul Freedman. Involves Jewish preteens in a meaningful religious, educational, and social environment; fosters a sense of identity and commitment to the Jewish community and the Conservative movement; conducts synagogue-based chapter programs and regional Kadima days and weekends. *Mitzvah of the Month; Kadima Kesher; Chagim; Advisors Aid; Games;* quarterly *Kadima* magazine.

———, NATIONAL ASSOCIATION OF SYNAGOGUE ADMINISTRATORS (1948). 155 Fifth Ave., NYC 10010. (212)533-7800. Pres. Thomas Jablonski. Aids congregations affiliated with the United Synagogue of America to further the aims of Conservative Judaism through more effective administration (Program for Assistance by Liaisons to Synagogues—PALS); advances professional standards and promotes new methods in administration; cooperates in United Synagogue placement services and administrative surveys. *NASA Newsletter; NASA Journal.*

———, UNITED SYNAGOGUE YOUTH OF (1951). 155 Fifth Ave., NYC 10010. (212)-533-7800. Pres. David Bianco; Exec. Dir. Rabbi Paul Freedman. Seeks to strengthen identification with Conservative Judaism, based on the personality development, needs, and interests of the adolescent, in a Mitzvah framework. *Achshav; Tikun Olam; A.J. Heschel Honor Society Newsletter; SATO Newsletter; USY Alumni Assn. Newsletter; USY Program Bank; Hamadrich Newsletter for Advisors.*

VAAD MISHMERETH STAM (1976). 4902 16th Ave., Brooklyn, NY 11204. (718) 438-4963. Exec. Dir. Rabbi Yakov Basch. A nonprofit consumer-protection agency dedicated to preserving and protecting the halakhic integrity of Torah scrolls, phylacteries, and *mezuzot.* Makes presentations and conducts examination campaigns in schools and synagogues. *The Jewish Quill.*

WEST COAST TALMUDICAL SEMINARY (Yeshiva Ohr Elchonon Chabad) (1953). 7215 Waring Ave., Los Angeles, CA 90046. (213)937-3763. Dean Rabbi Ezra Schochet. Provides facilities for intensive Torah education as well as Orthodox rabbinical training on the West Coast; conducts an accredited college preparatory high school combined with a full program of Torah-talmudic training and a graduate talmudical division on the college level. *Torah Quiz; Kobetz Migdal Ohr.*

WOMEN'S LEAGUE FOR CONSERVATIVE JUDAISM (1918). 48 E. 74 St., NYC 10021. (212)628-1600. Pres. Evelyn Auerbach; Exec. Dir. Bernice Balter. Constitutes parent body of Conservative (Masorti) women's groups in U.S., Canada, Puerto Rico, Mexico, and Israel; provides them with programs and resources in Jewish education, social action, Israel affairs, Canadian public affairs, leadership training, services to the disabled, community affairs, and publicity techniques; publishes books of Jewish interest; contributes to support of Jewish Theological Seminary of America and its residence halls. *Women's League Outlook; Ba'Olam.*

WORLD COUNCIL OF SYNAGOGUES (1957). 155 Fifth Ave., NYC 10010 (212)533-7693. Pres. Rabbi Zachary Heller; Exec. Dir. Bernard Barsky. International representative of Conservative organizations and congregations; promotes the growth and development of the Conservative movement in Israel and throughout the world; supports educational institutions overseas; holds biennial international conventions; represents the world Conservative movement on the Executive of the World Zionist Organization. *World Spectrum.*

WORLD UNION FOR PROGRESSIVE JUDAISM, LTD. (1926). 838 Fifth Ave., NYC 10021. (212)249-0100. Pres. Donald Day; Exec. Dir. Rabbi Richard G. Hirsch; N. Amer. Dir. Martin Strelzer; Dir. Internatl. Relations & Development Rabbi Clifford Kulwin. International umbrella organization of Liberal Judaism; promotes and coordinates efforts of Liberal congregations throughout the world; starts new congregations, recruits rabbis and rabbinical students for all countries; organizes international conferences of Liberal Jews. *Ammi; Rodnik; Newsupdates.*

YAVNE HEBREW THEOLOGICAL SEMINARY (1924). PO Box 185, Brooklyn, NY 11218. (718)436–5610. Pres. Nathan Shapiro; Exec. Dir. Rabbi Solomon K. Shapiro. School for higher Jewish learning; maintains Machon Maharshal branch in Jerusalem for higher Jewish education and for an exchange student program. *Otzar Hashe'elot Vehateshuvot; Yavne Newsletter.*

YESHIVA UNIVERSITY (1886). 500 W. 185 St., NYC 10033. (212)960–5400. Pres. Norman Lamm; Chmn. Bd. of Trustees Ludwig Jesselson. In its second century, the nation's oldest and largest independent university founded under Jewish auspices, with a broad range of undergraduate, graduate, and professional schools, a network of affiliates, a widespread program of research and community outreach, publications, and a museum. Curricula lead to bachelor's, master's, doctoral, and professional degrees. Undergraduate schools provide general studies curricula supplemented by courses in Jewish learning; graduate schools prepare for careers in medicine, law, social work, Jewish education, psychology, Jewish studies, Semitic languages, literatures, and cultures, and other fields. It has six undergraduate schools, seven graduate and professional schools, and three affiliates, with its four main centers located in Manhattan and the Bronx. *Alumni Review/Inside YU.*

Undergraduate schools for men at Main Center: Yeshiva College (Dean Norman S. Rosenfeld) provides liberal arts and sciences curricula; grants BA degree. Isaac Breuer College of Hebraic Studies (Dean Rabbi Jacob M. Rabinowitz) awards Hebrew teacher's diploma, AA, BA, and BS. James Striar School of General Jewish Studies (Dir. Rabbi Benjamin Yudin) grants AA degree. Yeshiva Program/ Mazer School of Talmudic Studies (Dean Rabbi Zevulun Charlop) offers advanced course of study in talmudic texts and commentaries.

Undergraduate school for women at Midtown Center, 245 Lexington Ave., NYC 10016 (212)340–7700: Stern College for Women (Dean Karen Bacon), includes Teachers Institute for Women; offers liberal arts and sciences curricula supplemented by Jewish studies courses; awards BA, AA, and Hebrew teacher's diploma.

Sy Syms School of Business at Main Center (Dean Michael Schiff) offers undergraduate business curricula in conjunction with study at Yeshiva College or Stern College; grants BS degree.

Sponsors one high school for boys (Manhattan) and one for girls (Queens).

Universitywide programs serving the community and the nation include the Irving and Hanni Rosenbaum Aliyah Incentive Fund; Jacob E. Safra Institute of Sephardic Studies; Ivan L. Tillem Program for Special Services for the Jewish Elderly; Holocaust Studies Program; Interdisciplinary Conference on Bereavement and Grief; Yeshiva University Museum; Yeshiva University Press.

———, ALBERT EINSTEIN COLLEGE OF MEDICINE (1955). Eastchester Rd. & Morris Pk. Ave., Bronx, NY 10461. (212)430–2000. Pres. Norman Lamm; Chmn. Bd. of Overseers Burton P. Resnick; Dean Dr. Dominick P. Purpura. Prepares physicians and conducts research in the health sciences; awards MD degree; includes Sue Golding Graduate Division of Medical Sciences (Dir. Dr. Leslie A. Leinwand), which grants PhD degree. Einstein College's clinical facilities, affiliates, and resources encompass Jack D. Weiler Hospital of Albert Einstein College of Medicine, Bronx Municipal Hospital Center, Montefiore Medical Center, and the Rose F. Kennedy Center for Research in Mental Retardation and Human Development. *Einstein; AECOM Today; Einstein Quarterly Journal of Biology and Medicine.*

———, ALUMNI OFFICE, 500 W. 185 Street, NYC 10033. 212)960–5373. Dir. E. Yechiel Simon. Seeks to foster a close allegiance of alumni to their alma mater by maintaining ties with all alumni and servicing the following associations: Yeshiva College Alumni (Pres. Solomon Shoulson); Stern College for Women Alumnae (Pres. Rachel Oppenheim); Albert Einstein College of Medicine Alumni (Pres. Dr. Arthur Schapiro); Ferkauf Graduate School of Psychology Alumni (Pres. Alvin I. Schiff); Wurzweiler School of Social Work Alumni

(Pres. Ilene Stein Himber); Bernard Revel Graduate School—Harry Fischel School Alumni (Pres. Bernard Rosensweig); Rabbinic Alumni (Pres. Rabbi Myron Rakowitz); Benjamin N. Cardozo School of Law Alumni (Pres. Rhonda Weingarten). Alumni Council (Chmn. Abraham S. Guterman) offers guidance to Pres. and Bd. of Trustees on university's academic development and service activities. *Alumni Review/Inside YU; AECOM Alumni News; Jewish Social Work Forum.*

———, BELFER INSTITUTE FOR ADVANCED BIOMEDICAL STUDIES (1978). Eastchester Rd. & Morris Pk. Ave., Bronx, NY 10461. (212)430–2801. Dir. Dr. Ernst R. Jaffé. Integrates and coordinates the Medical College's postdoctoral research and training-grant programs in the basic and clinical biomedical sciences. Awards certificate as Research Fellow or Research Associate on completion of training.

———, BENJAMIN N. CARDOZO SCHOOL OF LAW (1976). 55 Fifth Ave., NYC 10003. (212)790–0200. Pres. Norman Lamm; Bd. Chmn. Jacob Burns; Dean Monroe E. Price. Provides innovative courses of study within a traditional legal framework; program includes judicial internships; grants Doctor of Law (JD) degree. Programs and services include Bet Tzedek Legal Services Clinic; Jacob Burns Institute for Advanced Legal Studies; Leonard and Bea Diener Institute of Jewish Law; Samuel and Ronnie Heyman Center on Corporate Governance; Howard M. Squadron Program in Communications Law; Center for Professional Development; International Law and Human Rights Program. *Cardozo Studies in Law and Literature; Cardozo Law Review; Arts and Entertainment Law Journal; Women's Annotated Legal Bibliography; International Law Student Association Journal of International Law; Cardozo Law Forum.*

———, BERNARD REVEL GRADUATE SCHOOL (1937). 500 W. 185 St., NYC 10033. (212)960–5253. Dean Leo Landman. Offers graduate programs in Judaic studies and Semitic languages, literatures, and cultures; confers MS, MA, and PhD degrees.

———, BROOKDALE INSTITUTE FOR THE STUDY OF GERONTOLOGY (WURZWEILER SCHOOL OF SOCIAL WORK) (1976). 500 W. 158th St., NYC 10033. (212)960–0820. Dir. Samuel M. Goldstein. Offers an interdisciplinary program for professionals holding master's degrees in such fields as social work, psychology, counseling, nursing, or the clergy; grants post-master's certificate.

———, DAVID J. AZRIELI GRADUATE INSTITUTE OF JEWISH EDUCATION AND ADMINISTRATION (1945). 245 Lexington Ave., NYC 10016. (212)340–7705. Dir. Yitzchak S. Handel. Offers MS degree in Jewish elementary and secondary education; specialist's certificate and EdD in administration and supervision of Jewish education. Block Education Program, initiated under a grant from the Jewish Agency's L.A. Pincus Fund for the Diaspora, provides summer course work to complement year-round field instruction in local communities; grants MS, specialist's certificate and EdD degrees.

———, FERKAUF GRADUATE SCHOOL OF PSYCHOLOGY (1957). 1300 Morris Pk. Ave., NYC 10461. (212)430–4201. Dean Barbara G. Melamed. Offers MA in general psychology; PsyD in clinical and school psychology; and PhD in clinical, school, developmental, and experimental psychology (with a concentration in health psychology). Programs and services include Robert M. Beren Center for Psychological Intervention; Marcus Family Project for the Study of the Disturbed Adolescent; Center for Psychological and Psychoeducational Services.

———, HARRY FISCHEL SCHOOL FOR HIGHER JEWISH STUDIES (1945). 500 W. 185 St., NYC 10033. (212)960–5253. Dean Leo Landman. Offers summer graduate programs in Judaic studies and Semitic languages, literatures, and cultures; confers MS, MA, and PhD degrees.

———, (affiliate) RABBI ISAAC ELCHANAN THEOLOGICAL SEMINARY (1896). 2540 Amsterdam Ave., NYC 10033. (212)960–5344. Chmn. Bd. of Trustees Judah Feinerman; V.-Pres. for Administration & Professional Education Rabbi Robert S. Hirt; Dean Rabbi Zevulun Charlop. Leading school in the Western Hemisphere for preparing Orthodox rabbis; grants *semikhah* (ordination) and the degrees of Master of Religious Education, Master of Hebrew Literature, Doctor of Religious Education, and Doctor of Hebrew Literature.

PHILIP AND SARAH BELZ SCHOOL OF

JEWISH MUSIC (19540. 526 W. 187 St., NYC 10033. (212)960–5353. Dir. Cantor Bernard Beer. Provides professional training of cantors and courses for others with an interest in Jewish liturgical music; offers classes for students of all ages, maintains a specialized library, and conducts outreach; awards associate cantor's certificate and cantorial diploma.

The seminary includes Rabbi Joseph B. Soloveitchik Center of Rabbinic Studies; Morris and Nellie L. Kawaler Rabbinic Training Program; Caroline and Joseph S. Gruss Institute in Jerusalem (Dir. Rabbi Aharon Lichtenstein); Caroline and Joseph S. Gruss Kollel Elyon (Post-Graduate Kollel Program) (Dir. Rabbi Aharon Kahn); Marcos and Adina Katz Kollel (Institute for Advanced Research in Rabbinics) (Dir. Rabbi Hershel Schachter); Kollel L'Horaah (Yadin Yadin) (Dir. Rabbi J. David Bleich); Chaver Program (Dir. Rabbi J. David Bleich). Brookdale Chaplaincy Internship Program trains prospective rabbis to work effectively with the elderly. Maybaum Sephardic Fellowship Program trains rabbis for service in Sephardic communities here and abroad. Gindi Program for the Enhancement of Professional Rabbinics serves rabbis "in the field" throughout North America with support services, conferences, and counseling. The service arm of the Seminary, Max Stern Division of Communal Services (Dir. Rabbi Robert S. Hirt), provides personal and professional service to the rabbinate and related fields, as well as educational, consultative, organizational, and placement services to congregations, schools, and communal organizations around the world.

Other Seminary programs are the Stone-Sapirstein Center for Jewish Education, identifying and training future educators through programs of learning, service, and internship; National Commission on Torah Education, a lay group concerned with Torah education in all of its ramifications; Sephardic Community Activities Programs, enriching Sephardic communal life by focusing on the spiritual, educational, and cultural aspects of this distinctive heritage; Dr. Joseph and Rachel Ades Sephardic Community Outreach Program, administering youth retreats as well as lecture and outreach programs to strengthen Sephardic life. Camp Morasha (Dir. Zvi Reich) offers Jewish studies program.

———, WOMEN'S ORGANIZATION (1928). 500 W. 185 St., NYC 10033. (212)960–0855. Natl. Presidium: Judy Kirshenbaum, Inge Rennert, Alice Turobiner; Dir. Joy Malka. Supports Yeshiva University's national scholarship program for students training in education, community service, law, medicine, and other professions, and its development program. *YUWO News Briefs.*

———, WURZWEILER SCHOOL OF SOCIAL WORK (1957). 500 W. 185 St., NYC 10033. (212)960–0800. Pres. Norman Lamm; Chmn. Bd. of Govs. Herbert H. Schiff; Dean Samuel M. Goldstein. Offers graduate programs in social group work, social casework, community social work; grants MSW and DSW degrees and post-master's certificate in gerontology through the Brookdale Institute for the Study of Gerontology; two-year, full-time Concurrent Plan combines classroom study and supervised field instruction; Extended Plan permits some MSW candidates up to five years to complete requirements; Accelerated Plan grants MSW in 14 months to qualified students; Plan for Employed Persons is designed for those working in social agencies; Block Education Plan (Dir. Frances A. Sosnoff) designed for students living outside New York, provides field instruction in agencies in the U.S., Canada, Israel, and Europe; Clergy Plan provides training in counseling for clergy of all denominations. Part-Time Professional Education Plan enables human services professionals and others to take up to 12 credits as nondegree students, with credits applied to the MSW if students later matriculate. *Jewish Social Work Forum.*

———, (affiliate) YESHIVA UNIVERSITY OF LOS ANGELES (1977). 9760 W. Pico Blvd., Los Angeles, CA 90035. (213)553–4478. Dean Rabbi Marvin Hier; Bd. Chmn. Samuel Belzberg; Dir. Academic Programs Rabbi Sholom Tendler. Grants BA degree in Jewish studies. Has university program and graduate studies department. Also provides Jewish studies program for beginners. Affiliates are high schools, Jewish Studies Institute for Adult Education, and Simon Wiesenthal Center.

SIMON WIESENTHAL CENTER (1977). 9760 W. Pico Blvd., Los Angeles, CA 90035. (213)553–9036. Dean Rabbi Marvin Hier; Assoc. Dean Rabbi Abraham Cooper; Dir. Gerald Margolis. Branch

Offices: 320 N. Michigan Ave., Suite 1005, Chicago, IL 60601, (312)704-0027; 342 Madison Ave., Suite #320, NYC, 10017 (212)370-0320. Dedicated to preserving the memory of the Holocaust through education and awareness. Programs: museum; library; archives; "Testimony for the Truth" oral history; educational outreach; Scholars' Forum; International Social Action. *Simon Wiesenthal Center Annual; Response Magazine; Page One* (syndicated weekly radio news magazine presenting contemporary Jewish issues).

YESHIVATH TORAH VODAATH AND MESIVTA RABBINICAL SEMINARY (1918). 425 E. 9 St., Brooklyn, NY 11218. (718)- 941-8000. Bd. Chmn. Chaim Leshkowitz. Offers Hebrew and secular education from elementary level through rabbinical ordination and postgraduate work; maintains a teachers institute and community-service bureau; maintains a dormitory and a nonprofit camp program for boys. *Chronicle; Mesivta Vanguard; Thought of the Week; Torah Vodaath News.*

———, ALUMNI ASSOCIATION (1941). 425 E. 9 St., Brooklyn, NY 11218. (718)941- 8000. Pres. Marcus Saffer; Bd. Chmn. Seymour Pluchenik. Promotes social and cultural ties between the alumni and the schools through fund raising; offers vocational guidance to students; operates Camp Torah Vodaath; sponsors research fellowship program for boys. *Annual Journal; Hamesivta Torah periodical.*

SOCIAL, MUTUAL BENEFIT

ALPHA EPSILON FRATERNITY(1913). 8815 Wesleyan Rd., Indianapolis, IN 46268- 1185. (317)876-1913. Natl. Pres. Stanford Odesky; Exec. V.-Pres. Sidney N. Dunn. International Jewish fraternity active on over 100 campuses in the U.S. and Canada; encourages Jewish students to remain loyal to their heritage and to assume leadership roles in the community; active in behalf of Soviet Jewry, the State of Israel, and other Jewish causes. *The Lion of Alpha Epsilon Pi* (quarterly magazine).

AMERICAN FEDERATION OF JEWS FROM CENTRAL EUROPE, INC. (1938). 570 Seventh Ave., NYC 10018. (212)921-3871. Pres. K. Peter Lekisch; Bd. Chmn. Curt C. Silberman; Exec. Asst. Katherine Rosenthal. Seeks to safeguard the rights and interests of American Jews of Central European descent, especially in reference to restitution and indemnification; through its Research Foundation for Jewish Immigration sponsors research and publications on the history, immigration, and acculturation of Central European Jewry in the U.S.; sponsors social programs for needy Nazi victims in the U.S.; undertakes cultural activities, annual conferences, publications, and lecture programs; member, Council of Jews from Germany.

AMERICAN SEPHARDI FEDERATION (1973). 515 Park Ave., #515, NYC 10022. (212)- 308-3455. Pres. Leon Levy; Exec. V.- Pres. Hal M. Lewis. Central umbrella organization for all Sephardic congregations, organizations, and agencies. Seeks to preserve and promote Sephardic culture, education, and traditions. Disseminates resource material on all aspects of Sephardic life. Strives to bring a Sephardic agenda and perspective to American Jewish life. *Sephardic Highlights.*

AMERICAN VETERANS OF ISRAEL (1949). c/o Samuel E. Alexander, 548 E. Walnut St., Long Beach, NY 11561. (516)431- 8316. Pres. Lola Sprinzeles; Sec. Samuel E. Alexander. Maintains contact with American and Canadian volunteers who served in Aliyah Bet and/or Israel's War of Independence; promotes Israel's welfare; holds memorial services at grave of Col. David Marcus; is affiliated with World Mahal. *Newsletter.*

ASSOCIATION OF YUGOSLAV JEWS IN THE UNITED STATES, INC. (1941). 130 E. 59 St., Suite 1202, NYC 10022. (212)371- 6891. Pres. Mary Levine; Exec. Off. Emanuel Salom; Treas./V.-Pres. Mirko Goldschmidt. Assists all Jews originally from Yugoslavia; raises funds for Israeli agencies and institutions. *Bulletin.*

BNAI ZION—THE AMERICAN FRATERNAL ZIONIST ORGANIZATION (1908). 136 E. 39 St., NYC 10016. (212)725-1211. Pres. Werner Buckold; Exec. V.-Pres. Mel Parness. Fosters principles of Americanism, fraternalism, and Zionism; offers life insurance and other benefits to its members. Sponsors various projects in Israel: settlements, youth centers, medical clinics, Bnai Zion Home for Retarded Children (in Rosh Ha'ayin), B'nai Zion Medical Center (in Haifa), and the Herman Z. Quittman Center in Ha'kfar Hashwedi in Jerusalem. Has Young Leadership Division. *Bnai*

Zion Voice; Bnai Zion Foundation Newsletter; The Challenge; Haifa Happenings.

BRITH ABRAHAM (1859; reorg. 1887). 136 E. 39 St., NYC 10016. (212)725–1211. Grand Master Robert Freeman. Protects Jewish rights and combats anti-Semitism; supports Soviet and Ethiopian emigration and the safety and dignity of Jews worldwide; furnishes regular financial assistance to Bnai Zion in Haifa, Haifa Medical Center, and other institutions to relieve the social burdens on the Israeli economy; aids and supports various programs and projects in the U.S.: Hebrew Excellence Program—Gold Medal presentation in high schools and colleges; Camp Loyaltown; Brith Abraham and Bnai Zion Foundations. *Voice.*

BRITH SHOLOM (1905). 3939 Conshohocken Ave., Philadelphia, PA 19131. (215)878–5696. Pres. Harold Sklar; Exec. Dir. Mervin L. Krimins. Fraternal organization devoted to community welfare, protection of rights of Jewish people, and activities which foster Jewish identity and provide support for Israel; sponsors Brith Sholom House for senior citizens in Philadelphia and Brith Sholom Beit Halochem in Haifa, a rehabilitation center for Israel's permanently war-wounded. *Brith Sholom Presents; monthly news bulletin.*

CENTRAL SEPHARDIC JEWISH COMMUNITY OF AMERICA (1941). 8 W. 70 St., NYC 10023. (212)787–2850. Pres. Emilie Levy; Treas. Victor Tarry. Pres. Women's Div. Irma Cardozo; Treas. Laura Capelluto. Promotes Sephardic culture by awarding scholarships to qualified needy students in New York and Israel; raises funds for hospital and religious institutions in U.S. and Israel. *Annual journal.*

FREE SONS OF ISRAEL (1849). 180 Varick St., 14th fl., NYC 10014. (212)924–6566. Grand Master Robert Grant; Grand Sec. Stanley Siflinger. The oldest Jewish fraternal order in the U.S.; helps Israel through UJA and Israel Bonds; subsidizes old-age-homes, hospitals, camps, and other institutions for handicapped, underprivileged, and disabled children and adults. Maintains scholarship fund for members and children of members, insurance fund, and credit union. *Free Sons Reporter.*

JEWISH LABOR BUND (Directed by WORLD COORDINATING COMMITTEE OF THE BUND) (1897; reorg. 1947). 25 E. 21 St., NYC 10010. (212)475–0059. Exec. Sec. Joel Litewka. Coordinates activities of Bund organizations throughout the world and represents them in the Socialist International; spreads the ideas of socialism as formulated by the Jewish Labor Bund; publishes books and periodicals on world problems, Jewish life, socialist theory and policy, and on the history, activities, and ideology of the Jewish Labor Bund. *Unser Tsait* (U.S.); *Lebns-Fragn* (Israel); *Unser Gedank* (Australia); *Unser Shtimme* (France).

SEPHARDIC JEWISH BROTHERHOOD OF AMERICA, INC. (1915). 97–29 64th Rd., Rego Park, NY 11374. (718)459–1600. Pres. Bernard Ouziel; Sec. Michael Cohen. A benevolent fraternal organization seeking to further social, religious, and cultural goals of its members; offers funeral and burial benefits to members, scholarships, and aid to the needy. *Sephardic Brother.*

UNITED ORDER TRUE SISTERS, INC. (UOTS) (1846). 212 Fifth Ave., NYC 10010. (212)679–6790. Pres. Laurette Blumenkrantz; Exec. Admin. Dorothy B. Giuriceo. Philanthropic, community service, especially for indigent cancer victims; supports camps for children with cancer. *Echo.*

WORKMEN'S CIRCLE (1900). 45 E. 33 St., NYC 10016. (212)889–6800. Pres. Harold Ostroff; Exec. Dir. Robert A. Kaplan. Provides fraternal benefits and activities, Jewish educational programs, secularist Yiddish schools, and summer camps; promotes public-affairs activities in the U.S. on international and national issues. Underwrites "Folksbiene" theater; sponsors Yiddish cultural, music, and theatrical festivals in U.S. and Canada. Allied to *Jewish Forward* and WEVD. *Workmen's Circle Call; Kultur un Leben.*

SOCIAL WELFARE

AMC CANCER RESEARCH CENTER (formerly JEWISH CONSUMPTIVES' RELIEF SOCIETY, 1904; incorporated as AMERICAN MEDICAL CENTER AT DENVER, 1954). 1600 Pierce St., Denver, CO 80214. (303)233–6501. Dir. Dr. Joseph Cullen; Pres./CEO Bob R. Baker. A nationally recognized leader in the fight against cancer; employs a three-pronged, interdisciplinary approach that combines laboratory, clinical, and community cancer-control research to advance the prevention, early detection, diagnosis, and treatment of the disease. *Quarterly bulletin; annual report.*

AMERICAN JEWISH CORRECTIONAL CHAPLAINS ASSOCIATION, INC. (formerly NATIONAL COUNCIL OF JEWISH PRISON CHAPLAINS) (1937). 10 E. 73 St., NYC 10021–4194. (212)879–8415. (Cooperates with the New York Board of Rabbis and Jewish Family Service.) Pres. Rabbi Irving Koslowe; Exec. Off. Rabbi Moses A. Birnbaum. Supports spiritual, moral, and social services for Jewish men and women in corrections; stimulates support of correctional chaplaincy; provides spiritual and professional fellowship for Jewish correctional chaplains; promotes sound standards for correctional chaplaincy; schedules workshops and research to aid chaplains in counseling and with religious services for Jewish inmates. Constituent, American Correctional Chaplains Association. *Chaplains Manual.*

AMERICAN JEWISH SOCIETY FOR SERVICE, INC. (1949). 15 E. 26 St., Rm. 1304, NYC 10010. (212)683–6178. Pres. Arthur Lifson; Exec. Dir. Elly Saltzman. Conducts voluntary work-service camps each summer to enable high school juniors and seniors to perform humanitarian service.

ASSOCIATION OF JEWISH COMMUNITY ORGANIZATION PERSONNEL (1969). c/o Jewish Community Federation of Cleveland, 1750 Euclid Ave., Cleveland, OH 44115. (216)566–9200. Pres. Alan Gill; Exec. Dir. Howard Berger. An organization of professionals engaged in areas of fund raising, endowments, budgeting, social planning, financing, administration and coordination of services. Objectives are to develop and enhance professional practices in Jewish communal work; to maintain and improve standards, practices, scope and public understanding of the field of community organization, as practiced through local federations, national agencies, other organizations, settings, and private practitioners. *ProLog newsletter.*

ASSOCIATION OF JEWISH FAMILY AND CHILDREN'S AGENCIES (1972). 3084 State Hwy. 27, Suite 1—PO Box 248, Kendall Park, NJ 08824–0248. (201)821–0909; (800)634–7346. Pres. John L. Goldman; Exec. Dir. Bert J. Goldberg. The national service organization for Jewish family and children's agencies in Canada and the U.S. Reinforces member agencies in their efforts to sustain and enhance the quality of Jewish family and communal life. Operates the Elder Support Network for the National Jewish Community. *Bulletin* (bimonthly); *Directory; Professional Opportunities Bulletin.*

ASSOCIATION OF JEWISH FAMILY AND CHILDREN'S AGENCY PROFESSIONALS (1965). 730 Broadway, NYC 10003–9543. (212)704–9275. Pres. Melvin Cohen. Brings together Jewish caseworkers and related professionals in Jewish family, children's, and health services. Seeks to improve personnel standards, further Jewish continuity and identity, and strengthen Jewish family life; provides forums for professional discussion at national conference of Jewish communal service and regional meetings; takes action on social-policy issues. *Newsletter.*

BARON DE HIRSCH FUND (1891). 130 E. 59 St., NYC 10022. (212)836–1358. Pres. Francis F. Rosenbaum, Jr.; Mng. Dir. Lauren Katzowitz. Aids Jewish immigrants and their children in the U.S. and Israel by giving grants to agencies active in educational and vocational fields; has limited program for study tours in U.S. by Israeli agriculturists.

B'NAI B'RITH INTERNATIONAL (1843). 1640 Rhode Island Ave., NW, Washington, DC 20036. (202)857–6600. Pres. Seymour D. Reich; Exec. V.-Pres. Thomas Neumann. International Jewish organization with affiliates in 43 countries. Offers programs designed to insure the preservation of Jewry and Judaism: Jewish education, community volunteer service to aid the needy, expansion of human rights, assistance to Israel, housing for the elderly, leadership training for youths and adults, rights of Soviet Jews and Jews of other countries to emigrate. *International Jewish Monthly; Shofar; Insider.*

———, ANTI-DEFAMATION LEAGUE OF (*see* p. 536)

———, CAREER AND COUNSELING SERVICES (1938). 1640 Rhode Island Ave., NW, Washington, DC 20036. (202)857–4992; (1–800)321–1026 (for appointments information). Chmn. Kenneth L. Bloom; Natl. Dir. Max F. Baer. Offers educational and career testing/counseling to Jewish youth and adults on a group and individual basis in New York, North Jersey, and Greater Philadelphia.

———, HILLEL FOUNDATIONS, INC. (see p. 547)

———, KLUTZNICK MUSEUM (see p. 540)

———, YOUTH ORGANIZATION (see p. 548)

B'NAI B'RITH WOMEN (1897). 1640 Rhode Island Ave., NW, Washington, DC 20036. (202)857–1300. Pres. Hyla S. Lipsky; Exec. Dir. Elaine K. Binder. Promotes social advancement through education, service, and action. Offers programs that contribute to preservation of Jewish life and values; supports treatment of emotionally disturbed boys in BBW Residential Treatment Centers in Israel; advocates for Israel and for family issues. *Women's World.*

CITY OF HOPE NATIONAL MEDICAL CENTER AND BECKMAN RESEARCH INSTITUTE (1913). 1500 E. Duarte Rd., Duarte, CA 91010. (818)359–8111. Pres. and Chief Exec. Off. Dr. Sanford M. Shapero; Bd. Chmn. Richard Fiman. Offers care to those with cancer and major diseases, medical consultation service for second opinions, and pilot research programs in genetics, immunology, and the basic life process. *From the Top, City of Hope Cancer Center Report.*

CONFERENCE OF JEWISH COMMUNAL SERVICE (1899). 3084 State Hwy. 27, Suite 1, Kendall Park, NJ 08824–1657. (201)821–1871. Pres. Daniel Thursz; Exec. Dir. Joel Ollander. Serves as forum for all professional philosophies in community service, for testing new experiences, proposing new ideas, and questioning or reaffirming old concepts; umbrella organization for seven major Jewish communal service groups. Concerned with advancement of professional personnel practices and standards. *Concurrents; Journal of Jewish Communal Service.*

COUNCIL OF JEWISH FEDERATIONS, INC. (1932). 730 Broadway, NYC 10003. (212)-475–5000. Pres. Mandell Berman; Exec. V.-Pres. Martin Kraar. Provides national and regional services to more than 200 associated federations embracing 800 communities in the U.S. and Canada, aiding in fund raising, community organization, health and welfare planning, personnel recruitment, and public relations. *Directory of Jewish Federations, Welfare Funds and Community Councils; Directory of Jewish Health and Welfare Agencies* (biennial); *What's New in Federations; Newsbriefs; annual report.*

HOPE CENTER FOR THE DEVELOPMENTALLY DISABLED (1965). 3601 Martin L. King Blvd., Denver, CO 80205. (303)388–4801. Bd. Chmn. Albert Cohen; Exec. Dir. George E. Brantley; Sec. Helen Fonda. Provides services to developmentally disabled of community: preschool training, day training and work activities center, speech and language pathology, occupational arts and crafts, recreational therapy, and social services.

INTERNATIONAL COUNCIL ON JEWISH SOCIAL AND WELFARE SERVICES (1961). c/o American Jewish Joint Distribution Committee, 711 Third Ave., NYC 10017. (NY liaison office with UN headquarters.) (212)687–6200. Chmn. David Cope-Thompson; Exec. Sec. Cheryl Mariner. Provides for exchange of views and information among member agencies on problems of Jewish social and welfare services, including medical care, old age, welfare, child care, rehabilitation, technical assistance, vocational training, agricultural and other resettlement, economic assistance, refugees, migration, integration and related problems, representation of views to governments and international organizations. Members: six national and international organizations.

JEWISH BRAILLE INSTITUTE OF AMERICA, INC. (1931). 110 E. 30 St., NYC 10016. (212)889–2525. Pres. Jane Evans; Exec. V.-Pres. Gerald M. Kass. Provides Judaic materials in braille, talking books, and large print for blind, visually impaired, and reading-disabled adults and children; special services for the blind and visually impaired of Israel, including low-vision clinic, sound-studio facilities, libraries, and special funding for seminars for the advancement of the blind; counseling for clients, their families, and others who work on their behalf, such as communal workers and educators. *Jewish Braille Review; JBI Voice; Likkutim.*

JEWISH CONCILIATION BOARD OF AMERICA, INC. (A DIVISION OF THE JEWISH BOARD OF FAMILY AND CHILDREN'S SERVICES (1920). 235 Park Ave. S., NYC 10003. (212)460–0900. Cochmn. Milton J. Schubin and Ruth Daniel; Dir. Betty E. Sinowitz. Offers dispute-resolution services to families, individuals, and organizations. Social-work, rabbinic, and legal expertise are available for family and divorce mediation and arbitration. Fee—sliding scale.

JEWISH FUND FOR JUSTICE (1984). 920 Broadway, Suite 605, NYC 10010. (212)-677-7080. Bd. Chmn. Lawrence S. Levine; Exec. Dir. Marlene Provizer. A national grant-making foundation supporting efforts to combat the root causes of poverty in the U.S. Provides diverse opportunities to individual, family, and synagogue involvement through memorial, youth endowment, and synagogue challenge funds; works cooperatively with other denominational funders and philanthropies promoting social and economic justice. *Newsletter; Five-Year Report.*

JWB (1917). 15 E. 26 St., NYC 10010–1579. (212)532–4949. Pres. Donald R. Mintz; Exec. V.-Pres. Arthur Rotman. Central leadership agency for 275 Jewish community centers, YM-YWHAs, and camps in the U.S. and Canada, serving over one million Jews. Provides informal Jewish educational and cultural experiences through JWB Jewish Book and Music Councils and Lecture Bureau and many projects related to Israel. U.S. government-accredited agency for the religious, Jewish educational, and recreational needs of Jewish military personnel, their families and hospitalized VA patients through JWB Jewish Chaplains Council. *JWB Circle; JWBriefing; Zarkor; JWB Personnel Reporter.*

———, JEWISH BOOK COUNCIL (see p. 542)

———, JEWISH CHAPLAINS COUNCIL (formerly COMMISSION ON JEWISH CHAPLAINCY) (1940). 15 E. 26 St., NYC 10010–1579. Chmn. Rabbi Aaron Landes; Dir. Rabbi David Lapp. Recruits, endorses, and serves Jewish military and Veterans Administration chaplains on behalf of the American Jewish community and the major rabbinic bodies; trains and assists Jewish lay leaders where there are no chaplains, for service to Jewish military personnel, their families, and hospitalized veterans. *CHAPLINES newsletter.*

———, JEWISH MUSIC COUNCIL (see p. 542)

———, LECTURE BUREAU (see p. 542)

LEVI HOSPITAL (sponsored by B'nai B'rith) (1914). 300 Prospect Ave., Hot Springs, AR 71901. (501)624–1281. Pres. Steven Kirsch; CEO Patrick G. McCabe, Jr. Maintains a nonprofit, nonsectarian hospital for treatment of arthritis patients; rehabilitation for stroke, arthritis, and joint replacement patients; a mental health/psychiatric unit; a work hardening center; and a hospice program. *Levi Hospital Progress Chart.*

NATIONAL ASSOCIATION OF JEWISH FAMILY, CHILDREN'S AND HEALTH PROFESSIONALS (see Association of Jewish Family and Children's Agency Professionals)

NATIONAL ASSOCIATION OF JEWISH VOCATIONAL SERVICES (formerly JEWISH OCCUPATIONAL COUNCIL) (1939). 160 Lexington Ave., New York, NY 10016. (212) 779–2612. Pres. Pat P. Fine; Exec. Dir. Richard M. Africk. Acts as coordinating body for all Jewish agencies in U.S., Canada, and Israel, having programs in educational-vocational guidance, job placement, vocational rehabilitation, skills-training, sheltered workshops, and occupational research. *Newsletter; NAJVS Reports.*

NATIONAL CONGRESS OF JEWISH DEAF (1956; inc. 1961). 4960 Sabal Palm Blvd., Bldg. 7, Apt. 207, Tamarac, FL 33319. TTY (305)977–7887. Pres. Dr. Martin Florsheim; Exec. Dir. Alexander Fleischman. Congress of Jewish congregations, service organizations, and associations located throughout the U.S. and Canada, advocating religious spirit and cultural ideals and fellowship for the Jewish deaf. Affiliated with World Organization of Jewish Deaf. Publishes *Signs of Judaism,* a guide to sign language of Judaism. *NCJD Quarterly; Jewish Deaf Trivia.*

NATIONAL COUNCIL OF JEWISH PRISON CHAPLAINS, INC. (see American Jewish Correctional Chaplains Association, Inc.)

NATIONAL COUNCIL OF JEWISH WOMEN (1893). 53 W. 23 St., NYC 10010. (212)-645–4048. Pres. Lenore Feldman; Exec. Dir. Dadie Perlov. Furthers human welfare through program of community service, education, advocacy for children and youth, aging, women's issues, constitutional rights, Jewish life and Israel. Promotes education for the disadvantaged in Israel through the NCJW Research Institute for Innovation in Education at Hebrew University, Jerusalem. Promotes welfare of children in U.S. through Center for the Child. *NCJW Journal; Washington Newsletter.*

NATIONAL INSTITUTE FOR JEWISH HOSPICE (1985). 8723 Alden Drive, ASB/1 Bldg., Suite 652, Los Angeles, CA 90048. (213) HOSPICE. Pres. Rabbi Maurice Lamm; Exec. Dir. LaWana Skaggs-McMaster. Serves as a national Jewish hospice resource center. Through conferences, research, publications, video training courses, referral, and counseling services offers guidance, training, and information to patients, family members, clergy of all faiths, professional caregivers, and volunteers who work with seriously ill Jews. *Jewish Hospice Times.*

NATIONAL JEWISH CENTER FOR IMMUNOLOGY AND RESPIRATORY MEDICINE (formerly NATIONAL JEWISH HOSPITAL/NATIONAL ASTHMA CENTER) (1899). 1400 Jackson St., Denver, CO 80206. (303)388-4461; (1-800)222-LUNG (for information). Pres. Michael Schonbrun; Chmn. Bd. Dirs. Edward Robinson. Nonprofit and nonsectarian world-renowned specialty care facility focusing on chronic lung and immune-system disorders, engaged in research, education, and patient care. *New Direction* (quarterly); *Lung Line Letter* (quarterly); *Medical Scientific Update; annual report.*

NATIONAL JEWISH COMMITTEE ON SCOUTING (Boy Scouts of America) (1926). 1325 Walnut Hill La., Irving, TX 75015-2079. (214)580-2059. Chmn. Robert G. Kurzman; Dir. Fred Tichauer. Assists Jewish institutions in meeting their needs and concerns through use of the resources of scouting. Works through local Jewish committees on Scouting to establish Tiger Cub groups (1st grade), Cub Scout packs, Boy Scout troops, and coed Explorer posts in synagogues, Jewish community centers, day schools, and other Jewish organizations wishing to draw Jewish youth. Support materials and resources on request. *Hatzofe* (quarterly).

NATIONAL JEWISH GIRL SCOUT COMMITTEE (1972). Synagogue Council of America, 327 Lexington Ave., NYC 10016. (212)686-8670. Chmn. Rabbi Herbert W. Bomzer; Field Chmn. Adele Wasko. Under the auspices of the Synagogue Council of America, serves to further Jewish education by promoting Jewish award programs, encouraging religious services, promoting cultural exchanges with the Israel Boy & Girl Scouts Federation, and extending membership in the Jewish community by assisting councils in organizing Girl Scout troops and local Jewish Girl Scout committees. *Newsletter.*

NORTH AMERICAN ASSOCIATION OF JEWISH HOMES AND HOUSING FOR THE AGING (1960). 2525 Centerville Rd., Dallas, TX 75228. (214)327-4503. Pres.Mary Ellen Lavery; Exec. V.-Pres. Herbert Shore. Represents a community of not-for-profit charitable homes and housing for the Jewish aging; promotes excellence in performance and quality of service through fostering communication and education and encouraging advocacy for the aging. *Perspectives* (newsletter); *Directory.*

WORLD CONFEDERATION OF JEWISH COMMUNITY CENTERS (1947). Litt. Bldg., 12 Hess St., Jerusalem, Israel 94185. (02)-221265. Pres. Ralph Goldman; Exec. Dir. Don Scher. Composed of national center movements in Europe, Israel, Latin America, and North America; seeks to strengthen cooperation among center associations and individual centers; provides programs to enhance Jewish educational opportunities for lay leaders of centers and professional staffs. *Bamerkaz.*

ZIONIST AND PRO-ISRAEL

ALYN—AMERICAN SOCIETY FOR HANDICAPPED CHILDREN IN ISRAEL (1934). 19 W. 44 St., NYC 10036. (212)869-8085. Chmn. Simone P. Blum; Exec. Dir. Joan R. Mendelson. Supports the work of ALYN Orthopaedic Hospital and Rehabilitation Center for Physically Handicapped Children, located in Jerusalem.

AMERICA-ISRAEL CULTURAL FOUNDATION, INC. (1939). 41 E. 42 St., Suite 608, NYC 10017. (212)557-1600. Bd. Chmn. Isaac Stern; Pres. Carl Glick; Acting Exec. Dir. Stanley Grayson. Raises funds to encourage the growth of culture in Israel through support of the arts; provides scholarships to gifted students and professionals in all the arts—music, dance, theater, the visual and plastic arts, film, and television. *Hadashot.*

AMERICA-ISRAEL FRIENDSHIP LEAGUE, INC. (1971). 134 E. 39 St., NYC 10016. (212)213-8630. Pres. Herbert Tenzer; Exec. V.-Pres. Ilana Artman. A nonsectarian, nonpartisan organization which seeks to broaden the base of support for Israel among Americans of all faiths and backgrounds. Activities include educational exchanges, tours of Israel for American leadership groups, symposia and public education activities, and the dissemination of printed information. *Newsletter.*

AMERICAN ASSOCIATES, BEN-GURION UNIVERSITY OF THE NEGEV (1973). 342 Madison Ave., Suite 1924, NYC 10173. (212)687–7721. Pres. Michael W. Sonnenfeldt; Bd. Chmn. Irwin H. Goldenberg; Chancellor Ambassador Yosef Tekoah. Serves as the university's publicity and fund-raising link to the U.S. The Associates are committed to publicizing university activities and curricula, securing student scholarships, transferring contributions, and encouraging American interest in the university. *AABGU Reporter; BGU Bulletin; Negev; Overseas Study Program Catalog.*

AMERICAN COMMITTEE FOR SHAARE ZEDEK HOSPITAL IN JERUSALEM, INC. (1949). 49 W. 45 St., Suite 1100, NYC 10036. (212)354–8801. Pres. Charles Bendheim; Bd. Chmn. Ludwig Jesselson; Sr. Exec. V.-Pres. Morris Talansky. Raises funds for the various needs of the Shaare Zedek Medical Center, Jerusalem, such as equipment and medical supplies, nurse training, and research; supports exchange program between Shaare Zedek Medical Center and Albert Einstein College of Medicine, NY. *Heartbeat Magazine.*

AMERICAN COMMITTEE FOR SHENKAR COLLEGE IN ISRAEL, INC. (1971). 855 Ave. of the Americas, NYC 10001. (212)-947–1597. Pres. David Pernick; Exec. Dir. Charlotte Fainblatt. Raises funds for capital improvement, research and development projects, laboratory equipment, scholarships, lectureships, fellowships, and library/archives of fashion and textile design at Shenkar College in Israel, Israel's only fashion and textile technology college. Accredited by the Council of Higher Education, the college is the chief source of personnel for Israel's fashion and apparel industry. *Shenkar News.*

AMERICAN COMMITTEE FOR THE WEIZMANN INSTITUTE OF SCIENCE (1944). 515 Park Ave., NYC 10022. (212)752–1300. Chmn. Bram Goldsmith; Pres. Alan A. Fischer; Exec. V.-Pres. Bernard N. Samers. Through 12 regional offices in the U.S. raises funds for the Weizmann Institute in Rehovot, Israel, and disseminates information about the scientific research under way there. *Rehovot; Interface; Research.*

AMERICAN FRIENDS OF BETH HATEFUTSOTH (1976). 515 Park Ave., NYC 10022. (212)752–0246. Pres. Philip M. Klutznick; V.-Pres. Sam E. Bloch; Exec. Dir. Gloria Golan. Supports the maintenance and development of Beth Hatefutsoth, the Nahum Goldmann Museum of the Jewish Diaspora in Tel Aviv, and its cultural and educational programs for youth and adults. Circulates its traveling exhibitions and provides various cultural programs to local Jewish communities. Includes the Douglas E. Goldman Jewish Genealogy Center (DOROT); the Center for Jewish Music and the Grunstein Shamir Photodocumentation Center. *Beth Hatefutsoth* quarterly newsletter.

AMERICAN FRIENDS OF EZRATH NASHIM HOSPITAL-JERUSALEM, INC. (1895). 10 E. 40 St., Suite 2701, NYC 10016. (212)725–8175. Pres. Burton G. Greenblatt; Exec. Dir. Mira Berman. Supports research, education, and patient care at Ezrath Nashim Hospital in Jerusalem, which includes a 250-bed hospital, comprehensive outpatient clinic, drug-abuse clinic, geriatric center, and the Jacob Herzog Psychiatric Research Center; Israel's only nonprofit, voluntary psychiatric hospital; used as a teaching facility by Israel's major medical schools. *Friend to Friend; To Open the Gates of Healing.*

AMERICAN FRIENDS OF HAIFA UNIVERSITY (1972). 168 Fifth Ave., 5th fl., NYC 10010. (212)627–4488. Pres. Burton Haahren; Exec. V.-Pres. Michael Weisser. Promotes, encourages, and aids higher and secondary education, research, and training in all branches of knowledge in Israel and elsewhere; aids in the maintenance and development of Haifa University; raises and allocates funds for the above purposes; provides scholarships; promotes exchanges of teachers and students. *Newsletter.*

AMERICAN FRIENDS OF THE HAIFA MARITIME MUSEUM, INC. (1977). 236 Fifth Ave., NYC 10001. (212)696–8084. Chmn. and Treas. Bernard Weissman; Pres. Stephen K. Haber. Supports National Maritime Museum in Haifa. Promotes interest in maritime life among American Jews.

AMERICAN FRIENDS OF THE HEBREW UNIVERSITY (1925; inc. 1931). 11 E. 69 St., NYC 10021. (212)472-9800. Pres. Herbert D. Katz; Exec. V.-Pres. Robert A. Pearlman; Bd. Chmn. Harvey L. Silbert. Fosters the growth, development, and maintenance of the Hebrew University of Jerusalem; collects funds and conducts programs of information throughout the U.S., interpreting the work of the university and its significance; administers American student programs and arranges exchange professorships in the U.S. and Israel. *News from the Hebrew University of Jerusalem; Scopus magazine.*

AMERICAN FRIENDS OF THE ISRAEL MUSEUM (1972). 10 E. 40 St., Suite 1208, NYC 10016. (212)683-5190. Pres. Maureen Cogan; Exec. Dir. Michele Cohn Tocci. Raises funds for special projects of the Israel Museum in Jerusalem; solicits works of art for exhibition and educational purposes. *Newsletter.*

AMERICAN FRIENDS OF THE SHALOM HARTMAN INSTITUTE (1976). 1029 Teaneck Rd., Teaneck, NJ 07666. (201)837-0887. Pres. Robert P. Kogod; Dir. Rabbi Donniel Hartman; Admin. Dorothy Minchin. Supports the Shalom Hartman Institute, Jerusalem, an institute of higher education and research center, devoted to applying the teachings of classical Judaism to the issues of modern life. Founded in 1976 by David Hartman, the institute includes a Beit Midrash and centers for philosophy, theology, *Halakhah,* political thought, and medical science, an experimental school, and programs for lay leadership. *A Word from Jerusalem.*

AMERICAN FRIENDS OF THE TEL AVIV MUSEUM (1974). 133 E. 58 St., Suite 704, NYC 10022. (212)593-5771. Chmn. Milton J. Schubin; Exec. Dir. Ursula Kalish. Raises funds for the Tel Aviv Museum of Art in Tel Aviv, Israel.

AMERICAN FRIENDS OF THE TEL AVIV UNIVERSITY, INC. (1955). 360 Lexington Ave., NYC 10017. (212)687-5651. Board Chmn. Stewart Colton; Pres. Saul B. Cohen; Exec. V.-Pres. Jules Love. Promotes, encourages, and advances higher education at Tel Aviv University, the largest in Israel, and in Israel generally. The university has a law school, medical school, dental school, and more than 50 research institutes, including the Moshe Dayan Center for Middle East & African Studies and the Jaffe Center for Strategic Studies. *Tel Aviv University News; Tau Fax Flash; Tel Aviv University Report.*

AMERICAN ISRAEL PUBLIC AFFAIRS COMMITTEE (AIPAC) (1954). 440 First St., NW, Washington, DC 20001. (202)639-5200. Pres. Ed Levy, Jr.; Exec. Dir. Thomas A. Dine. Registered to lobby on behalf of legislation affecting U.S.-Israel relations; represents Americans who believe support for a secure Israel is in U.S. interest. Works for a strong U.S.-Israel relationship. *Near East Report; AIPAC Papers on U.S.-Israel Relations.*

AMERICAN-ISRAELI LIGHTHOUSE, INC. (1928; reorg. 1955). 30 E. 60 St., NYC 10022. (212)838-5322. Pres. Mrs. Leonard F. Dank; Sec. Frances Lentz. Provides education and rehabilitation for the blind and physically handicapped in Israel to effect their social and vocational integration into the seeing community; built and maintains Rehabilitation Center for the Blind (Migdal Or) in Haifa. *Tower.*

AMERICAN JEWISH LEAGUE FOR ISRAEL (1957). 30 E. 60 St., NYC 10022. (212)-371-1583. Pres. Rabbi Reuben M. Katz; Bd. Chmn. Joseph Landow. Seeks to unite all those who, notwithstanding differing philosophies of Jewish life, are committed to the historical ideals of Zionism; works, independently of class, party, or religious affiliation, for the welfare of Israel as a whole. Not identified with any political parties in Israel. Member, World Confederation of United Zionists. *Bulletin of the American Jewish League for Israel.*

AMERICAN PHYSICIANS FELLOWSHIP, INC. FOR MEDICINE IN ISRAEL (1950). 2001 Beacon St., Brookline, MA 02146. (617)-232-5382. Pres. Dr. Edward H. Kass; Exec. Dir. Daniel C. Goldfarb. Helps Israel become a major world medical center; secures fellowships for selected Israeli physicians and arranges lectureships in Israel by prominent American physicians; runs medical seminars in Israel and U.S.; coordinates U.S. and Canadian medical and paramedical emergency volunteers to Israel; supports research and health care projects in Israel. *APF News.*

AMERICAN RED MAGEN DAVID FOR ISRAEL, INC. (1940). 888 Seventh Ave., Suite 403, NYC 10106. (212)757-1627. Pres. Robert L. Sadoff, M.D.; Natl. Chmn.

Louis Cantor; Exec. V.-Pres. Benjamin Saxe. An authorized tax-exempt organization; the sole support arm in the U.S. of Magen David Adom, Israel's Red Cross Service; raises funds for MDA's emergency medical services for Israel's military and civilian population, supplies ambulances, bloodmobiles, and mobile cardiac rescue units serving all hospitals and communities throughout Israel; supports MDA's 73 emergency medical clinics and helps provide training and equipment for volunteer emergency paramedical corps. *Lifeline.*

AMERICAN SOCIETY FOR TECHNION-ISRAEL INSTITUTE OF TECHNOLOGY (1940). 810 Seventh Ave., NYC 10019. (212)262–6200. Pres. Leonard H. Sherman; Exec. V.-Pres. Melvyn H. Bloom. Supports the work of the Technion-Israel Institute of Technology, Haifa, which trains nearly 10,000 students in 20 departments and a medical school, and conducts research across a broad spectrum of science and technology. *Technion USA; Technion Magazine; ATS Women's Division Newsletter.*

AMERICAN SOCIETY FOR THE PROTECTION OF NATURE IN ISRAEL (1986). 330 Seventh Ave., NYC 10001. (212)947–2820. Hon. Pres. Samuel W. Lewis; Exec. Dir. Tamar C. Podell. Seeks to increase the American public's awareness of, and support for, the critical conservation efforts conducted in Israel by the Society for the Protection of Nature in Israel (SPNI). Conducts educational programs and outdoor activities in the U.S. *Israel Land and Nature* (published quarterly in Israel).

AMERICAN ZIONIST FEDERATION (1939; reorg. 1949 and 1970). 515 Park Ave., NYC 10022. (212)371–7750. Pres. Simon Schwartz; Exec. Dir. Karen Rubinstein. Coordinates the work of the Zionist constituency in the areas of education, *aliyah*, youth and young leadership and public and communal affairs. Seeks to involve the Zionist and broader Jewish community in programs and events focused on Israel and Zionism (e.g., Zionist Shabbat, Scholars-in-Residence, Yom Yerushalayim) and through these programs to develop a greater appreciation for the Zionist idea among American Jewry. Composed of 16 national Zionist organizations, 10 Zionist youth movements, and affiliated organizations. Offices in Chicago, Los Angeles, New York. Groups in Baltimore, Detroit, Philadelphia, Pittsburgh, Rochester, Washington, DC. *HaMakor.*

AMERICAN ZIONIST YOUTH FOUNDATION, INC. (1963). 515 Park Ave., NYC 10022. (212)751–6070. Pres. Leon Levy; Exec. Dir. Ruth Kastner. Heightens Zionist awareness among Jewish youth through programs and services geared to high-school and college-age youngsters. Sponsors educational tours to Israel, study in leading institutions; sponsors field workers on campus and in summer camps; prepares and provides specialists who present and interpret the Israel experience for community centers and federations throughout the country. *Activist Newsletter; Guide to Education and Programming Material; Programs in Israel.*

AMERICANS FOR A SAFE ISRAEL (1971). 114 E. 28 St., NYC 10016. (212)696–2611. Chmn. Herbert Zweibon; Exec. Dir. Joseph Puder. Seeks to educate Americans in Congress, the media, and the public in general about Israel's role as a strategic asset for the West; through meetings with legislators and the media, in press releases and publications, promotes the notion of Jewish rights to Judea and Samaria and the concept of "peace for peace" as an alternative to "territory for peace." *Outpost.*

AMERICANS FOR PROGRESSIVE ISRAEL (1952). 150 Fifth Ave., Suite 911, NYC 10011. (212)255–8760. Pres. Mark Gold. A socialist Zionist movement that calls for a just and durable peace between Israel and its Arab neighbors; works for the liberation of all Jews; seeks the democratization of Jewish communal and organizational life; promotes dignity of labor, social justice, and a deeper understanding of Jewish heritage. Affiliate of American Zionist Federation, World Union of Mapam, Hashomer Hatzair, and Kibbutz Artzi Fed. of Israel. *Israel Horizons; API Newsletter.*

AMIT WOMEN (formerly AMERICAN MIZRACHI WOMEN) (1925). 817 Broadway, NYC 10003. (212)477–4720. Pres. Daisy Berman; Exec. Dir. Marvin Leff. The State of Israel's official *reshet* (network) for religious secondary technological education; conducts social service, child care, Youth Aliyah villages, and vocational-educational programs in Israel in an environment of traditional Judaism; promotes cultural activities for the purpose of disseminating Zionist ideals and strengthening traditional Judaism in America. *AMIT Woman.*

AMPAL—AMERICAN ISRAEL CORPORATION (1942). 10 Rockefeller Plaza, NYC 10020. (212)586-3232. Pres. Michael Arnon. Finances and invests in Israeli economic enterprises; mobilizes finance and investment capital in the U.S. through sale of own debenture issues and utilization of bank credit lines. *Annual report; prospectuses.*

ARZA—ASSOCIATION OF REFORM ZIONISTS OF AMERICA (1977). 838 Fifth Ave., NYC 10021. (212)249-0100. Pres. Norman D. Schwartz; Exec. Dir. Rabbi Eric Hoffie. Individual Zionist membership organization devoted to achieving Jewish pluralism in Israel and strengthening the Israeli Reform movement. Chapter activities in the U.S. concentrate on these issues and on strengthening American public support for Israel. *ARZA Newsletter.*

BAR-ILAN UNIVERSITY IN ISRAEL (1955). 130 East 59 St., NYC 10022.. (212)832-0095. Chancellor Emanuel Rackman; Pres. Michael Albeck; Chmn. Global Bd. of Trustees Ludwig Jesselson; Pres. Amer. Bd. of Overseers Belda Lindenbaum. Supports Bar-Ilan University, a traditionally oriented liberal arts and sciences institution, where all students must take Basic Jewish Studies courses as a requirement of graduation; located in Ramat-Gan, Israel, and chartered by the Board of Regents of the State of NY. *Update; Bar-Ilan News.*

BETAR ZIONIST YOUTH ORGANIZATION (1935). 38 East 23 St., NYC 10010. (212)-353-8033. Central Shaliach Eli Cohen. Organizes youth groups across North America to teach Zionism, Jewish pride, and love of Israel; sponsors summer programs in Israel for Jewish youth ages 13-21; sponsors Tagar Zionist Student Activist Movement on college campuses. *Etgar.*

BOYS TOWN JERUSALEM FOUNDATION OF AMERICA INC. (1948). 91 Fifth Ave., Suite 601, NYC 10003. (212)242-1118. Pres. Michael J. Scharf; Chmn. Josh S. Weston; V.-Chmn. Alexander S. Linchner; Exec. V.-Pres. Rabbi Ronald L. Gray. Raises funds for Boys Town Jerusalem, which was established in 1948 to offer a comprehensive academic, religious, and technical education to disadvantaged Israeli and immigrant boys from over 45 different countries, including Ethiopia and Iran. Enrollment: over 1,500 students in jr. high school, academic and technical high school, and a college of applied engineering. *BTJ Newsbriefs; Your Town Magazine.*

COUNCIL FOR A BEAUTIFUL ISRAEL ENVIRONMENTAL EDUCATION FOUNDATION (1973). 350 Fifth Ave., 19th fl., NYC 10118. (212)947-5709. Pres. Anita Kaskel Roe; Admin. Dir. Donna Lindemann. A support group for the Israeli body, whose activities include education, town planning, lobbying for legislation to protect and enhance the environment, preservation of historical sites, the improvement and beautification of industrial and commercial areas, and renovating bomb shelters into parks and playgrounds. *Yearly newsletter.*

DROR—YOUNG KIBBUTZ MOVEMENT—HABONIM (1977). 27 W. 20 St., 9th fl., NYC 10011. (212)675-1168. Exec. Dir. Yoel Skolnick. Provides an opportunity for individuals who have spent time in Israel, on a kibbutz program, to continue their contact with the kibbutz movement through regional and national activities and seminars; sponsors two *garinim* to kibbutz each year and a teenage summer program. *New Horizons.*

———, CHAVURAT HAGALIL (1978). Exec. Dir. Yoel Skolnick. Aids those aged 27-35 in making *aliyah* to a kibbutz. Affiliated with TAKAM kibbutz association.

———, GARIN YARDEN, YOUNG KIBBUTZ MOVEMENT (1976). Exec. Dir. Yoel Skolnick. Aids those aged 20-30 interested in making *aliyah* to a kibbutz; affiliated with TAKAM kibbutz association.

EMUNAH WOMEN OF AMERICA (formerly HAPOEL HAMIZRACHI WOMEN'S ORGANIZATION) (1948). 7 Penn Plaza, NYC 10001 (212)564-9045. Pres. Gladys Baruch; Exec. Dir. Shirley Singer. Maintains and supports 200 educational and social-welfare institutions in Israel within a religious framework, including nurseries, day-care centers, vocational and teacher-training schools for the underprivileged, a community college complex, and Holocaust study center. Also involved in absorption of Ethiopian immigrants. *The Emunah Woman; Lest We Forget; Emunah Connection.*

FEDERATED COUNCIL OF ISRAEL INSTITUTIONS—FCII (1940). 4702 15th Ave., Brooklyn, NY 11219. (718)972-5530. Bd. Chmn. Z. Shapiro; Exec. V.-Pres. Rabbi

Julius Novack. Central fund-raising organization for over 100 affiliated institutions; handles and executes estates, wills, and bequests for the traditional institutions in Israel; clearinghouse for information on budget, size, functions, etc., of traditional educational, welfare, and philanthropic institutions in Israel, working cooperatively with the Israeli government and the overseas department of the Council of Jewish Federations. *Annual financial reports and statistics on affiliates.*

FRIENDS OF LABOR ISRAEL (1987). 28 Ramban, Jerusalem, Israel 92268. (02)664342. Membership Services Office: PO Box 17305, Milwaukee, WI 53217–99. Chmn. Rabbi Daniel Polish; Exec. Dir. Rabbi Stanley A. Ringler. American organization committed to a program of education in America and Israel on behalf of institutions, organizations, and projects in Israel designed to promote democracy, pluralism, social justice and peace. FLI is an affinity group of the Israel Labor party and represents the concerns of progressive American Jews in Labor party circles. *Labor Political Briefs; Folio newsletter.*

FRIENDS OF THE ISRAEL DEFENSE FORCES (1981). 21 W. 38 St., 5th fl., NYC 10018. (212)575–5030. Bd. Chmn. Henry Plitt. Supports the *Agudah Lema'an Hahayal,* Israel's Assoc. for the Well-Being of Soldiers, founded in the early 1940s, which provides social, recreational, and educational programs for soldiers, special services for the sick and wounded, and much more. *Newsletter.*

FUND FOR HIGHER EDUCATION (1970). 1768 S. Wooster St., Los Angeles, CA 90035. (213)202–1879. Chmn. Amnon Barness; Chmn. Exec. Com. Max Candiotty. Raises funds and disseminates information in the interest of institutions of higher education in the U.S. & Israel. Over $18 million distributed to over 100 institutions of higher learning, including over $11 million in Israel and $6 million in the U.S. *In Response.*

GIVAT HAVIVA EDUCATIONAL FOUNDATION, INC. (1966). 150 Fifth Ave., Suite 911, NYC 10011. (212)255–2992. Chmn. Martin Mensch. Supports programs in Israel to further Jewish-Arab rapprochement, narrow economic and educational gaps within Israeli society, and improve educational opportunities for various disadvantaged youth. Affiliated with the Givat Haviva Center of the Kibbutz Artzi Federation, the Menachem Bader Fund, and other projects. In the U.S., GHEF, Inc. sponsors educational seminars, public lectures and parlor meetings with Israeli speakers, as well as individual and group trips to Israel. *News from Givat Haviva; special reports.*

GOLDA MEIR ASSOCIATION (1984). 33 E. 67 St., NYC 10021. (212)570–1443. Chmn. Alfred H. Moses; Pres. Robert C. Klutznick; Exec. Dir. Avner Tavori. North American support group for the Israeli association, whose large-scale educational programs address the issues of democracy in Israel, Sephardi-Ashkenazi integration, religious pluralism, the peace process, and relations between Israeli Jews and Arabs. Its "Project Democracy" is the largest program dealing with the tide of extremism sweeping Israel's youth. *Newsletter.*

HABONIM-DROR NORTH AMERICA (1934). 27 W. 20 St., 9th fl., NYC 10011. (212)-255–1796. Sec.-Gen. Chuck Buxbaum; Exec. Off. Yaron Raz. Fosters identification with pioneering in Israel; stimulates study of Jewish life, history, and culture; sponsors community-action projects, seven summer camps in North America, programs in Israel, and *garinei aliyah* to Kibbutz Ravid. *Batnua; Progressive Zionist Journal; Bimat Hamaapilim.*

HADASSAH, THE WOMEN'S ZIONIST ORGANIZATION OF AMERICA, INC. (1912). 50 W. 58 St., NYC 10019. (212)355–7900. Pres. Carmela E. Kalmanson; Exec. Dir. Aileen Novick. In America helps interpret Israel to the American people; provides basic Jewish education as a background for intelligent and creative Jewish living; sponsors Young Judaea/Hashachar, largest Zionist youth movement in U.S., which has four divisions: Young Judaea, Intermediate Judaea, Senior Judaea, and Hamagshimim; operates six Zionist youth camps in this country; supports summer and all-year courses in Israel. Maintains in Israel Hadassah-Hebrew University Medical Center for healing, teaching, and research; Hadassah Institute of Technology; and Hadassah Career Counseling Institute. Is largest organizational contributor to Youth Aliyah and to Jewish National Fund for land purchase and reclamation. *Update; Headlines; Hadassah Magazine; Textures; Bat Kol; The Catalyst; The American Scene.*

———, YOUNG JUDAEA/HASHACHAR (1909; reorg. 1967). 50 W. 58 St., NYC 10019. (212)355-7900. Pres. of Sr. Judaea (high-school level) Eitan Mendelowitz; Coord. Hamagshimim (college level) Michael Balaban; Natl. Dir. Glen Karonsky. Seeks to educate Jewish youth from the ages of 9-27 toward Jewish and Zionist values, active commitment to and participation in the American and Israeli Jewish communities; maintains summer camps and year programs in Israel. *Hamagshimim Journal; Kol Hat'nua; The Young Judaean.*

HASHOMER HATZAIR, SOCIALIST ZIONIST YOUTH MOVEMENT (1923). 150 Fifth Ave., Suite 911, NYC 10011. (212)929-4955. Sec. Morrie Hermon; Central Shaliach Chaim Broom. Seeks to educate Jewish youth to an understanding of Zionism as the national liberation movement of the Jewish people. Promotes *aliyah* to *kibbutzim*. Affiliated with AZYF and Kibbutz Artzi Federation. Espouses socialist-Zionist ideals of peace, justice, democracy, and brotherhood. *Young Guard.*

ISRAEL HISTADRUT FOUNDATION (1960). 276 Fifth Ave., Suite 901, NYC 10001. (212)683-5454. Pres. Herbert Rothman; Exec. V.-Pres. Alvin Smolin. Specializes in the field of deferred giving, which includes testamentary bequests, charitable trusts, and endowment funds that benefit over 85% of the people of Israel through the social-service agencies of the Histadrut. These agencies consist of 17 Kupat Holim major general hospitals, over 1,300 medical clinics, 4 schools of nursing, 158 Amal vocational trade schools, 6 Mishan senior-citizen geriatric centers, 5 Mishan children's village homes, and 4 colleges.

JEWISH COMMITTEE FOR ISRAELI-PALESTINIAN PEACE (1982). PO Box 4991, Washington, DC 20008. (301)963-5673. Seth Grimes, Ellen Siegel, representatives. Promotes a two-state solution to the Israeli-Palestinian conflict to be achieved through negotiations with the PLO in order to ensure Israeli security and Palestinian rights. Sponsors educational and dialogue programs, writes articles and editorials, assists the Israeli peace movement, and holds a yearly Jewish-Palestinian Friendship Dinner. *Israeli-Palestinian Digest.*

JEWISH NATIONAL FUND OF AMERICA (1901). 42 E. 69 St., NYC 10021. (212)-879-9300. Pres. Joseph P. Sternstein; Exec. V.-Pres. Samuel I. Cohen. Exclusive fund-raising agency of the world Zionist movement for the afforestation, reclamation, and development of the land of Israel, including construction of roads, parks, and recreational areas, preparation of land for new communities and industrial facilities; helps emphasize the importance of Israel in schools and synagogues throughout the U.S. *JNF Almanac; Land and Life.*

JEWISH PEACE LOBBY (1989). 4431 Lehigh Rd., Suite 141, College Park, MD 20740. (301)589-8764. Pres. Jerome M. Segal. A legally registered lobby promoting changes in U.S. policy vis-à-vis the Israeli-Palestinian conflict. Supports Israel's right to peace within secure borders; a political settlement based on mutual recognition of the right of self-determination of both peoples; a two-state solution as the most likely means to a stable peace.

KEREN OR, INC. (1956). 1133 Broadway, NYC 10010. (212)255-1180. Bd. Chmn. Dr. Edward L. Steinberg; Pres. Dr. Albert Hornblass; Exec. Dir. Paul H. Goldenberg. Funds the Keren Or Center for Multihandicapped Blind Children, in Jerusalem, providing long-term basic training, therapy, rehabilitative, and early childhood education to the optimum level of the individual; with major hospitals, involved in research into causes of multihandicapped blind birth; campaign under way for new multipurpose building on government landgrant in Ramot.

LABOR ZIONIST ALLIANCE (formerly FARBAND LABOR ZIONIST ORDER; now uniting membership and branches of POALE ZION—UNITED LABOR ZIONIST ORGANIZATION OF AMERICA and AMERICAN HABONIM ASSOCIATION) (1913). 33 E. 67 St., NYC 10021. (212)628-0042. Pres. Menachem Z. Rosensaft; Exec. Dir. Sarrae G. Crane. Seeks to enhance Jewish life, culture, and education in U.S. and Canada; aids in building State of Israel as a cooperative commonwealth, and its Labor movement organized in the Histadrut; supports efforts toward a more democratic society throughout the world; furthers the democratization of the Jewish community in America and the welfare of Jews everywhere; works with labor and liberal forces in America. *Jewish Frontier; Yiddisher Kempfer.*

LEAGUE FOR LABOR ISRAEL (1938; reorg. 1961). 33 E. 67 St., NYC 10021. (212)628-0042. Pres. Menachem Z. Rosensaft; Exec. Dir. Sarrae Crane. Conducts Labor Zionist educational and cultural activities, for youth and adults, in the American Jewish community. Promotes educational travel to Israel.

LIKUD-HERUT ZIONISTS OF AMERICA, INC. (1925). 38 E. 23 St., NYC 10010. (212)-353-9552. Exec. Dir. Glenn Mones. Educates the Jewish community and the American public about the views of Israel's Likud party; encourages support for a strong, secure State of Israel in all of its territory. *The Likud Letter.*

MERCAZ (1979). 155 Fifth Ave., NYC 10010. (212)533-7800. Pres. Goldie Kweller; Exec. Dir. Hindy Kisch. The U.S. Zionist political organization for Conservative/Masorti Judaism; works to attain religious rights for the Masorti movement in Israel; fosters Zionist education and *aliyah* among its constituents and develops young leadership. *Mercaz News & Views.*

NA'AMAT USA, THE WOMEN'S LABOR ZIONIST ORGANIZATION OF AMERICA, INC. (formerly PIONEER WOMEN/NA'AMAT) (1925; reorg. 1985). 200 Madison Ave., Suite 1808, NYC 10016. (212)725-8010. Pres. Harriet Green. Part of a world movement of working women and volunteers, NA'AMAT USA helps provide social, educational, and legal services for women, teenagers, and children in Israel. It also advocates legislation for women's rights and child welfare in the U.S., furthers Jewish education, and supports Habonim-Dror, the Labor Zionist youth movement. *NA'AMAT Woman magazine.*

NATIONAL COMMITTEE FOR LABOR ISRAEL—HISTADRUT (1923). 33 E. 67 St., NYC 10021. (212)628-1000. Pres. Bruce C. Vladeck; Exec. V.-Pres. Eliezer Rafaeli; Chmn. Trade Union Council Morton Bahr. Promotes relations and understanding between American trade unions and the Israeli labor movement-Histadrut; offers educational programs on Israeli labor in the Jewish community and among the general public; raises funds for the educational, health, social and cultural projects of Histadrut for working people, Jews, and Arabs in Israel and for Histadrut's programs in the Third World. *Backdrop Histadrut; Amal Newsletter.*

NEW ISRAEL FUND (1979). 111 W. 40 St., Suite 2300, NYC 10018. (212)302-0066. Pres. Mary Ann Stein; Exec. Dir. Norman Rosenberg. Supports the citizens'-action efforts of Israelis working to achieve social justice and to protect and strengthen the democratic process in Israel. Also seeks to enrich the quality of the relationships between Israelis and North American Jews through deepened mutual understanding. Publishes background booklets on civil rights, women's status, Jewish-Arab coexistence, religious pluralism, and community action in Israel. *A Guide to Arab-Jewish Peacemaking in Israel; quarterly newsletter; annual report.*

PEC ISRAEL ECONOMIC CORPORATION (formerly PALESTINE ECONOMIC CORPORATION) (1926). 511 Fifth Ave., NYC 10017. (212)687-2400. Pres. Joseph Ciechanover; Exec. V.-Pres. Frank J. Klein; Sec.-Asst. Treas. William Gold. Primarily engaged in the business of organizing, financing, and administering business enterprises located in or affiliated with enterprises in the State of Israel, through holdings of equity securities and loans. *Annual report.*

PEF ISRAEL ENDOWMENT FUNDS, INC. (1922). 41 E. 42 St., Suite 607, NYC 10017. (212)599-1260. Chmn. Sidney Musher; Sec. Harvey Brecher. Uses funds for Israeli educational and philanthropic institutions and for constructive relief, modern education, and scientific research in Israel. *Annual report.*

PIONEER WOMEN/NA'AMAT (*see* NA'AMAT USA)

POALE AGUDATH ISRAEL OF AMERICA, INC. (1948). 3190 Bedford Ave., Brooklyn, NY 11210. (718)377-4111. Pres. Rabbi Fabian Schonfeld; Exec. V.-Pres. Rabbi Moshe Malinowitz. Aims to educate American Jews to the values of Orthodoxy and *aliyah;* supports *kibbutzim,* trade schools, *yeshivot, moshavim, kollelim,* research centers, and children's homes in Israel. *PAI News; She'arim; Hamayan.*

———, WOMEN'S DIVISION OF (1948). Pres. Aliza Widawsky; Presidium: Sarah Ivanisky, Miriam Lubling, Bertl Rittenberg. Assists Poale Agudath Israel to build and support children's homes, kindergartens, and trade schools in Israel. *Yediot PAI.*

PROGRESSIVE ZIONIST CAUCUS (1982). 27 W. 20 St., NYC 10011. (212)675–1168. Shlihim Yaron Raz, David Koran; Dir. Beth Martin. A campus-based grass-roots organization committed to a progressive Zionist agenda. Students organize local and regional educational, cultural, and political activities, such as speakers, films, *Kabbalot Shabbat,* and Arab-Jewish dialogue groups. The PZC Kvutzat Aliyah is a support framework for individuals interested in *aliyah* to a city or town. *La'Inyan; Makor.*

RELIGIOUS ZIONISTS OF AMERICA. 25 W. 26 St., NYC 10010. (212)689–1414.

———, BNEI AKIVA OF NORTH AMERICA (1934). 25 W. 26 St., NYC 10010. (212)-889–5260. Pres. Yitz Feigenbaum; V.-Pres. Admin. Jerry Yudkowsky. Seeks to interest youth in *aliyah* to Israel and social justice through pioneering *(halutziut)* as an integral part of their religious observance; sponsors five summer camps, a leadership training camp for eleventh graders, a work-study program on a religious kibbutz for high school graduates, summer tours to Israel; establishes nuclei of college students for kibbutz or other settlement. *Akivon; Hamvaser; Pinkas Lamadrich; Daf Rayonot; Ma'Ohalai Torah; Zraim.*

———, MIZRACHI-HAPOEL HAMIZRACHI (1909; merged 1957). 25 W. 26 St., NYC 10010. (212)689–1414. Pres. Hermann Merkin; Exec. V.-Pres. Israel Friedman. Disseminates ideals of religious Zionism; conducts cultural work, educational program, public relations; raises funds for religious educational institutions in Israel, including *yeshivot hesder* and Bnei Akiva. *Newsletters; Kolenu.*

———, MIZRACHI PALESTINE FUND (1928). 25 W. 26 St., NYC 10010. Chmn. Joseph Wilon; Sec. Israel Friedman. Fundraising arm of Mizrachi movement.

———, NATIONAL COUNCIL FOR TORAH EDUCATION OF MIZRACHI-HAPOEL HAMIZRACHI (1939). 25 W. 26 St., NYC 10010. Pres. Rabbi Israel Schorr; Dir. Rabbi Meyer Golombek. Organizes and supervises *yeshivot* and Talmud Torahs; prepares and trains teachers; publishes textbooks and educational materials; organizes summer seminars for Hebrew educators in cooperation with Torah Department of Jewish Agency; conducts *ulpan. Hazarkor; Chemed.*

———, NOAM-MIZRACHI NEW LEADERSHIP COUNCIL (formerly NOAM-HAMISHMERET HATZEIRA) (1970). 25 W. 26 St., NYC 10010. (212)684–6091. Chmn. Rabbi Marc Schneier; V.-Chmn. Sheon Karol; Dir. Jeffrey M. Weisberg. Develops new religious Zionist leadership in the U.S. and Canada; presents young religious people with various alternatives for settling in Israel through *garinei aliyah* (core groups); meets the religious, educational, and social needs of Jewish young adults and young couples. *Forum.*

SOCIETY OF ISRAEL PHILATELISTS (1948). 27436 Aberdeen, Southfield, MI 48076. (313)557–0887. Pres. Howard Chapman; Exec. Sec. Irvin Girer. Promotes interest in, and knowledge of, all phases of Israel philately through sponsorship of chapters and research groups, maintenance of a philatelic library, and support of public and private exhibitions. *Israel Philatelist; monographs; books.*

STATE OF ISRAEL BONDS (1951). 730 Broadway, NYC 10003. (212)677–9650. Internatl. Chmn. David B. Hermelin; Pres. Ambassador Meir Rosenne; Exec. V.-Pres. Morris Sipser. Seeks to provide large-scale investment funds for the economic development of the State of Israel through the sale of State of Israel bonds in the U.S., Canada, Western Europe, and Latin America.

THEODOR HERZL FOUNDATION (1954). 515 Park Ave., NYC 10022. (212)752–0600. Chmn. Kalman Sultanik; Sec. Isadore Hamlin. Cultural activities, lectures, conferences, courses in modern Hebrew and Jewish subjects, Israel, Zionism, and Jewish history. *Midstream.*

———, HERZL PRESS. Chmn. Kalman Sultanik. Serves as "the Zionist Press of record," publishing books that are important for the light they shed on Zionist philosophy, Israeli history, contemporary Israel and the Diaspora, and the relationship between them. Many of these volumes, because of their specialized nature, would not be attractive to commercial publishers, but are important as contributions to Zionist letters and history. *Midstream.*

———, THEODOR HERZL INSTITUTE. Chmn. Jacques Torczyner; Dir. Philip S. Gutride. Program geared to review of contemporary problems on Jewish scene here and abroad, presentation of Jewish heritage values in light of Zionist experience of the ages, study of modern Israel, and Jewish social research with particular consideration of history and impact of Zionism. Lectures, forums, Encounter with Creativity; musicales, recitals, concerts; holiday celebrations; visual art programs, Nouveau Artist Introductions. *Annual Program Preview; Herzl Institute Bulletin.*

UNITED CHARITY INSTITUTIONS OF JERUSALEM, INC. (1903). 1141 Broadway, NYC 10001. (212)683-3221. Chmn. Rabbi Zevulun Charlop; Sec. Sam Gabel. Raises funds for the maintenance of schools, kitchens, clinics, and dispensaries in Israel; free loan foundations in Israel.

UNITED ISRAEL APPEAL, INC. (1925). 515 Park Ave., NYC 10022. (212)688-0800. Chmn. Henry Taub; Exec. V.-Chmn. Herman Markowitz. As principal beneficiary of the United Jewish Appeal, serves as link between American Jewish community and Jewish Agency for Israel, its operating agent; assists in resettlement and absorption of refugees in Israel, and supervises flow of funds and expenditures for this purpose.

UNITED STATES COMMITTEE SPORTS FOR ISRAEL, INC. (1948). 1926 Arch St., Philadelphia, PA 19103. (215)561-6900. Pres. Robert E. Spivak; Exec. Dir. Barbara G. Lissy. Sponsors U.S. participation in, and fields and selects U.S. team for, World Maccabiah Games in Israel every four years; promotes education and sports programs in Israel; provides funds and technical and material assistance to Wingate Institute for Physical Education and Sport in Israel; sponsors coaching programs in Israel. *USCSFI Newsletter;* commemorative Maccabiah Games journal.

WOMEN'S LEAGUE FOR ISRAEL, INC. (1928). 515 Park Ave., NYC 10022. (212)838-1997. Pres. Trudy Miner; Sr. V.-Pres. Annette Kay; Exec. Dir. Dorothy Leffler. Promotes the welfare of young people in Israel; built and maintains homes in Jerusalem, Haifa, Tel Aviv; Natanya Vocational Training and Rehabilitation Center; the Orah Workshop for the Blind and Handicapped, and the National Library of Social Work. Also many facilities and programs on the campuses of the Hebrew University. *WLI Bulletin.*

WORLD CONFEDERATION OF UNITED ZIONISTS (1946; reorg. 1958). 30 E. 60 St., NYC 10022. (212)371-1452. Copres. Bernice S. Tannenbaum, Kalman Sultanik, Melech Topiol. Promotes Zionist education, sponsors nonparty youth movements in the Diaspora, and strives for an Israel-oriented creative Jewish survival in the Diaspora. *Zionist Information Views.*

WORLD ZIONIST ORGANIZATION—AMERICAN SECTION (1971). 515 Park Ave., NYC 10009. (212)752-0600. Chmn. Bernice S. Tannenbaum; Exec. V.-Chmn. Zelig Chinitz. As the American section of the overall Zionist body throughout the world, it operates primarily in the field of *aliyah* from the free countries, education in the Diaspora, youth and Hechalutz, organization and information, cultural institutions, publications; conducts a worldwide Hebrew cultural program including special seminars and pedagogic manuals; disperses information and assists in research projects concerning Israel; promotes, publishes, and distributes books, periodicals, and pamphlets concerning developments in Israel, Zionism, and Jewish history. *Midstream; Five Fifteen.*

———, DEPARTMENT OF EDUCATION AND CULTURE (1948). 515 Park Ave., NYC 10022. (212)752-0600. Exec. Dir. Asher Rivlin. Renders educational services to boards and schools: study programs, books, AV aids, instruction, teacher in-service training, Judaic and Hebrew subjects. Annual Bible and Israel contests; Israel summer and winter programs for teachers and students; Ulpan centers in Greater N.Y. area; preparation for Isaeli matriculation examinations.

———, NORTH AMERICAN ALIYAH MOVEMENT (1968). 515 Park Ave., NYC 10022. (212)752-0600. Pres. Lois Kitchen; Exec. Dir. Jo-Ann Sandler. Promotes and facilitates *aliyah* and *klitah* from the U.S. and Canada to Israel; serves as a social framework for North American immigrants to Israel. *Aliyon; NAAM Newsletter; Coming Home.*

———, ZIONIST ARCHIVES AND LIBRARY OF THE (1939). 515 Park Ave., NYC 10022. (212)753-2167. Dir. and Librarian

Esther Togman. A depository for books, pamphlets, newspapers, periodicals, ephemera, and archival material; a primary center in the U.S. for research and authentic information on Israel, Zionism, the Middle East, and Jewish life in the Diaspora.

ZIONIST ORGANIZATION OF AMERICA (1897). ZOA House, 4 E. 34 St., NYC 10016. (212)481–1500. Pres. Sidney Silverman; Exec. V.-Pres. Paul Flacks. Seeks to safeguard the integrity and independence of Israel, assist in its economic development, and foster the unity of the Jewish people and the centrality of Israel in Jewish life in the spirit of General Zionism. In Israel, owns and maintains both the ZOA House in Tel Aviv, a cultural center, and the Kfar Silver Agricultural and Technical High School in Ashkelon, with a full-time student enrollment of 700 students. Kfar Silver, under the supervision of the Israel Ministry of Education, focuses on academic studies, vocational training, and programs for foreign students. *American Zionist Magazine; Zionist Information Service Weekly News Bulletin (ZINS); Public Affairs Action Guidelines; Public Affairs Action Report for ZOA Leaders.*

PROFESSIONAL ASSOCIATIONS*

AMERICAN ASSOCIATION OF RABBIS (Religious, Educational)

AMERICAN CONFERENCE OF CANTORS, UNION OF AMERICAN HEBREW CONGREGATIONS (Religious, Educational)

AMERICAN JEWISH CORRECTIONAL CHAPLAINS ASSOCIATION, INC. (Social Welfare)

AMERICAN JEWISH PRESS ASSOCIATION (Cultural)

AMERICAN JEWISH PUBLIC RELATIONS SOCIETY (1957). 234 Fifth Ave., NYC 10001. (212)697–5895. Pres. Henry R. Hecker; Treas. Hyman Brickman. Advances professional status of workers in the public-relations field in Jewish communal service; upholds a professional code of ethics and standards; serves as a clearinghouse for employment opportunities; exchanges professional information and ideas; presents awards for excellence in professional attainments, including the "Maggid Award" for outstanding achievement which enhances Jewish life. *AJPRS Newsletter; AJPRS Directory.*

ASSOCIATION OF HILLEL/JEWISH CAMPUS PROFESSIONALS (Religious, Educational)

ASSOCIATION OF JEWISH CENTER WORKERS (Community Relations)

ASSOCIATION OF JEWISH COMMUNITY ORGANIZATION PERSONNEL (Social Welfare)

ASSOCIATION OF JEWISH COMMUNITY RELATIONS WORKERS (Community Relations)

CANTORS ASSEMBLY (Religious, Educational)

CENTRAL CONFERENCE OF AMERICAN RABBIS (Religious, Educational)

CONFERENCE OF JEWISH COMMUNAL SERVICE (Social Welfare)

COUNCIL OF JEWISH ORGANIZATIONS IN CIVIL SERVICE (Community Relations)

INTERNATIONAL JEWISH MEDIA ASSOCIATION (Cultural)

JEWISH CHAPLAINS COUNCIL, JWB (Social Welfare)

JEWISH EDUCATORS ASSEMBLY, UNITED SYNAGOGUE OF AMERICA (Religious, Educational)

JEWISH MINISTERS CANTORS ASSOCIATION OF AMERICA, INC. (Religious, Educational)

JEWISH TEACHERS ASSOCIATION—MORIM (Religious, Educational)

NATIONAL ASSOCIATION OF HEBREW DAY SCHOOL ADMINISTRATORS, TORAH UMESORAH (Religious, Educational)

NATIONAL ASSOCIATION OF SYNAGOGUE ADMINISTRATORS, UNITED SYNAGOGUE OF AMERICA (Religious, Educational)

NATIONAL ASSOCIATION OF TEMPLE ADMINISTRATORS, UNION OF AMERICAN HEBREW CONGREGATIONS (Religious, Educational)

NATIONAL ASSOCIATION OF TEMPLE EDUCATORS, UNION OF AMERICAN HEBREW CONGREGATIONS (Religious, Educational)

---

*For fuller listing see under categories in parentheses.

NATIONAL CONFERENCE OF YESHIVA PRINCIPALS, TORAH UMESORAH (Religious, Educational)

RABBINICAL ASSEMBLY (Religious, Educational)

RABBINICAL COUNCIL OF AMERICA (Religious, Educational)

RECONSTRUCTIONIST RABBINICAL ASSOCIATION, JEWISH RECONSTRUCTIONIST FOUNDATION (Religious, Educational)

UNION OF ORTHODOX RABBIS OF THE U.S. AND CANADA (Religious, Educational)

WORLD CONFERENCE OF JEWISH COMMUNAL SERVICE (Community Relations)

WOMEN'S ORGANIZATIONS*

AMIT WOMEN (Zionist and Pro-Israel)

B'NAI B'RITH WOMEN (Social Welfare)

BRANDEIS UNIVERSITY NATIONAL WOMEN'S COMMITTEE (1948). PO Box 9110, Waltham, MA 02254–9110. (617)-736–4160. Natl. Pres. Estelle W. Jacobs; Exec. Dir. Harriet J. Winer. Provides financial support for the Brandeis Libraries and works to enhance the imgage of Brandeis, a Jewish-sponsored, nonsectarian university. Offers its members opportunity for intellectual pursuit, continuing education, community service, social interaction, personal enrichment, and leadership development. *Imprint.*

HADASSAH, THE WOMEN'S ZIONIST ORGANIZATION OF AMERICA (Zionist and Pro-Israel)

NA'AMAT USA, THE WOMEN'S LABOR ZIONIST ORGANIZATION OF AMERICA (Zionist and Pro-Israel)

NATIONAL COUNCIL OF JEWISH WOMEN (Social Welfare)

NATIONAL FEDERATION OF TEMPLE SISTERHOODS, UNION OF AMERICAN HEBREW CONGREGATIONS (Religious, Educational)

UOTS (Social, Mutual Benefit)

WOMEN'S AMERICAN ORT, AMERICAN ORT FEDERATION (Overseas Aid)

WOMEN'S BRANCH OF THE UNION OF ORTHODOX JEWISH CONGREGATIONS OF AMERICA (Religious, Educational)

WOMEN'S DIVISION OF POALE AGUDATH ISRAEL OF AMERICA (Zionist and Pro-Israel)

WOMEN'S DIVISION OF THE JEWISH LABOR COMMITTEE (Community Relations)

WOMEN'S DIVISION OF THE UNITED JEWISH APPEAL (Overseas Aid)

WOMEN'S LEAGUE FOR CONSERVATIVE JUDAISM (Religious, Educational)

WOMEN'S LEAGUE FOR ISRAEL, INC. (Zionist and Pro-Israel)

WOMEN'S ORGANIZATION, YESHIVA UNIVERSITY (Religious, Educational)

YOUTH AND STUDENT ORGANIZATIONS*

AMERICAN ZIONIST YOUTH FOUNDATION (Zionist and Pro-Israel)

B'NAI B'RITH HILLEL FOUNDATIONS (Religious, Educational)

B'NAI B'RITH YOUTH ORGANIZATION (Religious, Educational)

BNEI AKIVA OF NORTH AMERICA, RELIGIOUS ZIONISTS OF AMERICA (Zionist and Pro-Israel)

BNOS AGUDATH ISRAEL, AGUDATH ISRAEL OF AMERICA, GIRLS' DIVISION (Religious, Educational)

DROR—YOUNG KIBBUTZ MOVEMENT—HABONIM (Zionist and Pro-Israel)

HABONIM-DROR NORTH AMERICA (Zionist and Pro-Israel)

HASHOMER HATZAIR, SOCIALIST ZIONIST YOUTH MOVEMENT (Zionist and Pro-Israel)

KADIMA, UNITED SYNAGOGUE OF AMERICA (Religious, Educational)

NATIONAL CONFERENCE OF SYNAGOGUE YOUTH, UNION OF ORTHODOX JEWISH CONGREGATIONS OF AMERICA (Religious, Educational)

NOAM-MIZRACHI NEW LEADERSHIP COUNCIL, RELIGIOUS ZIONISTS OF AMERICA (Zionist and Pro-Israel)

---

*For fuller listing see under categories in parentheses.

NORTH AMERICAN FEDERATION OF TEMPLE YOUTH, UNION OF AMERICAN HEBREW CONGREGATIONS (Religious, Educational)

NORTH AMERICAN JEWISH STUDENTS APPEAL (1971). 165 Pidgeon Hill Rd., Huntington Station, NY 11746. (516)385–8771. Pres. Cindy Rubin; Chmn. Magda S. Leuchter; Exec. Dir. Brenda Gevertz. Serves as central fund-raising mechanism for six national, independent Jewish student organizations; insures accountability of public Jewish communal funds used by these agencies; assists Jewish students undertaking projects of concern to Jewish communities; advises and assists Jewish organizations in determining student project feasibility and impact; fosters development of Jewish student leadership in the Jewish community. Beneficiaries include local and regional Jewish student projects; current constituents include Jewish Student Press Service, Student Struggle for Soviet Jewry, *Response Magazine,* Yugntruf Youth for Yiddish, Progressive Zionist Caucus, and the newest constituent, Project Orchim for outreach on campus.

NORTH AMERICAN JEWISH STUDENTS' NETWORK (1969). 501 Madison Ave., 17th fl., NYC 10022. (212)888–8417. Pres. Jacob Davidson; Natl. Chmn. Helene Donna Drobenare; Admin. Dir. Sandy Lawrence Edry. Coordinates information and programs among all Jewish student organizations in North America; promotes development of student-controlled Jewish student organizations; maintains contacts and coordinates programs with Jewish students throughout the world through the World Union of Jewish Students (WUJS); sponsors regional, national, and North American conferences. *Network: A Forum for the Jewish Student.*

STUDENT STRUGGLE FOR SOVIET JEWRY (Community Relations)

YOUNG JUDAEA/HASHACHAR, HADASSAH (Zionist and Pro-Israel)

YUGNTRUF YOUTH FOR YIDDISH (1964). 200 W. 72 St., Suite 40, NYC 10023. (212)-787–6675. Chmn. Itzek Gottesman; Editor Paul Glasser. A worldwide, nonpolitical organization for high school and college students with a knowledge of, or interest in, Yiddish. Spreads the love and use of the Yiddish language; organizes artistic and social activities, including annual conference for young adults; sponsors Yiddish-speaking preschool for non-Orthodox children; disseminates new Yiddish teaching materials. *Yugntruf.*

ZEIREI AGUDATH ISRAEL, AGUDATH ISRAEL OF AMERICA, YOUNG MEN'S DIVISION (Religious, Educational)

CANADA

B'NAI BRITH CANADA (1875). 15 Hove St., Suite 200, Downsview, ONT M3H 4Y8. (416)633–6224. Pres. Moishe Smith; Exec. V.-Pres. Frank Dimant. Canadian Jewry's senior organization; makes representations to all levels of government on matters of Jewish concern; promotes humanitarian causes and educational programs, community volunteer projects, adult Jewish education, and leadership development; dedicated to human rights; sponsors youth programs of B'nai Brith Youth Org. (serving youth ages 13–18) and B'nai Brith Hillel Foundations (serving college and university students). *Covenant; Communiqué; Hillel Voice.*

———, INSTITUTE FOR INTERNATIONAL AND GOVERNMENTAL AFFAIRS (1987). 15 Hove St., Downsview, Ont. M3H 4YB. (416)633–6224. Natl. Chmn. Brian Morris; Natl. Dir. Paul Marcus. Identifies and protests the abuse of human rights throughout the world. Monitors the condition of Jewish communities worldwide and advocates on their behalf when they experience serious violations of their human rights. *Comment.*

———, LEAGUE FOR HUMAN RIGHTS (1970). 15 Hove St., Downsview, Ont. M3H 4Y8. (416)633–6227. Natl. Chmn. Hershie Frankel; Natl. Dir. Karen Mock. Dedicated to monitoring human rights, combating racism and racial discrimination, and preventing bigotry and anti-Semitism through education and community relations. Sponsors Holocaust Education Programs, the R. Lou Ronson Research Institute on Anti-Semitism; distributor of Anti-Defamation League materials in Canada. *Review of Anti-Semitism.*

CANADA-ISRAEL SECURITIES, LTD., STATE OF ISRAEL BONDS (1953). 1255 University St., Suite 200, Montreal, PQ H3B 3B2. (514)878–1871. Pres. Melvyn A. Dobrin; Exec. V.-Pres. Julius Briskin. Sells Israel bonds and notes.

CANADIAN ASSOCIATION FOR LABOR ISRAEL (HISTADRUT) (1944). 7005 Kildare Rd., Suite 14, Cote St. Luc, Que. H4W 1C1. (514)484-9430. Pres. Harry J. F. Bloomfield; Exec. Dir. Leonard Waldman. Conducts fund-raising and educational activities on behalf of Histadrut, Kupat Holim, and Amal schools in Israel.

CANADIAN FOUNDATION FOR JEWISH CULTURE (1965). 4600 Bathurst St., Willowdale, ONT M2R 3V2. (416)635-2883. Pres. Mira Koschitzky; Exec. Sec. Edmond Y. Lipsitz. Promotes Jewish studies at university level and encourages original research and scholarship in Jewish subjects; awards annual scholarships and grants-in-aid to scholars in Canada.

CANADIAN FRIENDS OF THE ALLIANCE ISRAÉLITE UNIVERSELLE (1958). PO Box 578, Victoria Station, Montreal, PQ H3Z 2Y6. (514)481-3552. Pres. Joseph Nuss. Supports the educational work of the Alliance.

CANADIAN FRIENDS OF THE HEBREW UNIVERSITY (1944). 3080 Yonge St., Suite 5024, Toronto, ONT M4N 3P4. Pres. Edward J. Winant; Exec. V.-Pres. Shimon Arbel. Represents and publicizes the Hebrew University in Canada; serves as fundraising arm for the university in Canada; processes Canadians for study at the university. *Scopus; Dateline Jerusalem.*

CANADIAN JEWISH CONGRESS (1919; reorg. 1934). 1590 Dr. Penfield Ave., Montreal, PQ H3G 1C5. (514)931-7531. Pres. Les Scheininger; Exec. V.-Pres. Alan Rose. The official voice of Canadian Jewish communities at home and abroad; acts on all matters affecting the status, rights, concerns and welfare of Canadian Jewry; internationally active on behalf of Soviet Jewry, Jews in Arab lands, Holocaust remembrance and restitution; largest Jewish archives in Canada. *National Small Communities Newsletter; Intercom; Ottawa Digest; National Soviet Jewry Newsletter; National Archives Newsletter; Community Relations Newsletter; regional newsletters.*

CANADIAN ORT ORGANIZATION (Organization of Rehabilitation Through Training) (1942). 5165 Sherbrooke St. W., Suite 208, Montreal, PQ H4A 1T6. (514)481-2787. Pres. Bernard Gross; Exec. Dir. Mac Silver. Carries on fund-raising projects in support of the worldwide vocational-training-school network of ORT. *ORT Reporter.*

———, WOMEN'S CANADIAN ORT (1948). 3101 Bathurst St., Suite 604, Toronto, ONT M6A 2A6. (416)787-0339. Natl. Pres. Joann Smith; Natl. Exec. Dir. Diane Uslaner. Chapters in 11 Canadian cities raise funds for ORT's nonprofit global network of schools where Jewish students learn a wide range of marketable skills, including the most advanced high-tech professions. *Focus Magazine.*

CANADIAN SEPHARDI FEDERATION (1973). c/o Or Haemet School, 210 Wilson Ave., Toronto, ONT M5M 3B1. (416)483-8968. Pres. Maurice Benzacar; Sec. Laeticia Benabou. Preserves and promotes Sephardic identity, particularly among youth; works for the unity of the Jewish people; emphasizes relations between Sephardi communities all over the world; seeks better situation for Sephardim in Israel; supports Israel by all means. Participates in *La Voix Sépharade, Le Monde Sépharade,* and *Sephardi World.*

CANADIAN YOUNG JUDAEA (1917). 788 Marlee Ave., Suite 205, Toronto, ONT M6B 3K1. (416)787-5350. Exec. Dir. Samuel Gotkin; Natl. Shaliach Avi Gur. Strives to attract Jewish youth to Zionism, with goal of *aliyah;* educates youth about Jewish history and Zionism; prepares them to provide leadership in Young Judaea camps in Canada and Israel and to be concerned Jews. *Judaean; The Young Judaean.*

CANADIAN ZIONIST FEDERATION (1967). 5250 Decarie Blvd., Suite 500, Montreal, PQ H3X 2H9. (514)486-9526. Pres. David J. Azrieli. Umbrella organization of all Zionist and Israel-related groups in Canada; carries on major activities in all areas of Jewish life through its departments of education and culture, *aliyah,* youth and students, public affairs, and fund raising for the purpose of strengthening the State of Israel and the Canadian Jewish community. *Canadian Zionist.*

———, BUREAU OF EDUCATION AND CULTURE (1972). Pres. David J. Azrieli. Provides counseling by pedagogic experts, in-service teacher-training courses and seminars in Canada and Israel; national pedagogic council and research center; distributes educational material and teaching aids; conducts annual Bible contest and Hebrew-language courses for adults. *Al Mitzpe Hachinuch.*

FRIENDS OF PIONEERING ISRAEL (1950s). 1111 Finch Ave. W., Suite 154, Downsview, ONT M3J 2E5 (416)736–0977. Pres. Joe Podemsky. Supports progressive organizations and activities in Israel.

HADASSAH—WIZO ORGANIZATION OF CANADA (1917). 1310 Greene Ave., Suite 900, Montreal, PQ H3Z 2B8. (514)937–9431. Natl. Pres. Naomi Frankenburg; Exec. V.-Pres. Lily Frank. Extends material and moral support to the people of Israel requiring such assistance; strengthens and fosters Jewish ideals; encourages Hebrew culture in Canada and promotes Canadian ideals of democracy. *Orah Magazine.*

JEWISH IMMIGRANT AID SERVICES OF CANADA (JIAS) (1919). 5151 Cote Ste. Catherine Rd., Suite 220, Montreal, PQ H3W 1M6.(514)342–9351. Natl. Pres. Sheldon Sper; Natl. Exec. Dir. Susan Davis. Serves as a national agency for immigration and immigrant welfare. *JIAS Bulletin.*

JEWISH NATIONAL FUND OF CANADA (KEREN KAYEMETH LE'ISRAEL, INC.) (1901). 1980 Sherbrooke St. W., Suite 500, Montreal, PQ H3H 1E8. (514)934–0313. Pres. Neri J. Bloomfield; Exec. V.-Pres. Morris Zilka. Fund-raising organization affiliated with the World Zionist Organization; involved in afforestation, soil reclamation, and development of the land of Israel, including the construction of roads and preparation of sites for new settlements; provides educational materials and programs to Jewish schools across Canada.

LABOR ZIONIST ALLIANCE OF CANADA (1909).7005 Kildare Rd., Suite 10, Cote St. Luc, PQ H3W 1C1. (514)484–1789. Pres. David Kofsky; Chmn. Toronto City Committee Harry Weinstock; Chmn. Montreal City Committee Harry Froimovitch. Associated with the World Labor Zionist movement and allied with the Israel Labor party. Provides recreational and cultural programs, mutual aid, and fraternal care to enhance the social welfare of its membership; actively promotes Zionist education, cultural projects, and forums on aspects of Jewish and Canadian concern.

MIZRACHI-HAPOEL HAMIZRACHI ORGANIZATION OF CANADA (1941). 159 Almore Ave., Downsview, ONT M3H 2H9. (416)-630–7575. Natl. Pres. Kurt Rothschild; Natl. Exec. V.-Pres. Rabbi Menachem Gopin. Promotes religious Zionism, aimed at making Israel a state based on Torah; maintains Bnei Akiva, a summer camp, adult education program, and touring department; supports Mizrachi-Hapoel Hamizrachi and other religious Zionist institutions in Israel which strengthen traditional Judaism. *Mizrachi Newsletter; Or Hamizrach Torah Quarterly.*

NATIONAL COUNCIL OF JEWISH WOMEN OF CANADA (1897). 1110 Finch Ave. W., #518, Downsview, ONT M3J 2T2. (416)-665–8251. Pres. Gloria Strom; Exec. Dir. Eleanor Appleby. Dedicated to furthering human welfare in Jewish and non-Jewish communities, locally, nationally, and internationally; provides essential services, and stimulates and educates the individual and the community through an integrated program of education, service, and social action. *New Edition.*

NATIONAL JOINT COMMUNITY RELATIONS COMMITTEE OF CANADIAN JEWISH CONGRESS (1936). 4600 Bathurst St., Willowdale, ONT M2R 3V2 (416)635–2883. Chmn. Joseph J. Wilder; Exec. Dir. Manuel Prutschi. Seeks to safeguard the status, rights, and welfare of Jews in Canada; to combat anti-Semitism and promote understanding and goodwill among all ethnic and religious groups. *Community Relations Report.*

Jewish Federations, Welfare Funds, Community Councils

UNITED STATES

ALABAMA

BIRMINGHAM
BIRMINGHAM JEWISH FEDERATION (1936; reorg. 1971); PO Box 130219 (35213); (205)-879–0416. FAX: (205)879–0466. Pres. Steven Brickman; Exec. Dir. Richard Friedman.

MOBILE
MOBILE JEWISH WELFARE FUND, INC. (inc. 1966); One Office Park, Suite 219 (36609); (205)343–7197. Pres. Nancy Silverboard; Admin. Barbara V. Paper.

MONTGOMERY
JEWISH FEDERATION OF MONTGOMERY, INC. (1930); PO Box 20058 (36120); (205)-277–5820. Pres. Jake Mendel; Exec. Dir. Beverly Lipton.

ARIZONA

PHOENIX
JEWISH FEDERATION OF GREATER PHOENIX (1940); 32 W. Coolidge, Suite 200 (85013); (602)274–1800. FAX: (602)266–7875. Pres. Andi Minkoff; Exec. Dir. Harold Morgan.

TUCSON
JEWISH FEDERATION OF SOUTHERN ARIZONA (1942); 635 N. Craycroft (85711); (602)327–7957. FAX: (602)323–2189. Pres. Harold Greenberg; Exec. V. Pres. Richard Fruchter.

ARKANSAS

LITTLE ROCK
JEWISH FEDERATION OF ARKANSAS (1911); 4942 W. Markham, Suite 5 (72205); (501)-663–3571. Pres. Jane B. Mendel; Exec. Dir. Ariel Barak Imber.

CALIFORNIA

LONG BEACH
JEWISH FEDERATION OF GREATER LONG BEACH AND W. ORANGE COUNTY (1937; inc. 1946); 3801 E. Willow St. (90815); (213)-426–7601. FAX: (213)426–3915. Pres. Morton Stuhlbarg; Exec. Dir. Sandi Goldstein.

LOS ANGELES
JEWISH FEDERATION COUNCIL OF GREATER LOS ANGELES (1912; reorg. 1959); 6505 Wilshire Blvd. (90048); (213)852–1234. FAX: (213)655–4458. Pres. George Caplan; Exec. V. Pres. Wayne Feinstein.

OAKLAND
JEWISH FEDERATION OF THE GREATER EAST BAY (Alameda and Contra Costa Counties) (1918); 401 Grand Ave. (94610); (415)839–2900. FAX: (415)839–3996. Pres. Dr. Miles Adler; Exec. V. Pres. Ami Nahshon.

This directory is based on information supplied by the Council of Jewish Federations.

ORANGE COUNTY
JEWISH FEDERATION OF ORANGE COUNTY (1964; inc. 1965); 1385 Warner Ave., Suite. A, Tustin (92680–6442); (714)259–0655. FAX: (714)259–1635. Pres. Jeff Schulein; Exec. Dir. Merv Lemmerman.

PALM SPRINGS
JEWISH FEDERATION OF PALM SPRINGS (1971); 255 El Cielo N., Suite 430 (19962); (619)325–7281. Pres. Sondra Landau; Exec. Dir. Irving Ginsberg.

SACRAMENTO
JEWISH FEDERATION OF SACRAMENTO (1948); PO Box 254589 (95865); (916)486–0906. FAX: (916)486–0816. Pres. Barbara Ansel; Exec. Dir. Arnold Feder.

SAN DIEGO
UNITED JEWISH FEDERATION OF SAN DIEGO COUNTY (1936); 4797 Mercury St. (92111–2102); (619)571–3444. FAX: (619)-571–0701. Pres. Shearn Platt; Exec. V. Pres. Stephen M. Abramson.

SAN FRANCISCO
JEWISH COMMUNITY FEDERATION OF SAN FRANCISCO, THE PENINSULA, MARIN, AND SONOMA COUNTIES (1910; reorg. 1955); 121 Steuart St. (94105); (415)777–0411. FAX: (415)495–6635. Pres. Annette Dobbs; Exec. Dir. Rabbi Brian Lurie.

SAN JOSE
JEWISH FEDERATION OF GREATER SAN JOSE (incl. Santa Clara County except Palo Alto and Los Altos) (1930; reorg. 1950); 14855 Oka Rd., Los Gatos (95030); (408)-358–3033. FAX: (408)356–0733. Pres. Bernie Kotansky; Exec. Dir. Michael Papo.

SANTA BARBARA
SANTA BARBARA JEWISH FEDERATION (org. 1974); PO Box 90110, Santa Barbara (93190); (805)966–7860. Pres. Steven A. Amerikaner; Exec. Dir. Ina F. Frank.

COLORADO

DENVER
ALLIED JEWISH FEDERATION OF DENVER (1936); 300 S. Dahlia St. (80222); (303)321–3399. FAX: (303)322–8328. Pres. Larry Siegel; Exec. Dir. Sheldon Steinhauser.

CONNECTICUT

BRIDGEPORT
JEWISH FEDERATION OF GREATER BRIDGEPORT, INC. (1936; reorg. 1981); 4200 Park Ave. (06604); (203)372–6504. FAX: (203)-374–0770. Pres. Selig Danzig; Exec. Dir. Gerald A. Kleinman.

DANBURY
JEWISH FEDERATION OF GREATER DANBURY (1945); 54 Main St., Suite E (06810); (203)792–6353. Pres. S. Benedict Levin; Exec. Dir. Sharon Garelick.

EASTERN CONNECTICUT
JEWISH FEDERATION OF EASTERN CONNECTICUT, INC. (1950; inc. 1970); 28 Channing St., PO Box 1468, New London (06320); (203)442–8062. FAX: (203)444–0759. Pres. Reuben Levin; Exec. Dir. Jerome E. Fischer.

GREENWICH
GREENWICH JEWISH FEDERATION (1956); 600 W. Putnam Ave. (06830); (203)622–1434. FAX: (203)622–1237. Pres. Paula Lustbader; Exec. Dir. Rabbi Melvin Libman.

HARTFORD
GREATER HARTFORD JEWISH FEDERATION (1945); 333 Bloomfield Ave., W. Hartford (06117); (203)232–4483. FAX: (203)232–5221. Pres. Robert Siskin; Exec. Dir. Don Cooper.

NEW HAVEN
NEW HAVEN JEWISH FEDERATION (1928); 419 Whalley Ave. (06511); (203)562–2137. FAX: (203)787–1524. Pres. Mary Lou Winnick; Exec. Dir. Susan Shimelman.

NORWALK
(See Westport)

STAMFORD
UNITED JEWISH FEDERATION (inc. 1973); 1035 Newfield Ave., PO Box 3038 (06905); (203)322–6935. FAX: (203)322–3277. Pres. Benson Zinbarg; Exec. Dir. Sheila L. Romanowitz.

WATERBURY
JEWISH FEDERATION OF WATERBURY, INC. (1938); 359 Cooke St. (06710); (203)756–7234. FAX: (203)573–0368. Pres. Dr. Alan Stein; Exec. Dir. Eli J. Skora.

WESTPORT–WESTON–WILTON–NORWALK
UNITED JEWISH APPEAL/FEDERATION OF WESTPORT-WESTON-WILTON-NORWALK (inc. 1980); 49 Richmondville Ave. (06880); (203)266–8197. Pres. Michael Stashower; Exec. Dir. Robert Kessler.

JEWISH FEDERATIONS, FUNDS, COUNCILS / 587

DELAWARE

WILMINGTON
JEWISH FEDERATION OF DELAWARE, INC. (1934); 101 Garden of Eden Rd. (19803); (302)478-6200. FAX: (302)478-5374. Pres. William N. Topkis; Exec. V. Pres. Robert N. Kerbel.

DISTRICT OF COLUMBIA

WASHINGTON
UNITED JEWISH APPEAL-FEDERATION OF GREATER WASHINGTON, INC. (1935); 6101 Montrose Rd., Rockville, MD 20852. (301)-230-7200. FAX: (301)230-7272. Pres. Edward Kaplan; Exec. V. Pres. Ted B. Farber.

FLORIDA

DAYTONA BEACH
JEWISH FEDERATION OF VOLUSIA & FLAGLER COUNTIES, INC.; 533 Seabreeze Blvd., Suite 300 (32118-3977); (904)255-6260. Pres. Gary Greenfield.

FT. LAUDERDALE
JEWISH FEDERATION OF GREATER FT. LAUDERDALE (1968); 8358 W. Oakland Park Blvd. (33351); (305)748-8400. FAX: (305)748-6332. Pres. Harold L. Oshry; Exec. Dir. Kenneth B. Bierman.

JACKSONVILLE
JACKSONVILLE JEWISH FEDERATION (1935); 8505 San Jose Blvd. (32217); (904)-448-5000. FAX: (904)448-5715. Pres. Joan Levin; Exec. V. Pres. Isaac Lakritz.

LEE COUNTY
JEWISH FEDERATION OF LEE COUNTY (1974); 3628 Evans Ave., Ft. Myers (33901); (813)275-3554. Pres. Mark Geisler; Exec. Dir. Helene Kramer.

MIAMI
GREATER MIAMI JEWISH FEDERATION, INC. (1938); 4200 Biscayne Blvd. (33137); (305)576-4000. FAX: (305)573-8115. Pres. Donald E. Lefton; Exec. V. Pres. Myron J. Brodie.

ORLANDO
JEWISH FEDERATION OF GREATER ORLANDO (1949); 851 N. Maitland Ave., PO Box 941508, Maitland (32794-1508); (305)-645-5933. FAX: (407)645-1172. Pres. Betty Monroe; Exec. Dir. Jordan Harburger.

PALM BEACH COUNTY
JEWISH FEDERATION OF PALM BEACH COUNTY, INC. (1962); 501 S. Flagler Dr., Suite 305, W. Palm Beach (33401); (407)832-2120. FAX: (407)832-0562. Pres. Alec Engelstein; Exec. Dir. Jeffrey L. Klein.

PINELLAS COUNTY
JEWISH FEDERATION OF PINELLAS COUNTY, INC. (incl. Clearwater and St. Petersburg) (1950; reincorp. 1974); 301 S. Jupiter Ave., Clearwater (34615); (813) 446-1033. FAX: (813)461-0700. Pres. James Soble; Exec. Dir. Robert F. Tropp.

SARASOTA
SARASOTA-MANATEE JEWISH FEDERATION (1959); 580 S. McIntosh Rd. (34232); (813)-371-4546. FAX: (813)378-2947. Pres. Doris Loevner; Exec. Dir. Norman Olshansky.

SOUTH BROWARD
JEWISH FEDERATION OF SOUTH BROWARD, INC. (1943); 2719 Hollywood Blvd., Hollywood (33020); (305)921-8810. FAX: (305)-921-6491. Pres. Dr. Howard Barron; Exec. Dir. Sumner G. Kaye.

SOUTH PALM BEACH COUNTY
SOUTH PALM BEACH COUNTY JEWISH FEDERATION (inc. 1979); 336 NW Spanish River Blvd., Boca Raton (33431); (407) 368-2737. FAX: (407)368-5240. Pres. Marvin Zale; Exec. Dir. Rabbi Bruce S. Warshal.

TAMPA
TAMPA JEWISH FEDERATION (1941); 2808 Horatio (33609); (813)875-1618. FAX: (813)875-1843. Pres. Walter H. Kessler; Exec. V. Pres. Gary S. Alter.

GEORGIA

ATLANTA
ATLANTA JEWISH FEDERATION, INC. (1905; reorg. 1967); 1753 Peachtree Rd. NE (30309); (404)873-1661. FAX: (404)874-7043. Pres. William E. Schatten; Exec. Dir. David I. Sarnat.

AUGUSTA
AUGUSTA JEWISH FEDERATION (1937); PO Box 3251, Sibley Rd. (30904); (404)736-1818. Pres. Matt Marks.

COLUMBUS
JEWISH WELFARE FEDERATION OF COLUMBUS, INC. (1941); PO Box 6313 (31907); (404)568-6668. Pres. Jack Hirsch; Sec. Irene Rainbow.

SAVANNAH
SAVANNAH JEWISH FEDERATION (1943); PO Box 23527 (31403); (912)355-8111. FAX: (912)355-8116. Pres. Ricky Eichholz; Exec. Dir. Stan Ramati.

HAWAII
HONOLULU
JEWISH FEDERATION OF HAWAII (1956); 677 Ala Moana, Suite 803 (96813); (808)531-4634. FAX: (808)531-4631. Pres. Richard I. Kersten; Exec. Dir. Barbara Fischlowitz.

ILLINOIS
CHAMPAIGN-URBANA
CHAMPAIGN-URBANA JEWISH FEDERATION (1929); 503 E. John St., Champaign (61820); (217)367-9872. Pres. Helen Levin; Exec. Dir. Janie Yairi.

CHICAGO
JEWISH FEDERATION OF METROPOLITAN CHICAGO (1900); 1 S. Franklin St. (60606-4694); (312)346-6700. FAX: (312)444-2086. Pres. John C. Colman; Exec. V. Pres. Steven B. Nasatir.

JEWISH UNITED FUND OF METROPOLITAN CHICAGO (1900); 1 S. Franklin St. (60606-4694); (312)346-6700. FAX: (312)444-2086. Pres. John C. Colman; Exec. Dir. Steven B. Nasatir.

DECATUR
DECATUR JEWISH FEDERATION (1942); c/o Temple B'nai Abraham, 1326 W. Eldorado (62522); (217)429-5740. Pres. Cheri Kalvort; Treas. Marvin Tick.

ELGIN
ELGIN AREA JEWISH WELFARE CHEST (1938); 330 Division St. (60120); (312)741-5656. Pres. Dr. Albert Simon; Treas. Richard Cutts.

PEORIA
JEWISH FEDERATION OF PEORIA (1933; inc. 1947); 3100 N. Knoxville, Suite 19 (61603); (309)686-0611. Pres. Morey Slodki; Exec. Dir. Barry Nove.

QUAD CITIES
JEWISH FEDERATION OF QUAD CITIES (incl. Rock Island, Moline, Davenport, Bettendorf) (1938; comb. 1973); 224 18 St., Suite 303, Rock Island (61201); (309)793-1300. Pres. Jerald Greenblatt; Exec. Dir. Ida Kramer.

ROCKFORD
JEWISH FEDERATION OF GREATER ROCKFORD (1937); 1500 Parkview Ave. (61107); (815)399-5497. Pres. Jay Kamin; Exec. Dir. Tony Toback.

SOUTHERN ILLINOIS
JEWISH FEDERATION OF SOUTHERN ILLINOIS, SOUTHEASTERN MISSOURI AND WESTERN KENTUCKY (1941); 6464 W. Main, Suite 7A, Belleville (62223); (618)398-6100. Pres. Ronald Rubin; Exec. Dir. Gary Cohn.

SPRINGFIELD
SPRINGFIELD JEWISH FEDERATION (1941); 730 E. Vine St. (62703); (217)528-3446. Pres. Howard Feldman; Exec. Dir. Lenore Loeb.

INDIANA
EVANSVILLE
EVANSVILLE JEWISH COMMUNITY COUNCIL, INC. (1936; inc. 1964); PO Box 5026 (47715); (812)477-7050. Pres. Jon Goldman; Exec. Sec. Maxine P. Fink.

FORT WAYNE
FORT WAYNE JEWISH FEDERATION (1921); 227 E. Washington Blvd. (46802); (219)422-8566. Pres. Carol Sandler; Exec. Dir. Vivian Lansky.

INDIANAPOLIS
JEWISH FEDERATION OF GREATER INDIANAPOLIS, INC. (1905); 615 N. Alabama St., Suite 412 (46204-1430); (317)637-2473. FAX: (317)637-2477. Pres. Stanley Talesnick; Exec. V. Pres. Harry Nadler.

LAFAYETTE
FEDERATED JEWISH CHARITIES (1924); PO Box 708 (47902); (317)742-9081. FAX: (317)742-4379. Pres. Arnold Cohen; Finan. Sec. Louis Pearlman, Jr.

MICHIGAN CITY
MICHIGAN CITY UNITED JEWISH WELFARE FUND; 2800 S. Franklin St. (46360); (219)-874-4477. Pres. & Treas. Harold Leinwand.

NORTHWEST INDIANA
THE JEWISH FEDERATION, INC. (1941; reorg. 1959); 2939 Jewett St., Highland (46322); (219)972-2250. Pres. Jerome Gardberg; Exec. Dir. Marty Erann.

SOUTH BEND
JEWISH FEDERATION OF ST. JOSEPH VALLEY (1946); 105 Jefferson Centre, Suite 804

JEWISH FEDERATIONS, FUNDS, COUNCILS / 589

(46601); (219)233–1164. FAX: (219)288–4103. Pres. Dr. Martin I. Jacobs; Exec. V. Pres. Kimball Marsh.

IOWA

DES MOINES
JEWISH FEDERATION OF GREATER DES MOINES (1914); 910 Polk Blvd. (50312); (515)277–6321. FAX: (515)255–1920. Pres. Harry Bookey; Exec. Dir. Elaine Steinger.

SIOUX CITY
JEWISH FEDERATION (1921); 525 14th St. (51105); (712)258–0618. Pres. Michael Potash; Exec. Dir. Doris Rosenthal.

KANSAS

WICHITA
MID-KANSAS JEWISH FEDERATION, INC. (1935); 400 N. Woodlawn, Suite 8 (67208); (316)686–4741. Pres. Ivonne Goldstein; Exec. Dir. Beverly Jacobson.

KENTUCKY

LEXINGTON
CENTRAL KENTUCKY JEWISH FEDERATION (1976); 333 Waller, Suite 5 (40504); (606)-252–7622. Pres. Michael Ades; Exec. Dir. Linda Ravvin.

LOUISVILLE
JEWISH COMMUNITY FEDERATION OF LOUISVILLE, INC. (1934); 3630 Dutchman's Lane (40205); (502)451–8840. FAX: (502)-458–0702. Pres. Ronald W. Abrams; Exec. Dir. Dr. Alan S. Engel.

LOUISIANA

ALEXANDRIA
THE JEWISH WELFARE FEDERATION AND COMMUNITY COUNCIL OF CENTRAL LOUISIANA (1938); 1227 Southhampton (71303); (318)445–4785. Pres. Alvin Mykoff; Sec.-Treas. Roeve Weill.

BATON ROUGE
JEWISH FEDERATION OF GREATER BATON ROUGE (1971); 11744 Haymarket Ave., Suite B; PO Box 80827 (70898); (504) 291–5895. Pres. Dr. Steven Cavalier; Exec. Dir. Louis Goldman.

NEW ORLEANS
JEWISH FEDERATION OF GREATER NEW ORLEANS (1913; reorg. 1977); 1539 Jackson Ave. (70130); (504)525–0673. FAX: (504)-568–9290. Pres. Dr. Julius L. Levy, Jr.; Exec. Dir. Jane Buchsbaum.

SHREVEPORT
SHREVEPORT JEWISH FEDERATION (1941; inc. 1967); 2032 Line Ave. (71104); (318)-221–4129. Pres. Neal Nierman; Exec. Dir. Monty Pomm.

MAINE

LEWISTON-AUBURN
LEWISTON-AUBURN JEWISH FEDERATION (1947); 74 Bradman St., Auburn (04210); (207)786–4201. Pres. Scott Nussinow.

PORTLAND
JEWISH FEDERATION COMMUNITY COUNCIL OF SOUTHERN MAINE (1942); 57 Ashmont St. (04103); (207)773–7254. Pres. Lisa Cohen; Exec. Dir. Meyer Bodoff.

MARYLAND

BALTIMORE
ASSOCIATED JEWISH CHARITIES & WELFARE FUND, INC. (1920; reorg. 1969); 101 W. Mt. Royal Ave. (21201); (301) 727–4828. FAX: (301)752–1177. Chmn. Suzanne F. Cohen,; Pres. Darrell D. Friedman.

MASSACHUSETTS

BERKSHIRE COUNTY
JEWISH FEDERATION OF THE BERKSHIRES (1940); 235 East St., Pittsfield (01201); (413)-442–4360. Pres. Joel Greenberg; Exec. Dir. Richard Davis.

BOSTON
COMBINED JEWISH PHILANTHROPIES OF GREATER BOSTON, INC. (1895; inc. 1961); One Lincoln Plaza (02111); (617)330–9500. FAX: (617)330–5197. Pres. Edward M. Sidman; Exec. V. Pres. Barry Shrage.

FRAMINGHAM (Merged with Boston)

LEOMINSTER
LEOMINSTER JEWISH COMMUNITY COUNCIL, INC. (1939); 268 Washington St. (01453); (617)534–6121. Pres. Dr. Milton Kline; Sec.-Treas. Howard J. Rome.

MERRIMACK VALLEY
MERRIMACK VALLEY UNITED JEWISH COMMUNITIES (1988); (Serves Lowell, Lawrence, Andover, Haverhill, Newburyport, and 22 surrounding communities); 805 Turnpike St., N. Andover (01845); (508)688–0466. Pres. Larry Ansin; Exec. Dir. Howard Flagler.

NEW BEDFORD
JEWISH FEDERATION OF GREATER NEW BEDFORD, INC. (1938; inc. 1954); 467 Hawthorn St., N. Dartmouth (02747); (508)997-7471. FAX: (508)997-7730. Pres. Elliot Rosenfield; Exec. Dir. Jerry S. Neimand.

NORTH SHORE
JEWISH FEDERATION OF THE NORTH SHORE, INC. (1938); 4 Community Rd., Marblehead (01945); (617)598-1810. FAX: (617)639-1284. Pres. Lawrence Slater; Exec. Dir. Bruce Yudewitz.

SPRINGFIELD
JEWISH FEDERATION OF GREATER SPRINGFIELD, INC. (1925); 1160 Dickinson St. (01108); (413)737-4313. FAX: (413)737-4348. Pres. Betsy Gaberman; Exec. Dir. Joel Weiss.

WORCESTER
WORCESTER JEWISH FEDERATION, INC. (1947; inc. 1957); 633 Salisbury St. (01609); (508)756-1543. FAX: (508)798-0962. Pres. Michael Sleeper; Exec. Dir. Joseph Huber.

MICHIGAN

ANN ARBOR
JEWISH COMMUNITY ASSOCIATION/ UNITED JEWISH APPEAL (1986); 2939 Birch Hollow Dr. (48108). (313)677-0100. Pres. Dr. Irving Smokler; Interim Dir. Nancy N. Margolis.

DETROIT
JEWISH WELFARE FEDERATION OF DETROIT (1899); Fred M. Butzel Memorial Bldg., 163 Madison (48226); (313)965-3939. FAX: (313)965-5778 (executive offices); (313)965-8217 (all other departments). Pres. Mark E. Schlussel; Exec. V. Pres. Robert P. Aronson.

FLINT
FLINT JEWISH FEDERATION (1936); 619 Wallenberg St. (48502); (313)767-5922. FAX: (313)767-9024. Pres. Gary Hurand; Exec. Dir. David Nussbaum.

GRAND RAPIDS
JEWISH COMMUNITY FUND OF GRAND RAPIDS (1930); 2609 Berwyck SE (49506); (616)956-9365. Pres. Joseph N. Schwartz; Admin. Dir. Judy Joseph.

MINNESOTA

DULUTH-SUPERIOR
JEWISH FEDERATION & COMMUNITY COUNCIL (1937); 1602 E. Second St. (55812); (218)-724-8857. Pres. David Blustin; Sec. Admin. Gloria Vitullo.

MINNEAPOLIS
MINNEAPOLIS FEDERATION FOR JEWISH SERVICE (1929; inc. 1930); 7600 Wayzata Blvd. (55426); (612)593-2600. FAX: (612)-593-2544. Pres. Herbert Goldenberg; Exec. Dir. Max L. Kleinman.

ST. PAUL
UNITED JEWISH FUND AND COUNCIL (1935); 790 S. Cleveland, Suite 201 (55116); (612)690-1707. Pres. Allen Freeman; Exec. Dir. Sam Asher.

MISSISSIPPI

JACKSON
JACKSON JEWISH WELFARE FUND, INC. (1945); 5315 Old Canton Rd. (39211-4625); (601)956-6215. Pres. Ruth Friedman; V. Pres. Erik Hearon.

MISSOURI

KANSAS CITY
JEWISH FEDERATION OF GREATER KANSAS CITY (1933); 5801 W. 115th St., Overland Park, KS (66211-1824); (913)469-1340. FAX: (913)451-9358. Pres. Ann R. Jacobson; Exec. Dir. A. Robert Gast.

ST. JOSEPH
UNITED JEWISH FUND OF ST. JOSEPH (1915); 509 Woodcrest Dr. (64506); (816)-279-7154. Pres. Dorathea Polsky; Exec. Sec. Martha Rothstein.

ST. LOUIS
JEWISH FEDERATION OF ST. LOUIS (incl. St. Louis County) (1901); 12 Millstone Campus Dr. (63146); (314)432-0020. FAX: (314)-432-1277. Pres. Alyn V. Essman; Exec. V. Pres. William Kahn.

NEBRASKA

LINCOLN
LINCOLN JEWISH WELFARE FEDERATION, INC. (1931; inc. 1961); PO Box 80014 (68501); (402)423-5695. Co-Pres. Ruth & Irwin Goldenberg; Exec. Dir. Robert Pitlor.

JEWISH FEDERATIONS, FUNDS, COUNCILS / 591

OMAHA
JEWISH FEDERATION OF OMAHA (1903); 333 S. 132nd St. (68154-2198); (402)334-8200. Pres. Saranne Gitnick; Exec. Dir. Howard Bloom.

NEVADA

LAS VEGAS
JEWISH FEDERATION OF LAS VEGAS (1973); 1030 E. Twain Ave. (89109); (702)732-0556. FAX: (702)732-3228. Pres. Hal Ober; Exec. Dir. Norman Kaufman.

NEW HAMPSHIRE

MANCHESTER
JEWISH FEDERATION OF GREATER MANCHESTER (1974); 698 Beech St. (03104); (603)627-7679. Pres. Dr. David Stahl; Acting Exec. Dir. Lillian G. Crockett.

NEW JERSEY

ATLANTIC COUNTY
FEDERATION OF JEWISH AGENCIES OF ATLANTIC COUNTY (1924); 505-507 Tilton Rd., Northfield (08225); (609)646-7077. FAX: (609)646-6441.Pres. Lynn Kramer; Exec. Dir. Bernard Cohen.

BERGEN COUNTY
UNITED JEWISH COMMUNITY OF BERGEN COUNTY (inc. 1978); 111 Kinderkamack Rd., PO Box 4176, N. Hackensack Station, River Edge (07661); (201)488-6800. FAX: (201)-488-1507. Pres. Paula Cantor; Exec. V. Pres. James Young.

CENTRAL NEW JERSEY
JEWISH FEDERATION OF CENTRAL NEW JERSEY (1940; merged 1973); Green Lane, Union (07083); (201)351-5060. FAX: (201)-351-7060. Pres. Leonard Posnock; Exec. V. Pres. Burton Lazarow.

CLIFTON-PASSAIC
JEWISH FEDERATION OF GREATER CLIFTON-PASSAIC (1933); 199 Scoles Ave., Clifton (07012). (201)777-7031. FAX: (201)777-6701. Pres. Jon Gurkoff; Exec. Dir. Yosef Muskin.

CUMBERLAND COUNTY
JEWISH FEDERATION OF CUMBERLAND COUNTY (inc. 1971); 629 Wood St., Suite 204, Vineland (08360); (609)696-4445. Pres. Gerald Batt; Exec. Dir. Daniel Lepow.

ENGLEWOOD
(Merged with Bergen County)

JERSEY CITY
UNITED JEWISH APPEAL (1939); 71 Bentley Ave. (07304); (201)332-6644. Gen. Chmn. Mel Blum; Exec. Sec. Madeline Mazer.

MERCER COUNTY
JEWISH FEDERATION OF MERCER AND BUCKS COUNTIES NJ/PA; (1929; reorg. 1982); 999 Lower Ferry Rd., Trenton (08628); (609)883-5000. FAX: (609)883-2563. Pres. Richard Dickson; Exec. Dir. Haim Morag. (Also see listing under Pennsylvania.)

METROWEST NEW JERSEY
UNITED JEWISH FEDERATION OF METROWEST (1923); 60 Glenwood Ave., E. Orange (07017); (201)673-6800; (212)943-0570. FAX: (201)673-4387. Pres. Sam Oolie; Exec. V. Pres. Howard E. Charish.

MIDDLESEX COUNTY
JEWISH FEDERATION OF GREATER MIDDLESEX COUNTY (org. 1948; reorg. 1985); 100 Metroplex Dr., Suite 101, Edison (08817); (201)985-1234. FAX: (201)985-3295. Pres. James Stahl; Exec. V.-Pres. Michael Shapiro.

MONMOUTH COUNTY
JEWISH FEDERATION OF GREATER MONMOUTH COUNTY (1971); 100 Grant Ave., PO Box 210, Deal (07723-0210); (201)531-6200-1. Pres. Sharon Portman; Exec. Dir. Marvin Relkin.

MORRIS-SUSSEX COUNTY
(Merged with MetroWest NJ)

NORTH JERSEY
JEWISH FEDERATION OF NORTH JERSEY (1933); One Pike Dr., Wayne (07470); (201)-595-0555. FAX: (201)595-1532. Pres. Joanne Sprechman; Exec. Dir. Barry Rosenberg.

NORTHERN MIDDLESEX COUNTY
(See Middlesex County)

OCEAN COUNTY
OCEAN COUNTY JEWISH FEDERATION (1977); 301 Madison Ave., Lakewood (08701); (201)363-0530. FAX: (201)363-2097. Pres. Zev Rosen; Exec. Dir. Michael Ruvel.

PRINCETON
PRINCETON AREA UJA-FEDERATION; PO Box 385, Princeton (08542); (609)924-6859.

Pres. Dr. Eliot Freeman; Exec. Dir. Jerilyn Zimmerman.

RARITAN VALLEY
(See Middlesex County)

SOMERSET COUNTY
JEWISH FEDERATION OF SOMERSET, HUNTERDON, & WARREN COUNTIES (1960); 120 Finderne Ave., Bridgewater (08807); (201)-725-6994. Pres. George Blank; Exec. Dir. Alan J. Nydick.

SOUTHERN NEW JERSEY
JEWISH FEDERATION OF SOUTHERN NEW JERSEY (incl. Camden, Burlington, and Gloucester counties) (1922); 2393 W. Marlton Pike, Cherry Hill (08002); (609)665-6100. FAX: (609)665-0074. Pres. Dr. Robert Paul; Exec. V. Pres. Stuart Alperin.

NEW MEXICO

ALBUQUERQUE
JEWISH FEDERATION OF GREATER ALBUQUERQUE, INC. (1938); 12800 Lomas NE, Suite F (87112); (505)292-1061. Pres. Shirlee R. Londer; Exec. Dir. Joel Brooks.

NEW YORK

ALBANY
(Merged with Schenectady; see Northeastern New York)

BROOME COUNTY
JEWISH FEDERATION OF BROOME COUNTY (1937; inc. 1958); 500 Clubhouse Rd., Binghamton (13903); (607)724-2332. Pres. Howard Rittberg; Exec. Dir. Victoria Rouff.

BUFFALO
JEWISH FEDERATION OF GREATER BUFFALO, INC. (1903); 787 Delaware Ave. (14209); (716)886-7750. FAX: (716)886-1367. Pres. Stuart G. Lerman; Exec. Dir. Harry Kosansky.

DUTCHESS COUNTY
JEWISH FEDERATION OF DUTCHESS COUNTY; 110 S. Grand Ave., Poughkeepsie (12603); (914)471-9811. Pres. Morris Krakinowski; Exec. Dir. Ira Minot.

ELMIRA
ELMIRA JEWISH WELFARE FUND, INC. (1942); Grandview Rd. Ext., PO Box 3087 (14905); (607)734-8122. Pres. Arnold Rosenberg; Exec. Dir. Cy Leveen.

KINGSTON
JEWISH FEDERATION OF GREATER KINGSTON, INC. (inc. 1951); 159 Green St. (12401); (914)338-8131. Pres. Dr. Howard Rothstein.

NEW YORK
UJA-FEDERATION OF JEWISH PHILANTHROPIES OF NEW YORK, INC. (incl. Greater NY; Westchester, Nassau, and Suffolk counties) (Fed. org. 1917; UJA 1939; merged 1986); 130 E. 59th St. (10022); (212)980-1000. FAX: (212)888-7538. Pres. David G. Sacks; Chmn. Joseph Gurwin; Exec. V. Pres. Stephen D. Solender.

NIAGARA FALLS
JEWISH FEDERATION OF NIAGARA FALLS, NY, INC. (1935); Temple Beth Israel, Rm. #5, College & Madison Ave. (14305); (716)-284-4575. Pres. Howard Rushner.

NORTHEASTERN NEW YORK
UNITED JEWISH FEDERATION OF NORTHEASTERN NEW YORK (1986); Latham Circle Mall, 800 New Loudon Rd., Latham (12110); (518)783-7800. FAX: (518)783-1557. Pres. Rabbi Martin Silverman; Exec. Dir. Norman J. Schimelman.

ORANGE COUNTY
JEWISH FEDERATION OF GREATER ORANGE COUNTY (1977); 360 Powell Ave., Newburgh (12550); (914)562-7860. Pres. Richard Levin; Exec. Dir. Nancy Goldman.

ROCHESTER
JEWISH COMMUNITY FEDERATION OF ROCHESTER, NY, INC. (1939); 441 East Ave. (14607); (716)461-0490. FAX: (716)461-0912. Pres. Linda Cornell Weinstein; Exec. Dir. Lawrence W. Fine.

ROCKLAND COUNTY
UNITED JEWISH COMMUNITY OF ROCKLAND COUNTY (1985); 240 W. Nyack Rd., W. Nyack (10994-1711). (914)627-3700. FAX: (914)627-7881. Pres. Mark Karsch; Exec. Dir. Michael A. Bierman.

SCHENECTADY
(Merged with Albany; see Northeastern New York)

SYRACUSE
SYRACUSE JEWISH FEDERATION, INC. (1918); 101 Smith St.; PO Box 510, DeWitt (13214-0510); (315)445-0161. FAX: (315)-445-1559. Pres. Helen Marcum; Exec. V. Pres. Barry Silverberg.

TROY
(Merged with Albany-Schenectady; see Northeastern New York)

UTICA
JEWISH FEDERATION OF UTICA, NY, INC. (1933; inc. 1950); 2310 Oneida St. (13501); (315)733-2343. Pres. Richard Dinerstein; Exec. Dir. Meyer L. Bodoff.

NORTH CAROLINA

ASHEVILLE
WESTERN NORTH CAROLINA JEWISH FEDERATION (1935); 236 Charlotte St. (28801); (704)253-0701. FAX: (704)251-9144. Pres. Robert J. Deutsch; Exec. Dir. David Seidenberg.

CHARLOTTE
CHARLOTTE JEWISH FEDERATION (1938); PO Box 13369 (28211); (704)366-5007. Pres. Emily Zimmerman; Exec. Dir. Michael Minkin.

DURHAM-CHAPEL HILL
DURHAM-CHAPEL HILL JEWISH FEDERATION & COMMUNITY COUNCIL (1979); 1310 LeClair St., Chapel Hill (27514); (919)967-1945. Pres. Barry Nakell.

GREENSBORO
GREENSBORO JEWISH FEDERATION (1940); 713-A N. Greene St. (27401); (919)272-3189. Pres. Bernard Gutterman; Exec. Dir. Marilyn Chandler.

WAKE COUNTY
WAKE COUNTY JEWISH FEDERATION, INC. (1987); 3900 Merton Dr., Suite 108, Raleigh (27609); (919)787-0666. Pres. Joseph Woodland.

OHIO

AKRON
AKRON JEWISH COMMUNITY FEDERATION (1935); 750 White Pond Dr. (44320); (216)-867-7850. Pres. Joseph Kanfer; Exec. Dir. Michael Wise.

CANTON
CANTON JEWISH COMMUNITY FEDERATION (1935; reorg. 1955); 2631 Harvard Ave., NW (44709); (216)452-6444. FAX: (216)-452-4487. Pres. Robert Narens; Exec. Dir. Jay Rubin.

CINCINNATI
JEWISH FEDERATION OF CINCINNATI (1896; reorg. 1967); 1811 Losantiville, Suite 320 (45237); (513) 351-3800. FAX: (513)351-3863. Pres. Stanley M. Chesley; Exec. V. Pres. Aubrey Herman.

CLEVELAND
JEWISH COMMUNITY FEDERATION OF CLEVELAND (1903); 1750 Euclid Ave. (44115); (216)566-9200. FAX: (216)861-1230. Pres. Max R. Friedman; Exec. Dir. Stephen H. Hoffman.

COLUMBUS
COLUMBUS JEWISH FEDERATION (1926); 1175 College Ave. (43209); (614)237-7686. FAX: (614)237-2221. Pres. Benjamin L. Zox; Exec. Dir. Alan H. Gill.

DAYTON
JEWISH FEDERATION OF GREATER DAYTON (1910); 4501 Denlinger Rd. (45426); (513)854-4150. FAX: (513)854-2850. Pres. Lawrence T. Burick; Exec. V. Pres. Peter H. Wells.

STEUBENVILLE
JEWISH COMMUNITY COUNCIL (1938); 300 Lovers Lane (43952); (614)264-5514. Pres. Morris Denmark; Exec. Sec. Jennie Bernstein.

TOLEDO
JEWISH FEDERATION OF GREATER TOLEDO (1907; reorg. 1960); 6505 Sylvania Ave., PO Box 587, Sylvania (43560); (419)885-4461. FAX: (419)885-3207. Pres. James J. Akers; Exec. Dir. Steven J. Edelstein.

YOUNGSTOWN
YOUNGSTOWN AREA JEWISH FEDERATION (1935); PO Box 449, 505 Gypsy Lane (44501); (216)746-3251. FAX: (216)746-7926. Pres. Esther L. Marks; Exec. V. Pres. Sam Kooperman.

OKLAHOMA

OKLAHOMA CITY
JEWISH FEDERATION OF GREATER OKLAHOMA CITY (1941); 2800 Quail Plaza Dr. (73120). (405)752-7307. Pres. Jerry Bendorf; Exec. Dir. Garth Potts.

TULSA
JEWISH FEDERATION OF TULSA (1938); 2021 E. 71st St. (74136); (918)495-1100. FAX: (918)495-1220. Pres. Curtis S. Green; Exec. Dir. David Bernstein.

OREGON

PORTLAND
JEWISH FEDERATION OF PORTLAND (incl. state of Oregon and adjacent Washington communities) (1920; reorg. 1956); 6651 SW Capitol Highway (97219); (503)245-6219. FAX: (503)245-6603. Pres. Stanley D. Geffen; Exec. Dir. Charles Schiffman.

PENNSYLVANIA

ALLENTOWN
JEWISH FEDERATION OF ALLENTOWN (1948); 702 N. 22nd St. (18104); (215)821-5500. FAX: (215)821-8946. Pres. Leonard Abrams; Exec. Dir. Ivan C. Schonfeld.

ALTOONA
FEDERATION OF JEWISH PHILANTHROPIES (1920; reorg. 1940; inc. 1944); 1308 17th St. (16601); (814)944-4072. Pres. Morley Cohn.

BUCKS COUNTY
JEWISH FEDERATION OF MERCER AND BUCKS COUNTIES NJ/PA (1929; reorg. 1982); 999 Lower Ferry Rd., Trenton, NJ (08628); (609)883-5000. FAX: (609)883-2563. Pres. Richard Dickson; Exec. Dir. Haim Morag. (Also see listing under New Jersey.)

ERIE
JEWISH COMMUNITY COUNCIL OF ERIE (1946); 701 G. Daniel Baldwin Bldg., 1001 State St. (16501); (814)455-4474. Pres. Richard Levick.

HARRISBURG
UNITED JEWISH COMMUNITY OF GREATER HARRISBURG (1941); 100 Vaughn St. (17110); (717)236-9555. FAX: (717)236-8104. Pres. Morton Spector; Exec. Dir. Elliot Gershenson.

JOHNSTOWN
UNITED JEWISH FEDERATION OF JOHNSTOWN (1938); 601 Wayne St. (15905); (814)-539-9891 (home). Pres. Isadore Suchman.

PHILADELPHIA
FEDERATION OF JEWISH AGENCIES OF GREATER PHILADELPHIA (includes Bucks, Chester, Delaware, Montgomery, and Philadelphia counties) (1901; reorg. 1956); 226 S. 16th St. (19102); (215)893-5600. FAX: (215)735-7977. Pres. Miriam A. Schneirov; Exec. V. Pres. Robert P. Forman.

PITTSBURGH
UNITED JEWISH FEDERATION OF GREATER PITTSBURGH (1912; reorg. 1955); 234 McKee Pl. (15213); (412)681-8000. FAX: (412)681-3980. Pres. David S. Shapira; Exec. V. Pres. Howard M. Rieger.

READING
JEWISH FEDERATION OF READING, PA., INC. (1935; reorg. 1972); 1700 City Line St. (19604); (215)921-2766. Pres. Alma Lakin; Exec. Dir. Daniel Tannenbaum.

SCRANTON
SCRANTON-LACKAWANNA JEWISH FEDERATION (incl. Lackawanna County) (1945); 601 Jefferson Ave. (18510); (717)961-2300. Pres. Joseph Dubin; Exec. Dir. Seymour Brotman.

WILKES-BARRE
JEWISH FEDERATION OF GREATER WILKES-BARRE (1935); 60 S. River St. (18702); (717)-822-4146. Pres. Connie Roth; Exec. Dir. Robert S. Capin.

RHODE ISLAND

PROVIDENCE
JEWISH FEDERATION OF RHODE ISLAND (1945); 130 Sessions St. (02906); (401)421-4111. FAX: (401)331-7961. Pres. Norman Tilles; Exec. V. Pres. Elliot Cohan.

SOUTH CAROLINA

CHARLESTON
CHARLESTON JEWISH FEDERATION (1949); 1645 Raoul Wallenberg Blvd., PO Box 31298 (29407); (803)571-6565. FAX: (803)556-6206. Pres. Ellis I. Kahn; Exec. Dir. Michael Wise.

COLUMBIA
COLUMBIA JEWISH FEDERATION (1960); 4540 Trenholm Rd., PO Box 6968 (29260); (803)787-0580. Pres. Samuel Tenenbaum; Exec. Dir. Alexander Grossberg.

SOUTH DAKOTA

SIOUX FALLS
JEWISH WELFARE FUND (1938); National Reserve Bldg., 513 S. Main Ave. (57102); (605)336-2880. Pres. Laurence Bierman; Exec. Sec. Louis R. Hurwitz.

TENNESSEE

CHATTANOOGA
CHATTANOOGA JEWISH FEDERATION (1931); 5326 Lynnland Terrace, PO Box 8947 (37411); (615)894-1317. Pres. Charles B. Lebovitz; Exec. Dir. Louis B. Solomon.

JEWISH FEDERATIONS, FUNDS, COUNCILS / 595

KNOXVILLE

KNOXVILLE JEWISH FEDERATION (1939); 6800 Deane Hill Dr., PO Box 10882 (37939-0882); (615)693-5837. Pres. Barbara Bernstein; Exec. Dir. Conrad J. Koller.

MEMPHIS

MEMPHIS JEWISH FEDERATION (incl. Shelby County) (1935); 6560 Poplar Ave. (38138); (901)767-7100. FAX: (901)767-7128. Pres. Jerome Makowsky; Exec. Dir. Gary Siepser.

NASHVILLE

JEWISH FEDERATION OF NASHVILLE & MIDDLE TENNESSEE (1936); 801 Percy Warner Blvd. (37205); (615)356-3242. FAX: (615)352-0056. Pres. Nedda Pollack; Exec. Dir. Jay M. Pilzer.

TEXAS

AUSTIN

JEWISH FEDERATION OF AUSTIN (1939; reorg. 1956); 11713 Jollyville Rd. (78759); (512)331-1144. FAX: (512)331-7059. Pres. Rafael Pelc; Exec. Dir. Wayne Silverman.

DALLAS

JEWISH FEDERATION OF GREATER DALLAS (1911); 7800 Northaven Rd., Suite A (75230); (214)369-3313. FAX: (214)369-8943. Pres. Sanford Fagadau; Exec. Dir. Morris A. Stein.

EL PASO

JEWISH FEDERATION OF EL PASO, INC. (incl. surrounding communities) (1937); 405 Wallenberg Dr., PO Box 12097 (79913-0097); (915)584-4437. FAX: (915)584-0243. Pres. Joan Johnson; Exec. Dir. David Brown.

FORT WORTH

JEWISH FEDERATION OF FORT WORTH AND TARRANT COUNTY (1936); 6801 Dan Danciger Rd. (76133); (817)292-3081. FAX: (817)292-3214. Pres. David Beckerman; Exec. Dir. Bruce Schlosberg.

GALVESTON

GALVESTON COUNTY JEWISH WELFARE ASSOCIATION (1936); PO Box 146 (77553); (409)763-5241. Pres. Harold Levine; Treas. Joe Nussenblatt.

HOUSTON

JEWISH FEDERATION OF GREATER HOUSTON (1936); 5603 S. Braeswood Blvd. (77096-3999); (713)729-7000. FAX: (713)-721-6232. Pres. Sandra Weiner; Exec. Dir. Hans Mayer.

SAN ANTONIO

JEWISH FEDERATION OF SAN ANTONIO (incl. Bexar County) (1922); 8434 Ahern Dr. (78216); (512)341-8234. FAX: (512)341-2842. Pres. Joe Westheimer, Jr.; Exec. Dir. Robert Posner.

WACO

JEWISH FEDERATION OF WACO AND CENTRAL TEXAS (1949); PO Box 8031 (76714-8031); (817)776-3740. Pres. Mike Stupak; Exec. Sec. Martha Bauer.

UTAH

SALT LAKE CITY

UNITED JEWISH COUNCIL AND SALT LAKE JEWISH WELFARE FUND (1936); 2416 E. 1700 South (84108); (801)581-0098. Pres. Fred Tannenbaum; Exec. Dir. Martha Solomon.

VIRGINIA

NEWPORT NEWS-HAMPTON-WILLIAMSBURG

UNITED JEWISH COMMUNITY OF THE VIRGINIA PENINSULA, INC. (1942); 2700 Spring Rd., Newport News (23606); (804)930-1422. Pres. Dr. Steven Seltzer; Exec. Dir. Barbara Rostov.

RICHMOND

JEWISH COMMUNITY FEDERATION OF RICHMOND (1935); 5403 Monument Ave., PO Box 17128 (23226); (804)288-0045. FAX: (804)282-7507. Pres. Dr. Walter N. Rabhan; Exec. Dir. Robert S. Hyman.

TIDEWATER

UNITED JEWISH FEDERATION OF TIDEWATER (incl. Norfolk, Portsmouth, and Virginia Beach) (1937); 7300 Newport Ave., PO Box 9776, Norfolk (23505); (804)489-8040. FAX: (804)489-8230. Pres. Dr. Charles J. Goldman; Exec. V. Pres. Gary N. Rubin.

WASHINGTON

SEATTLE

JEWISH FEDERATION OF GREATER SEATTLE (incl. King County, Everett, and Bremerton) (1926); 2031 Third Ave. (98121); (206)443-5400. FAX: (206)443-0303. Pres. Herbert Pruzan; Exec. Dir. Michael Novick.

WEST VIRGINIA

CHARLESTON

FEDERATED JEWISH CHARITIES OF CHARLESTON, INC. (1937); PO Box 1613

(25326); (304)346–7500. Pres. Carl Lehman; Exec. Sec. William H. Thalheimer.

WISCONSIN

KENOSHA

KENOSHA JEWISH WELFARE FUND (1938); 8041 48th Ave. (53142); (414)694–6695. Pres. Richard Selsberg; Sec.-Treas. Steven Barasch.

MADISON

MADISON JEWISH COMMUNITY COUNCIL, INC. (1940); 310 N. Midvale Blvd., Suite 325 (53705); (608)231–3426. Pres. Lawrence Shapiro; Exec. Dir. Steven H. Morrison.

MILWAUKEE

MILWAUKEE JEWISH FEDERATION, INC. (1902); 1360 N. Prospect Ave. (53202); (414)-271–8338. Pres. R. Todd Lappin; Exec. Dir. Rick Meyer.

CANADA

ALBERTA

CALGARY

CALGARY JEWISH COMMUNITY COUNCIL (1962); 1607 90th Ave. SW (T2V 4V7); (403)-253–8600. FAX: (403)253–7915. Pres. Hal Joffe; Exec. Dir. Drew J. Staffenberg.

EDMONTON

JEWISH FEDERATION OF EDMONTON (1954; reorg. 1982); 7200 156th St. (T5R 1X3); (403)487–5120. FAX: (403)481–3463. Pres. Sheldon Maerov; Exec. Dir. Sidney Indig.

BRITISH COLUMBIA

VANCOUVER

JEWISH FEDERATION OF GREATER VANCOUVER (1932; reorg. 1987); 950 W. 41st Ave. (V5Z 2N7); (604)266–7115. Pres. Daniel U. Pekarsky; Exec. Dir. Steve Drysdale.

MANITOBA

WINNIPEG

WINNIPEG JEWISH COMMUNITY COUNCIL (1938; reorg. 1973); 370 Hargrave St. (R3B 2K1); (204)943–0406. FAX: (204)956–0609. Pres. Sidney Halpern; Exec. Dir. Robert Freedman.

ONTARIO

HAMILTON

JEWISH FEDERATION OF HAMILTON, WENTWORTH & AREA (1932; merged 1971); PO Box 7258, 1030 Lower Lion Club Rd., Ancaster (L9G 3N6); (416)648–0605. FAX: (416)648–8388. Pres. Gerald Swaye Q.C.; Exec. Dir. Mark Silverberg.

LONDON

LONDON JEWISH FEDERATION (1932); 536 Huron St. (N5Y 4J5); (519)673–3310. FAX: (519)673–1161. Pres. Gloria Gilbert; Exec. Dir. Gerald Enchin.

OTTAWA

JEWISH COMMUNITY COUNCIL OF OTTAWA (1934); 151 Chapel St. (K1N 7Y2); (613)232–7306. FAX: (613)563–4593. Pres. Dr. Eli Rabin; Exec. Dir. Gerry Koffman.

TORONTO

TORONTO JEWISH CONGRESS (1917); 4600 Bathurst St.; Willowdale (M2R 3V2); (416)-635–2883. FAX: (416)635–1408. Pres. Charles S. Diamond; Exec. Dir. Steven Ain.

WINDSOR

JEWISH COMMUNITY COUNCIL (1938); 1641 Ouellette Ave. (N8X 1R9); (519)973–1772. FAX: (519)973–1774. Pres. Alan R. Orman; Exec. Dir. Allen Juris.

QUEBEC

MONTREAL

ALLIED JEWISH COMMUNITY SERVICES (1965); 5151 Cote St. Catherine Rd. (H3W 1M6); (514)735–3541. FAX: (514)735–8972. Pres. Maxine Sigman; Exec. Dir. John Fishel.

Jewish Periodicals[1]

UNITED STATES

ARIZONA

ARIZONA POST (1946). 635 N. Craycroft, #202, Tucson, 85711. (602)325-5864. Sandra R. Heiman. Fortnightly. Jewish Federation of Southern Arizona.

GREATER PHOENIX JEWISH NEWS (1947). PO Box 26590, Phoenix, 85068. (602)870-9470. Flo Eckstein. Weekly.

CALIFORNIA

B'NAI B'RITH MESSENGER (1897). PO BOX 35915, Los Angeles, 90035. (213)659-2952. Rabbi Yale Butler. Weekly.

HADSHOT L.A. (1988). 13535 Ventura Blvd., Suite 200, Sherman Oaks, 91423. (818)-783-3090. Meir Doron. Weekly. Hebrew.

HERITAGE-SOUTHWEST JEWISH PRESS (1914). 2130 S. Vermont Ave., Los Angeles, 90007. (213) 737-2122. Dan Brin. Weekly. (Also SAN DIEGO JEWISH HERITAGE, [weekly]; ORANGE COUNTY JEWISH HERITAGE, [weekly]; CENTRAL CALIFORNIA JEWISH HERITAGE [monthly].) Heritage Group.

JEWISH JOURNAL (1986). 3660 Wilshire Blvd., Suite 204, Los Angeles, 90010. (213)738-7778. Gene Lichtenstein. Weekly.

JEWISH NEWS & ISRAEL TODAY (1973). 11071 Ventura Blvd., Studio City, 91604. (818)786-4000. Phil Blazer. Monthly.

JEWISH SPECTATOR (1935). 4391 Park Milano, Calabasas, 91302. (818)883-5141. Robert Bleiweiss. Quarterly. American Friends of Center for Jewish Living and Values.

JEWISH STAR (1956). 109 Minna St., Suite 323, San Francisco, 94105. (415)421-4874. Nevon Stuckey. Bimonthly.

NORTHERN CALIFORNIA JEWISH BULLETIN (1946). 88 First St., Suite 300, San Francisco, 94105. (415)957-9340. Marc S. Klein. Weekly. San Francisco Jewish Community Publications Inc.

SAN DIEGO JEWISH TIMES (1979). 2592 Fletcher Pkwy., El Cajon, 92020. (619)-463-5515. Carol Rosenberg. Biweekly.

TIKKUN (1986). 5100 Leona St., Oakland, 94619. (415)482-0805. Michael Lerner. Bimonthly. Institute for Labor & Mental Health.

WESTERN STATES JEWISH HISTORY (1968). 2429 23rd St., Santa Monica, 90405. (213)-450-2946. Norton B. Stern. Quarterly. Western States Jewish History Association.

COLORADO

INTERMOUNTAIN JEWISH NEWS (1913). 1275 Sherman St., Suite 214, Denver, 80203. (303)861-2234. Miriam H. Goldberg. Weekly.

CONNECTICUT

CONNECTICUT JEWISH LEDGER (1929). 2475 Albany Ave., West Hartford, 06117. (203)233-2148. Berthold Gaster. Weekly.

DISTRICT OF COLUMBIA

B'NAI B'RITH INTERNATIONAL JEWISH MONTHLY (1886 under the name MENORAH). 1640 Rhode Island Ave., NW,

---

[1]The information in this directory is based on replies to questionnaires circulated by the editors. For organization bulletins, see the directory of Jewish organizations.

Washington, 20036. (202)857-6645. Jeff Rubin. Ten times a year. B'nai B'rith.

JEWISH VETERAN (1896). 1811 R St., NW, Washington, 20009. (202)265-6280. Warren S. Dolny. Bimonthly. Jewish War Veterans of the U.S.A.

MOMENT (1975). 3000 Connecticut Ave., NW, Suite 300, Washington, 20008. (202)-387-8888. Hershel Shanks. Bimonthly. Jewish Educational Ventures, Inc.

NEAR EAST REPORT (1957). 440 First St., NW, Suite 607, Washington, 20001. (202)-639-5300. Mitchell G. Bard. Weekly. Near East Research, Inc.

UCSJ QUARTERLY REPORT. 1819 H Street, NW, Suite 230, Washington, 20006. (202)-775-9770. Stacy Burdett. Quarterly. Union of Councils for Soviet Jews.

WASHINGTON JEWISH WEEK. *See under* MARYLAND.

FLORIDA

JEWISH FLORIDIAN (1929). 120 NE 6 St., Miami, 33132. (305)373-4605. Fred K. Shochet. Weekly.

JEWISH JOURNAL (1977). PO Box 189006, Plantation, 33318. (305)581-2244. Steven Sands. Weekly. South Florida Newspaper Network.

JEWISH PRESS OF PINELLAS COUNTY (1986). 301 Jupiter Ave. S., Clearwater, 34615. (813)441-4500. FAX: (813)461-0700. Jim Dawkins. Biweekly. Wolfson-Dawkins Publications.

JEWISH PRESS OF TAMPA. 2808 Horatio St., Tampa, 33609. (813)871-2332. FAX: (813)461-0700. Karen Wolfson Dawkins. Biweekly. Wolfson-Dawkins Publications.

JEWISH WORLD (1982). 2405 Mercer Ave., Suite 8, W. Palm Beach, 33401. (407)833-8331. Martin Pomerance. Weekly.

MIAMI JEWISH TRIBUNE (1986). 3550 Biscayne Blvd., Suite 600, 3rd fl., Miami, 33137-3845. (305)576-9500. Andrew Polin. Weekly. Jewish Media Group, Inc.

SOUTHERN JEWISH WEEKLY (1924). PO Box 3297, Jacksonville, 32206. (904)634-1469. Isadore Moscovitz. Weekly. Southern Independent Operators, Inc.

GEORGIA

ATLANTA JEWISH TIMES (1925); (formerly SOUTHERN ISRAELITE). 1575 Northside Dr., NW, Atlanta, 30318. (404)352-2400. Vida Goldgar. Weekly.

JEWISH CIVIC PRESS (1972). 3330 Peachtree Rd. NE, Suite 500, Atlanta, 30326. (404)-231-2194. Abner L. Tritt. Monthly.

ILLINOIS

CHICAGO JUF NEWS (1972). One S. Franklin St., Chicago, 60606. (312)444-2853. Joseph Aaron. Monthly. Jewish Federation of Metropolitan Chicago.

JEWISH COMMUNITY NEWS (1941). 6464 W. Main, Suite 7A, Belleville, 62223. (618)-398-6100. Rabbi Zalman Stein. Irregularly. Jewish Federation of Southern Illinois.

THE SENTINEL (1911). 175 W. Jackson Blvd., Suite 1927, Chicago, 60604. (312)-663-1101. J. I. Fishbein. Weekly.

INDIANA

ILLIANA NEWS (1975). 2939 Jewett St., Highland, 46322. (219)972-2250. Sharon Blumberg. Ten times a year (not July/August). Jewish Federation, Inc./Northwest Indiana.

INDIANA JEWISH POST AND OPINION (1935). PO Box 449097; 2120 N. Meridian, Indianapolis, 46202. (317)927-7800. Sarah Baker. Weekly.

NATIONAL JEWISH POST AND OPINION (1932). 2120 N. Meridian St., Indianapolis, 46202. (317)927-7800. Gabriel Cohen. Weekly.

KANSAS

KANSAS CITY JEWISH CHRONICLE. *See under* MISSOURI.

KENTUCKY

KENTUCKY JEWISH POST AND OPINION (1931). 1551 Bardstown Rd., Louisville, 40205. (502)459-1914. Gabriel Cohen. Weekly.

LOUISIANA

COMMUNITY (1989). 924 Valmont St., New Orleans, 70115. (504)895-8784. Michael Blackman. Semiweekly. Jewish Federation of Greater New Orleans.

JEWISH CIVIC PRESS (1965). PO Box 15500, 924 Valmont St., New Orleans, 70115. (504)895-8785. Abner Tritt. Monthly.

MARYLAND

BALTIMORE JEWISH TIMES (1919). 2104 N. Charles St., Baltimore, 21218. (301)752-3504. Gary Rosenblatt. Weekly.

WASHINGTON JEWISH WEEK (1930, as the NATIONAL JEWISH LEDGER). 12300 Twinbrook Pkwy., Suite 250, Rockville, 20852. (301)230-2222. Martin Pomerance. Weekly.

MASSACHUSETTS

AMERICAN JEWISH HISTORY (1893). 2 Thornton Rd., Waltham, 02154. (617)891-8110. FAX: (617)899-9208. Marc Lee Raphael. Quarterly. American Jewish Historical Society.

BOSTON JEWISH TIMES (1945). 169 Norfolk Ave., Boston, 02119. (617)442-9680. Sten Lukin. Fortnightly.

GENESIS 2 (1970). 99 Bishop Allen Dr., Cambridge, 02139. (617)576-1801. Lawrence Bush. Quarterly.

JEWISH ADVOCATE (1902). 1168-70 Commonwealth Ave., Boston, 02134. (617)-277-8988. Bernard M. Hyatt. Weekly.

JEWISH REPORTER (1970). 76 Salem End Rd., Framingham, 01701. (508)879-3302. Jodie B. Holzwasser. Monthly.

JEWISH WEEKLY NEWS (1945). PO Box 1569, Springfield, 01101. (413)739-4771. Leslie B. Kahn. Weekly.

JOURNAL OF THE NORTH SHORE JEWISH COMMUNITY (1977). 324 B Essex St., Swampscott, 01970. (508)581-7110. Barbara Wolf. Biweekly (one issue in July). Jewish Federation of the North Shore.

MICHIGAN

DETROIT JEWISH NEWS (1942). 20300 Civic Center Dr., Suite 240, Southfield, 48076. (313)354-6060. Gary Rosenblatt. Weekly.

HUMANISTIC JUDAISM (1968). 28611 W. Twelve Mile Rd., Farmington Hills, 48018. (313)478-7610. M. Bonnie Cousens, Ruth D. Feldman. Quarterly. Society for Humanistic Judaism.

MINNESOTA

AMERICAN JEWISH WORLD (1912). 4509 Minnetonka Blvd., Minneapolis, 55416. (612)920-7000. Marshall Hoffman. Weekly.

MISSOURI

KANSAS CITY JEWISH CHRONICLE (1920). 7373 W. 107 St., Suite 250, Overland Park, KS 66212. (913)648-4620. Ruth Baum Bigus. Weekly. Sun Publications.

MISSOURI JEWISH POST (1948). 9531 Lackland, Suite 207, St. Louis, 63114. (314)-423-3088. Kathie Sutin. Weekly.

ST. LOUIS JEWISH LIGHT (1947). 12 Millstone Campus Dr., St. Louis, 63146. (314)-432-3353. Robert A. Cohn. Weekly. Jewish Federation of St. Louis.

NEBRASKA

JEWISH PRESS (1921). 333 S. 132 St., Omaha, 68154. (402)334-8200. Morris Maline. Weekly. Jewish Federation of Omaha.

NEVADA

JEWISH REPORTER (1976). 1030 E. Twain Ave., Las Vegas, 89109. (702)732-0556. Marla Gerecht. Monthly. Jewish Federation of Las Vegas.

LAS VEGAS ISRAELITE (1965). PO Box 14096, Las Vegas, 89114. (702)876-1255. Michael Tell. Biweekly.

NEW JERSEY

AVOTAYNU (1985). 1485 Teaneck Rd., Teaneck, 07666. (201)837-2701. Sallyann Amdur Sack. Quarterly.

JEWISH COMMUNITY VOICE (1941). 2393 W. Marlton Pike, Cherry Hill, 08002. (609)-665-6100. Harriet Kessler. Biweekly. Jewish Federation of Southern NJ.

JEWISH HORIZON (1981). 1391 Martine Ave., Scotch Plains, 07076. (201)889-9200. Fran Gold. Weekly.

JEWISH RECORD (1939). 1525 S. Main St., Pleasantville, 08232. (609)383-0999. Martin Korik. Weekly.

JEWISH STANDARD (1931). 385 Prospect Ave. Hackensack, 07601. (201)342-1115. Rebecca Kaplan Boroson. Weekly.

JEWISH STAR (1975). 100 Metroplex Dr., Edison, 08817. (201)985-1234. Mindy

Belfer. Bimonthly. Jewish Federation of Greater Middlesex County.

JOURNAL OF JEWISH COMMUNAL SERVICE (1899). 3084 State Hwy. 27, Suite 1, Kendall Pk, NJ 08824. (201)821-1871. Gail Naron Chalew. Quarterly. Conference of Jewish Communal Service.

METROWEST JEWISH NEWS (1947). 60 Glenwood Ave., E. Orange, 07017. (201)-678-3900. David Frank. Weekly. United Jewish Federation of MetroWest.

NEW YORK

AFN SHVEL (1941). 200 W. 72 St., Suite 40, NYC, 10023. (212)787-6675. Mordkhe Schaechter. Quarterly. Yiddish. League for Yiddish, Inc.

ALGEMEINER JOURNAL (1972). 404 Park Ave. S., NYC, 10016. (212)689-3390. Gershon Jacobson. Weekly. Yiddish-English.

AMERICAN JEWISH YEAR BOOK (1899). 165 E. 56 St., NYC, 10022. (212)751-4000. David Singer, Ruth R. Seldin. Annually. American Jewish Committee and Jewish Publication Society.

AMERICAN ZIONIST (1910). 4 E. 34 St., NYC, 10016. (212)481-1500. Paul Flacks. Quarterly. Zionist Organization of America.

AMIT WOMAN (1925). 817 Broadway, NYC, 10003. (212)477-4720. Micheline Ratzersdorfer. Five times a year. AMIT Women (formerly American Mizrachi Women).

AUFBAU (1934). 2121 Broadway, NYC, 10023. (212)873-7400. Henry Marx. Fortnightly. German. New World Club, Inc.

BITZARON (1939). PO Box 623, Cooper Station, NYC, 10003. (212)998-8985. Hayim Leaf. Bimonthly. Hebrew; English abstracts. Hebrew Literary Foundation.

BUFFALO JEWISH REVIEW (1918). 15 E. Mohawk St., Buffalo, 14203. (716)854-2192. Harlan C. Abbey. Weekly. Kahaal Nahalot Israel.

COMMENTARY (1945). 165 E. 56 St., NYC, 10022. (212)751-4000. Norman Podhoretz. Monthly. American Jewish Committee.

CONGRESS MONTHLY (1933). 15 E. 84 St., NYC, 10028. (212)879-4500. Maier Deshell. Seven times a year. American Jewish Congress.

CONSERVATIVE JUDAISM (1945). 3080 Broadway, NYC, 10027. (212)678-8049. Rabbi Shamai Kanter. Quarterly. Rabbinical Assembly.

CONTEMPORARY JEWRY (1974 under the name JEWISH SOCIOLOGY AND SOCIAL RESEARCH). Center for Jewish Studies, CUNY Graduate School and University Center, 33 W. 42 St., NYC, 10036. (212)-790-4404. Paul Ritterband. Semiannually. Association for the Social Scientific Study of Jewry.

ECONOMIC HORIZONS (1953). 350 Fifth Ave., Suite 1919, NYC, 10118. (212)971-0310. Ronny Bassan. Annually. American-Israel Chamber of Commerce and Industry, Inc.

HADAROM (1957). 275 Seventh Ave., NYC, 10001. (212)807-7888. Rabbi Gedalia Dov Schwartz. Annually. Hebrew. Rabbinical Council of America.

HADASSAH MAGAZINE (1921). 50 W. 58 St., NYC, 10019. (212)303-8014. Alan M. Tigay. Monthly (except for combined issues of June-July and Aug.-Sept.). Hadassah, the Women's Zionist Organization of America.

HADOAR (1921). 1841 Broadway, Rm. 510, NYC, 10023. (212)581-5151. Shlomo Shamir, Yael Feldman. Weekly. Hebrew. Hadoar Association, Inc.

ISRAEL HORIZONS (1952). 150 Fifth Ave., Suite 911, NYC, 10011. (212)255-8760. Arieh Lebowitz. Quarterly. Americans for Progressive Israel.

ISRAEL QUALITY (1976). 350 Fifth Ave., Suite 1919, NYC 10118. (212)971-0310. Beth Belkin. Quarterly. Government of Israel Trade Center and American-Israel Chamber of Commerce and Industry.

JEWISH ACTION MAGAZINE (1950). 45 W. 36 St., 9th fl., NYC, 10018. (212)244-2011. Heidi Tenzer. Quarterly. Union of Orthodox Jewish Congregations of America.

JEWISH BOOK ANNUAL (1942). 15 E. 26 St., NYC, 10010. (212)532-4949. Jacob Kabakoff. English-Hebrew-Yiddish. JWB Jewish Book Council.

JEWISH BOOK WORLD (1945). 15 E. 26 St., NYC, 10010. (212)532-4949. William

JEWISH PERIODICALS / 601

Wollheim. Quarterly. JWB Jewish Book Council.

JEWISH BRAILLE INSTITUTE VOICE (1978). 110 E. 30 St., NYC, 10016. (212)889–2525. Jacob Freid. Monthly (except May/June, July/Aug.) (audio cassettes). Jewish Braille Institute of America, Inc.

JEWISH BRAILLE REVIEW (1931). 110 E. 30 St., NYC, 10016. (212)889–2525. Jacob Freid. Monthly, except May/June, July/Aug. English braille. Jewish Braille Institute of America, Inc.

JEWISH CURRENT EVENTS (1959). 430 Keller Ave., Elmont, 11003. Samuel Deutsch. Biweekly.

JEWISH CURRENTS (1946). 22 E. 17 St., Suite 601, NYC, 10003. (212)924–5740. Morris U. Schappes. Monthly (July/Aug. combined). Association for Promotion of Jewish Secularism, Inc.

JEWISH EDUCATION (1929). 426 W. 58 St., NYC, 10019. (212)713–0290. Alvin I. Schiff. Quarterly. Council for Jewish Education.

JEWISH FORWARD (1897). 45 E. 33 St., NYC, 10016. (212)889–8200. Mordechai Strigler. Weekly. Yiddish-English. Forward Association, Inc.

JEWISH FRONTIER (1934). 33 East 67 St., NYC 10021. (212)645–8121. Nahum Guttman. Bimonthly. Labor Zionist Letters, Inc.

JEWISH JOURNAL (1969). 8723 Third Ave., Brooklyn, 11209. (718)238–6600. Irving Ruderman. Weekly.

JEWISH LEDGER (1924). 2535 Brighton-Henrietta Town Line Rd., Rochester, 14623. (716)427–2434. Barbara Morgenstern. Weekly.

JEWISH MUSIC NOTES (1945). 15 E. 26 St., NYC, 10010. (212)532–4949. Debra Wachsberger, Norman Summers. Bi-annually. JWB Jewish Music Council.

JEWISH OBSERVER (1963). 84 William St., NYC, 10038. (212)797–9000. Rabbi Nisson Wolpin. Monthly (except July and Aug.). Agudath Israel of America.

JEWISH OBSERVER (1978). PO Box 510, DeWitt, 13214. (315)445–0161. Mollie Leitzes Collins. Biweekly. Syracuse Jewish Federation, Inc.

JEWISH POST AND RENAISSANCE (1977). 57 E. 11 St., NYC, 10003. (212)420–0042. Charles Roth. Bimonthly.

JEWISH PRESS (1950). 338 Third Ave., Brooklyn, 11215. (718)330–1100. Rabbi Sholom Klass. Weekly.

JEWISH SOCIAL STUDIES (1939). 2112 Broadway, Rm. 206, NYC, 10023. (212)-724–5336. Tobey B. Gitelle. Quarterly. Conference on Jewish Social Studies, Inc.

JEWISH TELEGRAPHIC AGENCY COMMUNITY NEWS REPORTER (1962). 330 Seventh Ave., 11th fl., NYC 10001–5010. (212)643–1890. FAX: (212)643–8498. Mark Joffe, Elli Wohlgelernter, Mark A. Seal. Weekly.

JEWISH TELEGRAPHIC AGENCY DAILY NEWS BULLETIN (1917). 330 Seventh Ave., 11th fl., NYC 10001–5010. (212)-643–1890. FAX: (212)643–8498. Mark Joffe, Elli Wohlgelernter, Mark A. Seal. Daily.

JEWISH TELEGRAPHIC AGENCY WEEKLY NEWS DIGEST (1933). 330 Seventh Ave., 11th fl., NYC 10001–5010. (212)643–1890. FAX: (212)643–8498. Mark Joffe, Elli Wohlgelernter, Mark A. Seal. Weekly.

JEWISH WEEK (1876; reorg. 1970). 1457 Broadway, NYC, 10036. (212)921–7822. Sheldon Engelmayer. Weekly.

JEWISH WORLD (1965). 1104 Central Ave., Albany, 12205. (518)459–8455. Laurie J. Clevenson. Weekly.

JOURNAL OF REFORM JUDAISM (1953). 192 Lexington Ave., NYC, 10016. (212)684–4990. Samuel Stahl. Quarterly. Central Conference of American Rabbis.

JUDAISM (1952). 15 E. 84 St., NYC, 10028. (212)879–4500. Robert Gordis. Quarterly. American Jewish Congress.

JWB CIRCLE (1946). 15 E. 26 St., NYC, 10010. (212)532–4949. Shirley R. Frank. Quarterly. JWB.

KIBBUTZ JOURNAL (1984). 27 W. 20 St., 9th fl., NYC, 10011. (800)444–7007. Avshalom Horowitz. Annually. English-Hebrew. Kibbutz Aliya Desk.

KOL HAT'NUA (VOICE OF THE MOVEMENT) (1975). 50 W. 58 St., NYC, 10019. (212)-303–8256. Daniel A. Miller. Bimonthly. Young Judaea-Hashachar.

KOSHER DIRECTORY (1925). 45 W. 36 St., NYC, 10018. (212)563-4000. Tziporah Spear. Every two years. Union of Orthodox Jewish Congregations of America.

KOSHER DIRECTORY, PASSOVER EDITION (1923). 45 W. 36 St., NYC, 10018. (212)-563-4000. Tziporah Spear. Annually. Union of Orthodox Jewish Congregations of America.

KULTUR UN LEBN—CULTURE AND LIFE (1967). 45 E. 33 St., NYC, 10016. (212)889-6800. Joseph Mlotek. Quarterly. Yiddish. Workmen's Circle.

LAMISHPAHA. (1963). 1841 Broadway, Rm. 510, NYC, 10023. (212)581-5151. Hanita Brand. Monthly (except July and Aug.). Hebrew. Histadruth Ivrith of America.

LIKUTIM (1981). 110 E. 30 St., NYC, 10016. (212)889-2525. Joanne Jahr. Two to four times a year (audio cassettes). Hebrew. Jewish Braille Institute of America, Inc.

LILITH—THE JEWISH WOMEN'S MAGAZINE (1976). 250 W. 57 St., #2432, NYC, 10107. (212)757-0818. Susan Weidman Schneider. Quarterly.

LONG ISLAND JEWISH WORLD (1971). 115 Middle Neck Rd., Great Neck, 11021. (516)829-4000. Jerome W. Lippman. Weekly.

MARTYRDOM AND RESISTANCE (1974). 48 W. 37 St., 9th fl., NYC 10018-4708. (212)-564-1865. Eli Zborowski. Bimonthly. International Society for Yad Vashem.

MELTON JOURNAL (1982). 3080 Broadway, NYC, 10027. (212)678-8031. Eduardo Rauch, Barry W. Holtz. Biannually. Melton Research Center for Jewish Education.

MIDSTREAM (1954). 515 Park Ave., NYC, 10022. (212)752-0600. Murray Zuckoff. Monthly. Theodor Herzl Foundation, Inc.

MODERN JEWISH STUDIES ANNUAL (1977). Queens College, Kiely 802, 65-30 Kissena Blvd., Flushing, 11367. (718)520-7067. Joseph C. Landis. Annually. American Association of Professors of Yiddish.

NA'AMAT WOMAN (1926). 200 Madison Ave., Suite 2120, NYC, 10016. (212)725-8010. Judith A. Sokoloff. Five times a year. English-Yiddish-Hebrew. NA'AMAT USA, the Women's Labor Zionist Organization of America.

OLOMEINU—OUR WORLD (1945). 6101 16th Ave., Brooklyn, NY 11204. (718)259-1223. Rabbi Yaakov Fruchter, Rabbi Nosson Scherman. Monthly. English-Hebrew. Torah Umesorah-National Society for Hebrew Day Schools.

PEDAGOGIC REPORTER (1949). 730 Broadway, NYC, 10003. (212)529-2000. Mordecai H. Lewittes. Quarterly. English-Hebrew. Jewish Education Service of North America, Inc.

PROCEEDINGS OF THE AMERICAN ACADEMY FOR JEWISH RESEARCH (1920). 3080 Broadway, NYC, 10027. (212)678-8864. Annually. English-Hebrew-French-Arabic-Persian-Greek. American Academy for Jewish Research.

RABBINICAL COUNCIL RECORD (1953). 275 Seventh Ave. NYC, 10001. (212)807-7888. Rabbi Louis Bernstein. Quarterly. Rabbinical Council of America.

REFORM JUDAISM (1972; formerly DIMENSIONS IN AMERICAN JUDAISM). 838 Fifth Ave., NYC, 10021. (212)249-0100. Aron Hirt-Manheimer. Quarterly. Union of American Hebrew Congregations.

REPORTER (1972). 500 Clubhouse Rd., Binghamton, 13903. (607)724-2360. Marc Goldberg. Weekly. Jewish Federation of Broome County.

RESPONSE (1967). 27 W. 20 St., 9th fl., NYC, 10011. (212)675-1168. Cindy Rubin. Quarterly.

SHEVILEY HA-HINNUKH (1939). 426 W. 58 St., NYC, 10019. (212)713-0290. Zvulun Ravid. Quarterly. Hebrew. Council for Jewish Education.

SH'MA (1970). Box 567, 23 Murray Ave., Port Washington, 11050. (516)944-9791. FAX: (516)767-9315. Eugene B. Borowitz. Biweekly (except June, July, Aug.).

SHMUESSEN MIT KINDER UN YUGENT (1942). 770 Eastern Pkwy., Brooklyn, 11213. (718)493-9250. Nissan Mindel. Monthly. Yiddish. Merkos L'Inyonei Chinuch, Inc.

SYNAGOGUE LIGHT (1933). 47 Beekman St., NYC, 10038. (212)227-7800. Rabbi Meyer Hager. Semiannually. Union of Chassidic Rabbis.

TALKS AND TALES (1942). 770 Eastern Pkwy., Brooklyn, 11213. (718)774-4000 or

6000. Nissan Mindel. Monthly (also Hebrew, French, and Spanish editions). Merkos L'Inyonei Chinuch, Inc.

TRADITION (1958). 275 Seventh Ave., NYC, 10001. (212)807-7888. Rabbi Emanuel Feldman. Quarterly. Rabbinical Council of America.

TRENDS (1982). 730 Broadway, NYC, 10003. (212)529-2000. Leora W. Isaacs. Semiannually. Jewish Education Service of North America, Inc.

UNITED SYNAGOGUE REVIEW (1943). 155 Fifth Ave., NYC, 10010. (212)533-7800. Lois Goldrich. Biannually. United Synagogue of America.

UNSER TSAIT (1941). 25 E. 21 St., NYC, 10010. (212)475-0059. Editorial committee. Monthly. Yiddish. Jewish Labor Bund.

WOMEN'S AMERICAN ORT REPORTER (1966). 315 Park Ave. S., NYC, 10010. (212)505-7700. Eve M. Jacobson. Quarterly. Women's American ORT, Inc.

WOMEN'S LEAGUE OUTLOOK (1930). 48 E. 74 St., NYC, 10021. (212)628-1600. Lynne Heller. Quarterly. Women's League for Conservative Judaism.

WORKMEN'S CIRCLE CALL (1933). 45 E. 33 St., NYC, 10016. (212)889-6800. Walter L. Kirschenbaum. Bimonthly. Workmen's Circle.

YEARBOOK OF THE CENTRAL CONFERENCE OF AMERICAN RABBIS (1890). 192 Lexington Ave., NYC, 10016. (212)684-4990. Elliot L. Stevens. Annually. Central Conference of American Rabbis.

YIDDISH (1973). Queens College, Kiely 802, 65-30 Kissena Blvd., Flushing, 11367. (718)520-7067. Joseph C. Landis. Quarterly. Queens College Press.

DI YIDDISHE HEIM (1958). 770 Eastern Pkwy., Brooklyn, 11213. (718)493-9250. Rachel Altein. Quarterly. English-Yiddish. Neshei Ub'nos Chabad.

YIDDISHE KULTUR (1938). 1133 Broadway, Rm. 1023, NYC, 10010. (212)691-0708. Itche Goldberg. Monthly (except June-July, Aug.-Sept.). Yiddish. Yiddishe Kultur Farband, Inc.—YKUF.

DOS YIDDISHE VORT (1953). 84 William St., NYC, 10038. (212)797-9000. Joseph Friedenson. Monthly. Yiddish. Agudath Israel of America.

YIDDISHER KEMFER (1900). 275 Seventh Ave., NYC, 10001. (212)675-7808. Mordechai Strigler. Weekly. Yiddish. Labor Zionist Alliance.

YIDISHE SHPRAKH (1941). 1048 Fifth Ave., NYC, 10028. (212)231-7905. Mordkhe Schaechter. Irregularly. Yiddish. Yivo Institute for Jewish Research, Inc.

YIVO ANNUAL OF JEWISH SOCIAL SCIENCE (1946). 1048 Fifth Ave., NYC, 10028. (212)535-6700. Deborah Dash Moore. Annually. Yivo Institute for Jewish Research, Inc.

YIVO BLETER (1931). 1048 Fifth Ave., NYC, 10028. (212)535-6700. David E. Fishman. Irregularly. Yiddish. Yivo Institute for Jewish Research, Inc.

YOUNG ISRAEL VIEWPOINT (1952). 3 W. 16 St., NYC, 10011. (212)929-1525. Peter Nuchims. Six times a year. National Council of Young Israel.

YOUNG JUDAEAN (1910). 50 W. 58 St., NYC, 10019. (212)303-8271. Mordecai Newman. 4 times a year between Sept. and June. Hadassah Zionist Youth Commission.

YUGNTRUF (1964). 200 W. 72 St., Suite 40, NYC 10023. Paul Glasser. Quarterly. Yiddish. Yugntruf Youth for Yiddish.

NORTH CAROLINA

AMERICAN JEWISH TIMES OUTLOOK (1934; reorg. 1950). PO Box 33218, Charlotte, 28233. (704)372-3296. Ruth Goldberg. Monthly. The Blumenthal Foundation.

OHIO

THE AMERICAN ISRAELITE (1854). 906 Main St., Rm. 505, Cincinnati, 45202. (513)621-3145. Phyllis R. Singer. Weekly.

AMERICAN JEWISH ARCHIVES (1948). 3101 Clifton Ave., Cincinnati, 45220. (513)221-1875. Jacob R. Marcus, Abraham J. Peck. Semiannually. American Jewish Archives of Hebrew Union College-Jewish Institute of Religion.

CLEVELAND JEWISH NEWS (1964). 3645 Warrensville Rd., Shaker Hts., 44122. (216)991-8300. FAX: (216)991-9556.

Cynthia Dettelbach. Weekly. Cleveland Jewish Publication Co.

DAYTON JEWISH CHRONICLE (1961). 118 Salem Ave., Dayton, 45406. (513)222-0783. Leslie Cohen Zukowsky. Weekly.

INDEX TO JEWISH PERIODICALS (1963). PO Box 18570, Cleveland Hts., 44118. (216)-321-7296. Miriam Leikind, Jean H. Foxman. Semiannually.

OHIO JEWISH CHRONICLE (1922). 1600 Brice Rd., Reynoldsburg, 43068. (614)-860-9060. Judith Franklin. Weekly.

STARK JEWISH NEWS (1920). 2631 Harvard Ave. NW, Canton, 44709. (216)452-6444. Adele Gelb. Monthly. Canton Jewish Community Federation.

STUDIES IN BIBLIOGRAPHY AND BOOKLORE (1953). 3101 Clifton Ave., Cincinnati, 45220. (513)221-1875. Herbert C. Zafren. Irregularly. English-Hebrew-German. Library of Hebrew Union College–Jewish Institute of Religion.

TOLEDO JEWISH NEWS (1987). 6505 Sylvania Ave., Sylvania, 43560. (419)885-4461. Fred Flox. Monthly. Jewish Federation of Greater Toledo.

OKLAHOMA

SOUTHWEST JEWISH CHRONICLE (1929). 314-B N. Robinson St., Oklahoma City, 73102. (405)236-4226. E. F. Friedman. Quarterly.

TULSA JEWISH REVIEW (1930). 2021 E. 71 St., Tulsa, 74136. (918)495-1100. Dianna Aaronson. Bimonthly. Jewish Federation of Tulsa.

PENNSYLVANIA

JEWISH CHRONICLE OF PITTSBURGH (1962). 5600 Baum Blvd., Pittsburgh, 15206. (412)687-1000. Joel Roteman. Weekly. Pittsburgh Jewish Publication and Education Foundation.

JEWISH EXPONENT (1887). 226 S. 16 St., Philadelphia, 19102. (215)893-5740. Albert Erlick. Weekly. Jewish Publishers Group of Greater Philadelphia.

JEWISH QUARTERLY REVIEW (1910). 420 Walnut St., Philadelphia, 19149. (215)-238-1290. Leon Nemoy, Bernard Lewis, David M. Goldenberg, Vera B. Moreen. Quarterly. Annenberg Research Institute.

JEWISH TIMES OF THE GREATER NORTHEAST (1925). 103A Tomlinson Rd., Huntingdon Valley, 19006. (215)738-1177. Leon E. Brown. Weekly. Federation of Jewish Agencies of Greater Philadelphia.

NEW MENORAH (1979). 7318 Germantown Ave., Philadelphia, PA 19119-1793. (215)-242-4074. Arthur Waskow. Quarterly. P'nai Or Religious Fellowship.

RECONSTRUCTIONIST (1935). Church Rd. & Greenwood Ave., Wyncote, 19095. (215)-887-1988. Joy Levitt. Bimonthly. Federation of Reconstructionist Congregations and Havurot.

RHODE ISLAND

RHODE ISLAND JEWISH HISTORICAL NOTES (1954). 130 Sessions St., Providence, 02906. (401)331-1360. Judith Weiss Cohen. Annually. Rhode Island Jewish Historical Association.

TENNESSEE

THE HEBREW WATCHMAN (1925). 4646 Poplar Ave., Suite 232, Memphis, 38117. (901)763-2215. Herman I. Goldberger. Weekly.

THE OBSERVER (1934). 801 Percy Warner Blvd., Nashville, 37205. (615)356-3242. Judith A. Saks. Bimonthly (except July). Jewish Federation of Nashville.

TEXAS

JEWISH CIVIC PRESS (1965). PO Box 35656, Houston, 77235. (713)721-8901. Abner Tritt. Monthly.

JEWISH HERALD-VOICE (1908). PO Box 153, Houston, 77001-0153. (713)630-0391. Joseph W. Samuels. Weekly.

JEWISH JOURNAL OF SAN ANTONIO (1973). 8434 Ahern, San Antonio, 78216. (512)-341-8234. Marion H. Bernstein. Monthly (11 issues). Jewish Federation of San Antonio.

TEXAS JEWISH POST (1947). 3120 S. Expressway, Fort Worth, 76110. (817) 927-2831. 11333 N. Central Expressway, Dallas, 75243. (214)692-7283. Jimmy Wisch. Weekly.

VIRGINIA

RENEWAL MAGAZINE (1984). 7300 Newport Ave., Norfolk, 23505. (804)489-8040. FAX: (804)489-8230. Reba Karp. Quarterly. United Jewish Federation of Tidewater.

UJF VIRGINIA NEWS (1959). 7300 Newport Ave., Norfolk, 23505. (804)489-8040. FAX: (804)489-8230. Reba Karp. 21 issues yearly. United Jewish Federation of Tidewater.

WASHINGTON

JEWISH TRANSCRIPT (1924). 2031 Third Ave., Suite 200, Seattle, 98121. (206)441-4553. Craig Degginger. Fortnightly. Jewish Federation of Greater Seattle.

WISCONSIN

WISCONSIN JEWISH CHRONICLE (1921). 1360 N. Prospect Ave., Milwaukee, 53202. (414)271-2992. Andrew Muchin. Weekly. Milwaukee Jewish Federation.

INDEXES

INDEX TO JEWISH PERIODICALS (1963). PO Box 18570, Cleveland Hts., 44118. (216)-321-7296. Miriam Leikind, Jean H. Foxman. Semiannually.

NEWS SYNDICATES

JEWISH TELEGRAPHIC AGENCY, INC. (1917). 330 Seventh Ave., 11th fl., NYC., 10001-5010. (212)643-1890. FAX: (212)-643-8498. Mark Joffe, Elli Wohlgelernter, Mark A. Seal. Daily.

CANADA

CANADIAN JEWISH HERALD (1977). 17 Anselme Lavigne Blvd., Dollard des Ormeaux, PQ H9A 1N3. (514)684-7667. Dan Nimrod. Irregularly. Dawn Publishing Co., Ltd.

CANADIAN JEWISH NEWS (1971). 10 Gateway Blvd., #420, Don Mills, ONT M3C 3A1. (416)422-2331. Patricia Rucker. Weekly.

CANADIAN JEWISH OUTLOOK (1963). 6184 Ash St., #3, Vancouver, BC V5Z 3G9. (604) 324-5101. Henry M. Rosenthal. Monthly. Canadian Jewish Outlook Society.

CANADIAN ZIONIST (1934). 5250 Decarie Blvd., Suite 550, Montreal, PQ H3X 2H9. (514)486-9526. Five times a year. Canadian Zionist Federation.

DIALOGUE (1989). 1590 Dr. Penfield Ave., Montreal, PQ H3G 1C5. (514)931-7531. Semiannually. French-English. Canadian Jewish Congress, Quebec Region.

JEWISH EAGLE (1907). 4180 De Courtrai, Rm. 218, Montreal, PQ H3S 1C3. (514)-735-6577. B. Hirshtal. Weekly. Yiddish-Hebrew-French.

JEWISH POST & NEWS (1987). 117 Hutchings St., Winnipeg, MAN R2X 2V4. (204)694-3332. Matt Bellan. Weekly.

THE JEWISH STANDARD (1930). 77 Mowat Ave., Suite 016, Toronto, ONT M6K 3E3. (416)537-2696. Julius Hayman. Fortnightly.

JEWISH WESTERN BULLETIN (1930). 3268 Heather St., Vancouver, BC V5Z 3K5. (604) 879-6575. Samuel Kaplan. Weekly.

JOURNAL OF PSYCHOLOGY AND JUDAISM (1976). 1747 Featherston Dr., Ottawa, ONT K1H 6P4. (613)731-9119. Reuven P. Bulka. Quarterly. Center for the Study of Psychology and Judaism.

OTTAWA JEWISH BULLETIN & REVIEW (1954). 151 Chapel St., Ottawa, ONT K1N 7Y2. (613)232-7306. Cynthia Engel. Biweekly. Jewish Community Council of Ottawa.

UNDZER VEG (1932). 272 Codsell Ave., Downsview, ONT M3H 3X2. (416)636-4024. Joseph Kage. Irregularly. Yiddish-English. Achdut HaAvoda-Poale Zion of Canada.

WINDSOR JEWISH COMMUNITY BULLETIN (1942). 1641 Ouellette Ave., Windsor, ONT N8X 1K9. (519)973-1772. Allen Juris. Quarterly. Windsor Jewish Community Council.

Obituaries: United States[1]

ALPERIN, ARON, journalist; b. Lodz, Poland, (?), 1901; d. Manhasset, N.Y., May 4, 1988; in U.S. since 1941. Edited and wrote for Yiddish newspapers in Poland, 1920–28; editor in chief of Yiddish-language *La Journée Parisien*, Paris, 1928–39; correspondent for Hebrew daily *Ha'aretz*, Tel Aviv, 1930–40; joined the *Jewish Day*, NYC, 1941; edited the merged *Day-Morning Journal* until it ceased publication in 1970. Author: *History of the Jews of Lodz*.

ARONSON, DAVID, rabbi, communal worker; b. Vitebsk, Russia, Aug. 1, 1892; died Los Angeles, Calif., Oct. 20, 1988; in U.S. since 1906. Educ.: NYU; Columbia U.; Jewish Theol. Sem. of Amer. Rabbi: Camp Upton, 1917–19; Salt Lake City, Utah, 1920–22; Duluth, Minn., 1922–24; Beth El Syn., Minneapolis, Minn., 1924–59, emer. thereafter; prof. of Talmud, U. of Judaism, Los Angeles, 1960 on. Mem.: Minn. Governor's Human Relations Comm., 1943–59; Mayor's Council on Human Relations; Citizens' Charter Comm. Assoc. ed., *Amer. Jewish World*, 1920–59; pres., Rabbinical Assembly, 1948–50; mem., bd. of overseers, JTS. Author: *The Jewish Way of Life* and numerous articles on Jewish affairs. Recipient: Mayor's Service Award, City of Minneapolis; Outstanding Service Award, Minneapolis Jewish Fed.; Solomon Schechter Award, JTS; Prime Minister's Award, State of Israel; Mordecai Kaplan Medal, U. of Judaism.

ASOFSKY, ISAAC L., communal worker; b. Slutzk, Russia, Dec. 10, 1889; d. NYC, Jan. 18, 1988. Began working for the Hebrew Immigrant Aid Society (HIAS) as a clerk in 1911, became gen. mgr. in 1923, and dir. during WWII, retiring in 1952.

BEN-HORIN, MEIR, professor; b. Koenigsberg, E. Prussia, Dec. 31, 1918; d. Cleveland, Ohio, Jan. 7, 1988; in U.S. since 1938 (?). Educ.: Gymnasium, Danzig; Hebrew U., Jerusalem; Jewish Theol. Sem. of Amer.; Columbia U. (PhD). Served U.S. Army, WWII; reserve officer, 1948–74, achieving rank of col. Field dir., W. Europe, Jewish Cultural Reconstruction, 1949–50; asst. prof., Boston Hebrew Teachers Coll., 1951–57; prof. and chmn., dept. of educ., Dropsie Coll., 1957–; also, prof. and pres., Cleveland Coll. Jewish Studies; consultant, Reconstructionist Rabbinical Coll. Managing ed., *Jewish Social Studies*, 1957 on; contributing ed.: *Reconstructionist*, *Judaism*, *Jewish Social Studies*, *Jewish Education*, *Hadoar*; v.-pres., Natl. Council of Jewish Educ.; mem. exec. com., Histadruth Ivrith; bd. mem., Phila. ZOA; mem., com. on J. educ., Phila. Fed. of Jewish Agencies. Author: *Max Nordau: Philosopher of Human Solidarity*; *Common Faith—Uncommon People*; and other works; over 300 articles and papers; coed.: *Emancipation and Counter-Emancipation* (with A. G. Duker); *Judaism and the Jewish School* (with J. Pilch).

BENSTON, THERESE SIEGEL, librarian; b. NYC, Dec. 29, 1906; d. NYC, Oct. 26, 1988. Educ.: Columbia U. Cataloger, Columbia U. library, 1926–41; asst. librarian

---

[1] Including Jewish residents of the United States who died between January 1 and December 31, 1988.

and cataloger, Amer. Jewish Com. library, 1942–71; library volunteer, 92nd St. Y, 1975–86.

BERMAN, LAWRENCE V., professor; b. Cincinnati, Ohio, May 5, 1929; d. Palo Alto, Calif., Oct. 7, 1988. Educ.: Mesivta Chaim Berlin, Brooklyn, N.Y.; Coll. of Jewish Studies, Chicago; Brandeis U., Sorbonne; Hebrew U., Jerusalem (PhD). Served U.S. Marine Corps, Korean War. Instr., asst. prof., assoc. prof., Arabic and Islamic studies, Dropsie Coll., 1960–67; assoc. prof., religious studies, Stanford U., 1967–82 and prof., 1982 on; visiting prof.: U. California/Berkeley, Hebrew U., U. Paris. Regarded as a leading scholar in Islamic and Jewish political philosophy. Bd. mem.: Assoc. for J. Studies; mem.: internatl. com., Hebrew sect., *Opera Averrois*; exec. com., Soc. for Judaeo-Arabic Studies. Author: *Ibn Bajjah and Maimonides: A Chapter in the History of Political Philosophy*; a critical edition of the Hebrew transl. of the lost commentary of Averroes on the Nichomachean Ethics; and numerous scholarly articles. A new transl. and commentary on Judah Halevi's *Kuzari* was substantially completed before his death. Recipient: fellow, Amer. Acad. for Jewish Research; sr. fellowship, Natl. Endowment for the Humanities.

BERNSTEIN, MICHAEL, attorney; b. NYC, July 3, 1952; d. Lockerbie, Scotland (Pan Am Flight 103 crash), Dec. 21, 1988. Educ.: U. Michigan; Johns Hopkins U., U. Chicago Law School. Assoc., Covington & Burling, Washington, DC, 1979–85; joined staff of Office of Special Investigations, U.S. Dept. of Justice, 1985; named asst. deputy dir., spring 1988, investigating cases of Nazi war criminals in U.S. Recipient: Justice Dept.'s Special Achievement Award (1987); Yad Vashem Heroes & Martyrs Medal (posthumous); law library, Criminal Div., Dept. of Justice, named in his memory; and other honors.

BIRNBAUM, PHILIP, translator, author, b. Kielce, Poland, Apr. 15, 1904; d. NYC, Mar. 19, 1988; in U.S. since 1923. Educ.: Howard Coll.; Dropsie Coll. (PhD). Best known as the translator-editor of *HaSiddur HaShalem*, the daily prayer book ("The Birnbaum Siddur"), published by Hebrew Publishing Co. in 1949, which has since sold over 300,000 copies, he also wrote textbooks and works popularizing Jewish concepts and knowledge. Bd. mem.: Histadruth Ivrith; mem.: ZOA; Farband Labor Israel; Natl. Council of Jewish Education; Natl. Assoc. Professors of Hebrew; Amer. Acad. for Jewish Research. Author: major works included *The Arabic Commentary of Yefet ben Ali the Karaite on Book of Hosea*; *Maimonides' Mishneh Torah*; *HaSiddur HaShalem*; *Mahzor HaShalem*; *The Passover Haggadah*; *A Treasury of Judaism*; *Encyclopedia of Jewish Concepts*; *Fluent Hebrew*; *High Holyday Prayer Book*; Heb.-Eng. ed. Maimonides' *Mishneh Torah*; *The Torah and the Haftarot*. Recipient: Mordechai Ben-David Award, Yeshiva U.; Body of Works Citation, Jewish Book Council.

BRAUDE, WILLIAM G., rabbi, scholar; b. Telsiai, Lithuania, Apr. 25, 1907, d. Providence, R.I., Feb. 24, 1988; in U.S. since 1920. Educ.: U. Cincinnati; Hebrew Union Coll.; Brown U. (PhD). Rabbi: Temple Beth-El, Rockford, Ill., 1931–32; Cong. Sons of Israel and David-Temple Beth-El, Providence, R.I., 1932–75; emer. thereafter. Lect., Brown U., 1935–40; visiting prof.: Providence Coll., Yale U., Hebrew U., Leo Baeck Coll.-London, U. Conn. A founder and v.-pres., Providence Urban League; commissioner, Providence Human Rights Comm.; pres., R.I. World Affairs Council. Mem.: Central Conf. Amer. Rabbis; Rabbinical Assembly; R.I. Bd. of Rabbis; Amer. Acad. for Jewish Research.; bd. govs., HUC-JIR; Comm. on Jewish Educ., Union of Amer. Hebrew Congs. Contributing ed., *Judaism*; mem. editorial bd., *Journal of Reform Judaism*. Author: transls. of *Tanna debe Eliy'yahu* and *Pesikta de-Rab Kahana* (both with Israel J. Kapstein); *Pesikta Rabbati*; *Midrash on Psalms*; *Sefer Ha-aggadah, The Book of Jewish Lore*; articles on Midrash and other subjects in scholarly volumes and journals. Recipient: hon. doctorates: Brown U., HUC-JIR, U. Rhode Island, Providence Coll.; Jewish Book Council Award for transl. of a Jewish classic.

CITRIN, MARTIN E., businessman, communal worker; b. Detroit, Mich., Nov. 16, 1928; d. Detroit, Mich., Apr. 7, 1988. Petroleum marketing exec. Pres., Jewish Welfare Fed. of Detroit, 1975–78; chmn., CJF-UJA campaign task force; mem., bd. of govs., Jewish Agency for Israel, 1981–87; pres., Council of Jewish Feds., 1981–84. Recipient: Fred Butzel Memorial Award, Spirit of Detroit Award, and honors from the Boy Scouts of Amer. and Natl. Oil Jobbers Council.

COHEN, NOAH J., intelligence analyst, communal worker; b. Brooklyn, N.Y., Sept. 13, 1917; d. Silver Spring, Md., June 30, 1988. Educ.: NYU; Catholic U. (PhD). Served WWII with OSS in India and China; in army reserve, attained rank of lt. col. and taught at U.S. Army Intelligence School. Foreign-affairs analyst, CIA, postwar to 1971; sr. staff mem., div. of archaeology, dept. of classical studies, Tel Aviv U., 1971 on. A founder of Washington chap., Union of Orthodox Jewish Congs. of Amer., its pres. and chmn. its youth comm.; bd. mem.: Hebrew Acad. of Greater Washington; Beth Sholom Cong.; Midrasha Community H.S.; a founder and chmn., bd. of educ., Washington Highlands Jewish Center; mem.: Natl. Assoc. Professors of Hebrew; World Bible Soc.; Israel Exploration Soc.; Amer. Schools of Oriental Research; Biblical Archaeol. Soc. Author: *The Jay Treaty of 1794*; *Tsa'ar Ba'ale Hayim: The Prevention of Cruelty to Animals, Its Bases, Development and Legislation in Hebrew Literature*; and articles in scholarly journals and encyclopedias. Recipient: Chinese Decoration (1945); Merit Achievement Award, Natl. Conf. Synagogue Youth; Community Service and Leadership Award, UOJC; Merit Service Award, US Army Intelligence School.

COWAN, PAUL, journalist; b. Chicago, Ill., Sept. 21, 1940; d. NYC, Sept. 26, 1988. Educ.: Harvard U.; U. Chicago. A journalist since high school, began writing political articles for *Esquire* and *Dissent* in the early '60s, and for the *Village Voice* in 1965, often drawing on his experiences in the Peace Corps in Ecuador, the civil-rights movement in the South, and the movement against the Vietnam War. The writing of an article on poor Jews on the Lower East Side (1972) started him on an exploration of Judaism, to which he drew other assimilated young Jews with whom he established a *havurah* on the West Side of Manhattan. His book *An Orphan in History* was credited with influencing many young Jews to reclaim their heritage. Author: *The Making of an Un-American* (1970); *The Tribes of America* (1978); *An Orphan in History* (1982); coauthor, *Mixed Blessings* (1987), about intermarriage.

CRYSTAL, MORRIS, journalist; b. Ukraine, (?), 1908; d. NYC, Apr. 15, 1988; in U.S. since 1922. Writer and ed., the Yiddish-language *Forward*, 1943–70; known for writings on culture and politics.

DAUM, ANNETTE, educator, communal worker; b. NYC, June 29, 1926; d. Syosset, N.Y., Dec. 19, 1988. Educ.: Hunter Coll.; Hebrew Union Coll.-Jewish Inst. of Religion (teacher, master teacher, and principal certificates). On staff of Union of Amer. Hebrew Congs. over 25 years: assoc. dir., Comm. on Social Action of Reform Judaism and dir., Dept. of Interreligious Affairs. UAHC rep. to: Internatl. Jewish Com. on Interreligious Affairs (World Council of Churches and Vatican Comm. for Religious Relations); NJCRAC (Comm. on Church-State and Interreligious Relations, Comm. on Equal Opportunity, and Task Force on Equal Opportunity for Women); JCRAC-N.Y. (Task Force on Missionaries and Cults); Synagogue Council of Amer. (Interreligious Com., Domestic Affairs Com.); Catholic-Jewish Relations Com., Archdiocese of N.Y. Bd. mem. Kivie Kaplan Inst. Active in many bodies concerned with interreligious affairs, feminism, and equal rights. Mem. edit. advisory bd., *Lilith* magazine; founder, Feminists of Faith. Pres., North Shore Synagogue, Syosset, N.Y. Author: numerous articles in Jewish and Christian publications.

EPSTEIN, JUDITH, communal worker; b. Worcester, Mass., Oct. 31, 1895; d. NYC, Oct. 27, 1988. Educ.: Hunter Coll. Taught English for one year, Julia Richman H.S., NYC. A leader of Hadassah for over 70 years, she worked with Henrietta Szold to develop the organization in its early days. Twice natl. pres.: 1937–39 and 1943–47; chmn., *Hadassah* magazine, 1956–60; Hadassah UN liaison, 1965–69. Chmn., dept. of information and public relations, Amer. Zionist Council, 1963; 1st natl. chmn., women's div., Israel Bonds; named hon. fellow, Zionist Genl. Council of the World Zionist Cong., 1969; mem., Society for the Advancement of Judaism, NYC.

ETLINGER, FRANCINE SCHNITZER, editor, translator; b. Antwerp, Belgium, Nov. 29, 1936; d. NYC, Dec. 17, 1988; in U.S. since 1948. Educ.: CCNY; Jewish Theol. Sem. of Amer.; Sorbonne (dipl.). Ed. and research assoc., Inst. of Contemporary Jewry, Hebrew U., Jerusalem, 1960–71; ed., Am Oved Publishers, Tel Aviv, 1971–79; assoc. dir., publications, Anti-Defamation League, 1979–81; sr. ed., Amer. Jewish Com., 1981–88.

FALK, LEON, JR., businessman, philanthropist; b. Pittsburgh, Pa., Sept. 23, 1901; d. Pittsburgh, Pa., June 9, 1988. Educ.: Yale U. Served in WWII as v.-pres., Commodity Credit Corp. and chief, fats and oils bureau, War Foods Admin. Pres., Webster Hall Hotel; bd. chmn., Midtown Motors. A dir. of Pa. Industrial Chemical Corp., Natl. Steel Corp., Duquesne Light, and other companies, he also raised Polled Hereford cattle. Trustee, v.-pres. (for 40 years), U. Pittsburgh; pres., Community Chest; v.-pres., United Fund; trustee, Presbyterian U. Hosp.; mem. exec. com., Allegheny Conf. on Community Devel.; bd. chmn., Maurice and Laura Falk Found. Longtime supporter, Amer. Jewish Joint Distrib. Com.; pres., Fed. of Jewish Philanthropies; chmn., United Jewish Fund. Recipient: hon. doctorate, U. Pittsburgh.

FEIN, ISAAC, educator, author; b. Benderi, Bessarabia, Russia, Apr. 18, 1899; died Boston, Mass., May 16, 1988; in U.S. since 1923. Educ.: U. Vienna; Dropsie Coll. (PhD). Principal and dir. of Arbeiter Ring and Sholem Aleichem schools, 1923–43; prof., Jewish hist., Baltimore Hebrew Coll., 1943–64; curator, Maryland Jewish Hist. Soc., 1960–70; lect., Harvard Inst. for Learning in Retirement, 1978–88. Mem.: acad. council, Amer. Jewish Hist. Soc.; Farband; ACLU; Natl. Council for Jewish Educ. Author: *The Making of an American Jewish Community* (a history of Baltimore Jewry); *Boston: Where It All Began*; numerous articles in scholarly journals and in the Yiddish-Hebrew press. Recipient: hon. doctorate, Baltimore Hebrew Coll.; Distinguished Alumnus Award, Dropsie Coll.

FEYNMAN, RICHARD P., theoretical physicist; b. Far Rockaway, N.Y., May 11, 1918; d. Los Angeles, Calif., Feb. 15, 1988. Educ.: MIT; Princeton U. (PhD). Member, Manhattan Project, Los Alamos, N.M., 1942–45; assoc. prof., Cornell U., 1945–50; prof., Calif. Inst. of Technology, 1950–88. Regarded as one of the most original and influential scientific minds of his time, he devised the "Feynman diagram" for mapping complicated behavior of particles; revised the theory of quantum electrodynamics; created a theory for weak interactions; and provided explanations of the behavior of liquid helium and the behavior of electrons in high-energy collisions. Author: *QED: The Strange Theory of Light and Matter*; *Surely You're Joking, Mr. Feynman*, (with Ralph Leighton), a book of memoirs; *Quantum Electrodynamics*; *The Character of Physical Law*; *The Feynman Lectures on Physics*, 3 vols.; and other works. Recipient: co-winner, Nobel Prize (1965), for work in quantum electrodynamics; Albert Einstein Award; Oersted Medal; Niels Bohr Internatl. Gold Medal; and many other honors.

FREEDMAN, THEODORE, communal worker; b. Staten Island, N.Y., Jan. 5, 1922; d. Houston, Tex., Oct. 21, 1988. Educ.: Emory U. Served U.S. Army, WWII. Joined staff of Anti-Defamation League in 1949, where he held various positions: as Southwest area dir. and head of Houston regional office; dir., natl. intergroup relations div. (responsible for depts. of education, radio and film, publications, and interfaith affairs); dir., European office since 1986, serving as liaison to the Vatican. Wrote extensively on human relations and lectured at universities and to law-enforcement and military personnel.

FREEMAN, CYNTHIA (BEATRICE CYNTHIA FREEMAN FEINBERG), novelist; b. NYC, ca. 1915; d. San Francisco, Calif., Oct. 22, 1988. Raised in San Francisco, left school after 6th grade, married at 18 (a doctor), and worked as an interior decorator for 25 years. The romantic novels she began writing at age 50 (her only previous experience was writing skits and plays for Temple Emanu-El Sisterhood Guild, Hadassah, and other Jewish groups), in which a common theme was the struggle of Jewish immigrants to rise in American society, sold more than 20 million copies and were translated into 33 languages. Author: *A World Full of Strangers*, *Come Pour the Wine*, *Portraits*, *No Time for Tears*, *Illusions of Love*, *Seasons of the Heart*, *The Last Princess*.

GEFFEN, JOEL S., rabbi; b. Kovno, Lithuania, Aug. 8, 1902; d. NYC, July 2, 1988; in U.S. since 1903. Educ.: Emory U.; N.Y. State Teachers Coll.; Jewish Theol. Sem. of Amer. Chaplain to Jewish naval cadets, Rensselaer Poly. Inst., WWII. Founding rabbi: Temple Beth El, Harrisburg, Pa., 1926–29; Temple Beth El, Troy, N.Y., 1929–44. Served on admin. of JTS from 1944 until his retirement in 1985 in various capacities: dir., dept. of field activities and community educ.; advisor, bd. of overseers; spiritual advisor, Natl. Fed. of Jewish Men's Clubs, 1944 on; dir., N.Y.

Metropolitan Region, United Syn. of Amer., 1953–65; dir., Natl. Patrons Soc., JTS, since 1965; a founder, Camp Ramah in the Berkshires, which dedicated a Torah Center in his honor; ed., *Torch* magazine. Bd. mem.: World Council of Syns.; Amer. Jewish History Center; Natl. Acad. for Adult Jewish Studies; Mercaz; mem.: Amer. Acad. for Jewish Research; Natl. Jewish Com. on Scouting. Author: articles in *Amer. Jewish Historical Quarterly*; coed., *Roads to Jewish Survival*. Recipient: hon. doctorate, JTS, and other honors, including Distinguished Service Award, Natl. Fed. of Jewish Men's Clubs; Special Citation, B'nai B'rith District 1.

GEVIRTZ, STANLEY, professor; b. Brooklyn, N.Y., Jan. 27, 1929; d. Santa Monica, Calif., July 29, 1988. Educ.: Brooklyn Coll.; U. Chicago (PhD). Served N.Y. and Ill. Natl. Guard, 1948–55. Faculty mem., dept. of Oriental (Near Eastern) languages and civilizations, U. Chicago: lect., 1956–58; instr., 1958–62; asst. prof., 1962–65; assoc. prof., 1965–72; prof. of Bible and ancient Near Eastern civilizations, Hebrew Union Coll.-Jewish Inst. of Religion (Los Angeles), 1972–88. Mem.: Amer. Oriental Soc.; Amer. Schools of Oriental Research; Assoc. for Jewish Studies; Soc. of Biblical Lit. and Exegesis. Author: *Patterns in the Early Poetry of Israel* and articles in various scholarly publications.

GOLDBERG, ROMAYNE, communal worker; b. Scranton, Pa., Jan. 19, 1907; d. Newton, Mass., May 3 (?), 1988. Educ.: Wellesley Coll. Pres., Boston chap., Hadassah, 1948–51; pres., N.E. region, 1957- 59; mem. natl. bd., 1948–59. Pres., women's div., Combined Jewish Appeal, 1954–56, and life trustee. Trustee and fellow, Brandeis U.; natl. pres. its women's com., 1960. V.-pres., Boston chap., Amer. Jewish Com. Treas., 25th, 45th, and 55th Wellesley Coll. class reunions and cochmn., 50th reunion.

GOODMAN, ABRAHAM, businessman, philanthropist; b. Gritsev, Ukraine, Apr. 1, 1890; d. Fort Lee, N.J., Apr. 8, 1988; in U.S. since 1907 (?). Educ.: NYU. Financed his accounting studies by selling combs, which he and family members expanded into a business, Goodman & Sons, later Goody Products, producers of hair-care accessories, of which he was president until 1977. In 1929 acquired a half interest in the Foster Grant Co., producer of sunglasses and combs, and became its chmn. A life-long Zionist, was a leader of the ZOA and treas. of the Jewish Agency for Israel. Helped found the Reconstructionist Rabbinical Coll. (Philadelphia); Herzliah Jewish Teachers Sem. (NYC); and Mt. Sinai Hosp. (Miami Beach). Pres., bd. chmn., and trustee for over 25 years, Hebrew Arts School, NYC, and principal donor of its Abraham Goodman House.

GRAND, SAMUEL, educator, author; b. NYC, Aug. 28, 1912; d. NYC, Jan. 15, 1988. Educ.: CCNY; Jewish Theol. Sem. of Amer.; Hebrew U., Jerusalem; Columbia U. (PhD). Principal: Forest Hills Jewish Center, NYC, 1936–37; Park Ave. Syn., NYC, 1938–41; exec. sec., Amer. Assoc. for Jewish Educ., 1941–42; dist. consultant, Jewish Educ. Com. of N.Y., 1946–52; dir., audio-visual aids and experimental educ., Union of Amer. Hebrew Congs., 1952–65; free-lance producer of a-v aids, consultant, lect., and writer, 1965 on. A founder, Natl. Assoc. of Temple Educators; v.-pres., Natl. Conf. of Jewish Communal Services; mem. and off., Jewish Peace Fellowship; exec. bd. mem.: Natl. Council on Jewish Audio-Visual Materials; Natl. Bible Contest. Producer of over 150 filmstrips on Jewish subjects. Author: *Hebrew Prayer Skills*; *The Jews Settle in New Amsterdam-1654*; coauthor: *Hebrew the Audio-Lingual Way*; *The Children of Israel*; *Jews in Distant Lands*. Recipient: awards from Council for Jewish Educ.; Natl. Assoc. of Temple Educators.

HALPERN, PERETZ, rabbi; b. NYC, Apr. 11, 1905; d. Swampscott, Mass., Feb. 29, 1988. Educ.: Herzliah Hebrew Teachers Sem., Columbia U. (Teachers Coll.); Jewish Theological Sem. of Amer. Rabbi: Temple B'nai Sholom, Rockville Center, NY 1945–56; Temple Israel, Swampscott, Mass., 1956–77. Pres.: N.E. region, Rabbinical Assembly; N. Shore Rabbinical Assoc. Mem.: Rabbinic Cabinet, JTS; joint comm. on Jewish educ., Rabbinical Assembly and United Syn. of Amer. Recipient: hon. doctorate, JTS; Distinguished Alumnus Citation, Herzliah Hebrew Teachers Sem.

HIRSH, MARILYN, author, illustrator; b. Chicago, Ill., Jan. 1, 1944; d. NYC, Oct. 17, 1988. Educ.: Carnegie-Mellon Inst.; NYU Inst. of Fine Arts. A historian of Indian and Buddhist art; teacher, NYU Inst. of Fine Arts and Cooper Union. Author-illustrator of over 30 children's books, incl. *Where is Yonkela? Could Anything Be*

Worse? One Little Goat, *Captain Jiri and Rabbi Jacob*, and *I Love Hanukkah*. Illustrator: *The Best of Ktonton*; author: *Joseph Who Loved the Sabbath*. Recipient: 1st Sydney Taylor Award for Jewish Children's Lit., Assoc. of Jewish Libraries.

JACOBSON, HENRIETTA, actress; b. Chicago, Ill., Mar. 27, 1906; d. NYC, Oct. 9, 1988. Member of a prominent Yiddish theatrical family, made her debut at age 3 in Chicago and went on to become a star of the Yiddish stage. Her frequent costar was her husband, Julius Adler, with whom she also produced and directed plays. In English, she appeared in Neil Simon's *Come Blow Your Horn* on Broadway, in the film *Hero at Large*, and in dinner-theater shows across the country. Life mem., Hebrew Actors Union. Recipient: (with her husband) Golden Goldy Award for lifetime achievement in the theater, Cong. for Jewish Culture.

KENEN, ISAIAH L. ("Si"), journalist, lobbyist; b. St. Stephen, New Brunswick, Canada, Mar. 7, 1905; d. Washington, D.C., Mar. 23, 1988; in U.S. since 1926. Educ.: U. Toronto; Cleveland Law School. Political writer, Cleveland (Ohio) *News*, 1926–43; information dir., Amer. Zionist Emergency Com., 1943; public relations dir. and exec. sec., Amer. Jewish Conference, 1943–47; information dir., Jewish Agency delegation at UN, 1947–48; information dir. and alt. rep., 1st Israeli UN delegation, 1948–50. Founder, Amer. Zionist Com., Washington, 1951, to lobby for support for Israel; in 1954 it became the American Israel Public Affairs Com.(AIPAC), which he served as exec. dir. and registered lobbyist until 1973 and chmn., 1973–75. Founder and 1st ed., *Near East Report*, 1957–73; pres., Near East Research, 1973 on; Washington correspondent: Jerusalem *Post*, 1965–69; London *Jewish Chronicle*, 1965–69 and 1975–79. Founded Young Judaea chap., Toronto, 1917; Sunday school teacher, Euclid Ave. Temple, Cleveland, 1929–43; chmn., public relations com., Cleveland Jewish Welfare Fed., 1933–43; pres., Cleveland Zionist Dist., 1940–43; mem., Temple Sinai, Washington. Active in American Newspaper Guild: a founder of 1st Cleveland local, 1933; pres. of local, 1937; chmn., ANG constitution com., 5 years; internatl. v.-pres., 1938–40; bd. mem., Cleveland City Club, 1933–36. Author: *Israel's Defense Line*; *All My Causes*; and numerous articles. Recipient: Cleveland Newspaper Guild Award; Heywood Broun Memorial Award; hon. doctorate, HUC-JIR; hon. fellow, Hebrew University, Jerusalem; and awards from many Jewish organizations.

LEHRMAN, HAL, foreign correspondent; b. NYC, Jan. 7, 1911; d. NYC, Oct. 31, 1988. Educ.: Cornell U. Reporter, AP-Paris, 1934–35; asst. natl. affairs ed., *Newsweek*, 1935–36; cable news ed., Havas News Agency, 1936–39; night cable ed., NY *Daily News*, 1939–41. Chief, U.S. Off. of War Information, Istanbul, 1942–43; OWI ed. bd., 1943–44. Free-lance writer and special correspondent, 1944 to mid-'70s, covering Europe, Africa, and the Middle East for the N.Y. *Times*, *Wall St. Journal*, N.Y. *Post*, *Reader's Digest*, *Commentary*, *Harper's*, and many other publications. Founding mem., gov., v.-pres., and pres., Overseas Press Club, NYC; mem., Council on Foreign Relations. Author: *Israel, the Beginning and Tomorrow*; *Russia's Europe*. Recipient: Guggenheim fellowship for reporting on Israel and the Middle East (1951, 1953); George Polk Award for Outstanding Foreign Reporting (1951); Overseas Press Club Citation; Amer. Security Council Award.

LUBIN, CHARLES W., businessman, philanthropist; b. Chicago, Ill., Nov. 16, 1903; d. Chicago, Ill., July 15, 1988. Educ.: through 8th grade. Apprenticed to a baker at age 14, in the 1930s bought three small bakeries; in 1949 founded Kitchens of Sara Lee (named for his daughter), where he invented the process for baking, freezing, shipping, and selling the cake in the same container; sold company to Consolidated Foods in 1956, remaining pres. until 1964. Mem., bd. of govs., and benefactor, Weizmann Inst. of Science, and hon. v.-chmn., Amer. Com. for the Weizmann Inst. of Science. Recipient: Horatio Alger Award (1968); Igloo Award, Frozen Food Assoc.; Fellowship Award, Brandeis U.; hon. doctorate, Weizmann Inst. of Science.

MANCHER, HARRY R., accountant, communal worker; b. NYC, Dec. 3, 1917; d. NYC, Oct. 5, 1988. Educ.: CCNY (Baruch Coll.). Joined S.D. Leidesdorf & Co., 1943; partner, 1957; managing partner, 1969; sr. managing partner, 1973; v.-chmn. and regional partner, Ernst & Whinney (after merger), 1978–82. Pres., N.Y. Fed. of Jewish Philanthropies, 1977–80; bd. mem., v.-pres., UJA of Greater N.Y.; treas., UJA-Fed. Joint Campaign; bd. and exec. com. member: Natl. UJA; Amer. Jewish Joint Distribution Com.; CLAL; Council of Jewish Feds.; Amer. Israel Cultural Found.; pres., Altro Health and Rehab. Services; treas., bd. mem., Mt. Sinai Med. Center; trustee, Bet Am Shalom Syn., White Plains, N.Y.; bd. mem.: Council of the Amer. Inst. of CPAs; N.Y. State Soc. of CPAs. Recipient: Public Service Award, N.Y. State Soc. of CPAs; King Solomon Award, Amer.-Israel Cultural Found.; and other honors.

MARGOLIES, ISRAEL RAPHAEL, rabbi; b. Brooklyn, N.Y., (?), 1916; d. Teaneck, N.J., Feb. 11, 1988. Educ.: Jewish Inst. of Religion. Rabbi: Temple Emanu-el, Englewood, N.J., 1937–53; Beth Am, the People's Temple, NYC, 1953–81. An activist in the civil rights and anti-Vietnam movements; founding mem., N.J. chap., SANE.

MEYERHOFF, LYN P., communal worker; b. Chicago, Ill., Aug. 5, 1927; d. Baltimore, Md., Apr. 6, 1988. As Maryland chmn. of "The Campaign to Remember," was, with her husband, Harvey Meyerhoff, a leading supporter of the U.S. Holocaust Memorial Museum in Washington. An active Republican, she was a member of the U.S. Mission to the 38th UN Genl. Assembly (1984). Chmn., Jeanne Kirkpatrick Forum for Public Leadership and Public Policy, Tel Aviv U.; mem. exec. com.: Baltimore Symphony Orch.; Assoc. Jewish Charities; mem. adv. com., School of Internatl. Studies, Johns Hopkins U.; trustee: Natl. Aquarium in Baltimore; Walters Art Gallery; Planned Parenthood Assoc. of Md.

MILLER, JOSEPH K., accountant, communal worker; b. Brooklyn, N.Y., May 27, 1932; d. Lockerbie, Scotland (Pan Am Flight 103 crash), Dec. 21, 1988. Educ.: Baruch Coll.; N.Y. Law School. Sr. partner, Miller-Ellin and Co.; bd. chmn., S & S Industries. Treas., Union of Orthodox Jewish Congs.; chmn., Amer. Friends of Shamir; v.-pres., Gesher Found.; fellow: Stern Coll. and Rabbi Isaac Elchanan Theol. Sem.; chmn., bd. of govs., Amer. Friends of Yeshivat Sha'alvim.

MINTZ (SATZ), ELI, actor; b. Lemberg, Austria, Aug. 1, 1904; d. Pt. Pleasant, N.J., June 8, 1988; in U.S. since 1927. Made his debut as a child actor in Europe; in U.S., played numerous roles on Yiddish stage, 1929–48 (changed his name early in his career because his brother, Ludwig Satz, was already a well-known Yiddish actor). Among the many English stage productions he appeared in were *The Fifth Season*, *I Was Dancing*, *Catch Me If You Can*, *Friends and Enemies*; his Hollywood films included *Stardust Memories*, *Boardwalk*, *Murder, Inc.*, and *The Proud Rebel*. Best known for his portrayal of "Uncle David" in the stage (1948–49), movie (1951), and television (1950–58) versions of *The Goldbergs*.

MORSE, EARL, businessman, communal worker; b. Milwaukee, Wis., Mar. 19, 1907; d. NYC, Feb. 19, 1988. Educ.: U. Wisconsin; Harvard Law School. Private law practice, 1930–35; atty., Fed. Communications Comm., 1935–37; dir. and exec. v.-pres., Doughnut Corp. of Amer. (DCA Food Industries), 1937–72. Chmn., bd. of trustees, Union of Amer. Hebrew Congs., 1967–71; mem., bd. of govs., Hebrew Union Coll.-Jewish Inst. of Religion, 1963–77; bd. mem. and hon. trustee, Jewish Museum, NYC; pres., Natl. Found. for Jewish Culture, 1972–75; mem. exec., Amer. Section, World Jewish Congress; bd. mem.: Amer. Friends of Alliance Israélite Universelle; hon. bd. mem., Board of Jewish Educ. of Greater N.Y.; hon. trustee, Central Syn., NYC. Benefactor, mem. visiting com. on Far Eastern art, Metropolitan Museum of Art; mem.: China Art Soc.; Horticultural Soc. of N.Y. Recipient: hon. doctorate, HUC-JIR.

NEVELSON, LOUISE, sculptor; b. Kiev, Russia, Sept. 23 (?), 1899; d. NYC, Apr. 17, 1988; in U.S. since 1902. A pioneer creator of environmental sculpture; studied art privately; achieved recognition only in her late 50s, when she was included in a group exhibition at the Museum of Modern Art in 1958; represented U.S. at Venice Biennale, 1962; a major retrospective was mounted at the Whitney Museum in 1967, followed by a large traveling exhibition of her work in 1973–75. Among her numerous public commissions was a 55-foot wall for Temple Beth-El, Great Neck, N.Y. Author: *Dawns and Dusks* (autobiog.).

PRINZ, JOACHIM, rabbi, communal worker; b. Burkhardsdorf, Germany, May 10, 1902; d. W. Orange, N.J., Sept. 30, 1988; in U.S. since 1937. Educ.: U. Berlin; U. Giessen (PhD); Jewish Theol. Sem., Breslau. Rabbi: Jewish Community of Berlin, 1926–37;

Temple B'nai Abraham, Newark and Livingston, N.J., 1939–77; emer. thereafter. Pres., Amer. Jewish Cong., 1956–64; chmn., Conf. of Presidents of Major Amer. Jewish Orgs., 1963–67; v.-pres. and chmn. gov. bd., World Jewish Cong., since 1960; dir., Conf. on Jewish Material Claims Against Germany, 1958 on; chmn., World Conf. Jewish Orgs., since 1976. Expelled from Germany after repeated arrests because of his public criticism of the Hitler regime, became a vocal advocate of liberal causes in the U.S. A founding chmn., 1963 March on Washington for civil rights, and an activist in civil-rights causes. Author: Several works in German on Bible and Jewish history; *The Dilemma of the Modern Jew*; *Popes from the Ghetto*; *The Secret Jews*; and other works. Recipient: hon. doctorates, HUC-JIR; Hofstra U.; Upsala Coll.; and other honors.

RABI, ISIDOR ISAAC, research physicist; b. Rymanow, Austria-Hungary, July 29, 1898; d. NYC, Jan. 11, 1988; in U.S. since 1900. Educ.: Cornell U.; Columbia U. (PhD); postdoctoral work in Europe with Niels Bohr and other leading physicists. Appointed lect. at Columbia, 1929 (the first Jew in that dept.), advanced to asst. prof., prof., and prof. emer.; named Columbia's 1st univ. prof. in 1964; a chair in physics named for him in 1985. By 1937 had developed the technique for measuring the magnetic properties of atoms, molecules, and atomic nuclei for which he was awarded the Nobel Prize in 1944. In WWII, worked to develop radar; served as sr. adviser on Manhattan Project, which developed the atom bomb, albeit with reservations. Postwar, joined with Enrico Fermi in opposing devel. of the hydrogen bomb and worked for internatl. control of atomic energy. Headed Genl. Advisory Com. of Atomic Energy Comm.; mem., President's Science Adv Com., 1952–68. Defended J. Robert Oppenheimer at loyalty hearings in 1954. Regarded as a voice of conscience of the scientific community, who sought ways to channel knowledge of the atom to peaceful uses. Pres. Amer. Phys. Soc.; mem.: science advisory com., Bar-Ilan U.; bd. govs. and hon. fellow, Weizmann Inst. of Science; adv. com., Technion Soc. (N.Y.); trustee, Mt. Sinai Medical Center. Recipient: Nobel Prize, 1944; U.S. Medal of Merit; Atoms for Peace Award; Niels Bohr Internatl. Gold Medal; Comdr., French Legion of Honor; hon. doctorates from Hebrew U., Bar-Ilan U., Technion-Israel Inst. of Technology, and many other honors. Author: *My Life and Times as a Physicist*, in addition to scientific articles.

RABINOWITZ, ISAAC, professor; b. Brooklyn, N.Y., July 3, 1909; d. Ithaca, N.Y., Sept. 11, 1988. Educ.: U. California/Berkeley; Yale U. (PhD). Served OSS, WWII. Public-school teacher, St. Louis, 1932–33; dir., youth educ., Union of Amer. Hebrew Congs., 1935–38; dir., Hillel Foundations: U. Michigan, 1938–40; Brooklyn Coll., 1940–44; U. Pa. and Temple U., 1944–45; natl. dir., B'nai B'rith Boys Work, 1945–46; exec. dir., East N.Y. YM-YWHA, 1946–55; prof., Wayne State U., 1955–57; prof., biblical and Hebrew studies, Cornell U., 1957–70 and chmn., dept. of Semitic languages and literatures (Near Eastern Studies), 1965–70. Mem.: Amer. Oriental Soc.; Soc. Bibl. Lit.; Amer. Schools of Oriental Research. Author: *Towards a Valid Theory of Biblical Hebrew*; numerous articles on the Dead Sea Scrolls, Semitic epigraphy, Bible, and related subjects; transl., *The Book of the Honey Comb's Flow*, a 15th-century Hebrew work by Judah Messer Leon. Recipient: fellowships from the Guggenheim Found., Amer. Council of Learned Societies, Natl. Endowment for the Humanities.

RECHTZEIT, JACK, actor; b. (?), 1903, Warsaw, Poland; d. NYC, July 24, 1990; in U.S. since 1923. Acted in Yiddish theater in Poland, Romania, France, Belgium, London, Israel, and S. America, as well as in U.S., where his last appearance was in 1985–86 in NYC, in the Folksbiene production of *Broome St., America*. Pres., Hebrew Actors Union; v.-pres., Assoc. Actors and Artists of Amer.; mem. exec., Yiddish Theatrical Alliance.

REISS, LIONEL S., artist; b. Jaroslav, Galicia, (?), 1894; d. NYC, Apr. 16, 1988; in U.S. since childhood. Studied commercial art; bicycled through Europe, Africa, and Middle East in 1920s, making portraits of Jews and Jewish landmarks, which were published in a 1938 volume, *My Models Were Jews*. A similar journey resulted in *New Lights and Old* (1954). Among the many books he illustrated were an English ed. of Bialik's poems (1948) and *A World of Twilight* (1972), a portrait of Jewish communities in E. Europe before WWII, with text by I.B. Singer and Milton Hindus. His works are in the collections of the Brooklyn Museum, Jewish Museum, Natl. Portrait Gallery, Tel Aviv and Bezalel Museums in Israel, and others.

RIVKIN, NACHA, educator,; b. Kalisz, Poland, May 19, 1900; d. Brooklyn, N.Y., July 14, 1988; in U.S. since 1929. Educ.: Gymnasium, Rostov, Russia; studied in Jerusalem with Profs. Joseph and Elizedek Klausner. A founder of the Shulamith School for Girls, Brooklyn, and teacher, 1929–45; teacher, Yeshivah Ohel Moshe, Brooklyn, 1945–65; also an artist who had several exhibitions. Author: *Reishis Chochmah*, widely used Hebrew textbooks, first published in 1954 and reprinted yearly thereafter; 3 vols. of original Hebrew songs for children.

SIEGEL, SEYMOUR, rabbi, professor; b. Chicago, Ill., Sept. 12, 1927; d. NYC, Feb. 24, 1988. Educ.: U. Chicago; Jewish Theol. Sem. of Amer. (ord.; DHL). Registrar, postgrad. dept., JTS, 1951–59; assoc. prof., theology, JTS, 1959–67; prof., ethics and rabbinic thought, 1967–76; named Ralph Simon Prof. of Ethics and Theology, 1976. Visiting sr. research fellow, Kennedy Inst. for Bioethics at Georgetown Univ.; visiting scholar, Woodrow Wilson Center for Scholars; visiting prof.: Medical Coll. of Pa., CCNY, Union Theol. Sem., Carleton Coll., Seminario rabinico latinoamericano (Buenos Aires); fellow: Conf. on Science, Philosophy and Religion; Soc. for Religion in Higher Educ. Mem.: Amer. Acad. of Religion; Amer. Acad. for Jewish Research. Chmn., com. on Jewish law and standards, Rabbinical Assembly; sec., R.A.; mem. exec. com., N.Y. Jewish Comm. Relations Advisory Council; pres., Amer. Jewish Forum; bd. mem., Jewish Museum. Ed., div. of modern Jewish scholarship, *Encyclopedia Judaica*; mem. edit. bd.: Jewish Publication Soc., *Shma*, *Linacre Quarterly*, *Worldview Magazine*; *Encyclopedia of Bio-Med. Ethics*, and other publications; mem.: bioethics com., Amer. Hosp. Assoc.; U.S. Holocaust Council (and its exec. dir. for 2 years); President's Comm. on Ethics in Medicine and Biomedical Research; Advisory Council on Human Concerns, Republican Natl. Com. Author: hundreds of articles; *The Jewish Dietary Laws*; *Medical Ethics in a Jewish Perspective*; ed.: *Conservative Judaism and Jewish Law*; *God in the Teachings of Conservative Judaism*.

SILBERSCHLAG, EISIG, professor, poet; b. Stryj, Austria, Jan. 8, 1903; d. Austin, Tex., Sept. 30, 1988; in U.S. since 1920. Educ.: U. Vienna (PhD). Prof., Hebrew lang., Boston Hebrew Teachers Coll., beginning 1944; named dean 1947 and pres. 1968, retiring in 1970; visiting prof., Emmanuell Coll., Boston, 1970–73; visiting prof., Judaic Studies, U. Texas at Austin, 1973–85. Visiting lect.: Columbia, Brandeis, NYU, Hebrew U.-Jerusalem, U. Wisconsin, U. Capetown, Oxford Center for Postgrad. Hebrew Studies. Pres., Natl. Assoc. Professors of Hebrew; mem., World Union Hebrew Studies; trustee, Boston Hebrew Coll. Author: *Hebrew Literature: An Evaluation*; *Saul Tchernichovski—Poet of Revolt*; *From Renaissance to Renaissance: Hebrew Literature, 1492–1970*; *Hebrew Literature in Israel 1870–1970*; several books of poetry in Hebrew; transl.: Aristophanes, *Comedies*; Carl de Haas, *Berenice*. Recipient: Florence Kovner Memorial Award (for Hebrew poetry); City of Tel Aviv Tchernichovski Prize (for transl. from Greek); fellow: Middle East Studies Assoc.; Amer. Acad. for Jewish Research.

SOLOMON, AARON L., attorney, communal worker; b. Newark, N.J., March 26, 1908; d. NYC, July 12, 1988. Educ.: Columbia U.; Brooklyn Law School. Attorney in private practice, specializing in labor relations. Mem., United Hosp. Fund Manpower Comm.; Amer. Arbitration Assn. A founder, pres., and life trustee, L.I. Jewish Hospital-Hillside Medical Center; pres., Natl. Com. for Labor Israel-Histadrut; founding trustee and bd. mem., Jewish Assoc. for the Aged, NYC; mem. bd. govs., ADL; mem., Cong. Emanu-El, NYC.

SPACK, ABRAHAM, educator; b. Volin, Poland, Feb. 9, 1909; d. Newark, N.J., Nov. 26, 1988; in U.S. since 1921. Educ.: Tufts U.; Harvard U.; Boston Hebrew Teachers Coll. Teacher, Menorah Inst., Roxbury, 1927–39, and principal, 1940–48; educ. dir., Cong. Kehillath Israel, Brookline, 1948–62; principal, Temple B'nai Abraham, Newark and South Orange, N.J., 1962–72. Consultant, United Syn. comm. on educ.; a founder and v.-pres., Jewish Educators Assembly; dir., Tel Noar Lodge, 1940s; cultural dir.: Camp Tevya, 1950s, and Cejwin Camps, 1960s. Recipient: Benj. Shevach Memorial Prize, Boston Hebrew Coll.; hon. doctorate, JTS; Man of the Year, Solomon Schechter Day School of Essex and Union counties, N.J.

SPELLMAN, GLADYS NOON, politician; b. NYC, Mar. 2, 1918; d. Washington, D.C., June 19, 1988. Educ.: George Washington U. Elected to Congress in 1974 from a suburban Washington district, served three full terms and was reelected to a fourth, but was unable to fill it because of a disabling illness. In Congress, was a staunch advocate of Israel and the struggle for Soviet Jews.

TEPFER, JOHN J., rabbi, professor; b. London, England, Mar. 25, 1894; d. NYC, Mar. 12, 1988; in U.S. since 1918 (?). Educ.: Jews Coll., London; London U.; Temple U.; Jewish Inst. of Religion. Rabbi: Selma, Ala., 1931; Scranton, Pa., 1931–34. Joined faculty of JIR, 1936, as instr. of Talmud, history, homiletics, liturgy, philosophy; prof., HUC-JIR, 1950–86; acting dean, 1956–58; dean, 1958–60. JWB lecturer, 1928–50; mem., rabbinic mission to USSR, 1966. Coed.: *Jewish Institute Quarterly*; *Avukah Annual* (1925–30). Author: *Martin Buber and Neo-Mysticism*. Recipient: hon. doctorates, JIR; HUC-JIR.

WERNER, ERIC, professor, musicologist; b. Ludenberg, Austria, Aug. 1, 1901; d. NYC, July 28, 1988; in U.S. since 1938. Educ.: U.'s of Graz, Vienna, Prague, Berlin, Göttingen, Strasbourg (PhD). Teacher, Saarbrücken Conservatory and Gymnasium, 1926–33; Jewish Gymnasium and Rabbinical Sem., Breslau, 1935–38; prof., liturgical music, Hebrew Union Coll.-Jewish Inst. of Religion, Cincinnati, 1939–67, where he was also responsible for the music of its worship services, acting as organist and choral conductor. A founder and faculty mem., School of Sacred Music, HUC-JIR, in NYC; prof. emer. since 1967; chmn., dept. of musicology, Tel Aviv U., 1967–72. An authority on comparative liturgy, especially the place of synagogue music and liturgy in the early church; was the 1st Jewish scholar to lecture at the Vatican's Pontifical Inst. of Sacred Music; guest lect., U.'s of Cologne and Heidelberg and the Eastman School of Music (Rochester). Pres.: 1st Internatl. Cong. of Jewish Music, Paris, 1957, and of 1978 cong. Author: *The Sacred Bridge* (2 vols.); *A Voice Still Heard: The Sacred Songs of the Ashkenazic Jews*; *Mendelssohn: A New Image of the Composer and His Age*, and other works, as well as articles in *Grove's Dictionary* on various aspects of Jewish music and scores of contributions to scholarly and Jewish publications. Recipient: Natl. Jewish Music Award, JWB Jewish Music Council; dedication to him of Hebrew University's 1st yearbook of Jewish music (1968); fellow, Amer. Acad. for Jewish Research.

WIEN, LAWRENCE A., attorney, philanthropist; b. NYC, May 30, 1905; d. Westport, Conn., Dec. 10, 1988. Educ.: Columbia Coll., Columbia U. Law School. Founder and sr. partner, Wien Malkin & Bettex. A pioneer in real-estate investment syndication, his groups controlled major NYC properties, incl. the Empire State Bldg., the Lincoln Bldg., and leading hotels, as well as properties in other cities. Known as a man who enjoyed giving money away, he was a patron of the arts and a major contributor to a wide range of philanthropies. Trustee, Brandeis U., 1957–84, chmn., 1967–71, and a major benefactor; among his many gifts, the Wien Internatl. Scholarships and a statue of Justice Brandeis. Trustee, Columbia U., 1964–70, where he created a scholarship fund at the Law School, in addition to other benefactions. V.-chmn. and trustee, Lincoln Center for the Performing Arts, NYC; cochmn. its Directors Emeriti Council and a major benefactor of the center and the NYC Ballet and NYC Opera. Mayoral appointee, NYC Council Against Poverty; trustee: Inst. of Internatl. Educ.; WNET/13; founder, Com. to Increase Corporate Philanthropic Giving. Pres., N.Y. Fed. of Jewish Philanthropies, 1960–63, bd. chmn., 1970–72, hon. chmn. 1974–86; mem., Cong. Emanu-El, NYC.

Calendars

SUMMARY JEWISH CALENDAR, 5750–5754 (Sept. 1989–Aug. 1994)

HOLIDAY	5750 1989			5751 1990			5752 1991			5753 1992			5754 1993		
Rosh Ha-shanah, 1st day	Sa	Sept.	30	Th	Sept.	20	M	Sept.	9	M	Sept.	28	Th	Sept.	16
Rosh Ha-shanah, 2nd day	S	Oct.	1	F	Sept.	21	T	Sept.	10	T	Sept.	29	F	Sept.	17
Fast of Gedaliah	M	Oct.	2	S	Sept.	23	W	Sept.	11	W	Sept.	30	S	Sept.	19
Yom Kippur	M	Oct.	9	Sa	Sept.	29	W	Sept.	18	W.	Oct.	7	Sa	Sept.	25
Sukkot, 1st day	Sa	Oct.	14	Th	Oct.	4	M	Sept.	23	M	Oct.	12	Th	Sept.	30
Sukkot, 2nd day	S	Oct.	15	F	Oct.	5	T	Sept.	24	T	Oct.	13	F	Oct.	1
Hosha'na' Rabbah	F	Oct.	20	W	Oct.	10	S	Sept.	29	S	Oct.	18	W	Oct.	6
Shemini 'Azeret	Sa	Oct.	21	Th	Oct.	11	M	Sept.	30	M	Oct.	19	Th	Oct.	7
Simhat Torah	S	Oct.	22	F	Oct.	12	T	Oct.	1	T.	Oct.	20	F	Oct.	8
New Moon, Heshwan, 1st day	S	Oct.	29	F	Oct.	19	T	Oct.	8	T	Oct.	27	F	Oct.	15
New Moon, Heshwan, 2nd day	M	Oct.	30	Sa	Oct.	20	W	Oct.	9	W.	Oct.	28	Sa	Oct.	16
New Moon, Kislew, 1st day	T	Nov.	28	S	Nov.	18	Th	Nov.	7	Th.	Nov.	26	S	Nov.	14
New Moon, Kislew, 2nd day	W	Nov.	29				F	Nov.	8				M	Nov.	15
Hanukkah, 1st day	Sa	Dec.	23	W	Dec.	12	M	Dec.	2	s	Dec.	20	Th	Dec.	9
New Moon, Ṭevet, 1st day	Th	Dec.	28	M	Dec.	17	Sa	Dec.	7	F	Dec.	25	T	Dec.	14
New Moon, Ṭevet, 2nd day	F	Dec.	29	T	Dec.	18	S	Dec.	8				W	Dec.	15
		1990									1993				
Fast of 10th of Ṭevet	S	Jan.	7	Th	Dec.	27	T	Dec.	17	S	Jan.	3	F	Dec.	24

	1990		1991		1992		1993		1994	
New Moon, Shevat	Sa	Jan. 27	W	Jan. 16	M	Jan. 6	Sa	Jan. 23	Th	Jan. 13
Hamishshah-'asar bi-Shevat	Sa	Feb. 10	W	Jan. 30	M	Jan. 20	Sa	Feb. 6	Th	Jan. 27
New Moon, Adar I, 1st day	S	Feb. 25	Th	Feb. 14	T	Feb. 4	S	Feb. 21	F	Feb. 11
New Moon, Adar I, 2nd day	M	Feb. 26	F	Feb. 15	W	Feb. 5	M	Feb. 22	Sa	Feb. 12
New Moon, Adar II, 1st day					Th	Mar. 5				
New Moon, Adar II, 2nd day					F	Mar. 6				
Fast of Esther	Th	Mar. 8	W	Feb. 27	W	Mar. 18	Th	Mar. 4	Th	Feb. 24
Purim	S	Mar. 11	Th	Feb. 28	Th	Mar. 19	S	Mar. 7	F	Feb. 25
Shushan Purim	M	Mar. 12	F	Mar. 1	F	Mar. 20	M	Mar. 8	Sa	Feb. 26
New Moon, Nisan	T	Mar. 27	Sa	Mar. 16	Sa	Apr. 4	T	Mar. 23	S	Mar. 13
Passover, 1st day	T	Apr. 10	S	Mar. 30	S	Apr. 18	T	Apr. 6	S	Mar. 27
Passover, 2nd day	W	Apr. 11	M	Mar. 31	M	Apr. 19	W	Apr. 7	M	Mar. 28
Passover, 7th day	M	Apr. 16	S	Apr. 5	S	Apr. 24	M	Apr. 12	M	Apr. 2
Passover, 8th day	T	Apr. 17	M	Apr. 6	M	Apr. 25	T	Apr. 13	T	Apr. 3
Holocaust Memorial Day	S	Apr. 22	Sa	Apr. 11	Sa	Apr. 30	S	Apr. 18	S	Apr. 8*
New Moon, Iyar, 1st day	W	Apr. 25	Th	Apr. 14	Th	May 3	W	Apr. 21	W	Apr. 11
New Moon, Iyar, 2nd day	Th	Apr. 26	S	Apr. 15	S	May 4	Th	Apr. 22	T	Apr. 12
Israel Independence Day	M	Apr. 30	M	Apr. 19*	M	May 8*	M	Apr. 26	T	Apr. 16
Lag Ba-'omer	S	May 13	F	Apr. 19*	F	May 21	S	May 9	Sa	Apr. 29
Jerusalem Day	W	May 23	Th	May 2	Th	May 31	W	May 19	F	May 9
New Moon, Siwan	F	May 25	S	May 12	S	Jun 2	F	May 21	M	May 11
Shavu'ot, 1st day	W	May 30	T	May 14	T	Jun 7	W	May 26	M	May 16
Shavu'ot, 2nd day	Th	May 31	W	May 15	S	Jun 8	Th	May 27	T	May 17
New Moon, Tammuz, 1st day	Sa	June 23	M	May 20	M	July 1	Sa	June 19	T	June 9
New Moon, Tammuz, 2nd day	S	June 24	W	May 29	W	July 2	S	June 20	F	June 10
Fast of 17th of Tammuz	T	July 10	Th	June 13	Th	July 19	S	July 6	S	June 26
New Moon, Av	M	July 23	S	July 12	S	July 31	M	July 19	Sa	July 9
Fast of 9th of Av	T	July 31	F	July 21	F	Aug. 9	T	July 27	S	July 17
New Moon, Elul, 1st day	T	Aug. 21	Sa	Aug. 10	Sa	Aug. 29	S	Aug. 17	S	Aug. 7
New Moon, Elul, 2nd day	W	Aug. 22	S	Aug. 11	S	Aug. 30	W	Aug. 18	M	Aug. 8

*Observed Thursday, a day earlier, to avoid conflict with the Sabbath.

CONDENSED MONTHLY CALENDAR
(1989–1992)

1988, Dec. 9–Jan. 6, 1989]   ṬEVET (29 DAYS)   [5749

Civil Date	Day of the Week	Jewish Date	SABBATHS, FESTIVALS, FASTS	PENTATEUCHAL READING	PROPHETICAL READING
Dec. 9	F	Ṭevet 1	New Moon; Hanukkah, sixth day	Num. 28:1–15 Num. 7:42–47	
10	Sa	2	Mi-ḳez; Hanukkah, seventh day	Gen. 41:1–44:17 Num. 7:48–53	Zechariah 2:14–4:7
11	S	3	Hanukkah, eighth day	Num. 7:54–8:4	
17	Sa	9	Wa-yiggash	Gen. 44:18–47:27	Ezekiel 37:15–28
18	S	10	Fast of 10th of Ṭevet (morning and afternoon)	Exod. 32:11–14 Exod. 34:1–10	Isaiah 55:6–56:8 (afternoon only)
24	Sa	16	Wa-yeḥi	Gen. 47:28–50:26	I Kings 2:1–12
31	Sa	23	Shemot	Exod. 1:1–6:1	Isaiah 27:6–28:13 29:22–23 *Jeremiah 1:1–2:3*

Italics are for Sephardi Minhag.

1989, Jan. 7–Feb. 5] SHEVAṬ (30 DAYS) [5749

Civil Date	Day of the Week	Jewish Date	SABBATHS, FESTIVALS, FASTS	PENTATEUCHAL READING	PROPHETICAL READING
Jan. 7	Sa	Shevat 1	Wa-'era'; New Moon	Exod. 6:2–9:35 Num. 28:9–15	Isaiah 66:1–24
14	Sa	8	Bo'	Exod. 10:1–13:16	Jeremiah 46:13–28
21	Sa	15	Be-shallaḥ (Shabbat Shirah); Ḥamishshah-'asar bi-Shevaṭ	Exod. 13:17–17:16	Judges 4:4–5:31 *Judges 5:1–31*
28	Sa	22	Yitro	Exod. 18:1–20:23	Isaiah 6:1–7:6 9:5–6 *Isaiah 6:1–13*
Feb. 4	Sa	29	Mishpaṭim	Exod. 21:1–24:18	I Samuel 20:18–42
5	S	30	New Moon, first day	Num. 28:1–15	

Italics are for Sephardi Minhag.

1989, Feb. 6–Mar. 7] ADAR I (30 DAYS) [5749

Civil Date	Day of the Week	Jewish Date	SABBATHS, FESTIVALS, FASTS	PENTATEUCHAL READING	PROPHETICAL READING
Feb. 6	M	I Adar 1	New Moon, second day	Num. 28:1–15	
11	Sa	6	Terumah	Exod. 25:1–27:19	I Kings 5:26–6:13
18	Sa	13	Teẓawweh	Exod. 27:20–30:10	Ezekiel 43:10–27
25	Sa	20	Ki tissa'	Exod. 30:11–34:35	I Kings 18:1–39 *I Kings 18:20–39*
Mar. 4	Sa	27	Wa-yakhel (Shabbat Shekalim)	Exod. 35:1–38:20 Exod. 30:11–16	II Kings 12:1–17 *II Kings 11:17–12:17*
7	T	30	New Moon, first day	Num. 28:1–15	

1989, Mar. 8–Apr. 5] ADAR II (29 DAYS) [5749

Civil Date	Day of the Week	Jewish Date	SABBATHS, FESTIVALS, FASTS	PENTATEUCHAL READING	PROPHETICAL READING
Mar. 8	W	II Adar 1	New Moon, second day	Num. 28:1–15	
11	Sa	4	Pekude	Exod. 38:21–40:38	I Kings 7:51–8:21 *I Kings 7:40–50*
18	Sa	11	Wa-yikra' (Shabbat Zakhor)	Levit. 1:1–5:26 Deut. 25:17–19	I Samuel 15:2–34 *I Samuel 15:1–34*
20	M	13	Fast of Esther	Exod. 32:11–14 Exod. 34:1–10 (morning and afternoon)	Isaiah 55:6–56:8 (afternoon only)
21	T	14	Purim	Exod. 17:8–16	Book of Esther (night before and in the morning)
22	W	15	Shushan Purim		
25	Sa	18	Ẓaw (Shabbat Parah)	Levit. 6:1–8:36 Num. 19:1–22	Ezekiel 36:16–38 *Ezekiel 36:16–36*
Apr. 1	Sa	25	Shemini (Shabbat Ha-ḥodesh)	Levit. 9:1–11:47 Exod. 12:1–20	Ezekiel 45:16–46:18 *Ezekiel 45:18–46:15*

Italics are for Sephardi Minhag.

1989, Apr. 6–May 5] NISAN (30 DAYS)

Civil Date	Day of the Week	Jewish Date	SABBATHS, FESTIVALS, FASTS	PENTATEUCHAL READING	PROPHETICAL READING
Apr. 6	Th	Nisan 1	New Moon	Num. 28:1–15	
8	Sa	3	Tazria'	Levit. 12:1–13:59	II Kings 4:42–5:19
15	Sa	10	Mezora' (Shabbat Ha-gadol)	Levit. 14:1–15:33	Malachi 3:4–24
19	W	14	Fast of Firstborn		
20	Th	15	Passover, first day	Exod. 12:21–51 Num. 28:16–25	Joshua 5:2–6:1, 27
21	F	16	Passover, second day	Levit. 22:26–23:44 Num. 28:16–25	II Kings 23:1–9, 21–25
22	Sa	17	Hol Ha-mo'ed, first day	Exod. 33:12–34:26 Num. 28:19–25	Ezekiel 37:1–14
23	S	18	Hol Ha-mo'ed, second day	Exod. 13:1–16 Num. 28:19–25	
24	M	19	Hol Ha-mo'ed, third day	Exod. 22:24–23:19 Num. 28:19–25	
25	T	20	Hol Ha-mo'ed, fourth day	Num. 9:1–14 Num. 28:19–25	
26	W	21	Passover, seventh day	Exod. 13:17–15:26 Num. 28:19–25	II Samuel 22:1–51
27	Th	22	Passover, eighth day	Deut. 15:19–16:17 Num. 28:19–25	Isaiah 10:32–12:6
29	Sa	24	Aḥare mot	Levit. 16:1–18:30	Amos 9:7–15
May 2	T	27	Holocaust Memorial Day		
5	F	30	New Moon, first day	Num. 28:1–15	

Italics are for Sephardi Minhag.

1989, May 6–June 3]   IYAR (29 DAYS)   [5749

Civil Date	Day of the Week	Jewish Date	SABBATHS, FESTIVALS, FASTS	PENTATEUCHAL READING	PROPHETICAL READING
May 6	Sa	Iyar 1	Ḳedoshim; New Moon, second day	Levit. 19:1–20:27 Num. 28:9–15	Isaiah 66:1–24
10	W	5	Israel Independence Day		
13	Sa	8	Emor	Levit. 21:1–24:23	Ezekiel 44:15–31
20	Sa	15	Be-har	Levit. 25:1–26:2	Jeremiah 32:6–27
23	T	18	Lag Ba-'omer		
27	Sa	22	Be-ḥukkotai	Levit. 26:3–27:34	Jeremiah 16:19–17:14
June 2	F*	28	Jerusalem Day		
3	Sa	29	Be-midbar	Num. 1:1–4:20	I Samuel 20:18–42

*Observed Thursday, a day earlier, to avoid conflict with the Sabbath.

1989, June 4–July 3]   SIWAN (30 DAYS)   [5749

Civil Date	Day of the Week	Jewish Date	SABBATHS, FESTIVALS, FASTS	PENTATEUCHAL READING	PROPHETICAL READING
June 4	S	Siwan 1	New Moon	Num. 28:1–15	
9	F	6	Shavu'ot, first day	Exod. 19:1–20:23 Num. 28:26–31	Ezekiel 1:1–28 3:12
10	Sa	7	Shavu'ot, second day	Deut. 15:19–16:17 Num. 28:26–31	Habbakuk 3:1–19 *Habbakuk 2:20–3:19*
17	Sa	14	Naso'	Num. 4:21–7:89	Judges 13:2–25
24	Sa	21	Be-ha'alotekha	Num. 8:1–12:16	Zechariah 2:14–4:7
July 1	Sa	28	Shelaḥ lekha	Num. 13:1–15:41	Joshua 2:1–24
3	M	30	New Moon, first day	Num. 28:1–15	

Italics are for Sephardi Minhag.

1989, July 4–Aug. 1]   TAMMUZ (29 DAYS)   [5749

Civil Date	Day of the Week	Jewish Date	SABBATHS, FESTIVALS, FASTS	PENTATEUCHAL READING	PROPHETICAL READING
July 4	T	Tammuz 1	New Moon, second day	Num. 28:1–15	
8	Sa	5	Ḳoraḥ	Num. 16:1–18:32	I Samuel 11:14–12:22
15	Sa	12	Ḥuḳḳat, Balaḳ	Num. 19:1–25:9	Micah 5:6–6:8
20	Th	17	Fast of 17th of Tammuz	Exod. 32:11–14 Exod. 34:1–10 (morning and afternoon)	Isaiah 55:6–56:8 (afternoon only)
22	Sa	19	Pineḥas	Num. 25:10–30:1	Jeremiah 1:1–2:3
29	Sa	26	Maṭṭot, Mas'e	Num. 30:2–36:13	Jeremiah 2:4–28 3:4 *Jeremiah 2:4–28* *4:1–2*

Italics are for Sephardi Minhag.

1989, Aug. 2–Aug. 31] AV (30 DAYS) [5749

Civil Date	Day of the Week	Jewish Date	SABBATHS, FESTIVALS, FASTS	PENTATEUCHAL READING	PROPHETICAL READING
Aug. 2	W	Av 1	New Moon	Num. 28:1–15	
5	Sa	4	Devarim (Shabbat Ḥazon)	Deut. 1:1–3:22	Isaiah 1:1–27
10	Th	9	Fast of 9th of Av	Morning: Deut. 4:25–40 Afternoon: Exod. 32:11–14 34:1–10	(Lamentations is read the night before.) Jeremiah 8:13–9:23 (morning) Isaiah 55:6–56:8 (afternoon)
12	Sa	11	Wa-ethannan (Shabbat Naḥamu)	Deut. 3:23–7:11	Isaiah 40:1–26
19	Sa	18	'Eḳev	Deut. 7:12–11:25	Isaiah 49:14–51:3
26	Sa	25	Re'eh	Deut. 11:26–16:17	Isaiah 54:11–55:5
31	Th	30	New Moon, first day	Num. 28:1–15	

1989, Sept. 1–Sept. 29] ELUL (29 DAYS) [5749

Civil Date	Day of the Week	Jewish Date	SABBATHS, FESTIVALS, FASTS	PENTATEUCHAL READING	PROPHETICAL READING
Sept. 1	F	Elul 1	New Moon, second day	Num. 28:1–15	
2	Sa	2	Shofeṭim	Deut. 16:18–21:9	Isaiah 51:12–52:12
9	Sa	9	Ki teẓe'	Deut. 21:10–25:19	Isaiah 54:1–10
16	Sa	16	Ki tavo'	Deut. 26:1–29:8	Isaiah 60:1–22
23	Sa	23	Niẓẓavim, Wa-yelekh	Deut. 29:9–31:30	Isaiah 61:10–63:9

1989, Sept. 30–Oct. 29]   TISHRI (30 DAYS)   [5750

Civil Date	Day of the Week	Jewish Date	SABBATHS, FESTIVALS, FASTS	PENTATEUCHAL READING	PROPHETICAL READING
Sept. 30	Sa	Tishri 1	Rosh Ha-shanah, first day	Gen. 21:1–34 Num. 29:1–6	I Samuel 1:1–2:10
Oct. 1	S	2	Rosh Ha-shanah, second day	Gen. 22:1–24 Num. 29:1–6	Jeremiah 31:2–20
2	M	3	Fast of Gedaliah	Exod. 32:11–14 Exod. 34:1–10 (morning and afternoon)	Isaiah 55:6–56:8 (afternoon only)
7	Sa	8	Ha'azinu (Shabbat Shuvah)	Deut. 32:1–52	Hosea 14:2–10 Micah 7:18–20 Joel 2:15–27 *Hosea 14:2–10* *Micah 7:18–20*
9	M	10	Yom Kippur	Morning: Levit. 16:1–34 Num. 29:7–11 Afternoon: Levit. 18:1–30	Isaiah 57:14–58:14 Jonah 1:1–4:11 Micah 7:18–20
14	Sa	15	Sukkot, first day	Levit. 22:26–23:44 Num. 29:12–16	Zechariah 14:1–21
15	S	16	Sukkot, second day	Levit. 22:26–23:44 Num. 29:12–16	I Kings 8:2–21
16–19	M–Th	17–20	Hol Ha-mo'ed, first to fourth days	M Num. 29:17–25 T Num. 29:20–28 W Num. 29:23–31 Th Num. 29:26–34	
20	F	21	Hosha'na' Rabbah	Num. 29:26–34	
21	Sa	22	Shemini 'Azeret	Deut. 14:22–16:17 Num. 29:35–30:1	I Kings 8:54–66
22	S	23	Simhat Torah	Deut. 33:1–34:12 Gen. 1:1–2:3 Num. 29:35–30:1	Joshua 1:1–18 *Joshua 1:1–9*
28	Sa	29	Be-re'shit	Gen. 1:1–6:8	I Samuel 20:18–42
29	S	30	New Moon, first day	Num. 28:1–15	

Italics are for Sephardi Minhag.

1989, Oct. 30–Nov. 28] HESHWAN (30 DAYS) [5750

Civil Date	Day of the Week	Jewish Date	SABBATHS, FESTIVALS, FASTS	PENTATEUCHAL READING	PROPHETICAL READING
Oct. 30	M	Heshwan 1	New Moon, second day	Num. 28:1–15	
Nov. 4	Sa	6	Noah	Gen. 6:9–11:32	Isaiah 54:1–55:5 *Isaiah 54:1–10*
11	Sa	13	Lekh lekha	Gen. 12:1–17:27	Isaiah 40:27–41:16
18	Sa	20	Wa-yera'	Gen. 18:1–22:24	II Kings 4:1–37 *II Kings 4:1–23*
25	Sa	27	Hayye Sarah	Gen. 23:1–25:18	I Kings 1:1–31
28	T	30	New Moon, first day	Num. 28:1–15	

1989, Nov. 29–Dec. 28] KISLEW (30 DAYS) [5750

Civil Date	Day of the Week	Jewish Date	SABBATHS, FESTIVALS, FASTS	PENTATEUCHAL READING	PROPHETICAL READING
Nov. 29	W	Kislew 1	New Moon, second day	Num. 28:1–15	
Dec. 2	Sa	4	Toledot	Gen. 25:19–28:9	Malachi 1:1–2:7
9	Sa	11	Wa-yeze'	Gen. 28:10–32:3	Hosea 12:13–14:10 *Hosea 11:7–12:12*
16	Sa	18	Wa-yishlah	Gen. 32:4–36:43	Hosea 11:7–12:12 *Obadiah 1:1–21*
23	Sa	25	Wa-yeshev; Hanukkah, first day	Gen. 37:1–40:23 Num. 7:1–17	Zechariah 2:14–4:7
24–27	S–W	26–29	Hanukkah, second to fifth days	S Num. 7:18–29 M Num. 7:24–35 T Num. 7:30–41 W Num. 7:36–47	
28	Th	30	New Moon, first day; Hanukkah, sixth day	Num. 28:1–15 Num. 7:42–47	

Italics are for Sephardi Minhag.

1989, Dec. 29–Jan. 26, 1990] ṬEVET (29 DAYS) [5750

Civil Date	Day of the Week	Jewish Date	SABBATHS, FESTIVALS, FASTS	PENTATEUCHAL READING	PROPHETICAL READING
Dec. 29	F	Ṭevet 1	New Moon, second day; Ḥanukkah, seventh day	Num. 28:1–15 Num. 7:48–53	
30	Sa	2	Mi-ḳez; Ḥanukkah, eighth day	Gen. 41:1–44:17 Num. 7:54–8:4	I Kings 7:40–50
Jan. 6	Sa	9	Wa-yiggash	Gen. 44:18–47:27	Ezekiel 37:15–28
7	S	10	Fast of 10th of Ṭevet	Exod. 32:11–14 Exod. 34:1–10 (morning and afternoon)	Isaiah 55:6–56:8 (afternoon only)
13	Sa	16	Wa-yeḥi	Gen. 47:28–50:26	I Kings 2:1–12
20	Sa	23	Shemot	Exod. 1:1–6:1	Isaiah 27:6–28:13 29:22–23 *Jeremiah 1:1–2:3*

Italics are for Sephardi Minhag.

1990, Jan. 27–Feb. 25]   SHEVAṬ (30 DAYS)   [5750

Civil Date	Day of the Week	Jewish Date	SABBATHS, FESTIVALS, FASTS	PENTATEUCHAL READING	PROPHETICAL READING
Jan. 27	Sa	Shevaṭ 1	Wa-'era'; New Moon	Exod. 6:2–9:35 Num. 28:9–15	Isaiah 66:1–24
Feb. 3	Sa	8	Bo'	Exod. 10:1–13:16	Jeremiah 46:13–28
10	Sa	15	Be-shallaḥ (Shabbat Shirah); Ḥamishshah-'asar bi-Shevaṭ	Exod. 13:17–17:16	Judges 4:4–5:31 *Judges 5:1–31*
17	Sa	22	Yitro	Exod. 18:1–20:23	Isaiah 6:1–7:6 9:5–6 *Isaiah 6:1–13*
24	Sa	29	Mishpaṭim (Shabbat Sheḳalim)	Exod. 21:1–24:18 Exod. 30:11–16	II Kings 12:1–17 *II Kings 11:17–12:17* I Samuel 20:18,42
25	S	30	New Moon, first day	Num. 28:1–15	

Italics are for Sephardi Minhag.

1990, Feb. 26–Mar. 26]   ADAR (29 DAYS)   [5750

Civil Date	Day of the Week	Jewish Date	SABBATHS, FESTIVALS, FASTS	PENTATEUCHAL READING	PROPHETICAL READING
Feb. 26	M	Adar 1	New Moon, second day	Num. 28:1–15	
Mar. 3	Sa	6	Terumah	Exod. 25:1–27:19	I Kings 5:26–6:13
8	Th	11	Fast of Esther	Exod. 32:11–14 Exod. 34:1–10 (morning and afternoon)	Isaiah 55:6–56:8 (afternoon only)
10	Sa	13	Teẓawweh (Shabbat Zakhor)	Exod. 27:20–30:10 Deut. 25:17–19	I Samuel 15:2–34 *I Samuel 15:1–34*
11	S	14	Purim	Exod. 17:8–16	Book of Esther (night before and in the morning)
12	M	15	Shushan Purim		
17	Sa	20	Ki tissa' (Shabbat Parah)	Exod. 30:11–34:35 Num. 19:1–22	Ezekiel 36:16–38 *Ezekiel 36:16–36*
24	Sa	27	Wa-yaḳhel, Peḳude (Shabbat Ha-ḥodesh)	Exod. 35:1–40:38 Exod. 12:1–20	Ezekiel 45:16–46:18 *Ezekiel 45:18–46:15*

Italics are for Sephardi Minhag.

1990, Mar. 27–Apr. 25]   NISAN (30 DAYS)   [5750

Civil Date	Day of the Week	Jewish Date	SABBATHS, FESTIVALS, FASTS	PENTATEUCHAL READING	PROPHETICAL READING
Mar. 27	T	Nisan 1	New Moon	Num. 28:1–15	
31	Sa	5	Wa-yikra'	Levit. 1:1–5:26	Isaiah 43:21–44:24
Apr. 7	Sa	12	Zaw (Shabbat Ha-gadol)	Levit. 6:1–8:36	Malachi 3:4–24
9	M	14	Fast of Firstborn		
10	T	15	Passover, first day	Exod. 12:21–51 Num. 28:16–25	Joshua 5:2–6:1, 27
11	W	16	Passover, second day	Levit. 22:26–23:44 Num. 28:16–25	II Kings 23:1–9, 21–25
12	Th	17	Hol Ha-mo'ed, first day	Exod. 13:1–16 Num. 28:19–25	
13	F	18	Hol Ha-mo'ed, second day	Exod. 22:24–23:19 Num. 28:19–25	
14	Sa	19	Hol Ha-mo'ed, third day	Exod. 33:12–34:26 Num. 28:19–25	Ezekiel 37:1–14
15	S	20	Hol Ha-mo'ed, fourth day	Num. 9:1–14 Num. 28:19–25	
16	M	21	Passover, seventh day	Exod. 13:17–15:26 Num. 28:19–25	II Samuel 22:1–51
17	T	22	Passover, eigth day	Deut. 15:19–16:17 Num. 28:19–25	Isaiah 10:32–12:6
21	Sa	26	Shemini	Levit. 9:1–11:47	II Samuel 6:1–7:17 *II Samuel 6:1–19*
22	S	27	Holocaust Memorial Day		
25	W	30	New Moon, first day	Num. 28:1–15	

Italics are for Sephardi Minhag.

1990, Apr. 26–May 24] IYAR (29 DAYS) [5750

Civil Date	Day of the Week	Jewish Date	SABBATHS, FESTIVALS, FASTS	PENTATEUCHAL READING	PROPHETICAL READING
Apr. 26	Th	Iyar 1	New Moon, second day	Num. 28:1–15	
28	Sa	3	Tazria', Mezora'	Levit. 12:1–15:33	II Kings 7:3–20
30	M	5	Israel Independence Day		
May 5	Sa	10	Aḥare mot, Ḳedoshim	Levit. 16:1–20:27	Amos 9:7–15 *Ezekiel 20:2–20*
12	Sa	17	Emor	Levit. 21:1–24:23	Ezekiel 44:15–31
13	S	18	Lag Ba-'omer		
19	Sa	24	Be-har, Be-ḥuḳḳotai	Levit. 25:1–27:34	Jeremiah 16:19–17:14
23	W	28	Jerusalem Day		

1990, May 25–June 23] SIWAN (30 DAYS) [5750

Civil Date	Day of the Week	Jewish Date	SABBATHS, FESTIVALS, FASTS	PENTATEUCHAL READING	PROPHETICAL READING
May 25	F	Siwan 1	New Moon	Num. 28:1–15	
26	Sa	2	Be-midbar	Num. 1:1–4:20	Hosea 2:1–22
30	W	6	Shavu'ot, first day	Exod. 19:1–20:23 Num. 28:26–31	Ezekiel 1:1–28 3:12
31	Th	7	Shavu'ot, second day	Deut. 15:19–16:17 Num. 28:26–31	Habbakuk 3:1–19 *Habbakuk 2:20–3:19*
June 2	Sa	9	Naso'	Num. 4:21–7:89	Judges 13:2–25
9	Sa	16	Be-ha'alotekha	Num. 8:1–12:16	Zechariah 2:14–4:7
16	Sa	23	Shelaḥ lekha	Num. 13:1–15:41	Joshua 2:1–24
23	Sa	30	Ḳoraḥ; New Moon, first day	Num. 16:1–18:32 Num. 28:9–15	Isaiah 66:1–24 *Isaiah 66:1–24* *I Samuel 20:18, 42*

Italics are for Sephardi Minhag.

1990, June 24–July 22] TAMMUZ (29 DAYS) [5750

Civil Date	Day of the Week	Jewish Date	SABBATHS, FESTIVALS, FASTS	PENTATEUCHAL READING	PROPHETICAL READING
June 24	S	Tammuz 1	New Moon, second day	Num. 28:1–15	
30	Sa	7	Hukkat	Num. 19:1–22:1	Judges 11:1–33
July 7	Sa	14	Balak	Num. 22:2–25:9	Micah 5:6–6:8
10	T	17	Fast of 17th of Tammuz	Exod. 32:11–14 Exod. 34:1–10 (morning and afternoon)	Isaiah 55:6–56:8 (afternoon only)
21	Sa	21	Pinehas	Num. 25:10–30:1	Jeremiah 1:1–2:3
28	Sa	28	Mattot, Mas'e	Num. 30:2–36:13	Jeremiah 2:4–28 3:4 *Jeremiah 2:4–28 4:1–2*

Italics are for Sephardi Minhag.

1990, July 23–Aug. 21]   AV (30 DAYS)   [5750

Civil Date	Day of the Week	Jewish Date	SABBATHS, FESTIVALS, FASTS	PENTATEUCHAL READING	PROPHETICAL READING
July 23	M	Av 1	New Moon	Num. 28:1–15	
28	Sa	6	Devarim (Shabbat Hazon)	Deut. 1:1–3:22	Isaiah 1:1–27
31	T	9	Fast of 9th of Av	Morning: Deut. 4:25–40 Afternoon: Exod. 32:11–14 Exod. 34:1–10	(Lamentations is read the night before.) Jeremiah 8:13–9:23 (morning) Isaiah 55:6–56:8 (afternoon)
Aug. 4	Sa	13	Wa-ethannan (Shabbat Nahamu)	Deut. 3:23–7:11	Isaiah 40:1–26
11	Sa	20	'Ekev	Deut. 7:12–11:25	Isaiah 49:14–51:3
18	Sa	27	Re'eh	Deut. 11:26–16:17	Isaiah 54:11–55:5
21	T	30	New Moon, first day	Num. 28:1–15	

1990, Aug. 22–Sept. 19]   ELUL (29 DAYS)   [5750

Civil Date	Day of the Week	Jewish Date	SABBATHS, FESTIVALS, FASTS	PENTATEUCHAL READING	PROPHETICAL READING
Aug. 22	W	Elul 1	New Moon, second day	Num. 28:1–15	
25	Sa	4	Shofetim	Deut. 16:18–21:9	Isaiah 51:12–52:12
Sept. 1	Sa	11	Ki teze'	Deut. 21:10–25:19	Isaiah 54:1–10
8	Sa	18	Ki tavo'	Deut. 26:1–29:8	Isaiah 60:1–22
15	Sa	25	Nizzavim, Wa-yelekh	Deut. 29:9–31:30	Isaiah 61:10–63:9

1990, Sept. 20–Oct. 19] TISHRI (30 DAYS) [5751

Civil Date	Day of the Week	Jewish Date	SABBATHS, FESTIVALS, FASTS	PENTATEUCHAL READING	PROPHETICAL READING
Sept. 20	Th	Tishri 1	Rosh Ha-shanah, first day	Gen. 21:1–34 Num. 29:1–6	I Samuel 1:1–2:10
21	F	2	Rosh Ha-shanah, second day	Gen. 22:1–24 Num. 29:1–6	Jeremiah 31:2–20
22	Sa	3	Ha'azinu (Shabbat Shuvah)	Deut. 32:1–52	Hosea 14:2–10 Micah 7:18–20 Joel 2:15–27 *Hosea 14:2–10* *Micah 7:18–20*
23	S	4	Fast of Gedaliah	Exod. 32:11–14 Exod. 34:1–10 (morning and afternoon)	Isaiah 55:6–56:8 (afternoon only)
29	Sa	10	Yom Kippur	Morning: Levit. 16:1–34 Num. 29:7–11 Afternoon: Levit. 18:1–30	Isaiah 57:14–58:14 Jonah 1:1–4:11 Micah 7:18–20
Oct. 4	Th	15	Sukkot, first day	Levit. 22:26–23:44 Num. 29:12–16	Zechariah 14:1–21
5	F	16	Sukkot, second day	Levit. 22:26–23:44 Num. 29:12–16	I Kings 8:2–21
Oct. 6	Sa	Tishri 17	Hol Ha-mo'ed, first day	Exod. 33:12–34:26 Num. 29:17–22	Ezekiel 38:18–39:16
7–9	S–T	18–20	Hol Ha-mo'ed, second to fourth days	S Num. 29:20–28 M Num. 29:23–31 T Num. 29:26–34	
10	W	21	Hosha'na' Rabbah	Num. 29:26–34	
11	Th	22	Shemini 'Azeret	Deut. 14:22–16:17 Num. 29:35–30:1	I Kings 8:54–66
12	F	23	Simḥat Torah	Deut. 33:1–34:12 Gen. 1:1–2:3 Num. 29:35–30:1	Joshua 1:1–18 *Joshua 1:1–9*
13	Sa	24	Be-re'shit	Gen. 1:1–6:8	Isaiah 42:5–43:10 *Isaiah 42:5–21*
19	F	30	New Moon, first day	Num. 28:1–15	

Italics are for Sephardi Minhag.

1990, Oct. 20–Nov. 17] ḤESHWAN (29 DAYS) [5751

Civil Date	Day of the Week	Jewish Date	SABBATHS, FESTIVALS, FASTS	PENTATEUCHAL READING	PROPHETICAL READING
Oct. 20	Sa	Ḥeshwan 1	Noah; New Moon, second day	Gen. 6:9–11:32 Num. 28:9–15	Isaiah 66:1–24
27	Sa	8	Lekh lekha	Gen. 12:1–17:27	Isaiah 40:27–41:16
Nov. 3	Sa	15	Wa-yera'	Gen. 18:1–22:24	II Kings 4:1–37 *II Kings 4:1–23*
10	Sa	22	Ḥayye Sarah	Gen. 23:1–25:18	I Kings 1:1–31
17	Sa	29	Toledot	Gen. 25:19–28:9	I Samuel 20:18–42

1990, Nov. 18–Dec. 17] KISLEW (30 DAYS) [5751

Civil Date	Day of the Week	Jewish Date	SABBATHS, FESTIVALS, FASTS	PENTATEUCHAL READING	PROPHETICAL READING
Nov. 18	S	Kislew 1	New Moon	Num. 28:1–15	
24	Sa	7	Wa-yeze'	Gen. 28:10–32:3	Hosea 12:13–14:10 *Hosea 11:7–12:12*
Dec. 1	Sa	14	Wa-yishlaḥ	Gen. 32:4–36:43	Hosea 11:7–12:12 *Obadiah 1:1–21*
8	Sa	21	Wa-yeshev	Gen. 37:1–40:23	Amos 2:6–3:8
12–14	W–F	25–27	Hanukkah, first to third days	W Num. 7:1–17 Th Num. 7:18–29 F Num. 7:24–35	
15	Sa	28	Mi-kez; Hanukkah, fourth day	Gen. 41:1–44:17 Num. 7:30–35	Zechariah 2:14–4:7
16	S	29	Hanukkah, fifth day	Num. 7:36–47	
17	M	30	New Moon, first day; Hanukkah, sixth day	Num. 28:1–15 Num. 7:42–47	

Italics are for Sephardi Minhag.

1990, Dec. 18–Jan. 15, 1991] TEVET (29 DAYS) [5751

Civil Date	Day of the Week	Jewish Date	SABBATHS, FESTIVALS, FASTS	PENTATEUCHAL READING	PROPHETICAL READING
Dec. 18	T	Tevet 1	New Moon, second day; Hanukkah, seventh day	Num. 28:1–15 Num. 7:48–53	
19	W	2	Hanukkah, eighth day	Num. 7:54–8:4	
22	Sa	5	Wa-yiggash	Gen. 44:18–47:27	Ezekiel 37:15–28
27	Th	10	Fast of 10th of Tevet	Exod. 32:11–14 43:1–10 (morning and afternoon)	Isaiah 55:6–56:8 (afternoon only)
29	Sa	12	Wa-yehi	Gen. 47:28–50:26	I Kings 2:1–12
Jan. 5	Sa	19	Shemot	Exod. 1:1–6:1	Isaiah 27:6–28:13 29:22–23 *Jeremiah 1:1–2:3*
12	Sa	26	Wa-'era'	Exod. 6:2–9:35	Ezekiel 28:25–29:21

Italics are for Sephardi Minhag.

1991, Jan. 16–Feb. 14] SHEVAṬ (30 DAYS) [5751

Civil Date	Day of the Week	Jewish Date	SABBATHS, FESTIVALS, FASTS	PENTATEUCHAL READING	PROPHETICAL READING
Jan. 16	W	Shevaṭ 1	New Moon	Num. 28:1–15	
19	Sa	4	Bo'	Exod. 10:1–13:16	Jeremiah 46:13–28
26	Sa	11	Be-shallaḥ (Shabbat Shirah)	Exod. 13:17–17:16	Judges 4:4–5:31 *Judges 5:1–31*
30	W	15	Ḥamishshah-'asar bi-Shevaṭ		
Feb. 2	Sa	18	Yitro	Exod. 18:1–20:23	Isaiah 6:1–7:6 9:5, 6 *Isaiah 6:1–13*
9	Sa	25	Mishpaṭim (Shabbat Shekalim)	Exod. 21:1–24:18 Exod. 30:11–16	II Kings 12:1–17 *II Kings 11:17–12:17*
14	Th	30	New Moon, first day	Num. 28:1–15	

Italics are for Sephardi Minhag.

1991, Feb. 15–Mar. 15] ADAR (29 DAYS) [5751

Civil Date	Day of the Week	Jewish Date	SABBATHS, FESTIVALS, FASTS	PENTATEUCHAL READING	PROPHETICAL READING
Feb. 15	F	Adar 1	New Moon, second day	Num. 28:1–15	
16	Sa	2	Terumah	Exod. 25:1–27:19	I Kings 5:26–6:13
23	Sa	9	Teẓawweh (Shabbat Zakhor)	Exod. 27:20–30:10 Deut. 25:17–19	I Samuel 15:2–34 *I Samuel 15:1–34*
27	W	13	Fast of Esther	Exod. 32:11–14 Exod. 34:1–10 (morning and afternoon)	Isaiah 55:6–56:8 (afternoon only)
28	Th	14	Purim	Exod. 17:8–16	Book of Esther (night before and in the morning)
Mar. 1	F	15	Shushan Purim		
2	Sa	16	Ki tissa'	Exod. 30:11–34:35	I Kings 18:1–39 *I Kings 18:20–39*
9	Sa	23	Wa-yakhel, Peḳude (Shabbat Parah)	Exod. 35:1–40:38 Num. 19:1–22	Ezekiel 36:16–38 *Ezekiel 36:16–36*

Italics are for Sephardi Minhag.

1991, Mar. 16–Apr. 14]   NISAN (30 DAYS)   [5751

Civil Date	Day of the Week	Jewish Date	SABBATHS, FESTIVALS, FASTS	PENTATEUCHAL READING	PROPHETICAL READING
Mar. 16	Sa	Nisan 1	Wa-yikra' (Shabbat Ha-hodesh); New Moon	Levit. 1:1–5:26 Exod. 12:1–20 Num. 28:9–15	Ezekiel 45:16–46:18 *Ezekiel 45:18–46:15*
23	Sa	8	Zaw (Shabbat Ha-gadol)	Levit. 6:1–8:36	Malachi 3:4–24
29	F	14	Fast of Firstborn		
30	Sa	15	Passover, first day	Exod. 12:21–51 Num. 28:16–25	Joshua 5:2–6:1, 27
31	S	16	Passover, second day	Levit. 22:26–23:44 Num. 28:16–25	II Kings 23:1–19, 21–25
Apr. 1	M	17	Hol Ha-mo'ed, first day	Exod. 13:1–16 Num. 28:19–25	
2	T	18	Hol Ha-mo'ed, second day	Exod. 22:24–23:19 Num. 28:19–25	
3	W	19	Hol Ha-mo'ed, third day	Exod. 34:1–26 Num. 28:19–25	
4	Th	20	Hol Ha-mo'ed, fourth day	Num. 9:1–14 Num. 28:19–25	
5	F	21	Passover, seventh day	Exod. 13:17–15:26 Num. 28:19–25	II Samuel 22:1–51
6	Sa	22	Passover, eighth day	Deut. 15:19–16:17 Num. 28:19–25	Isaiah 10:32–12:6
11	Th	27	Holocaust Memorial Day		
13	Sa	29	Shemini	Levit. 9:1–11:47	I Samuel 20:18–42
14	S	30	New Moon, first day	Num. 28:1–15	

Italics are for Sephardi Minhag.

1991, Apr. 15–May 13]   IYAR (29 DAYS)   [5751

Civil Date	Day of the Week	Jewish Date	SABBATHS, FESTIVALS, FASTS	PENTATEUCHAL READING	PROPHETICAL READING
Apr. 15	M	Iyar 1	New Moon, second day	Num. 28:1–15	
19	F*	5	Israel Independence Day		
20	Sa	6	Tazria', Mezora'	Levit. 12:1–15:33	II Kings 7:3–20
27	Sa	13	Ahare mot, Kedoshim	Levit. 16:1–20:27	Amos 9:7–15 *Ezekiel 20:2–20*
May 2	Th	18	Lag Ba-'omer		
4	Sa	20	Emor	Levit. 21:1–24:23	Ezekiel 44:15–31
11	Sa	27	Be-har, Be-hukkotai	Levit. 25:1–27:34	Jeremiah 16:19–17:14
12	S	28	Jerusalem Day		

*Observed Thursday, a day earlier, to avoid conflict with the Sabbath.

Italics are for Sephardi Minhag.

1991, May 14–June 12]   SIWAN (30 DAYS)   [5751

Civil Date	Day of the Week	Jewish Date	SABBATHS, FESTIVALS, FASTS	PENTATEUCHAL READING	PROPHETICAL READING
May 14	T	Siwan 1	New Moon	Num. 28:1–15	
18	Sa	5	Be-midbar	Num. 1:1–4:20	Hosea 2:1–22
19	S	6	Shavu'ot, first day	Exod. 19:1–20:23 Num. 28:26–31	Ezekiel 1:1–28 3:12
20	M	7	Shavu'ot, second day	Deut. 15:19–16:17 Num. 28:26–31	Habbakuk 3:1–19 *Habbakuk 2:20–3:19*
25	Sa	12	Naso'	Num. 4:21–7:89	Judges 13:2–25
June 1	Sa	19	Be-ha'alotekha	Num. 8:1–12:16	Zechariah 2:14–4:7
8	Sa	26	Shelah lekha	Num. 13:1–15:41	Joshua 2:1–24
12	W	30	New Moon, first day	Num. 28:1–15	

1991, June 13–July 11]   TAMMUZ (29 DAYS)   [5751

Civil Date	Day of the Week	Jewish Date	SABBATHS, FESTIVALS, FASTS	PENTATEUCHAL READING	PROPHETICAL READING
June 13	Th	Tammuz 1	New Moon, second day	Num. 28:1–15	
15	Sa	3	Korah	Num. 16:1–18:32	I Samuel 11:14–12:22
22	Sa	10	Hukkat	Num. 19:1–22:1	Judges 11:1–33
29	Sa	17	Balak	Num. 22:2–25:9	Micah 5:6–6:8
30	S	18	Fast of 17th of Tammuz	Exod. 32:11–14 Exod. 34:1–10 (morning and afternoon)	Isaiah 55:6–56:8 (afternoon only)
July 6	Sa	24	Pinehas	Num. 25:10–30:1	Jeremiah 1:1–2:3

Italics are for Sephardi Minhag.

1991, July 12–Aug. 10]   AV (30 DAYS)   [5751

Civil Date	Day of the Week	Jewish Date	SABBATHS, FESTIVALS, FASTS	PENTATEUCHAL READING	PROPHETICAL READING
July 12	F	Av 1	New Moon	Num. 28:1–15	
13	Sa	2	Maṭṭot, Mas'e	Num. 30:2–36:13	Jeremiah 2:4–28 3:4 *Jeremiah 2:4–28 4:1–2*
20	Sa	9	Devarim (Shabbat Ḥazon)	Deut. 1:1–3:22	Isaiah 1:1–27
21	S	10	Fast of 9th of Av	Morning: Deut. 4:25–40 Afternoon: Exod. 32:11–14 Exod. 34:1–10	(Lamentations is read night before.) Jeremiah 8:13–9:23 (morning) Isaiah 55:6–56:8 (afternoon)
27	Sa	16	Wa-ethannan (Shabbat Naḥamu)	Deut. 3:23–7:11	Isaiah 40:1–26
Aug. 3	Sa	23	'Eḳev	Deut. 7:12–11:25	Isaiah 49:14–51:3
10	Sa	30	Re'eh; New Moon, first day	Deut. 11:26–16:17 Num. 28:9–15	Isaiah 66:1–24 I Samuel 20:18, 42

1991, Aug. 11–Sept. 8]   ELUL (29 DAYS)   [5751

Civil Date	Day of the Week	Jewish Date	SABBATHS, FESTIVALS, FASTS	PENTATEUCHAL READING	PROPHETICAL READING
Aug. 11	S	Elul 1	New Moon, second day	Num. 28:1–15	
17	Sa	7	Shofeṭim	Deut. 16:18–21:9	Isaiah 51:12–52:12
24	Sa	14	Ki teze'	Deut. 21:10–25:19	Isaiah 54:1–10
31	Sa	21	Ki tavo'	Deut. 26:1–29:8	Isaiah 60:1–22
Sept. 7	Sa	28	Niẓẓavim	Deut. 29:9–30:20	Isaiah 61:10–63:9

Italics are for Sephardi Minhag.

TISHRI (30 DAYS)

Civil Date	Day of the Week	Jewish Date	SABBATHS, FESTIVALS, FASTS	PENTATEUCHAL READING	PROPHETICAL READING
Sept. 9	M	Tishri 1	Rosh Ha-shanah, first day	Gen. 21:1–34 Num. 29:1–6	I Samuel 1:1–2:10
10	T	2	Rosh Ha-shanah, second day	Gen. 22:1–24 Num. 29:1–6	Jeremiah 31:2–20
11	W	3	Fast of Gedaliah	Exod. 32:11–14 Exod. 34:1–10 (morning and afternoon)	Isaiah 55:6–56:8 (afternoon only)
14	Sa	6	Wa-yelekh (Shabbat Shuvah)	Deut. 31:1–30	Hosea 14:2–10 Micah 7:18–20 Joel 2:15–27 *Hosea 14:2–10* *Micah 7:18–20*
18	W	10	Yom Kippur	Morning: Levit. 16:1–34 Num. 29:7–11 Afternoon: Levit. 18:1–30	Isaiah 57:14–58:14 Jonah 1:1–4:11 Micah 7:18–20
21	Sa	13	Ha'azinu	Deut. 32:1–52	II Samuel 22:1–51
23	M	15	Sukkot, first day	Levit. 22:26–23:44 Num. 29:12–16	Zechariah 14:1–21
24	T	16	Sukkot, second day	Levit. 22:26–23:44 Num. 29:12–16	I Kings 8:2–21
25–27	W-F	17–19	Hol Ha-mo'ed, first to third days	W Num. 29:17–25 Th Num. 29:20–28 F Num. 29:23–31	
28	Sa	20	Hol Ha-mo'ed, fourth day	Exod. 33:12–34:26 Num. 29:26–31	Ezekiel 38:18–39:16
29	S	21	Hosha'na' Rabbah	Num. 29:26–34	
30	M	22	Shemini 'Azeret	Deut. 14:22–16:17 Num. 29:35–30:1	I Kings 8:54–66
Oct. 1	T	23	Simhat Torah	Deut. 33:1–34:12 Gen. 1:1–2:3 Num. 29:35–30:1	Joshua 1:1–18 *Joshua 1:1–9*
5	Sa	27	Be-re'shit	Gen. 1:1–6:8	Isaiah 42:5–43:10 *Isaiah 42:5–21*
8	T	30	New Moon, first day	Num. 28:1–15	

Italics are for Sephardi Minhag.

1991, Oct. 9–Nov. 7]   HESHWAN (30 DAYS)   [5752

Civil Date	Day of the Week	Jewish Date	SABBATHS, FESTIVALS, FASTS	PENTATEUCHAL READING	PROPHETICAL READING
Oct. 9	W	Heshwan 1	New Moon, second day	Num. 28:1–15	
12	Sa	4	Noah	Gen. 6:9–11:32	Isaiah 54:1–55:5 *Isaiah 54:1–10*
19	Sa	11	Lekh lekha	Gen. 12:1–17:27	Isaiah 40:27–41:16
26	Sa	18	Wa-yera'	Gen. 18:1–22:24	II Kings 4:1–37 *II Kings 4:1–23*
Nov. 2	Sa	25	Hayye Sarah	Gen. 23:1–25:18	I Kings 1:1–31
7	Th	30	New Moon, first day	Num. 28:1–15	

1991, Nov. 8–Dec. 7]   KISLEW (30 DAYS)   [5752

Civil Date	Day of the Week	Jewish Date	SABBATHS, FESTIVALS, FASTS	PENTATEUCHAL READING	PROPHETICAL READING
Nov. 8	F	Kislew 1	New Moon, second day	Num. 28:1–15	
9	Sa	2	Toledot	Gen. 25:19–28:9	Malachi 1:1–2:7
16	Sa	9	Wa-yeze'	Gen. 28:10–32:3	Hosea 12:13–14:10 *Hosea 11:7–12:12*
23	Sa	16	Wa-yishlah	Gen. 32:4–36:43	Hosea 11:7–12:12 *Obadiah 1:1–21*
30	Sa	23	Wa-yeshev	Gen. 37:1–40:23	Amos 2:6–3:8
Dec. 2–6	M–F	25–29	Hanukkah, first to fifth days	M Num. 7:1–17 T Num. 7:18–29 W Num. 7:24–35 Th Num. 7:30–41 F Num. 7:36–47	
7	Sa	30	Mi-kez; New Moon, first day; Hanukkah, sixth day	Gen. 41:1–44:17 Num. 28:9–15 Num. 7:42–47	Zechariah 2:14–4:7

Italics are for Sephardi Minhag.

1991, Dec. 8–Jan. 5 1992]   ṬEVET (29 DAYS)   [5752

Civil Date	Day of the Week	Jewish Date	SABBATHS, FESTIVALS, FASTS	PENTATEUCHAL READING	PROPHETICAL READING
Dec. 8	S	Tevet 1	New Moon, second day; Hanukkah, seventh day	Num. 28:1–15 Num. 7:48–53	
9	M	2	Hanukkah, eighth day	Num. 7:54–8:4	
14	Sa	7	Wa-yiggash	Gen. 44:18–47:27	Ezekiel 37:15–28
17	T	10	Fast of 10th of Ṭevet	Exod. 32:11–14 Exod. 34:1–10 (morning and afternoon)	Isaiah 55:6–56:8 (afternoon only)
21	Sa	14	Wa-yeḥi	Gen. 47:28–50:26	I Kings 2:1–12
28	Sa	21	Shemot	Exod. 1:1–6:1	Isaiah 27:6–28:13 29:22–23 *Jeremiah 1:1–2:3*
Jan. 4	Sa	28	Wa-'era'	Exod. 6:2–9:35	Ezekiel 28:25–29:21

Italics are for Sephardi Minhag.

SELECTED ARTICLES OF INTEREST IN RECENT VOLUMES OF THE AMERICAN JEWISH YEAR BOOK

The American Jewish Family Today	Steven Martin Cohen 82:136–154
Attitudes of American Jews Toward Israel: Trends Over Time	Eytan Gilboa 86:110–125
The Bitburg Controversy	Deborah E. Lipstadt 87:21–37
California Jews: Data from the Field Polls	Alan M. Fisher and Curtis K. Tanaka 86:196–218
A Century of Conservative Judaism in the United States	Abraham J. Karp 86:3–61
A Century of Jewish History, 1881–1981: The View from America	Lucy S. Dawidowicz 82:3–98
The "Civil Judaism" of Communal Leaders	Jonathan S. Woocher 81:149–169
Counting Jewish Populations: Methods and Problems	Paul Ritterband, Barry A. Kosmin, and Jeffrey Scheckner 88:204–221
The Demographic Consequences of U.S. Jewish Population Trends	U.O. Schmelz and Sergio DellaPergola 83:141–187
The Demography of Latin American Jewry	U.O. Schmelz and Sergio DellaPergola 85:51–102
The Impact of Feminism on American Jewish Life	Sylvia B. Fishman 89:3–62
Israelis in the United States: Motives, Attitudes, and Intentions	Dov Elizur 80:53–67
Jewish Education Today	Walter I. Ackerman 80:130–148
Jewish Survival: The Demographic Factors	U.O. Schmelz 81:61–117
Jews in the United States: Perspectives from Demography	Sidney Goldstein 81:3–59

The Labor Market Status of American Jews: Patterns and Determinants	Barry R. Chiswick 85:131–153
Latin American Jewry Today	Judith Laikin Elkin 85:3–49
Los Angeles Jewry: A Demographic Portrait	Bruce A. Phillips 86:126–195
The National Gallup Polls and American Jewish Demography	Alan M. Fisher 83:111–126
New Perspectives in American Jewish Sociology	Nathan Glazer 87:3–19
The 1981–1982 National Survey of American Jews	Steven Martin Cohen 83:89–110
The Population of Reunited Jerusalem, 1967–1985	U.O. Schmelz 87:39–113
Recent Jewish Community Population Studies: A Roundup	Gary A. Tobin and Alvin Chenkin 85:154–178
Recent Trends in American Judaism	Jack Wertheimer 89:63–162
Reform and Conservative Judaism in Israel: A Social and Religious Profile	Ephraim Tabory 83:41–61
Religiosity Patterns in Israel	Calvin Goldscheider and Dov Friedlander 83:3–39
The Social Characteristics of the New York Area Jewish Community, 1981	Paul Ritterband and Steven M. Cohen 84:128–161
South African Jewry: A Sociodemographic Profile	Sergio DellaPergola and Allie A. Dubb 88:59–140
South African Jews and the Apartheid Crisis	Gideon Shimoni 88:3–58
Trends in Jewish Philanthropy	Steven Martin Cohen 80:29–51

OBITUARIES

Leo Baeck	By Max Gruenewald 59:478–82
Jacob Blaustein	By John Slawson 72:547–57
Martin Buber	By Seymour Siegel 67:37–43
Abraham Cahan	By Mendel Osherowitch 53:527–29
Albert Einstein	By Jacob Bronowski 58:480–85
Felix Frankfurter	By Paul A. Freund 67:31–36
Louis Ginzberg	By Louis Finkelstein 56:573–79
Jacob Glatstein	By Shmuel Lapin 73:611–17
Sidney Goldmann	By Milton R. Konvitz 85:401–03
Hayim Greenberg	By Marie Syrkin 56:589–94
Abraham Joshua Heschel	By Fritz A. Rothschild 74:533–44
Horace Meyer Kallen	By Milton R. Konvitz 75:55–80
Mordecai Kaplan	By Ludwig Nadelmann 85:404–11
Herbert H. Lehman	By Louis Finkelstein 66:3–20
Judah L. Magnes	By James Marshall 51:512–15
Alexander Marx	By Abraham S. Halkin 56:580–88
Reinhold Niebuhr	By Seymour Siegel 73:605–10
Joseph Proskauer	By David Sher 73:618–28
Maurice Samuel	By Milton H. Hindus 74:545–53
Leo Strauss	By Ralph Lerner 76:91–97
Max Weinreich	By Lucy S. Dawidowicz 70:59–68
Chaim Weizmann	By Harry Sacher 55:462–69
Stephen S. Wise	By Philip S. Bernstein 51:515–18
Harry Austryn Wolfson	By Isadore Twersky 76:99–111

Index

Abbas, Mohammed Abu al-, 251
Abed, Shukri B., 414
Aberbach, David, 332
Abrahams, Alfred, 334
Abram, Morris, 208, 231, 259, 260, 261, 265, 266, 267
Abramovich, Pavel, 329, 384
Abramsky, Harry, 320
Abuhatzeira, Aharon, 85
Abu Jihad, 233, 248, 324, 486
abu-Lughod, Ibrahim, 247, 446
Achille Lauro, 251
Adamec, Ladislav, 389
Adhami, Ali, 322
Adiv, Assaf, 413
Adler, Chaim, 3, 60, 71, 117
Adler, Hans Gunther, 334
Affo, Abd al-Nasser al-, 416
Afn Shvel, 600
Agudath Israel of America, 546
    Agudah Women of American-N'Shei Agudath Israel, 546
    Children's Division—Pirchei Agudath Israel, 546
    Girls' Division-Bnos Agudath Israel, 546
    Young Men's Division—Zeirei Agudath Israel, 546
Agudath Israel World Organization, 546
Ahimeir, O., 106
Akale, Shlomo, 502
Akzin, Benjamin, 81
Alba, Richard D., 105
Alderman, Geoffrey, 333
Aldoubi, Roman, 430, 431, 432
Algemeiner Journal, 600

Alkallay, Rachel, 318
Allchild, Charles, 334
Allen, Jim, 325
Allen, Woody, 258
Alliance, David, 331, 334
Almagor, Gila, 510
Aloni, Shulamit, 463
Alperin, Aron, 606
Alpha Epsilon Pi Fraternity, 565
Alter, Viktor, 392
ALYN—American Society for Handicapped Children in Israel, 570
AMC Cancer Research Center, 566
America-Israel Cultural Foundation, 570
America-Israel Friendship League, 570
American Academy for Jewish Research, 539
American Associates, Ben-Gurion University of the Negev, 571
American Association for Ethiopian Jews, 544
American Association of Rabbis, 546
American Biblical Encyclopedia Society, 539
American Committee for Shaare Zedek Hospital in Jerusalem, 571
American Committee for Shenkar College in Israel, 571
American Committee for Weizmann Institute of Science, 571
American Council for Judaism, 535
American Federation of Jews from Central Europe, 565
American Friends of Alliance Israélite Universelle, 544
American Friends of Beth Hatefutsoth, 571

American Friends of Ezrath Nashim Hospital-Jerusalem, 571
American Friends of Haifa Maritime Museum, 571
American Friends of Haifa University, 571
American Friends of Hebrew University, 572
American Friends of Israel Museum, 572
American Friends of Shalom Hartman Institute, 572
American Friends of Tel Aviv Museum, 572
American Friends of Tel Aviv University, 572
American Israeli Lighthouse, 572
American Israelite, 603
American Israel Public Affairs Committee (AIPAC), 256, 271, 272, 572
American Jewish Alternatives to Zionism, 535
American Jewish Archives, 550, 603
American Jewish Committee, 227, 271, 272, 275, 276, 350, 374, 535
American Jewish Congress, 258, 259, 272, 276, 536
American Jewish Correctional Chaplains Association, 567
American Jewish Historical Society, 539
American Jewish History, 599
American Jewish Joint Distribution Committee, JDC, 544
American Jewish League for Israel, 572
American Jewish Periodical Center, 550
American Jewish Philanthropic Fund, 544
American Jewish Press Association, 539
American Jewish Public Relations Society, 580
American Jewish Society for Service, 567
American Jewish Times Outlook, 603
American Jewish World, 599
American Jewish Year Book, 600
American ORT Federation, 544
  American and European Friends of ORT, 544
  American Labor ORT, 545
  Business and Professional ORT, 545
  National ORT League, 545
  Women's American ORT, 545
American Physicians Fellowship for Medicine in Israel, 572
American Red Magen David for Israel, 572
American Sephardi Federation, 565
Americans for Progressive Israel, 573
Americans for a Safe Israel, 573
American Society for Jewish Music, 539
American Society for Protection of Nature in Israel, 573
American Veterans of Israel, 565
American Zionist, 600
American Zionist Federation, 573
American Zionist Youth Foundation, 573
Amir, Y., 65
Amit Women, 573, 600
Amital, Yehudah, 462
Ampal—American Israel Corporation, 574
Anctil, Pierre, 318
Anda, Torleiv, 488
Andersson, Sten, 453, 455, 488
Andreevna, Nina, 383
Andreotti, Giulio, 346, 347
Andriko, Miklos, 490
Angelico, Irene, 317
Anne Frank Foundation, 342, 343
Annenberg Research Institute, 546
Anti-Defamation League (ADL), 213, 214, 215, 218, 223, 262, 272, 536
Appelfeld, Aharon, 333
Arad, Moshe, 208, 224, 231, 471
Arad, Nili, 412
Arafat, Yasir, 209, 228, 247, 249, 250, 251, 252, 261, 262, 328, 346, 394, 401, 406, 437, 441, 450, 451, 452, 453, 454, 455, 456, 461, 463, 464, 473, 480, 487
Archer, Peter, 326
Arens, Moshe, 241, 246, 447, 459, 471, 476, 477, 485
Argentina, 491, 523
Arian, Asher, 86, 479

Arieli, Yehoshua, 413
Arizona Post, 597
Armacost, Michael, 486
Aronson, David, 606
Arouri, Ribhi, 413
Aryan Nations, 214, 307
ARZA—Association of Reform Zionists of America, 574
Ashkenazy, Ruth, 320
Asofsky, Isaac L., 606
Aspler Baila, 319
Assad, Hafez al-, 238, 239, 240, 447
Association for Civil Rights in Israel, 419, 423, 439
Association for Jewish Studies, 547
Association for Social Scientific Study of Jewry, 539
Association of Hillel/Jewish Campus Professionals, 547
Association of Jewish Book Publishers, 540
Association of Jewish Center Professionals, 536
Association of Jewish Community Organization Personnel, 567
Association of Jewish Community Relations Workers, 536
Association of Jewish Family and Children's Agencies, 567
Association of Jewish Family and Children's Agency Professionals, 567
Association of Jewish Genealogical Societies, 540
Association of Jewish Libraries, 540
Association of Orthodox Jewish Scientists, 547
Association of Yugoslav Jews in the United States, 565
Atamukas, Solomonas, 388
Atlanta Jewish Times, 598
Attewell, Bill, 302
Aufbau, 600
Ausländer, Rose, 369
Australia, 393–400, 491, 530
Avineri Shlomo, 372
Avner, Uri, 83, 98
Avner, Yehuda, 322
Avotaynu, 599

Awad, Mubarak, 212, 233, 417, 418
Ayed, Muhammad al-, 425

Bachi, Roberto, 3, 4, 51, 60
Bacon, Josephine, 332
Bahbout, Mino, 354
Baker, Mark, 400
Baker, Zachary, 318
Bakr, Mustafa Abu, 426
Baldwin, James, 223
Ball, George, 272
Baltimore Hebrew University, 547
  Bernard Manekin School of Undergraduate Studies, 547
  Perggy Meyerhoff Pearlstone School of Graduate Studies, 547
  Baltimore Institute for Jewish Communal Service, 547
Baltimore Jewish Times, 268, 599
Bangemann, Martin, 356
Banks, Lynne Reid, 333
Barak, Aharon, 413
Barak, Ehud, 231, 476, 478
Baram, Uzi, 458, 473, 474
Bar-Ilan University in Israel, 574
Bar-Joseph, Uri, 332
Barkoff, Edward, 320
Bar Lev, Haim, 231, 476, 477
Baron de Hirsch Fund, 567
Barrett, Dave, 301
Barschel, Uwe, 357
Baruch, Jacques, 343
Bar Yossef, Rivka, 3, 81
Bashi, J., 65
Bashri, Avshalom, 481
Bassiouny, Muhammad, 493
Baum, Gerhard, 357
Bauman, Janina, 333
Baz, Ibrahim al-, 338
Beatrix, Queen (Netherlands), 338, 342
Beatty, Perrin, 305
Becuson, David, 319
Begin, Binyamin, 459, 475
Begin, Menahem, 418
Begun, Yosef (Yosif), 265, 315, 382, 384, 502, 503
Beilin, Yosef (Yossi), 391, 474, 476, 488
Bein, Alexander, 512

Bein, Yochanan, 489
Beit-Hallahmi, Benjamin, 332
Belgium, 488, 524
Belz School of Jewish Music, 563
Ben Aharon, Yosef, 256, 486
Ben Ami, Oved, 513
Ben Chorin, Schalom, 369
Ben Dov, Yaakov, 342
Ben Efrat, Roni, 413
Ben Efrat, Ya'akov, 413
Ben Gal, Avigdor, 461
Ben-Gurion, David, 95, 497
Ben-Gurion University of the Negev, American Associates, 571
Ben Horin, Meir, 606
Ben Meir, Yehuda, 83
Ben Moshe, E., 26
Ben Natan, Asher, 366
Ben Porat, Miriam, 512
Ben Rafael, Eliezer, 106, 118
Bensimon, Doris, 524
Ben Sira, Zeev, 114
Benston, Therese Siegel, 606
Bentsen, Lloyd, 251
Ben Yair, Miriam, 434
Ben Zvi, Yitzhak, 510
Berenbaum, Michael, 271, 272
Berend, Ivan, 390
Beresford, Jerry and Shirley, 499
Berger, David, 301
Berger, Harry, 320
Berman, Lawrence V., 607
Bernstein, Howard, 304
Bernstein, Leonard, 510
Bernstein, Michael, 607
Besser, Gedalia, 509
Betar Zionist Youth Organization, 574
Beth Hatefutsoth, American Friends of, 571
Beth Medrosh Elyon (Academy of Higher Learning and Research), 547
Bialik, Chaim Nachman, 387
Bilinsky, Ignatius, 210
Binder, Harry, 320
Birnbaum, Philip, 607
Birnberg, Naomi, 334
Bitzaron, 600

Blatas, Arbit, 387
Blatter, Janet, 333
Blaustein, Jacob, 271
Blondet, Maurizio, 349
Bloomfield, Douglas, 272
Bloomfield, Neri, 319
Blue, Lionel, 332
Blum, Benny, 341
Blüm, Norbert, 357
Blum, Yehuda Z., 332
Blumenfeld, Hans, 320
B'nai Brith Canada, 303, 582
  Institute for International and Governmental Affairs, 582
  League for Human Rights, 307, 582
B'nai B'rith Hillel Foundations, 547
B'nai B'rith International, 271, 567
  Anti-Defamation League of, 567
  Career and Counseling Services, 567
  Hillel Foundations, 568
  Klutznick Museum, 568
  Youth Organization, 568
B'nai B'rith International Jewish Monthly, 597
B'nai B'rith Klutznick Museum, 540
B'nai B'rith Messenger, 597
B'nai B'rith Women, 568
B'nai B'rith Youth Organization, 548
Bnai Zion, 565
Bnei Akiva of North America, 578
Board of Deputies of British Jews, 322, 323, 325, 326, 327, 328
Bois, Curt, 369
Bolivia, 491
Bolkestein, Frits, 335
Bookbinder, Hyman, 210, 268, 269
Borukhov, E., 31
Boschwitz, Rudy, 241
Boston Jewish Times, 599
Botha, P.W., 328
Bourgal, Mukhias, 435
Boys Town Jerusalem Foundation of America, 574
Bradley, Tom, 223
Brailovsky, Viktor, 329
Bramson ORT Technical Institute, 548
Brandeis-Bardin Institute, 548
Brandeis University, 548

Brandeis University National Women's Committee, 581
Brandt, Willy, 356
Braude, William G., 607
Brazil, 523
Brenner, Frederic, 332
Brentar, Jerome, 210
Breuer, Mordechai, 368
Brichto, Sidney, 330
Brinkman, Elco, 340
Britain, 487, 524
Brith Abraham, 566
Brith Sholom, 566
Brittan, Leon, 334
Broadbent, Ed, 304
Brodsky, Joseph, 333, 379
Bromberg, Charney, 224
Bronfman, Charles, 310
Bronfman, Edgar, 266, 310, 315, 349, 372, 375, 387, 399
Brookner, Anita, 333
Brown, Katie, 319
Bruce, David, 328
Brucker, Robert, 340
Bruno, Michael, 496
B'Tselem, 457
Buffalo Jewish Review, 600
Bukozba, Yitzhak, 497
Bulgaria, 490, 527
Bush, George, 210, 234, 237, 246, 250, 252, 263, 269, 270, 272, 381
Busse, Horst, 376
Butler, Eric, 396

Cahen, Joel, 343
CAJE, Coalition for the Advancement of Jewish Education, 548
Canada, 301–320, 522, 523
Canada-Israel Committee (CIC), 303, 304
Canada-Israel Securities, Ltd., State of Israel Bonds, 582
Canadian Association for Labor Israel (Histadrut), 583
Canadian Foundation for Jewish Culture, 583
Canadian Friends of the Alliance Israélite Universelle, 583

Canadian Friends of the Hebrew University, 583
Canadian Jewish Congress (CJC), 302, 305, 308, 310, 312, 314, 583
Canadian Jewish Herald, 605
Canadian Jewish News, 605
Canadian Jewish Outlook, 605
Canadian ORT Organization, 583
 Women's Canadian ORT, 583
Canadian Sephardi Federation, 583
Canadian Young Judaea, 583
Canadian Zionist, 605
Canadian Zionist Federation, 310, 583
 Bureau of Education and Culture, 583
Cantors Assembly, 274, 275, 548
Capanna, Mario, 346
Caplan, Albert, 320
Caplan, Leslie, 400
Caplan, Percy, 320
Caplan, Simon, 331
Cappucci, Hilarion, 338
Carlebach, Julius, 369
Carlucci, Frank, 256, 486
Carmon, Yigal, 512
Carr, Jim, 302
Carr, Shirley, 302
Carter, Jimmy, 418
Caspi, D., 82
Ceausescu, Nicolae, 392
Center for Contemporary Jewish Documentation (CDEC), 350, 351
Center for Holocaust Studies, Documentation & Research, 540
Center for Jewish Community Studies, 536
Central Conference of American Rabbis, 276, 548
Central Sephardic Jewish Community of America, 566
Central Yiddish Culture Organization (CYCO), 540
Chagall, Marc, 317
Chaiken, Miriam, 317
Chalmers, William, 325
Charles, Samuel, 334
Chayen, Israel, 334
Chelouche, David, 502

Cherrick, Bernard, 512
Chertoff, Mordecai, 3
Cheysson, Claude, 236
Chicago JUF News, 598
Chile, 524
China, 491
Chlenov, Mikhail, 386
Chnoupek, Bohuslav, 389, 490
Christie, Douglas, 302, 307
Chumak, Paul, 501
Ciapanna, Cesco, 348
Citrin, Martin E., 607
Citroen, Joop, 343
Citroen, Sofie, 343
City of Hope National Medical Center and Beckman Research Institute, 568
CLAL—National Jewish Center for Learning and Leadership, 276, 548
Clark, Joe, 303, 304, 310
Cleveland College of Jewish Studies, 548
Cleveland Jewish News, 603
Coalition for the Advancement of Jewish Education (CAJE), 548
Cohen, Eli, 432
Cohen, George, 320
Cohen, Marie Berdugo, 318
Cohen, N., 106
Cohen, Noah J., 608
Cohen, Rex, 334
Cohen, Steven M., 207, 214, 218
Cohen, Yolande, 318
Cokely, Steve, 223
Collins, Joseph, 334
Collins, Kenneth, 333
Colombia, 491
Colotka, Petr, 389
Colthof, Simon A., 344
Commentary, 270, 600
Commission on Social Action of Reform Judaism, 536
Community, 598
Conference of Jewish Communal Service, 568,
Conference of Jewish Federations of North America, 472
Conference of Presidents of Major American Jewish Organizations, 208, 213, 259, 505, 536,

Conference on Jewish Material Claims Against Germany, 361, 364, 371, 545
Conference on Jewish Social Studies, 540
Congregation Bina, 540
Congress Monthly, 600
Congress of Secular Jewish Organizations, 549
Connecticut Jewish Ledger, 597
Conservative Judaism, 600
Consultative Council of Jewish Organizations-CCJO, 536
Contemporary Jewry, 600
Conway, John, 308
Coordinating Board of Jewish Organizations, 537
Copisarow, Alcon, 334
Corneille, Roland de, 302
Cossigan, Francesco, 346
Cotler, Irwin, 315
Council for a Beautiful Israel Environmental Education Foundation, 574
Council for Jewish Education, 549
Council of Jewish Federations, 266, 267, 276, 277, 472, 473, 568
Council of Jewish Organizations in Civil Service, 537
Cowan, Paul, 608
Cranston, Alan, 241
Crelinsten, Michael, 320
Crystal, Morris, 608,
Curtis, Michael, 3
Cutner, Solomon, 334
Cymerman, Joseph, 334
Czechoslovakia, 389, 527

Dagan, Nehemiah, 404
Damari, Shoshana, 508
Danieli, David, 433
Dantecaridi, Jose, 491
Dantsig, M., 385
Daoud, Mounira, 430, 432
Daoud, Moussa Salah, 430
Dar, Y., 65, 79
Darousha, Abdel Wahab, 463, 507
Daum, Annette, 608
Davids, Leo, 318
Davies, Alan, 308

Davis, D., 65
Dayton Jewish Chronicle, 604
Delarosa, David, 433
DellaPergola, S., 12, 31, 38, 58, 71, 522, 524
De Mita, Ciriaco, 345, 346
Demjanjuk, John, 221, 263, 500, 501
Deri, Arye, 475, 477
Derksen, S. G., 343
Deschenes, Jules, 307
Deshen, Shlomo, 3
De'Sommi, Leone, 353
Detroit Jewish News, 599
Dialogue, 605
Diner, Dan, 361
Dinitz, Simcha, 490
Dinstein, Yoram, 329
Diskin, Abraham, 79, 82, 87, 93, 104
Di Yiddishe Heim, 603
Doesburg, Johan, 339
Dolin, Marty, 302
Dolman, Dick, 337, 341
Dorner, Dalia, 500
Dos Yiddishe Vort, 603
Dropsie College (Annenberg Research Institute), 546
Dror—Young Kibbutz Movement—Habonim, 574
  Chavurat Hagalil, 574
  Garin Yarden, Young Kibbutz Movement, 574
Dubinsky, Isadore, 320
Dubuc, Alain, 314
Dukakis, Kitty, 263
Dukakis, Michael, 209, 210, 211, 263, 269, 383
Dumas, Roland, 487

East Germany, 371–377, 527
Eban, Abba, 270, 332, 459, 468
Economic Horizons, 600
Edelman, Marek, 392
Edri, Rafael, 476, 477
Efrat, Elisha, 332
Egypt, 443, 448, 450, 492, 493, 511
Ehrenberg, Henry, 369
Eichmann, Adolf, 221
Eilon, Menachem, 512
Einan, Menahem, 478

Eisen, David, 320
Eisenbach, Zvi, 37
Eisenstadt, Shmuel N., 3, 80, 81, 106, 404
Eitan, Dov, 501
Eitan, Rafael, 463, 470
Elazar, Daniel J., 81, 86
Elbaz, André, 318
Elias, Norbert, 369
Eliav, Arye Lova, 508
Elizur, Yuval, 102
Elkin, Judith Laikin, 333, 524
Ellenoff, Theodore, 212, 261, 271
Emunah Women of America, 574
Engelmann, Bernd, 377
Epstein, Judith, 608
Eran, Oded, 484
Ericksen, Eugene, 105
Erlich, Henryk, 392
Essas, Eliahu, 503
Ethiopia, 527
Ethiopian Jews (*see* American Association for Ethiopian Jews and North American Conference on Ethiopian Jewry)
Etlinger, Francine S., 608
Ettinger, Shmuel, 404, 513
Evseev, Evgeny, 382
Ezrath Nashim Hospital-Jerusalem, American Friends of, 571

Fackenheim, Emil, 367
Faerber, Meir Marcell, 372
Fahd, King, 238
Fainlight, Ruth, 333
Falk, Hermann, 372
Falk, Leon, Jr., 609
Farrakhan, Louis, 208, 223
Fassbinder, Rainer Werner, 339
Faurisson, Robert, 306
Federal Republic of Germany, 356–370, 381
Federated Council of Israel Institutions—FCII, 574
Federation of Jewish Men's Clubs, 549
Federation of Reconstructionist Congregations and Havurot, 552
Fedorak, Bohdan, 210
Feher, Ilona, 512

Feigin, Leonid, 329
Fein, Isaac, 609
Fein, Leonard, 268, 269
Feinermann, Emanuel, 369
Feinstein, Elaine, 333
Feldman, Brian, 319
Feldman, Moshe Ze'ev, 477
Fellowship of Traditional Orthodox Rabbis, 274
Feynman, Richard P., 609,
Filbinger, Karl, 363
Finestone, Sheila, 301
Finta, Imre, 307, 308
Fischer, Oskar, 371
Fishbein, Irwin H., 275, 276
Fisher, Max, 272
Fishman, William J., 333
Fitzwater, Marlin, 237, 241
Flapan, Simha, 332
Flatto-Sharon, Shmuel, 85
Foxman, Abraham, 261, 263
France, 487, 524, 530
Frank, Elsie, 320
Frankel, Dan, 334
Frankel, William, 332
Frankenstein, Carl, 3
Freedman, Theodore, 609
Freeman, Cynthia, 609
Free Sons of Israel, 566
Fried, Erich, 370
Friedlander, Albert H., 365
Friedlander, Dov, 3, 26, 50, 56, 83, 114
Friends of the Israel Defense Forces, 575
Friends of Labor Israel, 575
Friends of Pioneering Israel, 584
Fund for Higher Education, 575
Fürst, Michael, 359
Furth, Eva Halverstad, 344

Gaft, B., 385
Galdau, Florian, 210
Galinski, Heinz, 358, 359, 361, 363, 364, 367, 372, 375
Gallay, Joseph, 320
Galnoor, Itzhak, 79
Gandhi, Rajiv, 491
Ganiram, Yitzhak, 498
Gaon, Benny, 495
Gavish, Yeshayahu, 495
Gay, Peter, 333
Gay-Rotstein, Nancy, 319
Gecas, Antanas, 326
Geffen, Joel S., 609
Genesis 2, 599
Genscher, Hans-Dietrich, 356, 357, 487
German Democratic Republic, 371–377, 527
Gerol, Ilya, 319
Gevirtz, Stanley, 610,
Ghali, Butrus, 250
Ghanem, Rabeh Hussein, 429
Ghattas, Basep, 508
Gidal, Nachum T., 368
Gierowski, Jozef, 391
Gies, Jan, 343
Gies, Miep, 333, 343
Gil, Benjamin Z., 27
Gilad, Ya'acov, 510
Gilad, Zerubavel, 512
Gill, Anton, 332
Ginsberg, Y., 31
Ginsburg, Alexander, 364
Gitelman, Zvi, 333
Giuliani, Massimo, 349
Givat Haviva Educational Foundation, 575
Gladman, Pearl, 320
Glanville, Brian, 333
Glaser, Joseph, 276
Glasser, Ralph, 333
Glatt, Josef, 342
Glick, August, 317
Glick, Srul Irving, 317
Glikson, P., 31, 38
Glustein, Yechiel, 320
Goebbels, Josef, 356
Goiss-Lau, Eva, 368
Gold, Bertram, 504
Gold, Mark, 260
Golda Meir Association, 575
Goldberg, Eliezer, 459, 460, 463
Goldberg, Romayne, 610
Goldbloom, Victor, 317
Goldfarb, Lionel, 320
Goldfarb, Martin, 305

Goldovsky, Ziva, 433
Goldscheider, Calvin, 3, 50, 56, 83, 114
Goldstein, Aaron, 226
Goldstein, Allan, 317
Goldstein, Sidney, 522
Gombrich, Ernst, 334
Gonen, Amiram, 31, 82
Goodman, Abraham, 610
Goodman, Jerry, 265, 267
Gorbachev, Mikhail, 244, 248, 265, 266, 329, 356, 378, 379, 381, 394, 399, 489
Gordis, Robert, 274
Gordon, Meron, 489
Gordon, Milton, 105
Goren, Shmuel, 234, 448
Goria, Giovanni, 345, 346
Gorki, Maxim, 387
Goss, Isaac, 334
Gotlieb, Allan, 319
Gottheil, Allan, 318
Goulding, Marack, 492
Gradus, Yehuda, 31
Granatstein, J.L., 319
Grand, Samuel, 610
Granot, Elazar, 491
Granovsky, Phil, 320
Gratz College, 549
Gray, Herb, 301
Great Britain, 321–334
Greater Phoenix Jewish News, 597
Greenberg, Irving, 264
Greenwood, Robert, 395
Grinberg, Lev, 103
Gross, David C., 332
Grossman, David, 332, 354
Grossman, Larry, 319
Grossman, Vassily,, 388
Grosz, Karoly, 389, 390, 490
Grunfeld, I., 332
Guarino, Philip, 210
Günter, Julius, 370
Gur, Mordechai, 447, 476, 477
Guth, Klaus, 368
Gutierrez, Guillermo Bedregal, 491
Gutmann, E., 81, 82
Guttman, Irving, 319

Guttman, Louis, 87
Gysi, Klaus, 367, 371

Haberman, Steven, 524
Habib, Philip, 237, 242
Habonim-Dror North America, 575
Hacohen, Menachem, 499
Hadarom, 600
Hadassah Magazine, 600
Hadassah-WIZO Organization of Canada, 584
Hadassah, Women's Zionist Organization of America, 575
  Young Judaea/Hashachar, 576
Haddow, Daphne, 334
Hadoar, 600
Hadshot L.A., 597
Haifa Maritime Museum, American Friends of, 571
Haifa University, American Friends of, 571
Halpern, Ben, 332
Halpern, Irving, 319
Halpern, Moishe Leib, 318
Halpern, Peretz, 610
Halpern, Peter, 340
Hamadei, Abbas, 357
Hamadei, Mohammed Ali, 357
Hamilton, Max, 334
Hammer, Zevulun, 462, 476, 477
Harden, Maximilian, 369
Harel, Yisrael, 427
Harish, Yitzhak, 439
Harish, Yosef, 232
Harkabi, Yehoshafat, 332
Harmelin, Yosef, 512
Harnick, Louis, 320
Harnoi, Yosef, 430
Hartt, Stanley, 319
Hashomer Hatzair, Socialist Zionist Youth Movement, 576
Hauser, Rita, 251, 261
Hawatmeh, Nayef (Naif), 413, 435
Hawke, Bob, 393, 394, 395, 399
Hayden, Bill, 491
Hazan, John, 334
Hebrew Arts Center (N.Y.), 540
Hebrew College (Boston), 549

Hebrew Culture Foundation, 541
Hebrew Immigrant Aid Society (HIAS), 267, 545
Hebrew Theological College, 549
Hebrew Union College—Jewish Institute of Religion, 276, 549
 American Jewish Archives, 550
 American Jewish Periodical Center, 550
 Edgar F. Magnin School of Graduate Studies, 550
 Jerome H. Louchheim School of Judaic Studies, 550
 Nelson Glueck School of Biblical Archaeology, 550
 Rhea Hirsch School of Education, 550
 School of Education, 550
 School of Graduate Studies, 550
 School of Jewish Communal Service, 550
 School of Jewish Studies, 551
 School of Sacred Music, 551
 Skirball Museum, 551
Hebrew University, American Friends of, 572
Hebrew Watchman, 604
Heritage-Southwest Jewish Press, 597C
Hershkovitz, Sara, 31
Herstig, Arturo, 433
Hertz, Leah, 334
Hertzberg, Arthur, 504
Herzberg, Judith, 344
Herzl Press, 578
Herzliah-Jewish Teachers Seminary, 551
 Graduate School of Jewish Studies, 551
 Jewish People's University of the Air, 551
Herzog, Chaim, 410, 469, 472, 473, 487, 497, 498, 504, 505, 512
Herzog, Hanna, 103, 113
Hesselbach, Walter, 358
Hetherington, Thomas, 325
Heym, Stefan, 377
Hiale, Makdes Mekonen, 502

HIAS (Hebrew Immigrant Aid Society), 545
Hillel Foundations, B'nai B'rith, 547, 568
Himmelfarb, H.S., 71
Hindi, Jamal Ahati al-, 416
Hirsch, Burkhard, 357
Hirschprung, Pinchas, 311
Hirsh, Marilyn, 610
Histadrut (Israel Federation of Labor), 463, 495, 496
Histadruth Ivrith of America, 541
Hoenlein, Malcolm, 261
Holocaust Center of the United Jewish Federation of Greater Pittsburgh, 541
Holocaust Memorial Resource & Education Center of Central Florida, 541
Honecker, Erich, 367, 371
Hope Center for the Developmentally Disabled, 568
Horowitz, Dan, 81
Houwaart, Dick, 342
Howe, Geoffrey, 322, 323
Howe, Irving, 270, 504
Humanistic Judaism, 599
Hungary, 381, 389, 390, 490, 527
Hunter, Basya, 317
Hurvitz, Ya'ir, 512
Hussein, King, 228, 235, 237, 238, 240, 243, 244, 246, 249, 250, 322, 443, 447, 449, 461
Husseini, Faisal al-, 408, 419, 457
Hymers, Robert, 225

Ilan, Menachem, 430, 431
Illiana News, 598
Index to Jewish Periodicals, 604, 605
India, 491, 527
Indiana Jewish Post and Opinion, 598
Inouye, Daniel, 226
Institute for Computers in Jewish Life, 551
Intermountain Jewish News, 597
International Conference of Jewish Communal Service (*see* World

Conference of Jewish Communal Service), 537
International Council on Jewish Social and Welfare Services, 568
International Jewish Media Association, 541
Iotti, Nilde, 346
Irving, David, 306
Israel, 401–513
Israel Histadrut Foundation, 576
Israel Horizons, 600
Israel Museum, American Friends of the, 572
Israel Quality, 600
Italy, 345–355, 524
Ivanov, Vladimir, 329

Jabara, Abdeen, 209
Jaber, Hatam Ahmed al-, 431
Jäckel, Eberhard, 368
Jackson, Jesse, 207, 208, 209, 211, 222, 223, 263, 269, 502
Jacobs, June, 327
Jacobson, Henrietta, 611
Jacobson, Sidney, 334
Jäger, Michael, 360
Jakobovits, Immanuel, 328, 329, 330, 334
Jaldati, Lin, 344
James, Robert Rhodes, 326
Janner, Greville, 333
Japan, 491
Japhet, Roger, 334
JDC (*see* American Jewish Joint Distribution Committee), 544
Jehoschua, Abraham B., 377
Jenninger, Philipp, 357, 359
JESNA, Jewish Education Service of North America, 551
Jewish Academy of Arts and Sciences, 541
Jewish Action Magazine, 600
Jewish Advocate, 599
Jewish Book Annual, 600
Jewish Book Council, JWB, 542
Jewish Book World, 600
Jewish Braille Institute of America, 568
Jewish Braille Institute Voice, 601

Jewish Braille Review, 601
Jewish Chautauqua Society, 551
Jewish Chronicle of Pittsburgh, 604
Jewish Civic Press (Ga.), 598
Jewish Civic Press (La.), 599
Jewish Civic Press (Tex.), 604
Jewish Committee for Israeli-Palestinian Peace, 576
Jewish Community News, 598
Jewish Community Voice, 599
Jewish Conciliation Board of America, 568
Jewish Current Events, 601
Jewish Currents, 601
Jewish Eagle, 605
Jewish Education, 601
Jewish Education in Media, 551
Jewish Education Service of North America (JESNA), 551
Jewish Exponent, 604
Jewish Floridian Group, 598
Jewish Forward, 601
Jewish Frontier, 601
Jewish Fund for Justice, 569
Jewish Herald-Voice, 604
Jewish Horizon, 599
Jewish Immigrant Aid Services of Canada (JIAS), 584
Jewish Journal, 597, 598, 601
Jewish Journal of San Antonio, 604
Jewish Labor Bund, 566
Jewish Labor Committee, 537
National Trade Union Council for Human Rights, 537
Jewish Ledger, 601
Jewish Ministers Cantors Association of America, 552
Jewish Museum, 541
Jewish Music Council, JWB, 542
Jewish Music Notes, 601
Jewish National Fund of America, 576
Jewish National Fund of Canada, 584
Jewish News & Israel Today, 597
Jewish Observer, 601
Jewish Peace Fellowship, 537
Jewish Peace Lobby, 576
Jewish People's University of the Air, 551

Jewish Post & News, 605
Jewish Post and Renaissance, 601
Jewish Press (N.Y.), 601
Jewish Press (Neb.), 599
Jewish Press of Pinellas County, 598
Jewish Press of Tampa, 598
Jewish Publication Society, 541
Jewish Quarterly Review, 604
Jewish Reconstructionist Foundation, 552
  Federation of Reconstructionist Congregations and Havurot, 552
  Reconstructionist Rabbinical Association, 552
  Reconstructionist Rabbinical College, 552
Jewish Record, 599
Jewish Reporter, 599
Jewish Restitution Successor Organization, 545
Jewish Social Studies, 601
Jewish Spectator, 597
Jewish Standard (N.J.), 599
Jewish Standard (Toronto), 605
Jewish Star (Calif.), 597
Jewish Star (N.J.), 599
Jewish Teachers Association—Morim, 552
Jewish Telegraphic Agency, 605
Jewish Telegraphic Agency Community News Reporter, 601
Jewish Telegraphic Agency Daily News Bulletin, 601
Jewish Telegraphic Agency Weekly News Digest, 601
Jewish Theological Seminary of America, 274, 552
  Albert A. List College of Jewish Studies, 552
  Cantors Institute and Seminary College of Jewish Music, 552
  Department of Radio and Television, 552
  Graduate School, 553
  Jerusalem Campus, JTS, 553
  Jewish Museum, 553
  Library of the Jewish Theological Seminary, 553
  Louis Finkelstein Institute for Religious and Social Studies 553,
  Melton Research Center, 553
  National Ramah Commission, 553
  Prozdor, 553
  Rabbinical School, 553
  Saul Lieberman Institute of Jewish Research, 553
  Schocken Institute for Jewish Research, 553
  University of Judaism, 553
Jewish Theological Society of Canada, 316
Jewish Times of the Greater Northeast, 604
Jewish Transcript, 605
Jewish Veteran, 598
Jewish War Veterans of the United States of America, 537
  National Memorial, 537
Jewish Week, 601
Jewish Weekly News, 599
Jewish Western Bulletin, 605
Jewish World, 598, 601
Jibril, Ahmed, 481
Joffre, Joseph, 320
John Paul II, Pope, 220, 225, 352
Joint Distribution Committee, American Jewish, 544
Jong, Louis de, 336
Jordan, 322, 323, 401, 443, 485
Joseph, Edward Walter, 334
Joseph, Henry Oscar, 334
Joseph, Howard, 317
Josephs, Zoe, 333
Journal of Jewish Communal Service, 600
Journal of the North Shore Jewish Community, 599
Journal of Psychology and Judaism, 605
Journal of Reform Judaism, 601
Judah L. Magnes Museum—Jewish Museum of the West, 541
Judaica Captioned Film Center, 542
Judaism, 601
Juliani, Richard N., 105
Just, Helmut, 369
Just-Dahlmann, Barbara, 369

JWB, 328, 569
  Jewish Book Council, 569
  Jewish Chaplains Council, 569
  Jewish Music Council, 569
  JWB Circle, 601
  JWB Lecture Bureau, 542

Kadar, Janos, 389
Kaddoumi, Farouk, 324
Kahane, Meir, 97, 460, 461, 497,
Kalikow, Peter, 277
Kalmanovich, Dov, 428
Kalmanovitch, Shabtai, 483
Kanovitch, Grigory, 386
Kansas City Jewish Chronicle, 599
Kaplan, Robert, 301
Kappler, Annalise, 351
Kappler, Herbert, 351
Kass, Drora, 251, 261
Katz, Dovid, 334,
Katz, Elihu, 497
Katz, Israel, 501
Katz, Moshe, 432
Katzav, Moshe, 477, 494
Katznelson, Berl, 497
Katz-Oz, Avraham, 476, 477
Kaufman, Gerald, 323, 324
Kaufman, Max, 370
Kazantzakis, Nikos, 225
Kedem, Perry, 83
Kedmi, Yaakov, 489
Keegstra, James, 302, 306, 307
Kelman, Wolfe, 225
Kemelman, Haim, 320
Kenen, Isaiah L., 611
Kennedy, Edward, 241
Kennedy, Eugene, 223
Kentucky Jewish Post and Opinion, 598
Kenya, 491
Keren Or, 576
Kesar, Israel, 102, 466
Kfir, D., 71, 73
Khalidi, Walid, 323
Khalil, Samiha, 416
Khan, Inamullah, 325
Kharchev, Konstantin, 380
Kholmiansky, Alexander, 329, 384
Kibbutz Journal, 601

Kimche, David, 506
King, Don, 224
Kinnock, Neil, 321, 323, 487
Kirchner, Peter, 367, 372
Kissinger, Henry, 247, 341, 454
Kiszczak, Czeslaw, 391
Klaff, Vivian Z., 31, 108
Klaperman, Gilbert, 208
Klein, Ernest, 319
Klinghoffer, Leon, 251
Klug, Aaron, 334
Klutznick Museum, B'nai B'rith, 540,
Knight, Bryan, 318
Knobloch, Charlotte, 366
Knobloch, Heinz, 368
Koch, Edward, 208, 209
Koch, Rudolf, 360
Kochubievsky, Feliks, 384
Koffman, Gerry, 320
Kohl, Helmut, 356, 357, 358, 359, 363, 365
Kohn, Avrohom, 334
Kohnstamm-van Voolen, Henny, 344
Kol Hat'nua, 601
Kollek, Teddy, 409, 410, 508
Komoroczy, Geza, 390
Kompaneets, Zinovy, 388
Konstantin, Nikolai, 490
Kook, Simcha, 381
Koonz, Claudia, 333
Kops, Bernard, 333
Koren, Yael, 343
Korff, Modest, 360
Kornberg, Jakob, 332
Kosharovsky, Yuli, 219, 384
Kosher Directory, 602
Kosher Directory, Passover Edition, 602
Kosmin, Barry, 271, 522, 524
Kotler, Oded, 509
Kovnats, Abe, 302
Kowarsky, Paul, 317
Krantz, Frederick, 310
Krause, Udo, 376
Krausz, Ernest, 3, 79, 81
Kristol, Irving, 269, 270
Krüger, Ralf, 358
Krzywinski, Ulrike, 368
Kühnen, Michael, 360

Kulas, Eli, 465
Kultur un Lebn—Culture and Life, 602
Kurz, Rudolff, 220
Kushner, Gordon, 317

Labor Zionist Alliance, 576-77,
Labor Zionist Alliance of Canada, 584
Lahad, Antoine, 480
La Malfa, Giorgio, 346
Lambert, Phyllis, 319
Lamishpaha, 602
Lamm, Norman, 273, 274, 277
Lammers, Johan, 342
Lampert, Irwin, 319
Landau, Julian J., 332
Langbein, Laura Irwin, 86
Lange, David, 394
Lanser, J., 343
Laqueur, Walter, 333
LaRouche, Lyndon, 215, 361
Laski, Marghanita, 334
Lastman, Mel, 302
Las Vegas Israelite, 599
Lauder, Ronald, 263
Lazarus, Felix, 320
League for Human Rights of B'nai Brith Canada, 305
League for Labor Israel, 577
League for Yiddish, 542
LeBlanc, Gerald, 314
Lecture Bureau, JWB, 542
Lederman, Sol, 319
Lee, John, 487
Lehrman, Hal, 611
Leib, Mani, 318
Leibler, Isi, 399
Leibler, Mark, 398, 400
Lenz, Siegfried, 358
Leo Baeck Institute, 542
Lerner, Alexander, 329, 384, 502
Lerner, Michael, 270
Leslie, Alison, 333
Lester, Julius, 223
Levenbuk, Aleksandr, 385
Levene, Peter, 334
Levi Hospital, 569
Levin, Arie, 489
Levin, Carl, 241

Levin, Dov, 500
Levine, Howard, 302
Levine, Martin, 312
Levinger, Moshe, 429
Levinson, Burton, 258
Levinson, Peter, 363
Levita, Elijah Bahur, 354
Levoy, Myron, 376
Levy, Caren, 524
Levy, David, 444, 459, 471, 476, 477, 511
Levy, Joseph, 318
Levy, Moshe, 102
Lewin, Abraham, 332
Lewin, Chaim, 320
Lewis, Frank, 340
Lewittes, Mendell, 319
Leydesdorff, Selma, 343
Libai, David, 476
Lichtman, Allan J., 87
Ligachev, Yegor, 381
Likud-Herut Zionists of America, 577
Likutim, 602
Lilith—The Jewish Women's Magazine, 217, 602
Limentani, Giacoma, 354
Lindwer, Willy, 343, 344
Linnik, V., 383
Lipman, Beata, 332
Lipman, Eugene, 276
Lipshitz, Gabriel, 29
Lissak, Moshe, 3, 81, 106
Litani, Yehuda, 426
Litvinoff, Barnet, 333
A Living Memorial to the Holocaust-Museum of Jewish Heritage, 542
Loewe, Raphael, 332
Löffler, Kurt, 367, 371
Loncar, Budimir, 490
Long Island Jewish World, 602
Loonstein, Herman, 344
Lorenz, Ina, 368
Lubavitcher Hassidim (Chabad), 227
Lubavitcher Rebbe (M. M. Schneerson), 467, 468
Lubbers, Rudolf (Ruud), 335, 336, 337, 487
Lubin, Charles W., 611,

Luitjens, Jacob, 308
Lukacs, Georg, 377
Luks, Harold Paul, 257
Lurie, Note, 388
Lustiger, Arno, 369
Luzzatto, Shmuel David, 354

Maalot, 542
Machne Israel, 554
Magarik, Alexei, 384, 502
Magonet, Jonathan, 332
Maikovskis, Boleslav, 221
Malek, Frederic V., 211
Malewski, Monette, 314
Malloth, Anton, 351, 361
Malz, Yaakov, 512
Mancher, Harry R., 611,
Mansour, Wasfi, 435
Margolies, Israel Raphael, 612
Margriet, Princess (Netherlands), 342
Marmur, Dow, 316
Marrus, Michael, 308, 319
Marshall, Louis, 271
Martilla and Kiley Organization, 213
Martyrdom and Resistance, 602
Martyrs Memorial & Museum of the Holocaust, 542
Maslin, Simeon, 276
Maslowsky, Barbara, 320
Masri, Taher al-, 239
Matas, David, 307
Matras, Judah, 3, 37, 87
Maxwell, Robert, 332
Mayer, Gerda, 333
Mayer-Vorfelder, Gerhard, 360
Maynard, Fredelle Bruser, 319
Mazar, Amihai, 511
McDougall, Barbara, 302
Medding, Peter Y., 3, 79, 93, 118
Medvedev, Vadim, 381
Meguid, Esmat Abdel, 239, 246, 450
Meijer, Ischa, 339
Meijers, Pinchas, 340
Meiman, Naum (Nahum), 384, 502
Mellor, David, 322, 323, 487
Melnikoff, Pamela, 333
Melton Journal, 602

Melton Research Center for Jewish Education, 553
Memorial Foundation for Jewish Culture, 330, 390, 542
Mendels, Josepha, 344
Menuhin, Yehudi, 369
Mercaz, 577
Meridor, Dan, 475, 477
Merkos L'Inyonei Chinuch, 554
Merks, Gilbert W., 333, 524
Mesivta Yeshiva Rabbi Chaim Berlin Rabbinical Academy, 554
MetroWest Jewish News, 600
Metzenbaum, Howard, 241
Mexico, 523
Meyer, Daniel, 389
Meyerhoff, Lyn P., 612
Miami Jewish Tribune, 598
Michelman, Henry, 225
Michman, D., 343
Michman, J., 343
Midstream, 602
Mikardo, Ian, 333
Mikhoels, Solomon, 384
Miklos, Imre, 390, 490
Milano, Paolo, 355
Miller, Buzi, 388
Miller, Israel, 371
Miller, Joseph K., 612
Miller, Shoshana, 499
Milo, Roni, 475, 476, 477
Milton, Sybil, 333
Minkowich, A., 65
Mintz, Eli, 612
Miransky, Peretz, 319
Miroschejdi, Pierre de, 511
Missouri Jewish Post, 599
Mitterrand, Francois, 487
Mitzna, Amram, 404, 405, 409, 418, 427, 430, 432, 436, 458
Mizrachi-Hapoel Hamizrachi, 578
Mizrachi-Hapoel Hamizrachi Organization of Canada, 584
Modai, Yitzhak, 474, 476, 477
Modern Jewish Studies Annual, 602
Moed, Yitzhak, 341
Mohammad, Mahmoud, 305
Molina, Rafael Samudio, 491

Molyneaux, Geoffrey, 319
Moment, 269, 275, 276, 598
Mondale, Walter, 211
Montand, Yves, 509
Montreal Allied Jewish Community Services (AJCS), 311
Moos, Alfred, 369
Moosberg, Kurt, 358
Morag-Talmon, Pnina, 118
Moranville, Kendall, 486
Mordechai, Yitzhak, 427
Mormons, 500
Morning Freiheit, 602
Morocco, 530
Morrison, Peter, 334
Morse, Earl, 612
Mosco, Maisie, 333
Moscowitch, Gail, 499
Moskowitz, Meshulam, 428
Moynihan, Daniel Patrick, 241
Mubarak, Hosni, 235,-240, 322, 486, 492, 493
Muller, Leopold, 334
Mulroney, Brian, 301, 303
Murphy, Richard, 234, 237, 238, 245, 442, 448
Mustapha, Abdul, 322

Na'amat USA, 577
Na'amat Woman, 602
Nabokov, Vladimir, 379
Nachmani, Amikam, 332
Nachmann, Werner, 362, 363, 364, 365
Nafeh, Bashir, 412
Nagler, Michael, 340
Nahon, Yaacov, 60, 71, 106, 109, 110
Naimark, Arnold, 319
Naor, Arye, 506
Nathan, G., 12, 31, 56
National Association of Jewish Family, Children's and Health Professionals (*see* Association of Jewish Family and Children's Agency Professionals), 569
National Association of Jewish Vocational Services, 569
National Committee for Furtherance of Jewish Education, 554
National Committee for Labor Israel—Histadrut, 577
National Conference of Synagogue Youth, 560
National Conference on Soviet Jewry, 264, 265, 266, 267, 537
  Soviet Jewry Research Bureau, 538
National Congress of Jewish Deaf, 569
National Council of Jewish Prison Chaplains, Inc. (*see* American Jewish Correctional Chaplains Association, Inc.) 569
National Council of Jewish Women, 569
National Council of Jewish Women of Canada, 584
National Council of Young Israel, 259, 554
National Foundation for Jewish Culture, 543
National Hebrew Culture Council, 543
National Institute for Jewish Hospice, 570
National Jewish Center for Immunology and Respiratory Medicine, 570
National Jewish Center for Learning and Leadership (*see* CLAL), 555
National Jewish Coalition, 538
National Jewish Commission on Law and Public Affairs (COLPA), 222, 538
National Jewish Committee on Scouting, 570
National Jewish Community Relations Advisory Council, 259, 266, 538
National Jewish Girl Scout Committee, 570
National Jewish Hospitality Committee, 555
National Jewish Information Service for the Propagation of Judaism, 555
National Jewish Post and Opinion, 598
National Joint Community Relations Committee of Canadian Jewish Congress, 584
National Ramah Commission, 553
National Yiddish Book Center, 543
National Young Leadership Conference of the United Jewish Appeal, 260

Navon, Yitzhak, 102, 392, 476, 477, 490, 494
Near East Report, 272, 598
Nedava, Yosef, 512
Ne'eman, Yuval, 463, 479, 480
Nefsky, Marilyn, 308
Neikik, Abbey, 317
Nelson, Rafi, 512
Nemeth, Miklos, 389
Nemetz, Nathan, 319
Ner Israel Rabbinical College, 555
Netanyahu, Benjamin, 475, 476
Netherlands, 335–344, 487, 524
Neuman, Isaac, 374
Neusner, Jacob, 270
Nevelson, Louise, 612
New Israel Fund, 577
New Jewish Agenda, 538
Newman, Aubrey, 333
Newman, Peter C., 319
New Menorah, 604
New Zealand, 394, 530
Nir, Amiram, 512
Nir, Barak, 498
Nissim, Moshe, 476, 477, 493, 494, 496, 506, 507
Nitikman, Israel, 320
Niv, Orna Ben-Dor, 510
Nixon, Richard, 211
Niznik, Chaim, 319
Noam-Mizrachi New Leadership Council, 578
Nobleman, Ben, 302
Nolte, Ernst, 368
Noriega, Manuel, 215
Norman, Hilary, 333
North American Aliyah Movement, 579
North American Association of Jewish Homes and Housing for the Aging, 570
North American Conference on Ethiopian Jewry (NACOEJ), 545
North American Jewish Data Bank, 271
North American Jewish Students Appeal, 582
North American Jewish Students' Network, 582
Northern California Jewish Bulletin, 597

Norway, 488
Nosenko, Vladimir, 383
Novak, Michael, 105
Novik, Nimrod, 238
Nudel, Ida, 329, 347, 502, 503

Oakley, Phyllis, 248
The Observer, 604
O'Connor, John Cardinal, 264
O'Connor, Sandra Day, 225
Ogonyok, 382, 383
Ohio Jewish Chronicle, 604
Okun, Herbert S., 230, 232
Olechowski, Tadeusz, 391, 490
Olmert, Ehud, 238, 475, 476, 477
Olomeinu—Our World, 602
Ongor, Johan, 490
Oppenheim-Barnes, Sally, 334
The Order, 214
Orenstein, Eugene, 318
Orlikow, David, 301
Orr, Ori, 461
ORT (*see* Canadian ORT Organization), 583
ORT (*see* American ORT Federation), 544
Orthodox Rabbinical Council of Canada, 311
Ottawa Jewish Bulletin & Review, 605
Ovadiah ben Abraham Yare, 353
Oweida, Faisal, 327
Owen, David, 322
Oz, Amos, 332, 404
Ozar Hatorah, 555
Oziel, Moses, 320

Pagani, Herbert, 355
Paikin, Marnie, 319
Palmer, Mark, 390
Palzur, Mordechai, 490
Papandreou, Andreas, 488
Pappe, Ilan, 332
Parfitt, Tudor, 332
Paritsky, Alexander, 384
Pasternak, Boris, 379
Pasztor, Lazio, 210
Patt, Gideon, 477
Patten, John, 326

Pätzold, Kurt, 377
Pazner, Aviezer, 417, 456
Pearl, Chaim, 332
PEC Israel Economic Corporation, 577
Peck, Gregory, 509
Pedagogic Reporter, 602
Pedatzur, Reuven, 480
PEF Israel Endowment Funds, 577
Pelletier, Gerard, 313, 314
Pelletreau, Jr., Robert H., 253, 456
Penn and Schoen Organization, 213
Penner, Roland, 302
Penniman, Howard R., 81, 86
Percy, Charles, 272
Peres, Shimon, 235, 238, 240, 243, 245, 246, 252, 253, 260, 322, 346, 389, 390, 442, 445, 446, 447, 448, 450, 454, 456, 458, 462, 463, 464, 466, 468, 471, 472, 473, 474, 476, 477, 482, 483, 484, 487, 490, 491, 492, 493, 496, 512
Peres, Yochanan, 112
Peretz, Yitzhak, 475, 477, 499
Pérez de Cuellar, Javier, 236, 237, 492
Peritz, Eric, 56, 83
Perlis, Morris, 319
Permutti, Gavriel, 481
P'eylim—American Yeshiva Student Union, 555
Pezzana, Angelo, 348
Philip and Sarah Belz School of Jewish Music, 563
Piccoli, Flaminio, 346
Pickering, Thomas, 234, 247, 257, 448, 484
Pioneer Women/Na'amat (*see* Na'amat USA), 577
Poale Agudath Israel of America, 577
  Women's Division of, 577
Poale Zion, 327
Pogrebin, Letty Cottin, 270
Poirier, Marie, 318
Poland, 381, 390, 391, 392, 527
Poliker, Yehuda, 510
Pollock, David, 208
Popkin, Ruth, 504
Porat, Tirza, 431
Porat, Uri, 451

Pratt, Richard, 398, 400
Prestin, Vladimir, 329
Prinz, Joachim, 612
Pripstein, Chaim, 320
Proceeedings of the American Academy for Jewish Research, 602
Progressive Zionist Caucus, 578
Proligheuer, Hans, 369
Proskauer, Joseph, 271
Puvogel, Ulrike, 369

Quayle, Dan, 251
Quester, George, 482

Raab, Ernest, 308
Rabadi, Nidal, 410
Rabbi Isaac Elchanan Theological Seminary, 563
Rabbinical Alliance of America (Igud Harabonim), 555
Rabbinical Assembly, 556
Rabbinical College of Telshe, 556
Rabbinical Council of America, 259, 260, 277, 556
Rabbinical Council Record, 602
Rabbo, Yasir Abed, 253
Rabi, Isidor Isaac, 613
Rabin, Yitzhak, 231–234, 246, 256, 258, 388, 403–406, 415, 418, 428, 438, 440, 441, 444, 448, 451, 454, 456, 463, 464, 466, 471, 472, 476, 477, 481, 482, 484, 486, 504, 507
Rabinowitz, Isaac, 613
Rabkin, Yakov, 315
Rafih, Abd al-Aziz Uda, 416
Rahm, Victor, 434
Rakowski, Mieczyslaw, 391
Ramon, Haim, 476
Rapaport, Yakov, 384
Rappaport, Ira, 498
Rasky, Frank, 319
Ratzinger, Joseph Cardinal, 225, 226
Reagan, Ronald, 218, 219, 222, 227, 230, 232, 234, 237, 240, 242, 243, 245, 246, 253, 254, 256, 262, 265, 381, 443, 444, 445, 448, 450, 455, 485, 486, 505
Rechtzeit, Jack, 613

Reconstructionism (*see* Jewish Reconstructionist Foundation), 552
Reconstructionist, 604
Reconstructionist Rabbinical Association, 552
Reconstructionist Rabbinical College, 556
Redman, Charles, 230, 231, 232, 233, 243, 250, 252, 454
Reform Judaism, 602
Regev, Arie, 322
Reich, Seymour, 261
Reichmann, Eva G., 369
Reiss, Lionel S., 613
Reitman, Dorothy, 303
Religious Zionists of America, 578
  Bnei Akiva of North America, 578
  Mizrachi Palestine Fund, 578
  National Council for Torah Education of Mizrachi-Hapoel Hamizrachi, 578
  Noam-Mizrachi New Leadership Council, 578
Renewal Magazine, 604
Renglich, Szloma, 319
Reporter, 602
Research Foundation for Jewish Immigration, 543
Research Institute of Religious Jewry, 556
Resh, N., 65, 79
Response, 602
RE'UTH Women's Social Service, 545
Revesz, Herbert, 333
Reyers, A., 342
Rhode Island Jewish Historical Notes, 604
Richterich, Rivka, 368
Rifai, Zaid al-, 235
Ritterband, Paul, 522
Rivkin, Nacha, 614
Robertson, Pat, 207, 208, 210
Robertson, Ritchie, 332
Robic, Louise, 314
Robinson, W.S., 86
Roegholt, Richter, 343
Rogov, Sergei, 383
Rohwer, Jürgen, 368

Romanenko, A.Z., 382, 383
Romania, 392, 527
Rome, David, 318
Ronel, Nurit, 3
Roper Organization (poll), 213, 217, 218, 222
Rose, Jack, 320
Rosen, Moses David, 392
Rosenberg, Hans, 370
Rosenberg, Suzanne, 319
Rosenfeld, Henry, 507
Rosensaft, Menachem, 251, 260, 261
Rosenstein, Gershon Zvi, 502
Roskies, David, 318
Roskies, Jonathan, 320
Rosovsky, Henry, 504
Ross, Dennis, 246
Ross, Malcolm, 306
Rotenstreich, Yehoshua, 512
Roth, Joseph, 369
Roth, Stephen J., 332
Rothschild, Dorothy de, 334
Rothschild, Evelyn de, 334
Rotstein, Sigmund, 367, 373
Rozenshtain, Grigory, 384
Rozsa, Endre, 390
Rubin, Yaacov, 329
Rubinek, Saul, 317
Rubinstein, Eli, 238
Rubinstein, Richard, 269
Rudin, James, 219
Rujoub, Jibril al-, 408
Rulli, Giovanni, 349
Runge, Irene, 377
Rushdie, Salman, 329
Ryan, Claude, 314

Safdie, Moshe, 318
Safieh, Afif, 337
Saguy, Uri, 478
Saguy, Yehoshua, 479
Said, Edward, 247, 446
St. Louis Center for Holocaust Studies, 543
St. Louis Jewish Light, 599
Sakharov, Andrei, 379
Salomon, Kathryn, 333
Salpeter, Eliahu, 102

Salutin, Rick, 319
Salzmann, Dov, 340
San Diego Jewish Times, 597
Sandor, Anna, 308
Saudi Arabia, 322, 486, 487
Savidor, Menachem, 513
Sawyer, Eugene, 223
Sbeihat, Samir, 412
Scandinavia, 526
Schach, Menachem Eliezer, 85, 462, 468
Scheckner, Jeffrey, 522
Schecter, David, 317
Schelekens, Y., 26
Schiff, Jacob, 271
Schifter, Richard, 232, 233, 267, 448
Schindler, Alexander, 231, 258, 259, 504
Schlee, Emil, 361
Schlesinger, Eliezer, 432
Schmelz, U.O., 4, 10, 12, 20, 26, 31, 38, 51, 56, 58, 515, 522, 524
Schmidt, Henry, 377
Schnabel, Ernst, 333
Schneerson, M. M. (Lubavitcher Rebbe), 467, 468
Schneier, Arthur, 266
Schönduve, Loeki, 342
Schonfeld, Hugh, 334
Schönhuber, Franz, 361
Schorsch, Ismar, 274, 275, 316
Schreier, Max, 277
Schrijver, Hans, 344
Schulweis, Harold, 269
Schwartz, Howard, 333
Schwartz, Michal, 413
Schwartz, Yossi, 310
Scorsese, Martin, 225, 510
Segal, Jerome, 249
Seidelman, William, 308
Selbee, Kelvin, 37
The Sentinel, 598
Sephardic House, 543
Sephardic Jewish Brotherhood of America, 566
Shaare Zedek Hospital in Jerusalem, American Committee for, 571
Shahaf, Yigal, 435
Shahal, Moshe, 457, 476, 477
Shahar, Arie, 31
Shakdiel, Leah, 499
Shaki, Avner, 462, 477
Shalom, Avraham, 512
Shalom Center, 538
Shalom Hartman Institute, American Friends of, 572
Shamgar, Meir, 417, 420, 460
Shami, Hani al-, 440
Shamir, Michal, 103
Shamir, Shimon, 493
Shamir, Yitzhak, 233, 235, 236, 238, 239, 240, 241, 242, 245, 246, 247, 252, 253, 254, 255, 259, 260, 261, 276, 310, 311, 323, 324, 337, 346, 350, 359, 381, 390, 401, 402, 411, 417, 441–447, 449, 451–454, 456, 457, 459, 462, 463, 465, 466, 468–477, 483, 485, 486, 488, 490, 492, 498, 505
Shanan, Leah, 31
Shapiro, Laura, 217
Shapiro, Lev, 502
Shapiro, Milton, 261
Shapiro, Yonatan, 81
Sharaa, Farouk al-, 239
Sharan, S., 65
Sharansky, Natan, 329, 333, 502, 503
Sharett, Moshe, 497
Sharif (Sherif), Bassam Abu, 248, 323, 448, 449
Sharir, Avraham, 392, 431, 484, 490
Sharon, Ariel, 93, 257, 392, 431, 435, 459, 461, 464, 471, 474, 476, 477, 490
Shavit, Y., 71, 73
Shavit, Zeev, 86
Sheffer, Eliezer, 481
Shefman, Alan, 319
Sheftel, Yoram, 221, 501
Sheinbaum, Stanley, 251, 261
Shemer, Sara, 112
Shenkar College in Israel, American Committee for, 571
Sher, Antony, 333
Shevardnadze, Eduard, 236, 356, 381, 489
Sheviley Ha-Hinnukh, 602
Shifman, Hya, 387

Shilon, Dan, 463
Shimon, Tova, 314
Shlaim, Avi, 332
Sh'ma, 271, 602
Shmuessen Mit Kinder Un Yugent, 602
Shokeid, Moshe, 3
Sholem Aleichem Folk Institute, 556
Shomron, Dan, 406, 407, 411, 418, 420, 438, 458, 481
Shratzky, Rina, 434
Shternshtam, Iosif, 387
Shternshtam, Luiza, 387
Shultz, George, 230, 232, 235, 237–249, 251–256, 260, 262, 264, 268, 442–448, 450, 453, 455, 458, 483, 484, 485, 505
Sichrovsky, Peter, 333
Siedner, Amir, 481
Siegel, Mark, 209
Siegel, Seymour, 614
Siegman, Henry, 258, 261
Sierra, Sergio, 354
Silberschlag, Eisig, 614
Silkin, Jon, 333
Silverman, Ira, 261
Simon, Akiva Ernst, 512
Simon, Hermann, 375
Simon, Ulrich, 333
Simon Wiesenthal Center, 271, 325, 564
Singer, Israel, 375
Singer, Lynn, 265
Siniora, Hanna, 327, 402
Skirball Museum, 550
Skoblo, Roman, 368
Slater, Ruth, 316
Slepak, Vladimir, 329
Smith, David, 226
Smith, Hanoch, 231
Smooha, Sammy, 3, 103, 106
Snow, Ralph, 303
Sobol, Yehoshua, 339, 509
Society for the History of Czechoslovak Jews, 543
Society for Humanistic Judaism, 556
Society of Friends of the Touro Synagogue, National Historical Shrine, 556
Society of Israel Philatelists, 578

Sofaer, Abraham, 492
Sofer, Sasson, 333
Sokol, Yuri, 386
Solarz, Stephen, 226
Solender, Sanford, 271
Solis, Daniel da Silva, 344
Solomon, Aaron L., 614
Soloveitchik, Aaron, 277
Sonis, Michael, 31
South Africa, 397, 527
Southern Jewish Weekly, 598
Southwest Jewish Chronicle, 604
Soviet Jewry, National Conference on, 264, 265, 267, 537
Soviet Jewry Research Bureau, 538
Soviet Jewry, Student Struggle for, 265
Soviet Jews, Union of Councils for, 265, 267, 538
Soviet Union, 356, 378–388, 397, 526
Sowan, Ismail, 322
Spack, Abraham, 614,
Spadolini, Giovanni, 346
Spain, 526
Spanier, Ginette, 334
Späth, Lothar, 356, 263
Spector, Cyril, 333
Spellman, Gladys Noon, 614
Spencer, Gary, 216
Spertus College of Judaica, 556
Spivak, Sidney, 303,304
Stark Jewish News, 604
State of Israel Bonds, 578
Steinberg, Blema, 310
Steinsaltz, Adin, 315, 390, 347, 387, 508
Stern, G. B., 333
Stern, Moshe, 316
Sternberg, Sigmund, 325
Stevens, Elliot, 275
Stewart, Ian, 326
Strashnow, Amnon, 404, 419, 440, 441
Strauss, Franz-Josef, 356, 357
Strougal, Lubomir, 389
Stuart, G. H. Cohen, 343
Stuart, Mary, 342
Student Struggle for Soviet Jewry (SSSJ), 265, 538
Studies in Bibliography and Booklore, 604

Suasso, Francisco Lopez, 342
Suffoth, Zeev, 338
Sununu, John H., 211, 212
Suttner, Raymond, 328
Suzman, Helen, 369
Sweden, 488
Swetschinski, Daniel, 342
Switzerland, 526
Synagogue Council of America, 263, 557
Synagogue Light, 602
Syria, 443, 448, 527
Szirtes, George, 333

Taba, 492
Tabori, George, 339
Tagger, Siona, 512
Tal, Zvi, 500, 501
Talks and Tales, 602
Talmage, Frank, 320
Tambo, Oliver, 357
Tamir, Avraham, 332, 491
Tanenbaum, Marc, 226
Tannenbaum, Jacob, 221
Tauchner, Maximilian, 369
Technion-Israel Institute of Technology, American Society for, 573,
Tel Aviv Museum, American Friends of, 572
Tel Aviv University, American Friends of, 572
Tepfer, John J., 614
Teveth, Shabtai, 333
Texas Jewish Post, 604
Thalmann, Rita, 369
Thanks to Scandinavia, 545
Thatcher, Margaret, 236, 322, 323, 326, 329, 487
Theiner, George, 334
Theodor Herzl Foundation, 578
  Herzl Press, 578
  Theodor Herzl Institute, 579
Thornburgh, Richard, 268
Tichauer, Shlomo, 375
Tikkun, 597
Toaff, Elio, 352
Toledano, Dayan Pinchas, 332
Toledo Jewish News, 604

Torah Schools for Israel—Chinuch Atzmai, 557
Torah Umesorah—National Society for Hebrew Day Schools, 557
  Institute for Professional Enrichment, 557
  National Association of Hebrew Day School Administrators, 557
  National Association of Hebrew Day School Parent-Teacher Associations, 557
  National Conference of Yeshiva Principals, 557
  National Yeshiva Teachers Board of License, 557
Torgov, Morley, 317
Toronto Jewish Congress, 308, 311
Touro College, 557
  Barry Z. Levine School of Health Sciences and Center for Biomedical Education, 558
  College of Liberal Arts and Sciences, 558
  Graduate School of Jewish Studies, 558
  Institute of Jewish Law, 558
  Jacob D. Fuchsberg Law Center, 558
  Jewish People's University of the Air, 558
  School of General Studies, 558
  Shulamith School, 558
Tradition, 603
Trends, 603
Trenter, George, 334
Troper, Harold,, 318
Troster, Lawrence, 316
Truman, Harry, 263
Tshervizov, Andrei, 383
Tsitverblit, Naftaly, 329
Tulsa Jewish Review, 604
Tunisia, 530
Turkey, 527
Turner, Barry, 333
Turner, John, 304
Twerski, Aaron, 273, 274
Tzaban, Yair, 457, 463
Tzur, Yaakov, 477, 501, 503

UCII (Union of Italian Jewish Communities), 350, 351
UCSJ Quarterly Report, 598
UJF Virginia News, 605
Ullendorff, Edward, 332
Undzer Veg, 605
Union of American Hebrew Congregations, 271, 558
  American Conference of Cantors, 558
  Commission on Jewish Education of the Union of of American Hebrew Congregations, Central Conference of American Rabbis and National Association of Temple Educators, 558
  Commission on Social Action of Reform Judaism, 559
  Commission on Synagogue Management, 559
  National Association of Temple Administrators, 559
  National Association of Temple Educators, 559
  National Federation of Temple Brotherhoods, 559
  National Federation of Temple Sisterhoods, 559
  National Federation of Temple Youth, 559
Union of Councils for Soviet Jews (UCSJ), 265, 267, 538
Union of Orthodox Jewish Congregations of America, 274, 559
  National Conference of Synagogue Youth, 560
  Women's Branch, 560
Union of Orthodox Rabbis of the United States and Canada, 315, 560
Union of Sephardic Congregations, 560
United Charity Institutions of Jerusalem, 579
United Israel Appeal (UIA), 311, 312, 472
United Jewish Appeal, 263, 276, 546, 579
United Lubavitcher Yeshivoth, 560
United Order True Sisters (UOTS), 566
United States Committee Sports for Israel, 579
United States Holocaust Memorial Council, 387, 543
United Synagogue of America, 275, 560
  Commission on Jewish Education, 560
  Committee on Social Action and Public Policy, 560
  Jewish Educators Assembly, 561
  Kadima, 561
  National Association of Synagogue Administrators, 561
  United Synagogue Youth of, 561
United Synagogue Review, 603
University of Judaism, 553
Uno, Sousuke, 491
Unser Tsait, 603
Urban, Jerzy, 490
Uruguay, 523
USSR, 488, 489

Vaad Mishmereth Stam, 561
van Aardenne, G., 338
van de Kamp, Lody, 340
van den Berg, A., 343
van den Broek, Hans, 336, 337, 487
van der Linden, René, 335
van der Molen, Henk, 343
van der Zee, Nanda, 343
van Dijk, Willem, 340
van Eekelen, Willem F., 335
van Thijn, Ed, 341
van Tonningen, Flora Rost, 336
Vanunu, Mordechai, 482
Vardi, Aharon, 490
Varella, Julia and Claudio, 499
Varkonyi, Peter, 490
Vecht, Constant, 343
Veil, Simone, 502
Velikhov, Evgeny, 387
Venezuela, 524
Venger, Baruch, 512
Verbelen, Robert Jan, 221
Vermes, Pamela, 332
Vigod, Bernie, 320
Vilnai, Ze'ev, 512
Vilsker, Leib, 388

Vineberg, Arthur, 320
Vineberg, Ethel Shane, 320
Vishnitzer Hassidim, 313
Vital, David, 332
Vitta, Edoardo, 354
Vogel, Hans-Jochen, 356
Vogel, Rolf, 369
Volvovsky, Ari and Ludmilla, 502
Volvovsky, Leonid, 329, 384
von Dohnanyi, Klaus, 369
von Weizsäcker, Richard, 357, 358, 363
Vorspan, Albert, 259, 261

Wa Botende, Lamponda, 491
Wagenaar, Willem A., 333
Wajda, Andrzej, 391, 509
Wajsberg, Henoch, 341
Waldegrave, William, 323
Waldheim, Kurt, 220, 262, 326, 349
Walesa, Lech, 391
Wallace, Mike, 272
Wallach, Yehuda, 220
Wallerstein, Pinhas, 429
Wallmann, Walter, 358
Walters, Vernon A., 230
Walzer, Michael, 270, 504
Warburg, Eric M.
Washington Jewish Week, 210, 599
Wasserman, Lew, 225
Wazir, Khalil al- (Abu Jihad), 322, 406, 437
Weil, Wolf, 370
Weiner, Gerry, 301, 302
Weinfeld, Morton, 318
Weingrod, Alex, 3, 31
Weinreb, Friedrich, 344
Weiss, Avi, 265
Weiss, Rachel, 432, 433
Weiss, Szewach, 103
Weizman, Ezer, 438, 465, 476, 477
Weizmann Institute of Science, American Committee for, 571
Werczberger, E., 31
Werner, Eric, 614
West Coast Talmudical Seminary, 561
Western States Jewish History, 597
West Germany, 487, 524
Wetzel, Juliane, 369
Whitehead, John, 234, 392, 484

Wien, Lawrence A., 614
Wiesel, Elie, 220, 358, 399
Wieseltier, Leon, 310
Wiesenthal, Simon, 210, 351
Wiesenthal (Simon) Center, 564
Willebrands, Johannes, 352
Willmot, Bob, 319
Wilson, Derek, 333
Winant, Edward, 319
Windsor Jewish Community Bulletin, 605
Winograd, Eliahu, 495
Wisconsin Jewish Chronicle, 605
Wisse, Ruth, 318, 319
Wohlfarth, Peter, 334
Wolfstein-Frölich, Rosi, 370
Women's American ORT Reporter, 603
Women's League for Conservative Judaism, 561
Women's League for Israel, 579
Women's League Outlook, 603
Workmen's Circle, 566
Workmen's Circle Call, 603
World Confederation of Jewish Community Centers, 570
World Confederation of United Zionists, 579
World Conference of Jewish Communal Service, 539
World Council of Synagogues, 561
World Jewish Congress (WJC), 266, 363, 372, 387, 399, 539
World Jewish Population, 514–532
World Union for Progressive Judaism, 561
World Zionist Organization—American Section, 579
  Department of Education and Culture, 579
  North American Aliyah Movement, 579
  Zionist Archives and Library of the, 579
Wörner, Manfred, 360
Wurzweiler School of Social Work, 564

Yaakobi, Gad, 457, 477
Yadin, Yigael, 82
Yaffe, Leo, 319

Yahav, David, 423
Yancey, William L., 105
Yariv, Aharon, 479
Yaroslavsky, Zev, 223
Yavne Hebrew Theological Seminary, 562
Yearbook of the Central Conference of American Rabbis, 603
Yedidya, Eli, 440
Yegar, Moshe, 504
Yehezkeli, Israel, 501
Yehoshua, A.B., 332, 377, 404
Yeshiva University, 274, 562
  Albert Einstein College of Medicine, 562
  Alumni Office, 562
  Belfer Institute for Advanced Biomedical Studies, 563
  Benjamin N. Cardozo School of Law, 563
  Bernard Revel Graduate School, 563
  Brookdale Institute for the Study of Gerontology, 563
  David J. Azrieli Graduate Institute of Jewish Education and Administration, 563
  Ferkauf Graduate School of Psychology, 563
  Harry Fischel School for higher Jewish Studies, 563
  Rabbi Isaac Eichanan Theological Seminary, 563
  Philip and Sarah Belz School of Jewish Music, 563
  Women's Organization, 564
  Wurzweiler School of Social Work, 564
Yeshiva University Museum, 544
Yeshivath Torah Vodaath and Mesivta Rabbinical Seminary, 565
  Alumni Association, 565
Yeutter, Clayton, 212
Yiddish, 603
Yiddishe Kultur, 603
Dos Yiddishe Vort, 603
Yiddisher Kemfer, 603
Yiddisher Kulter Farband—YKUF, 544
Yidishe Shprakh, 603
YIVO Bleter, 603
YIVO Institute for Jewish Research, 544
  Max Weinreich Center for Advanced Jewish Studies, 544
Yoffe, Alexander, 384, 502
Yogev, A., 71, 73
Yorke, Valerie, 332
Yosef, Ovadia, 85, 462
Young Israel, National Council of, 554
  American Friends of Young Israel Synagogues in Israel, 554
  Armed Forces Bureau, 554
  Employment Bureau, 554
  Institute for Jewish Studies, 554
  Young Israel Collegiates and Young Adults, 554
  Young Israel Youth, 554
Young Israel Viewpoint, 603
Young Judaea/Hashachar, 576
Young Judaean, 603
Yugntruf, 603
Yugntruf Youth for Yiddish, 582
Yugoslavia, 527

Zaire, 491
Zakout, Fat'hi, 435
Ze'ev, Israel, 429
Ze'evi, Rehavam, 460, 461, 497
Zerker, Sally, 304
Zevi, Tullia, 350, 351, 352
Zilbershtain, Ilya, 388
Zingeris, Emanuelis, 386
Zionist Organization of America, 259, 260, 262, 579
Ziyada, Muhammad, 435
Zuckerman, Alan, 103
Zundel, Ernst, 302, 306, 307

3 1542 00147 1667

296.05 A512
1990
American Jewish year book.

WITHDRAWN

Trexler Library
Muhlenberg College
Allentown, PA 18104